Cover Image:
South American, Incan ceremonial tunic (c. 1500).

Wool and cotton.

Stuart Franklin/Magnum Photos

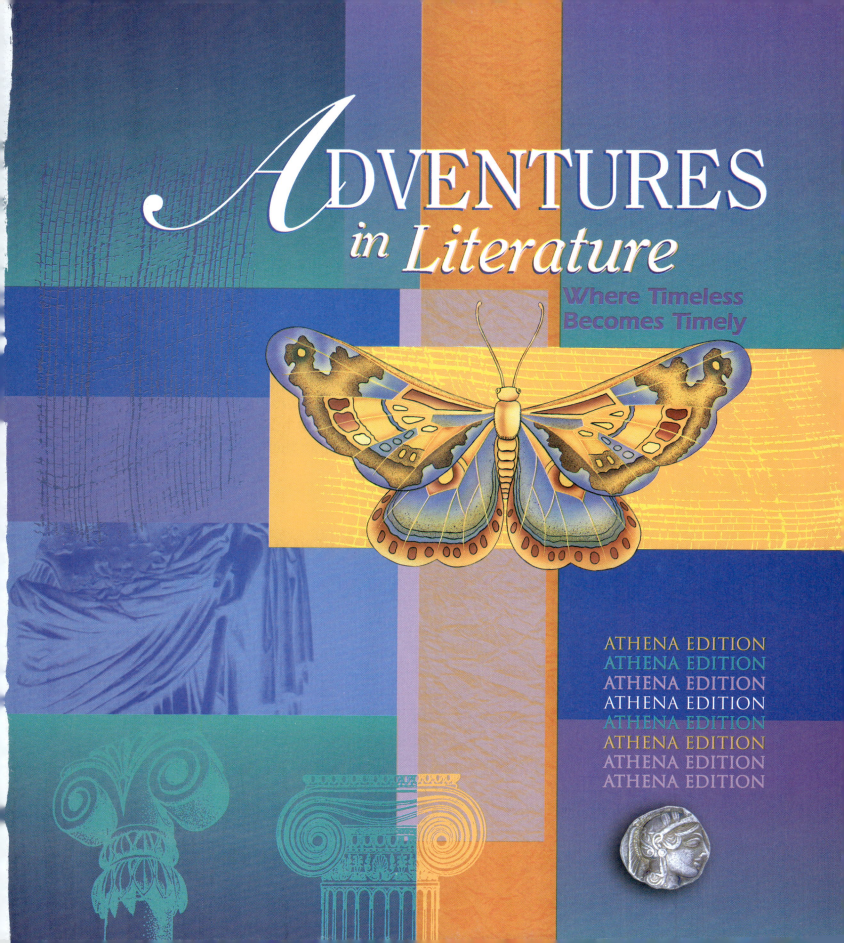

Classic Tales and

Classic literature is timeless and timely—forever lifting time-bound travelers beyond the boundaries of their ages with supreme grace and beauty.

For nearly 70 years, **Adventures in Literature** has helped teachers to bring about this transformation in their classrooms.

LITERATURE SOARS TO NEW HEIGHTS

Our Athena Edition ©1996, for grades 6 through 12, expands upon the traditional flight of the imagination and travels along some new and exciting paths.

You'll find

- Time-honored classics you love to teach and new selections to further enlighten and engage students
- Cross-cultural connections to elevate student awareness of literature's global reach
- Interdisciplinary bridges that make selections more relevant to students
- Stimulating activities to develop and improve students' writing skills
- Special critical-reading and thinking features to enhance students' literary insight

New Adventures

These well-organized support materials not only meet your students' needs, but also will save you valuable lesson planning time by enhancing students' learning experiences, integrating language arts skills, and offering multiple assessment options.

TIMELY MATERIALS FOR TODAY'S CLASSROOM

Pupil's Edition

Annotated Teacher's Edition

Teaching Resources with Organizer
- Teaching Resources Booklets
  - Teacher's Notes and Answer Keys
  - Reading Checks
  - Reading Focus Worksheets (Grade 6)
  - Study Guides
  - Language Skills Worksheets
  - Building Vocabulary Worksheets
  - Selection Vocabulary Tests
  - Selection Tests
  - Mastery Tests
  - Analogy Lessons
  - Analogy Tests
  - Revision Worksheets (Grade 6); Composition Tests (Grades 7-12)
- Portfolio Assessment and Professional Support Materials
- Teaching Resource Organizer

Test Generator
- IBM® PC and Compatibles
- Macintosh® Computers

Audiovisual Resources Binder
- Fine Art and Instructional Transparencies with Teacher's Notes and Blackline Masters
- Many Voices: Selection Audiocassettes with Teacher's Notes

ANNOTATED TEACHER'S EDITION

Adventures for Readers
AN INTRODUCTION

ATHENA EDITION

HOLT, RINEHART AND WINSTON
Harcourt Brace & Company

Austin • New York • Orlando • Atlanta • San Francisco • Boston • Dallas • Toronto • London

Copyright © 1996 by Holt, Rinehart and Winston, Inc.

All rights reserved. No part of this publication may be reproduced or transmitted in any form or by any means, electronic or mechanical, including photocopy, recording, or any information storage and retrieval system, without permission in writing from the publisher.

Requests for permission to make copies of any part of the work should be mailed to: Permissions Department, Holt, Rinehart and Winston, Inc., 6277 Sea Harbor Drive, Orlando, Florida 32887-6777.

Material from earlier edition: copyright © by Harcourt Brace & Company. All rights reserved.

For permission to reprint copyrighted material, grateful acknowledgment is made to the following sources:

Atheneum Books for Young Readers, an imprint of Simon & Schuster Children's Publishing Division: From "Beach Stones" from *Something New Begins* by Lilian Moore. Copyright © 1982 by Lilian Moore. Excerpt (Retitled: "Jody's Discovery") from *The Yearling* by Marjorie Kinnan Rawlings. Copyright 1938 by Marjorie Kinnan Rawlings; copyright renewed © 1966 by Norton Baskin.

Creative Arts Book Company: From "Momotaro: Boy-of-the-Peach" from *The Dancing Kettle and Other Japanese Folk Tales* by Yoshiko Uchida. Copyright © 1986 by Yoshiko Uchida.

Farrar, Straus & Giroux, Inc.: From "The Toaster" from *Laughing Time* by William Jay Smith. Copyright © 1990 by William Jay Smith.

HarperCollins Publishers, Inc.: From *Sounder* by William H. Armstrong. Text copyright © 1969 by William H. Armstrong. From "Cynthia in the Snow" from *Bronzeville Boys and Girls* by Gwendolyn Brooks. Copyright © 1956 by Gwendolyn Brooks Blakely.

Heidelberg Graphics and Leroy V. Quintana: From "Legacy II" by Leroy V. Quintana from *The Face of Poetry*, edited by L. H. Clark and Mary MacArthur. Copyright © 1979 by Heidelberg Graphics.

Bobbi Katz: From "Things To Do If You Are a Subway" by Bobbi Katz. Copyright © 1970 by Bobbi Katz. All rights reserved.

William Morrow and Company, Inc.: From "Knoxville, Tennessee" from *Black Feeling, Black Talk, Black Judgment* by Nikki Giovanni. Copyright © 1968, 1970 by Nikki Giovanni.

Penguin Books Ltd.: From "A Heavy Cart Rumbles" by Kuroyanagi Shoha and from "A Chilling Moon" by Tan Taigi from *The Penguin Book of Japanese Verse,* translated by Geoffrey Bownas and Anthony Thwaite (Penguin Books, 1964). Translation copyright © 1964 by Geoffrey Bownas and Anthony Thwaite.

Third Woman Press, Berkeley, CA: From "Abuelito Who" from *My Wicked, Wicked Ways* by Sandra Cisneros. Copyright © 1987 by Sandra Cisneros.

University of Arkansas Press: From "Interview" from *Story Hour* by Sara Henderson Hay. Copyright © 1982 by Sara Henderson Hay.

Printed in the United States of America

ISBN 0-03-098627-3

2 3 4 5 041 97 96 95

Critical Readers and Contributors

H. Edward Deluzain
A. Crawford Mosley
High School
Panama City, Florida

Mary Grace
School District of Janesville
Janesville, Wisconsin

Beverly Grossman
Austin, Texas

Annie Hartnett
Austin, Texas

Theresa Holloway
George Washington
Intermediate School
Honolulu, Hawaii

Emily Licate
West Junior High School
Ashtabula, Ohio

Carolee Lanier
Rockville, Maryland

Nancy Nowlin
Austin, Texas

Donna Rawlins
McGuffey Intermediate School
Claysville, Pennsylvania

Donna Townsend
Austin, Texas

Trudy Williams
Austin, Texas

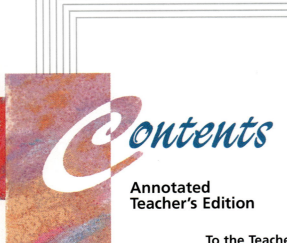

Contents

Annotated Teacher's Edition

To the Teacher T14

Unit 1

A GALLERY OF CHARACTERS

| **Teaching Guide** . . . . 1A |

Close Reading of a Selection 2
Guidelines for Close Reading 2
    Jean Craighead George . . . . . FROM *Julie of the Wolves* 3
Looking at Yourself as a Reader 7
Thinking About Words . . . . Using Context Clues 8

    C. S. Lewis . . . . Mr. Tumnus
                                                  FROM *The Lion, the Witch*
                                                   and the Wardrobe 10
    Ann Petry . . . . Harriet Tubman
                                                 FROM *Harriet Tubman, Conductor*
                                                 on the Underground Railroad 22

▪▪ **Literature and History: The Underground Railroad** 34
    Gary Soto . . . . The Jacket 35
    Mark Twain . . . . FROM *The Adventures of Tom Sawyer* . . . 42

No Questions Asked
    John R. Erickson . . . . FROM *Hank the Cowdog* 56

■■ **Focus on Reading and Critical Thinking: Making Generalizations** 62
■■ **Focus on Writing: Writing a Personal Narrative** 63

Unit 2

QUESTS

| **Teaching Guide** .... | 65A |

Close Reading of a Selection 68
Guidelines for Close Reading 68
    Scott O'Dell .... FROM Carlota 69
Looking at Yourself as a Reader 75
Thinking About Words .... How to Own a Word 76

Anne McCaffrey .... The Smallest Dragonboy 78

■■ **Connecting Cultures: Myths About Dragons** 96

Gary Paulsen .... FROM Hatchet 99
William Armstrong .... FROM Sounder 114
Marjorie Kinnan
    Rawlings .... Jody's Discovery
                         FROM *The Yearling* 129
No Questions Asked
    M. R. Cox .... The Algonquin Cinderella 147

■■ **Focus on Reading and Critical Thinking: Exploring Connotations** 152

■■ **Focus on Writing: Writing a Description** 153

Unit 3

SHORT STORIES

Teaching Guide 155A

Close Reading of a Short Story 158
Guidelines for Close Reading 158
   Quentin Reynolds .... A Secret for Two 159
Looking at Yourself as a Reader 165

PLOT
   John Gardner .... Dragon, Dragon 166

CHARACTER
   Robert Cormier .... President Cleveland, Where Are You? .. 178

THEME
   Ray Bradbury .... All Summer in a Day 194
▪▪ **Literature and Science: Fact Versus Fiction** 205
   Lloyd Alexander .... The Stone 206

POINT OF VIEW
   James Berry .... Becky and the Wheels-and-Brake Boys ... 220

SETTING
   Elizabeth Enright .... Nancy 233
   Olaf Baker .... Where the Buffaloes Begin 252

No Questions Asked
   Lensey Namioka .... The All-American Slurp 264
▪▪ **Focus on Reading and Critical Thinking: Evaluating Short Stories** ... 274
   Robin Kinkead .... Rolls for the Czar 275
▪▪ **Focus on Writing: Writing a Short Story** 277

Unit 4

POETRY

Teaching Guide 279A

Eve Merriam	Inside a Poem	281
Close Reading of a Poem		282
Jack Prelutsky	The Darkling Elves	282
Looking at Yourself as a Reader		283

STORY POEMS 284

Dr. Seuss		
(Theodor Geisel)	The Sneetches	285
Edward Lear	The Jumblies	295

SOUND EFFECTS 300

Gwendolyn Brooks	Cynthia in the Snow	301
Maya Angelou	Life Doesn't Frighten Me	303
Arthur Guiterman	Habits of the Hippopotamus	307
T. S. Eliot	The Rum Tum Tugger	310
E. E. Cummings	who knows if the moon's	314
Gwendolyn Brooks	Narcissa	318

USING YOUR SENSES 321

Lilian Moore	Beach Stones	323
Pat Mora	Petals	326
Dorthi Charles	Concrete Cat	328
Shōha, Taigi,		
Bonchō, Ryōta	Haiku	330

MAKING COMPARISONS 333

James Reeves	The Sea	335
William Jay Smith	The Toaster	338
Bobbi Katz	Things To Do If You Are a Subway	340
Sandra Cisneros	Abuelito Who	345
Langston Hughes	Dream Variations	350

IDEAS AND FEELINGS 353

Robert Frost	A Minor Bird	354
David Kherdian	That Day	356
Leroy V. Quintana	Legacy II	360
Nikki Giovanni	Knoxville, Tennessee	365
Carl Sandburg	Phizzog	368
Sara Henderson Hay	Interview	370

No Questions Asked
    Shel Silverstein . . . . Sarah Cynthia Sylvia Stout Would
                                            Not Take the Garbage Out 372

Portraits of Imagination 374
  Focus on Reading and Critical Thinking:
  Relating Sound to Meaning 380
    Theodore Roethke . . . . The Waking 380
  Focus on Writing: Writing a Poem 381

Unit 5

NONFICTION

Teaching Guide 383A

Close Reading of Nonfiction 386
Guidelines for Close Reading 386
  Dian Fossey . . . . FROM Gorillas in the Mist 387
Looking at Yourself as a Reader 391

BIOGRAPHY AND AUTOBIOGRAPHY
  Anne Frank . . . . FROM The Diary of a Young Girl . . . 393
  Russell Freedman . . . . A Backwoods Boy
                              FROM *Lincoln: A Photobiography* 402

HISTORY

Huynh Quang Nhuong ..... The Land I Lost 411
Brent Ashabranner .... The Most Vulnerable People
                                   FROM *Into a Strange Land* 422

SCIENCE

Patricia Lauber .... Volcano
                                   FROM *Volcano: The Eruption
                                   and Healing of Mt. St. Helens* 431

■ Literature And Science: Myths and Scientific Words 445

THE PERSONAL ESSAY

James Thurber .... Snapshot of a Dog 446

No Questions Asked

Bill Cosby .... Fatherhood 453

■ Focus on Reading and Critical Thinking:
Understanding Cause and Effect 458

■ Focus on Writing: Writing an Informative Paper 459

Unit 6

PLAYS

Teaching Guide 461A

Close Reading of a Play 464
Guidelines for Close Reading 464
Rod Serling .... FROM *The Monsters Are Due
                                   on Maple Street* 465
Looking at Yourself as a Reader 470
Thinking About Words .... Comparing Words: Semantic Features .. 472
Blanche Hanalis .... The Secret Garden *based on the novel by
                                   Frances Hodgson Burnett* 474

No Questions Asked: A Scene for Classroom Theater

Patricia Gray .... Riddles in the Dark *based on the novel
                                   The Hobbit by J.R.R. Tolkien* 534

■ Focus on Reading and Critical Thinking: Drawing Inferences 544

■ Focus on Writing: Writing a Scene 545

Unit 7

MYTHS AND FOLK TALES

Teaching Guide		547A
Close Reading of a Folk Tale		550
Guidelines for Close Reading		550
Kim So-un	The Pheasant's Bell (A Korean Folk Tale)	551
Looking at Yourself as a Reader		555
Thinking About Words	Using Context Clues	556
THREE HEROES OF MYTH		557
Richard Erdoes and Alfonso Ortiz	Glooscap Fights the Water Monster (A Micmac Myth)	558
Robert Graves	Perseus (A Greek Myth)	567
Amy Cruse	Quetzalcoatl (A Mexican Myth)	576
"HOW AND WHY" STORIES		585
Zora Neale Hurston	How the Possum Lost the Hair on Its Tail FROM *Mules and Men* (An African American Folk Tale)	586
Harold Courlander	Paul Bunyan's Cornstalk (An American Tall Tale)	589
▪▪ Connecting Cultures: Tales About Giants		593
Rudyard Kipling	How the Whale Got His Throat FROM *Just So Stories*	595
Chinua Achebe	Why Tortoise's Shell Is Not Smooth FROM *Things Fall Apart* (An African Folk Tale)	601

TALES THAT AMUSE AND AMAZE 607

    Elisabeth Gille . . . . Ali Baba and the Forty Thieves
                                       FROM *Tales from the Arabian Nights*
                                       (A Middle Eastern Folk Tale) 609

    Yoshiko Uchida . . . . Momotaro: Boy-of-the-Peach
                                       (A Japanese Folk Tale) 618

    Hans Baumann . . . . Nana Miriam
                                       (An African Folk Tale) 633

No Questions Asked
    Jenny Leading Cloud . . . . . . The End of the World
                                       (A Sioux Myth) 638

❚❚ **Focus on Reading and Critical Thinking:**
    Identifying the Main Idea 640
    Claude Brown . . . . Two Frogs and the Milk Vat 640

❚❚ **Focus on Writing: Writing a Book Report** 641

Unit 8

THE NOVEL

Teaching Guide 643A

Close Reading of a Novel 646
Guidelines for Close Reading 646
Thinking About Words . . . . How to Own a Word 647
    Betsy Byars . . . . The Summer of the Swans 648

❚❚ **Focus on Reading and Critical Thinking:**
    Distinguishing Between Facts and Opinions 718
    Seymour Simon . . . . FROM Wetlands 718

❚❚ **Focus on Writing: Writing a Persuasive Essay** 719

Books for Further Reading 722

WRITING ABOUT LITERATURE

Reasons for Writing About Literature 726
Using the Writing Process 727
Writing on a Topic of Your Own: A Character Sketch 731
Prewriting 732
Writing 733
Evaluating and Revising Papers 735
Proofreading and Publishing 735

Literary Terms and Techniques 738
Handbook for Revision 750
    Model Essays 752
    Sentence Structure 760
    Pronouns 761
    Verbs 762
    Comma Usage 765
    Style 767
    Glossary of Usage 769
    Grammar Reference Guide 775
    Mechanics 778

Glossary 786
Outline of Concepts and Skills 806
Index of Contents by Types 810
Index of Fine Art and Illustrations 812
Photo Credits 813
Index of Authors and Titles 814

Note to Teachers

EXCERPTED LITERARY WORKS USED IN THIS TEXT

The following selections are excerpts from larger works. Excerpts were chosen on the basis of key literary or thematic elements.

FROM *Julie of the Wolves*
FROM *The Lion, the Witch and the Wardrobe*
FROM *Harriet Tubman, Conductor on the Underground Railroad*
FROM *The Adventures of Tom Sawyer*
FROM *The Original Adventures of Hank the Cowdog*
FROM *Carlota*

FROM *Hatchet*
FROM *Sounder*
FROM *The Yearling*
FROM *Gorillas in the Mist*
FROM *The Diary of A Young Girl*
FROM *Lincoln: A Photobiography*
FROM *Volcano: The Eruption and Healing of Mt. St. Helens*

FROM *Into a Strange Land*
FROM *Fatherhood*
FROM *The Monsters Are Due on Maple Street*
FROM *Mules and Men*
FROM *Things Fall Apart*
FROM *Tales from the Arabian Nights*
FROM *Manchild in the Promised Land*
FROM "*Wetlands*"

Index of Titles by Themes

Animal Friends

from *Hank the Cowdog,* John R. Erickson, 56
from *Sounder,* William Armstrong, 114
Jody's Discovery, from *The Yearling,* Marjorie Kinnan Rawlings, 129
Secret for Two, A, Quentin Reynolds, 159
Habits of the Hippopotamus, Arthur Guiterman, 307
Rum Tum Tugger, The, T.S. Eliot, 310
Concrete Cat, Dorthi Charles, 328
Snapshot of a Dog, James Thurber, 446

Challenges

from *Julie of the Wolves,* Jean Craighead George, 3
from *Hatchet,* Gary Paulsen, 99
Life Doesn't Frighten Me, Maya Angelou, 303
Ali Baba and the Forty Thieves, Elisabeth Gille, 609
Two Frogs and the Milk Vat, Claude Brown, 640
The Summer of the Swans, Betsy Byars, 648

Changes/Transformations

Algonquin Cinderella, The, M.R. Cox 147
Dragon, Dragon, John Gardner, 166
That Day, David Kherdian, 356
The Pheasant's Bell, Kim So-un, 551
Glooscap Fights the Water Monster, Richard Erdoes and Alfonso Ortiz, 558
How the Whale Got His Throat, from *Just So Stories,* Rudyard Kipling, 595
Why Tortoise's Shell Is Not Smooth, from *Things Fall Apart,* Chinua Achebe, 601

Coming of Age

Jacket, The, Gary Soto, 35
from *Carlota,* Scott O'Dell, 69
from *Hatchet,* Gary Paulsen, 99
President Cleveland, Where Are You?, Robert Cormier, 178
The Stone, Lloyd Alexander, 206
Legacy II, Leroy V. Quintana, 360
The Summer of the Swans, Betsy Byars, 648

Fantasy and Science Fiction

Mr. Tumnus, from *The Lion, the Witch and the Wardrobe,* C.S. Lewis, 10
Smallest Dragonboy, The, Anne McCaffrey, 78
Dragon, Dragon, John Gardner, 166
All Summer in a Day, Ray Bradbury, 194
The Stone, Lloyd Alexander, 206
The Darkling Elves, Jack Prelutsky, 282
Sneetches, The, Dr. Seuss, 285
Jumblies, The, Edward Lear, 295
Things To Do If You Are a Subway, Bobbi Katz, 340
from *The Monsters Are Due on Maple Street,* Rod Serling, 465
Riddles in the Dark, based on *The Hobbit,* J.R.R. Tolkein, 534

A Gallery of Characters

from *Julie of the Wolves,* Jean Craighead George, 3
Mr. Tumnus, from *The Lion, the Witch and the Wardrobe,* C.S. Lewis, 10
Harriet Tubman, from *Harriet Tubman, Conductor on the Underground Railroad,* Ann Petry, 22
Jacket, The, Gary Soto, 35
from *The Adventures of Tom Sawyer,* Mark Twain, 42
from *Hank the Cowdog,* John R. Erickson, 56
Secret for Two, A, Quentin Reynolds, 159
Becky and the Wheels-and-Brake Boys, James Berry, 220
Nancy, Elizabeth Enright, 233
Abuelito Who, Sandra Cisneros, 345
Sarah Cynthia Sylvia Stout Would Not Take the Garbage Out, Shel Silverstein, 372
Snapshot of a Dog, James Thurber, 446
Nana Miriam, Hans Baumann, 633

Humor/The Comic Vision

from *The Adventures of Tom Sawyer,* Mark Twain, 42
from *Hank the Cowdog,* John R. Erickson, 56
All-American Slup, The, Lensey Namioka, 264
Sneetches, The, Dr. Seuss, 285
Jumblies, The, Edward Lear, 295
Habits of the Hippopotamus, Arthur Guiterman, 307
Rum Tum Tugger, The, T.S. Eliot, 310
Interview, Sara Henderson Hay, 370
Sarah Cynthia Sylvia Stout Would Not Take the Garbage Out, Shel Silverstein, 372
from *Fatherhood,* Bill Cosby, 453
How the Possum Lost the Hair on Its Tail, from *Mules and Men,* Zora Neale Hurston, 586
Paul Bunyan's Cornstalk, Harold Courlander, 589

Lessons from History

Harriet Tubman, from *Harriet Tubman, Conductor on the Underground Railroad,* Ann Petry, 22
from *The Diary of a Young Girl,* Anne Frank, 393
A Backwoods Boy, from *Lincoln: A Photobiography,* Russell Freedman, 402
The Land I Lost, Huynh Quang Nhuong, 411
The Most Vulnerable People, from *Into a Strange Land,* Brent Ashabranner, 422

Mythic and Legendary Heroes

Where the Buffaloes Begin, Olaf Baker, 252
Glooscap Fights the Water Monster, Richard Erdoes and Alfonso Ortiz, 558
Perseus, Robert Graves, 567
Quetzalcoatl, Amy Cruse, 576
Momotaro: Boy-of-the-Peach, Yoshiko Uchida, 618
Nana Miriam, Hans Baumann, 633

The Natural World

from *Hatchet,* Gary Paulsen, 99
Cynthia in the Snow, Gwendolyn Brooks, 301
Beach Stones, Lilian Moore, 323
The Sea, James Reeves, 335
A Minor Bird, Robert Frost, 354
The Waking, Theodore Roethke, 380
from *Gorillas in the Mist,* Dian Fossey, 387
Volcano, from *Volcano: The Eruption and Healing of Mt. St. Helens,* Patricia Lauber, 431

The Power of Love

from *Sounder,* William Armstrong, 114
Jody's Discovery, from *The Yearling,* Marjorie Kinnan Rawlings, 129
President Cleveland, Where Are You?, Robert Cormier, 178
The Secret Garden, Blanche Hanalis, 474
The Summer of the Swans, Betsy Byars, 648

Quests

from *Carlota,* Scott O'Dell, 69
Smallest Dragonboy, The, Anne McCaffrey, 78
from *Hatchet,* Gary Paulsen, 99
from *Sounder,* William Armstrong, 114
Algonquin Cinderella, The, M.R. Cox 147
Dragon, Dragon, John Gardner, 166
Where the Buffaloes Begin, Olaf Baker, 252
Perseus, Robert Graves, 567
Momotaro: Boy-of-the-Peach, Yoshiko Uchida, 618

To the Teacher—

This **Annotated Teacher's Edition** for *ADVENTURES FOR READERS: AN INTRODUCTION* includes all the Pupil's Edition pages, slightly reduced in size to create top and side margins. Each unit of this Annotated Teacher's Edition includes a **Teaching Guide** at the beginning, **Teaching Features** in the top margins of every selection, and **Side-Margin Features** and **Annotations** that offer information about the content for all selections. The reduced pupil's pages contain notes for teachers.

New to This Edition

Features Added to the Teaching Guide

- **Planning Guide Chart**—provides a list of ancillary material available for each selection to aid in developing daily lesson plans and in planning units of instruction.
- **Transparency Listing**—fine art and instructional transparencies from the *Audiovisual Resources Binder* are listed.
- **Student Learning Options**—suggests activities for the whole unit as well as for individual selections. Many of these activities may be suitable as projects that allow for alternative assessment.

Features Added to the Top and Side Margin

- **Meeting Individual Needs: ESL/LEP (English as a Second Language/Limited English Proficient)**—aids students for whom English is a second language or other students who may be challenged in understanding literature. Focuses upon idioms, dialect, and other aspects of the literature that students might have trouble with.
- **Meeting Individual Needs: Learning Styles**—provides activities appropriate to students with various learning styles (visual, auditory, kinesthetic).
- **Cultural Diversity**—explores the sociological, political, historical, literary, and other characteristics and achievements of various cultures as they relate to the literature being studied.
- **Curriculum/Community Link**—includes activities that link literature to other subjects in the curriculum or to the community.
- **Cooperative Learning**—provides suggestions for structured collaborative activities.
- **Portfolio Assessment**—suggests a variety of projects suitable for student portfolios.
- **Transparency Listing**—cross-references fine art and instructional transparencies from the *Audiovisual Resources Binder*.
- **Literary Elements** and **Guided Reading** are color coded with overscreens.

Adventures for Readers
AN INTRODUCTION

ATHENA EDITION

HOLT, RINEHART AND WINSTON
Harcourt Brace & Company

Austin • **New York** • Orlando • Atlanta • San Francisco • Boston • Dallas • Toronto • London

Staff Credits

EDITORIAL
Project Director: Fannie Safier
Editorial Coordinator: Katie Vignery
Editorial Staff: Lynda Abbott, Sally Ahearn, Judith Austin-Mills, Laura Baci, Amanda Beard, Richard Blake, Susan Britt, Robert Carranza, Kathleen Daniel, Daniela Guggenheim, Scott Hall, Bobbi Hernandez, Constance D. Israel, Susan Lynch, Mary Malone, Jennifer Osborne, Marie Hoffman Price, Sara Schroeder, Amy D.D. Simpson, Atietie O. Tonwe
Editorial Support: Carla M. Beer, Ruth Hooker, Margaret Guerrero
Editorial Permissions: Carrie Jones
Software Development: Armin Gutzmer, Lydia Doty

DESIGN AND PHOTO RESEARCH
Design: Pun Nio, *Senior Art Director;* Richard Metzger, *Design Supervisor;* Diane Motz, *Senior Designer;* Anne Wright, *Designer*
Photo: Debra Saleny, *Photo Research Manager;* V. Sing Griffin Bitzer, Yvonne Gerin, Ann Gillespie, Jeannie Taylor, *Photo Researchers*

PRODUCTION
Beth Prevelige, *Senior Production Manager;* Simira Davis, *Production Assisstant;* Sergio Durante, *Secretary;* George Prevelige, *Production Manager;* Rose Degollado, *Production Coordinator*
Electronic Publishing: Carol Martin, *Electronic Publishing Manager;* Kristy Sprott, *Electronic Publishing Supervisor;* Debra Schorn, *Electronic Publishing Senior Coordinator;* Lana Castle, Denise Haney, David Hernandez, Maria Homic, Barbara Hudgens, Mercedes Newman, Monica Shomos, *Electronic Publishing Staff*

Cover Design: Design 5

Copyright © 1996 by Holt, Rinehart and Winston, Inc.

All rights reserved. No part of this publication may be reproduced or transmitted in any form or by any means, electronic or mechanical, including photocopy, recording, or any information storage and retrieval system, without permission in writing from the publisher.

Requests for permission to make copies of any part of the work should be mailed to: Permissions Department, Holt, Rinehart and Winston, Inc., 6277 Sea Harbor Drive, Orlando, Florida 32887-6777.

Material from earlier edition: copyright © by Harcourt Brace & Company.
All rights reserved.

Acknowledgments appear on pages iv–v, which are an extension of the copyright page.

Printed in the United States of America

ISBN 0-03-098625-7   3 4 5   040   97 96

Contributors AND Critical Readers

Kay Bevino
Bruner Middle School
Fort Walton Beach, Florida

Scott J. Ewald
Roosevelt Elementary School
Watertown, South Dakota

Barbara Francis
New York, New York

Nancy A. Frese
St. Thomas the Apostle School
Florissant, Missouri

Jan Freeman
Florence, Massachusetts

Patti Grady
St. Thomas More School
Lynnwood, Washington

V. Pauline Hodges
Forgan Public Schools
Forgan, Oklahoma

Linda Ann Lee
Holcomb Bridge Middle School
Alpharetta, Georgia

Carroll Moulton
Formerly of Duke University
Durham, North Carolina

Mary Elizabeth Thomas
Sandy Springs Middle School
Atlanta, Georgia

Acknowledgments

For permission to reprint copyrighted material, grateful acknowledgment is made to the following sources:

American Library Association: From comment by Lloyd Alexander from *Top of the News,* "Editors Notes," January 1968. Copyright © 1968 by the American Library Association.

Arte Público Press: "Petals" by Pat Mora from *Chants* (Houston: Arte Público Press–University of Houston, 1985).

Brent Ashabranner: "The Most Vulnerable People" from *Into a Strange Land* by Brent Ashabranner. Copyright © 1987 by Brent Ashabranner and Melissa Ashabranner.

Atheneum Publishers, an imprint of Macmillan Publishing Company: "Our Washing Machine" from *The Apple Vendor's Fair* by Patricia Hubbell. Copyright © 1963 by Patricia Hubbell. "Beach Stones" from *Something New Begins* by Lilian Moore. Copyright © 1982 by Lilian Moore. "Since Hanna Moved Away" from *If I Were in Charge of the World* by Judith Viorst. Copyright © 1981 by Judith Viorst.

Toni Cade Bambara: From "Rapping About Story Forms" from *Tales and Stories for Black Folks,* edited by Toni Cade Bambara. Copyright © 1971 by Toni Cade Bambara.

Susan Bergholz Literary Services: Comment on "Abuelito Who" by Sandra Cisneros. Copyright © 1991 by Sandra Cisneros.

Georges Borchardt, Inc. for the Estate of John Gardner: "Dragon, Dragon" from *Dragon, Dragon and Other Tales* by John Gardner. Copyright © 1993 by Boskydell Artists Ltd.

Bradbury Press, an Affiliate of Macmillan, Inc.: From *Volcano: The Eruption and Healing of Mount St. Helens* by Patricia Lauber. Text copyright © 1988 by Patricia Lauber. From *Hatchet* by Gary Paulsen. Copyright © 1987 by Gary Paulsen.

Betsy Byars: From comment by Betsy Byars from *Something About the Author,* Volume 1. Copyright © 1976 by Betsy Byars. Published by Gale Research Company.

Clarion Books/Houghton Mifflin Co.: From *Lincoln: A Photobiography* by Russell Freedman. Copyright © 1987 by Russell Freedman. All rights reserved.

Ruth Cohen, Inc. on behalf of Lensey Namioka: "The All-American Slurp" by Lensey Namioka. Copyright © 1987 by Lensey Namioka.

Don Congdon Associates, Inc.: "All Summer in a Day" by Ray Bradbury. Copyright © 1954 and renewed © 1982 by Ray Bradbury.

Harold Courlander: "Paul Bunyan's Cornstalk" from *Ride with the Sun* by Harold Courlander. Copyright © 1955 and renewed © 1988 by Harold Courlander.

Creative Arts Book Company: "Momotaro: Boy-of-the-Peach" from *The Dancing Kettle and Other Japanese Folk Tales* by Yoshiko Uchida. Copyright © 1986 by Yoshiko Uchida.

The Crossroad/Continuum Publishing Group: From comment by Maya Angelou from *Black Women Writers at Work,* edited by Claudia Tate. Copyright © 1983 by The Crossroad/Continuum Publishing Group.

Delacorte Press, a division of Bantam Doubleday Dell Publishing Group, Inc.: "The Jacket" from *Small Faces* by Gary Soto. Copyright © 1986 by Gary Soto.

Doubleday, a division of Bantam Doubleday Dell Publishing Group, Inc.: "Good Morning Opponents" and "Who Dressed This Mess?" from *Fatherhood* by Bill Cosby. Copyright © 1986 by William H. Cosby. From *The Diary of Anne Frank: The Critical Edition.* Copyright © 1986 by Anne Frank-Fonds, Basle/Switzerland, for all texts of Anne Frank. "The Waking" from *The Collected Poems of Theodore Roethke.* Copyright 1948 by Theodore Roethke and renewed © 1976 by Beatrice Roethke, Administratrix of the Estate of Theodore Roethke.

The Dramatic Publishing Company: "Act One, Scene Three" (Retitled: "Riddles in the Dark") from *J.R.R. Tolkien's The Hobbit,* dramatized by Patricia Gray. Copyright © 1967 by The Dramatic Publishing Company.

Farrar, Straus & Giroux, Inc.: "The Toaster" from *Laughing Time* by William Jay Smith. Copyright © 1990 by William Jay Smith.

Gale Research Inc.: Comment from Lloyd Alexander (Vol. 49), Langston Hughes (Vol. 33), Gary Paulsen (Vol. 54), and Yoshiko Uchida (Vol. 1) from *Something About the Author,* edited by Anne Commire. Copyright © 1973, 1976, 1977, 1983, 1987 by Gale Research Inc.

Nikki Giovanni: Comment on "Knoxville, Tennessee" by Nikki Giovanni. Copyright © 1991 by Nikki Giovanni.

Greenwillow Books, a division of William Morrow & Company, Inc.: "The Darkling Elves" from *The Headless Horseman Rides Tonight* by Jack Prelutsky. Copyright © 1980 by Jack Prelutsky.

Gulf Publishing Company: From *The Original Adventures of Hank the Cowdog* by John R. Erikson. Copyright © 1980 by John Erikson.

Harcourt Brace & Company: Adapted definitions from *HBJ School Dictionary,* Second Edition. Copyright © 1985 by Harcourt Brace & Company. "The Rum Tum Tugger" from *Old Possum's Book of Practical Cats* by T. S. Eliot. Copyright 1939 by T. S. Eliot; copyright renewed © 1967 by Esme Valerie Eliot. From "It All Began with a Picture" from *Of Other Worlds: Essays and Stories* by C. S. Lewis, edited by Walter Hooper. Copyright © 1966 by the Executors of the Estate of C. S. Lewis. "Phizzog" from *Good Morning, America* by Carl Sandburg. Copyright 1928 and renewed © 1956 by Carl Sandburg. "The Algonquin Cinderella" from *World Tales, The Extraordinary Coincidence of Stories Told in All Times, in All Places* by Idries Shah. Copyright © 1979 by Technographia, S.A. and Harcourt Brace & Company.

HarperCollins Publishers, Inc.: From *Sounder* by William H. Armstrong. Text copyright © 1969 by William H. Armstrong. "Cynthia in the Snow" and "Narcissa" from *Bronzeville Boys and Girls* by Gwendolyn Brooks. Copyright © 1956 by Gwendolyn Brooks Blakely. From *Julie of the Wolves* by Jean Craighead George. Text copyright © 1972 by Jean Craighead George. "How the Possum Lost the Hair Off His Tail" from *Mules and Men* by Zora Neale Hurston. Copyright 1935 by Zora Neale Hurston; copyright renewed © 1963 by John C. Hurston and Joel Hurston. From *The Land I Lost* by Huynh Quang Nhuong. Text copyright © 1982 by Huynh Quang Nhuong. "January" from *Chicken Soup with Rice: A Book of Months* by Maurice Sendak. Copyright © 1962 by Maurice Sendak. "Sarah Cynthia Sylvia Stout Would Not Take the Garbage Out" and illustrations from *Where the Sidewalk Ends* by Shel Silverstein. Copyright © 1974 by Evil Eye Music, Inc.

HarperCollins Publishers Ltd.: From *The Lion, the Witch and the Wardrobe* (Retitled: "Mr. Tumnus") by C. S. Lewis. Copyright 1950 and renewed © 1978 by the Estate of C. S. Lewis.

Heidelberg Graphics and Leroy V. Quintana: "Legacy II" by Leroy V. Quintana from *The Face of Poetry,* edited by L. H. Clark and Mary MacArthur. Copyright © 1979 by Heidelberg Graphics.

William Heinemann, a division of Reed Book Services: "Why Tortoise's Shell Is Not Smooth" from *Things Fall Apart* by Chinua Achebe. Copyright © 1958 by Chinua Achebe.

Holiday House: Cartoon and riddle from *The Dinosaur Princess and Other Prehistoric Riddles* by David A. Adler, illustrated by Loreen Leedy. Text copyright © 1988 by David A. Adler. Illustrations copyright © 1988 by Loreen Leedy.

Henry Holt and Company, Inc.: "The Stone" from *The Foundling and Other Tales of Prydain* by Lloyd Alexander. Copyright © 1973 by Lloyd Alexander. "A Minor Bird" from *The Poetry of Robert Frost,* edited by Edward Connery Lathem. Copyright 1928 and renewed © 1956 by Robert Frost; copyright © 1969 by Holt, Rinehart and Winston. From "When I Was One-and-Twenty" from "A Shropshire Lad" - Authorized Edition - from *The Collected Poems of A. E. Housman.* Copyright 1939,

1940, © 1965 by Holt, Rinehart and Winston, Inc. Copyright © 1967, 1968 by Robert E. Symons.

The Horn Book, Inc., 14 Beacon St., Boston MA 02108: From "Did You Really Write That for Children?" by Brent Ashabranner from *The Horn Book Magazine,* November/December 1988, pp. 749-754.

Houghton Mifflin Co.: From *Gorillas in the Mist* by Dian Fossey. Copyright © 1983 by Dian Fossey. All rights reserved. From *Carlota* by Scott O'Dell. Copyright © 1977 by Scott O'Dell. All rights reserved.

The Johns Hopkins University Press: From "What Makes an Appealing and Readable Science Book?" by Patricia Lauber from *The Lion and the Unicorn,* Vol. 6, 1982. Copyright © 1982 by The Johns Hopkins University Press.

International Creative Management: Quote by Theodor Geisel from "The Miracle of Dr. Seuss" by Cynthia Lindsay from *Good Housekeeping,* December 1960. Copyright © 1960 by The Hearst Corporation.

Bobbi Katz: "Things To Do If You Are a Subway" by Bobbi Katz. Copyright © 1970 by Bobbi Katz. All rights reserved.

David Kherdian: Comment on "That Day" by David Kherdian. Copyright © 1991 by David Kherdian.

Alfred A. Knopf, Inc.: "Dream Variations" from *Selected Poems* by Langston Hughes. Copyright 1926 by Alfred A. Knopf, Inc.; copyright renewed 1954 by Langston Hughes.

Liveright Publishing Corporation: "who knows if the moon's" from *Complete Poems, 1904-1962* by E. E. Cummings, edited by George J. Firmage. Copyright © 1923, 1925, 1926, 1931, 1935, 1938, 1939, 1940, 1944, 1945, 1946, 1947, 1948, 1949, 1950, 1951, 1952, 1953, 1954, 1955, 1956, 1957, 1958, 1959, 1960, 1961, 1962 by E. E. Cummings; copyright © 1972, 1973, 1974, 1975, 1976, 1977, 1978, 1979, 1980, 1981, 1982, 1983, 1984, 1985, 1986, 1987, 1988, 1989, 1990, 1991 by the Trustees for the E. E. Cummings Trust.

Macmillan Publishing Company: From *Manchild in the Promised Land* (Retitled: "Two Frogs and the Milk Vat") by Claude Brown. Copyright © 1965 by Claude Brown. Definition for "Stroodle" from *Sniglets* by Rich Hall and Friends. Copyright © 1984 by Not the Network Company, Inc.

Anne McCaffrey and her agent, Virginia Kidd: "The Smallest Dragonboy" by Anne McCaffrey. Copyright © 1973 by Anne McCaffrey. First appeared in *Science Fiction Tales.*

William Morrow and Company, Inc.: "Knoxville, Tennessee" from *Black Feeling, Black Talk, Black Judgment* by Nikki Giovanni. Copyright © 1968, 1970 by Nikki Giovanni.

The New Yorker Magazine, Inc.: From "Thoughts on Progress" by David Daiches from *The New Yorker,* August 28, 1954. Copyright © 1954, 1982 by The New Yorker Magazine, Inc. "Rolls for the Czar" by Robin Kinkead. Copyright © 1937 and renewed © 1965 by The New Yorker Magazine, Inc. Drawing by Shanahan from *The New Yorker,* February 13, 1989. Copyright © 1989 by The New Yorker Magazine, Inc.

Harold Ober Associates Incorporated: From "Wetlands" by Seymour Simon from *The Big Book for Our Planet,* edited by Ann Durell, Jean Craighead George, and Katherine Paterson. Copyright © 1993 by Seymour Simon.

Orchard Books, New York: "Becky and the Wheels-and-Brake Boys" from *A Thief in the Village and Other Stories* by James Berry. Copyright © 1987 by James Berry.

The Overlook Press, Lewis Hollow Road, Woodstock, NY 12498: "That Day" from *I Remember Root River* by David Kherdian. Copyright © 1978 by David Kherdian.

Pantheon Books, a division of Random House, Inc.: "Nana Miriam" from *The Stolen Fire* by Hans Baumann, translated by Stella Humphries. Text copyright © 1974 by Random House, Inc. From Introduction and "President Cleveland, Where Are You?" from *Eight Plus One* by Robert Cormier. Copyright © 1980 by Robert Cormier. "The End of the World" and "Glooscap Fights the Water Monster" from *American Indian Myths and Legends* by Richard Erdoes and Alfonso Ortiz. Copyright © 1984 by Richard Erdoes and Alfonso Ortiz.

Penguin Books Ltd.: "Winter Rain" by Nozawa Boncho, "Bad-tempered, I Got Back" by Oshima Ryota, "A Heavy Cart Rumbles" by Kuroyanagi Shoha, and "A Chilling Moon" by Tan Taigi from *The Penguin Book of Japanese Verse,* translated by Geoffrey Bownas and Anthony Thwaite (Penguin Books, 1964). Translation copyright © 1964 by Geoffrey Bownas and Anthony Thwaite.

Random House, Inc.: "Life Doesn't Frighten Me" from *And Still I Rise* by Maya Angelou. Copyright © 1978 by Maya Angelou. "Ali Baba and the Forty Thieves" from *Tales from the Arabian Nights* by Elisabeth Gille, translated by Merle S. Haas. Copyright © 1964 by Random House, Inc. "The Sneetches" from *The Sneetches and Other Stories* by Dr. Seuss. TM and copyright © 1961 by The 1984 Geisel Trust.

The James Reeves Estate: "The Sea" from *The Wandering Moon and Other Poems* (Puffin Books) by James Reeves. Copyright © 1950 by James Reeves.

Marian Reiner: "Inside a Poem" from *It Doesn't Always Have to Rhyme* by Eve Merriam. Copyright © 1964 and renewed © 1992 by Eve Merriam. "Rags" from *Flashlight and Other Poems* by Judith Thurman. Copyright © 1976 by Judith Thurman.

Marian Reiner for the author, Lilian Moore: Comment on "Beach Stones" by Lilian Moore. Copyright © 1991 by Lilian Moore.

Beatrice Reynolds, Administratrix for the Estate of Quentin Reynolds: "A Secret for Two" by Quentin Reynolds. Copyright 1936 by Crowell-Collier Publishing Company.

Rosemont Productions, Ltd.: *The Secret Garden,* written for television by Blanche Hanalis, based on the novel by Frances Hodgson Burnett. Copyright © 1987 by Rosemont Productions, Ltd.

Russell & Volkening, Inc. as agents for Elizabeth Enright: "Nancy" from *The Moment Before the Rain* by Elizabeth Enright. Copyright © 1947 and renewed © 1975 by Elizabeth Enright.

Russell & Volkening, Inc. as agents for Ann Petry: "Harriet Tubman" from *Harriet Tubman: Conductor of the Underground Railroad* by Ann Petry. Copyright © 1955 and renewed © 1983 by Ann Petry.

Louise H. Sclove: "Habits of the Hippopotamus" from *Gaily the Troubador* by Arthur Guiterman.

Charles Scribner's Sons, an imprint of Macmillan Publishing Company: From *The Yearling* (Retitled: "Jody's Discovery") by Marjorie Kinnan Rawlings. Copyright 1938 by Marjorie Kinnan Rawlings; copyright renewed © 1966 by Norton Baskin.

The Rod Serling Trust: "The Monsters Are Due on Maple Street" by Rod Serling. Copyright © 1960 by Rod Serling; copyright renewed © 1988 by Carolyn Serling, Jodi Serling, and Ann Serling. All rights reserved.

Arnie Ten: Illustration for "Stroodle" from *Sniglets* by Rich Hall and Friends. Copyright © 1984 by Arnie Ten.

Third Woman Press, Berkeley, CA: "Abuelito Who" from *My Wicked, Wicked Ways* by Sandra Cisneros. Copyright © 1987 by Sandra Cisneros.

Rosemary A. Thurber: "Snapshot of a Dog" and illustration from *The Middle-Aged Man on the Flying Trapeze* by James Thurber. Copyright © 1935 by James Thurber; copyright renewed © 1963 by Helen W. Thurber and Rosemary A. Thurber. Published by HarperCollins.

Charles E. Tuttle Company: "The Pheasant's Bell" by Kim So-un from *The Story Bag: A Collection of Korean Folk Tales,* translated by Setsu Higashi. Copyright © 1955 by Charles E. Tuttle Company.

University of Arkansas Press: "Interview" from *Story Hour* by Sara Henderson Hay. Copyright © 1982 by Sara Henderson Hay.

University Press of New England: "The City" from *Poems 1934-1969* by David Ignatow. Copyright © 1970 by David Ignatow.

Viking Penguin, a division of Penguin Books USA Inc.: *The Summer of the Swans* by Betsy Byars. Copyright © 1970 by Betsy Byars.

A. P. Watt Ltd. on behalf of The Trustees of the Robert Graves Copyright Trust: "Perseus" from *Greek Gods and Heroes* by Robert Graves. Copyright © 1960 by Robert Graves.

Charlotte Zolotow: "Scene" from *River Winding: Poems by Charlotte Zolotow.* Text copyright © 1970 by Charlotte Zolotow.

UNIT 1 ◆ TEACHING GUIDE

A GALLERY OF CHARACTERS

OVERVIEW OF THE UNIT

Of all the elements of literature, none is more important than character. This anthology begins with a unit on character not only because it is an easy way to introduce the study of literature, but also because it is the most natural. The unit presents characters from fiction and nonfiction, from novels (including fantasy), biography, and autobiography. Many of these characters are young people with whom students can readily identify and sympathize.

The unit introduces, in a very simple way, the literary technique of **characterization**. Students should be able to describe how writers make their characters come alive. The Introduction on page 1 lists six methods writers use to reveal character. The study of characterization in this unit prepares students for Unit Three, Short Stories, which focuses on the elements of the short story, including the essential element of character.

CHARACTER TYPES

In stories from around the world, certain **character types** appear again and again. Some of these general types will be familiar to students from television, from movies, from comic strips, and, of course, from books. Before you start the unit, you might talk about characters. Students may know more about character types than you would expect.

1. The Hero. The hero (either male or female) usually undergoes a complex adventure that demands a show of strength and courage. (Unit 2, Quests, focuses on this part of the hero's story.) The hero embodies traits that we value and aspire to. In traditional myths, the hero is superhuman and has magic powers. Superman, Batman, Wonder Woman, and Hercules are examples.

2. The Villain. We shudder as we encounter this totally evil, diabolical character. (The shudder is pleasurable, for we know that the villain on a printed page or movie screen cannot harm us.) The villain embodies character traits we shun, such as selfishness, greed, and cruelty. The Wicked Witch in *The Wizard of Oz,* Darth Vader in *Star Wars,* the aliens that Captain Kirk faces in *Star Trek,* the wicked stepmothers in "Snow White" and "Hansel and Gretel"—students should have no trouble thinking of villains.

3. The Ordinary Person. The everyday problems and adventures of this character type are certainly not heroic, but they teach us something about what it means to cope with being human and therefore not always perfect. On television, *Roseanne, The Wonder Years,* and the *Cosby Show* are all about ordinary people coping. This character type prevails in juvenile fiction (see, for example, Sara in *The Summer of the Swans*).

Some other character types include the **wise old man or woman**, the **good friend**, the **trickster/rascal hero**, the **young lovers**, the **innocent child**.

OBJECTIVES OF THE UNIT

The aims of this unit for students are
- To monitor their own reading
- To make inferences
- To draw conclusions
- To predict outcomes
- To infer a character's traits
- To recognize methods of character development
- To evaluate characters
- To distinguish fantasy from realism
- To put events in chronological order
- To interpret similes and metaphors
- To use context clues to arrive at word meaning
- To understand dialect
- To write a description
- To dramatize a short work of fiction
- To write creatively and critically about the selections

CONCEPTS AND SKILLS

The following concepts and skills are treated in this unit:

CLOSE READING OF A SELECTION
Guidelines for Close Reading 2
One Reader's Response 3
Looking at Yourself as a Reader 7

THINKING ABOUT WORDS
Using Context Clues 8

FOCUS ON READING AND CRITICAL THINKING
Distinguishing Between Realism and Fantasy 18
Identifying the Sequence of Events 32
Making Inferences 40, 52
Making Generalizations 62

LITERARY ELEMENTS
Character 19, 32, 40, 52

LANGUAGE AND VOCABULARY
Glossary and Footnotes 19
Multiple Meanings 32
Similes 40
Metaphors 53

PLANNING GUIDE

FOR UNIT PLANNING
- Transparencies 1–6: *Audiovisual Resources Binder*
- *Portfolio Assessment and Professional Support Materials*
- Test Generator
- Mastery Tests: Teaching Resources A, pp. 75, 77
- Analogy Lessons: Teaching Resources A, pp. 80–88
- Analogy Test: Teaching Resources A, p. 89
- Revision Worksheet: Teaching Resources A, p. 90

SELECTION (Pupil's Page)	TEACHING RESOURCES A (page numbers shown below)								AV BINDER
	Teacher's Notes	Reading Check	Reading Focus	Study Guide	Language Skills	Building Vocabulary	Selection Vocab. Test	Selection Test	Audio-cassette
A GALLERY OF CHARACTERS *Introduction* (p. 1)	1								
Close Reading of a Selection Jean Craighead George from *Julie of the Wolves* (p. 3)	1								
C. S. Lewis *Mr. Tumnus* (p. 10)	2	5	6	7, 8	9, 12	15	17	18	
Ann Petry *Harriet Tubman* (p. 22)	20	23	24	25, 26	27	30	32	33	
Gary Soto *The Jacket* (p. 35)	35	38	39	40, 41	42	45	47	48	
Mark Twain from *The Adventures of Tom Sawyer* (p. 42)	50	53	54	55, 56	57, 60	63	65	66	TAPE 1 SIDE A
John R. Erickson from *Hank the Cowdog* (p. 56)	68				69				

OPPORTUNITIES FOR WRITING

Focus on Personal Narrative
Choosing a Topic 19
Gathering Details 32
Using Chronological Order 41
Using Vivid Language 54
Writing a Personal Narrative 63

CONNECTIONS

Literature and History 34

SPEAKING AND LISTENING

Dramatizing a Story 53
Reading Aloud 56

FINE ART TRANSPARENCIES

Theme: Meeting New People
1 *Summer Evening Harmony*, Beverly Blacksheep
2 *Portrait of the Artist with the Idol*, Paul Gauguin

READER RESPONSE

3 Design a Badge
4 Hi! Let Me Tell You About This Story

LITERARY ELEMENTS

5 Characterization

WRITING PROCESS

6 Writing a Personal Narrative

TRANSPARENCIES

The following unit support materials with specific correlations to literature selections are available in the **Fine Art and Instructional Transparencies with Teacher's Notes and Blackline Masters** section of your *Audiovisual Resources Binder*.

INTRODUCING THE UNIT

1. **Discussing Character Traits.** Make sure students understand what a **character trait** is—a quality such as kindness, shyness, or courage. Have students work in small groups to develop two lists of character traits: good traits and bad traits. When groups have

finished their lists, compile two classroom summary lists on the chalkboard. See if everyone agrees on the classification of traits as either good or bad. (This activity gives practice in the critical thinking skill of classification.)

When the lists of traits are finished, ask for an example of behavior that "shows" each trait. Study with students the **character wheel** in the section Writing About Literature at the back of the book.

2. **Compiling a Gallery of Characters.** Students can work in small groups or as a class to list memorable characters. Suggest they consider characters from books, comic strips, television, and movies. Have them sort these into categories—perhaps good guys and bad guys, animals, superhuman beings, successful people, strange people, lovable people, and others.

3. **Discussing Famous Real-Life Characters.** Have students name some men and women—past or present—and tell in a sentence or two what they admire about each person. Students might select ten favorites to learn more about.

4. **Writing About Character.** For advanced classes, ask students to write a single paragraph about a real-life person they know and admire. Ask them to explain why they admire the person and to give at least one example of the behavior they admire.

PORTFOLIO ASSESSMENT

Suggestions for use of portfolios as support for this unit are described in the *Portfolio Assessment and Professional Support Materials* booklet accompanying this program. Specific suggestions are provided for a variety of student projects that may be suitable for inclusion in a portfolio. In addition, copying masters are provided for guides that may be used for evaluation and assessment of student projects.

SELECTION NOTES

Following are vocabulary lists of words from each selection that are included in the Building Vocabulary Worksheets and Selection Vocabulary Tests; Reading Check tests (which are also available in blackline masters); and answers to questions in the Language and Vocabulary sections that follow the selections.

"Mr. Tumnus" (page 10)
Vocabulary

inquisitive	reign(s)	bawl(ed)	heartily
melancholy	cavern(s)	lull(ing)	
eternal	distress	wretched	

Reading Check

Have students judge each statement as true or false.
1. Mr. Tumnus asks Lucy if she is a daughter of Eve.   **True**
2. When Lucy arrives in Narnia, it is spring there.   **False**
3. Lucy asks to see Mr. Tumnus's home, but Mr. Tumnus refuses.   **False**
4. Mr. Tumnus had planned to kidnap Lucy.   **True**
5. Mr. Tumnus helps Lucy escape from the White Witch.   **True**

Language and Vocabulary: Glossary and Footnotes (page 19)

1. Bacchus
2. fauns
3. nymphs
4. Silenus
5. dwarfs
6. dryads

"Harriet Tubman" (page 22)
Vocabulary

intention	frantic	legitimate	destination
reluctant	elude	defiant	
retort(ed)	seizure(s)	concealment	

Reading Check

Have students judge each statement as true or false.
1. Harriet Tubman's first escape attempt is a failure.   **True**
2. She turns back because she is afraid.   **False**
3. Harriet uses a song to tell her sister she is running away.   **True**
4. The people on the Underground Railroad help Harriet because they know her well.   **False**
5. At the time of the story, slavery is legal in the state of Pennsylvania.   **False**

Language and Vocabulary: Multiple Meanings (page 32)

Answers will vary. Examples are given.
1. It was a bitter winter. The drink tastes bitter. Gilbert is a bitter loser.
2. The fence post is broken. Do not post signs. The soldier left his post. He went to post a letter.
3. The dog's bark is frightening. Birch bark makes good kindling. Ships are sometimes called barks.
4. Each new blow sent the boxer to the mat. Lucinda will blow out the birthday candles.
5. Apples and tomatoes are in the produce section. The singer will produce three new records. (Different pronunciations)
6. The strong wind stripped the trees of leaves. Please wind the clock. (Different pronunciations)

"The Jacket" (page 35)
Vocabulary

profile	terrorist	gossip	shrivel(ed)	casual(ly)

Reading Check

Ask students to respond with short answers.
1. What kind of jacket does the boy want?   **A black leather jacket with studs**
2. What color is his jacket?   **Olive green (the color of guacamole)**
3. How does the new jacket fit him?   **It is far too big.**
4. How does he feel when he wears the jacket to school for the first time?   **Embarrassed**
5. Who is the narrator's "ugly brother"?   **His jacket**

Language and Vocabulary: Similes (page 40)

Answers will vary. Sample answers are given.
1. a. He is comparing himself to a young tree.
   b. Responses will vary. He is probably very thin with long skinny arms and legs, like a young tree's branches.
2. a. The girls are compared to loose flowers.
   b. Responses will vary. He probably thinks they are beautiful and fragile and colorful. (Dust would suggest deadness, emptiness, grayness.)
3. a. He compares his forearms to the necks of turtles.
   b. Responses will vary. They are probably long and very skinny.

"The Adventures of Tom Sawyer" (page 42)

Vocabulary

intervene(ing)	exertion(s)	impulse	yield(ed)
captivity	admirable	jubilant	
vague	compensation(s)	succession	

Reading Check

Have students supply a word or phrase to complete these sentences. Wording of answers may vary.
1. First, Tom tells Aunt Polly that he has a _____. **mortified toe**
2. Aunt Polly uses a silk thread to _____. **pull out Tom's loose tooth**
3. Tom trades _____ for Huckleberry Finn's tick. **his tooth**
4. As his punishment, Tom must sit next to _____. **Becky Thatcher** or **the new girl**
5. On his slate, Tom writes this message to Becky: _____. **"I love you."**

Language and Vocabulary: Metaphors (page 53)

1. a. *Throned* suggests a comparison with a king.
   b. He runs the classroom as if he is king. He probably gives orders and demands obedience and respect.
2. a. Study is compared to the buzzing of bees
   b. Students might be saying their lessons or reading out loud in low voices. Notice that *buzz* is onomatopoetic.

Student Learning Options

A Gallery of Characters

1. Picturing a Character
Ask students to select the characters they like best in the stories in the unit and to draw pictures of them. As an alternative to drawing, have students locate in newspapers or magazines pictures of people who remind them of their favorite characters. Students can explain why the people in the pictures seem to have the same traits as the characters they select.

2. Playing the "Facts" Game
Have students work in groups to draw up twenty factual questions based on the stories in the unit. One student from each group takes the questions to each of the other groups and asks them the questions. The group with the highest number of correct answers wins.

3. Making a Vocabulary Chart
Let students work in groups of three or four to locate in the stories all of the words that they are not familiar with. Then ask three or four students to make a master list and to create a vocabulary chart with words and definitions. The chart can stay on display in the classroom, and students can add to it in future units.

4. Designing Costumes
Ask students to select characters from the unit and to design costumes for them. You can also have students find in magazines clothing that they think the characters might like to wear.

5. Selecting a Personal Symbol
Ask students to select characters they like and then to select an object, color, word, or gesture they feel symbolizes the characters. Students may then present their symbols to the class, explaining why they chose them.

6. Exploring Setting
The setting of *Julie of the Wolves* plays an important part in the story. Have students look up information about the climate and geography of Alaska for a report to the class.

7. Drawing a Map
Using information they glean from reading "Mr. Tumnus," students can draw a map of Narnia. Put the maps on display in the classroom.

8. Writing a Letter
Harriet Tubman wants to say goodbye to her sister Mary, but she does not get a chance to see her before she leaves. Have students write a letter from Harriet to Mary, telling about her escape and her reasons for wanting to be free.

9. Brainstorming Suggestions
Have students work in groups of three or four to brainstorm ideas about how the boy in "The Jacket" could decorate the jacket to make it "cool." If students have old jackets their parents are willing to let them use for the project, they might decorate jackets and show them off for the class.

10. Moving Characters Through Time
Ask students to imagine what Mark Twain's characters would be like today. Have them write brief character sketches that include information on the characters' favorite movies, TV shows, sports, video games, foods, songs, and ways to spend Saturday afternoon.

11. Choosing a New Title
Ask students to select new titles for "Hank the Cowdog" and to explain why each title is appropriate. Before they begin work on this option, you might want to discuss characteristics of a good title.

PORTFOLIO ASSESSMENT

Suggestions for journal inclusions are found in the "Before You Read" section of selections in the unit. In addition to including journals in their portfolios, students may want to write a collection of sketches of the main characters in the selections. Collections may be organized in scrapbook fashion, complete with mounted illustrations, pressed flowers, photographs, decorative crafts, doilies, or other forms of memorabilia that remind students of the character. Consult with students to help them plan inclusions for their portfolios for the unit. Suggest a means of self-assessment. (For more information on student portfolios, see the *Portfolio Assessment and Professional Support Materials* booklet in your teaching resources.)

VISUAL CONNECTIONS

According to Mexican tradition, St. John's Eve (June 23) is celebrated with bonfires (to commemorate St. John the Baptist). This young girl is Dorotea Herrera at the age of twelve. The daughter of Hurd's foreman, she is on her way to a church festival.

In the British Isles, huge bonfires are lit on June 21 to mark the summer solstice. In both traditions, fire symbolizes the triumph of light over darkness, life over death.

If you create a character in class (see opposite), you might base her on this young girl. Have students describe what this girl looks like, what she might say to the horseman in the distance, what she is thinking as she looks at the candle lit for the holyday, what she is going to do next, and what her friends think of her. Ask students how many sources of light they can find in the painting. (The candle; the house lights; the setting sun)

About the Artist
Peter Hurd (1904–1984) was born in New Mexico and was a rancher there. Another of Hurd's paintings is on page 361. Some of his murals can be seen in the post office in Dallas, Texas.

The Eve of St. John by Peter Hurd (1960). Tempera on board.

San Diego Museum of Art.
(Gift of Mr. and Mrs. Norton S. Walbridge)

UNIT ONE

A Gallery of Characters

Why do we read? For many readers, the answer to that question is, "To meet new people. To have new experiences. To get information." This unit, like a picture gallery, gives you portraits of several people. One character is a real person who led a dangerous, heroic life. One is a real person whose life is very ordinary. Two are memorable fictional characters. One is even a dog—one of the many unforgettable animal characters in literature.

Writers create lifelike characters for us in six ways:

1. By describing a character's appearance.
2. By letting us hear the character talk.
3. By telling us what the character thinks.
4. By showing us the character's actions.
5. By letting us know how others respond to the character.
6. By telling us directly what the character is like (good, evil, kind, and so on).

Watch for the ways the characters in this unit come alive. Do any of them remind you of people you know—or of yourself?

TEACHING RESOURCES A
Teacher's Notes, p. 1

INTRODUCING A GALLERY OF CHARACTERS

Throughout this unit, encourage students to talk about characters from books, movies, television, and real life. Discussing what they admire or dislike about these characters makes a good introduction to the study of memorable characters in literature.

Here are some kinds of characters that students often admire. Ask them to name some people—either real or fictional—in each category. They may also want to think of other categories of people they respect:

1. A person who excels in some field of work
2. A person who gets what he or she wants
3. A person who helps others
4. A person who creates something new
5. A person who succeeds despite overwhelming odds

You could also use the list on this page to work with students to create a description of a character they have imagined collectively. You might start by saying: Give me three adjectives that could describe someone's appearance.

FOCUS/MOTIVATION

Building on Prior Knowledge. Ask students to give some examples of the traditional Native Alaskan way of life. (Students should mention igloos, hunting, fishing, kayaks.) They should be able to locate Alaska and northern Canada as the home of these native peoples. (Note that many have moved to big cities.)

Ask students to tell what they know about wolves. (They are wild, look like dogs, live in groups, and hunt animals for food.)

Establishing a Purpose for Reading. Ask students to predict from the title what they think the story will be about.

Prereading Journal. If you want to assign a journal entry, ask students to imagine that they are alone in the wilderness shown on pages 4–5. Have them write about what they could do to survive.

TEACHING RESOURCES A
Teacher's Notes, p. 1

Close Reading OF A SELECTION

When you read, you may be sitting quietly, not making a sound. But if you are reading actively, a lot is going on in your head. There are different purposes for reading. When you read a science textbook, for example, you usually read for facts. Your purpose may be to learn how plants convert water and carbon dioxide into sugars and starches. When you read a math book, you may be looking for the information you will need to solve a specific problem.

You may have more than one purpose in reading. You can read a story for pure enjoyment. You can also read to enrich your understanding of other people and yourself.

Guidelines for Close Reading

1. Read actively. Ask questions as you read. Ask about unfamiliar words. Ask about clues that the writer drops. Ask about language or situations that puzzle you.
2. Make predictions as you read. Ask yourself, "What is going to happen next?"
3. Relate what you are reading to your own life and experience. Put yourself in the character's place. Ask yourself how you might act in a similar situation.
4. Put all your responses together. Answer the questions you raised during reading. Find out if your predictions were accurate. Think about the main idea of the selection. Think about your responses to the characters and events.

Here is an excerpt from a novel called *Julie of the Wolves*. The comments in the margin show how one reader has responded to the selection. Note that the reader's very first question has to do with the book's title. If you wish, cover up these comments and take notes of your own as you read. Then compare your responses with the printed comments.

2   A Gallery of Characters

LIBRARY LINK
As students begin reading the selections in the textbook, you might want to suggest that they keep a list of books, authors, or subjects that capture their attention. When students show interest in a particular author, suggest other books or selections they might want to read.

When students enjoy a chapter from a longer book, encourage them to check the library for the complete work. You might suggest that students share information about the availability of library books or pass books from student to student.

When you read nonfiction selections, you might remind students to jot down ideas about subjects they would like to know more about so that when they are searching for writing ideas or are reading related material in other subject areas, they can refer to their notes for ideas.

1. BACKGROUND
These are the opening pages of the novel. Wasting no time, the author plunks the reader into a suspenseful, dramatic situation. Only later do we learn that Julie (Miyax's English name) is thirteen and running away from an arranged marriage. She is trying to reach San Francisco, where her pen pal lives. Note how the author hooks our interest by purposely withholding this information.

2. LITERARY ELEMENTS:
Setting
Which details of setting create a sense of isolation and fear? Barren slope, three hundred miles, eight hundred miles, no roads, winds scream.

---

from
Julie of the Wolves
JEAN CRAIGHEAD GEORGE

Miyax pushed back the hood of her sealskin parka and looked at the Arctic sun. It was a yellow disc in a lime-green sky, the colors of six o'clock in the evening and the time when the wolves awoke. Quietly she put down her cooking pot and crept to the top of a dome-shaped frost heave, one of the many earth buckles that rise and fall in the crackling cold of the Arctic winter. Lying on her stomach, she looked across a vast lawn of grass and moss and focused her attention on the wolves she had come upon two sleeps ago. They were wagging their tails as they awoke and saw each other.

Her hands trembled and her heartbeat quickened, for she was frightened, not so much of the wolves, who were shy and many harpoon-shots away, but because of her desperate predicament. Miyax was lost. She had been lost without food for many sleeps on the North Slope of Alaska. The barren slope stretches for three hundred miles from the Brooks Range to the Arctic Ocean, and for more than eight hundred miles from the Chukchi to the Beaufort Sea. No roads cross it; ponds and lakes freckle its immensity. Winds scream across it, and the view in every direction is exactly the same. Somewhere in this cosmos was Miyax; and the very life in her body, its spark and warmth, depended upon these wolves for survival. And she was not so sure they would help.

The Eskimo peoples of Alaska are known for their carving of ivory figures, such as the walrus shown here.
© Chris Arend. Courtesy of Alaska State Council/Alaska Stock Images.

ONE READER'S RESPONSE

How do you say this name? Is she an Eskimo? Who is Julie? 1

A lime-green sky is weird.

What is a frost heave? (OK. Defined here.)
Is she alone?
Not a lawn like ours. This is the Arctic.

Two sleeps? Must mean two nights.

She's scared.

Why is she lost? I can't imagine going without food for several days!

A horrible place to be. How did she get here? 2

Wow—I thought wolves ate people. How could she be dependent on them for food?

Close Reading of a Selection

1
Caribou are a kind of deer related to the reindeer.

2. GUIDED READING:
Making Inferences
Notice how this reader makes inferences about the character of Miyax based on her actions.

Close Reading
OF A SELECTION

How can you tell a wolf you need food?

She is an Eskimo.

But how did he "tell" the wolf?

Well, I see she doesn't know either.

So her father has disappeared. Why is she in this terrible place? Did she get lost hunting? Was she abandoned?

2 *She must know a lot about animals. She is also patient—two days watching wolves!*

Miyax stared hard at the regal black wolf, hoping to catch his eye. She must somehow tell him that she was starving and ask him for food. This could be done, she knew, for her father, an Eskimo hunter, had done so. One year he had camped near a wolf den while on a hunt. When a month had passed and her father had seen no game, he told the leader of the wolves that he was hungry and needed food. The next night the wolf called him from far away and her father went to him and found **1** a freshly killed caribou. Unfortunately, Miyax's father never explained to her how he had told the wolf of his needs. And not long afterward he paddled his kayak into the Bering Sea to hunt for seal, and he never returned.

She had been watching the wolves for two days, trying to discern which of their sounds and movements expressed good will and friendship. Most animals had such signals. The little Arctic ground squirrels flicked their tails sideways to notify others of their kind that they were friendly. By imitating this signal with her forefinger, Miyax had lured many a squirrel to her hand. If she could discover such a gesture for the wolves,

Migrating Alaskan caribou.

©Larry B. Jennings/Photo Researchers

4 A Gallery of Characters

EXTENSION AND ENRICHMENT

Speaking. Have students work in pairs to create voices for Lucy and Mr. Tumnus. Then have them read aloud parts of the dialogue on pages 12–13 or 15–17 in the voices they have created.

Interpreting Meanings

6. Some may predict that the White Witch finds out about Lucy and punishes the faun by turning him into a horse or statue as he foresees on page 16. (This is, in fact, what happens in the novel.) Others may predict that the faun regrets he has let Lucy go and goes through the wardrobe to catch her.

7. The trip to the cave is more relaxed as Lucy is unaware of her danger. The journey back to the lamppost is more exciting to the reader and more dangerous for the characters because they both fear the Wicked Witch.

8. Possible answers: Spare Oom and War Drobe; the titles of Mr. Tumnus's books; the scene where Mr. Tumnus's tears make a puddle; Lucy's words "You are the nicest faun I've ever met." (She's never met any others.)

Applying Meanings

9. Students may also mention the tesseract that leads to Camazotz in *A Wrinkle in Time* (a nightmare world), *Tom's Midnight Garden* (a wish world), *Gulliver's Travels* (both nightmare and wish worlds). Remind them also of books like Maurice Sendak's *In the Night Kitchen*.

"This is the land of Narnia, . . . all that lies between the lamppost and the great castle of Cair Paravel on the eastern sea."

Illustration by Pauline Baynes.

7. Contrast the trip to the cave with the journey back to the lamppost. Which journey is more relaxed? Which is more exciting? Which is more dangerous?

8. One humorous picture in the story is that of a shaggy faun serving a very proper English tea. Did you find any other details in the story funny?

APPLYING MEANINGS

9. What other stories or movies do you know of in which a character enters another world or dimension? What kind of world does each character discover? (Is it a wish world or a nightmare world?) Think of Alice in Wonderland and Dorothy in Oz for two starters.

Focus on Reading

DISTINGUISHING BETWEEN REALISM AND FANTASY

A **realistic detail** is a true-to-life detail that could be found in the real world. A **fantastic detail** is one that could never be found in real life. *Wearing a red woolen muffler* is a realistic detail. We could see it in real life. But *a faun wearing a red woolen muffler* is a detail that could exist only in fantasy.

A fantasy like *The Lion, the Witch and the Wardrobe* includes both realistic and fantastic details. The realistic details, like snow falling in a wood, make the setting believable. But the fantastic details, like an endless winter controlled by a witch, make

ART LINK

Have students compare the illustrations of Narnia, Mr. Tumnus, and Lucy on pages 11 and 18. What elements are in both illustrations? Which picture has the most illustrative details? Which seems more fantastic? Which do students like best? You might encourage students to create their own illustrations of the meeting of the child and the faun, either small drawings on their own or a mural with a group of students.

---

the story strange and exciting. Fantastic details spark your imagination.

Write down three fantastic details from this story. Then write down three realistic details that make the setting seem familiar. Add two details of your own telling how you visualize Narnia. Are they fantastic or realistic?

Literary Elements

CHARACTER

At one point in the story, Mr. Tumnus calls himself "a bad faun." Is he really bad? Think of what Mr. Tumnus says, where he lives, and how he behaves. Which of the following words would you use to describe Mr. Tumnus's **character**?

1. Friendly
2. Honest
3. Weak
4. Home-loving
5. Brave
6. Fearful
7. Deceitful
8. Company-loving

Mr. Tumnus is a fantasy character who could not live in the world as we know it. Still, do you think people like him live in our world?

Language and Vocabulary

GLOSSARY AND FOOTNOTES

Here is a list of characters from myths and fairy tales referred to in "Mr. Tumnus." Use the story clues, the Glossary, and the footnotes to match each character with the description on the next page. When you are finished, you might enjoy illustrating each description.

fauns (p. 10)
Bacchus (p. 14)
dwarfs (p. 14)
dryads (p. 14)
nymphs (p. 13)
Silenus (p. 13)

1. The god of wine: _____.
2. Creatures that are part man and part goat: _____.
3. Spiritlike creatures of nature who live in the mountains, water, and woods: _____.
4. Leader of the fauns, who has horse's ears and a tail: _____.
5. Very tiny men who are skilled at mining and crafting precious stones and metals: _____.
6. Beautiful woodland spirits who live in trees: _____.

Focus on Personal Narrative

CHOOSING A TOPIC

How do you think Lucy would have told the story of her meeting with Mr. Tumnus? What do you think Lucy's personal account of her remarkable adventure would have been like?

In a **personal narrative,** you tell about an important experience in your own life. To share this experience, you use details to tell about events in the order in which they happened. In this kind of writing, you normally tell about real events rather than made-up or fantastic ones.

When you choose a topic for a personal narrative, here are guidelines to follow:

1. Write about an experience you remember well.
2. Write about an experience that was important to you.
3. Write about an experience that is not too private to share.

Mr. Tumnus 19

FOCUS ON READING
Distinguishing Between Realism and Fantasy
Some fantastic details: a wardrobe that leads to a fantasy world; a talking faun; a lamppost in the middle of a forest; a White Witch; permanent winter; trees that can spy. Some realistic details: the forest; the snow; the cave furnishings; the tea; Lucy.

Details that students add will vary. Encourage their imaginations.

LITERARY ELEMENTS
Character
Answers may vary about which traits apply. A case can be made for all of them.
1. Friendly. The faun's original friendliness is part of a strategy to trap Lucy, so it's difficult to know at this point if he's genuinely friendly.
2. Honest. He shows a strong honest streak. Although he attempts deceit, he can't go through with it.
3. Weak. The faun is weak in agreeing to serve the White Witch and abducting the innocent Lucy.
4. Home-loving. His cave and the tea he serves show he appreciates the comforts of home.
5. Brave. Despite his fears of the White Witch, the faun does bravely help Lucy escape.

6. Fearful. He is certainly afraid of the White Witch.
7. Deceitful. At first he deceives Lucy, but his later honesty shows that he's not truly deceitful.
8. Company-loving. He entertains Lucy with great ease and has a chair for a friend, so it seems as if he does like company.

Many people share Mr. Tumnus's complex character. All of us probably hover at times between fear and bravery, honesty and deceit.

LANGUAGE AND VOCABULARY
Glossary and Footnotes
For answers, see the **Teaching Guide** at the beginning of the unit.

FOCUS ON PERSONAL NARRATIVE
Choosing a Topic
If students are having trouble listing memories, you may want to give them time to talk with relatives or friends about memorable events. Students might also look through family photo albums or watch home videos if available.

Start to find a topic for a personal narrative by listing ideas and memories on a chart like the one below. You may change one or more of the categories if you wish. Save your notes.

Meetings	_____
Scares	_____
Travels	_____
Animals	_____
Holidays	_____

Illustration by Pauline Baynes.

C. S. Lewis (1898–1963) was born in Belfast, Ireland. As children, Lewis and his brother pretended that each one "owned" a country. Lewis's brother ruled a real country—India. Lewis, who loved to draw "dressed animals," possessed an imaginary place—Animal-Land.

When Lewis was seven, his family moved to a very large house in the country, much like the old professor's house in *The Lion, the Witch and the Wardrobe*. The "New House," as Lewis always called it, was one of the most important places in his life.

"The New House is almost a major character in my story," Lewis once wrote. "I am the product of long corridors, empty sunlit rooms, upstairs indoor silences, attics explored in solitude, distant noises of gurgling cisterns and pipes, and the noise of wind under the tiles. Also, of endless books. . . . In the seemingly endless rainy afternoons, I took volume after volume from the shelves."

This imaginative boy grew up to become a respected medieval scholar and writer. One day, at the age of forty, he found himself writing a story for children. The idea for the story came from a picture he had carried in his head for a long time: "a faun carrying an umbrella and parcels in a snowy wood." The story, of course, became the award-winning novel *The Lion, the Witch and the Wardrobe*. Its success led to six more adventures of Narnia. Lewis said the Narnia books should be read in this order: (1) *The Magician's Nephew*, (2) *The Lion, the Witch and the Wardrobe*, (3) *The Horse and His Boy*, (4) *Prince Caspian*, (5) *The Voyage of the "Dawn Treader,"* (6) *The Silver Chair*, and (7) *The Last Battle*. Of the many books C. S. Lewis wrote, *The Chronicles of Narnia* have proved to be the most memorable and the most popular.

Behind the Scenes

"It all began with a picture..."

You must not believe all that authors tell you about how they wrote their books. This is not because they mean to tell lies. It is because a man writing a story is too excited about the story itself to sit back and notice how he is doing it. In fact, that might stop the works; just as, if you start thinking about how you tie your tie, the next thing is that you find you can't tie it. And afterward, when the story is finished, he has forgotten a good deal of what writing it was like.

One thing I am sure of. All my seven Narnian books, and my three science fiction books, began with seeing pictures in my head. At first they were not a story, just pictures. The *Lion* all began with a picture of a faun carrying an umbrella and parcels in a snowy wood. This picture had been in my mind since I was about sixteen. Then one day, when I was about forty, I said to myself: "Let's try to make a story about it."

At first I had very little idea how the story would go. But then suddenly Aslan [a noble lion, the hero of the Narnia stories] came bounding into it. I think I had been having a good many dreams of lions about that time. Apart from that, I don't know where the lion came from or why he came. But once he was there he pulled the whole story together, and soon he pulled the six other Narnian stories in after him.

So you see that, in a sense, I know very little about how this story was born. That is, I don't know where the pictures came from. And I don't believe anyone knows exactly how he "makes things up." Making up is a very mysterious thing. When you "have an idea" could you tell anyone exactly *how* you thought of it?

—C. S. Lewis

TEACHING RESOURCES A

Teacher's Notes, p. 20
Reading Check, p. 23
Reading Focus, p. 24
Study Guide, pp. 25, 26
Language Skills, p. 27
Building Vocabulary, p. 30
Selection Vocabulary Test, p. 32
Selection Test, p. 33

VISUAL CONNECTIONS

When artists paint a portrait, they try to express the sitter's personality. The colors in the portrait and the clothing the subject is wearing contribute to the emotional effect.

1. What characteristics of Tubman's are expressed in this portrait? (List some.)

2. How do the colors in the portrait affect you? (Are they vibrant and bright, or solemn and dark?)

3. If you had to compose a caption for this portrait, what would you call it? (You might find a caption in the biography.)

About the Artist
Robert Savon Pious (1908–1983) was born in Meridian, Mississippi. He moved to St. Louis in 1914 and later to Chicago. There he attended the Chicago Art Institute while working full time in the pressroom of a newspaper. Pious's primary interest was in portrait painting, but he also worked as an illustrator and cartoonist; during the 1940s he worked for the U.S. Office of War. Like many African American artists, Pious came under the influence of the great Augusta Savage (see her sculpture on page 351).

OBJECTIVES

Students will infer a character's traits and cite actions that exemplify each trait. They will list a series of events in chronological order and evaluate a biographer's ability to make the subject "come alive."

TRANSPARENCIES 1 & 2

Fine Art
Theme: *Meeting New People* – invites students to examine artwork that reveals specific recognizable character traits.

Harriet Tubman

ANN PETRY

Harriet Tubman by Robert Savon Pious (1951). Oil on canvas.

22 A Gallery of Characters

FOCUS/MOTIVATION

Building on Prior Knowledge. The headnote gives information about the history of slavery in the United States. Have students share additional details. The nation was divided into free states, where slavery was illegal, and slave states. The question of whether slavery should be extended into the Western territories divided the nation from 1820 to 1860 and was one cause of the Civil War. In 1849 when this story takes place, a runaway slave crossing into a free state was considered free. By 1850, however, federal fugitive slave laws decreed that runaway slaves were not safe until they reached Canada.

Establishing a Purpose for Reading. Discuss these questions in class: Was it easy to run away from slavery? Why didn't everybody run away? What made escape so difficult? Have students read to discover the qualities of character that helped a runaway slave reach freedom.

Before You Read

This true story takes place during the mid-1800s in the United States, when most Southern states still allowed the practice of slavery. Slavery, or the complete ownership of one person by another person, had been established in the United States in 1619. (Slavery was not abolished until 1865.) The early slaves were brought over to the New World from Africa. They and their descendants had to work hard for their owners and had no rights of their own.

Eventually, many Americans who hated slavery started the Underground Railroad. This was not a railroad and neither was it underground. It was made up of people from the North and South who offered shelter, food, and protection to slaves escaping to freedom in the North. To keep the route secret, the organization used railroad terms, such as "stations" for the houses along the way and "conductors" for the people who offered help.

Harriet Tubman was a slave who became one of the most famous conductors on the Railroad. She helped more than three hundred men, women, and children along the perilous road to freedom.

This is an extract from a *biography*, a story of someone's life. We are introduced to Harriet Tubman when she is a field hand at the Brodas plantation in Maryland. As a young girl, Harriet had received a crushing blow when she refused to help tie up a runaway slave. The injury left a deep scar on her forehead; it also made her fall asleep quite suddenly and uncontrollably. Harriet's husband, John Tubman, was a free man. But, as this excerpt opens, he has made it clear that he will turn his wife in if she tries to escape. Harriet is tormented by fears of being sold off to slave owners farther South.

Before you read, write in your journal how you would feel if you were held in slavery. What would you be unable to do? What dangers and sorrows would you and your family face?

1. GUIDED READING:
Understanding Word Derivation
Write the word *abolitionist* on the board, and show how it comes from *abolish*. Quakers, free African Americans, and others who worked to abolish slavery called themselves abolitionists.

2. BACKGROUND
Note that this excerpt describes Harriet's own journey to freedom. She did not become a conductor on the Underground Railroad until later when she returned to the south to lead others to freedom.

3. BACKGROUND
Students may not understand how there could have been free African Americans at the time of slavery. John Tubman, Harriet's husband, was free because his parents were freed by their master at the time of his death. Later in the story Harriet is sheltered by a family of free African Americans. If they had enough money (which was nearly impossible), some slaves could purchase their freedom.

Prereading Journal. Have students read the last paragraph in the headnote on page 23 and then respond to the headnote questions in their journals.

READING THE SELECTION
The selection is on level; average and more advanced classes should read it without difficulty. You might read aloud in class through Harriet's return with her three brothers (page 26, top right column) and ask students to read the rest of the selection silently in class or as homework. With slower classes, read the whole story aloud in class.

1. GUIDED READING:
Making Inferences
What do you infer the woman is talking about? From the headnote, students should be able to infer that she's referring to Harriet's escape.

2. GUIDED READING:
Understanding Literal and Figurative Language
Note that the expression "slave driver," used literally here, has taken on the more general meaning of a hard or merciless taskmaster. A teacher who gives three hours of homework, for example, is called a "slave driver."

3. BACKGROUND
At any time a master could sell his slaves, since they were considered simply property. Husbands and wives, parents and children, brothers and sisters were often separated in this way and were never reunited.

Language and Vocabulary

Many English words have multiple meanings. In the third paragraph of this story, for example, the writer says there is fear "in the quarter." The definition of *quarter* in this context is not "a coin worth twenty-five cents." Here, *quarter* means "a district or section of a town or city." This quarter is the place on the plantation where the slaves live. In your reading, when you come across a word that has more than one meaning, the word's context will help you decide which meaning is intended.

One day, in 1849, when Harriet was working in the fields, near the edge of the road, a white woman wearing a faded sunbonnet went past, driving a wagon. She stopped the wagon, and watched Harriet for a few minutes. Then she spoke to her, asked her what her name was, and how she had acquired the deep scar on her forehead.

Harriet told her the story of the blow she had received when she was a girl. After that, whenever the woman saw her in the fields, she stopped to talk to her. She told Harriet that she lived on a farm, near Bucktown. Then one day she said, not looking at Harriet, but looking instead at the overseer,¹ far off at the edge of the fields, "If you ever need any help, Harriet, ever need any help, why you let me know."

That same year the young heir to the Brodas² estate died. Harriet mentioned the fact of his death to the white woman in the faded sunbonnet, the next time she saw her. She told her of the panic-stricken talk in the quarter, told her that the slaves were afraid that the master, Dr. Thompson, would start selling them. She said that Doc Thompson no longer permitted any of them to hire their time.³ The woman nodded her head, clucked to the horse, and drove off, murmuring, "If you ever need any help——"

The slaves were right about Dr. Thompson's <u>intention</u>. He began selling slaves almost immediately. Among the first

---

1. **overseer:** a person who supervises workers; in this case, a slave driver.
2. Edward Brodas, the previous owner of the plantation, died and left his property to his heir, who was not yet old enough to manage it. In the meantime, the plantation was placed in the hands of the boy's guardian, Dr. Thompson.
3. **hire their time:** Some slave owners allowed their slaves to hire themselves out, for pay, to other plantation owners who needed extra help.

24 A Gallery of Characters

MEETING INDIVIDUAL NEEDS

ESL/LEP • Model the pronunciation of the word *heir*, calling attention to the silent *h*. Write the word *air* on the chalkboard and point out that the two words are pronounced exactly the same. You may want to ask the class to define the word *heir* (a person who inherits or receives the property of someone who has died).

---

ones sold were two of Harriet Tubman's sisters. They went South with the chain gang[4] on a Saturday.

1 When Harriet heard of the sale of her sisters, she knew that the time had finally come when she must leave the plantation. She was reluctant to attempt the long trip North alone, not because of John Tub-
2 man's threat to betray her, but because she was afraid she might fall asleep somewhere along the way and so would be caught immediately.

She persuaded three of her brothers to go with her. Having made certain that John was asleep, she left the cabin quietly, and met her brothers at the edge of the plan-
3 tation. They agreed that she was to lead the way, for she was more familiar with the woods than the others.

The three men followed her, crashing through the underbrush, frightening themselves, stopping constantly to say, "What was that?" or "Someone's coming."

She thought of Ben[5] and how he had said, "Any old body can go through a woods crashing and mashing things down like a cow." She said sharply, "Can't you boys go quieter? Watch where you're going!"

One of them grumbled, "Can't see in the dark. Ain't got cat's eyes like you."

"You don't need cat's eyes," she retorted. "On a night like this, with all the stars out, it's not black dark. Use your own eyes."

She supposed they were doing the best they could, but they moved very slowly. She kept getting so far ahead of them that she had to stop and wait for them to catch up with her, lest they lose their way. Their progress was slow, uncertain. Their feet got tangled in every vine. They tripped over fallen logs, and once one of them fell flat on his face. They jumped, startled, at the most ordinary sounds: the murmur of the wind in the branches of the trees, the twittering of a bird. They kept turning around, looking back.

They had not gone more than a mile when she became aware that they had stopped. She turned and went back to them. She could hear them whispering. One of them called out, "Hat!"

"What's the matter? We haven't got time to keep stopping like this."

"We're going back."

"No," she said firmly. "We've got a good start. If we move fast and move quiet——"

Then all three spoke at once. They said the same thing, over and over, in frantic hurried whispers, all talking at once.

They told her that they had changed their minds. Running away was too dangerous. Someone would surely see them and recognize them. By morning, the master would know they had "took off." Then the handbills advertising them would be posted all over Dorchester County. The patterollers[6] would search for them. Even

---

4. **chain gang:** literally, a gang of people (slaves or prisoners) chained together.
5. Ben is Harriet's father. Her mother is called Old Rit.
6. **patterollers:** patrollers.

---

1. GUIDED READING:
Making Inferences
What does Harriet's reaction reveal about her character? She is a woman of action; she will not wait until the same thing happens to her.

2. BACKGROUND
These sleeping fits were deep trancelike states that came without warning. Harriet was injured several years before when an overseer threw a two-pound weight after a fleeing slave. The weight hit Harriet in the forehead, leaving her with chronic headaches, sudden sleeping fits, and a deep scar.

3. GUIDED READING:
Drawing Conclusions
What leadership qualities does Harriet show? She has knowledge; she makes decisions; she is determined and willing to take risks to achieve her goal.

HISTORY LINK

To help students understand the long-term impact of slavery in the United States, you might suggest that students make a time line of slavery, beginning with the introduction of slaves in 1619 and ending with the enactment of the constitutional amendments passed after the Civil War. They could include important events on the top line and pertinent people on the bottom line. Have small groups of students present what they learn to the class, and as they do, note the length of time and the many people involved before slavery was abolished and lasting freedoms and civil liberties were affirmed.

1. GUIDED READING:
Understanding Motives
Why do you think the brothers became angry? They probably were ashamed that a woman was braver than they, but were afraid to express these feelings. Perhaps they sincerely feared for her safety and wanted to protect her.

2. GUIDED READING:
Using Context Clues
What does pinioning *mean?* "To stop someone by binding or tying the arms." (See the Glossary.)

3. GUIDED READING:
Drawing Conclusions
Is Harriet being fair to her brothers here? Is it a "small risk"? No. The chances of being caught are great; the punishments are cruel.

4. GUIDED READING:
Understanding Main Ideas
Ask students to put this key statement into their own words: "If I can't be free, I'd rather die."

---

if they were lucky enough to elude the patrol, they could not possibly hide from the bloodhounds. The hounds would be baying after them, snuffing through the swamps and the underbrush, zigzagging through the deepest woods. The bloodhounds would surely find them. And everyone knew what happened to a runaway who was caught and brought back alive.

She argued with them. Didn't they know that if they went back they would be sold, if not tomorrow, then the next day, or the next? Sold South. They had seen the chain gangs. Was that what they wanted? Were they going to be slaves for the rest of their lives? Didn't freedom mean anything to them?

"You're afraid," she said, trying to shame them into action. "Go on back. I'm going North alone."

1 Instead of being ashamed, they became angry. They shouted at her, telling her that she was a fool and they would make her go back to the plantation with them. Suddenly they surrounded her, three men, her own brothers, jostling her, push- **2** ing her along, pinioning her arms behind her. She fought against them, wasting her strength, exhausting herself in a furious struggle.

She was no match for three strong men. She said, panting, "All right. We'll go back. I'll go with you."

She led the way, moving slowly. Her **3** thoughts were bitter. Not one of them was willing to take a small risk in order to be free. It had all seemed so perfect, so simple, to have her brothers go with her, sharing the dangers of the trip together, just as a family should. Now if she ever went North, she would have to go alone.

Two days later, a slave working beside Harriet in the fields motioned to her. She bent toward him, listening. He said the water boy had just brought news to the field hands, and it had been passed from one to the other until it reached him. The news was that Harriet and her brothers had been sold to the Georgia trader, and that they were to be sent South with the chain gang that very night.

Harriet went on working but she knew a moment of panic. She would have to go North alone. She would have to start as soon as it was dark. She could not go with the chain gang. She might die on the way, because of those inexplicable sleeping seizures. But then she—how could she run away? She might fall asleep in plain view along the road.

But even if she fell asleep, she thought, the Lord would take care of her. She murmured a prayer, "Lord, I'm going to hold steady onto You and You've got to see me through."

Afterward, she explained her decision to run the risk of going North alone, in these words: "I had reasoned this out in **4** my mind; there was one of two things I had a *right* to, liberty or death; if I could not have one, I would have the other; for no man should take me alive; I should fight for my liberty as long as my strength lasted, and when the time came for me to go, the Lord would let them take me."

26 A Gallery of Characters

GEOGRAPHY LINK
You might want to have a map or globe available so students can locate Harriet's home in Maryland; Georgia, where she would go with the trader; and routes to the north and freedom. You might even have students trace an outline of the eastern United States so they can color code the southern and the northern states as they developed into Union (anti-slavery) and Confederate (pro-slavery) states during the Civil War.

Slave Market in Richmond, Virginia, by Eyre Crowe (1852–1853). Oil on canvas.

Mrs. H. J. Heinz III

VISUAL CONNECTIONS
Slaves wait while the white men make bids to the auctioneer. The slaves have been dressed beautifully by their owners to make them attractive to the buyers. Our attention is drawn to the women and man on the benches; the white men are shadowy figures in the background. Notice the suggestion of separation in the fact that the man is sitting apart. These children might not be with their mothers for long, and if this man is the husband of one of the women, he might soon be forced to part from her. Most slaves were never taught to read and write, so once separated, families usually lost touch forever.

About the Artist
Eyre Crowe (1824–1910) was an English painter and writer who travelled in America for two years. When he was in Richmond he sat inside the slave house waiting for the auction to begin and made a sketch that was the basis of this painting.

At dusk, when the work in the fields was over, she started toward the Big House.[7] She had to let someone know that she was going North, someone she could trust. She no longer trusted John Tubman, and it gave her a lost, lonesome feeling. Her sister Mary worked in the Big House, and she planned to tell Mary that she was going to run away, so someone would know.

As she went toward the house, she saw the master, Doc Thompson, riding up the drive on his horse. She turned aside and went toward the quarter. A field hand had no legitimate reason for entering the kitchen of the Big House—and yet—there must be some way she could leave word so that afterward someone would think about it and know that she had left a message.

As she went toward the quarter, she began to sing. Dr. Thompson reined in his horse, turned around and looked at her. It was not the beauty of her voice that made

---
7. **Big House:** the plantation owner's house.

Harriet Tubman 27

Music Link

Students might want to find out about other spirituals that were popular with slaves in the South. You might suggest that they search through song books or music encyclopedias for selections. If they have access to a large library, they might find a copy of *Folksingers and Folksongs in America* by Ray Lawless, which designates spirituals as religious folk songs.

If you have students who can read music or have access to a piano (a one-finger melody line would suffice), you might have someone play or sing the songs. If students have music class, you might suggest to the music teacher that they learn some spirituals.

1. GUIDED READING:
Interpreting Meaning
Which lines convey Harriet's message to her sister? "I'm going to leave you, / I'm bound for the promised land, / Friends, I'm going to leave you." Many African American spirituals were really "code songs" and they often used the Jews' escape from Egyptian slavery as a metaphor for their own escape from slavery. The Promised Land was Israel in the Bible; to the singers of the spirituals, it was freedom. Crossing the Jordan literally meant crossing the River Jordan to the land of Israel; to the singers of spirituals it meant going North. Harriet Tubman, in fact, was later called Moses, a code name that suggested her identification with the deliverer of the Jews.

---

him turn and watch her, frowning; it was the words of the song that she was singing, and something defiant in her manner, that disturbed and puzzled him.

> 1 When that old chariot comes,
>   I'm going to leave you,
>   I'm bound for the promised land,
>   Friends, I'm going to leave you.
>
>   I'm sorry, friends, to leave you,
>   Farewell! Oh, farewell!
>   But I'll meet you in the morning,
>   Farewell! Oh, farewell!
>
>   I'll meet you in the morning,
>   When I reach the promised land;
>   On the other side of Jordan,
>   For I'm bound for the promised land.

That night when John Tubman was asleep, and the fire had died down in the cabin, she took the ashcake that had been baked for their breakfast, and a good-sized piece of salt herring, and tied them together in an old bandanna. By hoarding this small stock of food, she could make it last a long time, and with the berries and edible roots she could find in the woods, she wouldn't starve.

She decided that she would take the quilt[8] with her, too. Her hands lingered over it. It felt soft and warm to her touch. Even in the dark, she thought she could tell one color from another, because she knew its pattern and design so well.

---

8. This is the quilt that Tubman painstakingly stitched together before her wedding.

Then John stirred in his sleep, and she left the cabin quickly, carrying the quilt carefully folded under her arm.

Once she was off the plantation, she took to the woods, not following the North Star, not even looking for it, going instead toward Bucktown. She needed help. She was going to ask the white woman who had stopped to talk to her so often if she would help her. Perhaps she wouldn't. But she would soon find out.

When she came to the farmhouse where the woman lived, she approached it cautiously, circling around it. It was so quiet. There was no sound at all, not even a dog barking, or the sound of voices. Nothing.

She tapped on the door, gently. A voice said, "Who's there?" She answered, "Harriet, from Dr. Thompson's place."

When the woman opened the door, she did not seem at all surprised to see her. She glanced at the little bundle that Harriet was carrying, at the quilt, and invited her in. Then she sat down at the kitchen table, and wrote two names on a slip of paper, and handed the paper to Harriet.

She said that those were the next places where it was safe for Harriet to stop. The first place was a farm where there was a gate with big white posts and round knobs on top of them. The people there would feed her, and when they thought it was safe for her to go on, they would tell her how to get to the next house, or take her there. For these were the first two stops on the Underground Railroad—going North, from the Eastern Shore of Maryland.

28   A Gallery of Characters

> **TRANSPARENCY 3**
> **Reader Response**
> *Design a Badge* – invites students to design identifying badges that describe who characters are.

1 Thus Harriet learned that the Underground Railroad that ran straight to the North was not a railroad at all. Neither did it run underground. It was composed of a loosely organized group of people who offered food and shelter, or a place of concealment, to fugitives[9] who had set out on the long road to the North and freedom.

Harriet wanted to pay this woman who had befriended her. But she had no money. **2** She gave her the patchwork quilt, the only beautiful object she had ever owned.

That night she made her way through the woods, crouching in the underbrush whenever she heard the sound of horses' hoofs, staying there until the riders passed. Each time she wondered if they were already hunting for her. It would be so easy to describe her, the deep scar on her forehead like a dent, the old scars on the back of her neck, the husky speaking voice, the lack of height, scarcely five feet tall. The master would say she was wearing rough clothes when she ran away, that she had a bandanna on her head, that she was muscular and strong.

She knew how accurately he would describe her. One of the slaves who could read used to tell the others what it said on those handbills that were nailed up on the **3** trees, along the edge of the roads. It was easy to recognize the handbills that advertised runaways, because there was always a picture in one corner, a picture of a black man, a little running figure with a stick over his shoulder, and a bundle tied on the end of the stick.

Whenever she thought of the handbills, she walked faster. Sometimes she stumbled over old grapevines, gnarled and twisted, thick as a man's wrist, or became entangled in the tough, sinewy[10] vine of the honeysuckle. But she kept going.

In the morning, she came to the house where her friend had said she was to stop. She showed the slip of paper that she carried to the woman who answered her knock at the back door of the farmhouse. The woman fed her, and then handed her a broom and told her to sweep the yard.

Harriet hesitated, suddenly suspicious. Then she decided that with a broom in her hand, working in the yard, she would look as though she belonged on the place; certainly no one would suspect that she was a runaway.

That night the woman's husband, a farmer, loaded a wagon with produce. Harriet climbed in. He threw some blankets over her, and the wagon started.

It was dark under the blankets, and not exactly comfortable. But Harriet decided that riding was better than walking. She was surprised at her own lack of fear, wondered how it was that she so readily trusted these strangers who might betray her. For all she knew, the man driving the wagon might be taking her straight back to the master.

She thought of those other rides in wag-

---

9. **fugitive** (fyōō′jə·tiv): a person who is fleeing (here, from slavery and capture).

10. **sinewy** (sin′yoo·ē): strong, firm, tough.

---

1. BACKGROUND
According to one source, the name originated about 1831. Slaveholders expressing their frustration at the great number of successful runaways said that they "must have gone on an underground railroad." Abolitionists took up the railroad metaphor and began using the terms *depot, station, station master, conductor, train.*

2. GUIDED READING:
Making Inferences
What does this gesture reveal about Harriet? She is deeply grateful and incredibly generous. The quilt is not only the only beautiful thing she's ever owned, but it also took her countless hours to make. It also is associated with her marriage.

3. BACKGROUND
Many whites, as well as African Americans, could not read. This figure was a symbol alerting people that the handbill described a runaway slave.

PORTFOLIO ASSESSMENT

The poignant faces on the journeying individuals in the painting below suggest hardship and suffering. A monologue is a dramatic scene in which only one person speaks. Some students may be interested in writing a short monologue in which they tell the story behind one person's plight from the point of view of that individual. Suggest that they use sensory words to help create an interest in the character. Students may want to present orally their monologues to the class. Consult with students individually to agree on how their monologues will be assessed. (See *Portfolio Assessment and Professional Support Materials* for additional information on student portfolios.)

VISUAL CONNECTIONS

This famous painting is the result of an evening visit the artist made to the home of a famous abolitionist couple, Levi and Catherine Coffin. (The Coffins are shown here with another famous abolitionist, Hannah Haydock.) Many other details in the painting were inspired by Levi Coffin's journal: the straw-filled cart; the blankets wrapped around the women and children; the basket of food. Notice how similarly the fugitives and the abolitionists are dressed: in the painting, everyone is equal.

Students could write a paragraph telling "what is happening" in this scene. They should describe the people, weather, time of day, feelings suggested by the scene. (Are the fugitives relieved, scared, or something else?)

About the Artist

Charles T. Webber (1825–1911) was born in New York state and later moved to Cincinnati where he founded the McMicken School of Art and Design. Cincinnati offered educational opportunities to African Americans before the Civil War, and Webber did the portraits of several abolitionist leaders. This is his most famous painting.

The Underground Railroad by Charles T. Webber (1891 or 1893). Oil on canvas.

The Cincinnati Art Museum. Subscription Fund purchase.

ons, when she was a child, the same clop-clop of the horses' feet, creak of the wagon, and the feeling of being lost because she did not know where she was going. She did not know her destination this time either, but she was not alarmed. She thought of John Tubman. By this time he must have told the master that she was gone. Then she thought of the plantation and how the land rolled gently down toward the river, thought of Ben and Old Rit, and that Old Rit would be inconsolable because her favorite daughter was missing. "Lord," she prayed, "I'm going to hold steady onto You. You've got to see me through." Then she went to sleep.

The next morning, when the stars were still visible in the sky, the farmer stopped the wagon. Harriet was instantly awake.

He told her to follow the river, to keep following it to reach the next place where people would take her in and feed her. He

CLOSURE

Have students write one sentence telling which trait of Harriet Tubman's impresses them most, and why. (Her determination? her courage? her religious beliefs? her ability to keep her faith in human nature, given all she had suffered?)

EXTENSION AND ENRICHMENT

History Projects. Have students work in pairs or small groups to prepare brief oral reports on several related historical events and figures: Harriet Tubman's later accomplishments; Sojourner Truth; Frederick Douglass; the Dred Scott decision; the Emancipation Proclamation; the Atlanta bus boycott.

Film. You might show the video of the powerful movie *Glory* (1989), about the first African American Union regiment (the 54th Massachusetts Infantry) that fought during the Civil War.

---

said that she must travel only at night, and she must stay off the roads because the patrol would be hunting for her. Harriet climbed out of the wagon. "Thank you," she said simply, thinking how amazing it was that there should be white people who were willing to go to such lengths to help a slave get to the North.

When she finally arrived in Pennsylvania, she had traveled roughly ninety miles from Dorchester County. She had slept on the ground outdoors at night. She had been rowed for miles up the Choptank River by a man she had never seen before. She had been concealed in a haycock,[11] and had, at one point, spent a week hidden in a potato hole in a cabin which belonged to a family of free Negroes. She had been hidden in the attic of the home of a Quaker. She had been befriended by stout German farmers, whose guttural[12] speech surprised her and whose well-kept farms astonished her. She had never before seen barns and fences, farmhouses and outbuildings, so carefully painted. The cattle and horses were so clean they looked as though they had been scrubbed.

When she crossed the line into the free state of Pennsylvania, the sun was coming up. She said, "I looked at my hands to see if I was the same person now I was free. There was such a glory over everything, the sun came like gold through the trees, and over the fields, and I felt like I was in heaven."

---

11. **haycock:** a pile of hay in a field.
12. **guttural** (gut′ər·əl): harsh, rasping.

For Study and Discussion

IDENTIFYING FACTS

1. What did Harriet Tubman discover that made her want to escape?
2. Describe her first attempt to escape. Why did it fail?
3. Why did she decide that she must try to escape again, and this time alone?
4. How did Tubman learn about the Underground Railroad?
5. What did Tubman compare freedom to at the end of her journey?

INTERPRETING MEANINGS

6. Look back at what you wrote in your journal. Would you change anything after reading this biography?
7. The African American slaves used songs as codes to communicate certain forbidden messages. What message was Tubman giving to her sister when she sang about leaving on the chariot? What feelings was she also communicating through the song?

APPLYING MEANINGS

8. The politician Patrick Henry is famous for declaring (in 1775) "Give me liberty, or give me death!" Henry was urging the colonists to arm themselves against the British. Harriet Tubman says (page 26) that "there was one of two things I had a *right* to, liberty or death; if I could not have one, I would have the other; for no man should take me alive." Do you know of other people, in history or living today, who risk death in order to be free?

Harriet Tubman **31**

FOR STUDY AND DISCUSSION

Identifying Facts

1. She discovered that her two sisters had been sold South.
2. She first tried to escape with her three brothers, but they panicked and forced her to return with them.
3. She learned that she and her brothers had been sold. She went alone because she had no one she trusted to go with her.
4. She learned about the Underground Railroad when she went to the home of the white woman who had offered to help her.
5. She compared being free to entering heaven. Even the sun is transformed to gold.

Interpreting Meanings

6. Answers will vary.
7. She told her sister she was running away to the North. The song expressed sorrow at leaving and her great longing for freedom.

Applying Meanings

8. Students may suggest Martin Luther King, Jr., and other civil rights activists; Gandhi; people in eastern Europe today; the students of Tiananmen Square.

VISUAL CONNECTIONS
About the Artist
Jacob Lawrence (1917–) is one of the best known of the artists working in the 1920s and 1930s who asserted their African American heritage. Another painting by Lawrence is on page 644.

FOCUS ON READING
Identifying the Sequence of Events
Let students look back at the story if they want: 2, 1, 3, 6, 5, 4.

LITERARY ELEMENTS
Character
1. **Bravery**—Tubman's escape attempts, especially the second time alone, show great courage.
2. **Closeness to family**—She wants her three brothers to escape with her; she leaves a message for her sister; she thinks of her parents.
3. **Determination**—She tries to convince her brothers to go on and fights them to continue alone; she vows she will be free or die.
4. **Intelligence**—She knows the woods and how to survive in them. She is quick to understand the dangerous situation at the plantation.
5. **Faith in God**—She is deeply religious and trusts in God to protect her.

Other heroes may include people in politics, sports, entertainment, science. It is likely that they will not share all of Tubman's traits.

LANGUAGE AND VOCABULARY
Multiple Meanings
For answers, see the **Teaching Guide** at the beginning of the unit.

32

Focus on Reading

IDENTIFYING THE SEQUENCE OF EVENTS
Following are six main events from this biography. Number the events in the order in which they happened, starting with (1).

_____ Harriet Tubman and three of her brothers attempt to escape.
_____ Tubman first meets the white woman in the faded sunbonnet.
_____ Tubman sings a song to tell her sister she is going North to freedom.
_____ Tubman arrives in Pennsylvania.
_____ Tubman hitches a ride with a farmer in a wagon of produce.
_____ The woman in the sunbonnet directs Tubman to the first two stops on the Underground Railroad.

Literary Elements

CHARACTER
Think of what you learned about Harriet Tubman in this excerpt. Which of her words, thoughts, or actions reveal these **character traits**?

1. Bravery
2. Closeness to her family
3. Determination
4. Intelligence
5. Faith in God

Think of other heroes you know from stories or from real life. Do they all share these character traits?

Language and Vocabulary

MULTIPLE MEANINGS
Many English words have more than one meaning. Sometimes these multiple meanings are related, but sometimes they are not. Use each of the following words from the story of Harriet Tubman in two sentences that show two distinct meanings. (Which words are spelled the same but pronounced differently?)

bitter   bark   produce
post   blow   wind

Harriet Tubman worked as a water girl to cotton pickers; she also worked at plowing, carting, and hauling logs. From *The Harriet Tubman Series* (1939–1940) by Jacob Lawrence. Tempera on hardboard.

Hampton University Museum, Hampton, Virginia.

Focus on Personal Narrative

GATHERING DETAILS
If you want your readers to share and enjoy a personal narrative, you must supply

32   A Gallery of Characters

Literary Elements
Characterization — examines the concept of characterization and six ways an author might reveal character.

enough **details** so that the experience you tell about becomes clear and vivid. When you write, think about two kinds of details.

Action details tell what happened and how it happened. These details can also include **dialogue,** or the words that people say. For example, notice how Ann Petry uses dialogue and other details to describe Harriet's first attempt to escape with her brothers (page 25).

Sensory details make the experience vivid by appealing to one or more of the five senses: sight, hearing, taste, smell, and touch. Petry uses sensory details in the paragraph beginning "She decided she would take the quilt with her" (page 28).

Choose one of the topics you explored for the writing assignment on page 19, or select a new topic. Gather details by filling in a chart like the one below. Save your notes.

Topic of Narrative: _____
Action Details/Dialogue
_____
_____
_____
Sensory Details
_____
_____
_____

About the Author

Ann Petry (1911–   ) was born in Connecticut. After she graduated from college, she worked as a pharmacist, a reporter, a writer and salesperson for an advertising agency, and an editor. Her first novel, *The Street,* was published in 1946. It was the first novel written by an African American woman to describe the lives of African American women in urban areas. She has written two biographies about slavery for young readers: *Harriet Tubman: Conductor on the Underground Railroad* and *Tituba of Salem Village*. About her biography of Harriet Tubman Petry says, "I came across some references to Harriet Tubman, an escaped slave, who led other slaves to freedom before the Civil War. She seemed to me the epitome [ĭ•pĭtə•mē] of everything that is indomitable in the human spirit. . . ." In addition to biographies and novels, Petry has written short stories and poems.

FOCUS ON PERSONAL NARRATIVE
Gathering Details
You may want to choose a topic as a model for students and fill in the chart on the chalkboard. When listing action details, discuss with students the value of vivid verbs. Then explain to students that any dialogue they include should advance the narrative and sound natural. When listing sensory details, include all five senses and encourage students to try to do the same in their charts.

LITERATURE AND HISTORY
Making Connections: Activities

As an alternative activity, divide students into small groups who will act as members of a present-day Underground Railroad. Their purpose is to establish a route, including each of their houses, that escaping slaves could follow to freedom. First, students should determine the slaves' point of origin and the destination that marks freedom. With these two locations in mind, students can decide whose house should be the first stop, the second stop, and so forth. Just like the people who helped Harriet Tubman, students should prepare careful directions that include distinguishing features of each stop. Depending on the distance between stops, students may want to arrange for some type of clandestine transportation. If time permits, ask each group to share its route with the rest of the class.

Literature and History

The Underground Railroad

Although organized methods of helping runaway slaves were known as early as 1804, the term *Underground Railroad* was first used in 1831 when a runaway slave mysteriously disappeared just as he was about to be caught. At first the number of routes was limited, but by 1850 numerous lines of the Underground Railroad were in place. An amazing number of people risked imprisonment, financial hardship, and bodily harm in an effort to help slaves find freedom in the North.

Everyone involved in the Underground Railroad understood the great need for secrecy. To evade slave catchers, the routes had to be constantly changed. Many fugitives traveled by foot. Others were disguised and placed on boats and trains. Several accounts tell of slaves being shipped to free states in boxes and crates. Elaborate signals were devised so fugitives could recognize a "safe" house. Slaves were told to look for such things as a quilt hanging on a porch or a smoking chimney. The song "Follow the Drinking Gourd," which was spread from one plantation to the next, contained clues revealing a route to the North. The "Drinking Gourd" represented the constellation of stars known as the "Big Dipper." Upon identifying the Big Dipper, one could find the North Star, which pointed the way to free states in the North.

Many people active in the anti-slavery cause were involved in the Underground Railroad as conductors, like Harriet Tubman and Levi Coffin, an influential Quaker. Others contributed to the abolitionist cause by speaking and writing against the inhumanities of slavery. Frederick Douglass, an escaped slave, was among those whose personal accounts swayed public opinion against slavery. Harriet Beecher Stowe's bestselling novel, *Uncle Tom's Cabin* (1851–1852), angered numerous slaveowners who argued that Stowe's description of slavery was exaggerated.

Making Connections: Activities

1. Many authors have dramatized the story of fugitive slaves and the Underground Railroad. *When the Rattlesnake Sounds,* a play by Alice Childress, is based on Harriet Tubman's efforts to raise money to help runaway slaves. Read about the Underground Railroad. Two sources are *The Underground Railroad,* by Shaaron Cosner, and *Get on Board: The Story of the Underground Railroad,* by Jim Haskins. Write a short play or a poem based on a historical incident that interests you. If you write a play, create characters and a setting based on events in the life of a historical person, such as Harriet Tubman, Frederick Douglass, or Levi Coffin. Have classmates act in your play.

2. Find a copy of the song "Follow the Drinking Gourd." With a group of other students, identify the clues hidden in the song. Create a series of pictures that show fugitives following the North Star and other specific landmarks detailed in the song. Try to imagine what the journey was like and how slaves felt as they made their way north. Display your art work in the classroom.

34 A Gallery of Characters

OBJECTIVES

Students will infer a character's traits and cite specific details to support each trait; understand similes; make inferences; and write a paragraph with a clear sequence of events.

FOCUS/MOTIVATION

Building on Prior Knowledge. Begin a class discussion by having students respond to the question posed in the headnote (page 35). Ask students how important they think it is to wear "what everyone else is wearing." You might discuss who sets "style" for them.

Establishing a Purpose for Reading. Ask students to read to decide how much they sympathize with the narrator.

Prereading Journal. Have students write a few sentences describing some item of clothing they either loved or hated.

> **TEACHING RESOURCES A**
> Teacher's Notes, p. 35
> Reading Check, p. 38
> Reading Focus, p. 39
> Study Guide, pp. 40, 41
> Language Skills, p. 42
> Building Vocabulary, p. 45
> Selection Vocabulary Test, p. 47
> Selection Test, p. 48

The Jacket

GARY SOTO

Before You Read

Have you ever had to wear something that you hated? The narrator of this true story tells about a jacket that he wore long ago—and which he has never forgotten. Notice how the boy's feelings about his clothes reveal a lot about the kind of person he is—or once was.

After you read the first four paragraphs, look back and write down three adjectives that you would use to describe this boy as you know him so far. Do you think you would like him?

READING THE SELECTION
Read aloud the first four paragraphs (to the middle of column 1, page 37). Then stop so students can write three adjectives as the headnote directs. Discuss the adjectives they've chosen. (They may suggest *disappointed, polite, honest, angry.*)

For slower classes, continue reading aloud. Average and advanced classes will be able to read the selection independently. All students should be encouraged to talk about Soto's figurative language.

LANGUAGE LINK
After you discuss similes with students, you might want to allow them to write some of their own. You could give them a list of things that might be compared in a simile, such as rows of teeth—stacks of dishes, or baseball—globe. Ask students how the items could be compared. What is one trait that

1. LANGUAGE AND VOCABULARY
Read aloud this box on similes and tell students they have a minute to think of more examples. You might note that *simile* and *similar* come from a Latin word that means "likeness." Many common expressions—so common they are now trite—are similes, such as "fat as a pig," "hard as a rock," "cold as ice."

Stress that making similes is fun. Part of the pleasure of reading poetry comes from the writer's use of imaginative figures of speech. Gary Soto is a poet, and his similes are often astonishing.

2. GUIDED READING:
Making Inferences
Food references (guacamole here and tortillas on page 39) provide almost the only clues that the writer is Mexican American. His experience is universal.

3. LITERARY ELEMENTS:
Simile
Note this especially apt comparison. By the end of the selection, this "stranger" has become an "ugly brother."

> 1
>
> ## Language and Vocabulary
>
> **A simile is a comparison between two unlike things that uses the words *like* or *as.*** When we say "John's voice is like a trumpet," or "Diane is as tall as a giraffe," we are using similes. In the first paragraph of this story, the writer uses a simile when he says the nondancers felt "bitter as a penny toward the happy couples." Have you ever caught the taste of a penny? It has a very ugly and bitter taste. The writer here is comparing the bitter taste of a penny to the boys' unhappiness and bitter envy. Watch for the many similes in this story. Try to visualize their comparisons as you read.

My clothes have failed me. I remember the green coat that I wore in fifth and sixth grades, when you either danced like a champ or pressed yourself against a greasy wall, bitter as a penny toward the happy couples.

When I needed a new jacket and my mother asked what kind I wanted, I described something like bikers wear: black leather and silver studs with enough belts to hold down a small town. We were in the kitchen, steam on the windows from her cooking. She listened so long while stirring dinner that I thought she understood for sure the kind I wanted. The next day when I got home from school, I discovered draped on my bedpost a jacket the color of 2 day-old guacamole.[1] I threw my books on the bed and approached the jacket slowly, 3 as if it were a stranger whose hand I had to shake. I touched the vinyl sleeve, the collar, and peeked at the mustard-colored lining.

From the kitchen Mother yelled that my jacket was in the closet. I closed the door to her voice and pulled at the rack of clothes in the closet, hoping the jacket on the bedpost wasn't for me but my mean brother. No luck. I gave up. From my bed, I stared at the jacket, I wanted to cry because it was so ugly and so big that I knew I'd have to wear it a long time. I was a small kid, thin as a young tree, and it would be years before I'd have a new one. I stared at the jacket, like an enemy, thinking bad things before I took off my old jacket whose sleeves climbed halfway to my elbow.

I put the big jacket on. I zipped it up and down several times, and rolled the cuffs up so they didn't cover my hands. I put my hands in the pockets and flapped the jacket like a bird's wings. I stood in

---

1. **guacamole** (gwä′kə·mō′lē): a thick sauce made of puréed avocado. The sauce has an olive-green color.

A Gallery of Characters

makes the items in each group similar? Have students use the pairs to make their own similes. Then see if students can compare items they select in a simile of their own.

> **TRANSPARENCIES 1 & 2**
> **Fine Art**
> Theme: *Meeting New People* — invites students to examine artwork that reveals specific recognizable character traits.

front of the mirror, full face, then profile, and then looked over my shoulder as if someone had called me. I sat on the bed, stood against the bed, and combed my hair to see what I would look like doing something natural. I looked ugly. I threw it on my brother's bed and looked at it for a long time before I slipped it on and went out to **1** the backyard, smiling a "thank you" to my mom as I passed her in the kitchen. With my hands in my pockets I kicked a ball against the fence, and then climbed it to sit looking into the alley. I hurled orange peels at the mouth of an open garbage can, and when the peels were gone, I watched the white puffs of my breath thin to nothing.

I jumped down, hands in my pockets, and in the backyard on my knees I teased my dog, Brownie, by swooping my arms while making bird calls. He jumped at me and missed. He jumped again and again, until a tooth sunk deep, ripping an L-shaped tear on my left sleeve. I pushed Brownie away to study the tear as I would a cut on my arm. There was no blood, only a few loose pieces of fuzz. Darn dog, I thought, and pushed him away hard when **2** he tried to bite again. I got up from my knees and went to my bedroom to sit with my jacket on my lap, with the lights out.

That was the first afternoon with my **3** new jacket. The next day I wore it to fifth grade and got a *D* on a math quiz. During the morning recess, Frankie T., the playground terrorist, pushed me to the ground and told me to stay there until recess was over. My best friend, Steve Negrete, ate an apple while looking at me, and the girls turned away to whisper on the monkey bars. The teachers were no help: they looked my way and talked about how foolish I looked in my new jacket. I saw their heads bob with laughter, their hands half covering their mouths.

Even though it was cold, I took off the jacket during lunch and played kickball in a thin shirt, my arms feeling like Braille[2] **4** from goose bumps. But when I returned to class, I slipped the jacket on and shivered until I was warm. I sat on my hands, heating them up, while my teeth chattered like a cup of crooked dice. Finally warm, I slid out of the jacket but a few minutes later put it back on when the fire bell rang. We paraded out into the yard where we, the fifth-graders, walked past all the other grades to stand against the back fence. Everybody saw me. Although they didn't say out loud, "Man, that's ugly," I heard the buzz-buzz of gossip and even laughter that I knew was meant for me.

And so I went, in my guacamole jacket. So embarrassed, so hurt, I couldn't even do my homework. I received *C*'s on quizzes, and forgot the state capitals and the rivers of South America, our friendly neighbor. Even the girls who had been friendly blew away like loose flowers to follow the boys in neat jackets.

I wore that thing for three years until the sleeves grew short and my forearms stuck out like the necks of turtles. All during that time no love came to me—no little

---

2. **Braille** (brāl): a system of printing and writing for the blind, in which letters are indicated by raised dots which are felt by the fingers.

---

1. GUIDED READING:
Making Inferences
Why doesn't the narrator tell his mother how he feels? Maybe he doesn't want to hurt her feelings. He knows she wanted to buy what he wants but can't afford a more expensive jacket.

2. GUIDED READING:
Interpreting Meaning
What do you suppose the narrator is thinking? Students will probably agree he's feeling bad and very disappointed. He's worried about how others will react to the jacket, and he's probably even worried about what his mother will say about the tear.

3. GUIDED READING:
Understanding Cause and Effect
The boy thinks the jacket caused all the bad things that happened to him. How valid is his reasoning? Students should realize that Soto is exaggerating; all of these things might have happened anyway.

4. LITERARY ELEMENTS:
Simile
You might stop to admire this ingenious comparison. The exaggeration makes it humorous.

The Jacket   37

MEETING INDIVIDUAL NEEDS
Visual Learners • As you discuss traits of the main character in this story, you might draw a jacket outline on the chalkboard and add the character trait words to the jacket as designs. You might use large parts of the jacket for major character traits and small elements, such as a pocket or collar, for less obvious or less developed traits.

1. GUIDED READING:
Making Inferences
What are these propellers of grass? They are long blades of grass, split and bent. It's not easy to make them whirl like a propeller. In the next column, the boys spin the propellers to blot out what they don't want to see—happy couples.

2. LITERARY ELEMENTS:
Simile
Note this ingenious simile. (Ask what the girls are doing.)

dark girl in a Sunday dress she wore on Monday. At lunchtime I stayed with the ugly boys who leaned against the chain-link fence and looked around with propellers of grass spinning in our mouths. We saw girls walk by alone, saw couples, hand in hand, their heads like bookends pressing air together. We saw them and spun our propellers so fast our faces were blurs.

I blame that jacket for those bad years. I blame my mother for her bad taste and her cheap ways. It was a sad time for the

CLOSURE

Have three students give their opinions about how accurately Gary Soto has described a fifth or sixth grader and all his insecurities and fears. Have a fourth student explain whether or not the boy in this essay could just as well have been a girl.

---

heart. With a friend I spent my sixth-grade year in a tree in the alley, waiting for something good to happen to me in that jacket, which had become the ugly brother who tagged along wherever I went. And it was about that time that I began to grow. My chest puffed up with muscle and, strangely, a few more ribs. Even my hands, those fleshy hammers, showed bravely through the cuffs, the fingers already hardening for the coming fights. But that L-shaped rip on the left sleeve got bigger; bits of stuffing coughed out from its wound after a hard day of play. I finally Scotch-taped it closed, but in rain or cold weather the tape peeled off like a scab and more stuffing fell out until that sleeve shriveled into a palsied arm.[3] That winter the elbows began to crack and whole chunks of green began to fall off. I showed the cracks to my mother, who always seemed to be at the stove with steamed-up glasses, and she said that there were children in Mexico who would love that jacket. I told her that this was America and yelled that Debbie, my sister, didn't have a jacket like mine. I ran outside, ready to cry, and climbed the tree by the alley to think bad thoughts and watch my breath puff white and disappear.

But whole pieces still casually flew off my jacket when I played hard, read quietly, or took vicious spelling tests at school. When it became so spotted that my brother began to call me "camouflage," I flung it over the fence into the alley. Later, however, I swiped the jacket off the ground and went inside to drape it across my lap and mope.

I was called to dinner: Steam silvered my mother's glasses as she said grace; my brother and sister, with their heads bowed, made ugly faces at their glasses of powdered milk. I gagged too, but eagerly ate big rips of buttered tortilla that held scooped up beans. Finished, I went outside with my jacket across my arm. It was a cold sky. The faces of clouds were piled up, hurting. I climbed the fence, jumping down with a grunt. I started up the alley and soon slipped into my jacket, that green ugly brother who breathed over my shoulder that day and ever since.

---

3. **palsied arm:** *Palsy* is a form of paralysis resulting in weak muscles. A palsied arm would look limp and thinner than a healthy arm.

For Study and Discussion

IDENTIFYING FACTS

1. Describe the jacket the narrator asks his mother to buy for him. What kind of jacket does she actually buy?

2. What is the narrator's reaction when he first sees the jacket?

3. List the things that happen to the boy the first day he wears the new jacket to school.

INTERPRETING MEANINGS

4. Why do you think the narrator's mother bought him the jacket she did instead of the one he described to her?

5. Why didn't the boy just get another jacket?

FOR STUDY AND DISCUSSION

Identifying Facts

1. He asks for a black leather jacket with silver studs and belts but gets one that is olive-green vinyl.
2. He feels like crying because it's so big and ugly.
3. He gets a *D* on a math quiz. He is knocked down by a bully, and he thinks everyone is laughing at his jacket.

Interpreting Meanings

4. She could not afford the jacket he wanted.
5. He didn't have the money to buy another one, and he didn't want to make his mother feel bad.
6. The narrator must surely be wrong in imagining that *everyone* was laughing at his jacket, although some students might have been.

Yes, people can be horribly sensitive about their clothing and about what other people think of them.

7. The jacket represents his feelings of insecurity, failure to "fit in," embarrassment—feelings perhaps he still has from time to time. (There is an element of exaggeration in the essay.)

Applying Meanings

8. Everyone should be able to identify with Soto's problem.

The Jacket 39

EXTENSION AND ENRICHMENT

Listening/Literature. You might read aloud some of Soto's poems. "Oranges" can be found in many literature anthologies. Students will enjoy the following poems addressed to his little daughter Mariko: "Evening Walk," "Teaching Numbers," and "Eating Bread" (from his recent collection *A Fire in My Hands,* Scholastic, 1990).

FOCUS ON READING
Making Inferences

1. True. The boy must take some responsibility for his grades and failure to do his homework. Also, some of his problems (like his lack of girlfriend) are typical of adolescence.

2. False. The boy mistakenly imagines a simple cause-effect relationship: he thinks the jacket causes everything that happens (or doesn't happen) to him.

3. True. He knows his mother can't afford a different jacket and that complaining won't do him any good. He also doesn't want to hurt her feelings.

4. False. She probably bought the jacket because it was the best she could afford. Also she seems too busy to be concerned about his feelings about the jacket. She might also have bought the jacket in haste.

LITERARY ELEMENTS
Character

These are possible answers.

1. Shy and insecure. He imagines other people are laughing at him, he yields to the bully, and he seems afraid to approach girls. He doesn't immediately express his disappointment to his mother but

---

6. Do you think people *really* were talking about the boy and laughing at him in his jacket? Do people often get these feelings that they are being laughed at because of what they are wearing?

7. What do you think the narrator means when he describes the jacket as "that green ugly brother who breathed over my shoulder that day and ever since"? How could the jacket still bother him?

APPLYING MEANINGS
8. Have you ever been embarrassed to wear a piece of clothing? (If this has never happened to you, how do you think you would handle the situation if it did?)

Focus on Reading

MAKING INFERENCES
An **inference** is a conclusion based on some kind of evidence. If you see footprints crossing a snowy field, you can **infer** that someone has been walking on the snow. If you see puddles on the sidewalk when you get up in the morning, you can **infer** that it rained overnight. When you read, you naturally make inferences about things the writer *suggests* but does not state directly.

You probably made a lot of inferences as you read "The Jacket." Which of the following inferences about this story are true? (Can you point to evidence in the story that supports each inference?)

1. The ugly green jacket was not the only reason for the boy's troubles in fifth and sixth grades.

2. The playground terrorist Frankie T., the boy's friend Steve, the rest of the fifth grade, and all the teachers laughed at the boy and made his life miserable because they thought he looked hideous in his green jacket.

3. The boy knows that he must wear the jacket until he grows out of it and that he shouldn't complain.

4. His mother bought him the jacket because she thought he needed to be taught a lesson.

Literary Elements

CHARACTER
This true story is told by an adult who is looking back on his childhood. How would you describe this boy's **character**? Is he likeable? Shy? Outgoing? Angry? Unsure of himself? Selfish? Locate at least one detail in the story to support your answer. Look for examples in the boy's words and actions. Look also at the ways other people respond to the boy.

Is this boy's response to his hated jacket believable? Would you, or would most people you know, have felt this way?

Language and Vocabulary

SIMILES
Similes (sim'ə·lēs) are comparisons of unlike things that use words such as *like* or *as.* Writers use similes to create pictures in our minds. Similes can make us see a familiar object in a new and different way. Below are some similes from "The Jacket." Read them and answer the questions that follow.

1. "I was a small kid, thin as a young tree."

a. What is the narrator comparing himself to?
b. Describe what you think he looked like.

2. "Even the girls who had been friendly blew away like loose flowers . . ."
   a. What are the girls compared to?
   b. What does this comparison suggest about the way the writer feels about the girls? (Suppose the writer had said they'd blown away like clumps of dust?)

3. ". . . my forearms stuck out like the necks of turtles."
   a. What does the narrator compare his arms to?
   b. What do you think his arms look like?

Focus on Personal Narrative

USING CHRONOLOGICAL ORDER

The narrator in Gary Soto's "The Jacket" uses chronological order to tell his story. In **chronological** or **time order,** you tell events in the order in which they happened.

To help your readers follow your story, use **transitional words and phrases.** Transitions show the connections of events and ideas in your writing. Here is a list of useful transitions for time order:

after	often
before	soon
finally	then
first, second, third	when
next	

Write a paragraph or two telling about something funny or interesting that happened at school. Use time order and transitions to make the sequence of events clear. Save your writing.

Gary Soto (1952–   ) was born in Fresno, California. When he was a boy, he worked as a migrant worker. His book *Small Faces,* from which "The Jacket" is taken, describes many of his experiences and feelings growing up as a Mexican American. Other collections of stories are *Baseball in April* and *Local News*. Soto has written poetry as well as essays and short fiction. Soto says he did not have "any literary aspirations as a kid. In fact, we were a pretty illiterate family. We didn't have books, and no one encouraged us to read. So my wanting to write poetry was sort of a fluke." He became interested in writing when he found a book in the library called *The New American Poetry*. "I discovered this poetry and thought, This is terrific; I'd like to do something like this."

Photo of Gary Soto taken by his wife, Carolyn.

The Jacket 41

OBJECTIVES

Students will recognize details of characterization and make inferences. They will also write a paragraph using vivid action verbs and metaphors, interpret metaphors, and dramatize a story.

Teaching Resources A
Teacher's Notes, p. 50
Reading Check, p. 53
Reading Focus, p. 54
Study Guide, pp. 55, 56
Language Skills, pp. 57, 60
Building Vocabulary, p. 63
Selection Vocabulary Test, p. 65
Selection Test, p. 66

AV Resources Binder
Audiocassette 1, Side A

1. BACKGROUND
In his preface to the novel, Twain wrote, "Most of the adventures recorded in this book really occurred; one or two were experiences of my own, the rest those of boys who were schoolmates of mine. Huck Finn is drawn from life; Tom Sawyer also, but not from an individual—he is a combination of the characteristics of three boys whom I knew, and therefore belongs to the composite order of architecture. The odd superstitions touched upon were all prevalent . . . in the West at the period of this story . . ."

Geography Link
You might have students locate the Mississippi River on a United States map and look along the river for St. Petersburg, where this story is supposed to have taken place. When students are unable to locate the town, you might point out that Twain renamed his home town of Hannibal, Missouri, St. Petersburg, for his tales of Tom Sawyer and Huck Finn. After students locate Hannibal, you might have them speculate about why he renamed his home town in his stories.

from The Adventures of Tom Sawyer

MARK TWAIN

Before You Read

Some of the most popular programs on TV are comedies about characters growing up in America. But the most famous of all American stories about growing up was written by Mark Twain in 1876.

1   The title of Twain's novel is *The Adventures of Tom Sawyer.* The story takes place in a very small Mississippi River town called St. Petersburg. Tom and his friends go through many of the ordeals that the young characters on TV go through today: They have problems in school, they have conflicts at home, they fall in love, they face prejudice and even violence.

Tom lives with his Aunt Polly, his half-brother Sid, and his cousin Mary. Sid is always good; Tom is always in trouble. Aunt Polly is an unmarried lady who loves Tom dearly, but she often has difficulty understanding him.

After you read the first paragraph of this episode from the novel, stop and be sure you know the answer to this question: What is Tom's problem?

42   A Gallery of Characters

FOCUS/MOTIVATION

Building on Prior Knowledge. See what students already know about Mark Twain and *Tom Sawyer*. Some will be familiar with the whitewashing episode (Chapter 2) and will have heard of Huckleberry Finn. The episodes in the text are from Chapter 6.

Establishing a Purpose for Reading. Have students read the first paragraph to answer the question posed in the headnote: What is Tom's problem? Ask students to read the story to decide which of Tom's problems could happen to a young person today.

Prereading Journal. Ask students to write several sentences describing three ways they imagine their lives would be different if they lived in the year 1876 (the year *Tom Sawyer* was published).

Painting by Norman Rockwell.

Courtesy The Heritage Club, Norwalk, Connecticut.
Richard Cerretti for Mark Twain Museum, Hannibal, Missouri.

from *The Adventures of Tom Sawyer*

READING THE SELECTION

Twain's language is rich in metaphors, irony, and understatement, literary techniques that pose a challenge for some sixth-graders. For this reason, you might read aloud the section "Dentistry" and stop to discuss it. Advanced students should be able to read the sections "Huck Finn" and "Becky" independently, but you might continue reading aloud with slower classes. Despite the difficulty in language and the nineteenth-century setting of the story, students overwhelmingly respond to Tom's adventures.

> **TRANSPARENCY 3**
> **Reader Response**
> *Design a Badge* – invites students to design identifying badges that describe who characters are.

1. LANGUAGE AND VOCABULARY

Read aloud this feature on metaphor and make sure students realize that they use figures of speech in their own conversation all the time. You might spend five minutes writing some popular examples on the chalkboard.

Twain wrote *Tom Sawyer* more than a hundred years ago, so it contains some "difficult" words and some expressions that are no longer common. You can overcome any difficulties by reading the story aloud. Remind students to use the footnotes and Glossary.

2. GUIDED READING:
Using Context Clues
What clues help you guess what canvassed *means?* Found *and* investigated *suggest that* canvassed *means "examined thoroughly."*

3. GUIDED READING:
Paraphrasing
Ask students to restate this passage in their own words. ("One of his upper front teeth was loose, and Tom thought this was lucky because he could use it as an excuse to stay home. He was about to start groaning when it occurred to him that if he told his aunt about the loose tooth she would pull it out and that would hurt.")

Language and Vocabulary

Metaphors are a special kind of imaginative language in which one thing is compared to something very different. Metaphors are not literally true. If you say "That movie was a bomb," you are using a metaphor. If you say "New York is the Big Apple," you are using a metaphor. Like most talented writers, Twain uses many metaphors. In the first paragraph, for example, he suggests that Tom's school is a prison. Notice that Twain talks of school in terms of "captivity" and "fetters" (chains). When you read a writer like Mark Twain, you have to let your imagination go. Once you learn to trust your own instincts, most of Twain's language will become clear to you. If you are like millions of other readers, you will also find it very funny.

Dentistry

Monday morning found Tom Sawyer miserable. Monday morning always found him so—because it began another week's slow suffering in school. He generally began that day with wishing he had had no intervening holiday, it made the going into captivity and fetters again so much more odious.[1]

Tom lay thinking. Presently it occurred to him that he wished he was sick; then he could stay home from school. Here was a vague possibility. He canvassed his system. No ailment was found, and he investigated again. This time he thought he could detect colicky symptoms,[2] and he began to encourage them with considerable hope. But they soon grew feeble, and presently died wholly away. He reflected further. Suddenly he discovered something. One of his upper front teeth was loose. This was lucky; he was about to begin to groan, as a "starter," as he called it, when it occurred to him that if he came into court[3] with that argument, his aunt would pull it out, and that would hurt. So he thought he would hold the tooth in reserve for the present, and seek further. Nothing offered for some little time, and then he remembered hearing the doctor tell about a certain thing that laid up a patient for two or three weeks and threatened to make him lose a finger. So the boy eagerly

---

1. **odious** (ō'dē·əs): hateful, disgusting.
2. **colicky** (kŏl'i·kē) **symptoms:** pains in the stomach.
3. In other words, "if he came before his aunt." (Twain is comparing Tom's aunt to a judge in court.)

44 A Gallery of Characters

MEETING INDIVIDUAL NEEDS

ESL/LEP • Huck's groaning *makes* Sid's *flesh crawl*. Ask the class what this expression means. How many other ways can we say the same thing? Write student suggestions on the chalkboard. (Examples might include

Huck's groaning *gave* Sid *goosebumps*.
Huck's groaning *sent chills down* Sid's spine.)

Encourage students to give examples of things that make their *flesh crawl*. (For example, a fingernail drawn across a chalkboard.)

---

1 drew his sore toe from under the sheet and held it up for inspection. But now he did not know the necessary symptoms. However, it seemed well worth while to chance it, so he fell to groaning with considerable spirit.

But Sid slept on unconscious.

2 Tom groaned louder and fancied that he began to feel pain in the toe.

No result from Sid.

Tom was panting with his exertions by this time. He took a rest and then swelled himself up and fetched a succession of admirable groans.

Sid snored on.

Tom was aggravated. He said, "Sid, Sid!" and shook him. This course worked well, and Tom began to groan again. Sid yawned, stretched, then brought himself up on his elbow with a snort, and began to stare at Tom. Tom went on groaning. Sid said:

"Tom! Say, Tom!" (No response.) "Here, Tom! *Tom!* What is the matter, Tom?" And he shook him and looked in his face anxiously.

Tom moaned out:

"Oh, don't, Sid. Don't joggle me."

"Why, what's the matter, Tom? I must call Auntie."

3 "No—never mind. It'll be over by and by, maybe. Don't call anybody."

"But I must! *Don't* groan so, Tom, it's awful. How long you been this way?"

"Hours. Ouch! Oh, don't stir so, Sid, you'll kill me."

"Tom, why didn't you wake me sooner? Oh, Tom, *don't!* It makes my flesh crawl to hear you. Tom, what *is* the matter?"

"I forgive you everything, Sid. (Groan.) Everything you've ever done to me. When I'm gone——"

"Oh, Tom, you ain't dying, are you? Don't, Tom—oh, don't. Maybe——"

"I forgive everybody, Sid. (Groan.) 4 Tell 'em so, Sid. And Sid, you give my window sash and my cat with one eye to that new girl that's come to town, and tell her——"

But Sid had snatched his clothes and gone. Tom was suffering in reality, now, so handsomely was his imagination working, and so his groans had gathered quite a genuine tone.

Sid flew downstairs and said:

"Oh, Aunt Polly, come! Tom's dying!"

"Dying!"

"Yes'm. Don't wait—come quick!"

"Rubbage! I don't believe it!"

But she fled upstairs, nevertheless, with Sid and Mary at her heels. And her face grew white, too, and her lip trembled. When she reached the bedside she gasped out, "You, Tom! Tom, what's the matter with you?"

"Oh, Auntie, I'm——"

"What's the matter with you—what *is* the matter with you, child?"

"Oh, Auntie, my sore toe's mortified!"

The old lady sank down into a chair and laughed a little, then cried a little, then did both together. This restored her and she said:

"Tom, what a turn you did give me.

---

1. GUIDED READING:

Predicting Outcomes
What do you predict will happen? Students will guess that shrewd Aunt Polly will see through Tom's pretense.

2
Fancied means "imagined."

3. GUIDED READING:

Understanding Motivation
Why does Tom tell Sid not to call anybody? He's using "reverse psychology," telling Sid not to do exactly what he wants him to do.

4. LITERARY ELEMENTS:

Exaggeration
Note how Twain makes the situation humorous by taking it to the extreme: Tom is playing a deathbed scene. Tom collects things (here he bequeaths a window sash, or frame, and a cat).

from *The Adventures of Tom Sawyer*

1. LITERARY ELEMENTS:
Characterization
What traits does Tom display here? He's a quick thinker and doesn't give up easily. When he sees one trick won't work, he quickly switches.

2. GUIDED READING:
Self-Questioning
Students will be puzzled by Aunt Polly's directions. A chunk of fire is a red-hot coal or a piece of wood burning at one end. She's going to yank Tom's tooth out with the thread.

Now you shut up that nonsense and climb out of this."

The groans ceased and the pain vanished from the toe. The boy felt a little foolish, and he said:

1 "Aunt Polly, it *seemed* mortified, and it hurt so I never minded my tooth at all."

"Your tooth, indeed! What's the matter with your tooth?"

"One of them's loose, and it aches perfectly awful."

"There, there, now, don't begin that groaning again. Open your mouth. Well— your tooth *is* loose, but you're not going to die about that. Mary, get me a silk thread 2 and a chunk of fire out of the kitchen."

Tom said:

"Oh, please, Auntie, don't pull it out.

"Tom, Tom, I love you so, and you seem to try every way you can to break my old heart with your outrageousness."

From the movie *The Adventures of Tom Sawyer* (1938).

46   A Gallery of Characters

It don't hurt anymore. I wish I may never stir if it does. Please don't, Auntie. I don't want to stay home from school."

"Oh, you don't, don't you? So all this row[4] was because you thought you'd get to stay home from school and go a-fishing? Tom, Tom, I love you so, and you seem to try every way you can to break my old heart with your outrageousness." By this time the dental instruments were ready. The old lady made one end of the silk thread fast to Tom's tooth with a loop and tied the other to the bedpost. Then she seized the chunk of fire and suddenly thrust it almost into the boy's face. The tooth hung dangling by the bedpost now.

But all trials bring their compensations. As Tom wended[5] to school after breakfast, he was the envy of every boy he met because the gap in his upper row of teeth enabled him to expectorate[6] in a new and admirable way. He gathered quite a following of lads interested in the exhibition; and one that had cut his finger, and had been a center of fascination and homage up to this time, now found himself suddenly without an adherent,[7] and shorn of his glory. His heart was heavy, and he said with a disdain which he did not feel that it wasn't anything to spit like Tom Sawyer. But another boy said, "Sour grapes!" and he wandered away a dismantled hero.

Huck Finn

Shortly, Tom came upon the juvenile pariah[8] of the village, Huckleberry Finn, son of the town drunkard. Huckleberry was cordially hated and dreaded by all the mothers of the town, because he was idle and lawless and vulgar and bad—and because all their children admired him so, and delighted in his forbidden society, and wished they dared to be like him. Tom was like the rest of the respectable boys in that he envied Huckleberry his gaudy[9] outcast condition, and was under strict orders not to play with him. So he played with him every time he got a chance. Huckleberry was always dressed in the castoff clothes of full-grown men, and they were in perennial bloom and fluttering with rags. His hat was a vast ruin with a wide crescent lopped out of its brim; his coat, when he wore one, hung nearly to his heels and had the rearward buttons far down the back; but one suspender supported his trousers; the seat of the trousers bagged low and contained nothing; the fringed legs dragged in the dirt when not rolled up.

Huckleberry came and went at his own free will. He slept on doorsteps in fine weather and in empty hogsheads[10] in wet; he did not have to go to school or to church, or call any being master or obey anybody; he could go fishing or swimming

---

4. **row** (rou): noise and quarreling.
5. **wended:** traveled.
6. **expectorate** (ik·spek′tə·rāt′): spit.
7. **adherent** (əd·hir′ənt): follower.
8. **pariah** (pə·rī′ə): outcast.
9. **gaudy** (gô′dē): bright and showy, but not considered in "good taste."
10. **hogsheads:** very large barrels.

from *The Adventures of Tom Sawyer*

COOPERATIVE LEARNING

Twain states that the person upon which he based the character of Huckleberry Finn had become a very respectable kind of person as an adult, despite the fact that he incurred adult disapproval. He suggests that no matter how other people brand a person, his or her fate is not sealed by the opinions of others.

You might ask students to project how a character's early life and events could be overcome. Divide the class into groups of three or four and have students discuss what the future might bring for a character they have read about. You could assign each group a character or have students in the group decide upon one. Each person in the group should write a sentence proposing what the person might become. Have a spokesperson for each group present the findings to the class. Ask students to decide which circumstance they believe is truest to the character and which exhibits the most potential for change.

1. GUIDED READING:
Making Judgments
Do you think Huck really had everything that makes life "precious"? Huck's freedom seems enviable to the other boys, but Twain is being ironic (or romantic). Huck has no home, no family, no decent clothing. Some may wonder what kind of a future Huck can have without schooling. See Twain's comment on the model for Huck Finn, page 55.

2. GUIDED READING:
Reading Dialect
Point out how Twain imitates pronunciation through spelling, and ask students to read examples. (*Sho, 'em, becuz, less, genuwyne*)

3. GUIDED READING:
Understanding Implied Ideas
Why does Tom tell the truth? Tom is a quick thinker. He *wants* to sit next to the girl with the yellow hair and knows this will be part of his punishment. (How should these words be said aloud?)

---

when and where he chose, and stay as long as it suited him; nobody forbade him to fight; he could sit up as late as he pleased; he was always the first boy that went barefoot in the spring and the last to resume leather in the fall; he never had to wash, nor put on clean clothes; he could swear

1 wonderfully. In a word, everything that goes to make life precious, that boy had. So thought every harassed, hampered, respectable boy in St. Petersburg.

Tom hailed the romantic outcast: "Hello, Huckleberry! . . . Say—what's that?"

"Nothing but a tick."

"Where'd you get him?"

"Out in the woods."

"What'll you take for him?"

"I don't know. I don't want to sell him."

"All right. It's a mighty small tick, anyway."

"Oh, anybody can run a tick down that don't belong to them. I'm satisfied with it. It's a good enough tick for me."

2 "Sho, there's ticks a-plenty. I could have a thousand of 'em if I wanted to."

"Well, why don't you? Becuz you know mighty well you can't. This is a pretty early tick, I reckon. It's the first one I've seen this year."

"Say, Huck—I'll give you my tooth for him."

"Less see it."

Tom got out a bit of paper and carefully unrolled it. Huckleberry viewed it wistfully. The temptation was very strong. At last he said, "Is it genuwyne?"

Tom lifted his lip and showed the vacancy.

"Well, all right," said Huckleberry, "it's a trade."

Tom enclosed the tick in the percussion-cap box that had lately been the pinch bug's prison,[11] and the boys separated, each feeling wealthier than before.

Becky

When Tom reached the little isolated frame schoolhouse, he strode in briskly, with the manner of one who had come with all honest speed. He hung his hat on a peg and flung himself into his seat with businesslike alacrity.[12] The master, throned on high in his great splint-bottom armchair, was dozing, lulled by the drowsy hum of study. The interruption roused him.

"Thomas Sawyer!"

Tom knew that when his name was pronounced in full, it meant trouble.

"Sir!"

"Come up here. Now, sir, why are you late again, as usual?"

Tom was about to take refuge in a lie, when he saw two long tails of yellow hair hanging down a back that he recognized by the electric sympathy of love. And by that form was *the only vacant place* on the girls' side of the schoolhouse. He instantly said:

"I STOPPED TO TALK WITH HUCKLE- **3** BERRY FINN!"

---

11. Tom collects all sorts of things, including bugs and dead cats and teeth.
12. **alacrity** (ə·lak′rə·tē): eagerness and readiness.

48 A Gallery of Characters

The master's pulse stood still, and he stared helplessly. The buzz of study ceased. The pupils wondered if this foolhardy boy had lost his mind. The master said:

"You—you did what?"

"Stopped to talk with Huckleberry Finn."

There was no mistaking the words.

"Thomas Sawyer, this is the most astounding confession I have ever listened to. No mere ferule[13] will answer for this offense. Take off your jacket."

1 The master's arm performed until it was tired and the stock of switches notably diminished. Then the order followed:

"Now, sir, go and sit with the *girls!* And let this be a warning to you."

2 The titter that rippled around the room appeared to abash[14] the boy; but in reality, that result was caused rather more by his worshipful awe of his unknown idol and the dread pleasure that lay in his high good fortune. He sat down upon the end of the pine bench, and the girl hitched herself away from him with a toss of her head. Nudges and winks and whispers traversed the room, but Tom sat still, with his arms upon the long, low desk before him, and seemed to study his book.

By and by, attention ceased from him, and the accustomed school murmur rose upon the dull air once more. Presently, the 3 boy began to steal furtive glances at the girl. She observed it, made a mouth at him and gave him the back of her head for the space of a minute. When she cautiously faced around again, a peach lay before her. She thrust it away. Tom gently put it back. She thrust it away again, but with less animosity.[15] Tom patiently returned it to its place. Then she let it remain. Tom scrawled on his slate,[16] "Please take it—I got more." The girl glanced at the words but made no sign. Now the boy began to draw something on the slate, hiding his work with his left hand. For a time, the girl refused to notice. But her human curiosity presently began to manifest itself by hardly perceptible[17] signs. The boy worked on, 4 apparently unconscious. The girl made a sort of noncommittal attempt to see, but the boy did not betray that he was aware of it. At last she gave in and hesitatingly whispered, "Let me see it."

Tom partly uncovered a dismal caricature[18] of a house with two gable ends to it and a corkscrew of smoke issuing from the chimney. Then the girl's interest began to fasten itself upon the work, and she forgot everything else. When it was finished, she gazed a moment, then whispered, "It's nice—make a man."

The artist erected a man in the front

---

13. **ferule** (fer′ōōl): ruler or flat stick, used to hit children. (In those days, students could be whipped in school by the teacher. For serious offenses, the teacher used a light switch taken from a tree.)
14. **abash:** embarrass.
15. **animosity** (an′ə·mos′ə·tē): dislike.
16. **slate:** In those days, schoolchildren wrote on small chalkboards (or slates) that they carried with them. They did not use paper, as we do today.
17. **perceptible** (pər·sep′tə·bəl): noticeable.
18. **caricature** (kar′i·kə·chōōr): an exaggerated picture, like a cartoon.

from *The Adventures of Tom Sawyer*

1, GUIDED READING:
Making Inferences
What is happening here? The teacher is whipping Tom. Twain expresses the fact indirectly.

2. GUIDED READING:
Interpreting Meaning
What is Tom really feeling? Tom seems embarrassed by the class's laughter, but he is really awed at the thought of sitting next to Becky.

3. GUIDED READING:
Making Inferences
Alert students to Tom's masterful use of psychology in the scene that follows. He persists with the peach, pretends he doesn't want Becky to see his drawing and message, and manages to declare his love.

4. GUIDED READING:
Drawing Conclusions
Is Tom really "unconscious" of what's going on? No. He knows he can pique Becky's curiosity by pretending not to notice her.

MEETING INDIVIDUAL NEEDS

ESL/LEP • Tom's conversation with Becky contains forms that may prove confusing for some students learning standard English. You may want to call attention to the following:
1. Substitution of *learn* for *teach*
   I'll **learn** you.
2. Use of *lick me by* to mean *punish me with*
   That's the name they **lick me by.**
3. Substitution of *ain't* for *isn't*
   Oh, it **ain't** anything.

1. GUIDED READING:
Drawing Conclusions
Note the humor here. Instead of just saying that Tom can't draw, Twain describes exactly what he drew and lets us draw our own conclusions.

2. GUIDED READING:
Recognizing Dialect
Here's a Midwestern expression that seems to have disappeared. *That's a whack* means "That's a deal."

3. LITERARY ELEMENTS:
Characterization
Help students to appreciate Tom Sawyer's mastery of reverse psychology. With one exception (Aunt Polly), everyone (Sid, Huck, the teacher, and Becky) reacts in exactly the way Tom wants.

4
Deed is a shortened form of *indeed*. Ask students what they would say to solemnize a serious promise. (Cross my heart and hope to die?)

---

yard, which resembled a derrick.[19] He could have stepped over the house.

But the girl was not hypercritical. She was satisfied with the monster, and whispered, "It's a beautiful man—now make me coming along."

1 Tom drew an hourglass with a full moon and straw limbs to it and armed the spreading fingers with a portentous[20] fan.

The girl said, "It's ever so nice—I wish I could draw."

"It's easy," whispered Tom, "I'll learn you."

"Oh, will you? When?"

"At noon. Do you go home to dinner?"

"I'll stay if you will."

2 "Good—that's a whack. What's your name?"

"Becky Thatcher. What's yours? Oh, I know. It's Thomas Sawyer."

"That's the name they lick me by. I'm Tom when I'm good. You call me Tom, will you?"

"Yes."

3 Now Tom began to scrawl something on the slate, hiding the words from the girl. But she was not backward this time. She begged to see.

Tom said, "Oh, it ain't anything."

"Yes it is."

"No it ain't. You don't want to see."

"Yes I do, indeed I do. Please let me."

"You'll tell."

"No I won't—deed and deed and double deed I won't." **4**

"You won't tell anybody at all? Ever, as long as you live?"

"No, I won't ever tell *any*body. Now let me."

"Oh, *you* don't want to see!"

"Now that you treat me so, I *will* see." And she put her small hand upon his and a little scuffle ensued, Tom pretending to resist in earnest but letting his hand slip by degrees till these words were revealed: "*I love you*."

"Oh, you bad thing!" And she hit his hand a smart rap, but reddened and looked pleased nevertheless.

Just at this juncture[21] the boy felt a slow, fateful grip closing on his ear and a steady lifting impulse. In that vise[22] he was borne across the house and deposited in his own seat, under a peppering fire of giggles from the whole school. Then the master stood over him during a few awful moments, and finally moved away to his throne without saying a word. But although Tom's ear tingled, his heart was jubilant.

As the school quieted down, Tom made an honest effort to study, but the turmoil within him was too great. In turn, he took his place in the reading class and

---

19. **derrick:** a tall tapering framework used to support machinery (like an oil derrick).
20. **portentous** (pôr·ten′təs): large; marvelous.

21. **juncture** (jungk′chər): point in time.
22. **vise** (vīs): a carpenter's tool. Usually, a vise is attached to a workbench and used to grip firmly some object the carpenter is working on. Here, the grip of the schoolmaster is compared to the grip of a vise.

A Gallery of Characters

CLOSURE
Have students make up a list of adjectives that describe Tom Sawyer.

EXTENSION AND ENRICHMENT
Dramatizing the Story. You might read aloud or have students dramatize another episode from *Tom Sawyer* for a classroom theater. Try the whitewashing scene from Chapter 2, or the Pain Killer episode from Chapter 12.

1. GUIDED READING:
Making Inferences
What new fact about Tom does this sentence reveal? He's been the champion speller for months. Many students will be surprised because Tom seems to dislike school so much, but we've certainly seen evidence of Tom's intelligence. We might also be suspicious that Tom has won this medal through some trickery.

"*Let me see it.*"   Illustration by Worth Brehm.

made a botch of it. Then in the geography class, he turned lakes into mountains, mountains into rivers, and rivers into continents, till chaos was come again. Then in the spelling class, he got "turned down" by a succession of mere baby words, till he brought up the foot[23] and yielded up the pewter medal which he had worn with ostentation for months.

---
23. Tom ended up last in class. Notice that this meant he had to give up a medal he had shown off earlier. (*Ostentation* means "showing off.")

from *The Adventures of Tom Sawyer*

FOR STUDY AND DISCUSSION

Identifying Facts

1. Tom's problem is that he hates going to school, especially on Monday mornings.

   He feigns illness so he can stay at home.

2. Aunt Polly ties a silk thread around his tooth and ties the other end to a bed post. When Tom jerks backward from the chunk of fire that Aunt Polly thrusts into his face, the tooth is yanked out.

3. The mothers hate him because he is "idle and lawless and vulgar and bad." They fear his influence on their children.

   They want to play with him because they like him, envy his freedom, and want to defy their mothers.

4. He sends Tom to sit on the girls' side as a punishment for being late and stopping to talk with Huck Finn.

Interpreting Meanings

5. He loves it: He wants to sit next to Becky Thatcher, whom he loves.

6. Nothing can keep Tom from being happy about his conversation with Becky.

7. Answers will vary. In truth, Beckys abound in classrooms today.

8. Tom confuses the names and locations of

For Study and Discussion

IDENTIFYING FACTS

1. Tom is a character who always seems to have a **problem**. What is his problem as "Dentistry" opens? How does he try to solve his difficulties?

2. Explain how Tom finally loses his tooth.

3. Explain why all the mothers in town hate and dread Huck Finn. Why do all the "respectable" boys want to play with him?

4. Why does the schoolmaster send Tom to sit on the girls' side of the schoolroom?

The romantic outcast, Huck Finn.
Illustration by E. W. Kemble (1884).

INTERPRETING MEANINGS

5. Describe how Tom feels about being sent to sit next to the girls.

6. At the end of the story, the schoolmaster has just dragged Tom by the ear over to his own seat. Why, then, is Tom so jubilant, or happy?

7. Did you find Becky's **character** believable in this excerpt? Why or why not?

8. Tom botches his geography lesson. What does it mean that he turns "lakes into mountains, mountains into rivers, and rivers into continents"? Why does Tom make all these errors?

APPLYING MEANINGS

9. Today, would a teacher punish a boy by sending him to sit with the *girls*? What other things that happened in this schoolroom would *not* happen today?

Focus on Reading

MAKING INFERENCES

An **inference** is an "educated guess." That means that an inference is a conclusion that is based on certain evidence.

Here are some passages from the story about Tom Sawyer. First find each passage and read it in context (that is, read the passages immediately before and after it). Then answer the questions that follow.

1. "Then she seized the chunk of fire and suddenly thrust it almost into the boy's face. The tooth hung dangling by the bedpost now." (Page 47)
   a. What happened when Aunt Polly thrust the fire in Tom's face?

52 A Gallery of Characters

b. Write a sentence supplying the details that are missing between sentences 1 and 2 here.

2. "[Huckleberry] was always the first boy that went barefoot in the spring and the last to resume leather in the fall." (Page 48)
    a. What does Twain mean by "leather" here?
    b. What did the boys wear on their feet in the summer?

3. "The master's arm performed until it was tired and the stock of switches notably diminished." (Page 49)
    a. What is the master doing here?
    b. Explain the action in your own words.

Literary Elements

CHARACTER

Mark Twain's greatest character is Huck Finn. Later, in another novel, Twain lets Huck tell his own story. Look back now at the passage on page 47 where Twain introduces Huck. Make a list of the details that help Huck come alive. Organize your details under these headings:

1. Huck's **appearance.**
2. Huck's **speech.**
3. Huck's **actions.**
4. What **other people** think about Huck.
5. What the writer tells you **directly** about Huck.

Twain says that Huck has "everything that goes to make life precious." In what ways is this definitely not true? Are there children like Huck Finn in our society today?

Language and Vocabulary

METAPHORS

Metaphors are imaginative comparisons which are not literally true. Metaphors compare two things that are basically unlike. For example, in paragraph 2, approaching Aunt Polly with a complaint about a loose tooth is compared with going into court to complain to a judge. (Tom knows he won't win in Polly's court!) Here are some other metaphors in this story.

1. "The master, throned on high in his great splint-bottom armchair, was dozing. . . ."
    a. Which word in this passage suggests a comparison between the schoolmaster and a king?
    b. What does this suggest about the way the master ran his schoolroom?

2. "The buzz of study ceased."
    a. What does Twain compare the sound of studying to?
    b. How might students in a classroom "buzz"?

Dramatizing a Story

(A Group Activity)

Tom Sawyer is great fun to dramatize. Select one of the scenes presented here and write a dramatization for a classroom theater. Here is what you'll have to consider:

1. How many **characters** do you need? List them and write a description of each one.
2. Describe where the **scene** will be set. What scenery will you need?
3. What **costumes** will you need?

the geographical features he is asked to identify. (You might ask for examples: Appalachian Lake, Mississippi Mountains, Ohio Sea.)

Tom makes all these errors because he is dazed by his love for Becky. (He is "spaced out.")

Applying Meanings
9. Few teachers today would punish a boy by having him sit with the girls. (Girls would rebel; also, in most classrooms, boys and girls sit together, and boys would not consider this a punishment.)

No teacher today would be allowed to beat a student as Tom was beaten. Slates aren't used. Girls and boys are not separated. A child wouldn't be beaten for having talked to another child. Students do not sit on long benches.

FOCUS ON READING
Making Inferences
1.a. Tom pulled away from the fire, and his tooth came out.
  b. Possible answer: Tom jerked his head back to avoid the fire and made the silk thread taut, yanking the thread so that the loose tooth came out.
2.a. *Leather* means "shoes."
  b. The boys went barefoot in the summer.
3.a. He is whipping Tom.

from *The Adventures of Tom Sawyer*

b. He whipped Tom until his arm was tired. He used many/several different switches.

LITERARY ELEMENTS
Character

1. Huck's appearance: dressed in ragged hand-me-downs; hat is a ruin; coat hangs nearly to his heels; one suspender supports his trousers; seat of the trousers are baggy; fringed legs drag in the dirt when not rolled up; Huck is unwashed.

2. Huck's speech: Huck swears like an adult and speaks in dialect.

3. Huck's actions: Huck sleeps out of doors; doesn't go to school or church; fishes and swims whenever he wants; is under no authority; can fight and sit up as late as he pleases; goes around barefoot most of the year.

4. What other people think about Huck: the mothers hate him and fear his influence on their children; the boys admire and envy him and enjoy his company.

5. Twain doesn't characterize Huck directly except to say, ironically, that he has "everything that goes to make life precious." This romantic view of Huck's life does not reflect the grim realities of poverty and of being the

4. You will have to assign an individual or a group to write **dialogue**. You should try to use as much of Twain's own dialogue as possible. For a model of how dramatic dialogue is written, see Unit Six.

5. Will you use **music** or any other **sound effects?**

6. What **props** do you need? (*Props* are "properties," or small movable objects used by the actors. Huck's tick is a prop.) Make a list.

Focus on Personal Narrative

USING VIVID LANGUAGE

Mark Twain uses vivid language to bring Tom Sawyer's adventures to life. Here are two kinds of vivid language that will make your own narrative more lively:

Metaphors: imaginative comparisons which are not literally true—for example, "the electric sympathy of love" (page 48) or "a peppering fire of giggles" (page 50).

Vivid action verbs: for example, *rippled, abash, hitched, traversed* in the paragraph on page 49 beginning with "The titter that rippled around the room."

Write a paragraph in which you describe an adventure with a classmate or another friend. Use as many vivid action verbs as you can. Try to include at least two or three metaphors. Save your writing.

About The Author

Mark Twain (1835–1910) is America's greatest comic writer and the author of two famous novels about growing up: *The Adventures of Tom Sawyer* and *The Adventures of Huckleberry Finn.*

"Mark Twain" was born Samuel Langhorne Clemens on the Missouri frontier, and

Mark Twain, 15 years old.

From the Mark Twain Papers. The Bancroft Library, University of California, Berkeley.

he grew up in a town on the Mississippi River. As a boy, he thrived on the teeming river traffic. As an adult, he took his famous pen name from the cry the boatmen made when the water reached the safe depth of two fathoms: "Mark twain!" He later wrote *Life on the Mississippi,* a book about his experiences as a cub pilot on a Mississippi River steamboat.

Twain wrote over a dozen other books and stories. His tales brought him wealth and fame. But he also knew failure and tragedy. Several of his businesses went bankrupt, and he was crushed by the deaths of his wife and two of his three young daughters. As he grew older, the great humorist found it more and more difficult to write.

But today Twain is remembered for the gift of wit and laughter he gave to the American people. He once said that laughter is the best weapon we have against the troubles of life.

Behind the Scenes

Is the Story True?

In his autobiography, Mark Twain talks about some of the experiences from his own life that he used in his novels. Here is how he remembers the boy who inspired the character of Huckleberry Finn. His name was Tom Blankenship.

. . . I have drawn Tom Blankenship exactly as he was. He was ignorant, unwashed, insufficiently fed; but he had as good a heart as ever any boy had. His liberties were totally unrestricted. He was the only really independent person— boy or man—in the community, and by consequence he was tranquilly and continuously happy and was envied by all the rest of us. We liked him; we enjoyed his society. And as his society was forbidden us by our parents, . . . we sought and got more of his society than of any other boy's. I heard, four years ago, that he was justice of the peace in a remote village in Montana and was a good citizen and greatly respected.

—Mark Twain

son of the town drunkard. In truth, Huck is beaten by his drunken father and eventually runs away.

Yes, sadly, there are children like Huck in our society. They are children of the homeless or children surviving alone.

LANGUAGE AND VOCABULARY
Metaphors
For answers, see the **Teaching Guide** at the beginning of the unit.

DRAMATIZING A STORY
Encourage students to present their skits before this or other classes.

FOCUS ON PERSONAL NARRATIVE
Using Vivid Language
Including metaphors in paragraphs might be difficult for students, so you may want to model the process before assigning the activity. First, discuss with students the **Language and Vocabulary** activity on p. 53. Then, with the help of students, write a paragraph on the board that includes several metaphors. You may want to include vivid verbs to model that aspect of the assignment as well.

OBJECTIVES
Students will read aloud to enjoy the story and the unusual "voice" of this tough law enforcer, Hank.

TEACHING RESOURCES A
Teacher's Notes, p. 68
Language Skills, p. 69

PRESENTATION
True to the banner headline, we ask no questions on this lighthearted story. You can use it any way you wish—even as a way of getting students into the unit, if you want to start out with Hank. The story is very simple. Students will not only read it quickly, they'll also want to read more.

NO QUESTIONS ASKED

from Hank the Cowdog

JOHN R. ERICKSON

Before You Read

The next character you'll meet, Hank the Cowdog, will tell you what it's like to have the all-important job of "Head of Ranch Security." As Hank will explain, a cowdog is used on farms and ranches to protect the livestock from coyotes. It's a tough job, and Hank doesn't fool around. You might recognize Hank and his friends from the cartoon made from this book.

After reading the excerpt through once so you're familiar with Hank's lively personality, take turns "being Hank" and read his story aloud. (You'll need one person to play the timid Drover.) Have fun disguising your voices to make the characters of this tough cowdog and his bumbling assistant come to life in your classroom.

56 A Gallery of Characters

MEETING INDIVIDUAL NEEDS
Visual Learners • If you plan to have students take turns reading the story aloud, you might involve other students in making the reading more interesting with a scrolled TV presentation. Students could divide the story into small segments for illustration and several students could draw pictures for the story. Students could then glue the illustrated sheets of paper together in a continuous horizontal length. They could construct a television model from a cardboard box, insert dowels in holes cut on each side of a cut-out screen, and roll the illustrated story around each side of the dowel sticks inside the television screen. As students read the story, two volunteers can roll the dowel sticks and show the pictures corresponding to the tale.

Bloody Murder

It's me again, Hank the Cowdog. I just got some terrible news. There's been a murder on the ranch.

I know I shouldn't blame myself. I mean, a dog is only a dog. He can't be everywhere at once. When I took this job as Head of Ranch Security, I knew that I was only flesh and blood, four legs, a tail, a couple of ears, a pretty nice kind of nose that the women really go for, two bushels of hair and another half-bushel of Mexican sandburs.

You add that all up and you don't get Superman, just me, good old easy-going Hank who works hard, tries to do his job, and gets very little cooperation from anyone else around here.

I'm not complaining. I knew this wouldn't be an easy job. It took a special kind of dog—strong, fearless, dedicated, and above all, smart. Obviously Drover didn't fit. The job fell on my shoulders. It was my destiny. I couldn't escape the broom of history that swept through . . . anyway, I took the job.

Head of Ranch Security. Gee, I was proud of that title. Just the sound of it made my tail wag. But now this, a murder, right under my nose. I know I shouldn't blame myself, but I do.

I got the report this morning around dawn. I had been up most of the night patrolling the northern perimeter of ranch headquarters. I had heard some coyotes yapping up there and I went up to check it out. I told Drover where I was going and he came up lame all of a sudden, said he needed to rest his right front leg.

I went alone, didn't find anything. The coyotes stayed out in the pasture. I figured there were two, maybe three of them. They yapped for a couple of hours, making fun of me, calling me ugly names, and daring me to come out and fight.

Well, you know me. I'm no dummy. There's a thin line between heroism and stupidity, and I try to stay on the south side of it. I didn't go out and fight, but I answered them bark for bark, yap for yap, name for name.

The coyote hasn't been built who can outyap Hank the Cowdog.

A little before dawn, Loper, one of the

The coyote hasn't been built who can outyap Hank the Cowdog.

Courtesy Maverick Books.

EXTENSION AND ENRICHMENT

There's a lot you can do with Hank.

Dramatizing the Story. Prepare the story for a classroom theater. Students should write dialogue based on the dialogue here. They will have to assign roles, costume the characters, design a few simple sets, and make a list of the necessary props. If they are particularly creative, they might even provide musical background (country and western? rock? classical?). Be sure someone designs a poster to advertise the show.

Rapping the Story. Rap is, after all, a kind of "street poetry" or music. Students who have mastered the rap technique could let Hank tell his tale to a rap beat. They might want to change Hank's background a bit and make him a visitor from New York.

Drawing a Cartoon. The illustrations here are from the novel itself. Students who like to draw might base their cartoon on these illustrations.

---

sneaky, you've got to watch 'em every minute."

Drover squinted at the tracks. "Are you sure those are coon tracks? They sure look like coyote to me."

"You don't go by the *look,* son, you go by the *smell*. This nose of mine don't lie. If it says coon, you better believe there's a coon at the end of them tracks. And I'm fixing to clean house on him. Stay behind me and don't get hurt."

I threaded my way through the creek willows, over the sand, through the water. I never lost the scent. In the heat of a chase, all my senses come alive and point like a blazing arrow toward the enemy.

In a way I felt sorry for the coon, even though he'd committed a crime and become my mortal enemy. With me on his trail, the little guy just didn't have a chance. One of the disadvantages of being as big and deadly as I am is that you sometimes find yourself in sympathy with the other guy.

But part of being Head of Ranch Security is learning to ignore that kind of emotion. I mean, to hold down this job, you have to be cold and hard.

The scent was getting stronger all the time, and it didn't smell exactly like any coon I'd come across before. All at once I saw him. I stopped dead still and Drover, the little dummy, ran right into me and almost had a heart attack. I guess he thought I was a giant coon or something. It's hard to say what he thinks.

The coon was hiding in some bushes about five feet in front of me. I could hear him chewing on something, and that smell was real strong now.

"What's that?" Drover whispered, sniffing the air.

"Coon, what do you think?" I glanced back at him. He was shaking with fear. "You ready for some combat experience?"

"Yes," he squeaked.

"All right, here's the plan. I'll jump him and try to get him behind the neck. You come in the second wave and take what you can. If you run away like you did last time, I'll sweep the corral with you and give you a whupping you won't forget. All right, let's move out."

I crouched down and crept forward, every muscle in my highly conditioned body taut and ready for action. Five feet, four feet, three feet, two. I sprang through the air and hit right in the middle of the biggest porcupine I ever saw.

It was kind of a short fight.
Courtesy Maverick Books.

MEETING INDIVIDUAL NEEDS

Visual Learners • If you plan to have students take turns reading the story aloud, you might involve other students in making the reading more interesting with a scrolled TV presentation. Students could divide the story into small segments for illustration and several students could draw pictures for the story. Students could then glue the illustrated sheets of paper together in a continuous horizontal length. They could construct a television model from a cardboard box, insert dowels in holes cut on each side of a cut-out screen, and roll the illustrated story around each side of the dowel sticks inside the television screen. As students read the story, two volunteers can roll the dowel sticks and show the pictures corresponding to the tale.

Bloody Murder

It's me again, Hank the Cowdog. I just got some terrible news. There's been a murder on the ranch.

I know I shouldn't blame myself. I mean, a dog is only a dog. He can't be everywhere at once. When I took this job as Head of Ranch Security, I knew that I was only flesh and blood, four legs, a tail, a couple of ears, a pretty nice kind of nose that the women really go for, two bushels of hair and another half-bushel of Mexican sandburs.

You add that all up and you don't get Superman, just me, good old easy-going Hank who works hard, tries to do his job, and gets very little cooperation from anyone else around here.

I'm not complaining. I knew this wouldn't be an easy job. It took a special kind of dog—strong, fearless, dedicated, and above all, smart. Obviously Drover didn't fit. The job fell on my shoulders. It was my destiny. I couldn't escape the broom of history that swept through . . . anyway, I took the job.

Head of Ranch Security. Gee, I was proud of that title. Just the sound of it made my tail wag. But now this, a murder, right under my nose. I know I shouldn't blame myself, but I do.

I got the report this morning around dawn. I had been up most of the night patrolling the northern perimeter of ranch headquarters. I had heard some coyotes yapping up there and I went up to check it out. I told Drover where I was going and he came up lame all of a sudden, said he needed to rest his right front leg.

I went alone, didn't find anything. The coyotes stayed out in the pasture. I figured there were two, maybe three of them. They yapped for a couple of hours, making fun of me, calling me ugly names, and daring me to come out and fight.

Well, you know me. I'm no dummy. There's a thin line between heroism and stupidity, and I try to stay on the south side of it. I didn't go out and fight, but I answered them bark for bark, yap for yap, name for name.

The coyote hasn't been built who can outyap Hank the Cowdog.

A little before dawn, Loper, one of the

The coyote hasn't been built who can outyap Hank the Cowdog.

Courtesy Maverick Books.

Hank the Cowdog 57

MEETING INDIVIDUAL NEEDS
ESL/LEP • Erickson's language may require clarification for students learning standard English. Ask the class to supply standard forms for the following examples:
(p.58)
Them coyotes yipped louder than ever....
... the ugliest, dumbest, **worthlessest** cur ...
He **don't** know a cow from a sow....
(p. 59)
Well, I **throwed** open one eye....
... I **seen** his tracks down on the creek....
... but I take this stuff pretty **serious.**
Them's coon tracks....
(p. 60)
This nose of mine **don't** lie.

---

cowboys on this outfit, stuck his head out the door and bellered, "Shut up that yapping, you idiot!" I guess he thought there was only one coyote out there.

They kept it up and I gave it back to them. Next time Loper came to the door, he was armed. He fired a gun into the air and squalled, something about how a man couldn't sleep around here with all the daddanged noise. I agreed.

Would you believe it? Them coyotes yipped louder than ever, and I had no choice but to give it back to them.

Loper came back out on the porch and fired another shot. This one came so close to me that I heard the hum. Loper must have lost his bearings or something, so I barked louder than ever to give him my position, and, you know, to let him know that I was out there protecting the ranch.

The next bullet just derned near got me. I mean, I felt the wind of it as it went past. That was enough for me. I shut her down for the night. If Loper couldn't aim any better than that, he was liable to hurt somebody.

I laid low for a while, hiding in the shelter belt, until I was sure the artillery had gone back to bed. Then I went down for a roll in the sewer, cleaned up, washed myself real good, came out feeling refreshed and ready to catch up on my sleep. Trotted down to the gas tanks and found Drover curled up in my favorite spot.

I growled him off my gunny sack. "Beat it, son. Make way for the night patrol."

He didn't want to move so I went to sterner measures, put some fangs on him. That moved him out, and he didn't show no signs of lameness either. I have an idea that where Drover is lamest is between his ears.

I did my usual bedtime ritual of walking in a tight circle around my bed until I found just exactly the spot I wanted, and then I flopped down. Oh, that felt good! I wiggled around and finally came to rest with all four paws sticking up in the air. I closed my eyes and had some wonderful twitching dreams about . . . don't recall exactly the subject matter, but most likely they were about Beulah, the neighbor's collie. I dream about her a lot.

What a woman! Makes my old heart pound just to think about her. Beautiful brown and white hair, big eyes, nose that tapers down to a point (not quite as good as mine, but so what?), and nice ears that flap when she runs.

Only trouble is that she's crazy about a spotted bird dog, without a doubt the ugliest, dumbest, worthlessest cur I ever met. What could be uglier than a spotted short-haired dog with a long skinny tail? And what could be dumber or more worthless than a dog that goes around chasing *birds*?

They call him Plato. I don't know why, except maybe because his eyes look like plates half the time, empty plates. He don't know a cow from a sow, but do you think that makes him humble? No sir. He thinks that birdchasing is hot stuff. What really hurts, though, is that Beulah seems to agree.

58 A Gallery of Characters

Don't understand that woman, but I dream about her a lot.

Anyway, where was I? Under the gas tanks, catching up on my sleep. All at once Drover was right there beside me, jumping up and down and giving off that high-pitched squeal of his that kind of bores into your eardrums. You can't ignore him when he does that.

Well, I threw open one eye, kept the other one shut so that I could get some halfway sleep. "Will you please shut up?"

"Hank, oh Hankie, it's just terrible, you wouldn't believe, hurry and wake up, I seen his tracks down on the creek, get up before he escapes!"

I threw open the other eye, pushed myself up, and went nose-to-nose with the noisemaker. "Quit hopping around. Quit making all that racket. Hold still and state your business."

"Okay, Hank, all right, I'll try." He tried and was none too successful, but he did get the message across. "Oh Hank, there's been a killing, right here on the ranch, and we slept through it!"

"Huh?" I was coming awake by then, and the word *killing* sent a jolt clean out to the end of my tail. "Who's been killed?"

"They hit the chickenhouse, Hank. I don't know how they got in but they did, busted in there and killed one of those big leghorn hens, killed her dead, Hank, and oh, the blood!"

Well, that settled it. I had no choice but to go back on duty. A lot of dogs would have just turned over and gone back to sleep, but I take this stuff pretty serious.

We trotted up to the chickenhouse, and Drover kept jumping up and down and talking. "I found some tracks down by the creek. I'm sure they belong to the killer, Hank, I'm just sure they do."

"What kind of tracks?"

"Coyote."

"Hmm." We reached the chickenhouse and, sure enough, there was the hen lying on the ground, and she was still dead. I walked around the body, sniffing it good and checking the signs.

I noticed the position of the body and memorized every detail. The hen was lying on her left side, pointing toward the northeast, with one foot out and the other one curled up under her wing. Her mouth was open and it appeared to me that she had lost some tail feathers.

"Uh huh, I'm beginning to see the pattern."

"What, tell me, Hank, who done it?"

"Not yet. Where'd you see them tracks?" There weren't any tracks around the corpse, ground was too hard. Drover took off in a run and I followed him down into the brush along the creek.

He stopped and pointed to some fresh tracks in the mud. "There they are, Hank, just where I found them. Are you proud of me?"

I pushed him aside and studied the sign, looked it over real careful, sniffed it, gave it the full treatment. Then I raised up.

"Okay, I've got it now. It's all clear. Them's coon tracks, son, not coyote. I can tell from the scent. Coons must have attacked while I was out on patrol. They're

EXTENSION AND ENRICHMENT

There's a lot you can do with Hank.

Dramatizing the Story. Prepare the story for a classroom theater. Students should write dialogue based on the dialogue here. They will have to assign roles, costume the characters, design a few simple sets, and make a list of the necessary props. If they are particularly creative, they might even provide musical background (country and western? rock? classical?). Be sure someone designs a poster to advertise the show.

Rapping the Story. Rap is, after all, a kind of "street poetry" or music. Students who have mastered the rap technique could let Hank tell his tale to a rap beat. They might want to change Hank's background a bit and make him a visitor from New York.

Drawing a Cartoon. The illustrations here are from the novel itself. Students who like to draw might base their cartoon on these illustrations.

---

sneaky, you've got to watch 'em every minute."

Drover squinted at the tracks. "Are you sure those are coon tracks? They sure look like coyote to me."

"You don't go by the *look,* son, you go by the *smell*. This nose of mine don't lie. If it says coon, you better believe there's a coon at the end of them tracks. And I'm fixing to clean house on him. Stay behind me and don't get hurt."

I threaded my way through the creek willows, over the sand, through the water. I never lost the scent. In the heat of a chase, all my senses come alive and point like a blazing arrow toward the enemy.

In a way I felt sorry for the coon, even though he'd committed a crime and become my mortal enemy. With me on his trail, the little guy just didn't have a chance. One of the disadvantages of being as big and deadly as I am is that you sometimes find yourself in sympathy with the other guy.

But part of being Head of Ranch Security is learning to ignore that kind of emotion. I mean, to hold down this job, you have to be cold and hard.

The scent was getting stronger all the time, and it didn't smell exactly like any coon I'd come across before. All at once I saw him. I stopped dead still and Drover, the little dummy, ran right into me and almost had a heart attack. I guess he thought I was a giant coon or something. It's hard to say what he thinks.

The coon was hiding in some bushes about five feet in front of me. I could hear him chewing on something, and that smell was real strong now.

"What's that?" Drover whispered, sniffing the air.

"Coon, what do you think?" I glanced back at him. He was shaking with fear. "You ready for some combat experience?"

"Yes," he squeaked.

"All right, here's the plan. I'll jump him and try to get him behind the neck. You come in the second wave and take what you can. If you run away like you did last time, I'll sweep the corral with you and give you a whupping you won't forget. All right, let's move out."

I crouched down and crept forward, every muscle in my highly conditioned body taut and ready for action. Five feet, four feet, three feet, two. I sprang through the air and hit right in the middle of the biggest porcupine I ever saw.

It was kind of a short fight.
Courtesy Maverick Books.

A Gallery of Characters

Combining Stories. You might have students do a skit in which Hank the Cowdog is inserted into C. S. Lewis's Narnia where he meets Mr. Tumnus and tries to help him solve his problem with the White Witch.

PORTFOLIO ASSESSMENT
Suggest that students now take the time to reflect about what they have collected and selected for inclusion in their portfolios. Ask students to write a self-evaluation of their portfolios, pointing out what they think are strong inclusions, what they would like to improve, and how they would improve selections that need revision.

Quills: Just Part of the Job

It was kind of a short fight. Coming down, I seen them quills aimed up at me and tried to change course. Too late. I don't move so good in mid-air.

I lit right in the middle of him and *bam*, he slapped me across the nose with his tail, sure did hurt too, brought tears to my eyes. I hollered for Drover to launch the second wave but he had disappeared.

Porcupine took another shot at me but I dodged, tore up half an acre of brush, and got the heck out of there. As I limped back up to the house on pin-cushion feet, my thoughts went back to the murder scene and the evidence I had committed to memory.

It was clear now. The porcupine had had nothing at all to do with the murder because porcupines don't eat anything but trees. Drover had found the first set of tracks he had come to and had started hollering about coyotes. I had been duped into believing the runt.

Yes, it was all clear. I had no leads, no clues, no idea who had killed the hen. What I *did* have was a face-full of porcupine quills, as well as several in my paws. . . .

About the Author

John R. Erickson (1943–   ) was born in Midland, Texas. *Hank the Cowdog* is the first in the series of Hank the Cowdog books. Erickson has written more than twenty books about the adventures of Hank. Describing his books, Erickson says: "I write my stories to be like an amusement park water slide— once you're on, you can't get off and before you know it, it's over." In addition to writing, Erickson likes ranching and playing a five-string banjo. Two recent books by Erickson are *The Case of the Car-Barkaholic Dog* and *Hank the Cowdog: The Case of the Hooking Bull*.

Hank the Cowdog 61

OBJECTIVES

The overall aim is for students to use evidence and reasoning to identify and state the theme of a literary selection as a generalization.

PRESENTATION

You might introduce the concept of making generalizations by writing on the chalkboard the theme of "The Jacket" as stated in the text. Use the questions in the book to model how this theme applies to the story. Students might then work in small groups with the questions to analyze either of the suggested stories and write a statement of theme. Ask groups to share orally with the class their responses to the questions and their generalization. You might want to emphasize that often themes are universal statements to which many people can relate experiences from their own lives.

MAKING GENERALIZATIONS

The theme of a story is usually not stated directly. In addition to examining details in the story, insightful readers might discover the theme by thinking about their feelings as they read and about how the events remind them of things in their own lives. Good stories may have several themes which students can explore.

Answers

Answers will vary. Themes for "Mr. Tumnus" might include the following: A person should not forsake his or her own idea of what is right; friendship can create a powerful bond. For "Harriet Tubman," students might say the following: A person must make great sacrifices to be free; or help often comes from unexpected sources; or a person must believe in himself or herself.

FOCUS ON Reading and Critical Thinking

MAKING GENERALIZATIONS

The **theme** of a story is its main idea or basic meaning. The theme is not the same as the subject. You can usually state the subject of a story in a word or phrase: for example, "childhood" or "escape to freedom." The theme is something the writer wants to reveal about the subject. Use a complete sentence to state a theme.

A **generalization** about the theme of a work is a broad statement that sums up the work's central meaning. The ability to make a generalization can help you enjoy literature more. It can also help you to sum up the meaning of an experience you tell about in a **personal narrative.**

To make a generalization, you need to use sufficient evidence and sound reasoning. Here are some questions to ask when you are trying to find the theme of a story:

- *What is the writer's central purpose?* What is the writer trying to show about life or human nature?
- *How do the characters change through the story?* For example, does a character learn a new lesson or undergo a change in attitude?
- *What major conflicts occur, and how are they resolved?* Do the conflicts end with the characters understanding more about themselves? Do the characters overcome challenges?
- *Does the title give a clue to the theme?*

After you identify the theme of a story, state it in a complete sentence as a generalization about life or human nature. This means that the statement will apply to many people, not just to the characters in the story. For example, the theme of Gary Soto's "The Jacket" (page 35) might be stated as the following generalization: *When we feel insecure, even the smallest problems can seem major.*

Write a complete sentence stating the theme of *one* of the following selections: C. S. Lewis' "Mr. Tumnus" (page 10) or Ann Petry's "Harriet Tubman" (page 22). You can use the questions above as guidelines to help state the theme as a generalization.

A Gallery of Characters

OBJECTIVES

The overall aim is for students to write a personal narrative about an experience from their lives.

PRESENTATION

You might want to use this writing activity to emphasize the importance of writing as a process. Point out to students that their journals can become good places to apply the prewriting stage. Then have students review their notes from the sections titled "Focus on Personal Narratives" and explain that they already have the beginnings for a personal narrative. They can use these ideas or begin again. Increase students' awareness of the writing process and its recursiveness by writing with the students and using your narrative to model the steps. Be careful to show students that the revisions stage should be

---

FOCUS ON Writing

WRITING A PERSONAL NARRATIVE

*I*n a **personal narrative** you write about an experience from your own life. In this kind of writing, you tell about events in a clear order. You also express the thoughts and feelings you had about the experience.

Prewriting

1. You will find these hints helpful when you choose a subject for a personal narrative:
   - Choose an experience that is still sharp and clear in your memory.
   - Choose an experience that was important to you.
   - Choose an experience that you are willing to share.

   You can use a chart like the one below to get ideas about topics. What memories does the word at the top of each column prompt in you? (Feel free to use different memory prompts if you wish.)

Movies	Clothes	Family
Teams	Songs	Challenges

[See **Focus** assignment on page 19.]

2. Think about your purpose and audience. Your **purpose** in a personal narrative is to share one of your experiences with your readers. Make notes while you prewrite about your memories, thoughts, and feelings.

   Your **audience** will probably be your classmates and your teacher. Remember that they may need some background information in order to understand your experience. Make notes about the details that your audience may need.

3. Gather **action details** and **sensory details** that will make your narrative clear and lively. Action details tell what happened and how it happened. These details also include **dialogue,** or the words that people said. Try to use dialogue as often as you can to tell about a situation. You can turn a situation into dialogue by following these simple steps:
   - Visualize the situation as vividly as you can
   - Think about what the people involved in the situation said
   - Consider *how* the people spoke: cheerfully, sadly, quickly, slowly, hesitantly, and so on

   Sensory details appeal to the five senses of sight, hearing, taste, smell, and touch. You can list these details on a chart like the one on the next page.

Focus on Writing   63

HOLT WRITER'S WORKSHOP

This computer program provides help for all types of writing through guided instruction for each step of the writing process. (Program available separately.)

See **Elements of Writing, Introductory Course,** Chapter 3, for more instruction on expressive writing.

WRITING A PERSONAL NARRATIVE

Precision of word choice is important in creating detailed narrative writing. Students need time to experiment and play with words. Now may be the time to introduce students to the thesaurus or have students create their own lists of active verbs and sensory words and phrases.

Prewriting

After students have had plenty of time to gather their ideas in the charts, you might have them share their notes in small groups. Students should read their charts aloud and tell briefly about their experience, and then the listeners can ask questions and offer their own

63

viewed not as a punishment, but as a luxury. Tell students that good writers often feel that time does not allow them to revise as much as they want. Use the proofreading stage to demonstrate the need for students to make their writing easy to understand and to ensure that their readers are not distracted by mistakes. Point out that writers want their audiences to remember their words and ideas, not their errors. Students might benefit from always knowing how their writing will be published in the early stages of writing so that they can become more aware of their audience.

CLOSURE

Ask students to identify the steps of the writing process and to list what they did to their narratives at each stage.

---

insights about each other's narratives.

Writing

Remind students that a first draft is often one of discovery. Encourage students not to get bogged down with organization or words. Instead they should just write as naturally as possible, trying to use their own "voices" to tell about their experiences. As students write, you might plan conferences to help them with organization and language.

Evaluating and Revising

When students are ready to evaluate their drafts, encourage them to read their narratives aloud to a small group. The listeners should be prepared to make positive comments about each other's papers—what they like and what is good—before they begin to make suggestions for improvements. Students might help each other make a few revisions on these drafts and then use the **Checklist for Evaluation and Revision** for additional follow-up. For individual revision, have students experiment with different ways to use dialogue.

Details Chart

Action Details	Sensory Details
_____	_____
_____	_____
_____	_____
_____	_____

[See **Focus** assignment on page 32.]

4. Reflect on why the experience was important to you. What were you like before the experience? How did it change you? What did you learn from it? Make a few notes on the overall meaning of the experience.

Writing

1. Follow an outline like the one below to write your narrative.

    I. Beginning: Grab reader's attention and introduce topic.
    II. Body: Tell events in order, giving details, thoughts, and feelings.
    III. Ending: Show the meaning the experience had for you.

    Use **chronological** or **time order** in the body of your narrative. Also plan to use **transitional words and phrases** to show the connections of events and ideas. Some helpful transitions include the following: *after, before, finally, first, next, often, second, soon, then, third,* and *when*. [See **Focus** assignment on page 41.]

2. Make your language as vivid as you can. For example, you can use **metaphors,** or imaginative comparisons that are not literally true. You can also use **vivid action verbs** to help your readers *see* the action. [See **Focus** assignment on page 54.]

Evaluating and Revising

1. When you have finished your first draft, trade papers with a classmate. Read each other's narratives. Then give each other comments and suggestions. Is the order of events clear? Does the narrative help the reader "see" the characters and situations? Does the narrative help the reader understand the meaning of the experience?

    Here is how one writer revised a paragraph from a personal narrative.

Writer's Model

That Saturday morning I dressed *like an express train and tore* quickly. I went into the kitchen. I was so excited that I couldn't hardly eat breakfast. Uncle Harry was coming at seven o'clock to drive us all to the opening of the state fair in Raleigh. The fair is the most popular entertainment event in our area. I had carefully made a list of the main events and rides. I

---

64   A Gallery of Characters

overslept. The clock face said 6:45. At first I had no idea what day it was, but soon I realized it was the big weekend I'd been waiting for ever since spring began.

2. You may find the following checklist helpful as you revise your narrative.

Checklist for Evaluation and Revision

- Does the beginning get the reader's attention and tell the topic?
- Do I tell the events in their chronological order?
- Do I use vivid action verbs and lively language?
- Does the narrative include dialogue to show what people actually said?
- Do I include details that show my own thoughts and feelings?
- Do I tell or show the overall meaning of the experience?

Proofreading and Publishing

1. Proofread your personal narrative and correct any errors you find in grammar, usage, and mechanics. (Here you may find it helpful to refer to the **Handbook for Revision** on pages 750–785.) Then prepare a final version of your narrative by making a clean copy.
2. Consider some of the following publication methods for your narrative:
   - read your narrative orally in a story theater for younger students
   - share a copy of your narrative with a relative or friend
   - illustrate your narrative with drawings or other art work and then join with a small group to make a collection of narratives

Portfolio If your teacher approves, you may wish to keep a copy of your work in your writing folder or portfolio.

Proofreading and Publishing

You might want to do a few mini-lessons on punctuation, capitalization, and paragraphing of dialogue so that students can focus on these mechanics as they proofread their papers. You might create small editing groups and model how to proofread. Students should also be conscious of fragments, run-on sentences, and spelling errors.

Unit 2 ◆ Teaching Guide

QUESTS

OVERVIEW OF THE UNIT

The focus of this unit is the motif of the quest. For two reasons, the quest is especially appropriate for young students. First, most students are already familiar with the quest as an important element of the stories they came to know so well as children. Second, because quests are also a part of everyday life, students can use this unit to see the connection between literature and their own existence.

WHAT IS A QUEST?

A quest is a search for something of great value—a lost treasure, a hidden kingdom, a missing child. The sought-after person or thing must be important. Unless you were trying to be funny, you wouldn't use the word quest to describe a search for a missing button.

Some quests are internal. In many modern stories, especially, a character embarks on a quest for answers to the questions "Who am I?" and "What kind of life should I lead?"

Most of us think of quests as the journeys that King Arthur's knights once undertook to test their strength and wisdom and all-around worthiness. But, in fact, stories of quests are very, very old and they are told in all corners of the world. There are quest stories in the great myths of Sumeria, Greece, Egypt, Ireland, India, China, and Persia. In Africa and the Americas, every native culture has its quest stories. The quest is a prominent motif in European, African, and Asian fairy tales. There are quest stories in today's novels and in tomorrow's movies from Hollywood. For sheer storytelling power, there is nothing quite like a quest. If students think of the stories and movies that command attention today, they're likely to find a quest at the center.

THE ELEMENTS OF A QUEST STORY

1. The Goal. The quest takes shape when an individual (Indiana Jones, Superman, Dorothy in the Oz story) sets out on a journey to seek some goal. The goal might be a plane that has vanished from sight, an explorer who has been swallowed by a storm, or a child last seen leaving school. Dorothy's quest, for example, is to find the Wizard of Oz so she can get back home to Kansas. In the great mythic quest, the goal is usually to save a kingdom or a people who are in great danger.

2. The Perilous Journey. Quest stories involve a journey (either actual or figurative) that is full of peril. Heroes and heroines of literature fight many enemies on their quests: dragons, raging rivers, treacherous guides, false friends, tempters who try to stop the quest. Very often the quester must also face fear, doubt, mockery, or loneliness. In fact, it is usually when the person conquers these inner conflicts that he or she realizes the true value of the quest.

3. The Reward. If the quest is successful, the hero or heroine is rewarded or exalted at the end of the journey. Sometimes the person discovers that what is most important is not the pile of treasure or the fabulous kingdom. What often comes to be important is the quest itself—and what it has shown the hero or heroine to be capable of.

WHY ARE QUEST STORIES SO POPULAR?

The answer to this question might be that everyone's life can be seen as a quest story. All of us are on a "journey," searching for something of value: for love, perhaps, or happiness, peace, justice, or beauty. Some people believe, in fact, that the quest story has to do with our overriding quest to discover what it means to be truly human. And that discovery of the human identity may be the most important quest that any of us will ever undertake.

QUEST STORIES IN THIS BOOK

So key is the quest in literature that you can find a quest in almost every narrative in this book. Here are some selections in other units that you might want to discuss at some point, in terms of the quest:

"Julie of the Wolves" (page 3): a quest for survival in the wilderness
"Harriet Tubman" (page 22): a quest for freedom
"Dragon, Dragon" (page 166): a quest to save a threatened kingdom (a parody of the old romantic quest stories)
"President Cleveland, Where Are You?" (page 178): a quest to win something of material worth (a baseball mitt), which turns into a search for something of genuine human value (generosity, selflessness)
"Becky and the Wheels-and-Brake Boys" (page 220): a quest for a bicycle
"Nancy" (page 233): a quest for freedom (to be one's self)
"Where the Buffaloes Begin" (page 252): a quest to find a sacred lake, which turns into a quest to save a threatened people
The Secret Garden (page 474): a quest for love
"Glooscap Fights the Water Monster" (page 558): a god's quest to slay a monster and save a people
"Perseus" (page 567): a quest to slay a monster
The Summer of the Swans (page 648): a quest to find a lost brother, which turns into a quest for what is truly valuable in life

OBJECTIVES OF THE UNIT

The aims of this unit for students are
◆ To monitor their own reading
◆ To make inferences
◆ To draw conclusions
◆ To identify details that support conclusions
◆ To identify a narrative sequence
◆ To recognize and respond to descriptive details
◆ To predict outcomes
◆ To identify major events
◆ To use context clues to arrive at word meaning
◆ To identify a dialect
◆ To recognize a quest story

PLANNING GUIDE

For Unit Planning
- Transparencies 7–11: *Audiovisual Resources Binder*
- *Portfolio Assessment and Professional Support Materials*
- Test Generator
- Mastery Tests: Teaching Resources A, pp. 157, 159
- Analogy Test: Teaching Resources A, p. 163
- Revision Worksheet: Teaching Resources A, p. 164

SELECTION (Pupil's Page)	Teacher's Notes	Reading Check	Reading Focus	Study Guide	Language Skills	Building Vocabulary	Selection Vocab. Test	Selection Test	AV Binder Audio-cassette
QUESTS Introduction (p. 67)	91								
Close Reading of a Selection Scott O'Dell from *Carlota* (p. 69)	91								
Anne McCaffrey *The Smallest Dragonboy* (p. 78)	92	95	96	97, 98	99	102	104	105	
Gary Paulsen from *Hatchet* (p. 99)	107	110	111	112, 113	114, 117	120	122	123	
William Armstrong from *Sounder* (p. 114)	125	127	128	129, 130	131	134	136	137	Tape 1 Side A
Marjorie Kinnan Rawlings *Jody's Discovery* (p. 129)	139	142	143	144, 145	146	149	151	152	
M. R. Cox *The Algonquin Cinderella* (p. 147)	154								Tape 1 Side B

- To identify conflict
- To infer character traits
- To write a narrative
- To write creatively and critically about the selections

CONCEPTS AND SKILLS

The following concepts and skills are treated in this unit:

Close Reading of a Selection
Guidelines for Close Reading 68
One Reader's Response 69
Looking at Yourself as a Reader 75

Thinking About Words
How to Own a Word 76

Focus on Reading and Critical Thinking
Drawing Conclusions 95, 144
Identifying the Sequence of Events 111
Supporting General Statements 126
Exploring Connotations 152

Literary Elements
Conflict 95, 111
Character 145

Language and Vocabulary
Description and Mood 112
Dialect 126, 145

Opportunities for Writing
Focus on Descriptive Writing
Finding a Focus 96
Using Exact Words 112
Using Sensory Details 126
Organizing a Description 145
Writing a Description 153

Connections
Connecting Cultures 96

Speaking and Listening
An Oral Reading of Dialect 145
Classroom Theater 147

TRANSPARENCIES

The following unit support materials with specific correlations to literature selections are available in the **Fine Art and Instructional Transparencies with Teacher's Notes and Blackline Masters** section of your *Audiovisual Resources Binder*.

FINE ART TRANSPARENCIES

Theme: Searching for Something of Value
7 *Alexander Observing the Ichthyophagi,* Anonymous
8 *Harriet Tubman Series No. 22,* Jacob Lawrence

READER RESPONSE
9 Focus on Conflict

LITERARY ELEMENTS
10 Conflict

WRITING PROCESS
11 Writing a Description

INTRODUCING THE UNIT

1. Putting Together a Reading List. Encourage students to start assembling a bibliography of fiction and nonfiction narratives that involve a quest. Students could write brief reviews of the stories they select and post them on the class bulletin board so that other students can refer to them. (See a list of suggested readings on page 722).

2. Writing an Original Quest Story. Have students write the outline of an original story in which a character or characters embark on a quest. Encourage them to expand their outlines into stories. Some students will want to share their stories with the class.

3. Discussing Quests on TV. Capitalize on popular television programs by asking students to list their favorite shows and to discuss the quests that are often at the center of their plots.

PORTFOLIO ASSESSMENT

Suggestions for use of portfolios as support for this unit are described in the **Portfolio Assessment and Professional Support Materials** booklet accompanying this program. Specific suggestions are provided for a variety of student projects that may be suitable for inclusion in a portfolio. In addition, copying masters are provided for guides that may be used for evaluation and assessment of student projects.

SELECTION NOTES

Following are vocabulary lists of words from each selection that are included in the Building Vocabulary Worksheets and Selection Vocabulary Tests; Reading Check tests (which are also available in blackline masters); and answers to questions in the Language and Vocabulary sections that follow the selections.

"THE SMALLEST DRAGONBOY" (PAGE 78)

Vocabulary

transparent	replenish(ed)	unwieldy	incredulous
resume(d)	dispute	retrieve	
disgrace	indifference	exhalation	

Reading Check

Have students judge each statement as true or false.

1. The people of Benden Weyr must protect themselves against attacks of Thread.   **True**
2. The dragons are chosen by the dragonriders.   **False**
3. Keevan breaks his leg in an argument with Beterli.   **True**
4. Keevan is finally Impressed by a green dragon.   **False**
5. Beterli is Impressed by a bronze dragon.   **False**

Language and Vocabulary: A Glossary (page 80)

backwinging: flying backward.
Benden drink: a kind of beverage served with meals.
dragonrider: one of an elite corps that protects Pern.
firestone: a kind of fuel fed to dragons to create flames.
Hatching Day: day when the dragon eggs hatch.
Hatching Ground: hot cavern where dragon's eggs are hatched.
hatchling: small, newly born dragon.
Impress: to make telepathic communication with an infant dragon, during which he chooses you as his rider.
numb weed: plant that acts as an anesthetic.
rockbarrow: wheelbarrow used to carry black rock.
Thread: evil, destructive force that threatens Pern.
tuffed out: eliminated.
watchpair: dragon and its rider who guard Pern.
weyrleader: chief of the weyr, or cave colony.
weyrling: young member of the colony.
wher-hide: skin of a wher, used to make boots.
wingsecond: second-in-command of a group of dragonriders.

"HATCHET" (PAGE 99)

Vocabulary

delicate(ly)	embed(ded)	register(ed)	gratify(ied)
initial	ignite	intense	
gesture(s)	exasperation	consume(ing)	

Reading Check

Have students judge each statement as true or false.

1. Brian kills the bear with his hatchet.   **False**
2. A coyote enters Brian's cave.   **False**
3. Brian starts a fire with his matches.   **False**
4. Brian considers the fire to be a friend.   **True**

Language and Vocabulary: Description and Mood (page 112)

You might ask students to read aloud passages from the selection that appeal to the five senses.

Sight: "It was some form of chalky granite, or a sandstone, but imbedded in it were large pieces of a darker stone . . ." (page 106)
Sound: "Then he heard the slithering. A brushing sound, a slithering brushing sound near his feet . . ." (page 103)
Touch: "His fingers gingerly touched a group of needles that had been driven through his calf. They were stiff and very sharp on the ends that stuck out . . ." (page 103)
Taste: "The berries were full and ripe, and he tasted one to find it sweet, and with none of the problems of the gut cherries." (page 100)

Remind students to use word pictures that appeal to one or more of the five senses in their own descriptive sentences. Some sample descriptions: "The roar of the soccer team echoed from the metal lockers." "The street lights still glowed yellow in the morning fog." "The smell of sizzling bacon reached all the way to the parking lot."

"Sounder" (page 114)

Vocabulary

jeer(ed)	mellow	parch(ed)	waver(ing)
commotion	wilt(ed)	mimic(ked)	
pursuit	drought	distinct	

Reading Check

Have students judge each statement as true or false.

1. The boy is able to read his big book with ease. False
2. The man who helps the boy nurse his injured hand is a schoolteacher. True
3. The shelves in the man's cabin are filled with books. True
4. The boy's mother forbids him to go live with and be taught by the old man. False
5. Sounder dies before the father returns. False

Language and Vocabulary: Dialect (page 126)

1. "It has words that I am not used to reading. I can read words on signs in stores."
2. "You have been a very good friend to take me in like this. My fingers don't hurt anymore."
3. "Who has tended your injuries?"
4. "Why are you walking so fast? Have you found him? Is your hand hurt badly? Is that a Bible that someone has mistreated?"

"Jody's Discovery" (page 129)

Vocabulary

contortion(s)	falter(ed)	emit	catastrophe
vitality	deliberation	vigil	endure
futile	desolate		

Reading Check

Have students judge each statement as true or false.

1. The Baxter's two hunting dogs kill the rattlesnake. False
2. Jody runs to the Forresters to get help for his father. True
3. Jody tells Doc Wilson, "We Baxters are all tall and strong." False
4. Penny recovers immediately from the snakebite. False
5. Jody finds the fawn in the scrub. True

Language and Vocabulary: Dialect (page 145)

Remind the students to study carefully the passage they select. They should read the words aloud several times for their sound as well as for their content. Be sure they do not mock these characters.

Student Learning Options

Quests

1. Building a Model
Ask students to work in groups of three to build papier-mâché models of objects mentioned in one of the stories in the unit. Possibilities include a burro clam, a dragon or dragon egg, or an Algonquin wigwam.

2. Writing a Newspaper
The stories in this unit feature events that are newsworthy. Have students write a four-page newspaper with articles about the "news" in each of the stories. Students can include advertisements, pictures, and other items that newspapers contain.

3. Making a Report
There are many animals featured in the stories in this unit, and students are probably not familiar with most of them. Have students look up information, including pictures if possible, about the animals in the stories. They can report their findings to the class.

4. Improvising a Homecoming
Ask students to improvise the scene from *Sounder* in which the father returns from jail. You can divide the class into groups and let each group act out the scene, or you can select several students to do the improvisation for the whole class.

5. Exploring the Quest Theme
Ask your school librarian to prepare a book cart of works that deal with the quest theme. Bring the cart to the classroom and let students browse through the books. Encourage them to check out a book and to read it on their own.

6. Creating a Poster
Have students work in small groups to create posters advertising the stories in the unit. The posters should include an illustration from the story, a list of characters, with a brief description of each, and quotations from the story that attract the attention of potential readers. Display the posters in the classroom.

7. Drawing a Mural
Assign students to groups of three or four, and divide a story from the unit into as many parts as there are groups. Ask each group to read their assigned section carefully and then to design and execute a picture that represents what happens in their section of the story. Put all of the group pictures together to form a mural of the whole story, and use it to decorate the classroom.

8. Producing a Video
Ask small groups of students to select scenes from the stories in the unit and have each group act out their scene. Videotape the scenes and let the class decide on best actor, best actress, and best video.

9. Exploring Vocabulary
Give students a list of vocabulary words (such as the list provided in the teacher's material at the beginning of the unit) and have them look up the words. Then, have them look through old magazines to find the words used in headlines. They can cut out the headlines for use on a vocabulary collage.

10. Writing Titles
Have students write titles for the selections in the unit that are excerpted from books. Ask them to explain their titles in a brief paragraph or orally for the whole class.

65D

FOCUS/MOTIVATION

Background. The story of Carlota de Zubarán is based in part on the life of Luisa Montero, a real Spanish woman who lived in Southern California in the early 1800s. The object of Carlota's quest in this part of the novel is gold. The sunken ship is one of the great galleons that had, in the 1600s, carried fabulous treasures from South America and the Indies. Many of these galleons had sunk off the California coast. Others had hidden from pirates by pulling into the sheltered lagoons and then for some reason had been unable to return to sea. In one of these galleons, Carlota and her father have found two chests filled with pure gold minted in Lima, Peru, in 1612. Remember that at this time, California is owned by Mexico.

Establishing a Purpose for Reading. Ask students to try to visualize the setting and the perils Carlota must face in her underwater quest.

TEACHING RESOURCES A
Teacher's Notes, p. 91

Close Reading OF A SELECTION

*A*ctive readers are always thinking as they read. You are reading actively if you ask questions as you go along: "What will happen next?" or "How could she get herself into this mess?" or "What does that word mean?" Active readers make a lot of guesses, too, and as you know, it's a great feeling when you discover that you've guessed correctly. Active readers draw conclusions from many different clues.

Guidelines for Close Reading

1. Figure out the meaning of an unfamiliar word by using context clues, the words and phrases surrounding the word.
2. Visualize the scene. Use your imagination to picture the time and place of action.
3. Draw conclusions as you read. Look for direct and indirect clues to meaning.

The following excerpt is from the novel *Carlota* by Scott O'Dell. The main character in this novel, Carlota, lives with her father, Don Saturnino (sä•tōōr•nē′nō), a wealthy Spanish landowner in California. Her brother Carlos was killed by rivals of their Spanish colony before Carlota was born. Her father named Carlota after his dead son and has brought her up almost as her brother's replacement. As this episode begins, Carlota and her father are making one of their many trips to Blue Beach, where they have found a sunken ship full of gold. The story takes place in the 1800s. Carlota is telling the story.

The comments in the margin show one reader's response to the selection. Ask questions of your own as you read.

68 Quests

Prereading Journal. Have students write a few sentences describing what they think it must be like to be trapped underwater. What thoughts might go through their minds?

from
Carlota
SCOTT O'DELL

There were many things to do before the chests could be reached. Usually it took me half a day to bring up a pouch of coins from the sunken ship.

The place where I dove, which was surrounded by jagged rocks and driftwood, was too narrow for my father. He had tried to squeeze through when we first discovered the galleon, but partway down he got stuck and I had to pull him back. It was my task, therefore, to go into the cavelike hole. My father stood beside it and helped me to go down and to come up.

I buckled a strong belt around my waist and to it tied a riata that was ten *varas* long and stout enough to hold a stallion. I fastened my knife to my wrist—a two-edged blade made especially for me by our blacksmith—to protect myself against spiny rays and the big eels that could sting you to death. In the many dives I had made, I never had seen a shark.

Taking three deep breaths, I prepared to let myself down into the hole. In one hand I held a sink-stone, heavy enough to weigh me down. I let out all the air in my chest, took a deep breath, and held it. Then I began the descent.

The sink-stone would have taken me down fast, but the edges of the rocky hole were sharp. I let myself down carefully, one handhold at a time. It took me about a minute to reach the rotted deck where the chests lay. I now had two minutes to pry the coins loose and carry them to the surface. We had tried putting the coins in a leather sack and hoisting them to the surface. But we had trouble with this because of the currents that swept around the wreck.

The coins lay in a mass, stuck together, lapping over each other and solid as rock. They looked, when I first saw them, like something left on the stove too long. I always expected

ONE READER'S RESPONSE

Sunken treasure! This is my kind of adventure. The girl is doing the diving?

What's a galleon? Another word for ship?

"Jagged rocks," "driftwood," "cavelike"— she must be brave. The diving is dangerous. **1**
Is riata rope in Spanish? Varas—must be some kind of measurement. **2**

Maybe this is a hint that she'll meet a shark during this dive. Another danger. **3**

I'm trying to picture these jagged rocks under the water. It's a little confusing. **4**
She can hold her breath for three minutes?! I can only hold mine for forty seconds. **5**

Why are the coins stuck together? The ship must have been sunk for a long time.

1. GUIDED READING:
Making Inferences
Note that this reader has made an inference about Carlota—that she is brave—based on her actions and the threatening underwater setting.

2. GUIDED READING:
Using Context Clues
What clues help this reader guess the meaning of the word varas*? The words* ten *and* long *are clues.*

3. LITERARY ELEMENTS:
Foreshadowing and Suspense
This mention of sharks foreshadows possible danger ahead and builds up the reader's suspense.

4. GUIDED READING:
Visualizing the Setting
This detail is important to the story. You might ask students to draw the rocks and the sunken ship to see if they all can visualize the scene. Do they understand the reason for the "sink-stone"? (What do divers use today?)

5. GUIDED READING:
Using Prior Knowledge
Notice how reader uses her own experience to evaluate Carlota's ability.

Close Reading of a Selection

COOPERATIVE LEARNING

For her dive, Carlota used only a riata, a double-edged knife, and a sink-stone. Have students work together in small groups to research modern scuba equipment and to compare it to the equipment Carlota had on her dive. (Most encyclopedias have entries for *scuba* or *scuba diving*.) Extend this activity by asking students to find out about recent expeditions to explore sunken vessels. What are the divers' goals and what equipment do they use to achieve those goals?

1. GUIDED READING:
Making Inferences
Does anyone else besides Carlota and her father know about the gold? What makes you think this? Nobody else knows. Carlota and her father speak of the coins as though they are a secret.

2. GUIDED READING:
Drawing Conclusions
Notice that the reader draws a conclusion based on the information in the sentence.

3. GUIDED READING:
Predicting Outcomes
The reader expects trouble and predicts that it will come in the form of a shark.

Close Reading
OF A SELECTION

I can see her walking on the ship's deck with that rocky tunnel above. (It must be hard to walk under water.)

He's smart—I would have agreed with Carlota.

2 *That's nice—they must have a close relationship.*

What are barnacles?

I didn't know that. It must be a hard trip up to the surface with all that extra weight.

3 *She does see a shark... Oh, but it's not dangerous. So far, so good.*

---

to find them gone, but now as I walked toward the chests, with the stone holding me down, I saw that they were still there. No one had come upon them during the seven months since our last visit.

The first time I had dived and brought up a handful of coins, I said to my father that we should empty both the chests and take the coins home.

"Then everyone would talk," Don Saturnino said. "As soon as they saw the gold coins, the news would spread the length of California."

"We don't need to tell anyone. I can hide them in my chest at home."

1 "The news would fly out before the sun set. At the ranch there are many eyes."

I still thought it was a better idea to empty the chests before someone else did, but I could see that my father enjoyed these days when the two of us went to the Blue Beach, so I said no more.

The sun was overhead and its rays slanted down through the narrow crevice. There were many pieces of debris on the deck and I had to step carefully. With my knife I pried loose a handful of coins. They were of a dark green color and speckled here and there with small barnacles. I set the coins aside.

My lungs were beginning to hurt, but I had not felt the tug of the riata yet, the signal from my father that I had been down three minutes. I pried loose a second handful and put my knife away. Before the tug came, I dropped my sink-stone and took up the coins. Gold is very heavy, much heavier than stones of the same size.

Fish were swimming around me as I went up through the hole of rocks and tree trunks, but I saw no sting rays or eels. I did see a shark lying back on a ledge, but he was small and gray, a sandshark, which is not dangerous.

On my third trip down, I hauled up about the same number of coins as the other times. The pouch we had brought was now full. I asked my father if we had enough.

"Are you tired?" he said

70 Quests

SOCIAL STUDIES LINK
Invite students to learn more about the galleons that sank off the Pacific coast of California in the 1600s. Other students might want to learn about Luisa Montero, the woman on whom the character of Carlota is based. Have students give a short oral presentation on what they learned to the class.

Encourage interested students to read *Island of the Blue Dolphins* by Scott O'Dell, another story based on a historical incident on the Pacific coast.

1. GUIDED READING:
Predicting Outcomes
Again, the reader expects trouble and responds to the hints dropped by the storyteller.

"Yes, a little."
"Can you go down again?"
"Yes."
"Then go."

I dived twice more. It was on the last dive that I had the trouble. The tug on the riata had not come, but I was tired, so I started away from the chest with one handful of coins. Close to the chests, between them and the hole, I had noticed what seemed to be two pieces of timber covered with barnacles. They looked as if they might be part of a third and larger chest.

I still held my knife and I thrust it at a place where the two

I wonder if he's greedy, or maybe he is just enjoying the adventure of it all.

Now the trouble is coming. What will it be— another shark? **1**

Close Reading of a Selection 71

1. LITERARY ELEMENTS:
Suspense
One of the time-honored methods of creating suspense is to have a character work against the clock. This reader knows from an earlier detail that Carlota can hold her breath for only three minutes.

2. LITERARY ELEMENTS:
Suspense
We want to know what has caught Carlota and we fear she will drown if she can't hold her breath any longer. The repulsive words describing what Carlota sees when she looks into the murky water add to the suspense. What could this "long fleshy tongue" belong to?

3. GUIDED READING:
Using Prior Knowledge
The reader estimates the size of the clam by using information from the text and what she knows about the size of the average man.

4. GUIDED READING:
Noting Details
Notice, above, the mention of the fishermen who had "lost their lives in the burro's jaws."

Close Reading
OF A SELECTION

What is it? She's caught.

1 *This means she's been down for three minutes.*

I was right—a riata is a rope. Two tugs must be a distress signal.

Horrible! What could be licking her?

3 *Half the height of a man—that means about three feet. A three-foot clam?!*

She has to get air soon. She must be about to pass out.

Almost sounds like a science fiction movie. I would be terrified. A maw? Maybe a mouth (a huge mouth).

She's free—I can breathe again.

---

gray timbers seemed to join. It was possible that I had found another chest filled with coins.

As the knife touched them, the two timbers moved a little. Instantly, I felt pressure upon my wrist. I drew back the hand that held the knife. Rather, I tried to draw it back, but it would not move. The tide had shifted the timbers somehow and I was caught. So I thought.

I felt the tug upon the riata fastened to my waist. It was the signal from my father to come to the surface. I answered him with two quick tugs of the leather rope.

2 Now I felt a hot pain run up my arm. I tried to open my fingers to drop the knife, but my hand was numb. Then as I stared down into the murky water, I saw a slight movement where my hand was caught. At the same moment I saw a flash of pink, a long fleshy tongue sliding along my wrist.

I had never seen a burro clam, but I had heard the tales about them, for there were many on our coast. Attached to rocks or timbers, they grew to half the height of a man, these gray, silent monsters. Many unwary fishermen had lost their lives in the burros' jaws.

The pain in my arm was not so great now as the hot pains in my chest. I gave a long, hard tug on the riata to let my father know that I was in trouble. Again I saw a flash of pink as the burro opened its lips a little, and the fat tongue slid back and forth.

4 I dropped the coins I held in my other hand. The burro had closed once more on my wrist. But shortly it began to open again, and I felt a sucking pressure, as if the jaws were trying to draw me inside the giant maw.

Putting my knees against the rough bulge of the shell, as the jaws opened and then began to close, I jerked with all my strength. I fell slowly backward upon the ship's deck. My hand was free. With what breath I had I moved toward the hole. I saw the sun shining above and climbed toward it. The next thing I saw was my father's face and I was lying on the river's sandy bank. He took my knife in his hand.

After I told him what had happened, my father said, "The

knife saved your life. The burro clamped down upon it. See the mark here. The steel blade kept its jaws open. Enough to let you wrench yourself free."

1 He pulled me to my feet and I put on my leather pants and coat.

"Here," he said, passing the reins of his bay gelding to me, "ride Santana. He goes gentler than Tiburón."

"I'll ride my own horse," I said.

"Good, if you wish it."

"I wish it," I said, knowing that he didn't want me to say that my hand was numb.

"Does the hand hurt?"

"No."

"Some?"

"No."

"You were very brave," he said.

My father wanted me to be braver than I was. I wanted to say I was scared, both when the burro had hold of me and now, at this moment, but I didn't because he expected me to be as brave as Carlos. It was at times like this that I was angry at my father and at my dead brother, too.

"It was good fortune," I said.

"Fortune and bravery often go together," Don Saturnino said. "If you do not hurt, let us go."

These must be the horses' names. I guess a bay gelding must be a kind of horse.

Maybe numbness is a sign that the clam might have done lasting damage. Why doesn't her father want her to say it?

She's lying. Trying to be brave for her father?

Imagine trying to compete with a dead brother! I guess she must be angry with her brother for dying, but why is she angry with her father?

Well, at least they got some gold. I wonder if her hand gets better.

1. LITERARY ELEMENTS:
Setting
Setting involves place and time. It also involves lifestyles, culture, food, and clothing. These leather pants, mentioned in a story set in the 1800s, show how daring Carlota was—to wear the leather pants of a Spanish *vaquero*. Remember, too, that her father is raising her as if she were a boy.

VISUAL CONNECTIONS
Ask students to trace the outlines of this clam on a piece of paper and draw an arm beside it, to help them visualize Carlota's perilous situation. (How large would the arm be in relation to the clam?)

Close Reading of a Selection

SOCIAL STUDIES LINK
Encourage interested students to read other historical fiction by Scott O'Dell, such as *Sarah Bishop,* a story set in the Revolutionary War period, and *Sing Down the Moon,* a true account of the Navajo people in 1864.

SCIENCE LINK
Invite interested students to find out how modern-day scientists restore, preserve, and catalog treasures found in sunken ships. How have the processes changed in this age of advanced technology? Who keeps the treasures once they are found and restored? Students could look for information in encyclopedias under *galleons, salvage, sunken treasure,* or *treasure hunting.*

VISUAL CONNECTIONS
See the note on page 68 about the California lagoons, in which the great Spanish galleons often hid from marauding American and English pirates. This photograph shows a lagoon that could be the one Carlota is exploring.

Close Reading OF A SELECTION

CLOSURE

Have one volunteer describe Carlota's quest, telling (1) what its object was and (2) what its perils were.

PORTFOLIO ASSESSMENT

Students who found it helpful to keep a journal during their study of the first unit may want to keep a reader's journal as they study the selections in this unit. In their reading journals, students may include summaries, important words or phrases, unfamiliar words, questions, doodle art, and other responses to the literature. As they finish each selection, students may want to write a statement that tells what they think was the author's purpose in writing. Journals may be decorated and included in their portfolios. (For more information on student portfolios, see the *Portfolio Assessment and Professional Support Materials* booklet.)

Looking at Yourself as a Reader

As you look back over this reader's comments, you'll notice:

1. **The reader asks questions about vocabulary.** This reader correctly guesses that *riata* (rē·ä′tä) is the Spanish word for a type of rope. And *varas* is a measurement—equal to about 33 inches. Most of the time, this reader is able to make a good guess at unfamiliar words by using the **context clues,** or the words and phrases surrounding the word. For instance, a *galleon* is a kind of ship—in fact, a large Spanish ship made in the fifteenth and sixteenth centuries. The word *maw* means "oral cavity," or mouth. It is used to refer to the mouth of a large animal.

2. **The reader visualizes the scene.** As she pictures the rocks, she understands the danger of Carlota's quest.

3. **This reader also draws conclusions.** For example, she figures that the ship must have been sunk quite a while for the coins to be stuck together. She calculates the half-height of a man. She concludes that numbness could mean serious trouble after an attack by a burro clam.

Read the excerpt again, this time writing down your own thoughts. After you finish, answer these questions.

1. What kind of person is Carlota? Do you think that she likes being brave and strong and her father's favorite?
2. This reader didn't know why Carlota was angry with her father. What do you think?
3. What might happen next?

LOOKING AT YOURSELF AS A READER

1. Carlota is certainly strong, brave, resourceful, and obedient.
2. Carlota complains that her father might want her to be braver than she really is. She thinks that her father may measure her unfairly against Carlos, her dead brother.
3. Many things could happen next: Carlota's father could send her diving again for coins and she could hurt herself. Enemies could steal the coins. Her father could be killed. Carlota could rebel.

It seems impossible that she will not survive because she is telling the story and so is presumably alive at the writing. Ask students if the story would be more suspenseful if it were told not by Carlota but by an omniscient narrator, someone not in the story at all.

Close Reading of a Selection

How to Own a Word

The word *maw*, mentioned on pages 72 and 75, is interesting, and students might enjoy trying to use it themselves. Encourage them to fill in a chart something like this one:

Which animals would you say have "maws"?
-
-
-

Which animals would you say do *not* have "maws"?
-
-
-

What would a person be like if you described his or her mouth as a "maw"?
-
-
-

THINKING ABOUT WORDS

HOW TO OWN A WORD

What does it mean to know the meaning of a word? You can know nothing or just a little about a word, or you can know a lot about it. When you know a lot about a word, you may feel that you "own" it. To own a word means that you find it easy to understand—not only when you read it, but also when you speak it or write it.

Part of owning a word is figuring out what you already know about it. For instance, *condescend* (kon'di·send') is a word you may know something about. Maybe you've heard someone described as *condescending*. You may realize that people who are *condescending* talk or behave in ways that show they think they are superior to other people.

ORGANIZING WHAT YOU KNOW ABOUT A WORD

Below is a cluster diagram that organizes some ideas about *condescend*. Think of other ideas you might add.

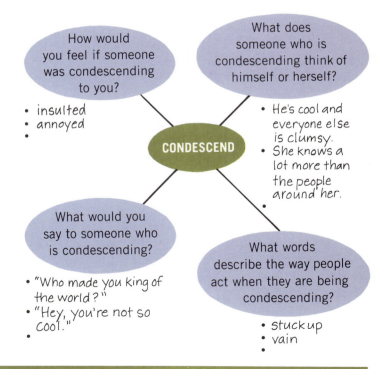

READING THE SELECTION

Most students who read on level will be familiar with fantasy, either from stories they've read as children or from movies or television. They should be able to read this story silently in one class sitting, after you've discussed the headnote and reviewed the illustrations.

Slower students may have trouble with the length of the story and with the vocabulary. For them, you may wish to divide the story into two parts: (1) up to the dragonriders' discussion of whether or not to eliminate the youngest candidates from Impression (pages 80–86); and (2) from the day following that discussion to the end of the story (pages 86–94). Remind them that the Glossary at the back of the book will help them with difficult words.

Before You Read

Somewhere in outer space lies the planet Pern, an imaginary world created by Anne McCaffrey. The planet is continually threatened by a deadly force and is protected by the great dragons and their riders who rule its skies. Many of McCaffrey's novels and short stories take place on Pern.

The deadly threat to Pern comes from a dangerous Red Star that rains threadlike plant spores on Pern every two hundred years or so. If the hungry Thread falls on Pern soil and grows there, it will devour every living thing.

To protect their planet, colonists on Pern have developed a race of great winged dragons. These dragons have the telepathic power to travel instantly from one place to another to fight Thread. When fed a special rock called *firestone,* the dragons of Pern breathe flaming tongues of fire that char Thread to ashes in midair. During Threadfall, the dragons and their dragonriders charge into airborne battle, while the other colonists hide safely in their Holds, or cave towns. During the Intervals between Threadfalls, Pern's protectors live inside the cones of old volcanoes, in cave colonies called *weyrs.* The following short story takes place in Benden Weyr, a dragonrider colony in the Benden Mountains.

As the story opens, young Keevan and his fellow candidates for dragonrider are awaiting important news from the Hatching Ground. A clutch of dragon eggs is about to hatch. It is the custom for each newborn dragon to choose its own rider—and lifelong partner—through a kind of telepathic communication called *Impression.*

Impressing a dragon at his first Hatching is vital to Keevan, the youngest dragonboy. How else can he silence the other boys' jeers that he is only "a babe"?

As you read this short story, keep a notepad handy. Write down all the questions you have about Keevan and his quest to become a dragonrider.

MEETING INDIVIDUAL NEEDS

ESL/LEP • Aside from the Pernian vocabulary, the author uses several words in a different context from what students might normally encounter. Before students read the story, write the following words on the chalkboard:

spanking
(fast moving; rapid) (page 80)

turns
(years; a term that signals a change in time) (page 85)

clutch
(a nest of eggs; a group of animals gathered together) (page 85)

Ask the class to define each word according to common usage and to use the word in a sentence. Then encourage students to guess the meaning of the word as the author uses it in the story.

1. LANGUAGE AND VOCABULARY

The Pernian vocabulary should not block students' enjoyment of this famous fantasy. Assure students that they should be able to figure out the meanings of most Pernian words from context clues. They will become familiar with other words as the story goes on; part of the pleasure in reading "The Smallest Dragonboy" comes from gradually understanding what these Pernian words mean.

Before they read, you might have the class as a whole decide on the way they'll pronounce the Pernian names: Keevan, Beterli, Mende, F'lar, Mnementh, K'last, L'vel.

2. GUIDED READING:
Making Inferences
What can you infer about Keevan's size? He is small, with short legs.

3. GUIDED READING:
Drawing Conclusions
What could "tail fork-end" mean? Since these are potential dragonriders, and since dragons have forked tails, the writer is probably playing with the more common phrase "tail end," meaning "last." This might be a Pernian figure of speech.

80

Language and Vocabulary

1 Pern has its own people, plants, animals, geography, and weather. To make this imaginary world believable, the writer has created new names, like Keevan, and new words, like *weyr*. She has also combined some familiar English words to make new words, like *dragonrider*. These invented words help you to enter the strange and dangerous world of Pern.

As you read the story, figure out the meanings of the invented words from their **context,** or the words around them. You might make a list of these words to put in a "Pernian" dictionary.

2 Although Keevan lengthened his walking stride as far as his legs would stretch, he couldn't quite keep up with the other candidates. He knew he would be teased again.

Just as he knew many other things that his foster mother told him he ought not to know, Keevan knew that Beterli, the most senior of the boys, set that spanking pace just to embarrass him, the smallest dragon-**3** boy. Keevan would arrive, tail fork-end of the group, breathless, chest heaving, and maybe get a stern look from the instructing wingsecond.

Dragonriders, even if they were still only hopeful candidates for the glowing eggs which were hardening on the hot sands of the Hatching Ground cavern, were expected to be punctual and prepared. Sloth[1] was not tolerated by the weyrleader of Benden Weyr. A good record was especially important now. It was very near hatching time, when the baby dragons would crack their mottled[2] shells and stagger forth to choose their lifetime companions. The very thought of that glorious moment made Keevan's breath catch in his throat. To be chosen—to be a dragonrider! To sit astride the neck of the winged beast with the jeweled eyes; to be his friend in telepathic communion[3] with him for life; to be his companion in good times and fighting extremes; to fly effortlessly over the lands of Pern! Or, thrillingly, *between* to any point anywhere on the world! Flying *between* was done on dragonback or not at all, and it was dangerous.

---
1. **sloth:** laziness.
2. **mottled:** marked with blotches and spots.
3. **telepathic** (tel'ə·path'ik) **communion:** communication between minds without speaking.

80 Quests

MEETING INDIVIDUAL NEEDS
Visual and Kinesthetic Learners • Have students create dioramas or murals of a favorite scene in the story or of a place on Pern, such as the Hatching Ground or Feeding Ground. Remind them to look back over the story for details to include. Encourage students who wish to work together on this project to do so.

Display completed projects in the classroom.

---

1 Keevan glanced upward, past the black mouths of the weyr caves in which grown dragons and their chosen riders lived, toward the Star Stones that crowned the ridge of the old volcano that was Benden Weyr. On the height, the blue watch dragon, his rider mounted on his neck, stretched the great transparent pinions[4] that carried him on the winds of Pern to fight the evil Thread that fell at certain times from the sky. The many-faceted rainbow jewels of his eyes glistened momentarily in the greeny sun. He folded his great wings to his back, and the watchpair resumed their statuesque pose of alertness.

Then the enticing view was obscured as Keevan passed into the Hatching Ground cavern. The sands underfoot were hot, even through heavy wher-hide boots. How the bootmaker had protested having to sew so small! Keevan was forced to wonder again why being small was reprehensible.[5] People were always calling him "babe" and shooing him away as being "too small" or "too young" for this or **2** that. Keevan was constantly working, twice as hard as any other boy his age, to prove himself capable. What if his muscles weren't as big as Beterli's? They were just as hard. And if he couldn't overpower anyone in a wrestling match, he could outdistance everyone in a footrace.

"Maybe if you run fast enough," Beterli had jeered on the occasion when Keevan had been goaded to boast of his swiftness, "you could catch a dragon. That's the only way you'll make a dragonrider!" **3**

"You just wait and see, Beterli, you just wait," Keevan had replied. He would have liked to wipe the contemptuous smile from Beterli's face, but the guy didn't fight fair even when the wingsecond was watching. "No one knows what Impresses a dragon!"

"They've got to be able to *find* you first, babe!"

Yes, being the smallest candidate was not an enviable position. It was therefore imperative that Keevan Impress a dragon in his first hatching. That would wipe the smile off every face in the cavern, and accord him the respect due any dragonrider, even the smallest one.

Besides, no one knew exactly what Impressed the baby dragons as they struggled from their shells in search of their lifetime partners.

"I like to believe that dragons see into **4** a man's heart," Keevan's foster mother, Mende, told him. "If they find goodness, honesty, a flexible mind, patience, courage—and you've that in quantity, dear Keevan—that's what dragons look for. I've seen many a well-grown lad left standing on the sands, Hatching Day, in favor of someone not so strong or tall or handsome. And if my memory serves me" (which it usually did—Mende knew every word of every Harper's tale worth telling, although Keevan did not interrupt her to say so), "I don't believe that F'lar, our weyrleader,

---
4. **pinions** (pin′yənz): wings.
5. **reprehensible** (rep′ri·hen′sə·bəl): deserving of blame.

The Smallest Dragonboy 81

---

1. GUIDED READING:
Visualizing
This is a fantastic description. Encourage students to describe what they see. Some might illustrate the scene. Would it make a good book cover?

2. GUIDED READING:
Making Inferences
What does this passage reveal about Keevan? It shows that Keevan is determined, that he tries very hard, and that he cares what others think of him.

3. LITERARY ELEMENTS:
Conflict
This establishes the conflict between Keevan and Beterli over Keevan's chances of becoming a dragonrider.

4. GUIDED READING:
Identifying Main Ideas
What is Mende saying? The values of goodness, honesty, flexibility, patience, and courage are more important to the dragons than physical strength or impressive size or looks. Dragons have the ability to see into the human heart and to judge character.

> **TRANSPARENCIES 7 & 8**
> **Fine Art**
> Theme: *Searching for Something of Value* – highlights artworks depicting people engaged in challenging, even dangerous, pursuits in order to achieve a goal.

1. GUIDED READING:
Drawing Conclusions
Note that there will be more candidates matched to green dragons than to bronze ones.

Green dragons are more numerous than bronze ones. Be sure students understand that the bronze dragons are the most desirable. Keevan has set his sights on a green—the easiest dragon of all to Impress.

2. GUIDED READING:
Making Inferences
What does this passage reveal about Beterli? The other candidates are afraid of Beterli. He is a bully and is capable of physical violence. He's also selected the most desirable kind of dragon—a bronze—as his own. He is arrogant.

1 was all that tall when bronze Mnementh chose him. And Mnementh was the only bronze dragon of that hatching."

Dreams of Impressing a bronze were beyond Keevan's boldest reflections; although that goal dominated the thoughts of every other hopeful candidate. Green dragons were small and fast and more numerous. There was more prestige to Impressing a blue or a brown than a green. Being practical, Keevan seldom dreamed as high as a big fighting brown, like Canth, F'nor's fine fellow, the biggest brown on all Pern. But to fly a bronze? Bronzes were almost as big as the queen, and only they took the air when a queen flew at mating time. A bronze rider could aspire to become weyrleader! Well, Keevan would console himself, brown riders could aspire to become wingseconds, and that wasn't bad. He'd even settle for a green dragon; they were small, but so was he. No matter! He simply had to Impress a dragon his first time in the Hatching Ground. Then no one in the weyr would taunt him anymore for being so small.

"Shells," thought Keevan now, "but the sands are hot!"

"Impression time is imminent,[6] candidates," the wingsecond was saying as everyone crowded respectfully close to him. "See the extent of the striations on this promising egg." The stretch marks *were* larger than yesterday.

Everyone leaned forward and nodded thoughtfully. That particular egg was the one Beterli had marked as his own, and no other candidate dared, on pain of being beaten by Beterli on the first opportunity, to approach it. The egg was marked by a large yellowish splotch in the shape of a dragon backwinging to land, talons outstretched to grasp rock. Everyone knew that bronze eggs bore distinctive markings. And naturally, Beterli, who'd been presented at eight Impressions already and

---

6. **imminent** (im′ə·nənt): about to happen.

82 Quests

was the biggest of the candidates, had chosen it.

"I'd say that the great opening day is almost upon us," the wingsecond went on, and then his face assumed a grave expression. "As we well know, there are only forty eggs and seventy-two candidates. Some of you may be disappointed on the great day. That doesn't necessarily mean you aren't dragonrider material, just that *the* dragon for you hasn't been shelled. You'll have other hatchings, and it's no disgrace to be left behind an Impression or two. Or more."

Keevan was positive that the wingsecond's eyes rested on Beterli, who'd been stood off at so many Impressions already. Keevan tried to squinch down so the wingsecond wouldn't notice him. Keevan had been reminded too often that he was eligible to be a candidate by one day only. He, of all the hopefuls, was most likely to be left standing on the great day. One more reason why he simply had to Impress at his first hatching.

"Now move about among the eggs," the wingsecond said. "Touch them. We don't know that it does any good, but it certainly doesn't do any harm."

Some of the boys laughed nervously, but everyone immediately began to circulate among the eggs. Beterli stepped up officiously to "his" egg, daring anyone to come near it. Keevan smiled, because he had already touched it . . . every inspection day . . . as the others were leaving the Hatching Ground, when no one could see him crouch and stroke it.

1
Grave means "serious," or "solemn." You could ask them at what other times someone might look grave.

2
Officiously (ə·fish′əs·lē) means "in a self-important manner." What other people sometimes behave officiously? Why is an officious person annoying?

The Smallest Dragonboy

1. GUIDED READING:
Making Comparisons
In what way is the egg like Keevan? It is apart from the other eggs, much as Keevan is apart from the other candidates because of his size and his age. Keevan feels that this egg, like himself, is not very desirable.

2. GUIDED READING:
Making Inferences
What does this passage reveal about Keevan? Keevan is not afraid to stand up for himself.

3. GUIDED READING:
Recognizing Cause and Effect
Note that the dragonriders are able to relax because there will be no Thread attack for three more days.

4. GUIDED READING:
Drawing Conclusions
Notice that without firestone, the dragons would be unable to destroy Thread and Pern would perish.

---

1 Keevan had an egg he concentrated on, too, one drawn slightly to the far side of the others. The shell bore a soft greenish-blue tinge with a faint creamy swirl design. The consensus was that this egg contained a mere green, so Keevan was rarely bothered by rivals. He was somewhat perturbed then to see Beterli wandering over to him.

"I don't know why you're allowed in this Impression, Keevan. There are enough of us without a babe," Beterli said, shaking his head.

"I'm of age." Keevan kept his voice level, telling himself not to be bothered by mere words.

"Yah!" Beterli made a show of standing on his toe tips. "You can't even see over an egg. Hatching Day, you better get in front or the dragons won't see you at all. 'Course, you could get run down that way in the mad scramble. Oh, I forget, you can run fast, can't you?"

2 "You'd better make sure a dragon sees *you* this time, Beterli," Keevan replied. "You're almost overage, aren't you?"

Beterli flushed and took a step forward, hand half raised. Keevan stood his ground, but if Beterli advanced one more step, he would call the wingsecond. No one fought on the Hatching Ground. Surely Beterli knew that much.

Fortunately, at that moment the wingsecond called the boys together and led them from the Hatching Ground to start on evening chores.

There were "glows" to be replenished in the main kitchen caverns and sleeping cubicles, the major hallways, and the queen's apartment. Firestone sacks had to be filled against Thread attack, and black rock brought to the kitchen hearths. The boys fell to their chores, tantalized by the odors of roasting meat. The population of the weyr began to assemble for the evening meal, and the dragonriders came in from the Feeding Ground or their sweep checks.

It was the time of day Keevan liked best. Once the chores were done, before dinner was served, a fellow could often get close to the dragonriders and listen to their talk. Tonight Keevan's father, K'last, was at the main dragonrider table. It puzzled Keevan how his father, a brown rider and a tall man, could *be* his father—because he, Keevan, was so small. It obviously never puzzled K'last when he deigned[7] to notice his small son: "In a few more turns, you'll be as tall as I am—or taller!"

3 K'last was pouring Benden drink all around the table. The dragonriders were relaxing. There'd be no Thread attack for three more days, and they'd be in the mood to tell tall tales, better than Harper yarns, about impossible maneuvers they'd done a-dragonback. When Thread attack was closer, their talk would change to a discussion of tactics of evasion, of going *between*, how long to suspend there until the burning but fragile Thread would freeze and crack and fall harmlessly off dragon and man. **4** They would dispute the exact moment to feed firestone to the dragon so he'd have the best flame ready to sear Thread midair

---

7. **deigned** (dānd): here, lowered himself.

84 Quests

and render it harmless to ground—and man—below. There was such a lot to know and understand about being a dragonrider that sometimes Keevan was overwhelmed. How would he ever be able to remember everything he ought to know at the right moment? He couldn't dare ask such a question; this would only have given additional weight to the notion that he was too young yet to be a dragonrider.

"Having older candidates makes good sense," L'vel was saying, as Keevan settled down near the table. "Why waste four to five years of a dragon's fighting prime until his rider grows up enough to stand the rigors?" L'vel had Impressed a blue of Ramoth's first clutch. Most of the candidates thought L'vel was marvelous because he spoke up in front of the older riders, who awed them. "That was well enough in the Interval when you didn't need to mount the full weyr complement to fight Thread. But not now. Not with more eligible candidates than ever. Let the babes wait."

"Any boy who is over twelve turns has the right to stand in the Hatching Ground," K'last replied, a slight smile on his face. He never argued or got angry. Keevan wished he were more like his father. And oh, how he wished he were a brown rider! "Only a dragon . . . each particular dragon . . . knows what he wants in a rider. We certainly can't tell. Time and again the theorists"—and K'last's smile deepened as his eyes swept those at the table—"are surprised by dragon choice. *They* never seem to make mistakes, however."

"Now, K'last, just look at the roster[8] of this Impression. Seventy-two boys and only forty eggs. Drop off the twelve youngest, and there's still a good field for the hatchlings to choose from. Shells! There are a couple of weyrlings unable to see over a wher egg, much less a dragon! And years before they can ride Thread."

"True enough, but the weyr is scarcely under fighting strength, and if the youngest Impress, they'll be old enough to fight when the oldest of our current dragons go *between* from senility."

"Half the weyrbred lads have already been through several Impressions," one of the bronze riders said then. "I'd say drop some of *them* off this time. Give the untried a chance."

"There's nothing wrong in presenting a clutch with as wide a choice as possible," said the weyrleader, who had joined the table with Lessa, the weyrwoman.

"Has there ever been a case," she said, smiling in her odd way at the riders, "where a hatchling didn't choose?"

Her suggestion was almost heretical[9] and drew astonished gasps from everyone, including the boys.

F'lar laughed. "You say the most outrageous things, Lessa."

"Well, *has* there ever been a case where a dragon didn't choose?"

"Can't say as I recall one," K'last replied.

"Then we continue in this tradition,"

---

8. **roster:** list.
9. **heretical** (hə·ret′i·kəl): against the established views.

The Smallest Dragonboy 85

SPEECH LINK
Divide the class into three teams to continue the dragonriders' debate of whether or not all the candidates should be allowed to stand in the Hatching Ground. One team could argue that all candidates should be allowed to stand, another team could argue that the youngest should be eliminated, and a third team could argue that those who had passed several impressions unchosen should be eliminated. Students may also wish to hold a debate about whether or not girls should be allowed to stand in the Hatching Ground.

1. GUIDED READING:
Summarizing
If you stop here, have students summarize the story so far. Summaries should explain the setting, characters, and major events: (a) Keevan lives in Pern, a planet in outer space that is protected by fabulous dragons and their riders. (b) His rival is Beterli, another boy, who taunts him for being small and young. (c) Keevan wants to be chosen a dragonrider at a Hatching of new dragons. The dragons choose their own riders. (d) Keevan has set his sights low, on a green dragon. A bronze is the most desirable dragon. (e) Beterli has marked a bronze egg as the one he wants. (f) The dragonriders discuss limiting the Impression to older candidates. (g) Keevan fears he'll be eliminated because of his age.

2. GUIDED READING:
Identifying Pronoun Referents
To whom does the pronoun he *refer?* To Keevan.

Lessa said firmly, as if that ended the matter.

But it didn't. The argument ranged from one table to the other all through dinner, with some favoring a weeding out of the candidates to the most likely, lopping off those who were very young or who had had multiple opportunities to Impress. All the candidates were in a swivet,[10] though such a departure from tradition would be to the advantage of many. As the evening progressed, more riders were favoring eliminating the youngest and those who'd passed four or more Impressions unchosen. Keevan felt he could bear such a dictum[11] only if Beterli was also eliminated. But this seemed less likely than that Keevan would be tuffed out, since the weyr's need was for fighting dragons and riders.

By the time the evening meal was over, no decision had been reached, although the weyrleader had promised to give the matter due consideration.

He might have slept on the problem, but few of the candidates did. Tempers were uncertain in the sleeping caverns next morning as the boys were routed out of their beds to carry water and black rock and cover the "glows." Mende had to call Keevan to order twice for clumsiness.

"Whatever is the matter with you, boy?" she demanded in exasperation when he tipped black rock short of the bin and sooted up the hearth.

---
10. **swivet** (swiv′ət): condition of irritation, annoyance.
11. **dictum:** authoritative pronouncement.

"They're going to keep me from this Impression."

"What?" Mende stared at him. "Who?"

"You heard them talking at dinner last night. They're going to tuff the babes from the hatching."

Mende regarded him a moment longer before touching his arm gently. "There's lots of talk around a supper table, Keevan. And it cools as soon as the supper. I've heard the same nonsense before every hatching, but nothing is ever changed."

"There's always a first time," Keevan answered, copying one of her own phrases.

"That'll be enough of that, Keevan. Finish your job. If the clutch does hatch today, we'll need full rock bins for the feast, and you won't be around to do the filling. All my fosterlings make dragonriders."

"The first time?" Keevan was bold enough to ask as he scooted off with the rockbarrow.

Perhaps, Keevan thought later, if he hadn't been on that chore just when Beterli was also fetching black rock, things might have turned out differently. But he had dutifully trundled the barrow to the outdoor bunker for another load just as Beterli arrived on a similar errand.

"Heard the news, babe?" asked Beterli. He was grinning from ear to ear, and he put an unnecessary emphasis on the final insulting word.

"The eggs are cracking?" Keevan all but dropped the loaded shovel. Several anxieties flicked through his mind then: He

TRANSPARENCY 10
Literary Elements
Conflict – explores the four common types of conflict introduced in this unit.

MEETING INDIVIDUAL NEEDS

ESL/LEP • Keevan believed he had been dropped from the candidacy when someone sniggered. *Snigger* is a variation of *snicker*, meaning to laugh in an ugly way that makes fun of someone. Ask the class to demonstrate what a snicker might look and sound like. Beterli is described as *snarling* while he yanks the shovel from Keevan. How is a snarl different from a snicker? What kinds of animals snarl?

1. GUIDED READING:
Making Inferences
Keevan thinks the news is that he has been disqualified from the upcoming Impression.

2. GUIDED READING:
Making Inferences
Why does Beterli use the word "babe" twice? He wants to make Keevan angrier, to provoke Keevan into a fight and then humiliate him by winning it.

3. GUIDED READING:
Making Inferences
What can you infer from Mende's words? Either Keevan or Beterli or both have been eliminated from the hatching.

4. GUIDED READING:
Recalling Key Events
Tell what happened at the blackrock bunker. Beterli taunted Keevan and implied that he'd been eliminated. Beterli grabbed the shovel from Keevan, Keevan grabbed it back, Beterli rammed the handle into Keevan's chest. Keevan fell, broke his leg, and lost consciousness.

---

was black with rock dust—would he have time to wash before donning the white tunic of candidacy? And if the eggs were hatching, why hadn't the candidates been recalled by the wingsecond?

"Naw! Guess again!" Beterli was much too pleased with himself.

1 With a sinking heart Keevan knew what the news must be, and he could only stare with intense desolation at the older boy.

"C'mon! Guess, babe!"

"I've no time for guessing games," Keevan managed to say with indifference. He began to shovel black rock into his barrow as fast as he could.

"I said, 'Guess.' " Beterli grabbed the shovel.

"And I said I'd no time for guessing games."

Beterli wrenched the shovel from Keevan's hands. "Guess!"

"I'll have the shovel back, Beterli." Keevan straightened up, but he didn't come up to Beterli's bulky shoulder. From somewhere, other boys appeared, some with barrows, some mysteriously alerted to the prospect of a confrontation among their numbers.

2 "Babes don't give orders to candidates around here, babe!"

Someone sniggered and Keevan knew, incredibly, that he must've been dropped from the candidacy.

He yanked the shovel from Beterli's loosened grasp. Snarling, the older boy tried to regain possession, but Keevan clung with all his strength to the handle, dragged back and forth as the stronger boy jerked the shovel about.

With a sudden, unexpected movement, Beterli rammed the handle into Keevan's chest, knocking him over the barrow handles. Keevan felt a sharp, painful jab behind his left ear, an unbearable pain in his right shin, and then a painless nothingness.

Mende's angry voice roused him, and startled, he tried to throw back the covers, thinking he'd overslept. But he couldn't move, so firmly was he tucked into his bed. And then the constriction of a bandage on his head and the dull sickishness in his leg brought back recent occurrences.

"Hatching?" he cried.

"No, lovey," said Mende, and her voice was suddenly very kind, her hand cool and gentle on his forehead. "Though **3** there's some as won't be at any hatching again." Her voice took on a stern edge.

Keevan looked beyond her to see the weyrwoman, who was frowning with irritation.

"Keevan, will you tell me what oc- **4** curred at the blackrock bunker?" Lessa asked, but her voice wasn't angry.

He remembered Beterli now and the quarrel over the shovel and . . . what had Mende said about some not being at any hatching? Much as he hated Beterli, he couldn't bring himself to tattle on Beterli and force him out of candidacy.

"Come, lad," and a note of impatience crept into the weyrwoman's voice. "I merely want to know what happened from you, too. Mende said she sent you for black

88 Quests

rock. Beterli—and every weyrling in the cavern—seems to have been on the same errand. What happened?"

"Beterli took the shovel. I hadn't finished with it."

"There's more than one shovel. What did he *say* to you?"

"He'd heard the news."

"What news?" The weyrwoman was suddenly amused.

"That . . . that . . . there'd been changes."

"Is that what he said?"

"Not exactly."

"What did he say? C'mon, lad. I've heard from everyone else, you know."

"He said for me to guess the news."

"And you fell for that old gag?" The weyrwoman's irritation returned.

"Consider all the talk last night at supper, Lessa," said Mende. "Of course the boy would think he'd been eliminated."

"In effect, he is, with a broken skull and leg." She touched his arm, a rare gesture of sympathy in her. "Be that as it may, Keevan, you'll have other Impressions. Beterli will not. There are certain rules that must be observed by all candidates, and his conduct proves him unacceptable to the weyr."

She smiled at Mende and then left.

1 "I'm still a candidate?" Keevan asked urgently.

"Well, you are and you aren't, lovey," his foster mother said. "Is the numb weed working?" she asked, and when he nodded, she said, "You just rest. I'll bring you some nice broth."

At any other time in his life, Keevan would have relished such cosseting,¹² but he lay there worrying. Beterli had been dismissed. Would the others think it was his fault? But everyone was there! Beterli provoked the fight. His worry increased, because although he heard excited comings and goings in the passageway, no one tweaked back the curtain across the sleeping alcove he shared with five other boys. Surely one of them would have to come in sometime. No, they were all avoiding him. And something else was wrong. Only he didn't know what.

Mende returned with broth and beachberry bread.

"Why doesn't anyone come see me, Mende? I haven't done anything wrong, have I? I didn't ask to have Beterli tuffed out."

2 Mende soothed him, saying everyone was busy with noontime chores and no one was mad at him. They were giving him a chance to rest in quiet. The numb weed made him drowsy, and her words were fair enough. He permitted his fears to dissipate. **3** Until he heard the humming. It started low, too low to be heard. Rather he felt it in the broken shin bone and his sore head. And thought, at first, it was an effect of the numb weed. Then the hum grew, augmented¹³ by additional sources. Two things registered suddenly in Keevan's groggy mind: The only white candidate's **4** robe still on the pegs in the chamber was

---

12. **cosseting** (kos′it·ing): pampering.
13. **augmented** (ôg·ment′əd): increased.

The Smallest Dragonboy 89

1. LITERARY ELEMENTS:
Suspense
How does Mende's response create suspense? It doesn't answer Keevan's question, so we wonder about his status.

2. GUIDED READING:
Interpreting Meaning
Is Mende telling the truth? No. We can infer that the other boys are actually at the Impression.

3
Dissipate means "to go away."

4. GUIDED READING:
Drawing Conclusions
How does Keevan know the Impression has begun? His is the only candidate's robe still in the chamber. He hears humming and knows that dragons hum when a clutch is being hatched.

1. GUIDED READING:
Recognizing Multiple Meanings
Note that this *clutch* means "hold on to." Elsewhere in this story, in Pernian lingo, *clutch* means "a group of eggs."

2. GUIDED READING:
Predicting Outcomes
What do you think Keevan will do next? He will go to the Impression.

3. GUIDED READING:
Making Inferences
Notice the detail suggesting that life on Pern is not technologically sophisticated. (No automatic washing machines)

---

his; and dragons hummed when a clutch was being laid or being hatched. Impression! And he was flat abed.

Bitter, bitter disappointment turned the warm broth sour in his belly. Even the small voice telling him that he'd have other opportunities failed to alleviate his crushing depression. *This* was the Impression that mattered! This was his chance to show *everyone* from Mende to K'last to L'vel and even the weyrleaders that he, Keevan, was worthy of being a dragonrider.

He twisted in bed, fighting against the tears that threatened to choke him. Dragonmen don't cry! Dragonmen learn to live with pain. . . .

Pain? The leg didn't actually pain him as he rolled about on his bedding. His head felt sort of stiff from the tightness of the bandage. He sat up, an effort in itself since the numb weed made exertion difficult. He touched the splinted leg, but the knee was unhampered. He had no feeling in his bone, really. He swung himself carefully to the side of his bed and slowly stood. The room wanted to swim about him. He closed his eyes, which made the dizziness worse, and **1** he had to clutch the bedpost.

Gingerly he took a step. The broken leg dragged. It hurt in spite of the numb weed, but what was pain to a dragonman? **2** No one had said he couldn't go to the Impression. "You are and you aren't," were Mende's exact words.

Clinging to the bedpost, he jerked off his bedshirt. Stretching his arm to the utmost, he jerked his white candidate's tunic from the peg. Jamming first one arm and then the other into the holes, he pulled it over his head. Too bad about the belt. He couldn't wait. He hobbled to the door, hung on to the curtain to steady himself. The weight on his leg was unwieldy. He'd not get very far without something to lean on. Down by the bathing pool was one of **3** the long crook-necked poles used to retrieve clothes from the hot washing troughs. But it was down there, and he was on the level above. And there was no one nearby to come to his aid. Everyone would be in the Hatching Ground right now, eagerly waiting for the first egg to crack.

90 Quests

1. GUIDED READING:
Making Inferences
What do you think this means? It means that the time of hatching is even closer than it was before.

1   The humming increased in volume and tempo, an urgency to which Keevan responded, knowing that his time was all too limited if he was to join the ranks of the hopeful boys standing about the cracking eggs. But if he hurried down the ramp, he'd fall flat on his face.

He could, of course, go flat on his rear end, the way crawling children did. He sat down, the jar sending a stab of pain through his leg and up to the wound on the back of his head. Gritting his teeth and blinking away the tears, Keevan scrabbled down the ramp. He had to wait a moment at the bottom to catch his breath. He got to one knee, the injured leg straight out in front of him. Somehow he managed to push himself erect, though the room wanted to tip over his ears. It wasn't far to the crooked stick, but it seemed an age before he had it in his hand.

Then the humming stopped!

The Smallest Dragonboy   91

**1. GUIDED READING:
Identifying the Author's Purpose**
Why do you think the author included this passage? Perhaps she wants to emphasize the difficulties Keevan must overcome to get to the Hatching Ground. She wants to increase our tension and suspense—the humming has stopped, the Impression is starting. Will Keevan make it?

**2. LITERARY ELEMENTS:
Suspense**
Notice that this question asks the same question we are asking ourselves.

3
Speculation means "guessing."

---

1 Keevan cried out and began to hobble frantically across the cavern, out to the bowl of the weyr. Never had the distance between the living caverns and the Hatching Ground seemed so great. Never had the weyr been so silent, breathless. As if the multitude of people and dragons watching the hatching held every breath in suspense. Not even the wind muttered down the steep sides of the bowl. The only sounds to break the stillness were Keevan's ragged breathing and the thump-thud of his stick on the hard-packed ground. Sometimes he had to hop twice on his good leg to maintain his balance. Twice he fell into the sand and had to pull himself up on the stick, his white tunic no longer spotless. Once he jarred himself so badly he couldn't get up immediately.

Then he heard the first exhalation of the crowd, the ooohs, the muted cheer, the susurrus[14] of excited whispers. An egg had cracked, and the dragon had chosen his rider. Desperation increased Keevan's **2** hobble. Would he never reach the arching mouth of the Hatching Ground?

Another cheer and an excited spate of applause spurred Keevan to greater effort. If he didn't get there in moments, there'd be no unpaired hatchling left. Then he was actually staggering into the Hatching Ground, the sands hot on his bare feet.

No one noticed his entrance or his halting progress. And Keevan could see nothing but the backs of the white-robed candidates, seventy of them ringing the area around the eggs. Then one side would surge forward or back and there'd be a cheer. Another dragon had been Impressed. Suddenly a large gap appeared in the white human wall, and Keevan had his first sight of the eggs. There didn't seem to be *any* left uncracked, and he could see the lucky boys standing beside wobble-legged dragons. He could hear the unmistakable plaintive crooning of hatchlings and their squawks of protest as they'd fall awkwardly in the sand.

Suddenly he wished that he hadn't left his bed, that he'd stayed away from the Hatching Ground. Now everyone would see his ignominious[15] failure. He scrambled now as desperately to reach the shadowy walls of the Hatching Ground as he had struggled to cross the bowl. He mustn't be seen.

He didn't notice, therefore, that the shifting group of boys remaining had begun to drift in his direction. The hard pace he had set himself and his cruel disappointment took their double toll on Keevan. He tripped and collapsed sobbing to the warm sands. He didn't see the consternation[16] in the watching weyrfolk above the Hatching Ground, nor did he hear the excited whispers of speculation. He didn't know that **3** the weyrleader and weyrwoman had dropped to the arena and were making their way toward the knot of boys slowly moving in the direction of the archway.

---

14. **susurrus** (sə·sur′əs): rustling sound.
15. **ignominious** (ig′nə·min′ē·əs): shameful; disgraceful.
16. **consternation** (kon′stər·nā′shən): great shock or fear that makes one confused or helpless.

PORTFOLIO ASSESSMENT

Sequels tell what happens to the characters in the future. Interested students may want to write a short sequel to "The Smallest Dragonboy" in which they tell what happens to Keevan and Beterli as a result of the Impression where a dragon chooses Keevan but not Beterli. Will Keevan become a weyrleader? Will Beterli's attitude change? What will happen during the next thread attack? Remind students to be consistent with Anne McCaffrey's development of the characters and plot. Consult with students individually to mutually agree how their sequels will be assessed. (See *Portfolio Assessment and Professional Support Materials* for additional information on student portfolios.)

---

1 "Never seen anything like it," the weyrleader was saying. "Only thirty-nine riders chosen. And the bronze trying to leave the Hatching Ground without making Impression!"

"A case in point of what I said last night," the weyrwoman replied, "where a hatchling makes no choice because the right boy isn't there."

"There's only Beterli and K'last's young one missing. And there's a full wing of likely boys to choose from. . . ."

"None acceptable, apparently. Where is the creature going? He's not heading for the entrance after all. Oh, what have we there, in the shadows?"

Keevan heard with dismay the sound of voices nearing him. He tried to burrow into the sand. The mere thought of how he would be teased and taunted now was unbearable.

2 *Don't worry! Please don't worry!* The thought was urgent, but not his own.

Someone kicked sand over Keevan and butted roughly against him.

"Go away. Leave me alone!" he cried.

Why? was the injured-sounding question inserted into his mind. There was no voice, no tone, but the question was there, perfectly clear, in his head.

Incredulous, Keevan lifted his head and stared into the glowing jeweled eyes of **3** a small bronze dragon. His wings were wet; the tips hung drooping to the sand. And he sagged in the middle on his unsteady legs, although he was making a great effort to keep erect.

Keevan dragged himself to his knees, oblivious to the pain of his leg. He wasn't even aware that he was ringed by the boys passed over, while thirty-one pairs of resentful eyes watched him Impress the dragon. The weyrleaders looked on, amused and surprised at the draconic[17] choice, which could not be forced. Could not be questioned. Could not be changed.

Why? asked the dragon again. *Don't you like me?* His eyes whirled with anxiety, and his tone was so piteous that Keevan staggered forward and threw his arms around the dragon's neck, stroking his eye ridges, patting the damp, soft hide, opening the fragile-looking wings to dry them, and assuring the hatchling wordlessly over and over again that he was the most perfect, most beautiful, most beloved dragon in the entire weyr, in all the weyrs of Pern.

"What's his name, K'van?" asked Lessa, smiling warmly at the new dragonrider. K'van stared up at her for a long moment. Lessa would know as soon as he did. Lessa was the only person who could "receive" from all dragons, not only her own Ramoth. Then he gave her a radiant smile, recognizing the traditional shortening of his name that raised him forever to the rank of dragonrider.

My name is Heath, thought the dragon **4** mildly and hiccuped in sudden urgency. *I'm hungry.*

"Dragons are born hungry," said Lessa, laughing. "F'lar, give the boy a hand. He can barely manage his own legs, much less a dragon's."

---

17. **draconic** (drə·kă′nĭk): dragon-like.

The Smallest Dragonboy   93

---

1. GUIDED READING:
Making Inferences
What can you infer about bronze hatchlings? No one has ever seen a bronze hatchling not make an Impression.

2. GUIDED READING:
Predicting Outcomes
Whose thought do you think this is? Some students will predict correctly that it is the thought of the as yet un-Impressed bronze dragon. Remember that dragons and their riders share telepathic communication.

3. GUIDED READING:
Seeing Connections
How are Keevan and the hatchling alike? Both have unsteady legs and find it difficult to remain erect, but are making a great effort. Both are insecure. The connection suggests they are well matched.

4
Dragons' names seem to end in *-th*. (Ramoth, Canth, Mnementh, Heath) Encourage students to make up some dragon names of their own.

CLOSURE
Have students define *quest* and tell how this is a quest story. They should define the hero, the object of the quest, the perils faced by the hero, the outcome.

RETEACHING
Have students identify at least one conflict from television or movies. Who is the hero or heroine? Who is the enemy? Does the hero or heroine also struggle to resolve an internal conflict?

EXTENSION AND ENRICHMENT
Art. Students may enjoy working in small groups to make an illustrated map showing the various places in Benden Weyr mentioned in the story.

FOR STUDY AND DISCUSSION
Identifying Facts
1. Keevan wants to Impress a newborn dragon so that he can become a dragonrider.
   He fears he may not succeed because he is the smallest and youngest candidate.
2. The newly hatched dragons see into the candidates' hearts and measure their character.
   Keevan fears he will be kept from this Impression because he is a "babe": he is very young and physically small. There are only 40 dragon eggs, but there are 72 candidates. Also, Keevan has heard the elders discuss cutting down on the number of candidates.
3. Beterli tries to make Keevan believe that he has been eliminated from candidacy. The two quarrel over a shovel, and Beterli seriously injures Keevan, breaking his skull and his leg.
4. The unprecedented event is that one dragon, and a bronze at that, refuses to choose a rider.
   Just when Keevan is most unhappy and discouraged, the small bronze dragon named Heath chooses him.

K'van remembered his stick and drew himself up. "We'll be just fine, thank you."

"You may be the smallest dragonrider ever, young K'van, but you're the bravest," said F'lar.

And Heath agreed! Pride and joy so leaped in both chests that K'van wondered if his heart would burst right out of his body. He looped an arm around Heath's neck and the pair—the smallest dragonboy, and the hatchling who wouldn't choose anybody else—walked out of the Hatching Ground together forever.

For Study and Discussion

IDENTIFYING FACTS

1. What does Keevan want, as the story opens? Why does he fear he won't get it?
2. Describe how the dragonriders are chosen. Why does Keevan fear he'll be kept from this Impression?
3. How does the bully Beterli try to ruin Keevan's chances on Hatching Day?
4. What happens at the Impression that never happened before? What happens to Keevan at the Impression, just when he is most unhappy and discouraged?

INTERPRETING MEANINGS

5. What does shortening Keevan's name to K'van signify?
6. Describe Keevan's **quest** at this stage of his life. What larger quest will he embark on when he is a dragonrider?
7. How do you **predict** Keevan will perform with Heath as a dragonrider? How did you feel about Keevan and Heath?
8. Why do you think no dragon has ever chosen Beterli? Why do you think F'lar called Keevan the bravest dragonboy?

APPLYING MEANINGS

9. List all the women in this story. Do they have powerful positions in Pern society? Or do only men hold power?
10. Pretend you live on Pern and are a candidate for Impression. Which color dragon would you like to Impress? What would be its name? Make up a Pern name for yourself.

Focus on Reading

DRAWING CONCLUSIONS

One of the challenges of this fantasy is trying to figure out the meanings of the words referring to life on Pern. The writer doesn't tell us directly, for example, what a dragonrider is. But you probably figured out that a dragonrider is someone who has been chosen by a dragon to be its rider for life. Dragonriders fight an enemy called Thread.

1. Based on what you have learned from clues in the story, tell all that you know about Thread. What conclusions would you draw about Thread and its threat to Pern? What do you imagine Thread looks like? (Could you illustrate Thread?)
2. Based on clues in the story, what conclusions can you come to about the dragons of Pern? Compare them with the dragons in old stories, like the one on page 66.

Literary Elements

CONFLICT

Conflict exists in all stories, and especially in stories of quests. **Conflict** is a struggle between two opposing forces. Some conflicts take place between two people. Some take place between a person and a force of nature. Sometimes a person is in conflict with a whole society. At times, a conflict takes place within a person's mind and heart. This might happen when a person has to struggle with fear or sadness or insecurity.

1. What person is Keevan in conflict with?
2. What feelings about himself are causing conflict for Keevan?

The Smallest Dragonboy

Interpreting Meanings

5. The shortening of Keevan's name signifies that he has been raised to the status of dragonrider (their names all seem to be shortened). He has attained his goal.
6. His quest at this stage is to prove that he has the courage and ability to be a dragonrider.

When Keevan becomes a dragonrider, he will embark on the great quest of protecting Pern against the menace of Thread.

7. Most students will probably say that Keevan will at least be brave, based on his character and actions so far.

Most will say they feel sympathy for Keevan, especially because of the way he endured the bully's attack, and that they feel pleasure because he has won the very likable little dragon Heath.

8. No dragon has chosen Beterli because he is a bully and lacks the qualities of character necessary in a true dragonrider.

F'lar called Keevan the bravest because Keevan endured and triumphed over the scorn of the other boys, the taunts of the bully, and his own physical pain.

Applying Meanings

9. The women in the story are Mende (Keevan's foster mother) and Lessa, the leader or weyrwoman. Mende's position is not clear, though we are shown that she is very wise and knows many secrets and all the Harpers' tales (which must be the ancient tales of Pern). Lessa occupies a position of special power in Pern society. She inquires into the quarrel between the boys, and only she has the power to "receive" thoughts from all dragons. There is also a queen on Pern (see page 84).

10. Encourage students to give their reasons.

Point out that dragon names end in *-th* and their Pern name should have a short form, like F'lar, L'vel, K'last, or K'van.

FOCUS ON READING
Drawing Conclusions
1. Thread is an evil physical entity that destroys all things by devouring them. It is destroyed by dragon fire. See page 79.

Thread might be a kind of acid rain, poison gas, or virus. Maybe it looks like long pieces of thread.

2. The dragons are noble, wise, kind, fearless, and telepathic. They have jeweled eyes and transparent wings. The dragons come in colors: green (small, fast, numerous), blue, brown, and bronze (the

3. What force is the whole society of Pern in conflict with?

This story is a fantasy. But do conflicts similar to these happen in real life?

Focus on Descriptive Writing

FINDING A FOCUS
In the final paragraph on page 89, the details give a vivid picture of Keevan's thoughts and feelings as he lies sick in bed. This paragraph is an example of **descriptive writing.**

In a description, you use vivid details and exact words to create a clear picture of a subject. You may also use sensory images and figures of speech.

When you plan a description, you need to find a specific focus for your topic. Make a focusing diagram like the one below.

Places at school
Cafeteria
Lunch time at the cafeteria

Make a list of familiar people, places, and objects. Pick one or two that you would like to describe. Make a focusing diagram to limit each topic you choose. Save your notes.

About the Author

Anne McCaffrey (1926–   ) is known to her many readers as "the Dragon lady." Among her numerous stories about dragons are *Dragonsong, Dragonsinger,* and *Dragondrums*—a series of science fantasy novels for young adults about the dragons of Pern. When asked why she defends dragons, McCaffrey said, "Dragons have always had a bad press. And I liked the thought of them being so big, and controlled by a bond of love." Anne McCaffrey grew up in Essex County, New Jersey. As a "lonely tomboy," she decided early on two things she most wanted. "When I was a very young girl, I promised myself fervently (usually after I'd lost another battle with one of my brothers) that I would become a famous author and I'd own my own horse." McCaffrey's books are now known all over the world and have been translated into many languages. Since she moved to County Wicklow in Ireland, she has owned her own horse—a black and white mare she calls "Pi." McCaffrey lives and works in Ireland at her home called "Dragonhold-Underhill."

Connecting Cultures

Myths About Dragons
Dragons have played an important role in the mythologies of various people. They were not always considered evil. In ancient

Greece and Rome, for example, dragons were often thought of as guardians, like the dragons of Pern in "The Smallest Dragonboy." In the classical legend of Jason and the Argonauts, the fabulous Golden Fleece is protected by a terrifying dragon. In order to steal the Fleece, Jason and Medea must first put the dragon to sleep.

Dragons are usually described as winged reptiles with lion's claws, eagle's wings, and a serpent's tail. Their breath is almost always fiery. Some dragons are she-monsters. The Chimaera (kī·mîr′ə) in Greek mythology has a lion's head, a goat's body, and a serpent's tail.

Many famous heroes in myths are dragonslayers. According to legend, Saint George, the patron saint of England, used a magic sword to save the king's daughter from being sacrificed to a dragon.

Making Connections: Activities

1. In an unabridged dictionary, find the origins of the word *dragon.* The etymology of a word is often shown within square brackets at the beginning of a dictionary entry. What different meanings did the word *dragon* have in other languages? Find out what connection there is between our word *dragon* and the name *Pendragon* in Arthurian legends.

2. Find out how the dragon was used as an emblem by the ancient Roman and Chinese empires and by the Welsh (the dragon is the national symbol of Wales). Discuss with class members possible sources you could use for research. Plan to bring illustrations to class when you share your findings.

3. In Norse mythology, Fafnir is an evil dragon that guards an ancient golden treasure. The hero Sigurd slays the dragon and receives the monster's magical powers. A good version of the story is found in *Legends of the North,* by Olivia Coolidge. In the Anglo-Saxon story of Beowulf, the hero receives his death wound during a fierce struggle with a dragon. The episode can be read in fast-moving verse in *Beowulf,* translated by Ian Seraillier. Learn how Bellerophon and his winged horse, Pegasus, destroy the Chimaera in classical mythology. You will find the story retold in many collections, including *Mythology* by Edith Hamilton.

Choose an effective passage from one of these myths to read aloud or perform as a drama.

4. Dragons are sometimes associated with myths of creation. In ancient Chinese mythology, for example, there was a huge flaming dragon with a human face and a red body. When it opened its eyes, there was daylight. When it closed them, it was dark. Its breath made the wind and the rain.

Find out by consulting a book of Norse myths what role was played by the dragon Nidhoggir.

5. Numerous stories have also been written about dragons. Two that you might enjoy are "The Fifty-first Dragon," by Heywood Broun, and "The Rule of Names," by Ursula Le Guin.

6. After you have completed your research on dragons, you might like to compose a letter to the author of "The Smallest Dragonboy," telling her what you have learned about these fabulous creatures.

largest and most desirable).

LITERARY ELEMENTS
Conflict
1. He is in conflict with Beterli.
2. He feels that he is small, young, and unfairly regarded as a "babe."
3. The whole society is in conflict with the evil forces of Thread.

Certainly, bullies like Beterli exist in actual life; smaller kids also get picked on in real life; and nuclear destruction or the greenhouse effect or pollution could be as threatening as Thread.

FOCUS ON DESCRIPTIVE WRITING
Finding a Focus
You may want to explain to students that they are moving from the general to the specific in a kind of mental funneling when they find a focus. Model the procedure for students by writing a general topic on the chalkboard and then narrowing it to a subject that would be appropriate for a descriptive paragraph.

CONNECTING CULTURES
As an alternative activity, have students work in small groups to write their own myths or stories about dragons.

OBJECTIVES

Students will identify external and internal conflict. They will also identify a narrative sequence and recognize descriptive details that create mood.

FOCUS/MOTIVATION

Establishing a Purpose for Reading. After they have read the headnote, ask students to predict what Brian's biggest problem will be as he tries to survive in the wilderness. Then have them read to find out if their predictions are accurate.

Prereading Journal. As the headnote suggests, have students write down three problems they might face if they were to find themselves stranded in the wilderness.

TEACHING RESOURCES A

Teacher's Notes, p. 107
Reading Check, p. 110
Reading Focus, p. 111
Study Guide, pp. 112, 113
Language Skills, pp. 114, 117
Building Vocabulary p. 120
Selection Vocabulary Test, p. 122
Selection Test, p. 123

READING THE SELECTION

This story is told from Brian's point of view, in an almost stream-of-consciousness style. This colloquial style helps us feel we *are* Brian as he responds to various threats to his life. The story should grip the interest of all students. To get them into the action, you might read aloud to the moment when the bear appears, on page 100, column 2. Stop reading aloud with the short dramatic sentence "Right there."

from Hatchet

GARY PAULSEN

Before You Read

The character's quest in the next story will keep you on the edge of your seat. As the novel *Hatchet* begins, Brian's parents have just been divorced. Thirteen-year-old Brian is the only passenger aboard a small plane, on his way to visit his father in Canada. Suddenly, with no warning, the pilot of the plane has a heart attack and dies. Brian—who has never flown a plane—is left alone. After a terrifying struggle to keep the plane in the air, he finally manages to crash-land in a lake and swim away from the sinking wreckage.

As this episode opens, Brian has spent two days in the Canadian wilderness with only the clothes on his back and the hatchet on his belt, a parting gift from his mother before he boarded the plane. He has succeeded in turning a rocky ledge into a makeshift shelter. The only food he has found so far are some strange-tasting berries he calls "gut cherries," but they make him violently ill.

Before you read this part of Brian's story, try to imagine what you would do if you suddenly found yourself alone in a wilderness. In your journal write down three problems you think you'd face.

Terry is Brian's good friend back in New York City.

MEETING INDIVIDUAL NEEDS

ESL/LEP • In referring to Brian's attempts to build a fire, the author describes the sparks by using images of water. How many images can students find? What are they?

shower
A **shower** of sparks (page 106)

stream
a **stream** of sparks (pages 107-108)

cloud
a **cloud** of sparks (page 108) (clouds hold rainshowers)

Why has the author chosen these words?

1. LANGUAGE AND VOCABULARY

The Language and Vocabulary note on this page alerts students to the rich descriptive details in this story. The Language and Vocabulary exercise on page 112 invites them to write their own descriptions to create particular moods.

2. GUIDED READING: Recognizing Descriptive Details

What details help you visualize the berries? "Full," "ripe," "sweet," "did not grow in clusters," "many of them," "easy to pick," "tiny tang."

3

Paulsen seems to have made up the word *wuffling*. It could mean "stuffing his mouth and whiffing or sniffling his nose at the same time."

Language and Vocabulary

1 **Description is a kind of writing that helps you see, hear, smell, or taste something, or feel its textures.** Even if you have never seen birch trees, you can "see" how they look from Gary Paulsen's vivid description: "They were a beautiful white with bark like clean, slightly speckled paper." As you read, use Paulsen's descriptions to help you visualize Brian's experiences. Does the writer help you feel that "you are there" in the wilderness?

Raspberries.

These he knew because there were some raspberry bushes in the park and he and Terry were always picking and eating them when they biked past.

2 The berries were full and ripe, and he tasted one to find it sweet, and with none of the problems of the gut cherries. Although they did not grow in clusters, there were many of them and they were easy to pick, and Brian smiled and started eating.

Sweet juice, he thought. Oh, they were sweet, with just a tiny tang, and he picked and ate and picked and ate and thought that he had never tasted anything this good. Soon, as before, his stomach was full, but now he had some sense and he did not gorge or cram more down. Instead he picked more and put them in his windbreaker, feeling the morning sun on his back and thinking he was rich, rich with food now, just rich, and he heard a noise to his rear, a slight noise, and he turned and saw the bear.

He could do nothing, think nothing. His tongue, stained with berry juice, stuck to the roof of his mouth and he stared at the bear. It was black, with a cinnamon-colored nose, not twenty feet from him and big. No, huge. It was all black fur and huge. He had seen one in the zoo in the city once, a black bear, but it had been from India or somewhere. This one was wild, and much bigger than the one in the zoo and it was right there.

Right there.

The sun caught the ends of the hairs along his back. Shining black and silky, the bear stood on its hind legs, half up, and studied Brian, just studied him, then lowered itself and moved slowly to the left, eating berries as it rolled along, wuffling **3** and <u>delicately</u> using its mouth to lift each

100 Quests

SCIENCE LINK

What are the chemical reactions that take place when a fire starts? What happens to something when it burns? Why does water put out fire? Challenge students to answer these and any other questions they might have about fire. You could begin by having students brainstorm a list of questions. Then divide the class into small groups to find their answers. Each group could explore the answer to one question and present its findings to the class.

---

berry from the stem, and in seconds it was gone. Gone, and Brian still had not moved. His tongue was stuck to the top of his mouth, the tip half out; his eyes were wide and his hands were reaching for a berry.

Then he made a sound, a low "Nnnnnnggg." It made no sense, was just a sound of fear, of disbelief that something that large could have come so close to him without his knowing. It just walked up to him and could have eaten him, and he could have done nothing. Nothing. And

1. GUIDED READING:
Making Inferences
Notice that Brian feels he has no control over his body. The clue is the repetition of the word *nothing*. Brian seems to have no control over his brain either.

from *Hatchet* 101

TRANSPARENCY 9
Reader Response
Focus on Conflict – invites students to consider the major character's foremost desire and the primary opposing forces—external or internal—to that goal.

1. GUIDED READING:
Identifying Pronoun Referents
To what does the word it *refer?* To the bear.

2. GUIDED READING:
Drawing Conclusions
What can you conclude about Brian's need for food compared to his fear of the bear? His fear of getting sick again from gut cherries is greater than his fear of the bear.

3. GUIDED READING:
Using Context Clues
See if students can make an educated guess that *rivulets* mean "little rivers." *Drenched* and *running down* are clues.

4. GUIDED READING:
Recognizing Descriptive Details
These words help us share the taste of the berry juice: *sweet, tangy, "like pop without the fizz."*

---

when the sound was half done, a thing happened with his legs, a thing he had nothing to do with, and they were running in the opposite direction from the bear, back toward the shelter.

He would have run all the way, in panic, but after he had gone perhaps fifty yards, his brain took over and slowed and, finally, stopped him.

If the bear had wanted you, his brain said, he would have taken you. It is something to understand, he thought, not something to run away from. The bear was eating berries.

Not people.

The bear made no move to hurt you, to threaten you. It stood to see you better, study you, then went on its way eating berries. It was a big bear, but it did not want you, did not want to cause you harm, and that is the thing to understand here.

He turned and looked back at the stand of raspberries. The bear was gone, the birds were singing, he saw nothing that could hurt him. There was no danger here that he could sense, could feel. In the city, at night, there was sometimes danger. You could not be in the park at night, after dark, because of the danger. But here, the bear had looked at him and had moved on and—this filled his thoughts—the berries were so good.

So good. So sweet and rich and his body was so empty.

And the bear had almost indicated that it didn't mind sharing—had just walked from him.

And the berries were so good.

And, he thought finally, if he did not go back and get the berries, he would have to eat the gut cherries again tonight.

That convinced him, and he walked slowly back to the raspberry patch and continued picking for the entire morning, although with great caution, and once when a squirrel rustled some pine needles at the base of a tree, he nearly jumped out of his skin.

About noon—the sun was almost straight overhead—the clouds began to thicken and look dark. In moments, it started to rain and he took what he had picked and trotted back to the shelter. He had eaten probably two pounds of raspberries and had maybe another three pounds in his jacket, rolled in a pouch.

He made it to the shelter just as the clouds completely opened and the rain roared down in sheets. Soon the sand outside was drenched and there were rivulets running down to the lake. But inside he was dry and snug. He started to put the picked berries back in the sorted pile with the gut cherries, but noticed that the raspberries were seeping through the jacket. They were much softer than the gut cherries and apparently were being crushed a bit with their own weight.

When he held the jacket up and looked beneath it, he saw a stream of red liquid. He put a finger in it and found it to be sweet and tangy, like pop without the fizz, and he grinned and lay back on the sand, holding the bag up over his face and letting the seepage drip into his mouth.

Outside the rain poured down, but

102 Quests

Brian lay back, drinking the syrup from the berries, dry and with the pain almost all gone, the stiffness also gone, his belly full and a good taste in his mouth.

For the first time since the crash he was not thinking of himself, of his own life. Brian was wondering if the bear was as surprised as he to find another being in the berries.

Later in the afternoon, as evening came down, he went to the lake and washed the sticky berry juice from his face and hands, then went back to prepare for the night.

While he had accepted and understood that the bear did not want to hurt him, it was still much in his thoughts, and as darkness came into the shelter, he took the hatchet out of his belt and put it by his head, his hand on the handle, as the day caught up with him and he slept.

At first he thought it was a growl. In the still darkness of the shelter in the middle of the night, his eyes came open and he was awake and he thought there was a growl. But it was the wind; a medium wind in the pines had made some sound that brought him up, brought him awake. He sat up and was hit with the smell.

It terrified him. The smell was one of rot, some musty rot that made him think only of graves with cobwebs and dust and old death. His nostrils widened and he opened his eyes wider, but he could see nothing. It was too dark, too hard dark, with clouds covering even the small light from the stars, and he could not see. But the smell was alive, alive and full and in the shelter. He thought of the bear, thought of Bigfoot and every monster he had ever seen in every fright movie he had ever watched, and his heart hammered in his throat.

Then he heard the slithering. A brushing sound, a slithering brushing sound near his feet—and he kicked out as hard as he could, kicked out and threw the hatchet at the sound, a noise coming from his throat. But the hatchet missed, sailed into the wall, where it hit the rocks with a shower of sparks, and his leg was instantly torn with pain, as if a hundred needles had been driven into it. "Unnnngh!"

Now he screamed, with the pain and fear, and skittered on his backside up into the corner of the shelter, breathing through his mouth, straining to see, to hear.

The slithering moved again, he thought toward him at first, and terror took him, stopping his breath. He felt he could see a low dark form, a bulk in the darkness, a shadow that lived, but now it moved away; slithering and scraping, it moved away and he saw or thought he saw it go out of the door opening.

He lay on his side for a moment, then pulled a rasping breath in and held it, listening for the attacker to return. When it was apparent that the shadow wasn't coming back, he felt the calf of his leg, where the pain was centered and spreading to fill the whole leg.

His fingers gingerly touched a group of needles that had been driven through his pants and into the fleshy part of his calf.

from *Hatchet*

1. GUIDED READING:
Making Inferences
Why do you think Brian pulls out four quills in rapid succession? If Brian stopped after each quill or every two quills, the pain would last longer and he would have to gather his strength and courage several times instead of only twice. We do this when we pull off adhesive bandages as fast as possible.

2. LITERARY ELEMENTS:
Figures of Speech
What is the pain compared with? The word *smear* suggests a comparison with a stain or a smear of blood or paint. You "smear" butter on bread or you "smear" paint on a wall. *Smear* suggests something random, loose, messy.

They were stiff and very sharp on the ends that stuck out, and he knew then what the attacker had been. A porcupine had stumbled into his shelter, and when he had kicked it the thing had slapped him with its tail of quills.

He touched each quill carefully. The pain made it seem as if dozens of them had been slammed into his leg, but there were only eight, pinning the cloth against his skin. He leaned back against the wall for a minute. He couldn't leave them in, they had to come out, but just touching them made the pain more intense.

So fast, he thought. So fast things change. When he'd gone to sleep he had satisfaction and in just a moment it was all different. He grasped one of the quills, held his breath, and jerked. It sent pain signals to his brain in tight waves, but he grabbed another, pulled it, then another quill. When he had pulled four of them, he stopped for a moment. The pain had gone from being a pointed injury pain to spreading in a hot smear up his leg, and it made him catch his breath.

Some of the quills were driven in deeper than others and they tore when they came out. He breathed deeply twice, let half of the breath out, and went back to work. Jerk, pause, jerk—and three more times before he lay back in the darkness, done. The pain filled his leg now, and with it came new waves of self-pity. Sitting alone in the dark, his leg aching, some mosquitoes finding him again, he started crying. It was all too much, just too much, and he couldn't take it. Not the way it was.

1 I can't take it this way, alone with no fire and in the dark, and next time it might be something worse, maybe a bear, and it wouldn't be just quills in the leg, it would be worse. I can't do this, he thought, again and again. I can't. Brian pulled himself up until he was sitting upright back in the corner of the cave. He put his head down on his arms across his knees, with stiffness taking his left leg, and cried until he was cried out.

2 He did not know how long it took, but later he looked back on this time of crying in the corner of the dark cave and thought of it as when he learned the most important rule of survival, which was that feeling sorry for yourself didn't work. It wasn't just that it was wrong to do, or that it was considered incorrect. It was more than that—it didn't work. When he sat alone in the darkness and cried and was done, was all done with it, nothing had changed. His leg still hurt, it was still dark, he was still alone, and the self-pity had accomplished nothing.

At last he slept again, but already his patterns were changing and the sleep was light, a resting doze more than a deep sleep, with small sounds awakening him twice in the rest of the night. In the last doze period before daylight, before he awakened finally with the morning light and the clouds of new mosquitoes, he dreamed. This time it was not of his mother, not of the Secret,[1] but of his father at first and then of his friend Terry.

In the initial segment of the dream, his father was standing at the side of a living room, looking at him, and it was clear from his expression that he was trying to tell Brian something. His lips moved but there was no sound, not a whisper. He waved his hands at Brian, made gestures in front of his face as if he were scratching something, and he worked to make a word with his mouth, but at first Brian could not see it. Then the lips made an *mmmmm* shape but no sound came. *Mmmmm—maaaa.* Brian could not hear it, could not understand it, and he wanted to so badly; it was so important to understand his father, to **3** know what he was saying. He was trying to help, trying so hard, and when Brian couldn't understand, he looked cross, the way he did when Brian asked questions more than once, and he faded. Brian's father faded into a fog place Brian could not see and the dream was almost over, or seemed to be, when Terry came.

He was not gesturing to Brian but was sitting in the park at a bench looking at a barbecue pit, and for a time nothing happened. Then he got up and poured some charcoal from a bag into the cooker, then some starter fluid, and he took a flick type of lighter and lit the fluid. When it was burning and the charcoal was at last getting hot, he turned, noticing Brian for the first time in the dream. He turned and smiled and

---

1. Brian doesn't want to tell his father that his mother is seeing another man.

from *Hatchet*

1. LITERARY ELEMENTS:
Internal Conflict
Note that Brian is suffering from loneliness, fear, and despair. His external conflict with the wilderness has resulted in internal suffering. In some respects, this is the point where the story becomes most interesting.

2. GUIDED READING:
Identifying the Main Idea
What is the main idea of this paragraph? Self-pity does not change anything. It does not make a bad situation better. (You might ask students how this idea could be extended to other difficulties in life.)

3. GUIDED READING:
Making Inferences
What inference can you make about Brian's father's ability to be patient? Although Brian's father tries very hard to help, he gets impatient when his son doesn't understand right away.

1. GUIDED READING:
Making Predictions
What could Brian use the hatchet for? He's going to use it to make a fire. See column 2.

2
Invented Words
What could scootched *mean? It seems to be made up. Let students demonstrate how Brian "scootched up." What words might* scootch *be made from?* Scramble, hitch, scoot, *etc.*

3. GUIDED READING:
Recognizing Main Events
What makes Brian realize that the hatchet is the key to fire—and survival? Sunlight hits the metal of the hatchet, causing a firelike flash of light.

---

pointed to the fire as if to say, see, a fire.

But it meant nothing to Brian, except that he wished he had a fire. He saw a grocery sack on the table next to Terry. Brian thought it must contain hot dogs and chips and mustard, and he could think only of the food. But Terry shook his head and pointed again to the fire, and twice more he pointed to the fire, made Brian see the flames, and Brian felt his frustration and anger rise, and he thought, all right, all right, I see the fire, but so what? I don't have a fire. I know about fire; I know I need a fire.

I know that.

His eyes opened and there was light in the cave, a gray dim light of morning. He wiped his mouth and tried to move his leg, which had stiffened like wood. There was thirst, and hunger, and he ate some raspberries from the jacket. They had spoiled a bit, seemed softer and mushier, but still had a rich sweetness. He crushed the berries against the roof of his mouth with his tongue and drank the sweet juice as it ran **1** down his throat. A flash of metal caught his eye and he saw his hatchet in the sand where he had thrown it at the porcupine in the dark.

2 He scootched up, wincing a bit when he bent his stiff leg, and crawled to where the hatchet lay. He picked it up and examined it and saw a chip in the top of the head.

The nick wasn't large, but the hatchet was important to him, was his only tool, and he should not have thrown it. He should keep it in his hand, and make a tool of some kind to help push an animal away. Make a staff, he thought, or a lance,² and save the hatchet. Something came then, a thought as he held the hatchet, something about the dream and his father and Terry, but he couldn't pin it down.

"Ahhh..." He scrambled out and stood in the morning sun and stretched his back muscles and his sore leg. The hatchet was still in his hand, and as he stretched and raised it over his head, it caught the **3** first rays of the morning sun. The first faint light hit the silver of the hatchet and it flashed a brilliant gold in the light. Like fire. That is it, he thought. What they were trying to tell me.

Fire. The hatchet was the key to it all. When he threw the hatchet at the porcupine in the cave and missed and hit the stone wall, it had showered sparks, a golden shower of sparks in the dark, as golden with fire as the sun was now.

The hatchet was the answer. That's what his father and Terry had been trying to tell him. Somehow he could get fire from the hatchet. The sparks would make fire.

Brian went back into the shelter and studied the wall. It was some form of chalky granite, or a sandstone, but <u>embedded</u> in it were large pieces of a darker stone, a harder and darker stone. It only took him a moment to find where the hatchet had struck. The steel had nicked into the edge of one of the darker stone pieces. Brian turned the head backward so he would strike with the flat rear of the

---

2. **lance:** long wooden shaft with a sharp metal spear.

Quests

		TRANSPARENCY 10
		Literary Elements
		Conflict – explores the four common types of conflict introduced in this unit.

hatchet and hit the black rock gently. Too gently, and nothing happened. He struck harder, a glancing blow, and two or three weak sparks skipped off the rock and died immediately.

He swung harder, held the hatchet so it would hit a longer, sliding blow, and the black rock exploded in fire. Sparks flew so heavily that several of them skittered and jumped on the sand beneath the rock, and he smiled and struck again and again.

There could be fire here, he thought. I will have a fire here, he thought, and struck again—I will have fire from the hatchet.

1 Brian found it was a long way from sparks to fire.

Clearly there had to be something for the sparks to ignite, some kind of tinder or kindling—but what? He brought some dried grass in, tapped sparks into it, and watched them die. He tried small twigs, breaking them into little pieces, but that was worse than the grass. Then he tried a combination of the two, grass and twigs.

Nothing. He had no trouble getting sparks, but the tiny bits of hot stone or metal—he couldn't tell which they were—just sputtered and died.

He settled back on his haunches in exasperation, looking at the pitiful clump of grass and twigs.

He needed something finer, something soft and fine and fluffy to catch the bits of fire.

Shredded paper would be nice, but he had no paper.

"So close," he said aloud, "so close . . ." **2**

He put the hatchet back in his belt and went out of the shelter, limping on his sore leg. There had to be something, had to be. Man had made fire. There had been fire for thousands, millions of years. There had to be a way. He dug in his pockets and found the twenty-dollar bill in his wallet. Paper. Worthless paper out here. But if he could get a fire going . . .

He ripped the twenty into tiny pieces, made a pile of pieces, and hit sparks into them. Nothing happened. They just wouldn't take the sparks. But there had to be a way—some way to do it.

Not twenty feet to his right, leaning out over the water, were birches, and he stood looking at them for a full half-minute before they registered on his mind. They **3** were a beautiful white with bark like clean, slightly speckled paper.

Paper.

He moved to the trees. Where the bark was peeling from the trunks, it lifted in tiny tendrils, almost fluffs. Brian plucked some of them loose, rolled them in his fingers. They seemed flammable, dry and nearly powdery. He pulled and twisted bits off the trees, packing them in one hand while he picked them with the other, picking and gathering until he had a wad close to the size of a baseball.

Then he went back into the shelter and arranged the ball of birch-bark peelings at the base of the black rock. As an afterthought he threw in the remains of the twenty-dollar bill. He struck and a stream

from *Hatchet* 107

1. GUIDED READING:
Interpreting Meaning
What does this sentence imply about Brian's success in making a fire? Brian's efforts to start a fire were unsuccessful. He's gotten sparks but no fire.

2. GUIDED READING:
Predicting Outcomes
Do you think Brian will give up? Why or why not? Given Brian's determination, most students will probably predict that he will keep trying to make a fire. (Remember that Brian is not telling this story. It's possible that he won't make it.)

3. GUIDED READING:
Recognizing Descriptive Details
Sight details include "white," "slightly speckled," "peeling," "tiny tendrils, almost fluffs." Touch details include "dry and nearly powdery."

1. GUIDED READING:
Following the Sequence of Events
Be sure students know what Brian is trying to do. He wants to get enough "kindling" together to catch and hold a flame.

2. BACKGROUND
The Cro-Magnons were a prehistoric race of people thought to be the ancestors of modern Europeans. They are named after a cave in France, where their remains were first found.

3. GUIDED READING:
Drawing Conclusions
Notice how Brian is thinking and behaving like a scientist. He imagines a solution, he tests it, and he evaluates it. He tries another. Notice the sequence of ideas that come into his head before he thinks of the key idea: *oxygen*.

---

of sparks fell into the bark and quickly died. But this time one spark fell on one small hair of dry bark—almost a thread of bark—and seemed to glow a bit brighter before it died.

The material had to be finer. There had to be a soft and incredibly fine nest for the sparks.

I must make a home for the sparks, he thought. A perfect home or they won't stay, they won't make fire.

He started ripping the bark, using his fingernails at first, and when that didn't work, he used the sharp edge of the hatchet, cutting the bark in thin slivers, hairs so fine they were almost not there. It was painstaking work, slow work, and he stayed with it for over two hours. Twice he stopped for a handful of berries and **1** once to go to the lake for a drink. Then back to work, the sun on his back, until at last he had a ball of fluff as big as a grapefruit—dry birchbark fluff.

He positioned his spark nest—as he thought of it—at the base of the rock, used his thumb to make a small depression in the middle, and slammed the back of the hatchet down across the black rock. A cloud of sparks rained down, most of them missing the nest, but some, perhaps thirty or so, hit in the depression, and of those six or seven found fuel and grew, smoldered and caused the bark to take on the red glow.

Then they went out.

Close—he was close. He repositioned the nest, made a new and smaller dent with his thumb, and struck again.

More sparks, a slight glow, then nothing.

It's me, he thought. I'm doing some- **2** thing wrong. I do not know this—a cave dweller would have had a fire by now, a Cro-Magnon man would have a fire by now—but I don't know this. I don't know how to make a fire.

Maybe not enough sparks. He settled the nest in place once more and hit the rock with a series of blows, as fast as he could. The sparks poured like a golden waterfall. At first they seemed to take; there were several, many sparks that found life and took briefly, but they all died.

Starved.

He leaned back. They are like me. They are starving. It wasn't quantity—there were plenty of sparks—but they needed more.

I would kill, he thought suddenly, for a book of matches. Just one book. Just one match. I would kill.

What makes fire? He thought back to **3** school. To all those science classes. Had he ever learned what made a fire? Did a teacher ever stand up there and say, "This is what makes a fire . . ."

He shook his head, tried to focus his thoughts. What did it take? You have to have fuel, he thought—and he had that. The bark was fuel. Oxygen—there had to be air.

He needed to add air. He had to fan on it, blow on it.

He made the nest ready again, held the hatchet backward, tensed, and struck four quick blows. Sparks came down and he

SPEECH LINK

Panels of three, four, or five students may want to discuss the dilemma in which both Brian and his parents find themselves when the plane that he is traveling in crashes. Remind students that the story is told from Brian's point of view and that what is happening to his parents is pure conjecture.

CLOSURE

Have one student explain how Brian used his hatchet to survive in the wilderness. Have a second student make a prediction about "what happens next." (In the novel, after 54 days in the wilderness, Brian is finally rescued by a fur buyer, whose plane is signaled by a transmitter Brian found when he explored the wreckage of his own plane.)

RETEACHING

Have a volunteer give examples of internal and external conflicts in everyday life. Then provide students with a list of conflicts and have them discuss which are external and which are internal.

FOR STUDY AND DISCUSSION

Identifying Facts

1. A large bear.
   Brian runs, but then he realizes that the bear probably meant him no harm. He is so hungry that he returns.
2. A porcupine.
   He is terrified. He thinks of bears, Bigfoot, and monster movies.
3. He realizes he can use the sparks that the hatchet makes when struck against the stone wall to make a fire. His problem is to capture enough sparks and to gather suitable fuel to catch the tiny flames. He tries small pieces of wood, shredded paper, and finally fine birch-bark fluff. Then he remembers that a fire needs oxygen, so he blows on the sparks to fan the flame.
4. It makes sparks against the rock, which Brian then uses to make a fire.

Interpreting Meanings

5. Brian is questing to conquer the wilderness and survive. (He must slay the dragons of fear, hunger, and loneliness. The bear is a real "dragon.")
6. The most important rule of survival is not to give in to self-pity.
   He reached this conclusion when he realized that

---

leaned forward as fast as he could and blew.

Too hard. There was a bright, almost intense glow, then it was gone. He had blown it out.

Another set of strikes, more sparks. He leaned and blew, but gently this time, holding back and aiming the stream of air from his mouth to hit the brightest spot. Five or six sparks had fallen in a tight mass of bark hair and Brian centered his efforts there.

The sparks grew with his gentle breath. The red glow moved from the sparks themselves into the bark, moved and grew and became worms, glowing red worms that crawled up the bark hairs and caught other threads of bark and grew until there was a pocket of red as big as a quarter, a glowing red coal of heat.

And when he ran out of breath and paused to inhale, the red ball suddenly burst into flame.

"Fire!" he yelled. "I've got fire! I've got it, I've got it, I've got it . . ."

But the flames were thick and oily and burning fast, consuming the ball of bark as fast as if it were gasoline. He had to feed the flames, keep them going. Working as fast as he could, he carefully placed the dried grass and wood pieces he had tried at first on top of the bark and was gratified to see them take.

But they would go fast. He needed more, and more. He could not let the flames go out.

He ran from the shelter to the pines and started breaking off the low, dead small limbs. These he threw in the shelter, went back for more, threw those in, and squatted to break and feed the hungry flames. When the small wood was going well, he went out and found larger wood and did not relax until that was going. Then he leaned back against the wood brace of his door opening and smiled.

I have a friend, he thought—I have a friend now. A hungry friend, but a good one. I have a friend named fire.

"Hello, fire . . ."

The curve of the rock back made an almost perfect drawing flue[3] that carried the smoke up through the cracks of the roof but held the heat. If he kept the fire small, it would be perfect and would keep anything like the porcupine from coming through the door again.

A friend and a guard, he thought.

So much from a little spark. A friend and a guard from a tiny spark.

He looked around and wished he had somebody to tell this thing, to show this thing he had done. But there was nobody.

Nothing but the trees and the sun and the breeze and the lake.

Nobody.

And he thought, rolling thoughts, with the smoke curling up over his head and the smile still half on his face, he thought: I wonder what they're doing now.

I wonder what my father is doing now.

I wonder what my mother is doing now.

I wonder if she is with him.

---

3. **flue:** passage for smoke, such as a chimney.

110 Quests

EXTENSION AND ENRICHMENT

Social Studies and Literature. Have students work in small groups to do research on these topics and prepare oral reports. Asterisks indicate assignments suitable for good readers.

1. How Brian was rescued. (Assign Paulsen's novel.)
*2. How Robinson Crusoe survived. (Assign the chapter "Crusoe Provides for Himself" from Defoe's famous novel.)
*3. How the heroes and heroines in these modern young adult novels are "Crusoe" figures: *Island of the Blue Dolphins* by Scott O'Dell (1960), *Julie of the Wolves* by Jean Craighead George (1972), *My Side of the Mountain* by Jean Craighead George (1959).

For Study and Discussion

IDENTIFYING FACTS

1. What big **problem** does Brian encounter when he is picking and eating raspberries? How does he deal with this problem?
2. On the night after Brian finds the raspberries, who is his midnight visitor? Describe Brian's reaction to the intruder.
3. Tell about Brian's efforts to make a fire.
4. In this episode from the novel, how does the hatchet help Brian to survive?

INTERPRETING MEANINGS

5. How would you describe Brian's **quest**? (What is he searching for?)
6. According to Brian, what is the most important rule of survival? How did he reach this conclusion?
7. Describe Brian's dream. In each segment of the dream, what do you think Terry and his father are trying to tell him? (What might his father's "Mmmmm-maaaa" mean?)
8. The ancient Greeks believed that a god named Prometheus (prə·mē'thē·əs) gave the gift of fire to humankind. What qualities of fire make it a precious gift? Why does Brian feel that his fire is his friend?

APPLYING MEANINGS

9. Brian's English teacher once told his class, "You are your most valuable asset. . . . *You* are the best thing you have." Do you agree with that advice or not? Do you think it might have helped Brian?

Focus on Reading

IDENTIFYING THE SEQUENCE OF EVENTS

The account of Brian's attempts to start a fire is important in this part of his story. Following are the key events in that account. Fill in the missing events in the sequence.

1. Tries to set a fire with grass.
2.
3. Tries to set a fire with grass and twigs.
4.
5. Tries birch bark.
6.
7. Blows on fire to give it oxygen.
8.
9. Feeds flames with branches.

Literary Elements

CONFLICT

Make a list of all of Brian's basic **conflicts**, or struggles, as he faces the wilderness. Be sure to mention the animals or forces of nature that he has to struggle with, which threaten his life and well being.

from *Hatchet* 111

"feeling sorry for yourself didn't work" (page 105).
7. The dream has two parts. In the first part, his father is standing in the living room, gesturing and trying to tell Brian something. In the second part, Brian's friend Terry is making a fire at a barbecue pit in the park.
   Maybe his father is trying to tell him to "Mmmmm-maaaa-make a fire." Or, maybe he is mouthing the word *match*, which sounds like *hatchet*.
8. Fire provides light in the darkness, heat, and protection from wild animals; it can also cook food so we don't have to eat it raw.
   Brian feels that fire is his friend because it will help him survive in the wilderness. He invests the fire with personality.

Applying Meanings
9. Answers will vary. The teacher's advice helped Brian to restore his sense of self-confidence and resourcefulness in a critically dangerous situation.

FOCUS ON READING
Identifying the Sequence of Events
2. Tries to set a fire with small twigs, breaking them into little pieces.
4. Tries to set a fire with

the shredded paper of a twenty-dollar bill.
6. Tries to set a fire with birch-bark fluff.
8. Feeds the flame with dry grass and wood pieces.

LITERARY ELEMENTS
Conflict
A list might include Brian vs. the bear, the porcupine, and the threat of starvation.

A list might include Brian vs. his own fear, despair, and loneliness; and his worries about his parents' divorce.

Many students will say that Brian's most frightening conflict would have to be the fear that he would die alone and in pain in the wilderness.

LANGUAGE AND VOCABULARY
Description and Mood
For answers, see the **Teaching Guide** at the beginning of the unit.

FOCUS ON DESCRIPTIVE WRITING
Using Exact Words
Because students might not have access to recently written postcards, first have students work in pairs to write postcards to each other. Then the partners can rewrite the postcards as the activity suggests, using exact

---

Then make a list of all the conflicts you can imagine that might exist in his heart and mind. Remember the worries he has about his parents.

Which conflicts of Brian's do you think are most frightening?

Robinson Crusoe with his own hatchet.

Language and Vocabulary

DESCRIPTION AND MOOD
When writers use **description,** they paint word pictures that appeal to our senses of *sight, hearing, touch, taste,* and *smell.* Descriptions often create a certain feeling, or **mood.** For example, when the author describes the bear's fur as "shining black and silky," the bear doesn't seem very threatening. If the writer had described the bear as having "tiny wicked yellow eyes and pointed dirty teeth," we'd feel scared and disgusted.

Try writing a description of your own that creates a mood. Write three sentences. You might describe a locker room, the street in morning, or a fast-food restaurant.

Exchange descriptions with a classmate. On your classmate's paper, write down the feeling that his or her description gives you. (Pleasant? tasty? scary? disgusting? secure? hopeful?)

Focus on Descriptive Writing

USING EXACT WORDS
Exact words help to create bright, clear pictures in a description. Here are some examples of exact words in the paragraph from *Hatchet* beginning with "He made it to the shelter" on page 102:

made it to the *shelter* (versus *place*)
the rain *roared* down (versus *came*)
the sand outside was *drenched* (versus *wet*)
he was dry and *snug* (versus *comfortable*)
the raspberries were *seeping* (versus *going*)

Rewrite the message on a postcard that you or someone you know received recently. Use exact nouns, verbs, adjectives, and adverbs. Save your writing.

About the Author

Gary Paulsen (1939–   ) was born in Minneapolis, but his father, who was in the military, moved the family around constantly. Paulsen has written over two hundred short stories and articles, as well as more than forty novels—many of them for adult readers. He is best known to young people for such novels as *The Voyage of the Frog, Tracker,* and *Dogsong.* He wrote *Dogsong* in camp at night while he was training his dogsled team to run a 1,200-mile race in Alaska. Like *Hatchet,* these are survival stories that also tell of adolescents struggling to find themselves. Both *Dogsong* and *Hatchet* have been acclaimed as Honor Books in the annual competition for the Newbery Award—the award given by the American Library Association to the author of the best children's book published in the United States each year. For Paulsen, such awards have a very personal meaning. "It's like things have come full circle," he explains. "I felt like nothing the first time I walked into a library, and now library associations are giving me awards. It means a lot to me." (See "Behind the Scenes" below.)

nouns, verbs, adjectives, and adverbs. You may want to circulate throughout the room to offer comments and suggestions to students as they write.

VISUAL CONNECTIONS
The illustration on page 112 shows Robinson Crusoe building his house, using *his* hatchet. Crusoe was wrecked in September 1659 and was rescued in December 1686. Author Daniel Defoe modeled Crusoe on a real sailor, Alexander Selkirk, who actually survived on a desert island for five years. Another excellent Crusoe-type novel students might enjoy is *The Sign of the Beaver* by Elizabeth Speare.

Behind the Scenes

A First Library Card

I went in to get warm and to my absolute astonishment the librarian walked up to me and asked if I wanted a library card. She didn't care if I looked right, wore the right clothes, dated the right girls, was popular at sports—none of those prejudices existed in the public library. When she handed me the card, she handed me the world. I can't even describe how liberating it was. She recommended westerns and science fiction but every now and then would slip in a classic. I roared through everything she gave me and in the summer read a book a day. It was as though I had been dying of thirst and the librarian had handed me a five-gallon bucket of water. I drank and drank.

—Gary Paulsen

OBJECTIVES

Students will idenfity the quest in the story, find passages that support general statements, write a letter expressing their feelings, and draw conclusions about the causes of cruelty.

FOCUS/MOTIVATION

Establishing a Purpose for Reading. Ask students to notice how the boy realizes that no "journey" taken in life is useless. What does he discover of value as he quests, without success, for his lost father?

Prereading Journal. As the headnote suggests, have students write down their own thoughts about why some people are cruel to others.

Teaching Resources A
Teacher's Notes p. 125
Reading Check, p. 127
Reading Focus, p. 128
Study Guide, pp. 129, 130
Language Skills, p. 131
Building Vocabulary, p. 134
Selection Vocabulary Test, p. 136
Selection Test, p. 137

AV Resources Binder
Audiocassette 1, Side A

from Sounder

WILLIAM ARMSTRONG

Before You Read

Sounder is a novel about the great power of love to carry people through tragedy. Except for the dog named Sounder, the characters in this fictional family are nameless—perhaps to make them stand for *all* families, everywhere. This family lives in the early 1900s in a nameless place in the rural South.

Sounder begins when the father is forced to steal meat to feed his hungry family. As the father is taken away to jail, the sheriff cruelly shoots the family's beloved dog, Sounder, who has tried to save his master. The mother is now left to support four young children. The oldest son takes his father's place in the fields and grieves and watches for Sounder, who disappeared after he was hurt. Finally, Sounder returns. The dog has healed himself in the woods, but he is changed. He is missing an eye, he is crippled, and he has lost the wonderful mellow voice that gave him his name.

But the father does not return. As the years pass, the boy from time to time searches for his father. All he knows is that his father has been sent far away with a prison work gang. Just before this part of the story opens, the boy had been standing outside the fence of a prison camp. He was searching the faces inside for his father, when a prison guard cruelly smashed his hand.

Read the first two paragraphs of the story, down to the words "He would carry it with him anyway." Pause to write down your own thoughts about why some people are cruel to others.

READING THE SELECTION

The story is told in dialect, contains allusions to the Bible, and raises some interesting questions about cruelty and the power of storytelling. It would probably be advisable to have students read the selection in class, allowing them to ask questions as necessary.

The stills are from the film Sounder, *made in 1972.*

Mattel/Radnitz.

VISUAL CONNECTIONS

The stills in this selection are from the 1972 movie *Sounder* with Cicely Tyson, Paul Winfield, Kevin Hooks, Carmen Mathews, and Taj Mahal (105 minutes). In the film, for obvious reasons, the characters are given names. The boy is David Lee. An interesting change from the novel is that the teacher is a woman, played by Janet MacLachlan. In his review of the film, Roger Ebert writes that *Sounder* "is one of the most compassionate and truthful of movies."

MEETING INDIVIDUAL NEEDS

ESL/LEP • In emphasizing the importance and legitimacy of dialect, explain that English, like all languages, may be thought of as a bicycle wheel. At the center, or hub, is standard English. Each spoke radiating out from the center is a different dialect. The wheel is not complete without all its parts.

1. LANGUAGE AND VOCABULARY

The Language and Vocabulary box on this page prepares students for the rich dialogue. The Language and Vocabulary exercise on page 126 gives students practice with dialect.

2. GUIDED READING: Paraphrasing

A possible paraphrase: "I have heard it said that cruelty comes from cowardice. I have found by experience that spitefulness and inhuman hatred are usually found in weak people. After all, it is only the lower animals like wolves and filthy bears that attack dying creatures that cannot fight back."

3. GUIDED READING: Recognizing Cause and Effect

What causes the boy's sadness? He has longed to own a book and now this one is too hard for him to understand. Notice that this is the first book the boy has ever had.

4. GUIDED READING: Making Connections

Both Joseph and David are young people who triumph over their enemies. Joseph, in addition, endures slavery. The boy's family is deeply religious.

Language and Vocabulary

1 **Dialect is a special way of speaking used by people who live in a particular part of the country or who belong to a particular group.** Dialects differ from standard English in their vocabulary, pronunciation, and grammar. Everybody speaks some kind of dialect. In *Sounder,* the boy and his mother speak a black dialect common to the rural South. For example, the mother says, "Scorchin' to be walkin' and totin' far today." How would your picture of the mother change if she said, "It's awfully hot to have to walk and carry something"?

Later that day, passing along a street in a strange and lonely town, the boy saw a man dump a box of trash into a barrel. He noticed that a large brown-backed book went in with the trash. He waited until the man went back into the building and then took the book from the barrel. It was a book of stories about what people think. There were titles such as Cruelty, Excellent Men, Education, Cripples, Justice, and many others. The boy sat down, leaned back against the barrel, and began to read from the story called Cruelty.

2 I have often heard it said that cowardice is the mother of cruelty, and I have found by experience that malicious and inhuman animosity and fierceness are usually accompanied by weakness. Wolves and filthy bears, and all the baser beasts, fall upon the dying.¹

The boy was trying to read aloud, for he could understand better if he heard the words. But now he stopped. He did not understand what it said; the words were too new and strange. He was sad. He 3 thought books would have words like the ones he had learned to read in the store signs, words like his mother used when she told him stories of the Lord and Joseph and 4 David.² All his life he had wanted a book. Now he held one in his hands, and it was only making his bruised fingers hurt more. He would carry it with him anyway.

He passed a large brick schoolhouse with big windows and children climbing on little ladders and swinging on swings. No one jeered at him or noticed him because he had crossed the street and was walking close up against the hedge on the other side. Soon the painted houses ran out, and he was walking past unpainted cabins. He

---

1. The writer is saying that cowardly and weak people can be the cruelest. A *malicious* person is mean. *Animosity* means "hatred."

2. The story of Joseph, who was sold into slavery in Egypt by his brothers, begins in Genesis 37. The boy David kills the giant Goliath with only a slingshot (1 Samuel 17).

116 Quests

1 always felt better on his travels when he came to the part of town where the unpainted cabins were. Sometimes people came out on the porch when he passed and talked to him. Sometimes they gave him a piece to eat on the way. Now he thought they might laugh and say, "What you carryin', child? A book?" So he held it close up against him.

"That's a school too," the boy said to himself as he stood facing a small unpainted building with its door at the end instead of the side, the way cabin doors were. Besides, he could always tell a school because it had more windows than a cabin.

At the side of the building two children were sloshing water out of a tin pail near a hand pump. One threw a dipper of water on a dog that came from underneath to bark at the boy. The school was built on posts, and a stovepipe came through the wall and stuck up above the rafters. A rusty tin pipe ran from the corner of the roof down to the cistern[3] where the children were playing.

The dog had gone back under the building, so the boy entered the yard and moved toward the children. If one of them
2 would work the pump handle, he could wash the dried blood off his hand. Just when he reached the cistern, a wild commotion of barking burst from under the floor of the school. Half a dozen dogs, which followed children to school and waited patiently for lunchtime scraps and for school to be over, burst from under the building in pursuit of a pig that had wandered onto the lot. In the wild chase around the building, the biggest dog struck the tin drainpipe, and it clattered down the wall and bounced on the cement top of the cistern. With a pig under the building and the dogs barking and racing in and out, the school day ended.

Two dozen or more children raced out the door, few of them touching the three steps that led from the stoop to the ground. Some were calling the names of dogs and looking under the building. The boy found himself surrounded by strange inquiring eyes. Questions came too fast to answer. "You new here?" "Where you moved to?" "That your book?" "You comin' here to school?" "Kin you read that big a book?" The boy had put his bruised hand into his pocket so no one could see it. Some of the children carried books too, but none were as big as the one he held close against his side.

Just when the commotion was quieting down, a man appeared at the schoolhouse door. The children scattered across the lot in four directions. "Tell your pa that he must keep his pig in the pen," he called to one child.

Then it was quiet. The boy looked at the man in the doorway. They were alone now. The dogs had followed the children. And the pig, hearing a familiar call from the corner of the lot, had come grunting from his sanctuary[4] and gone in the direction of the call.

---

3. **cistern** (sis′tərn): water tank.

4. **sanctuary** (sangk′choo·er′ē): safe, protected place.

**1. GUIDED READING:
Interpreting Meaning**
Why do you think the boy feels better in this part of town? Unpainted cabins suggest (at this time in history and in this place) that poor black people live there. Being poor and black himself, the boy feels more comfortable here. Probably these people are kinder to him.

2. BACKGROUND
The dried blood is from the injury inflicted on the boy by the cruel prison guard.

from *Sounder*

The boy's mother was played by Cicely Tyson in the 1972 film.

In his many journeyings among strangers the boy had learned to sniff out danger and spot orneriness⁵ quickly. Now, for the first time in his life away from home, he wasn't feared. The lean elderly man with snow-white hair, wearing Sunday clothes, came down the steps. "This pipe is always falling," he said as he picked it up and put it back in place. "I need to wire it up."

"I just wanted to wash my hand. It's got dried blood on it where I hurt my fingers."

"You should have run home."

"I don't live in these parts."

"Here, I'll hold your book, and I'll pump for you." And the mellow eyes of the man began to search the boy for answers, answers that could be found without asking questions.

"We need warm, soapy water," the teacher said. "I live right close. Wait 'til I get my papers and lock the door, and I'll take you home and fix it."

1 The boy wanted to follow the man into the schoolhouse and see what it was like inside, but by the time he got to the steps, the man was back again, locking the door. "I usually put the school in order after the children leave," he said, "but I'll do it in the morning before they get here."

At the edge of the school lot the man took the road that led away from the town. They walked without much talk, and the boy began to wish the man would ask him a lot of questions. When they had passed several cabins, each farther from the other as they went, the man turned off the road and said, "We're home. I live here alone. Have lived alone for a long time." Fingering the small wire hook on the neatly whitewashed gate which led into a yard that was green, the teacher stopped talking.

A cabin with a gate and green grass in the yard is almost a big house, the boy thought as he followed the man.

Inside the gate the man went along the fence, studying some plants tied up to stakes. **2** He began to talk again, not to the boy, but to a plant that was smaller than the others. "You'll make it, little one, but it'll take time to get your roots set again."

The boy looked at the white-haired old man leaning over like he was listening for the plant to answer him. "He's conjured,"⁶ the boy whispered to himself. "Lots of old folks is conjured or addled."⁷ He moved backward to the gate, thinking he'd better run away. "Conjured folks can conjure you," the boy's mother always said, "if you get yourself plain carried off by their soft spell-talk."

But before the boy could trouble his mind anymore, the man straightened up and began talking to him. "Some animal dug under the roots and tore them loose from the earth. It was wilted badly and might have died. But I reset it, and I water it every day. It's hard to reset a plant if it's

---

5. **orneriness** (ôr′nər·ē·nes): meanness.
6. **conjured** (kan′jərd): here, someone who practices magic.
7. **addled**: crazy.

from *Sounder*

1. GUIDED READING:
Noting Details
This detail and others reveal how desperately the boy wants an education.

2. GUIDED READING:
Noting Key Passages
Here is a statement referred to in question 7 on page 125. The plant and the boy both need their "roots" set again.

1. GUIDED READING:
Making Inferences
How is the boy feeling here? He is probably feeling angry, hurt, and ignored. The reality is that the teacher doesn't want to ask the boy questions that will be difficult or humiliating for him to answer.

2. GUIDED READING:
Making Inferences
What does this detail reveal about the boy? He's very poor—so poor that burning two lamps at once seems almost an unbelievable extravagance.

3. LITERARY ELEMENTS:
Theme
What is the message of this little story? A friend is more valuable than any material wealth. *Or:* Love can accomplish more than money can.

---

wilted too much; the life has gone out of it. But this one will be all right. I see new leaves startin'."

"What grows on it?" the boy asked, thinking it must be something good to eat if somebody cared that much about a plant.

"It's only a flower," the man said. "I'll water it when the earth has cooled a little. If you water a plant when the earth is too warm, it shocks the roots."

Inside the cabin the man started a fire in the cookstove and heated water. As he washed the boy's hand with a soft white rag, he said, "You musta slammed these fingers in a awful heavy door or gate." Before the boy could answer, the teacher began to talk about the plant he must remember to water.

1 He don't wanta know nothin' about me, the boy thought.

"When I saw your book, I thought you were coming to enroll for school. But you don't live in these parts, you say."

"I found the book in a trash barrel. It has words like I ain't used to readin'. I can read store-sign words and some newspaper words."

"This is a wonderful book," said the teacher. "It was written by a man named Montaigne,[8] who was a soldier. But he grew tired of being a soldier and spent his time studying and writing. He also liked to walk on country roads."

The teacher lit two lamps. The boy had never seen two lamps burning in the same 2 room. They made the room as bright as daylight.

"People should read his writings," the man continued. "But few do. He is all but forgotten." But the boy did not hear. He was thinking of a cabin that had two lamps, both lit at the same time, and two stoves, one to cook on and one to warm by.

The man sat in a chair between two tables that held the lamps. There were books on the tables too, and there were shelves filled not with pans and dishes, but with books. The mellow eyes of the man followed the boy's puzzled glances as they studied the strange warm world in which he had suddenly found himself.

"I will read you a little story from your book." The boy watched as the fingers of the man turned the pages one way and then the other until he found what he wanted to read.

3 "This is a very short story about a king named Cyrus,[9] who wanted to buy the prize horse that belonged to one of his soldiers. Cyrus asked him how much he would sell the horse for, or whether he would exchange him for a kingdom. The soldier said he would not sell his prize horse and he would not exchange him for a kingdom, but that he would willingly give up his horse to gain a friend. . . . But now I have told you the whole story so there's no use for me to read it."

---

8. **Montaigne** (män·tän'): Michel de Montaigne (1533–1592), a great French writer. Montaigne wrote personal essays on hundreds of topics. He is regarded as the "inventor" of the personal essay.

9. **Cyrus** (sī'rəs).

TRANSPARENCIES 7 & 8

Fine Art
Theme: *Searching for Something of Value* – highlights artworks depicting people engaged in challenging, even dangerous, pursuits in order to achieve a goal.

---

1 "You've been a powerful good friend to take me in like this," the boy said at last. "My fingers don't hurt no more."

"I am your friend," said the man. "So while I heat some water to soak your hand and make your cot for the night, you tell me all about yourself."

"I had a father and a dog named Sounder," the boy began. . . .

"Who's been kindly to your hurts?" the boy's mother asked as she looked down at the clean white rags that bandaged the boy's fingers. Rocking on the porch, she had seen the white dot swinging back and forth in the sun when the boy wasn't much more than a moving spot far down the road. "For a while I wasn't sure it was you," she said. "Why you walkin' fast? You done found him? Is your hand hurt bad? Is that a Bible somebody's done mistreated?" The woman's eyes had come to rest on the book the boy held in his good hand.

"No. It's a book. I found it in a trash can."

"Be careful what you carry off, child," his mother said. "It can cause a heap o' trouble."

"I got somethin' to tell," the boy said as he sat down on the edge of the porch and ran his bandaged fingers over the head of the great coon dog[10] who had stopped his jumping and whining and lay at the boy's feet with his head cocked to the side, looking up with his one eye. The younger children sat in a line beside the boy, waiting to hear.

"Is he poorly?" the woman asked **2** slowly. "Is he far?"

"It's about somethin' else," the boy said after a long spell of quiet. "I ain't found him yet."

The boy told his mother and the children about his night in the teacher's cabin. The teacher wanted him to come back and go to school. He had been asked to live in the teacher's cabin and do his chores. The children's eyes widened when they heard the cabin had two lamps, two stoves, and grass growing in a yard with a fence and a gate. He told how the teacher could read and that there were lots of books on shelves in the cabin.

"Maybe he will write letters to the road camps for you," the mother said, "'cause you'll be so busy with schoolin' and cleanin' the schoolhouse for him that you can't go searchin' no more."

"Maybe I'd have time," the boy said. "But he says like you, 'Better not to go. Just be patient and time will pass.'"

"It's all powerful puzzlin' and aggravatin', but it's the Lord's will." The boy noticed that his mother had stopped rocking; the loose boards did not rattle as the chair moved on them.

"The teacher said he'd walk all the **3** way and reason about it if you didn't want me to come to him. You don't want me to go, but I'll come home often as I can. And sometime I might bring word."

"It's a sign; I believes in signs." The

---

10. **coon dog:** "Coon" is a clipped form of raccoon, an animal that is a nuisance to farmers because it breaks into chicken coops and ruins corn crops. A coon dog tracks raccoons.

from *Sounder* 121

---

1. GUIDED READING:
Interpreting Meaning
Why do you think that of all the material in the book, the man chooses to read the story about Cyrus? Perhaps he senses that the boy is lonely and needs a friend. Perhaps the man wants to bring up the topic of friendship in an indirect way to let the boy know that he understands how important friends are.

2. GUIDED READING:
Interpreting Meaning
Who is "he"? The woman is referring to her missing husband, for whom the boy has been searching.

3. GUIDED READING:
Making Inferences
What can you infer about the teacher from the boy's words? The teacher believes that the boy is sincere in his desire to learn and that he has the ability. The teacher is generous and willing to put himself out to help someone else.

MEETING INDIVIDUAL NEEDS

Visual Learners • Have students compare the challenges faced by characters in the stories they read in Unit 2. Each student could create a chart describing for each story the type of challenge and how the character faced it.

Sample Chart:

Story Title	Description of Character's Challenge
The Smallest Dragonboy	Keevan is small for his age and often teased by his peers.
Hatchet	Brian is alone in the Canadian wilderness after a plane crash.

Method of Facing Challenge
Overcomes taunts of bully, physical pain, and inner conflicts by believing in himself.
Uses patience, persistence, and careful planning.

Students might want to add to their charts as they complete stories in the unit.

rocker began to move back and forth, rattling the loose boards in the porch floor. "Go, child. The Lord has come to you."

When he returned to the cabin with books on the shelves and the kind man with the white hair and the gentle voice, all the boy carried was his book with one cover missing—the book that he couldn't understand. In the summers he came home to take his father's place in the fields, for cabin rent had to be paid with field work. In the winter he seldom came because it took "more'n a day's walkin' and sleepin' on the ground."

"Ain't worth it," his mother would say.

Each year, after he had been gone for a whole winter and returned, the faithful Sounder would come hobbling on three legs far down the road to meet him. The great dog would wag his tail and whine. He never barked. The boy sang at his work in the fields; and his mother rocked in her chair and sang on the porch of the cabin. Sometimes when Sounder scratched fleas under the porch, she would look at the hunting lantern and the empty possum[11] sack hanging against the wall. Six crops of persimmons[12] and wild grapes had ripened. The possums and raccoons had gathered them unmolested. The lantern and possum sack hung untouched. "No use to nobody no more," the woman said.

The boy read to his brother and sisters when he had finished his day in the fields.

---

11. **possum:** short for opossum, a small furry animal that lives in trees and is hunted for food.
12. **persimmon** (pər·sim′ən): a kind of sweet fruit.

from *Sounder*

1. GUIDED READING:
Making Inferences
How long has the father been gone? The fact that six crops have ripened suggests that the father has been gone for six years.

1. BACKGROUND
Further Reading
You might have some students read Joseph's story, beginning in Genesis 37. One of the reasons the boy identifies so strongly with Joseph is that Joseph was taken away from home, sold into slavery, and cruelly imprisoned, but Joseph was also eventually rescued. References to the Joseph narrative recur throughout the novel. (It's a wonderful narrative to recommend to interested students.)

2. GUIDED READING:
Making Inferences
What does this decision reveal about the boy? He is sensitive and respectful of his mother. He doesn't want to make her feel inferior by showing off his new knowledge.

3. LITERARY ELEMENTS:
Foreshadowing
These details foreshadow the real reason for Sounder's erratic behavior. He's not mad; with a dog's uncanny perception, he senses that his long-lost master is nearby.

---

1 He read the story of Joseph over and over and never wearied of it. "In all the books in the teacher's cabin, there's no story as good as Joseph's story," he would say to them.

The woman, listening and rocking, would say, "The Lord has come to you, child. The Lord has certainly come to you."

Late one August afternoon the boy and his mother sat on the shaded corner of the porch. The heat and drought of dog days[13] had parched the earth, and the crops had been laid by. The boy had come home early because there was nothing to do in the fields.

"Dog days is a terrible time," the woman said. "It's when the heat is so bad **2** the dogs go mad." The boy would not tell her that the teacher had told him that dog days got their name from the Dog Star[14] because it rose and set with the sun during that period. She had her own feeling for the earth, he thought, and he would not confuse it.

"It sure is hot," he said instead. "Lucky to come from the fields early." He watched the heat waves as they made the earth look like it was moving in little ripples.

Sounder came around the corner of the cabin from somewhere, hobbled back and forth as far as the road several times, and then went to his cool spot under the porch.

---
13. **dog days:** the hot, rainless days of August. People used to think the heat drove dogs mad.
14. **Dog Star:** the brightest star in the heavens; also called *Sirius*.

"That's what I say about dog days," the woman said. "Poor creature's been addled with the heat for three days. Can't find no place to quiet down. Been down the road **3** nearly out o' sight a second time today, and now he musta come from the fencerows. Whines all the time. A mad dog is a fearful sight. Slobberin' at the mouth and runnin' every which way 'cause they're blind. Have to shoot 'em 'fore they bite some child. It's awful hard."

"Sounder won't go mad," the boy said. "He's lookin' for a cooler spot, I reckon."

A lone figure came on the landscape as a speck and slowly grew into a ripply form through the heat waves. "Scorchin' to be walkin' and totin' far today," she said as she pointed to the figure on the road.

A catbird fussed in the wilted lilac at the corner of the cabin. "Why's that bird fussin' when no cat's prowlin? Old folks has a sayin' that if a catbird fusses 'bout nothin', somethin' bad is comin'. It's a bad sign."

"Sounder, I reckon," the boy said. "He just passed her bush when he came around the cabin."

In the tall locust at the edge of the fence, its top leaves yellowed from lack of water, a mockingbird mimicked the catbird with half a dozen notes, decided it was too hot to sing, and disappeared. The great coon dog, whose rhythmic panting came through the porch floor, came from under the house and began to whine.

As the figure on the road drew near, it took shape and grew indistinct again in the

CLOSURE

Call on a volunteer to summarize how the boy's quest for his father turns out. What does the boy gain as a result of his quest?

RETEACHING

Review the idea of the quest, summarized for students on page 67. Have them discuss at least three examples of quests from the movies or TV and then apply what they've learned to the boy's quest in this story.

---

wavering heat. Sometimes it seemed to be a person dragging something, for little puffs of red dust rose in sulfurous[15] clouds at every other step. Once or twice they thought it might be a brown cow or mule, dragging its hooves in the sand and raising and lowering its weary head.

Sounder panted faster, wagged his tail, whined, moved from the dooryard to the porch and back to the dooryard.

The figure came closer. Now it appeared to be a child carrying something on its back and limping.

"The children still at the creek?" she asked.

"Yes, but it's about dry."

Suddenly the voice of the great coon hound broke the sultry[16] August deadness. The dog dashed along the road, leaving three-pointed clouds of red dust to settle back to earth behind him. The mighty voice rolled out upon the valley, each flutelike bark echoing from slope to slope.

"Lord's mercy! Dog days done made him mad." And the rocker was still.

Sounder was a young dog again. His voice was the same mellow sound that had ridden the November breeze from the lowlands to the hills. The boy and his mother looked at each other. The catbird stopped her fussing in the wilted lilac bush. On three legs, the dog moved with the same lightning speed that had carried him to the throat of a grounded raccoon.

Sounder's master had come home.

---

15. **sulfurous** (sul'fər·əs): here, fiery.
16. **sultry:** hot, still, and humid.

For Study and Discussion

IDENTIFYING FACTS

1. What wonderful thing does the boy discover in the trash?

2. What "powerful good friend" does the boy find on his travels? How does the friend help him?

3. What advice finally convinces the boy to stop his search?

4. Describe the father's homecoming. What wonderful change comes over Sounder?

INTERPRETING MEANINGS

5. Before he began his long **quest,** the boy makes this observation: ". . . in Bible-story journeys, ain't no journey hopeless. Everybody finds what they suppose to find." Although he didn't find his father, was the boy's quest hopeless? What did he find instead?

6. After he picks the book out of the trash, the boy reads a passage called Cruelty. Think about this passage (page 116). How would these words make the boy feel about the men who jailed and beat his father for stealing food to feed his hungry children? Do you agree with this analysis of cruelty?

7. On page 119 the teacher talks to a small plant. Which of his words to the little plant could apply to the boy himself?

APPLYING MEANINGS

8. Do you agree that no "journey" is hopeless—that if you make a great effort to do something, you will discover something of value? (Even if it's not what you set out to find.)

from *Sounder* 125

FOR STUDY AND DISCUSSION

Identifying Facts

1. He discovers a book of essays by the French writer Montaigne.

2. He finds the teacher. The teacher helps him by bandaging his wound, by reading to him, and by enrolling him in school.

3. The teacher advises the boy just to be patient and time will pass.

4. First we see a small, distorted figure far along down the road. We realize from Sounder's excitement that it's the father returning. Sounder races to greet his long-lost master.

Sounder acts like a young dog again, and his voice is heard echoing over the valley.

Interpreting Meanings

5. The boy's quest was not hopeless at all: he found two very important things—friendship and education.

6. The words might have explained why those men were so mindlessly cruel to his father and why the prison guard was so cruel to him.

Most students will agree that cruelty is inspired by resentful feelings caused by weakness and a sense of inferiority. Have them think of how immature or insecure children are often bullies. (Refer to Beterli in "The Smallest Dragonboy.")

7. "You'll make it, little one, but it'll take time to get your roots set again."

Applying Meanings

8. Some students will be able to see that every journey can yield a valuable result, even if the result is not exactly what we expect. (Sometimes it requires an act of faith or imagination to see it this way.) Others may argue that some journeys yield no value. Encourage lively discussion.

FOCUS ON READING
Supporting General Statements

1. "All his life he had wanted a book. Now he held one in his hands" (page 116).

2. He did not understand what it said; the words were too new and strange. . . . He thought books would have words like the ones he had learned to read in the store signs" (page 116).

3. "He always felt better on his travels when he came to the part of the town where the unpainted cabins were. Sometimes people came out on the porch when he passed and talked to him. Sometimes they gave him a piece to eat on the way" (pages 116–117).

126

Focus on Reading

SUPPORTING GENERAL STATEMENTS

Below are some general statements about this excerpt from *Sounder*. Find and read aloud the sentences from the story that support each statement.

1. The boy had never owned a book before.
2. The boy could read words, but not very well.
3. On his journeys, the boy feels better when he is traveling through the poorer parts of towns, because people there are kinder to him.
4. The teacher's house is more comfortable than the boy's own home.
5. The boy's mother has great religious faith.

Language and Vocabulary

DIALECT

A **dialect** is the form of a language spoken by people from a certain group or region. Dialects differ from standard English in grammar ("we was" instead of "we were"); in pronunciation ("lickin' " instead of "licking"); and in vocabulary ("I reckon" instead of "I guess"). The following sentences from *Sounder* are spoken by the boy or his mother. Read the sentences aloud and enjoy the sounds of the dialect. Then write the italicized dialect word or expression in standard English. (Some sentences may need rewriting.)

1. "It has words like *I ain't* used to *readin'*. I can read *store-sign* words . . ."
2. "You've been a *powerful good* friend to

126 Quests

take me in like this. . . . My fingers don't hurt *no more*."

3. "Who's been *kindly* to your hurts?"
4. "*Why you walkin'* fast? *You done found* him? Is your hand hurt *bad*? Is that a Bible somebody's *done mistreated*?"

Focus on Descriptive Writing

USING SENSORY DETAILS

Sensory details are words and phrases that appeal to the five senses:

sight   hearing   touch   taste   smell

For example, in the paragraph on page 123 beginning "Each year, after he had been gone for a whole winter," William Armstrong uses details that appeal to sight, hearing,

EXTENSION AND ENRICHMENT

Social Studies. Have students read in their history books or encyclopedias an account of life in the rural South in the years following the Civil War and into the early 1900s. What caused the poverty of sharecroppers like the boy's family? (They could check indexes under "South," "Sharecropping," and "Civil War Aftermath.")

Literature. Good readers might be directed to Book 17 of Homer's epic poem the *Odyssey,* in which the old dog Argus is the only one to recognize his master when he returns home after twenty years. See Armstrong's comment on page 128.

---

and touch to describe the family's life during the summer.

Working with a small group of your classmates, choose one of the four subjects below for a description. Fill out the **observation chart** with as many sensory details as you can. Save your notes.

a playground a kitchen
a party a circus

Observation Chart
Subject: _____

Sight	Hearing	Touch	Smell	Taste
___	___	___	___	___
___	___	___	___	___
___	___	___	___	___
___	___	___	___	___

About the Author

William H. Armstrong (1914–   ) spent many years teaching history to high-school students and writing books and articles on education. But he is best known for his award-winning novel *Sounder*—a story that has been read by countless children, translated into eight languages, and made into a popular Hollywood film.

William Armstrong was born on a farm in the historic Shenandoah Valley near Lexington, Virginia. There he acquired a love for history that has lasted all his life. He grew up riding his horse over the same hills once crossed by General Lee on his horse Traveler, after the Civil War.

When he began to write *Sounder,* Armstrong saw his novel as a kind of history—the personal history of an unforgettable African American teacher he once knew as a child. (See the section "Behind the Scenes" on page 128.)

In 1970, Armstrong's novel was awarded the Newbery Award as the outstanding book for children of that year. In accepting the award, Armstrong read aloud some letters he had received from children. One reader wrote of *Sounder:* "It made me feel very hollow inside. Because we are living comfortable while the boy's family lived uncomfortable. You made me feel like I was watching all this happening right in front of my eyes." Another wrote: "It was sad and a few of us cried silently. At first, I closed my ears to the book, but then I realized that I should listen."

---

4. "The boy had never seen two lamps burning in the same room. They made the room as bright as daylight" (page 120).

5. "'It's all powerful puzzlin' and aggravatin', but it's the Lord's will'" (page 121). "The woman, listening and rocking, would say, 'The Lord has come to you, child'" (page 124).

LANGUAGE AND VOCABULARY
Dialect
For answers, see the **Teaching Guide** at the beginning of the unit.

FOCUS ON DESCRIPTIVE WRITING
Using Sensory Details
Before students fill in their observation charts, you may want to work with the class to create a word bank of sensory details on the chalkboard. List the five senses as headings and have students offer suggestions. You could start with the following words: Sight—oblong, twisted, glittery; Hearing—shrill, rumble, chirp; Taste—salty, bitter, bland; Smell—musty, stale, rotten; Touch—rough, icy, sharp.

In addition, encourage students to keep word banks in a special section of their notebooks or journals. As they read or hear vivid sensory details, they can record them for later use.

Behind the Scenes

His History

Fifty years ago I learned to read at a round table in the center of a large, sweet-smelling, steam-softened kitchen. My teacher was a gray-haired black man who taught the one-room school several miles away from where we lived in the Green Hill district of the county. He worked for my father after school and in the summer. There were no radios or television sets, so when our lessons were finished, he told us stories. His stories came from Aesop, the Old Testament, Homer, and history.

There was a lasting, magnificent intoxication about the man that has remained after half a century. There was seldom a preacher at the white-washed, clapboard Baptist church in the Green Hill district, so he came often to our white man's church and sat alone in the balcony. Sometimes the minister would call on this eloquent, humble man to lead the congregation in prayer. He would move quietly to the foot of the balcony steps, pray with the simplicity of the Carpenter of Nazareth, and then return to where he sat alone, for no other black people ever came to join him.

He had come to our community from farther south, already old when he came. He talked little, or not at all, about his past. But one night at the great center table after he had told the story of Argus, the faithful dog of Odysseus, he told the story of Sounder, a coon dog.

It is the black man's story, not mine. It was not from Aesop, the Old Testament, or Homer. It was history—*his* history.

That world of long ago has almost totally changed. The church balcony is gone. The table is gone from the kitchen. But the story remains.

—W. H. Armstrong
(1970)

OBJECTIVES
Students will analyze details of character, select conclusions based on evidence, and write a descriptive paragraph.

FOCUS/MOTIVATION
Discuss with students books they may have read or television shows and movies they may have seen in which people respond to life-threatening situations. What did the people do? How must they have felt? Challenge students to face danger with Jody in the Florida scrub.

Prereading Journal. As the headnote on page 130 suggests, have students write about how they would respond to the disaster that strikes Jody's father. Read through to the words "Ol' Death goin' to git me yit" and stop to allow students to write.

VISUAL CONNECTIONS
You might rent and show the videotape of *The Yearling*, which was filmed on location in Florida in 1946. Your students will like Claude Jarman, Jr., who won a special Oscar for his portrayal of Jody. Other actors are Gregory Peck, Jane Wyman, Chill Wills, Margaret Wycherly, Henry Travers, Jeff York, Forrest Tucker, and June Lockhart.

Jody's Discovery

MARJORIE KINNAN RAWLINGS

The stills are from the film The Yearling, *made in 1946.*

Jody's Discovery 129

READING THE SELECTION

After you have familiarized students with the setting, dialect, and characters, begin the reading yourself, or let students read who have had the opportunity to study in advance. The narrative moves quickly with short sentences packed with action and suspense. High interest in Jody's struggles should motivate students to finish the reading at home. Suggest that they read all dialogue aloud if possible in preparation for oral reading in class the next day.

> **TEACHING RESOURCES A**
> Teacher's Notes, p. 139
> Reading Check, p. 142
> Reading Focus, p. 143
> Study Guide, pp. 144, 145
> Language Skills, p. 146
> Building Vocabulary, p. 149
> Selection Vocabulary Test, p. 151
> Selection Test, p. 152

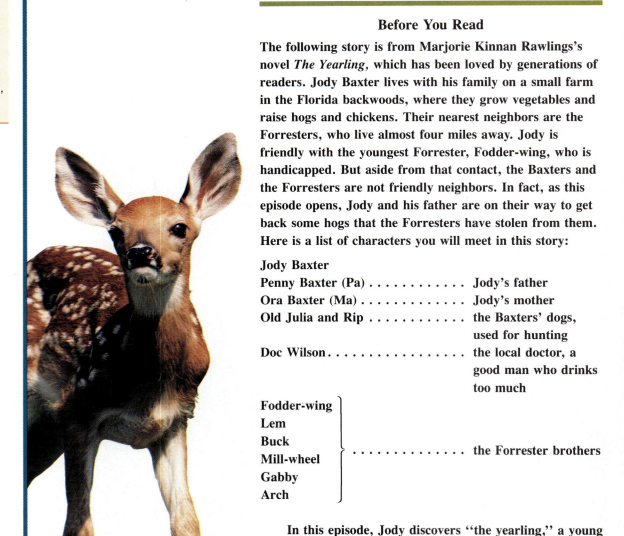

Before You Read

The following story is from Marjorie Kinnan Rawlings's novel *The Yearling*, which has been loved by generations of readers. Jody Baxter lives with his family on a small farm in the Florida backwoods, where they grow vegetables and raise hogs and chickens. Their nearest neighbors are the Forresters, who live almost four miles away. Jody is friendly with the youngest Forrester, Fodder-wing, who is handicapped. But aside from that contact, the Baxters and the Forresters are not friendly neighbors. In fact, as this episode opens, Jody and his father are on their way to get back some hogs that the Forresters have stolen from them. Here is a list of characters you will meet in this story:

Jody Baxter
Penny Baxter (Pa) . . . . Jody's father
Ora Baxter (Ma) . . . . Jody's mother
Old Julia and Rip . . . . the Baxters' dogs, used for hunting
Doc Wilson . . . . the local doctor, a good man who drinks too much

Fodder-wing
Lem
Buck
Mill-wheel } . . . . the Forrester brothers
Gabby
Arch

In this episode, Jody discovers "the yearling," a young deer with whom he develops a strong, mystical bond. As you read, think about Jody and his family. How would you have responded to the disaster that strikes Jody's father?

130

MEETING INDIVIDUAL NEEDS

ESL/LEP • The author's extensive use of dialect is especially challenging for students learning standard English. To provide assistance, at least in terms of spelling, write a few examples from the story on the chalkboard (*jest, keer, keetch, kin, hongry, leetle, mebbe, purty*). Then ask the class to supply the standard spellings.

Language and Vocabulary

Dialect is the form of a language spoken by people in a particular region or social group. The characters in *Sounder* (page 114) use a Southern black dialect of English. The characters in "Becky and the Wheels-and-Brake Boys" (page 220) speak in a Jamaican dialect. The characters in *The Yearling* use a different dialect, one spoken in the Florida backwoods. Penny Baxter uses dialect when he says, "I seed a man die—" and "Git a move on, young un." Penny uses *seed* for *saw*, *git* for *get*, and *un* for *one*. Sounds may be dropped from dialect words, as in *he'p* for *help* and *goin'* for *going*. Or sounds may be added, as when Jody says, "Hit's me!" Reading the characters' conversations aloud will help you understand their special dialect and hear how they sound. It will also help you to step into the backwoods with Jody and Penny and share their experiences.

1

A chill air moved across the scrub[1] and was gone, as though a vast being had blown a cold breath and then passed by. Jody shivered and was grateful for the hot air that fell in behind it. A wild grapevine trailed across the thin-rutted road. Penny leaned to pull it aside.

2 He said, "When there's trouble waitin' for you, you jest as good go to meet it."

The rattler struck him from under the grapevine without warning. Jody saw the flash, blurred as a shadow, swifter than a martin,[2] surer than the slashing claws of a bear. He saw his father stagger backward under the force of the blow. He heard him give a cry. He wanted to step back, too. He wanted to cry out with all his voice. He stood rooted to the sand and could not make a sound. It was lightning that had struck, and not a rattler. It was a branch **3** that broke, it was a bird that flew, it was a rabbit running——

Penny shouted, "Git back! Hold the dogs!"

The voice released him. He dropped back and clutched the dogs by the scruff of their necks. He saw the mottled shadow lift its flat head, knee-high. The head swung from side to side, following his father's slow motions. He heard the rattles hum. The dogs heard. They winded. The fur **4** stood stiff on their bodies. Old Julia whined and twisted out of his hand. She turned and slunk down the trail. Her long tail clung to her hindquarters. Rip reared on his hind feet, barking.

---

1. **scrub:** land covered with short, stunted trees or bushes.
2. **martin:** swallow.

Jody's Discovery **131**

---

1. LANGUAGE AND VOCABULARY
The Language and Vocabulary box helps to prepare students for the Florida backwoods dialect in this story. The Language and Vocabulary exercise on page 145 gives students practice in reading the dialect aloud.

2. LITERARY ELEMENTS: Foreshadowing
Pa is referring to his trouble with the Forresters, but his words foreshadow the rattler's attack.

3. GUIDED READING: Recognizing Inner Conflict
Why does Jody think of a breaking branch, a flying bird, and a running rabbit? He wants to believe the flash was one of these, not a striking rattler.

4
Winded: "detected a scent."

MEETING INDIVIDUAL NEEDS
Kinesthetic and Auditory Learners • Invite students to pretend that they are television or radio news anchors reporting on the events of the story. Students could develop a news script describing the events and could then present the newscast. They may wish to include fictional interviews with Penny, Jody, Jody's mother, Doc, and the Forresters.

He lifted his shotgun and leveled it at the head. (Gregory Peck is Penny in the film.)

Quests

HEALTH LINK
Have interested students report orally on the currently recommended first-aid procedures for dealing with snake bites. Suggest that they consult school personnel such as the school nurse or first-aid coordinator, or community resources such as the local chapter of the American Red Cross or the local Boy Scouts or Girl Scouts of America for information and materials on the subject.

---

1 As slowly as a man in a dream, Penny backed away. The rattles sung. They were not rattles—— Surely it was a locust humming. Surely it was a tree frog singing—— Penny lifted his gun to his shoulder and fired. Jody quivered. The rattler coiled and writhed in its spasms. The head was buried in the sand. The contortions moved down the length of the thick body, the rattles whirred feebly and were still. The coiling flattened into slow convolutions,[3] like a low tide ebbing. Penny turned and stared at his son.

He said, "He got me."

He lifted his right arm and gaped at it. His lips lifted dry over his teeth. His throat worked. He looked dully at two punctures in the flesh. A drop of blood oozed from each.

He said, "He was a big un."

Jody let go his hold on Rip. The dog ran to the dead snake and barked fiercely. He made sorties[4] and at last poked the coils with one paw. He quieted and snuffed about in the sand. Penny lifted his head **2** from his staring. His face was like hickory ashes.

He said, "Ol' Death goin' to git me yit."

He licked his lips. He turned abruptly and began to push through the scrub in the direction of the clearing. The road would be shorter going, for it was open, but he headed blindly for home in a direct line. He plowed through the low scrub oaks, the gallberries,[5] the scrub palmettos.[6] Jody panted behind him. His heart pounded so hard that he could not see where he was going. He followed the sound of his father's crashing across the undergrowth. Suddenly the denseness ended. A patch of higher oaks made a shaded clearing. It was strange to walk in silence.

Penny stopped short. There was a stirring ahead. A doe deer leaped to her feet. Penny drew a deep breath, as though **3** breathing were for some reason easier. He lifted his shotgun and leveled it at the head. It flashed over Jody's mind that his father had gone mad. This was no moment to stop for game. Penny fired. The doe turned a somersault and dropped to the sand and kicked a little and lay still. Penny ran to the body and drew his knife from its scabbard. Now Jody knew his father was insane. Penny did not cut the throat, but slashed into the belly. He laid the carcass wide open. The pulse still throbbed in the heart. Penny slashed out the liver. Kneeling, he changed his knife to his left hand. He turned his right arm and stared again at **4** the twin punctures. They were now closed. The forearm was thick-swollen and blackening. The sweat stood out on his forehead. He cut quickly across the wound. A dark blood gushed and he pressed the warm liver against the incision.

He said in a hushed voice, "I kin feel it draw——"

He pressed harder. He took the meat

---

3. **convolutions** (kon′və·lōō′shəns): twistings, coilings.
4. **sortie** (sôr′tē): sudden pounce. Rip thinks the snake is still alive.
5. **gallberries** (gôl′ber·rēz): berries on which a growth ("gall") has appeared.
6. **palmetto** (pal·met′ō): low-growing palm tree.

---

1. LITERARY ELEMENTS:
Point of View
We see Penny Baxter through Jody's eyes. The story is told from a limited third-person point of view, helping readers identify with Jody.

2. LITERARY ELEMENTS:
Similes
What color is Pa's face if it is "like hickory ashes"? It is pale gray.

3. LITERARY ELEMENTS:
Foreshadowing
Pa draws that deep breath because he knows the doe could help to save his life. Jody, of course, does not yet know Pa's plan.

4. BACKGROUND
The snake that bit Penny is a diamondback rattlesnake, the most poisonous snake in the United States. It can be as long as eight feet. An antiserum is now available for victims who report to medical centers soon enough.

Jody's Discovery

ECOLOGY LINK

Florida means "feast of flowers" in Spanish. Have students research the diverse geography, flora, and fauna of Florida, especially the unique ecology of the marshlands known as the Florida Everglades. Interested students may wish to look up *Everglades National Park* in an encyclopedia or other reference book and share information about the area with the class.

1. LITERARY ELEMENTS:
Similes
What simile describes Pa's terrible pain? Pa says it feels "like a hot knife was buried to the shoulder."

2. LITERARY ELEMENTS:
Imagery
What images tell readers how the fawn looks and sounds? The images are "A spotted fawn stood peering," "wavering on uncertain legs," "dark eyes . . . wide and wondering," "it tossed its small head, bewildered," "wobbled . . . and leaned to smell it," "it bleated."

---

away and looked at it. It was a venomous green. He turned it and applied the fresh side.

He said, "Cut me out a piece o' the heart."

Jody jumped from his paralysis. He fumbled with the knife. He hacked away a portion.

Penny said, "Another."

He changed the application again and again.

He said, "Hand me the knife."

He cut a higher gash in his arm where the dark swelling rose the thickest. Jody cried out.

"Pa! You'll bleed to death!"

"I'd ruther bleed to death than swell. I seed a man die——"

The sweat poured down his cheeks.

"Do it hurt bad, Pa?"

1 "Like a hot knife was buried to the shoulder."

The meat no longer showed green when he withdrew it. The warm vitality of the doe's flesh was solidifying in death. He stood up.

He said quietly, "I cain't do it no more good. I'm goin' on home. You go to the Forresters and git 'em to ride to the Branch for Doc Wilson."

"Reckon they'll go?"

"We got to chance it. Call out to 'em quick, sayin', afore they chunk somethin' at you or mebbe shoot."

He turned back to pick up the beaten trail. Jody followed. Over his shoulder he heard a light rustling. He looked back.

2 A spotted fawn stood peering from the edge of the clearing, wavering on uncertain legs. Its dark eyes were wide and wondering.

He called out, "Pa! The doe's got a fawn."

"Sorry, boy. I cain't he'p it. Come on."

An agony for the fawn came over him. He hesitated. It tossed its small head, bewildered. It wobbled to the carcass of the doe and leaned to smell it. It bleated.

Penny called, "Git a move on, young un."

Jody ran to catch up with him. Penny stopped an instant at the dim road.

"Tell somebody to take this road in to our place and pick me up in case I cain't make it in. Hurry."

The horror of his father's body, swollen in the road, washed over him. He began to run. His father was plodding with a slow desperation in the direction of Baxters' Island.[7]

Jody ran down the wagon trail to the myrtle thicket where it branched off into the main road to Forresters' Island. The road, much used, had no growth of weeds or grass to make a footing. The dry shifting sand caught at the soles of his feet and seemed to wrap clinging tentacles around the muscles of his legs. He dropped into a short dogtrot that seemed to pull more steadily against the sand. His legs moved,

---

[7] **Baxters' Island:** This island is not surrounded by water, but by scrub. In the Florida backwoods, a patch of rich soil in the midst of dense scrub is called an "island." Each family in the Florida scrub lives on its own "island."

but his mind and body seemed suspended above them, like an empty box on a pair of cartwheels. The road under him was a treadmill.[8] His legs pumped up and down, but he seemed to be passing the same trees and bushes again and again. His pace seemed so slow, so futile, that he came to a bend with a dull surprise. The curve was familiar. He was not far from the road that led directly into the Forrester clearing.

He came to the tall trees of the island. They startled him, because they meant that he was now so close. He came alive and he was afraid. He was afraid of the Forresters. And if they refused him help, and he got safely away again, where should he go? He halted a moment under the shadowy live oaks, planning. It was twilight. He was sure it was not time for darkness. The rain clouds were not clouds, but an infusion of the sky,[9] and had now filled it entirely. The only light was a strand of green across the west, the color of the doe's flesh with the venom on it. It came to him that he would call to his friend Fodder-wing. His friend would hear him and come, and he might be allowed to approach close enough to tell his errand. It eased his heart to think of it, to think of his friend's eyes gentle with sorrow for him. He drew a long breath and ran wildly down the path under the oak trees.

---

8. **treadmill:** an endless belt that moves backward as a person walks forward. (Jody feels as if he's getting nowhere.)
9. **infusion of the sky:** In other words, the clouds filled the sky completely.

He shouted, "Fodder-wing! Fodder-wing! Hit's Jody!"

In an instant now his friend would come to him from the house, crawling down the rickety steps on all fours, as he must do when in a hurry. Or he would appear from the bushes with his raccoon at his heels.

"Fodder-wing! Hit's me!"

There was no answer. He broke into the swept sandy yard.

"Fodder-wing!"

There was an early light lit in the house. A twist of smoke curled from the chimney. The doors and shutters were closed against the mosquitoes and against the nighttime. The door swung open. In the light beyond, he saw the Forrester men rise to their feet, one after the other, as though the great trees in the forest lifted themselves by their roots and stirred toward him. He stopped short. Lem Forrester advanced to the stoop. He lowered his head and turned it a little sideways until he recognized the intruder.

"You leetle varmint. What you after here?"

Jody faltered, "Fodder-wing——"

"He's ailin'. You cain't see him noways."

It was too much. He burst out crying. He sobbed, "Pa—— He's snake-bit."

The Forresters came down the steps and surrounded him. He sobbed loudly, with pity for himself and for his father, and because he was here at last and something was finished that he had set out to do. There was a stirring among the men, as

Jody's Discovery **135**

---

1. GUIDED READING: Identifying Cause and Effect
Why does Jody think he is on a treadmill? It's hard for him to run in the sand. More important, he is so anxious to bring help for his father that his best effort seems slow and futile.

2. LITERARY ELEMENTS: Imagery
The strand of green light in the sky reminds Jody of "the color of the doe's flesh with the venom on it." Note the appropriateness of the image to Jody's uneasy state of mind as he nears the Forresters' house.

3. GUIDED READING: Making Inferences About Character
Why does Lem address Jody as "You leetle varmint"? Lem, like the other Forrester men, regards the Baxters with dislike. He calls Jody the equivalent of "little pest animal." In the scene that follows, Lem is the Forrester with the hardest heart.

1. GUIDED READING:
Identifying Cause and Effect
Do you think the men are stirring because they pity Jody? Answers will vary. They may feel some pity. They are aroused by the news that a common enemy, a rattlesnake, has bitten someone they know.

2. GUIDED READING:
Interpreting Dialect
Translate Mill-wheel's words. "I would help a dog if a snake had bitten it. Don't thank me."

3. GUIDED READING:
Recognizing Humor
What does Gabby mean? With rough humor Gabby says if Doc has drunk all his whiskey, he can still give Penny a portion of it by breathing on him. (Giving whiskey to the victim of a rattlesnake is a folk remedy of doubtful value.)

4. GUIDED READING:
Summarizing
What are the reasons that Jody is terribly frightened? He has seen for himself how badly Penny was bitten. He has heard the Forresters' disheartening comments, and he realizes they think that hurrying to the rescue would be futile. Jody is terrified his father is dying.

---

though the leavening[10] quickened in a bowl of bread dough.

"Where's he at? What kind o' snake?"

"A rattlesnake. A big un. He's makin' it for home, but he don't know kin he make it."

"Is he swellin'? Where'd it git him?"

"In the arm. Hit's bad swelled a'ready. Please ride for Doc Wilson. Please ride for him quick, and I won't he'p Oliver[11] agin you no more. Please."

Lem Forrester laughed.

"A skeeter[12] promises he won't bite," he said.

Buck said, "Hit's like not to do no good. A man dies right now, bit in the arm. He'll likely be dead afore Doc kin git to him."

"He shot a doe deer and used the liver to draw out the pizen. Please ride for Doc."

1 Mill-wheel said, "I'll ride for him."
Relief flooded him like the sun.

"I shore thank you."

2 "I'd he'p a dog, was snake-bit. Spare your thanks."

Buck said, "I'll ride on and pick up Penny. Walkin's bad for a man is snake-bit. . . . Fellers, we ain't got a drop o' whiskey for him!"

Gabby said, "Ol' Doc'll have some. If he's purty tol'able sober, he'll have some **3** left. If he's drunk all he's got, he kin blow

---

10. **leavening:** a substance, such as yeast, that helps bread dough rise and become light and fluffy.
11. **Oliver,** a friend of the Baxters, got into a fight with the Forresters, and both Penny and Jody jumped in to help Oliver.
12. **skeeter:** slang for mosquito.

---

his breath, and that'll make a powerful portion."

Buck and Mill-wheel turned away with torturing deliberation to the lot to saddle their horses. Their leisureliness frightened Jody as speed would not have done. If there was hope for his father, they would be hurrying. They were as slow and unconcerned as though they were burying Penny, not riding for assistance. He stood, desolate. He would like to see Fodder-wing just a moment before he went away. The remaining Forresters turned back up the steps, ignoring him.

Lem called from the door, "Git goin', Skeeter."

Arch said, "Leave the young un be. Don't torment him, and his daddy likely dyin'." . . .

Frightened as he has never been before, **4**
Jody runs the four miles home in a driving rainstorm. He is terrified that his father has died of the snake bite. He finds the Forresters in his cabin, sitting by the empty hearth. . . .

Jody was faint. He dared not ask them the question. He walked past them and into his father's bedroom. His mother sat on one side of the bed and Doc Wilson sat on the other. Old Doc did not turn his head. His mother looked at him and rose without speaking. She went to a dresser and took out a fresh shirt and breeches and held them out to him. He dropped his wet bundle and stood the gun against the wall. He walked slowly to the bed.

136 Quests

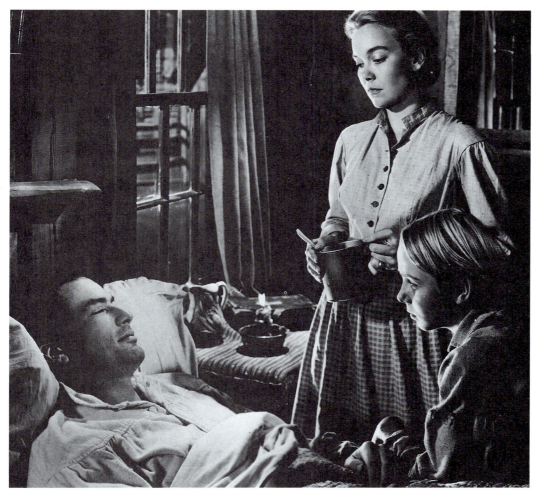

"If he's not dead now, he'll not die."

1. GUIDED READING:
Making Inferences
What is the purpose of the brick wrapped in flannel? The brick is heated, wrapped, and placed near the patient to warm him and treat him for shock.

He thought, "If he's not dead now, he'll not die."

In the bed, Penny stirred. Jody's heart leaped like a rabbit jumping. Penny groaned and retched. Doc leaned quickly and held a basin for him and propped his head. Penny's face was dark and swollen. He vomited with the agony of one who has nothing to emit, but must vomit still. He fell back panting. Doc reached inside the covers and drew out a brick wrapped in flannel. He handed it to Ma Baxter. She laid Jody's garments at the foot of the bed and went to the kitchen to heat the brick again.

Jody whispered, "Is he bad?"

"He's bad, a'right. Looks as if he'd make it. Then again, looks as if he won't."

Jody's Discovery 137

1. LITERARY ELEMENTS:
Imagery
What images show Pa's physical condition? The images are "puffed eyes," pupils so dilated that "his eyes seemed black," and his arm swollen "as thick as a bullock's thigh."

2. GUIDED READING:
Making Inferences About Character
What traits does Jody show in this speech? He shows courage, determination, and love for his father. He also shows that his father has helped to make him as strong as a young boy can be under the circumstances.

3. LITERARY ELEMENTS:
Similes
In what ways could the rolling of clouds be "like battalions of marching Spaniards"? The clouds could be advancing in orderly columns and could be as brightly colored as soldiers' dress uniforms.

4. LITERARY ELEMENTS:
Similes
What simile tells the color of Pa's face? It is "like a frog's belly."

---

1 Penny opened his puffed eyes. The pupils were dilated[13] until his eyes seemed black. He moved his arm. It was swollen as thick as a bullock's[14] thigh.

He murmured thickly, "You'll ketch cold."

Jody fumbled for his clothes and pulled them on. Doc nodded.

"That's a good sign, knowin' you. That's the first he's spoken."

A tenderness filled Jody that was half pain, half sweetness. In his agony, his father was concerned for him. Penny could not die. Not Penny.

2 He said, "He's obliged to make it, Doc, sir." He added, as he had heard his father say, "Us Baxters is all runty and tough."

Doc nodded.

He called to the kitchen, "Let's try some warm milk now."

With hope, Ma Baxter began to sniffle. Jody joined her at the hearth.

She whimpered, "I don't see as we'd deserve it, do it happen."

He said, "Hit'll not happen, Ma." But his marrow[15] was cold again.

He went outside for wood to hurry the fire. The storm was moving on to the west.

3 The clouds were rolling like battalions[16] of marching Spaniards. In the east, bright spaces showed, filled with stars. The wind blew fresh and cool. He came in with an armful of fatwood.

He said, "Hit'll be a purty day tomorrow, Ma."

"Hit'll be a purty day iffen he's yit alive when day comes." She burst into tears. They dropped on the hearth and hissed. She lifted her apron and wiped her eyes. "You take the milk in," she said. "I'll make Doc and me a cup o' tea. I hadn't et nothin', waitin' for you-all, when Buck carried him in."

He remembered that he had eaten lightly. He could think of nothing that would taste good. The thought of food on his tongue was a dry thought, without nourishment or relish. He carried the cup of hot milk carefully, balancing it in his hands. Doc took it from him and sat close to Penny on the bed.

"Now, boy, you hold his head up while I spoon-feed him."

Penny's head was heavy on the pillow. Jody's arms ached with the strain of lifting it. His father's breathing was heavy, like the Forresters' when they were drunk. His **4** face had changed color. It was green and pallid, like a frog's belly. At first his teeth resisted the intruding spoon.

Doc said, "Open your mouth before I call the Forresters to open it."

The swollen lips parted. Penny swallowed. A portion of the cupful went down. He turned his head away.

Doc said, "All right. But if you lose it, I'm comin' back with more."

Penny broke into a sweat.

Doc said, "That's fine. Sweatin's fine,

---

13. **dilated:** expanded.
14. **bullock** (bŏol′ək): male cow or ox.
15. **marrow:** tissue that fills bone. Jody is chilled to the bone.
16. **battalions** (bə·tal′yəns): large companies of soldiers.

> **TRANSPARENCY 10**
> **Literary Elements**
> *Conflict* – explores the four common types of conflict introduced in this unit.

for poison. Lord of the jaybirds, if we weren't all out of whiskey, I'd make you sweat."

Ma Baxter came to the bedroom with two plates with cups of tea and biscuits on them. Doc took his plate and balanced it on his knee. He drank with a mixture of gusto and distaste.

He said, "It's all right, but 'tain't whiskey."

He was the soberest Jody had ever heard of his being.

"A good man snake-bit," he said mournfully, "and the whole county out of whiskey."

Ma Baxter said dully, "Jody, you want somethin'?"

1 "I ain't hongry."

His stomach was as queasy as his father's. It seemed to him that he could feel the poison working in his own veins, attacking his heart, churning in his gizzard.[17]

Doc said, "Blest if he ain't goin' to keep that milk down."

Penny was in a deep sleep.

2 Ma Baxter rocked and sipped and nibbled.

She said, "The Lord watches the sparrer's fall. Mought be He'll take a hand for the Baxters."[18] . . .

Night comes and everyone tries to sleep. Jody goes to his father's bedroom.

It seemed to Jody that he was alone with **3** his father. The vigil was in his hands. If he kept awake, and labored for breath with the tortured sleeper, breathing with him and for him, he could keep him alive. He drew a breath as deep as the ones his father was drawing. It made him dizzy. He was light-headed and his stomach was empty. He knew he would feel better if he should eat, but he could not swallow. He sat down on the floor and leaned his head against the side of the bed. He began to think back over the day, as though he walked a road backward. He could not help but feel a greater security here beside his father than in the stormy night. Many things, he realized, would be terrible alone that were not terrible when he was with Penny. Only the rattlesnake had kept all its horror.

He recalled the triangular head, the lightning flash of its striking, the subsidence[19] into alert coils. His flesh crawled. It seemed to him he should never be easy in the woods again. He recalled the coolness of his father's shot, and the fear of the dogs. He recalled the doe and the horror of her warm meat against his father's wound. He remembered the fawn. He **4** sat upright. The fawn was alone in the night, as he had been alone. The catastrophe that might take his father had made it motherless. It had lain hungry and bewil-

---

17. **gizzard:** here, his stomach.
18. Ma is referring to a passage from the Bible about God's love. Jesus reminds the people that not even a sparrow falls to the ground without God's notice (Matthew 10:29).
19. **subsidence** (səb·sīd′əns): sinking or falling back.

---

1. GUIDED READING:
Making Inferences About a Character
Why isn't Jody hungry? He is so anxious about his father that he seems to feel the poison attacking himself.

2. GUIDED READING:
Making Inferences About a Character
How does Ma Baxter endure the strain of her husband's ordeal? After doing all she can to help, she rocks, takes some nourishment, and quotes comforting scripture.

3. GUIDED READING:
Making Inferences
Why does Jody keep a vigil in his father's bedroom? He wants to struggle with his father. He wants to feel the comfort of his father's presence.

4. GUIDED READING:
Making Inferences
What parallel does Jody recognize in his own experience and the fawn's? Both have kept vigil beside a parent. Both have known the presence of death. Both have felt a terrible aloneness.

Jody's Discovery

"*Ol' Death gone thievin' elsewhere.*" Illustration by N. C. Wyeth.

dered through the thunder and rain and lightning, close to the devastated body of its dam,[20] waiting for the stiff form to arise and give it warmth and food and comfort. He pressed his face into the hanging covers of the bed and cried bitterly. He was torn with hate for all death and pity for all aloneness. . . .

The next morning Penny is better, and the Forresters are ready to return home. Jody slips in to his father's bedside.

Jody said, "How you comin', Pa?"

1 "Jest fine, son. Ol' Death gone thievin' elsewhere. But wa'n't it a close squeak!"

"I mean."

Penny said, "I'm proud of you, boy, the way you kept your head and done what was needed."

"Pa——"

"Yes, son."

"Pa, you recollect the doe and the fawn?"

"I cain't never forget 'em. The pore doe saved me, and that's certain."

"Pa, the fawn may be out there yit. Hit's hongry, and likely mighty skeert."

"I reckon so."

"Pa, I'm about growed and don't need no milk. How about me goin' out and seein' kin I find the fawn?"

"And tote it here?"

"And raise it."

Penny lay quiet, staring at the ceiling.

---

20. **dam:** mother of a four-legged animal.

"Boy, you got me hemmed in." **2**

"Hit won't take much to raise it, Pa. Hit'll soon git to where it kin make out on leaves and acorns."

"Dogged if you don't figger the farrest of ary young un I've ever knowed."

"We takened its mammy, and it wa'n't no-ways to blame."

"Shore don't seem grateful to leave it starve, do it? Son, I ain't got it in my heart to say 'No' to you. I never figgered I'd see daylight, come dawn today."

"Kin I ride back with Mill-wheel and see kin I find it?"

"Tell your Ma I said you're to go."

He sidled back to the table and sat down. His mother was pouring coffee for everyone.

He said, "Ma, Pa says I kin go bring back the fawn."

She held the coffeepot in midair.

"What fawn?"

"The fawn belonged to the doe we kilt, to use the liver to draw out the pizen and save Pa."

She gasped.

"Well, for pity sake——"

"Pa says hit'd not be grateful to leave it starve."

Doc Wilson said, "That's right, Ma'am. Nothing in the world don't ever come quite free. The boy's right and his daddy's right."

Mill-wheel said, "He kin ride back with me. I'll he'p him find it."

She set down the pot helplessly.

"Well, if you'll give it your milk—— We got nothin' else to feed it."

---

1. LITERARY ELEMENTS:
Personification
Soon after the rattlesnake struck him (page 133) Pa said, "Ol' Death goin' to git me yit." Now that he is recovering, he says, "Ol' Death gone thievin' elsewhere." This personification of Death as a familiar old enemy shows Pa as a courageous fighter.

2. GUIDED READING:
Interpreting Meaning
What does Pa mean when he says Jody has him hemmed in? He means that he can't refuse Jody's plea. Penny owes his life to the fawn's mother and to Jody. The fawn would die without Jody's care.

PORTFOLIO ASSESSMENT
Comparisons often describe both likenesses and differences. Students may want to watch the film *The Yearling* to compare the excerpt from the novel found here to the portion of the film that contains the same material. Suggest that students organize their comparisons and present them in the form of short informative speeches. Provide a lectern or music stand for students, and remind them of appropriate posture and stage presence before they begin to plan. Consult with students individually to agree on how their speeches will be assessed. (See *Portfolio Assessment and Professional Support Materials*, especially the section entitled **Suggestions for Portfolio Projects**.)

1. GUIDED READING:
Making Inferences
Why doesn't Jody want Mill-wheel to go with him? Answers will vary. At times a person likes to try to do something alone so that no one else will see the disappointment or share the secret joy.

2. GUIDED READING:
Drawing Conclusions
What is your opinion of Mill-wheel? For a Forrester, he is a quite decent man, concerned about Jody's safety and giving him sound advice.

3. LITERARY ELEMENTS:
Suspense
Earlier in the narrative, readers were kept in suspense about whether Jody's father would live or die. Now readers are in suspense as Jody looks for the endangered fawn.

"That's what I aim to do. Hit'll be no time, and it not needin' nothin'." . . .

Mill-wheel and Jody set off on a horse. Mill-wheel asks Jody where he wants to get off.

1 Suddenly Jody was unwilling to have Mill-wheel with him. If the fawn was dead, or could not be found, he could not have his disappointment seen. And if the fawn was there, the meeting would be so lovely and so secret that he could not endure to share it.

He said, "Hits not fur now, but hit's powerful thick for a horse. I kin make it a-foot."

"But I'm daresome to leave you, boy. Suppose you was to git lost, or snake-bit, too?"

"I'll take keer. Hit'll take me likely a long time to find the fawn, if he's wandered. Leave me off right here."

2 "All right, but you go mighty easy now, pokin' in them palmeeters. This is rattlesnake heaven in these parts. You know north here, and east?"

"There, and there. That fur tall pine makes a bearin'."

"That's right. Now do things go wrong again, you or Buck, one, ride back for me. So long."

"So long, Mill-wheel. I'm shore obliged."

He waved after him. He waited for the sound of the hooves to end, then cut to the right. The scrub was still. Only his own crackling of twigs sounded across the silence. He was eager almost past caution, 3 but he broke a bough and pushed it ahead of him where the growth was thick and the ground invisible. Rattlers got out of the way when they had a chance. Penny had gone farther into the oak thicket than he remembered. He wondered for an instant if he had mistaken his direction. Then a buzzard rose in front of him and flapped into the air. He came into the clearing under the oaks. Buzzards sat in a circle around the carcass of the doe. They turned their heads on their long scrawny necks and hissed at him. He threw his bough at them and they flew into an adjacent tree. Their wings creaked and whistled like rusty pump handles. The sand showed large cat prints, he could not tell whether of wildcat or of panther. But the big cats killed fresh, and they had left the doe to the carrion birds.[21] He asked himself whether the sweeter meat of the fawn had scented the air for the curled nostrils.

He skirted the carcass and parted the grass at the place where he had seen the fawn. It did not seem possible that it was only yesterday. The fawn was not there. He circled the clearing. There was no sound, no sign. The buzzards clacked their wings, impatient to return to their business. He returned to the spot where the fawn had emerged and dropped to all fours, studying the sand for the small hoofprints. The night's rain had washed away all tracks except those of cat and buzzards. But the

---

21. **carrion birds:** birds that feed on *carrion,* the flesh of a dead body.

CLOSURE

Draw a large, five-spoked wheel on the board. Have students, working as a class, decide on Jody's five most important character traits, as revealed by his words and actions. Write each of the traits on a spoke. Have volunteers fill in the spaces between the spokes with details from the story that support each trait.

1. GUIDED READING:
Drawing Conclusions
How do you think the fawn has avoided being attacked by predators? Apparently it has been hiding among scrub palmettos, protected by its coloration and its stillness.

FOR STUDY AND DISCUSSION
Identifying Facts
1. He kills the doe. He makes an incision on his arm near the bite and then applies the liver. Then he uses the heart. Then he gashes his arm to let out the poison. Then he runs for home.
   Penny has to kill the doe because he needs its liver to draw out the snake's poison.
2. The scene in the Baxter cabin is tense with fear that Penny will die.
   The first hopeful sign is that he speaks to Jody, saying that the boy will catch cold.
3. Jody wants to find and raise the fawn. He argues that it won't take much to feed the fawn and that it is alone because Penny had to kill the doe.
4. Jody makes Mill-wheel leave him because, if the fawn is dead or cannot be found, Jody does not want anyone to see his disappointment. Also, if the fawn is there, "the meeting would be so lovely and

"It's me." Illustration by N. C. Wyeth.

cat sign had not been made in this direction. Under a scrub palmetto he was able to make out a track, pointed and dainty as the mark of a ground dove. He crawled past the palmetto.

Movement directly in front of him startled him so that he tumbled backward. The fawn lifted its face to his. It turned its head with a wide, wondering motion and shook him through with the stare of its liquid eyes. It was quivering. It made no effort to rise or run. Jody could not trust himself to move.

He whispered, "It's me."

Jody's Discovery 143

EXTENSION AND ENRICHMENT
Science. The Florida backwoods setting of more than fifty years ago is rich in wildlife topics for research. Ask each student to prepare a short report based on library reading on one of these topics: martins, the American black bear, the eastern diamondback rattlesnake, tree frogs, palmettos, deer, locusts, buzzards, wildcats, panthers, or doves.

---

so secret that he could not endure to share it" (page 142.)

Interpreting Meanings
5. Fear that his father may die and pity for the lonely fawn are troubling Jody.
6. Jody faces the danger of a possible attack by a rattlesnake or by a wildcat or panther.
   Most students will say that they felt joyful.
7. Most students will say that Jody's feeling of such a strong bond arose from an instinctive sense that he, like the fawn, might lose a parent to death.
   Some students will say that they would share Jody's feelings. Others might have no sensitivity to animals. Be prepared for both answers.

Applying Meanings
8. Some students will say that this part of the story is gory or violent. Help them see that the writer has described the events in a sensitive and caring way. She has not used the violence just to make us feel horror for the sake of horror (or to sell her book). She knows we must understand what a terrible conflict Penny is enduring.
9. Answers will vary. One of the famous older examples is Mary O'Hara's "My Friend Flicka." Also

For Study and Discussion

IDENTIFYING FACTS
1. List the steps Penny takes to fight the poison from the snakebite. Why does he have to kill the doe?

2. Describe the scene in the Baxter cabin when Penny is ill. What is the first hopeful sign that he may recover?

3. After his father gets well, what does Jody want to do? What arguments does he use to convince his father to let him do it?

4. Why does Jody make Mill-wheel leave him when they reach the area where the fawn should be?

INTERPRETING MEANINGS
5. As Jody is sitting by his father's bed, the writer says, "He was torn with hate for all death and pity for all aloneness" (page 141). What is troubling Jody?

6. Jody sets off on a **quest** for the abandoned fawn. Characters on quests often have to face dangers. What dangers does Jody face? How did you feel when he found the fawn?

7. Why do you think Jody feels such a strong bond with an animal he has barely seen? Do you think you would have felt the same way?

APPLYING MEANINGS
8. How did you feel when you read the part of the story about the snakebite and the doe's death? Did you feel it was too violent? Or did you feel that the writer described the events in a sensitive and caring way?

9. Name some other stories or movies or TV shows that focus on a young person who nearly loses (or does lose) a person who is greatly loved. Do you know of other stories about a young person who rescues an animal? Talk about how all these stories make you feel.

Focus on Reading

DRAWING CONCLUSIONS
As you read a story, you understand certain things even though they are not stated directly. You draw these **conclusions** from evidence in the story. For each passage below, choose the conclusion that best fits the evidence.

1. On page 131, when Penny is first bitten, Jody thinks "It was lightning that had struck, and not a rattler. It was a branch that broke, it was a bird that flew, it was a rabbit running—"
   a. Jody is seeing things.
   b. Jody believes that lightning struck his father.
   c. Jody wishes something else had happened, instead of the strike of a deadly snake.

2. On page 136, when Jody gets home after appealing to the Forresters to aid his father, he finds everyone in the cabin. We read: "Jody was faint. He dared not ask them the question."
   a. The question is "Is my father alive?"
   b. The question is "Is there any supper?"
   c. The question is "Did the Forresters fetch Doc Wilson?"

Literary Elements

CHARACTER
There are many strong and memorable characters in *The Yearling*. As you know from Unit One, we can get to know characters by watching their actions, by listening to what they say, and by hearing their thoughts. Think of the details in this story that reveal to you what the people are really like:

1. How does Jody's mother show her faith in God?
2. How do the Forresters show generosity of spirit when their enemy is in trouble?
3. How does Penny show great love for his young son?
4. How does Jody show courage and responsibility?

Did the writer make you care for these characters? Did you dislike any of them?

Language and Vocabulary

DIALECT (An Oral Activity)
With a partner or a small group, choose a **dialogue,** or conversation, from the story that appeals to you. Then prepare this dialogue for oral reading, using as many readers as you need. As you practice your dialogue, be aware of *what* the words are saying. Listen for the rhythm of the speech. Try to make your reading reflect the characters' personalities and feelings. Before you present your "scene" to the class, be sure you have read the conversation aloud at least once. (Don't forget that, depending on your passage, you may have to choose a narrator.)

Focus on Descriptive Writing

ORGANIZING A DESCRIPTION
If you organize the details of your description clearly, you will make it easy to follow. Here are two ways to arrange your details:

Spatial Order: Organize details according to their location: for example, from top to bottom (or bottom to top), or from near to far (or far to near). You will often find this method helpful for describing places and objects.

Order of Importance: Arrange details according to the importance or emphasis you want to give them. You can give the most important detail first or last in order to create the strongest impression on your

Jody's Discovery 145

Eric Knight's *Lassie Come-Home.*

FOCUS ON READING
Drawing Conclusions
1. c
2. a

LITERARY ELEMENTS
Character
1. When she says, "The Lord watches the sparrer's fall. Mought be He'll take a hand for the Baxters" (page 139).
2. When Mill-wheel volunteers to ride for Doc and when Arch tells the others not to torment Jody.
3. When he says from his sickbed that Jody will catch cold and when he agrees to allow Jody to raise the fawn. He also tells Jody, "I'm proud of you, boy, the way you kept your head and done what was needed" (page 141).
4. By running to get help from the Forresters and by braving the scrub and risking encountering another snake to rescue the fawn. He shows responsibility by keeping watch by his father's sickbed and by taking on the task of finding and raising the motherless fawn.

Students' feelings for the characters will vary.

145

LANGUAGE AND VOCABULARY
Dialect
For answers, see the **Teaching Guide** at the beginning of the unit.

FOCUS ON DESCRIPTIVE WRITING
Organizing a Description
You may want to discuss with students how the purpose of a description can affect the arrangement of details. Spatial order generally works well with objective descriptions when a reporting of facts is adequate. When using order of importance, however, the writer usually decides what he or she wants the reader to feel and arranges the details accordingly.

readers. This method is often useful for describing people or animals. Rawlings uses order of importance in her description of the fawn, where she saves the most important detail for last (see page 143).

Write a paragraph in which you describe a favorite object or animal. Arrange the details of your description in a logical order. Try to create a strong overall impression through specific, vivid details. Save your writing.

About the Author

Marjorie Kinnan Rawlings (1896–1953) introduced millions of readers to the special character of the Florida backwoods in her novel *The Yearling,* which won the Pulitzer Prize in 1939. Rawlings was raised in a big city, where she first worked as a journalist. When she grew unhappy with city living, she bought a huge orange grove near Hawthorn, Florida. Her new home was called Cross Creek. There she began to write short stories and novels inspired by the Florida "piney woods," their people, and their particular way of life. In her book called *Cross Creek,* she wrote: "For myself, the Creek satisfies a thing that had gone hungry and unfed since childhood days. I am often lonely. Who is not? But I should be lonelier in the heart of a city." Both *Cross Creek* and *The Yearling* have been made into successful movies.

OBJECTIVE
Students will read to enjoy the story.

PRESENTATION
As the headnote indicates, this is the Algonquin version of the traditional European Cinderella story. You might prepare students for reading by suggesting that, as they read, they compare and contrast this version of the story with the traditional version. Except for the Algonquin name of the Cinderella figure (Oochigeaskw), the story poses no reading problems. If you choose not to present the story as classroom theater (see headnote), students may read with enjoyment silently or aloud.

TEACHING RESOURCES A
Teacher's Notes, p. 154

AV RESOURCES BINDER
Audiocassette 1, Side B

1. BACKGROUND
Students who have read Elizabeth George Speare's *The Sign of the Beaver* (1983) will have some knowledge of Algonquin culture and may enjoy sharing it with other students.

NO QUESTIONS ASKED

The Algonquin Cinderella

Retold by M. R. COX

Buckskin gloves made by the Eastern Woodland Native Americans.

Courtesy Colter Bay Indian Arts Museum, Grand Teton National Park, Wyoming.

Before You Read

People who study literature have discovered that many stories told in different parts of the world are surprisingly similar. No one is certain why this is so. Some people think that certain wishes and fears are so universal that everyone wants to express them in story form.

One of the stories found in many cultures is the Cinderella story. Here is a "Cinderella" story told by the Algonquin (al·gong′kwin) people who lived in the Ottawa River region of Canada.

Before you read this story, take a moment to recall the traditional story. Remember the girl who lived among the ashes and who wanted to attend the prince's ball? What were the other elements of the story? (Remember the cruel stepsisters; the fairy godmother; the girl's ragged clothing; the magical changes?)

This story would be fun to present in a classroom theater. You would need a narrator and these characters:

The sister of the Invisible One
The other girls who try to "see" the Invisible One
Oochigeaskw's sisters
The Invisible One

After you read the story, you might talk in class about the fears or wishes the story expresses.

The Algonquin Cinderella 147

Cultural Diversity

It is important to remember that students from different cultures have different cultural referents. That is, not all students have grown up reading the tale of Cinderella. Before assigning the Algonquin version, discuss the traditional Cinderella story as a whole-class activity. Invite students to discuss stories, myths, fairy tales, from their own or other cultures that share similar themes.

1. GUIDED READING:
Comparing and Contrasting Stories
The test in the traditional version is the ability to wear a small glass slipper. (The stepsisters trim their heels or toes to force their large feet into the dainty shoe.)

2. GUIDED READING:
Comparing and Contrasting Stories
In the traditional version, the stepsisters insist on trying on the glass slipper even though their large feet could not possibly fit into the shoe. Students might note that the girls' deceit reveals character traits of dishonesty and arrogance.

A Micmac birchbark box with porcupine quills.
Courtesy The Heard Museum, Phoenix, Arizona.

There was once a large village belonging to the Micmac Indians of the Eastern Algonquins, built beside a lake. At the far end of the settlement stood a lodge, and in it lived a being who was always invisible. He had a sister who looked after him, and everyone knew that the girl who could see him might marry him. There were very few girls who did not try to marry him, but it was very long before anyone succeeded.

1 This is the way in which the test of sight was carried out. At evening time, when the Invisible One was due to return home, his sister would walk with any girl who might come down to the lakeshore. She, of course, could see her brother, since he was always visible to her. As soon as she saw him coming, she would say to the girls:

"Do you see my brother?"

"Yes," they would generally reply—though some of them did say "No."

2 To those who said that they could indeed see him, the sister would ask, "What is his shoulder strap made of?"

Or, some people say that she would inquire, "What is his moose-runner's haul?" or "What does he draw his sled with?"

And they would answer, "A strip of rawhide" or "A green flexible branch," or something like that.

Then the sister, knowing that they had not told the truth, would say, "Very well, let us return to the wigwam!"

When they went in, she would tell the girls not to sit in a certain place, because it belonged to the Invisible One. Then, af-

Snowshoes made by Eastern Canadian Native Americans.
Courtesy Colter Bay Indian Arts Museum, Grand Teton National Park, Wyoming.

148 Quests

MEETING INDIVIDUAL NEEDS
Visual and Kinesthetic Learners • Provide students with pictures of American Indian lodges and wigwams from encyclopedias and other reference materials. Students could then create small models of these dwellings out of clay, papier-mâché, or other materials.

---

ter they had helped to cook the supper, they would wait with great curiosity to see him eat. They could be sure that he was a real person, for when he took off his moccasins they became visible, and his sister hung them up. But beyond this, they saw nothing of him, not even when they stayed in the place all night, as many of them did.

Now there lived in the village an old man who was a widower, and his three daughters. The youngest girl was very small, weak, and often ill. And yet her sisters, especially the elder, treated her **1** cruelly. The second daughter was kinder and sometimes took her side. But the wicked sister would burn the younger girl's hands and feet with hot cinders. The girl was covered with scars from this treatment. She was so marked that people called her Oochigeaskw, the Rough-Faced-Girl.

When her father came home and asked why the youngest girl had such burns, the bad sister would say at once that it was the girl's own fault, for she had disobeyed orders and gone near the fire and fallen into it.

These two elder sisters decided one day to try their luck at seeing the Invisible One. So they dressed themselves in their finest clothes and tried to look their prettiest. They found the Invisible One's sister and took the usual walk by the water.

When the brother came, and when they were asked if they could see him, they answered, "Of course." And when asked about the shoulder strap or sled cord, they answered, "A piece of rawhide."

Leather pouch with beads and quills made by the Eastern Woodland Native Americans.
Courtesy Colter Bay Indian Arts Museum, Grand Teton National Park, Wyoming.

But of course they were lying like the others, and they got nothing for their pains.

The next afternoon, when the father returned home, he brought with him many of the pretty little shells from which wampum was made, and the sisters set to work to string them.

That day, poor little Oochigeaskw, who had always gone barefoot, got a pair of her father's moccasins, old ones, and put them into water to soften them so that she could wear them. Then she begged her

1. GUIDED READING:
Comparing and Contrasting Stories
The similarities between this story and the traditional version are remarkable. In the traditional version, one of the stepsisters is also kinder than the other. Perhaps this detail is meant to humanize the story somewhat by illustrating that most people are a mixture of good and evil.

The Algonquin Cinderella 149

COOPERATIVE LEARNING

Divide students into small groups to learn more about the Algonquins. Have one group of students use information from any encyclopedia entry for *Algonquin* to make a time line of important events in the history of these American Indian people. Ask another group to find out about the Algonquins' respect for natural resources and living things. How did they express this respect in their everyday lives? Have other groups learn about Algonquin foods, holidays, folk medicines, arts, and language. When research is completed, have students share what they have learned through oral, written, illustrated, or dramatic presentations.

1. BACKGROUND

In most folk tales and myths, true nobility is spiritual rather than physical. In the Camelot myth, for example, Arthur, though young and physically weaker than other knights, is able to extract the sword from the stone because he is the true king. Students might enjoy discussing the question "What is true nobility?"

2. LITERARY ELEMENTS:
Imagery
You might point out to students how the Algonquins draw their imagery from nature. The Invisible One is a kind of sky god.

Re-created wigwam made of tree bark.

American Indian Archaeological Institute, Washington, Connecticut.

sisters for a few wampum shells. The elder called her a little pest, but the younger one gave her some. Now, since she had no clothes other than her usual rags, the poor little thing went into the woods and got herself some sheets of birch bark. From these, she made a dress and put marks on it for decoration, in the style of long ago. She also made a petticoat and a loose gown, a cap, leggings, and a handkerchief. She put on her father's large old moccasins, which were far too big for her, and went forth to try her luck. She would try, she thought, to see the Invisible One.

She did not begin very well. As she set off, her sisters shouted and hooted, hissed and yelled, and tried to make her stay. And the loafers around the village, seeing the strange little creature, called out "Shame!"

The poor little girl in her strange clothes, with her face all scarred, was an awful sight, but she was kindly received by the sister of the Invisible One. And this **1** was, of course, because this noble lady understood far more about things than simply the mere outside which all the rest of the world knows. As the brown of the evening sky turned to black, the lady took the girl down to the lake.

"Do you see him?" the Invisible One's sister asked.

"I do, indeed—and he is wonderful!" said Oochigeaskw.

The sister asked, "And what is his sled string?"

The little girl said, "It is the Rain- **2** bow."

"And, my sister, what is his bow string?"

150   Quests

CLOSURE

Have students work together to make a list of the likenesses and differences between this story and the traditional Cinderella version.

PORTFOLIO ASSESSMENT

Students may be interested in creating collages to illustrate the story of "The Algonquin Cinderella." Suggest that students use pictures cut from magazines, along with twigs, bark, beads, beans, and other materials to produce an appropriate scene for their illustrative collage. Remind them to plan their project before they begin to glue anything. Some students may want to work with a partner. Consult with students individually or in pairs to agree on how their collages will be assessed. (See *Portfolio Assessment and Professional Support Materials.*)

"It is the Spirit's Road—the Milky Way."

"So you *have* seen him," said his sister. She took the girl home with her and bathed her. As she did so, all the scars
1 disappeared from the girl's body. Her hair grew again, as it was combed, long, like a blackbird's wing. Her eyes were now like stars: In all the world there was no other such beauty. Then, from her treasures, the lady gave her a wedding garment and adorned her.

Then she told Oochigeaskw to take the *wife*'s seat in the wigwam, the one next to where the Invisible One sat, beside the entrance. And when he came in, terrible and beautiful, he smiled and said:

"So we are found out!"

2 "Yes," said his sister. And so Oochigeaskw became his wife.

Mint, a Pretty Girl by George Catlin (1832). Oil on canvas.

National Museum of American Art, Washington DC/Art Resource, NY

Cradled in the Wind by Luke Simon. Contemporary Micmac sculpture made of buffed clay.

Courtesy Institute of American Indian Art, Santa Fe, New Mexico.

About the Authors

The **Algonquins** lived in the parts of Canada now called Quebec and Ontario. The Algonquins lived in groups of twenty-five or more close relatives, each group living together in one lodge. They believed in a *great spirit,* a very powerful god. They also believed that their lives were influenced by the spirits of plants, animals, and other elements of nature. In 1640, the Algonquins were defeated by their rivals, the Iroquois. Some four thousand Algonquins still live in parts of Canada today.

1. LITERARY ELEMENTS:
Similes
The simple similes "like a blackbird's wing" and "like stars" help us see the girl's beauty.

2. GUIDED READING:
Interpreting Meaning
Students might enjoy discussing whether the wish to be transformed into a great beauty and married to a powerful man is a wish of all women. If so, what do all men wish for? Remind students that Oochigeaskw proves her inner beauty before her appearance is transformed. Perhaps one wish that we *all* share is to be rewarded for our goodness, patience, kindness, and endurance of pain.

The Algonquin Cinderella 151

OBJECTIVES
The overall aim is for students to explore connotations of words in a literary selection.

PRESENTATION
Introduce this activity by writing on the chalkboard the three words from the text, and have students respond to the questions and explain their answers. Students might also look up and discuss the denotative definitions of the words. Then ask a student volunteer to read the passage from *Hatchet* aloud while students consider their associations with the underlined words. Divide the class into five groups, each one taking one question under **Exploring Connotations** to discuss. Groups can share their responses with the class.

EXPLORING CONNOTATIONS
The major difference between words with closely related denotations is in their connotations. Even though dictionaries often try to include the various shades of meaning of words, the best way to explore connotations of words is to become aware of how people actually use them. Good writers have to be careful in their word choices to make sure their attitudes are clear to their readers and fair to the subjects.

Answers
Answers will vary.
1. *Target* suggests something to be aimed at, hit or miss. *Home* implies nurturing and growing.
2. *Placed* creates a quick, almost unconscious act, whereas *positioned* conveys careful, thoughtful image.
3. *Slammed* implies a loud, forceful action; *hit* doesn't convey as much power.
4. *Burned* presents an image of going up quickly in flames, unlike *smoldered*, which indicates a slower process with little smoke and no flame.
5. *Prehistoric* is not as specific as *Cro-Magnon*, which allows the reader to visualize the author's comparison.

152

FOCUS ON *Reading and Critical Thinking*

EXPLORING CONNOTATIONS

The **denotation** of a word is its dictionary definition. A word's **connotations** are the emotions or associations that it has for readers. For example, the three adjectives *thin, slim,* and *skinny* might all be used to describe the same person. Which word would sound most favorable to you? Which word would sound least favorable?

Read the following passage from Gary Paulsen's *Hatchet*, paying special attention to the underlined words. Then use a separate sheet of paper to answer the questions below.

> I must make a <u>home</u> for the sparks, he thought. A perfect <u>home</u> or they won't stay, they won't make fire. . . .
>
> He <u>positioned</u> his spark nest—as he thought of it—at the base of the rock, used his thumb to make a small depression in the middle, and <u>slammed</u> the back of the hatchet down across the black rock. A cloud of sparks rained down, most of them missing the nest, but some, perhaps thirty or so, hit in the depression, and of those six or seven found fuel and grew, <u>smoldered</u> and caused the bark to take on the red glow.
>
> Then they went out.
>
> Close—he was close. He repositioned the nest, made a new and smaller dent with his thumb, and struck again.
>
> More sparks, a slight glow, then nothing.
>
> It's me, he thought. I'm doing something wrong. I do not know this—a cave dweller would have had a fire by now, a <u>Cro-Magnon</u> man would have a fire by now—but I don't know this. I don't know how to make a fire.

Exploring Connotations

1. What different associations would you have if Paulsen had used the word *target* rather than *home* in the first paragraph?

2. Explain how the word *placed* (versus *positioned*) would create a different effect at the beginning of the second paragraph.

3. What associations do you have with the verb *slammed?* How would the verb *hit* be different?

4. If the verb *burned* were substituted for *smoldered* toward the end of the second paragraph, what difference would the change make?

5. What if Paulsen had used the word *prehistoric*, rather than *Cro-Magnon*, in the last paragraph?

OBJECTIVES
The overall aim is for students to write a description of a subject of their choice.

PRESENTATION
You might begin this segment by having students re-examine the selections in the unit for effective descriptive passages. Ask a few volunteers to share their passages aloud with the class and to explain why they find them effective. Then students can enter into the prewriting stage by using notes taken for the strategies discussed in the unit. You may want students to state their audiences and purposes so that they will have a focus for collecting their details. During the writing stage, students might benefit from examining some models of descriptive writing that may help them with their introductions and organization. Students might enjoy publish-

FOCUS ON Writing

WRITING A DESCRIPTION

*I*n **descriptive writing,** you use words to create a picture or image of a subject. You can use description in many different forms for a variety of writing purposes. For example, you might want to express yourself in a journal entry, or persuade a friend to see a new movie. You could also use description in a lost-and-found notice or in a piece of creative writing such as a short story. During this unit, you have seen some of the key elements of description. Now you will have the chance to describe a subject of your own choice.

Prewriting

1. Use these guidelines when you start to plan a description:
   - Choose a familiar person, place, or thing.
   - Choose a subject that you can observe directly.
   - Focus and limit your subject so that you have enough space to cover all the important details.

   [See **Focus** assignment on page 96.]

2. Think about your purpose and audience. In a description, your **purpose** is usually to express yourself or to create a mood or feeling. Your **audience** may be your classmates and your teacher. Think about what they may know already about your subject. What might they like to know?

3. Use these techniques to gather details for your description:
   - observing
   - recalling
   - imagining

   Pay special attention to **sensory** details—words and phrases that appeal to the five senses: sight, hearing, touch, taste, and smell. Sensory details are especially important in descriptive writing because they help your readers to see your subject concretely and vividly. You may wish to use a chart like the one below in order to list sensory details about your subject.

   Subject of Description: _____

Sight	Hearing	Touch	Smell	Taste
___	___	___	___	___
___	___	___	___	___
___	___	___	___	___
___	___	___	___	___

   [See **Focus** assignment on page 126.]

4. Organize the details for your description in a logical way. Choose one of the two methods listed below:
   - **Spatial Order:** Present details in the order you see them: top to bottom, near to far, left to right.
   - **Order of Importance:** Place the most important details either first or last.

   [See **Focus** assignment on page 145.]

HOLT WRITER'S WORKSHOP

This computer program provides help for all types of writing through guided instruction for each step of the writing process. (Program available separately.)

See **Elements of Writing, Introductory Course,** Chapter 34, for more instruction on descriptive writing.

WRITING A DESCRIPTION
Description occurs in all kinds of writing—fiction and nonfiction, poetry and prose. The most common weakness in descriptive writing is the writer's reliance on generalizations to do the work that should be done by details. Writers must provide readers with verbal images of the particular viewpoint that separates

Focus on Writing 153

ing their descriptions in a class anthology, which they can display in the classroom.

their subject matter from anything else like it.

Prewriting
Encourage students to immerse themselves in their subject while they prewrite. They might make a sensory trip with the topic as they fill in their detail charts. You might take students outside, play music for them, or have them draw pictures to stimulate their senses. You may want to check students' charts before they write their first drafts. Also, remind students that their subjects and the details they have selected may dictate the organizational method they use.

Writing
Encourage students not to use too many figures of speech. They might experiment with them and then choose the very best ones to use in just the right place. Remind students that their descriptions should have a beginning, a middle, and an end.

Evaluating and Revising
You might want students to think of revising their description in two phases. First, they revise for content, looking at the big picture: the organization, number and kind of details, unity and transitions. Second, students

Writing

1. As you write the first draft of your description, try to make your words as exact as possible. Using **exact words**—nouns, verbs, adjectives, and adverbs—will help you to present a sharp, vivid picture of the subject. Avoid vague, general words like *move*, *thing*, *pretty*, *rather*, *very*, *nice*, and *interesting*. [See **Focus** assignment on page 112.]

2. Use **figures of speech** in your description where they can create special effects. Figures of speech are imaginative comparisons that are not meant to be taken literally.
   - A **simile** compares two unlike things, using a word such as *like*, *as*, *resembles*, or *than*: "The storm scattered the trees like bowling pins."
   - A **metaphor** is a direct comparison between two unlike things in which one thing becomes another thing: "Fame is a trumpet blast."

3. Be sure that all the details you include in your description contribute to a main feeling or overall impression. Leave out any details that do not fit your focus or the mood you are trying to create in your essay.

4. Use **transitional words and phrases** to show the connections between ideas in your paper. Below is a list of useful transitions:

above	first	most important
across	here	over
around	inside	then
before	into	there
behind	last	under
down	mainly	up

Evaluating and Revising

1. After you have finished a first draft of your description, put it aside for a while. Then evaluate your draft with fresh eyes. Have you chosen exact words to describe your subject? Do all the details in your paper contribute to a single impression or mood?

2. You may find the following checklist helpful as you revise your writing.

Checklist for Evaluation and Revision
- Have I limited my subject so that I can cover it?
- Do I clearly identify my subject in the introduction?
- Do I help readers "see" my subject by using exact words and sensory details?
- Have I used fresh, vivid figures of speech?
- Have I organized my details in a logical way that is easy to follow?
- Do all the details contribute to a single main impression?

TRANSPARENCY 11
Writing Process
Writing a Description – helps students plan and write an effective description.

Here is an example of how one writer revised a paragraph in a description.

Writer's Model

Russell ~~came slowly~~ *sauntered* out the door and ~~stood~~ *paused* on the porch. He casually glanced at the driveway and then caught his breath in surprise. The brand-new bike's chrome handlebars ~~were bright~~ *flashed* in the warm May sunshine. Where had this beautiful bike come from? He had no idea! it certainly hadn't been in the Winkler driveway an hour before. As he walked around the bicycle, his nose caught the smell of the leather seat. Then he saw the best part of all: the license plate that was made to order with gold letters on a black background, spelling out "RUSSELL 1." (tr) The rear reflector was *a fiery sparkle.* ~~red.~~

Proofreading and Publishing

1. Proofread your paper to correct errors in grammar, usage, capitalization, and punctuation. (You may find it helpful to refer to the **Handbook for Revision** on pages 750–785.) Then prepare a final version of your paper by making a clean copy.

2. Consider some of the following ways of publishing and sharing your paper:
   - illustrate your description with drawings or photos and then display your essay on the class bulletin board
   - submit your essay to the school newspaper or magazine
   - together with your classmates, make your essays the basis for a class "radio show" by tape recording your descriptions
   - deliver an oral reading of your paper in class

Portfolio If your teacher approves, you may wish to keep a copy of your work in your writing folder or portfolio.

revise for style and tone by looking at specific words and phrases or their titles. The **Checklist for Evaluation and Revision** will be a useful guide for students in this process.

Proofreading and Publishing
You might create small editing circles and have students check each other's papers for subject-verb agreement, comma usage, and spelling. Ask students to pass their papers around the circle and to focus on only one kind of error at a time in each paper.

Focus on Writing 155

UNIT 3 ◆ TEACHING GUIDE

SHORT STORIES

OVERVIEW OF THE UNIT

The short story is particularly useful in teaching students the literary elements found in longer works, like the novel. With the short story, students can more easily follow the development of a theme or chart the course of a plot. Having done this, they are better prepared to tackle longer works of fiction with confidence.

THE ELEMENTS OF A SHORT STORY

While style, technique, and vision have all varied considerably since Edgar Allan Poe first defined the modern short story in 1842, the essential elements of the short story have remained very much the same: plot (and conflict), character, setting, and theme.

1. Plot. The elements of plot (exposition of conflict and character, complications, climax, and resolution), though not as important as in longer works, are still important. The various kinds of conflict (person vs. nature; person vs. person; person vs. society; person vs. himself or herself) are often useful starting points in studying the short story.

2. Character. Because of their brevity, short stories often focus on a single character, who may be a human or an animal. The writer develops this main character by telling us about his or her appearance, words, thoughts, and actions, or by telling us how other people in the story respond to this person. What happens to this character often gives the reader an insight into life.

3. Setting. The setting is the story's time and place. In short stories, as in novels, the setting can contribute to the story's mood.

4. Theme. The central idea that forms the core of the story may be directly stated by the author or left to the reader to discover on his or her own. In some stories, theme is often edifying, even moralistic. In more modern fiction, the theme is more complex, and readers may have widely divergent interpretations of a work's meaning.

OBJECTIVES OF THE UNIT

The aims of this unit for students are
- To monitor their own reading
- To identify exaggeration, character traits, and sensory details
- To distinguish between fantastic and realistic details and between fact and opinion
- To use vivid verbs
- To describe a conflict and make inferences about it
- To draw conclusions about a character
- To use context clues and word parts to determine word meaning
- To write a statement of theme
- To predict outcomes
- To analyze and write similes
- To rewrite paragraphs from a different point of view
- To "translate" dialect
- To analyze a story's title and setting
- To rewrite imagery to create a different mood
- To write creatively and critically about the selections

CONCEPTS AND SKILLS

The following concepts and skills are treated in this unit:

CLOSE READING OF A SHORT STORY

Guidelines for Close Reading 158
One Reader's Response 159
Looking at Yourself as a Reader 165

FOCUS ON READING AND CRITICAL THINKING

Drawing Conclusions About Characters 190
Predicting Outcomes 203, 216
Distinguishing Between Fact and Opinion 250
Following a Sequence of Events 262
Evaluating Short Stories 274

LITERARY ELEMENTS

A Story Map 175
Character 190
Theme 204, 216
Point of View 229
Setting 262

LANGUAGE AND VOCABULARY

Vivid Verbs 176
Context Clues 191
Similes 204
Prefixes and Suffixes 217
Dialect 230
Imagery and Feelings 250
Sensory Details 263

OPPORTUNITIES FOR WRITING

Focus on Writing a Short Story
Building a Plot from a Story Idea 176
Imagining Characters 191
Exploring a Theme 204
Experimenting with Point of View 231
Listing Details of Setting 251
Writing a Short Story 277

Writing About Literature
Describing a Wish That Goes Wrong 217
Writing from a Different Point of View 263

CONNECTIONS

Literature and Science 205
Connecting Cultures 218

SPEAKING AND LISTENING

Dramatizing the Story 176
Reading Aloud 229, 265

PLANNING GUIDE

FOR UNIT PLANNING
- Transparencies 12–17: *Audiovisual Resources Binder*
- Portfolio Assessment and Professional Support Materials
- Test Generator
- Mastery Tests: Teaching Resources B, pp. 107, 109
- Analogy Test: Teaching Resources B, p. 113
- Revision Worksheet: Teaching Resources B, p. 114

SELECTION (Pupil's Page)	TEACHING RESOURCES B (page numbers shown below)								AV BINDER
	Teacher's Notes	Reading Check	Reading Focus	Study Guide	Language Skills	Building Vocabulary	Selection Vocab. Test	Selection Test	Audio-cassette
SHORT STORIES Introduction (p. 157)	1								
Guidelines for Close Reading Quentin Reynolds *A Secret for Two* (p. 159)	1								
John Gardner *Dragon, Dragon* (p. 166)	2	5	6	7, 8	9	12	14	15	TAPE 1 SIDE B
Robert Cormier *President Cleveland, Where Are You?* (p. 178)	17	20	21	22, 23	24	27	29	30	
Ray Bradbury *All Summer in a Day* (p. 194)	32	35	36	38, 39	40	43	45	46	
Lloyd Alexander *The Stone* (p. 206)	48	51	52	53, 54	55	59	61	62	
James Berry *Becky and the Wheels-and-Brake Boys* (p. 220)	64	66		67, 68	69	72	73	74	
Elizabeth Enright *Nancy* (p. 233)	76	79	80	81, 82	83	86	88	89	TAPE 2 SIDE A
Olaf Baker *Where the Buffaloes Begin* (p. 252)	91	93	94	95, 96	97	100	101	102	TAPE 2 SIDE A
Lensey Namioka *The All-American Slurp* (p. 264)	104								

TRANSPARENCIES

The following unit support materials with specific correlations to literature selections are available in the **Fine Art and Instructional Transparencies with Teacher's Notes and Blackline Masters** section of your *Audiovisual Resources Binder*.

FINE ART TRANSPARENCIES
Theme: Tales of Changes and Challenges
12 *The Problem We All Live With*, Norman Rockwell
13 *Self-Portrait with Seven Fingers*, Marc Chagall

READER RESPONSE
14 Plotting with a Storyboard

LITERARY ELEMENTS
15 Plot
16 Story Map

WRITING PROCESS
17 Writing a Short Story

INTRODUCING THE UNIT

1. Discussing a Cartoon Story. Show a videotaped cartoon to the class with no comment. Then, introduce the basic literary elements of plot, conflict, character, and setting. Have students discuss which elements can be applied to the cartoon. Then, reshow the cartoon, having students discuss how each element is revealed in the cartoon.

2. Identifying Elements of a Story. Use stories that the students have written themselves for practice in identifying the basic elements (see Focus on Writing: Writing a Short Story on pages 277–279).

3. Developing Plot Outlines. Have students, working individually or in small groups, develop plot outlines for stories. They can then discuss the basic elements and how they would develop the elements further in their stories.

PORTFOLIO ASSESSMENT

Suggestions for use of portfolios as support for this unit are described in the *Portfolio Assessment and Professional Support Materials* booklet accompanying this program. Specific suggestions are provided for a variety of student projects that may be suitable for inclusion in a portfolio. In addition, copying masters are provided for guides that may be used for evaluation and assessment of student projects.

SELECTION NOTES

Following are vocabulary lists of words from each selection that are included in the Building Vocabulary Worksheets and Selection Vocabulary Tests; Reading Check tests (which are also available in blackline masters); and answers to questions in the Language and Vocabulary sections that follow the selections.

"Dragon, Dragon" (page 166)

Vocabulary

plague(d)	envious(ly)	Meek(ly)	crane(d)
ravage(d)	timid(ly)	lunge(d)	blister(ing)
beam(ed)	sly(ly)		

Reading Check

Have students judge each statement as true or false.
1. The dragon switches all the kingdom's roads.   True
2. The king's knights fight the dragon.   False
3. The cobbler's eldest son runs from the dragon.   False
4. The youngest son recites a poem to the dragon.   True
5. At the end of the story, the queen is soaking wet.   True

Language and Vocabulary: Vivid Verbs (page 176)

Answers to all questions will vary. Possible answers:
1. roared, shouted, growled
2. hates, detests, loathes
3. wacks off, hacks off, lops off
4. races out, dances out, catapults out

"President Cleveland, Where Are You?" (page 178)

Vocabulary

regulation(s)	competition	divulge	harass(ed)
console(ing)	dismal	compassion	dejection
indignant	desperation		

Reading Check

Have students respond with words or phrases.
1. What is the time setting of the story?   1930s
2. What do Jerry and his friends collect?   cards
3. Where does Jerry's father work?   a comb factory
4. What does Armand need for the dance?   shoes and a corsage
5. At the end, who has the new baseball glove? Rollie Tremaine

Language and Vocabulary: Context Clues (page 191)

1. exposed—made visible, revealed (clue: *naked*)
2. assortments—a collection including a wide variety (clue: *fresh batch*)
3. layoff—temporary dismissal of employees (clue: *out of work*)
4. corsage—a small bouquet of flowers to be pinned to a dress (clue: *flowers*)

"All Summer in a Day" (page 194)

Vocabulary

intermix(ed)	surge(d)	immense	wail
gush	bore	suspend(ed)	solemn
feverish	tremor		

Reading Check

Have students judge each statement as true or false.
1. Margot wouldn't play with the other children.   True
2. Scientists had predicted the sun's reappearance.   True
3. Margot was born on Venus.   False
4. It was William's idea to lock up Margot.   True
5. Margot was beating on the door when the children returned to let her out.   False

Language and Vocabulary: Similes (page 204)

1. a. It is compared to a warm iron.
   b. Possible answer: The sun burnt like a hot iron.
2. a. They were compared to leaves before a hurricane.
   b. Possible answer: The children ran like rocks in an avalanche.
3. Possible answers:
   a. I am like an iris.
   b. I am as amusing as an entertainment center.
   c. At times I resemble a cruising Corvette.
   d. I can attack like a falcon.

"The Stone" (page 206)

Vocabulary

feeble	plight	sheepish	rue	mire(d)
delve(d)	jubilation	stammer(ed)	regret(fully)	fallow

Reading Check

Have students judge each statement as true or false.
1. Maibon is frail and feeble.   False
2. Doli is unable to turn himself invisible.   True
3. Maibon doesn't listen to Doli's warning.   True
4. Maibon blames Doli for Maibon's problems.   True
5. At the end, Maibon is proud of his white hair.   True

Language and Vocabulary: Prefixes and Suffixes (page 217)

Possible anwers include:
1. I would write *unseen* or *invisible*.
2. I would write *fearless*.
3. I would call it a *piglet*.
4. I would use the word *grateful*.
5. I would use the word *ungrateful*.
6. Someone who is *antiwar* is against war.
7. A *prewar* house was built before the war.

"Becky and the Wheels-and-Brake Boys" (page 220)

Vocabulary

veranda   menace   barge(d)   quarrel   interfere

Reading Check

Have students judge each statement as true or false.
1. Becky is the youngest child in her family.   **False**
2. Granny-Liz says all girls should have bikes.   **False**
3. Becky's mother says Becky looks like she just escaped from a hair-pulling battle.   **True**
4. Becky tries to sell her dad's sun helmet.   **True**
5. Becky's cousin Ben teaches her to ride.   **True**

Language and Vocabulary: Dialect (page 230)

Possible answers:
1. "Even though I was so considerate of Granny's need for a cool drink, she started scolding me."
2. " 'Haven't I told you I don't want you keeping company with those awful boys on their bikes?' "
3. " 'And one day perhaps I'll even have a son of my own, one like you.' "
4. "I could see Mum really didn't have much money."
5. "I knew anything of Dad's—anything—would be worth a lot."

"Nancy" (page 233)

Vocabulary

conventional	guttural	abruptly	riotous(ly)
appreciative(ly)	exhilarate(d)	random	reproach(es)
mutual	substantial		

Reading Check

Have students judge each statement as true or false.
1. Fiona's grandmother is Fiona's favorite relative.   **False**
2. Fiona runs away while her nurse sleeps.   **True**
3. Fiona complains about being called Nancy.   **False**
4. The Fadgins and Fiona play exciting games like hide-and-seek and gangsters.   **True**
5. Darlene's mother and Fiona's nurse have a neighborly chat about the children.   **False**

Language and Vocabulary: Imagery and Feelings (page 250)

Possible answers:
1. *small, stuffy, open suitcases and travel guides, clean, neat, the furniture was buried under stacks of shorts and swimsuits, a cat settled happily on a pile of beach robes.*
2. *stale, unused smell, neglect, bare, uncluttered, except for an old mattress, radio was silent, white as a ghost, eating grapes.*

"Where the Buffaloes Begin" (page 252)

Vocabulary

| eerie(ly) | shimmer | margin | bellow(ing) | retreat |
| desert(ed) | expanse | stealth(ily) | heave | shrill(y) |

Reading Check

Have students judge each statement as true or false.
1. Little Wolf was ten when he led the buffalo.   **True**
2. Little Wolf thought that the dim spot he saw was the herd of buffalo he was seeking.   **False**
3. The buffaloes received a message from Little Wolf that even he didn't understand.   **True**
4. Little Wolf's pony was trampled by stampeding buffaloes.   **False**
5. Little Wolf became part of the legend about the buffaloes.   **True**

Language and Vocabulary: Sensory Details (page 263)

Possible answers:
1. The words *blazing campfires, moaned eerily, thickets of juniper and fir, in the Indian tongue,* and *waters never rest* helped me see and hear the scene.
2. There are prairie grouse, larks, sparrows, and wild roses. It makes me like the prairie.
3. The words are *a gray sheet with a glint of silver, glimmering under the sun, the prairies lay utterly deserted,* and *in the white shimmer of the air.*
4. The words are *trampling, snorting, the flash of the water,* and *the sharp moist smell of the great beasts as they crowded in on one another.* The writer made me feel awe, excitement, and suspense.

Student Learning Options

Short Stories

1. Exploring Card Collecting
The boy in "President Cleveland, Where Are You?" collects president cards to get a baseball glove, but many people collect various kinds of cards as a serious hobby. Invite a speaker knowledgeable about card collecting to talk to the class about the hobby, or ask your students who are card collectors to tell the class about the hobby.

2. Locating Story Settings
Using a world map, students can use pins to mark the settings of the stories they have read in this unit. Keep the map on display in the classroom, and have students add to it each time they read another literary work.

3. Building a Model
When students read "All Summer in a Day," have them build a model of the solar system, with special emphasis on Venus. Ask them to write information about parts of the model for "exhibit cards" that viewers can read.

4. Choosing Mood Music
Have students choose songs or other musical works to reflect the themes or moods of the stories in this unit. Play recordings of the songs, and ask the class to choose the one they think best represents the story for which it was chosen.

VISUAL CONNECTIONS

Use this famous painting by Benton to talk about the elements of storytelling, especially the element of conflict. Have students use their imaginations to guess at what has caused the train wreck and what will happen next to the people at the crossroads.

If you want to emphasize point of view, you might have one group of students write this story from the point of view of the train's engineer, and another group write it from the point of view of the people in the cart.

About the Artist
Thomas Hart Benton (1889–1975) is now recognized as one of the foremost American artists whose imagination focused on familiar Midwestern scenes. Like many painters of his day, Benton painted many murals for public buildings. You can see his pictures on the walls of the New School for Social Research in New York City and the Missouri State Capitol building.

UNIT THREE

Short Stories

Storytelling is natural to people, just as eating and sleeping are. There is not a group of people on earth who have not told stories. All over the world, stories are built on certain elements. The **plot** is "what happens" in the story. The most important element in the plot is **conflict**, or struggle. This means that a character wants something very much and meets resistance trying to get it. The **characters** in a story are also important. The best stories, in fact, are the ones that create interesting, lifelike characters. Most stories also have a **setting**, a particular time and place in which the action occurs. When you finish a story, you frequently ask: "But what does it MEAN?" What you are looking for is the story's **theme**, or what the story reveals about life. The best stories help us see ourselves and our lives more clearly.

The Wreck of the Ole '97 by Thomas Hart Benton (1943). Egg tempera on gessoed masonite.

Hunter Museum of Art, Chattanooga, Tennessee.
Gift of the Benwood Foundation.

TEACHING RESOURCES B
Teacher's Notes, p. 1

INTRODUCING THE SHORT STORY

Help students to understand that when we care about a main character, we empathize with him or her in the struggle to solve a problem or overcome an obstacle. We see how the character is influenced and sometimes hindered by the time and place and cultural setting of the story. When the conflict is at last resolved for better or worse, we are left with the realization that we have learned something new and important. A good story may move us to laughter or tears, to a sense of wonder or of horror.

FOCUS/MOTIVATION
Until fairly recently, a milkman left glass bottles of milk on the doorstep every morning in many communities. Though milk has been delivered by truck for many years, in earlier times it was brought in wagons pulled by horses. Montreal is home to a large French-Canadian community, of which Pierre and Jacques are members.

Establishing a Purpose for Reading. Ask students to look for clues as they read that foreshadow what will happen at the end of the story. These clues will help them make predictions about the story's outcome.

Prereading Journal Have students write a few sentences about a close relationship they have had with an animal or one they have read about or seen on TV or in the movies. Do they think that some animals can act almost like people?

Close Reading OF A SHORT STORY

Think of how you read the listing of television programs in a weekly guide or the recipe for a favorite dessert or a letter from a pen pal. You read each of these things in a different way.

Reading literature also requires special skills. Follow these guidelines to become an active reader.

Guidelines for Close Reading

1. Ask questions as you read. Respond to clues and draw inferences from them. Guess at the meaning of unfamiliar words. Draw conclusions from what you have read.
2. Make predictions. Think about what is going to happen next.
3. Relate what you read to your own life and experiences. Put yourself in the main character's place.
4. Try to state the author's overall purpose in your own words.
5. Consider your own responses. What questions remain unanswered? Did your predictions come true? Do you understand your own feelings and actions after reading the selection?

Here is a brief story that has been read carefully by one reader. The comments in the margin show how this reader has responded to the story. If you would like, make notes of your own on a separate sheet of paper, covering up the printed notes as you read. You may wish to compare your responses with these printed comments at a later point.

158 Short Stories

GEOGRAPHY LINK

Encourage students to create a map of Pierre's milk delivery route in Montreal, based on specific information from the story. Have them label streets, locations, and landmarks. Extend this activity by having students locate Montreal, Canada's largest city, on a world map. Have students make entries in their journals or learning logs, giving the province in which Montreal is located (Quebec) and then listing the other nine provinces of Canada (Alberta, British Columbia, Manitoba, New Brunswick, Newfoundland, Nova Scotia, Ontario, Prince Edward Island, Saskatchewan).

TEACHING RESOURCES B
Teacher's Notes, p. 1

1. LITERARY ELEMENTS:
Suspense
The title is good because it causes the reader to make predictions about what the secret is and who shares it. It helps involve the reader with the story from the very beginning.

2. GUIDED READING:
Using Prior Knowledge
The reader has recognized St. Joseph from the New Testament. Since he was Mary's husband, St. Joseph was Jesus' earthly father. He is revered as a gentle, kind man, the patron saint of workers, husbands and fathers, and families. By giving the horse this name, Pierre is suggesting that the horse has some of the same qualities.

3. GUIDED READING:
Drawing Conclusions
The reader has guessed already that Pierre and Joseph are the "two" mentioned in the title.

A Secret for Two

QUENTIN REYNOLDS

Montreal is a very large city, but, like all cities, it has some very small streets. Streets, for instance, like Prince Edward Street, which is only four blocks long, ending in a cul-de-sac.[1] No one knew Prince Edward Street as well as did Pierre Dupin, for Pierre had delivered milk to the families on the street for thirty years now.

During the past fifteen years the horse which drew the milk wagon used by Pierre was a large white horse named Joseph. In Montreal, especially in that part of Montreal which is very French, the animals, like children, are often given the names of saints. When the big white horse first came to the Provincale Milk Company he didn't have a name. They told Pierre that he could use the white horse henceforth. Pierre stroked the softness of the horse's neck; he stroked the sheen of its splendid belly and he looked into the eyes of the horse.

"This is a kind horse, a gentle and a faithful horse," Pierre said, "and I can see a beautiful spirit shining out of the eyes of the horse. I will name him after good St. Joseph, who was also kind and gentle and faithful and a beautiful spirit."

Within a year Joseph knew the milk route as well as Pierre. Pierre used to boast that he didn't need reins—he never touched them. Each morning Pierre arrived at the stables of the Provincale Milk Company at five o'clock. The wagon would be loaded and Joseph hitched to it. Pierre would call *"Bonjour, vieil ami,"*[2] as he climbed into his seat and Joseph would turn his head and the other drivers would smile and say that the horse would smile at Pierre. Then Jacques, the foreman, would say, "All right, Pierre, go on," and Pierre would call softly to Joseph, *"Avance, mon ami,"*[3] and this splendid

---

1. **cul-de-sac** (kul′də·sak′): dead-end street.
2. **Bonjour, vieil ami** (bōn·zhōō′ vē·ā′ ä·mē′): French for "Good morning, old friend."
3. **Avance, mon ami** (ä·väns′ mōn ä·mē): French for "Go forward, my friend."

ONE READER'S RESPONSE

It's a good title. What is the secret? Who are the "two" people? **1**

The story is set in Canada.

This must be a long time ago, when milk was delivered to people's homes by a horse and wagon.

I know who St. Joseph was. **2**

Two characters so far: a milkman named Pierre and a horse named Joseph. The horse is practically a saint.

Pierre and Joseph are good friends. Joseph is like a human. (They are probably the "two" in the title. What's their secret?) **3**

Close Reading of a Short Story 159

1. LITERARY ELEMENTS:
Foreshadowing
The author does not make the foreshadowing so obvious that the ending is given away. Here, what seems at first to be hyperbole turns out to be no more than the literal truth.

2. GUIDED READING:
Self-Questioning
Suggest to students that when they don't like some element or feature of a story, they should question themselves closely to determine whether their dislike is merely a matter of taste or whether it might possibly result from a misjudgment on the author's part or a lack of sympathy or experience on their part. In this case, it may well be the reader's lack of experience that leads to his or her irritation with the use of French, which actually serves to add color and verisimilitude to the narrative.

3. GUIDED READING:
Interpreting Meaning
Here, students can readily see how much more of the author's meaning can be interpreted in a second reading.

Close Reading
OF A SHORT STORY

1 Joseph knows the route as well as Pierre does.

[When I reread the story, I found this clue.]

2 I don't like all this French.

3 [When I reread the story, I saw that there is more truth in this than Jacques realizes.]

Pierre can't read or write! [When I reread the story, I saw that this is a hint about the surprise ending.]

---

combination would stalk proudly down the street.

The wagon, without any direction from Pierre, would roll three blocks down St. Catherine Street, then turn right two blocks along Roslyn Avenue; then left, for that was Prince Edward Street. The horse would stop at the first house, allow Pierre perhaps thirty seconds to get down from his seat and put a bottle of milk at the front door and would then go on, skipping two houses and stopping at the third. So down the length of the street. Then Joseph, still without any direction from Pierre, would turn around and come back along the other side. Yes, Joseph was a smart horse.

Pierre would boast at the stable of Joseph's skill. "I never touch the reins. He knows just where to stop. Why, a blind man could handle my route with Joseph pulling the wagon."

So it went on for years—always the same. Pierre and Joseph both grew old together, but gradually, not suddenly. Pierre's huge walrus mustache was pure white now and Joseph didn't lift his knees so high or raise his head quite as much. Jacques, the foreman of the stables, never noticed that they were both getting old until Pierre appeared one morning carrying a heavy walking stick.

"Hey, Pierre," Jacques laughed. "Maybe you got the gout,[4] hey?"

"*Mais oui*,[5] Jacques," Pierre said a bit uncertainly. "One grows old. One's legs get tired."

"You should teach that horse to carry the milk to the front door for you," Jacques told him. "He does everything else."

He knew every one of the forty families he served on Prince Edward Street. The cooks knew that Pierre could neither read nor write, so instead of following the usual custom of leaving a note in an empty bottle if an additional quart of milk was needed they would sing out when they heard the rumble of his wagon wheels over the cobbled street, "Bring an extra quart this morning, Pierre."

---
4. **gout** (gowt): a painful swelling of the feet or hands; like arthritis.
5. *Mais oui* (mā wē′): French for "But yes."

160   Short Stories

1. GUIDED READING:
Making Inferences
You may want to stop here to determine whether your students have picked up on these clues and have inferred that Jacques cannot see.

2. LITERARY ELEMENTS:
Conflict
The reader is aware of the essential elements of plot and is hunting for conflict. Although the conflict is often delineated at the beginning of a short story, this is not always the case.

Close Reading
OF A SHORT STORY

[This is also a clue, but I didn't get it till the end of the story.]

1 [Another clue: Pierre doesn't have to make out bills. He doesn't have to use his eyes.]

Here is a clue to the title. [At the end of the story you know what this means.]

2 I don't see any conflict in this story so far. What's going to be its point?

"So you have company for dinner tonight," he would call back gaily.

Pierre had a remarkable memory. When he arrived at the stable he'd always remember to tell Jacques, "The Paquins took an extra quart this morning; the Lemoines bought a pint of cream."

Jacques would note these things in a little book he always carried. Most of the drivers had to make out the weekly bills and collect the money, but Jacques, liking Pierre, had always excused him from this task. All Pierre had to do was to arrive at five in the morning, walk to his wagon, which was always in the same spot at the curb, and deliver his milk. He returned some two hours later, got down stiffly from his seat, called a cheery, "Au 'voir"[6] to Jacques and then limped slowly down the street.

One morning the president of the Provincale Milk Company came to inspect the early morning deliveries. Jacques pointed Pierre out to him and said: "Watch how he talks to that horse. See how the horse listens and how he turns his head toward Pierre? See the look in that horse's eyes? You know, I think those two share a secret. I have often noticed it. It is as though they both sometimes chuckle at us as they go off on their route. Pierre is a good man, Monsieur[7] President, but he gets old. Would it be too bold of me to suggest that he be retired and be given perhaps a small pension?" he added anxiously.

"But of course," the president laughed. "I know his record. He has been on this route now for thirty years and never once has there been a complaint. Tell him it is time he rested. His salary will go on just the same."

But Pierre refused to retire. He was panic-stricken at the thought of not driving Joseph every day. "We are two old men," he said to Jacques. "Let us wear out together. When Joseph is ready to retire—then I, too, will quit."

Jacques, who was a kind man, understood. There was

---
6. **Au 'voir** (ō vwär'): French for "good-bye."
7. **Monsieur** (mis·yər'): French word for "sir."

something about Pierre and Joseph which made a man smile tenderly. It was as though each drew some hidden strength from the other. When Pierre was sitting in his seat, and when Joseph was hitched to the wagon, neither seemed old. But when they finished their work, then Pierre would limp down the street slowly, seeming very old indeed, and the horse's head would drop and he would walk very wearily to his stall.

Then one morning Jacques had dreadful news for Pierre when he arrived. It was a cold morning and still pitch-dark. The air was like iced wine that morning and the snow which had fallen during the night glistened like a million diamonds piled together.

Jacques said, "Pierre, your horse, Joseph, did not wake up this morning. He was very old, Pierre, he was twenty-five and that is like being seventy-five for a man."

"Yes," Pierre said, slowly. "Yes. I am seventy-five. And I cannot see Joseph again."

"Of course you can," Jacques soothed. "He is over in his stall, looking very peaceful. Go over and see him."

Pierre took one step forward then turned. "No . . . no

[This is so true! But you don't know till the end.]

Something is wrong! I wonder what?

Joseph has died. How sad! Now what will become of Pierre? 1

1. GUIDED READING:
Interpreting Meaning
It is not explicitly stated that Joseph has died. The reader has inferred this from the euphemistic phrase "did not wake up this morning" and the references to his age.

Close Reading of a Short Story

1. GUIDED READING:
Interpreting Meaning
Because the reader has been paying careful attention to how this story is crafted, he or she is aware that the surface meaning—that Pierre is sad—may not be the full explanation for the way his eyes look.

Close Reading
OF A SHORT STORY

What doesn't Jacques understand? [You know at the end of the story.]

1 Are his eyes this way because he is sad? Or is something wrong with them? [You know at the end.]

Is Pierre deaf? No, he heard Jacques talk to him.

What are cataracts?

How did Jacques know the horse knew? It's a sad story, but I really like it. I wish it didn't have so many French words.

". . . you don't understand, Jacques."

Jacques clapped him on the shoulder. "We'll find another horse just as good as Joseph. Why, in a month you'll teach him to know your route as well as Joseph did. We'll . . ."

The look in Pierre's eyes stopped him. For years Pierre had worn a heavy cap, the peak of which came low over his eyes, keeping the bitter morning wind out of them. Now Jacques looked into Pierre's eyes and he saw something which startled him. He saw a dead, lifeless look in them. The eyes were mirroring the grief that was in Pierre's heart and his soul. It was as though his heart and soul had died.

"Take today off, Pierre," Jacques said, but already Pierre was hobbling off down the street, and had one been near one would have seen tears streaming down his cheeks and have heard half-smothered sobs. Pierre walked to the corner and stepped into the street. There was a warning yell from the driver of a huge truck that was coming fast and there was the scream of brakes, but Pierre apparently heard neither.

Five minutes later an ambulance driver said, "He's dead. Was killed instantly."

Jacques and several of the milk-wagon drivers had arrived and they looked down at the still figure.

"I couldn't help it," the driver of the truck protested, "he walked right into my truck. He never saw it, I guess. Why, he walked into it as though he were blind."

The ambulance doctor bent down, "Blind? Of course the man was blind. See those cataracts? This man has been blind for five years." He turned to Jacques, "You say he worked for you? Didn't you know he was blind?"

"No . . . no . . ." Jacques said, softly. "None of us knew. Only one knew—a friend of his named Joseph. . . . It was a secret, I think, just between those two."

Short Stories

PORTFOLIO ASSESSMENT
For this unit's portfolio project, students may want to write their own short short stories of about one hundred words. Suggest that they create simple plots from their own experience. Have students make a brief outline that includes the major points. Remind students that a well-written short story requires careful word choice. They may want to use a thesaurus or dictionary. Consult with students individually to agree on how their short short stories will be assessed. (See *Portfolio Assessment and Professional Support Materials,* especially the section entitled **Suggestions for Portfolio Projects.**)

Looking at Yourself as a Reader

Suppose you were this reader, and suppose that now you are reviewing your responses to look for something to write about.

1. You will notice that most of your responses have to do with clues that **foreshadow** or hint at the story's surprise ending. If you want to write about the use of foreshadowing in the story, you might start with this sentence:

   > In "A Secret for Two," Quentin Reynolds drops several clues that foreshadow the surprise ending. Here are the clues. (I found most of them only after the story was over.)

2. You might also write about the story's **title.** Notice that you asked right away what the title meant—what *is* the "secret"?

3. Your notes also show that the story had a strong **emotional effect** on you. This could be another topic for a composition. You could also tell if the story reminded you of your own experiences with animals. You might open with this statement:

   > After I had finished "A Secret for Two" by Quentin Reynolds, I felt sad about the fates of the two characters who loved each other so much.

LOOKING AT YOURSELF AS A READER
Point out that a good writing topic can often help to bring together all of a reader's thoughts about a story. Readers may focus on a literary technique (such as foreshadowing), something in the selection (such as one passage or the title), or the reader's own responses. Explain that a writing topic could also focus on a plot element, a character, or the setting.

Close Reading of a Short Story

OBJECTIVES
Students will identify examples of exaggeration, complete a story map, create an original conflict and plot, and rewrite sentences using vivid verbs.

TEACHING RESOURCES B
Teacher's Notes, p. 2
Reading Check, p. 5
Reading Focus, p. 6
Study Guide, pp. 7, 8
Language Skills, p. 9
Building Vocabulary, p. 12
Selection Vocabulary Test, p. 14
Selection Test, p. 15

AV RESOURCES BINDER
Audiocassette 1, Side B

FOCUS/MOTIVATION
Building on Prior Knowledge. Build on knowledge of fairy tales by asking for descriptions of typical characters, settings, and plots. Ask students what usually happens to dragons and how this end is achieved. (They might list character types such as princesses, wizards, knights; castle settings; and happily-ever-after plots. They may say that dragons are slain in armed battle.)

Prereading Journal. Have students write a few sentences telling what they think a fairy tale called "Dragon, Dragon" will be about.

PLOT

Dragon, Dragon

JOHN GARDNER

Before You Read

In most of the old fairy tales we loved to read when we were very young, a big strong hero surprises the evil dragon and kills it with a magic sword. In this story, however, the writer has fun with these old fairy tales. For one thing, cars and their spark plugs appear right alongside the dragon and wizard. For another thing, the wizard, supposedly the brains of the kingdom, has a terrible memory. In what other ways does this story spoof the old fairy tales? You'll find glaring examples in the first paragraph.

READING THE STORY

Before they begin this story, students from other cultures may benefit from reading a few fairy tales (to help them catch on to Gardner's spoof). Then have students read this story orally, so they can share the humor. They can also begin thinking about how to dramatize the story (see Dramatizing the Story, page 176).

Language and Vocabulary

Verbs are words that express action or that help make a statement. The action verbs in this story are so vivid they make the action come alive. For example, in the first two paragraphs, the dragon is described as *plaguing* the kingdom and *ravaging* the countryside. *Plaguing* (plāg'ing) means "bringing terrible troubles to." It makes us think of those disgusting diseases (called *plagues*) that used to kill thousands of people (and in some places still do). *Ravaging* (rav'ij·ing) means "violently destroying something." So, a dragon that plagued and ravaged would be pretty bad news.

There was once a king whose kingdom was plagued by a dragon. The king did not know which way to turn. The king's knights were all cowards who hid under their beds whenever the dragon came in sight, so they were of no use to the king at all. And the king's wizard could not help either because, being old, he had forgotten his magic spells. Nor could the wizard look up the spells that had slipped his mind, for he had unfortunately misplaced his wizard's book many years before. The king was at his wit's end.

Every time there was a full moon, the dragon came out of his lair and ravaged the countryside. He frightened maidens and stopped up chimneys and broke store windows and set people's clocks back and made dogs bark until no one could hear himself think.

He tipped over fences and robbed graves and put frogs in people's drinking water and tore the last chapters out of novels and changed house numbers around . . .

He stole spark plugs out of people's cars and put firecrackers in people's cigars and stole the clappers from all the church bells and sprung every bear trap for miles around so the bears could wander wherever they pleased.

And to top it all off, he changed around all the roads in the kingdom so that people could not get anywhere except by starting out in the wrong direction.

"That," said the king in a fury, "is enough!" And he called a meeting of everyone in the kingdom.

Now it happened that there lived in the kingdom a wise old cobbler[1] who had a wife and three sons. The cobbler and his family came to the king's meeting and stood way in back by the door, for the cobbler had a feeling that since he was nobody important there had probably been some mistake, and no doubt the king had

---
1. In most parts of this country, cobblers are called *shoemakers*.

Dragon, Dragon

---

1. LANGUAGE AND VOCABULARY
The Language and Vocabulary box on this page helps students to recognize vivid verbs. The Language and Vocabulary exercise on page 176 provides practice in using them.

2. GUIDED READING:
Using Prior Knowledge
How do these characters differ from those in traditional fairy tales? The knights are cowardly instead of brave, the wizard is forgetful instead of clever.

3. LITERARY ELEMENTS:
Setting
Gardner uses anachronisms for their humorous effect. Students should be able to identify elements (such as spark plugs) that do not fit the given setting.

4. GUIDED READING:
Understanding Cause and Effect
Which one of the dragon's tricks makes the king so angry that he calls a meeting? The dragon has changed around all the roads in the kingdom.

MEETING INDIVIDUAL NEEDS
Visual and Kinesthetic Learners • Have students create dioramas of the castle, the cobbler's home, or the dragon's lair. Encourage students to look back at the story for specific details about these locations to include in their projects.

CREATIVE WRITING LINK
Invite students to write Help Wanted ads that might be placed in the local newspaper by the king in his search for a qualified dragon slayer. Ads should include necessary experience and skills, along with qualities that might be useful for the job, such as bravery and cleverness.

---

1. GUIDED READING:
Making Inferences About Character
What kind of man is the cobbler? He is sensible and realistic as shown by his thoughts and speech.

2. LITERARY ELEMENTS:
Vivid Verbs
Point out that *racked* is more vivid than *worked* or *searched*. It means "tortured," as though on a rack (an instrument of torture, on which victims were stretched apart till they died).

3. GUIDED READING:
Distinguishing Between Fantasy and Reality
The cobbler sounds more like a practical modern man than a king's lowly subject in a fairy tale. Cite examples of his practicality. He says that an ordinary person could not support a princess. He points out that some people are already married. He even turns down the chance to win half the kingdom because "it's too much responsibility" (page 169). He speaks plainly in a modern idiom.

---

intended the meeting for everyone in the kingdom except his family and him.

"Ladies and gentlemen," said the king when everyone was present, "I've put up with that dragon as long as I can. He has got to be stopped."

All the people whispered amongst themselves, and the king smiled, pleased with the impression he had made.

1 But the wise cobbler said gloomily, "It's all very well to talk about it—but how are you going to do it?"

And now all the people smiled and winked as if to say, "Well, King, he's got you there!"

The king frowned.

"It's not that His Majesty hasn't tried," the queen spoke up loyally.

"Yes," said the king, "I've told my knights again and again that they ought to slay that dragon. But I can't *force* them to go. I'm not a tyrant."

"Why doesn't the wizard say a magic spell?" asked the cobbler.

"He's done the best he can," said the king.

The wizard blushed and everyone looked embarrassed. "I used to do all sorts of spells and chants when I was younger," the wizard explained. "But I've lost my spell book, and I begin to fear I'm losing my memory too. For instance, I've been trying for days to recall one spell I used to do. I forget, just now, what the deuce[2] it was for. It went something like–

---

2. **what the deuce:** an expression meaning something like "what in the world."

Bimble,
Wimble,
Cha, Cha
CHOOMPF!

Suddenly, to everyone's surprise, the queen turned into a rosebush.

"Oh dear," said the wizard.

"Now you've done it," groaned the king.

"Poor Mother," said the princess.

"I don't know what can have happened," the wizard said nervously, "but don't worry, I'll have her changed back in a jiffy." He shut his eyes and racked his 2 brain for a spell that would change her back.

But the king said quickly, "You'd better leave well enough alone. If you change her into a rattlesnake, we'll have to chop off her head."

Meanwhile the cobbler stood with his hands in his pockets, sighing at the waste of time. "About the dragon . . ." he began.

"Oh yes," said the king. "I'll tell you what I'll do. I'll give the princess's hand in marriage to anyone who can make the dragon stop."

"It's not enough," said the cobbler. 3 "She's a nice enough girl, you understand. But how would an ordinary person support her? Also, what about those of us that are already married?"

"In that case," said the king, "I'll offer the princess's hand or half the kingdom or both—whichever is most convenient."

The cobbler scratched his chin and considered it. "It's not enough," he said at

168 Short Stories

last. "It's a good enough kingdom, you understand, but it's too much responsibility."

"Take it or leave it," the king said.

"I'll leave it," said the cobbler. And he shrugged and went home.

But the cobbler's eldest son thought the bargain was a good one, for the princess was very beautiful and he liked the idea of having half the kingdom to run as he pleased. So he said to the king, "I'll accept those terms, Your Majesty. By tomorrow morning the dragon will be slain."

"Bless you!" cried the king.

"Hooray, hooray, hooray!" cried all the people, throwing their hats in the air.

The cobbler's eldest son beamed with pride, and the second eldest looked at him enviously. The youngest son said timidly, "Excuse me, Your Majesty, but don't you think the queen looks a little unwell? If I were you, I think I'd water her."

"Good heavens," cried the king, glancing at the queen who had been changed into a rosebush, "I'm glad you mentioned it!"

Now the cobbler's eldest son was very clever and was known far and wide for how quickly he could multiply fractions in his head. He was perfectly sure he could slay the dragon by somehow or other playing a trick on him, and he didn't feel that he needed his wise old father's advice. But he thought it was only polite to ask, so he went to his father, who was working as usual at his cobbler's bench, and said, "Well, Father, I'm off to slay the dragon. Have you any advice to give me?"

The cobbler thought a moment and replied, "When and if you come to the dragon's lair, recite the following poem:

Dragon, dragon, how do you do?
I've come from the king to murder you.

Say it very loudly and firmly, and the dragon will fall, God willing, at your feet."

"How curious!" said the eldest son. And he thought to himself, "The old man is not as wise as I thought. If I say something like that to the dragon, he will eat me up in an instant. The way to kill a dragon is to outfox him." And keeping his opinion to himself, the eldest son set forth on his quest.

When he came at last to the dragon's lair, which was a cave, the eldest son slyly disguised himself as a peddler and knocked on the door and called out, "Hello there!"

"There's nobody home!" roared a voice.

The voice was as loud as an earthquake, and the eldest son's knees knocked together in terror.

"I don't come to trouble you," the eldest son said meekly. "I merely thought you might be interested in looking at some of our brushes. Or if you'd prefer," he added quickly, "I could leave our catalogue with you and I could drop by again, say, early next week."

"I don't want any brushes," the voice roared, "and I especially don't want any brushes next week."

Dragon, Dragon 169

1. **GUIDED READING:**
Predicting Outcomes
Do you think the eldest son will slay the dragon? Possible answer: No, this doesn't happen in fairy tales. Also, the eldest son is too confident and proud.

2. **GUIDED READING:**
Recognizing Humor
How do you think the rosebush queen looks? Probably her leaves look dry and her petals look withered.

3. **GUIDED READING:**
Making Inferences About Character
What is your opinion of the cobbler's eldest son? Since he decides to disregard his father's advice, he is probably too clever for his own good.

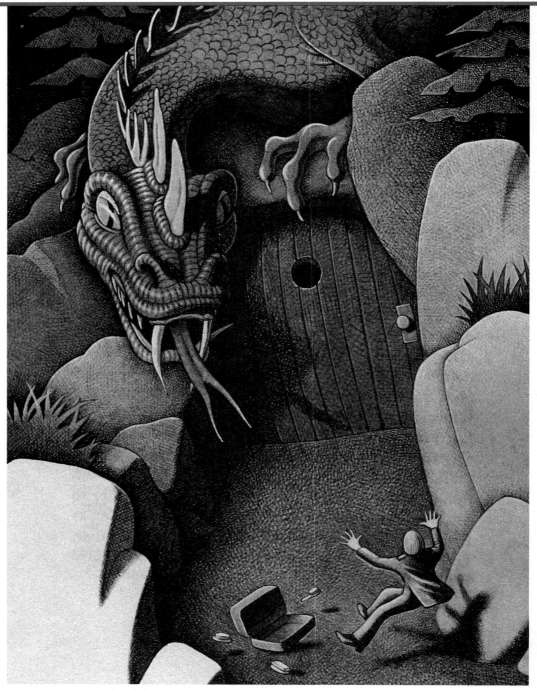

Suddenly a great shadow fell over him . . .

Illustration by Charles Shields.

MEETING INDIVIDUAL NEEDS

ESL/LEP • Refer to page 171 to review the use of adverbs. Ask students to name the ending that marks an adverb. (-ly) To what part of speech is the -ly suffix joined? (adjective) How many adverbs can students find on this page? (badly, bitterly, personally, perfectly, simply, loudly, firmly, terribly) In one of these, a final -e is omitted from the adjective before adding -ly. Which one? (simply)

"Oh," said the eldest son. By now his knees were knocking together so badly that he had to sit down.

Suddenly a great shadow fell over him, and the eldest son looked up. It was the dragon. The eldest son drew his sword, but the dragon lunged and swallowed him in a single gulp, sword and all, and the eldest son found himself in the dark of the dragon's belly. "What a fool I was not to listen to my wise old father!" thought the eldest son. And he began to weep bitterly.

"Well," sighed the king the next morning, "I see the dragon has not been slain yet."

"I'm just as glad, personally," said the princess, sprinkling the queen. "I would have had to marry that eldest son, and he had warts."

1 Now the cobbler's middle son decided it was his turn to try. The middle son was very strong and was known far and wide for being able to lift up the corner of a church. He felt perfectly sure he could slay the dragon by simply laying into him, but he thought it would be only polite to ask his father's advice. So he went to his father and said to him, "Well, Father, I'm off to slay the dragon. Have you any advice for me?"

The cobbler told the middle son exactly what he'd told the eldest.

"When and if you come to the dragon's lair, recite the following poem:

Dragon, dragon, how do you do?
I've come from the king to murder you.

Say it very loudly and firmly, and the dragon will fall, God willing, at your feet."

"What an odd thing to say," thought the middle son. "The old man is not as wise as I thought. You have to take these dragons by surprise." But he kept his opinion to himself and set forth.

2 When he came in sight of the dragon's lair, the middle son spurred his horse to a gallop and thundered into the entrance, swinging his sword with all his might.

3 But the dragon had seen him while he was still a long way off, and being very clever, the dragon had crawled up on top of the door so that when the son came charging in, he went under the dragon and onto the back of the cave and slammed into the wall. Then the dragon chuckled and got down off the door, taking his time, and strolled back to where the man and the horse lay unconscious from the terrific blow. Opening his mouth as if for a yawn, the dragon swallowed the middle son in a single gulp and put the horse in the freezer to eat another day.

"What a fool I was not to listen to my wise old father," thought the middle son when he came to in the dragon's belly. And he, too, began to weep bitterly.

That night there was a full moon, and the dragon ravaged the countryside so terribly that several families moved to another kingdom.

"Well," sighed the king in the morning, "still no luck in this dragon business, I see."

"I'm just as glad, myself," said the princess, moving her mother, pot and all,

Dragon, Dragon   171

---

1. GUIDED READING:
Predicting Outcomes
What trait of the cobbler's middle son will probably cause him trouble? He relies too much on his physical strength.

2. LITERARY ELEMENTS:
Vivid Verbs
Point out verbs that make the narration lively. Some of these are *spurred, thundered,* and *swinging.* There are others in the next paragraph.

3. GUIDED READING:
Making Inferences About Character
What does this action show about the dragon? He is tremendously large, clever, mean, and thrifty. Readers may feel sorry for the horse.

TRANSPARENCY 15
Literary Elements
Plot – invites students to explore the concept of a plot as a sequence of events.

1. LITERARY ELEMENTS:
Imagery
Why does the youngest son drag his sword along behind his horse "like a plow"? It is too heavy for him to carry any other way. Note the amusing visual image created by this simile. Students who are familiar with the Bible may recall the saying "hammer their swords into plowshares" (Isaiah 2:4). Knowing this quotation increases the irony of the situation.

2. GUIDED READING:
Contrasting Characters
How does the youngest son differ from his brothers? He is neither clever nor strong, but decent, honest, and obedient to his father, even when his father's advice makes him uneasy.

3. GUIDED READING:
Visualizing a Scene
Have students shut their eyes and imagine how the boy and dragon look in this scene.

---

to the window where the sun could get at her. "The cobbler's middle son was a kind of humpback."

Now the cobbler's youngest son saw that his turn had come. He was very upset and nervous, and he wished he had never been born. He was not clever, like his eldest brother, and he was not strong, like his second-eldest brother. He was a decent, honest boy who always minded his elders.

He borrowed a suit of armor from a friend of his who was a knight, and when the youngest son put the armor on, it was **1** so heavy he could hardly walk. From another knight he borrowed a sword, and that was so heavy that the only way the youngest son could get it to the dragon's lair was to drag it along behind his horse like a plow.

When everything was in readiness, the youngest son went for a last conversation with his father.

"Father, have you any advice to give me?" he asked.

"Only this," said the cobbler. "When and if you come to the dragon's lair, recite the following poem:

Dragon, dragon, how do you do?
I've come from the king to murder you.

Say it very loudly and firmly, and the dragon will fall, God willing, at your feet."

2 "Are you certain?" asked the youngest son uneasily.

"As certain as one can ever be in these matters," said the wise old cobbler.

And so the youngest son set forth on his quest. He traveled over hill and dale[3] and at last came to the dragon's cave.

The dragon, who had seen the cobbler's youngest son while he was still a long way off, was seated up above the door, inside the cave, waiting and smiling to himself. But minutes passed and no one came thundering in. The dragon frowned, puzzled, and was tempted to peek out. However, reflecting that patience seldom goes unrewarded, the dragon kept his head up out of sight and went on waiting. **3** At last, when he could stand it no longer, the dragon craned his neck and looked. There at the entrance of the cave stood a trembling young man in a suit of armor twice his size, struggling with a sword so heavy he could lift only one end of it at a time.

At sight of the dragon, the cobbler's youngest son began to tremble so violently that his armor rattled like a house caving in. He heaved with all his might at the sword and got the handle up level with his chest, but even now the point was down in the dirt. As loudly and firmly as he could manage, the youngest son cried—

Dragon, dragon, how do you do?
I've come from the king to murder you.

"What?" cried the dragon, flabbergasted.[4] "You? *You?* Murder *Me???*" All at once he began to laugh, pointing at the little cobbler's son. *"He he he ho ha!"* he

---

3. **dale:** valley.
4. **flabbergasted:** greatly surprised.

Short Stories

"Dragon, dragon, how do you do?"   Illustration by Charles Shields.

COOPERATIVE LEARNING

Have students read another humorous retelling of a familiar tale, Jon Scieszka's *The True Story of The Three Little Pigs.* Then have students work in small groups to write and share orally their own humorous interpretations of a traditional fairy tale or folk tale.

1. LITERARY ELEMENTS:

Plot

Does this story have a typical fairy tale ending? No, it is not entirely happy. The king is running away from a wet and angry queen.

---

roared, shaking all over, and tears filled his eyes. *"He he he ho ho ho ha ha!"* laughed the dragon. He was laughing so hard he had to hang onto his sides, and he fell off the door and landed on his back, still laughing, kicking his legs helplessly, rolling from side to side, laughing and laughing and laughing.

The cobbler's son was annoyed. "I *do* come from the king to murder you," he said. "A person doesn't like to be laughed at for a thing like that."

"*He he he!*" wailed the dragon, almost sobbing, gasping for breath. "Of course not, poor dear boy! But really, *he he,* the *idea* of it, *ha ha ha!* And that simply *ridiculous poem!*" Tears streamed from the dragon's eyes and he lay on his back perfectly helpless with laughter.

"It's a good poem," said the cobbler's youngest son loyally. "My father made it up." And growing angrier, he shouted, "I want you to stop that laughing, or I'll— I'll——" But the dragon could not stop for the life of him. And suddenly, in a terrific rage, the cobbler's son began flopping the sword end over end in the direction of the dragon. Sweat ran off the youngest son's forehead, but he labored on, blistering mad, and at last, with one supreme heave, he had the sword standing on its handle a foot from the dragon's throat. Of its own weight the sword fell, slicing the dragon's head off.

"*He he ho huk,*" went the dragon— and then he lay dead.

The two older brothers crawled out and thanked their younger brother for saving their lives. "We have learned our lesson," they said.

Then the three brothers gathered all the treasures from the dragon's cave and tied them to the back end of the youngest brother's horse, and tied the dragon's head on behind the treasures, and started home. "I'm glad I listened to my father," the youngest son thought. "Now I'll be the richest man in the kingdom."

There were hand-carved picture frames and silver spoons and boxes of jewels and chests of money and silver compasses and maps telling where there were more treasures buried when these ran out. There was also a curious old book with a picture of an owl on the cover, and inside, poems and odd sentences and recipes that seemed to make no sense.

When they reached the king's castle, the people all leaped for joy to see that the dragon was dead, and the princess ran out and kissed the youngest brother on the forehead, for secretly she had hoped it would be him.

"Well," said the king, "which half of the kingdom do you want?"

"My wizard's book!" exclaimed the wizard. "He's found my wizard's book!" He opened the book and ran his finger along under the words and then said in a loud voice, "Glmuzk, shkzmlp, blam!"

Instantly the queen stood before them in her natural shape, except she was soaking wet from being sprinkled too often. She glared at the king.

"Oh dear," said the king, hurrying toward the door.

174   Short Stories

CLOSURE

Have students make up endings for the following sentences about the story. In their endings, students should use both exaggeration and vivid verbs.

1. The dragon was so annoying to the people in the kingdom that _____.
2. The youngest son was so frightened by the dragon that _____.
3. The queen was so angry about being turned into a rosebush that _____.

For Study and Discussion

IDENTIFYING FACTS

1. Name four things that this dragon does to annoy people.
2. Describe what happens when the wizard tries to remember one of his old spells.
3. What advice does the cobbler give his sons before they go off to fight the dragon? How do they feel about the father and his advice?
4. Tell why the youngest son is successful. What is his reward?
5. One of the comical things about this fairy tale is that it combines details from modern life with regular fairy-tale details. Find three details that are out of place in a fairy tale (like the novels and house numbers in paragraph 3).

INTERPRETING MEANINGS

6. What do you think the queen will do next?
7. The **plots** of most fairy tales end happily ever after. Does this one? What happens to the two older brothers? the dragon killer? the queen? the wizard?
8. Characters and their actions often seem funny because the writer uses **exaggeration**. For example, this wizard is clumsy. If he were clumsy in an ordinary way, he might just have stayed in his palace room all day trying to remember his spells. But, instead, he is *so* clumsy that when he bungles a spell, he turns the queen into a rosebush. Tell about another character in the story who is funny because some characteristic is exaggerated.

APPLYING MEANINGS

9. This story teaches a **message** about wisdom. In real life, is it always the experts (like this wizard) who are wise? Or does wisdom often come from humble, unexpected sources? Who is wise in this story? Talk about the wise people you know.

Literary Elements

A STORY MAP

Just as you can draw a map of a section of the world to show its main features, so can you draw a map of a story to show its main elements. Following is a chart containing an outline for a "story map." Write this outline on a separate piece of paper and fill in the details. When you have finished, compare your story map to those of your classmates. Do your maps agree on the details?

Story Map
Title and author:
Setting:
Characters:
Main events in the plot: 1. 2. 3. and so on.
Conflict faced by the characters:
Solution to the conflict:
Story's message to me:

Dragon, Dragon   175

FOR STUDY AND DISCUSSION

Identifying Facts
1. The dragon ravages the countryside, frightens maidens, stops up chimneys, breaks store windows, sets clocks back, makes dogs bark, tips over fences, robs graves, puts frogs in drinking water, tears out the endings of novels, changes house numbers, steals spark plugs, puts firecrackers in cigars, steals clappers from church bells, springs bear traps, and changes roads around.
2. He accidentally turns the queen into a rosebush.
3. He tells them to recite a poem in front of the dragon's lair.

The first two sons conclude that their father isn't as wise as they thought. The youngest son is uneasy.

4. The youngest son is successful because he follows his father's advice.

His reward is half the kingdom and the princess's hand in marriage.

5. Out-of-place details include store windows, spark plugs, firecrackers, cigars, a democratic meeting, and a door-to-door salesman with a catalogue.

Interpreting Meanings
6. Perhaps berate the king; insist that the wizard

EXTENSION AND ENRICHMENT

Art. Students may enjoy working together to create a life-size mural showing the middle son crashing into the dragon's cave, while the dragon watches.

be dismissed; water the king.

7. Except for the queen, the plot ends happily.

The older brothers return to life, the dragon killer earns his reward, the queen regains her human shape, and the wizard finds his spell book.

8. The dragon is perhaps the foremost comic character. His exaggerated idea of his own power is the source of much of the humor.

Applying Meanings

9. In real life, wisdom comes from both sources.

In this story, the cobbler and his youngest son are both wiser than the reputed wizard. (Fairy tales often confound our expectations.)

Make sure students supply specific details.

LITERARY ELEMENTS
A Story Map
Title and Author: "Dragon, Dragon," John Gardner.
Setting: fairytale kingdom.
Characters: a dragon; a king, queen, and princess; a wizard; a cobbler and his three sons.
Main events: 1. The king calls a meeting; 2. The cobbler gives advice; 3. The two sons are defeated; 4. the third son kills the dragon.

176

Language and Vocabulary

VIVID VERBS

"Dragon, Dragon" uses striking verbs that make the humorous details in the story come alive. For instance, the writer says that the middle son "*thundered* into the entrance" of the dragon's cave. If he had written that the son "rode into the entrance," the action would have been the same. But the verb *thundered* makes us imagine that the son galloped into the cave with a lot of noise (like thunder).

The verbs in the following sentences are underlined. All of them are weak, tame verbs. Rewrite each sentence using a stronger verb—one that makes the action juicier, noisier, more exciting, more active. Exchange your papers in class. How many vivid verbs has your class thought of for each tame verb?

1. The dragon <u>said</u>, "I am the fiercest, toughest dragon around!"
2. The queen <u>dislikes</u> being a rosebush.
3. The youngest son <u>cuts off</u> the dragon's head.
4. The princess <u>comes out</u> of the palace to greet her hero.

Focus on Writing a Short Story

BUILDING A PLOT FROM A STORY IDEA

John Gardner builds his story on old fairy tales. To find your own story ideas, think first about your own experiences. Here are some possible sources for story ideas:

176   Short Stories

events you have witnessed
people you have met or imagined
stories you have heard
daydreams
pictures in magazines or albums

The characters in good stories usually face a **conflict** or problem. The **plot** of a story reaches a **climax,** or turning point, when the outcome of the conflict is decided one way or another. This is the point of greatest excitement or tension. In Gardner's story, the climax occurs when the cobbler's youngest son kills the dragon.

Working with a partner, brainstorm some story ideas together with a main conflict. Try building a plot around this conflict by filling out a chart like the one below. Save your notes.

Introduction	
Conflict	Climax
	Resolution

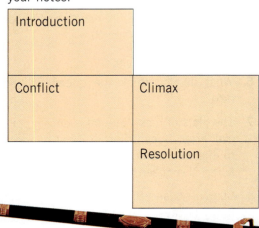

Dramatizing the Story

(A Group Activity)
This dragon-slaying story would be fun to act out in the classroom. Before you present the play, you will have to take the following steps:

1. List the **characters** you will need. Write a brief description of what each one should look like.
2. Block out your **scenes**. For example, you might decide to have these scenes:
   a. An opening scene in which a narrator tells the audience the background for the action.
   b. Scene 1: The Meeting
   c. Scene 2: The Eldest Son
   d. Scene 3: The Middle Son
   e. Scene 4: The Youngest Son
   f. Scene 5: Back at the Castle
3. Write your **dialogue.** Be sure to include some descriptions of how people are to say their lines (such as angrily, meekly, stupidly).
4. List your **props** (short for "properties"). These are all the movable items the actors will need (for example, the rosebush that was once the queen).
5. Plan your **costumes.** One of your challenges will be dressing the dragon.

Examples of plays can be found in Unit Six.

About the Author

John Gardner (1933–1982) is best known as a scholar and novelist. The story you have just read is from *Dragon, Dragon, and Other Tales*, his first collection for young readers. Each of the four stories in the collection gives a traditional fairy tale a humorous twist. For instance, in "The Tailor and the Giant," the beautiful princess is won not by the handsome prince but by the "timid little

tailor." Gardner also wrote the popular *Child's Bestiary*, a collection of humorous verses about animals. His famous book for adults, *Grendel*, is based on the well-known old English epic tale *Beowulf*. The tale is about the hero Beowulf, who battles and finally defeats the monster Grendel. Like his fairy tale spoofs, Gardner twists this tale by telling *his* story from the monster's point of view. Gardner said that his favorite authors when he was young were Charles Dickens and Walt Disney. He said "both created wonderful cartoon images, told stories as direct as fairy tales, knew the value of broad comedy, spiced up with a little weeping." He kept a statue of Dickens's head in his study "to keep me honest." Gardner was only forty-nine years old when he died in a motorcycle accident.

Conflict: The dragon is ravaging the kingdom.
Solution: The third son makes the dragon helpless with laughter and kills it.
Message: Perhaps: Honest goodness overcomes cleverness.

LANGUAGE AND VOCABULARY
Vivid Verbs
For answers, see the **Teaching Guide** at the beginning of the unit.

FOCUS ON WRITING A SHORT STORY
Building a Plot from a Story Idea
You may want to use one of the conflicts suggested in the activity and model for students how to build a plot around the conflict. Duplicate on the chalkboard the sample chart and fill in the **Conflict** box. Then work through the process of filling in the **Introduction, Climax,** and **Resolution** boxes.

DRAMATIZING THE STORY
The characters are the dragon, the king, the queen, the princess, the cobbler, the cobbler's three sons, the wizard, and extra knights and townspeople. Props include a sword, treasures, and a spell book.

OBJECTIVES

Students will describe conflicts and make inferences about the story. They will also draw conclusions about a character and use context clues to determine word meaning.

FOCUS/MOTIVATION

Building on Prior Knowledge. Ask your students what their grandparents or other elderly relatives or friends have told them about the Depression of the 1930s.

Prereading Journal. Have students write in response to the suggestion in the last paragraph of the headnote: Tell about something that you once wanted so very badly that it almost hurt.

TEACHING RESOURCES B
Teacher's Notes, p. 17
Reading Check, p. 20
Reading Focus, p. 21
Study Guide, pp. 22, 23
Language Skills, p. 24
Building Vocabulary, p. 27
Selection Vocabulary Test, p. 29
Selection Test, p. 30

CHARACTER

President Cleveland, Where Are You?

ROBERT CORMIER

Before You Read

This is a story about *want*. It takes place during the Depression of the 1930s, a period when many businesses failed and many people were out of work. It was a period when the whole nation was "in want." This story concerns eleven-year-old Jerry, who wants a particular thing.

Jerry's "want" creates the simple conflict that draws us into the story. We all know that feeling of wanting something so badly it hurts. Most of us have believed at one time or another that if only we could have that baseball mitt or that skateboard or that red dress, our life would become happy.

You'll see that in many ways, life was different in the 1930s. Boys and girls didn't collect baseball cards; they collected cowboy cards. Cowboys in the movies were big heroes then, just as sports figures are today. It costs Jerry only ten cents to see a movie, and only five cents to buy a candy bar.

Before you read about Jerry, write in your journal at least three sentences telling about something you once wanted so very badly it almost hurt.

178

READING THE STORY

Students could begin this story by taking turns reading aloud. After they identify with the likeable narrator, they can complete the reading as a homework assignment. Cormier is a popular young adult writer and the story should hook their interest.

Language and Vocabulary

Context refers to all the words or phrases or sentences that surround a particular word. You will probably come across some unfamiliar words in this story. Don't let this discourage you. Grappling with new words is the best way to increase your vocabulary. If a dictionary isn't handy, you can often guess a word's meaning by looking carefully at its context. Here are two kinds of context clues:

1. Sometimes a synonym (sin′ə·nim) of the word appears in the sentence. **Synonyms** are words with the same or nearly the same meanings.

2. Sometimes an antonym (an′tə·nim) appears in the sentence. **Antonyms** are words with opposite meanings. For example, in the third paragraph, Jerry says that Rollie Tremaine "did not live in a tenement but in a big white birthday cake of a house on Laurel Street." If you don't know what a *tenement* is, the context of this whole paragraph will give you a general idea. The sentence says that a tenement is different from a "big white birthday cake of a house." You can figure that a tenement is a place to live, and that it is not as desirable as that big white fancy house.

LANGUAGE AND VOCABULARY

The Language and Vocabulary box gives instruction on synonym and antonym context clues, both of which are found in this story. Students will find practice using synonym context clues in the Language and Vocabulary exercise at the end of the story, page 191.

President Cleveland, Where Are You?

Cultural Diversity

Students coming from cultures outside the United States may not be familiar with the Depression of the 1930s. Explain that this period in American history, beginning in 1929 and continuing through the 1930s, is also known as the Great Depression. The word *depression* refers to the fact that the economy was depressed or weakened, which meant unemployment, hunger, and suffering for millions of Americans.

1. GUIDED READING:
Making Inferences
Why does the narrator describe the cards in such detail? Apparently they are important to the characters.

2. LITERARY ELEMENTS:
Point of View
Who is telling the story? One of the boys, a first-person narrator (later identified as Jerry).

3. GUIDED READING:
Summarizing
What reasons does the narrator give for his statement that "you could almost hate Rollie Tremaine"? Rollie is the only son of a prosperous merchant and lives in a fine house. He is too fat to help the neighborhood team. He shows off his spending money and his cowboy cards.

1 That was the autumn of the cowboy cards—Buck Jones and Tom Tyler and Hoot Gibson and especially Ken Maynard. The cards were available in those five-cent packages of gum: pink sticks, three together, covered with a sweet white powder. You couldn't blow bubbles with that particular gum, but it couldn't have mattered less. The cowboy cards were important—the pictures of those rock-faced men with eyes of blue steel.

On those wind-swept, leaf-tumbling afternoons, we gathered after school on the sidewalk in front of Lemire's Drugstore, across from St. Jude's Parochial School, **2** and we swapped and bargained and matched for the cards. Because a Ken Maynard serial was playing at the Globe every Saturday afternoon, he was the most popular cowboy of all, and one of his cards was worth at least ten of any other kind. Rollie Tremaine had a treasure of thirty or so, and he guarded them jealously. He'd match you for the other cards, but he risked his Ken Maynards only when the other kids threatened to leave him out of the competition altogether.

3 You could almost hate Rollie Tremaine. In the first place, he was the only son of Auguste Tremaine, who operated the Uptown Dry Goods Store, and he did not live in a tenement but in a big white birthday cake of a house on Laurel Street. He was too fat to be effective in the football games between the Frenchtown Tigers and the North Side Knights, and he made us constantly aware of the jingle of coins in his pockets. He was able to stroll into Lemire's and casually select a quarter's worth of cowboy cards while the rest of us watched, aching with envy.

Once in a while I earned a nickel or dime by running errands or washing windows for blind old Mrs. Belander, or by finding pieces of copper, brass, and other valuable metals at the dump and selling them to the junkman. The coins clutched in my hand, I would race to Lemire's to buy a cowboy card or two, hoping that Ken Maynard would stare boldly out at me as I opened the pack. At one time, before a disastrous matching session with Roger Lussier (my best friend, except where the cards were involved), I owned five Ken Maynards and considered myself a millionaire, of sorts.

One week I was particularly lucky; I had spent two afternoons washing floors

MATH LINK

Invite interested students to make charts comparing the cost of goods and services during the 1930s with the cost of those same items today. Students could start with prices of goods and services mentioned in the story, such as baseball trading cards, movies, and children's compensation for household chores. How much have costs increased? The following chart headings might be used: Cost in 1930s, Cost Today, Percent Increase.

1. LITERARY ELEMENTS:
Simile
This colorful simile, which is explained in a footnote, will remind students of some of their friends.

for Mrs. Belander and received a quarter. Because my father had worked a full week at the shop, where a rush order for fancy combs had been received, he allotted[1] my brothers and sisters and me an extra dime along with the usual ten cents for the Saturday afternoon movie. Setting aside the movie fare, I found myself with a bonus of thirty-five cents, and I then planned to put Rollie Tremaine to shame the following Monday afternoon.

Monday was the best day to buy the cards because the candy man stopped at Lemire's every Monday morning to deliver the new assortments. There was nothing more exciting in the world than a fresh batch of card boxes. I rushed home from school that day and hurriedly changed my clothes, eager to set off for the store. As I burst through the doorway, letting the screen door slam behind me, my brother Armand blocked my way.

He was fourteen, three years older than I, and a freshman at Monument High School. He had recently become a stranger to me in many ways—indifferent to such matters as cowboy cards and the Frenchtown Tigers—and he carried himself with a mysterious dignity that was fractured now and then when his voice began shooting off in all directions like some kind of vocal fireworks.[2]

"Wait a minute, Jerry," he said. "I want to talk to you." He motioned me out

---

1. **allotted:** gave as a share.

2. **vocal fireworks:** many different levels of sounds— very deep one minute, high the next. (Armand's voice is changing because of his age.)

President Cleveland, Where Are You?

MEETING INDIVIDUAL NEEDS

ESL/LEP • The English language contains many idioms, expressions that cannot be understood from the individual meaning of each word. Some idiomatic expressions make reference to parts of the body. Two such idioms appear on pages 182 and 185 (earshot, by heart). Write the idiomatic expressions on the chalkboard and ask the class to restate each in simple, literal terms. Can students think of other idioms that refer to parts of the body?
Examples might include the following expressions:

That's no sweat off my back.
I'll give you a hand.
He volunteered to foot the bill.
She always sticks her nose into everyone else's business.
They elbowed their way through the crowd.

---

1. LITERARY ELEMENTS:
Conflict
What conflicts does this passage establish? It establishes the external conflict between the brothers over money and the more important internal conflict between Jerry's desire to buy cards and his need to be a generous son and brother.

2. LITERARY ELEMENTS:
Internal Conflict
Although Jerry has given Armand a total of fifteen cents for their father's present, he is keeping twenty cents for the cards he wants. For the time being the cards are winning out over family devotion.

3. LITERARY ELEMENTS:
Foreshadowing
How does Jerry know that something disastrous has happened? Roger is disconsolately kicking a tin can, and Rollie is sitting sullenly on the steps of the store.

---

of earshot of my mother, who was busy supervising the usual after-school skirmish in the kitchen.

I sighed with impatience. In recent months Armand had become a figure of authority, siding with my father and mother occasionally. As the oldest son he sometimes took advantage of his age and experience to issue rules and regulations.

"How much money have you got?" he whispered.

"You in some kind of trouble?" I asked, excitement rising in me as I remembered the blackmail plot of a movie at the Globe a month before.

1 He shook his head in annoyance. "Look," he said, "it's Pa's birthday tomorrow. I think we ought to chip in and buy him something . . ."

I reached into my pocket and caressed the coins. "Here," I said carefully, pulling out a nickel. "If we all give a nickel, we should have enough to buy him something pretty nice."

He regarded me with contempt.³ "Rita already gave me fifteen cents, and I'm throwing in a quarter. Albert handed over a dime—all that's left of his birthday money. Is that all you can do—a nickel?"

"Aw, come on," I protested. "I haven't got a single Ken Maynard left, and I was going to buy some cards this afternoon."

"Ken Maynard!" he snorted. "Who's more important—him or your father?"

His question was unfair because he knew that there was no possible choice—"my father" had to be the only answer. My father was a huge man who believed in the things of the spirit. . . . He had worked at the Monument Comb Shop since the age of fourteen; his booming laugh—or grumble—greeted us each night when he returned from the factory. A steady worker when the shop had enough work, he quickened with gaiety on Friday nights . . . and he was fond of making long speeches about the good things in life. In the middle of the Depression, for instance, he paid cash for a piano, of all things, and insisted that my twin sisters, Yolande and Yvette, take lessons once a week.

I took a dime from my pocket and **2** handed it to Armand.

"Thanks, Jerry," he said. "I hate to take your last cent."

"That's all right," I replied, turning away and consoling myself with the thought that twenty cents was better than nothing at all.

When I arrived at Lemire's I sensed **3** disaster in the air. Roger Lussier was kicking disconsolately⁴ at a tin can in the gutter, and Rollie Tremaine sat sullenly on the steps in front of the store.

"Save your money," Roger said. He had known about my plans to splurge on the cards.

"What's the matter?" I asked.

"There's no more cowboy cards," Rollie Tremaine said. "The company's not making any more."

---

3. **contempt:** (kən·tempt′): disgust or scorn.

4. **disconsolately** (dis·kon′sə·lit·lē): unhappily.

182 Short Stories

"They're going to have President cards," Roger said, his face twisting with disgust. He pointed to the store window. "Look!"

A placard in the window announced: "Attention, Boys. Watch for the New Series. Presidents of the United States. Free in Each 5-Cent Package of Caramel Chew."

"President cards?" I asked, dismayed.

I read on: "Collect a Complete Set and Receive an Official Imitation Major League Baseball Glove, Embossed[5] with Lefty Grove's Autograph."

Glove or no glove, who could become excited about Presidents, of all things?

Rollie Tremaine stared at the sign. "Benjamin Harrison,[6] for crying out loud," he said. "Why would I want Benjamin Harrison when I've got twenty-two Ken Maynards?"

I felt the warmth of guilt creep over me. I jingled the coins in my pocket, but the sound was hollow. No more Ken Maynards to buy.

"I'm going to buy a Mr. Goodbar," Rollie Tremaine decided.

I was without appetite, indifferent even to a Baby Ruth, which was my favorite. I thought of how I had betrayed Armand and, worst of all, my father.

"I'll see you after supper," I called over my shoulder to Roger as I hurried away toward home. I took the shortcut behind the church, although it involved leaping over a tall wooden fence, and I zigzagged recklessly through Mr. Thibodeau's garden, trying to outrace my guilt. I pounded up the steps and into the house, only to learn that Armand had already taken Yolande and Yvette uptown to shop for the birthday present.

I pedaled my bike furiously through the streets, ignoring the indignant horns of automobiles as I sliced through the traffic. Finally I saw Armand and my sisters emerge from the Monument Men's Shop. My heart sank when I spied the long, slim package that Armand was holding.

"Did you buy the present yet?" I asked, although I knew it was too late.

"Just now. A blue tie," Armand said. "What's the matter?"

"Nothing," I replied, my chest hurting.

He looked at me for a long moment. At first his eyes were hard, but then they softened. He smiled at me, almost sadly, and touched my arm. I turned away from him because I felt naked and exposed.

"It's all right," he said gently. "Maybe you've learned something." The words were gentle, but they held a curious dignity, the dignity remaining even when his voice suddenly cracked on the last syllable.

I wondered what was happening to me, because I did not know whether to laugh or cry.

Sister Angela was amazed when, a week before Christmas vacation, everybody in the class submitted a history essay worthy

---

5. **embossed** (im·bôst'): printed with letters that are raised above the surface.
6. **Benjamin Harrison:** the twenty-third President of the United States. (He served from 1889 to 1893.)

---

1. GUIDED READING:
Making Inferences About Character
Why isn't Jerry hungry for a Baby Ruth? He feels guilty and wants to contribute his money for his father's present after all.

2. GUIDED READING:
Recognizing Cause and Effect
Why does Jerry's chest hurt? It hurts because he has raced so fast and because he is sorry to be too late to give Armand more money.

3. GUIDED READING:
Making Inferences About Character
Why do you think Armand speaks gently? He knows that Jerry already feels miserable and sorry. Armand is by nature and by experience an understanding older brother.

President Cleveland, Where Are You?

**1. LITERARY ELEMENTS:
Characterization**
Does the author make Sister Angela seem real? Yes, she is a teacher with firm convictions and wise strategy.

**2. LITERARY ELEMENTS:
Plot**
What complication makes it hard for the boys to collect a complete set of Presidents? Entire boxes are often devoted to a single President.

**3. LITERARY ELEMENTS:
Plot**
Who has the strongest desire for the glove? Rollie Tremaine wants it so much he is willing to pay for extra cards or for the glove itself.

1 of a high mark—in some cases as high as *A*-minus. (Sister Angela did not believe that anyone in the world ever deserved an *A*.) She never learned—or at least she never let on that she knew—we all had become experts on the Presidents because of the cards we purchased at Lemire's. Each card contained a picture of a President, and on the reverse side, a summary of his career. We looked at those cards so often that the biographies imprinted themselves on our minds without effort. Even our street-corner conversations were filled with such information as the fact that James Madison was called "The Father of the Constitution," or that John Adams had intended to become a minister.

The President cards were a roaring success and the cowboy cards were quickly forgotten. In the first place we did not receive gum with the cards, but a kind of chewy caramel. The caramel could be tucked into a corner of your mouth, bulging your cheek in much the same manner as wads of tobacco bulged the mouths of baseball stars. In the second place the competition for collecting the cards was fierce and frustrating—fierce because everyone was intent on being the first to send away for a baseball glove, and frustrating because although there were only thirty-two Presidents, including Franklin Delano Roosevelt,[7] the variety at Lemire's was at a minimum. When the deliveryman

---

7. **Franklin Delano Roosevelt:** Roosevelt was elected to the presidency four different times. (He died in 1944 during his fourth term.)

left the boxes of cards at the store each Monday, we often discovered that one entire box was devoted to a single President—two weeks in a row the boxes contained nothing but Abraham Lincolns. One week Roger Lussier and I were the heroes of Frenchtown. We journeyed on our bicycles to the North Side, engaged three boys in a matching bout and returned with five new Presidents, including Chester Alan Arthur, who up to that time had been missing.

Perhaps to sharpen our desire, the card company sent a sample glove to Mr. Lemire, and it dangled, orange and sleek, in the window. I was half sick with longing, thinking of my old glove at home, which I had inherited from Armand. But Rollie Tremaine's desire for the glove outdistanced my own. He even got Mr. Lemire to agree to give the glove in the window to the first person to get a complete set of cards, so that precious time wouldn't be wasted waiting for the postman.

We were delighted at Rollie Tremaine's frustration, especially since he was only a substitute player for the Tigers. Once after spending fifty cents on cards—all of which turned out to be Calvin Coolidge—he threw them to the ground, pulled some dollar bills out of his pocket and said, "The heck with it. I'm going to buy a glove!"

"Not that glove," Roger Lussier said. "Not a glove with Lefty Grove's autograph. Look what it says at the bottom of the sign."

We all looked, although we knew the words by heart: "This Glove Is Not For Sale Anywhere."

Rollie Tremaine scrambled to pick up the cards from the sidewalk, pouting more than ever. After that he was quietly obsessed with the Presidents, hugging the cards close to his chest and refusing to tell us how many more he needed to complete his set.

I, too, was obsessed with the cards, because they had become things of comfort

President Cleveland, Where Are You? 185

SOCIAL STUDIES LINK
Suggest that interested students find out what happened on October 24, 1929, when the stock market in the United States collapsed. What effect did this collapse have on the United States economy? Is this something that could happen today? Why or why not? Ask students to record what they learn in their journals or learning logs or to share the information with the class in informal oral reports.

1. GUIDED READING:
Making Inferences About Character
What does this passage tell you about Jerry's father? He prefers to work, but he maintains his family during the layoff with his sound credit, personal economy, and wry humor. He is a proud man.

2. GUIDED READING:
Using Context Clues
What does muckalize mean? Apparently Armand has coined this word to mean "make muck of" or "smear." The context shows *muckalize* to be something terrible Armand will do to Jerry if Jerry tells his secret. As you know, most boys and girls use exaggerated threats.

3. GUIDED READING:
Self-Questioning
Do you agree with Jerry that love is an unnecessary waste of time? (Answers will vary considerably.)

---

in a world that had suddenly grown dismal. After Christmas a layoff at the shop had thrown my father out of work. He received no paycheck for four weeks, and the only income we had was from Armand's after-school job at the Blue and White Grocery Store—a job he lost finally when business dwindled[8] as the layoff continued.

1 Although we had enough food and clothing—my father's credit had always been good, a matter of pride with him—the inactivity made my father restless and irritable.... The twins fell sick and went to the hospital to have their tonsils removed. My father was confident that he would return to work eventually and pay off his debts, but he seemed to age before our eyes.

When orders again were received at the comb shop and he returned to work, another disaster occurred, although I was the only one aware of it. Armand fell in love.

I discovered his situation by accident, when I happened to pick up a piece of paper that had fallen to the floor in the bedroom he and I shared. I frowned at the paper, puzzled.

"Dear Sally, When I look into your eyes the world stands still . . ."

The letter was snatched from my hand before I finished reading it.

"What's the big idea, snooping around?" Armand asked, his face crimson. "Can't a guy have any privacy?"

He had never mentioned privacy before. "It was on the floor," I said. "I didn't know it was a letter. Who's Sally?"

2 He flung himself across the bed. "You tell anybody and I'll muckalize you," he threatened. "Sally Knowlton."

"A girl from the North Side?" I asked, incredulous.[9]

He rolled over and faced me, anger in his eyes, and a kind of despair too.

"What's the matter with that? Think she's too good for me?" he asked. "I'm warning you, Jerry, if you tell anybody . . ."

3 "Don't worry," I said. Love had no particular place in my life; it seemed an unnecessary waste of time. And a girl from the North Side was so remote that for all practical purposes she did not exist. But I was curious. "What are you writing her a letter for? Did she leave town, or something?"

"She hasn't left town," he answered. "I wasn't going to send it. I just felt like writing to her."

I was glad that I had never become involved with love—love that brought desperation to your eyes, that caused you to write letters you did not plan to send. Shrugging with indifference, I began to search in the closet for the old baseball glove. I found it on the shelf, under some old sneakers. The webbing was torn and the padding gone. I thought of the sting I would feel when a sharp grounder slapped into the glove, and I winced.[10]

---

8. **dwindled** (dwin′dəld): steadily shrank.

9. **incredulous** (in·krej′ə·ləs): unbelieving.
10. **winced:** twisted his face with pain.

186   Short Stories

PORTFOLIO ASSESSMENT

Conversations in "President Cleveland, Where Are You?" contain slang expressions used in the 1930s that are no longer in use today. Examples include "heck" and "muckalize." Computer-literate students may want to use a database program to create a small dictionary of currently used slang and colloquial words. Remind them that a dictionary contains short standard-English definitions. Some students may want to set up their database to sort alphabetically by slang term or by key word in its definition. Consult with students to agree on how their slang dictionaries will be assessed. (See *Portfolio Assessment and Professional Support Materials*, especially the section entitled **Suggestions for Portfolio Projects**.)

"You tell anybody about me and Sally and I'll—"

"I know. You'll muckalize me."

I did not divulge his secret and often shared his agony, particularly when he sat at the supper table and left my mother's special butterscotch pie untouched. I had never realized before how terrible love could be. But my compassion was short-lived because I had other things to worry about: report cards due at Eastertime; the loss of income from old Mrs. Belander, who had gone to live with a daughter in Boston; and, of course, the Presidents.

Because a stalemate[11] had been reached, the President cards were the dominant force in our lives—mine, Roger Lussier's, and Rollie Tremaine's. For three weeks, as the baseball season approached, each of us had a complete set—complete except for one President, Grover Cleveland. Each time a box of cards arrived at the store, we hurriedly bought them (as hurriedly as our funds allowed) and tore off the wrappers, only to be confronted by James Monroe or Martin Van Buren or someone else. But never Grover Cleveland, never the man who had been the twenty-second *and* the twenty-fourth President of the United States. We argued about Grover Cleveland. Should he be placed between Chester Alan Arthur and Benjamin Harrison as the twenty-second President, or did he belong between Benjamin Harrison and William McKinley as the twenty-fourth President? Was the card company playing fair? Roger Lussier brought up a horrifying possibility—did we need *two* Grover Clevelands to complete the set?

Indignant, we stormed Lemire's and protested to the harassed storeowner, who had long since vowed never to stock a new series. Muttering angrily, he searched his bills and receipts for a list of rules.

"All right," he announced. "Says here you only need one Grover Cleveland to finish the set. Now get out, all of you, unless you've got money to spend."

Outside the store, Rollie Tremaine picked up an empty tobacco tin and scaled it across the street. "Boy," he said. "I'd give five dollars for a Grover Cleveland."

When I returned home I found Armand sitting on the piazza[12] steps, his chin in his hands. His mood of dejection mirrored my own, and I sat down beside him. We did not say anything for a while.

"Want to throw the ball around?" I asked.

He sighed, not bothering to answer.

"You sick?" I asked.

He stood up and hitched up his trousers, pulled at his ear, and finally told me what the matter was—there was a big dance next week at the high school, the Spring Promenade, and Sally had asked him to be her escort.

I shook my head at the folly of love. "Well, what's so bad about that?"

---

11. **stalemate:** a draw where neither side can win.

12. **piazza** (pē·az′ə): in the United States, a large, covered porch.

---

1. GUIDED READING: Understanding Explicit Ideas
Does Jerry continue to feel compassion for Armand? No, he has other things to worry about.

2. GUIDED READING: Making Inferences About Character
Can you understand why Mr. Lemire is angry? Answers will vary. He wants to make money, but he has to spend too much time trying to satisfy the boys.

3. LITERARY ELEMENTS: Plot
Rollie Tremaine's willingness to pay five dollars for a Grover Cleveland is a significant detail of the plot.

MEETING INDIVIDUAL NEEDS

ESL/LEP • English has borrowed many words from other languages. Two examples on these pages include *corsage* and *piazza*.

Corsage, from the French language, means a small bouquet of flowers for a woman to wear. In Italy, a *piazza* is an open public square. It may also be used, as in the story, to mean a large covered porch. What other French and Italian words can students think of that are commonly used in English? Examples might include the following terms:
French—*bouquet, petite, crochet, boulevard, costume*
Italian—*pizza, cappuccino, opera, crescendo, pasta*

1. GUIDED READING:
Drawing Conclusions
At this point in the story, which brother has the more important problem? Answers may vary, but most students will feel sympathy for Armand.

2. GUIDED READING:
Making Inferences About Character
What does this speech tell you about Armand? He is the kind of older brother almost anyone would appreciate.

1   "How can I take Sally to a fancy dance?" he asked desperately. "I'd have to buy her a corsage . . . and my shoes are practically falling apart. Pa's got too many worries now to buy me new shoes or give me money for flowers for a girl."

I nodded in sympathy. "Yeah," I said. "Look at me. Baseball time is almost here, and all I've got is that old glove. And no Grover Cleveland card yet . . ."

"Grover Cleveland?" he asked. "They've got some of those up on the North Side. Some kid was telling me there's a store that's got them. He says they're looking for Warren G. Harding."

"Holy smoke!" I said. "I've got an extra Warren G. Harding!" Pure joy sang in my veins. I ran to my bicycle, swung into the seat—and found that the front tire was flat.

"I'll help you fix it," Armand said.   2

Within half an hour I was at the North Side Drugstore, where several boys were matching cards on the sidewalk. Silently but blissfully, I shouted, "President Grover Cleveland, here I come!"

After Armand had left for the dance, all dressed up as if it were Sunday, the small green box containing the corsage under his

188   Short Stories

CLOSURE

Ask students if they would have believed Jerry if he had concluded his story by saying, "As soon as I gave Armand the five dollars, I felt noble and happy." Why is the actual ending more true to life? Why do conflicts sometimes continue even after we have made the best decisions we can?

RETEACHING

After students have analyzed Jerry's internal conflict, you might ask if other characters in the story are also feeling internal conflicts. From what Jerry says about them, we can gather that Jerry's father feels internal conflict during the layoff and that Armand feels internal conflict when he falls in love. What struggle is going on in the father's mind? In Armand's mind? What change in point of view would help us understand the father? Armand?

---

arm, I sat on the railing of the piazza, letting my feet dangle. The neighborhood was quiet because the Frenchtown Tigers were at Daggett's Field, practicing for the first baseball game of the season.

1 I thought of Armand and the ridiculous expression on his face when he'd stood before the mirror in the bedroom. I'd avoided looking at his new black shoes. "Love," I muttered.

Spring had arrived in a sudden stampede of apple blossoms and fragrant breezes. Windows had been thrown open and dust mops had banged on the sills all day long as the women busied themselves with housecleaning. I was puzzled by my lethargy.[13] Wasn't spring supposed to make everything bright and gay?

I turned at the sound of footsteps on the stairs. Roger Lussier greeted me with a sour face.

"I thought you were practicing with the Tigers," I said.

"Rollie Tremaine," he said. "I just couldn't stand him." He slammed his fist against the railing. "Jeez, why did *he* have to be the one to get a Grover Cleveland? You should see him showing off. He won't let anybody even touch that glove . . ."

I felt like Benedict Arnold[14] and knew that I had to confess what I had done.

"Roger," I said, "I got a Grover Cleveland card up on the North Side. I sold it to Rollie Tremaine for five dollars."

---
13. **lethargy** (leth′ər·jē): a condition of feeling dull, tired, lifeless.
14. **Benedict Arnold**: a famous traitor in the American Revolutionary War.

"Are you crazy?" he asked.

"I needed that five dollars. It was an—an emergency."

"Boy!" he said, looking down at the ground and shaking his head. "What did you have to do a thing like that for?"

I watched him as he turned away and began walking down the stairs.

"Hey, Roger!" I called.

He squinted up at me as if I were a stranger, someone he'd never seen before.

"What?" he asked, his voice flat.

"I had to do it," I said. "Honest."

He didn't answer. He headed toward the fence, searching for the board we had loosened to give us a secret passage.

I thought of my father and Armand and Rollie Tremaine and Grover Cleveland and wished that I could go away someplace far away. But there was no place to go.

Roger found the loose slat in the fence and slipped through. I felt betrayed: Weren't you supposed to feel good when you did something fine and noble?

2 A moment later two hands gripped the top of the fence and Roger's face appeared. "Was it a real emergency?" he yelled.

"A real one!" I called. "Something important!"

His face dropped from sight and his voice reached me across the yard: "All right."

"See you tomorrow!" I yelled.

I swung my legs over the railing again. The gathering dusk began to soften the sharp edges of the fence, the rooftops, the **3** distant church steeple. I sat there a long time, waiting for the good feeling to come.

President Cleveland, Where Are You? 189

---

1. GUIDED READING:
Making Inferences About Character
Jerry mentions the "ridiculous expression" on his brother's face. How do you suppose Armand looks? He probably looks proud, happy, and dreamy.

2. GUIDED READING:
Making Inferences
Do you understand why Roger and Jerry are best friends? Answers will vary. They share many interests and attitudes. The ending of the story shows they can trust each other.

3. LITERARY ELEMENTS:
Internal Conflict
Why doesn't Jerry feel happy? Although he has helped Armand, he has had to sell his Grover Cleveland card to a boy he dislikes. He feels he has denied his own interests and betrayed his friends. Even though Jerry has done the right thing, he still suffers from the loss of something he wanted very much. (Life is not simple.)

EXTENSION AND ENRICHMENT

Social Studies. Have students interview their grandparents or their great-grandparents or other older people who know something about the Great Depression of the 1930s. Prepare for the interview by composing a class list of suitable questions. By making careful notes or transcribing from tape recorders, students can write the interview with many direct quotations—in other words, first-person reminiscences. Let students read the interviews aloud, and perhaps print them in a class magazine.

FOR STUDY AND DISCUSSION

Identifying Facts

1. Jerry feels that way because Rollie is rich, bad at sports, and insensitive to the other boys' envy.
2. Presidents became the topic of conversation and essays.
3. The two disasters were that Jerry's father lost his job and that his brother Armand fell in love.
4. Jerry sells the card to Rollie for five dollars for Armand's sake.

Interpreting Meanings

5. Armand wants to take Sally to the dance but feels he can't afford to.
6. Jerry feels guilty because he had been withholding his money from Armand in order to buy trading cards, which are now useless. "I jingled the coins . . . but the sound was hollow. No more Ken Maynards to buy" (page 183).
7. Jerry feels guilty for having held back money from his brother while leading Armand to believe that Jerry had already given him Jerry's "last cent" (page 182).
8. Jerry learned that he cared more about his father than about trading cards. More broadly, he learned that human relationships are more important than possessions.

For Study and Discussion

IDENTIFYING FACTS

1. Jerry says that "you could almost hate Rollie Tremaine." List the reasons Jerry gives for feeling this way about Rollie.
2. After the cowboy cards were phased out, what was the topic of street-corner talk and essays for Sister Angela?
3. Name the two disasters that occurred while Jerry was busy collecting President cards.
4. What does Jerry finally do with the President card he had so longed for?

INTERPRETING MEANINGS

5. Describe Armand's **conflict** when Sally asks him to the Spring dance. (What does he want? What is keeping him from getting it?)
6. Describe Jerry's **conflicts**. (What does he want? What keeps him from getting it?)
7. When Jerry learns that Lemire's store will sell President cards rather than cowboy cards, he says, "I felt the warmth of guilt creep over me." (Page 183) Why does Jerry feel guilty?
8. When Jerry catches up with Armand and finds that his brother and sisters have already bought their father's gift, Armand says, "Maybe you've learned something." (Page 183) What might Jerry have learned?
9. An **inference** is a guess you make based on evidence in the story. What inference can you make about why Jerry sold the President Cleveland card to Rollie?
10. At the end, Jerry says, "I sat there a long time, waiting for the good feeling to come." Why doesn't he feel good right away? Do you think eventually he *will* feel good about what he did?

APPLYING MEANINGS

11. In this story, Jerry makes a great sacrifice for his brother. Did you find his action believable? Did Armand deserve this good turn?

Focus on Reading

DRAWING CONCLUSIONS ABOUT CHARACTERS

A **conclusion** is a general statement about people and events. You make ("or draw") a conclusion based on what you learn in the story. For example, the list below gives information about Jerry's father's actions:

1. He works hard at the comb shop.
2. He buys his twin daughters a piano and pays for their lessons even though there is little money in the family.
3. When he works a full week, he gives his children an extra dime.

What can you conclude about Jerry's father?
Share your ideas with others in the class. You might want to edit your own conclusions after hearing what others have to say.

Literary Elements

CHARACTER

As you recall from Unit One, writers can create characters in six ways. Think of how Robert Cormier created Jerry's character. Fill in the chart that follows with details that bring Jerry to life. Can you find at least one detail for every box?

You might want to brainstorm in class and fill out the chart as a group.

How the writer reveals Jerry's character	
1. His appearance.	
2. His speech.	
3. His thoughts.	
4. His actions.	
5. The way he affects other people.	
6. Telling us directly what Jerry is like.	

Language and Vocabulary

CONTEXT CLUES
Use context clues to figure out the meanings of these italicized words from the story. Look for (1) synonyms for the unfamiliar word, and (2) definitions contained right in the sentence. Your guesses will be rough; be sure to check them in a dictionary.

1. "He smiled at me, almost sadly, and touched my arm. I turned away from him because I felt naked and *exposed*."
2. "Monday was the best day to buy the cards because the candy man stopped at Lemire's every Monday morning to deliver the new *assortments*. There was nothing more exciting in the world than a fresh batch of card boxes."
3. "After Christmas a *layoff* at the shop had thrown my father out of work."
4. " 'How can I take Sally to a fancy dance?' he asked desperately. 'I'd have to buy her a *corsage* . . . and my shoes are practically falling apart. Pa's got too many worries now to buy me new shoes or give me money for flowers for a girl.' "

Focus on Writing a Short Story

IMAGINING CHARACTERS
In his story Robert Cormier uses many details to help you "see" the main characters: Jerry, Armand, Roger, and Rollie. When you plan your own story, try to form a mental picture of the characters. Feel free to use people you know in real life as models for characters in your story. Describe their looks, speech, and actions as vividly as you can.

Review the notes you made for the assignment on page 176 or choose another story idea. Create at least two characters for your story by filling out a chart like the **Literary Elements** chart for Jerry on the left. Save your notes.

About the Author

Robert Cormier (1925–) is well known for his novels and stories for young adults. In his novels, heroes who find themselves isolated from friends and adults must struggle to cope with difficult problems on their own. For example, in *The Chocolate War* (1974), the hero, also called Jerry, attends a private school. Each year, the students sell chocolates to raise money for the school,

9. We can infer that Jerry sold the card to Rollie in order to help his brother Armand.
10. Possible answer: If a sacrifice is truly a sacrifice, we won't feel good right away.

Possible answer: I think that Jerry will eventually feel that he made the right decision and even come to feel good about it.

Applying Meanings
11. Most students will find Jerry's action believable in view of Jerry's character and will feel that Armand deserved the good turn.

FOCUS ON READING
Drawing Conclusions About Characters
Possible answer: Jerry's father is industrious and generous. He is willing to make sacrifices for his children and desires their happiness.

Possible answers: Jerry is a typical eleven-year-old in many ways, but he also shows a special sensitivity to others. Like his father, he cares about other people's happiness.

LITERARY ELEMENTS
Character
Possible answers:
1. Defenseless
2. and 3. Have students look for a speech that reveals values, and a key

thought. (Perhaps about the betrayal of his father, page 183)
4. Gives up something of value to help his brother
5. Trusted and valued by Armand and Roger
6. Feels guilty when he knows he has done something wrong

LANGUAGE AND VOCABULARY
Context Clues
For answers, see the **Teaching Guide** at the beginning of the unit.

FOCUS ON WRITING A SHORT STORY
Imagining Characters
After students have created characters by filling in their charts, have them work in pairs to determine whether the characters are believable and lifelike. In addition, by discussing their story ideas, partners can offer suggestions about how to improve the characters in the context of the story.

BEHIND THE SCENES
Comments in Robert Cormier's "A Marvelous Moment" are worth special attention. Ask students why Cormier felt like Columbus sighting land. Why is "a big white birthday cake of a house" the right image for Jerry's story?

---

even though they dislike doing it. One year, however, Jerry takes a stand and refuses to sell the candy. Two of Cormier's novels, *I am the Cheese* and *The Chocolate War*, have been made into movies.

Cormier is often recognized for his outstanding writing by such publications as *The New York Times*. He lives today in Leominster, Massachusetts.

Behind the Scenes

A Marvelous Moment

There's a sentence in "President Cleveland, Where Are You?" which is probably the most significant I have written in terms of my development as a writer. The sentence echoes back to a lost and half-forgotten story I wrote in the days when I was scribbling stories in pencil at the kitchen table. The story was about a boy from the poorer section of a town who falls desperately in love with a girl from the other side of town where the people live, or so he thinks, grandly and affluently. The story was told in the first person, the narrator was a twelve-year-old boy.

The problem concerned description. The narrator (and I, the writer) faced the problem of describing the girl's house, a thing of grandeur and beauty, white and shining, alien to the three-story tenement building in which the boy lived. How to describe such a house? I knew little about architecture, next to nothing at all. The house had an aura of graceful antiquity—was it a relic of some earlier era? It seemed that I had seen such houses in books—but what books? I knew nothing about researching such a subject and, anyway, I didn't want to burden the narrative with a long description of the house. In fact, this would not only be fatal to the forward thrust of the story, but would also not be consistent with what a twelve-year-old boy would know about architecture. Yet, I wanted to describe it as more than just a big white house.

The problem brought the story to a complete halt. I walked my hometown streets, desolated by the thought of all the things I did not know. How could someone so ignorant about so much ever become a writer? Back home, chewing at the pencil, I read and reread the words I had written. The lean clean prose of Ernest Hemingway and the simplicity of William Saroyan had affected me deeply, and I always told myself: Keep it simple, don't get too technical. So, let's apply those principles to the girl's house. Forget architecture—what did the house look like? Not what did it *really* look like, but what did it look like to this twelve-year-old boy?

Yes, that was the key—the viewpoint of the boy and not the writer. And from somewhere the description came. It looked like a big white birthday cake of a house! I knew this was exactly the kind of image I had sought. I felt the way Columbus must have felt when he sighted land.

In that moment, I had discovered simile and metaphor, had learned that words were truly tools, that figures of speech were not just something fancy to dress up a piece of prose but words that could evoke scene and event and emotion. Until that discovery at the kitchen table, I had been intimidated [frightened] by much of what I encountered in books of grammar, including the definitions of similes and metaphors. Suddenly, the definitions didn't matter. What mattered was using them to enrich my stories—not in a "Look, Ma, how clever I am" way, but to sharpen images, pin down emotions, create shocks of recognition in the reader.

At any rate, the story of the boy and the birthday cake of a house has been lost through the years. I doubt if it was ever published. In "President Cleveland, Where Are You?" I resurrected the description. It occurs in the second sentence of the third paragraph, a tribute to a marvelous moment in my hesitant journey toward becoming a writer.

—Robert Cormier

OBJECTIVES
Students will write a statement of theme. They will also predict outcomes and analyze and write similes.

FOCUS/MOTIVATION
Prereading Journal. As the headnote suggests, have students read almost to the end of column 1 on page 197. Then have them write down their predictions about how the story will end.

Establishing a Purpose for Reading. Have students read to determine whether their predictions are accurate.

TEACHING RESOURCES B
Teacher's Notes, p. 32
Reading Check, p. 35
Reading Focus, p. 36
Study Guide, pp. 38, 39
Language Skills, p. 40
Building Vocabulary, p. 43
Selection Vocabulary Test, p. 45
Selection Test, p. 46

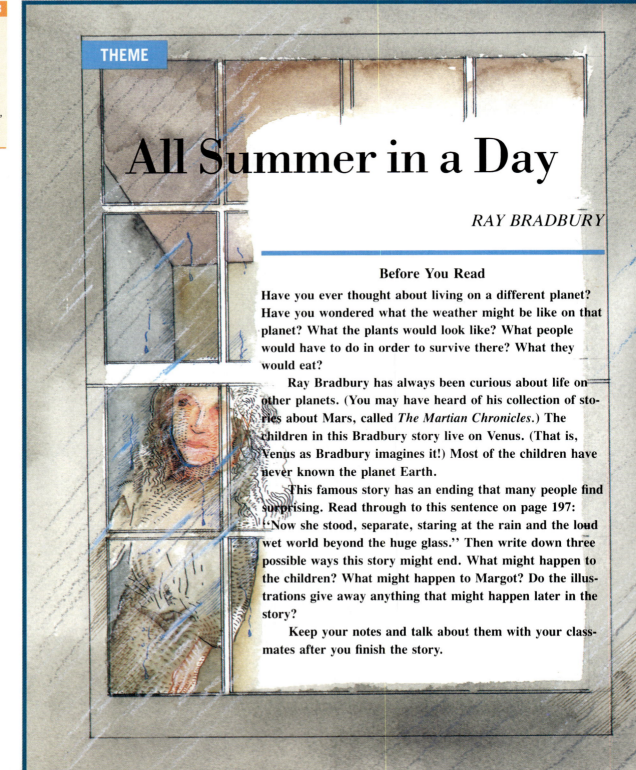

THEME

All Summer in a Day

RAY BRADBURY

Before You Read

Have you ever thought about living on a different planet? Have you wondered what the weather might be like on that planet? What the plants would look like? What people would have to do in order to survive there? What they would eat?

Ray Bradbury has always been curious about life on other planets. (You may have heard of his collection of stories about Mars, called *The Martian Chronicles*.) The children in this Bradbury story live on Venus. (That is, Venus as Bradbury imagines it!) Most of the children have never known the planet Earth.

This famous story has an ending that many people find surprising. Read through to this sentence on page 197: "Now she stood, separate, staring at the rain and the loud wet world beyond the huge glass." Then write down three possible ways this story might end. What might happen to the children? What might happen to Margot? Do the illustrations give away anything that might happen later in the story?

Keep your notes and talk about them with your classmates after you finish the story.

194

READING THE STORY

This is a challenging selection because students must visualize an unfamiliar imaginary setting and work through language that is filled with images and figures of speech. For this reason, you may want to have student volunteers read the story aloud.

MEETING INDIVIDUAL NEEDS

ESL/LEP • The introduction describes Margot "staring at the rain and the loud wet world." To reinforce this image, Bradbury uses many "wet" words on pages 196–197. Create small study groups and ask each group to make a list of these words. Then have a member of each group write their findings on the chalkboard. Here are a few examples:

rained	storms
raining	tidal waves
rain	washed
gush	wet
water	drenched
showers	

195

ART LINK
To foster students' appreciation of the power of figurative language, you might have them turn the similes in this story into art. First, they might locate all the similes they can find in the story and decide which they would like to visually interpret. You might suggest that they use construction paper and marking pens or colored pencils to depict the similes. Encourage students to show both the literal and the figurative meanings in their artistic interpretations. Have them label their artwork with the similes they depict. You could display their work under the title of the story.

1. LANGUAGE AND VOCABULARY
The Language and Vocabulary box on this page gives students help in using the many similes in this story to visualize its setting. For practice using similes, see the Language and Vocabulary exercise on page 204.

2. LITERARY ELEMENTS: Setting
How does Bradbury give a sense of the effects of all the rain? He uses vivid language and imagery to paint a scene of a planet buffeted by rain.

3. GUIDED READING: Making Inferences About Character
What does this sentence about Margot suggest about her character? Because she is the first character to be named, it makes her seem important. That she stands apart suggests that she may be in conflict with the other children.

Language and Vocabulary

1 This story contains many **similes** (sim'ə·lēs), that is, comparisons between two unlike things using the words *like* or *as*. Margot uses a simile when she says that the sun is "like a penny." This may seem an odd comparison at first. But think of the shape and color of a brand-new penny—it is round, coppery, and glints just like the sun. Watch for other similes as you read. Use them to visualize the story's setting. Do the similes sometimes make the story sound like poetry?

"**R**eady?"

"Ready."

"Now?"

"Soon."

"Do the scientists really know? Will it happen today, will it?"

"Look, look; see for yourself!"

The children pressed to each other like so many roses, so many weeds, intermixed, peering out for a look at the hidden sun.

It rained.

2 It had been raining for seven years; thousands upon thousands of days compounded and filled from one end to the other with rain, with the drum and gush of water, with the sweet crystal fall of showers and the concussion[1] of storms so heavy they were tidal waves come over the islands. A thousand forests had been crushed under the rain and grown up a thousand times to be crushed again. And this was the way life was forever on the planet Venus, and this was the schoolroom of the children of the rocket men and women who had come to a raining world to set up civilization and live out their lives.

"It's stopping, it's stopping!"

"Yes, Yes!"

Margot stood apart from them, from 3 these children who could never remember a time when there wasn't rain and rain and rain. They were all nine years old, and if there had been a day, seven years ago, when the sun came out for an hour and showed its face to the stunned world, they could not recall. Sometimes, at night, she heard them stir, in remembrance, and she knew they were dreaming and remembering gold or a yellow crayon or a coin large enough to buy the world with. She knew they thought they remembered a warmness, like a blushing in the face, in the body, in the arms and legs and trembling hands. But then they always awoke to the tatting drum, the endless shaking down of clear bead necklaces upon the roof, the walk, the gardens, the forests, and their dreams were gone.

All day yesterday they had read in

---

1. **concussion** (kən·kush'ən): violent shaking.

196 Short Stories

MEETING INDIVIDUAL NEEDS
Visual Learners • You might have students design a bulletin board, with a sun symbol prominent in the background, that would present their ideas about the theme of the story. Students could write their summaries of the themes on slips of paper, and each summary could be displayed on the bulletin board.

---

class about the sun. About how like a lemon it was, and how hot. And they had written small stories or essays or poems about it:

I think the sun is a flower,
That blooms for just one hour.

That was Margot's poem, read in a quiet voice in the still classroom while the rain was falling outside.

"Aw, you didn't write that!" protested one of the boys.

"I did," said Margot. "I *did*."

"William!" said the teacher.

But that was yesterday. Now the rain was slackening,² and the children were crushed in the great thick windows.

"Where's teacher?"

"She'll be back."

"She'd better hurry, we'll miss it!"

They turned on themselves, like a <u>feverish</u> wheel, all tumbling spokes.

Margot stood alone. She was a very frail girl who looked as if she had been lost in the rain for years and the rain had washed out the blue from her eyes and the red from her mouth and the yellow from her hair. She was an old photograph dusted from an album, whitened away, and if she spoke at all, her voice would be a ghost. Now she stood, separate, staring at the rain and the loud wet world beyond the huge glass.

"What're *you* looking at?" said William.

Margot said nothing.

---

2. **slackening:** falling off, lessening.

"Speak when you're spoken to." He gave her a shove. But she did not move; rather, she let herself be moved only by him and nothing else.

They edged away from her; they would not look at her. She felt them go away. And this was because she would play no games with them in the echoing tunnels of the underground city. If they tagged her and ran, she stood blinking after them and did not follow. When the class sang songs about happiness and life and games, her lips barely moved. Only when they sang about the sun and the summer did her lips move as she watched the drenched windows.

And then, of course, the biggest crime **1** of all was that she had come here only five years ago from Earth, and she remembered the sun and the way the sun was and the sky was when she was four in Ohio. And they, they had been on Venus all their lives, and they had been only two years old when last the sun came out and had long since forgotten the color and heat of it and the way it really was. But Margot remembered.

"It's like a penny," she said once, eyes closed.

"No it's not!" the children cried.

"It's like a fire," she said, "in the stove."

"You're lying, you don't remember!" cried the children.

But she remembered and stood quietly apart from all of them and watched the patterning windows. And once, a month **2** ago, she had refused to shower in the school shower rooms, had clutched her

---

1. LITERARY ELEMENTS:
Point of View
Whose thoughts does this paragraph express? It expresses the thoughts of the other children about Margot.

2. GUIDED READING:
Interpreting Meaning
Why didn't Margot want to shower? Possible answer: She hated water because it reminded her of the endless rain.

All Summer in a Day

SCIENCE LINK

As students read this science-fiction story about life on another planet, you might interest them in learning more about Venus and the other planets. Locate a map of the solar system and use it to talk about the planets, their relative distances from the sun and from one another, and what astronomers have learned about their climates and other characteristics.

You might also discuss space exploration and the information that space probes have given us about Venus. (In 1962 the first planetary probe, *Mariner 2,* flew by Venus. In 1975 *Pioneers 10* and *11* photographed Venus.)

1. GUIDED READING:
Making Inferences
Why were the children smiling? Possible answer: They thought they had finally given Margot what she deserved.

2. GUIDED READING:
Interpreting the Text
It is arguable that the children were so taken up with seeing the sun that they forgot that they were not "all here" or that they were lying as a group. Discuss which explanation your students think best fits the story.

3. LITERARY ELEMENTS:
Imagery
To help students get a sense of what the Venusian children experienced when the rain stopped, you might wish to bring in hand-held musical instruments such as cymbals or gongs. Have students play them all at once and then have them stop on your signal.

---

hands to her ears and over her head, screaming the water mustn't touch her head. So after that, dimly, dimly, she sensed it, she was different and they knew her difference and kept away.

There was talk that her father and mother were taking her back to Earth next year. It seemed vital to her that they do so, though it would mean the loss of thousands of dollars to her family. And so, the children hated her for all these reasons of big and little consequence.[3] They hated her pale snow face, her waiting silence, her thinness, and her possible future.

"Get away!" The boy gave her another push. "What're you waiting for?"

Then, for the first time, she turned and looked at him. And what she was waiting for was in her eyes.

"Well, don't wait around here!" cried the boy savagely. "You won't see nothing!"

Her lips moved.

"Nothing!" he cried. "It was all a joke, wasn't it?" He turned to the other children. "Nothing's happening today. *Is it?*"

They all blinked at him and then, understanding, laughed and shook their heads. "Nothing, nothing!"

"Oh, but," Margot whispered, her eyes helpless. "But this is the day, the scientists predict, they say, they *know,* the sun . . ."

"All a joke!" said the boy, and seized her roughly. "Hey, everyone, let's put her in a closet before teacher comes!"

"No," said Margot, falling back.

They surged about her, caught her up and bore her, protesting, and then pleading, and then crying, back into a tunnel, a room, a closet, where they slammed and locked the door. They stood looking at the door and saw it tremble from her beating and throwing herself against it. They heard her muffled cries. Then, smiling, they turned and went out and back down the tunnel, just as the teacher arrived.

"Ready, children?" She glanced at her watch.

"Yes!" said everyone.

"Are we all here?"

"Yes!"

The rain slackened still more.

They crowded to the huge door.

The rain stopped.

It was as if, in the midst of a film concerning an avalanche, a tornado, a hurricane, a volcanic eruption, something had, first, gone wrong with the sound apparatus,[4] thus muffling and finally cutting off all noise, all of the blasts and repercussions and thunders, and then, second, ripped the film from the projector and inserted in its place a peaceful tropical slide which did not move or tremor. The world ground to a standstill. The silence was so immense and unbelievable that you felt

---

3. **consequence** (kän′sə·kwens′): importance.

4. **apparatus** (ap′ə·rat′əs): device. (The author refers to the part of the film projector that controls sound.)

198 Short Stories

COOPERATIVE LEARNING

After students have read what Bradbury writes about his high school predictions, you might divide the class into a number of groups to make their own predictions about the future. Groups might warm up by listing some of the inventions and changes that have taken place during their lives. Then, they could think about those items in terms of future changes.

For example, CD-ROMs and cellular phones are relatively recent inventions that have come into general use during students' lifetimes. What creations in related fields do students think will be dreamed up next? After they have had time to work in a group, have students present their ideas to the class. Award small-inventor prizes to the groups with the most creative or most unusual ideas.

MEETING INDIVIDUAL NEEDS

Visual Learners • The illustrations for this story, somewhat unusual in their interpretation, might present a good opportunity for students to critique the artwork. You could ask them a series of questions to lead them into their evaluation, such as "Are the drawings useful in understanding the story? How or why are they helpful (or not helpful)? Why do you think the artist chose this particular style to draw the children? Why do you think the artist uses the unusual marks? the disproportionate bodies? the gray and muted colors? the empty landscapes?"

If you'd like students to write their evaluations, you might include the questions on evaluation sheets. Or several students might work together on their interpretations and present their findings to the class in a brief panel discussion with the theme "A picture is worth a thousand words."

1. GUIDED READING:
Interpreting Meaning
How does the actual appearance of the sun compare to Margot's description of it and what does this mean? It is very close to Margot's description which shows that she is truthful.

2. GUIDED READING:
Paraphrasing
Have students paraphrase this passage. How are the children feeling? (Ecstatic)

your ears had been stuffed or you had lost your hearing altogether. The children put their hands to their ears. They stood apart. The door slid back and the smell of the silent, waiting world came in to them.

The sun came out.

1 It was the color of flaming bronze and it was very large. And the sky around it was a blazing blue tile color. And the jungle burned with sunlight as the children, released from their spell, rushed out, yelling, into the springtime.

"Now, don't go too far," called the teacher after them. "You've only two hours, you know. You wouldn't want to get caught out!"

But they were running and turning **2** their faces up to the sky and feeling the sun on their cheeks like a warm iron; they were taking off their jackets and letting the sun burn their arms.

"Oh, it's better than the sun lamps, isn't it?"

"Much, much better!"

200 Short Stories

They stopped running and stood in the great jungle that covered Venus, that grew and never stopped growing, tumultuously,[5] even as you watched it. It was a nest of octopi,[6] clustering up great arms of flesh-like weed, wavering, flowering in this brief spring. It was the color of rubber and ash, this jungle, from the many years without sun. It was the color of stones and white cheeses and ink, and it was the color of the moon.

The children lay out, laughing, on the jungle mattress, and heard it sigh and squeak under them, resilient[7] and alive. They ran among the trees, they slipped and fell, they pushed each other, they played hide-and-seek and tag, but most of all they squinted at the sun until tears ran down

---

5. **tumultuously** (to͞o·mul′cho͞o·wəs·lē): wildly.
6. **octopi** (ok′tə·pī): the plural of *octopus*.

7. **resilient** (ri·zil′yənt): springy. (See page 165.)

All Summer in a Day **201**

CLOSURE
Have students discuss the predictions they made about the ending of the story. Which of the predictions seems the most logical, based on clues in the first part of the story (to bottom of column 1, page 197)?

EXTENSION AND ENRICHMENT
Science. Have students research the actual climate on Venus and compare it to the climate pictured by Bradbury.

1. GUIDED READING:
Drawing Conclusions
How do the children feel at the end? Possible answer: Since they learned that Margot had told them the truth about the sun and that it was as wonderful as she said, they might feel sympathetic toward her and her need for the sun and embarrassed and guilty about their own actions.

FOR STUDY AND DISCUSSION
Identifying Facts
1. The children are excited because on this day, for only the second time in their lives, the perpetual rain will stop briefly and the sun will shine.
2. The teacher had spent the whole preceding day teaching about the sun, and Margot has told them about it.
3. The sun only shines briefly every seven years. The rest of the time there is heavy rain.
4. Margot is different in several important ways. Unlike the other children, she spent four years on Earth, so she remembers the sun clearly. Also, she does not thrive in the climate of Venus and she hates and fears the rain.
   She looks frail and washed out by the rain.

---

their faces, they put their hands up to that yellowness and that amazing blueness and they breathed of the fresh, fresh air and listened and listened to the silence which suspended them in a blessed sea of no sound and no motion. They looked at everything and savored[8] everything. Then, wildly, like animals escaped from their caves, they ran and ran in shouting circles. They ran for an hour and did not stop running.

And then——

In the midst of their running, one of the girls wailed.

Everyone stopped.

The girl, standing in the open, held out her hand.

"Oh, look, look," she said, trembling.

They came slowly to look at her opened palm.

In the center of it, cupped and huge, was a single raindrop.

She began to cry, looking at it.

They glanced quietly at the sky.

"Oh. Oh."

A few cold drops fell on their noses and their cheeks and their mouths. The sun faded behind a stir of mist. A wind blew cool around them. They turned and started to walk back toward the underground house, their hands at their sides, their smiles vanishing away.

A boom of thunder startled them, and like leaves before a new hurricane, they tumbled upon each other and ran. Lightning struck ten miles away, five miles away, a mile, a half-mile. The sky darkened into midnight in a flash.

They stood in the doorway of the underground for a moment until it was raining hard. Then they closed the door and heard the gigantic sound of the rain falling in tons and avalanches, everywhere and forever.

"Will it be seven more years?"

"Yes. Seven."

Then one of them gave a little cry.

"Margot!"

"What?"

"She's still in the closet where we locked her."

"Margot."

They stood as if someone had driven them, like so many stakes, into the floor. They looked at each other and then looked away. They glanced out at the world that was raining now and raining and raining steadily. They could not meet each other's glances. Their faces were solemn and pale. They looked at their hands and feet, their faces down.

"Margot."

One of the girls said, "Well . . . ?"

No one moved.

"Go on," whispered the girl.

They walked slowly down the hall in the sound of cold rain. They turned through the doorway to the room in the sound of the storm and thunder, lightning on their faces, blue and terrible. They walked over to the closet door slowly and stood by it.

Behind the closet door was only silence.

They unlocked the door, even more slowly, and let Margot out.

---

8. **savored:** delighted in.

For Study and Discussion

IDENTIFYING FACTS
1. At the beginning of the story, why are the children so excited?
2. Most of the children have not seen the sun for seven years. How do they know about the sun?
3. The children in this story live on Venus. What is the most important fact about this **setting**?
4. How is Margot different from the other children? Describe what Margot looks like.
5. What happens on the outside while Margot is in the closet?

INTERPRETING MEANINGS
6. Describe what you think Margot will say or do now. What would you do if you were in her situation?
7. Differences among people often cause **conflicts,** or problems. What causes the conflict between Margot and the other children? Why does Margot keep to herself?
8. **Characters** in a story usually behave in certain ways for certain reasons. Why do you think the children lock Margot in the closet when they know how much the sun means to her?
9. On page 202, the children remember that Margot is still in the closet. The narrator says that the children's faces "were solemn and pale. They looked at their hands and feet, their faces down." What does this tell you about how the children feel?

APPLYING MEANINGS
10. The narrator says that Margot's parents may soon take Margot back to Earth. Leaving Venus, however, will cost them "thousands of dollars." Which would be more important to you: going home to the sunshine, or setting up a civilization on Venus, where the money is?
11. Do you think the hardships faced by pioneers like these people on Venus are worth it? Would you volunteer to be a colonist on a distant planet?

Focus on Reading

PREDICTING OUTCOMES
When you start to read a story, you almost automatically begin to predict its outcome. This means that you begin to make guesses at how the conflict will end. You begin to guess about what will become of various characters. Making predictions is one of the great pleasures of reading.

When you make predictions, you look for clues left by the writer. If the story is illustrated, you also look for clues in the illustrations. (Some people "cheat" and read the last paragraph of a story to find out before they start how the story ends!)

What predictions did you make before you completed this story? What clues did you base them on? Did the illustrations affect your predictions?

Do you like any of your predictions better than Bradbury's conclusion?

Suppose the ending was different. How would that affect your feelings about the story?

5. The sun comes out, and the other children run and play under it.

Interpreting Meanings
6. Students' answers should take account of the character traits that Margot has exhibited in the story. You may want to encourage students to discuss whether or not Margot will recognize the change that has occurred in the other children.
7. The conflict is partly caused by the children's jealousy that Margot knows something they do not. They are also reacting to Margot's own sense of aloneness and to the fact that she acts differently from what they consider to be normal behavior.

Margot keeps to herself because she knows that she is different and that the other children dislike her for that reason.
8. Students may answer that they want to pay her back for what they perceive as her bragging about her knowledge of the sun.
9. They feel embarrassed and guilty. They now realize what they have made Margot miss.

Applying Meanings
10. Students should give convincing reasons to support whichever choice they prefer.

11. Students may say that it is worthwhile to face hardships because it is so important to have alternative places for people to live, where they have food, shelter, and education. Or they may say that it is better to invest the effort to make things work on our own planet.

FOCUS ON READING
Predicting Outcomes
Students will likely respond that they predicted that *something* would happen to Margot.

Students should mention specific quotations from the story as clues.

The illustrations, by prominent illustrator Alan Cober, may have given the students some idea that the story has a dark side.

Students may find Bradbury's ending too "unfinished" to be satisfactory and may, therefore, prefer their own conclusions.

A happy Margo at the story's end would change the impact of the story completely.

LITERARY ELEMENTS
Theme
Students may say that a group might hurt an outsider when its members feel threatened or embarrassed.

Students may respond that cruelty is more often acted out by a group than by individuals.

Literary Elements

THEME
Theme is the heart of a story. Theme is what the story reveals about our lives. Theme is different from plot. **Plot** is "what happens" in a story. **Theme** is what a story means. When you are asked to summarize a plot, you can start out by saying, "The major events in this story are . . ." When you are asked to summarize a theme, you can start out by saying "This story revealed to me that . . ."

Some stories have stronger themes than others. This story has a particularly strong theme. Write at least one sentence telling what the story reveals about the reasons people sometimes hurt one another.

Always think about how a theme relates to your own life. Think about whether you agree with the theme. (You don't have to agree with what every writer says.) Can you think of times in real life when a group would hurt an outsider like Margot?

Do you think it is easier to be cruel to someone when you are a member of a group than when you are acting alone?

Language and Vocabulary

SIMILES
A **simile** compares two very different things, using words such as *like* or *as*. Below are two sentences from "All Summer in a Day" that use similes. Answer the questions about each simile.

1. "But they were running and turning their faces up to the sky and feeling the sun on their cheeks like a warm iron. . . ."
   a. What is the sun compared to?
   b. Write another simile about an iron that would be unpleasant.
2. "A boom of thunder startled them, and like leaves before a new hurricane, they tumbled upon each other and ran."
   a. What are the running children compared to?
   b. Make up another simile describing how the running children looked.
3. Write some similes of your own. You might start out like this:
   a. I am like a _____ (name a flower or a tree).
   b. I am as _____ as a _____ (name a piece of furniture).
   c. At times I resemble _____ (you might base your simile on cars, foods, or mechanical objects).
   d. I can _____ (name some action) like a _____ (think of an animal or bird).

Focus on Writing a Short Story

EXPLORING A THEME
The **theme** of a story is its central idea about life. Some writers start a story with a theme in mind. Others discover a theme part way through the writing process.

Choose a theme for a short story of your own. Here are some ideas:

Never give up.
Love is stronger than hate.
Look before you leap.

Make some notes about a plot and some characters that you might use to develop the theme you have chosen into a story. Save your notes.

About the Author

Ray Bradbury (1920–   ) has been called the world's greatest science fiction writer. Encouraged by his teachers, Bradbury was sending science fiction stories to magazines by the time he was fifteen. He even began his own little magazine. Since then, Bradbury has written more than thirty books and hundreds of stories, poems, and radio, television, and movie scripts. He has been a frequent writer for the TV series *Alfred Hitchcock Presents* and Rod Serling's *The Twilight Zone.* He is best known for his books *The Martian Chronicles, The Illustrated Man,* and *Fahrenheit 451.*

Unlike many science fiction writers, Bradbury is not much concerned with the machines and gadgets of the future. Instead, he often writes about the loneliness that might await us in the world of the future. Bradbury encourages young people to explore the universe. "The stars are yours," he says, "if you have the head, the hands, and the heart for them."

Literature and Science

Fact Versus Fiction

In "All Summer in a Day," Bradbury creates an imaginary setting for the planet Venus. Because Venus lacks oxygen, an important element in the water molecule, the average temperature on the planet is above 850 degrees Fahrenheit! If water did exist on Venus, it would boil away immediately. Scientists now speculate that Venus may at one time have had oceans and life forms but that the "greenhouse effect"—a process in which heat becomes trapped at the planet's surface—may have changed the face of Venus.

Making Connections: Activities

1. Imagine that people could take trips to Venus or another planet and, while unable to land or stay very long, they could orbit its surface. After collecting information in the library, create a travel brochure or pamphlet that describes the interesting things people would see and experience while orbiting Venus. On the front of your brochure, provide a colored illustration of the planet. Describe Venus' surface and conditions (weather, temperature, sunlight, clouds, gases). See if other members of the class would like to do similar projects for other planets.

2. Astronomers and scientists have speculated that Venus may have had swamps and living things millions of years ago, but the planet underwent drastic changes. Many people fear that Earth is now undergoing a "greenhouse effect." Working with a partner or a group of students, prepare a report that explains the process and efforts to stop its damaging effects on Earth.

All Summer in a Day **205**

LANGUAGE AND VOCABULARY
Similes
For answers, see the **Teaching Guide** at the beginning of the unit.

FOCUS ON WRITING A SHORT STORY
Exploring a Theme
To help students understand the concept of theme, you may want to review some of the stories that the class has read and discuss the themes of the stories. Lead students to see that most stories' themes are not stated directly; instead, the reader must infer the theme.

LITERATURE AND SCIENCE
Explain to students that science fiction is a form of writing based on imaginative adventures in time, space, and other dimensions. It speculates on a world that, given what we now know of science, might just one day be possible. As an alternative activity, you may want to divide students into small groups and assign a "What if?" science-fiction situation to each group. For example, you might ask one group, "What if robots became practical and affordable?" Allow the groups time to brainstorm and take notes, and then have each group report its ideas to the rest of the class. Encourage students to save their notes as future story ideas.

OBJECTIVES
Students will identify the theme of the story and predict outcomes. They will also use prefixes and suffixes to determine word meanings.

FOCUS/MOTIVATION
Establishing a Purpose for Reading. Have students read the headnote. Tell them to read this story to see how Maibon uses his wish.
Prereading Journal. See the suggestion in the headnote.

READING THE STORY
Many cultures have stories with lazy, foolish husbands who are at odds with their industrious, clever wives. Invite students from other cultures to share such a story with the class before they read this on-level story silently.

TEACHING RESOURCES B
Teacher's Notes, p. 48
Reading Check, p. 51
Reading Focus, p. 52
Study Guide, pp. 53, 54
Language Skills, p. 55
Building Vocabulary, p. 59
Selection Vocabulary Test, p. 61
Selection Test, p. 62

The Stone

LLOYD ALEXANDER

Before You Read
Have you ever asked your friends, "If you were granted one wish, what would it be?" It's a question that could keep you thinking for hours. The next story starts out normally enough, until the main character has a chance to change his life with a wish. Before you read the story, write in your journal your response to this question: How would you like to remain forever at the age you are now?

HEALTH LINK

To get students thinking about how much they grow in a day, you might ask a few students to search through their health books or check library resources to find out how much someone in their age bracket actually grows in a day. For example, how many new skin cells replace those sloughed off in a day? How much does a human hair grow in a day? How fast do bones grow, and how much can someone expect to increase in height in only a day? Have students report what they find out to the class.

Language and Vocabulary

One of the ways you can analyze words is by examining their parts. For example, this story opens on a day that is "cloudless." You probably know that *-less* is a **suffix** meaning "not, or without," and that *cloudless* means "without clouds." The suffix *-less* is used quite a lot in this story. You'll find a toothless baby, a calfless cow, and a fruitless tree. In fact, the whole story is about what it means to be "changeless." Do you know what *that* would be like?

1. LANGUAGE AND VOCABULARY
The Language and Vocabulary box on this page gives students help in determining the meanings of words with the suffix *-less*. The Language and Vocabulary exercise on page 217 gives students practice in using prefixes and suffixes to determine word meaning.

2. GUIDED READING:
Contrasting Characters
What contrasts do you see between Maibon and his wife? He talks and complains instead of working. She is practical and sensible.

There was a cottager named Maibon, and one day he was driving down the road in his horse and cart when he saw an old man hobbling along, so frail and feeble he doubted the poor soul could go many more steps. Though Maibon offered to take him in the cart, the old man refused; and Maibon went his way home, shaking his head over such a pitiful sight, and said to his wife, Modrona:

"Ah, ah, what a sorry thing it is to have your bones creaking and cracking, and dim eyes, and dull wits. When I think this might come to me, too! A fine, strong-armed, sturdy-legged fellow like me? One day to go tottering, and have his teeth rattling in his head, and live on porridge, like a baby? There's no fate worse in all the world."

"There is," answered Modrona, "and that would be to have neither teeth nor porridge. Get on with you, Maibon, and stop borrowing trouble. Hoe your field or you'll have no crop to harvest, and no food for you, nor me, nor the little ones."

Sighing and grumbling, Maibon did as his wife bade him. Although the day was fair and cloudless, he took no pleasure in it. His ax-blade was notched, the wooden handle splintery; his saw had lost its edge; and his hoe, once shining new, had begun to rust. None of his tools, it seemed to him, cut or chopped or delved as well as they once had done.

"They're as worn out as that old codger I saw on the road," Maibon said to himself. He squinted up at the sky. "Even the sun isn't as bright as it used to be, and doesn't warm me half as well. It's gone threadbare as my cloak. And no wonder, for it's been there longer than I can remember. Come to think of it, the moon's been looking a little wilted around the edges, too.

"As for me," went on Maibon, in dismay, "I'm in even a worse state. My appetite's faded, especially after meals. Mornings, when I wake, I can hardly keep myself from yawning. And at night, when I go to bed, my eyes are so heavy I can't

The Stone 207

MEETING INDIVIDUAL NEEDS

ESL/LEP • The author often uses pairs of *-ing* words to describe characters and objects. For example:

laughing and crowing (p. 210)
fretting and fuming (p. 212)
winking and glittering (p. 213)
rattling and clattering (p. 213)

All of these pairs, except one, describe sound. Which pair describes the way something looks rather than the way it sounds? (*winking* and *glittering*) You may want to explain the use of the word *crowing*. Ask students to name a farmyard animal that crows. (rooster) The verb *crow*, like the rooster, is associated with proud, boastful behavior. Invite the class to demonstrate the sound of *crowing*. You may also want to discuss the difference between *rattling* and *clattering*. Ask the class to suggest daily objects that rattle and clatter.

1. GUIDED READING:
Understanding Cause and Effect
If Doli could have made himself invisible, what would have happened? Maibon wouldn't have seen him and wouldn't have gotten a wish.

hold them open. If that's the way things are now, the older I grow, the worse it will be!"

In the midst of his complaining, Maibon glimpsed something bouncing and tossing back and forth beside a fallen tree in a corner of the field. Wondering if one of his piglets had squeezed out of the sty and gone rooting for acorns, Maibon hurried across the turf. Then he dropped his ax and gaped in astonishment.

There, struggling to free his leg which had been caught under the log, lay a short, thickset figure: a dwarf with red hair bristling in all directions beneath his round, close-fitting leather cap. At the sight of Maibon, the dwarf squeezed shut his bright red eyes and began holding his breath. After a moment, the dwarf's face went redder than his hair; his cheeks puffed out and soon turned purple. Then he opened one eye and blinked rapidly at Maibon, who was staring at him, speechless.

"What," snapped the dwarf, "you can still see me?"

"That I can," replied Maibon, more than ever puzzled, "and I can see very well you've got yourself tight as a wedge under that log, and all your kicking only makes it worse."

At this, the dwarf blew out his breath and shook his fists. "I can't do it!" he shouted. "No matter how I try! I can't make myself invisible! Everyone in my family can disappear—Poof! Gone! Vanished! But not me! Not Doli! Believe me, if I could have done, you never would have found me in such a plight. Worse luck! Well, come on. Don't stand there goggling like an idiot. Help me get loose!"

At this sharp command, Maibon began tugging and heaving at the log. Then he

208   Short Stories

stopped, wrinkled his brow, and scratched his head, saying:

"Well, now, just a moment, friend. The way you look, and all your talk about turning yourself invisible—I'm thinking you might be one of the Fair Folk."

"Oh, clever!" Doli retorted. "Oh, brilliant! Great clodhopper! Giant beanpole! Of course I am! What else! Enough gabbling. Get a move on. My leg's going to sleep."

1 "If a man does the Fair Folk a good turn," cried Maibon, his excitement growing, "it's told they must do one for him."

"I knew sooner or later you'd come round to that," grumbled the dwarf. "That's the way of it with you ham-handed, heavy-footed oafs. Time was, you **2** humans got along well with us. But nowadays, you no sooner see a Fair Folk than it's grab, grab, grab! Gobble, gobble, gobble! Grant my wish! Give me this, give me that! As if we had nothing better to do!

"Yes, I'll give you a favor," Doli went on. "That's the rule, I'm obliged to. Now, get on with it."

Hearing this, Maibon pulled and pried and chopped away at the log as fast as he could, and soon freed the dwarf.

Doli heaved a sigh of relief, rubbed his shin, and cocked a red eye at Maibon, saying:

"All right. You've done your work, you'll have your reward. What do you want? Gold, I suppose. That's the usual. Jewels? Fine clothes? Take my advice, go for something practical. A hazelwood twig to help you find water if your well ever goes dry? An ax that never needs sharpening? A cook pot always brimming with food?"

"None of those!" cried Maibon. He bent down to the dwarf and whispered eagerly, "But I've heard tell that you Fair Folk have magic stones that can keep a man young forever. That's what I want. I claim one for my reward."

Doli snorted. "I might have known you'd pick something like that. As to be expected, you humans have it all muddled. There's nothing can make a man young again. That's even beyond the best of our skills. Those stones you're babbling about? Well, yes, there are such things. But greatly overrated. All they'll do is keep you from growing any older."

"Just as good!" Maibon exclaimed. "I want no more than that!"

Doli hesitated and frowned. "Ah—between the two of us, take the cook pot. Better all around. Those stones—we'd sooner not give them away. There's a difficulty——" **3**

"Because you'd rather keep them for yourselves," Maibon broke in. "No, no, you shan't cheat me of my due. Don't put me off with excuses. I told you what I want, and that's what I'll have. Come, hand it over and not another word."

Doli shrugged and opened a leather pouch that hung from his belt. He spilled a number of brightly colored pebbles into his palm, picked out one of the larger stones, and handed it to Maibon. The dwarf then jumped up, took to his heels, raced across the field, and disappeared into a thicket.

---

1. BACKGROUND
This is a well-known rule in fairy tales. That Maibon has taken so long to formulate it reinforces how stupid he is.

2. GUIDED READING:
Understanding Contrast
What is Doli suggesting about people in this passage? They have become much greedier and more selfish than they once were.

3. GUIDED READING:
Drawing Conclusions
Maibon states what he thinks Doli was going to claim as the difficulty. What do you think Doli was going to say?

1. GUIDED READING:
Contrasting Characters
How do Modrona's ideas for wishes contrast with Maibon's? They are practical and useful. Most of them address the needs of the whole family rather than one member.

2. GUIDED READING:
Drawing Conclusions
Is the dwarf really dishonest? How can you tell? Possible answer: There is not enough information to draw a valid conclusion yet. But it is clear that Maibon's logic is faulty.

3. GUIDED READING:
Predicting Outcomes
What do you think has happened to the chickens? See if students can connect the unhatched eggs with Maibon's ungrown beard.

Laughing and crowing over his good fortune and his cleverness, Maibon hurried back to the cottage. There, he told his wife what had happened, and showed her the stone he had claimed from the Fair Folk.

"As I am now, so I'll always be!" Maibon declared, flexing his arms and thumping his chest. "A fine figure of a man! Oho, no gray beard and wrinkled brow for me!"

Instead of sharing her husband's jubilation, Modrona flung up her hands and burst out:

1 "Maibon, you're a greater fool than ever I supposed! And selfish into the bargain! You've turned down treasures! You didn't even ask that dwarf for so much as new jackets for the children! Nor a new apron for me! You could have had the roof mended. Or the walls plastered. No, a stone is what you ask for! A bit of rock no better than you'll dig up in the cow pasture!"

2 Crestfallen and sheepish, Maibon began thinking his wife was right, and the dwarf had indeed given him no more than a common field stone.

"Eh, well, it's true," he stammered, "I feel no different than I did this morning, no better nor worse, but every way the same. That redheaded little wretch! He'll rue the day if I ever find him again!"

So saying, Maibon threw the stone into the fireplace. That night he grumbled his way to bed, dreaming revenge on the dishonest dwarf.

Next morning, after a restless night, he yawned, rubbed his eyes, and scratched his chin. Then he sat bolt upright in bed, patting his cheeks in amazement.

"My beard!" he cried, tumbling out and hurrying to tell his wife. "It hasn't grown! Not by a hair! Can it be the dwarf didn't cheat me after all?"

"Don't talk to me about beards," declared his wife as Maibon went to the fireplace, picked out the stone, and clutched it safely in both hands. "There's 3 trouble enough in the chicken roost. Those

eggs should have hatched by now, but the hen is still brooding on her nest."

"Let the chickens worry about that," answered Maibon. "Wife, don't you see what a grand thing's happened to me? I'm not a minute older than I was yesterday. Bless that generous-hearted dwarf!"

"Let me lay hands on him and I'll bless him," retorted Modrona. "That's all well and good for you. But what of me? You'll stay as you are, but I'll turn old and gray, and worn and wrinkled, and go doddering into my grave! And what of our little ones? They'll grow up and have children of their own. And grandchildren, and great-grandchildren. And you, younger than any of them. What a foolish sight you'll be!"

But Maibon, gleeful over his good luck, paid his wife no heed, and only tucked the stone deeper into his pocket. Next day, however, the eggs had still not hatched.

The Stone 211

1. GUIDED READING:
Making Inferences
If possible, have students identify the exact place in the story at which they realized that the stone was having an effect on all of Maibon's property.

2. GUIDED READING:
Interpreting Meaning
Why do you think the stone came back? Maibon didn't really want to let it go.

1 "And the cow!" Modrona cried. "She's long past due to calve, and no sign of a young one ready to be born!"

"Don't bother me with cows and chickens," replied Maibon. "They'll all come right, in time. As for time, I've got all the time in the world!"

Having no appetite for breakfast, Maibon went out into his field. Of all the seeds he had sown there, however, he was surprised to see not one had sprouted. The field, which by now should have been covered with green shoots, lay bare and empty.

"Eh, things do seem a little late these days," Maibon said to himself. "Well, no hurry. It's that much less for me to do. The wheat isn't growing, but neither are the weeds."

Some days went by and still the eggs had not hatched, the cow had not calved, the wheat had not sprouted. And now Maibon saw that his apple tree showed no sign of even the smallest, greenest fruit.

"Maibon, it's the fault of that stone!" wailed his wife. "Get rid of the thing!"

"Nonsense," replied Maibon. "The season's slow, that's all."

Nevertheless, his wife kept at him and kept at him so much that Maibon at last, and very reluctantly, threw the stone out **2** the cottage window. Not too far, though, for he had it in the back of his mind to go later and find it again.

Next morning he had no need to go looking for it, for there was the stone sitting on the window ledge.

"You see?" said Maibon to his wife. "Here it is back again. So, it's a gift meant for me to keep."

"Maibon!" cried his wife. "Will you get rid of it! We've had nothing but trouble since you brought it into the house. Now the baby's fretting and fuming. Teething, poor little thing. But not a tooth to be seen! Maibon, that stone's bad luck and I want no part of it!"

Protesting it was none of his doing that the stone had come back, Maibon carried it into the vegetable patch. He dug a hole, not a very deep one, and put the stone into it.

212 Short Stories

1 Next day, there was the stone above ground, winking and glittering.

"Maibon!" cried his wife. "Once and for all, if you care for your family, get rid of that cursed thing!"

Seeing no other way to keep peace in the household, Maibon regretfully and unwillingly took the stone and threw it down the well, where it splashed into the water and sank from sight.

But that night, while he was trying vainly to sleep, there came such a rattling and clattering that Maibon clapped his hands over his ears, jumped out of bed, and went stumbling into the yard. At the well, the bucket was jiggling back and forth and up and down at the end of the rope; and in the bottom of the bucket was the stone.

Now Maibon began to be truly distressed, not only for the toothless baby, the calfless cow, the fruitless tree, and the hen sitting desperately on her eggs, but for himself as well.

2 "Nothing's moving along as it should," he groaned. "I can't tell one day from another. Nothing changes, there's nothing to look forward to, nothing to show for my work. Why sow if the seeds don't sprout? Why plant if there's never a harvest? Why eat if I don't get hungry? Why go to bed at night, or get up in the morning, or do anything at all? And the way it looks, so it will stay for ever and ever! I'll shrivel from boredom if nothing else!"

"Maibon," pleaded his wife, "for all our sakes, destroy the dreadful thing!"

Maibon tried now to pound the stone to dust with his heaviest mallet; but he could not so much as knock a chip from it. He put it against his grindstone without so much as scratching it. He set it on his anvil and belabored it with hammer and tongs, all to no avail.

At last he decided to bury the stone again, this time deeper than before. Picking up his shovel, he hurried to the field. But he suddenly halted and the shovel dropped from his hands. There, sitting cross-legged on a stump, was the dwarf.

"You!" shouted Maibon, shaking his fist. "Cheat! Villain! Trickster! I did you a good turn, and see how you've repaid it!"

The dwarf blinked at the furious Maibon. "You mortals are an ungrateful crew. I gave you what you wanted."

"You should have warned me!" burst out Maibon.

"I did," Doli snapped back. "You wouldn't listen. No, you yapped and yammered, bound to have your way. I told you we didn't like to give away those stones. When you mortals get hold of one, you stay just as you are—but so does everything around you. Before you know it, you're **3** mired in time like a rock in the mud. You take my advice. Get rid of that stone as fast as you can."

"What do you think I've been trying to do?" blurted Maibon. "I've buried it, thrown it down the well, pounded it with a hammer—it keeps coming back to me!"

"That's because you really didn't want to give it up," Doli said. "In the back of your mind and the bottom of your heart, you didn't want to change along with the

---

1. LITERARY ELEMENTS:
Conflict
What conflict has developed in this story? The conflict involves Maibon's efforts to get rid of the stone and his desire to keep it.

2. LITERARY ELEMENTS:
Characterization
It is his own sufferings from not being part of the growing, changing world that finally convince Maibon that his wish wasn't wise. Being out of the cycle of change has rendered life dull and meaningless.

3. LITERARY ELEMENTS:
Similes
What comparison does Doli use to explain the effects of the stone? He says you are "mired in time like a rock in the mud" (page 213).

The Stone 213

CLOSURE

Have students write one-sentence statements of the theme of this story.

RETEACHING

Have students look back at "The Algonquin Cinderella" and try to identify its theme by answering the following questions: What are the two older sisters like? How would you characterize the younger sister? How does the story end? What is the message?

EXTENSION AND ENRICHMENT

Science. Students may enjoy researching the topic *Alchemists* in encyclopedias or in books on the Middle Ages. They should note the ways that the alchemists tried to create gold.

rest of the world. So long as you feel that way, the stone is yours."

"No, no!" cried Maibon. "I want no more of it. Whatever may happen, let it happen. That's better than nothing happening at all. I've had my share of being young, I'll take my share of being old. And when I come to the end of my days, at least I can say I've lived each one of them."

"If you mean that," answered Doli, "toss the stone onto the ground, right there at the stump. Then get home and be about your business."

Maibon flung down the stone, spun around, and set off as fast as he could. When he dared at last to glance back over his shoulder, fearful the stone might be bouncing along at his heels, he saw no sign of it, nor of the redheaded dwarf.

Maibon gave a joyful cry, for at that same instant the fallow field was covered with green blades of wheat, the branches of the apple tree bent to the ground, so laden were they with fruit. He ran to the cottage, threw his arms around his wife and children, and told them the good news. The hen hatched her chicks, the cow bore her calf. And Maibon laughed with glee when he saw the first tooth in the baby's mouth.

Never again did Maibon meet any of the Fair Folk, and he was just as glad of it. He and his wife and children and grandchildren lived many years, and Maibon was proud of his white hair and long beard as he had been of his sturdy arms and legs.

"Stones are all right, in their way," said Maibon. "But the trouble with them is, they don't grow." **1**

The Stone 215

1. LITERARY ELEMENTS: Theme
How can you tell that this statement concerns the theme? The idea of growing and changing or of not growing and changing has been the central idea in the story so far. The stone represents the idea of not growing and changing.

LIBRARY AND ART LINK

After students have read Alexander's description of his hunger as a reader, you might plan a bulletin board (or paper mural) showing the reading tastes of class members. Students could draw or cut out a large table for the bulletin board or mural, spread it with serving plates, and design name tags for the guests. Each student could then draw a stack of book covers that show his or her particular reading tastes or favorite books. Students could paste their book stacks onto the serving plates and write their names on the name tags to complete the literary feast.

FOR STUDY AND DISCUSSION

Identifying Facts

1. He thinks the worst thing is to grow old.
2. Doli is one of the Fair Folk who are obliged to grant a favor to anyone who does them a good turn.
3. Doli suggests that Maibon wish for something practical like a twig to find water, an ax that never needs sharpening, or a cook pot that is always full.
   Maibon insists on having a stone that keeps its owner from growing any older.
4. The stone makes the owner and everything else around stay just as it is.
   The stone keeps Maibon's beard from growing, the chickens' eggs from hatching, the cow from calving, the wheat seeds from sprouting, the apple trees from bearing fruit, and the baby's teeth from coming in.
5. When Maibon really wants to get rid of the stone, he is able to do so, and things are able to change and grow again.

Interpreting Meanings

6. Maibon is selfish, impulsive, lazy, and foolish. He is also self-pitying, and he thinks he is clever.
   Unlike her husband, Modrona is practical.

For Study and Discussion

IDENTIFYING FACTS

1. What does Maibon think is the worst thing that can happen to him?
2. Who is Doli, and why does he grant Maibon a wish?
3. What does Doli suggest Maibon wish for? What wish does Maibon insist on?
4. How does the magic stone work? List all the effects it has on Maibon's household.
5. How does Maibon finally resolve his **conflict,** or problem?

INTERPRETING MEANINGS

6. How would you describe Maibon's **character**? (Is he impulsive? stupid? selfish? hard-working?) How is Maibon's wife different?
7. Maibon's troubles start when he sees a wizened old man in the road. Do you agree that Maibon "borrows trouble," as his wife puts it?
8. Doli makes some guesses about what Maibon will wish for. What does Doli think about human values, or at least the values of Maibon's society? How would Doli be surprised if Modrona had rescued him and had been granted the wish?

APPLYING MEANINGS

9. On a sheet of paper, write the heading "Doli, the Wish Granter, will grant one wish to each of those below." Pass the paper around and have your classmates write down their wishes. Are any wishes the same? Would Doli approve or disapprove of these wishes?

Focus on Reading

PREDICTING OUTCOMES

As you read this story, did you guess that Maibon's wish might not turn out the way he expected? Did you guess how the magic stone was actually keeping him from changing? As we read, we naturally make guesses about what's going to happen next. Look back over the story now and make a list of all the clues you found at the beginning of the story that **foreshadowed,** or hinted at, Maibon's foolishness. Then make a list of the clues that told you that the stone was working its magic. One reader has already filled in two clues, below.

Maibon's wish will be a mistake
1. Doli, who has experience in wish-making, thinks Maibon's choice is dumb.
2.
3.

The stone *is* magic
1. The first thing Maibon notices is that his beard doesn't grow.
2.
3.

Literary Elements

THEME

The **theme** of a story is its main idea, or the message the writer is sending you. This story has a very strong theme that should be easy to pick up. In fact, the story concludes with a statement that almost sums up its theme. To put you on the right track as you try to discover the story's theme, answer the questions below.

1. Why does Maibon quickly become disenchanted with his immortality?
2. When is Maibon truly able to throw the stone away without its coming back to him?
3. Explain what Maibon means when he says at the end, "Stones are all right, in their way. But the trouble with them is, they don't grow."
4. State the theme of "The Stone" in your own words. (A theme always has to be stated in a complete sentence.)
5. What do you think of the story's message or theme? If you were Maibon, how would you have felt about living forever?

Language and Vocabulary

PREFIXES AND SUFFIXES

As you know, **prefixes** are added to the front of words to alter their meanings. **Suffixes** are added to the ends of words to alter their meanings. Here are some useful prefixes and suffixes:

Prefixes:
in- "in, into," or "not"
un- "not, to do the opposite of"
pre- "before"
ante- "before"
anti- "against"

Suffixes:
-less "not, without"
-ish "of, belonging to, like"
-let "small, little, ornament"
-ful "full of, able to"

Use these prefixes and suffixes to answer the following questions:

1. How would you use a prefix to describe someone who cannot be seen?
2. How would you use a suffix to describe someone who is not at all scared?
3. What would you call a very small pig?
4. How would you use a suffix to describe someone who is full of gratitude?
5. How would you use a prefix and suffix to describe someone who has no feelings of gratitude at all?
6. If someone is said to be *antiwar,* is that person *against* war, or was that person born *before* a war?
7. If someone has a *prewar* house, was the house built *before* or *after* the war?

Writing About Literature

DESCRIBING A WISH THAT GOES WRONG

Doli advises Maibon to wish for something practical and then gives him several suggestions. Choose one of Doli's suggestions, and write a story about how that wish could go wrong. (For instance, would the hazelwood twig find water not only when Maibon needed it but also when he didn't?) Make up your own "wish that goes wrong" if you don't want to use one of Doli's. You can use Maibon and his wife as the characters in your story if you like, or you can invent new characters.

There is reason to believe that she is also generous, hard-working, and clever.
7. Possible answer: Yes, I agree, because if he hadn't started worrying about growing old, none of the problems would have happened. He should have just mended his tools and done his work.
8. Doli thinks humans are greedy and vain.
Modrona would have surprised him by being as practical as he could wish.

Applying Meanings
9. You might assign several students to act, in turn, as Doli and pass judgment on the class's wishes. In fairy tales, wishes almost always turn out badly; can students think of wishes that are certain to bring them what they really want? To be sure that no feelings are hurt or that privacy is not disturbed, you should ask for anonymous wishes.

FOCUS ON READING
Predicting Outcomes
Possible answer: I guessed that Maibon's wish wouldn't turn out well because he was so clearly a fool and didn't make good choices.
Possible answer: Yes, it was clear that nothing on his whole farm was changing.
Maibon's wish will be a mistake: 2. Doli says that

nothing can make a man young again. 3. Doli says the stones are overrated. 4. Maibon has proved he is pretty stupid anyway.

The stone is magic: 2. The chickens, cow, wheat, apple trees, and baby aren't growing and changing. 3. He can't get rid of the stone; it keeps coming back.

LITERARY ELEMENTS
Theme
1. He quickly becomes disenchanted because nothing changes and there's nothing to look forward to. (Page 213)
2. He is able to get rid of it when he is really willing to change along with the rest of the world.
3. He means that stones are not alive and cannot experience the kind of natural growth that people experience; from the cradle to the grave, we are always "growing" and changing.
4. Possible answer: Growing old is part of the change that is necessary to being human.
5. Possible answer: I think it is true.
   Possible answer: I would have felt it wasn't worth it when I saw what the consequences were. (Be ready for arguments.)

LANGUAGE AND VOCABULARY
For answers, see the **Teaching Guide** at the beginning of the unit.

About the Author

Lloyd Alexander (1924–   ) decided to become a poet at the early age of fifteen. His parents were unable to send him to college, so he found a job as a messenger in a bank after he graduated from high school. He spent most of his free time writing and trying to get his stories published. In 1943 he joined the army because, as he put it, "Adventure, I decided, was the best way to learn writing." After the war, Alexander wrote for a total of seventeen years before he found success by writing fantasy books for children. His most popular series is called the *Prydain Chronicles.* "The Stone" is taken from *The Foundling and Other Tales of Prydain.*

Alexander says he likes to write fantasy books because ". . . a wish is certainly a good way to start. There's no law in the fantasy world or in the real world that says some wishes can't come true. If fantasy is a kind of hopeful dream, it's nevertheless one that we made up ourselves."

Some of Alexander's recent titles are *The Hedera Adventure, The Philadelphia Adventure,* and *The Remarkable Journey of Prince Jen.*

Connecting Cultures

Wishes in Folklore
The wish is a familiar theme in the folklore of many cultures. A popular figure in the Russian *Baba Yaga* tales is the wise old woman who lives in the woods and has the power to make wishes come true. A similar character named Adivinadora appears in the folk tales of Spain. The genie in the Arabian tale "Aladdin and the Wonderful Lamp" is perhaps one of the most famous wish granters in literature.

Sometime during the nineteenth century, the Grimm brothers in Germany collected many popular European folk tales. Several of these classics center on the fulfillment of a wish, such as the tales about Cinderella, Sleeping Beauty, and Rumpelstiltskin.

Other folk tales you might like to read are China's "Chen Ping and His Magic Axe," Africa's "Pot Full of Luck" (Ashanti), and the Cherokee legend "Ahyoka and the Talking Leaves."

Making Connections: Activities
1. Read one of the stories listed above or one of the following. In a short report describe the character whose wish comes true. How does the granting of the wish change the character's life?

   Tuck Everlasting, a novel by Natalie Babbit
   "The Monkey's Paw," a short story by W. W. Jacobs
   "The Fisherman and His Wife," a fairy tale by Jakob and Wilhelm Grimm
   The Greek myth about King Midas (available in many collections of Greek mythology)

2. Choose a story that you and a few friends know well, such as the tale of Cinderella or Rumpelstiltskin. Using a cassette player, record the story as you remember it. Let each person tell a different part of the story. Compare the group's version with a printed version of the tale. What new and interesting details are introduced in the oral retelling of a familiar story?

Behind the Scenes

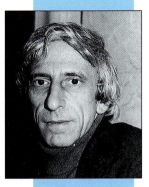

A Hungry Reader

I was always a hungry reader—in more ways than one. I gobbled up stories and never had my fill. At the same time, I wanted a real taste of whatever food the people in the stories were eating. Reading about the Mad Tea Party in *Alice in Wonderland*, I pleaded for a cup of tea, bread and butter, and treacle. (Treacle, I guessed, was something like pancake syrup.) My poor mother! How did she ever find patience to put up with her son's reading-and-eating habits!

In *Treasure Island* (you'll be reading it soon), bloodthirsty pirates nearly find young Jim Hawkins hiding in an apple barrel. So, of course, I had to munch an apple. . . .

However, when Robin Hood and his Merry Men dined on venison washed down with flagons of brown October ale, I could only make believe with a hamburger and a glass of root beer. A dish of cornmeal mush took the place of Indian maize when, sitting cross-legged under our living room lamp, I devoured *The Song of Hiawatha*. Our neighborhood grocer never sold—nor had we money to buy—anything like the rich feasts at *King Arthur's Round Table*. Instead of the roast goose of *A Christmas Carol*, I gnawed a chicken leg. The pages of *Winnie-the-Pooh*, along with my fingers, got sticky with honey. My mother's cookbook held no recipe for the nectar and ambrosia of Greek mythology; I settled for corn flakes and grape juice. Zeus must have smiled at that.

In time, to sighs of relief from my parents, I lost the habit of eating what I read about, but never my hunger for reading. I think the stories we love as children stay with us, somewhere in our hearts, to feed our imaginations. We never outgrow our need for them, any more than we outgrow our need for food. But, to me, the books I love are better than a feast.

—Lloyd Alexander

WRITING ABOUT LITERATURE
Describing a Wish That Goes Wrong
Suggest that students make the wish seem to work out at first and then give hints that foreshadow how things will go wrong.

CONNECTING CULTURES
As an alternative activity, have students work in small groups to write modern tales in which a character's wish is granted. In planning the story, students should create a main character who desires something and a wish-granter who has unique powers. Students should also specify why the wish is important and explain how the wish changes the main character's life. Encourage students to share their tales with the rest of the class.

OBJECTIVES
Students will analyze conflict and setting, rewrite five paragraphs from a different point of view, and "translate" dialect.

TEACHING RESOURCES B
Teacher's Notes, p. 64
Reading Check, p. 66
Study Guide, pp. 67, 68
Language Skills, p. 69
Building Vocabulary, p. 72
Selection Vocabulary Test, p. 73
Selection Test, p. 74

FOCUS/MOTIVATION
Establishing a Purpose. As Becky watches the Wheels-and-Brake Boys riding their bicycles, she longs for a bike of her own. Her widowed mother, who supports the family by sewing, and her Granny-Liz lecture Becky. They try to convince her that a girl shouldn't want a bike, but Becky says, "I want it and want it and want it." How can she change their minds and earn enough money to buy the beautiful bike of her dreams?

Prewriting Journal. Have students write their own answers to the questions at the end of the headnote.

POINT OF VIEW

Becky and the Wheels-and-Brake Boys

JAMES BERRY

READING THE STORY
Read aloud the first several paragraphs yourself so that students can enjoy the sound and sense of the lilting Jamaican dialect. Help them to interpret Becky's way of expressing herself. Be sure that boys as well as girls identify with Becky in knowing "total-total" how satisfying it would be to fufill a dream. Let students continue reading aloud or silently.

Before You Read

Like the earlier story by Robert Cormier, this story about a Jamaican girl is about *want*. Becky has a terrible craving for a bicycle and for the boys' world it will open for her. In spite of her family's lack of money, and the sensible advice of her mother and grandmother, Becky goes right on wanting—and in the end, working out a clever plan to try to get what she wants.

Jamaica is an island in the Caribbean Sea. Much of the island consists of farms where sugarcane, bananas, and coconut palm trees are grown. Becky's father used to work on one of these farms, but he has died before this story opens.

Before you read, write in your journal a response to this question: In your world, what activities do people feel girls should *not* do? What activities do they feel boys *should*, and *should not*, do? Or aren't there any differences?

Becky and the Wheels-and-Brake Boys 221

GEOGRAPHY LINK

After you introduce this story, you might want to have students locate Jamaica and the Caribbean Sea on a map or globe. Point out Jamaica's relationship to Mexico, Central America, Cuba, and the United States. Ask students what kind of climate they think Jamaica has, judging by its location. What would it be like to live on an island?

1. LANGUAGE AND VOCABULARY

The Language and Vocabulary box on this page gives students help with the Jamaican dialect in the story. The Language and Vocabulary exercise on page 230 gives students practice in "translating" the dialect.

The Jamaican dialect should not block students' enjoyment of this entertaining story. Assure students that they should be able to figure out the meanings of most of the dialect from context clues. Part of the pleasure in reading this selection comes from the lifelike speech and lilting vocal patterns.

2. GUIDED READING:
Understanding Dialect
No fair reason means "not fair that."

3. GUIDED READING:
Understanding Dialect
Total-total means "totally" or "absolutely."

4. LITERARY ELEMENTS:
Plot
What are the two reasons Becky's mother is not ready to buy Becky a bike? Her mother thinks bikes are for boys, and they cost too much.

Language and Vocabulary

1 **Dialect is a special form of a language spoken by people in a particular region (the Midwest, Brooklyn) or by people in a special group (teenagers, Irish immigrants).** In this story, the writer imitates the special way Jamaicans speak English. The story is written in the first person (using the pronoun *I*), so that you can almost hear Becky talking to you. You'll come across some strange expressions in this story, such as "I know total-total." And some words are pronounced in unusual ways, such as "dohn" for "don't" and "bwoy" for "boy." Read the story aloud. This will help you to understand the dialect. It will also make you feel as if you are in Jamaica, in Becky's world.

Even my own cousin Ben was there—riding away, in the ringing of bicycle bells down the road. Every time I came to watch them—see them riding round and round enjoying themselves—they scooted off like crazy on their bikes.

They can't keep doing that. They'll see!

I only want to be with Nat, Aldo, **2** Jimmy, and Ben. It's no fair reason they don't want to be with me. Anybody could go off their head for that. Anybody! A girl can not, not, let boys get away with it all the time.

Bother! I have to walk back home, alone.

3 I know total-total that if I had my own bike, the Wheels-and-Brake Boys wouldn't treat me like that. I'd just ride away with them, wouldn't I?

Over and over I told my mum I wanted **4** a bike. Over and over she looked at me as if I was crazy. "Becky, d'you think you're a boy? Eh? D'you think you're a boy? In any case, where's the money to come from? Eh?"

Of course I know I'm not a boy. Of course I know I'm not crazy. Of course I know all that's no reason why I can't have a bike. No reason! As soon as I get indoors I'll just have to ask again—ask Mum once more.

At home, indoors, I didn't ask my mum.

It was evening time, but sunshine was still big patches in yards and on housetops. My two younger brothers, Lenny and Vin, played marbles in the road. Mum was taking measurements of a boy I knew, for his new trousers and shirt. Mum made clothes for people. Meggie, my sister two years younger than me, was helping Mum on the veranda.¹ Nobody would be pleased with me not helping. I began to help.

Granny-Liz would always stop fanning herself to drink up a glass of ice water. I gave my granny a glass of ice water, there in her rocking chair. I looked in the kitchen to find shelled coconut pieces to cut into small cubes for the fowls' morning feed. But Granny-Liz had done it. I came and started tidying up bits and pieces of cut-off material around my mum on the floor. My sister got nasty, saying she was already helping Mum. Not a single good thing was happening for me.

With me even being all so thoughtful of Granny's need of a cool drink, she started up some botheration against me.

Listen to Granny-Liz: "Becky, with you moving about me here on the veranda, I hope you dohn have any centipedes or scorpions in a jam jar in your pocket."

"No, mam," I said sighing, trying to be calm. "Granny-Liz," I went on, "you forgot. My centipede and scorpion died." All the same, storm broke against me.

"Becky," my mum said. "You know I don't like you wandering off after dinner. Haven't I told you I don't want you keeping company with those awful riding-about bicycle boys? Eh?"

"Yes, mam."

"Those boys are a menace. Riding bicycles on sidewalks and narrow paths together, ringing bicycle bells and braking at people's feet like wild bulls charging anybody, they're heading for trouble."

"They're the Wheels-and-Brake Boys, mam."

"The what?"

"The Wheels-and-Brake Boys."

"Oh! Given themselves a name as well, have they? Well, Becky, answer this. How d'you always manage to look like you just escaped from a hair-pulling battle? Eh? And don't I tell you not to break the backs down and wear your canvas shoes like slippers? Don't you ever hear what I say?"

"Yes, mam."

"D'you want to end up a field laborer? Like where your father used to be overseer?"²

"No, mam."

"Well, Becky, will you please go off and do your homework?"

Everybody did everything to stop me. I was allowed no chance whatsoever. No chance to talk to Mum about the bike I dream of day and night! And I knew exactly the bike I wanted. I wanted a bike like Ben's bike. Oh, I wished I still had even my scorpion on a string to run up and down somebody's back!

I answered my mum. "Yes, mam." I went off into Meg's and my bedroom.

I sat down at the little table, as well as I might. Could homework stay in anybody's head in broad daylight outside? No. Could I keep a bike like Ben's out of my

---

1. **veranda** (və·ran′də): a long, open, outdoor porch.
2. **overseer**: someone who supervises laborers at their work.

Becky and the Wheels-and-Brake Boys 223

MEETING INDIVIDUAL NEEDS
Visual and Auditory Learners • To help students connect the colorful language to the colorful sights on the island of Jamaica, you might want to bring in some pictures of Jamaican people and their bright-colored clothing and homes for students to look at as you read and discuss this story. (Try back copies of *National Geographic* as a starting point.)

Then, you could use the predominant colors from the photos and any pictures that can be cut out as a start for a bulletin board entitled, "The Colorful Language of Jamaica." Students could select some of their favorite expressions from the story, write them on strips of paper, and add them to the bulletin board. Encourage students to explain why the language appeals to them. What makes words colorful?

---

1. LITERARY ELEMENTS:
Character
Becky fantasizes about an extraordinary bike, longs for the father who would have granted her wish, and then tumbles on a great idea. Note how resourceful and determined she is.

2. GUIDED READING:
Understanding Cause and Effect
What is the real cause of Granny-Liz's frustration? She wishes she were physically capable of doing more work to help her daughter support the family.

3. GUIDED READING:
Understanding Cause and Effect
Why don't the boys race away this time? They notice that Becky looks different. They enjoy showing off for a girl who admires them and looks nice.

---

1 head? Not one bit. That bike took me all over the place. My beautiful bike jumped every log, every rock, every fence. My beautiful bike did everything cleverer than a clever cowboy's horse, with me in the saddle. And the bell, the bell was such a glorious gong of a ring!

If Dad was alive, I could talk to him. If Dad was alive, he'd give me money for the bike like a shot.

I sighed. It was amazing what a sigh could do. I sighed and tumbled on a great idea. Tomorrow evening I'd get Shirnette to come with me. Both of us together would be sure to get the boys interested to teach us to ride. Wow! With Shirnette they can't just ride away!

Next day at school, everything went sour. For the first time, Shirnette and me had a real fight, because of what I hated most.

Shirnette brought a cockroach to school in a shoepolish tin. At playtime she opened the tin and let the cockroach fly into my blouse. Pure panic and disgust nearly killed me. I crushed up the cockroach in my clothes and practically ripped my blouse off, there in open sunlight. Oh, the smell of a cockroach is the nastiest ever to block your nose! I started running with my blouse to go and wash it. Twice I had to stop and be sick.

I washed away the crushed cockroach stain from my blouse. Then the stupid Shirnette had to come into the toilet, falling about laughing. All right, I knew the cockroach treatment was for the time when I made my centipede on a string crawl up Shirnette's back. But you put fair-is-fair aside. I just barged into Shirnette.

When it was all over, I had on a wet blouse, but Shirnette had one on, too.

Then, going home with the noisy flock of children from school, I had such a new, new idea. If Mum thought I was scruffy, Nat, Aldo, Jimmy, and Ben might think so, too. I didn't like that.

After dinner I combed my hair in the bedroom. Mum did her machining on the veranda. Meggie helped Mum. Granny sat **2** there, wishing she could take on any job, as usual.

I told Mum I was going to make up a quarrel with Shirnette. I went, but my friend wouldn't speak to me, let alone come out to keep my company. I stood alone and watched the Wheels-and-Brake Boys again.

This time the boys didn't race away **3** past me. I stood leaning against the tall coconut palm tree. People passed up and down. The nearby main road was busy with traffic. But I didn't mind. I watched the boys. Riding round and round the big flame tree, Nat, Aldo, Jimmy, and Ben looked marvelous.

At first each boy rode round the tree alone. Then each boy raced each other round the tree, going round three times. As he won, the winner rang his bell on and on, till he stopped panting and could laugh and talk properly. Next, most reckless and fierce, all the boys raced against each other. And, leaning against their bicycles, talking and joking, the boys popped soft drinks open, drank, and ate chipped bananas.

TRANSPARENCY 15
Literary Elements
Plot – invites students to explore the concept of plot as a sequence of events.

CLOSURE
Have two students explain the main conflict in the story, one from the point of view of Becky's mother and one from that of Granny-Liz.

EXTENSION AND ENRICHMENT
Listening. Have students listen for expressions in dialects other than their own and copy these in their journals to share with classmates. Sources might be students' conversations, television, movies, live performances, and dialogue read aloud from books. You may discover some students with special talent in close listening and mimicry.

1. GUIDED READING:
Understanding Cause and Effect
Why do the boys become "silent and serious" and ride away? Probably because Becky's grin and her wise comments have made them think.

2. LITERARY ELEMENTS:
Conflict
What prevents the conflict in Becky's life from being resolved in this passage? First Becky is about to persuade Mum to help her get a bike despite the cost, but then Granny-Liz argues in opposition.

I walked up to Nat, Aldo, Jimmy, and Ben and said, "Can somebody teach me to ride?"

"Why don't you stay indoors and learn to cook and sew and wash clothes?" Jimmy said.

I grinned. "I know all that already," I said. "And one day perhaps I'll even be mum to a boy child, like all of you. Can you cook and sew and wash clothes, Jimmy? All I want is to learn to ride. I want you to teach me."

1 I didn't know why I said what I said. But everybody went silent and serious.

One after the other, Nat, Aldo, Jimmy, and Ben got on their bikes and rode off. I wasn't at all cross with them. I only wanted to be riding out of the playground with them. I knew they'd be heading into the town to have ice cream and things and talk and laugh.

Mum was sitting alone on the veranda. She sewed buttons onto a white shirt she'd made. I sat down next to Mum. Straightaway, "Mum," I said, "I still want to have 2 a bike badly."

"Oh, Becky, you still have that foolishness in your head? What am I going to do?"

Mum talked with some sympathy. Mum knew I was honest. "I can't get rid of it, mam," I said.

Mum stopped sewing. "Becky," she said, staring in my face, "how many girls around here do you see with bicycles?"

"Janice Gordon has a bike," I reminded her.

"Janice Gordon's dad has acres and acres of coconuts and bananas, with a business in the town as well."

I knew Mum was just about to give in. Then my granny had to come out onto the veranda and interfere. Listen to that Granny-Liz. "Becky, I heard you mother tell you over and over she cahn[3] afford to buy you a bike. Yet you keep on and on. Child, you're a girl."

"But I don't want a bike because I'm a girl."

"D'you want it because you feel like a bwoy?" Granny said.

---

3. **cahn:** can't.

226 Short Stories

"No. I only want a bike because I want it and want it and want it."

Granny just carried on. "A tomboy's like a whistling woman and a crowing hen, who can only come to a bad end.[4] D'you understand?"

I didn't want to understand. I knew Granny's speech was an awful speech. I went and sat down with Lenny and Vin, who were making a kite.

By Saturday morning, I felt real sorry for Mum. I could see Mum really had it hard for money. I had to try and help. I knew anything of Dad's—anything—would be worth a great mighty hundred dollars.

I found myself in the center of town, going through the busy Saturday crowd. I hoped Mum wouldn't be too cross. I went into the fire station. With lots of luck I came face to face with a round-faced man in uniform. He talked to me. "Little miss, can I help you?"

I told him I'd like to talk to the head man. He took me into the office and gave me a chair. I sat down. I opened out my brown paper parcel. I showed him my dad's sun helmet. I told him I thought it would make a good fireman's hat. I wanted to sell the helmet for some money toward a bike, I told him.

The fireman laughed a lot. I began to laugh, too. The fireman put me in a car and drove me back home.

Mum's eyes popped to see me bringing home the fireman. The round-faced fireman laughed at my adventure. Mum laughed, too, which was really good. The fireman gave Mum my dad's hat back. Then—mystery, mystery—Mum sent me outside while they talked.

My mum was only a little cross with me. Then—mystery and more mystery—my mum took me with the fireman in his car to his house.

The fireman brought out what? A bicycle! A beautiful, shining bicycle! His nephew's bike. His nephew had been taken away, all the way to America. The bike had been left with the fireman-uncle for him to sell it. And the good, kind fireman-uncle decided we could have the bike—on small payments. My mum looked uncertain. But in a big, big way, the fireman knew it was all right. And Mum smiled a little. My mum had good sense to know it was all right. My mum took the bike from the fireman Mr. Dean.

And guess what? Seeing my bike much, much newer than his, my cousin Ben's eyes popped with envy. But he took on the big job. He taught me to ride. Then he taught Shirnette.

I ride into town with the Wheels-and-Brake Boys now. When she can borrow a bike, Shirnette comes too. We all sit together. We have patties and ice cream and drink drinks together. We talk and joke. We ride about, all over the place.

And, again, guess what? Fireman Mr. Dean became our best friend, and Mum's especially. He started coming around almost every day.

---

4. **tomboy's . . . end:** an old expression meaning that just as a hen does not crow, a woman shouldn't whistle. (Whistling was thought to be unladylike.)

---

1. GUIDED READING:
Drawing Conclusions
Do you think it's true that anything that belonged to Becky's dad is necessarily worth a lot of money? No, Becky's love for him makes her think so, however.

2. GUIDED READING:
Drawing Conclusions
Can you explain the actions that Becky calls mysteries? Yes, the fireman impresses Mum with his good humor and generosity. They are both interested in making Becky happy, and they are attracted to each other.

3. GUIDED READING:
Making Inferences About Character
Why does Ben teach Becky and Shirnette to ride? He admires Becky's new bike. Also he may be getting old enough to be interested in girls.

Becky and the Wheels-and-Brake Boys

PORTFOLIO ASSESSMENT

"Becky and the Wheels-and-Brake Boys" is a kind of stream-of-consciousness writing in which the natural flow of the storyteller's feelings, reflections, memories, and mental images are revealed as if they are just happening. Some students who want to experiment with this type of writing may want to write an autobiographical sketch in first person, similar to the next-to-last paragraph in the story. Students may want to exchange sketches with a partner and give anonymous dramatic readings of them. Readings may be audiotaped. Consult with students to agree on how their sketches and readings will be assessed. (See *Portfolio Assessment and Professional Support Materials,* especially the section entitled **Suggestions for Portfolio Projects.**)

FOR STUDY AND DISCUSSION

Identifying Facts

1. The Wheels-and-Brake Boys are a group of boys in Becky's neighborhood who ride bicycles together.
2. Becky wants a bicycle—because others have bicycles, and simply for fun.
   Lack of money and her mother's and grandmother's opposition keep her from getting one.
3. Becky tries to persuade her mother to buy a bicycle. She also tries to get the boys to teach her to ride. Then, she tries to sell her father's helmet in order to get money.
   At the end, Becky gets a bike, is taught by Ben to ride it, and becomes a frequent companion of the Wheels-and-Brake Boys. In addition, it appears that the fireman will become her stepfather.

Identifying Meanings

4. As a result of Becky's meeting with the fireman, Becky gets a bicycle and "Fireman Mr. Dean became our best friend, and Mum's especially" (page 227).
5. First, her mother asks Becky, "Where's the money to come from?" (page 222). Second, her mother points out that the father of the one other girl who owns a bike is very prosperous (page 226).

For Study and Discussion

IDENTIFYING FACTS

1. The story has an unusual **title.** Who are the Wheels-and-Brake Boys?
2. What does Becky want so badly? Why does she want it? What keeps her from getting it?
3. What steps does Becky take to solve her problem, or **conflict?** How does life change for her at the story's end?

INTERPRETING MEANINGS

4. Name two good things that result from Becky's meeting with the fireman.
5. Becky knows that her family doesn't have much money. Yet she keeps asking her mother for the bike. Make a list of the events that lead up to Becky's thinking, "I could see Mum really had it hard for money." (Page 227)
6. Granny says to Becky, "A tomboy's like a whistling woman and a crowing hen . . ." (Page 227) What is Granny's message? Why does Becky say it was an "awful speech"? Do you agree?
7. Other characters in this story besides Granny have firm ideas about the roles males and females should play. What are some of these ideas? How does Becky rebel against them?

APPLYING MEANINGS

8. Many people in this story think that Becky should not have a bicycle because she is a girl. Name other things that some people believe girls should *not* have. Then name things that some people think *boys* should not have. What do you think of these ideas?
9. This story is **set** in Jamaica. Could it happen where you live? What details in the story would change if its setting were your own town or city?
10. If you want to play a trick on a friend in Jamaica, you can pick up a bug on the way to school. What jokes do children play on each other in your neighborhood? Can any of them become cruel or harsh?

228 Short Stories

Focus on Reading

READING ALOUD (A Group Project)

Prepare this story for oral reading. First, you will have to decide how many readers you will need. You might want to assign one narrator to read Becky's voice and have separate readers read each of the other characters' lines.

Next, be sure you practice the dialect before you present your reading. How will one character's voice be different from another's?

Finally, decide who your audience will be. Your presentation to a group of younger children might be quite different from your presentation to parents or a group of boys and girls who are your own age.

Literary Elements

POINT OF VIEW

Point of view refers to the vantage point from which a story is told. Many stories are told from an **omniscient** (om·nish′ənt) point of view, that is, by someone who knows everything about every character and every event, past, present, and future. *Omniscient* means "all-knowing." The omniscient narrator is just that: all-knowing, like a god.

Many stories are told from the **first-person** point of view. This means that an "I" tells the story, someone who is a character in the story. Becky tells this story using the first-person pronoun *I*.

Becky's story would be very different if it were told by an omniscient narrator.

Third, her Granny-Liz reminds her that her mother has told Becky that they can't afford a bike (page 226).

6. Granny's message is that females should stay within traditional roles.

Becky says it was an "awful speech" both because she disagrees and because it was antagonistic to her.

Most students today will agree with Becky.

7. Mum shares Granny's views about gender roles, though her views are less rigid, and Jimmy says, "Why don't you stay indoors and learn to cook and sew and wash clothes?" (page 226).

Becky rebels by persevering in her pursuit of a bicycle.

Applying Meanings

8. Some common ideas include these: girls should not play active sports, girls should not like math and computers, boys should not play with dolls, boys should not be gentle, boys should not like the arts.

Students' opinions about these stereotypes may vary.

9. Though specific details may vary greatly, the basic conflicts in the story (child vs. parents; boys vs. girls) never change, nor does the fact that all of us want things desperately from

MEETING INDIVIDUAL NEEDS
Auditory Learners • Students who are not familiar with the Jamaican dialect may not appreciate the lyric quality of the language until it is read aloud to them. If you are not able to pronounce the dialect comfortably, you might try locating someone who is from Jamaica or who is familiar with dialects and could effectively mimic the tone of voice and the turns of phrase. Another possibility is finding a recording of Jamaican music, which could also demonstrate the lilting sounds of the dialect.

time to time, just as Becky wanted that bicycle.

10. Traditional American school-age pranks include hiding hats, lunchboxes, briefcases, and balls.

Most students will agree that any prank can turn cruel. (Refer to "All Summer in a Day" on page 194.)

FOCUS ON READING
Reading Aloud
The students who read Mum's and Fireman Dean's lines should sound mature, and the student who reads Granny's lines should be able to mimic an elderly person. An audience of children might need an introduction to dialect.

LITERARY ELEMENTS
Point of View
Look for understanding of the concept of point of view, including consistent substitution of *she* for *I* and *her* for *my* and use of standard English instead of dialect.

"President Cleveland, Where Are You?" is told from the first-person point of view, as the use of *I* shows. In rewriting "Dragon, Dragon," possible first-person viewpoints include the dragon, the king, the princess, the wizard, the cobbler, the cobbler's third son, or, less likely, one of the other sons, a knight or other citizen, or the queen.

Take the first five paragraphs of the story, down to "I'd just ride away with them, wouldn't I?" Rewrite these paragraphs as if they are being told by an omniscient narrator. You will have to drop the "I." You will have to drop Becky's dialect. Here is how the opening could be rewritten:

Even Becky's own cousin Ben was there.

Which point of view is "President Cleveland, Where Are You?" (page 178) told from? How can you tell?

"Dragon, Dragon" (page 166) is told by an omniscient narrator. Take the first five paragraphs of that story and retell them in the first person. Who will be the first-person narrator, or the "I" of your story? Will it be the dragon, or some other character?

Language and Vocabulary

DIALECT
Dialect is a way of speaking that is particular to a region or group of people. If you know anyone who was born in the Caribbean islands, you'll know that James Berry is very good at imitating the musical way Jamaicans speak English. If this story had been written in standard English, we would have had a very different feel for Becky and her world. For instance, the Jamaican Becky says in the third paragraph, "It's no fair reason they don't want to be with me. Anybody could go off their head for that." A Becky in Missouri might have said instead, "It's not fair that they don't want to be with me. Anybody would be upset about that." See how a

230 Short Stories

change in dialect makes Becky a different person?

In the following passages from the story, some expressions characteristic of Jamaican dialect are underlined. How would you "translate" these expressions into your own dialect, or way of speaking?

1. "With me <u>even being all so thoughtful of Granny's need of a cool drink, she started up some botheration against me.</u>"
2. " 'Haven't I told you I don't want you keeping company with those awful <u>riding-about bicycle boys?</u>' "
3. " 'And one day perhaps I'll even be <u>mum to a boy child</u>, like all of you.' "
4. "I could see Mum really <u>had it hard for money</u>."
5. "I knew anything of Dad's—anything— would be worth <u>a great mighty</u> hundred dollars."

Focus on Writing a Short Story

EXPERIMENTING WITH POINT OF VIEW

Choose a story idea. For example, you might want to retell the story of a movie or TV show you saw recently. Then write the first paragraph for your story in two different ways. In one version, use **first-person point of view** by having a character in your tale tell the story. In the second version, use **omniscient point of view**—that is, refer to the characters either by their names or with third-person pronouns like *she, he,* and *they.*

Get together with a classmate to compare paragraphs. Save your writing.

About the Author

James Berry (1925–), who was born in Jamaica, writes short stories, children's fiction, and poetry. "Becky and the Wheels-and-Brake Boys" is from a collection of short stories he wrote for children called *A Thief in the Village and Other Stories.* In a review of this collection, one critic wrote that the nine stories in this collection evoke in precise detail Caribbean village life, where young people carry wood and water before they go to school, the arrival of the city bus gives shape to the day, and people wash their donkeys in the sea early on Sunday morning. Another popular book by Berry is a collection of West Indian folk tales called *Anancy—Spiderman.*

LANGUAGE AND VOCABULARY
For answers, see the **Teaching Guide** at the beginning of the unit.

FOCUS ON WRITING A SHORT STORY
Experimenting with Point of View
You may want to model this activity for students before asking them to complete it independently. As you write your paragraph in the first-person point of view, explain to students that only the thoughts and feelings of the narrator can be revealed, but that this point of view helps to create a personal tone. As you rewrite the paragraph using omniscient point of view, explain that the thoughts and feelings of any or all of the characters can be revealed.

Becky and the Wheels-and-Brake Boys

ARCHITECTURE LINK
Some of your students may be intrigued by the elaborate decorations and colorful details on both the Victorian-home photographs in this story. You might have students find out about architectural features that are prominent in Victorian homes (popular from the mid–nineteenth century to the early twentieth century). They could find examples of designs such as these: cupolas, dormer windows, paired (or triple) windows, mansard roofs, cornices, hooded windows, brackets, friezes, shingled walls, spindlework, gables, and towers. You might also ask a spokesperson from a local historical preservation group to speak to the class about Victorian homes.

OBJECTIVES
Students will analyze the title of the story, describe the setting, and identify character traits. They will also distinguish between fact and opinion and change imagery to create a different mood.

FOCUS/MOTIVATION
Building on Prior Knowledge. Point out that the main character in this story is seven years old. Emphasize that since the students are much older, they can use their experience and insight to help them evaluate her experience.

Prereading Journal. Have students think about their own experiences as they answer the questions posed in the first paragraph of the headnote.

TEACHING RESOURCES B
Teacher's Notes, p. 76
Reading Check, p. 79
Reading Focus, p. 80
Study Guide, pp. 81, 82
Language Skills, p. 83
Building Vocabulary, p. 86
Selection Vocabulary Test, p. 88
Selection Test, p. 89

AV RESOURCES BINDER
Audiocassette 2, Side A

SETTING

Nancy

ELIZABETH ENRIGHT

Before You Read

This is a story about outsiders. Before you read, write a few ideas in your journal about outsiders. What is an outsider? Why do some individuals feel like outsiders? Can whole families or groups of people feel like outsiders? This is also a story about our need for friends. In your journal, describe the way you'd feel if you were seven years old and lonely for friends.

Though this story takes place many years ago, Fiona is just like children you know today. As you read, notice the differences between Fiona's home life and the Fadgins' home life. Why do you think the writer calls the story "Nancy" instead of "Fiona"?

Nancy 233

READING THE STORY
This selection, written for young adults, could be challenging for slower readers. You will probably want to begin reading the story orally in class. Take enough time to discuss the staid lifestyle of the family and Fiona's inner conflict as revealed at the beginning of the story. After Fiona escapes and finds the Fadgins' home (bottom of column 2, page 238), you might assign the rest of the story for home reading.

MATH LINK
Check students' math skills by asking them to figure the differences between Fiona's age and the ages of her parents and her nurse. You might also ask them to determine the number of years that have now passed since Fiona's mother was a girl in 1914.

1. LANGUAGE AND VOCABULARY
The imagery in this selection is essential in helping the reader visualize the two contrasting settings. The Language and Vocabulary box on this page gives students help in understanding those images. The Language and Vocabulary exercise on page 250 reinforces the concept through practice in rewriting imagery.

2. GUIDED READING:
Making Inferences About Character
How do you think Fiona's upbringing affects her relationship with other children? Possible answer: They think she is odd and old-fashioned; they think she thinks she is better than they are; they don't like her because she is different.

3. GUIDED READING:
Making Inferences About Character
Why do you think Fiona ruins her dolls? Possible answer: She is taking out all her frustration from her loneliness and her suppressed emotions on them.

Language and Vocabulary

1 **The use of words to describe sights, sounds, tastes, smells, and textures is called imagery.** As Fiona lies down to take a nap, she notices sounds and smells around her. She hears the snoring of the adults and the rattling of Nana's newspaper. Through the window, she hears the sound of insects and she smells the grass. As you read, notice all the images that help you visualize Fiona's grandparents' house. Then look for contrasting images that help you experience life at the Fadgins' house. Try to put yourself into these two settings.

Fiona Farmer was seven years old. Her mother was forty-six, her father was fifty-five, her nurse was sixty-one, and her grandmother and grandfather, with whom they were all spending the summer, had reached such altitudes of age that no one 2 remembered what they were. From these great heights, Fiona was loved and directed.

She wore her hair as her mother had worn it in 1914, braided tight and tied back in pretzel loops with big stiff ribbons. In winter, she was the only girl at school to wear a flannel petticoat and underwear with sleeves. Her mother read her all the books she had loved in her childhood: *Rebecca of Sunnybrook Farm*, and *The Five Little Peppers*, and *Under the Lilacs*. Her grandmother read her the books *she* had loved as a child: *Macé's Fairy Tales*, and *Grimm's Fairy Tales*, and *The Princess and Curdie*. On this mixed diet of decorum[1] and brutality, Fiona was rapidly turning into a "quaint little creature." She was a pensive[2] child with large attentive eyes and rather elderly manners; all her play was quiet, accompanied at times by nothing noisier than a low continuous murmuring, so it was 3 strange that the ranks of dolls on her nursery shelves were scalped and eyeless.

"What on earth does she do to them?" her mother said to Nana, the nurse. "Why, when I was little, my dollies were really like babies to me. I took such *care* of them, I *loved* them so. . . ."

"I honestly don't know, Mrs. Farmer," Nana said. "She'll be as quiet as a mouse in here for hours at a time, and then I'll come in and find all this—this destruction! It seems so unlike her!"

Fiona's grandmother reproached her quietly. "How would you like it if your dear mother pulled all your hair out of your head and broke your arms and legs? Your

---

1. **decorum** (di·kôr′əm): proper behavior.

2. **pensive** (pen′siv): thoughtful.

Short Stories

dolls are your little responsibilities, your *children* in a way. . . ."

Her admonishments,³ though frequent, were always mild. When Fiona scratched her head or picked her nose, she would say, "That's not very pretty, dear, is it? We don't do those things, do we?" She was a lofty, dignified, conventional lady, and she smelled like an old dictionary among whose pages many flowers have been dried and pressed. She taught Fiona how to make a sachet and a pomander ball and play Parcheesi.⁴

Fiona liked her grandfather the best. He was a man of wonderful patience and politeness, deaf as a post. Every morning she followed him out to the vegetable garden where, in his old loose button-down-the-front sweater and his white canvas golf hat that sagged in a ruffle around his head, he worked along the rows of beets and cabbages with his hoe and rake. Fiona followed at his heels, speaking ceaselessly. It did not matter to her that he never heard a word she said; she told him everything. Now and then, he would stop, resting on his hoe handle, and look down at her appreciatively. "Well," he would say. "You're a pleasant little companion, aren't you?" Then he would reach out his old parched hand (he was so old that he never sweated anymore) and give her a brittle tap or two on the shoulder or head, and he and Fiona would smile at each other out of a mutual feeling of benevolence.⁵

Sooner or later, though, Nana's voice would begin to caw, "Fee-ona! Fee-ona!" and she would have to go back to the house to pick up her toys, or change her dress, or eat a meal, or do some other dull thing.

Her grandparents' house was big and cool inside. All the rooms were full of greenish light reflected from the maple trees outdoors; the floors were dark and gleaming, the carpets had been taken up for the summer, and the furniture had linen dresses on. There was no dust anywhere, not even in the corners of the empty fireplaces, for Cora and Mary, the maids who had been there for thirty years, spent their lives seeing that there was not.

Cora had arthritis, and on Sundays when Fiona had noon dinner with the whole family, she marveled at the extreme slowness with which the maid moved about the table, like a running-down toy. Her face looked very still and concentrated then, relaxing only when she served Fiona, whispering, "Eat it all up now, dear, every bit, so I can tell Mary."

Oh, food! People were always speaking of food to Fiona; the Sunday dinners were a trial to toil through. "Eat it all up, dear," and "Clean your plate" were phrases that were ugly in her ears.

After Sunday dinner everyone went to

---

3. **admonishments** (ad·mon′ish·mənts): mild scoldings.
4. A **sachet** (sa·shā′) is a bag of perfumed powder; a **pomander** (pō′man·dər) **ball** is a mixture of sweet-smelling substances shaped like a ball; and **Parcheesi** (pär·chē′zē) is a board game played with dice.
5. **benevolence** (bə·nev′ə·ləns): goodwill.

---

1. GUIDED READING:
Drawing Conclusions
Does Fiona get a chance to enjoy anything? Possible answer: Every activity in her life is subjected to intense scrutiny. It seems that she only enjoys being with her grandfather.

COOPERATIVE LEARNING
You might have students examine the origins of names and their significance to their owners. To get students started, divide the group into pairs and have each pair research the significance of their given names and, if possible, determine the origins. Students can begin by looking in a dictionary to investigate the meanings of many given names.

Students can also interview family members to find out more about their names. Is the student's given name one that was handed down by family members or a name that appealed to the parents? Is it a common name or an unusual name? Was it chosen to go well with the last name, perhaps using alliteration as Fiona Farmer's name does? Is it a name that has special meaning for people in a particular culture?

Do students have nicknames or pet family names that they also use? Which name do they like better? Which name seems to fit the person better? After students learn as much

---

1. GUIDED READING:
Drawing Conclusions
Why does Fiona have to nap? It seems to be the habit of the household that she is forced to join. It certainly doesn't seem that she herself needs a nap.

2. GUIDED READING:
Distinguishing Between Fantasy and Reality
Does a real "voice from on high" speak to Fiona? No, she imagines the voice because she wants to run away.

3. GUIDED READING:
Making Inferences About Character
What does this passage tell you about Fiona? She is imaginative and capable of amusing herself with fantasies, but she can't sustain them for very long.

---

sleep for a while and the house droned with different pitches of snoring. Wearing nothing but a pink wrapper, Fiona would lie on the big white bed while Nana sat in an armchair by the window rattling the Sunday paper. Out of doors the cicadas[6] sounded hot as drills. The lazy air coming in the window brought a smell of grass, and **1** Fiona wished that Nana would fall asleep so that she could get up and find something to play with, but Nana would not fall asleep.

But once she did.

Once on Sunday after the usual slow, massive[7] dinner, as Fiona lay in the extremity of boredom counting mosquito bites and listening to herself yawn, she heard another sound: a new one that might promise much. Quietly she raised herself to her elbows, hardly daring to believe, and saw that the impossible had happened at last. Nana lay in the armchair, abandoned, with her head thrown back and her hair coming down and her mouth wide open like that of a fish. A faint guttural sound came out of it each time she breathed.

2 A great light seemed to flood the room, and a voice from on high addressed Fiona: "Get up and dress, but do not put on your shoes. Carry them in your hand till you get outside, and close the front door quietly behind you."

Fiona got up at once, dressed with the silence and speed of light, and departed.

---

6. **cicadas** (si·kā′dəs): large insects with transparent wings. The males make shrill sounds, like crickets.
7. **massive**: large, heavy.

The upstairs hall hummed and trumpeted with the noises of sleeping; no one heard her running down the stairs.

Out of doors it was bright and hot; she sat on the front step and put on her sandals with her heart galloping in her chest. Though old, the members of her family were tall, their legs were long as ladders, and if they came after her, they would surely catch her. Leaving the sandal straps unbuckled, Fiona ran out of the gate and down the street, terrified and exhilarated. She ran till she was giddy[8] and breathless, but when at last she stopped and looked behind her, the street on which she found herself was still and empty; steeped[9] in Sunday.

She walked for a long time. Her heart stopped racing and her breathing became comfortable again. Her fear, too, gave way to pleasure and pride. It was a beautiful afternoon. The street was very high with elms. The light that came through their roof **3** of leaves was green and trembling like light through water. Fiona became a little crab crawling among the roots of seaweed. The parked cars were fishes which would eat her up, danger was everywhere. . . . She walked sideways, made claws out of her thumbs, hid behind trees, and felt that her eyes grew out on stems. But not for long. Suddenly, as sometimes happened, the fancy[10] collapsed, betrayed her completely. There was no danger; the cars were cars

---

8. **giddy** (gid′ē): here, dizzy.
9. **steeped**: here, absorbed.
10. **fancy**: imaginative idea. (Fiona was creating a make-believe world.)

as they can about one another's names, have the partners report to the class what's in a name.

Gertrude by Frank Weston Benson (1899). Museum of Fine Arts, Boston, Massachusetts. Gift of Mrs. William Rodman Fay.

VISUAL CONNECTIONS

Use this painting and the painting on page 244 together, to discuss contrasts. Notice that one girl is dressed beautifully in elegant and rather fussy clothes. The other girl is ruddy and slightly disheveled. Which girl looks like Fiona? Which girl might be one of the Fadgins? Ask students what the mood of each portrait is—that is, does one girl suggest thoughtfulness and quiet, while the other suggests robustness and energy? Which girl would they rather be?

You might use these portraits to assign a composition presenting contrasts. Writers should focus on the girls' moods, clothing, and coloration.

TRANSPARENCY 16
Literary Elements
Story Map – asks students to identify the basic elements of fiction in a story and to create a story map.

1. LITERARY ELEMENTS:
Conflict
What conflict in Fiona's mind is revealed here? Fiona's desire for an exciting or even dangerous experience is battling with the reality of her restricted life.

2. LITERARY ELEMENTS:
Foreshadowing
What kind of outcome does the setting suggest? The setting suggests that Fiona is coming to a place where her dreams will be realized. The shabby houses, "gilded road," and lively wind suggest a place different from any Fiona has been in before.

3. LITERARY ELEMENTS:
Setting
Have students close their eyes and visualize the house in its state of disrepair. (The illustration on pages 240–241 will help.)

1 only. Nothing was any better than real. In the end, somebody would catch her and take her home, or she would return of her own accord, driven by hunger or conscience, and everything would be as it had always been.

The houses sat back from their green laps of lawn, silent and substantial, regarding her like people wearing glasses. There was a smell of privet[11] and hot asphalt in the still air; a boring smell. Intolerable[12] boredom amounting to anguish drove Fiona to turn abruptly and kick the iron palings[13] of a fence that she was passing—a kick that hurt right through her shoe.

The big street came to an end finally at a small Civil War monument and branched out beyond it in three roads. She chose the right-hand one because there was a dog asleep on the sidewalk there; but when she got to him, she saw the flies strolling up and down his face and he looked up at her balefully[14] with a low ripple of sound in his throat, and she hurried on.

2 This street had few trees; it was broader, and the houses, while farther apart, were shabbier. The afternoon sun was in her eyes, drawing her along the gilded[15] road. The wind had sprung up, too, warm and lively, blowing from the west.

On the outskirts of the town she came upon her destination, though at first she did not realize it. For some time the wind had been bringing her great blasts of radio music; and she saw now that these had their source in a gray frame house that fairly trembled with melody. Though not small, **3** this was the seediest of all the houses. It stood in the middle of a yard as full of tall grass as a field. There were paths through the field and bald patches where people had stamped and trampled, and many souvenirs abandoned and half grown over: a rusted little wagon with no wheels, somebody's shoe, an old tire.

The house had a queer shape, fancy, but with everything coming off or breaking. Some of the shutters hung by one hinge only; the cupola[16] on top was crooked, and so was the porch from which half the palings were gone. The fence, too, had lost many of its pickets and stood propped against the tangle like a large comb with teeth missing. But it had kept its gate, and hanging onto this and swinging slowly back and forth were three little girls. Fiona walked more slowly.

One of the girls had a bandanna tied tightly around her head, but the other two regarded her from under untrimmed dusty bangs, like animals peering out from under ferns. The gate gave a long snarl of sound as they pushed it forward.

---

11. **privet** (priv′it): a kind of hedge that has a strong odor.
12. **intolerable** (in·tol′ər·ə·bəl): unbearable.
13. **palings** (pā′lingz): pickets of a fence.
14. **balefully** (bāl′fəl·lē): threateningly.
15. **gilded** (gild′id): as if inlaid with gilt, or gold.
16. **cupola** (kyōō′pə·lə): a circular dome-shaped roof.

238 Short Stories

"Where are you going?" said the tallest one.

Fiona could not be sure of the tone of this question: Was it a friendly or a hostile challenge? She moved still more slowly, touching each picket with her forefinger.

"No place," she said guardedly.

1 "What's your name?" demanded the girl with the bandanna. She smelled of kerosene.[17]

"Fiona Farmer," said Fiona.

"That's a funny name. My name's Darlene, and hers is Pearl, and *hers* is Merle. Nancy is a nice name."

Fiona saw that all of them were wearing red nail polish and asked a question of her own.

"Are you all three sisters?"

"Yes, and there's more of us. *Them*," said Pearl, the tallest girl, jerking her head. "In the swing."

Beyond the house Fiona now saw for the first time an old double-rocker swing full of boys.

"There's Norman and Stanley and Earl," Darlene said. "And in the house we got a baby sister named Marilyn, and down to the picture theater we got a big sister named Deanna. Come on in."

"Will they let me swing in the swing?" said Fiona.

"Sure they will. *What* did you say your name was?"

"Fiona," she admitted. "Fiona Farmer."

"Gee," said Pearl.

"We'll call her Nancy," said Darlene, who, though younger, seemed to be a leader in her way. "Come on, Nancy, you wanna swing on the gate? Get off, Merle."

Merle got off obediently, sucking her thumb.

"I would like to swing in the *swing*," Fiona said.

She came into the yard, gazing up at the tipsy cupola. "Can you get up there into that kind of little tower?"

"Sure," said Darlene. "Come on up and we'll show you."

2 Fiona followed them through the interesting grass in which she now saw a broken doll, somebody's garter, somebody's hat, and many weathered corncobs and beer cans.

On the porch which swayed when they walked on it there was a tough-looking baby buggy, two sleds, a bent tricycle, a lot of chairs and boxes and bushel baskets and peck baskets and a baby pen and a wagon wheel and some kindling wood. The screen door was full of holes, and instead of a doorknob, there was a wooden thread spool to turn.

3 The noise of music was stunning as they went indoors; it kept the Mason jars[18] ringing on the shelves. They walked right into it, into the thrilling heart of noise which was the kitchen, where a woman was sitting nursing a baby and shouting random conversation at an old, old woman with a beak nose.

---

17. **kerosene:** fuel oil that is sometimes used as a home treatment for head lice.

18. **Mason jars:** jars used for preserving fruits and vegetables.

1. GUIDED READING:
Appreciating Humor
What is funny about these introductions? Fiona's polite greetings and curtsy seem incongruous in the casual household.

2. LITERARY ELEMENTS:
Simile
What simile describes the old lady's hand? Fiona thinks the hand feels "like a few twigs in a glove." Apparently the hand is thin and shriveled.

3. GUIDED READING:
Making Inferences About Character
What do you infer about Darlene's father? The strong smell and the all-day sleeping suggest that he is an alcoholic. Darlene's language indicates long familiarity with the situation.

The music ceased with a flourish and the radio announcer's tremendous tones replaced it, but this did not stop the shouted discourse of the woman with the baby. As the girls crossed the kitchen, she turned for a moment to look at them, saw Fiona, and said, "Who's she?"

"She's Nancy," called Darlene, against the radio.

"Who?"

"Nancy! She dropped in."

"That's Mom," Pearl said.

1 Fiona went over to the lady to shake her hand. She made her usual curtsy and said, "How do you do?"

Mom's hand felt limp and rather damp and startled. She was a big woman with a wide face and tired blue eyes.

"The old one's Gramma," Darlene said, so Fiona curtsied to the old lady too, 2 and shook her hand, which felt like a few twigs in a glove.

3 "And that's my father," Darlene added a few seconds later when they had gone up the loud bare stairs to the next floor. Fiona peeked in the doorway of the dim, strong-smelling room, but all she saw of *him* was the soles of his socks, and she heard him snoring.

"Just like at home," she said. "Sunday afternoon they all sleep."

"He sleeps all *day* on Sundays," Darlene said, and Fiona felt a little humiliated for her own father.

"This is Gramma's room." Pearl threw open the door. "She likes flowers."

The room was a jungle steeped in musky twilight. A vine of some kind had crawled all over the window and parts of the wall, and on the sill, the sash, and the floor below were pots and jars and coffee tins in which stout lusty plants were growing and flowering.

"How does she open the window at night?" Fiona wondered.

"*She* don't open no windows day or night," Darlene said. "She's *old*, she's gotta stay *warm*."

They went up another flight of stairs,

1. GUIDED READING:
Making Inferences
What are the advantages and disadvantages of such a bedroom? Answers will vary. Some readers may deplore the uncomfortable bed and crowded conditions. Others may say the little girls are companionable with their "quarreling or giggling" and their profusion of comic books.

narrow steep ones, crowded with magazines and articles of clothing and decayed toys. "Up here's where we sleep," Darlene said. "Us girls, all of us except Marilyn. Pearl and me and Merle sleep in the big bed and Deanna she sleeps in the cot. This is the attic like."

The big bed was made of iron with the post knobs missing. It dipped in the middle like a hammock, and there, Fiona knew, the little girls would lie at night, dumped together in a tangle, quarreling or giggling in whispers.

"Look at all the comic books!" she cried, and indeed they lay everywhere in tattered profusion, a drift of stained, disordered leaves.

"We got about a hundred or a thousand of 'em, I guess," Pearl said. "You want some?"

"Could I really, Pearl? Could you spare them?"

Nancy 241

1. GUIDED READING:
Understanding Contrast
How does Mrs. Fadgin's treatment of her daughters contrast with Fiona's previous experience? Mrs. Fadgin is much more involved with her children than Fiona's mother or grandmother. She allows them a great deal of freedom and is perhaps too easygoing, but she punishes them when she judges that their behavior is dangerous. To some students, her shouts and slaps may not seem as cruel as the "mild" admonishments of Fiona's grandmother.

"*Atom Annie*'s a good one," Pearl said. "We got a lot about her, and here's one called *Hellray* that's real good, real scary. Take these."

Fiona looked at them longingly. "I don't know if my mother—she doesn't like for me to have comics."

"Heck, why not?"

"Well, maybe this time she won't mind," Fiona said, taking the books, determined that everything would be all right for once. "Thank you very, very much, Darlene and Pearl."

"Here's the stairs to the lookout," Darlene said. "Get out of the way, Merle, you wait till last."

They climbed the ladder steps in the middle of the room, Pearl pushed open the trap door, and one by one they ascended into the tiny chamber.

It was a tipped little cubicle like a ship's cabin in stiff[19] weather, and stiflingly hot. It seemed remote, high, cozy, and its four soiled windows showed four different views of the town, faded and reduced as pictures in an old book. Flies buzzed and butted at the hot glass. Fiona felt disappointed when she saw the steeple of the church that stood across the street from her grandfather's house. She had not thought it was so near.

"Jump!" cried Darlene. They all began to jump, and the cupola jarred and trembled under the pounding.

"Won't it break?" cried Fiona, pounding with the rest. "Won't it fall off?"

"Naw, it won't break," Darlene called back. "It never did yet."

"But it might someday, though," shouted Pearl encouragingly.

It was fun to jump riotously and yell, as the tiny tower rocked and resounded.

There was an interruption from below. **1**

"Get out of there!" bawled Mom up the stairs. "How many times I told you kids to stay down out of there! You want to get your backs broke? You want to get killed? You scram down!"

"Get out of the way, Merle, let Nancy go first," Pearl said.

Mom stood at the foot of the steps wearing the baby around her neck. Anxiety had made her furious. "That place ain't safe, you know that!" she cried. "How many times have I told you?" She gave Pearl a slap on the cheek and would have given one to Darlene, too, if Darlene had not bent her neck adroitly.[20]

"You let me catch you up there one more time and I'll get your father to lick you good!"

"Aw, climb a tree," said Darlene.

Fiona was aghast. What would happen now?

But nothing happened. Merle still quietly sucked her thumb, Darlene and Pearl seemed cool and jaunty, and as they descended through the house, Mom's anger dried up like dew.

"You kids want a snack?" she said. "You didn't eat since breakfast."

"Can Nancy stay?"

---

19. **stiff:** rough.

20. **adroitly** (ə·droit′lē): skillfully.

"Why, sure, I guess. Why not?"

"Oh, thank you very, very much. . . ."

The kitchen, like the rest of the house, had a rich, bold, musty smell. It smelled of constant usage and memories of usage. It was crowded and crusted with objects: pots, pans, kettles, boxes, jars, cans, buckets, dippers. There were two alarm clocks, one lying on its side, and both asserting a different hour, and four big Coca-Cola calendars on the wall, none for the current year. The radio was still thundering music, and close beside it warming herself at the noise sat Gramma, dark as a crow, chewing and chewing on her empty gums.

The stove was named Ebony Gem, and behind it in a cardboard box there was something alive; something moved. . . .

"It's kittens," said Merle, removing her thumb from her mouth and speaking for the first time. "Our cat had kittens."

"Oh, let me see!" Fiona knelt by the box. There inside it lay a bland[21] and happy group: mother cat with her yellow eyes half closed and her paws splayed out in pleasure; kittens lined up all along her, sucking.

Merle put out her little forefinger with its chipped red nail polish, stroking first one infant, then the next. "The black one's name is Blackie and the white one's name is Whitey and we call *this* one Butch because he's so——"

"My father usually drowns them, all but one," Darlene interrupted. She bent her kerchiefed head close to Fiona's, so that there was a blinding smell of kerosene. "Tomorrow probly," she whispered. "We don't tell Merle, it makes her feel so bad." Then she raised her voice. "She knows it's going to happen but she don't know when, huh, Merle?"

"You could take one, Nancy," Merle said, still gazing at the kittens. "You could keep it and be good to it."

"Do you mean honestly and truly?" Fiona's joy was suffocating.

"Any one? Any one at all?"

"Except Butch," Darlene said. "We're going to keep him to help with the rats."

"Could I have Blackie? Really for keeps?"

Merle plucked the dark little thing from the mother as if she were plucking off a burr and gave it to Fiona.

"I can feel its little tiny heart," Fiona said. "I'll give it milk all the time and brush its fur and it can sleep in the doll cradle. Oh look at its ears, oh Merle, oh thank you!"

Shamed by gratitude, Merle put her thumb back in her mouth and looked away.

"You kids get out from under my feet," Mom said. "Sit up to the table now, it's all ready. Come on, Mama, come on, *boys!*" She opened the screen door and put her head out, shouting so hard that great cords stood out on her neck.

They sat around the big table with its oilcloth cover, everything in easy reach: cereal in paper boxes, sugar, catsup. . . . They had cornflakes and milk, Swiss cheese sandwiches with catsup, cream

---

21. **bland**: mild.

---

1. GUIDED READING:
Drawing Conclusions
Why is Fiona so excited about the kitten? Having a pet would give her something alive to be attached to apart from her family, something to play with and something of her own. Having a kitten beats learning to make sachets and pomander balls (see page 235).

2. GUIDED READING:
Comparing and Contrasting
This passage states that on the table sat "everything in easy reach." How do you think Fiona's grandmother would describe the table? Students should recognize that her grandmother would consider the table a cluttered and horrendous mess.

Art Link

You might assess students' ability to read and interpret details by having them create pictures of one of the families in this descriptive story. Students could sketch drawings of either the Fadgin family with their tumble-down house or the Farmer family with their elegant, stately home. Encourage students to use the details in the story to help them draw. They could add color or pen and ink strokes to finish the drawings. You might want students to create an illustration of both families so that they can contrast the two.

VISUAL CONNECTIONS

See the note on page 237, suggesting that this portrait and the portrait on that page be used together as a study in contrasts. Note the dates of the two paintings: Only 14 years separates these two girls, yet which portrait looks more "modern"?

Young Mary O'Donnell was probably one of thousands of young Irish girls who arrived in Boston as immigrants in the early years of the twentieth century. At one point, prejudice against people like Mary was so virulent in Boston that signs were posted in shops saying "No Irish need apply." Nana in Enright's story might be reflecting similar prejudice against the "outsiders" called Fadgin.

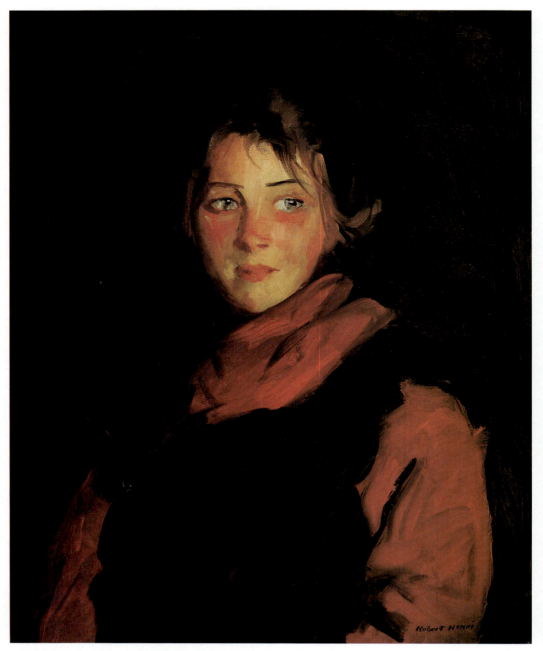

Irish Girl (Mary O'Donnell) by Robert Henri (1913).

Museum of Fine Arts, Boston, Massachusetts. John T. Spaulding Collection.

244 Short Stories

soda in bottles, and little cakes out of a box with pink and green beads on them. Fiona ate everything.

"Nancy eats good, don't she, Mom?" Darlene said.

"I never had catsup before," said Fiona. "My, it certainly is delicious, isn't it?"

The table was a family battlefield. Fiona had never seen anything like it in her life. Stanley and Norman threw pieces of sandwich at each other; Earl took one of Merle's cakes and Merle cried and Mom slapped Earl; Darlene stole big swigs from Pearl's soda bottle, was loudly accused, and loudly defended herself.

"You kids shut up," Mom said, eating over Marilyn's head and giving her occasional bits of cake dipped in tea. Gramma was the only quiet one; she sat bent over, all wrapped and absorbed in her old age, gazing into her cup as she drank from it with a long purring sound. Blackie was quiet too, asleep in Fiona's lap. She kept one hand on his little velvet back.

Mom pointed at Fiona with her spoon. "Looks like Margaret O'Brien[22] used to, don't she? The ribbons and all."

"Margaret who?" said Fiona.

"O'Brien. *You* know, the kid in the movies," Darlene said.

"Oh, I never go to movies," said Fiona. "I'm not allowed."

"Not allowed!" cried Darlene incredulously. "We go all the time, don't we, Mom? Even Deanna goes. We could take Nancy with us sometimes, couldn't we, Mom?"

"Maybe, if her folks say yes."

"Oh, if I went with *you*, it would be all right, I'm sure," cried Fiona joyously. Drunk with noise, strange flavors, gifts, and new friendship, she really believed this.

Afterward, still with catsup on their upper lips, they went outdoors to play hide-and-seek.

"You be her partner, Stanley," ordered Darlene, who was "it." "You kind of look after her, she don't know our places to hide."

Then she hid her eyes with her arm, cast herself against a tree like a girl in grief, and began to count out loud.

"The cellar," hissed Stanley, grabbing Fiona's hand. He was a big eight-year-old boy, and still clutching the kitten, Fiona ran with him willingly, hesitating only for a second at sight of the dark abyss.[23] On the steps were many cans and crates, but Stanley led her safely down among these and into the black deep tunnel beyond. Fiona could feel that there were solid things all around them—probably more boxes, more crates—but she could see nothing. Stanley's hand was warm and firm, it just fitted hers, and she liked having him lead her.

---

22. **Margaret O'Brien**: a child movie star in the 1940s and 1950s. (She often wore her hair in looped braids tied with ribbons.)

23. **abyss** (ə·bis'): bottomless space.

---

1. GUIDED READING:
Understanding Contrast
How does this meal differ from Sunday dinner at Fiona's grandmother's? At the Fadgins, Fiona eats everything without being chided. She enjoys the meal. The manners are nonexistent and the atmosphere exciting. The meal at Fiona's was served by maids, the atmosphere was quiet and decorous, and the meal was described as "massive" (probably a Sunday roast). At the Fadgins, the meal consists of what we'd call junk food, or packaged food, and breakfast food. The Fadgins' meal is a battlefield, food is thrown around, voices are loud.

2. LITERARY ELEMENTS:
Character
Do you think Fiona's family would really allow her to go to the movies with Darlene's family? No, her family would thoroughly disapprove of the Fadgins. Fiona wishes it were true that she might go to the movies with Darlene. She doesn't see the Fadgin family as we know her family would view them.

1. **GUIDED READING:**
Understanding Feelings
How does Fiona feel about scraping her knee and the other discomforts she has suffered? She doesn't seem to mind at all because she is having such a good time.

2. **LITERARY ELEMENTS:**
Climax
How does the "gangster" game with the Fadgins bring Fiona to a great peak of pleasure? During this game she is totally accepted and involved with her new friends. In contrast to her fantasy with the crab, which was fizzled out by dull reality, this imaginary play with others is lively and satisfying.

"We can stop now," he said, "but keep quiet."

Darlene could still be heard, faintly. Her counting voice sounded deserted and defiant: "*Ninety*-five, *ninety*-six, *ninety*-seven"... The blackness throbbed and shimmered and the air had a dense aged smell.

"Coming, ready or not!" called the faraway defiant voice.

"We're safe here anyways," Stanley said. "She won't come down *here*, she's scared to." He laughed silently and gave Fiona's hand a squeeze. "There's rats down here."

"Oh no, oh no! Oh, Stanley, let's go up again," cried Fiona, tears of panic in her voice.

But Stanley held onto her hand. "You going to be a sissy, too?" he demanded. "We got the *cat,* ain't we?"

Fiona strained the tiny kitten to her chest. Her heart was banging terribly and she wanted to cry, but she would not. All around the rats were closing in, large as dogs and smiling strangely; smiling like people. She almost sobbed when Stanley said, "Now we can go, hurry up, and keep still!"

They were the first ones back.

For a long time they played and Stanley always was her partner. He knew the best places to hide: up in the boughs of a pear tree, under the porch steps, in the fearful little dark privy with its different-sized "family accommodations," and flat on their stomachs under the folded-back cellar door. Darlene was "it" till she caught Merle, and Merle was "it" for hours. Fiona got spiderwebs in her mouth and gnats up her nose, tore her dress, scraped her knee, lost one hair ribbon, and gave the other to Merle, who had admired it.

When they were through with hide-and-seek, they all got into the rocker swing and played gangsters. The swing leapt to and fro, to and fro, screaming wildly at the joints; surely it would break, and soon! That was the thrilling thing about this place: So many features of it—the tower, the swing, the porch—trembled at the edge of ruin, hung by a thread above the fatal plunge.

Earl and Stanley and Norman leaned over the back of one of the seats firing at the enemy. "Step on it, you guys," yelled Stanley, "they got a gat!"

"They got a rod!" yelled Norman. "They got a lotta rods!"

"What's a rod?" cried Fiona. "What's a gat?"

"Guns he means," Darlene told her. "Rods and gats is guns."

"Shoot 'em, Stanley," yelled Fiona. "With your gat, shoot the eyes out of 'em!"

Clutching the clawing kitten to her collarbone, her hair in her open mouth, she bawled encouragement to them. The swing accelerated ever more wildly. Soon it would take off entirely, depart from its hinges, fly through the air, burn a hole through the sky! . . .

"Fee-ona Farmer!"

The cry was loud enough to be heard

above all sounds of war and wind and radio music.

Beside the swing stood Nana, so tall, so highly charged with hurry and emotion, that the children stopped their play at once.

"Who's she?" Stanley asked.

"She's my nurse," Fiona murmured.

"Your nurse! What's the matter, are you sick?"

"No . . . she just—takes care of me."

"Takes *care* of you!"

"You get out of that swing and come this in-stant!"

Having struck the bottom of disgrace, Fiona stepped down and slowly went to Nana. From the swing the others watched as still as children posing for a photograph.

"Put down that cat and come at once."

"Oh no!" Fiona said. "It's mine, they gave it to me."

"Put. Down. That. Cat."

Darlene came to stand beside Fiona. "But we did give it to her. We want for her to have it."

Nana struck the kitten from Fiona's arms. "You will not take that creature home! It's filthy, it has fleas!"

"Oh my kitty!" shrieked Fiona, diving after Blackie, but Nana caught her wrist.

"You come!"

Fiona pulled, struggled, cast a glare of anguish at all the rapt[24] photograph-faces in the swing.

"You should be punished. You should be whipped. Whipped!" Nana whistled the cruel words; Nana, who was never cruel! Her fingers on Fiona's wrist were hard.

"Let me say good-bye to them, Nana, let me say good-bye to their *mother!* You said I should *always* say good-bye to the mother!"

"Not this time, this time it doesn't matter," Nana said. "You're going straight home and into the tub. Heavens knows what you will have caught!" Upon Fiona's friends she turned a single brilliant glance like one cold flash from a lighthouse.

There was nothing to commend Fiona's departure; dragged by the hand, whimpering, she looked back at her friends in desperation. "Oh, Darlene!"

But it was easy to see that Darlene had detached herself. "Good-bye, Nancy," she said, not without a certain pride. She did not smile or say anything else, but her attitude showed Fiona and Nana that she had no need for either of them, could not be hurt by them, and would not think of them again. As they went out the gate, she turned her back and skipped away, and Fiona heard the rocker swing resume its screaming tempo.

Halfway home, Nana's recriminations[25] began to modify, gradually becoming reproaches: "How could you have, Fiona, run away like that. Why it's only by the grace of God I ever found you at all! And all the time I was half sick with worry I never said a word to your father and mother! I didn't want *them* to worry!"

Somewhere deep inside her Fiona

---

24. **rapt**: absorbed.

25. **recriminations** (ri·krim′ə·nā′shəns): accusations.

---

1. GUIDED READING:
Contrasting Characters
How has Nana changed and why? She has become cruel and is forcing Fiona to ignore rules of social conduct that she had carefully taught her. Fiona cannot account for this difference, but we know it is because the Fadgins are slovenly and easygoing—unacceptable role models for the delicately reared Fiona.

2. GUIDED READING:
Contrasting Characters
How does Darlene's attitude in this passage contrast with how you think Fiona feels? Fiona will probably remember this day as long as she lives. She does not have Darlene's pride and would probably say that she needs friends desperately.

3. LITERARY ELEMENTS:
Character
Is Nana's statement the truth or what she wants Fiona to believe? Nana is afraid of losing her job because she did not take proper care of Fiona. That is the real reason she didn't tell Fiona's parents that Fiona was missing.

PORTFOLIO ASSESSMENT
The word *homesick* evokes different images depending on memories of home. Some students may be interested in writing an essay in which they describe what the word *homesick* means to them. Suggest that they use words that appeal to all the senses, sight, smell, taste, feeling, and hearing, to produce sensory images of their home. They will also need to evaluate and label their emotions connected to missing their home. Consult with students individually to agree on how their essays will be assessed. (See *Portfolio Assessment and Professional Support Materials,* especially the section entitled **Suggestions for Portfolio Projects.**)

1. GUIDED READING:
Drawing Conclusions
Are the Fadgins poor? Nana says they are, but Fiona says they aren't. They are clearly poor in the economic sense, but their possessions, pets, and companionship make them rich in other ways, ways in which Fiona is poor.

2. GUIDED READING:
Forming Valid Opinions
Is Fiona, in fact, a baby? No, and the fact that her mother calls her that shows us how out-of-touch Fiona's mother is with Fiona's needs.

3. GUIDED READING:
Drawing Conclusions
How can Fiona be homesick at home? Because she longs for the things in which the Fadgin family is rich, the Fadgins' home seems more homelike to Fiona than her grandmother's house.

---

understood exactly why Nana had said nothing to her parents, but she just kept on saying, "I want my kitty, I want my kitty."

Finally Nana said, "If you're a good girl, maybe we'll get you another kitten."

"I don't want another, I want that one."

"Oh for pity's sakes, it had fleas; or worse. Anything belonging to the Fadgins would be bound to have—"

"Do *you* know them?"

"I know *about* them, everybody does. They're the dirtiest, the shiftlessest, the most down-at-the-heel tribe in this whole town!"

"They are not, they're nice, I love them!"

Nana relented a little. "Maybe it's hard not to be shiftless when you're that poor."

"*They* aren't poor. You should see all the things they've got! More than Grandmother's got in her whole house!"

"All right now, dearie, all right. We'll forget about it, shall we? It will be our secret and we'll never tell anyone because we don't want them to worry, do we? But you must promise me never, never to do such a thing again, hear?"

"I want my kitty," droned Fiona.

Her grandparents' house smelled cool and sweetish. There was a bowl of white and pink stock[26] on the hall table, and her grandmother's green linen parasol leaned in a corner among the pearly company of her grandfather's canes.

In the shaded living room, Fiona saw her mother knitting and her grandmother at the piano playing the same kind of music she always played, with the loose rings clicking on her fingers.

"Is that my baby?" called her mother—but Nana answered hastily, "I'm getting her right into her bath, Mrs. Farmer. She's sim-ply fil-thy."

Upstairs Nana went in to run the water in the tub. Fiona kicked off one sandal, then the other. A terrible pain took hold of her; it began in her mind and spread down to her stomach. She had never been homesick before and did not know what ailed her. She knew only that she wanted to sleep at night in a big twanging bed full of children and to eat meals at a crowded table where people threw bread at each other and drank pop. She wanted Stanley's hand to guide her and Darlene's voice to teach her and Blackie's purr to throb against her chest. . . .

Beyond the window she saw her grandfather's wilted golf hat bobbing among the cornstalks, and escaped again, running on bare feet down the back stairs and out of doors across the billowing lawn which seemed to be colliding with the trees and sky and shadows, all flooded and dazzled with tears. Blindly she flung open the garden gate and pushed her way through the green-paper corn forest to her grandfather, who dropped his hoe and held out his arms when he saw her face.

"Come here now," he said in his gentle deaf voice. "Well, well, this won't do, no it won't, not at all. Come sit here with

---

26. **stock:** a kind of flower.

CLOSURE

Have students discuss how the author uses contrasting settings (Fiona's grandmother's house and the Fadgins' house) in this story. Have students list specific images in the story that reveal the contrasts. Students might look, for example, at the description of Fiona's grandmother's house on page 235 and at the description of the Fadgins' house and yard on page 238. Use the photographs on pages 232–233 and 240–241.

Grandpa, sit here in the arbor. Did you hurt yourself?"

He led her to the seat under the green grape trellis where he sometimes rested from the hot sun. He put his arm around her shoulders, offering himself as a support for grief, and Fiona howled against his waistcoat till the wet tweed chapped her cheek and there was not a tear left in her. He did not interrupt or ask questions but kept patting her shoulder in a sort of sympathetic accompaniment to her sobs, which he could not hear but which he felt. What's the cause of it all, he wondered. A broken toy? A scolding? Children's tragedies, he thought, children's little tragedies. There are bigger ones in store for you, Fiona, a world of them. The thought did not move him deeply, everyone must suffer, but for an instant he was not sorry to be old.

Fiona leaned against him and after a while, between the hiccups left from sobbing, she could hear the ancient heart inside his chest tick-tocking steadily, as tranquil and unhurried as he was himself. All the wild performance of her sorrow had not quickened its tempo by a single beat, and this for some reason was a comfort.

The sound of her grandmother's music, sugary and elegant, came sparkling from the house, and upstairs in the bedroom or the hall Nana began to call. "Fee-ona?" she cried. "Oh, Fee-ona?" There was a hint of panic in her voice now, but no response came from under the green trellis: Fiona's grandfather could not hear the calling, and Fiona, for the time being, did not choose to answer.

For Study and Discussion

IDENTIFYING FACTS

1. One **setting** in the story is the grandparents' house. Explain why Fiona finds life there boring.

2. We see a very different **setting** when we get to the Fadgins' house. Describe their house and yard.

3. Fiona has many new experiences with the Fadgin children. Name three or four of her adventures. How does she respond to her newfound friends?

4. Fiona's nurse says that she "knows about" the Fadgins. What does she know about them?

INTERPRETING MEANINGS

5. This is a story about several outsiders. How are the Fadgins outsiders? How is Fiona also an outsider?

6. Fiona's grandparents and the Fadgins have very different lifestyles. Describe the meal at the grandparents' house. Then describe "snacktime" at the Fadgins' house. Why do you think Fiona so loves being with the disorderly Fadgins?

7. A **character trait** is a quality that describes how a person thinks, feels, or behaves. (For example, a character can be outgoing, shy, or clever.) List at least three character traits that could describe Fiona. What traits does she show when she becomes "Nancy"?

8. Why do you think Fiona from time to time destroys her dolls? (What could this show about her feelings?)

Nancy **249**

FOR STUDY AND DISCUSSION

Identifying Facts
1. She finds it formal, silent, old-fashioned, lonely.
2. The house is seedy and ramshackle. The yard is unkempt and filled with clutter. A radio is blasting. Students may add numerous details.
3. She swings in a swing, explores the attic, reads comic books, jumps in the cupola, plays with a kitten, eats ketchup, plays hide-and-seek, and plays gangsters.

She responds with love, joy, excitement, amazement, envy.
4. The nurse knows the Fadgins' reputation for poverty and shiftlessness.

Interpreting Meanings
5. Look for definitions that describe "outsider" as someone who does not belong in a given group.

The Fadgins are outsiders from the point of view of Fiona's family because they are poor, shiftless, and none too clean.

Fiona is an outsider in her family because she is a child and fun-loving and an outsider among the Fadgins because she is from a rich family.

EXTENSION AND ENRICHMENT
Drama. Students may enjoy acting out some of the scenes from the story. An interesting contrast could result from having one group act out dinner at the grandparents' house (with the grandmother, grandfather, mother, father, Nana, Fiona, Cora, and Mary) and one of the scenes at the Fadgins' house (with the grandmother, mother, six children, the baby, and Fiona). Extra students could be directors.

6. Meals at the grandparents' house are "slow, massive" (page 236), silent, boring, served by a servant, and followed by naps.
Fadgin snacktimes are "like a family battlefield" (page 245)—extremely casual and messy.
Fiona likes the Fadgins because of the contrast with her grandparents' house.
7. Fiona might be described as "pensive" (page 234), quiet, unhappy, unworldly, bored.
As "Nancy," she is still relatively quiet compared to her playmates, but no longer unhappy or bored.
8. She probably destroys her dolls because she is angry at her parents and grandparents and possibly angry at herself too.
9. The author chose the title "Nancy" to emphasize the change in Fiona in her new environment. "Nancy" is a very real part of Fiona that had previously been unknown.

Applying Meanings
10. Most students will agree that people like Nana often disapprove of people like the Fadgins—perhaps out of ignorance, perhaps out of fear of becoming like the Fadgins or of being rejected by others.

9. Why do you think the author chose "Nancy" for the **title** of this story?

APPLYING MEANINGS
10. Do you think it's true that people like Fiona's Nana often disapprove of people like the Fadgins? What are the various reasons we sometimes reject or fear other people?

Focus on Reading

DISTINGUISHING BETWEEN FACT AND OPINION
A **fact** is a statement that can be proved right or wrong. The proof may be taken from details in the story, from your own experience, or from some outside source, like an encyclopedia or newspaper. It is a fact, for example, that Nancy's mother is forty-six years old. This is stated in the first paragraph of the story.
An **opinion,** on the other hand, is a personal belief. It cannot be proved right or wrong. One reader's opinion might be: "It's not fair that Fiona's parents keep her cooped up in the house all day." Sometimes two people look at the very same facts and have different opinions. That's when things get interesting.
Identify each statement below as fact (F) or opinion (O). Do all your classmates agree?

1. The Fadgins' house is falling apart because they are lazy.
2. The Fadgins' yard is littered with a hat, a broken doll, and some corncobs.
3. The Fadgins lead exciting and adventurous lives.
4. The Fadgins are poor.
5. Three of the Fadgin girls sleep in the same bed.
6. It's wrong that Darlene Fadgin talks back to her mother.
7. Darlene has head lice.

Language and Vocabulary

IMAGERY AND FEELINGS
Images are words that describe sights, sounds, smells, and tastes. They also describe textures, or things that you touch. The author of this story uses images to help you create mental pictures of two settings. Images often reveal a writer's feelings. Images can reveal pleasure or disgust, happiness or sadness.
The images are underlined in the passages below. For each underlined word or group of words, substitute different words to change the feeling of the image. For instance, in the first sentence in the first passage, you might say "Her grandparents' house was tiny and hot inside."

1. "Her grandparents' house was big and cool inside. All the rooms were full of greenish light reflected from the maple trees outdoors; the floors were dark and gleaming, the carpets had been taken up for the summer, and the furniture had linen dresses on. There was no dust anywhere. . . ."

2. "The kitchen, like the rest of the house, had a rich, bold, musty smell. It smelled of constant usage and memories of usage. It was crowded and crusted with objects: pots, pans, kettles, boxes, jars, cans, buckets, dippers. . . . The radio was still thundering music, and close beside it warming herself at the noise sat Gramma, dark as a crow, chewing and chewing on her empty gums."

Focus on Writing a Short Story

LISTING DETAILS OF SETTING

Setting is the time and place of a story. The setting can help to create atmosphere or mood. For example, compare the mood in the description of Fiona's grandparents' house (page 235) with the mood created by the details about the Fadgins' kitchen (page 243).

Create a setting for a short story of your own by filling out a chart like the one below. List as many descriptive details as you can. Save your notes.

Setting Chart
Place: _____
Time: _____
Weather: _____
Time of Year/Time of Day: _____
Objects: _____
Sights/Sounds/Smells: _____
_____
_____
Overall Atmosphere/Mood: _____

About the Author

Elizabeth Enright (1909–1968) wrote books about children who have unusual adventures. Four of those books, *The Saturdays, The Four-Story Mistake, Spiderweb for Two,* and *Then There Were Five* are about the Melendy children. Four of the Melendy children grow up in a home without a mother near New York City. In describing the children's adventures, Enright writes, "They discovered a secret room, built a tree house, found a diamond, escaped from dangers, effected rescues . . . got lost, and did many other striking things. . . ."

FOCUS ON READING
Distinguishing Between Fact and Opinion
1. O 2. F 3. O 4. F 5. F.
6. O 7. F.

The above are probable answers, but there is some room for disagreement.

LANGUAGE AND VOCABULARY
For answers, see the **Teaching Guide** at the beginning of the unit.

FOCUS ON WRITING A SHORT STORY
Listing Details of Setting
You may want to demonstrate to students how changing the descriptive details of a place can affect the overall atmosphere or mood. Recreate the chart on the board and fill in a place such as a classroom. First, fill in the chart to create a happy, carefree mood. Then, using the same place, fill in the chart to create a sad, lonely mood.

As students fill out their charts, suggest that they determine an overall atmosphere or mood after they choose a place. Then they can fill in the remaining descriptive details to create that mood.

OBJECTIVES
Students will analyze settings, list narrative clue words and phrases, and identify sensory details.

Teaching Resources B
Teacher's Notes, p. 91
Reading Check, p. 93
Reading Focus, p. 94
Study Guide, pp. 95, 96
Language Skills, p. 97
Building Vocabulary, p. 100
Selection Vocabulary Test, p. 101
Selection Test, p. 102

AV Resources Binder
Audiocassette 2, Side A

FOCUS/MOTIVATION
Building on Prior Knowledge. Help students build on prior knowledge by asking them to list facts about the Plains Indians. (They should mention the Indians' relationship to the buffalo—they used it for food, shelter, and clothing—and to their ponies. They might also know that only the men hunted and that there was intertribal warfare among different groups of the Native Americans who lived on the Plains. These facts are all brought out in the story.)

Where the Buffaloes Begin

OLAF BAKER

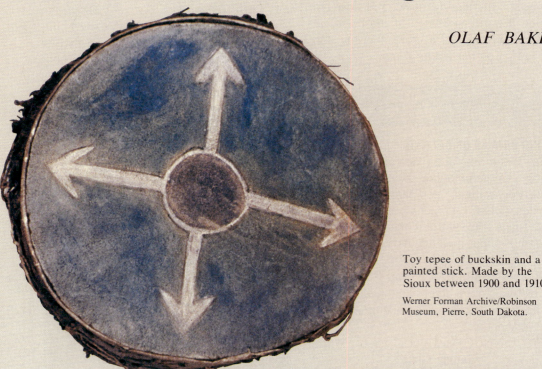

Toy tepee of buckskin and a painted stick. Made by the Sioux between 1900 and 1910.

Werner Forman Archive/Robinson Museum, Pierre, South Dakota.

Dance drum made out of painted hide from South Dakota.

Robinson Museum, Pierre, South Dakota/Museum of the American Indian, Heye Foundation.

Before You Read
This story tells how a boy becomes a hero to his people. Little Wolf lives long ago on the great western prairie of North America. He has heard a tale about where the buffaloes came from, and one day he sets off on a quest to find out if the old tale is true. The strange things that happen to Little Wolf become an addition to the old legend.

Before you read, describe in your journal your favorite setting. What is the weather like there? What do you see and hear there? How does this place make you feel?

Prereading Journal. Have students write a few sentences in response to the suggestion in the second paragraph of the headnote: Describe your favorite setting. You might want to expand the assignment to include a place where the students have not actually been but would like to go.

TRANSPARENCIES 12 & 13
Fine Art
Theme: *Tales of Changes and Challenges* — invites students to explore artworks that show people exploring new settings or meeting challenges.

READING THE STORY
Students will enjoy this story especially if you read it aloud to them. In class, you might help students construct a detailed story map to make certain they understand "what happens."

SOCIAL STUDIES LINK
To encourage students to discover the geographical areas inhabited by the Plains Indians, have them look for maps showing the lands of the Native American peoples. To begin, you might help students find a map that shows the Great Plains. Then help them locate maps showing the names of the Indian groups that lived within the area. (The National Geographic Society has an excellent wall map, "Indians of North America," which might prove helpful for the classroom.)

This might also be a good opportunity to point out the American Indian names that became part of the geography, such as Cheyenne, Omaha, Iowa, and Missouri.

1. GUIDED READING:
Paraphrasing
What does the legend say? If you go to the sacred spot from which the buffaloes began at the right time, you can see them come out of the lake.

2. GUIDED READING:
Making Inferences
How do the Indians regard the legend Nawa tells? They believe that it has great authority and believe that it is true.

> ### Language and Vocabulary
> **Description is the use of language that appeals to our senses of sight, smell, taste, hearing, and touch.** Description often creates a mood or feeling. This writer uses specific details to appeal to your five senses and to create a powerful mood or feeling. As you read, let the descriptive details work their magic. Let them help you experience what it was like to live with Little Wolf and his people on this vast windy prairie, in a world of nature that has almost disappeared with the shaggy buffaloes themselves.

Over the blazing campfires, when the wind moaned eerily through the thickets of juniper and fir, they spoke of it in the Indian tongue—of the strange lake to the south whose waters never rest. And Nawa, the wise man, who had lived such countless moons that not even the oldest member of the tribe could remember a time when Nawa was not old, declared

1 *that if you arrived at the right time, on the right night, you would see the buffaloes rise out of the middle of the lake and come crowding to the shore; for there, he said, was the sacred spot where the buffaloes began. It was not only Nawa who*

2 *declared that the buffaloes had their beginnings beneath the water and were born in the depths of the lake. The Indian legend, far older even than Nawa, said the same thing. Nawa was only the voice that kept the legend alive.*

Often in the winter, when the wind drove with a roar over the prairies and came thundering up the creek, making the tepees shudder and strain, Little Wolf would listen to the wind and think it was the stampede of the buffaloes. Then he would snuggle warmly under the buffalo robe that was his blanket and would be thankful for the shelter of his home. And sometimes he would go very far down the shadow ways of sleep and would meet the buffaloes as they came up from the lake, with the water shining on their shaggy coats and their black horns gleaming in the moon. And the buffaloes would begin by being very terrible, shaking their great heads at him as if they intended to kill him there and then. But later they would come up close, and smell him, and change their minds, and be friendly after all.

Little Wolf was only ten years old, but he could run faster than any of his friends. And the wildest pony was not too wild for him to catch and ride. But the great thing about him was that he had no fear. He knew that if an angry bull bison or a pack of prairie wolves ran him down, there would be nothing left of him but his bones. And he was well aware that if he fell into the hands of his people's enemies, the Assiniboins,[1] he would be killed and scalped as neatly as could be. Yet none of these things terrified him. Only, being wise for his age, he had a clear understanding that, for the present, it was better to keep out of their way.

But of all the thoughts that ran this way and that in his quick brain, the one that galloped the hardest was the thought of the great lake to the south where the buffaloes began. And as the days lengthened and he could smell springtime on the warm blowing air, the thought grew bigger and bigger in Little Wolf's mind. At last it was so very big that Little Wolf could not bear it any longer. And so, one morning, very early, before the village was awake, he crept out of the tepee and stole along below the junipers and tall firs till he came to the spot where the ponies were hobbled.[2]

The dawn was just beginning to break, and in the gray light the ponies looked like dark blotches along the creek. But Little Wolf's eyes were very sharp, and soon he had singled out his own pony, because it had a white forefoot and a white patch on its left side. When Little Wolf spoke, calling softly, the animal whinnied in answer and allowed itself to be caught. Little Wolf unhobbled the pony, slipped on the bridle he had brought with him, and leaped lightly upon its back. A few minutes afterward, horse and rider had left the camp behind them and were out on the prairie, going due south.

When the sun rose, they had already traveled far. Little Wolf's eyes constantly swept the immense horizon, searching for danger, moving or in half-concealed ambush. Far off, just on the edge of his sight, there was a dim spot on the yellowish gray of the prairie. Little Wolf reined in his pony and watched to see if it moved. If it did, it crept so slowly as to seem absolutely still. He decided that it was a herd of antelope feeding and that there was nothing to fear.

On he went, hour after hour, never ceasing to watch. The prairie grouse[3] got up almost under the pony's feet. Larks and sparrows filled the air with their singing, and everywhere wild roses were in bloom. It seemed as if nothing but peace would ever find its way among these singing birds and flowers. Yet Little Wolf knew well that his enemies, the Assiniboins, could come creeping along the hollows of the prairie

---

1. **Assiniboins** (ə·sin′ə·boins): members of the Sioux group of people, who lived in northeast Montana and parts of Canada.
2. **hobbled:** Two of a pony's legs would be tied loosely together, which prevented the pony from running away.
3. **grouse** (grous): plump birds.

Where the Buffaloes Begin 255

SCIENCE LINK

Students who love animals might be interested in finding out how the buffalo has almost become extinct. You might want to point out before they begin their research that what we call the buffalo is actually a bison *(American Bison bison)*. Students can find out about the bison in North America, the reasons for the near extinction of the animal, and the measures that have been taken to bring back the herds. If several students work on the project, have them collaborate to present what they find out for the class.

1. LITERARY ELEMENTS:
Point of View
Is the narrator blaming Little Wolf for not warning Little Wolf's people? Possible answer: No, because the narrator says that "If he had known," Little Wolf probably would have warned them, and this passage shows that he didn't know.

2. LITERARY ELEMENTS:
Plot
How does Little Wolf face this seeming defeat in his attempts to find the buffaloes? He is very patient and prepared to wait a long time to get what he wants.

like wolves, and that there is no moment more dangerous than when there is no hint of danger.

All this time he had not seen a single buffalo, but he told himself that this was because the herds had taken some other way and that he would probably not see them until he was near the lake. He lost sight of the shadowy spot that had been so far away. If he had known that it was a party of Assiniboins on the way to his village, he would have thought twice about continuing to the lake and would probably have returned along the trail to give warning to his people. But his head was too full of the singing of birds and the breath of roses, and, above all, of the great thought of the buffaloes, fighting below the lake.

It was late in the afternoon when, at last, he sighted the lake. It lay, a gray sheet with a glint of silver, glimmering under the sun. Little Wolf looked eagerly on all sides for any sign of buffaloes, but far and wide the prairies lay utterly deserted, very warm and still in the white shimmer of the air. As he drew nearer, however, he saw trails, many trails, all going in one direction and leading toward the lake. Antelope and coyote, wolf and buffalo—all had left traces behind them as they went to the water and returned. But it was the buffalo trails that were most numerous and most marked, and Little Wolf noted them above all the others.

When he was quite close to the lake, he dismounted; hobbling the pony, he turned it loose to graze. Then Little Wolf lay down behind some tussocks[4] of prairie grass, above the low bank at the edge of the lake, and waited. From this position he could overlook the lake without being seen. He gazed far over its glittering expanse, very still now under the strong beams of the sun. It was disappointingly still. Scarcely a ripple broke on the shore. Little Wolf could not possibly imagine that the buffaloes were struggling underneath. Where was the movement and the mysterious murmur of which Nawa had spoken? But Little Wolf was not impatient. He could afford to wait and listen for hours, if need be.

The time went on. Slowly the sun dipped westward, and the shadows of the

---
4. **tussocks:** clumps.

grass grew longer. The lake kept its outward stillness, and nothing happened. At last the sun reached the horizon; it lay there a few moments, a great ball of flame, then sank out of sight. Twilight fell, and all over the vast wilderness crept a peculiar silence, like a wild creature stealing from its lair. Far in the west there lingered the strange orange light that belongs to the prairie skies alone when the sun is down and the night winds sigh along the grass. Little Wolf could not tell whether it was the sighing of the wind or not, but there came to him along the margin of the lake a strange, low murmur that died away and rose again. As the night deepened, the sound grew clearer; Little Wolf was certain now that it was not the wind but a murmur that came from the center of the lake. For hours he lay and listened, but the mysterious murmur never ceased. Sometimes it was a little louder, sometimes a little softer; but always it was plain to hear—a wonderful and terrible thing in the silence of the night. And as Little Wolf lay watching under the stars, the words of Nawa kept singing in his head:

> Do you hear the noise that never ceases?
> It is the Buffaloes fighting far below.
> They are fighting to get out upon the prairie.
> They are born below the Water but are fighting for the Air,
> In the great lake in the Southland where the Buffaloes begin!

Suddenly, Little Wolf lifted himself up. He could not tell whether he had been asleep or not, but there in the lake he saw a wonderful sight: *the buffaloes!*

There they were, hundreds and hundreds of them, rising out of the water. He could not see the surface anymore. Instead, he saw a lake of swaying bodies and heads that shook; and on their horns and tossing heads the water gleamed in the moonlight, as it had done in his dreams.

Little Wolf felt the blood run along his body. He clutched at the prairie grass, crushing it in his hot hands. With staring eyes he drank in the great vision. And not only with his eyes but also with his ears and his nose: for his ears were filled with the trampling and snorting of the herd and the flash of the water as it moved under their hooves. And his nose inhaled the sharp moist smell of the great beasts as they crowded in on one another—the smell the wolves know well when it comes dropping down the wind.

Little Wolf never knew what came to him, what spirit of the wild whispered in his ear; but suddenly he leaped to his feet and cried out. And when he cried, he flung his arms above his head. And then he cried out again.

At the first cry, a shiver passed through the herd. As if they were one beast, the buffaloes threw up their heads and listened, absolutely still. Above the margin of the lake they saw, in the white light of the moon, a little wild boy making swift motions with his arms. He seemed to speak with his arms—to talk to them with

---

1. LITERARY ELEMENTS: Setting
Students should notice the sensory details, including the simile, that evoke the eerie setting.

2. GUIDED READING: Making Inferences
Do you think Little Wolf has correctly identified the murmuring sound he hears? Possible answer: Yes, since the Indians believe the legend is true, then Nawa's words about the noise must be true, too.

3. LITERARY ELEMENTS: Character
How does Little Wolf react when his goal is realized? He is overwhelmed; he is aware of the buffaloes with all his senses and is inspired to cry out and motion to them.

SOCIAL STUDIES LINK
You might have students find out as much as they can about the culture of the Plains Indians for a presentation. Students could work in groups, gathering information about subjects such as these: clothing, ceremonies, language, legends or stories, enemies, daily life, and arts and handiwork.

VISUAL CONNECTIONS
About the Artist
George Catlin (1796–1872) gave up a career in law and spent six summers traveling west in Indian territory making portraits and sketches of almost fifty Native American tribes. Many of his paintings can be seen today in the Smithsonian Institution in Washington, D.C.

You might have interested students do a research project on George Catlin. Students could report on Catlin's early life; on his travels in the American West among the Native American tribes; and on the subjects of some of his paintings. Note that Catlin's paintings serve as a record of a way of life that was even in his time very near extinction.

Buffalo Hunt by George Catlin (1835). Oil on canvas.

258 Short Stories

The Smithsonian Institution, Washington, D.C./Art Resource.

the ripple of his muscles and the thrust of his fingers in the air. They had never seen such a thing before. Their eyes fastened on the boy excitedly, and shot out sparks of light. And when he cried out again, there swept through the stillness of the herd a stir, a movement, a ripple that Little Wolf could see. And the ripple became a wave, and the wave a swell. It was a swell of buffaloes that began on the outskirts of the herd and broke along the margin of the lake in a terrifying roar.

It was a wonderful sound, that roar of the buffaloes on the edge of a stampede. It rolled far out on the prairie in the hollow silence of the night. Wandering wolves caught it, threw their long noses to the moon, and howled an answering cry.

It was the hour when, on the lonely prairie, sound carries an immense distance. But the ears it might have warned—the quick ears of Assiniboin warriors—did not catch it, for they were too far away on the northern trail.

On moccasins noiseless as the padded feet of the wolves, as intent, and almost more cruel, these painted warriors were stealthily approaching the camp of Little Wolf's people, determined to wipe them out before the Dog Star faded in the dawn.

But now the buffaloes had received the strange message that the Indian boy waved to them from the margin of the lake. Little Wolf did not understand this message. He had cried out to the buffaloes because he could not help himself, because he loved them as the creatures of his dreams. But when he saw and heard their answer, when

1. LITERARY ELEMENTS:
Foreshadowing
What do you think will happen to the Assiniboin? Possible answer: The buffalo will attack them.

2. GUIDED READING:
Paraphrasing
What do the Assiniboin intend to do? They intend to kill all of Little Wolf's tribe in a predawn attack.

3. GUIDED READING:
Interpreting Meaning
What do you think was the message that Little Wolf waved to the buffaloes? Possible answer: The message might have been to help him protect his people.

Where the Buffaloes Begin

PORTFOLIO ASSESSMENT
Students may be interested in creating their own versions of some of the art and crafts pictured in this selection. They may want to see more examples of American Indian art before they begin their own project. Suggest that they create a drawing or a craft of something familiar to them. They may want to enlist their art teacher's assistance in the planning. Display students' artwork and crafts in designated areas around the classroom. Consult with students individually to agree on how their art or craft will be assessed. (See *Portfolio Assessment and Professional Support Materials*, especially the section entitled **Suggestions for Portfolio Projects**.)

1. GUIDED READING:
Making Inferences
What did Little Wolf fear would happen? He feared that the buffaloes would trample him to death.

2. GUIDED READING:
Identifying Sequence of Events
What actually happened after Little Wolf jumped on his pony? Little Wolf tried to escape from the buffaloes, but could not outrun them because his pony was tired. The buffaloes began to gain, and the herd drew abreast of him. Soon they were all around him, but rather than trampling him, they rallied to his cry and ran with him.

---

they came surging out of the lake like a mighty flood, <u>bellowing</u> and stamping and tossing their heads, a wild excitement possessed him. For the first time in his life, he knew the meaning of fear.

1   Swift as the wolf for whom he was named, he darted toward his pony. To unhobble it and leap upon its back took but a moment. Then he was off, riding for his life!

Behind him came the terrible sound of the buffaloes as they swept out of the lake. Little Wolf threw a quick glance behind to see which way they took and saw the dark surging mass <u>heave</u> itself onto the prairie and gallop due north.

Chee-ah-ka-tchee, Wife of Not-to-way by George Catlin (1835–1836). Oil on canvas.

National Museum of American Art, Washington DC/Art Resource, NY

Little Wolf tried to escape the middle 2 rush of the herd by turning the pony's head slightly westward. Once the buffaloes surrounded him, he did not know what might happen. If the pony had been fresh, Little Wolf could easily have outstripped them, but after a long day the animal was tired, and was going at half its usual speed. Little Wolf again glanced over his shoulder. The buffaloes were gaining! He cried out to the pony—little, short cries that made a wild note in the night.

As they swept along, the leaders of the left flank of the herd drew so close that Little Wolf could hear the snorting sound of their breath. Then they were beside him, and the pony and the buffaloes were galloping together. Yet they did nothing to harm him. They did not seem to have any other desire but to gallop on into the night.

Soon Little Wolf was completely surrounded by the buffaloes. In front, behind, and on both sides of him, a heaving mass of buffaloes billowed like the sea. Again, as when he had cried out beside the lake, a wild feeling of excitement seized him, and he felt the blood stir along his scalp. And once again he shouted a cry—a long, ringing cry—flinging his arms above his head. And the buffaloes replied, bellowing a wild answer that rolled like thunder along the plains.

Northward the great gallop swept—down the hollows, over the swells of the prairie, below the lonely ridges with their piles of stones that mark where Indians leave their dead. Crashing through the alder thickets beside the creeks and

260   Short Stories

CLOSURE

Have students identify the passages in the story that contributed most forcibly to their sense of the setting. Have them point out the sensory details that helped them visualize the setting.

RETEACHING

Review the concept of point of view. Have students retell one main event in the story from the point of view of someone else, perhaps Nawa, a buffalo, an Assiniboin, Little Wolf's mother, Little Wolf himself speaking in first person, or an objective observer. Have students consider how the events and setting might have a different significance to each different narrator.

Carved statue of a buffalo. Made by the Plains Native Americans. Green quartzite.

through the shallow creeks themselves, churning the water into a muddy foam, the mighty herd rolled on its way; and the thunder of its coming spread terror far and wide. The antelopes were off like the wind; the badgers and coyotes slunk into their holes. Even the wolves heeded the warning, vanishing shadowlike along the hollows to the east and west.

Little Wolf was beside himself with excitement and joy. It seemed as if he, too, were a member of the herd, as if the buffaloes had adopted him and made him their own.

Suddenly he saw something ahead. He could not see clearly because of the buffaloes in front of him, but it looked like a band of men. They were not mounted but were running swiftly on foot, as if to regain their ponies. At first, Little Wolf thought they were his own people; he knew by the outline of the country that the camp could not be far off. But then he saw that the men were not running toward the camp but away from it. Very swiftly, the thought flashed on him: They were Assiniboins, the deadly enemies of his tribe. They must have left their ponies some distance away in order to approach the camp unseen through the long grass and attack Little Wolf's people as they slept!

Little Wolf knew well that unless his enemies reached their ponies in time, the buffaloes would cut off their retreat. Once that great herd hurled itself upon them, nothing could save them from being trampled. He saw the Assiniboins making desperate efforts to escape. He cried shrilly, hoping that it would excite the buffaloes even more. The buffaloes seemed to answer his cries. They bore down upon the fleeing men at a terrible gallop, never slackening speed. One by one the Assiniboins were overtaken, knocked down, and trampled underfoot.

Suddenly, Little Wolf's pony went down too. The boy leaped clear as the animal fell. By this time they were on the outskirts of the herd, and before Little Wolf could get to his fallen pony, the last buffalo had passed. The pony struggled to its feet, trembling but unharmed, and with his arm around its neck, Little Wolf watched the herd disappear into the night . . .

Over the blazing campfires, when the wind moans eerily through the thickets of juniper and fir, they still speak of the great lake to the south where the buffaloes begin. But now they always add the name of Little Wolf to the legend, for he is the boy who led the buffaloes and saved his people.

FOR STUDY AND DISCUSSION

Identifying Facts

1. The buffaloes began in the middle of a lake.
2. Little Wolf kept thinking about the lake until he couldn't bear it anymore and had to go see it.
3. Little Wolf cries out to the buffaloes, making them stampede.
4. Little Wolf saves his people from their enemies by guiding the buffalo stampede to run the enemies down before they reach Little Wolf's village.

Interpreting Meanings

5. Little Wolf's visit to the lake, his inciting the buffalo stampede, his perilous ride in the midst of the stampede, and the buffaloes' running down of the Assiniboin could all have happened in the world as we know it. The buffaloes' rising from the middle of a lake could not have happened.
6. One explanation might be that Little Wolf really encountered a herd of buffalo near the lake and did stampede them toward his own country, where they luckily killed a band of Little Wolf's enemies. The rising of the buffalo from the lake could be an inference Little Wolf made based on his beliefs, without actually seeing it.

Where the Buffaloes Begin

EXTENSION AND ENRICHMENT

Social Studies. Some students may wish to do research to learn more about the culture of the Plains Indians. Be sure they find out how the buffalo was essential to their culture.

Applying Meanings

7. Many students will say that heroes today are sports heroes, or TV heroes. Some might argue that we do have heroes who save lives at the risk of their own or who accomplish important acts at some risk.

Be sure they can explain why certain people become heroes.

8. Doubtless, Little Wolf today would be a leader. He probably would excel at sports (which ones?).

9. Modern heroes include astronauts, athletes, leaders such as Martin Luther King, Jr., and Lech Walesa who have fought for freedom against great odds.

An example of a sports legend is Babe Ruth's "calling" of a home run by pointing to the stands before the pitch.

FOCUS ON READING

Following a Sequence of Events

1. At last; one morning, very early, before the village was awake
2. Late in the afternoon; at last
3. Suddenly

LITERARY ELEMENTS

Setting

1. If "Mr. Tumnus" took place in Miami in the year 2000, details of lifestyle and dialect would change. Would it be eternal winter in Narnia, if Lucy lived in Miami?
2. If Tom Sawyer took

For Study and Discussion

IDENTIFYING FACTS

1. According to the legend, where did the buffaloes begin?
2. Explain why Little Wolf rides to the lake one morning.
3. What causes the buffaloes to stampede out of the water?
4. Tell how Little Wolf saves his people from their enemies.

INTERPRETING MEANINGS

5. Which events in this story of Little Wolf could really have happened? Which events could not happen in the world as we know it?
6. Suppose you wanted to tell this as a realistic story. How would you explain the fantastic details of Little Wolf's experience?

APPLYING MEANINGS

7. How do you think heroes are created today? Name three people you think are heroes or heroines.
8. Suppose that Little Wolf were living today. Suppose, in fact, that he has always lived in your town and that he attends your school. What kind of a "modern" boy do you think he might be?
9. Look through a newspaper; ask some of your relatives. Can you find a modern story of a heroic deed that might someday make a good legend? Do you know of any heroic legends that people keep passing on today?

Focus on Reading

FOLLOWING A SEQUENCE OF EVENTS

In a story, or **narrative,** clue words and phrases like *first, later, the next day,* and *at last* help you know when each event takes place. List the clue words and phrases that signal when the following events take place.

1. "At last it was so very big that Little Wolf could not bear it any longer. And so, one morning, very early, before the village was awake, he crept out of the tepee . . ."
2. "It was late in the afternoon when, at last, he sighted the lake."
3. "Suddenly, Little Wolf lifted himself up."

Literary Elements

SETTING

A few stories could take place in any setting at all, but most stories take place in very particular settings. In fact, most stories would not be the same if they were set someplace else. Review the following stories. Tell where each one is set. Could any of these stories be set someplace else and still be the same? (Use the **Index of Authors and Titles** at the back of this book to locate the page on which each story begins.)

1. "Mr. Tumnus": could this story take place in Miami, Florida, in the year 2000?
2. "The Adventures of Tom Sawyer": could this story take place anywhere in the United States in the year 2000?
3. "Sounder": could this story take place in any modern city?

4. "All Summer in a Day": could this story take place in a modern suburb in the United States?

Language and Vocabulary

SENSORY DETAILS

Writers use description to create a feeling or mood. Vivid description is made up of **sensory details,** that is, words and phrases that appeal to your senses of sight, hearing, touch, taste, and smell.

Beaded moccasins. Made by the Dakota, Blackfoot, or Assiniboin people.
National Museum of the American Indian, Smithsonian Institution.

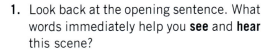

1. Look back at the opening sentence. What words immediately help you **see** and **hear** this scene?
2. Look back at the seventh paragraph beginning "On he went." What do you **see** and **hear** on the prairie? How does this description make you **feel** about the prairie setting?
3. Look back at the ninth paragraph, beginning "It was late in the afternoon." What words make you **see, hear,** and **feel** what it would be like to stand with Little Wolf on this late afternoon and look at the lake?
4. Look at the paragraph on page 257 that opens "Little Wolf felt the blood . . ." In this paragraph and the following ones, find the words that help you **see** and **hear** and **smell** the buffaloes and the great stampede. How does the writer make you **feel** about these great beasts?

Writing About Literature

WRITING FROM A DIFFERENT POINT OF VIEW

Imagine that you are a twelve-year-old Assiniboin who went along on the raiding party. You are the only one who managed to escape the buffalo stampede. You struggle back to your own camp. Write a paragraph telling what you would say to your people there.

Use the first-person pronoun *I*. Tell your people what happened. Try to use descriptive details telling what you **saw, heard, smelled,** and **felt** during the stampede.

About the Author

Olaf Baker was born in England in the 1870s. After leaving school, he traveled to the United States and spent many years traveling throughout the West. One of his favorite places was the vast Northern Plains area of the Midwest, which had been the territory of the Blackfoot, Crow, Sioux, Assiniboin, and Pawnee peoples. Baker wrote several stories and novels about Native Americans. "Where the Buffaloes Begin" was first published in 1915 by *St. Nicholas Magazine,* a very popular children's magazine of the time. When the story was republished in book form in 1981, it won the Caldecott Medal for its illustrations.

Where the Buffaloes Begin   263

---

place in the U.S. in the year 2000, details of American schools and fads would change.
3. The rural setting and era are crucial to *Sounder,* though it's possible that details of urban poverty could be substituted. But the boy would probably not be travelling to find his father: The prison locale would be known today.
4. A story about children locking a classmate in a closet so she'll miss a longed-for event is certainly conceivable in an American suburb. The difference would lie in the impact of what she has missed through a random act of cruelty.

LANGUAGE AND VOCABULARY
For answers, see the **Teaching Guide** at the beginning of the unit.

WRITING ABOUT LITERATURE
Writing from a Different Point of View
Look for sensory words. Student paragraphs should express awe, terror or grief.

Cultural Diversity

Every culture has its own customs. When we look closely at these customs, even if they seem strange at first, there are usually very good reasons that they exist. For example, according to the story, it is Chinese custom to behave in the following ways:

eat your soup by slurping (page 270)

protest when somone offers a compliment (page 270)

eat only one "dish" of food at a time (page 271)

Invite the class to discuss possible reasons for each of these customs.

TEACHING RESOURCES B
Teacher's Notes, p. 104

NO QUESTIONS ASKED

The All-American Slurp

LENSEY NAMIOKA

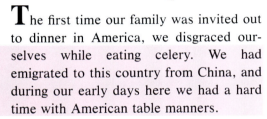

Before You Read

This comical short story is told by a young Chinese American girl. Her story is divided into six parts. You might use several readers and present parts of the story to the class. Before you present the story, decide how you will say the word *slurp*. How will you imitate the sounds of people eating celery *(crunch)*, or the sounds of threads coming off the celery stalk *(z-z-zip)*? How will you say *shloop*, which is the sound of a slurp in any language?

The first time our family was invited out to dinner in America, we disgraced ourselves while eating celery. We had emigrated to this country from China, and during our early days here we had a hard time with American table manners.

In China we never ate celery raw, or any other kind of vegetable raw. We always had to disinfect the vegetables in boiling water first. When we were presented with our first relish tray, the raw celery caught us unprepared.

We had been invited to dinner by our neighbors, the Gleasons. After arriving at the house, we shook hands with our hosts and packed ourselves into a sofa. As our family of four sat stiffly in a row, my younger brother and I stole glances at our parents for a clue as to what to do next.

Mrs. Gleason offered the relish tray to Mother. The tray looked pretty, with its tiny red radishes, curly sticks of carrots, and long, slender stalks of pale green celery. "Do try some of the celery, Mrs. Lin," she said. "It's from a local farmer, and it's sweet."

Mother picked up one of the green stalks, and Father followed suit. Then I picked up a stalk, and my brother did too. So there we sat, each with a stalk of celery in our right hand.

Mrs. Gleason kept smiling. "Would you like to try some of the dip, Mrs. Lin? It's my own recipe: sour cream and onion flakes, with a dash of Tabasco sauce."

Most Chinese don't care for dairy products, and in those days I wasn't even ready to drink fresh milk. Sour cream sounded perfectly revolting. Our family shook our heads in unison.

Mrs. Gleason went off with the relish tray to the other guests, and we carefully watched to see what they did. Everyone seemed to eat the raw vegetables quite happily.

Mother took a bite of her celery. *Crunch.* "It's not bad!" she whispered.

Father took a bite of his celery. *Crunch.* "Yes, it *is* good," he said, looking surprised.

I took a bite, and then my brother. *Crunch, crunch.* It was more than good; it

The All-American Slurp 265

MEETING INDIVIDUAL NEEDS
Auditory Learners • You might have students in your classroom who are quite good at making lively sounds that demonstrate the use of onomatopoeia in language. (In fact, you may have students who spend quite a lot of time making noises in the classroom.) Harness their energy and encourage them to imitate the crunch, z-z-zip, and schloop sounds that Namioka uses in the story. Then encourage students to recall other words that imitate sounds they are familiar with, such as *zip, pop, bark, yap,* and *meow.* Have them use their best imitative prowess to create realistic sounds.

1. GUIDED READING:
Visualizing
Encourage students to visualize this embarrassing moment.

2. LITERARY ELEMENTS:
Resolution
The narrator finds a resolution to the conflict in the shared attitudes of the two mothers.

3. GUIDED READING:
Contrasting Characters
Students should notice the contrasting styles of learning English (see page 267 for the parents' approaches).

---

was delicious. Raw celery has a slight sparkle, a zingy taste that you don't get in cooked celery. When Mrs. Gleason came around with the relish tray, we each took another stalk of celery, except my brother. He took two.

There was only one problem: Long strings ran through the length of the stalk, and they got caught in my teeth. When I help my mother in the kitchen, I always pull the strings out before slicing celery.

1 I pulled the strings out of my stalk. Z-z-zip, z-z-zip. My brother followed suit. Z-z-zip, z-z-zip, z-z-zip. To my left, my parents were taking care of their own stalks. Z-z-zip, z-z-zip, z-z-zip.

Suddenly I realized that there was dead silence except for our zipping. Looking up, I saw that the eyes of everyone in the room were on our family. Mr. and Mrs. Gleason, their daughter Meg, who was my friend, and their neighbors the Badels—they were all staring at us as we busily pulled the strings off our celery.

That wasn't the end of it. Mrs. Gleason announced that dinner was served and invited us to the dining table. It was lavishly covered with platters of food, but we couldn't see any chairs around the table. So we helpfully carried over some dining chairs and sat down. All the other guests just stood there.

Mrs. Gleason bent down and whispered to us, "This is a buffet[1] dinner. You help yourselves to some food and eat it in the living room."

---
1. **buffet** (boo·fā′).

Our family beat a retreat back to the sofa as if chased by enemy soldiers. For the rest of the evening, too mortified to go back to the dining table, I nursed a bit of potato salad on my plate.

Next day Meg and I got on the school bus together. I wasn't sure how she would feel about me after the spectacle our family made at the party. But she was just the same as usual, and the only reference she made to the party was, "Hope you and your folks got enough to eat last night. You certainly didn't take very much. Mom never tries to figure out how much food to prepare. She just puts everything on the table and hopes for the best."

2 I began to relax. The Gleasons' dinner party wasn't so different from a Chinese meal after all. My mother also puts everything on the table and hopes for the best.

Meg was the first friend I had made after we came to America. I eventually got acquainted with a few other kids in school, but Meg was still the only real friend I had.

3 My brother didn't have any problems making friends. He spent all his time with some boys who were teaching him baseball, and in no time he could speak English much faster than I could—not better, but faster.

I worried more about making mistakes, and I spoke carefully, making sure I could say everything right before opening my mouth. At least I had a better accent than my parents, who never really got rid of their Chinese accent, even years later. My parents had both studied English in

266 Short Stories

school before coming to America, but what they had studied was mostly written English, not spoken.

Father's approach to English was a scientific one. Since Chinese verbs have no tense, he was fascinated by the way English verbs changed form according to whether they were in the present, past imperfect, perfect, pluperfect, future, or future perfect tense. He was always making diagrams of verbs and their inflections,[2] and he looked for opportunities to show off his mastery of the pluperfect and future perfect tenses, his two favorites. "I shall have finished my project by Monday," he would say smugly.

Mother's approach was to memorize lists of polite phrases that would cover all possible social situations. She was constantly muttering things like "I'm fine, thank you. And you?" Once she accidentally stepped on someone's foot, and hurriedly blurted, "Oh, that's quite all right!" Embarrassed by her slip, she resolved to do better next time. So when someone stepped on *her* foot, she cried, "You're welcome!"

In our own different ways, we made progress in learning English. But I had another worry, and that was my appearance. My brother didn't have to worry, since Mother bought him blue jeans for school, and he dressed like all the other boys. But she insisted that girls had to wear skirts.

---

2. **inflections** (in·flek'shəns): changes in the form of a verb to indicate things like tense or speaker (*am, are, was, were,* for examples, are just a few of the inflections of the verb *to be*).

By the time she saw that Meg and the other girls were wearing jeans, it was too late. My school clothes were bought already, and we didn't have money left to buy new outfits for me. We had too many other things to buy first, like furniture, pots, and pans.

The first time I visited Meg's house, she took me upstairs to her room, and I wound up trying on her clothes. We were pretty much the same size, since Meg was shorter and thinner than average. Maybe that's how we became friends in the first place. Wearing Meg's jeans and T-shirt, I looked at myself in the mirror. I could almost pass for an American—from the back, anyway. At least the kids in school wouldn't stop and stare at me in the hallways, which was what they did when they saw me in my white blouse and navy blue skirt that went a couple of inches below the knees.

When Meg came to my house, I invited her to try on my Chinese dresses, the ones with a high collar and slits up the sides. Meg's eyes were bright as she looked at herself in the mirror. She struck several sultry poses, and we nearly fell over laughing.

The dinner party at the Gleasons' didn't stop my growing friendship with Meg. Things were getting better for me in other ways too. Mother finally bought me some jeans at the end of the month, when Father got his paycheck. She wasn't in any hurry about buying them at first, until I worked on her. This is what I did. Since we didn't

---

1. GUIDED READING:
Self-Questioning
Students will probably have an easy time imagining how it would feel to be out-of-fashion.

The All-American Slurp

1. GUIDED READING:
Making Inferences
Students should notice that after a slow start, the Americanization of the Lin family proceeds rapidly.

2. GUIDED READING:
Predicting Outcomes
You may wish to encourage students to imagine what might happen to the Lin family at this elegant restaurant.

have a car in those days, I often ran down to the neighborhood store to pick up things for her. The groceries cost less at a big supermarket, but the closest one was many blocks away. One day, when she ran out of flour, I offered to borrow a bike from our neighbor's son and buy a ten-pound bag of flour at the big supermarket. I mounted the boy's bike and waved to Mother. "I'll be back in five minutes!"

Before I started pedaling, I heard her voice behind me. "You can't go out in public like that! People can see all the way up to your thighs!"

"I'm sorry," I said innocently. "I thought you were in a hurry to get the flour." For dinner we were going to have pot-stickers (fried Chinese dumplings), and we needed a lot of flour.

"Couldn't you borrow a girl's bicycle?" complained Mother. "That way your skirt won't be pushed up."

"There aren't too many of those around," I said. "Almost all the girls wear jeans while riding a bike, so they don't see any point buying a girl's bike."

1 We didn't eat pot-stickers that evening, and Mother was thoughtful. Next day we took the bus downtown and she bought me a pair of jeans. In the same week, my brother made the baseball team of his junior high school, Father started taking driving lessons, and Mother discovered rummage sales. We soon got all the furniture we needed, plus a dart board and a 1,000-piece jigsaw puzzle (fourteen hours later, we discovered that it was a 999-piece jigsaw puzzle). There was hope that the Lins might become a normal American family after all.

Then came our dinner at the Lakeview restaurant.

The Lakeview was an expensive restaurant, one of those places where a headwaiter dressed in tails[3] conducted you to your seat, and the only light came from candles and flaming desserts. In one corner of the room a lady harpist played tinkling melodies.

Father wanted to celebrate, because he had just been promoted. He worked for an electronics company, and after his English started improving, his superiors decided to appoint him to a position more suited to his training. The promotion not only brought a higher salary but was also a tremendous boost to his pride.

Up to then we had eaten only in Chinese restaurants. Although my brother and I were becoming fond of hamburgers, my parents didn't care much for western food, other than chow mein.

2 But this was a special occasion, and Father asked his coworkers to recommend a really elegant restaurant. So there we were at the Lakeview, stumbling after the headwaiter in the murky dining room.

At our table we were handed our menus, and they were so big that to read mine I almost had to stand up again. But why bother? It was mostly in French, anyway.

Father, being an engineer, was always

---

3. **tails:** short for coattails. The expression refers to the long coattails on formal suit jackets.

268 Short Stories

1. LITERARY ELEMENTS:
Humor
This passage is humorous because of the incongruity between Mr. Lin's assurance that he can approach life in a scientific, systematic way and the failure of this method.

1 systematic. He took out a pocket French dictionary. "They told me that most of the items would be in French, so I came prepared." He even had a pocket flashlight, the size of a marking pen. While Mother held the flashlight over the menu, he looked up the items that were in French.

"*Pâté en croûte*,"[4] he muttered. "Let's see . . . *pâté* is paste . . . *croûte* is crust . . . hmm . . . a paste in crust."

The waiter stood looking patient. I squirmed and died at least fifty times.

At long last Father gave up. "Why don't we just order four complete dinners at random?" he suggested.

"Isn't that risky?" asked Mother.

"The French eat some rather peculiar things, I've heard."

"A Chinese can eat anything a Frenchman can eat," Father declared.

The soup arrived in a plate. How do you get soup up from a plate? I glanced at the other diners, but the ones at the nearby tables were not on their soup course, while the more distant ones were invisible in the darkness.

Fortunately, my parents had studied books on western etiquette before they came to America. "Tilt your plate," whispered my mother. "It's easier to spoon the soup up that way."

She was right. Tilting the plate did the trick. But the etiquette book didn't say anything about what you did after the soup

---

4. *pâté en croûte* (pä·tā′ onh kro͞ot).

The All-American Slurp 269

1. GUIDED READING:
Self-Questioning
You may want to encourage students to consider what they would have done in this situation.

1 reached your lips. As any respectable Chinese knows, the correct way to eat your soup is to slurp. This helps to cool the liquid and prevent you from burning your lips. It also shows your appreciation.

We showed our appreciation. *Shloop*, went my father. *Shloop*, went my mother. *Shloop, shloop*, went my brother, who was the hungriest.

The lady harpist stopped playing to take a rest. And in the silence, our family's consumption of soup suddenly seemed unnaturally loud. You know how it sounds on a rocky beach when the tide goes out and the water drains from all those little pools? They go *shloop, shloop, shloop*. That was the Lin family, eating soup.

At the next table a waiter was pouring wine. When a large *shloop* reached him, he froze. The bottle continued to pour, and red wine flooded the tabletop and into the lap of a customer. Even the customer didn't notice anything at first, being also hypnotized by the *shloop, shloop, shloop*.

It was too much. "I need to go to the toilet," I mumbled, jumping to my feet. A waiter, sensing my urgency, quickly directed me to the ladies' room.

I splashed cold water on my burning face, and as I dried myself with a paper towel, I stared into the mirror. In this perfumed ladies' room, with its pink-and-silver wallpaper and marbled sinks, I looked completely out of place. What was I doing here? What was our family doing in the Lakeview restaurant? In America?

The door to the ladies' room opened. A woman came in and glanced curiously at me. I retreated into one of the toilet cubicles and latched the door.

Time passed—maybe half an hour, maybe an hour. Then I heard the door open again, and my mother's voice. "Are you in there? You're not sick, are you?"

There was real concern in her voice. A girl can't leave her family just because they slurp their soup. Besides, the toilet cubicle had a few drawbacks as a permanent residence. "I'm all right," I said, undoing the latch.

Mother didn't tell me how the rest of the dinner went, and I didn't want to know. In the weeks following, I managed to push the whole thing into the back of my mind, where it jumped out at me only a few times a day. Even now, I turn hot all over when I think of the Lakeview restaurant.

But by the time we had been in this country for three months, our family was definitely making progress toward becoming Americanized. I remember my parents' first PTA meeting. Father wore a neat suit and tie, and Mother put on her first pair of high heels. She stumbled only once. They met my homeroom teacher and beamed as she told them that I would make honor roll soon at the rate I was going. Of course, Chinese etiquette forced Father to say that I was a very stupid girl and Mother to protest that the teacher was showing favoritism toward me. But I could tell they were both very proud.

The day came when my parents announced that they wanted to give a dinner party. We

270 Short Stories

had invited Chinese friends to eat with us before, but this dinner was going to be different. In addition to a Chinese-American family, we were going to invite the Gleasons.

"Gee, I can hardly wait to have dinner at your house," Meg said to me. "I just *love* Chinese food."

That was a relief. Mother was a good cook, but I wasn't sure if people who ate sour cream would also eat chicken gizzards stewed in soy sauce.

Mother decided not to take a chance with chicken gizzards. Since we had western guests, she set the table with large dinner plates, which we never used in Chinese meals. In fact we didn't use individual plates at all, but picked up food from the platters in the middle of the table and brought it directly to our rice bowls. Following the practice of Chinese-American restaurants, Mother also placed large serving spoons on the platters.

The dinner started well. Mrs. Gleason exclaimed at the beautifully arranged dishes of food: the colorful candied fruit in the sweet-and-sour pork dish, the noodle-thin shreds of chicken meat stir-fried with tiny peas, and the glistening pink prawns[5] in a ginger sauce.

At first I was too busy enjoying my food to notice how the guests were doing. But soon I remembered my duties. Sometimes guests were too polite to help themselves and you had to serve them with more food.

---

5. **prawns:** shellfish, something like large shrimp.

I glanced at Meg, to see if she needed more food, and my eyes nearly popped out at the sight of her plate. It was piled with food: The sweet-and-sour meat pushed right against the chicken shreds, and the chicken sauce ran into the prawns. She had been taking food from a second dish before she finished eating her helping from the first!

Horrified, I turned to look at Mrs. Gleason. She was dumping rice out of her bowl and putting it on her dinner plate. Then she ladled prawns and gravy on top of the rice and mixed everything together, the way you mix sand, gravel, and cement to make concrete.

I couldn't bear to look any longer, and I turned to Mr. Gleason. He was chasing a pea around his plate. Several times he got it to the edge, but when he tried to pick it up with his chopsticks, it rolled back toward the center of the plate again. Finally, he put down his chopsticks and picked up the pea with his fingers. He really did! A grown man!

All of us, our family and the Chinese guests, stopped eating to watch the activities of the Gleasons. I wanted to giggle. Then I caught my mother's eyes on me. She frowned and shook her head slightly, and I understood the message: The Gleasons were not used to Chinese ways, and they were just coping the best they could. For some reason I thought of celery strings.

When the main courses were finished, Mother brought out a platter of fruit. "I hope you weren't expecting a sweet des-

---

1. GUIDED READING:
Understanding Contrast
Point out that this dinner party is going to be a counterpart of the dinner party at the Gleasons' described at the beginning of the story.

2. GUIDED READING:
Making Inferences About Character
Perhaps because of her experience at the Gleasons', Mrs. Lin is sensitive to cultural differences and makes concessions to western tastes and customs in planning her party.

The All-American Slurp

COOPERATIVE LEARNING
Ethnic feasts can be fun and can help students to develop an appreciation of others' cultures. Groups of five or six students may want to provide appetizer-sized portions of ethnic foods for the class to sample and enjoy. The group may also want to present a panel discussion in which they talk about such things as table manners, customs, utensils, and staple foods of an ethnic culture. Suggest that each member of the group share a particular expertise, such as manners or staple foods.

1. LITERARY ELEMENTS:
Theme
This last incident neatly ties up the selection. Namioka has shown that members of any culture have customs that make sense only to themselves and which are misinterpreted by others, but tolerance and understanding of the different ways different peoples act can smooth over the embarrassing situations that result.

sert," she said. "Since the Chinese don't eat dessert, I didn't think to prepare any."

"Oh, I couldn't possibly eat dessert!" cried Mrs. Gleason. "I'm simply stuffed!"

Meg had different ideas. When the table was cleared, she announced that she and I were going for a walk. "I don't know about you, but I feel like dessert," she told me, when we were outside. "Come on, there's a Dairy Queen down the street. I could use a big chocolate milkshake!"

Although I didn't really want anything more to eat, I insisted on paying for the milkshakes. After all, I was still hostess.

Meg got her large chocolate milkshake and I had a small one. Even so, she was finishing hers while I was only half done. Toward the end she pulled hard on her straws and went *shloop, shloop*.

"Do you always slurp when you eat a milkshake?" I asked, before I could stop myself.

Meg grinned. "Sure. All Americans slurp."

About the Author

Lensey Namioka (1929–   ) was born in Beijing, China, and came to the United States with her parents when she was nine. As a child, she liked to make up stories about princes, dragons, and magical powers. Namioka studied and taught mathematics before she began writing stories for young people. She has written a series of novels about two young samurai warriors, Matsuko and Zenta, in feudal Japan. She is also the author of *Who's Hu?*, a humorous story about a Chinese American teenager, and *The Phantom of Tiger Mountain,* a mystery set in China. A recent book, *The Loyal Cat,* is based on a story told by her husband's uncle, a priest at a "cat temple" in Japan.

OBJECTIVES

The overall aim is for students to apply a set of standards in evaluating short stories.

PRESENTATION

You might want to assign a small group of students to each standard—plot, character, setting, point of view, and theme—and have them use the questions to evaluate that particular literary element of the stories. Each group can explain to the class the standard they have been assigned and then report their evaluations of the stories. Then you might read the new story aloud to the class and have the students work independently to apply the various criterions, or you might reassign the groups to work on each standard and to share their ideas orally with the class.

EVALUATING SHORT STORIES

Because an evaluation is really a type of opinion, it can never be proved absolutely true. But an evaluation can be judged by looking at the kind of evidence that is used to back it up. Students should be prepared to use good examples from the stories to support their evaluations.

Answers

Answers will vary.
1. Gardner presents his events in chronological order with plenty of foreshadowing to create suspense.
2. Cormier uses first-person point of view to reveal Jerry's internal feelings and motivations for his actions.
3. It is through the setting that Fiona finds out about prejudice and isolation. The two settings provide the contrast between the two worlds and bring about Fiona's loss of innocence.
4. From Maibon's point of view, the reader might not have known about the other characters' feelings. We would see and understand only what Maibon sees and comprehends.
5. Theme of "All Summer in a Day" might be as follows: People often resent those who are different or those who have had expe-

---

FOCUS ON Reading and Critical Thinking

EVALUATING SHORT STORIES

You have studied some key elements of short stories in this unit. Below are some standards that you can use to **evaluate**, or judge, the quality of any short story you read. Use a separate sheet of paper to answer the questions marked with this symbol: ■.

Plot

1. *Is the conflict in the story clear and believable? Does the plot hold the reader's interest?* Even stories with elements of fantasy, such as John Gardner's "Dragon, Dragon," should include a well-developed conflict.

   ■ What structure does Gardner use in "Dragon, Dragon" (page 166) to draw out the conflict and to create suspense?

Character

2. *Do the characters' actions match their words and thoughts? Are their actions clearly motivated by events in the story? Are the characters lifelike and believable?*

   ■ Think about Jerry in "President Cleveland, Where Are You?" (page 178). How does Robert Cormier reveal Jerry as a complex individual, different from any other character in the story?

Setting

3. *What role does the setting play? Is the setting realistic or fantastic? Does the setting have an important connection to the plot, or could the story have been set in any time and place?*

   ■ In Elizabeth Enright's "Nancy" (page 233), how is the setting related to the central conflict of the story? How does the setting help to create atmosphere or mood in this story?

Point of View

4. *What point of view is used and what is its purpose?* For example, James Berry uses first-person point of view in "Becky and the Wheels-and-Brake Boys" (page 220) to help us understand why Becky wants a bicycle.

   ■ How do you think Lloyd Alexander's "The Stone" (page 206) might have been different if Maibon had told the story from his own point of view?

Theme

5. *Does the story offer an important idea or message about people or about life?* Some stories are written purely for entertainment. From others, however, the reader can draw an important or valuable lesson. More often than not, readers draw a conclusion about the theme from what happens in the story.

   ■ Choose *one* of the following stories: Ray Bradbury's "All Summer in a Day" (page 194) or Olaf Baker's "Where the Buffaloes Begin" (page 252). How

would you state the message or theme of the story you have chosen? Test your statement by seeing if it includes all the important aspects of the story.
- Do you think Lensey Namioka's story "The All-American Slurp" (page 264) is purely humorous entertainment? Or does a more serious theme lie behind the comedy? How would you state Namioka's central message?

Use the questions on page 274 to evaluate the following story.

Rolls for the Czar
Robin Kinkead

This is a tale of the days of the Czars, of ermine and gold and pure white bread.

In Saint Petersburg[1] the Czar held his court with pomp and ceremony that dazzled peasants and ambassadors alike. His Winter Palace covered acres by the side of the frozen Neva.[2] It had pillars of lapis lazuli[3] and of rare stone from the Urals. Its halls held treasures from all the world.

Once a year the Czar paid a visit of state to Moscow, where the rich merchants lived, trade center of the Imperial Domain. Here he would sit in the throne room of the Kremlin,[4] where his ancestors once ruled warring Muscovy.[5]

---

1. **Saint Petersburg:** city in northwest Russia.
2. **Neva** (Nē′və, nyĕ·vă′): a river.
3. **lapis lazuli** (lăp′ĭs lăz′yōō·lē): an azure-blue gemstone.
4. **Kremlin** (krĕm′lən): the fortress of Moscow.
5. **Muscovy** (mŭs′kə·vē): the Russian Empire.

There was another great man in Moscow—a baker, Markov by name. The master bakers of the city were famous, and Markov was prince among them. His cakes and pastry were renowned throughout all the Russias, but his rolls were the best of all: pure white, like the driven snow of the steppes, a crust just hard enough to crunch, the bread not too soft, but soft enough to hold the melted butter.

Merchant princes from the gold rivers of Siberia, chieftains from the Caucasus in high fur hats, nobles from their feudal estates in the country, all came to Moscow to eat Markov's rolls.

The Czar himself was a mighty eater and especially fond of Markov's delicacies. So one day in February, when it came time for a visit to Moscow, he was thinking of Markov and his art, anticipating the rolls. His private car bore the imperial coat of arms. The rest of the train was filled with grand dukes, princes of the blood, and noble ladies. The railroad track ran straight as an arrow five hundred miles through the snow, the white birch forests, and the pines.

The train chuffed into the Moscow station, into a morning of sun and frost. The sun sparkled on the gold domes of churches, it glittered on the cuirasses[6] of a regiment of guards, all men of noble birth.

---

6. **cuirasses** (kwĭ·răs′əs): armor for the breast and back.

Smoke rose straight up from chimneys. Twin jets of steam snorted from the nostrils of the three horses of the Czar's troika.[7] The Czar has a fine appetite.

The horses' hoofs kicked up gouts of snow as they galloped over the moat and through the gate in the Kremlin wall. The Czar walked up the royal staircase, carpeted in red and lined with bowing servants. He was thinking of the rolls.

He went through the formal greetings with a distracted look, then sat down eagerly at the breakfast table. Not a glance did he give the caviar, the smoked sterlets,[8] the pheasant in aspic. He watched the door. When a royal footman came through carrying a silver platter loaded with rolls, the Czar smiled. All was well.

The Czar rubbed his hands and took a steaming roll. He broke it open and the smile vanished from his face. A dead fly lay embedded in the bread. Courtiers crowded around to look.

"Bring Markov here!" said the Czar, with one of his terrible glances.

The banquet room was silent in tense horror. Markov came in puffing slightly but bearing himself with the pride of a master artist.

"Look at this, Markov," said the Czar, pointing at the fly, "and tell me what it is."

Markov looked and stood frozen for a moment. Princes, nobles, and servants all leaned forward waiting for doom to strike him. The Czar could bend horseshoes in his bare hands. A word from him and the bleak wastes of Siberia lay waiting.

No man could tell what Markov thought, but they knew that a fly had endangered his life. He reached to the platter and picked up the fly. He put it in his mouth and ate it. Every eye watched him swallow.

"It is a raisin, Sire," he said.

Wrath faded from the Czar's face. He broke out laughing and the nobles relaxed.

"Markov," he said, "we grant you a coat of arms with a fly as the motif.[9] A fly imperiled your life and a fly saved your life."

And the Czar went on with his rolls.

---

7. **troika** (troi′kə): a small carriage drawn by a team of three horses.
8. **sterlets** (stûr′līts): sturgeon, a source of caviar.

9. **motif** (mō·tēf′): main figure in the design.

OBJECTIVES

The overall aim is for students to incorporate the important elements of short stories into a story of their own.

PRESENTATION

You might want to have students use ideas from their journals to begin their prewriting. Or you might want to ask students to bring pictures of people from magazines and newspapers to class. Paste these on construction paper or tagboard and let students choose two or more characters in the pictures and create a short dialogue between them. To the dialogue they can add setting, plot, point of view, and theme. Students might also enjoy role-playing to generate dialogue which can be recorded. Then they can transcribe the dialogue, revise it, proofread it, and publish it.

FOCUS ON Writing

WRITING A SHORT STORY

In a **short story** you entertain your readers by creating lifelike characters, together with a well-developed plot and a specific setting. In this unit you have studied some of the important elements of short stories. Now you will have the chance to write a story of your own.

Prewriting

1. Start to find a story idea by thinking of familiar people, places, and situations. Notice a person or problem—and give your imagination free rein. You might want to ask yourself some "What if?" questions such as the following:

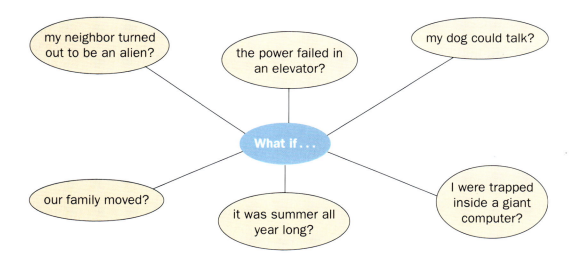

You can also use these methods to find a story idea:
- brainstorming with classmates
- reviewing notes for this unit
- looking at family albums
- skimming news stories
- observing people in a park or mall

2. Work on turning your story idea into a **plot** by making some notes on the following key plot elements:
   - introduction
   - conflict
   - climax
   - resolution

Pay special attention to the main **conflict** or problem. Plan to introduce this conflict early in your story in order to grab the reader's attention. Here are

 HOLT WRITER'S WORKSHOP

This computer program provides help for all types of writing through guided instruction for each step of the writing process. (Program available separately.)

See **Elements of Writing, Introductory Course,** Chapter 5, for more instruction on creative writing.

WRITING A SHORT STORY

The central element of any good story is conflict, which is all around us. As the cornerstone of their stories, writers often explore the major conflicts that are closest to them—within their own families and communities. One reason to read and to write such stories, beyond the pleasure they give, is to gain understanding of what life is all about.

Prewriting

Encourage students not to skip any of the prewriting strategies. With plenty of notes and ideas, students will find that their stories will almost write themselves. You might want to remind students that their stories must be linked so that one happening causes another. When students are ready to create their story maps, you might want to talk about

Focus on Writing 277

> **TRANSPARENCY 17**
> **Writing Process**
> *Writing a Short Story* – helps students to formulate and organize creative ideas for a short story.

cause and effect and have students make sure that the events of their plots are linear and propelled forward by other events. Students might share their story maps with a small group to check for gaps in their story lines.

Writing

Remind students to be conscious of and consistent in the point of view they have chosen and not to shift the point of view as they write. Students might need to look at some of the stories in this unit for methods of beginning and ending their stories. Then have students brainstorm ideas and write them down to display in the room while they write. Emphasize for students the importance of a good title.

---

three types of conflict to consider:

- a person versus another person (external conflict)
- a person versus a force of nature (external conflict)
- a struggle or problem within a character's mind (internal conflict)

When you have identified the key conflict of your story, decide what the **climax** or **high point** will be—the point where the conflict is settled one way or the other. This is usually the point of greatest excitement or tension: for example, the moment in Lloyd Alexander's "The Stone" when Maibon is finally able to throw away the magic stone (page 215). [See **Focus** assignment on page 176.]

3. Make some notes about the **characters** for your story. Fill out a character chart like the one below for each person you create:

Character Chart
Name: _____ Age: _____
Physical Appearance: _____
Way of Moving and Speaking: _____
Personality Traits: _____
Likes and Dislikes: _____
Habits: _____

[See **Focus** assignment on page 191.]

4. Make a list of details for the **setting** of your story—the time and place of the events. Pay special attention to **sensory details** when you imagine the setting: details that appeal to sight, hearing, taste, smell, and touch. Think about the possible relationship between setting and mood in your story. [See **Focus** assignment on page 251.]

5. Decide on the **point of view,** or vantage point, from which you will tell your story. In **first-person point of view,** your narrator will be a character in the story and will use the first-person pronouns *I, me,* and *my.* In **third-person point of view,** the narrator will be outside the story. The narrator will be an omniscient or "all-knowing" storyteller who knows everything about the characters and their problems. If you choose this point of view, you will refer to your characters with third-person pronouns such as *he, she,* and *they.* [See **Focus** assignment on page 231.]

6. Use all the notes you have made so far to create a **story map,** a plan that lists all the main elements of your story. [For a sample story map, see **Literary Elements** on page 175.]

Writing

1. When you write your story, use **chronological** or **time order** to tell events. Remember that **transitions** can help your readers to follow your story better. Here are some helpful **transitional words and phrases:**

after	finally	soon
at once	first	suddenly
before	meanwhile	then
eventually	next	when

2. You can make your story more lifelike if you use **dialogue,** or the words that characters actually say. Say the words

278 Short Stories

CLOSURE

Call on students to identify the story elements as they used them in their own short stories.

---

aloud, and decide if they sound like real conversation. When you write dialogue, feel free to use brief phrases, contractions, and slang.

3. Remember that **vivid action verbs** and **sensory details** are two powerful tools a writer has to make a story lively.

Evaluating and Revising

1. When you have finished your first draft, put it aside for a while. Then reread your writing; remember that your audience wants to be entertained. Pay attention to using exact, vivid words. Here is how one writer revised a passage from a short story.

Writer's Model

Raven knew that he might have only ~~a short time~~ *minutes* to save the President's life. He ~~looked at~~ *frantically scanned* the computer printout, ~~He~~ *Searching* ~~looked~~ for initials that matched the code letters for the world's top terrorists. ~~He~~ *When* came up blank, ~~He~~ took a deep breath. "Something's ~~strange~~ *wrong*," he murmured. "I'm just not ~~understanding~~ *getting* one piece of ~~this situation~~ *puzzle*."

2. You may find the following checklist helpful as you revise your short story.

Checklist for Evaluation and Revision

✔ Do I grab the reader's attention at the beginning?
✔ Do I present a strong conflict for one of the main characters?
✔ Are the characters lifelike and believable?
✔ Do I tell the events in chronological order?
✔ Is there a clear climax or turning point?
✔ Is the setting clear?
✔ Does the resolution of the story make sense?

Proofreading and Publishing

1. Proofread your short story and correct any errors you find in grammar, usage, and mechanics. (Here you may find it helpful to refer to the **Handbook for Revision** on pages 750–785.) Then prepare a final version of your story by making a clean copy.

2. Consider some of the following publication methods for your story:
   - join with classmates to produce a "story hour" for younger children
   - illustrate your story with drawings or other art work and post it on the class bulletin board
   - submit your story to the school or community newspaper

Portfolio If your teacher approves, you may wish to keep a copy of your work in your writing folder or portfolio.

Evaluating and Revising

Remind students that a good story should have a message or theme. To begin evaluating their stories, students should write down the theme of their stories. If they are unclear about their themes, then they need to revise for content, maybe rethinking the conflict and character motivation and growth or change. Students might need to emphasize their themes through details in their story endings: some dialogue, a detail about setting, or a thought in the mind of the main character or narrator. Students can work in small groups to read their stories aloud and apply the questions in the **Checklist for Evaluation and Revision.** Students might also share their stories with family members for additional ideas for improvement.

Proofreading and Publishing

Students should proofread their stories, paying close attention to punctuation and paragraphing, especially in dialogue. Working with a partner, students can check each other's stories for correct spelling, capitalization, and verb usage.

Focus on Writing

UNIT 4 ◆ TEACHING GUIDE

POETRY

OVERVIEW OF THE UNIT

What is a poem? There is no single, all-inclusive definition of poetry. Poets and critics have discussed the question for thousands of years. Most agree that most poems have certain features in common. In a poem, both sound and sense are important. Poems usually have a rhythmical quality, whether or not there is a regular pattern of meter. Poems usually have sounds that please our ears, whether or not there is rhyme. Repetition is one important means of creating poetic rhythm. Most of the verbal devices we associate with poetry—end rhyme, internal rhyme, alliteration, onomatopoeia, rhythm, refrain—are ways of repeating specific kinds of sounds. Yet, perhaps paradoxically, compactness is an equally important feature of poetry. In a good poem, every word is there for a reason, sometimes for more than one reason.

ABOUT THIS UNIT

The poetry in this unit is divided into five sections, which represent five major elements of poetry, or five ways of looking at poetry. In the section Story Poems, students will read aloud narrative verse in the form of two classics of nonsense: Dr. Seuss's "The Sneetches" and "The Jumblies" by Edward Lear. In the section Sound Effects, students will respond to such ear-pleasing aspects of poetry as rhyme, refrain, alliteration, and onomatopoeia. The section Using Your Senses introduces students to the world of imagery. A highlight of this unit is a cycle of four classic Japanese haiku. In the section Making Comparisons, students will become acquainted with figurative language—simile and metaphor. In the section Ideas and Feelings, students will respond to the themes and personal expressions of the poets. A special feature of this unit is Portraits of Imagination, a collection of fifteen poems written by imaginative sixth graders who have contributed to this textbook.

OBJECTIVES OF THE UNIT

The aims of this unit for students are
- To monitor their own reading
- To gain skills in reading poetry aloud
- To recognize and to use the elements of poetry, such as imagery, figurative language, rhythm, rhyme, alliteration, onomatopoeia, wordplay, and tone
- To recognize some techniques of free verse
- To identify a poem's speaker
- To identify and to use portmanteau words, prefixes, slang, and cognates in other languages
- To imitate a poet's style
- To illustrate a poem
- To write their own poems
- To write creatively and critically about poetry

CONCEPTS AND SKILLS

The following concepts and skills are treated in this unit:

CLOSE READING OF A POEM
One Reader's Response 282
Looking at Yourself as a Reader 283

FOCUS ON READING AND CRITICAL THINKING
Relating Sound to Meaning 380

LITERARY ELEMENTS
Rhythm 292, 316
Alliteration 299
Refrain 304
Rhyme Scheme 308
Rhymes and Alliteration 319

Imagery 321, 324
Simile and Metaphor 333
Metaphors 346, 358
Couplets 355
Free Verse 358, 362, 366

LANGUAGE AND VOCABULARY
Wordplay 292
Sounds and Spellings 312
Slang 316
Concrete Words 329
Onomatopoeia 337

Homophones 339
Prefixes 342
Names in Other Languages 346
Spanish Words 362

OPPORTUNITIES FOR WRITING

Focus on Writing a Poem
Finding a Subject 299
Experimenting with Refrain 304
Exploring Rhymes in Couplets 304
Playing with Words 308
Experimenting with Sound Effects 313
Experimenting with Visual Effects 317

Writing About Literature
Describing a Fantastic Creature 292
Creating Metaphors 337
Letting an Object Speak 339
Writing a Journal Entry 355
Interviewing an Older Person 363
Describing Your Phizzog 369

SPEAKING AND LISTENING
Reading Aloud 300, 307, 372
Choral Reading 310

ART/MUSIC
Illustrating a Fantastic Creature 292
Illustrating the Poem 327
Setting a Poem to Music 351

PLANNING GUIDE

FOR UNIT PLANNING
- Transparencies 18–23: *Audiovisual Resources Binder*
- *Portfolio Assessment and Professional Support Materials*
- Test Generator
- Mastery Tests: Teaching Resources B, pp. 214, 216
- Analogy Test: Teaching Resources B, p. 219
- Revision Worksheet: Teaching Resources B, p. 220

SELECTION (Pupil's Page)	TEACHING RESOURCES B (page numbers shown below)								AV BINDER
	Teacher's Notes	Reading Check	Reading Focus	Study Guide	Language Skills	Building Vocabulary	Selection Vocab. Test	Selection Test	Audio-cassette
POETRY Introduction (p. 281) Eve Merriam *Inside a Poem* (p. 281)	115								TAPE 2 SIDE B
Close Reading of a Poem Jack Prelutsky *The Darkling Elves* (p. 282)	115								TAPE 2 SIDE B
Dr. Seuss (Theodor Geisel) *The Sneetches* (p. 285)	116			119, 121		123	125	126	
Edward Lear *The Jumblies* (p. 295)	116			120, 122		123	125	126	TAPE 2 SIDE B
Gwendolyn Brooks *Cynthia in the Snow* (p. 301)					143				TAPE 2 SIDE B
Maya Angelou *Life Doesn't Frighten Me* (p. 303)	128			129, 130	143			149	TAPE 2 SIDE B
Arthur Guiterman *Habits of the Hippopotamus* (p. 307)	131			133, 135	143	146	148	149	TAPE 2 SIDE B
T. S. Eliot *The Rum Tum Tugger* (p. 310)	131			134, 136		146	148	149	TAPE 2 SIDE B
E. E. Cummings *who knows if the moon's* (p. 314)	137			139, 141	143			149	TAPE 2 SIDE B
Gwendolyn Brooks *Narcissa* (p. 318)	137			140, 142	143	146	148	149	TAPE 2 SIDE B
Lilian Moore *Beach Stones* (p. 323)	151			152, 154		161	163	164	TAPE 2 SIDE B
Pat Mora *Petals* (p. 326)	151			153		161	163	164	TAPE 2 SIDE B
Dorthi Charles *Concrete Cat* (p. 328)	155			157, 159				164	
Shōha, Taigi, Bonchō, Ryōta *Haiku* (p. 330)	155			158, 160		161	163	164	
James Reeves *The Sea* (p. 335)	166			168, 171	179	182	183	184	TAPE 2 SIDE B
William J. Smith *The Toaster* (p. 338)	166			169, 172				184	TAPE 2 SIDE B

SELECTION (Pupil's Page)	TEACHING RESOURCES B (CONTINUED) (page numbers shown below)								AV BINDER
	Teacher's Notes	Reading Check	Reading Focus	Study Guide	Language Skills	Building Vocabulary	Selection Vocab. Test	Selection Test	Audio-cassette
Bobbi Katz *Things To Do If You Are a Subway* (p. 340)	166			170, 173		182	183	184	Tape 2 Side B
Sandra Cisneros *Abuelito Who* (p. 345)	174			176, 178				184	Tape 2 Side B
Langston Hughes *Dream Variations* (p. 350)	174			177	179	182	183	184	Tape 2 Side B
Robert Frost *A Minor Bird* (p. 354)	186			188, 190	198	207	208	209	Tape 2 Side B
David Kherdian *That Day* (p. 356)	186			189, 191		207	208	209	Tape 2 Side B
Leroy V. Quintana *Legacy II* (p. 360)	192			194, 196	198	207	208	209	
Nikki Giovanni *Knoxville, Tennessee* (p. 365)	192			195, 197	198			209	Tape 2 Side B
Carl Sandburg *Phizzog* (p. 368)	201			203, 205		207	208	209	Tape 2 Side B
Sara Henderson Hay *Interview* (p. 370)	201			204, 206		207	208	209	Tape 2 Side B
Shel Silverstein *Sarah Cynthia Sylvia Stout Would Not Take the Garbage Out* (p. 372)	211								Tape 2 Side B

TRANSPARENCIES

The following unit support materials with specific correlations to literature selections are available in the **Fine Art and Instructional Transparencies with Teacher's Notes and Blackline Masters** section of your *Audiovisual Resources Binder*.

FINE ART TRANSPARENCIES
Theme: Fewer Words, More Meaning
18 *Marbles VII*, Charles Bell
19 *Red Canna*, Georgia O'Keeffe

READER RESPONSE
20 Responding with Head or Heart?
21 From My Scrapbook

LITERARY ELEMENTS
22 Sound Effects in Poetry

WRITING PROCESS
23 Writing a Poem

INTRODUCING THE UNIT

What Do They Already Know? You might begin by asking students "What poems do you remember reading?" Encourage students to name poems read in previous grades and to think of popular songs, patriotic songs, holiday songs or carols, hymns, and school cheers. They might also remember Mother Goose rhymes, jump-rope chants, singing games, and rhyming books that were read to them when they were very young. Invite students to bring in their favorite poems to share.

SELECTION NOTES

Following are vocabulary lists of words from poems that are included in the Building Vocabulary Worksheets and Selection Vocabulary Tests for each of the five sections in this unit and answers to questions in the Language and Vocabulary sections that follow individual poems.

STORY POEMS (PAGES 284–299)
Vocabulary

guarantee(d) clamber(ed) contraption warble(d) peculiar

"The Sneetches"
Language and Vocabulary: Wordplay (page 292)

Line 4: *thars* rhymes with *stars*.
Line 40: *berked* rhymes with *jerked*.
Line 57: *eaches* rhymes with *beaches*.
Rhyming lines will vary. A sample line might be
  "Though her mother had cooked her some porrange."

SOUND EFFECTS (PAGES 300–320)
Vocabulary

| principles | disobliging | sneer(s) | muddle | pomp |

"The Rum Tum Tugger"

Language and Vocabulary: Sounds and Spellings (page 312)

Possible rhymes include *abbot* and *davit*.

"who knows if the moon's"

Language and Vocabulary: Slang (page 316)

A "keen" knife would be sharp; someone with a "keen" intelligence would be very bright.

Slang words will vary. Be sure that students try to define their words and use them in original sentences.

USING YOUR SENSES (PAGES 321–332)
Vocabulary

| glint(ed) | Callous(ed) | Magenta | rumble(s) |
| fleck(ed) | turquoise | stroke | clatter |

"Concrete Cat"

Language and Vocabulary: Concrete Words (page 329)

Answers will vary. These are sample answers.
1. *sight:* sunset, glimmer
2. *smell:* cigar, gas
3. *taste:* bacon, chocolate
4. *hearing:* roar, purr
5. *touch:* velvet, silk, ice

MAKING COMPARISONS (PAGES 333–352)
Vocabulary

| clash(ing) | bound(s) | express | fling |
| gnaw(s) | scarcely | variation(s) | |

"The Sea"

Language and Vocabulary: Onomatopoeia (page 337)

Examples include *moans* (stanza 1); *snuffs, sniffs, howls,* and *hollos* (stanza 2); and *snores* (stanza 3).

Answers will vary. Possibilities include the following words:
1. sizzles, pops
2. roars, hoots, claps
3. buzzes
4. howls, whispers

"The Toaster"

Language and Vocabulary: Homophones (page 339)

Sample homophones are as follows: red / read; bread / bred; one / won; by / bye / buy; sees / seas / seize.

Sentences will vary.

"Things To Do If You Are a Subway"

Language and Vocabulary: Prefixes (page 342)

1. c   2. e   3. h   4. f   5. b   6. d   7. a   8. g

"Abuelito Who"

Language and Vocabulary: Names in Other Languages (page 346)

Spanish word for "little grandma" is *abuelita*.

First-name research will vary. Students with non-English names might look up their English equivalents.

IDEAS AND FEELINGS (PAGES 353–373)
Vocabulary

minor	generation(s)	dreary	interview
gesture	exchange(d)	bog	deny(ies)
fabric	banish		

"Legacy II"

Language and Vocabulary: Spanish Words (page 362)

Cafeteria comes from the Spanish word *café* (coffee). Related words are *coffee, caffeine*.

Stampede comes from the Spanish word *estampida* (uproar). Related word is *stamp*.

Bonanza comes from the Spanish word *bueno* (good). Related words are *bonus, bona fide*.

Student Learning Options

POETRY

1. Playing the Alliteration Game
A student (or the teacher) writes on the chalkboard a word that starts with a consonant sound. The next student adds before or after the first word a word that alliterates with the first word and that makes sense. Keep this up with additional students as long as they can continue thinking of alliterative words. Students who cannot think of an alliterative word are "out." Students can add *is* or *are*, prepositions, and articles without being out as long as they also add alliterative words.

2. Creating a Poetry Anthology
Ask students to create their own collection of favorite poems and to write a brief explanation of why they have included each poem. They can use other textbooks or library books in addition to this textbook.

3. Making an Illustrated Manuscript
Ask students to recopy a poem in their best handwriting on a sheet of construction paper or drawing paper and then to illustrate the poem with decorations and pictures that are appropriate for the content of the poem.

4. Finding Poems
Have students locate poetic expressions in popular songs or in newspaper and magazine advertisements. Put these on display on a bulletin board or on posters.

5. Supplying Rhyming Words
Give students a copy of a rhyming poem with the last word in each line omitted. Ask students to supply the missing words, making sure they pay close attention to the meaning. You can let students work individually or in small groups on this activity. You can consider giving a small prize or a bonus point to students who get all the words correct.

ART LINK
Celebrate the poetry unit by inviting students to select their favorite lines or stanzas from poems in the unit. Then, challenge students to share these in artistic ways. Students may choose to paint banners, make mobiles or collages, embroider fabric, dance, or make music. Give students an opportunity to share what they have created.

VISUAL CONNECTIONS
Ask students quickly to jot down in their journals three or four words describing how these rhythmic waves and the view of Mt. Fuji make them feel or how they think the fisherman feels. They will practice this kind of spontaneous writing again, and meet Hokusai again, in "Haiku" (page 330).

About the Artist
Hokusai (1760–1849) was one of the great Japanese printmakers who made *ukiyo-e*—"pictures of the floating world." These pictures show the lives of ordinary people such as innkeepers, fishermen, and actresses, rather than of royalty. Disdained at first because of their everyday subject matter, *ukiyo-e* are now among the world's art treasures.

UNIT FOUR

Poetry

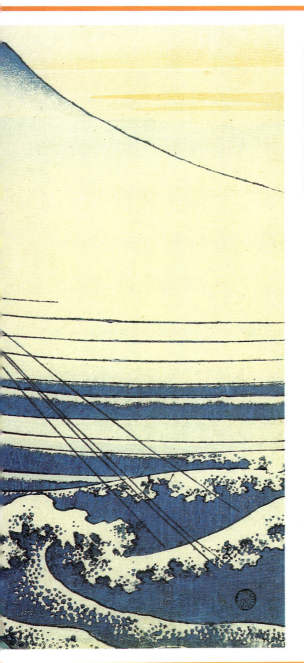

Inside a Poem
EVE MERRIAM

It doesn't always have to rhyme,
but there's the repeat of a beat,
    somewhere
an inner chime that makes you want to
tap your feet or swerve in a curve;
a lilt, a leap, a lightning-split:—
thunderstruck the consonants jut,
while the vowels open wide as waves in
    the noon-blue sea.

You hear with your heels, your eyes feel
what they never touched before:
fins on a bird, feathers on a deer;
taste all colors, inhale
memory and tomorrow and always the
    tang is today.

Mt. Fuji from Kajikazawa in the Province of Kai, from *The Thirty-six Views of Fuji* by Hokusai.

The Metropolitan Museum of Art, New York, Rogers Fund, 1922. (JP1327)

FOCUS/MOTIVATION

Have students read the headnote before reading the poem silently by themselves. Invite them to compare their first impressions with those of the reader whose responses are written in the marginal notes. When students have discussed the poem and the marginal notes, have them think about the question posed in the headnote: Do you agree that the poem might have more than one meaning? (The poem can refer to real, tiny creatures in the woods, such as bats and mosquitoes, and to imaginary ones, such as elves, at the same time.)

Prereading Journal. Have students imagine that they are in dense, dark woods and that they feel things brushing against them from the air. Have them describe how they feel and what is happening.

> **TEACHING RESOURCES B**
> Teacher's Notes, p. 115
>
> **AV RESOURCES BINDER**
> Audiocassette 2, Side B

1. LITERARY ELEMENTS:
Sound Effects
The reader is responding to the unusual rhyme scheme (aaab, cccb, dddb, eeeb) and the alliteration, as in the first line of stanzas 1–3.

2. LITERARY ELEMENTS:
Repetition
The refrain makes the poem scary, since the reader is the one the elves are hungry for.

3. GUIDED READING:
Interpreting Meaning
Students often have difficulty with the concept that there is no one "right" way to respond to poetry and that a poem may have more than one meaning. A good beginning point is to discuss how the poem makes the students feel. If there are mixed feelings, then the poem may well have more than one meaning.

282

Close Reading OF A POEM

*P*oetry is the shortest kind of writing, but it can be the most demanding to read. This is because poets pack a lot of meaning into a very few words. Here is how one reader responded to this very short poem. Do you think it has more than one layer of meaning?

The Darkling Elves
JACK PRELUTSKY

ONE READER'S RESPONSE

What does "darkling" mean? Dark? Are elves good or bad?

1 I like the sounds of the poem.

I like the beat. It's fun.

Good pictures in the poem. (What is "garish"?)

Gross! They eat you?

2 Hungry for what? This is repeated.

The rhymes are good.

Again. Same line. They eat people? Or bite them?

They must be tiny. Whom is the poet talking to?

3 Again! I just had an idea. Maybe these elves are mosquitoes? Or bats? Maybe the poem is meant to be funny? Or is it really scary? What do others think?

In wildest woods, on treetop shelves,
sit evil beings with evil selves—
they are the dreaded darkling elves
and they are always hungry.

In garish garb of capes and hoods, 5
they wait and watch within their woods
to peel your flesh and steal your goods
for they are always hungry.

Through brightest days and darkest nights
these terrifying tiny sprites 10
await to strike and take their bites
for they are always hungry.

Watch every leaf of every tree,
for once they pounce you cannot flee—
their teeth are sharp as sharp can be . . . 15
and they are always hungry.

282 Poetry

CLOSURE
Ask individual students to respond to this question: Does the poem change the way you think about small animals that may bite, such as mosquitoes?

COOPERATIVE LEARNING
Have students work in small groups to rewrite this narrative poem as a story. For example, students might begin, "I was walking in the dark woods when I had a strange feeling that I was being watched by some elves." After composing their stories, groups could share them and compare different versions.

TRANSPARENCY 22

Literary Elements
Sound Effects in Poetry – explores the poetic concepts introduced in the unit, such as rhyme, rhythm, refrain, alliteration, and onomatopoeia.

Looking at Yourself as a Reader
Suppose you were this reader. How would you sum up this little poem?

1. You might say that it has **sounds** you like. You noticed that the poem **rhymes** and that it has a good **beat**.
2. You might say that you noticed that one line is **repeated** four times. The line gave you a scary feeling.
3. You might say that at the end of the poem you had an idea: You thought that maybe the poet was talking about mosquitoes or bats that attack people in the woods.

Read the poem over again, this time aloud. Do you have any other ideas about it?

Compare your response with the responses of your classmates. What do you agree on? What do you disagree about? Would you recommend the poem to anyone else?

VISUAL CONNECTIONS
Ask students where this tree is being viewed from: the ground or the sky. Like a poem, the painting is deliberately ambiguous.

About the Artist
Georgia O'Keeffe (1887–1986) was one of the most individualistic and important American artists of this century. Born in Sun Prairie, Wisconsin, she taught and studied in Texas and New York and married the great photographer Alfred Steiglitz. She is known for her strong, stylized representations of flowers, barns, city skylines, and of the Southwest landscape where she lived in seclusion during the last decades of her life.

The Lawrence Tree by Georgia O'Keeffe (1929). Oil on canvas. Wadsworth Atheneum, Hartford, Connecticut. The Ella Gallup Sumner and Mary Catlin Sumner Collection.

Close Reading of a Poem

OBJECTIVES

Students will interpret the "lesson" of the poem on the next page; they will practice reading aloud to emphasize rhythm; and they will recognize the use of wordplay.

INTRODUCING STORY POEMS

Point out to your students that stories were told long before writing was invented. When pre-literate storytellers composed their tales, they often used some form of repetition as a memory device. It is generally easier to remember a few lines of verse than an equal amount of prose. (Encourage your students to try it.) Ancient bards—including Homer and his colleagues—could memorize epic poems that were hundreds of lines long. In some very ancient civilizations, even laws were originally put to verse. When writing began to replace the oral tradition in ancient Greece, the great philosopher Socrates worried that people's memory would become weaker if they were no longer forced to memorize. You might discuss this question with your students. Urge them to memorize poems of their choice.

FOCUS/MOTIVATION

Building on Prior Knowledge. Ask if students have read any books by Dr. Seuss. Encourage them to share their sense of what makes his books fun. Ask volunteers to bring in Dr. Seuss books from home or the library, or bring them in yourself.

Prereading Journal. Give students one minute to write down all the words they can think of that rhyme with *Sneetch*. (Beach, beech, bleach, leach, peach, impeach, preach, reach, beseech, screech, speech, teach) You might list students' suggested words on the chalkboard.

STORY POEMS

Centuries ago, all stories were told in poetry. In ancient Greece, stories about the post-war wanderings of the soldier Odysseus were told in poetry. At one time in the United States, people used to read long stories in poetry the way we read best-selling novels today. Story poems often have a strong beat and strong rhymes. They often use a lot of repetition. All of these elements help the storyteller remember the lines. They also help keep the listener interested. Here are two lively story poems, which are also wonderful nonsense. Be sure to read them aloud.

READING THE POEM
Since the poem is so easy to read and understand, let students enjoy it by taking turns reading orally. You might teach them a few good oral reading techniques that they can use in presenting the poem to pre-schoolers or primary students: lively presentation, a feeling for the rhythm, accurate pronunciation, emphasis on the italicized words, observance of the punctuation, occasional eye contact with their audience, and humorous or exaggerated expression.

TEACHING RESOURCES B
Teacher's Notes, p. 116
Study Guide, pp. 119, 121
Building Vocabulary, p. 123
Selection Vocabulary Test, p. 125
Selection Test, p. 126

1. LITERARY ELEMENTS:
Alliteration
Be sure the students exaggerate the *sn* sounds in this line.

2. GUIDED READING:
Reading for Meaning
Notice this hint that the problem in this story poem is not going to be totally nonsensical. Do students notice a situation here that is perilously close to what happens on playgrounds all over the world? (One child or another is excluded from play because he or she is "different." In a classroom tryout of this poem, one group of students noted that modern-day equivalents of the Star-Bellies and the Plain-Bellies would be kids who had designer sneakers and those who did not.)

Before You Read
Fantastic creatures are the characters in this poem, which moves at a gallop from start to finish, with lots of hilarious action along the way. You've probably guessed, if you haven't already peeked, that the poet is Dr. Seuss. "The Sneetches," like some of his other poems, is meant for both children and adults. Perhaps you read this poem when you were a little child. But did you realize that under the clever wordplay there is a very important idea? "The Sneetches" must be read aloud. Perhaps you can share it with a younger student.

The Sneetches   *DR. SEUSS (THEODOR GEISEL)*

Now, the Star-Belly Sneetches
Had bellies with stars.
The Plain-Belly Sneetches
Had none upon thars.

Those stars weren't so big. They were really so small   5
You might think such a thing wouldn't matter at all.

But, because they had stars, all the Star-Belly Sneetches
Would brag, "We're the best kind of Sneetch on the beaches."
With their snoots in the air, they would sniff and they'd snort   **1**
"We'll have nothing to do with the Plain-Belly sort!"   10
And whenever they met some, when they were out walking,
They'd hike right on past them without even talking.

When the Star-Belly children went out to play ball,   **2**
Could a Plain Belly get in the game . . . ? Not at all.
You only could play if your bellies had stars   15
And the Plain-Belly children had none upon thars.

The Sneetches   285

MEETING INDIVIDUAL NEEDS
ESL/LEP • Because Dr. Seuss uses language in a nonsensical way, parts of this poem may be especially challenging for non-native speakers. Explain to students that some words have been changed, such as *thars* to mean *theirs* and *eaches* for *each,* in order to make the poem rhyme. Explain that Dr. Seuss also made up or created new words, such as *klonked* and *berked* (page 288).

1. VISUAL CONNECTIONS
The biography on page 293 notes that an art teacher once told Dr. Seuss that he would never learn to draw. Ask students if they think the teacher was right. Notice that though they may think Dr. Seuss never learned to draw like anyone else, his drawings are uniquely his own. (It's probable that he could draw like everyone else if he wanted to.)

2. LITERARY ELEMENTS:
Sound Effects
What rhymes do you find in this stanza? There is end-rhyme in *Sneetches, beaches* and *stars, cars.* There is internal rhyme in line 24—*moping, doping.*

When the Star-Belly Sneetches had frankfurter roasts
Or picnics or parties or marshmallow toasts,
They never invited the Plain-Belly Sneetches.
They left them out cold, in the dark of the beaches.   20
They kept them away. Never let them come near.
And that's how they treated them year after year.

2   Then ONE day, it seems . . . while the Plain-Belly Sneetches
Were moping and doping alone on the beaches,
Just sitting there wishing their bellies had stars . . .   25
A stranger zipped up in the strangest of cars!

286   Poetry

Cultural Diversity

"The Sneetches" could provide a lead-in to class discussion of diversity. You could involve students by asking questions like these: What physical characteristics are seen by some as making certain people better than others? What are the consequences of such beliefs? What other differences sometimes divide people? What can we learn from the Sneetches?

"My friends," he announced in a voice clear and keen,
"My name is Sylvester McMonkey McBean.
And I've heard of your troubles. I've heard you're unhappy.
But I can fix that. I'm the Fix-it-Up Chappie.   30
I've come here to help you. I have what you need.
And my prices are low. And I work at great speed.
And my work is one hundred per cent guaranteed!"

Then, quickly, Sylvester McMonkey McBean
Put together a very peculiar machine.   35
And he said, "You want stars like a Star-Belly Sneetch . . . ?
My friends, you can have them for three dollars each!"

1. GUIDED READING:
Making Inferences
What kind of character is McBean? He is a fast-talking salesman who may become wealthy in this situation.

1. LITERARY ELEMENTS:
Sound Effects
Point out sound effects in this stanza. There is end rhyme. There is internal rhyme in *klonked, bonked* and *jerked, berked*, and *stars, thars*. There is also onomatopoeia in words such as *roared, klonked, bopped*, and *bonked*.

1 "Just pay me your money and hop right aboard!"
So they clambered inside. Then the big machine roared
And it klonked. And it bonked. And it jerked. And it berked   40
And it bopped them about. But the thing really worked!
When the Plain-Belly Sneetches popped out, they had stars!
They actually did. They had stars upon thars!

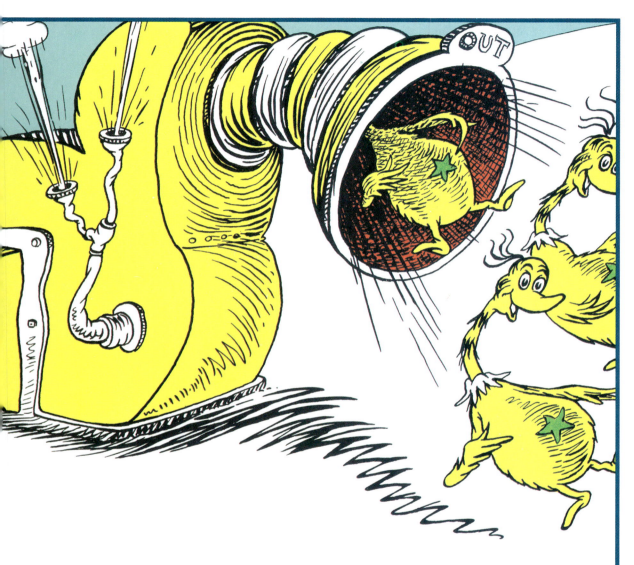

Then they yelled at the ones who had stars at the start,
"We're exactly like you! You can't tell us apart. 45
We're all just the same, now, you snooty old smarties!
And now we can go to your frankfurter parties."

"Good grief!" groaned the ones who had stars at the first.
"We're *still* the best Sneetches and they are the worst.
But, now, how in the world will we know," they all frowned, 50
"If which kind is what, or the other way round?"

The Sneetches

1. GUIDED READING:
Extending the Poem
Does the behavior of the Sneetches remind you of the way people behave in regard to fashions? Students should be able to describe Sneetch-like behavior with the latest clothes and hairstyles, and also with the "in" music, games, dances, slang, attitudes, and so on.

Then up came McBean with a very sly wink
And he said, "Things are not quite as bad as you think.
So you don't know who's who. That is perfectly true.
But come with me, friends. Do you know what I'll do? 55
I'll make you, again, the best Sneetches on beaches
And all it will cost you is ten dollars eaches."

"Belly stars are no longer in style," said McBean.
"What you need is a trip through my Star-*Off* Machine.
This wondrous contraption will take *off* your stars 60
So you won't look like Sneetches who have them on thars."
And that handy machine
Working very precisely
Removed all the stars from their tummies quite nicely.

1 Then, with snoots in the air, they paraded about 65
And they opened their beaks and they let out a shout,
"We know who is who! Now there isn't a doubt.
The best kind of Sneetches are Sneetches without!"

Then, of course, those with stars all got frightfully mad.
To be wearing a star now was frightfully bad. 70
Then, of course, old Sylvester McMonkey McBean
Invited *them* into his Star-Off Machine.

Then, of course from THEN on, as you probably guess,
Things really got into a horrible mess.

All the rest of that day, on those wild screaming beaches, 75
The Fix-it-Up Chappie kept fixing up Sneetches.
Off again! On again!
In again! Out again!
Through the machines they raced round and about again,
Changing their stars every minute or two. 80
They kept paying money. They kept running through
Until neither the Plain nor the Star-Bellies knew
Whether this one was that one . . . or that one was this one
Or which one was what one . . . or what one was who.

290 Poetry

Then, when every last cent 85
Of their money was spent,
The Fix-it-Up Chappie packed up
And he went.

And he laughed as he drove
In his car up the beach, 90
"They never will learn.
No. You can't teach a Sneetch!"

But McBean was quite wrong. I'm quite happy to say
That the Sneetches got really quite smart on that day,
The day they decided that Sneetches are Sneetches 95
And no kind of Sneetch is the best on the beaches.
That day, all the Sneetches forgot about stars
And whether they had one, or not, upon thars.

1. GUIDED READING:
Recognizing Cause and Effect
Why does the Fix-it-Up Chappie leave? He has taken all the Sneetches' money.

CLOSURE

Ask students to identify the made-up words and rhymes they enjoyed most in "The Sneetches."

EXTENSION AND ENRICHMENT

A Collaborative Poem. Divide the class into small groups and have each group collaborate on a four-line poem in the style of Dr. Seuss, using invented words and wacky characters and situations. Have a member of each group read its poem aloud. Encourage groups to give each other constructive feedback.

Drama. For extra credit, have volunteers stage "The Sneetches" as a play.

FOR STUDY AND DISCUSSION

Identifying Details

1. The Star-Bellies feel they are better because they have stars on their bellies.
   They will not talk to them on the beach; they will not let them join their ball games; they never invite them to their picnics.
2. McBean is a stranger who promises to help the Plain-Bellies for a fee.
   He says he can use a machine to give them stars.
   McBean thinks that the Sneetches will never learn because they can't be taught.
3. At the end, the Sneetches have decided that no Sneetch is really the best.
   They changed because they saw that their prejudices led to disaster.

Interpreting Meanings

4. Answers might be, "It is foolish for anyone to assume that he or she is better than anyone else," or "Prejudice is the result of superficial differences in people," or "People who think they are superior to others are very silly."
   Most students will agree that the poem teaches an important lesson.

292

For Study and Discussion

IDENTIFYING DETAILS

1. A **conflict** is introduced right at the beginning of this story poem. Why do the Star-Bellies feel that they are better than the Plain-Bellies? How do the Star-Bellies treat the Plain-Bellies?
2. Who is McBean? What does he say he can do for the Plain-Bellies? What does he think of the Sneetches?
3. At the end of the poem, how have the Sneetches changed? What caused them to change?

INTERPRETING MEANINGS

4. In your own words, explain this story poem's **lesson** or **moral**. Do you think it is an important lesson?

APPLYING MEANINGS

5. What real-life people behave like the Sneetches or like Sylvester McMonkey McBean?

Literary Elements

RHYTHM

The **rhythm** of a poem is the repetition of stressed and unstressed syllables in each line. In the following lines, the syllables that get heavy stresses are marked with a (´).

292 Poetry

Read the lines aloud and exaggerate the stressed sounds:

Now, the Stár-Bélly Snéetches
Had béllies with stárs.

"The Sneetches" is told in very regular sing-song rhythms. Read the poem aloud to feel its beat. Does the poem move quickly or slowly? Does its rhythm make the story more fun to read? Practice reading the poem aloud, as if you were going to read it to a young child. Can you vary the way you read some verses, making them either fast or slow, loud or soft?

Language and Vocabulary

WORDPLAY

To make his lines rhyme, and to add to the fun, Dr. Seuss sometimes changed a spelling, added a new ending sound, or even invented a word. Find the funny words that Dr. Seuss made up in lines 4, 40, and 57. What word does each made-up word rhyme with?

Make up another line of poetry to rhyme with the following line. (You will have to invent a rhyming word because no word in English rhymes with *orange*.)

Eva was eating an orange

Writing About Literature

DESCRIBING AND ILLUSTRATING A FANTASTIC CREATURE

Write three sentences describing a creature who lives on an imaginary world and who thinks he or she is superior to other creatures. Make up a name for your creature. If you like, draw its picture in the style of Dr. Seuss.

PORTFOLIO ASSESSMENT

Groups of students may have fun producing a dramatic interpretation of "The Sneetches." Students might videotape their project, acting out and giving a dramatic reading of the poem. Others may want to serve as a film crew. They will need to make some props, such as stars and McBean's star-on, star-off machine. Remind students that except for their stars, all sneetches look exactly alike. Consult individually with students in the planning stages to agree on how their individual contribution to the project will be assessed. Ask each to write a self-assessment for inclusion in portfolios. (See *Portfolio Assessment and Professional Support Materials* for additional information on student portfolios.)

About the Author

Dr. Seuss, whose real name was Theodor Seuss Geisel (1904–1991), was born in Springfield, Massachusetts. He began drawing fantastic animals while he was still a child. (His father ran the local zoo.) An art teacher told him that he would never learn to draw, and twenty-nine publishers rejected his first children's book, *And to Think That I Saw It on Mulberry Street.* But Dr. Seuss went on to write and illustrate more than forty books for children. Judged by the number of books he has sold—at least eighty million copies—he is perhaps the most popular writer in the world. ("Dr." is a title that he gave himself. He also wrote under the name Theo LeSieg—"Geisel" spelled backward.) When asked the question "What is rhyme?" Dr. Seuss replied, "A rhyme is something without which I would probably be in the dry-cleaning business!"

Applying Meanings
5. Students may suggest real-life people like snobs and conformists, or swindlers, con-men, and crooks.

LANGUAGE AND VOCABULARY
Wordplay
For answers, see the **Teaching Guide** at the beginning of the unit.

WRITING ABOUT LITERATURE
Describing and Illustrating a Fantastic Creature
Encourage students to be imaginative in their sentences and in the names they make up for their creatures. Ask students to share their sentences and their drawings.

Behind the Scenes

"Dr. Seuss"

The "Dr. Seuss" name is a combination of my middle name and the fact that I had been studying for my doctorate when I quit to become a cartoonist. My father had always wanted to see a Dr. in front of my name, so I attached it. I figured by doing that, I saved him about ten thousand dollars.

—Theodor Geisel

OBJECTIVES
Students will recognize and use alliteration and refrain; they will recognize and use wordplay and list possible subjects for poems.

FOCUS/MOTIVATION
Building on Prior Knowledge. Ask students to share knowledge of movies (*Honey, I Shrunk the Kids*) or books (*The Borrowers, Stuart Little*) about the adventures of tiny characters.

Prereading Journal. Have students imagine that they are going to sea in a sieve, and then have them write about what they would use to stop the leaks, to keep themselves dry, to serve as a sail and mast. Encourage outlandish ideas.

READING THE POEM
Because of its vocabulary and syntax, "The Jumblies" is a bit more challenging than "The Sneetches." You might guide a group of good readers in an oral presentation. You could also assign six good readers to present the six parts of the poem. The poem could also be read by a narrator and a group of "Jumblies."

MUSIC LINK
"The Jumblies" has lively rhythm and rhyme appropriate to song. Invite students to set the poem to music. Students may wish to compose their own melodies or use melodies they already know. Encourage students to perform their songs for the class.

TEACHING RESOURCES B
Teacher's Notes, p. 116
Study Guide, pp. 120, 122
Building Vocabulary, p. 123
Selection Vocabulary Test, p. 125
Selection Test, p. 126

AV RESOURCES BINDER
Audiocassette 2, Side B

1. LITERARY ELEMENTS:
Refrain
Here is the refrain that keeps echoing through the Jumblie saga. Students should begin to form their own images of what a Jumblie looks like. Each time it appears, the refrain might be said in a different tone of voice.

Before You Read
Most members of the middle and upper classes in nineteenth-century England were highly serious, proper folk. Then along came Edward Lear. Lear was a professional artist, but he also loved words and nonsense.

You probably have a sieve (siv) in your kitchen at home. It's also called a sifter or strainer. The main thing to know about a sieve is that it is full of holes.

The Jumblies
EDWARD LEAR

1

They went to sea in a Sieve, they did,
  In a Sieve they went to sea:
In spite of all their friends could say,
On a winter's morn, on a stormy day,
  In a Sieve they went to sea!   5
And when the Sieve turned round and round,
And everyone cried, "You'll all be drowned!"
They called aloud, "Our Sieve ain't big,
But we don't care a button! we don't care a fig!
  In a Sieve we'll go to sea!"   10
    Far and few, far and few,
      Are the lands where the Jumblies live;
    Their heads are green, and their hands are blue,
      And they went to sea in a Sieve.

2

They sailed away in a Sieve, they did,   15
  In a Sieve they sailed so fast,
With only a beautiful pea-green veil
Tied with a ribbon by way of a sail;
  To a small tobacco-pipe mast;
And everyone said, who saw them go,   20

The Jumblies   295

1
You might explain that a crockery jar is like a cookie jar. (The Jumblies are very tiny.)

2. GUIDED READING:
Recognizing Onomatopoeia
What words and phrases imitate sounds? Whistled, warbled, and echoing sound of a coppery gong.

"O won't they be soon upset, you know!
For the sky is dark, and the voyage is long,
And happen what may, it's extremely wrong
　　In a Sieve to sail so fast!"
　　　Far and few, far and few,　　　　　　　　25
　　　　Are the lands where the Jumblies live;
　　　Their heads are green, and their hands are blue,
　　　　And they went to sea in a Sieve.

3

The water it soon came in, it did,
　　The water it soon came in;　　　　　　　　30
So to keep them dry, they wrapped their feet
In a pinky paper all folded neat,
　　And they fastened it down with a pin.
1 And they passed the night in a crockery jar,
　　And each of them said, "How wise we are!　35
Though the sky be dark, and the voyage be long,
Yet we never can think we were rash or wrong,
　　While round in our Sieve we spin!"
　　　Far and few, far and few,
　　　　Are the lands where the Jumblies live;　40
　　　Their heads are green, and their hands are blue,
　　　　And they went to sea in a Sieve.

4

And all night long they sailed away;
　　And when the sun went down,
2 They whistled and warbled a moony song　　45
To the echoing sound of a coppery gong,
　　In the shade of the mountains brown.
"O Timballoo! How happy we are,
When we live in a Sieve and a crockery jar,
And all night long in the moonlight pale,　　　50
We sail away with a pea-green sail,
　　In the shade of the mountains brown!"
　　　Far and few, far and few,

296　Poetry

  Are the lands where the Jumblies live;
 Their heads are green, and their hands are blue,   55
  And they went to sea in a Sieve.

5

They sailed to the Western Sea, they did,
 To a land all covered with trees,
And they bought an Owl, and a useful Cart,
And a pound of Rice, and a Cranberry Tart,   60
 And a hive of silvery Bees.
And they bought a Pig, and some green Jackdaws,
And a lovely Monkey with lollipop paws,
And forty bottles of Ring-Bo-Ree,
 And no end of Stilton Cheese.   65
  Far and few, far and few,
  Are the lands where the Jumblies live;
 Their heads are green, and their hands are blue,
  And they went to sea in a Sieve.

1. LITERARY ELEMENTS:
Irony
Note the comic irony of the word *useful* in line 59. Usefulness scarcely counts as a reason for this voyage, and a cart would weigh down a seagoing sieve, which would sink anyway.

2
Stilton cheese is a rich, blue-veined cheese named for the place in England where it was first sold. (The Jumblies enjoy good food!)

The Jumblies

CLOSURE

Ask students to point out one or two examples of each of the following techniques from the poem: alliteration, refrain, and nonsense.

FOR STUDY AND DISCUSSION

Identifying Details

1. They are small creatures with green heads and blue hands.
2. Their boat is a sieve, full of holes, with a pea-green sail and a tobacco-pipe mast.
3. Lines 35–38 ("How wise we are!") and lines 48–53 ("How happy we are . . . ").
4. They landed at a place in the Western sea and visited the Lakes, the Torrible [Torrid?] Zone, and the hills of Chankly Bore. They bought an owl, a cart, a pound of rice, a cranberry tart, a hive of silvery bees, a pig, some green jackdaws, a monkey, forty bottles of Ring-Bo-Ree, and lots of Stilton cheese.

Interpreting Meanings

5. It is nonsensical that when the water pours in through the holes, the Jumblies keep their feet dry by wrapping them in neatly folded pink paper, fastened with a pin.

Nonsensical place names include the Torrible Zone (line 74) and the hills of Chankly Bore (line 75).

Students might suggest that a "moony song" would sound sad or sighing and that "lollipop paws" would look small

---

6

And in twenty years they all came back, 70
  In twenty years or more,
And everyone said, "How tall they've grown!
For they've been to the Lakes, and the Torrible Zone,
  And the hills of the Chankly Bore";
And they drank their health, and gave them a feast 75
Of dumplings made of beautiful yeast;
And everyone said, "If we only live,
We too will go to sea in a Sieve,—
  To the hills of the Chankly Bore!"
    Far and few, far and few, 80
      Are the lands where the Jumblies live;
    Their heads are green, and their hands are blue,
      And they went to sea in a Sieve.

For Study and Discussion

IDENTIFYING DETAILS

1. What do the Jumblies look like?
2. Describe the Jumblies' "boat."
3. Which lines tell how the sailing Jumblies feel about themselves?
4. Where did the Jumblies land and what did they buy there?

INTERPRETING MEANINGS

5. **Nonsense** is Lear's trademark. What is nonsensical about the Jumblies' boat and the way they keep their feet dry? Find two examples of nonsensical place names. How would you sing a "moony song" (line 45)? How would you illustrate "lollipop paws" (line 63)?

APPLYING MEANINGS

6. Many English people in Lear's day traveled to very exotic parts of the world. They brought back to England the most amazing souvenirs. How are the Jumblies like those travelers? Are the Jumblies like tourists today?

EXTENSION AND ENRICHMENT

Art. Artistically gifted students may wish to create new illustrations for "The Jumblies." All students may draw simple pictures showing what they think the Jumblies look like.

Literary Elements

ALLITERATION

Alliteration gives this story poem a lively, happy feeling. It also makes us laugh. **Alliteration** is the repetition of consonant sounds, especially at the beginning of words placed close together. An example of alliteration is the repeated s sound in:

> In a Sieve they went to sea

Find at least two other examples of alliteration in the **refrain,** the four lines that end each stanza. Can you find the alliteration in lines 32–33? In lines 44–45? In line 63?

Write three sentences of your own using silly alliteration.

Focus on Writing a Poem

FINDING A SUBJECT

You can find a subject for a poem of your own by thinking about people and things you know best. For example, "The Jumblies" is a poem about a journey. Would one of your own journeys be a good subject for a poem?

Here are some more examples of subjects you might consider:

riding a bike	an apple
a mouse	a snowflake
a crowded mall	playing baseball
a good friend	a relative

Make your own list of three possible subjects for a poem. Get together with a partner and exchange lists. Brainstorm with each other about how you might develop each subject. What words could you use to describe your subject? Save your notes.

About the Author

Many people believe that **Edward Lear** (1812–1888) is the world's greatest writer and illustrator of nonsense verse. Lear began writing funny verses as a hobby, but his nonsense became a safety valve for a life plagued by sickness and lack of money. Lear was the youngest of twenty-one children. He began earning his living as a commercial artist when he was only fifteen. Like the Jumblies, Lear loved to travel. He is said to have written letters regularly to 444 people. Lear's first *Book of Nonsense,* a collection of five-line humorous poems called **limericks,** was written to amuse a friend's children. "The Jumblies" is from his second book, *Nonsense Songs, Stories, Botany, and Alphabets.*

The Jumblies 299

and round and brightly colored.

Applying Meanings
6. The Jumblies, like tourists the world over, buy exotic souvenirs (see lines 59–65).

LITERARY ELEMENTS
Alliteration

Other examples of alliteration in the refrain are "Far and few, far and few"; "the lands where the Jumblies live"; "Their heads are green, and their hands are blue."

Students should note alliteration of the *p* and *f* sounds in lines 32–33, alliteration of the *w* sound in lines 44–45, and alliteration of the *l* and *p* sounds in line 63.

A sample sentence using silly alliteration: "Carla's cat capered on the calico carpet." (You might assign a different letter sound to each student.)

FOCUS ON WRITING A POEM
Finding a Subject

If students are having trouble listing possible subjects, suggest that they freewrite for five minutes. Then have them read through their freewriting and circle words, phrases, or lines that most interest them. If they are not satisfied with the circled choices as subjects for poems, suggest that students continue freewriting from the chosen phrases.

> **TRANSPARENCIES 18 & 19**
> **Fine Art**
> Theme: *Fewer Words, More Meaning* – invites students to explore everyday objects as subjects of works of art.

> **TRANSPARENCY 22**
> **Literary Elements**
> *Sound Effects in Poetry* – explores the poetic concepts introduced in the unit, such as rhyme, rhythm, refrain, alliteration, and onomatopoeia.

INTRODUCING SOUND EFFECTS

The examples in items, 1, 2, and 4 are from "The Darkling Elves" on page 282. You might have students turn back to that poem and identify the refrain.

Students respond enthusiastically to the idea of onomatopoeia, once they get over the hard word, and they should be encouraged to keep lists in their journal of good "echoic words."

1. LITERARY ELEMENTS:
Sound Effects
Of course, snow is silent. See if students agree that the poet echoes the sounds of silence. (Another poem by Brooks and a biography are on pages 318–320).

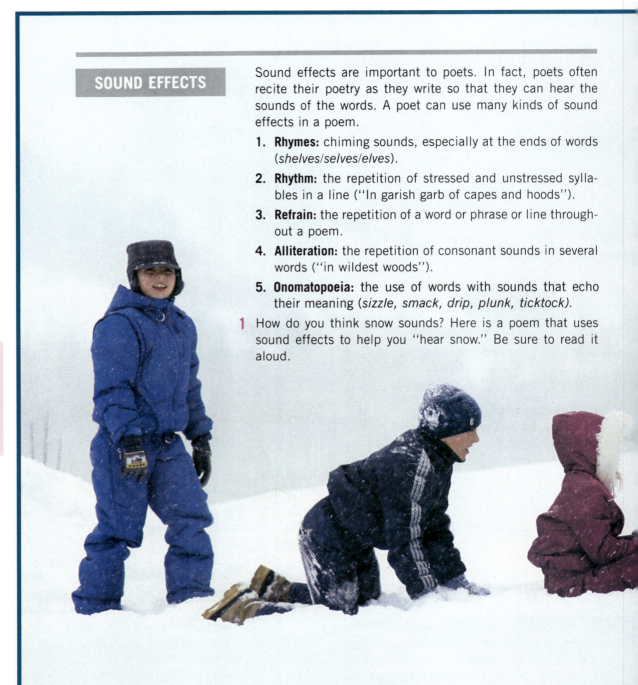

SOUND EFFECTS

Sound effects are important to poets. In fact, poets often recite their poetry as they write so that they can hear the sounds of the words. A poet can use many kinds of sound effects in a poem.

1. **Rhymes:** chiming sounds, especially at the ends of words (*shelves/selves/elves*).
2. **Rhythm:** the repetition of stressed and unstressed syllables in a line ("In garish garb of capes and hoods").
3. **Refrain:** the repetition of a word or phrase or line throughout a poem.
4. **Alliteration:** the repetition of consonant sounds in several words ("in wildest woods").
5. **Onomatopoeia:** the use of words with sounds that echo their meaning (*sizzle, smack, drip, plunk, ticktock*).

1 How do you think snow sounds? Here is a poem that uses sound effects to help you "hear snow." Be sure to read it aloud.

300   Poetry

COOPERATIVE LEARNING

Have students brainstorm a list of onomatopoetic words. Write students' suggestions on the chalkboard. Then, ask one student to begin a round-robin story by using one of the suggested words in a sentence such as "I was walking down the street when I heard a *crash*!" The next student should continue the story using another onomatopoetic word from the list in a sentence such as "I stopped suddenly and dropped my books with a loud *thud*!" Continue the story until all students have had a chance to contribute. You might want to have a student volunteer record the story for the class.

AV RESOURCES BINDER
Audiocassette 2, Side B

1. LITERARY ELEMENTS:
Sound Effects
Here are some of Brooks's sound effects: onomatopoeia and rhyme (*sushes* and *hushes*, *flitter* and *twitter*, *me* and *be*, *shirts* and *hurts*); alliteration (laughs a lovely whiteness; whitely whirs away).

Notice that the name *Cynthia* is soft and hushed like the snow. Suppose students were writing a poem about rain or bubbles or wind or hail: What names would echo those sounds? (Bobby, Hugh, Sarah, Florence, Ricky?)

You might talk with students about other aspects of the world that are "so beautiful they hurt."

Cynthia in the Snow
GWENDOLYN BROOKS

It SUSHES.
It hushes
The loudness in the road.
It flitter-twitters,
And laughs away from me.
It laughs a lovely whiteness,
And whitely whirs away,
To be
Some otherwhere,
Still white as milk or shirts.
So beautiful it hurts.

OBJECTIVE
Students will identify a refrain.

FOCUS/MOTIVATION
Prereading Journal. The headnote suggests that students make lists of three things that frighten most children. Depending on your class, you might also have students write about what makes childhood a happy time.

Because students from some cultures may not have heard of Mother Goose, explain that the name refers to a collection of nursery rhymes (poems for small children) first published in England in the eighteenth century and still very popular in this country.

VISUAL CONNECTIONS
Ask students about the mood of this little girl. Is her schoolroom brightly lit, or is it somber and dark? What do they see out the window? Why do they think she has been "kept in"?

The picture is one of four paintings that describe a one-room school district out of Cragsmoor, New York, in 1888. In 1873, the state had passed civil rights legislation that called on five large communities to integrate their schools. This child is isolated from her white classmates who play outside in the sunlight, her textbook abandoned on the floor. In terms of Angelou's poem, this little person might well be trying to reassure herself with the words "Life doesn't frighten me . . ."

About the Painter
Edward Lamson Henry (1841–1919), born in Charleston, South Carolina, lived in New York most of his life. He painted many rousing action scenes of the Civil War on commission.

Before You Read

Here is a bold little girl's voice telling everyone how brave she is. But *is* she as brave as she sounds? Before you read the poem, make a list of three things that you think frighten most small children—even those who really have nothing to be afraid of at all.

Kept In by Edward Lamson Henry (1888). Oil on canvas.

New York State Historical Association, Cooperstown.

302 Poetry

Life Doesn't Frighten Me

MAYA ANGELOU

Shadows on the wall
Noises down the hall
Life doesn't frighten me at all
Bad dogs barking loud
Big ghosts in a cloud   5
Life doesn't frighten me at all.

Mean old Mother Goose
Lions on the loose
They don't frighten me at all
Dragons breathing flame   10
On my counterpane°
That doesn't frighten me at all.

I go boo
Make them shoo
I make fun   15
Way they run
I won't cry
So they fly
I just smile
They go wild   20
Life doesn't frighten me at all.

Tough guys in a fight
All alone at night
Life doesn't frighten me at all.
Panthers in the park   25
Strangers in the dark
No, they don't frighten me at all.

That new classroom where
Boys all pull my hair
(Kissy little girls   30
With their hair in curls)
They don't frighten me at all.

Don't show me frogs and snakes
And listen for my scream,
If I'm afraid at all   35
It's only in my dreams.

I've got a magic charm
That I keep up my sleeve,
I can walk the ocean floor
And never have to breathe.   40

Life doesn't frighten me at all
Not at all
Not at all.
Life doesn't frighten me at all.

---

11. **counterpane:** quilt.

CLOSURE

Use the refrain as a launching pad for a discussion of the difference between "brave" and "fearless." Lead students to see that the speaker may have real fears, but she may be genuinely brave in overcoming them.

EXTENSION AND ENRICHMENT

Music. Invite students to share refrains from their (and your) favorite songs. Play the tapes if time permits. You might ask students to create a refrain for a song about your class.

> **TRANSPARENCY 22**
> **Literary Elements**
> *Sound Effects in Poetry* – explores the poetic concepts introduced in the unit, such as rhyme, rhythm, refrain, alliteration, and onomatopoeia.

FOR STUDY AND DISCUSSION

Identifying Details

1. She is not afraid of the following: shadows, noises down the hall, bad dogs barking, big ghosts, mean old Mother Goose, lions, dragons, tough guys in a fight, panthers, strangers, the new classroom, frogs and snakes, the ocean floor, and life.
2. She is afraid in her dreams.
3. It allows her to walk the ocean floor and never have to breathe.

Interpreting Meanings

4. Some students may suggest that her tough attitude may conceal inner fears.
5. Students may suggest that many Mother Goose rhymes include characters or events that are scary: Humpty Dumpty, for example. (Have them name others.)
6. She probably means sweet little girls who are popular in school. Or girls who are always good.
7. These fears might come from her imagination: shadows, noises, ghosts, Mother Goose, lions, dragons, and panthers. These fears might be real: bad dogs, tough guys, strangers, the classroom, frogs, and snakes.

304

For Study and Discussion

IDENTIFYING DETAILS

1. List all the things this brave girl is *not* afraid of.
2. When *is* she afraid?
3. What does her magic charm do?

INTERPRETING MEANINGS

4. Do you think that, with all her boldness and brave remarks, this speaker is not so brave after all? Talk about your responses.
5. Why do you think the speaker calls Mother Goose "mean"?
6. What do you think she means by "kissy little girls"?
7. Which of the little girl's fears might come from her imagination? Which are real?

APPLYING MEANINGS

8. Where do you think children's imaginary fears come from? What do you think of the old Mother Goose stories and fairy tales? Do you think that most small children are seriously frightened by them?

Literary Elements

REFRAIN

A **refrain** is a word or a phrase or a line that is repeated over and over again in a poem or song. Think of songs that are popular today, and you'll probably be able to find a refrain in every one. Can you make a list of at least three popular refrains?

Often refrains carry the main message of a song or poem.

304   Poetry

1. What is the refrain in this poem?
2. Do you think it carries the speaker's main message?
3. Would you recite the refrain exactly the same way each time it occurs?

Focus on Writing a Poem

EXPERIMENTING WITH REFRAIN

Have you ever found yourself humming a tune or repeating a phrase that you just couldn't get out of your head?

Working with a small group of partners, try building a short poem around a repeated phrase, or **refrain**. First, choose a phrase that the group likes. Then brainstorm to find images, examples, or incidents that fit the phrase. Save your notes.

If you wish, choose one phrase from the list below to get your group started:

They're so cool	Put on a smile
Life's a peach	Tell it out!
Baseball fever	Grrrr!

EXPLORING RHYMES IN COUPLETS

Not all poems have to rhyme, but exploring rhymes can be fun and can give you ideas for poems. You can explore rhymes by writing **couplets**, or pairs of rhyming lines like this one:

Dan, Dan, the ice cream man,
Drives a blue and silver van.

Write two or three couplets of your own and then share them with a partner. Save your writing.

PORTFOLIO ASSESSMENT

Some students may want to respond to "Life Doesn't Frighten Me" by writing a personal poem, while others may prefer to write an essay telling what about life does or does not frighten them. Regardless of which they choose, students will want to follow a logical plan of progression that ends by reinforcing their thesis (life does or does not frighten them). Suggest that they may find it easier to begin their plan with their thesis and then work on the supporting details. Consult with students individually to agree on how their poems or essays will be assessed. (See *Portfolio Assessment and Professional Support Materials* for additional information on student portfolios.)

About the Author

As everyone knows who has read the first volume of her autobiography, called *I Know Why the Caged Bird Sings,* **Maya Angelou** (1928–   ) grew up with her grandmother in the small town of Stamps, Arkansas. She went on to become a dancer, an actress, a writer, and a TV producer. The second and third volumes of her autobiography are called *Gather Together in My Name* and *Singin' and Swingin' and Gettin' Merry Like Christmas.* Four books of her poetry are called *Just Give Me a Cool Drink of Water 'Fore I Diiie, Oh Pray My Wings Are Gonna Fit Me Well, And Still I Rise,* and *Shaker, Why Don't You Sing?* Her lively titles show that Angelou loves words and the colorful rhythms and slang of everyday speech. Her titles also show that she was nourished on African American music, especially gospel songs, spirituals, and blues. In 1993 she recited her poem "On the Pulse of Morning" at President Clinton's inauguration.

Behind the Scenes

"All things are possible . . ."

I believe all things are possible for a human being, and I don't think there's anything in the world I can't do. Of course, I can't be five foot four because I'm six feet tall. I can't be a man because I'm a woman. The physical gifts are given to me, just like having two arms is a gift. In my creative source, wherever that is, I don't see why I can't sculpt. Why shouldn't I? Human beings sculpt. I'm a human being.

All my work, my life, everything is about survival. All my work is meant to say, "You may encounter many defeats, but you must not be defeated." In fact, the encountering may be the very experience which creates the vitality and the power to endure.

—Maya Angelou

Applying Meanings
8. Fears might come from their own sense of vulnerability—of being so small and defenseless.

Students may suggest that some children are frightened but that in general the fear is not serious. Psychologists suggest that fairy tales help children because they give voice to archetypal fears and desires.

LITERARY ELEMENTS
Refrain
1. The refrain consists of variations of "Life doesn't frighten me a tall."
2. The refrain certainly seems to convey the speaker's main message, which is, ironically, that the little girl is afraid and is trying not to show it. The refrain is like a magic incantation: If she says it enough, it'll be true.
3. Most students will suggest that the refrain should be varied. (Bold, tremulous, cocky)

FOCUS ON WRITING A POEM
Experimenting with Refrain
Before assigning students to groups, work through the exercise with the class to model the developing of a chosen refrain.
Exploring Rhymes in Couplets
You might point out to students that both lines of the example couplet share the same rhythm.

SCIENCE LINK

Ask students to use an encyclopedia to learn the real-life habits of hippopotamuses. What do hippopotamuses really eat? Have interested students make a chart comparing the fictional information given in the poem to the corresponding factual information.

Example:

	Fiction	Fact
Favorite Food	Hippopotomustard	
Behavior	True to principles; always tries to do best	

Before You Read

This nonsense poem about a real animal contains two British terms: *trams* are English streetcars and *omnibuses* are English buses. (This hippo seems to be English.) Read the poem aloud so that you can hear the words the poet has invented to create his comical rhymes.

Habits of the Hippopotamus

ARTHUR GUITERMAN

The hippopotamus is strong
    And huge of head and broad of bustle;
The limbs on which he rolls along
    Are big with hippopotomuscle.

He does not greatly care for sweets
    Like ice cream, apple pie, or custard,
But takes to flavor what he eats
    A little hippopotomustard.

The hippopotamus is true
    To all his principles, and just;
He always tries his best to do
    The things one hippopotomust.

He never rides in trucks or trams,
    In taxicabs or omnibuses,
And so keeps out of traffic jams
    And other hippopotomusses.

CLOSURE

Join with your students in inventing funny rhymes and new words for *elephant*, or for other animals such as *giraffe, gorilla, gnu,* or *chimpanzee*.

RETEACHING

To reinforce the concept of rhyme schemes, you might ask for rhyme schemes in "The Sneetches," page 285, and "The Jumblies," page 295.

FOR STUDY AND DISCUSSION

Identifying Details

1. He does not care for sweets but likes mustard; he is true to his principles and always does his best; he never rides in trucks, trams, taxicabs, or omnibuses.
2. Four silly portmanteau words are *hippopotomuscle* (line 4), *hippopotomustard* (line 8), *hippopotomust* (line 12), and *hippopotomusses* (line 16).

Interpreting Meanings

3. He means that it has a broad rear end.
4. We might expect a creature the size of a hippo to want more than "a little" mustard. A big tank-like hippo might not be expected to be so wary of crowds, or even so principled. We laugh at the image of a hippo in a bustle.

Perhaps rougher, cruder, pushier habits.

LITERARY ELEMENTS

Rhyme Scheme

The rhyme pattern in the other three stanzas is the same: cdcd, efef, ghgh.

308

For Study and Discussion

IDENTIFYING DETAILS

1. What *are* the habits of the hippopotamus?
2. Much of the humor in the poem comes from portmanteau (pôrt·man·tō′) words. A portmanteau is a suitcase that opens into two sections. **Portmanteau** words are invented by combining words. For example, *smog* is a portmanteau word; it is a combination of *smoke* and *fog*. Find four silly portmanteau words in the poem.

INTERPRETING MEANINGS

3. A bustle (bus′l) is a framework or padding worn many years ago by women to puff out their long skirts at the rear. Some bustles were huge. What does the poet mean when he says the hippo is "broad of bustle"?
4. Think of what a hippo looks like (see the handsome fellow on page 306). Is this the way you would expect a hippo to behave if it were a person? How would you have described the habits of the hippo?

Literary Elements

RHYME SCHEME

Words that rhyme end in the same sound or sounds, like *strong* and *along*. A **rhyme scheme** is the pattern of rhyming words at the ends of lines in a poem. Suppose you give each new rhyme in stanza 1 a letter. You will get this pattern of rhyme: **abab.** What is the rhyme scheme in the other three stanzas?

308 Poetry

Colored engraving by Gustave Doré.

Focus on Writing a Poem

PLAYING WITH WORDS

Some poets, as you see from Guiterman's verses, like to make up comical words. But we all have these impulses to play with language. The following story plays with words by exchanging the first letter of one word for the first letter of another. After you read this story aloud (if you can stand it), write your own fairy tale in Prinderella style.

Prinderella and the Cinch

Twonce upon a wime there was a gritty little pearl named Prinderella who lived with her two sugly isters and her sticked weptmother, who made her pine the shots and shans and do all the other wirty dirk around the house.

Well, one day the Ping issued a Kroclamation saying that all geligible irls were invited to the Palace for a drancy fess ball. Well the two sugly isters and the sticked weptmother were going but Prinderella couldn't go because she didn't have a drancy fess. But along came her Gary Fodmother and she changed a cumpkin into a poach and hice into morses and her rirty dags into a drancy fess. And she sent her off to the palace saying "Now, Prinderella, you come home at the moke of stridnight or—your drancy fess will be turned into rirty dags again." So Prinderella went to the stalace and she pranced all night with the Cinch.

But at the moke of stridnight she ran down the stalace peps and on the bottom pep she slopped her dripper—now wasn't that a shirty dame?

The next day the Ping issued another Kroclamation saying that all geligible irls should sly on the tripper. Well, the two sugly isters and the sticked weptmother, they slied on the tripper but it fiddent dit. Prinderella slied on the tripper and it fid dit.

So Prinderella and the Cinch mot garried and hived lappily ever after.

About the Author

Arthur Guiterman (gē′tər·man) (1871–1943) was born in Vienna, Austria, but his parents were American citizens. The family returned to New York before Guiterman started school. Even as a child, Guiterman loved animals. Many of his clever animal poems first appeared in *Life* magazine and *The New Yorker*. Guiterman also wrote the words for many songs and operas.

OBJECTIVES
Students will experiment with sound effects and will write pairs of homophones.

FOCUS/MOTIVATION
Discuss pets. Do students think pets have personalities?
Prereading Journal. Have students do a quick-write on how they feel about cats and why. When volunteers read their entries aloud, use an amusing one as a lead-in to Eliot's poem.

READING THE POEM
You might want to read the narrator's lines yourself, or choose a student. Have students read aloud in unison the last four lines of each stanza as a chorus.

TEACHING RESOURCES B
Teacher's Notes, p. 131
Study Guide, pp. 134, 136
Building Vocabulary, p. 146
Selection Vocabulary Test, p. 148
Selection Test, p. 149

AV RESOURCES BINDER
Audiocassette 2, Side B

1. GUIDED READING:
Using Context Clues
What does curious *mean here?* Here it means "strange" rather than "inquisitive."

2. LITERARY ELEMENTS:
Rhythm
Did Eliot forget to make lines 9–10 and 20–21 long enough? No, he placed a short refrain in each stanza for the fun of varying the rhythm.

Before You Read

The famous serious poet T. S. Eliot also wrote funny poems about cats. The Tugger is a British cat, so you should be alert for British terms, such as "flats" (apartments) and "larder" (a place to keep food). If you present a group reading, have fun with these comical rhymes and thumping rhythms.

The Rum Tum Tugger

T. S. ELIOT

1   Narrator   The Rum Tum Tugger is a Curious Cat:
     Girls' chorus If you offer him pheasant he would rather have grouse.°
                   If you put him in a house he would much prefer a flat,
                   If you put him in a flat then he'd rather have a house.
                   If you set him on a mouse then he only wants a rat,   5
                   If you set him on a rat then he'd rather chase a mouse.
     Narrator   Yes the Rum Tum Tugger is a Curious Cat—
                      And there isn't any call for me to shout it:
2   For he will do
                         As he do do   10
                   And there's no doing anything about it!

     Narrator   The Rum Tum Tugger is a terrible bore:
     Boys' chorus When you let him in, then he wants to be out;
                   He's always on the wrong side of every door,
                   And as soon as he's at home, then he'd like to get about.   15
                   He likes to lie in the bureau drawer,
                   But he makes such a fuss if he can't get out.
     Narrator   Yes the Rum Tum Tugger is a Curious Cat—
                      And it isn't any use for you to doubt it:
                         For he will do   20
                         As he do do
                            And there's no doing anything about it!

---

2. **pheasant . . . grouse:** birds used for food, considered delicacies.

The Cat by an unknown American painter (c. 1840). National Gallery of Art, Washington, D.C. Gift of Edgar William and Bernice Chrysler Garbisch.

Narrator	The Rum Tum Tugger is a curious beast:
Girls' chorus	His disobliging ways are a matter of habit.
	If you offer him fish then he always wants a feast; 25
	When there isn't any fish then he won't eat rabbit.
Boys' chorus	If you offer him cream then he sniffs and sneers,
	For he only likes what he finds for himself;
	So you'll catch him in it right up to the ears,
	If you put it away on the larder shelf. 30
Girls' chorus	The Rum Tum Tugger is artful and knowing,
	The Rum Tum Tugger doesn't care for a cuddle;
	But he'll leap on your lap in the middle of your sewing,
	For there's nothing he enjoys like a horrible muddle.
	Yes the Rum Tum Tugger is a Curious Cat— 35
Narrator	And there isn't any need for me to spout it:
	For he will do
	As he do do
	And there's no doing anything about it!

The Rum Tum Tugger

CLOSURE

Have students create rhyming lines of poetry using the homophones from the Language and Vocabulary exercise on pages 312–313. Example: It's such a bore / sitting by the door / waiting for a knock.

EXTENSION AND ENRICHMENT

Musical Theater. Bring in a recording of the Broadway Musical *CATS* from the public library and elicit student responses on how the music for "The Rum Tum Tugger" enhances the words and fits his personality.

FOR STUDY AND DISCUSSION

Identifying Details

1. He would rather have grouse if you offer him pheasant; he would prefer to be in a flat if you put him in a house; he only wants a rat if you set him on a mouse.
2. He is a bore because he wants to be out if you let him in, and vice versa. Also, he likes to live in the bureau drawer; however, he makes a fuss if he can't get out.
3. He shows this by being finicky in his eating habits and by choosing his own time to jump on his owner's lap.

Interpreting Meanings

4. Students might suggest that the Tugger is like an eccentric or unpredictable relative or friend.
5. How do they think he'd make out as a politician, a TV anchorman, a computer hack, a surgeon?

LANGUAGE AND VOCABULARY

Sounds and Spellings

For answers, see the **Teaching Guide** at the beginning of the unit.

For Study and Discussion

IDENTIFYING DETAILS

1. The Tugger is a curious cat (meaning an "odd" cat). Find at least three examples of the Tugger's peculiar behavior in stanza 1.
2. Why is the Tugger also a bore, according to stanza 2?
3. How does the Tugger show that he is not interested in obliging or pleasing his owner, according to stanza 3?

APPLYING MEANINGS

4. It is said that all of T. S. Eliot's cat poems are really about people. Do you know any people who are like the Tugger? Tell about them.
5. The long-running Broadway musical *CATS* is based on Eliot's cat poems. In the show, the Rum Tum Tugger is portrayed as a rock singer. What do you think of that? What other human occupation would the Tugger like?

Language and Vocabulary

SOUNDS AND SPELLINGS

You may think it is simple to find rhyming words, but it is not always easy to work good rhymes or funny rhymes into a poem. For example, in lines 24 and 26, Eliot rhymes *habit* and *rabbit*. Can you think of any other word in the whole English language that also rhymes with *habit/rabbit*?

Some words look as if they should *not* rhyme, but they do. Complete each entry in

Terry Mann as the Rum Tum Tugger in the Broadway Musical *CATS*.

312 Poetry

the list below with words that rhyme with *know* and *sew* or *door* and *bore*, but look as if they shouldn't.

1. know/sew/s_/n_/t_____/t__/g_/h__/J__
2. bore/door/f___/f__/o__/l___/n__/p___/r___

Focus on Writing a Poem

EXPERIMENTING WITH SOUND EFFECTS

If you participated in a group reading of "The Rum Tum Tugger," you know how important **sound effects** can be in a poem. Here are some sound effects that you can use in your own poems:

rhyme	repetition
rhythm	alliteration

Experiment with sound effects by choosing *two* of the four devices listed above. Write a few lines of prose or poetry in which you use each device.

For example, you might create a sentence with alliteration like the following: "Cheerfully Charles charged into the Chinese restaurant." If you choose rhythm, you might write two lines of verse like these:

Colder nights are lasting longer,
Winter's bite is in the air.

After you have finished, share your experiments with classmates. Save your writing.

About the Author

T. S. Eliot (1888–1965) was born in St. Louis, Missouri, and studied literature at Harvard, but he lived in England for most of his life. Eliot wrote the most famous poem of the twentieth century, called *The Wasteland*. Eliot collected his cat poems in a book called *Old Possum's Book of Practical Cats*. ("Old Possum" is the nickname given to him by his friend and fellow poet Ezra Pound.) These poems imitate the "thumping rhythms" of poetry he heard as a child. Eliot clearly loved and understood cats. His own pets had names like Pettipaws, Wiscus, and George Pushdragon.

FOCUS ON WRITING A POEM

Experimenting with Sound Effects

You may want to suggest that each student choose a specific subject for all the prose or poetry that they write for this activity. It might be one of the subjects for poems they chose in the activity on page 299. Through their experimentation, students might find the precise and fresh word choices for which poets strive.

The Rum Tum Tugger

OBJECTIVES
Students will write two lines of poetry imitating the poet's use of typography.

FOCUS/MOTIVATION
As the headnote indicates, the layout of this poem is different from that of most poems. Before students read the poem, ask them to identify specific points about its appearance that make it unusual (varying line lengths, lack of capitalization, jamming up of words and punctuation in lines 2, 5, and 15, and words run together in line 5).

Teaching Resources B
Teacher's Notes, p. 137
Study Guide, pp. 139, 141
Language Skills, p. 143
Selection Vocabulary Test, p. 148
Selection Test, p. 149

AV Resources Binder
Audiocassette 2, Side B

1. GUIDED READING:
Identifying the Main Idea
Are the people in the balloon or in the sky city? They are in both. They take the speaker and listener into the balloon and sail into the sky city.

2. GUIDED READING:
Understanding Punctuation Marks
Note where parentheses begin and end, lines 4 and 15. The parenthetical passage primarily describes the voyage; the other lines describe the moon and the city.

3. LITERARY ELEMENTS:
Rhythm
Notice how the rhythm would change if the lines were broken at different spots. Suppose 7 were added to the end of 6, and 14 to the end of 13?

Before You Read

Suppose that you are a very young child looking at the bright, full moon for the first time. You have no idea what the moon is. What might you imagine it to be? Jot down one or two ideas. Then see what this poet imagines the moon is.

You'll notice the unusual way this poem is printed on the page. It's as if the poem is saying "Pay attention to me! Look at each and every one of my words!"

who knows if the moon's
E. E. Cummings

who knows if the moon's
1 a balloon,coming out of a keen city
in the sky—filled with pretty people?
2 (and if you and i should

get into it,if they   5
should take me and take you into their balloon,
why then
we'd go up higher with all the pretty people

than houses and steeples and clouds:
go sailing   10
away and away sailing into a keen
city which nobody's ever visited,where

always
3   it's
         Spring)and everyone's   15
in love and flowers pick themselves

READING THE POEM

Before students read, point out that the poem really consists of two sentences. Have a volunteer read the first sentence (lines 1–3) aloud. Then discuss the question that the speaker asks in that sentence. Tell students, also, that the speaker talks about *you, i,* and *they* in the poem. Help them to understand the referents for these pronouns. You might want to read the entire poem aloud yourself first and then ask for volunteers for a second reading.

VISUAL CONNECTIONS

Encourage students to discuss how this dreamlike painting makes them feel—peaceful, merry, sad? Encourage imaginative answers to questions such as, "Who are the people?" (Note the title.) "Where are they coming from? Where are they going? Why are they in costume? What does the moon add to their evening and to this picture?" Connect the painting with the poem by pointing out that in both of them, the moon is a focus for romantic fancies—an object associated with love, escape, freedom from care.

About the Artist
Henri Rousseau (1844–1910) was a French customs officer and self-taught painter. He is known for his lush, dreamlike pictures of animals and of people who are often dressed in exotic outfits or placed in strange settings.

A Carnival Evening by Henri Rousseau. Oil on canvas.

Philadelphia Museum of Art. Stern Collection.

CLOSURE

Have students make a list of three slang words that Cummings might use in place of *keen* if he were writing the poem today. (*Far-out? neat? cool?*) Have students read the poem aloud, replacing *keen* with a word from their list. How is the effect of the poem changed? (The meaning that *keen* carries of "sharpness" is lost, and the long *e* sound is different.)

FOR STUDY AND DISCUSSION

Identifying Details

1. He suggests that the moon is a balloon.
 It comes from a city in the sky, filled with pretty people.
2. The speaker and his beloved would go sailing to the "keen city" in the sky.

Interpreting Meanings

3. Details include the pretty people, the fact that nobody's ever visited, the continual spring, the fact that everyone is in love, and the fact that flowers do not even have to be picked.
4. He may be talking to a woman he loves, or to the reader.
5. Cummings does not capitalize the pronoun *I* in line 4.
 The word that gets the most emphasis is *Spring* (line 15).

Applying Meanings

6. Spring suggests rebirth from winter's deadness; it makes you think of flowers, warmth, and hope.
 Ask students to explain the reasons for their choice of a season.

For Study and Discussion

IDENTIFYING DETAILS

1. What does the speaker suggest the moon is? Where does it come from?
2. Inside the parentheses, the speaker imagines a journey. Who would go on the journey? Where would they go?

INTERPRETING MEANINGS

3. What details make the "keen city" sound like a wonderful place?
4. Whom do you think the speaker is talking to in this poem?
5. Cummings capitalizes a word only if he wants to emphasize it. In line 4, which word, usually capitalized, does he *not* capitalize? Which word in the poem gets the most emphasis?

APPLYING MEANINGS

6. Why do you suppose poets usually associate love and joy with spring? If you were describing a perfect place, what season would you assign to it? Why?

Literary Elements

RHYTHM

E. E. Cummings wrote his poems so that they looked very unusual on the page. You are supposed to read some of Cummings's lines very fast, some very slowly.

Look at lines 2, 5, and 12. Why do you think the word following the comma bumps right up to it? Look at line 15. Why do you think the parenthesis is all jammed up between two words? Would you read these lines quickly, or slowly?

Which lines in the poem would you definitely read slowly?

Write two lines in imitation of Cummings. Write one line in such a way that the reader knows it should be read very fast. Write the other line so that the reader would know that it should be read very slowly.

Language and Vocabulary

SLANG

Slang is informal language that is often popular with certain groups. Many slang words are "in" (fashionable) for just a year or two. For example, *groovy* was a popular slang word in the 1960s, but it's not used today at all. Some other once-popular slang words are *cool, uptight, mellow, dig it, bug off, far-*

SCIENCE LINK

Show a movie or videotape of the first moon landing and moonwalk by Apollo 11 astronauts on July 20, 1969. The school librarian or audiovisual coordinator should be able to help you locate films and/or videotapes if they are not already available in your school or public library. Afterwards, discuss with students ways the moon landing affected people's ideas about the moon. For example, the moon would never again seem as mysterious and unattainable as it once was.

---

out. (Do you use any of these words today?) In "who knows if the moon's," Cummings uses the word *keen* as slang to mean "good" or "fine." Do you know anyone today who uses *keen* in this way? What do you mean when you say a knife is "keen"? Or when you say someone has a "keen intelligence"?

Think of three slang words popular today. (Perhaps use your favorite ones.) Write a definition of each slang word and use it in a sentence.

Focus on Writing a Poem

EXPERIMENTING WITH VISUAL EFFECTS

E. E. Cummings was a pioneer in his experiments with punctuation and capital letters. You have seen how the way a poem looks on the page can be related to what it means and how it should be read aloud.

Write a poem of your own describing either a pet or a wild animal with whose habits you are familiar. You can identify and organize details for your description by filling out a chart like the one below.

Details Chart
Animal's Name: _____
Setting/Habitat: _____
Physical Appearance: _____
_____
Action/Movements: _____
_____

In your poem, experiment with visual effects by running letters or words together, capitalizing important words, omitting punctuation, or arranging words to form a picture on the page. Save your writing.

About the Author

E. E. Cummings (1892–1962) was born in Cambridge, Massachusetts, and completed his education at Harvard. Cummings is famous for the unusual way his poems look on the page. By experimenting with punctuation and capital letters, he surprises readers into paying attention to every word. In his anthology *Sleeping on the Wing,* the poet Kenneth Koch writes this about Cummings: ". . . almost every poem seems like some kind of experiment, like another investigation into the use of words. His poetry constantly breaks all the rules. . . . His way of writing seems to call attention to the sense of each word, so that each word counts and is important in the poem."

LITERARY ELEMENTS
Rhythm

In lines 2, 5, and 12, the word following the comma bumps right up to it to suggest a quick pace.

In line 15, the parentheses are jammed up to suggest a quick pace.

Possibilities of lines to be read slowly include lines 7, 13, and 14.

Urge students to imitate Cummings's distinctive use of capitalization, punctuation, and varying line length.

LANGUAGE AND VOCABULARY
Slang

For answers, see the **Teaching Guide** at the beginning of the unit.

FOCUS ON WRITING A POEM
Experimenting with Visual Effects

Students are sometimes intimidated when the conventions of punctuation, capitalization, and form are removed from a writing assignment. You could help them get started by illustrating on the chalkboard several visual effects. For example, stretch out the word *long* as in *long tail.* Or write the word *jump* in a cascading fashion to illustrate *jump from a fence.* In addition, you could refer students to the poem "Concrete Cat" on page 328.

OBJECTIVES
Students will identify rhymes and alliteration.

FOCUS/MOTIVATION
Building on Prior Knowledge. Ask students about times when they may have preferred being alone rather than playing with others. Did other children ever feel that they were being "stuck up"?

Prereading Journal. Have students imagine that they are sitting alone while other children play. Have them write the thoughts they might think to make themselves feel better about being alone.

READING THE POEM
The language of the poem is simple, but the characterization of Narcissa is challenging. Read the poem aloud for the students. Then have them read silently to decide what kind of girl they think Narcissa is.

TEACHING RESOURCES B
Teacher's Notes, p. 137
Study Guide, pp. 140, 142
Language Skills, p. 143
Building Vocabulary, p. 146
Selection Vocabulary Test, p. 148
Selection Test, p. 149

AV RESOURCES BINDER
Audiocassette 2, Side B

VISUAL CONNECTIONS
After students have read "Narcissa," ask them which figure in the painting on the opposite page could be little Narcissa, and why. This scene is set in Boston in 1938. Do any details date the children?

About the Artist
Allan Rohan Crite (1910–) is an African American artist who has exhibited widely. He has also written and illustrated religious books and articles. Born in Plainfield, New Jersey, he earned his B.A. from Harvard University at the age of 58. He now lives in Boston.

Before You Read
In Greek mythology, Narcissus was a young man who was very proud of his own good looks and would not marry. Angry at his selfishness, the goddess of love made him fall in love with his reflection in a lake. Narcissus looked at himself for so long that he wasted away. The first narcissus flowers grew in the spot where he died.

Is this little Narcissa anything like that Greek boy?

Narcissa
GWENDOLYN BROOKS

Some of the girls are playing jacks.
Some are playing ball.
But small Narcissa is not playing
Anything at all.

Small Narcissa sits upon   5
A brick in her back yard
And looks at tiger lilies,
And shakes her pigtails hard.

First she is an ancient queen
In pomp and purple veil.   10
Soon she is a singing wind.
And, next, a nightingale.

How fine to be Narcissa,
A-changing like all that!
While sitting still, as still, as still   15
As anyone ever sat!

For Study and Discussion

IDENTIFYING DETAILS
1. Narcissa is not playing, but she is very busy all the same. What does small Narcissa "change" into?

INTERPRETING MEANINGS
2. To someone just looking at her, Narcissa seems to be "not playing / Anything at all." However, someone—like the speaker of the poem—who really knows Narcissa can tell what she is doing in her imagination. What game is Narcissa playing?

3. Do you see any connection between Narcissa and the boy in the Greek myth? Or do you think the poet chose this name just by accident? What do you think of the name?

318 Poetry

CLOSURE

Have students think up simple lines with repetition that describe each of these situations: (1) a baby asleep; (2) a small girl running to get a kite in the air; (3) a fire truck speeding to answer an alarm; (4) a small child lying in the grass looking at the stars. Example: She ran faster, faster, so much faster / To launch the paper bird.

> **TRANSPARENCY 22**
> *Literary Elements*
> *Sound Effects in Poetry* – explores the poetic concepts introduced in the unit, such as rhyme, rhythm, refrain, alliteration, and onomatopoeia.

Marble Players by Allan Rohan Crite (1938). Oil on canvas.

The Boston Athenaeum. Gift of the artist.

APPLYING MEANINGS

4. What qualities in Narcissa might someday help her to be a good writer, if that's what she wants to be?

Literary Elements

RHYMES AND ALLITERATION

The music of a poem is created by its rhymes and by other sound effects. Write out the words at the ends of the lines of this poem that rhyme. What **internal rhymes,** or rhymes within the lines, can you hear in lines 2–3 and 11–12?

Music in this poem is also created by **alliteration,** the repetition of consonant sounds. Find where the poet uses alliteration in lines 3, 5, 6, 7, 10, 11, 12, 15, and 16.

Read the lines aloud to hear the musical effects of all these repeated sounds.

FOR STUDY AND DISCUSSION

Identifying Details

1. Narcissa changes into an ancient queen, a singing wind, and a nightingale.

Interpreting Meanings

2. She is playing a game like "Let's pretend."
3. Point out that Narcissa, like Narcissus, is changing into something or someone *else*; but she is not admiring herself. Although Narcissa is not egotistical like the Greek boy, she is the main figure in her own dreams, just as he is the main focus of his dreams. (Names like this aren't insignificant. Brooks knows what she's doing.)

Applying Meanings

4. Qualities that might make a good writer include imagination, the ability to enjoy herself while she is alone, persistence, and vivid sense impressions.

LITERARY ELEMENTS

Rhymes and Alliteration

Words at the end of lines that rhyme: *ball* and *all*, *yard* and *hard*, *purple veil* and *nightingale*, *that* and *sat*.

Internal rhymes occur in lines 2–3 (*ball* and *small*) and in lines 11–12 (*singing* and *nightingale*).

There is alliteration of

the s sound in line 3; the s sound in line 5; the b sound in line 6; the l sound in line 7; the p sound in line 10; the s and n sounds in line 11; the n sound in line 12; and the s sound in lines 15 and 16.

FOCUS ON WRITING A POEM
Planning a Poem
Encourage students to answer the questions on the list and to fill out the chart when they plan their poems.

Focus on Writing a Poem

PLANNING A POEM

"Narcissa" is from a collection of poems for children called *Bronzeville Boys and Girls.* Each poem in this book tells about the thoughts and feelings of a different city child. The title of each poem is a child's name. For example, "Skipper" is about the way a child feels when his pet dies. Here is how you might plan a similar poem:

1. Think of an interesting name for a little boy or girl. (Do not use the name of anyone you know.)

2. Next, think about a feeling that your young child might have.

3. Then think about where (at what place or event) the child would have that feeling. For example, a child might feel happy about going to a birthday party, or angry about being left with a babysitter.

On a sheet of paper, copy this planning chart and fill it in. Using this information, you can now write your poem whenever you want.

Child's name (two or three ideas) _____
_____
Feeling _____
_____
Place or event _____
_____

About the Author

Gwendolyn Brooks (1917–) is a major American poet. The "Bronzeville" that she writes about is a black neighborhood in Chicago, a city she has lived in for most of her life. In her autobiography, *Report from Part One,* Brooks writes that she "dreamed a lot" when she was a child, perhaps just like Narcissa. "As a little girl I dreamed freely, often on the top step of the back porch—morning, noon, sunset, deep twilight. I loved clouds . . . I loved the gold worlds I saw in the sky . . . I was writing all the time." Brooks's many prizes include the Pulitzer Prize for poetry, which she received for *Annie Allen,* her collection of adult poems. In addition to writing, Brooks seeks out and encourages young poets. Her advice to young writers is to get as much education as possible, read widely, and "live richly with eyes open, and heart, too."

PORTFOLIO ASSESSMENT

Actions that we perform produce a sensory reaction. The children in the photograph probably feel the coarse sand, hear the sound of waves rippling, see the glowing beach, taste salt in the air, and smell a mild fish and salt aroma. Students may want to plan, write, and revise a poem or paragraph about how a favorite action produces reactions from all five of their senses. Suggest students choose actions that are commonplace to them. Allow time for planning, writing, peer editing, and revising. Consult with students individually to agree on how their poems or paragraphs will be assessed. (See *Portfolio Assessment and Professional Support Materials* for additional information on student portfolios.)

USING YOUR SENSES

Poets try to create very precise pictures of what they experience. This means that they search for words to create pictures in our minds. Words that create pictures are called **images.** Images can also appeal to other senses. They can help us hear how something sounds, tastes, or smells, or even how something feels to the touch (hot, cold, rough, smooth, slimy). As you read a poem, you want to enter the poet's world. Images will help you share the poet's imagination.

INTRODUCING USING YOUR SENSES

Talk with students about the five senses. What are they, and how do we use them to understand the world? One of the first tasks of poetry, perhaps even before it reveals ideas or feelings, is to make us aware of our senses and of the fascinating phenomena they connect us with. Words can stimulate our senses of sight, sound, touch, taste, and smell, even though we only see words on the page or hear them at a poetry reading. This is magic.

As a creative writing exercise, have students in small groups imagine some common object—an orange, a blade of grass, an old chair. Have each member of the group write a sentence describing that object as it is perceived by a different one of the five senses.

OBJECTIVES
Students will recognize alliteration and identify and write sense images.

FOCUS/MOTIVATION
Prereading Journal. Ask students to recall or imagine a beautiful object in nature—for example, waves, a mountain, a flower, stars. Have them jot down a list of words they would use to help a friend form an accurate mental picture of the object.

READING THE POEM
Some of the imagistic words in this poem are challenging (*tide-tumbled, moonsilver*) and may require paraphrasing. Aloud, the poem should be read slowly so that the images may form in students' minds.

Before You Read
Have you ever found something beautiful outside? This poet writes about an experience that has happened to many of us. Notice how she shows you a sequence of carefully drawn pictures. As you read, be aware of the feelings that each word-picture gives you.

Beach Stones

LILIAN MOORE

When these small
stones
were
in clear pools and
nets of weed   5

tide-tumbled
teased by spray

they glowed
moonsilver,
glinted sunsparks on   10
their speckled
skins.

Spilled on the
shelf
they were   15
wet-sand jewels
wave-green
still flecked with
foam.

Now   20
gray stones
lie
dry and dim.

Why did we bring them home?

CLOSURE

This poem is really about how we sometimes spoil beauty in an attempt to seize it or own it. Have three students give examples of how our attempts to seize or own something beautiful have actually only destroyed it. You might have another student suggest ways we should "handle" beauty if we are not to destroy it. (Think of beaches seized by developers and sold in parcels to people who want to "own" them; or think of forests, marshlands, the Everglades. The list, unfortunately, is long.)

TRANSPARENCIES 18 & 19
Fine Art
Theme: *Fewer Words, More Meaning* – invites students to explore everyday objects as subjects of works of art.

FOR STUDY AND DISCUSSION

Identifying Details

1. The stones lost their brilliant, glowing colors and became "dry and dim."
2. Examples might include alliteration of the *s* sound in lines 1–2, of the *t* sound in lines 6–7, of the *s* and *sp* sounds in lines 10–12, of the *f* sound in lines 18–19, and of the *d* sound in line 23.

Interpreting Meanings

3. The speaker feels puzzled, disappointed, and sad. The last line of the poem expresses these feelings.

Applying Meanings

4. Possibilities might include butterflies, birds' nests, and flowers. Notice how this speaker has spoiled beauty in an attempt to possess it.

LITERARY ELEMENTS

Imagery

Details that help readers to visualize the wet stones are "glowed moonsilver" (lines 8–9), "glinted sun-sparks" (line 10), "speckled skins" (lines 11–12), "wet-sand jewels" (line 16), and "wave-green / still flecked with / foam" (lines 17–19).

For Study and Discussion

IDENTIFYING DETAILS

1. What happened to the stones when they were brought home?

2. This poem doesn't have rhymes, but it does contain the kind of sound echoes called alliteration. **Alliteration** is the repetition of consonant sounds in words that are close together. Alliteration makes lines more musical and memorable. (Advertisers often use alliteration in their slogans.) Read aloud your favorite example of alliteration in this poem.

INTERPRETING MEANINGS

3. How does the speaker feel about the stones now? Which line of the poem tells you?

APPLYING MEANINGS

4. What other things can you think of that look beautiful when you see them in nature, but which change after you "bring them home"?

Literary Elements

IMAGERY

Images are details that help you **see** something, **smell** it, **hear** it, **taste** it, or **feel** its textures or temperatures. List three details that help you see what these stones looked like when they were wet.

Focus on Writing a Poem

GATHERING IMAGES

Choose a subject for a poem and make a chart like the one below. Save your notes.

Subject _____	
Sense	Image
sight	_____
hearing	_____
smell	_____
taste	_____
touch	_____

About the Author

Lilian Moore (1909–   ) was born in New York City, where she went to Hunter College and Columbia University. For many years, she was a teacher and a reading specialist in the New York City schools. She also wrote many stories and poems for young people. *See My Lovely Poison Ivy* is her collection of poems about ghosts and witches. Moore is a founding member of the Council on Interracial Books for Children.

Behind the Scenes

A Poem's Roots

Sometimes poems come with long roots. The poem "Beach Stones" comes out of feelings that go back to my childhood. I loved many things I found at the beach, but beach stones had a special fascination. As they lay washed up on the beach or in small tide pools, they seemed to be magically colored, and even then they looked to me like jewels of the sea. I gathered them eagerly and it was always hard to choose. One seemed more beautiful than another.

Several times I brought them home to have forever. What a disappointment to see them fade into plain gray stones! After a while I learned that some things can't be moved. They have to be enjoyed where they are.

—Lilian Moore

FOCUS ON WRITING A POEM

Gathering Images
After students fill in their charts, suggest that they use dictionaries, thesauruses, and dictionaries of synonyms to replace tired, overused words with vivid, descriptive words. You could also have students meet in small groups to share their charts and to offer comments and suggestions.

OBJECTIVE
Students will identify the images in the poem.

TEACHING RESOURCES B
Teacher's Notes, p. 151
Study Guide, p. 153
Building Vocabulary, p.161
Selection Vocabulary Test, p. 163
Selection Test, p. 164

AV RESOURCES BINDER
Audiocassette 2, Side B

VISUAL CONNECTIONS
Rivera has made the flowers the most eye-catching things in his painting, big in size and rich in color and form. Pat Mora does the same, in finding vivid words to describe her flowers. You might ask your students to write two sentences describing what they *see* in the painting. In a third sentence they should give their response to it. When they finish the poem, ask students how Mora's flowers are different from Rivera's. (Mora's are paper.)

About the Artist
Diego Rivera (1886–1957) was born in Mexico City and studied in Spain and France, where he was a friend of several Cubist painters. Best known for his controversial murals of Mexican life and history, Rivera also did many smaller easel paintings, such as this one of a flower seller.

FOCUS/MOTIVATION
Building on Prior Knowledge. As the headnote suggests, students may not think that old people once were young. In class discussion, talk about the oldest people students know.

Prereading Journal. Have students describe an old person. Then describe how the person might have looked when he or she was ten years old.

Before You Read
If you have ever traveled in Mexico or in parts of the Southwest, you might have seen older women selling souvenirs to tourists. See what the speaker in the poem thinks about an old woman selling paper flowers in an open-air market, probably in Mexico.

Calluses are those rough, hard places on our skin that are caused by things like hard labor or shoes that don't fit.

You have to read the title as the first line.

Petals PAT MORA

have calloused her hands,
brightly colored crepe paper: turquoise,
yellow, magenta, which she shapes
into large blooms for bargain-hunting tourists
who see her flowers, her puppets, her baskets,
but not her—small, gray-haired woman
wearing a white apron, who hides behind
blossoms in her stall at the market,
who sits and remembers collecting wildflowers
as a girl, climbing rocky Mexican hills
to fill a straw hat with soft blooms
which she'd stroke gently, over and over again
with her smooth fingertips.

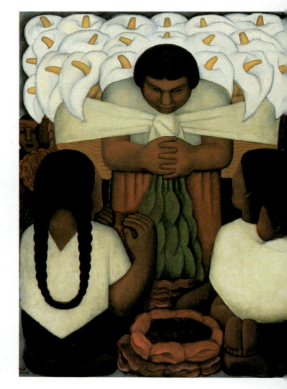

Flower Day by Diego Rivera (1925).
Encaustic on canvas.
Los Angeles County Museum of Art.
Los Angeles County Funds.

CLOSURE

As preparation for their illustrations of the poem, ask students what colors evoked their feelings about the flowers and the flower seller. Lead them to see that color imagery makes the woman seem drab and sad behind the vivid flowers.

For Study and Discussion

IDENTIFYING DETAILS

1. What does the woman in the marketplace sell? Whom does she sell to?
2. What have calloused her hands?
3. What **images** do the tourists see? What *don't* they see?
4. What does this woman remember? How were her hands different then?

INTERPRETING MEANINGS

5. How do you feel about the woman in this poem?
6. List the five **images** of color in the poem. What colors are similar to turquoise and magenta?

APPLYING MEANINGS

7. Can you think of other people like this flower seller, whose humanity is ignored by those who pass by?

Illustrating the Poem

This poem is full of color. You might collaborate with a group of classmates to produce a collage (kə·läzh′) illustrating the objects, people, and events you see in this little scene. Be sure to include the five colors in the poem. (A **collage** is made up of pictures and objects from all sources: photographs from magazines, words from newspapers, stones, flowers, sand, seeds, leaves, cloth, and so on. What makes a collage interesting is the way all these images are put together.)

About the Author

Pat Mora (1942–   ) is a Mexican American. Much of her poetry is about the blending of Hispanic culture into American society. Mora has a particular interest in writing for children. She says, "Writing is a way of thinking about what I see and feel. In words I save images of people and of scenes. Writing is not exactly like a picture album, though, because when I write I have to think about why I want to save those images, how I feel about them."

FOR STUDY AND DISCUSSION

Identifying Details

1. She sells flowers, puppets, and baskets to tourists.
2. The crepe paper has calloused them.
3. They see the woman's wares, but they don't see the woman herself.
4. She remembers collecting wild flowers as a girl.
   Her fingertips were smooth.

Interpreting Meanings

5. Students may feel pity or sympathy or love for her.
6. The five images are turquoise, yellow, and magenta paper flowers; gray-haired woman; and a white apron. Colors that are similar to turquoise are blue and green. Colors that are similar to magenta are purple and red.

Applying Meanings

7. Students might suggest salespeople in stores, employees who collect tolls on highways, and, of course, the homeless.

OBJECTIVE
Students will identify concrete words.

FOCUS/MOTIVATION
Ask students whether they have ever thought of a poem as something to look at rather than to read. Discuss the definition of *concrete* in the headnote, and then write the word *balloon* on the board. Ask students how the letters of the word can be arranged so that they represent the object. What other word might be associated with *balloon*? (*String*) How might the letters of this word be added to the balloon poem?

TEACHING RESOURCES B
Teacher's Notes, p. 155
Study Guide, pp. 157, 159
Selection Test, p. 164

Before You Read

Most poems are written to be read aloud. Here's one poem that you can't read aloud. Its meaning comes from the shape the words make on the page. The title "Concrete Cat" refers to the type of poetry that it is. "Concrete" means something real and solid, something that can be touched. A concrete poem is shaped like its subject. The words make a picture that is fun to look at.

Concrete Cat   DORTHI CHARLES

```
        A              A
      e   r          e   r
       eYe            eYe         stripestripestripestripe
   whisker         whisker           stripestripestripe      t
                                                              a
   whisker   m   h whisker         stripestripestripestripes   i  t a i l
              o   t                  stripestripestripe        l
              U                    stripestripestripestripe

         paw  paw             paw  paw                    ǝ s n o ɯ

      dishdish                         litterbox
                                       litterbox
```

328   Poetry

CLOSURE
Ask each student to give an example of (1) an abstract word and (2) a concrete word.

For Study and Discussion

INTERPRETING MEANINGS
1. List all the words the poet has used. Can you think of any that might be added? Where would you put them?
2. Why do you think the word *mouse* is upside down? Explain why *dishdish* and
   litterbox
   litterbox
   are printed the way they are.
3. What do you think the capital letters *A*, *Y*, and *U* represent?

APPLYING MEANINGS
4. What other subjects do you think might be good for a concrete poem? List three subjects that, in your opinion, would be *poor* choices for a concrete poem. (Do your classmates all agree?)

Language and Vocabulary

CONCRETE WORDS
You have learned that *concrete* is a word used to describe a poem that has the shape of an actual thing. *Concrete* is also used to describe words that refer to actual things that can be seen, touched, tasted, smelled, or heard. Concrete words are words like *cat*, *paw*, *mouse*, and *litterbox*. Each of these words names something that can be seen. The opposite of *concrete* is *abstract*. Abstract words name ideas or qualities. Some examples of abstract words are *beauty*, *power*, *democracy*, and *peace*. Poets are usually more interested in concrete words than in abstract ones.

Write down two concrete words or phrases that appeal to each of these senses.

1. sight
2. smell
3. taste
4. hearing
5. touch

Focus on Writing a Poem

WRITING A CONCRETE POEM
First, think of a subject. For your first concrete poem, you may want to use just one word, such as *dog*, *rain*, *slide*, *wave*, or *pizza*. Next, decide what kind of shape your subject suggests to you. Finally, think of words associated with your subject. Remember that how you arrange the words should have something to do with what they mean.

About the Author

Dorthi Charles is a penname that X. J. Kennedy (1929–   ) used when he began writing poems for young people. X. J. Kennedy's true first name is Joseph. He says he uses the initial X to distinguish himself from the Kennedys of political fame. X. J. Kennedy was born in New Jersey and began writing and publishing homemade comic books when he was in the seventh grade. He has taught in college and has written several best-selling textbooks. He and his wife, Dorothy M. Kennedy, began making up verses and stories to amuse their own five children. Their *Knock at a Star* introduces children to different types of poetry and encourages them to write their own poems. Two of X. J. Kennedy's books of poetry are *Brats* and *The Phantom Ice Cream Man*. His first novel for young people is called *The Owlstone Crown*.

Concrete Cat

FOR STUDY AND DISCUSSION
Interpreting Meanings
1. The words are *ear*, *eye*, *stripe*, *paw*, *dish*, *litterbox*, *mouse*, *whisker*, *mouth,* and *tail.*

They might add such words as *nose*, *back*, *fur*, *claw*, *collar*, *tongue*. (Would these details be more difficult to use than the ones in the poem?)
2. The cat has killed the mouse.

The words *dishdish* and *litterbox* suggest the relative size, shape, height, and position of the items.
3. The two capital *A*'s suggest the tips of the ears; the capital *Y* suggests the center or pupil of the eye; the capital *U* suggests the center of the cat's mouth.

Applying Meanings
4. Good subjects might include a dog, a giraffe, an elephant, scissors. Poor choices might be abstract words that can't be visualized, such as *friendship*, *admiration,* or *fear*.

FOCUS ON WRITING A POEM
Writing a Concrete Poem
Drawing a picture of the subject should suggest ideas for the arrangement of the words in the poem.

Before You Read

The most famous form of Japanese poetry is called *haiku* (hī′kōō). Haiku are always three lines long. Often they are about a particular season. Haiku try to capture a moment with a few quick, sharp pictures. As you read these haiku, try to put yourself in the scene along with the poet. What do you see? What do you hear? How do you feel about the moment expressed?

Haiku

A heavy cart rumbles,
And from the grass
Flutters a butterfly.
—Kuroyanagi Shōha

A chilling moon
As I walk alone:
Clatter of the bridge.
—Tan Taigi

Winter rain:
A farmhouse piled with firewood,
A light in the window.
—Nozawa Bonchō

Bad-tempered, I got back:
Then, in the garden,
The willow tree.
—Ōshima Ryōta

CLOSURE

As closure for the lesson, be sure each student produces at least one haiku he or she is pleased with. Many classes create a bulletin board display of their haiku, along with illustrations.

ART LINK

Students might enjoy learning about another distinctively Japanese art form—origami. Origami is the art of folding paper into various shapes of animals and objects. Students can find instructional books on origami in school or public libraries. Encourage students to create origami figures, and ask them to teach the skill to the rest of the class. If students are writing haiku, suggest that they create origami figures that relate to their haiku. Decorate the class by hanging the origami from the ceiling or beside students' haiku poems displayed on the bulletin board.

View of Kondrai by Hokusai. Woodcut. Museum Chiossone, Geneva, Switzerland.

VISUAL CONNECTIONS

Some students may wish to use this Japanese painting as a source of inspiration for the writing assignment on page 332. The simplicity of composition in this picture parallels the simplicity of the haiku. In both forms, a few, exactly right images are chosen. Many images are left out so that our imaginations can participate in the artist's scene.

About the Artist

We have met **Hokusai** (1760–1849) before on page 280. Your students may be interested to learn that he was a noted eccentric who changed his name more than thirty times and his residence more than ninety. In his work, people are often dwarfed by massive forces of nature. (It is said that in every Japanese painting of a natural scene, the viewer can find a human presence.)

Haiku

Cultural Diversity

Often the art forms created by a culture tell us something about that culture. The writing of a *haiku* is governed by some very specific rules. For example, each haiku must have exactly seventeen syllables. With this information, invite students to speculate on why this particular form of poetry was created. What can we infer about the people who invented it?

TRANSPARENCIES 18 & 19
Fine Art
Theme: *Fewer Words, More Meaning* – invites students to explore everyday objects as subjects of works of art.

FOR STUDY AND DISCUSSION
Interpreting Meanings
1. Possible seasons are (a) summer, (b) autumn, (c) winter, (d) spring.
2. Three images of sight are fluttering butterfly, moon, light in the window, willow tree.
   Two images of hearing are the "rumbling of the cart" and the "clatter of the bridge."
3. The first haiku presents the contrasting images of the heavy cart versus the light butterfly. The third haiku presents contrasting images of the winter rain (cold) versus the lighted farmhouse (warm). The fourth haiku presents contrasting images of bad temper versus the tender young willow leaves.
4. Loneliness might be suggested by the chilling moon; coziness by the lighted farmhouse; happiness by the willow tree; fear by the lonely walker.
   The fourth haiku shows how nature can change a person's bad mood.
5. Choices will vary.

FOCUS ON WRITING A POEM
Writing a Haiku
Look for vibrant images. The most challenging aspect of haiku writing is to imply feeling through a few sensory images without stating it directly.

For Study and Discussion

In the Japanese language, a haiku has just seventeen syllables: five syllables in lines 1 and 3 and seven syllables in line 2. The translators of these haiku have not tried to imitate the rule of seventeen syllables.

Here are some other "rules" for writing a haiku. (Not all haiku follow all these rules.)

1. A haiku is about daily life.
2. A haiku describes particular things, often two contrasting things.
3. A haiku records a moment of enlightenment—a sudden discovery about life.
4. A haiku is usually about a season of the year. Often a haiku contains a *kigo*, a "season" word.

That is quite a lot to get into only seventeen syllables! But to Japanese poets, the challenge of the haiku is part of its pleasure.

INTERPRETING MEANINGS
1. What season might each haiku describe?
2. List three **images** in these haiku that help you **see** something. List two **images** that help you **hear** sounds.
3. Which haiku present **contrasting images?**
4. Did any of the images make you feel lonely? Cozy? Happy? Fearful? Which haiku reveals how nature can change a person's bad mood?
5. In Japan, there are poetry contests in which judges award prizes to the best haiku. Suppose you are one of the judges. Which of these haiku would you give the prize to? Why?

Focus on Writing a Poem

WRITING A HAIKU

Haiku are fun to write. You may not be able to create a poem as forceful as one of these Japanese haiku, but you can still produce images that you will be pleased with. Before you write, review the "rules" for writing haiku. (You can skip the rule about the seventeen syllables.) Then keep filling out charts like the one below until you have images and a feeling that you think will work. You might try to open with a word stating your season. Be sure to list some contrasting images in your chart. One important rule: You must limit your poem to three lines.

Haiku ideas	
Season	
Sight images	
Sound images	
Touch images	
Smell images	
Taste images	
Feeling or discovery I want to express	

332   Poetry

MAKING COMPARISONS

We all use comparisons every day. We might say that somebody is "white as a ghost" or that someone "wormed out of an invitation" or that someone is "as light as a feather." In these everyday expressions, we are comparing someone's pale face to the whiteness of a ghost; we are comparing someone who gets out of a tight spot to a worm slithering out of a hole; we are comparing someone's weight with the lightness of a feather.

Here are the two major kinds of comparisons used by poets:

1. **Simile:** a comparison made between two very unlike things that uses a specific word of comparison such as *like* or *as* or *resembles* ("cheeks like roses," "skin like marble," "feet as big as boats").
2. **Metaphor:** a comparison made between two very unlike things that omits the specific word of comparison ("cheeks are roses," "skin is marble," "boats for feet").

Why do poets use so many comparisons? Some people believe it is because they want to show that everything in the world is "one."

INTRODUCING MAKING COMPARISONS

Analogy is one of the primary forms of human reasoning, and comparisons are a form of analogy. In our everyday prose lives, however, our comparisons tend to be similes: "He runs like a duck." "My car sounds like a dishwasher." Metaphor, though created through the mere omission of *like* or *as*, requires a leap of the imagination. Children, societies with a strong verbal tradition, and poets all show a special propensity for metaphor.

To prove to students that they are naturals at creating metaphors, keep having them turn similes into metaphors. Three examples occur on this page, in the comparisons about cheeks, skin, and feet. Discuss how metaphor adds force and even shock value to simile. "My love is a rose" is more forceful and startling than "My love is like a rose."

Notice how, in this famous photograph opposite, the photographer has seen a metaphor in a telescope. What has he made the telescope into? (A person's face)

OBJECTIVES

Students will identify an extended metaphor, create metaphors, and use onomatopoeia.

FOCUS/MOTIVATION

Building on Prior Knowledge. Have students share their sea experiences. Brainstorm to create a list of images to describe a stormy sea, a calm sea, a dead sea.

Prereading Journal. Have students write down what they think of when they hear the word *sea*.

READING THE POEM

Read the poem aloud. Once you have discussed the questions on page 336, have volunteers read aloud each of the three stanzas, emphasizing the sea's different moods.

VISUAL CONNECTIONS

Compare this detail from a nineteenth-century American portrayal of the sea and a shipwreck with the somewhat earlier Japanese print on page 331. Hokusai's and Bierstadt's life spans overlapped slightly. In class discussion, ask students to compare the moods of the sea in each painting. Which painting tries to make the sea look more "real"? In which painting (or both?) is the sea threatening?

About the Artist
Albert Bierstadt (1830–1902) was born in Germany but came to the United States at the age of two. He became famous for his huge landscapes of the West, realistic but awe-inspiring in their portrayals of mountains, rivers, wildlife, and Indian camps. This painting of the beautiful, translucent turquoise wave was based on a trip the painter made to the Bahamas in 1877.

The Shore of the Turquoise Sea (detail) by Albert Bierstadt (1878). Oil on canvas.

The Manoogian Collection, Detroit, Michigan.

SCIENCE LINK
Encourage students to research the daily and seasonal changes in ocean tides. Ask students to determine at what times of day and year the sea is most like "a hungry dog" and when it lies quietly like a dog "with his head between his paws." Students can find information about tides in books about the ocean or by looking in encyclopedias under *ocean, sea, waves,* or *tides.* Have students record what they learn about tides in their journals or learning logs, or ask them to share it orally with the class.

Before You Read

After you read the title of the next poem, stop for a moment. In your journal, describe the picture that comes to your mind. What sounds do you hear in your imagination? As you read the poem, compare the sights and sounds you saw and heard with the ones James Reeves gives you.

The Sea   JAMES REEVES

The sea is a hungry dog,
Giant and gray.
He rolls on the beach all day.
With his clashing teeth and shaggy jaws
Hour upon hour he gnaws   5
The rumbling, tumbling stones,
And "Bones, bones, bones!"
The giant sea dog moans,
Licking his greasy paws.

And when the night wind roars   10
And the moon rocks in the stormy cloud,
He bounds to his feet and snuffs and sniffs,
Shaking his wet sides over the cliffs,
And howls and hollos long and loud.

But on quiet days in May or June,   15
When even the grasses on the dune
Play no more their reedy tune,
With his head between his paws
He lies on the sandy shores,
So quiet, so quiet, he scarcely snores.   20

The Sea   335

TEACHING RESOURCES B
Teacher's Notes, p. 166
Study Guide, pp. 168, 171
Language Skills, p. 179
Building Vocabulary, p. 182
Selection Vocabulary Test, p. 183
Selection Test, p. 184

AV RESOURCES BINDER
Audiocassette 2, Side B

1. GUIDED READING:
Making Inferences
How might a hungry dog behave? A hungry dog would be very restless and growly; a dog that has just been fed tends to be quiet and sleepy.

2. LITERARY ELEMENTS:
Verbs
What vivid verbs help us see and hear the sea? Examples are *rolls, gnaws, moans,* and *licking.*

3. LITERARY ELEMENTS:
Imagery
What words in this stanza help us hear the sea? *Roars* (line 10), *snuffs* and *sniffs* (line 12), *howls* and *hollos* (line 14).

CLOSURE

Extend the poem's metaphors by playing a "chain metaphor" game. Going around the room, have each student use the second term of the preceding student's metaphor as the first term of a new metaphor. Start with line 1 of the poem.

FOR STUDY AND DISCUSSION

Identifying Details

1. In the first stanza the sea dog is hungry, gnaws the stones on the beach with "his clashing teeth and shaggy jaws," moans, and licks his "greasy paws." In the second stanza the dog bounds to his feet, sniffs, shakes his wet sides, and howls loudly. In the third stanza, the dog lies quietly on the sand, his head between his paws.

Interpreting Meanings

2. a. The sea is like a "hungry" dog because it attacks the stones and "eats" the beach.
  b. The sea would "roll" on the beach with the breaking of each wave.
  c. His "clashing teeth and shaggy jaws" would be the crashing waves covered with spume.
  d. The "bones" are the pebbles and stones on the beach.
  e. The sea spray is lapping the stones on the shore.
  f. He imagines that the spray is water that the dog has shaken off.
  g. The sea would be making loud sounds as the waves crashed against the shore.
  h. The dog's quiet snore is compared with the gentle lapping of the waves.

336

For Study and Discussion

IDENTIFYING DETAILS

1. A **metaphor** compares two things that are basically very different. The poet wants you to see how these two different things are similar in some way. In "The Sea," the poet identifies the sea as a dog. Describe what you see the sea dog doing in each stanza.

INTERPRETING MEANINGS

2. This poem is an **extended metaphor**—that is, it states a very unusual comparison and then extends it throughout several lines. See if you can find all the ways the sea is like a dog.
  a. How is the sea like a "hungry" dog?
  b. How would the sea "roll" on the beach?
  c. What would its "clashing teeth and shaggy jaws" be?
  d. What are the "bones" the sea dog gnaws?
  e. When the sea dog is "licking its greasy paws," what is the sea doing?
  f. In stanza 2, what does the poet imagine the sea spray is?
  g. When the sea dog "howls and hollos," what would the sea really be doing?
  h. What sound of the sea is compared to the dog's quiet snore?

3. If the sea is a "hungry" dog in the first two stanzas, what kind of dog is it in stanza 3? Find two details in the third stanza that are a striking contrast to details in stanzas 1 and 2.

APPLYING MEANINGS

4. Can you think of any other animals the sea might remind someone of? What animal would a volcano remind you of? How about a tornado?

336 Poetry

Language and Vocabulary

ONOMATOPOEIA

Onomatopoeia (on·ə·mat'ə·pē'ə) is a word that came into English from the Greek language. The Greek words that it comes from mean "name-making." In English, onomatopoeia refers to the use of a word whose sound suggests its meaning. For example, the words *bark, woof, ticktock,* and *crash* imitate the sounds they name. Poets use onomatopoeia to create sound effects that echo the meaning of a poem. Three of the words in "The Sea" that sound like what they mean are *clashing, roars,* and *rumbling.* Can you find one more example of onomatopoeia in each stanza?

Fill in the blank in each sentence below with a word that sounds like what it means. Then compare your choices with those of your classmates.

1. The bacon _____.
2. The crowd _____.
3. The bee _____.
4. The wind _____.

Writing About Literature

CREATING METAPHORS

Write a list of at least three metaphors, in which you say one thing *is* another very different thing (it has to be a noun).

A smile is . . .   Happiness is . . .
My brain is . . .   A walnut is . . .
My handwriting is . . . Jealousy is . . .
I am . . .   Love is . . .
My life is . . .   Home is . . .

About the Author

James Reeves (1909–   ) was born in a small town near London. As a child, he loved to read; he wrote his first poem when he was only eleven. For many years, Reeves was a teacher in England. He has had a lifelong interest in traditional stories of all kinds. His love of folk tales and myths led to his best-known prose works, *The Shadow of the Hawk* and *The Cold Flame.*

---

3. In the third stanza, the sea is a quiet, sleepy dog.

Two contrasting details include the dog lying on the sand (rather than rolling) and the dog scarcely snoring (rather than moaning).

Applying Meanings
4. The sea might remind someone of a whale, a lion, a dragon.

A volcano might suggest a dragon.

A tornado might suggest a trumpeting elephant.

LANGUAGE AND VOCABULARY
Onomatopoeia
For answers, see the **Teaching Guide** at the beginning of the unit.

WRITING ABOUT LITERATURE
Creating Metaphors
Sample answers: "A smile is sunshine / a turned-on light bulb / a happy song." Or, "My brain is a computer / an expressway / a spider's web." Remember that the metaphors have to compare *unlike* things.

OBJECTIVES
Students will recognize and use homophones. They will also personify an object.

FOCUS/MOTIVATION
Building on Prior Knowledge. Discuss with students personifications from everyday life. Think of how we personify an object, such as a bicycle or a car, by giving it a name and thinking of it as alive. Think of how products are personified on TV.

Prereading Journal. Before students read the poem, tell them that the poet personifies a toaster. Then have them write in their journals about an animal, real or imaginary, that might represent a toaster.

TEACHING RESOURCES B
Teacher's Notes, p. 166
Study Guide, pp. 169, 172
Selection Test, p. 184

AV RESOURCES BINDER
Audiocassette 2, Side B

1. GUIDED READING:
Drawing Conclusions
Notice that the fact that the dragon nicely returns the toasted bread indicates that he is friendly. (There are several dragons in this book. The ones in "The Smallest Dragonboy," page 78, are also friendly.)

Before You Read

Poets use imaginative comparisons to help you see the ordinary world in brand-new ways. The speaker in "The Sea" made you see the sea as a dog. The speaker in this poem gives you a different way of looking at something very ordinary—something you may use every day.

The Toaster

WILLIAM JAY SMITH

A silver-scaled Dragon with jaws flaming red
Sits at my elbow and toasts my bread.
I hand him fat slices, and then, one by one,
1 He hands them back when he sees they are done.

338 Poetry

CLOSURE

Brainstorm ways in which we personify objects around us in daily life. (We may see car headlights as eyes, a furnace or incinerator as a mouth, a tree's branches as fingers.)

For Study and Discussion

IDENTIFYING DETAILS
1. What is the speaker's action in this poem?

INTERPRETING MEANINGS
2. The speaker in "The Toaster" identifies the toaster as a dragon. What part of the toaster is the dragon's silver scales? What part of the toaster is the dragon's jaws?
3. Suppose this poem had no title. What clues would have helped you decide what this dragon really was?
4. According to legend, what can a dragon do that makes it easy—if somewhat surprising—to imagine one disguised as a toaster?

Language and Vocabulary

HOMOPHONES
Homophones are words that sound alike but have different meanings. Homophones are also spelled differently. For example, *to, too,* and *two* are homophones. You can usually figure out which spelling to use from the word's context (the words surrounding it in the sentence). "The Toaster" contains several words that have homophones. Think of homophones for the words *red, bread, one, by, sees*. Now make up three sentences using at least two homophones in each sentence. Here is an example:

> The dragon ate eight knights in two nights.

Writing About Literature

LETTING AN OBJECT SPEAK
Think of something like a garden hose, a refrigerator, a computer, or a TV. Write a brief paragraph in which you let the object speak as "I," revealing its true personality. Here are some details you might want the object to talk about:

> My true name (known only to me)
> Where I live
> What my family is like
> My work
> My appearance
> What I like about my job
> What I don't like about it
> What I wish I were
> What I like to do on weekends

About the Author

William Jay Smith (1918–   ) has Choctaw ancestors on his mother's side. His father was a corporal in the Sixth Infantry Band. In a few years, you might want to read *Army Brat*, the poet's fascinating account of growing up in an Army family. Smith attended Washington University in St. Louis. He also studied at Columbia University, Oxford University (where he was a Rhodes scholar), and the University of Florence. He has been a college teacher, a translator of Russian and French poetry, and a member of the Vermont legislature. *Laughing Time* is a collection of his poems. Smith is also co-editor (with Louise Bogan) of *The Golden Journey: Poems for Young People*.

FOR STUDY AND DISCUSSION

Identifying Details
1. The speaker is toasting slices of bread in a toaster.

Interpreting Meanings
2. The scales are the toaster's metallic sides. The jaws are the places where the slices of bread are inserted.
3. Students might suggest such clues as "toasts my bread" in line 2 or "I hand him fat slices" in line 3.
4. Legends say that a dragon can breathe fire.

LANGUAGE AND VOCABULARY

Homophones
For answers, see the **Teaching Guide** at the beginning of the unit.

WRITING ABOUT LITERATURE

Letting an Object Speak
Look for creative characterizations. If students have trouble thinking of a speaker, suggest that they just look at the objects near them, or think of what's in their kitchen.

OBJECTIVES
Students will identify onomatopoeia and imagery. They will also extend a metaphor and determine word meaning through prefixes.

TEACHING RESOURCES B
Teacher's Notes, p. 166
Study Guide, pp. 170, 173
Building Vocabulary, p. 182
Selection Vocabulary Test, p. 183
Selection Test, p. 184

AV RESOURCES BINDER
Audiocassette 2, Side B

1. LITERARY ELEMENTS:
Metaphor
By using metaphor, poets "pretend" that one thing is another. "Pretend you are a dragon" is Katz's way of saying, "A dragon is a metaphor for a subway."

2. LITERARY ELEMENTS:
Verbs
The verbs *roar, swallow, spit,* and *zoom* help us see and hear this dragon / subway.

3. GUIDED READING:
Drawing Conclusions
Why do you think these directions to the dragon / subway might appeal to young people? Because it is told to go fast and to make as much noise as it wants. These actions are the opposite of what most children are told they can do.

FOCUS/MOTIVATION
Building on Prior Knowledge. If you do not live in a place with a subway, ask students who have visited large cities to share what they know about subways. Have them describe how subway trains move and how they sound. The photograph here gives an idea of the subway's speed.

Establishing a Purpose for Reading. Have students read to discover whether the dragon in this poem is like or different from the dragon in "The Toaster" (page 338).

Before You Read
A subway is a train that runs under the ground of a city and takes people from station to station. When this poet worked in New York City, she rode the subway at least twice a day. As you read, compare this poem to "The Toaster."

Things To Do If You Are a Subway

BOBBI KATZ

1. Pretend you are a dragon.
   Live in underground caves.
2. Roar about underneath the city.
   Swallow piles of people.
   Spit them out at the next station.
   Zoom through the darkness.
   Be an express.
   Go fast.
3. Make as much noise as you please.

340 Poetry

READING THE POEM

Students can read the poem easily on their own. Ask for volunteers to read the poem aloud quickly and energetically in order to emphasize the dragon / subway's personality.

CLOSURE

In this poem, words echo loud sounds. Have students think of an object that could be associated with soft, low sounds, such as a canoe or a kite. Then have students list words that echo the soft sounds the object might make.

TECHNOLOGY LINK

Suggest that interested students find out more about subway trains. Students could research how they are powered, how fast they travel, how many people can ride inside them, and how they are operated. Students could record this information in their journals or learning logs and/or share it with the class. Do these facts about subway trains make them seem more like dragons or less?

FOR STUDY AND DISCUSSION

Identifying Details

1. Both "live" underground, make loud noises, swallow people and then spit them out, and travel fast.
2. Words that imitate the sounds the "dragon" makes include *spit* (line 5) and *zoom* (line 6).

Interpreting Meanings

3. The subway is taking on and letting off passengers.
4. The word should be a verb, perhaps *roar, swallow, spit,* or *zoom*.
5. The "you" is both the subway train and the reader.

Applying Meanings

6. The toaster dragon might say it has a safer nicer life, but the subway dragon might reply that *it* has much more fun and excitement. The subway dragon might say that the toaster dragon has sold out.

LANGUAGE AND VOCABULARY

For answers, see the **Teaching Guide** at the beginning of the unit.

For Study and Discussion

IDENTIFYING DETAILS

1. This poem is an **extended metaphor.** In what ways is a subway like a dragon?

2. *Roar,* in line 3, is an example of **onomatopoeia**—that is, a word that sounds like what it means. Find two more words in the poem that imitate sounds the "dragon" makes.

INTERPRETING MEANINGS

3. In lines 4–5, what do you see the subway doing?

4. Which word gives you the clearest, strongest **image** of the dragon-subway? Is the word a noun or a verb?

5. All the sentences in this poem are the same kind. If you know your grammar, you'll see that they are all imperative, which means they give orders. Who could the "you" in this poem be?

APPLYING MEANINGS

6. Suppose that this dragon-subway met the dragon-toaster (page 338). What do you think they might say to each other? What name might each dragon choose for himself or herself?

Language and Vocabulary

PREFIXES

A **prefix** is a letter or syllable added to the beginning of a word to change its meaning. Two very useful prefixes are *sub-* and *super-*. *Sub-* means "under, lower than, or lesser than." Its opposite is *super-*, meaning "over, above, or better than." Like many other prefixes, *sub-* and *super-* come from the Latin language. When you know what the prefix means, you can often figure out the meaning of a word. See if you can find the definition in the right column that best fits each of the numbered words in the left column.

1. subcompact
2. subconscious
3. subcontinent
4. submerge
5. superscript
6. supernatural
7. superstructure
8. supersonic

a. a building above the foundation
b. a sign written above a number
c. smaller than a compact car
d. outside the laws of nature
e. beneath the conscious mind
f. to place under water
g. greater than the speed of sound
h. a land mass smaller than a continent

Focus on Writing a Poem

EXTENDING A METAPHOR

You might want to try imitating this poem.

1. First of all, choose something that moves. Whatever you choose should be an object, not an animal. You might want to write about things to do if you are an airplane, a balloon, a kite, a computer, a fire engine, an ambulance, a steam shovel, a wrecking ball, or a truck.

2. Next (this is the hard part), think about an animal or other "creature" that moves and sounds like the object you have cho-

sen. This is what you will have your object "pretend" to be.

This is one way to start:

Title: Things to Do If You Are a Wrecking Ball
First line: Pretend you are an elephant.

Before you go on, you may want to jot down your ideas on a chart like this one.

Title	
Pretends to be	
Sounds it makes	
How it acts	
Strong verbs to use	

When you write your poem, choose your best ideas. Don't try to extend your metaphor too far. Remember, a three-line poem can be just as good as a long one.

About the Author

Bobbi Katz (1933–   ) was born in Newburgh, New York. She studied art history at Goucher College in Baltimore and at Hebrew University in Israel. She has been a creative writing consultant for several schools and has contributed her poems to magazines and anthologies. Katz says, "I write only for children because I desperately want to return childhood to them."

Reprinted by permission of UFS, Inc.

OBJECTIVES
Students will identify metaphors. They will locate a reference work to research the meanings of their names.

FOCUS/MOTIVATION
Setting a Purpose for Reading. Students should read to answer the question posed in the headnote: How does the speaker feel about her grandfather?

Prereading Journal. Have students write quickly about their memories of an older relative, such as a grandparent or great-grandparent.

344 Poetry

READING THE POEM

Before they read the poem, you may want students to read Cisneros's comment on pages 348–349. After they read the poem, the comment will strengthen their image of the central character. Whenever it is read, the comment will help overcome any cultural differences.

MEETING INDIVIDUAL NEEDS

Kinesthetic Learners • After students write in their Prereading Journal about a grandparent or great-grandparent, ask them to put into a small box several items that remind them of the people they have written about. After they have collected them, have students present the items, one by one, with explanations about what they represent.

Before You Read

Abuelito (ä·bwā·lē'tō) is Spanish for "Granddaddy." This poet has put a poem together from memories of her grandfather. How do you think she feels about him?

Abuelito Who

SANDRA CISNEROS

Abuelito who throws coins like rain 1
and asks who loves him
who is dough and feathers
who is a watch and glass of water
whose hair is made of fur
is too sad to come downstairs today
who tells me in Spanish you are my diamond
who tells me in English you are my sky
whose little eyes are string
can't come out to play
sleeps in his little room all night and day
who used to laugh like the letter *k*
is sick
is a doorknob tied to a sour stick
is tired shut the door
doesn't live here anymore
is hiding underneath the bed 2
who talks to me inside my head
is blankets and spoons and big brown shoes
who snores up and down up and down up and down
again
is the rain on the roof that falls like coins 3
asking who loves him
who loves him who?

TEACHING RESOURCES B

Teacher's Notes, p. 174
Study Guide, pp. 176, 178
Selection Test, p. 184

AV RESOURCES BINDER

Audiocassette 2, Side B

1. GUIDED READING: Identifying Pronouns

In lines 2 and 22–23, *who* is an interrogative pronoun. In all other lines, *who* or *whose* is a relative pronoun referring to Abuelito. The *who* in the title refers to Abuelito. Be sure students understand the referent of all these *who*'s.

2. GUIDED READING: Making Inferences

See if students can guess why Abuelito is hiding under the bed. He may be frightened or confused. Or, this may be the imagination of the speaker, who thinks her grandfather is under the bed because he won't play with her.

3. LITERARY ELEMENTS: Figures of Speech

Find the metaphor and simile in line 21. "Rain . . . that falls like coins" is the simile and "[Abuelito} is the rain" is the metaphor. Be sure students notice how adept Abuelito himself is at coining metaphors. See lines 7–8.

CLOSURE
Ask students to think about an older relative, such as a grandparent, whom they know well. Have them make up simple metaphors to describe the relative's familiar actions. Example: Nan laughs *like the sun in June.*

EXTENSION AND ENRICHMENT
Using the Spanish Language. Ask a Spanish-speaking student how to say *who* in Spanish, or point out yourself that *who* in Spanish is *quien* (kē·yen'). Lead students to hear how the word echoes the *k* sound of Abuelito's laughter.

FOR STUDY AND DISCUSSION
Identifying Details
1. Abuelito used to throw coins and play with the grandchildren. He asked his grandchildren who loved him. He used to call the speaker his diamond and his sky.
2. Abuelito has changed because he has grown old and sick.

Interpreting Meanings
3. The last three lines in the poem echo the first two lines by mentioning coins, rain, and love.
   Many students will say that the lines make them feel sad or tender.
4. Most students will say that the poet's feelings about Abuelito have not changed.
   The poet would probably say that *she* loves Abuelito. We know this because she writes of him in a loving and sympathetic way.

Applying Meanings
5. Good things might include love, memories, tales about old times, an adult to take your side when you quarrel with your parents. Some difficult things might include the elderly person's sickness or other disabilities, or overcrowding, lack of privacy.

For Study and Discussion

IDENTIFYING DETAILS
1. What did Abuelito used to do? What did he used to ask his grandchildren? What did he used to say to this speaker?
2. How has Abuelito changed? What changed him?

INTERPRETING MEANINGS
3. Look at the first two lines and the last three lines of the poem. How does the poem circle back to its beginning? What feelings do these lines give you?
4. Have the poet's feelings about Abuelito changed? How would she probably answer the question at the end? How do you know?

APPLYING MEANINGS
5. The poet knew her grandfather quite well. It sounds as if they lived in the same house. What might be some good things and some difficult things about sharing your house with an elderly relative? How do you think the poet felt about it?

Literary Elements

METAPHORS
A **metaphor**, as you have learned, is a direct comparison between two very different things. This poet does not say Abuelito is *like* dough and feathers. That would be a **simile**. Instead, she says in line 3 that he "*is* dough and feathers." Find two more metaphors that tell what Abuelito reminds the speaker of.

Language and Vocabulary

NAMES IN OTHER LANGUAGES
Like English, the Spanish language has many **suffixes**, syllables added to the ends of words to change their meanings. The *-ito* suffix, for instance, expresses smallness and affection. *Gato* means "cat"; *gatito* means "kitty." *Abuelo* means "grandfather"; when you add *-ito* to *abuel-*, it means "little grandpa" or "granddaddy." In Spanish, the word for "grandmother" is *abuela*. Most "male" nouns in Spanish end in *o*; "female" nouns end in *a*. Can you guess now what the Spanish word would be for "little grandma"?

The *-ito* or *-ita* suffix is often added to a child's name. For example, *Juan* (pronounced wän), which means "John," becomes *Juanito* ("Johnny"). *Juana*, which means "Joan" or "Joanna," becomes *Juanita* ("Joanie").

Try to find out if your first name has an equivalent in a foreign language. Then find out if your name would change when it is used for a child.

Start your research by asking at home. Perhaps one of your grandparents speaks another language. Many English dictionaries tell what language a name came from. At the library you can even find name dictionaries.

While you're looking up your name, find out what it means, too.

Invite Spanish-speaking students to bring to class favorite poems written in Spanish to read aloud. Encourage the class to listen to the rhythms and sounds of the words and to try to identify the poems' moods. Afterwards, ask students to translate the poems they have read.

Focus on Writing a Poem

USING FIGURES OF SPEECH

Figures of speech are words or phrases that describe one thing in terms of another but are not literally true. Poets use figures of speech to appeal to the imagination in unexpected ways.

The chart below shows three of the most common types of figures of speech.

Figures of Speech	
Simile: uses *like* or *as* to compare two different things	The patchwork quilt was like a paintbox.
Metaphor: compares two different things directly	The quilt was a riot of colors.
Personification: gives human qualities to something nonhuman	The quilt painted the bed in a hundred colors.

Choose a familiar subject: for example, a garden, a house, or a bird. Create a chart like the one above by making up three figures of speech to describe your subject: one simile, one metaphor, and one example of personification. Save your notes.

About the Author

Sandra Cisneros (1954–   ) was born in Chicago. She grew up there and in Mexico City, where her parents were born. Cisneros was the only daughter in a family of six sons. She grew up speaking both English and Spanish. She has taught creative writing and poetry to grade school, high school, and college students in San Antonio, Chicago, and cities in California. The books she has published so far are a novel, *The House on Mango Street*; and two collections of poems, *Bad Boys* and *My Wicked, Wicked Ways*. Cisneros now lives in Austin, Texas, where she is still writing and still teaching students how to write. In fact, she has used "Abuelito Who" to teach poetry to sixth graders.

Hispanic girl in costume at street dance

The poet seems to miss the old Abuelito and to have loved living with him. See her comment on pages 348–349.

LITERARY ELEMENTS
Metaphors
Metaphors include "who is a watch and a glass of water" (line 4), "whose little eyes are string" (line 9), "is a doorknob tied to a sour stick" (line 14), "is blankets and spoons and big brown shoes" (line 19), "is the rain on the roof that falls like coins" (line 21). The poet comments on her images and figures of speech on pages 348–349.

LANGUAGE AND VOCABULARY
Names in Other Languages
For answers, see the **Teaching Guide** at the beginning of the unit.

FOCUS ON WRITING A POEM
Using Figures of Speech
You may want to work through the chart with students before assigning it for independent practice. You might use the following examples:
Simile: Our backyard fence is like a row of soldiers at attention.
Metaphor: Our backyard fence is a guard on duty.
Personification: Our backyard fence ignores our desire for freedom.

EXTENSION AND ENRICHMENT
Good readers, especially your Mexican American students, will enjoy Sandra Cisneros's touching and funny novel *The House on Mango Street* (Arte Publico Press, 1986), which centers on the growing up of a spunky young girl named Esperanza (which means "hope" in Spanish).

1. GUIDED READING:
Responding to an Essay
Be sure students read and think about Cisneros's comments here, especially these comments about poetry. You could easily use this whole essay to introduce the poetry unit. Who but a poet could talk about the art of poetry so beautifully and so evocatively?

Behind the Scenes

The Story That Goes with the Poem

When I was little, my grandpa—my Abuelito, that is, which is sort of like Granddaddy, only sweeter—my Abuelito used to love to give all his grandchildren their *domingo* (literally "Sunday," because that's the day children receive it), that is, their allowance. But my Abuelito loved the ritual of asking in a loud voice, "Who loves Grandpa?" and we would answer, also in a loud voice, "We do!" Then he would take a handful of change he'd been saving all week for this purpose, Mexican coins which are thick and heavy, and toss them up in the air so that they'd fall like rain, like a *piñata* (pē·nyä′tä), and we'd scramble all over each other picking up as many coins as we could. To me it was much more fun to get our *domingo* this way instead of having it placed in our hands.

Well, it's this fun grandpa that this poem is about. And about the coins falling like rain, and rain falling like coins, that at times makes me think of him and miss him. I recall he became rather sick and cranky in his last years. I suppose that's what some of the images refer to, but I was grown and gone already, and my Abuelito in faraway Mexico City.

1 I'm not sure what exactly all the images refer to, and I'm not sure I ever knew. But that's what's so wonderful about poetry. It comes from some deep and true place inside you, the place where dreams come from. We don't always know what dreams mean, do we, and we don't have to always know to enjoy and experience them. That's how it is with poetry, too. When I write, I don't question where images are coming from. I write dictated by sound and directed by my heart. And these images—"dough and feathers," "little eyes are string," and "doorknob tied to a sour stick"—felt right then and still feel right as I read them now. "Dough and feathers" I suppose has to do with how he felt when I held him and he held me. He was soft

PORTFOLIO ASSESSMENT

Close family members usually share a deep affection or disaffection for one another. Sandra Cisneros communicates her deep affection for her grandfather in the poem "Abuelito Who." Students may want to write paragraphs in which they share their feelings about a close family member. Suggest that they write a clear purpose (thesis) statement about their affection or disaffection. Remind them that a paragraph has a beginning (thesis), middle (development of the thesis), and end (conclusion). Require a minimum of four sentences, and ask students to identify their thesis, development, and conclusion. (See *Portfolio Assessment and Professional Support Materials* for additional information on student portfolios.)

1. GUIDED READING:
Discussing Ideas

These comments about metaphors and the impossibility of pinpointing exactly what they mean are very important for students to absorb. Too often students lose that love of language they have as very young children. They become "prosaic." Everything must have a very precise meaning. Everything must be explainable. As Cisneros says here, everything is *not* explainable. This comment relates in a way to the impulse to write nonsense poetry. (See Dr. Seuss and Edward Lear who began this unit.) If you give your students encouragement, their natural love of nonsense and their playfulness with language will come to the surface.

---

and squishy as dough or feathers. But it could also mean the color of his skin and hair. The texture of his skin. The silliness of his being. They're all "right."

"Little eyes of string" is harder to pinpoint. Did I mean like a spiral of string, like when we are sick? Maybe. But then again, perhaps it's the way he looked at me when he was sick. And "doorknob tied to a sour stick." I recall a cane he had and how he changed when he was very old and cranky and waved it when he wanted to make a point. So I suppose he had "soured." Why tied to a doorknob? Who knows?

A few biographical tidbits. My grandfather *did* laugh like the letter *k*. A kind of "kkkk" sound when he chuckled, which, surprisingly, I've inherited.

And. He was very proud that he could speak English, even though he lived in Mexico City most of his life. And so he liked to show off his English to his grandchildren from the United States when they came to visit. "You are my diamond," my grandpa would say in typical Mexican fashion. But then he would mistranslate "You're my heaven" and instead come out with "You're my sky," because "sky" and "heaven" are the same word in Spanish. I remember thinking even as a child that it sounded wonderful—"You're my sky." How much better than *heaven*. All, all of that! Imagine. I've always been much more partial to sky and clouds, and am even now.

Finally, the older we grow, the younger we become as well, don't you think? That is, our Abuelito had to take naps, and he liked to play games, like the one with the coins, and he talked to us in a way that other adults didn't, and he couldn't climb the stairs very well, like my baby brothers. So in a way he was getting younger and younger and younger until he wasn't anymore.

—Sandra Cisneros

OBJECTIVES
Students will identify contrasts and similes. They will also match a poem to a piece of music.

FOCUS/MOTIVATION
Play recordings or tapes of vintage 1940s and 1950s jazz by artists such as Miles Davis, Thelonious Monk, Dizzy Gillespie, Charlie Parker, or Billie Holiday.
Prereading Journal. Have students list sight and sound images that come to mind as they listen to the music.

READING THE POEM
To be sure of an expressive but simple first reading, read this poem aloud yourself. Then have it read again by a student after discussion.

TEACHING RESOURCES B
Teacher's Notes, p. 174
Study Guide, p. 177
Language Skills, p. 179
Building Vocabulary, p. 182
Selection Vocabulary Test, p. 183
Selection Test, p. 184

AV RESOURCES BINDER
Audiocassette 2, Side B

Before You Read
When Langston Hughes was a young man and first writing poetry, he lived in Harlem, in New York City. At this time, several highly gifted musicians in Harlem were playing the new rhythm-and-blues music that became known as jazz. In "Dream Variations," Hughes tries to capture in words the feelings and sounds of jazz. Even the title comes from the changes and contrasts that jazz musicians make on a melody. As you read, think of how this poem might be set to music.

Dream Variations
LANGSTON HUGHES

To fling my arms wide
In some place of the sun,
To whirl and to dance
Till the white day is done.
Then rest at cool evening   5
Beneath a tall tree
While night comes on gently,
    Dark like me——
That is my dream!

To fling my arms wide   10
In the face of the sun,
Dance! Whirl! Whirl!
Till the quick day is done.
Rest at pale evening . . .
A tall, slim tree . . .   15
Night coming tenderly
    Black like me.

La Citadella-Freedom by Augusta Savage. Bronze.

The Permanent Collection. Gallery of Art, Howard University, Washington, D.C.

CLOSURE

Have students think of two occasions when they have contrasting moods. (On a schoolday, for example, they might feel disciplined and constrained, but on a summer Saturday they may feel free.) Then have them list metaphors or images that describe themselves at these times. On a schoolday, for example, they may be "a tightly wrapped package waiting to be opened."

For Study and Discussion

IDENTIFYING DETAILS

1. What does the speaker want to do during daytime? What does he dream of doing at night?

2. Notice the **contrasts**, the great differences in the poem. Day is bright with sunlight—hot, strong, and active. What is evening like?

3. Compare very carefully the first four lines of stanza 1 with the first four lines of stanza 2. What variations or changes do you find in the words?

INTERPRETING MEANINGS

4. Find the **similes** (comparisons using *like* or *as*) in the poem that describe what night is like. What adverbs describe how night comes on? Which do you think the poet identifies with: the whirl of day or the gentleness of night?

APPLYING MEANINGS

5. Suppose that "Dream Variations" were set to music. Which lines in each stanza might be played fast and loud? How do you think the rest of the poem might be played?

Setting a Poem to Music

Find a musical piece that you think might go well with one of the poems in this unit. The type of music is up to you. It may be popular, classical, jazz, patriotic, religious, country, rock—anything that pleases you. Try to ignore the words of the musical pieces you consider. Just look for a melody and

Dream Variations 351

FOR STUDY AND DISCUSSION

Identifying Details

1. During the daytime he wants to fling his arms wide in a sunny spot, whirl, and dance.

At night he dreams of resting beneath a tall tree.

2. Evening is gentle, tender, and dark.

3. Line 1 in each stanza is the same. Line 2 in stanza 2 substitutes "In the face" for "In some place." Line 3 in stanza 2 is the more agitated or energetic "Dance! Whirl! Whirl!," rather than just "To whirl and to dance." In line 4 of stanza 2, a "quick day" replaces a "white day."

Interpreting Meanings

4. Similes for night are "dark like me" (line 8) and "Black like me" (line 17).

The adverbs are *gently* (line 7) and *tenderly* (line 16).

Most will agree that the poet identifies with night.

Applying Meanings

5. Lines that might be played fast and loud include 1–4 and 10–13.

Lines 5–9 and 14–17 might be played slow and soft.

SETTING A POEM TO MUSIC

The haiku might also be particularly suitable for musical interpretation.

COOPERATIVE LEARNING

Have students read **Behind the Scenes** to learn how Langston Hughes began writing poetry. Then have them work together to write a poem, as Hughes did, about their class and school. If possible, have the poem published in the school newspaper for all students and faculty to enjoy.

---

rhythm that match the feeling in the poem you chose. Write three or four sentences telling which poem you have decided on, which musical piece you have chosen to go with it, and why you made that choice. Share your ideas in class. Have any of you set the same poem to very different music?

About the Author

Langston Hughes (1902–1967) was born in Joplin, Missouri. He was brought up by his mother, who was a schoolteacher, and his grandmother, who had attended Oberlin College before the Civil War. An avid reader since second grade, Hughes wrote his first poem when he was fourteen. When he was sixteen, he visited his father in Mexico and learned to speak and read Spanish. Later, Hughes moved to Harlem in New York City and attended Columbia University. Although his travels took him all over the world, Hughes always considered Harlem his home. His best writing was inspired by the people, music, and art he found there. Until he could support himself from his writing, Hughes worked as a seaman, dishwasher, busboy, cook, and café bouncer. Throughout his life, he encouraged and helped many young black poets, including Gwendolyn Brooks (see pages 301 and 318). Arna Bontemps, a poet and biographer, wrote about Hughes: "His sources are street music. . . . He is an American original."

Behind the Scenes

The Class Poet

I was the Class Poet. . . . The day I was elected, I went home and wondered what I should write. Since we had eight teachers in our school, I thought there should be one verse for each teacher, with an especially good one for my favorite teacher, Miss Ethel Welsh. And since the teachers were to have eight verses, I felt the class should have eight, too. So my first poem was about the longest poem I ever wrote—sixteen verses, which were later cut down. In the first half of the poem, I said that our school had the finest teachers there ever were. And in the latter half, I said our class was the greatest class ever graduated. So at graduation, when I read the poem, naturally everybody applauded loudly. That was the way I began to write poetry.

—Langston Hughes

IDEAS AND FEELINGS

Like all literature, poetry is about ideas. But the ideas in poetry are not morals or practical lessons; they do not tell us how to behave or how to make money. The ideas in poetry help us make sense of life. They help us see ourselves and our world more clearly.

Poetry is also about feelings. Many times a poet starts to write because of a strong emotion he or she wants to share and capture in words: perhaps love, sadness, awe, regret, jealousy, security, or terror.

A poem "works" when we have grasped the poet's "message" and have shared the poet's feeling. A poem works when we can say "I understand what you mean!" "I know how you felt!"

INTRODUCING IDEAS AND FEELINGS

The ideas in this section tend to focus on coming to terms with our self-images and with childhood memories. These preoccupations are characteristic of much recent poetry; they happen also to be subjects that young readers respond to.

Students may wonder why so much poetry is about sadness and loss. Try to help them understand that one of the profoundest experiences in life is working through pain or confusion, till we say, "Aha! That's been bothering me for a long time, but now I understand it." When something bothers us, one of the best ways of handling it is to turn it into art. Encourage students to think of subjects or feelings they would like to turn into art for this reason.

OBJECTIVES
Students will explain a poem's message and sum up a main idea.

FOCUS/MOTIVATION
Building on Prior Knowledge. If you are musical, you might sing or play a few bars in a major key and then in a minor key, or have a student musician demonstate. Ask them to notice if this bird in the poem is really a "minor" bird. (It's provided the speaker with a major discovery.)

READING THE POEM
Before students read the poem, tell them that it is written in couplets, and that the reader should pause slightly between pairs of lines. This is a good poem for student memorization. Frost is a great American poet and they'll be meeting him again and again as they go through school.

TEACHING RESOURCES B
Teacher's Notes, p. 186
Study Guide, pp. 188, 190
Language Skills, p. 198
Building Vocabulary, p. 207
Selection Vocabulary Test, p. 208
Selection Test, p. 209

AV RESOURCES BINDER
Audiocassette 2, Side B

---

1. GUIDED READING:
Interpreting Meaning
This poem is about a bird, but do we sometimes treat a person like this? Yes, we sometimes send away a person who is not a "major bird" in our lives or whose "song" we don't like.

FOR STUDY AND DISCUSSION
Identifying Details
1. He has wished that the bird would fly away and stop singing.
2. He dislikes its constant singing.
3. He says that he himself was partly at fault.
  The bird was not to blame for his key, and there has to be "something wrong" about "wanting to silence any song."

Interpreting Meanings
4. The message might be that when nature makes us happy or sad, it is really we ourselves who create the emotion. This poet

---

Before You Read

Robert Frost plays with the double meaning of the word *minor* in his title. *Minor* means "less important or lesser in rank (compared to others)." We have the *minor* leagues in baseball. You're a *minor* if you're under the legal adult age. But *minor* also refers to a minor key in music. A musical key is a series of related tones that form a scale. Most Western music is written in major keys. To some people, songs written in major keys sound happy. Minor keys, to the Western ear, tend to sound sad or haunting.

But Frost isn't really writing about music here. He is expressing an idea about something else. Look for what he learns in the second half of this poem.

A Minor Bird

ROBERT FROST

I have wished a bird would fly away,
And not sing by my house all day;

Have clapped my hands at him from the door
When it seemed as if I could bear no more.

The fault must partly have been in me.
The bird was not to blame for his key.

And of course there must be something wrong
1 In wanting to silence any song.

---

354   354 Poetry

CLOSURE

Have each student write one sentence explaining the message of the poem. Then have three volunteers tell what might be troubling the poet besides the bird. (When they are troubled themselves, do they want to destroy expressions of happiness from someone else?)

TRANSPARENCY 20
Reader Response
Responding with Head or Heart? — asks students to identify primary and secondary responses to a selection.

For Study and Discussion

IDENTIFYING DETAILS

1. What has the speaker wished?
2. What is it about the bird that the speaker dislikes?
3. Who does the speaker say is partly at fault? What two reasons does he give?

INTERPRETING MEANINGS

4. What do you think is the poet's **message** in "A Minor Bird"?
5. Describe the **feelings** the poet expresses in this poem. (Regret? Irritation? Self-blame? Delight?)

APPLYING MEANINGS

6. Do you agree with the last two lines of this poem? Tell why or why not.

Literary Elements

COUPLETS

Notice that each pair of lines in this poem is a couplet. A **couplet** is made up of two rhyming lines that follow one another and that form a complete unit. Sum up the idea in each of Frost's couplets.

Writing About Literature

WRITING A JOURNAL ENTRY

Suppose you are Frost and you have not yet written this poem. You are trying to work, and you hear a bird. Write a journal entry about your experience. Tell the season of the year, your mood, where you are, what the bird sounded like, and why it irritated you.

About the Author

Robert Frost (1874–1963) was born in San Francisco, but his ancestors had been New Englanders for nine generations. After the death of his father, eleven-year-old Robert moved to Massachusetts with his sister and mother. There in high school, he combined writing poetry with playing varsity football. Later, his grandfather gave him a small farm, and Frost tried to support his family by raising chickens for eleven long years. In 1912, after the deaths of two of his children, he and his family moved to England. There, Frost had success: His first two poetry collections were published. Frost eventually returned to New Hampshire and spent the rest of his long life writing poetry, lecturing, giving public readings, and farming. The plain speech and simple, everyday subjects of his poems disguise their complex thoughts. Frost won four Pulitzer Prizes. He is one of the few modern poets who appeal to a great variety of readers.

A Minor Bird 355

blames the bird for the irritation he feels, but the bird is not responsible for his "key."

5. Feelings might include annoyance, regret, self-blame, irony, sadness.

Applying Meanings

6. Most will agree; the word *song* usually connotes happiness or joy.

LITERARY ELEMENTS
Couplets
Summaries will vary. Couplet 1: Annoyed by the singing of a bird, the speaker wishes it would fly away. Couplet 2: He claps his hands to frighten the bird away. Couplet 3: He realizes he is partly to blame; the bird sings by nature. Couplet 4: It must be immoral or unjust to destroy nature or anything that is beautiful. Or, the speaker thinks: "There must be something wrong with *me* that I want to destroy something natural and beautiful."

WRITING ABOUT LITERATURE
Writing a Journal Entry
Encourage students to think of the poet as a real human being. You may want them to focus on Frost specifically or generalize as if they were any poet.

Before You Read

Suppose that you are grown up. What day from your childhood do you think you will remember most? As you read this poem, see if the day you remember is anything like the day that "stands out forever" in this poet's memory. (The poet's parents were Armenian.)

That Day

DAVID KHERDIAN

Just once
my father stopped on the way
into the house from work
and joined in the softball game
we were having in the street,   5
and attempted to play in *our*
game that *his* country had never
known.

Just once
and the day stands out forever   10
in my memory
as a father's living gesture
to his son,
that in playing even the fool
or clown, he would reveal   15
that the lines of their lives
were sewn from a tougher fabric
than the son had previously known.

Boy with Baseball by George Luks. Oil on canvas.

The Metropolitan Museum of Art. The Edward Joseph Gallagher III Memorial Collection. Gift of Edward J. Gallagher, Jr., 1954. (54.10.2)

READING THE POEM
You might have a different male student read each stanza aloud. The vocabulary of the poem is not difficult, but the metaphor in lines 16–18 may need close study.

CLOSURE
Have students write, as free verse, the first five sentences in "The Story Behind the Poem," page 359. Encourage students to break lines as they see fit and to repeat words or lines for emphasis ("an American stranger," for example). Have students share their free verse poems and discuss reasons for their line breaks and repetition.

VISUAL CONNECTIONS
Have students look at the picture and imagine that the boy portrayed is the boy in the poem. It is just after the incident in the poem, in which his father played ball with him. Have them describe what the boy is thinking and feeling about himself. About his father?

About the Artist
George Luks (1867–1933) was an influential teacher and personality in New York City early in this century. He often painted the city's slum life. A member of the group of painters called "The Eight," Luks also created a popular comic strip called "The Yellow Kid" for the New York *World*.

FOR STUDY AND DISCUSSION

Identifying Details

1. The speaker means the game of softball, which he and his childhood friends were playing in the street.

  We know that the speaker's father was born in a foreign country because the poet refers to a game that "*his* country had never known" (lines 7–8).

2. The day stands out because the speaker remembers it as the only time his father played ball with him.

Interpreting Meanings

3. The father's "living gesture" was a sign, through playing the game, that he was "sewn from a tougher fabric / than the son had previously known" (lines 17–18). The father was not afraid to look foolish playing a strange, unfamiliar game.

4. The father showed kindness and interest in his son and the son's childhood playmates.

  The son feels respectful and affectionate toward his father.

5. The metaphor suggests family strength.

Applying Meanings

6. Students may suggest that they would feel pride, embarrassment, amusement, or affection.

  Students might suggest

For Study and Discussion

IDENTIFYING DETAILS

1. Whose game does the speaker mean when he says "*our* game"? How do you know that the speaker's father was born in a different country?

2. Why does the day stand out forever in the speaker's memory?

INTERPRETING MEANINGS

3. A "gesture" is an action that shows a feeling or an idea. For example, in many countries, a bow is a gesture of respect. What was the father's "living gesture"?

4. What **feeling** did the father show for his son? How does the son feel about his father?

5. A **metaphor** at the end compares the life of this family with tough fabric. Does this suggest family strength? Or weakness?

APPLYING MEANINGS

6. Suppose your father or mother or guardian joined in a game with you and your friends and played badly enough to look silly. How would you feel? Can you think of other things parents or guardians might do as gestures of love and solidarity?

Literary Elements

FREE VERSE

This poem is a good example of free verse. **Free verse** is "free" of all regular patterns of rhythm. Often free verse is also free of a regular rhyme scheme. But poets writing in free verse still have to find ways of making

their poems sound rhythmical. You will notice in this poem that Kherdian uses repetition to create rhythm. Read the poem aloud. What words does he repeat? Variety in line length also can create rhythm. Where does Kherdian vary his lines?

Do you prefer free-verse poems? Or do you prefer poems with a strong pattern of rhythm, like that in "A Minor Bird" (page 354)?

Focus on Writing a Poem

IMITATING THE POEM

Imitate the structure of this poem and write a poem about something that happened with a member of your family that was especially memorable. Open with the poet's words:

> Just once
> and the day stands out forever
> in my memory:

Try to use one **metaphor** in your poem, that is, use some very unusual comparison that describes a person or feeling, or the way something looked or sounded on that memorable day.

Before you write, read what Kherdian says about poetry (opposite). Try to find an incident that *touched* you, in the way that this incident touched him.

About the Author

David Kherdian (1931–   ) was born in Racine, Wisconsin, and brought up in the Armenian culture of his parents. He learned English after he started school. Kherdian served in the Army and graduated from the University of Wisconsin. Between the ages of nineteen and thirty-eight, he remembers being always on the move: "the army and college and Europe and an endless series of odd jobs: unloading boxcars, shoe clerking, magazine selling, rug merchanting, office help . . . and always secretly scribbling: waiting for the stuff to become good enough to spring on the world."

Behind the Scenes

The Story Behind the Poem

In many ways my father and I were strangers to each other. At home I was his Armenian son, but in the streets I was an American stranger. I'm putting this a little bluntly. I'm exaggerating. So far as I knew, children did not play games in the Old Country. Therefore I did not believe that he understood any of the games I was involved in. And then, one day, while walking home from work, along the street where we were playing a pick-up game of softball, he stopped and either pitched the ball, or picked up the bat and tried to give the ball a hit. He was *intentionally* participating, he was joining in, and by doing so he was sharing with me something that was of value in my life that I did not believe had any importance in his life. I was deeply touched by this, though why I was touched, or where I was touched, or even how I was touched, was beyond my understanding at the time. Which brings me to poetry and why I write: but that's another story, and has to do with why I wrote *all* of my poems, not just the one you are looking at today.

—David Kherdian

---

helping with homework, sharing a meal, giving a special gift, organizing a family excursion, taking a walk together, doing a chore for a child.

LITERARY ELEMENTS
Free Verse
Repeated words include *just once, father, son, play,* and *playing.*

Kherdian varies his line lengths with short lines in lines 1, 8, 9, 11, and 13.

Answers will vary. Most students like rhyme and strong rhythms.

FOCUS ON WRITING A POEM
Imitating the Poem
Be sure students read what Kherdian says about poetry on this page. Encourage students to share their poems and to show them to their families at home. You might do the assignment yourself and share your poem with the class.

OBJECTIVES
Students will identify the speaker and explain the message of the poem. They will research the history of several Spanish words.

FOCUS/MOTIVATION
As the headnote suggests, discuss the "legacies" people can pass on.
Prereading Journal. Have students write about a nonmaterial legacy they have received or will receive from a grandparent or other older person.

READING THE POEM
Read this poem aloud to emphasize its conversational rhythms. The four directions can be read in any natural order ("El Norte—El Sur—Oriente—Poniente"). If you have Spanish-speaking students, they can present a second reading.

Teaching Resources B
Teacher's Notes, p. 192
Study Guide, pp. 194, 196
Language Skills, p. 198
Building Vocabulary, p. 207
Selection Vocabulary Test, p. 208
Selection Test, p. 209

1. GUIDED READING
Making Inferences
Do you think the speaker really regrets going to college? Probably not. He regrets losing touch with traditional ways, but college might have helped make him a poet, among other things.

Before You Read

Usually we think of a legacy as money or property handed down from a relative who has died. Before you read this poem, talk about all the kinds of "legacies" people might pass on. Can people pass on nonmaterial things—values like wisdom, faith, or honesty?

Quintana is a Mexican American; you will find four Spanish words in the poem.

Legacy II

LEROY V. QUINTANA

Grandfather never went to school
spoke only a few words of English,
a quiet man; when he talked
talked about simple things

planting corn or about the weather   5
sometimes about herding sheep as a child.
One day pointed to the four directions
taught me their names

   El Norte

Poniente   Oriente   10

   El Sur

He spoke their names as if they were
one of only a handful of things
a man needed to know

Now I look back   15
only two generations removed
realize I am nothing but a poor fool
who went to college

trying to find my way back
to the center of the world   20
where Grandfather stood
that day

360   Poetry

CLOSURE
Have students write a few sentences in the speaker's voice, stating directly in prose what he learned from his grandfather. Visually inclined students may do an illustration for the poem instead.

MEETING INDIVIDUAL NEEDS
Kinesthetic Learners • Illustrate the concept of leaving a nonmaterial legacy (see **Before You Read**) by asking each student to think of a legacy he or she might like to leave to a student coming into next year's class. Encourage students to be creative and humorous. Example: "I leave my ability to clean the hamster cage in record time!" Have students write their messages on slips of paper to be picked out of a hat by next year's class.

VISUAL CONNECTIONS
If you are in the Southwest, you and your students can easily identify with the vast landscape of this picture. If not, the painting will help you feel you "are there" in your imagination. Encourage students to relate the landscape of this picture to the very similar landscape in which the grandfather in "Legacy II" pointed out the four directions. Encourage comparisons of this landscape to the one your students know. What wisdom would a person gain from living in this Southwest landscape? (Would life be hard here?) What wisdom have people learned from your own landscape? (How do people make a living there?)

For a brief note on **Peter Hurd,** see the opening of Unit One.

FOR STUDY AND DISCUSSION
Identifying Details
1. A grandson is speaking.

He went to college but he considers himself a "poor fool" compared with his grandfather; he seems to have lost his way.
2. Grandfather never went to school, spoke Spanish, was quiet, talked about simple things, herded sheep as a child.

The Dry River by Peter Hurd. Egg tempera on board. Roswell Museum and Art Center. Roswell, New Mexico. Gift of Mr. and Mrs. Daniel Longwell. Photo by Richard Faller.

3. The speaker says he is "trying to find my way back / to the center of the world" (lines 19–20).

Interpreting Meanings
4. He feels tender, perhaps envious, regretful, respectful.
5. Grandfather's legacy may be an awareness of what is important in life, wisdom, confidence, the earth, and a strong sense of the value of tradition.
6. In lines 9–11, the shape of the lines helps us to understand that the Spanish words refer to the four directions, or cardinal points, of a compass: El Norte (North), Poniente (West), Oriente (East), and El Sur (South).

Applying Meanings
7. One statement of the poet's message might be, "Wisdom does not come from book learning. It comes from character and life experience. It comes from contact with the earth."

If they would like to share the wisdom of their grandparents, the message applies to their lives.

LITERARY ELEMENTS
Free Verse
Lead students to understand that line breaks in free verse follow speech rhythms. Often the lines are arranged in "breath groupings."

For Study and Discussion

IDENTIFYING DETAILS
1. Who is **speaking** to you in the poem? What do you find out about this person?
2. What do you learn about Grandfather?
3. What is the speaker trying to do now?

INTERPRETING MEANINGS
4. How does the speaker **feel** about his Grandfather?
5. What do you think Grandfather's legacy is?
6. Find the lines in the poem that look different from the other lines. How does the shape of these lines help you to understand the Spanish words? What do the words mean?

APPLYING MEANINGS
7. What is the **message** the poet is sharing with you? Does his message apply to your own life?

Literary Elements

FREE VERSE
This poem is written in **free verse.** This means that the lines don't have a regular rhythmic beat. Read the poem aloud. Does it sound natural—the way someone would speak? When you read the poem aloud, pause briefly at the ends of lines that do not have marks of punctuation. Make a nearly full pause when you come to a comma and a full pause when you reach a period. How would you read the four directions aloud?

Language and Vocabulary

SPANISH WORDS
Some Spanish words look and sound a little like English words. That's because Spanish and English belong to the same family of languages. Have you ever heard someone speaking Japanese, Finnish, or Arabic? It's more difficult for an English speaker to learn those languages because each of them belongs to a family of languages that is different from the English language family.

You probably had no trouble figuring out that *el norte* (nôr'tā) means "the north," and *el sur* (pronounced like "sore") means "the south." Grandfather chose two words that are beautiful ways of saying east and west in Spanish. *Oriente* (ôr·ē·en'tā) means not just "the east," but also "the beginning." *Poniente* (pōn·ē·en'tā) means not just "the west," but also "the setting or the ending."

At first glance, you may think that *oriente* and *poniente* aren't much like English. But here are some English words that are related to them:

Oriente: the Orient (the Far East—China, Japan, Indonesia)
to orient (to adjust to a situation)
orientation (a period of introduction and adjustment)

Poniente: position (from the Latin verb *ponere* meaning "to place")
ponderous (very weighty)

Many Spanish words have been adopted into the English language. We eat foods such as enchiladas and burritos. We watch broncos and rodeos. We yell "Adios!" to our friends. Because English and Spanish are related, we can often figure out the meaning of an unfamiliar Spanish word by thinking about English words that resemble it. Become a language detective. Find an English dictionary that tells what language words come from. Then look up the following Spanish words and (1) give the original Spanish word for each and (2) list one or two English words that resemble that word. To do this, you can either look in the dictionary or use your own experience with words.

Spanish Word	Origin	Related English Words
sombrero	sombra (shade)	somber umbrella
cafeteria		
stampede		
bonanza		

Writing About Literature

INTERVIEWING AN OLDER PERSON

Find out as much as you can about the way someone you know well lived at least fifty years ago. Perhaps you can interview one of your grandparents to discover what was important to him or her a half-century ago. Find out what this person liked to talk about. Think about what this person taught you. Then write a paragraph summarizing what you learned about this person's life. Before you conduct your interview, be sure to write down at least three questions you want to ask.

About the Author

Leroy V. Quintana (1944–   ) was born in Albuquerque, New Mexico. He has worked as a journalist, a counselor, and a teacher. In 1982 his book *Sangre* (Blood) received the American Book Award for poetry from the Before Columbus Foundation. Quintana says, "I was raised by my grandparents and my major form of entertainment was the old *cuentos* (stories) I was told. I have always enjoyed stories—I read comic books by the hundreds, went to the movies, and recited the stanzas in the back of the catechism religiously." Quintana uses Mexican folklore and traditional storytelling techniques in his poetry. "In many ways," he says, "I'm still basically a small-town New Mexico boy carrying on the oral tradition."

LANGUAGE AND VOCABULARY
Spanish Words
For answers, see the **Teaching Guide** at the beginning of the unit.

WRITING ABOUT LITERATURE
Interviewing an Older Person
Encourage students to make lists of questions such as the ones mentioned in the assignment before they conduct their interviews.

Legacy II

OBJECTIVES
Students will identify different types of sense images. They will read aloud a poem written in free verse.

VISUAL CONNECTIONS
Romare Bearden is well known for his colorful collages of African American life. He was strongly influenced by the Cubist painters of the early part of this century. You might tell students that the Cubist movement tried to break down objects into such geometric shapes as cubes, spheres, cylinders, cones. Pablo Picasso was a leader of the Cubist movement. Ask students if they can recognize the Cubist influence in this Bearden collage.

About the Artist
Bearden (1914–1988) was educated at New York University and studied art at the Art Students League and the Sorbonne, in Paris. His paintings hang today in such museums as the Metropolitan Museum in New York City, the Philadelphia Museum of Art, the Museum of Fine Arts in Boston, the Newark Museum, the St. Louis Art Museum, and the High Museum of Art in Atlanta, Georgia. If students are interested in doing a report on Bearden, they will find an article on the painter in the March 30, 1981, issue of *Newsweek*.

FOCUS/MOTIVATION
Building on Prior Knowledge. Have students discuss their past summers. As a class, make lists of summer activities and foods that they especially like. With students from different parts of the country, focus on geographical differences.

Prereading Journal. Use the questions in the first paragraph of the headnote to prompt a few minutes of writing. After a brief discussion of the responses, continue with the rest of the headnote to motivate reading.

Maudelle Sleet's Magic Garden by Romare Bearden (c. 1978). Collage on board.

Collection of Mr. and Mrs. Gerhard Stebich.
Courtesy The Estate of Romare Bearden.

364 Poetry

READING THE POEM
The poem reads so simply and clearly that students are likely to say, "I can write that way, too." You may want them to feel that they can, as they also appreciate the poem's artful construction.

Cultural Diversity
Some students may never have heard gospel music. Explain that although there are different kinds of gospel music, the poet is probably referring to a type of American music sung primarily in African American Baptist churches. In the church setting, the preacher supplies the text, or words, and the congregation sings a response. This musical dialogue, or conversation, between preacher and congregation is a kind of gospel music.

TEACHING RESOURCES B
Teacher's Notes, p. 192
Study Guide, pp. 195, 197
Language Skills, p. 198
Selection Test, p. 209

AV RESOURCES BINDER
Audiocassette 2, Side B

1. LITERARY ELEMENTS:
Free Verse
Why does the speaker use so many and*'s?* The repetition is appropriate for a child. It also creates an incantatory rhythm and propels the short, rhythmic lines forward.

2. BACKGROUND
Not all students understand the nature of gospel music. Since most gospel music is about the Christian doctrine of redemption, it is essentially life-affirming and joyous.

Before You Read

What's your favorite season? Imagine it is that season now. Close your eyes for a few seconds. What sounds do you hear? What tastes and smells do you connect with that time of year? What activities and people do you think of? When you read Nikki Giovanni's poem, see if she mentions any of your memories and associations.

This poet was born in Knoxville, Tennessee, but later moved to Cincinnati, Ohio. After the move, she loved to return to Knoxville in the summer. Her beloved grandmother lived there, and visiting her was always like coming home.

Knoxville, Tennessee

NIKKI GIOVANNI

I always like summer
best
you can eat fresh corn
from daddy's garden
and okra
and greens
and cabbage
and lots of
1 barbecue
and buttermilk
and homemade ice cream
at the church picnic
and listen to
gospel music 2
outside
at the church
homecoming
and go to the mountains with
your grandmother
and go barefooted
and be warm
all the time
not only when you go to bed
and sleep

CLOSURE

The list-poem that students will write in the Focus on Writing a Poem exercise on this page will be in free verse. For closure, have students read their own poems aloud, pausing to emphasize line breaks. Have them identify words that are repeated to create rhythm.

MEETING INDIVIDUAL NEEDS

Kinesthetic Learners • Have each student design a word-search puzzle related to the sights, sounds, and smells of one of the four seasons—spring, summer, fall, or winter. Word-search puzzles have words hidden horizontally, vertically, and diagonally in rows of letters. You may want to provide students with an example puzzle to help them get started. After students have completed their puzzles, they can trade with one another and try to find the hidden words and guess the seasons in the puzzles they receive.

FOR STUDY AND DISCUSSION

Identifying Details

1. Images are as follows: *Sight:* "go to the mountains" (line 18); *sound:* "listen to gospel music" (lines 13–14); *taste:* "eat fresh corn" (line 3); *touch:* "go barefooted and be warm" (lines 20–21).

Interpreting Meanings

2. The speaker feels affectionate and warm.
3. Yes, the word *warm* in line 21 could refer both to actual heat and to the warmth of love and security.

Applying Meanings

4. Most students will suggest that love makes people spiritually rich.

LITERARY ELEMENTS

Free Verse

1. There is no punctuation.
   In most cases, students will pause at the end of each line. They should make fuller pauses after lines 2 and 17.
2. Repeated words include *and, at the church,* and *and go.*
3. The first two and last four lines may be most important. Ask students to discuss their favorite lines and experiment with reading them aloud in different ways.

366

For Study and Discussion

IDENTIFYING DETAILS

1. Find an **image** or word-picture in this poem that appeals to each of these senses: sight, sound, taste, and touch.

INTERPRETING MEANINGS

2. How does the speaker feel about Knoxville and her grandmother?

3. Could the word *warm* in line 21 refer to the warmth of love and security, as well as to actual heat? Talk about your answers.

APPLYING MEANINGS

4. In a poem called "Nikki-Rosa," Giovanni writes that "Black love is Black wealth." How does that idea apply to "Knoxville, Tennessee"? How does it apply to all people?

Literary Elements

FREE VERSE

Like "That Day" (page 356), this poem is also written in **free verse,** that is, in poetry that is free from a regular pattern of rhythm. But how does this poet make her poem sound like a poem, and not like prose? Read the poem aloud.

1. Is there any punctuation in the poem at all? Would you pause at the end of each line? Or sometimes would you run your voice right on to the next line?

2. What words are repeated to create rhythm?

3. What are the most important lines?

366 Poetry

Focus on Writing a Poem

MAKING A LIST-POEM

Imitate the way Nikki Giovanni starts her poem. First, copy her opening sentence and fill in your own favorite season.

> I always like _____
> best

Then list the tastes, smells, sights, sounds, and activities that make this time of year special to you.

WRITING A FUNNY POEM

If you prefer to write a funny poem, here is one way to do it. First, think of the season you dislike most. Then list all of the reasons why you dislike it. Follow the same form that Giovanni used. Here is an example:

> I always like summer
> least
> there are so many mosquitoes
> my ice cream melts
> you can smell garbage
> rotting

About the Author

Nikki Giovanni (1943–   ) was born in Knoxville and grew up in Cincinnati, Ohio. She graduated with honors from Fisk University in Nashville, Tennessee. She has taught at Queens College in New York, at Rutgers University in New Jersey, and at Ohio State University. In addition to her own writing, she has edited and collected the writings of other African American authors. Three of her collections for children are *Spin a Soft Black Song, Ego Tripping & Other Poems for Young Readers,* and *Vacation Time.* Giovanni has recorded her poems, using gospel music as background.

Behind the Scenes

A Favorite Place

"Knoxville, Tennessee" is one of my favorite poems because it's one of my favorite places. Though I was born in Knoxville, our family moved to Cincinnati, Ohio, shortly after my birth. Knoxville always represented summer and warmth and sitting on porches overhearing the stories and gossip of my grandparents. Even though I liked snow and playing in it, I preferred the summer games, and still do, that take me outdoors.

I simply tried to recall and capture the summertime fun of reading books because I want to, not because they are school reports, making and baking clay figures (a few of which have survived) at camp. . . the summertime freedom that all adults know is all too short.

My language is really quite literal though I do believe literal language conveys figurative thoughts.

The poem is fun to me because the experience was fun. And sometimes happiness is a good enough reason to write a poem.

—Nikki Giovanni

FOCUS ON WRITING A POEM

Making a List-Poem
Look for vivid sensory details and original details. Ask volunteers to read their lists aloud.

Writing a Funny Poem
Small groups could collaborate to encourage originality and humor. Each group should read its poem aloud, perhaps in a choral reading. Both writing assignments could be extended to subjects other than seasons.

1. GUIDED READING:
Identifying Main Ideas
Here is another statement about the genesis of poetry. You might use this to introduce students to poetry. Poets often write out of a need to express some feeling or response to the world. That feeling is not always negative: It often is a feeling of happiness. You might skim the unit and find some poems that seem to have been spurred by happiness: Cummings's "who knows if the moon's" on page 314; the haiku by Shōha, Bonchō and Ryōta on page 330; "That Day" by David Kherdian on page 356.

OBJECTIVE	FOCUS/MOTIVATION	READING THE POEM
Students will explain and evaluate the poem's message.	Ask students what kind of face most people would want if they had the choice. Do they think people are often judged too much on appearance? **Prereading Journal.** Have students describe an ideal face (according to current standards) in a couple of sentences.	Have students read the poem silently. Then ask how they think it should sound when read aloud. Friendly? Casual? Sarcastic? Have a volunteer read aloud the poem.

TEACHING RESOURCES B
Teacher's Notes, p. 201
Study Guide, pp. 203, 205
Building Vocabulary, p. 207
Selection Vocabulary Test, p. 208
Selection Test, p. 209

AV RESOURCES BINDER
Audiocassette 2, Side B

1. LITERARY ELEMENTS:
Tone
In addition to the slang word *phizzog*, Sandburg uses other slang expressions, such as *This here*, to create a casual, conversational tone. This tone reflects on the message of the poem: We shouldn't be too serious about our faces, which, after all, were just handed to us.

2. GUIDED READING:
Making Inferences
How does the speaker want you to feel about yourself and your face? He wants you to smile, to make the best of what you have, and not take yourself too seriously.

FOR STUDY AND DISCUSSION
Identifying Details
1. People get their faces handed out to them by "Somebody."

Before You Read

"Phizzog" (fiz·og′) or "phiz" (fiz) was a slang word in the 1920s and 1930s. It was short for *physiognomy* (fiz′ē·og′nə·mē), which means "face." The word usually refers to facial features and expressions that are supposed to reveal character. Have you ever wished you could trade in your face for another one? Carl Sandburg thought about that question. As you read this poem, decide how he would answer it.

Phizzog

CARL SANDBURG

1 This face you got,
This here phizzog you carry around,
You never picked it out for yourself,
   at all, at all—did you?
This here phizzog—somebody handed it
   to you—am I right?
Somebody said, "Here's yours, now go see
   what you can do with it."
Somebody slipped it to you and it was like
   a package marked:
"No goods exchanged after being taken away"——
2 This face you got.

For Study and Discussion

IDENTIFYING DETAILS
1. According to the poet, how do people get their faces?

INTERPRETING MEANINGS
2. Who do you think Sandburg implies that "Somebody" is?

3. How do you think Sandburg feels about his own face?

4. What do you think is the **idea** behind this poem? Do you think the poem's message is important?

APPLYING MEANINGS
5. Suppose that someday plastic surgery costs very little. Do you think that most

CLOSURE

Have a panel of students take fifteen minutes to present views on the role that looks play in people's lives. Our faces tell people very little about what's inside, yet we are often judged, and we judge others, by these outer appearances (which we have done nothing to deserve or to earn). Is this fair? Is it unavoidable? Encourage lively discussion.

ART LINK

Encourage students to draw self-portraits on butcher paper. Once the self-portraits are completed, encourage students to discuss the process. Was it difficult or easy? Why?

Carl Sandburg by Edward Steichen (1936). Photographic montage.

National Portrait Gallery, Washington, D.C./Art Resource, NY/with permission of Joanna T. Steichen.

people would want to change their faces? Imagine that thousands of people choose the same face. What might happen then? (Rod Serling once wrote an episode on this idea for his long-running, eerie suspense series *The Twilight Zone*.)

Writing About Literature

DESCRIBING YOUR PHIZZOG

Bring to school a picture of yourself when you were a baby. Write about how you have changed in the past ten or eleven years. Be sure to include a description of how your face has changed. (If you can't find a baby picture of yourself, ask some of your relatives or family friends to describe how you looked when you were a baby.)

About the Author

Carl Sandburg (1878–1967) is one of the best-loved American poets. He was born in Galesburg, Illinois, the son of immigrants from Sweden. Forced to leave school at age thirteen, he rode trains all around the country looking for jobs. While working as a newspaper editor and writer in Chicago, he had several poems published. *Chicago Poems*, his collection of free-verse poetry about Chicago and its people, made him famous. The best-known poem in that book is the one about the fog in Chicago coming in on little cat feet. Sandburg traveled throughout the United States, reciting his poems, playing his guitar, and gathering folksongs that he later published in the book *American Songbag*. He was awarded the Pulitzer Prize in history for the last four volumes of his six-volume biography of Abraham Lincoln. Sandburg also received the Pulitzer Prize in poetry. His two books of poems for young people are called *Early Moon* and *Wind Song*. His autobiography is titled *Always the Young Strangers*. Sandburg once described what he wanted out of life: "to eat regular, . . . to get what I write printed, . . . a little love at home and a little nice affection hither and yon over the American landscape, . . . [and] to sing every day."

Interpreting Meanings
2. "Somebody" might be God.
3. Sandburg might feel proud or contented or resigned.
4. A possible statement of the poem's main idea is "What your face looks like is not nearly as important as what you accomplish and how you behave in life."

Most will agree that the message is important.

Applying Meanings
5. Many would opt for it if it were also painless and cheap.

WRITING ABOUT LITERATURE

Describing Your Phizzog
Encourage student comments that show self-esteem. Try to defuse student mockery of one another. You might bring in baby pictures of yourself or your own children to share with the class. If you have children in class who have no family and whose origins are not known, you will have to modify the assignment. You could ask the class in such instances to describe the way they *imagine* they looked as babies.

Phizzog 369

OBJECTIVES
Students will identify the speaker in the poem and interpret her tone.

FOCUS/MOTIVATION
You might review the Cinderella story. Students might refer to "The Algonquin Cinderella" on page 147 and to "Prinderella and the Cinch," a hilarious parody in mangled language, on page 309.

Prereading Journal. Ask students to write in their journals, quickly, two or three sentences describing Cinderella's stepmother and her two daughters.

TEACHING RESOURCES B
Teacher's Notes, p. 201
Study Guide, pp. 204, 206
Building Vocabulary, p. 207
Selection Vocabulary Test, p. 208
Selection Test, p. 209

AV RESOURCES BINDER
Audiocassette 2, Side B

1. GUIDED READING:
Making Inferences
According to this speaker, how did the original story of Cinderella's mistreatment get around? The stepmother claims that it was all lies spread by Cinderella.

FOR STUDY AND DISCUSSION
Identifying Details
1. Cinderella's stepmother.
   She is speaking to an interviewer.
   The stepmother's own daughters are present.
2. She tells her girls to be sweet and natural.
3. She dislikes Cinderella and is jealous of her.
   She thinks Cinderella spread lies about her.

Interpreting Meanings
4. Students may suggest that they disbelieve the stepmother because she is jealous. Some students may prefer to believe the stepmother's side of the story. (Ask for reasons.)
5. Most will say she is serious.

READING THE POEM
Have students follow silently as you read the poem aloud. Once they understand the stepmother's bitterness, have volunteers read the poem aloud again so that the tone is emphasized.

Before You Read
Do you remember Cinderella? According to the old fairy tale, Cinderella was treated very badly by her stepmother and two unattractive stepsisters. But since she was the heroine of a fairy tale, life turned out well for Cinderella. She married a handsome prince and lived happily ever after. This poem presents another point of view on Cinderella. The first thing you must do as you read is decide who the speaker is.

Interview

SARA HENDERSON HAY

Yes, this is where she lived before she won
The title Miss Glass Slipper of the Year,
And went to the ball and married the king's son.
You're from the local press, and want to hear
About her early life? Young man, sit down.   5
These are my *own* two daughters; you'll not find
Nicer, more biddable° girls in all the town,
And lucky, I tell them, not to be the kind

That Cinderella was, spreading those lies,
Telling those shameless tales about the way   10
We treated her. Oh, nobody denies
That she was pretty, if you like those curls.
But looks aren't everything, I always say.
Be sweet and natural, I tell my girls,
And Mr. Right will come along, someday.   15

7. **biddable:** eager to obey, docile.

370 Poetry

CLOSURE

Have students identify the speaker of the poem. Then have them describe how the tone of the poem would differ if another person were its speaker. Finally ask if this poem changed their perception of the Cinderella story.

EXTENSION AND ENRICHMENT

Library Research. You might ask interested students to trace the origins of some familiar fairy tales. The tale of "Cinderella," for example, goes back to a Chinese story told over a thousand years ago. It has since been retold with hundreds of variations in many lands. The best-known English version is a translation from Charles Perrault's *Tales of Mother Goose*. Note that in a Cinderella story told in Appalachia the title character is called Ashpet.

For Study and Discussion

IDENTIFYING DETAILS

1. Who is the speaker? Whom is this person speaking to? Who else is at the interview?
2. What advice does the speaker give her girls?
3. How does the speaker **feel** about Cinderella? Why would she feel this way?

INTERPRETING MEANINGS

4. Perhaps the **message** in this poem is that there are two sides to every story. Whose side of this story do you tend to believe? Explain why.
5. Do you think that the speaker really believes what she is saying about Cinderella and her own girls? What do you suppose her own girls look like?

APPLYING MEANINGS

6. One **idea** in this poem might be that stepmothers and stepsisters are portrayed unfairly in fairy tales. Talk about your responses to this idea.
7. Another Cinderella story appears on page 147. This one was told by the Algonquin people of North America. How do the two stories compare? Why do you think the Cinderella story is so popular?

Literary Elements

TONE

Tone is the speaker's or writer's attitude. When you listen to people, you can often tell from their voices and faces how they feel. You usually know whether they are bored, serious, sarcastic, worried, or self-satisfied. But when you read a poem or story, you have to depend on words alone to discover the speaker's attitude. After you've read this poem to yourself a couple of times, think about the character who is speaking.

1. Which word would you use to describe her tone in lines 1–3: sarcastic or admiring?
2. How would you describe her tone in lines 6–9: joking or serious?
3. How would you describe her tone in lines 11–13: sad or jealous?
4. In lines 14–15, is the speaker's tone optimistic or wishful?

Read the poem aloud to reveal the speaker's feelings. Decide how you will change your voice to show where the speaker's tone changes.

About the Author

Sara Henderson Hay (1906–1987) was born in Pittsburgh and lived there and in the South for most of her life. Hay published six collections of poetry. "Interview" is from the collection called *Story Hour*, which offers surprising and often humorous twists on several old stories. Another poem in that collection, "The Builders," tells the story of the Three Little Pigs from the point of view of the sensible pig who used bricks to build his home.

Her own two girls probably do not have Cinderella's pretty curls. They are, by implication and tradition, homely.

6. You might encourage students to discuss other fairy tales involving stepparents. ("Snow White" and "Rapunzel" are two.) The stepparents in these old stories represent the false parent, whom the child struggles to escape from. It is probably true that fairy tales have given stepparents a bad reputation.

7. The stories are remarkably similar: (a) The youngest girl is the heroine. (b) The elder sisters (or stepsisters) are cruel and tell lies. (c) The youngest is in rags. (d) The youngest wins the prince because of her virtue. (e) She is transformed by magic, her rags turning to beautiful dresses. (f) A "fairy godmother" transforms the girl. There is no ball and no stepmother in the Algonquin story.

The Cinderella story is popular because it embodies universal wishes and fears.

LITERARY ELEMENTS
Tone
1. Sarcastic.
2. Serious .
3. Jealous.
4. Wishful.

OBJECTIVE
Students will read aloud to enjoy the poem.

PRESENTATION
Students will be interested to know that they are about to read a poem about garbage! (Poetry can be about anything.) Before they read, you might have them list the most disgusting kinds of food they might find in a garbage can. Then have them compare their items with those in Sarah's pile. You might also, later, discuss constructive uses of Sarah's garbage through recycling.

Since the poem is written in couplets, take turns with oral reading around the class, having each student read a couplet.

TEACHING RESOURCES B
Teacher's Notes, p. 211

AV RESOURCES BINDER
Audiocassette 2, Side B

1. LITERARY ELEMENTS:
Sound Effects
The humorous qualities of the poem are reinforced by the regular rhyme scheme and meter.

2. LITERARY ELEMENTS:
Lists
This list of vivid sight images helps us see the garbage in living color and to react with an "Ugh!"

NO QUESTIONS ASKED

Before You Read

Do you think poetry has to be about beautiful things? If you've ever read any of Shel Silverstein's poems, you won't be surprised to find that he once wrote a poem about garbage. Read this poem aloud or you'll miss a lot of the fun.

Sarah Cynthia Sylvia Stout Would Not Take the Garbage Out

SHEL SILVERSTEIN

Sarah Cynthia Sylvia Stout
Would not take the garbage out!
She'd scour the pots and scrape the pans,
Candy the yams and spice the hams,
And though her daddy would scream and shout,   5
She simply would not take the garbage out.
And so it piled up to the ceilings:
Coffee grounds, potato peelings,
Brown bananas, rotten peas,
Chunks of sour cottage cheese.   10
It filled the can, it covered the floor,
It cracked the window and blocked the door
With bacon rinds and chicken bones,
Drippy ends of ice cream cones,
Prune pits, peach pits, orange peel,   15
Gloppy glumps of cold oatmeal,
Pizza crusts and withered greens,
Soggy beans and tangerines,
Crusts of black burned buttered toast,
Gristly bits of beefy roasts . . .   20

EXTENSION AND ENRICHMENT

Writing. Many poets love to write lists. Have students write lists of their own. Here are some ideas:

Great things
Bad things
Things to look forward to

Things that go together (like hot dogs and mustard)

Using Adjectives. As this poem proves, images are not always pretty. For each phrase that follows, students can suggest new adjectives that create an image of delicious food:

gloppy glumps of cold oatmeal
withered greens
soggy beans
cold french fries
black burned buttered toast
moldy melons
green baloney
rubbery blubbery macaroni

The garbage rolled on down the hall,
It raised the roof, it broke the wall . . .
Greasy napkins, cookie crumbs,
Globs of gooey bubble gum,
Cellophane from green baloney,   25
Rubbery blubbery macaroni,
Peanut butter, caked and dry,
Curdled milk and crusts of pie,
Moldy melons, dried-up mustard,
Eggshells mixed with lemon custard,   30
Cold french fries and rancid meat,
Yellow lumps of Cream of Wheat.
At last the garbage reached so high
That finally it touched the sky.
And all the neighbors moved away,   35
And none of her friends would come to play.
And finally Sarah Cynthia Stout said,
"OK, I'll take the garbage out!"
But then, of course, it was too late . . .
The garbage reached across the state,   40
From New York to the Golden Gate.
And there, in the garbage she did hate,
Poor Sarah met an awful fate,
That I cannot right now relate
Because the hour is much too late.   45
But children, remember Sarah Stout   **1**
And always take the garbage out!

Original illustrations by Shel Silverstein from *Where the Sidewalk Ends*, Harper & Row, Publishers © 1974.

1. LITERARY ELEMENTS:

Theme
This may be one of the most direct statements of theme in poetry.

About the Author

Shel Silverstein (1932–   ) was born in Chicago, where he still lives sometimes. He also lives in Key West, Florida, in New York City, and on a houseboat off the coast of California. Besides writing and illustrating poetry and prose for children and adults, Silverstein is a folksinger and songwriter. (His best-known song is "A Boy Named Sue.") His first poetry collection, *Where the Sidewalk Ends*, which includes "Sarah Cynthia Sylvia Stout . . .," converted many people of all ages who thought they didn't like poetry. His second collection of humorous verse, *A Light in the Attic*, was on *The New York Times* adult best-seller list for three years. His prose works include *The Giving Tree* and *A Giraffe and a Half*.

OBJECTIVES

Students will write metaphor poems, acrostic poems, Japanese-lantern poems, cinquains, sense poems, parts-of-speech poems, couplets, and limericks.

PRESENTATION

Remind students of poems they have already written during this unit: concrete poems, haiku, list-poems, and other forms. Tell students that poets like to write within the restrictions of a form. It is a challenge, just like playing tennis with a net, or playing football according to the rules.

Depending on your students, you may want them to write in pairs or small groups. All these exercises are well suited to collaborative writing.

METAPHOR POEMS

You might want students to work in pairs to create these poems. One student could name the first part of the metaphor, and the second student could complete it. You might make this a fun activity by having the second student complete the metaphor as quickly as possible, without thinking.

PORTRAITS OF IMAGINATION

WRITING YOUR OWN POEMS

A poem is like a portrait. You visualize something in your mind, and to share that vision with someone else, you may draw a picture or write about it. A poem or a picture shows your imagination at work.

Poets follow certain rules and use certain patterns to send their messages. Since poets work under these limitations, every word is important. As a poet, you want to paint that picture as carefully as possible so that your reader understands what you are trying to say.

Two elements are very important in poetry: one is the **image,** or a picture created by words. The other is the **metaphor,** or an unusual comparison made between two very different things. As you write your poems, images and metaphors will help you express your own unique imagination.

The following exercises are suggested to get you started, to help you share your imagination with your friends and classmates.

1. Metaphor Poems

Metaphors compare one thing with another very different thing. We go through life making all kinds of comparisons. Usually we use the words *like* or *as* to make a comparison; this produces a simile. A metaphor is a comparison that does not use *like* or *as.*

Similes: The child was as quiet as a mouse.
The road looked like a ribbon of black.

Metaphors: The child was a quiet mouse.
The road was a ribbon of black.
They drove along the black ribbon of highway.

Write a metaphor poem using the following structure, or something like it:

Line 1 says that you are something else.
Line 2 says that a friend is something else.
Line 3 says that your life is something else.

My days are a crowded mall
My life is an untied knot holding
 a brick
My brain is an overflowing
 pool.

—Elan Dobbs
6th grade

---

374 Poetry

Portfolio Assessment

Students who chose to make a scrapbook collection of favorite poems may want to take the time to reflect on their selections, replacing those that do not meet the purpose stated in their introductions. Suggest that they also take the time to create a decorated cover or book jacket that illustrates the thesis for their scrapbook. Ask students to write about what they learned by collecting, reflecting, and selecting poems for their scrapbooks. Provide a rubric for them to self-assess their project. (See *Portfolio Assessment and Professional Support Materials* for additional information on student portfolios.)

My handwriting is a junkyard
My friend's handwriting is a
   blooming flower
My hand is a grasping crane.
—Jim Philippou
6th grade

My eyes are the sky
My friend's eyes are dirt
My heart is a stomping foot.
—Megan Morelli
6th grade

2. Acrostic Poems

An **acrostic poem** is a series of lines in which the first, last, or special letters spell out a word or a phrase. The name poem is a kind of acrostic that describes *you*, the writer. First, write the letters of your name vertically, in very bold print. Skip a space between your first and your last name. Then write a characteristic of yourself beside each letter. The trick is to find something to say about yourself that begins with the right letter. You can choose physical characteristics, attitudes, or relationships.

Erica: That's me, I
Reject blondes
I also hate airheads
Can't stand the Cougars and boys
   named John
And I like:

Boys: Only the cute ones
Ongoing notes
Talking on the phone
Terrorizing Gus Splittorf especially
Sand, sun, surfing, and the stars.
—Erica Botts
6th grade

3. Japanese-Lantern Poems

A lantern gives off light. A Japanese-lantern poem is said to be light and airy, and a lantern can easily be drawn around it if you center each line. A lantern poem should create pictures with words. It should also create a feeling. The pattern of the poem is this:

Line 1 has one syllable.
Line 2 has two syllables.
Line 3 has three syllables.
Line 4 has four syllables.
Line 5 has one syllable, just like line 1.

Stars
Shining
Reflecting
Magnificent
Stars

—Melia Price
6th grade

ACROSTIC POEMS

For group writing of acrostic poems, you can make the acrostic word or phrase something other than an individual name. It might be the number of your classroom spelled out, the name of your town, the name of the group's favorite band or sports team, the name of a historical figure, or any other word or phrase that the group chooses.

JAPANESE-LANTERN POEMS

Students might work together in groups and brainstorm for ideas. They should write or say out loud all the words that their "object" makes them think of. They could even create group cluster diagrams. Then they can choose the words they like best to make their lantern.

Portraits of Imagination

CINQUAINS

Cinquains can be effectively written in groups of five students with each student contributing one line.

SENSE POEMS

In preparation for these poems, you might have students brainstorm a list of emotions and colors. A thesaurus is a good source of color words that may not be a part of students' everyday vocabulary.

4. Cinquains

A **cinquain** (sin'kān) has five lines. (The name comes from the French word for "five.") The inventor of the cinquain was influenced by the Japanese haiku. Each line of our cinquain will have a special function:

Line 1 is a title; it has one word with two syllables.
Line 2 has four syllables that describe the title.
Line 3 has six syllables and shows action.
Line 4 has eight syllables and expresses a feeling.
Line 5 has two syllables and gives another name for the title.

> Thunder
> loud claps scaring
> comes, goes, shrieks, scares, frightens
> dark, loud, lonely, sacred, lovely
> Beauty
>
> —Erica Botts
> 6th grade

> Reading
> Bathing the mind
> Interesting, still fun
> Expressing messages or thoughts
> Knowledge
>
> —Elan Dobbs
> 6th grade

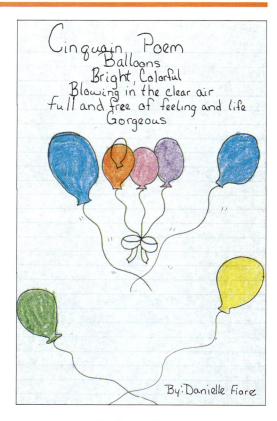

5. Sense Poems

A **sense poem** is good to write when you feel a strong emotion: when you are happy, sad, angry, mellow, excited—whatever. First, you name your emotion and give it a color. Second, you tell how it smells. Third, you tell how it tastes. Next, you tell how it sounds. Finally, you tell how it feels. In this poem, you can use **similes** (comparisons between two different things using *like* or *as*) or **metaphors** (comparisons between two different things without using *like* or *as*). Here are some student "sense" poems:

Embarrassment is pink.
It smells like vinegar.
It tastes like pickle juice out of a jar.
It sounds like a horn blowing in your ear.
And it feels like a mosquito bite that doesn't stop itching.
—Kelly Burke
6th grade

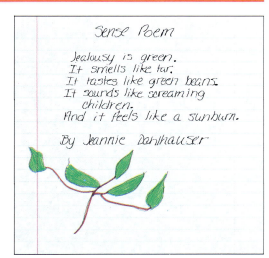

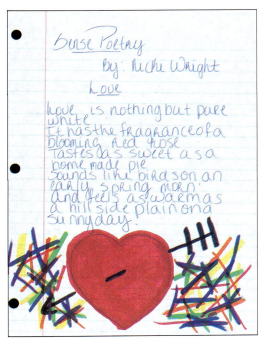

The students' poems on these pages were written for Jane Meyer Lee's classes at Safety Harbor Middle School, Pinellas County, Florida.

Friendship is violet.
It smells like blooming roses.
It tastes like candy.
It sounds like laughter.
It feels like a mother's kiss.
—Cindy Duncan
6th grade

Think of an emotion as a gift that you have. In your poem, you use this gift to let other people know how you feel about them or the world around you. In your poem, you are expressing real things that you like and do not like. Be truthful when you write this poem. Open the gift package that surrounds you.

6. Parts-of-Speech Poems

Parts-of-speech poems help reinforce your understanding of the eight parts of speech. You should follow this structure:

PARTS-OF-SPEECH POEMS

Students could work in groups of five, with one being responsible for each part of speech. Be sure students are familiar with these parts of speech.

Portraits of Imagination

COUPLETS

If students have not already read it, you may want them to look at the No Questions Asked poem, "Sarah Cynthia Sylvia Stout Would Not Take the Garbage Out," on page 372. "Sarah" is written in (hilarious) couplets.

Line 1 consists of an article and a noun.
Line 2 consists of two adjectives joined by a conjunction.
Line 3 has two verbs joined by a conjunction.
Line 4 has an adverb.
Line 5 has a noun that relates to the first line.

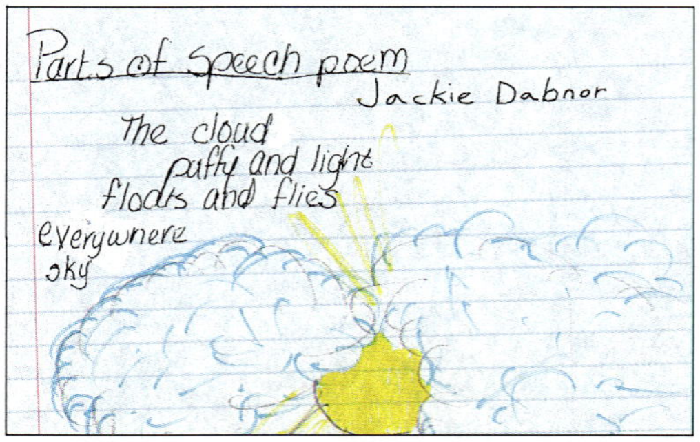

> Parts of speech poem
> Jackie Dabnor
> The cloud
> puffy and light
> floats and flies
> everywhere
> sky

> A tree
>   green and tall
> grows and dies
>   daily.
> Oak
> —Megan Morelli
>   6th grade

> An elephant
>   smelly and big
> tramples and stomps
>   constantly.
> Pacaderm
>   —Elan Dobbs
>   6th grade

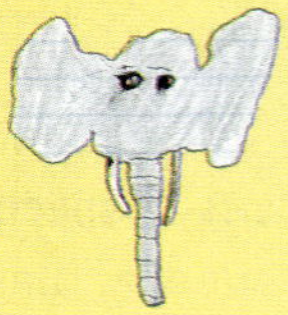

When you make up a parts-of-speech poem, you might color code each of the different parts of speech you use. Try to think of good words for your parts of speech. You might look for words that create vivid pictures, or that have fun sounds. Draw a picture to illustrate your creation.

7. Couplets

Couplets are the simplest rhymed poems. A couplet has two rhyming lines. Couplets are often funny. Here is one couplet by a famous humorous poet:

> The cow is of the bovine ilk;
> One end is moo, the other, milk.
> —Ogden Nash

Couplets can be put together to make a longer poem. Here is Nash again:

> Behold the duck.
> It does not cluck.
> A cluck it lacks.
> It quacks.
> It is specially fond
> Of a puddle or pond.
> When it dines or sups,
> It bottoms ups.
> —Ogden Nash

Here is a sixth grader's couplet poem:

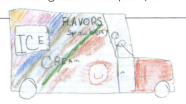

Dan Dan the ice cream man
He drives a purple polka dot van
He plays his music round the clock
But all it really is is rock
You can hear his bells all over
   town
His lights flash round and then
   down
Even though it's very scary
He only sells strawberry.
—Michelle Kraft
6th grade

8. Limericks

A **limerick** is a humorous verse form that takes its name from the City of Limerick, Ireland. No one knows how the limerick originated, but it is a five-line poem with a special rhythm and a definite rhyme pattern. Lines 1, 2, and 5 rhyme, and lines 3 and 4 rhyme. Lines 1, 2, and 5 have three strong beats, and lines 3 and 4 have only two.

> There once was a girl, oh so cool,
> She never thought much about school.
>   She stayed home a lot.
>   What she learned she forgot.
> Now all she can do is play pool.

Some nursery rhymes follow the pattern of a limerick. "Hickory Dickory Dock" is an example.

Many limericks put a place name at the end of their first line and open with the words "There once was." Here are two famous limericks:

> There once was a man from Nantucket
> Who kept all his cash in a bucket.
>   But his daughter named Nan
>   Ran away with a man,
> And as for the bucket, Nantucket.

> There was an old man of Tarentum,
> Who gnashed his false teeth till he bent
>   'em:
>   And when asked for the cost
>   Of what he had lost,
> Said, "I really can't tell, for I rent 'em."

LIMERICKS
Students who find limericks appealing may want to read some of Edward Lear's classic limericks, found in most school libraries. Students may remember Lear from his poem "The Jumblies" on page 295 of this anthology.

OBJECTIVES

The overall aim is for students to identify sound devices that help give meaning to a literary selection. For a complete list of objectives, see the **Teacher's Notes**.

PRESENTATION

You might want to begin this segment by listing the sound devices used in poetry on the chalkboard and asking students to define them orally. Then read aloud the poem in the text while students follow along. They should listen and look for the sound devices and maybe even make a few independent notes. Students can now work in small groups with the activity that follows the poem. Groups should share orally their responses.

RELATING SOUND TO MEANING

Answers

Answers will vary.
1. Alliteration: "Heat. . . happy" (4); "stones. . . sang" (9). Rhyme: There is no end rhyme, but students might see some internal rhyme in line 19, "dew loosened;" lines 23-24, "ears and early;" and line 27, "Sang. . . veins." Many repetitious sounds, such as *s, w, th, r,* occur throughout the poem. Refrain: "blossoms sang," "stones sang," "waters sang." Rhythm is regular with approximately four beats to each line, two stressed and two unstressed, giving the poem a lively and upbeat mood. Onomatopoeia: shimmered (6) and sighed (18).
2. The mood is cheerful, even joyful.
3. Themes might include the following ideas: A person can find great enjoyment in nature. The elements of nature can be our friends.
4. Some students might say that rhyming lines would restrict the sound effects and free-flowing style of the poem. Others might feel that rhyming lines would add to the poem's musical quality.

FOCUS ON Reading and Critical Thinking

RELATING SOUND TO MEANING

The sounds of the words in a poem are often closely related to the poem's meaning and mood. Sound devices in poetry include rhyme, repetition, alliteration, refrain, rhythm, and onomatopoeia.

Read the following poem aloud. Then join with a small group of classmates for the activity that follows.

The Waking

I strolled across
An open field;
The sun was out;
Heat was happy.

This way! This way!   5
The wren's throat shimmered,
Either to other,
The blossoms sang.

The stones sang,
The little ones did,   10
And flowers jumped
Like small goats.

A ragged fringe
Of daisies waved;
I wasn't alone   15
In a grove of apples.

Far in the wood
A nestling sighed;
The dew loosened
Its morning smells.   20

I came where the river
Ran over stones:
My ears knew
An early joy.

And all the waters   25
Of all the streams
Sang in my veins
That summer day.
—Theodore Roethke

Relating Sound to Meaning

1. Working in small groups, use a sheet of paper to list all the sound devices that contribute to the description in this poem. List one or more specific examples from the poem for each sound device. Identify each example you list by line number.

2. Discuss with your group how you would describe the speaker's mood in this poem.

3. Now discuss with the group what you think the poet's overall message or theme is in "The Waking."

4. Do you think this poem would have been more effective if the poet had used rhyming lines? Why or why not?

OBJECTIVES

The overall aim is for students to express their perspectives by writing a poem. For a complete list of objectives, see the **Teacher's Notes.**

PRESENTATION

You might have a read-around in which students sit in a circle and share something they have written during this poetry unit. Afterwards, tell students they will have an opportunity to use the writing process to write and publish a poem. You might incorporate the strategies discussed here with the **Portraits of Imagination** and let students experiment with several kinds of poems. They can choose the best one to revise and publish. During the process, students should have many opportunities to read their poetry aloud so that they can explore and play with language.

FOCUS ON Writing

WRITING A POEM

Poets use only a few words to offer their readers many layers of meaning. Poetry is fun to read and write because poems often present new ways of looking at the world. In this unit you have studied some of the basic elements of poetry. Now you will have the chance to express *your* way of looking at the world by writing a short poem.

Prewriting

1. Here are some techniques to use when you look for a subject:
   - brainstorm with a group of classmates
   - draw a sketch of a person or object
   - focus on visualizing a favorite memory

   Remember that almost anything can be a good subject for a poem. In fact, you may find it easier to write something fresh and original about an unexpected subject: a tomato, for instance!

   To jump-start your imagination, try listing the associations you have with the following:
   - a slice of pizza
   - ice-cold water
   - wearing a scarf
   - washing clothes
   - helping a friend
   - skateboarding
   - the color green
   - lightning
   - birds
   - shoveling snow
   - lions
   - a red hat

   [See **Focus** assignment on page 299.]

2. You can also get ideas for poems by exploring patterns for a poem's structure. Here are three kinds of patterns you can explore:

   Metaphor poems use a metaphor in all three lines.
   (See Poem 1b on page 383.)

   Sense poems name a strong emotion and give it a color in the first line. The next four lines use similes or metaphors to tell how that emotion smells, tastes, sounds, and feels.
   (See the poems on page 377.)

   Cinquains have five lines. (The name comes from the French word for "five.") Each line has a special function:
   Line 1 is a title; it has one word with two syllables.
   Line 2 has four syllables that describe the title.
   Line 3 has six syllables and shows action.
   Line 4 has eight syllables and expresses a feeling.
   Line 5 has two syllables and gives another name for the title.
   (See the poems on page 376.)

   Parts-of-speech poems have five lines and follow this pattern:
   Line 1 consists of an article and a noun.
   Line 2 consists of two adjectives joined by a conjunction.
   Line 3 consists of two verbs joined by a conjunction.

HOLT WRITER'S WORKSHOP

This computer program provides help for all types of writing through guided instruction for each step of the writing process. (Program available separately.)

See **Elements of Writing, Introductory Course,** Chapters 4 and 5, for more instruction on descriptive and creative writing.

WRITING A POEM

Writing poetry allows a kind of freedom that appeals to many students. They feel less intimidated by poetry than by prose because poetry is usually a brief writing experience. Students are often able to write and rewrite a complete draft in a class period and get immediate satisfaction from a finished piece.

Prewriting

Encourage students to use the prewriting techniques discussed in the text. They might start over with a new subject or take an idea they have already written about. As they experiment with the various techniques, you might put students in small groups to share and to receive other viewpoints for their image charts, figures of speech, sound effects, and possible organization methods.

Focus on Writing

TRANSPARENCY 23
Writing Process
Writing a Poem – helps students to plan and write a creative poem.

Writing

Remind students that content controls form. Therefore, in their first drafts students should be concerned with writing freely and honestly and should not try to fit their ideas into any particular structure. Once they have seen what they have to say and they have experimented with the language, they can concentrate on the appropriate form or shape.

Line 4 has an adverb.
Line 5 has a noun that relates to the first line.

Here is an example of a parts-of-speech poem:

> A tree
>   green and tall
>   grows and dies
>   daily.
> Oak

3. After you have chosen a subject, explore it further by listing some **sensory details.** Fill out an **image chart** like the one below:

Sense	Image
Sight	_____
Hearing	_____
Smell	_____
Taste	_____
Touch	_____

4. **Figures of speech** are words or phrases that describe one thing in terms of another. Think about how you could use one or more of the figures of speech below to make the language in your poem more interesting.

- **Simile** uses *like* or *as* to compare two different things.
    Example: The road looked like a ribbon of black.
- **Metaphor** compares two different things directly.
    Example: The road was a black ribbon.
- **Personification** gives human qualities to something nonhuman.
    Example: The road guided us steadily onward.

[See **Focus** assignment on page 347.]

5. Experiment with **sound effects.** Here are some of the devices you can use:

- repetition
- alliteration
- refrain
- rhythm
- rhyme
- onomatopoeia

[See **Focus** assignments on pages 304, 308, and 313.]

6. Use one of the following methods to organize the details for your poem. If you wish, make an **outline** of your poem in note form.

- chronological order
- spatial order
- order of importance

Writing

1. Write a first draft of your poem. You do not need to use rhyme or regular rhythm, although you can use either or both for special effects. As you write, concentrate on making every word count. Choose precise, specific words. Make your writing as vivid as you can.

2. Feel free to be as inventive as you want in your poem. Here are three ideas you can use:

- Make up some new words, like "hippopotomuscle" (page 307) or "phizzog" (page 368).
- Use foreign words for special effects, the way Leroy Quintana does in "Legacy II" (see page 360)

Poetry

- Experiment with punctuation, capitalization, and the layout of words on the page (see pages 314 and 328)
3. Make sure that all the details you include in your poem contribute to the same overall impression or main idea.
4. Give your poem a title that describes the subject or conveys your overall meaning.

Evaluating and Revising

1. Put your first draft aside for a while. Then reread it and evaluate it as objectively as you can. Add, cut, reorder, or replace words. Trade papers with a partner, and offer each other suggestions.

Compare these two versions of the poem that appears on page 374. Why is the second version better?

Writer's Model

1a. My days are a mall

   My life is a knot holding a brick

   My brain is overflowing.

1b. My days are a crowded mall

   My life is an untied knot holding a

   brick

   My brain is an overflowing pool.

2. You may find the following checklist helpful as you revise your poem:

Checklist for Evaluation and Revision

✔ Have I created a single main impression in the poem?
✔ Do I use precise, concrete words?
✔ Do I use fresh, clear images that appeal to the senses?
✔ Have I used figures of speech?
✔ Do I use sound effects that contribute to the meaning?

Proofreading and Publishing

1. Proofread your poem and correct any errors you find in grammar, usage, and mechanics. (Here you may find it helpful to refer to the **Handbook for Revision** on pages 750–785.) Then prepare a final version of your poem by making a clean copy.
2. Consider some of the following publication methods for your poem:
   - read your poem aloud to the class
   - post your poem on the class bulletin board
   - send your poem to the school newspaper or magazine
   - join with a group of classmates and create a poetry anthology

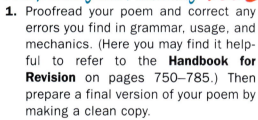 If your teacher approves, you may wish to keep a copy of your work in your writing folder or portfolio.

Focus on Writing 383

UNIT 5 ◆ TEACHING GUIDE

NONFICTION

OVERVIEW OF THE UNIT

Among readers of all ages, some prefer fiction, while others would much rather read about something real—a real person, events that actually happened, information about the world. This unit presents a sampling of nonfiction that should appeal to sixth graders' interest in real people and events. The unit contains an excerpt from one of the world's most famous diaries, two biographical excerpts, two personal narratives, a science article, and three essays.

THE AUTHOR'S PURPOSE

Writing is sometimes categorized according to the author's purpose. Two of these purposes—exposition and persuasion—are only found in nonfiction.

LITERARY MODES	FORMS OF WRITING	
	FICTION	NONFICTION
Narration is writing that tells a story.	Short Story Novel Drama	Biography Autobiography True narrative History
Description is writing that describes a person, place, or thing.	[Passages occur in all literary forms.]	
Exposition gives information or explores a subject.		Essay Newspaper and magazine articles History Science
Persuasion is writing that tries to persuade.		Editorials Critical reviews Advertisements

THE WRITER'S VOICE

Another way of categorizing nonfiction is to focus on the writer's voice. Nonfiction may be very **subjective** and **personal**, as it is in journals, diaries, and personal essays. *The Diary of a Young Girl,* "The Land I Lost," and "Snapshot of a Dog" are examples of this kind of personal writing.

Much nonfiction, on the other hand, is **impersonal** and **objective**. In fact, there is little "voice" at all; content is emphasized rather than the voice of the writer. Examples of this impersonal type of writing include "A Backwoods Boy," "The Most Vulnerable People," and "Volcano."

OBJECTIVES OF THE UNIT

The aims of this unit for students are
◆ To identify main ideas and supporting details
◆ To distinguish facts from opinions
◆ To gain information from graphic aids
◆ To identify factual sources for biography
◆ To identify an author's tone
◆ To recognize narrative elements in nonfiction
◆ To recognize irony
◆ To visualize descriptions
◆ To recognize internal and external conflicts
◆ To summarize a character
◆ To write creatively and critically in relation to the selections
◆ To use suffixes in words
◆ To use context clues to determine meanings of words
◆ To interpret figures of speech
◆ To make connections between literature and science
◆ To write an informative paper

CONCEPTS AND SKILLS

The following concepts and skills are treated in this unit:

CLOSE READING OF NONFICTION

Guidelines for Close Reading 386
One Reader's Response 387
Looking at Yourself as a Reader 391

FOCUS ON READING AND CRITICAL THINKING

Distinguishing Between Facts and Opinions 400
Visualizing Descriptions 420
Supporting Conclusions 428
Using Graphic Aids: Maps and Captions 443
Understanding Cause and Effect 458

LITERARY ELEMENTS

Tone 400   Conflict 428
Irony 408   Figures of Speech 443
A Narrative 420   Character 451

LANGUAGE AND VOCABULARY

Suffixes 408   Description 451
Context Clues 420

OPPORTUNITIES FOR WRITING

Focus on Informative Writing
Planning a Biographical Report 401
Organizing a Biographical Report 409
Exploring Cause and Effect 428
Explaining a Process 444
Writing an Informative Paper 459

PLANNING GUIDE

FOR UNIT PLANNING
- Transparencies 24–28: *Audiovisual Resources Binder*
- *Portfolio Assessment and Professional Support Materials*
- Test Generator
- Mastery Tests: Teaching Resources C, pp. 95, 97
- Analogy Test: Teaching Resources C, p. 99
- Revision Worksheet: Teaching Resources C, p. 100

SELECTION (Pupil's Page)	Teacher's Notes	Reading Check	Reading Focus	Study Guide	Language Skills	Building Vocabulary	Selection Vocab. Test	Selection Test	AV BINDER Audio-cassette
NONFICTION Introduction (p. 385)	1								
Close Reading of a Biography Dian Fossey from *Gorillas in the Mist* (p. 387)	1								
Anne Frank from *The Diary of a Young Girl* (p. 393)	2	5	6	7, 8	9	12	14	15	TAPE 3 SIDE A
Russell Freedman *A Backwoods Boy* (p. 402)	17	20	21	22, 23	24	27	29	30	
Huynh Quang Nhuong *The Land I Lost* (p. 411)	32	35	36	37, 38	39	42	44	45	TAPE 3 SIDE A
Brent Ashabranner *The Most Vulnerable People* (p. 422)	47	49	50	51, 52	53	56	58	59	
Patricia Lauber *Volcano* (p. 431)	61	64	65	67, 68	69	72	75	76	
James Thurber *Snapshot of a Dog* (p. 446)	78	80		81, 82	83	87	89	90	TAPE 3 SIDE A
Bill Cosby from *Fatherhood* (p. 453)	92								TAPE 3 SIDE A

Writing About Literature
Describing a Place 421
Writing Your Own Snapshot 451

CONNECTIONS
Literature and Science 445

SPEAKING AND LISTENING
Reading Aloud 453

TRANSPARENCIES

The following unit support materials with specific correlations to literature selections are available in the **Fine Art and Instructional Transparencies with Teacher's Notes and Blackline Masters** section of your *Audiovisual Resources Binder*.

FINE ART TRANSPARENCIES
Theme: Fact-Based Writing
24 *The Grinder*, Diego Rivera
25 *Akbar Crossing the Ganges*, Anonymous

READER RESPONSE
26 Charting Your Response

LITERARY ELEMENTS
27 Imagery

WRITING PROCESS
28 Writing an Informative Paper

INTRODUCING THE UNIT

You might introduce the unit with an activity that focuses on the various types of nonfiction.
1. With the librarian's help, assemble a classroom library of high-interest nonfiction. Include books and magazines on sports, nature, science, history, and hobbies. You might also include a daily newspaper.
2. You may wish to have students write very brief reviews of nonfiction books they read. Post these on the class bulletin board so that other students can refer to them. With your librarian's help, make available a list of recommended nonfiction that covers a wide range of subjects as well as forms. This is especially useful if selections are cross referenced: "If you enjoyed _____, be sure to try _____."
3. Have students write an autobiographical sketch, and encourage them to expand their sketches into fuller accounts. Volunteers may share their autobiographies with the class, but no one should be required to do so.

PORTFOLIO ASSESSMENT

Suggestions for use of portfolios as support for this unit are described in the *Portfolio Assessment and Professional Support Materials* booklet accompanying this program. Specific suggestions are provided for a variety of student projects that may be suitable for inclusion in a portfolio. In addition, copying masters are provided for guides that may be used for evaluation and assessment of student projects.

SELECTION NOTES

Following are vocabulary lists of words from each selection that are included in the Building Vocabulary Worksheets and Selection Vocabulary Tests; Reading Check tests (which are also available in blackline masters); and answers to questions in the Language and Vocabulary sections that follow the selections.

FROM THE DIARY OF A YOUNG GIRL (PAGE 393)

Vocabulary

vital	drone(ing)	penetrate(ing)	implore
stifle(d)	dependent	impenetrable	recede
impression	atmosphere		

Reading Check

Have students judge each statement as true or false.
1. Anne Frank is thirteen when the excerpt begins. **True**
2. Her diary is made up of letters to a classmate. **False**
3. The Frank family goes into hiding with another family. **True**
4. Anne takes her cat with her into hiding. **False**
5. Miep and Henk are friends who help the Frank family. **True**

"A BACKWOODS BOY" (PAGE 402)

Vocabulary

hostile	epidemic	luminous	sociable	complexion

Reading Check

Have students judge each statement as true or false.
1. Lincoln often boasted about his childhood. **False**
2. Lincoln came from a wealthy family. **False**
3. His mother died from "milk sickness." **True**
4. His stepmother was cruel to Abe and his sister. **False**
5. Lincoln was an expert working with an ax. **True**

Language and Vocabulary: Suffixes (page 408)
1. -dom (kingdom)
2. -less (windowless)
3. -ful (painful)
4. communism, totalitarianism, authoritarianism

"THE LAND I LOST" (PAGE 411)

Vocabulary

distinguish	inseparable	resent(ed)	tragic
edible	infest(ed)	avenge	hysterical
disrupt(ed)	wily		

Reading Check

Have students supply words or phrases to fill in the blanks in the following statements.
1. The narrator writes about his village in _____. **Vietnam**
2. In the story, Trung and Lan celebrate their _____. **wedding or marriage**
3. That night Lan is carried of by a(n) _____. **crocodile**
4. All night Trung thinks he hears _____. **Lan calling him or Lan's voice**
5. The next morning they discover Lan in a _____. **tree**

Language and Vocabulary: Context Clues (page 420)
1. inseparable—CLUE: "did not allow them to be alone together anymore." DEFINITION: incapable of being separated.
2. infested—CLUE: "Because crocodiles infested the river." DEFINITION: occupied in large numbers, causing danger or harm.
3. wily—CLUES: "avoided the barrier"; "sneaked up behind." DEFINITION: sly; cunning.
4. hallucination—CLUES: "Nobody doubted he thought he had heard her call, but they all believed that he was the victim of a hallucination"; "not believing him." DEFINITION: the impression of seeing or hearing something that isn't really there.
5. resented—CLUE: "He resented them for not believing him. . . ." DEFINITION: showed anger and ill will.
6. avenge—CLUE: ". . . kill the beast in order to . . . avenge your tragic death." DEFINITION: get revenge.

"THE MOST VULNERABLE PEOPLE" (PAGE 422)

Vocabulary

vulnerable	anchor(ed)	refugee
familiar	clutch(ed)	

Reading Check

Have students judge each statement as true or false.
1. Tran thinks his father is taking him fishing. **True**
2. Several members of Tran's family are on the boat. **False**
3. Tran's father gives him a plastic bag. **True**
4. Tran's mother does not want him to go to America. **False**
5. The people on the boat are going to a refugee camp in Thailand. **True**

"Volcano" (page 431)

Vocabulary

erupt	bulge	scald(ing)	churn(ed)
lumber(ed)	billow(ing)	scour(ing)	dome
fell(ed)	witness(es)		

Reading Check

Have students supply words to fill the blanks in the following sentences.
1. For 123 years Mount St. Helens was a sleeping _____. **volcano**
2. Mount St. Helens is in the state of _____. **Washington**
3. Scientists who study the earth are called _____. **geologists**
4. Several months before Mount St. Helens erupted, there was a large _____ followed by many smaller ones. **earthquake**
5. At 8:32 A.M. on May 18, 1980, Mount St. Helens _____. **erupted**

"Snapshot of a Dog" (page 446)

Vocabulary

nobility	tranquil	disposition	malice
dignity	vicious	strenuous	integrity
extravagant	turmoil		

Reading Check

Have students judge each statement as true or false.
1. Though Rex is a big dog, he is not very strong.   **False**
2. In a fight, Rex would hold on to the other dog's ear for hours.   **True**
3. One fight had to be broken up by the Fire Department.   **True**
4. Rex couldn't swim and feared the water.   **False**
5. The narrator thinks Rex died from a beating.   **True**

Student Learning Options

NONFICTION

1. Planning a Diary
Ask students to plan a diary or journal for themselves, like the one Anne Frank kept. Ask them to set a schedule for writing in the diary and to develop a list of topics they would like to write about. You can encourage students to keep their diaries for at least a few weeks to see whether they enjoy the activity.

2. Scheduling a Day
Have students work in groups to draw up a schedule for a day in the life of Dian Fossey, Anne Frank, or the young Abraham Lincoln. They should keep in mind the limitations and responsibilities their characters face. Let them share their schedules with the class and explain why they included each activity.

3. Exploring the Experiences of Refugees
If you know a refugee in your community from Vietnam or another country, invite that person to speak to your students about his or her experiences. If you are unable to invite a refugee, ask students who have moved to your area from another part of the country to share their experiences of coming to a new place.

4. Grading Nonfiction
Have students work in groups of three or four to grade each of the selections in the unit. Students should give grades of A, B, C, D, or F for the "entertainment value" and the "information value" of each selection. After the groups have graded the selections, rank them according to the grades they received.

5. Exploring Nonfiction Books
Ask the school librarian to prepare a cart of nonfiction books on a variety of subjects for you to use in the classroom. Let students spend time browsing through the books before they select one to report on. Students do not have to read the books at this point. Instead, they should prepare "quick reports" on the books by reading the dust jackets, studying the tables of contents or the indexes, and flipping through the book to read a paragraph here and there. Each report should last no more than a minute and should be geared toward arousing interest in potential readers. Students who are interested in a particular book can check it out and read it on their own.

6. Making a Model
Have students make a cross-sectional model of a volcano like the one illustrated on page 433. Ask them to label the parts of the volcano and to write brief explanations of each section of the model. You can put the models on display in the classroom or share them with a science teacher.

7. Mapping Vietnam
Ask students to draw a map of Vietnam and the part of Southeast Asia surrounding Vietnam. Have students include important rivers, mountains, and cities on their maps.

8. Developing a Chronology
Ask students to look up Abraham Lincoln in an encyclopedia and to develop a chronology, or time line, of the major events in his life. In a companion document, they can briefly describe the most important events.

VISUAL CONNECTIONS
This painting was based on a real whaler that was caught between masses of ice. Many such ships got trapped in the ice and were never able to escape. Bradford's paintings are known for their gorgeous colors and minute detail. Have students examine the painting and note the details. Ask them what the general mood of the painting is. (The mood is grim and somber.)

About the Artist
William Bradford (1827–1892) was born in New Bedford, Massachusetts, and taught himself how to paint. He painted the ships and marine views he saw along the coasts of Massachusetts, Labrador, and Nova Scotia. He went on several expeditions to the Arctic region, and was the first American painter to portray the frozen areas of the north.

UNIT FIVE

Nonfiction

Nonfiction is writing that is based on fact, but like other forms of literature, it appeals to the imagination. Nonfiction includes biography (the story of someone's life), autobiography (the story of the writer's own life), articles, diaries, journals, speeches, interviews, true adventures, and travel literature.

Imagine yourself at the scene shown in this painting of whalers trapped in ice somewhere in the Arctic. If you were one of the whalers keeping a record of your journey, how would you describe the scene shown here? Write a brief journal entry about what you see.

Compare your responses with those of other students. Evaluate your work. What details have others seen that you missed? Are you more aware of any elements in the painting after writing down your ideas and listening to others' responses?

Whalers Trapped in Arctic Ice by William Bradford (c. 1870–1880). Oil on canvas.

The Manoogian Collection, Detroit, Michigan.

FOCUS/MOTIVATION

Background. During her stay in the Virunga Mountains, Fossey encountered numerous hardships. One of her fiercest struggles was with poachers who killed gorillas to provide meat and trophies to the illegal market and captured live animals for sale to zoos. After being caught by poachers, both Coco and Pucker suffered from grief, wounds, and starvation in captivity. Because they were near death, Fossey was summoned. So, her difficult task included gaining their trust and then nursing the babies back to health. Her goal was to eventually return them to the forest of their birth as members of a new group. Unfortunately, they could not be returned to their real families because all the family members had died trying to defend the youngsters.

Establishing a Purpose for Reading. Ask students to try to visualize the setting and to predict the methods Fossey might use in training the baby gorillas.

Prereading Journal. If students have ever tried

> **TEACHING RESOURCES C**
> Teacher's Notes, p. 1

1
A *naturalist* studies nature, especially by direct observation.

Close Reading OF NONFICTION

The subjects of nonfiction are as broad as the world itself: people, animals, environment, exploration, adventure, science, arts, politics, current events, history, personal opinions. Nonfiction can take many forms. An autobiographical narrative, for example, may combine true adventure, scientific observations, historical accounts, and interpretations. When you read nonfiction, you must determine whether the facts and conclusions presented by the author are reliable and complete.

Guidelines for Close Reading

1. Read actively, asking questions as you read. Think about any details or passages that puzzle you. Ask yourself what might happen next.
2. Guess the meaning of unfamiliar words by using context clues. Look up any words or references you don't understand.
3. Think about how the selection relates to your own experience or to things you have already learned. What reactions do you have during and after reading?
4. What impression do you have of the writer? Do you agree or disagree with the writer's ideas?
5. Note the writer's use of language. Are there any images that appeal to you? Is the writer using formal language or a conversational style?
6. Ask yourself what the writer's overall purpose might be. Is it to give information, to entertain the reader, to present a particular interpretation, or some combination of these objectives?

The following excerpt is from *Gorillas in the Mist* by Dian
1 Fossey, a naturalist who spent a number of years observing mountain gorillas in a part of Africa. In addition to recording her

to train an animal, ask them to write a few sentences about their experience. If not, ask them to choose an animal and write about what they think it would be like to train it.

scientific observations and discoveries about gorillas, Fossey gives an account of her adventures. At one point she took care of two orphan gorillas, whom she named Pucker and Coco. Her object was to train these baby gorillas so that they could be returned to their natural home in the wild.

The notes in the margin represent one reader's responses. If you wish, cover these notes and write your own comments on a separate sheet of paper as you read. Then at a later point compare your own responses with the printed comments.

from
Gorillas in the Mist
DIAN FOSSEY

One day while walking in a new area, Pucker suddenly ran toward a large cluster of *Hagenia* trees on the edge of the forest leading to the mountain. Coco leapt from my arms in rapid pursuit—which was unusual. I thought they were making a dash for the mountain and was hastily taking out the bananas **2** when both infants halted below one of the largest trees. They peered up at the tree like children looking up a chimney on Christmas eve. I had never seen them so fascinated by a tree, nor could I determine what it was that so strongly attracted them. Suddenly the two began frenziedly climbing the huge trunk, leaving me even more puzzled. About thirty feet above the ground they stopped, pig-grunted at one another, and avidly started biting into a large bracket fungus. Previously I had noted these shelf-like growths, which protrude from *Hagenia* tree trunks and rather resemble overgrown solidified mushrooms. They are rare throughout the forest, and before acquiring Coco and Pucker I had never observed wild gorillas **3** being interested in them. Try as they might, neither Coco nor Pucker could pry the fungus from its anchorage on the trunk,

ONE READER'S RESPONSE

I guess the bananas would bring them back. **1**

I didn't know that gorillas eat fungus.

Close Reading of Nonfiction 387

1. GUIDED READING:
Making Inferences
Notice how this reader makes inferences about the gorillas based on the information given.

2. LITERARY ELEMENTS:
Simile
Note the humorous comparison.

3. GUIDED READING:
Using Context Clues
What clues help you guess what *anchorage* means? *Pry* and the root word *anchor* suggest that *anchorage* means "firm hold."

1. GUIDED READING:
Using Context Clues
Note that context clues cannot provide complete definition here. From a dictionary students can learn that an *elixir* is "a much sought-after preparation that supposedly maintains life indefinitely." Author shows humor in word choice.

2. GUIDED READING:
Recognizing Cause and Effect
Note that Fossey includes meat for gorillas because she now knows they prefer it over foliage or fruit.

3. LITERARY ELEMENTS:
Sensory Details
Identify details that appeal to each of the five senses. (Hearing: "boisterously banging"; Touch: "hugs"; Sight: "two separate pans bolted . . . to . . . playpen"; Taste: "bananas and wild blackberries"; Smell: "disinfectant.")

4. GUIDED READING:
Using Prior Knowledge
Notice how reader uses own experience to evaluate character's situation.

Close Reading
OF NONFICTION

1 What's an "elixir"?

This must have been an important discovery.

4 I like watching animals in a zoo, but I'm not sure I'd like to live next to them!

so they had to content themselves with gnawing chunks out of it. A half-hour later only a remnant remained. Reluctantly they descended, but as we walked on they gazed longingly back at the tree with the fungus elixir. Needless to say, the next day everyone in camp was asked to search the forest for bracket fungus!

Another rare food item that evoked squabbles between Coco and Pucker was the parasitic flowering shrub *Loranthus luteo-aurantiacus* belonging in the mistletoe family. Fortunately for the gorillas, the staff knew exactly where to find abundant supplies of the delicacy.

My studies with the gorillas showed that larvae and grub matter were often obtained from the inner hollow dead stalk material, but I was amazed to see the two captives ignore such treats as blackberries to search for worms and grubs. They often appeared to know exactly where to peel the slabs from live and dead tree trunks to find abundant deposits of larvae. Even while licking one slab clean, purring with pleasure over their feast, they were ripping off another slab for more burrowed protein sources. Worms, when discovered, were immediately torn in half—a rather revolting sight to watch—and each half was chewed with gusto, though not always ingested. After realizing that Coco and Pucker craved such **2** food I included boiled hamburger in their diet, which they ate before any of their cherished foliage or fruit.

Coco and Pucker's outdoor freedom carried over into the security of their room, where eventually nearly every conceivable item of natural gorilla food was introduced three times a day, along with medicine given on a routine schedule.

Usually the pair awoke voluntarily around 7:00 A.M. They weren't the least bit reticent about informing me they were awake by boisterously banging on the wire door between our **3** rooms. After the three of us exchanged good morning hugs, I gave them their milk formulas in two separate pans bolted down to the top of the playpen. Then, food such as bananas and wild blackberries was tossed into the outside run to get rid of the babies during the time it took us to scrub the floor

388 Nonfiction

and shelves of the room and discard every bit of vegetation and other debris left over from the previous day. During that time other members of the staff were collecting fresh vegetation for feeding and nesting purposes, so that when the runway door into the room was finally opened the gorillas could return to a "fresh forest," albeit one that smelled slightly of disinfectant.

If the weather was overcast or cold, they spent about an hour feeding contentedly before making their nests in the new vegetation. If it was sunny, they demanded to be taken outdoors, where they could unleash their pent-up energy in roughhouse wrestling, chasing, and tree-climbing.

Between 12:30 P.M. and 1:00 P.M. I would bring them back to the cabin to repeat the early morning routine of medication, favorite food, and fresh foliage. Afternoon activities were again dictated by weather, though the two ruffians were more content to rest during this time of day. At 4:00 P.M. old foliage was discarded for new along with piles of leafy *Vernonia* saplings for me, and later for them, to use as their night-nesting materials. The **1** 5:00 P.M. schedule was much the same except that the youngsters were left alone for an hour to feed. During this time their croons of pleasure and belch vocalizations nearly drowned out the noise of my typewriter in the adjoining room, lending an air of serenity and contentment to the near end of each day.

Once Coco and Pucker had eaten their fill, the four of us, including Cindy, set the cabin frame shaking as we chased, tumbled, and wrestled within the miniforest of their room. I recall those hours as some of the most joyful I have ever known at camp, because Pucker, somewhat inhibited during the day when other people were around the cabin, became ebullient and outgoing when just the four of us were alone together.

3   During these relaxed sessions I learned a great deal about

Dian Fossey shown with Pucker and Coco.

What are "belch vocalizations"? Have to look that up.

It sounds like they made a mess of the place but didn't get in trouble for it.

I think the word ebullient **2** must mean something like "enthusiastic." Will check.

1. LITERARY ELEMENTS:
Style
The author uses a variety of nouns to refer to the gorillas. Up to this point in the narrative, author has used their names *Coco* and *Pucker, infants, pair, babies, ruffians,* and *youngsters.*

2. GUIDED READING:
Context Clues
What clues help this reader guess the meaning of the word ebullient? *The words* inhibited *and* outgoing *are clues.*

3. GUIDED READING:
Paraphrasing
Ask students to restate this passage in their own words. (Because Coco and Pucker were used to her, author learned a lot more from them than she did from the gorillas she observed in the wild.)

Close Reading of Nonfiction

> **TRANSPARENCY 27**
> **Literary Elements**
> *Imagery* – examines the use of imagery to make unfamiliar things more clear to the reader.

1. GUIDED READING:
Making Connections
Notice how reader relates the selection to own experience.

2. LITERARY ELEMENTS:
Conflict
This reader recognizes Fossey's inner conflict.

Close Reading
OF NONFICTION

1 She found out that gorillas like to tickle each other. I'll have to watch for that when I visit the zoo.

2 She has mixed emotions—she doesn't want to lose them but knows how unfair it would be to keep them. I admire her.

gorilla behavior that I had not gained previously from the free-ranging animals who had yet to become totally habituated to my presence. Tickling between Coco and Pucker provoked many loud play chuckles and also lengthened their play sessions. Tentatively, I first tried out tickling Coco, and after receiving a very receptive response tried it later with Pucker. After a few weeks I changed approaches from mild "tickle-tickles" to drawn-out "oouchy-gouchy-goo-zoooom" tickles, much like those given by parents or grandparents when zeroing in with a teasing finger for a child's belly button. The term "oouchy-gouchy-goo-zoooom" is not in any dictionary, yet it seems to be an international and interspecific term that can evoke laughter and smiles from both human and nonhuman primates. Later I had occasion to tickle free-living gorilla youngsters in the same manner and was able to elicit the same delighted responses that Coco and Pucker had given. This was done very rarely for it was always necessary to keep in mind that the observer should not interfere with the behavior of the wild subjects.

When I felt that they were tiring from our strenuous sessions, I broke off the leafy tops of the *Vernonia* branches to place on fresh beds of moss on the highest storage shelf. The final positioning of the foliage signaled night-nest time to the infants. After about seven weeks, Coco and Pucker were able to construct their own night nests and showed selectivity in their choice of the fullest branches for their nests. That was exactly the type of independent behavior I had been hoping for, a necessity if the two were going to be reintroduced to the wild. During the night stillness I often was saddened by the thought of the inevitable separation between myself and the two captives, yet thrilled to imagine them as members of Group 8, free to spend the remainder of their lives in the forests of their birth.

Nonfiction

Looking at Yourself as a Reader

Think about your responses to this selection from Fossey's book. Did you enjoy reading it? Did you learn something from it? Would you be interested in reading more of this book?

If you wrote your own responses while you were reading the selection, compare your notes with the printed notes. Did you have similar reactions or not? Did the printed responses clarify any of your own reactions?

Which of the following statements best expresses the central idea of the selection? If you don't agree with any of the choices, state your own idea in a sentence or two.

1. Gorillas can be trained as house pets, just like cats and dogs.
2. Gorillas need to learn routines the way small children do.
3. A naturalist must guard against changing the natural behavior of creatures in the wild.
4. Gorillas eat a variety of foods besides fruit and vegetation.

OBJECTIVES
Students will distinguish facts from opinions. They will also identify the author's tone and recognize negative prefixes.

TEACHING RESOURCES C
Teacher's Notes, p. 2
Reading Check, p. 5
Reading Focus, p. 6
Study Guide, pp. 7, 8
Language Skills, p. 9
Building Vocabulary, p. 12
Selection Vocabulary Test, p. 14
Selection Test, p. 15

AV RESOURCES BINDER
Audiocassette 3, Side A

392 Nonfiction

FOCUS/MOTIVATION

Building on Prior Knowledge. Elicit more facts about World War II, such as when it occurred, which countries were on which side, who won. Students who have seen movies or television shows about the Holocaust may provide additional information. (The Nazis didn't persecute only the Jews; they killed six million Jews as well as gypsies, Poles, and other people they considered undesirable). Explain that Anne Frank's experiences occurred in Europe; a whole other part of World War II was being fought in Asia. A map would be helpful for locating Amsterdam, the Netherlands, and Germany.

Prereading Journal. Before students begin reading, have them write the journal assignment suggested at the bottom of page 393.

1. BACKGROUND

The Nazis invaded and controlled much of Europe: Austria and Czechoslovakia in 1938; Poland in 1939; Denmark and Norway the following spring. On May 10, 1940, the Germans invaded the Netherlands.

All Dutch Jews had to wear yellow stars. They were not allowed to ride public transportation or go to public schools. Within a short time, thousands of Jews were sent to concentration camps. In 1940 there were 140,000 Jews in Holland; only 35,000 survived.

BIOGRAPHY AND AUTOBIOGRAPHY

from The Diary of a Young Girl

ANNE FRANK

Before You Read

A diary is very private. In a diary, a writer can be as personal and honest as he or she wants to be. After all, a diary is not usually read by anyone except the writer. To keep their diaries private, some writers have even written them in a code that only they can read.

One of the most famous diaries in the world was kept by a teenaged girl, who hid in an attic during World War II. Anne Frank was a German Jewish girl whose family had fled to the Netherlands in 1933 to escape the Nazi persecutions against the Jews in Germany. Then trouble started in the Netherlands too. The freedom of Jews was brutally limited there by the occupying Nazis. Some Jewish families fled the country. Some went into hiding. Anne's diary, kept from June 14, 1942, till August 1, 1944, provides a touching human record of what it was like to hide, terrified, in a small crowded attic for two years.

Before you read, write in your own journal how you think you would feel if you had to hide for two years in a few small rooms on the top of an office building. You can never go outside. You are totally dependent on a few people who bring you food and news. How would you pass the time? What would you miss most?

READING THE SELECTION
Students of all ability levels will benefit from reading this selection aloud in class so that they can share their responses as they try to understand and empathize with the plight of Anne Frank and her family. In-class reading will also enable you to provide background information.

CREATIVE WRITING LINK
Invite students to keep an informal diary for a week. Suggest that students record individual observations, feelings, and comments about events and people, as Anne did in her diary. Students might also want to name their diaries as Anne did. At the end of the week, ask students whether or not they enjoyed this form of informal writing. Why or why not? How did it differ from other kinds of writing they have done?

1. GUIDED READING:
Identifying the Author's Purpose
Anne Frank states her purpose for keeping the diary.

2. GUIDED READING:
Interpreting Meaning
What do you think this saying means? You can take as much time as you need to get your thoughts just right when you write, but you cannot do so when you speak.

3. GUIDED READING:
Identifying Implied Ideas
What idea is implied by this repetition of the term "real friend"? She implies that a "real friend" is different—more special, more worthy—than a "regular friend."

4. GUIDED READING:
Making Inferences About Character
Based on this passage, what can you infer about Anne? She is unusual among her friends. She is serious-minded, sensitive, and inquisitive. She is also self-aware and plain-speaking.

Language and Vocabulary

Prefixes are word parts added to the front of a word. If you add the prefix *anti-* (meaning "against") to the word *war,* you get the word *antiwar,* "against war." Anne and her family were victims of *anti-Semitism,* which means "being against people because they are Jewish." The Franks often used to hear *antiaircraft* guns—guns directed "against" aircraft. Knowing prefixes will help you as you figure out the meanings of new words.

Saturday, June 20, 1942

I haven't written for a few days, because I wanted first of all to think about my diary. It's an odd idea for someone like me to keep a diary; not only because I have never done so before, but because it seems to me that neither I—nor for that matter anyone else—will be interested in the unbosomings¹ of a thirteen-year-old schoolgirl. Still, **1** what does that matter? I want to write, but more than that, I want to bring out all kinds of things that lie buried deep in my heart.

2 There is a saying that "paper is more patient than man"; it came back to me on one of my slightly melancholy days, while I sat chin in hand, feeling too bored and limp even to make up my mind whether to go out or stay at home. Yes, there is no doubt that paper is patient and as I don't intend to show this cardboard-covered notebook, bearing the proud name of "di- **3** ary," to anyone, unless I find a real friend, boy or girl, probably nobody cares. And now I come to the root of the matter, the reason for my starting a diary: it is that I have no such real friend.

Let me put it more clearly, since no one will believe that a girl of thirteen feels herself quite alone in the world, nor is it so. I have darling parents and a sister of sixteen. I know about thirty people who one might call friends—I have strings of boy friends, anxious to catch a glimpse of me and who, failing that, peep at me through mirrors in class. I have relations, aunts and uncles, who are darlings too, a good home, no—I don't seem to lack anything. But it's the same with all my friends, **4** just fun and joking, nothing more. I can never bring myself to talk of anything outside the common round. We don't seem to be able to get any closer, that is the root of the trouble. Perhaps I lack confidence, but anyway, there it is, a stubborn fact and I don't seem to be able to do anything about it.

Hence, this diary. In order to enhance in my mind's eye the picture of the friend for whom I have waited so long, I don't

---
1. **unbosomings** (un·bōōz′əm·ingz): confidences.

394 Nonfiction

COOPERATIVE LEARNING

Divide the class into small groups to discuss whether or not *The Diary of a Young Girl* should be required reading for students around the world. After they have had plenty of time to discuss the question, have each group work together to write an article for the school or local community newspaper. In their articles groups should share the results of their discussions, stating reasons given in support of and in opposition to the required reading of this selection.

---

want to set down a series of bald facts in a diary like most people do, but I want this diary itself to be my friend, and I shall call my friend Kitty.

Wednesday, July 8, 1942

Dear Kitty,

Years seem to have passed between Sunday and now. So much has happened, it is just as if the whole world had turned upside down. But I am still alive, Kitty, and that is the main thing, Daddy says.

Yes, I'm still alive, indeed, but don't ask where or how. You wouldn't understand a word, so I will begin by telling you what happened on Sunday afternoon.

At three o'clock (Harry[2] had just gone, but was coming back later) someone rang the front doorbell. I was lying lazily reading a book on the veranda in the sunshine, so I didn't hear it. A bit later, Margot appeared at the kitchen door looking very excited. "The S.S.[3] have sent a call-up notice for Daddy," she whispered. "Mummy has gone to see Mr. Van Daan already." (Van Daan is a friend who works with Daddy in the business.) It was a great shock to me, a call-up; everyone knows what that means. I picture concentration camps and lonely cells—should we allow him to be doomed to this? "Of course he won't go," declared Margot, while we waited together. "Mummy has gone to the Van Daans to discuss whether we should move into our hiding place tomorrow. The Van Daans are going with us, so we shall be seven in all." Silence. We couldn't talk anymore, thinking about Daddy, who, little knowing what was going on, was visiting some old people in the Joodse Invalide;[4] waiting for Mummy, the heat and suspense, all made us very overawed and silent.

Suddenly the bell rang again. "That is Harry," I said. "Don't open the door." Margot held me back, but it was not necessary as we heard Mummy and Mr. Van Daan downstairs, talking to Harry, then they came in and closed the door behind them. Each time the bell went, Margot or I had to creep softly down to see if it was Daddy, not opening the door to anyone else.

Margot and I were sent out of the room. Van Daan wanted to talk to Mummy alone. When we were alone together in our bedroom, Margot told me that the call-up was not for Daddy, but for her. I was more frightened than ever and began to cry. Margot is sixteen; would they really take girls of that age away alone? But thank goodness she won't go, Mummy said so herself; that must be what Daddy meant when he talked about us going into hiding.

Into hiding—where would we go, in a town or the country, in a house or a cottage, when, how, where . . . ?

These were questions I was not allowed to ask, but I couldn't get them out of my mind. Margot and I began to pack

---

2. **Harry:** a friend of Anne's.
3. **S.S.:** the dreaded Secret Police of the Nazis.
4. **Joodse Invalide** (yoodʹsə in·val·ēdʹ): the Jewish hospital.

**1
Using Context Clues**
What is a "call-up"? A person is told to report to authorities at a certain time and place. Then the person is taken away to a concentration camp. Many who were called up were killed immediately.

**2. GUIDED READING:
Making Inferences**
What can you infer from the fact that the Franks had a hiding place they could move into on a day's notice? They had anticipated that they would have to go into hiding and therefore had a place ready.

**3. GUIDED READING:
Making Inferences**
Why do you think Anne is more frightened when she learns about Margot's call-up? She probably sees her father as stronger and more able to take care of himself than a young, vulnerable girl. She may also be frightened that she, too, will be called up.

from The Diary of a Young Girl

1. GUIDED READING:
Identifying with Characters
If you were in Anne's situation, what would you take with you? Ask students to think about taking only what they could carry inconspicuously.

2. BACKGROUND
Note that Mr. Koophuis, Miep, and Henk are not Jewish. They risk severe punishments for helping to hide the Franks.

3. GUIDED READING:
Understanding Implied Ideas
Why wouldn't a Jew carry a suitcase? A Jew (remember they wore yellow stars) carrying a suitcase would attract attention and risk being arrested.

4. GUIDED READING:
Making Inferences
Why didn't Anne's parents tell her where the hiding place was? Maybe they felt she was too young to keep such an important secret. Or maybe they didn't want to burden her with knowledge that would have made her more anxious.

---

some of our most vital belongings into a school satchel. The first thing I put in was this diary, then hair curlers, handkerchiefs, schoolbooks, a comb, old letters; I put in the craziest things with the idea that we were going into hiding. But I'm not sorry, memories mean more to me than dresses.

At five o'clock Daddy finally arrived, and we phoned Mr. Koophuis[5] to ask if he could come around in the evening. Van Daan went and fetched Miep.[6] Miep has been in the business with Daddy since 1933 and has become a close friend, likewise her brand-new husband, Henk. Miep came and took some shoes, dresses, coats, underwear, and stockings away in her bag, promising to return in the evening. Then silence fell on the house; not one of us felt like eating anything, it was still hot and everything was very strange. We let our large upstairs room to a certain Mr. Goudsmit, a divorced man in his thirties, who appeared to have nothing to do on this particular evening; we simply could not get rid of him without being rude; he hung about until ten o'clock. At eleven o'clock Miep and Henk Van Santen arrived. Once again, shoes, stockings, books, and underclothes disappeared into Miep's bag and Henk's deep pockets, and at eleven-thirty they too disappeared. I was dog tired and although I knew that it would be my last night in my own bed, I fell asleep immediately and didn't wake up until Mummy called me at five-thirty the next morning. Luckily it was not so hot as Sunday; warm rain fell steadily all day. We put on heaps of clothes as if we were going to the North Pole, the sole reason being to take clothes with us. No Jew in our situation would have dreamed of going out with a suitcase full of clothing. I had on two vests, three pairs of pants, a dress, on top of that a skirt, jacket, summer coat, two pairs of stockings, lace-up shoes, woolly cap, scarf, and still more; I was nearly stifled before we started, but no one inquired about that.

Margot filled her satchel with schoolbooks, fetched her bicycle, and rode off behind Miep into the unknown, as far as I was concerned. You see I still didn't know where our secret hiding place was to be. At seven-thirty the door closed behind us. Moortje,[7] my little cat, was the only creature to whom I said farewell. She would have a good home with the neighbors. This was all written in a letter addressed to Mr. Goudsmit.

There was one pound of meat in the kitchen for the cat, breakfast things lying on the table, stripped beds, all giving the impression that we had left helter-skelter. But we didn't care about impressions, we only wanted to get away, only escape and arrive safely, nothing else. Continued tomorrow. . . .

Yours, Anne

---

5. **Mr. Koophuis** (kōp'hūs): a business associate of Mr. Frank's.
6. **Miep** (mēp).
7. **Moortje** (mōort'jə).

396 Nonfiction

"This is a photo as I would wish myself to look all the time. Then I would maybe have a chance to come to Hollywood."

Anne Frank, October 10, 1942

Monday, July 19, 1943

Dear Kitty,
North Amsterdam was very heavily bombed on Sunday. The destruction seems to be terrible. Whole streets lie in ruins, and it will take a long time before all the people are dug out. Up till now there are two hundred dead and countless wounded; the hospitals are crammed. You hear of children lost in the smoldering ruins, looking for their parents. I shudder when I recall the dull droning rumble in the distance, which for us marked the approaching destruction.

Yours, Anne

Friday, July 23, 1943

Dear Kitty,
Just for fun I'm going to tell you each person's first wish, when we are allowed to go outside again. Margot and Mr. Van Daan long more than anything for a hot bath filled to overflowing and want to stay in it for half an hour. Mrs. Van Daan wants most to go and eat cream cakes immediately. Dussel thinks of nothing but seeing Lotje, his wife; Mummy of her cup of coffee; Daddy is going to visit Mr. Vossen first; Peter the town and a cinema, while I should find it so blissful, I shouldn't know where to start! But most of all, I long for a home

from The Diary of a Young Girl

Cultural Diversity

The Nazis put to death millions of people whose cultural or religious backgrounds differed from their own, including Jews, Catholics, Gypsies, and so on. Invite the class to discuss the following questions: What causes people to be afraid of or to be angry with people they perceive as being different? Have you ever been afraid of or angry with someone whose language, religion, or dress differed from yours? What happened? Have you ever been treated badly because you were different? How did this feel? What can each of us do to prevent a tragedy like Anne Frank's from ever happening again?

1. GUIDED READING:
Interpreting Meaning
What do you think she is saying here? Everyone's moods are affected by the lack of freedom, poor food, and fear.

2. LITERARY ELEMENTS:
Irony
One kind of irony occurs when readers know something that a character doesn't. Have students read "About the Author" (page 401) and explain the tragic irony in this entry.

3. LITERARY ELEMENTS:
Simile
What is being compared in this extended simile? Ask students to identify the blue heaven ("Secret Annexe"), black clouds (the Nazis), people fighting below (the war outside).

---

of our own, to be able to move freely and to have some help with my work again at last, in other words—school. . . .

                              Yours, Anne

Monday evening, November 8, 1943

Dear Kitty,

If you were to read my pile of letters one after another, you would certainly be struck by the many different moods in which they are written. It annoys me that I am so dependent on the atmosphere here, but I'm certainly not the only one—we all find it the same. If I read a book that impresses me, I have to take myself firmly in hand, before I mix with other people; otherwise they would think my mind rather queer. At the moment, as you've probably noticed, I'm going through a spell of being depressed. I really couldn't tell you why it is, but I believe it's just because I'm a coward, and that's what I keep bumping up against.

This evening, while Elli was still here, there was a long, loud, penetrating ring at the door. I turned white at once, got a tummy ache and heart palpitations,[8] all from fear. At night, when I'm in bed, I see myself alone in a dungeon, without Mummy and Daddy. Sometimes I wander by the roadside or our "Secret Annexe" is on fire, or they come and take us away at night. I see everything as if it is actually taking place, and this gives me the feeling that it may all happen to me very soon! Miep often says she envies us for possessing such tranquillity here. That may be true, but she is not thinking about all our fears. I simply can't imagine that the world will ever be normal for us again. I do talk about "after the war," but then it is only a castle in the air, something that will never really happen. If I think back to our old house, my girl friends, the fun at school, it is just as if another person lived it all, not me.

I see the eight of us with our "Secret Annexe" as if we were a little piece of blue heaven, surrounded by heavy black rain clouds. The round, clearly defined spot where we stand is still safe, but the clouds gather more closely about us and the circle

The building where the Franks and their friends hid is now called the Anne Frank House.

---

8. **palpitations** (pal′pə·tā′shənz): rapid heartbeats.

CLOSURE

Have three volunteers read aloud passages from the three excerpts mentioned in "Tone" (pages 400–401). Have them try to communicate the writer's tone with their voices.

RETEACHING

Ask the students to define *fact* and *opinion*. Then have them find three examples of each in the selection. You might discuss whether the diary is mostly facts, mostly opinions, or a combination of both. How could one *prove* that the facts in the diary are true? (Historical records; the testimony of Anne's father and Miep)

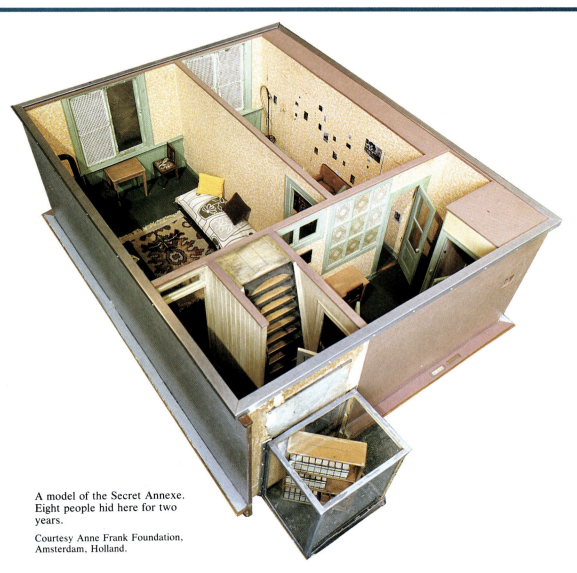

A model of the Secret Annexe. Eight people hid here for two years.

Courtesy Anne Frank Foundation, Amsterdam, Holland.

FOR STUDY AND DISCUSSION

Identifying Facts

1. She will use it as a substitute for a deep, intimate friendship.

2. A possible summary: The S.S. called up Margot. Mr. Frank wasn't home, so Mrs. Frank went to the Van Daans' home to discuss going into hiding. Margot and Anne packed, and Miep and Henk carried away some of their things. Early the next morning they dressed in as many clothes as they could. Margot left with Miep; the others followed, leaving Anne's cat behind.

3. North Amsterdam had been heavily bombed. Anne shudders when she recalls the rumbling noise before the bombing.

4. Anne wants to be in her own home with her family, to move about freely, and to go to school.

5. She fears the Nazis will discover them; that she will be separated from her family and imprisoned.

She sees them as a small piece of "blue heaven" surrounded by threatening clouds that are closing in.

Interpreting Meanings

6. Possible answers: Yes, because Anne confides in the diary just as she said she wanted to.

which separates us from the approaching danger closes more and more tightly. Now we are so surrounded by danger and darkness that we bump against each other, as we search desperately for a means of escape. We all look down below, where people are fighting each other, we look above, where it is quiet and beautiful, and meanwhile we are cut off by the great dark mass, which will not let us go upward, but which stands before us as an <u>impenetrable</u> wall; it tries to crush us, but cannot do so yet. I can only cry and <u>implore</u>: "Oh, if only the black circle could <u>recede</u> and open the way for us!"

Yours, Anne

from The Diary of a Young Girl

EXTENSION AND ENRICHMENT
Drama. Students may act out a scene from Frances Goodrich and Albert Hackett's play *The Diary of Anne Frank* (Doubleday, 1952).

Social Studies. Have students research and prepare brief oral reports on one aspect of World War II they would like to know more about. Call on volunteers to present their reports to the class.

Students may be interested in looking at Miep Gies's book about Anne Frank and her family, *Anne Frank Remembered* (Simon & Schuster, 1987).

Yes, the diary contains Anne's deepest thoughts and feelings.

Applying Meanings
7. Possible answer: It made me feel what a great loss—and how tragic and stupid—the death of this young girl was.
8. Responses will vary. You might ask volunteers to read aloud their entries.
9. Anne's story told in the third person would lose its immediacy and vividness. A biographer would not know Anne's feelings and thoughts.

FOCUS ON READING
Distinguishing Between Facts and Opinions
1. This is an opinion.
2. These are facts.
3. This is a fact.

Possible answers: "Memories mean more to me than dresses" (page 396); "But most of all, I long for a home of our own . . ." (page 397); "It annoys me that I am so dependent on the atmosphere here" (page 398).

LITERARY ELEMENTS
Tone
1. Answers will vary. Some may see it as comic or mildly ironic; others may think she is straightforward.
2. Possible answer: Her tone shows horror and fear.

400

For Study and Discussion

IDENTIFYING FACTS
1. On June 20, 1942, what reason does Anne give for starting a diary?
2. Summarize the events reported by Anne on July 8, 1942.
3. What happened on July 19, 1943, that made Anne shudder?
4. What did Anne wish on July 23, 1943?
5. What fears does Anne confide to her diary on November 8, 1943? Describe how she visualizes the eight people in the Secret Annexe.

INTERPRETING MEANINGS
6. Do you think "Kitty" did become the friend Anne longed for? Do you think Anne succeeded in bringing out things that lay buried in her heart?

APPLYING MEANINGS
7. How did this diary make you feel about Anne and about what eventually happened to her and her family? (See About the Author, page 401.)
8. Read your responses to the questions at the bottom of page 393. Are they the same as or different from Anne's responses?
9. How would Anne's story be different if it were told by a historian or biographer?

Focus on Reading

DISTINGUISHING BETWEEN FACTS AND OPINIONS
In her entry for June 20, 1942, Anne says "I don't want to set down a series of bald facts in a diary like most people do." Anne wants instead to "bring out all kinds of things that lie buried deep in my heart."

Below are several quotations from Anne's diary on July 8, 1942. Which are factual statements: that is, statements that could be proved true? Which are opinion statements: that is, statements that express Anne's feelings?

1. ". . . it is just as if the whole world had turned upside down."
2. "Miep has been in the business with Daddy since 1933 and has become a close friend . . ."
3. "At seven-thirty the door closed behind us."

Find three other expressions of Anne's feelings in these diary entries.

Literary Elements

TONE
Tone means a speaker's or writer's attitude. Here are some words that can describe tone: sarcastic, serious, critical.

When we speak, we can indicate tone by using our voices and facial expressions. In writing we can reveal tone only through words. We can't rely on our voices or facial expressions.

1. How would you describe Anne's tone when she says toward the end of the entry for July 8, 1942:
   "I was nearly stifled before we started, but no one inquired about that."
   Is she being sarcastic? Comic? Or just straightforward?

400 Nonfiction

2. How would you describe Anne's tone on July 19, 1943? (Frightened? Confident? Sarcastic?)

3. How would you describe Anne's tone on November 8, 1943? (Fearful? Hopeless? Angry?)

Focus on Informative Writing

PLANNING A BIOGRAPHICAL REPORT

In a **biographical report,** you present information about a person's life and achievements.

When you choose a subject for a report, ask yourself these questions:

What is interesting or special about the person?
What has the person accomplished?
Can I get the information I need?

To gather details for a report, you need to use **sources** about your subject. If she or he is a celebrity, you can use books or articles in newspapers and magazines. If you are writing about a family member or a friend, you may be able to **interview** the person.

Choose a subject for a biographical report: for example, a famous person from history such as Anne Frank, a current celebrity, or a family member or friend you admire. Fill out a chart like the one below. Save your notes.

Biographical Report Chart
Subject: _____
Date and Place of Birth: _____
Childhood/Education: _____
Job/Profession: _____
Achievements/Special Awards: _____
Opinions/Outlook on Life: _____
Statements/Quotations: _____
Overall Importance: _____

About the Author

The life of **Anne Frank** (1929–1945) was tragically short. She was born in Frankfurt-am-Main in Germany on June 12, 1929, and she died in a concentration camp in March 1945. Anne lived only 16 years. Tragically, only two months after Anne died, the Allies liberated her camp. The last entry in Anne's diary is August 1, 1944. It was three days after this date that the Nazis raided the Secret Annexe. All the occupants of the attic were sent off to concentration camps. Of all the occupants of the Secret Annexe, only Mr. Frank survived. Anne's red-checked diary was later found by Miep, lying among a pile of old books, magazines, and newspapers in the Secret Annexe. If you are interested in knowing more about Anne, you should read her diary. A play and a movie have also been made about Anne. Miep Gies tells the story in her own words in *Anne Frank Remembered.*

from The Diary of a Young Girl

OBJECTIVES
Students will organize a biographical report, distinguish between fact and opinion, and recognize irony and suffixes.

FOCUS/MOTIVATION
Building on Prior Knowledge. Write two headings—*Facts* and *Opinions*—on the chalkboard, and ask students to make some statements about Lincoln based on what they already know about him. The class should decide whether statements are facts or opinions, and then write each statement in the appropriate column.

> **TEACHING RESOURCES C**
> Teacher's Notes, p. 17
> Reading Check, p. 20
> Reading Focus, p. 21
> Study Guide, pp. 22, 23
> Language Skills, p. 24
> Building Vocabulary, p. 27
> Selection Vocabulary Test, p. 29
> Selection Test, p. 30

A Backwoods Boy

RUSSELL FREEDMAN

Before You Read

This is the second chapter of a Newbery-Award-winning "photobiography" of Abraham Lincoln. The book is called a "photobiography" because many historical photographs illustrate the text. Lincoln, as every American schoolchild knows, was born in the backwoods and became President of the United States in 1861. Before you begin reading, talk about the Presidents that you know something about. What were their backgrounds? Do you think a person born very, very poor could get to be President today?

A replica of Lincoln's Kentucky birthplace.
Illinois State Historical Library, Springfield

Establishing a Purpose for Reading. Ask students to form a single general statement that summarizes Lincoln's early life.
Prereading Journal. List what you think are the three most important things you know about Abraham Lincoln's life.

READING THE SELECTON
In class, read aloud and discuss the quotation on page 403. Make sure students understand what Lincoln is saying here. Ask them to decide whether they agree or disagree with Lincoln's summary of his life.

Because of its brevity and simple vocabulary, students of all ability levels should have no trouble reading the rest of this selection independently. You might assign it as homework.

Language and Vocabulary

A suffix is a word part that is added to the end of a word. Suffixes can create whole new words. (For example, a suffix makes the verb *toddle* into the noun *toddler* in the third paragraph of this selection.) Suffixes are often useful when you have to figure out the meaning of a new word. They are also useful in writing, since they can help you say something in fewer words. For example, it is much simpler to say "Abe Lincoln was still a toddler," than to say "Abe Lincoln was still a baby who would toddle around."

1. BACKGROUND
Here is the complete stanza from Thomas Gray's "Elegy Written in a Country Churchyard": Let not Ambition mock their useful toil, / Their homely joys, and destiny obscure; / Nor Grandeur hear with a disdainful smile / The short and simple annals of the poor."

2. GUIDED READING:
Understanding Implied Ideas
Why do you suppose Lincoln wouldn't talk about his early life? Perhaps it was too painful for him, or maybe he didn't want people to feel sorry for him.

3. GUIDED READING:
Distinguishing Facts from Opinions
Are these details facts or opinions? They are facts; they can be proved by checking reference books.

4. GUIDED READING:
Self-Questioning
Students will wonder what a "blab school" is. It is defined in the next sentence.

It is a great piece of folly to attempt to make anything out of my early life. It can all be condensed into a simple sentence,
1 *and that sentence you will find in Gray's "Elegy"—"the short and simple annals[1] of the poor." That's my life, and that's all you or anyone else can make out of it.*
—Abraham Lincoln

2 Abraham Lincoln never liked to talk much about his early life. A poor backwoods farm boy, he grew up swinging an ax on frontier homesteads in Kentucky, Indiana, and Illinois.

3 He was born near Hodgenville, Kentucky, on February 12, 1809, in a log cabin with one window, one door, a chimney, and a hardpacked dirt floor. His parents named him after his pioneer grandfather. The first Abraham Lincoln had been shot dead by hostile Indians in 1786, while planting a field of corn in the Kentucky wilderness.

Young Abraham was still a toddler when his family packed their belongings and moved to another log-cabin farm a few miles north, on Knob Creek. That was the first home he could remember, the place where he ran and played as a barefoot boy.

He remembered the bright waters of Knob Creek as it tumbled past the Lincoln cabin and disappeared into the Kentucky hills. Once he fell into the rushing creek and almost drowned before he was pulled out by a neighbor boy. Another time he caught a fish and gave it to a passing soldier.

Lincoln never forgot the names of his first teachers—Zachariah Riney followed by Caleb Hazel—who ran a windowless log schoolhouse two miles away. It was called **4** a "blab school." Pupils of all ages sat on rough wooden benches and bawled out

---
1. **annals** (an'əlz): yearly records.

A Backwoods Boy

MEETING INDIVIDUAL NEEDS

ESL/LEP • This story contains many compound words. Write the following words and definitions on the chalkboard, and ask students to find the corresponding compound words in the text: *photobiography*, a life history that includes many photographs; *schoolchild*, a child who attends school; *backwoods*, of the woods or countryside; *hardpacked*, packed together tightly; *schoolhouse*, a building used as a school; *kinfolk*, relatives.

MEETING INDIVIDUAL NEEDS

ESL/LEP • In describing Lincoln and his father, the author uses several adjectives that may be unfamiliar—*burly*, *barrel-chested*, *sociable*, *spindly*, and *unruly*. Write these on the chalkboard, and ask the class to suggest synonyms.

---

1. GUIDED READING:
Identifying Factual Sources
What source(s) might the author have used for this fact? A marriage certificate, a family Bible, a dated photograph, or a letter

2. GUIDED READING:
Recognizing Subjective Details
Although biographies consist mostly of objective, factual details, they can also contain subjective details, as in this statement of Lincoln's feelings.

3
Using Context Clues
What is a "lean-to"? It's a crude three-sided shelter. (It must have been freezing during the winter.)

4. LITERARY ELEMENTS:
Recognizing Metaphor
Ask students to identify the metaphor (a tall spider of a boy) and explain why it is in quotation marks. Somebody described Lincoln in this way; the source isn't cited.

---

their lessons aloud. Abraham went there with his sister Sarah, who was two years older, when they could be spared from their chores at home. Holding hands, they would walk through scrub trees and across creek bottoms to the schoolhouse door. They learned their numbers from one to ten, and a smattering of reading, writing, and spelling.

Their parents couldn't read or write at all. Abraham's mother, Nancy, signed her name by making a shakily drawn mark. He would remember her as a thin, sad-eyed woman who labored beside her husband in the fields. She liked to gather the children around her in the evening to recite prayers and Bible stories she had memorized.

His father, Thomas, was a burly, barrel-chested farmer and carpenter who had **1** worked hard at homesteading since marrying Nancy Hanks in 1806. A sociable fellow, his greatest pleasure was to crack jokes and swap stories with his chums. With painful effort, Thomas Lincoln could scrawl his name. Like his wife, he had grown up without education, but that wasn't unusual in those days. He supported his family by living off his own land, and he watched for a chance to better himself.

In 1816, Thomas decided to pull up stakes again and move north to Indiana, which was about to join the Union as the nation's nineteenth state. Abraham was **2** seven. He remembered the one-hundred-mile journey as the hardest experience of his life. The family set out on a cold morning in December, loading all their possessions on two horses. They crossed the Ohio River on a makeshift ferry, traveled through towering forests, then hacked a path through tangled underbrush until they reached their new homesite near the backwoods community of Little Pigeon Creek.

Thomas put up a temporary winter **3** shelter—a crude, three-sided lean-to of logs and branches. At the open end, he kept a fire burning to take the edge off the cold and scare off the wild animals. At night, wrapped in bearskins and huddled by the fire, Abraham and Sarah listened to wolves howl and panthers scream.

Abraham passed his eighth birthday in the lean-to. He was big for his age, "a tall **4** spider of a boy," and old enough to handle an ax. He helped his father clear the land. They planted corn and pumpkin seeds between the tree stumps. And they built a new log cabin, the biggest one yet, where Abraham climbed a ladder and slept in a loft beneath the roof.

Soon after the cabin was finished, some of Nancy's kinfolk arrived. Her aunt and uncle with their adopted son Dennis had decided to follow the Lincolns to Indiana. Dennis Hanks became an extra hand for Thomas and a big brother for Abraham, someone to run and wrestle with.

A year later, Nancy's aunt and uncle lay dead, victims of the dreaded "milk sickness" (now known to be caused by a poisonous plant called white snake root). An epidemic of the disease swept through the Indiana woods in the summer of 1818. Nancy had nursed her relatives until the

404 Nonfiction

MEETING INDIVIDUAL NEEDS

Visual, Auditory, and Kinesthetic Learners • Invite interested students to look in books such as *Bartlett's Familiar Quotations* for well known quotations by Lincoln that appear in this selection. Have students who are kinesthetic learners write the quotations on large banners, and hang the banners around the room. Students who are auditory learners could make audiotapes of the quotations. Extend the activity by asking students to collect quotations and to create banners and tapes for other former presidents.

Abraham Lincoln in June 1860, when he was a presidential candidate. Photograph by Alexander Hessler. Gelatin silver print.

National Portrait Gallery, Smithsonian Institution, Washington, D.C.

A Backwoods Boy 405

CLOSURE
Ask students to tell what they liked best about this biographical excerpt—the facts, the opinions, or the photographs.

RETEACHING
Have students identify the various factual sources a biographer can use for a subject long dead. Ask them to think of different sources a biographer might use when the subject is alive (interviews with subject, friends, relatives).

1. GUIDED READING:
Identifying Sources
Where could this quotation have come from? The quotation might have come from a letter or a diary Dennis Hanks wrote. It might have been written down by someone who heard him say it.

2. GUIDED READING:
Understanding Main Ideas
Ask students to state the paragraph's main idea in one sentence. (Possible answer: Sarah Bush Johnston was a good wife to Thomas Lincoln and a good stepmother to his children.)

Sarah Bush Lincoln.
Illinois State Historical Library, Springfield, Illinois.

Thomas Lincoln.
The Abraham Lincoln Museum, Harrogate, Tennessee.

end, and then she too came down with the disease. Abraham watched his mother toss in bed with chills, fever, and pain for seven days before she died at the age of thirty-four. "She knew she was going to die," Dennis Hanks recalled. "She called up the children to her dying side and told them to be good and kind to their father, to one another, and to the world."

Thomas built a coffin from black cherry wood, and nine-year-old Abraham whittled the pegs that held the wooden planks together. They buried Nancy on a windswept hill, next to her aunt and uncle. Sarah, now eleven, took her mother's place, cooking, cleaning, and mending clothes for her father, brother, and cousin Dennis in the forlorn and lonely cabin.

Thomas Lincoln waited for a year. Then he went back to Kentucky to find himself a new wife. He returned in a four-horse wagon with a widow named Sarah Bush Johnston, her three children, and all her household goods. Abraham and his sister were fortunate, for their stepmother was a warm and loving person. She took the motherless children to her heart and raised them as her own. She also spruced up the neglected Lincoln cabin, now shared by eight people who lived, ate, and slept in a single smoky room with a loft.

Abraham was growing fast, shooting

406 Nonfiction

EXTENSION AND ENRICHMENT

Speaking. Have students imagine themselves Lincoln's presidential campaign manager. Ask them to write a brief campaign speech in which they stress the fine qualities of character that Lincoln demonstrated in his boyhood.

Students should have a chance to try out their speeches in small groups to get some feedback. Give them time to revise and rehearse their speeches before calling on volunteers to deliver their speeches in class. You may wish to record speeches for playback later.

TRANSPARENCY 27

Literary Elements

Imagery – examines the use of imagery to make unfamiliar things more clear to the reader.

1 up like a sunflower, a spindly youngster with big bony hands, unruly black hair, a dark complexion, and luminous gray eyes. He became an expert with the ax, working alongside his father, who also hired him out to work for others. For twenty-five cents a day, the boy dug wells, built pigpens, split fence rails, felled trees. "My how he could chop!" exclaimed a friend. "His ax would flash and bite into a sugar tree or a sycamore, and down it would come. If you heard him felling trees in a clearing, you would say there were three men at work, the way the trees fell."

Meanwhile, he went to school "by littles," a few weeks one winter, maybe a month the next. Lincoln said later that all his schooling together "did not amount to one year." Some fragments of his schoolwork still survive, including a verse that he wrote in his homemade arithmetic book: "Abraham Lincoln/his hand and pen/he will be good but/god knows When." 2

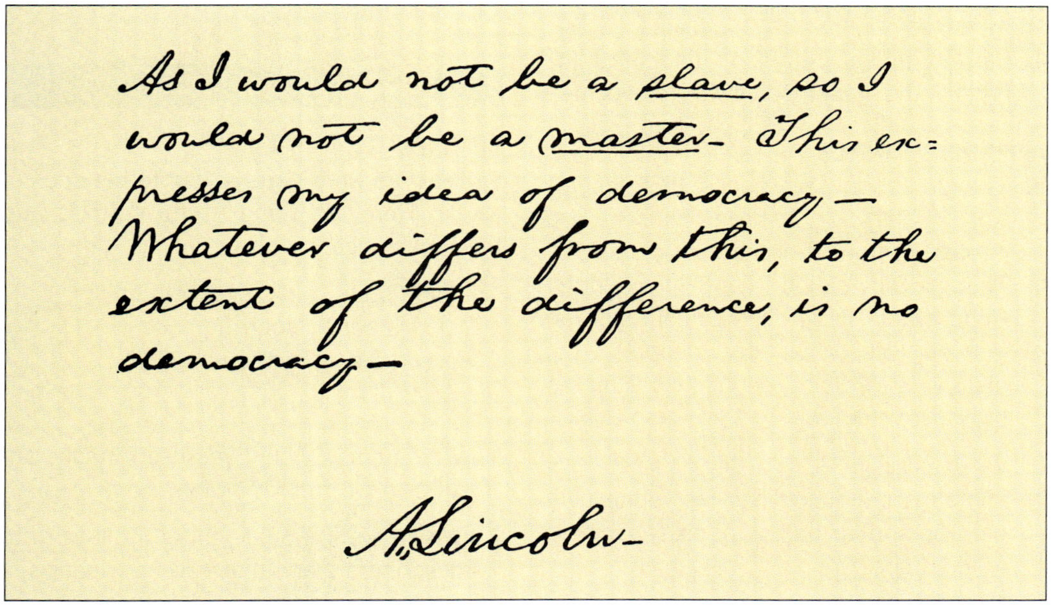

As I would not be a slave, so I would not be a master– This expresses my idea of democracy– Whatever differs from this, to the extent of the difference, is no democracy–

A. Lincoln–

A copy of a fragment of a manuscript containing Lincoln's idea of democracy. The fragment is undated but might have been written around 1858. No one knows where the original fragment is today.

1. LITERARY ELEMENTS: Recognizing Similes

What is the simile in this description? The simile is "shooting up like a sunflower." Students should also note the specific details of Lincoln's appearance (one of the ways of revealing character).

2

Using Context Clues

Note that the context defines "by littles," an expression no longer used.

PORTFOLIO ASSESSMENT

Biographies, or true stories about people, are usually, but not necessarily, written about famous people. Students may want to write a short episode of a biography about a person they particularly admire. The person may be living or dead, famous or virtually unknown. Ask students to plan how they will conduct their research before they begin and remind them to narrow their topics to short episodes in the person's life. Consult with students in the planning stages to agree on how their biographical episodes will be assessed. (For more information on student portfolios, see the *Portfolio Assessment and Professional Support Materials* booklet in your teaching resources.)

FOR STUDY AND DISCUSSION

Identifying Facts

1. Possible answers: During his childhood he lived in Kentucky and Indiana. His mother died when he was nine. He had less than a year of formal schooling.

Interpreting Meanings

2. Possible answers: Lincoln did not have an easy childhood. Or Lincoln's family was a typical pioneer family.
3. Answers will vary. Many students will think his mother's death was hardest.
4. Answers will vary. Most will say No. Others may think that the facts that he was a hard worker and that he tried to do his best in every task hint at his adult life.

Applying Meanings

5. He summed up his life as being the typical life of a poor person.
   Possible answers: Jesse Jackson, Lyndon Johnson, Bette Midler, Elvis Presley, Oprah Winfrey.
6. Answers will vary. Possible answer: Lincoln's story tells us that diligence, perseverance, and steadfastness can overcome hardships.
   Yes. Many boys and girls live in poverty; some are not able to go to school.

408

For Study and Discussion

IDENTIFYING FACTS

1. This biography of Lincoln is crammed with facts. Skim the selection again. Then close your book and write down three facts you learned about Lincoln's childhood.

INTERPRETING MEANINGS

2. Write down one **general statement** you would make about Lincoln's early life.
3. What do you think was the hardest part of Lincoln's early life?
4. Can you find any hints in Lincoln's childhood of the great man he was to become?

APPLYING MEANINGS

5. The quotation that opens this excerpt was written by Lincoln himself. He quotes in turn from a long poem by Thomas Gray called "Elegy in a Country Churchyard." How does Lincoln sum up his early life? What other people in the history of America could also sum up their lives this way?
6. What **message** do you think the story of Lincoln's childhood has for young people? Do similar hardships exist for boys or girls today?

Literary Elements

IRONY

We feel a sense of **irony** when *we* know something that a character does *not* know. For instance, suppose we read that Reggie Jackson as a young boy once said sadly, "I'll just never be able to hit that ball." *We* know that this boy went on to become a famous ballplayer. This knowledge gives us a sense of irony. We know something that the character did *not* know at the time. Lincoln wrote in his arithmetic book that he "will be good" sometime, "but god knows When." What do *we* know now, that Lincoln *didn't* know then?

We also feel irony when something happens that is totally different from what most people expect. For instance, Lincoln had about one year of school. What do most people expect would become of someone with so little formal education?

Language and Vocabulary

SUFFIXES

Suffixes are word parts added to the ends of words. Here are some useful suffixes and their meanings:

- *-dom* "state, rank, or condition"
- *-ism* "manner, doctrine"
- *-less* "lacking, without"
- *-ful* "full of"

1. Which suffix would you use to make another noun from the noun *king*?
2. Which suffix would you add to a word to describe a place that had no windows?
3. Which suffix would you add to a word to describe a situation that is full of pain?
4. What political systems are described using the suffix *-ism*?

408 Nonfiction

Focus on Informative Writing

ORGANIZING A BIOGRAPHICAL REPORT
When you write a biographical report, you should follow **chronological** or **time order.** With this method, you tell events in the order in which they happen.

You can help your reader follow your report more easily if you use **transitional words and phrases.** For example, notice how Russell Freedman uses these transitions to show time order in the paragraph describing Nancy's death: *a year later, until, then, before* (see pages 404–406).

Write an outline like the one below for a biographical report of three paragraphs. Save your notes.

I. Introduction
    A. Attention grabber: _____
    B. Statement of subject and main idea: _____

II. Body
    Facts/Anecdotes about subject: _____

III. Conclusion
    A. Restatement of main idea: _____
    B. Summary of person's importance: _____

About the Author

Russell Freedman (1929–   ) lives in New York City. He has written over thirty books for children and young adults, including *Children of the Wild West, Immigrant Kids,* and *Two Thousand Years of Space Travel.* His book on Lincoln won the Newbery Award for the most distinguished contribution to children's literature in 1988. Before writing that book, Freedman read widely, including all of Lincoln's letters and his notes. At the end of the book, Freedman has a section called "In Lincoln's Footsteps." There he lists all the historical sites he visited, places that played a part in Lincoln's life. You yourself can follow this Lincoln Heritage Trail through Kentucky, Indiana, Illinois, Pennsylvania, and Washington, D.C.

OBJECTIVES
Students will recognize narrative elements, visualize descriptions, write a description of life in a community, and use context clues for unfamiliar words.

FOCUS/MOTIVATION
Building on Prior Knowledge. Have someone read aloud what a history textbook (American history or world history for junior high students) says about the Vietnam war. Also use a world map to locate Vietnam.

Establishing a Purpose for Reading. The next two selections are about Vietnam. As they read, ask students to consider which kind of "history" of Vietnam (these personal narratives or the textbook history) they find more satisfying, and why.

> **TEACHING RESOURCES C**
> Teacher's Notes, p. 33
> Reading Check, p. 35
> Reading Focus, p. 36
> Study Guide, pp. 37, 38
> Language Skills, p. 39
> Building Vocabulary, p. 42
> Selection Vocabulary Test, p. 44
> Selection Test, p. 45
>
> **AV RESOURCES BINDER**
> Audiocassette 3, Side A

Prereading Journal. See the assignment in "Before You Read," this page. If you wish to give students a choice of assignments, you might ask them to list three things they know about crocodiles.

READING THE SELECTION
Most students will be able to read this selection in one class sitting. With slower classes you may want to divide the selection into two parts. Read aloud and discuss the introductory section (to "So Close," page 413). Then ask students to read silently through the point where Trung and his relatives realize that a crocodile has grabbed the young bride (bottom, page 416). You can assign the rest of the selection as homework, or read it aloud in class the next day.

HISTORY

The Land I Lost

HUYNH QUANG NHUONG

Before You Read

In 1961, the United States began sending military advisors to South Vietnam, a country in Southeast Asia. Within a few years, the United States was fully involved in South Vietnam's war against the Communists in North Vietnam. The war tore Vietnam apart. People in the United States were deeply divided over this country's involvement in the Vietnam war, and traces of this conflict still persist today. Here is one former South Vietnamese soldier's recollection of a more peaceful time in his beautiful country. These essays are from his book called *The Land I Lost*.

Before you read, write in your journal three things that you think of when you hear the word *Vietnam*.

(The writer's name is pronounced whyng quong nuong.)

The Land I Lost 411

SOCIAL STUDIES LINK
You may want to discuss with students some of the issues that arose from our country's involvement in the war in Vietnam. After students have read the material on page 411, ask them if they know why many people protested the United States' involvement in Vietnam. Have students interview people who remember the Vietnam era and/or invite a speaker into class to discuss the war and the anti-war movement. Culminate the activity with a second discussion to give students the opportunity to express their responses to and opinions about what they have learned.

1. LITERARY ELEMENTS:
Recognizing Autobiography
Since this is nonfiction, the pronoun *I* indicates that the narrator is the author and that this is an autobiographical account.

2. GUIDED READING:
Visualizing Setting
Have students try to picture the village from these descriptive details. The specific verbs *scattered* and *propped* help us visualize the houses' location.

3. GUIDED READING:
Making Comparisons
Note the villagers' clever, inexpensive way of protecting themselves. Ask students how people in our society protect themselves and their houses.

4. GUIDED READING:
Drawing Conclusions
Why did the people go to the jungle? They hunted animals for food. The rest of the paragraph is about food.

Language and Vocabulary

Context clues are clues contained in a sentence or passage which help you figure out the meaning of an unfamiliar word. If the context does not actually define an unfamiliar word, it will often give you enough information about the word so that you can make a pretty good guess about its meaning.

In the very first sentence of this story, for example, the writer says he lived in a small *hamlet*. If you do not know what a hamlet is, you will find clues in the first three paragraphs. There are houses in a hamlet. Some hamlets have shops and marketplaces. People travel to distant hamlets for certain supplies. By this time, you would be pretty sure that a hamlet is a town or village. As you read, use information in the context to help you figure out the meanings of any unfamiliar words.

1 I was born on the central highlands of Vietnam in a small hamlet on a riverbank that had a deep jungle on one side and a chain of high mountains on the other. Across the river, rice fields stretched to the slopes of another chain of mountains.

2 There were fifty houses in our hamlet, scattered along the river or propped against the mountainsides. The houses were made of bamboo and covered with coconut leaves, and each was surrounded by a deep trench to protect it from wild animals or **3** thieves. The only way to enter a house was to walk across a "monkey bridge"—a single bamboo stick that spanned the trench. At night we pulled the bridges into our houses and were safe.

There were no shops or marketplaces in our hamlet. If we needed supplies—medicine, cloth, soaps, or candles—we had to cross over the mountains and travel to a town nearby. We used the river mainly for traveling to distant hamlets, but it also provided us with plenty of fish.

During the six-month rainy season, nearly all of us helped plant and cultivate fields of rice, sweet potatoes, Indian mustard, eggplant, tomatoes, hot peppers, and corn. But during the dry season, we became hunters and turned to the jungle. **4**

Wild animals played a very large part in our lives. There were four animals we feared the most: the tiger, the lone wild hog, the crocodile, and the horse snake. Tigers were always trying to steal cattle. Sometimes, however, when a tiger became old and slow it became a maneater. But a lone wild hog was even more dangerous

412 Nonfiction

GEOGRAPHY LINK

Through the author's eyes, we get a glimpse of daily life in the highlands of Vietnam. Included in this scene are animals native to the area. Ask students to find out about the wild animals mentioned in the story. Suggest that students find information about and pictures of the tigers, wild hogs, crocodiles, monkeys, squirrels, birds, raccoons, and snakes found in the highlands of Vietnam. Students could work in small groups, each group focusing on one of the animals.

---

than a tiger. It attacked every creature in sight, even when it had no need for food. Or it did crazy things, such as charging into the hamlet in broad daylight, ready to kill or to be killed.

1 The river had different dangers: crocodiles. But of all the animals, the most hated and feared was the huge horse snake. It was sneaky and attacked people and cattle just for the joy of killing. It would either crush its victim to death or poison it with a bite.

Like all farmers' children in the hamlet, I started working at the age of six. My seven sisters helped by working in the kitchen, weeding the garden, gathering eggs, or taking water to the cattle. I looked after the family herd of water buffaloes. Someone always had to be with the herd because no matter how carefully a water buffalo was trained, it always was ready to nibble young rice plants when no one was looking. Sometimes, too, I fished for the family while I guarded the herd, for there were plenty of fish in the flooded rice fields during the rainy season.

I was twelve years old when I made my first trip to the jungle with my father. I learned how to track game, how to recog-
2 nize useful roots, how to distinguish edible mushrooms from poisonous ones. I learned that if birds, raccoons, squirrels, or monkeys had eaten the fruits of certain trees, then those fruits were not poisonous. Often they were not delicious, but they could calm a man's hunger and thirst.

My father, like most of the villagers, was a farmer and a hunter, depending upon the season. But he also had a college edu- 3 cation, so in the evenings he helped to teach other children in our hamlet, for it was too small to afford a professional schoolteacher.

My mother managed the house, but during the harvest season she could be found in the fields, helping my father get the crops home; and as the wife of a hunter, she knew how to dress and nurse a wound and took good care of her husband and his hunting dogs.

I went to the lowlands to study for a while because I wanted to follow my father as a teacher when I grew up. I always planned to return to my hamlet to live the rest of my life there. But war disrupted my dreams. The land I love was lost to me forever.

These stories are my memories. . . .

So Close

My grandmother was very fond of cookies made of banana, egg, and coconut, so my mother and I always stopped at Mrs. Hong's house to buy these cookies for her on our way back from the marketplace. My mother also liked to see Mrs. Hong because they had been very good friends since grade-school days. While my mother talked with her friend, I talked with Mrs. Hong's daughter, Lan. Most of the time Lan asked me about my older sister, who was married to a teacher and lived in a nearby town. Lan, too, was going to get married—to a young man living next door, Trung.

The Land I Lost 413

---

1. GUIDED READING:
Understanding the Main Idea
Which sentence expresses the paragraph's main idea? "But of all the animals, the most hated and feared was the huge horse snake." The sentences that follow give specific details that explain why.

2
Using Context Clues
Ask students to guess what *edible* means and to find context clues. (*Edible* means "can be eaten"; *distinguish . . . from* and *poisonous* are clues.)

3. GUIDED READING:
Understanding Implied Ideas
What idea is implied in this passage? The passage implies that a college education is rare among the villagers.

Art Link

In these essays, the author describes happy memories of his childhood in Vietnam. Invite students to illustrate special memories or impressions that have stayed with them through childhood. Ask each student to share his or her drawing and to explain the significance of the illustrated memory or impression.

1
Recognizing Prefixes
Tell students that the prefix *in-* means "not," and ask them to guess the meaning of *inseparable* ("not capable of being separated").

2. GUIDED READING:
Making Inferences
How did the fish get on the windowsill? Trung put it there.

3. GUIDED READING:
Making Comparisons
Ask students to compare the way couples in Vietnam and America become engaged.

1 Trung and Lan had been inseparable playmates until the day tradition did not allow them to be alone together anymore. Besides, I think they felt a little shy with each other after realizing that they were man and woman.

Lan was a lively, pretty girl who attracted the attention of all the young men of our hamlet. Trung was a skillful fisherman who successfully plied[1] his trade on the river in front of their houses. Whenever Lan's mother found a big fish on the kitchen windowsill, she would smile to herself. Finally she decided that Trung was a fine young man and would make a good husband for her daughter.

Trung's mother did not like the idea of her son giving good fish away, but she liked the cookies Lan brought her from time to time. Besides, the girl was very helpful; whenever she was not busy at her house, Lan would come over in the evening and help Trung's mother repair her son's fishing net.

Trung was happiest when Lan was helping his mother. They did not talk to each other, but they could look at each other when his mother was busy with her work. Each time Lan went home, Trung looked at the chair Lan had just left and secretly wished that nobody would move it.

One day when Trung's mother heard her son call Lan's name in his sleep, she decided it was time to speak to the girl's mother about marriage. Lan's mother

---

1. **plied** (plīd): worked at.

414   Nonfiction

TRANSPARENCIES 24 & 25
Fine Art
Theme: *Fact-Based Writing* – invites students to examine artwork that shows real people or real events.

TRANSPARENCY 26
Reader Response
Charting Your Response – prompts students to evaluate their reaction to the selection.

1. GUIDED READING:
Making Inferences
How do you suppose Trung's relatives feel when they realize Trung was right about Lan all along? They probably feel embarrassed, ashamed, and sorry for not having believed him.

2. LITERARY ELEMENTS:
Plot
Up until this point, we only know Trung's experiences. Now we hear Lan's side of the story.

1 discovered that the moving tree was, in fact, Lan. She had covered herself with leaves because she had no clothes on.

At first nobody knew what had really happened because Lan clung to Trung and cried and cried. Finally, when Lan could talk they pieced together her story. 2

Lan had fainted when the crocodile snapped her up. Had she not fainted, the crocodile surely would have drowned her

TRANSPARENCIES 24 & 25
Fine Art
Theme: *Fact-Based Writing* — invites students to examine artwork that shows real people or real events.

Cultural Diversity

Discuss the traditional Vietnamese courtship and marriage customs described in the story. Ask students how these customs are similar to and different from courtship and marriage customs in North America. List students' responses in two columns, headed "Similarities" and "Differences," on the chalkboard. Interested students might want to find out about customs in additional cultures and add that information to what has already been written on the chalkboard to create a chart.

1. GUIDED READING:
Making Comparisons
Ask students to compare the traditions the author describes with the wedding customs they are familiar with.

2. GUIDED READING:
Understanding Time Order
Ask students to identify words in the next three paragraphs that give time clues. (*first, then, after, before, that ended the day's celebrations, later*)

3. GUIDED READING:
Making Inferences About a Character
What does this suggest about Lan? Tradition is not as important to her as it is to the others.

4. LITERARY ELEMENTS:
Plot
Now the story gets exciting. What is the conflict here? Somebody needs to save Lan from the crocodile and certain death.

---

agreed they should be married and even waived[2] the custom whereby the bridegroom had to give the bride's family a fat hog, six chickens, six ducks, three bottles of wine, and thirty kilos[3] of fine rice, for the two families had known each other for a long time and were good neighbors.

The two widowed mothers quickly set the dates for the engagement announcement and for the wedding ceremony. Since their decision was immediately made known to relatives and friends, Trung and Lan could now see each other often. . . .

1 At last it was the day of their wedding. Friends and relatives arrived early in the morning to help them celebrate. They brought gifts of ducks, chickens, baskets filled with fruits, rice wine, and colorful fabrics. Even though the two houses were next to each other, the two mothers observed all the proper wedding day traditions.

2 First Trung and his friends and relatives came to Lan's house. Lan and he prayed at her ancestors' altars and asked for their blessing. Then they joined everyone for a luncheon.

After lunch there was a farewell ceremony for the bride. Lan stepped out of her house and joined the greeting party that was to accompany her to Trung's home. Tradition called for her to cry and to express her sorrow at leaving her parents behind and forever becoming the daughter of her husband's family. In some villages the bride was even supposed to cling so tightly to her mother that it would take several friends to pull her away from her home. But instead of crying, Lan smiled. **3** She asked herself, why should she cry? The two houses were separated by only a garden; she could run home and see her mother anytime she wanted to. So Lan willingly followed Trung and prayed at his ancestors' altars before joining everyone in the big welcome dinner at Trung's house that ended the day's celebrations.

Later in the evening of the wedding night Lan went to the river to take a bath. Because crocodiles <u>infested</u> the river, people of our hamlet who lived along the riverbank chopped down trees and put them in the river to form barriers and protect places where they washed their clothes, did their dishes, or took a bath. This evening, a <u>wily</u> crocodile had avoided the barrier by crawling up the riverbank and sneaked up behind Lan. The crocodile **4** grabbed her and went back to the river by the same route that it had come.

Trung became worried when Lan did not return. He went to the place where she was supposed to bathe, only to find that her clothes were there but she had disappeared. Panic-stricken, he yelled for his relatives. They all rushed to the riverbank with lighted torches. In the flickering light they found traces of water and crocodile claw prints on the wet soil. Now they knew that a crocodile had grabbed the young bride and dragged her into the river.

Since no one could do anything for the girl, all of Trung's relatives returned to the

---

2. **waived** (wāvd): gave up voluntarily.
3. **kilos** (kēl′ōz): A kilogram is about 2.2 pounds.

house, urging the bridegroom to do the same. But the young man refused to leave the place; he just stood there, crying and staring at the clothes of his bride.

Suddenly the wind brought him the sound of Lan calling his name. He was very frightened, for according to an old belief, a crocodile's victim must lure a new victim to his master; if not, the first victim's soul must stay with the beast forever.

Trung rushed back to the house and woke all his relatives. Nobody doubted he thought he had heard her call, but they all believed that he was the victim of a hallucination. Everyone pleaded with him and tried to convince him that nobody could survive when snapped up by a crocodile and dragged into the river to be drowned and eaten by the animal.

The young man brushed aside all their arguments and rushed back to the river. Once again, he heard the voice of his bride in the wind, calling his name. Again he rushed back and woke his relatives. Again they tried to persuade him that it was a hallucination, although some of the old folks suggested that maybe the ghost of the young girl was having to dance and sing to placate[4] the angry crocodile because she failed to bring it a new victim.

No one could persuade Trung to stay inside. His friends wanted to go back to the river with him, but he said no. He resented them for not believing him that there were desperate cries in the wind.

Trung stood in front of the deep river alone in the darkness. He listened to the sound of the wind and clutched the clothes Lan had left behind. The wind became stronger and stronger and often changed direction as the night progressed, but he did not hear any more calls. Still he had no doubt that the voice he had heard earlier was absolutely real. Then at dawn, when the wind died down, he again heard, very clearly, Lan call him for help.

Her voice came from an island about six hundred meters away. Trung wept and prayed: "You were a good girl when you were still alive, now be a good soul. Please protect me so that I can find a way to kill the beast in order to free you from its spell and avenge your tragic death." Suddenly, while wiping away his tears, he saw a little tree moving on the island. The tree was jumping up and down. He squinted to see better. The tree had two hands that were waving at him. And it was calling his name.

Trung became hysterical and yelled for help. He woke all his relatives and they all rushed to his side again. At first they thought that Trung had become stark mad. They tried to lead him back to his house, but he fiercely resisted their attempt. He talked to them incoherently[5] and pointed his finger at the strange tree on the island. Finally his relatives saw the waving tree. They quickly put a small boat into the river and Trung got into the boat along with two other men. They paddled to the island and

---

4. **placate** (plā'kāt): calm the anger of.

5. **incoherently** (in'kō·hir'ənt·lē): not clearly; in a confused way.

The Land I Lost

TRANSPARENCY 26

Reader Response
Charting Your Response – prompts students to evaluate their reaction to the selection.

1. GUIDED READING:
Making Inferences
How do you suppose Trung's relatives feel when they realize Trung was right about Lan all along? They probably feel embarrassed, ashamed, and sorry for not having believed him.

2. LITERARY ELEMENTS:
Plot
Up until this point, we only know Trung's experiences. Now we hear Lan's side of the story.

1 discovered that the moving tree was, in fact, Lan. She had covered herself with leaves because she had no clothes on.

At first nobody knew what had really happened because Lan clung to Trung and cried and cried. Finally, when Lan could 2 talk they pieced together her story.

Lan had fainted when the crocodile snapped her up. Had she not fainted, the crocodile surely would have drowned her

418   Nonfiction

CLOSURE
Call on volunteers to tell how reading this "snapshot" of life in a Vietnamese village has affected their understanding of Vietnam and the Vietnam war.

EXTENSION AND ENRICHMENT
Science. Have students work in small groups to research and prepare reports on crocodiles, alligators, tigers, and other dangerous animals. Encourage them to include photographs or drawings.

Social Studies. Students can describe engagement and wedding traditions they are familiar with, as well as marriage customs in other cultures.

before carrying her off to the island. Lan did not know how many times the crocodile had tossed her in the air and smashed her against the ground, but at one point, while being tossed in the air and falling back onto the crocodile's jaw, she regained consciousness. The crocodile smashed her against the ground a few more times, but Lan played dead. Luckily the crocodile became thirsty and returned to the river to drink. At that moment Lan got up and ran to a nearby tree and climbed up it. The tree was very small. Lan stayed very still for fear that the snorting, angry crocodile, roaming around trying to catch her again, would find her and shake her out of the tree. Lan stayed in this frozen position for a long time until the crocodile gave up searching for her and went back to the river. Then she started calling Trung to come rescue her.

Lan's body was covered with bruises, for crocodiles soften up big prey before swallowing it. They will smash it against the ground or against a tree, or keep tossing it into the air. But fortunately Lan had no broken bones or serious cuts. It was possible that this crocodile was very old and had lost most of its teeth. Nevertheless, the older the crocodile, the more intelligent it usually was. That was how it knew to avoid the log barrier in the river and to snap up the girl from behind.

Trung carried his exhausted bride into the boat and paddled home. Lan slept for hours and hours. At times she would sit up with a start and cry out for help, but within three days she was almost completely recovered.

Lan's mother and Trung's mother decided to celebrate their children's wedding a second time, because Lan had come back from the dead.

FOR STUDY AND DISCUSSION
Identifying Facts
1. Possible answers: The rainy season lasts six months. They grow rice, corn, and vegetables. They have to travel a long way for medicine, soap, and other supplies.
2. Possible answers: Parents arrange children's marriages. Bridegroom usually gives bride's family gifts of livestock, wine, and food. Wedding couple prays to their ancestors. Bride's family provides a lunch, groom's family a dinner.
3. Possible answers: They soften up big prey by smashing it or tossing it in the air. They can attack people.

Interpreting Meanings
4. The Vietnam war changed the land and the life he had planned. (Biography tells that he left Vietnam and came to the United States.)
5. Crocodiles are so deadly that no one escapes. If the crocodile hadn't gotten thirsty, she would have died.

The Land I Lost 419

Applying Meanings
6. Students may say they believe in love and marriage; loyalty to family and country; respect for traditions.
7. The selection makes students see the Vietnamese as individuals who have the same needs and concerns that they have.

FOCUS ON READING
Visualizing Descriptions
Emphasize that students won't be graded on their drawing ability. Look for specific details in the drawings.

LITERARY ELEMENTS
A Narrative
1. Trung is the hero; Lan is the heroine.
2. A crocodile had kidnapped Lan.
3. The setting is a small village in central Vietnam.
4. The enemy is a crocodile.
5. The crocodile is extremely strong and wily.
6. Lan plays dead, the crocodile goes for a drink, and she escapes.
   Opinions will vary on whether the story is entirely factual. Some may believe the facts have been manipulated to make a more suspenseful story.
   The story could be proved to be true by contacting the writer or by interviewing Lan, Trung, and the other villagers.

420

For Study and Discussion

IDENTIFYING FACTS
1. Name at least three facts you learned about life in the writer's hamlet.
2. What facts did you learn from the section called "So Close" about marriage customs in the Vietnam highlands?
3. What facts did you learn about crocodiles?

INTERPRETING MEANINGS
4. Tell how the writer lost the land he loved.
5. Why did the mothers feel that Lan had come back from the dead?

APPLYING MEANINGS
6. This selection is about a faraway land with customs very different from those in North America. What values and feelings do you share with Nhuong's people?
7. Look at the list of facts you wrote about Vietnam. How would your list change now that you have read this writer's account?

Focus on Reading

VISUALIZING DESCRIPTIONS
Were you able to visualize Nhuong's village? To see how well you are able to form pictures in your mind, draw a picture of what you see when you think of this village. Close your book when you make your drawing. Then check your images with Nhuong's description. Write down three things not included in your drawing.

420 Nonfiction

Literary Elements

A NARRATIVE
A **narrative** is a series of related events. A narrative is, in many ways, just like a short story, although a narrative can be either fictional or true-to-life. In this selection, Nhuong tells a narrative about a girl's ordeal with a crocodile. Within this narrative are many of the elements of storytelling.

1. Who are the **hero** and **heroine** of the story?
2. What is their problem, or **conflict**?
3. What is the narrative's **setting**?
4. Who is the **enemy**?
5. What are the enemy's **special powers** that make him hard to conquer?
6. How is the conflict **resolved**?

Do you think this narrative is totally factual? Or do you think some parts of it might be fictional, or imaginary? How could the story be proved to be true?

Language and Vocabulary

CONTEXT CLUES
This writer used some words that might have puzzled you. For example, did you know what these words mean?

> inseparable (page 414)
> infested (page 416)
> wily (page 416)
> hallucination (page 417)
> resented (page 417)
> avenge (page 417)

1. Skim the selection and find how each of these words is used in context. Working with a partner, find at least one clue in each word's context that will help you guess at each word's meaning.
2. Try out each guess in the sentence. Does it make sense?
3. Write out your definitions and check them with the definitions in the glossary at the back of this book. How close did you come?

Writing About Literature

DESCRIBING A PLACE

In the first section of his autobiography, Nhuong describes features of life in his village. Write a description of everyday life in your own town or neighborhood or rural area. Write as if you are going to publish your description in a different country, where they know nothing about your country—where people live, what they eat, how people make a living.

Open your description with the words "I was born in" (or "I live in"). End your description with a statement telling how you feel about this place.

About the Author

Huynh Quang Nhuong (1946–   ) was born in Mytho, Vietnam. He graduated from Saigon University, where he majored in chemistry. While serving in the South Vietnamese army, he was shot and paralyzed. He came to the United States to be treated for his injuries and now he lives in Columbia, Missouri. Nhuong has since earned additional university degrees in French and literature.

LANGUAGE AND VOCABULARY
For answers, see the **Teaching Guide** at the beginning of the unit.

WRITING ABOUT LITERATURE
Describing a Place
Students should include specific details that will interest people from other countries. Look for precise and vivid language, an opening phrase (such as "I was born in . . ."), and closing statements that tell about feelings.

OBJECTIVES
Students will recognize internal and external conflict and identify details that support conclusions.

FOCUS/MOTIVATION
Building on Prior Knowledge. If students have already read "The Land I Lost" (page 411), note that this selection deals with a Vietnamese boy during the period right after the Vietnam war ended.

Establishing a Purpose for Reading. Students should look for the conflicts, or struggles, that the main character faces.

> **TEACHING RESOURCES C**
> Teacher's Notes, p. 47
> Reading Check, p. 49
> Reading Focus, p. 50
> Study Guide, pp. 51, 52
> Language Skills, p. 53
> Building Vocabulary, p. 56
> Selection Vocabulary Test, p. 58
> Selection Test, p. 59

1. GUIDED READING:
Making Connections
If they know their family histories, ask volunteers to tell where their ancestors lived before they came to America, when they came, and how.

2. GUIDED READING:
Making Connections
Ask students what other "boat people" they have heard about. (Boat people leave Cuba and Haiti for the United States; many still flee from Vietnam to Hong Kong and Thailand.)

3. BACKGROUND
Into a Strange Land is a collection of true narratives about young unaccompanied refugees who came to America in an unusual way. The book, which Ashabranner worked on with his daughter, won an American Library Association Notable Book award and a Christopher Award.

The Most Vulnerable People

BRENT ASHABRANNER

Before You Read

The next selection is also a true story from Vietnam. The Vietnam war (1957–1979) ravaged the country. It left many people stripped of their possessions and desperate to leave the country. Like so many other refugees, many Vietnamese made the difficult voyage to America. Since 1975, thousands of refugees have come from Vietnam and other war-torn countries of Southeast Asia.

Most of the Vietnamese refugees escape their homeland in small fishing boats. They usually travel through the South China Sea to Thailand, where they stay temporarily in refugee camps. Though the boats are small and the trip is very dangerous, the passage is expensive. Often a Vietnamese family can only afford to send one person—usually, this is the oldest son. In this essay from his nonfiction book *Into a Strange Land,* Brent Ashabranner writes the true story of one Vietnamese boy, Tran, and what he endured to be free.

Before you read Tran's story, write two or three sentences in your journal telling what you think it would be like to be torn from your family suddenly, without warning. Do you know of any people who have had this experience?

422 Nonfiction

Prereading Journal. See the assignment suggested on page 422. For an alternate assignment, ask students to list some reasons why the United States is the destination of choice for so many refugees.

READING THE SELECTION
This short selection has a simple vocabulary and syntax that make it suitable for homework for students of all ability levels.

Before assigning it, you may wish to discuss some aspects of Vietnamese culture, especially reverence for family and homeland. It would also be helpful to give a brief overview of what happened in South Vietnam right after American troops left. (South Vietnamese leaders feared for their lives; many people tried to leave the country; "boat people" ended up in refugee camps.)

Cultural Diversity

Many Americans have ancestors that originally traveled to this country as refugees, that is, people seeking refuge from political or economic hardship. Have students interview their parents or other relatives to discover how their ancestors came to this country. How were their experiences similar to or different from Tran's?

1. LITERARY ELEMENTS:
Setting
Where is Tran? This is his third day at sea in a crowded boat somewhere near Vietnam.

2. LITERARY ELEMENTS:
Flashback
Note that the narrative goes back four days earlier to explain why Tran is alone on the boat.

1 The waves were not big now. Tran sat in the middle of the boat, crowded next to an old woman. She had put her arm around him during the night when the spray from the high waves was cold. He did not know her name. The boat was packed with people standing, sitting, a few lying down, but Tran could see no familiar face. Even now, on their third day at sea, he could not think clearly. He could not really believe what had happened. He knew he was not having a bad dream, but still he hoped he would wake up and be at his home in Vietnam.

The beginning had been good. Late in **2** the afternoon, four days ago, Tran's father had told him they were going fishing, just the two of them. Tran was very happy because he had never been fishing with his father before. Tran's brother, who was ten, and four years younger than Tran, cried

424 Nonfiction

MATH LINK
Many Vietnamese left their homeland and immigrated into the United States, as other groups of people before them have done. Ask students to find out where their ancestors or members of their families originally entered the United States. Did they arrive via land, air, or sea? Invite students who enjoy math to use this data to create a bar, line, or pie graph that shows the various types of entry and the number of families that used each type.

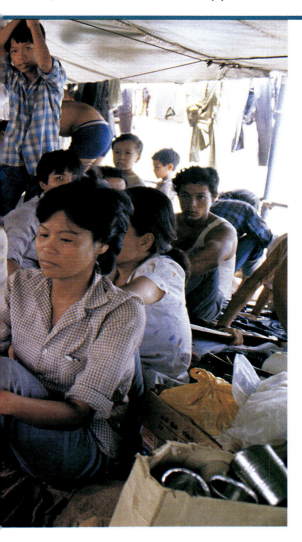

because his father would not let him come. Tran remembered that his mother stood in the doorway of their house and watched them leave.

An hour later, when it was almost dark, Tran's father led them to a place on the beach where a man was waiting in a small boat. "Hurry," the man said. "You are late."

Tran and his father got into the boat, and the man poled them away from the shore. After a while, Tran saw a big boat anchored in the bay. They headed toward it, and Tran saw other small boats going in the same direction.

"When are we going to fish?" Tran asked.

"Soon," his father said, "from the big boat."

Tran did not understand, but he said nothing more. Their boat came alongside the big boat; his father and the boatman grabbed a rope ladder from the big boat and pulled their own boat close. Tran's father handed Tran a small plastic bag.

"Climb up the ladder and do not lose the bag," he said.

Tran's eyes widened with fear. "No," he said. "I don't want to."

His father picked him up and swung him to the rope ladder. "I will follow," he said.

Then Tran climbed the ladder, gripping the bag tightly in one hand. When he reached the big boat's rail, two men waiting there swung him onto the deck. Tran saw that the deck was crowded with people. Most were men, but there were also women and children.

Tran looked down and saw that his father was still in the small boat. His father looked up at Tran and raised his hand. "Do not lose the bag," he said.

Then the boatman pushed the small boat away, and soon it was lost in the darkness. Tran cried out to his father, but one of the men standing beside him gripped him roughly by the shoulder. "Do not make noise," he said.

The Most Vulnerable People 425

1. LITERARY ELEMENTS:
Irony
Tran's father and the reader both know what Tran doesn't suspect yet—they are not going fishing at all.

2. GUIDED READING:
Motivation
Why do you think Tran's father says this? He senses that Tran is reluctant to go aboard. The father's words reassure the boy so he will get on the boat.

3. GUIDED READING:
Drawing Conclusions
Why does the man say this? Leaving Vietnam in this way is illegal. It is almost dark; if Tran makes noise, they may be stopped and punished for trying to leave.

CLOSURE
Ask students to compare what they learned about Vietnam from the two selections "The Land I Lost" and "The Most Vulnerable People." Have them tell which account they liked better and why.

RETEACHING
Have students form small groups to discuss the kinds of internal and external conflicts that make a story interesting. Encourage them to think of examples from television, movies, fiction, and real-life stories.

> **TRANSPARENCIES 24 & 25**
> *Fine Art*
> Theme: *Fact-Based Writing* – invites students to examine artwork that shows real people or real events.

1. GUIDED READING:
Making Inferences
What do you think Tran is feeling? What details support this inference? He is terrified, disbelieving, panicky. Note the details that support this inference: Tran "clutched" and "stared." "His heart pounded." He "spun away," "tried to run," "began to tremble."

2. GUIDED READING:
Recognizing Cause and Effect
What makes Tran sick? The rolling movement of the boat makes him seasick.

3. LITERARY ELEMENTS:
Flashback
Note that the flashback ends here. The narrative returns to Tran's third day at sea, the point at which it opened. Tran is huddled next to the old woman.

4. GUIDED READING:
Predicting Outcomes
What role do you think the old woman might play in Tran's life? Students may guess that she will take care of him on the boat and in the refugee camp.

426

---

1 Tran clutched the boat's rail and stared into the night. His heart pounded. Perhaps his father had forgotten something and would return. But in only a few minutes, the big boat's engine started up, and the boat moved quickly out to sea. Tran spun away from the rail and tried to run, but people were all around him, and he could hardly move. He held the plastic bag close, and he began to tremble.

2 After that, time ran together. During the dark night, the boat began to roll, and Tran became seasick. He vomited until there was nothing in his stomach and then continued to retch until all the muscles of his body hurt. He lay on the deck and called for his mother. All around him people were sick; he could hear their moans over the noise of the boat's engine.

When at last the sun came up, the sea was calmer, and the boat did not roll so much. Tran was no longer sick, but he was terribly thirsty. He whispered for water, but no one heard him or paid any attention. Finally, a man came around with a bucket of water and gave everyone a single cupful. Tran drank his in a few gulps and then he was sick again. Sometime after that another man came around with a bucket of rice. He gave Tran a cupful, but Tran could not eat even one bite.

Now the sun overhead was hot and burned into Tran's skin. He cradled his head in his arms and slept all day on the deck. That night, when the waves came high again, he crawled to the middle of the boat and found a place beside the old woman.

It was not until the third day that Tran opened the plastic bag, although it had not been out of his hand, even for a moment. Some of his clothes were in the bag, and there was an envelope. He opened it and found a picture of his family that had been taken last year. He was in the picture with his mother and father, his two sisters, and his brother, Sinh.

A letter from his mother was also in the bag. The letter said she was sorry they could not tell him he was going away. She said the boat would take him to a refugee camp[1] in a place called Thailand.[2] She told him to tell the people who ran the camp that he wanted to go to America. She said she hoped someday the whole family could come, or at least his brother when he was older.

Tran held the letter in his hand and stared at it. He knew about refugees. You could not live in Vietnam and not know about them. He had even thought that **3** someday he might be a refugee, but had never imagined that he would leave Vietnam without his family.

"Are you alone?" the old woman asked.

For a moment Tran could not speak. At last he said, "I want to go home."

"Pray that we reach the refugee **4** camp," the woman told him. "Do not even think about anything else.". . .

---

1. **refugee camp:** *Refugees* are people who flee their country because of persecution or danger. Many countries have *camps*, or places where refugees from a particular country are grouped together.
2. **Thailand** (tī'land): a country in southeast Asia, close to Vietnam.

426 Nonfiction

EXTENSION AND ENRICHMENT

Speaking. Have pairs of volunteers act out a conversation that might have taken place between Tran and the old woman just after the selection ends. Or have Tran read aloud a letter that he wrote from the refugee camp to his family.

Social Studies. Ask a volunteer to do a brief report on where "boat people" are coming from these days, where they go, and what happens to them.

FOR STUDY AND DISCUSSION

Identifying Facts
1. The story takes place on a boat in the South China Sea.
2. His family is sending him to a refugee camp in Thailand with the hope that he will reach America.

Interpreting Meanings
3. The letter explains why his parents sent him away. The picture and letter might be his only connection to his family for a long time.
4. *Vulnerable* people are weak and easily hurt.
   They are young and inexperienced; they have no one to protect them.
5. Answers will vary. Most will think that the parents sacrificed to help their son find a better life.

Applying Meanings
6. Like other refugees, Tran is on a quest for freedom, education, and the chance to earn a living and prosper.
7. Students may suggest being the lone survivor after a fire or natural disaster. Some may think of an African kidnapped during the days of the slave trade.

For Study and Discussion

IDENTIFYING FACTS
1. Where does this story take place?
2. Why is Tran on the boat?

INTERPRETING MEANINGS
3. Why do you think Tran's father was so anxious that Tran not lose the plastic bag?

4. Brent Ashabranner calls refugee children like Tran "the most vulnerable people." What does that title suggest to you? Why are refugee children like Tran so vulnerable to harm?

5. Tran's family suddenly uprooted him and sent him alone to a far-distant country. Do you think they were cruel to do this? Or do you think they were making a sacrifice to help their son? Explain.

The Most Vulnerable People 427

FOCUS ON READING
Supporting Conclusions
1. True. The trip is illegal, the seas are rough, the sun burns, and there is little food and water.
2. True. She puts her arm around him; she talks to him and gives him advice.
3. True. He thinks he is going fishing; his father lies to him; in her letter, his mother apologizes for not telling him the truth.
4. False. Nothing in the story supports this conclusion.

LITERARY ELEMENTS
Conflict
Answers will vary. Tran's sickness resulting from the rocking boat is an example of an external conflict.

Internal conflicts include Tran's feelings of fear and loneliness and his desire to be back in Vietnam.

Some may suggest that they would think about the future, plan to work hard, and hope to reunite the family.

Answers will vary about Tran's worst problem. Students may suggest loneliness and fear.

APPLYING MEANINGS
6. What common **quest** does Tran share with the millions of refugees who have come to America since 1620? That is, what does Tran's family want for him?
7. What other experiences from real life can you think of that could be compared with Tran's ordeal?

Focus on Reading

SUPPORTING CONCLUSIONS
Here are four conclusions that one reader has drawn about "The Most Vulnerable People." First, decide if each conclusion is true—that is, is there enough evidence in the article to support it? Once you decide which conclusions are valid, write down the evidence from the article that supports each one.

1. The boat trip to Thailand was very difficult and dangerous.
2. The old woman on the boat was protective of the boy.
3. Tran did not know his mother and father had planned to send him away.
4. Tran's family had to send him away because they were in political trouble with the rulers of Vietnam.

Literary Elements

CONFLICT
Tran endures many **conflicts,** or struggles, during his three days at sea. Describe at least one **external conflict**—that is, a conflict with forces that exist outside of Tran himself. Describe at least one **internal conflict**—that is, a conflict that exists in Tran's own heart and mind.

If you were in Tran's place, how would you deal with the conflicts facing you in this small boat, away from your family, bound for a land where you wouldn't even be understood?

In your opinion, what is Tran's worst problem?

Focus on Informative Writing

EXPLORING CAUSE AND EFFECT
A **cause-and-effect** paper is a type of informative writing in which you explore why something happens and what the results are. When you plan this kind of paper, you will often find that a single event or situation has more than one cause. Likewise, a single event can lead to more than one effect. Study the diagram below.

Causes
Fear for safety in Vietnam
Hope for a better life
Open escape route to Thailand

Decision of Tran's Parents to Send Tran Away

Breakup of family
Tran's sadness and loneliness
Effects

Make some notes for a cause-and-effect paper on a topic that interests you. To find a topic, ask yourself these questions:

Why did . . . happen?
What would happen if . . . ?

Save your notes.

About the Author

Brent Ashabranner (1921–   ) is an American writer who has a special interest in people of other cultures. Among his nonfiction books for young people are *Children of the Maya,* about Guatemalans living in the United States; *Dark Harvest,* about the experiences of migrant farm workers; and *To Live in Two Worlds,* about the experiences of young Native Americans.

Brent Ashabranner grew up in the small town of Shawnee, Oklahoma. He spent his childhood devouring books about exotic lands, including books by Rudyard Kipling. Looking back, Ashabranner says, "I have never had any doubt that the books I read as a boy influenced the direction of my life." That direction led Ashabranner to live and work in exotic countries such as Ethiopia, Libya, Nigeria, India, Indonesia, and the Philippines.

Behind the Scenes

A Firsthand Sense

When I describe the refugee boy in *Into a Strange Land* who spent sleepless nights preparing to make his first classroom talk in English and then, standing before his classmates, found that nothing but Vietnamese would come out of his mouth, I have at least some firsthand sense of what he felt. [He is describing what later happened to Tran.]

Not much more than ten years ago, as a Ford Foundation staff member in Indonesia, I made my first visit to a village on the island of Bali. I knew that I would be welcomed with a speech by the headman, and I had spent a considerable amount of time the night before rehearsing my reply in Indonesian. The word for *headman* in Indonesian is *kepala,* and it so happens that the word for coconut is *kelapa,* just a reversal of two syllables. It was, of course, inevitable that I should begin my words of thanks by addressing the headman as *kelapa.* Now, when you go into a Balinese village and begin by calling the revered leader of the people a coconut, you are not off to a good start. I do know what it is like to try to function in a strange culture, and I do know what the Vietnamese boy was going through.

—Brent Ashabranner

OBJECTIVES

Students should demonstrate an ability to obtain appropriate information from maps, diagrams, and captions; identify main ideas; explain a process; and analyze figures of speech.

TEACHING RESOURCES C
Teacher's Notes, p. 62
Reading Check, p. 64
Reading Focus, p. 65
Study Guide, pp. 67, 68
Language Skills, p. 69
Building Vocabulary, p. 72
Selection Vocabulary Test, p. 75
Selection Test, p. 76

FOCUS/MOTIVATION

Building on Prior Knowledge. Have students turn to the diagram on page 433 (bottom) and explain what it shows—based on what they already know about volcanoes. Tell them that the article they're going to read gives more information and a detailed close-up of the eruption of one volcano.

Many students may know that there are volcanoes in Hawaii and other parts of the world; they may be surprised to learn that there are volcanoes on the American mainland.

Establishing a Purpose for Reading. Have students look through the article to find the two headings "The Volcano Wakes" (page 432) and "The Big Blast" (page 436). (These are chapter titles in Lauber's book.) Have them read to find out what each heading refers to.

Prereading Journal. See the assignment at the end of the headnote, page 431.

SCIENCE

Volcano

PATRICIA LAUBER

1   **Before You Read**

How should you read scientific articles and books? Here are some suggestions:

1. Look for imaginative ways the writer explains or describes things that might be strange to you. Scientific writers, just like fiction writers, often use imaginative comparisons, or figures of speech, to clarify difficult ideas.
2. Look for cause-and-effect relationships. How is one event connected to another?
2 3. When you come across new scientific words, check the context for their definitions. Or, try to figure out their meanings from other clues in the passage.
4. Look for graphic aids—those tables, charts, graphs, photographs, diagrams, maps and their captions that will help you visualize what the author is saying.

Here is a section of an exciting, prize-winning book on volcanoes. Before you read, write down in your journal three facts you already know (or think you know) about that
3 monster of nature, the volcano.

1. GUIDED READING:

Making Connections
Read this headnote aloud. Its suggestions apply to reading history as well as to all types of science writing.

2

Using the Glossary
Remind students to use the Glossary or a dictionary if they cannot figure out meanings from context clues. In reading science materials, it is important that they know the precise meanings of scientific terms.

3. LITERARY ELEMENTS:

Metaphor
Ask students to name some other "monsters of nature." (Floods, earthquakes, hurricanes, tornadoes, blizzards, lightning, tidal waves)

Volcano   **431**

READING THE SELECTION
The selection is on grade level, but because it is long and contains many scientific terms, it will be challenging for average and slower classes. You may want to read much of it aloud in class, pausing after each paragraph to discuss main ideas and define terms.

Pay special attention to the graphic aids, asking questions based on captions and maps (see the Focus on Reading exercise on page 443).

1
Scientific Terms
The scientific term for a sleeping volcano is *dormant*, from a Latin word meaning "sleeping."

2. GUIDED READING:
Summarizing Main Ideas
Ask students to summarize the main idea of this paragraph. (When a volcano erupts, molten rock and gases from inside the earth come to the earth's surface.)

Language and Vocabulary

Many words in science have interesting histories. For example, some scientific words come from the names of gods, goddesses, and other characters from ancient Greek and Roman mythology. The word *volcano,* for example, comes from Vulcanus, the Roman god of fire. The Romans imagined that Vulcanus, or Vulcan, was the gods' blacksmith and that he lived and worked in a mountain in Italy. Blacksmiths work with hot iron, mostly to make shoes for horses. The ancient myth makers imagined that when Vulcan stirred the underground fires which he needed for his blacksmith's forge, terrible clanking, roaring noises, and steam, smoke, and fire came from the mountain. They imagined that when Vulcan pounded the iron on his anvil to shape it, the mountain exploded. As you read the following article, think about why the ancients imagined that a volcanic eruption was caused by the activity of Vulcan.

The Volcano Wakes

1 For many years the volcano slept. It was silent and still, big and beautiful. Then the volcano, which was named Mount St. Helens, began to stir. On March 20, 1980, it was shaken by a strong earthquake. The quake was a sign of movement inside St. Helens. It was a sign of a waking volcano that might soon erupt again.

2 Mount St. Helens was built by many eruptions over thousands of years. In each eruption hot rock from inside the earth forced its way to the surface. The rock was so hot that it was molten, or melted, and it had gases trapped in it. The name for such rock is magma. Once the molten rock reaches the surface it is called lava. In some eruptions the magma was fairly liquid. Its gases escaped gently. Lava flowed out of the volcano, cooled, and hardened. In other eruptions the magma was thick and sticky. Its gases burst out violently, carrying along sprays of molten rock. As it blasted into the sky, the rock cooled and hardened. Some of it rained down as ash—tiny bits of rock. Some rained down as pumice—frothy rock puffed up by gases.

Together the lava flows, ash, and pumice built a mountain with a bowl-shaped crater at its top. St. Helens grew to a height of 9,677 feet, so high that its peak was often hidden by clouds. Its big neighbors were built in the same way. Mount St. Helens is

432 Nonfiction

ART LINK

Invite students to create a mural that depicts different stages in the life of a waking or active volcano. Remind students to reread sections of the piece that give vivid descriptions of the stages that Mount St. Helens went through until the explosions finally stopped. Each interested student could choose a particular passage from the selection to illustrate.

part of the Cascade Range, a chain of volcanoes that runs from northern California into British Columbia.

In the middle 1800s a number of small eruptions took place. Between 1832 and 1857 St. Helens puffed out clouds of steam and ash from time to time. It also gave off small flows of lava. Then the mountain fell still.

For well over a hundred years the volcano slept. Each spring, as winter snows

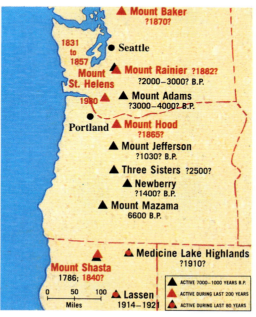

(*Opposite*) Map shows the Cascade Range in the United States and the periods in which each volcano last erupted. Question marks mean that dates are not certain. *B.P.* means "before present."

(*Below*) A volcano is a place where hot, molten rock from inside the earth comes to the surface. Mount St. Helens was built by many eruptions over thousands of years.

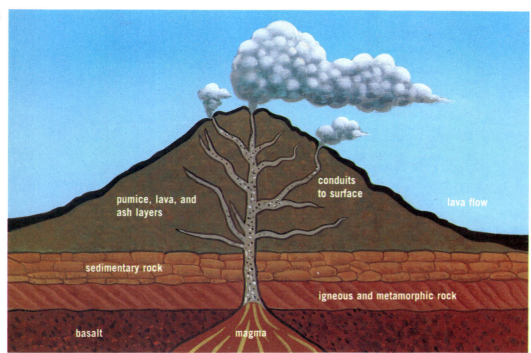

1. **GUIDED READING:**
Drawing Conclusions
For how many years was Mount St. Helens asleep before it erupted in 1980? Students should use their math: 123 years.

2. **GUIDED READING:**
Using Captions
Ask students what *B.P.* stands for (*before present*) and why there are question marks on the map (dates are uncertain).

3. **GUIDED READING:**
Using Maps
How many volcanoes on this map have been active during the last 80 years? During the last 200 years? (Students can answer this question by using the **map key.**)

4
Scientific Terms
As an activity, you might ask students to make a vocabulary list to accompany this diagram. Have them look up the words *basalt*, *sedimentary*, *conduits*, *igneous*, and *metamorphic*. (They can get definitions of *pumice* and *lava* and *magma* from the article.)

Volcano 433

MEETING INDIVIDUAL NEEDS

ESL/LEP • Students will encounter the verb *erupt* and its noun form, *eruption*. Explain that these words come from the Latin *erumpere*, meaning to break out (*e–*, out + *rumpere*, to break). Pair students, and ask them to find the origins and definitions of the words *interrupt, corrupt,* and *rupture* in a dictionary. In what way are all the words related to *erupt*? Invite students to make note of this relationship in their vocabulary journals and to use these words in context by writing original sentences.

1. VISUAL CONNECTIONS
If students have seen a mountain "in person," ask them to tell about their experiences. *Would you like to climb a mountain such as this one? Would you like to live near a mountain?* Students may change their minds after they read this article.

Before: Visitors enjoyed the sight of wild animals, forested slopes, and clear cold waters.

434 Nonfiction

CAREER LINK

As noted in the selection, geologists are scientists who study the earth. Ask interested students to brainstorm a list of other professionals who might be found working at the site of a dormant, waking, or active volcano. (Lists might include naturalists, meteorologists, media reporters and photographers, emergency medical teams, and cartographers.) Encourage students to look for clues in the selection to help them compile their list. Afterwards, ask each student to select one listed profession and to use a dictionary or an encyclopedia to find out about that profession.

---

melted, its slopes seemed to come alive. Wildflowers bloomed in meadows. Bees gathered pollen and nectar. Birds fed, found mates, and built nests. Bears lumbered out of their dens. Herds of elk and deer feasted on fresh green shoots. Thousands of people came to hike, picnic, camp, fish, paint, bird watch, or just enjoy the scenery. Logging crews felled tall trees and planted seedlings.

These people knew that Mount St. Helens was a volcano, but they did not fear it. To them it was simply a green and pleasant mountain, where forests and firs stretched up the slopes and streams ran clear and cold.

The mountain did not seem so trustworthy to geologists, scientists who study the earth. They knew that Mount St. Helens was dangerous. It was a young volcano and one of the most active in the Cascade Range. In 1975 two geologists finished a study of the volcano's past eruptions. They predicted that Mount St. Helens would erupt again within 100 years, perhaps before the year 2000.

The geologists were right. With the earthquake of March 20, 1980, Mount St. Helens woke from a sleep of 123 years. Magma had forced its way into the mountain, tearing apart solid rock. The snapping of that rock set off the shock waves that shook St. Helens. That quake was followed by many others. Most of them were smaller, but they came so fast and so often that it was hard to tell when one quake ended and another began.

On March 27, people near Mount St. Helens heard a tremendous explosion. The volcano began to blow out steam and ash that stained its snow-white peak. Small explosions went on into late April, stopped, started again on May 7, and stopped on May 14.

The explosions of late March opened up two new craters at the top of the mountain. One formed inside the old crater. The other formed nearby. The two new craters grew bigger. Soon they joined, forming one large crater that continued to grow during the next few weeks. Meanwhile, the north face of the mountaintop was swelling and cracking. The swelling formed a bulge that grew outward at a rate of five to six feet a day.

Geologists were hard at work on the waking volcano. They took samples of ash and gases, hoping to find clues to what was happening inside. They placed instruments on the mountain to record earthquakes and the tilting of ground. They kept measuring the bulge. A sudden change in its rate of growth might be a sign that the volcano was about to erupt. But the bulge grew steadily, and the ash and gases yielded no clues.

By mid-May the bulge was huge. Half a mile wide and more than a mile long, it had swelled out 300 feet.

On Sunday morning, May 18, the sun inched up behind the Cascades, turning the sky pink. By 8 A.M. the sun was above the mountains, the sky blue, the air cool. There was not one hint of what was to come.

At 8:32 Mount St. Helens erupted. Billowing clouds of smoke, steam, and ash hid

---

1. LITERARY ELEMENTS:
Irony
What is ironic about this description of the mountain? We know what the picnickers, hikers, and campers don't know—that Mount St. Helens isn't dead, only sleeping.

2
Using Context Clues
What is a geologist? (A scientist who studies the earth) Note the same Greek root *geo*, "earth," in *geography* and *geode*. In Greek mythology Gaea was the earth goddess.

3. GUIDED READING:
Understanding Cause and Effect
What caused the earthquake? Magma had torn apart and "snapped" solid rock inside the mountain.

4
Using Context Clues
What is a crater? A crater is a large bowl-shaped pit.

5. GUIDED READING:
Evaluating Ideas
Do you agree that there was not one hint? The huge bulge was a hint; so were the earthquakes.

MATH LINK
Have students use specific information and numbers from the selection to create a graph comparing "stone wind" and lava flow speeds to others, such as car speeds, walking and running speeds, and normal wind speeds. Students could consult an encyclopedia to find average walking and running speeds. Newspapers are good sources for collecting data on local wind velocities. Post the graph and challenge students to add to it periodically as they measure or learn other data in school and at home.

1. GUIDED READING:
Understanding Main Ideas
Tell students to look for the answers to these three questions in the next section, "The Big Blast."

2
An *avalanche* is a sudden sliding of snow, earth, or rock down the side of a mountain.

3
Ask students if they know the name of these instruments. (Seismograph)

the mountain from view and darkened the sky for miles.

The eruption went on until evening. By its end a fan-shaped area of destruction stretched out to the north, covering some 230 square miles. Within that area 57 people and countless plants and animals had died.

Geologists now faced two big jobs. One was to keep watch on the mountain, to find out if more eruptions were building up. If so, they hoped to learn how to predict the eruptions.

The other job was to find out exactly what had happened on May 18. Most vol‑
1 canic eruptions start slowly. Why had Mount St. Helens erupted suddenly? What events had caused the big fan-shaped area of destruction? What had become of the mountaintop, which was now 1,200 feet lower?

The answers to these questions came slowly, as geologists studied instrument records and photographs, interviewed wit‑ nesses, and studied the clues left by the eruption itself. But in time they pieced together a story that surprised them. This eruption turned out to be very different from the ones that built Mount St. Helens.

The Big Blast

The May 18 eruption began with an earth‑
2 quake that triggered an avalanche. At 8:32
3 A.M. instruments that were miles away registered a strong earthquake. The pilot and passengers of a small plane saw the north side of the mountain rippling and churning.

436 Nonfiction

After: The mountain disappeared in billowing clouds of hot gas, ash, and rock.

1. GUIDED READING:
Understanding Main Ideas
Ask students to restate the main idea of this paragraph in their own words. (Water under pressure can be heated beyond the boiling point. When the liquid suddenly changes to steam, it can cause an explosion.)

2. GUIDED READING:
Understanding Main Ideas
The "stone wind" was only one of the destructive forces caused by the eruption. Name some others. The heat of the explosion, the avalanche, the lava and ash.

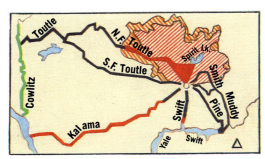

Red stripes mark the area of destruction caused by the blast. Yellow stripes mark the area where trees were left standing but were killed by heat. Solid red shows the avalanche path.

Shaken by the quake, the bulge was tearing loose. It began to slide, in a huge avalanche that carried along rock ripped from deep inside Mount St. Helens.

The avalanche tore open the mountain. A scalding blast shot sideways out of the opening. It was a blast of steam, from water heated by rising magma.

1 Normally, water cannot be heated beyond its boiling point, which is 212 degrees Fahrenheit at sea level. At boiling point, water turns to a gas, which we call steam. But if water is kept under pressure, it can be heated far beyond its boiling point and still stay liquid. (That is how a pressure cooker works.) If the pressure is removed, this superheated water suddenly turns, or flashes, to steam. As steam it takes up much more room—it expands. The sudden change to steam can cause an explosion.

Before the eruption, Mount St. Helens was like a giant pressure cooker. The rock inside it held superheated water. The water stayed liquid because it was under great pressure, sealed in the mountain. When the mountain was torn open, the pressure was suddenly relieved. The superheated water flashed to steam. Expanding violently, it shattered rock inside the mountain and exploded out the opening, traveling at speeds of up to 200 miles an hour.

The blast flattened whole forests of 180-foot-high firs. It snapped off or uprooted the trees, scattering the trunks as if they were straws. At first, this damage was puzzling. A wind of 200 miles an hour is not strong enough to level forests of giant trees. The explanation, geologists later discovered, was that the wind carried rocks ranging in size from grains of sand to blocks as big as cars. As the blast roared out of the volcano, it swept up and carried along the rock it had shattered.

The result was what one geologist described as "a stone wind." It was a wind **2** of steam and rocks, traveling at high speed. The rocks gave the blast its great force. Before it, trees snapped and fell. Their stumps looked as if they had been sandblasted. The wind of stone rushed on. It stripped bark and branches from trees and uprooted them, leveling 150 square miles of countryside. At the edge of this area other trees were left standing, but the heat of the blast scorched and killed them.

The stone wind was traveling so fast that it overtook and passed the avalanche. On its path was Spirit Lake, one of the most beautiful lakes in the Cascades. The blast stripped the trees from the slopes surrounding the lake and moved on.

Meanwhile, the avalanche had hit a ridge and split. One part of it poured into Spirit Lake, adding a 180-foot layer of rock and dirt to the bottom of the lake. The slide of avalanche into the lake forced the water out. The water sloshed up the slopes, then fell back into the lake. With it came thousands of trees felled by the blast.

The main part of the avalanche swept down the valley of the North Fork of the Toutle River. There, in the valley, most of the avalanche slowed and stopped. It covered 24 square miles and averaged 150 feet thick.

The blast itself continued for ten to fifteen minutes, then stopped. Minutes later, Mount St. Helens began to erupt upward. A dark column of ash and ground-up rock rose miles into the sky. Winds blew the ash eastward. Lightning flashed in the ash cloud and started forest fires. In Yakima, Washington, some 80 miles away, the sky turned so dark that street lights went on at noon. Ash fell like snow that would not melt. This eruption continued for nine hours.

Shortly after noon, the color of the ash column changed. It became lighter, a sign that the volcano was now throwing out mostly new magma. Until then, much of the ash had been made of old rock.

The blast leveled forests of huge firs. The tiny figures of two scientists (lower right) give an idea of scale.

TRANSPARENCY 27

Literary Elements
Imagery – examines the use of imagery to make unfamiliar things more clear to the reader.

1. GUIDED READING:
Understanding Implied Ideas
This passage helps to answer the third question in the passage on page 436: "What had become of the mountaintop, which was now 1,200 feet lower?" Some of the missing mountaintop was in this avalanche.

2. GUIDED READING:
Using Map Skills; Drawing Conclusions
Were the people in Seattle, Washington, affected by the ash? Have students use the map on page 433. Probably not. Seattle is north; the ash blew east.

VISUAL CONNECTIONS

In 1990 (ten years later) naturalists reported that 90 percent of the animals and about 70 percent of the plant species had returned to Mount St. Helens. However, it will take 100–200 years for an evergreen forest to cover the destroyed area.

The tourists have returned, too. There are a new visitor center and a popular viewing site on the east side of the mountain. Ask students whether they'd like to visit Mount St. Helens, and why or why not.

An eruption on March 19, 1982, melted snow and caused this mudflow. The smaller part of the flow went into Spirit Lake (lower left), while the larger part traveled down the Toutle River.

CLOSURE
Have three students tell what they think was the most important thing they learned from this article.

RETEACHING
Ask students to suppose that there was a printing error, and the text of "Volcano" was completely left out. Have them tell what they could learn from just looking at the photographs, captions, map, and diagram.

At the same time the volcano began giving off huge flows of pumice and ash. The material was very hot, with temperatures of about 1,000 degrees Fahrenheit, and it traveled down the mountain at speeds of 100 miles an hour. The flows went on until 5:30 in the afternoon. They formed a wedge-shaped plain of pumice on the side of the mountain. Two weeks later, temperatures in the pumice were still 780 degrees.

Finally, there were the mudflows, which started when heat from the blast melted ice and snow on the mountaintop. The water mixed with ash, pumice, ground-up rock, and dirt and rocks of the avalanche. The result was a thick mixture that was like wet concrete, a mudflow. The mudflows traveled fast, scouring the landscape and sweeping down the slopes into river valleys. Together, their speed and thickness did great damage.

The largest mudflow was made of avalanche material from the valley of the North Fork of the Toutle River. It churned down the river valley, tearing out steel bridges, ripping houses apart, picking up boulders and trucks and carrying them along. Miles away it choked the Cowlitz River and blocked shipping channels in the Columbia River.

When the sun rose on May 19, it showed a greatly changed St. Helens. The mountain was 1,200 feet shorter than it had been the morning before. Most of the old top had slid down the mountain in the avalanche. The rest had erupted out as shattered rock. Geologists later figured that

1. GUIDED READING:
Understanding Implied Ideas
To help students understand how hot these temperatures are, note that water boils at 212° Fahrenheit.

Ask students why they think the pumice was 780° two weeks later. (The pumice plain was so big and so deep that the air could not cool it quickly.)

2. GUIDED READING:
Understanding Main Ideas
Students should add the mudflow to their list of destructive forces (see page 438).

EXTENSION AND ENRICHMENT

Science/Speaking. Ask students to make a list of mountains, lakes, rivers, swamps, deserts in your state or region. Students can work in small groups to gather information about one of these features to present orally to the class.

Creative Writing. Ask students to write another short myth explaining the origin of something they have observed in nature: why there are seasons, stars, day and night, butterflies, and so on. They may work individually, in pairs, or in small groups.

Cartography. Tell students that the art of mapmaking is called cartography. You might assign a map of a region they are familiar with. They must provide a caption for the map. They might have to think of symbols for geographic features like mountains, deserts, pine barrens, marshes, rivers.

FOR STUDY AND DISCUSSION

Identifying Facts

1. The first sign was an earthquake on March 20, 1980.
2. They were built by the lava flows, ash, and pumice of "many eruptions over thousands of years."
3. (1) They had to watch the mountain to find out if more eruptions were coming and to learn how to predict them. (2) They had to find out exactly what happened on May 18.
4. Why had Mount St. Helens erupted so suddenly? What had caused the fan-shaped area of destruction? What had happened to the top 1200 feet of the mountain?

They studied instrument records and photographs, interviewed witnesses, and visited the scene.

They learned that the eruption was different from earlier ones.

5. *Magma:* molten rock from the earth's center.
Lava: magma after it reaches the surface.
Pumice: frothy rock puffed up by gases.

Interpreting Meanings

6. Images will vary. She contrasts the sleeping volcano "silent and still, big and beautiful" with the huge, noisy destruction of the erupting volcano. She

Crack in dome shows red-hot molten rock just below the surface.

the volcano had lost three quarters of a cubic mile[1] of old rock.

The north side of the mountain had changed from a green and lovely slope to a fan-shaped wasteland.

At the top of Mount St. Helens was a big, new crater with the shape of a horseshoe. Inside the crater was the vent, the opening through which rock and gases erupted from time to time over the next few years.

In 1980 St. Helens erupted six more times. Most of these eruptions were explosive—ash soared into the air, pumice swept down the north side of the mountain. In the eruptions of June and August, thick pasty lava oozed out of the vent and built a <u>dome</u>. But both domes were destroyed by the next eruptions. In October the pattern changed. The explosions stopped, and thick lava built a dome that was not destroyed. Later eruptions added to the dome, making it bigger and bigger.

During this time, geologists were learning to read the clues found before eruptions. They learned to predict what St. Helens was going to do. The predictions helped to protect people who were on and near the mountain.

Among these people were many natural scientists. They had come to look for survivors, for plants and animals that had lived through the eruption. They had come to look for colonizers, for plants and animals that would move in. Mount St. Helens had erupted many times before. Each time life had returned. Now scientists would have a chance to see how it did. They would see how nature healed itself.

---

1. **cubic mile:** the amount of space in a cube one mile long, one mile wide, and one mile high.

PORTFOLIO ASSESSMENT
Volcanoes, geysers, rain forests, the ozone layer, and endangered species are some science topics that may interest students. Suggest that they may want to discover an appropriate scientific association and write to it, asking for information about their chosen topic. Since this will be a business letter, the final draft should be typewritten. Students may want to use a word processor to write and revise their drafts and to print their final copy. Allow for peer editing of a second draft of the letter. Those familiar with on-line communications may want to send their letters using e-mail or some other service. (For more information on student portfolios, see the *Portfolio Assessment and Professional Support Materials* booklet in your teaching resources.)

For Study and Discussion

IDENTIFYING FACTS

1. What was the first sign that something was going on inside Mount St. Helens?

2. Describe the process which built Mount St. Helens and neighboring volcanoes.

3. After the eruption that took place on May 18, what two big jobs did the geologists face?

4. What three questions did the geologists want answered after the May 18 eruption? How did they get the answers? What did they learn?

5. This writer very carefully defines several scientific terms in **context**. Skim the opening of the selection to find where the following "volcano terms" are defined. Write out their definitions:
   a. magma
   b. lava
   c. pumice

INTERPRETING MEANINGS

6. The writer contrasts St. Helens before the eruption with St. Helens after the eruption. Describe some of these before-and-after **images**. How did the writer make you feel about what happened to people, animals, and land as a result of the explosion?

7. Just as fiction writers do, scientific writers build up **suspense**. They want to make us eager to read on to find out "what happens next." Where in this selection did the writer build up your suspense? At these moments, what questions did she plant in your mind?

8. Scientific writers, like all nonfiction writers, have to know their **audience**. This book about volcanoes was written for young adults. Do you think the writer succeeded in making difficult scientific concepts clear? Was anything unclear?

APPLYING MEANINGS

9. If you lived in the area around Mount St. Helens and were warned that it was going to erupt some time within the next five years, would you continue to live there? Explain.

Focus on Reading

USING GRAPHIC AIDS: MAPS AND CAPTIONS

To help you understand a science article, an author will usually include **graphic aids,** such as charts, graphs, diagrams, maps, and photographs. These graphic aids often are accompanied by **captions,** which explain what the aids are about.

Use the map and caption on page 433 to answer the following questions.

1. What does the map show?

2. Which is farther away from Mount Jefferson, Mount Shasta or Mount Rainier?

3. What do the letters *B.P.* stand for?

4. Which is closer to Mount Mazama, Lassen or Three Sisters?

5. Which volcano is between Mount Hood and Three Sisters?

Literary Elements

FIGURES OF SPEECH

When science writers need to explain ideas that are unfamiliar to their readers, they may

contrasts the green, peaceful images before with the ashy wasteland after.

Students may say they feel sympathetic, sad, shocked, frightened.

7. Possible answer: The subheading "The Volcano Wakes," the first paragraph (page 432), and the scientists' concerns helped build suspense.

Students might have been asking themselves, when will the volcano erupt? Will anyone be hurt? How bad will it be? Can it be stopped?

8. Most will agree the writer did a good job.

Applying Meanings

9. Some may say they would stay because of the beauty of the place. Others would say, "No way. It's too dangerous."

FOCUS ON READING
Using Graphic Aids: Maps and Captions

1. The map shows volcanoes in the Cascade Range in the United States and the periods in which each volcano last erupted.
2. Mount Shasta
3. *B.P.* stands for *before present*.
4. Three Sisters
5. Mount Jefferson

LITERARY ELEMENTS
Figures of Speech
1. "For well over a hundred years the volcano

TRANSPARENCY 26
Reader Response
Charting Your Response – prompts students to evaluate their reaction to the selection.

slept" (page 433). "With the earthquake of March 20, 1980, Mount St. Helens awoke from a sleep of 123 years" (page 435).
2. a. The mountain is compared to a pressure cooker.
 b. Yes. Both contained superheated steam under great pressure. If a pressure cooker is not used properly, it will explode.
3. a. They are compared to straws.
 b. Answers will vary. Possible answers: Yes, because it gives a clear idea of how strong the stone wind was.
4. Nature is compared to a plant or an animal; both can heal their wounds.

FOCUS ON INFORMATIVE WRITING
Explaining a Process
You may want to have students include lists of any materials necessary for their processes.

LITERATURE AND SCIENCE
Myths and Scientific Words
An **arachnid** is a small land animal of a group related to insects and including spiders. In Greek mythology Arachne is so proud of her skill in weaving that she challenges the goddess Athena to a contest. In anger, Athena changes Arachne into a spider, the myth thus explaining the origin of spiders.

444

---

compare those ideas to things their readers already know. Comparisons between two unlike things are called **figures of speech.**

The very first sentence of this selection uses a figure of speech when the writer says "For many years the volcano slept." Obviously, a volcano cannot close its eyes and snooze. This figure of speech makes us visualize the volcano as a sleeping giant—something that will be dangerous when it "wakes up."

1. Find other passages in which this writer describes the volcano in terms of a sleeping person.
2. "Before the eruption, Mount St. Helens was like a giant pressure cooker."
   a. What is the mountain compared with here?
   b. Is this a good comparison? Why?
3. "It snapped off or uprooted the trees, scattering the trunks as if they were straws."
   a. What are the tree trunks compared with?
   b. In your opinion, is this a good comparison? Why?
4. What do you think nature is compared with in the very last sentence?

Focus on Informative Writing

EXPLAINING A PROCESS
In a **process explanation,** you tell your readers how something works or how to do something. For example, in "Volcano" Patricia Lauber explains the process that leads to an eruption. She also explains how geologists work.

444 Nonfiction

To find a topic for a process explanation, ask yourself questions like these:
 What do I like to do?
 What can I do best?
 What might interest my audience?

Get together with a small group. Brainstorm with your classmates to find *two* topics for informative papers. One topic should focus on how to do something. The other should focus on how something works. Here are some possible topics for your group to consider:

How to do X	*How X Works*
how to make a kite	how blood circulates
how to make salsa	how VCRs work

For each topic your group chooses, make a chart like the one below. List each step or stage of the process in the correct order. Save your notes.

```
Topic: _____
Steps/Stages
  1. _____
  2. _____
  3. _____
  4. _____
```

About the Author

Patricia Lauber (1924–   ) is best known for her informational books on a variety of topics, including animals, rivers, planets, robots, and cattle ranching. She has been praised for her skill in presenting clearly and with colorful detail subjects that young people often think are boring. She says that the greatest reward in writing scientific books for young readers comes from children who write her letters asking for "more."

Literature and Science

Myths and Scientific Words

Many words in science have their beginnings in the mythologies of ancient Greece and Rome. You have already seen that the word *volcano* comes from the name of the Roman god Vulcan. Nearly all the planets in our solar system are named after Roman gods, and a number of constellations are named after Greek figures. The names of several chemical elements come from figures in Greek mythology.

Making Connections: Activities

Use a dictionary, an encyclopedia, or other reference book to discover how the meaning of each of the following words is associated with a figure in classical mythology. Can you add to this list other scientific words named after mythological persons?

arachnid	plutonium
heliosphere	chronometer
Mercury	selenium
ocean	typhoon
medusa	echidna

A **heliosphere** is a region around the sun over which the effect of solar wind extends. In Greek mythology, Helios is the sun god.

Mercury is the smallest planet. It was named for the swift messenger of ancient gods in Roman mythology.

The modern term **ocean** is derived from the Greek god Oceanus, who was a Titan and ruler of the seas before Poseidon.

Medusa, a type of jellyfish, takes its name from the character of the same name in greek mythology. Medusa was one of the Gorgons slain by Perseus.

Named for the Roman god of the underworld, Pluto, **plutonium** is a radioactive, metallic element.

Chronometer is the name for an accurate timepiece. The first part of the word is derived indirectly from the name of the greek god Cronos, who ruled the universe.

Named for Selene, the goddess of the moon in Greek mythology, **selenium** is a nonmetallic element related to sulfur.

A **typhoon** is a violent tropical cyclone or hurricane. In Greek mythology Typhon is father of the winds.

The **echidna,** commonly known as the spiny anteater, traces its name back to the Greek word for viper—same spelling.

Behind the Scenes

A "Spinachlike" Reputation

To many people an "appealing" science book is a contradiction in terms, for science tends to have a spinachlike reputation. . . . Readers of science books are unlikely to feel the hair rise on the backs of their necks or to laugh or cry, except perhaps for highly personal reasons. They may well have to work hard to understand the content. And so science is often viewed as being somewhat unpalatable [not tasty]—but good for you . . .

Yet, that is an adult view. Children are not born turned off by science, and if they grow up that way, it is because they have "caught" that attitude, along with the common cold and other scourges. Children are born curious, wanting and needing to understand the world around them, wanting to know why, how, and what: the very questions that scientists ask.

—Patricia Lauber

THE PERSONAL ESSAY

Snapshot of a Dog

JAMES THURBER

Before You Read

A famous animal character can be as vivid and memorable as a human character. Just think of the many well-known animals created in the movies (like Lassie), on television (like Alf), or in cartoons (like Garfield). What famous animals do you know from books you have read?

James Thurber characterized and even drew a "breed" of dog called the Thurber dog, or Thurberhound. In this essay he remembers a real dog his family once owned. Do you think these events are all absolutely true, or has Thurber exaggerated a little to make you smile?

After reading the first paragraph, sketch Rex. Compare your "snapshots" with those of your classmates.

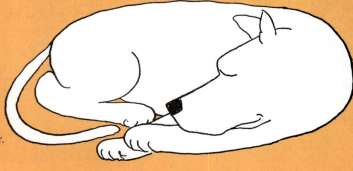

A sketch of Rex by James Thurber.
Courtesy Rosemary Thurber.

READING THE SELECTION
Some of the difficult words in this selection are footnoted. However, slower students may find the language challenging. Since it is short, you might read the whole piece aloud with students of lesser ability. The humor and the popularity of the subject (a pet) should capture the interest of all students.

> ## Language and Vocabulary
>
> **Descriptive details help us see something, taste it, smell it, hear its sounds, and feel its textures.** A snapshot is an informal picture taken with a camera. Here, Thurber is *writing* a snapshot, using descriptive details to help us form a clear, and comical, picture of his pet Rex. (Just looking at your drawings of Rex will show you how many details you picked up from Thurber's description.) As you read, be aware of the descriptions of Rex that make him come bounding off the page.

1. GUIDED READING:
Discussing Character
In what way can a dog be "noble" and "dignified"? A dog who doesn't bark madly and fuss might display these traits. He would stay calm and in control.

2. GUIDED READING:
Making Inferences
Besides his strength, what other qualities of Rex are revealed in this retrieval? He displays determination and cleverness.

I ran across a dim photograph of him the other day, going through some old things. He's been dead twenty-five years. His name was Rex (my two brothers and I named him when we were in our early teens) and he was a bull terrier. "An American bull terrier," we used to say, proudly; none of your English bulls. He had one brindle[1] eye that sometimes made him look like a clown and sometimes reminded you of a politician with derby hat and cigar. The rest of him was white except for a brindle saddle that always seemed to be slipping off and a brindle stocking on a hind leg. **1** Nevertheless, there was a nobility about him. He was big and muscular and beautifully made. He never lost his dignity even when trying to accomplish the extravagant tasks my brothers and myself used to set for him. One of these was bringing a ten-foot wooden rail into the yard through the back gate. We would throw it out into the alley and tell him to go get it. Rex was as powerful as a wrestler, and there were not many things that he couldn't manage somehow to get hold of with his great jaws and lift or drag to wherever he wanted to put them, or wherever we wanted them put. He could catch the rail at the balance[2] and lift it clear of the ground and trot with great confidence toward the gate. Of course, since the gate was only four feet wide or so, he couldn't bring the rail in broadside.[3] He found that out when he got a few terrific jolts, but he wouldn't give up. He finally **2** figured out how to do it, by dragging the rail, holding onto one end, growling. He got a great, wagging satisfaction out of his work. We used to bet kids who had never seen Rex in action that he could catch a baseball thrown as high as they could throw it. He almost never let us down. Rex

---
1. **brindle:** streaks or spots of a darker color.
2. **at the balance:** in the middle.
3. **broadside:** here, with the length of the pole facing front.

MEETING INDIVIDUAL NEEDS

ESL/LEP • Thurber uses several idiomatic expressions that may require explanation. These include *ran across* (found), *let us down* (disappointed us), *held up* (delayed), *on hand* (present), and *fell to* (began).

ART LINK
Invite students to draw their own imaginary breed of dog. To encourage students who have difficulty drawing, you may wish to point out the simplicity of Thurber's sketches. Encourage students to name their breeds, and post the drawings around the room. Extend this activity by teaming interested students to create comic strips starring their dogs.

1. LITERARY ELEMENTS:
Description
Description often appeals to our sense of hearing. *Point out three details of sound in this passage.* Snarling, screeching, plump.

2. LITERARY ELEMENTS:
Humor
Ask students to explain the humor of this passage. (The picture of fire engines and a fire hose trying to break up a dog fight is a funny one. Students should try to picture a hundred-yard distance—the distance of an entire football field, for example.)

---

could hold a baseball with ease in his mouth, in one cheek, as if it were a chew of tobacco.

He was a tremendous fighter, but he never started fights. I don't believe he liked to get into them, despite the fact that he came from a line of fighters. He never went for another dog's throat but for one of its ears (that teaches a dog a lesson), and he would get his grip, close his eyes, and hold on. He could hold on for hours. His longest fight lasted from dusk until almost pitch-dark, one Sunday. It was fought in East Main Street in Columbus with a large, snarly nondescript[4] that belonged to a big neighborhood handyman. When Rex finally got his ear grip, the brief whirlwind of snarling turned to screeching. It was frightening to listen to and to watch. The man boldly picked the dogs up somehow and began swinging them around his head, and finally let them fly like a hammer in a hammer throw, but although they landed ten feet away with a great plump, Rex still held on.

The two dogs eventually worked their way to the middle of the car tracks, and after a while two or three streetcars were held up by the fight. A motorman tried to pry Rex's jaws open with a switch rod; somebody lighted a fire and made a torch of a stick and held that to Rex's tail, but he paid no attention. In the end, all the residents and storekeepers in the neighborhood were on hand, shouting this, suggesting that. Rex's joy of battle, when battle was joined, was almost tranquil. He had a kind of pleasant expression during fights, not a vicious one, his eyes closed in what would have seemed to be sleep had it not been for the turmoil of the struggle. The Oak Street Fire Department finally had to be sent for—I don't know why nobody thought of it sooner. Five or six pieces of apparatus arrived, followed by a battalion[5] chief. A hose was attached and a powerful stream of water was turned on the dogs. Rex held on for several moments more while the torrent buffeted him about like a log in a freshet.[6] He was a hundred yards away from where the fight started when he finally let go.

The story of that Homeric[7] fight got all around town, and some of our relatives looked upon the incident as a blot on the family name. They insisted that we get rid of Rex, but we were very happy with him, and nobody could have made us give him up. We would have left town with him first, along any road there was to go. It would have been different, perhaps, if he'd ever started fights, or looked for trouble. But he had a gentle disposition. He never bit a person in the ten strenuous years that he lived, nor ever growled at anyone except prowlers. He killed cats, that is true, but

---

4. **nondescript:** here, no particular breed of dog.

5. **battalion:** here, a group of firefighters.
6. **freshet:** a sudden stream of water.
7. **Homer** was a Greek poet of the eighth century B.C. who was famous for a long story-poem called the *Iliad*, about a ten-year-long battle.

Nonfiction

MEETING INDIVIDUAL NEEDS

Kinesthetic Learners • Thurber uses exaggeration to make this essay humorous. The abilities of Rex the dog and many of the descriptive passages in the story are humorous exaggerations based on familiar situations. Have students work in pairs to dramatize exaggerations of familiar situations. Students might choose to exaggerate typical scenes from school, such as a conversation with a teacher or classmate, or from home, such as a family meal or an argument with a sibling.

---

1 quickly and neatly and without especial malice, the way men kill certain animals. It was the only thing he did that we could never cure him of doing. He never killed, or even chased, a squirrel. I don't know why. He had his own philosophy about such things. He never ran barking after wagons or automobiles. He didn't seem to see the idea in pursuing something you couldn't catch, or something you couldn't do anything with, even if you did catch it. A wagon was one of the things he couldn't tug along with his mighty jaws, and he knew it. Wagons, therefore, were not a part of his world.

Swimming was his favorite recreation. The first time he ever saw a body of water (Alum Creek), he trotted nervously along the steep bank for a while, fell to barking wildly, and finally plunged in from a height of eight feet or more. I shall always remember that shining, virgin dive. Then he swam upstream and back just for the pleasure of it, like a man. It was fun to see him battle upstream against a stiff current, struggling and growling every foot of the way. He had as much fun in the water as any person I have known. You didn't have to throw a stick in the water to get him to go in. Of course, he would bring back a stick to you if you did throw one in. He would even have brought back a piano if you had thrown one in.

That reminds me of the night, way after midnight, when he went a-roving in the light of the moon and brought back a small chest of drawers that he found somewhere—how far from the house nobody ever knew; since it was Rex, it could easily have been half a mile. There were no drawers in the chest when he got it home, and it wasn't a good one—he hadn't taken it out of anybody's house; it was just an old cheap piece that somebody had abandoned on a trash heap. Still, it was something he wanted, probably because it presented a nice problem in transportation. It tested his mettle.[8] We first knew about his achievement when, deep in the night, we heard him trying to get the chest up onto the porch. **2** It sounded as if two or three people were trying to tear the house down. We came downstairs and turned on the porch light. Rex was on the top step trying to pull the thing up, but it had caught somehow and he was just holding his own. I suppose he would have held his own till dawn if we hadn't helped him. The next day we carted the chest miles away and threw it out. If we had thrown it out in a nearby alley, he would have brought it home again, as a small token of his integrity in such matters. After all, he had been taught to carry heavy wooden objects about, and he was proud of his prowess.

I am glad Rex never saw a trained police dog jump. He was just an amateur jumper himself, but the most daring and tenacious I have ever seen. He would take on any fence we pointed out to him. Six feet was easy for him, and he could do eight by making a tremendous leap and hauling himself over finally by his paws, grunting and straining; but he lived and died without

---

8. **mettle:** spirit or courage.

---

1. GUIDED READING:
Understanding the Author's Purpose
Why does the author make this comparison? Thurber is making an ironic comment—killing cats is always bad, whether or not there is malicious intent. But he is continuing to defend his dog's character. He may also be aiming criticism at hunters.

2. LITERARY ELEMENTS:
Exaggeration
This is a good example of Thurber's use of exaggeration. You might have students be on the lookout for other examples. (See the answer to question 6, page 451).

CLOSURE

Have students sum up Rex's character, listing his chief character traits.

FOR STUDY AND DISCUSSION

Identifying Facts

1. He could bring a 10-foot rail through a 4-foot gate; he could hold a baseball in one cheek; he could jump an 8-foot fence.
2. The fight between Rex and the nondescript dog lasted from sunset until dark. Rex maintained his grip on the dog's ear despite being thrown ten feet, having his jaws pried by a switchrod, and having a torch held to his tail. Finally fire engines hosed the dogs apart and Rex landed 100 feet from where the fight began.
3. He suspects that Rex got the chest of drawers because it was a challenge to get it home.
4. Rex's last hours were spent fighting. He apparently was badly beaten by the owner of a dog he had just fought. He fought against death until his third master returned home.

Interpreting Meanings

5. Thurber loved, respected, and admired his pet. He was also deeply amused by him.

Answers will vary. Most students will also like and admire Rex and will feel a sense of sadness when reading about his valiant death.

450

---

knowing that twelve- and sixteen-foot walls were too much for him. Frequently, after letting him try to go over one for a while, we would have to carry him home. He would never have given up trying.

There was in his world no such thing as the impossible. Even death couldn't beat him down. He died, it is true, but only, as one of his admirers said, after "straight-arming[9] the death angel" for more than an hour. Late one afternoon he wandered home, too slowly and too uncertainly to be the Rex that had trotted briskly homeward up our avenue for ten years. I think we all knew when he came through the gate that he was dying. He had apparently taken a terrible beating, probably from the owner of some dog that he had got into a fight with. His head and body were scarred. His heavy collar with the teeth marks of many a battle on it was awry;[10] some of the big brass studs in it were sprung loose from the leather. He licked at our hands and, staggering, fell, but got up again. We could see that he was looking for someone. One of his three masters was not home. He did not get home for an hour. During that hour the bull terrier fought against death as he had fought against the cold, strong current of Alum Creek, as he had fought to climb twelve-foot walls. When the person he was waiting for did come through the gate, whistling, ceasing to whistle, Rex walked a few wobbly paces toward him, touched his hand with his muzzle, and fell down again. This time he didn't get up.

---

9. **straight-arming:** pushing away with the arm outstretched (like a tackler in football).

10. **awry** (ə·rī′): leaning or turned to one side.

A Thurberhound.
Courtesy Rosemary Thurber.

For Study and Discussion

IDENTIFYING FACTS

1. Describe Rex's extraordinary talents. What feats do Thurber and his brothers get Rex to accomplish?
2. Describe Rex's Homeric fight with the nondescript dog. What does it take to finally break them up?
3. Why does Thurber think Rex decided to bring home the chest of drawers?
4. Describe Rex's last hours. What was his final brave struggle?

INTERPRETING MEANINGS

5. How did Thurber feel about his pet? How did he make you feel about Rex?

450 Nonfiction

Portfolio Assessment

Students may be interested in creating a short album of photographs or caricatures of their own pets. Suggest that they brainstorm several ideas using the format suggested in Writing About Literature, below, and that they draw caricatures or take photographs of the pet that illustrate items in their list. Students may want to write short captions under mounted pictures, just as Thurber did under his illustrations. Remind students to sort their mounted pictures until they have an order they are comfortable with and then to create a cover and a title page for their album. Consult with students to agree on how their albums will be assessed. (For more information on student portfolios, see the *Portfolio Assessment and Professional Support Materials* booklet in your teaching resources.)

---

6. What descriptions or events do you think Thurber has **exaggerated** in this snapshot of Rex?

APPLYING MEANINGS

7. One of Thurber's famous dogs went around biting everyone and everything. His name was Muggs. When Muggs died, Thurber wrote this for his tombstone: "Cave canem," which means "Beware of the dog" in Latin. What would you write on Rex's tombstone? (It doesn't have to be in a foreign language.)

Literary Elements

CHARACTER

Think for a minute about Rex's unusual character. Then go back through the story and list at least three things Thurber says Rex *did*.

Next, list at least three things Thurber says Rex did *not* do.

Finally, list at least three direct statements that Thurber makes about Rex's character. (For example, at the beginning of the essay, Thurber says "there was a nobility about him.")

All of these details taken together should give you a good summary of Rex's character. Did Rex remind you of any pets you have known and loved?

Language and Vocabulary

DESCRIPTION

When you want to help a reader see something, or smell it, taste it, hear its sounds or feel its textures, you use **description**. Thurber uses many descriptive details to make Rex jump off the page, as if he were alive. Reread paragraphs 1, 2, and 3 from the essay. Then make a list of the descriptive details from one of these paragraphs that help you **see** Rex and **hear** the sounds that result from his adventures.

Writing About Literature

WRITING YOUR OWN SNAPSHOT

Pick a favorite animal (or far-out creature, if you like) and write your own "Snapshot of a _____." You can choose your animal or creature from real life, or from a movie, book, or TV show. Use Thurber's snapshot as a model. Start out by describing your animal's physical appearance. Then go on to describe some actions that will give your reader a good idea of your animal's character. Before you write, you might want to brainstorm some ideas in a chart such as the one below. One writer filled in a few details.

Name of animal or creature: _Sneegle_

Appearance	Actions
Has rolls of furry fat.	Is always getting stuck in small places. Once I had to pull him out of the neighbor's flowerpot.
Is orange-and-brown-striped.	
Has smart, beady eyes.	

---

6. Possible answers: Rex angling a 10-foot pole through a 4-foot gate; Rex fighting one dog for several hours, relinquishing his grip only after a fire hose is aimed at him; carrying a chest of drawers for half a mile; sounding like three people tearing a house down; leaping 8-foot walls.

Applying Meanings

7. Students might give humorous answers such as "The strongest dog that ever lived" or more serious ones such as "He enjoyed life."

LITERARY ELEMENTS

Character

Things Rex did: dragged a 10-foot pole through a 4-foot gate; held a baseball in his cheek; used an ear grip when fighting; fetched a stick thrown in a river; brought home a chest of drawers; fought off death for an hour.

Things Rex didn't do: never went for another dog's throat; didn't have a vicious expression during a fight; never chased a squirrel; never bit a person.

Direct statements: "he had a gentle disposition"; "he didn't seem to see the idea in pursuing something you couldn't catch";

"he was proud of his prowess"; "he would never have given up trying."

Students will undoubtedly have their own stories about pets they have known.

WRITING ABOUT LITERATURE
Writing Your Own Snapshot Consider the student's presentation of both physical features and personality traits. These traits should be revealed through actions and not just in direct statements. Students' snapshots should be imaginative and full of interesting details.

About the Author

James Thurber (1894–1961) was once asked to write an autobiographical sketch. He started out this way: "James Thurber was born on a night of wild portent and high wind in the year 1894, at 147 Parsons Avenue, Columbus, Ohio." Thurber grew up to be the greatest humorist of his time. In addition to humorous stories and essays, he was famous for his hilarious cartoons of people and animals. In 1925 he began his long-term association with *The New Yorker* magazine. Among his many famous works are "The Secret Life of Walter Mitty"; a children's fantasy called *Many Moons*; and a collection of essays called *The Middle-Aged Man on the Flying Trapeze*, from which this story about Rex is taken. Thurber loved dogs. "If I have any beliefs at all about immortality," he once said (exaggerating as usual), "it is that certain dogs I have known will go to heaven, and very, very few persons will be there. I am pretty sure that heaven will be densely populated with bloodhounds, for one thing."

A dog and a turtle by James Thurber.
Courtesy Rosemary Thurber.

OBJECTIVE
Students will read these two essays aloud to enjoy them.

PRESENTATION
Before they read, you might have students discuss what they know about Bill Cosby and what they think of him. (Students may not know that Cosby has a Ph.D. in education.) These two brief essays are from Cosby's best-seller *Fatherhood*. Although most students are familiar with Cosby's humor and delivery, you may wish to play some of his recordings to get them in the mood for reading these essays.

TEACHING RESOURCES C
Teacher's Notes, p. 92

AV RESOURCES BINDER
Audiocassette 3, Side A

NO QUESTIONS ASKED

Fatherhood

BILL COSBY

Before You Read

Who hasn't heard of Bill Cosby, the star of the TV show that was a top-running hit for many years? If you've seen the re-runs, do you remember how Bill Cosby is always running into family problems? (Usually they're funny ones—though not always.) In his best-selling book of essays called *Fatherhood,* he talks about similar situations that have happened in real life with his own five children. As you read aloud, you will surely hear Bill Cosby's own unique voice coming through. You will probably also find yourself imagining how these situations could take place right on *The Cosby Show.*

MEETING INDIVIDUAL NEEDS

Auditory Learners • You might want to play for students a recording of *Bill Cosby Himself* (Motown Records), Cosby's humorous descriptions of his childhood. Other Bill Cosby recordings students might enjoy are *To Russell, My Brother Whom I Slept With* and *Why Is There Air?*

1. GUIDED READING:
Interpreting Details
Note that he's referring to the fact that women live longer than men.

2. LITERARY ELEMENTS:
Humor
Students may want to talk about what makes the essay funny. Cosby uses slapstick here; when he wonders about the divorce laws (two paragraphs later), he's using exaggeration.

Good Morning, Opponents

If a family wants to get through the day with a minimum of noise and open wounds, the parents have to impose order on the domestic scene. And such order should start with breakfast, which we all know is the most important meal of the day. My wife certainly thinks so. A few weeks ago, she woke me at six o'clock in the morning and said, "I want you to go downstairs and cook breakfast for the children."

"But, dear," I said with an incredulous[1] look at the clock, "it's six in the morning."

"You tell time very nicely. Now go down and cook breakfast for the children. They have to go to school."

"But to eat at six . . . isn't that bad for the stomach? I mean, they just ate twelve hours ago."

"Bill, get out of this bed and go downstairs and cook breakfast for your children!"

I would like to repeat a point I made before: I am not the boss of my house. I don't know how I lost it and I don't know where I lost it. I probably never had it to begin with. My wife is the boss, and I do not understand how she is going to outlive me.

"But here's the thing, dear," I said, now a desperate man, "I don't know what they want to eat."

"It's *down* there."

I went back to sleep. I dreamed I was with Scott in the Antarctic, perhaps because my wife was pouring ice water over my head.

"Have you given any more thought to cooking breakfast?" she said as I awoke again.

And so, downstairs I went, wondering about the divorce laws in my state, and I started slamming things around. I had bacon, sausages, and eggs all lined up when my four-year-old arrived, looking so adorable with her cute face and little braids.

"Morning, Daddy," she said.

"Okay," I said, "what do *you* want for breakfast?"

"Chocolate cake," she replied.

"Chocolate *cake*? For *breakfast*? That's ridiculous."

Then, however, I thought about the ingredients in chocolate cake: milk and eggs and wheat, all part of good nutrition.

"You want chocolate cake, honey?" I said, cutting a piece for her. "Well, here it is. But you also need something to drink."

And I gave her a glass of grapefruit juice.

When the other four children came downstairs and saw the four-year-old eating chocolate cake, they wanted the same, of course; and since I wanted good nutrition for them too, I gave each of them a piece.

So there my five children sat, merrily eating chocolate cake for breakfast, occasionally stopping to sing:

Dad is the greatest dad you can make!
For breakfast he gives us chocolate cake!

---

1. **incredulous** (in·krej′ə·ləs): disbelieving.

The party lasted until my wife appeared, staggered slightly, and said, "Chocolate cake for *breakfast?* Where did you all get *that?*"

"*He* gave it to us! *He* made us eat it!" said my five adorable ingrates[2] in one voice; and then my eight-year-old added, "*We* wanted eggs and cereal."

Who Dressed This Mess?

The father of a daughter, especially one in her teens, will find that she doesn't like to be seen walking with him on the street. In fact, she will often ask him to walk a few paces behind. The father should not take this outdoor demotion personally; it is simply a matter of clothes. His are rotten. Every American daughter is an authority on fashion, and one of the things she knows is that her father dresses like somebody in the Mummers Parade.

In schools, you can always identify the children who were dressed by their fathers. Such children should have signs pinned on their strange attire that say:

Please do not scorn or mock me. I was dressed by my father, who sees colors the way Beethoven heard notes.[3]

Whenever I travel with my kids, the moment I open my suitcase in a hotel, I see the instructions from my wife:

The red blouse goes with the gray skirt.

Do not *let her wear the green striped shirt with the purple plaid pants.*

The pink paisley pants and pink paisley sweater go together.

They may jog or sleep in their sweat suits, but no *one is to wear a sweat suit into the hotel dining room.*

The problem is that men are less studied than women about the way they dress. They never see what a woman sees—for example, that those khaki pants do not cover their ankles. Therefore, the child who goes out to be seen by the public represents the mother; and if this child is out of fashion, an observer will say, "Who dressed that little girl? Some woman at Ringling Brothers?"

"No," will come the answer. "That is Mrs. Cosby's child."

"You're kidding! In spite of her choice of husband, I've always thought that woman had taste."

"It must have been Bill who dressed the child today."

"Oh no, he's not allowed to dress them."

Unless he happens to work for Halston,[4] the American father cannot be trusted to put together combinations of clothes. He is a man who was taught that the height of fashion was to wear two shoes that matched; and so, children can easily convince him of the elegance of whatever they do or don't want to wear.

---

2. **ingrates**: people who are ungrateful for something that's been done for them.
3. **Beethoven** (bā′tō·vən) (1770–1827) was a great German composer who became completely deaf.
4. **Halston** was a famous designer.

Bill Cosby and his TV family, the Huxtables.

"Dad, I don't want to wear socks today."

"Fine."

"Or a shirt."

"That's fine, too."

1 Mothers, however, are relentless in dressing children and often draw tears.

"Young lady, you are not going to wear red leotards outside this house unless you're on your way to dance *Romeo and Juliet*."

"But, Mom, everyone at *school* is wearing them."

"Then I'm helping you keep your individuality. You're wearing that nice gray skirt with the blue sweater and the white lace blouse."

"But, Mom, I *hate* that white lace blouse. It makes me look like a *waitress*."

"Which is what you will be if you don't wear it 'cause you won't be leaving the house to go to school, and a restaurant job will be *it*."

And now come the tears, which move a father deeply. His heart breaks for this child crying at seven in the morning, and he fears that this moment will leave a scar on her psyche. He wonders if Blue Cross covers psychiatry. Couldn't his wife back off a bit? After all, *he* would allow red leotards. He would *also* allow green combat boots.

2

However, a few minutes later at breakfast, where his darling little girl appears with swollen eyes, a runny nose, and the white lace blouse, she and her mother are getting along beautifully.

Of course, it is not hard to get along beautifully with my wife—certainly not for *me*. After twenty-two years of marriage, she is still as feminine as a woman can be; she has fine taste, especially in husbands; **3** and we have many things in common, the greatest of which is that we are both afraid of the children. (The sternness with which she disciplines them is just a front.) I am happiest when she is happy, which means I am happy most of the time. . . .

About the Author

Bill Cosby (1937–   ) was born and grew up in Philadelphia. He is most famous now for his TV comedy show about the Huxtable family. Cosby started his career as a stand-up comic in the coffeehouses in Philadelphia, playing for five dollars a night. Now four records feature his jokes, with such titles as *Bill Cosby Is a Very Funny Fellow . . . Right?* and *I Started Out as a Child*.

When Cosby was twenty-three, he enrolled in Temple University in Philadelphia on an athletic scholarship (despite his high IQ, he had dropped out of high school in the tenth grade). Cosby majored in physical education (he played halfback on Temple's football team), but he chose comedy over sports as his career.

As on his sitcom, Cosby in real life has five children, and all of their names begin with the letter "E." Cosby compares his humor to jazz solos: "To me, a joke is a tune that has a beginning, a middle, and an end. I'm the soloist, and my chord changes are the punch lines that make people laugh."

---

1. GUIDED READING:
Identifying Generalizations
Here's another generalization. Cosby's technique throughout is to generalize about men and women, fathers and mothers, and children.

2. BACKGROUND
To understand the humor here, students need to know that Blue Cross is a health insurance company and that psychiatry is the field of medicine that treats emotional and mental disorders.

3. LITERARY ELEMENTS:
Recognizing Humor
Note that Cosby's immodesty is humorous.

OBJECTIVES

The overall aim is for students to identify causes and effects in a literary passage. For a complete list of objectives, see the **Teacher's Notes**.

PRESENTATION

Review cause and effect with students by asking them to identify a situation from their own lives that involved cause and effect, such as possibly breaking a school rule. What caused them to break the rule, and what were the effects? Then, divide the class into small groups and ask them to read the passage in the text and to answer the questions that follow. Have a leader of each group share the responses with the class and discuss their ideas.

UNDERSTANDING CAUSE AND EFFECT

Students will find an understanding of cause and effect useful to them in their daily lives as they encounter situations that require them to make logical decisions. Also, analyzing cause and effect will improve students' comprehension in all their school subjects. Learning how to use cause and effect in their writing will help in their language arts, science, and social studies classes.

Answers
Answers may vary.
1. The water was under great pressure, sealed in the mountain.
2. The superheated water shattered rock inside the mountain and exploded out the opening; the blast flattened forests; and it swept up and carried along the rock it had shattered.
3. The wind produced from the blast carried rocks ranging in size from grains of sand to blocks as big as cars.

FOCUS ON Reading and Critical Thinking

UNDERSTANDING CAUSE AND EFFECT

A **cause** is a reason that something happens. An **effect** is a result of something that happens. Writers often develop their ideas by explaining or discussing causes and effects.

Read this passage from "Volcano" by Patricia Lauber carefully. Then answer the questions that follow.

> Before the eruption, Mount St. Helens was like a giant pressure cooker. The rock inside it held superheated water. The water stayed liquid because it was under great pressure, sealed in the mountain. When the mountain was torn open, the pressure was suddenly relieved. The superheated water flashed to steam. Expanding violently, it shattered rock inside the mountain and exploded out the opening, traveling at speeds of up to 200 miles an hour.
>
> The blast flattened whole forests of 180-foot-high firs. It snapped off the trunks as if they were straws. At first, this damage was puzzling. A wind of 200 miles an hour is not strong enough to level forests of giant trees. The explanation, geologists later discovered, was that the wind carried rocks ranging in size from grains of sand to blocks as big as cars. As the blast roared out of the volcano, it swept up and carried along the rock it had shattered.

Understanding Cause and Effect

1. What caused the water to stay liquid, even though it was superheated?
2. List *three* effects of the sudden relief of pressure when the mountain was torn open.
3. What explanation does the writer give for the fact that the wind could level forests of giant trees?

Nonfiction

WRITING AN INFORMATIVE PAPER
OBJECTIVES

The overall aim is for students to write an informative paper in the form of a how-to paper, a cause-and-effect paper, or a biographical report. For a complete list of objectives, see the **Teacher's Notes**.

PRESENTATION

From the questions in the text, create headings for long pieces of butcher paper and hang them around the classroom. Ask students to brainstorm responses to the headings, and volunteers can write the ideas on each of the butcher paper lists. Now students have visual charts of possible topics for their informative papers. After students have chosen their topics, you might want to do a quick check of topics and to group students according to the type of paper they are writing. These groups can help each other during the prewriting, revision, and proofreading stages. You may also need to plan library days or to give students time outside

---

FOCUS ON *Writing*

WRITING AN INFORMATIVE PAPER

*I*n **informative writing,** your purpose is to share information. In a **how-to paper,** you explain how to do a process or how something works. In a **cause-and-effect paper,** you explore the reasons and/or the results of an event or situation. In a **biographical report,** you share information about a person's life, personality, and achievements.

Prewriting

1. To find a subject for a process or "how-to" paper, ask yourself questions like these:
   - What do I like to do?
   - What do I do well?

   If you want to write a cause-and-effect explanation, start with these questions:
   - Have I ever wondered why . . . ?
   - What would happen if . . . ?

   If your assignment is to write a biographical report, ask:
   - What is special about this person?
   - What has this person done that would interest my readers?

2. Gather **details** for your informative paper. If you are writing a how-to explanation, list the steps or stages of a process carefully. Remember to list them in exact order. Then list any materials that people may need to perform the process. [See **Focus** assignment on page 444.]

   To identify details for a cause-and-effect explanation, fill out a chart like the one below.

Cause
_____
_____
_____
Event/Problem/Situation:
Effects
_____
_____
_____

   When you fill out your chart, remember that one event or situation may have more than one cause and may result in more than one effect. [See **Focus** assignment on page 428.]

   For a biographical report, fill out a chart like the one below.

Details Chart for a Biographical Report
Date and Place of Birth: _____
Education: _____
Job/Career: _____
Achievements/Special Awards: ____
Family Life: _____
Statements/Quotations: _____
Overall Importance: _____

   [See **Focus** assignment on page 401.]

3. Develop a **main idea** for your paper. Use the hints below to write your main idea in one sentence.

HOLT WRITER'S WORKSHOP

This computer program provides help for all types of writing through guided instruction for each step of the writing process. (Program available separately.)

See **Elements of Writing, Introductory Course,** Chapter 6, for more instruction on informative writing.

WRITING AN INFORMATIVE PAPER

Informative writing includes a broad range of nonfiction prose, from factual reporting to personal reminiscence. The term applies to any kind of writing that explains, and that explanation can take the form of description, narration, defining, or reasoning, and even have undertones of arguing and persuading. Whatever the form, the writer attempts to present the facts, comprehensively and objectively.

Prewriting

You may want students to determine who their audiences will be before they begin prewriting and then to write their main ideas before they begin to fill in their charts. Now they will have a focus for which to collect their details. Remind students that they

Focus on Writing

class to consult the necessary resources for adequate details.

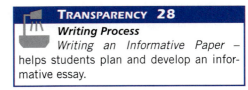

TRANSPARENCY 28
Writing Process
Writing an Informative Paper — helps students plan and develop an informative essay.

should collect details that are relevant to their topics and audiences.

Writing
Students might benefit from creating informal sentence or even paragraph outlines from the samples in the text. Then from their outlines they can write their drafts and add the appropriate transitional words and phrases.

Main Ideas in Informative Writing

How-to paper ⟶ state reason for learning process
"If you follow these simple steps, you can save money on groceries."

Cause-and-effect paper ⟶ summarize what follows
"There are three important reasons for not closing the playground."

Biographical report ⟶ state reason for person's importance
"Jack Benny was one of the most talented comedians of his time."

1. Follow an **outline** when you write your first draft. Below are three samples.

    Process Paper
    I. Introduction
        A. Grab reader's attention
        B. State reason for learning process
    II. Body
        A. List necessary materials
        B. Explain each step
    III. Conclusion
        Summarize value of process

    Cause-and-Effect Explanation
    I. Introduction
        A. Grab reader's attention
        B. State main idea
    II. Body
        Discuss causes/effects in a logical order
    III. Conclusion
        Sum up main points and add comment

    Biographical Report
    I. Introduction
        A. Grab reader's attention
        B. State main idea
    II. Body
        Give facts/anecdotes in chronological order
    III. Conclusion
        A. Restate main idea
        B. Summarize person's importance

2. Remember to arrange the details in the body of your paper in a logical order. In an informative paper, you will usually find it convenient to use **chronological** or time order. In a process paper, you explain the steps of a process in the exact order in which they occur. In a cause-and-effect explanation, you can help the reader to follow a sequence or chain of causes and effects by using time order. Finally, in a biographical report, you will usually want to give the facts and/or anecdotes about a person's life or achievements in correct time order.

3. Help your readers to understand the connections of facts and ideas in your paper by using **transitions.** Here are some useful words and phrases.

    Transitions in Informative Writing
    How-to paper: after, before, first, next, then, when
    Cause-and-effect paper: as a result, because, for, since, therefore
    Biographical report: after, before, finally, next, often, then, until
    [See **Focus** assignment on page 409.]

460 Nonfiction

Evaluating and Revising

1. When you have finished a first draft, put it aside for a while. Then look it over for places that need improvement. Pay special attention to evaluating your details and the order in which you present them. Have you included all the necessary details? Have you arranged them in a sensible order that is easy to follow?

   Here is how one writer revised a paragraph in an informative paper on washing clothes.

Checklist for Evaluation and Revision

- ✔ Do I grab the reader's interest at the beginning?
- ✔ Do I state my main idea in the first paragraph?
- ✔ Do I list any necessary materials that readers may need in order to perform a process?
- ✔ Do I present the details for my paper in a sensible order?
- ✔ Is all my information accurate?
- ✔ Do I conclude my paper with a clear summary statement?

Writer's Model

Place one load of clothes in the washing machine. ~~First separate the light-colored clothes from the dark-colored ones.~~ *Next,* Select the proper wash cycle. Wait two or three minutes until the load is completely wet. Then add detergent. at the end of the cycle remove the clothes from the washer promptly.

Proofreading and Publishing

1. Proofread your paper and correct any errors you find in grammar, usage, and mechanics. (Here you may find it helpful to refer to the **Handbook for Revision** on pages 750–785.) Then prepare a final version of your paper by making a clean copy.

2. Consider some of the following publication methods for your paper:
   - send your essay to the school newspaper or magazine
   - illustrate your essay with maps, diagrams, or charts, and then post it on the class bulletin board
   - stage a "How-to Day" or a "I Wonder Why Day" or a "Celebrity Day" in your class and read your essays aloud

   Portfolio If your teacher approves, you may wish to keep a copy of your work in your writing folder or portfolio.

2. Use the following checklist when you revise your paper.

CLOSURE
Ask students to identify the three types of informative writing, to explain how they are used, and to list the elements of each.

Evaluating and Revising
Students might read their papers aloud in small groups. As each writer reads, each listener is responsible for one part of the paper—the introduction, the body, and the conclusion. Groups can use the **Checklist for Evaluation and Revision** as a guide to evaluate the parts. Students can help each other revise any parts that are weak.

Proofreading and Publishing
You might want to provide students with a focus for their proofreading by asking them to make a list of their errors from previous papers and to choose two or three of those errors to work on for this paper. Be sure that students look for only one error at a time.

UNIT 6 ◆ TEACHING GUIDE

PLAYS

OVERVIEW OF THE UNIT

Watching dramatic presentations is one of the most common activities in your students' lives. Many of them may never have seen a live play, but virtually all of them have seen drama on television and in the movies. Some may also have listened to plays on the radio. Tell your students that in this unit, they'll be gaining a clearer understanding of an activity they've been enjoying since they were small. If any of them have ever thought of going into careers in video, film, theater, or advertising, this unit will deserve their special attention.

WHAT MAKES DRAMA SPECIAL?

Drama differs from the other forms of literature in that it is meant to be performed. Thus, although the greatest plays, such as those of Shakespeare, Chekhov, Ibsen, and O'Neill, are well worth simply reading, they gain an extra dimension from a good performance. In addition to playwrights, actors, directors, set designers and builders, prop persons, costume designers, makeup artists, stage managers, and many others collaborate to create a living event. In this unit, your students will mostly be reading, writing about, and talking about dramas in their literary aspect, but they will also have the chance to stage their own dramatic performances. Students with a variety of aptitudes can enjoy working on plays together.

HOW TO READ A PLAY

You might compare a play to a building. The playwright is the architect. The script, with its dialogue and stage directions, is the blueprint. The process of staging a play is the process of building the building. In this unit, your students will be learning about the architecture of plays. But in understanding a play, it's helpful to keep in mind that the playwright relies on the work of many other gifted people to make the play a reality. It's useful to keep in mind the question "How would this look onstage?"

Other questions that help us read plays include these: "What tone of voice is the character using?" "What is the character doing with his or her hands, face, body, while speaking these lines?" "What are the other actors doing while they aren't talking?" "What does the set look like?" "How are the characters dressed?" "What are their physical traits?"

THE FOUNDATIONS OF DRAMA

The foundations of a play are its characters, conflict, plot, and setting. In a play, as in a short story, we catch a group of interesting characters at a crucial point in their lives. The time span of a play is usually more extended than that of a short story and less extended than that of a novel, though this is only a general description, not a rule. The number of characters must be a number that's manageable on stage—usually between two and two dozen. The setting of a stage play is usually quite unified—many plays only have one locational setting, although the time setting often changes between acts, whether it's a gap of a few hours or several years. With the change of acts, there is also almost always some specific, noteworthy development in the characters' efforts to resolve their major conflict. At the play's end, some sort of satisfying resolution is usually achieved, if only in the characters' new insights into the ongoing problems of life.

THE MATERIALS OF DRAMA

The play's foundation is built into an edifice through the bricks and mortar of dialogue and stage directions. Dialogue is what we tend to notice more, and many readers are tempted to skip the longer stage directions, but that's a mistake. The stage directions tell us what is happening and how to picture it. Especially in film and television scripts and twentieth-century American plays, entire scenes can be developed with minimal dialogue. If a character says, for instance, "Good morning, Ned. How's the family?" it's important to know that she is wearing a business suit, carrying an attaché case, and striding briskly toward the exit without giving Ned so much as a glance.

Reading a play with the ability to visualize its scenes is especially important in the screen media, and two of the plays in this unit—*The Secret Garden* and *The Monsters Are Due on Maple Street*—are television plays. Encourage your students, as they read, to visualize the camera shots. Conversely, encourage them, as they watch television shows or movies, to think about the scripts. This will inevitably give them a better understanding of the drama form and heighten their enjoyment. (They'll even enjoy bad movies and TV shows more if they are able to take them apart in their minds and understand what makes them bad.) If they are seriously interested in this field, consciously developing the habit of reading and watching dramas in this way will nurture a strong intuitive grasp of how plays, movies, and television shows work.

OBJECTIVES OF THE UNIT

The aims of this unit for students are
- To monitor their own reading
- To recognize major events
- To recognize cause and effect
- To make inferences
- To interpret meaning
- To predict outcomes
- To identify a narrative sequence
- To recognize conflict in drama
- To recognize and appreciate descriptive details
- To appreciate dialogue
- To recognize and appreciate suspense
- To recognize foreshadowing
- To compare words using a semantic chart
- To write creatively and critically in relation to the selections
- To write a scene

PLANNING GUIDE

FOR UNIT PLANNING
- Transparencies 29–33: *Audiovisual Resources Binder*
- *Portfolio Assessment and Professional Support Materials*
- Test Generator
- Mastery Tests: Teaching Resources C, pp. 164, 166
- Analogy Test: Teaching Resources C, p. 169
- Revision Worksheet: Teaching Resources C, p. 170

SELECTION (Pupil's Page)	TEACHING RESOURCES C (page numbers shown below)								AV BINDER
	Teacher's Notes	Reading Check	Reading Focus	Study Guide	Language Skills	Building Vocabulary	Selection Vocab. Test	Selection Test	Audio-cassette
PLAYS *Introduction* (p. 463)	101								
Close Reading of a Play Rod Serling from *The Monsters are Due on Maple Street* (p. 465)	101								
Blanche Hanalis Based on the Novel by Frances Hodgson Burnett *The Secret Garden, Act One* (p. 477)	102	104		105	147, 150, 153	106	108	116	
The Secret Garden, Act Two (p. 487)	109	111		112	147, 150, 153	113	115	116	
The Secret Garden, Act Three (p. 496)	118	120		121	147, 150, 153	122	124	132	
The Secret Garden, Act Four (p. 504)	125	127		128	147, 150, 153	129	131	132	
The Secret Garden, Act Five (p. 512)	134	136		137	147, 150, 153	138	140	159	
The Secret Garden, Act Six (p. 523)	141	144		145, 146	147, 150, 153	156	158	159	
Patricia Gray Based on the Novel *The Hobbit* by J.R.R. Tolkien *Riddles in the Dark* (p. 534)	161								

CONCEPTS AND SKILLS

The following concepts and skills are treated in this unit:

CLOSE READING OF A PLAY
Guidelines for Close Reading 464
One Reader's Response 465
Looking at Yourself as a Reader 470

THINKING ABOUT WORDS
Comparing Words: Semantic Features 472

FOCUS ON READING AND CRITICAL THINKING
Drawing Inferences 544

LANGUAGE AND VOCABULARY
Teleplay Terms 476
A Semantic Chart (A Group Project) 532
Stage Terms 536

OPPORTUNITIES FOR WRITING
Focus on Writing a Scene
Using Improvisation to Explore a Scene 531
Writing a Scene 545

SPEAKING AND LISTENING
Acting It Out (A Group Activity) 532
Classroom Theater 535

ART
Making a Diorama 532

TRANSPARENCIES

The following unit support materials with specific correlations to literature selections are available in the **Fine Art and Instructional Transparencies with Teacher's Notes and Blackline Masters** section of your *Audiovisual Resources Binder*.

FINE ART TRANSPARENCIES

Theme: Bring Your Imagination with You

29 *Bust Portrait of the Actor Morita Kanya VIII as the Palanquin-Bearer Uguisu no Jirosaku*, Toshusai Sharaku

30 *Vaudeville*, Jacob Lawrence

READER RESPONSE

31 Critic's Choice

LITERARY ELEMENTS

32 Suspense

WRITING PROCESS

33 Writing a Scene

INTRODUCING THE UNIT

1. Using Pantomimes. Have students work in small groups to perform pantomimes. Allow them a few minutes to decide what situation they would like to act out and to rehearse their pantomimes. After students have performed, discuss with them the importance of nonverbal methods of communication, such as facial expressions, hand gestures, and body language.

2. Practicing "Tones of Voice." To help students appreciate how the meaning of a line of dialogue can change depending on the way an actor or actress interprets it, have students say the words "I really don't want to go now," first in an imploring tone, then in an angry tone, and finally in a tone of exhaustion.

3. Staging the Plays. All the works in this unit may be staged by your class, in whole or part. At the unit's end, ambitious students may want to perform *The Secret Garden* for other classes. (Cutting may be necessary for reasons of time.) Encourage students to search the library for other plays that would be suitable for individual reading, group-staged readings, or full-fledged performances.

PORTFOLIO ASSESSMENT

Suggestions for use of portfolios as support for this unit are described in the **Portfolio Assessment and Professional Support Materials** booklet accompanying this program. Specific suggestions are provided for a variety of student projects that may be suitable for inclusion in a portfolio. In addition, copying masters are provided for guides that may be used for evaluation and assessment of student projects.

SELECTION NOTES

Following are vocabulary lists of words from each act that are included in the Building Vocabulary Worksheets and Selection Vocabulary Tests; Reading Check tests for each act (which are also available in blackline masters); and answers to questions in the Language and Vocabulary section that follows Act Six.

THE SECRET GARDEN, ACT ONE (PAGE 477)

Vocabulary

imposing	arrogance	intrigue(d)	revelation
intrusion	enhance	chastise	illuminate(s)
disrepair	haughty		

Reading Check

Have students judge each statement as true or false.
1. Mary spent her early years in India. **True**
2. Mary's parents were killed by rioting Indians. **False**
3. Mrs. Medlock is a rich woman who has offered to take Mary in even though she is a stranger. **False**
4. Mary is nasty because she suffered from cholera as a child. **False**
5. Archibald Craven is the name of Mary's father's long-lost brother. **False**

THE SECRET GARDEN, ACT TWO (PAGE 487)

Vocabulary

curt	caustic	wistful(ly)	triumphant(ly)
wry	dry(ly)	grudging	grim
sarcastic	contemptuous		

Reading Check

Have students judge each statement as true or false.
1. Dickon is a boy who understands wild animals. **True**
2. Archibald Craven killed his wife. **False**
3. Archibald Craven had the secret garden locked up because he had been miserable in it. **False**
4. Lilias Craven had married Archibald even though she hadn't loved him. **False**
5. Mary discovers that the crying seems to come from behind a tapestry. **True**

THE SECRET GARDEN, ACT THREE (PAGE 496)

Vocabulary

emerge(s)	debris	anticipation	precede(s)
elate(d)	minimal	beckon(s)	
accumulation	adjacent	repulsive	

Reading Check

Have students judge each statement as true or false.
1. Mary gets the key to the secret garden by pleading with Dickon for it. **False**
2. In the secret garden, Mary finds an ugly tangle of dead vines and plants. **True**
3. Mary decides to work on improving the garden's appearance. **True**
4. Archibald Craven likes Mary because she is honest. **True**
5. At the end of the tapestry corridor, Mary discovers a crying girl about her own age. **False**

THE SECRET GARDEN, ACT FOUR (PAGE 504)

Vocabulary

petulant	overwhelm(ed)	tyrant	decisive
distraught	dedicate(d)	survey(ing)	
frail	confrontation	thrive	

Reading Check

Have students judge each statement as true or false.
1. Colin is a sickly child who is nasty to almost everyone. **True**
2. Mary is good for Colin because she lets him do whatever he wants. **False**
3. Dr. Craven is trying to kill Colin because he wants to inherit Misselthwaite Manor. **False**
4. Dickon has helped bring the secret garden back into bloom. **True**
5. Mary decides she wants to help Colin. **True**

THE SECRET GARDEN, ACT FIVE (PAGE 512)

Vocabulary

agitate(d)	tantrum	exquisite	anguish
astound(ed)	awe(d)	forlorn	
ailment(s)	radiant(ly)	eavesdrop(ping)	

Reading Check

Have students judge each statement as true or false.
1. Mary gets Colin to stop screaming by threatening to scream louder. **True**
2. Mary shares the secret of the garden with Colin. **True**
3. Dickon speaks a Yorkshire dialect. **True**
4. Colin refuses to do any garden work himself. **False**
5. Colin's leg muscles are weak because of an accident. **False**

THE SECRET GARDEN, ACT SIX (PAGE 523)

Vocabulary

despondent	envision	somber	tremulous(ly)
listless	commitment	cascade (verb)	
profusion	tentative(ly)	meander(s)	

Reading Check

Have students judge each statement as true or false.
1. Colin teaches himself to walk in secret. **True**
2. When Colin shows his father that he can walk, his father is angry and upset. **False**
3. Dickon was wrong when he predicted he and his friends would be separated. **False**
4. Dickon was killed in World War I. **True**
5. At the end of the play, Dickon and Mary agree to get married. **False**

Language and Vocabulary: A Semantic Chart (page 532)

Here are some sample semantic analysis charts. (Charts will vary, and you should expect arguments.)

Group 1	violent	discouraged	anxious	thwarted
angered	+	–	+	+
frustrated	–	+	+	+
annoyed	–	–	–	+

Group 2	proud	shallow	cold to other people	the kind of trait you look for in a friend
arrogant	+	–	+	–
superficial	–	+	–	–
indifferent	–	–	+	–

You could add to these lists by listing further features across the top. For example, you might add to the top of the Group 2 words the names of some people in the play (Mary, Colin, Mary's mother, Colin's father, Dickon).

Student Learning Options

PLAYS

1. Dramatizing Vocabulary
Assign a vocabulary word from one of the plays in the unit to each student and have students teach the word to the rest of the class by acting out the word's meaning. You can videotape the performances so students can refer to them later to study the words.

2. Building a Stage Set
Ask students to build a model set for one of the plays in the unit. They can use a cardboard box for the stage and doll-house furniture and other miniatures for the props. If building a model is not possible, let students draw the set, using perspective to create a three-dimensional effect.

3. Picturing the Secret Garden
Ask students to draw a color picture of the secret garden. It might be helpful to have on hand books with color photographs of gardens for students to look at.

4. Writing Screen Directions
After students have read the two teleplays in the unit, ask them to create the screen directions for a brief segment of a real TV show. Bring to class a videotape of a three-minute segment of a TV show and play it several times so that students can observe what happens before they write their directions. You might find it helpful to do this activity along with your students.

5. Writing a Play
Ask students to select a short story from Unit 3 of this textbook or from some other source and to rewrite it in play form. The play should include stage directions as well as dialogue.

6. Sculpting Characters
Have students use modeling clay or some other pliable substance to sculpt one or more of the characters in *Riddles in the Dark*. The cartoon characters pictured in the textbook can help students get ideas, but encourage them to be creative and to come up with their own ideas.

VISUAL CONNECTIONS

In this photograph, students can see a grown American woman in a costume on a stage, circa 1979; they can also see a young boy in a turn-of-the-century British fantasy story. The fact that we can see both things in the same person is part of the magic of the theater. In a way, every actor and actress is a walking metaphor: one person who is simultaneously another person.

The title character in James M. Barrie's *Peter Pan* has been played by women ever since Nina Boucicault created the role for the London stage in 1904. Fifty years later, Mary Martin did a classic performance on the American stage and on television. Another twenty-five years and it was Sandy Duncan's turn on Broadway. What fine actress will take on the role in 2004? Note that Peter Pan is a boy who never grows old.

The Broadway production of *Peter Pan*, with Sandy Duncan playing the lead (1979).

UNIT SIX

Plays

Martha Swope Photography, Inc.

Drama may be the oldest form of storytelling. We don't know how or when drama began, but we can guess that people as long ago as prehistoric times started acting out an exciting story. Like any story, drama has a plot, conflict, and characters. But reading a story is basically a private act. Drama, on the other hand, is meant to be performed. Bringing a drama to life requires the creative effort of many people—the playwright, actors, directors, set designers, and many others.

Today you can attend a live performance of a play, you can watch television, or you can go to a movie theater. Why do people love drama so much? Probably for the same reasons we enjoy any form of storytelling: Stories allow us to meet people, to witness actions, and to feel emotions that broaden our experience of life. But even more than that, dramas allow us to share the storytelling experience with the people who sit with us in the living room, the movie house, or the theater.

TEACHING RESOURCES C
Teacher's Notes, p. 101

INTRODUCING THE PLAY
Explain the link between the television shows and movies your students watch and the teleplays and screenplays from which those performances derive. This will help overcome any student reluctance to read plays. Discuss specific examples of impressive dramas your students have seen in any medium. What elements do students feel contribute most to a successful drama—dialogue, action, setting, performance, music, or others? In this unit, as they read plays, students will have the chance to think about the performance aspect as well.

Close Reading OF A PLAY

Just like a story or poem, a play demands active reading and the exercise of your imagination. The most important feature of a play is its dialogue—what the actors and actresses say. But there is more to reading a play than simply reading dialogue. You also have to read stage directions. Stage directions (or in the case of television plays and movie scripts, camera directions) reveal where the scene is set, how the characters read their lines, and how they should act.

Guidelines for Close Reading

1. Read actively and thoughtfully. Look for conflict and clues to characterization. Ask questions. Make predictions. Try to relate the play to your own experiences. When you're finished, see if all your questions have been answered. See if any of your predictions have come true. Think about your overall response to the play. Try to state the main idea of the play in one or two sentences.

2. Read the stage directions or camera directions carefully. These directions are usually in parentheses or brackets.

3. Use your imagination to visualize the play just as if you were watching it on stage or on the movie or television screen.

Here is the first act of a teleplay called *The Monsters Are Due on Maple Street*. This television play was produced in 1960 for the famous television series *The Twilight Zone*. Alongside the selection you will find one reader's response.

FOCUS/MOTIVATION

Establishing a Purpose for Reading. Ask students to look for the suspense in the play. What keeps them reading?

Prereading Journal. Ask students to write a paragraph telling how they think they would react to the landing of an alien spaceship in their neighborhood.

READING THE TELEPLAY

Because this might be your class's first exposure to teleplay form, have the teleplay read aloud by volunteers as the rest of the class follows along. Have one or two volunteers "play" the reader's comments.

---

from
The Monsters Are Due on Maple Street
ROD SERLING

Act One

Scene 1:
Fade-in on shot of the night sky. The various heavenly bodies stand out in sharp, sparkling relief. As the camera begins a slow pan across the heavens, we hear the narrator.

NARRATOR: (*offstage*) There is a fifth dimension beyond that which is known to man. It is a dimension as vast as space, and as timeless as infinity. It is the middle ground between light and shadow—between science and superstition. And it lies between the pit of man's fears and the summit of his knowledge. This is the dimension of imagination. It is an area which we call the Twilight Zone.

Scene 2:
The camera begins to pan down until it passes the horizon and stops on a sign which reads "Maple Street." It is daytime. Then we see the street below. It is a quiet, tree-lined, small-town American street. The houses have front porches on which people sit and swing on gliders, talking across from house to house. STEVE BRAND *is polishing his car, which is parked in front of his house. His neighbor,* DON MARTIN, *leans against the fender watching him. A Good Humor man riding a bicycle is just in the process of stopping to sell some ice cream to a couple of kids. Two women gossip on the front lawn. Another man is watering his lawn with a garden hose. At this moment* TOMMY, *one of the two boys buying ice cream from the vendor, looks up to listen to a tremendous screeching roar from overhead. A flash of light plays on the faces of both boys and then moves down the street and disappears. Various people leave*

ONE READER'S RESPONSE

I like it already. What kind of monsters will they be? Is this going to be funny or scary?

I don't know what a "slow pan" is—some kind of camera direction?

I think I've seen a few of these old shows on TV. They can be scary. **1**

I guess "pan" must mean the camera is moving.

"Gliders" must be like porch swings.

Good Humor man—I guess this is like an ice-cream truck. **2**
I'm getting a pretty good picture of this setting. Sounds like your regular small-town U.S.A. This must be the fifties or sixties. Seems pretty peaceful.
Is this a plane—what's the flash of light?

---

1. LITERARY ELEMENTS:
Atmosphere
What words in the narrator's dialogue make the reader think the play might be scary? The words include *shadow, superstition, pit of man's fears.*

2. GUIDED READING:
Making Inferences About Setting
What do you think the weather is like on this day? How do you know? It is most likely warm. There is much outdoor activity, such as the selling and buying of ice cream and the watering of lawns.

Close Reading of a Play 465

MEETING INDIVIDUAL NEEDS

Visual and Kinesthetic Learners • Encourage students to enlist the aid of the school librarian in finding newspaper and magazine articles about sightings of unidentified flying objects (UFOs) in the United States. Then, have students create a bulletin board display or a scrapbook of copies or their own reproductions of these articles. Have students include in the display a U.S. map showing where the sightings have occurred. Ask students to determine if there are more sightings in certain areas of the country or if there are any discernible patterns to the locations of sightings.

1. GUIDED READING:
Using Prior Knowledge
The reader has used his or her knowledge of old television shows and movies to predict that the light is from an alien spaceship. This prior understanding of the genre puts the reader a step ahead of the characters.

2. GUIDED READING:
Drawing Conclusions
The reader has used the information presented so far to answer the earlier question about whether the play is going to be funny or scary.

3. LITERARY ELEMENTS:
Dialogue
Woman One, Myra, and Voices One through Five all convey information about the power failure through dialogue.

4. GUIDED READING:
Using Prior Knowledge
The reader may know that telephone systems use a separate power supply. This is no ordinary blackout, as later clues show.

Close Reading
OF A PLAY

Do they see anything?

1 I bet it's a spaceship. The "monsters" are probably aliens from another planet. I wonder what they'll look like?

I can't believe they think it's a meteor.

2 Sounds like these people are in for something scary—it's not going to be a comedy.

3 The electricity's out.

4 Even the telephones are out. The spaceship—if that's what it was—did this. This is getting more weird.

---

their porches or stop what they are doing to stare at the sky. STEVE BRAND, *the man who has been polishing his car, stands there transfixed, staring upward. He looks at* DON MARTIN, *his neighbor from across the street.*

STEVE: What was that? A meteor?

DON: That's what it looked like. I didn't hear any crash though, did you?

STEVE: Nope. I didn't hear anything except a roar.

MYRA: (*from her porch*) Steve? What was that?

STEVE: (*raising his voice and looking toward the porch*) Guess it was a meteor, honey. Came awful close, didn't it?

MYRA: Too close for my money! Much too close.

[*The camera pans across the various porches to people who stand there watching and talking in low conversing tones.*]

NARRATOR: Maple Street. Six forty-four P.M. on a late September evening. (*A pause*) Maple Street in the last calm and reflective moment . . . before the monsters came!

[*The camera takes us across the porches again. A man is replacing a light bulb on a front porch. He gets down off his stool to flick the switch and finds that nothing happens. Another man is working on an electric power mower. He plugs in the plug, flicks the switch of the mower off and on; but nothing happens. Through a window we see a woman pushing her finger back and forth on the dial hook of a telephone. Her voice sounds far away.*]

WOMAN ONE: Operator, operator, something's wrong on the phone, operator!

[MYRA BRAND *comes out on the porch and calls to* STEVE.]

MYRA: (*calling*) Steve, the power's off. I had the soup on the stove and the stove just stopped working.

WOMAN ONE: Same thing over here. I can't get anybody on the phone either. The phone seems to be dead.

ART LINK

Have students create murals, dioramas, or other visual representations of what they think will happen next in the play. Encourage students to use information from the camera directions on page 465, which describe Maple Street in detail. Students may also wish to include the "monsters" they think the Maple Street residents might meet.

[*We look down again on the street. Small, mildly disturbed voices creep up from below.*]

VOICE ONE: Electricity's off.
VOICE TWO: Phone won't work.
VOICE THREE: Can't get a thing on the radio.
VOICE FOUR: My power mower won't move, won't work at all.
VOICE FIVE: Radio's gone dead!

[PETE VAN HORN, *a tall, thin man, is seen standing in front of his house.*]

PETE: I'll cut through the back yard . . . see if the power's still on, on Floral Street. I'll be right back!

[*He walks past the side of his house and disappears into the back yard. The camera pans down slowly until we are looking at ten or eleven people standing around the street and overflowing to the curb and sidewalk. In the background is* STEVE BRAND'S *car.*]

STEVE: Doesn't make sense. Why should the power go off all of a sudden *and* the phone line?
DON: Maybe some kind of an electrical storm or something.
CHARLIE: That don't seem likely. Sky's just as blue as anything. Not a cloud. No lightning. No thunder. No nothing. How could it be a storm?
WOMAN ONE: I can't get a thing on the radio. Not even the portable.

[*The people again murmur softly in wonderment.*]

CHARLIE: Well, why don't you go downtown and check with the police, though they'll probably think we're crazy or something. A little power failure and right away we get all flustered and everything——
STEVE: It isn't just the power failure, Charlie. If it was, we'd

These people are completely cut off now. If something happens, they can't get help.

I wonder if he'll come back? **1**

What's the portable?

I notice Charlie isn't going himself!

1. LITERARY ELEMENTS:
Suspense
Note how each new action raises a new suspenseful question. Suspense has shifted from who the visitors are to what will happen to Pete.

Close Reading of a Play **467**

ENVIRONMENT LINK

Encourage interested students to find out how much electricity and gas are used in an average American home each day. Then ask students to research energy-saving strategies such as alternatives to common electrical appliances. Students could then present their findings in the form of pamphlets, posters, or short presentations.

1. GUIDED READING:
Using Context Clues
The reader uses the context clue of "radio" to determine that a "portable" refers to a portable radio.

2. GUIDED READING:
Making Inferences
How does the reader know this? Steve is the "voice of reason" in this scene, making intelligent comments and taking useful actions.

3. GUIDED READING:
Using Prior Knowledge
Again, the reader is drawing on knowledge about a specific movie involving aliens that land on Earth. Point out that the makers of *Close Encounters* drew on their own familiarity with previous alien-contact stories—such as this famous episode from *The Twilight Zone*.

4. GUIDED READING:
Visualizing
Point out that if we were watching the show, we would actually see the look. As readers, we form pictures in our minds—which is both an advantage and a disadvantage of reading versus watching.

Close Reading
OF A PLAY

1 I guess a portable radio would be battery-operated. It shouldn't be affected by a power loss. What's going on?

2 Steve seems to be a major character. He seems like a good guy.

3 It definitely is more than just a power failure. The "monsters" must be doing this. They seem powerful. Something like this happened in that movie *Close Encounters of the Third Kind*.

I already figured that.

4 What's the look? Do they suspect something horrible?

Does he know something? How does he know?

---

still be able to get a broadcast on the portable.

[*There is a murmur of reaction to this.* STEVE *looks from face to face and then over to his car.*]

STEVE: I'll run downtown. We'll get this all straightened out.

[*He walks over to the car, gets in, and turns the key. Looking through the open car door, we see the crowd watching* STEVE *from the other side. He starts the engine. It turns over sluggishly and then stops dead. He tries it again, and this time he can't get it to turn over. Then very slowly he turns the key back to "off" and gets out of the car. The people stare at* STEVE. *He stands for a moment by the car and then walks toward them.*]

STEVE: I don't understand it. It was working fine before——
DON: Out of gas?
STEVE: (*shakes his head*) I just had it filled up.
WOMAN ONE: What's it mean?
CHARLIE: It's just as if . . . as if everything had stopped. (*Then he turns toward* Steve.) We'd better walk downtown.

[*Another murmur of assent to this.*]

STEVE: The two of us can go, Charlie. (*He turns to look back at the car.*) It couldn't be the meteor. A meteor couldn't do this.

[*He and* CHARLIE *exchange a look. Then they start to walk away from the group.* TOMMY *comes into view. He is a serious-faced young boy in spectacles. He stands halfway between the group and the two men who start to walk down the sidewalk.*]

TOMMY: Mr. Brand . . . you'd better not!
STEVE: Why not?
TOMMY: They don't want you to.

[STEVE *and* CHARLIE *exchange a grin and* Steve *looks back toward the boy.*]

468 Plays

Steve: *Who* doesn't want us to?
Tommy: (*jerks his head in the general direction of the distant horizon*) Them!
Steve: Them?
Charlie: Who are *them*?
Tommy: (*intently*) Whoever was in that thing that came by overhead.

[Steve *knits his brows for a moment, cocking his head questioningly. His voice is intense.*]

Steve: What?
Tommy: Whoever was in that thing that came over. I don't think they want us to leave here.

[Steve *leaves* Charlie, *walks over to the boy, and puts his hand on the boy's shoulder. He forces his voice to remain gentle.*]

Steve: What do you mean? What are you talking about?
Tommy: They don't want us to leave. That's why they shut everything off.
Steve: What makes you say that? Whatever gave you *that* idea?
Woman One: (*from the crowd*) Now isn't that the craziest thing you ever heard?
Tommy: (*persistent but a little frightened*) It's always that way, in every story I ever read about a ship landing from outer space.
Woman One: (*to the boy's mother*, Sally, *who stands on the fringe of the crowd*) From outer space yet! Sally, you better get that boy of yours up to bed. He's been reading too many comic books or seeing too many movies or something!
Sally: Tommy, come over here and stop that kind of talk.
Steve: Go ahead, Tommy. We'll be right back. And you'll see. That wasn't any ship or anything like it. That was just a . . . a meteor or something. Likely as not——(*He turns to the group, now trying very hard to sound more optimistic than he*

He's seen something. The **1**
monsters!

Did he see a spaceship?

Sure looks like it!

Steve is really nervous.

This is getting creepy.
Who is "they"?

It figures. No one ever **2**
believes kids.

1. GUIDED READING:
Self-Questioning
At this point, students may be asking themselves why Tommy has seen something when no one else has and how he can remain so calm.

2. GUIDED READING:
Making Generalizations
The reader is making a generalization about adults, which seems true in this specific case but may not be in other cases.

Close Reading of a Play

1. GUIDED READING:
Using Prior Knowledge
What often happens in a suspenseful drama when characters say they'll be right back? They won't be back for a long time, if at all.

2. GUIDED READING:
Using Context Clues
Context clues suggest that the idiom "raise Cain" means to cause a commotion. (In Genesis, Cain is the first murderer—he slew his brother, Abel. In raising Cain, his parents, Adam and Eve, raised a problem.)

3. GUIDED READING:
Predicting Outcomes
The reader is increasing his or her own suspense by predicting that Tommy is part of the monsters' plan. Note that readers, unlike characters, often hope for the worst, because it makes for excitement.

LOOKING AT YOURSELF AS A READER
1. Can answer b. (meteor), c. (Tommy), and d. (to check with the police).
2. Responses will vary. Possibilities include the title, the narrator's comment about the calmness before the monsters came, and Tommy's insistence that "they" do not want inhabitants of Maple

---

Close Reading
OF A PLAY

1 He's really nervous. He knows there's more to it than that.

2 I've heard this about sunspots. What does "raise Cain" mean?

I notice that this Don isn't volunteering to go! They're all scared.

I wonder if they'll make it back?

3 I can't wait to read what happens next. I hope the monsters are really horrible. Maybe Tommy is part of their plan to take over.

---

feels.) No doubt it did have something to do with all this power failure and the rest of it. Meteors can do some crazy things, like sunspots.

DON: (*picking up the cue*) Sure. That's the kind of thing—like sunspots. They raise Cain with radio reception all over the world. And this thing being so close—why, there's no telling the sort of stuff it can do. (*He wets his lips, smiles nervously.*) Go ahead, Charlie. You and Steve go into town and see if that isn't what's causing it all.

[STEVE *and* CHARLIE *walk away from the group down the sidewalk, as the people watch silently.* TOMMY *stares at them, biting his lips, and finally calls out again.*]

TOMMY: Mr. Brand!

[*The two men stop.* TOMMY *takes a step toward them.*]

TOMMY: Mr. Brand . . . please don't leave here.

Looking at Yourself as a Reader

1. After reading the first part of the play, which of these questions are you able to answer:
   a. What is the name of the town where the action takes place?
   b. What do the adults think has caused the bright light passing overhead?
   c. Which character insists that a ship has come from outer space?
   d. Why do Steve and Charlie go into town?
2. *Foreshadowing* is the use of hints or clues to suggest that something is going to happen. List three specific events that foreshadow the trouble that lies ahead on Maple Street.
3. *Suspense* is the feeling of uncertainty about what is going to happen next. Which character creates suspense toward the end of the excerpt?
4. What do you think will happen to the people on Maple Street? Share your predictions with a partner.

PORTFOLIO ASSESSMENT

Plays depend on dialogue and actions to convey their messages. Students who enjoy writing stories may be interested in converting one of their stories into a short, one-act play for inclusion in their portfolios. This project should last the duration of the unit, with deadlines for prewriting, writing the first draft, revising, and making a final copy. You may want to allow class time for peer editing. Suggest students follow the guidelines for writing a scene on page 546. Consult with students individually to agree on how their plays will be assessed. (For more information on student portfolios see the Portfolio Assessment and Professional Support Materials booklet in your teaching resources.)

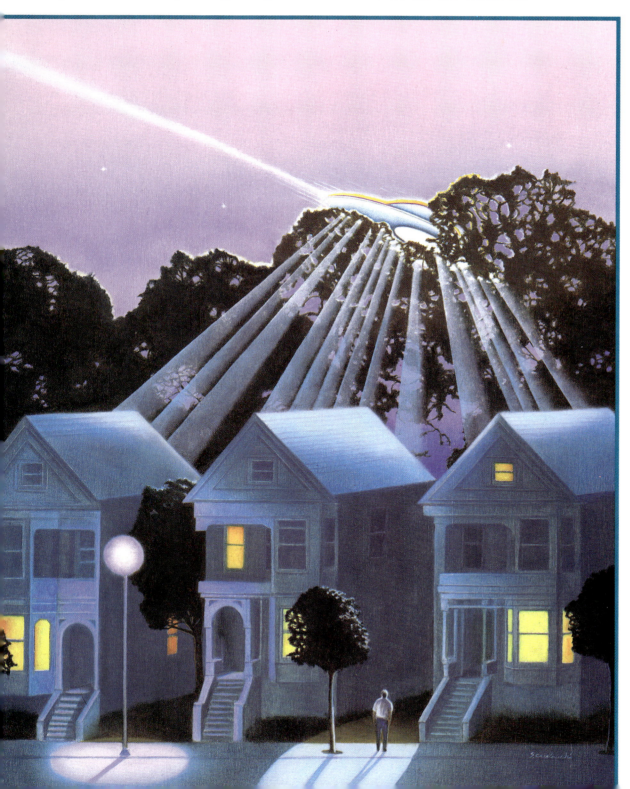

Street to leave.
3. Tommy.
4. Responses will vary. What really happens in the play is that the people become the "monsters." Through fear and suspicion they destroy themselves. The aliens do not have to do anything else to conquer them.

Thinking About Words

These charts are very useful and fun when done as a group or as a whole class. Students will argue about the exact meanings of words and about their applications. You might also do charts on other foods (vegetables, desserts, snacks) or even the application of slang words (wacky, cool, nerdy, creepy, finky, far out, etc.).

THINKING ABOUT WORDS

COMPARING WORDS: SEMANTIC FEATURES

Comparing words is a good way to learn about words. Doing a semantic features chart is an interesting way to compare words. A "semantic features chart" may sound hard, but it's really easy and can be fun to do.

Semantics means "the study of the meanings of words." To do a semantic features chart, you "take apart" the meanings of some words and compare the parts. If you do this carefully, you'll see that words that seem different can be alike in surprising ways. Or, you may see what is different about words that have similar meanings.

In a semantic features chart the words themselves are listed down the left-hand side. Various features, definitions, or meanings of the words are listed along the top. If a word usually has that feature or meaning, mark +. If it usually does *not* have that feature or meaning, mark −. Below is a semantic features chart comparing two very different foods that you probably know well.

	hot	delicious	sweet	spicy	good for breakfast	a good lunch
pizza	+	+	−	+	−	+
cocoa	+	+	+	−	+	−

Now let's try a semantic features analysis with some words you will meet as you read Unit Six. These are all words telling how characters can feel. Let's begin by taking a look at their definitions.

melancholy: "a strong feeling of quiet sadness that lasts a long time"
tranquillity: "a pleasant feeling of calm and peace"
frenzy: "a wildly excited or upset feeling"

Here is a semantic features analysis for these words. The chart helps you see that both *melancholy* and *tranquillity* are quiet feelings, but one feeling is sad while the other is peaceful. It also helps you see that both *melancholy* and *frenzy* are feelings people might have if something bad happens.

	sad	quiet	peaceful	wildly upset	the feeling you have when you hear soft music	the feeling you'd have if your pet ran away
melancholy	+	+	−	−	+	+
tranquillity	−	+	+	−	+	−
frenzy	−	−	−	+	−	+

DO IT YOURSELF

Now try to do a semantic chart of your own. The chart below uses two more words from Unit Six. A hint: The results of your chart will show that someone who is arrogant *can* be caustic. (Both words are defined in the Glossary at the back of the book.)

	proud	mean	feeling superior to others	intending to hurt someone
arrogant				
caustic				

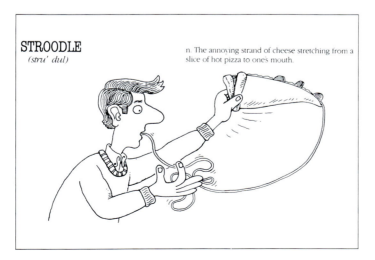

STROODLE
(stru' dul)

n. The annoying strand of cheese stretching from a slice of hot pizza to one's mouth.

Sniglets are those funny made-up words you use to describe something when a dictionary word just won't do. Here is a funny sniglet about pizza. (You might read some other funny ones Rich Hall comes up with in his book *Sniglets*.)

1. VOCABULARY:
Comparing Words
Try to do the same words with your class but put new features across the top. Two features you might use are "cozy and happy" and "ready to scream."

2. Do It Yourself
Arrogant: proud (+); mean (−); feeling superior to others (+); intending to hurt someone (−).

Caustic: proud (+); mean (+); feeling superior to others (+); intending to hurt someone (+).

Thinking About Words

OBJECTIVES

Students will recognize conflict in drama, recognize major events, interpret meanings, and make inferences. They will also use improvisation to explore a scene.

FOCUS/MOTIVATION

Establishing a Purpose for Reading. Tell students they are going to read about two characters they will hate at first. Mary and Colin are snobbish, dictatorial, cold, and obnoxious. The playwright, through authorial magic, will try to get us to like these characters by the time the play ends. Will the magic work? Tell students to look for the ways in which Mary and Colin change and for what causes the changes.

Prereading Journal. Have students answer the questions in the fourth paragraph of the headnote.

The Secret Garden

*Dramatized by BLANCHE HANALIS,
based on the novel by FRANCES HODGSON BURNETT*

Before You Read

This television play is based on a very popular young-adult novel. The play is one huge flashback. A flashback is an interruption in a story that flashes backward to tell you what happened at an earlier time. As the play opens, the main character, Mary, is an adult. She is returning to her childhood home in Yorkshire, a county in northern England. It is 1918, just at the end of World War I. The bulk of the play, however, takes place in the early 1900s, when Mary is a child.

As Act One begins, Mary is remembering her childhood. Her first memory is of her parents' home in New Delhi, the capital of India, a country that was then under British rule. At that time, many British officers, like Mary's father, were stationed in India. Their families lived in India with them, where they enjoyed lavish lifestyles and had many native Indians as their servants.

Epidemics of various diseases were common during those years. Without modern medicines, sicknesses spread easily and killed many people. Cholera (kol'ər·ə) epidemics, like the one at the beginning of this play, really happened. Cholera is an intestinal disease that is often fatal. It spreads quickly through food and drinking water and is even carried by flies.

Before you read, write your responses to this question in your journal: Suppose you were sent far away from home to a strange mansion, where there were no other children to play with and where you heard sounds of weeping at night. How would you feel?

READING THE SELECTION

Because many students will not be familiar with the format of a teleplay, you may wish to have them read aloud at least the first act in class. You can assign the remaining acts for homework. Throughout the play, British usage, including some Yorkshire dialect, may be a challenge for some students. Encourage students to use context clues to determine meanings. Encourage them also to say the words aloud; this will often clarify their meanings.

All stills illustrating the play are from the television production of *The Secret Garden* (November 30, 1987).

Rosemont Productions, Ltd., and CBS-TV Reading Program.

VISUAL CONNECTIONS

The photographs accompanying the teleplay of *The Secret Garden* will help students visualize the action. Encourage them to skim through the photos before beginning to read the play, just as they would look at the stills outside a movie theater before going in. At many points in their reading, a thoughtful look at the stills may clear up matters of setting, expression, gesture, and even character relationships.

The television production of *The Secret Garden* appeared on *Hallmark Hall of Fame* on November 30, 1987. *New York* magazine critic John Leonard said, "The garden is terrific" and had equally good words for the performers. Praising ten-year-old Gennie James's skill and magnetism as Mary, he said, "You want immediately to be her father." He concluded, "I cried."

MUSIC LINK
Interested students could select and play for the class recordings of music they think express the magic of the secret garden. Each student could select and play two pieces of music, one to express the mood of the secret garden when Mary first finds it and the other to express the magic of its transformation.

TEACHING RESOURCES C
Teacher's Notes, p. 102
Reading Check, p. 104
Study Guide, p. 105
Language Skills, pp. 147, 150, 153
Building Vocabulary, p. 106
Selection Vocabulary Test, p. 108
Selection Test, p. 116

1. GUIDED READING:
Scanning
Have students scan the list without memorizing the terms. Remind them to refer back to it as a way of visualizing scenes while reading the teleplay.

2. GUIDED READING:
Scanning
Mary, Mrs. Medlock, Dickon, Colin, and Archibald are the most important characters. Focus on them while going over this list with the class. Scan the others. Tell students to refer to the list as necessary during their reading, just as they refer to the scorecard at a ball game.

Teleplay Terms

Scripts written for television or the movies are different from scripts written for the stage. A **teleplay** (a script written for TV) or a **screenplay** (a script written for the movies) will contain these camera directions.

Fade-in: the picture appears on the screen.
Fade-out: the pictures goes away.
Cut to: a sudden change from one scene or character to another.
Tight shot: a close-up camera shot.
Ext.: exterior (outdoors).
Int.: interior (indoors).

Long shot: a camera shot from far off.
Pan: a swiveling movement of the camera, from one side to the other.
Montage: several images appear on the screen at once.
Beat: pause.
Day: daytime scene.
Night: nighttime scene.

Cast of Characters
(in order of appearance)

BEN WEATHERSTAFF: the gardener at Misselthwaite Manor in England.
MARY LENNOX: an orphaned English girl who is sent from India to live at Misselthwaite Manor.
CAPTAIN LENNOX } Mary's parents.
MRS. LENNOX
MRS. CRAWFORD: a friend of the Lennoxes in India.
COL. MCGRAW AND } British officers serving in India.
LIEUT. BARNEY
MRS. MEDLOCK: housekeeper for Archibald Craven.
JOHN: footman for Archibald Craven.
PITCHER: servant for Archibald Craven.
DICKON SOWERBY: a boy of about twelve. His family is large and poor and lives in a cottage near Misselthwaite Manor.
MARTHA SOWERBY: a servant for Archibald Craven; Dickon's sister.
BETTY: scullery maid at Misselthwaite Manor.
ARCHIBALD CRAVEN: master of Misselthwaite Manor; a bitter widower who is also an invalid.
COLIN CRAVEN: Archibald's only child, about twelve years old.
DR. CRAVEN: Colin's doctor; Archibald's cousin.
MRS. GORDY: cook at Misselthwaite Manor.
NURSE BOGGS: Colin's nurse.

Plays

FOCUS/MOTIVATION

To accustom your students to the teleplay format, ask them to discuss the ways movies and television dramas usually begin. There is usually a series of "establishing shots"—camera shots that show us where the drama takes place. Main characters are often introduced without dialogue at first. This happens during the first eight shots of this act.

READING ACT ONE

Make sure students can follow the flashback. Mary is an adult at the act's opening. Scene 11 begins the long flashback that dominates the teleplay. We then see Mary as a child.

Act One

1 **Fade-in:**
Opening titles appear over a succession of exterior shots.

1. *Ext.—Yorkshire moor—day*
   Wide on a moor with a stone gazebo[1] off in the distance.

2. *Ext. roadway—day*
   An open touring car[2] moves swiftly up the roadway toward the camera.

3. *Ext. signpost—day*
   The signpost reads: "Misselthwaite Manor." The touring car drives past and we see that the car bears a large Red Cross on the door.

4. *Ext. roadway—day*
   The car continues on its way, crossing a stone bridge.

2 5. *Ext. Misselthwaite Manor—day*
   A large imposing mansion that has seen better days. A tight shot of the centuries-old house reveals boarded windows and a building that is much in need of repair. The camera pans, and comes to a stop on BEN WEATHERSTAFF, who is holding a black cat in his arms. About eighty, BEN's rheumy[3] eyes and shaggy brows give him an almost sinister appearance. Watching the approaching car, he seems angered by the intrusion.

6. *Ext. roadway—day*
   The car continues on its way, passing the brick gazebo, which is also in a state of disrepair. BEN peeks out around the corner of the house, staring at the approaching car.

7. *Ext. touring car—day*
   Camera is tight on the driver of the car, MARY LENNOX, a beautiful young woman in her early twenties. The car comes to a stop outside the manor.

8. *Ext. Misselthwaite Manor—day*
   As she exits the car, we see that MARY **3** is wearing the uniform of a British Red Cross transport driver. BEN continues to watch MARY as she walks. Suddenly, the black cat he has been holding leaps from BEN's arms and streaks away.

9. *Ext. vegetable garden—day*
   As MARY passes through shot, the camera cuts to the cat moving along a wall—seemingly stalking MARY. MARY continues walking and there is suddenly heard the faint sound, filtered through time, of a little girl giggling. Again, the camera cuts to the cat as it continues to stalk MARY. MARY continues walking and there is suddenly the sound from the past of a **4** little girl's voice.

LITTLE GIRL'S VOICE: I never had any friends. When will it be spring? . . . We'll

---
1. **gazebo** (gə·zē'bō): outdoor roofed structure, like an open porch.
2. **touring car:** open, luxurious car. During World War I, these touring cars were donated to the Red Cross for use in transporting the wounded.
3. **rheumy** (ro͞om'ē): watery (a condition that often comes with old age).

1. GUIDED READING:
Visualizing
If you were watching this on television, what would you see? You would see the opening credits superimposed on the first several shots.

2. LITERARY ELEMENTS:
Setting and Mood
Where does the action take place? How would you describe the mood? What details help you to know? The setting is Misselthwaite Manor in Yorkshire. The mood is mysterious. Details include the condition of the mansion; Ben's "sinister" appearance and seeming anger at the "intrusion," and the presence of a black cat.

3. BACKGROUND
As many young women did in World War I and other wars, Mary is serving her country by driving wounded soldiers.

4. LITERARY ELEMENTS:
Drama
How can we tell that the girl's voice comes from the past? We infer it from the fact that there is no little girl in the visuals. On the screen, the actress playing Mary would look as if she were remembering something.

The Secret Garden, Act One

Cultural Diversity

To bring to life the language, dress, and cultural milieu of northern England (Yorkshire) in the early 1900s, you may want to show excerpts from the 1993 movie *The Secret Garden* directed by Agnieszka Holland. Particularly interesting are the scenes of Mary's arrival at Misselthwaite, which include a panorama of the moors, the horse-drawn carriage, the interior of the manor, and the introduction of the characters Martha and Dickon. Alert students that the movie is different from the play. For example, in the movie, Mary and Colin are cousins, and Mrs. Medlock is a sour, unsympathetic character.

MEETING INDIVIDUAL NEEDS
ESL/LEP • In developing Mary's character, the author uses the adjectives *curt, bitter, caustic, sarcastic, haughty,* and *contemptuous* to describe her. Write these words on the chalkboard, and invite the class to suggest definitions. Ask students to use each of the words in an original sentence. Write student sentences on the chalkboard.

---

be driven out, like from the Garden of Eden.

10. Ext. secret garden path—day

MARY moves to a brick wall, pushes the ivy aside, and pulls a loose brick out of the wall. Whatever she expected to find inside the niche isn't there. Disappointed, she replaces the brick, moves to a tree, and leans against it. Lost in revery, remembering another time, she touches the heart-shaped locket at her throat. Once again, there is the sound of a young girl speaking.

LITTLE GIRL'S VOICE: I shall wear it always.

[*Camera cuts to the cat, now in the tree just above* MARY *poising to leap. As the cat leaps, we hear a scream.*]

1 Cut to:

11. Int.—bedroom—(New Delhi, India, 1906)—on Mary—night

MARY, *ten years old, bolts upright in her bed, awakened by a scream. She's* **2** *a thin, dark-haired, rather "plain" little girl whose* arrogance *and imperious*[4] *manner do little to* enhance *her appearance.* MARY *calls her ayah:*[5]

MARY: Saidie?[6]

[*There's no response.*]

MARY: (*continuing*) Saidie? (*Angry now*) You're supposed to come when I call you!

---

4. **imperious** (im·pîr′ē·əs): proud and haughty.
5. **ayah** (ä′yə): native Indian nursemaid or lady's maid.
6. **Saidie** (sā′dē)

[*Frustrated and angry,* MARY *pushes the netting of her bed*[7] *aside and gets up from the bed. In the distance there is the sound of adult laughter. She slowly crosses the room and we see a collection of children's dolls. Clutch-* **3** *ing her robe, she starts for the door, then looks back at a photograph on the bureau. The photo is a picture of* MARY'S *parents,* CAPTAIN *and* MRS. LENNOX. MRS. LENNOX *is a luscious, dark-haired beauty.* CAPT. LENNOX, *a dashing young man in British Army dress uniform, is dark-haired with a waxed dark moustache.*]

12. Int. hallway—night

MARY *walks slowly down the hall as the laughter of the adults grows louder. She peeks through the slats of a door leading into a dining room area. Through the slats, the camera reveals a group of eight adults seated at a formal dinner setting. All the women wear lovely gowns and the men are in British Army dress uniforms.*

13. Int. dining room—night

MRS. LENNOX *sits at one end of the table,* CAPT. LENNOX *at the other.* MRS. LENNOX, *as superficial as she is* **4** *beautiful, ignores her other guests as she flirts with the handsome young officer to her right.* CAPT. LENNOX *is either oblivious or indifferent. His face*

---

7. People in India and other tropical climates put netting around their beds to protect them from mosquitoes.

---

1. GUIDED READING:
Understanding Time Order
The action shifts to the past and to India.

2. GUIDED READING:
Recognizing Detail
What does Mary look like? She is a "thin, dark-haired, rather 'plain' little girl . . ."

3. GUIDED READING:
Making Inferences
What does her looking at the photographs tell us about Mary as a character? It tells us she feels a lonely longing for her parents.

4. GUIDED READING:
Making Inferences About Character
In addition to being "superficial" and "beautiful," what else might you say about Mrs. Lennox? She is rude, insensitive, and vain. She neglects Mary. She ignores her husband.

The Secret Garden, Act One

ART LINK
Have students illustrate descriptive passages from the play. They might draw or paint Mary's secret garden as she first discovers it, dark and full of weeds, and then do another illustration of the garden as it appears after she and Dickon have brought it back to life.

1. GUIDED READING:
Making Inferences
What can you infer about the relationship between Mary and her parents? Mary and her mother don't have a good relationship. She prefers her father.

2. GUIDED READING:
Making Inferences
What does this scene show us about Mary? It shows that she can be both nasty and loving, like most children—most people.

3. LITERARY ELEMENTS:
Characterization
What kind of character would react this way to the news of a deadly plague? The reaction shows us that Mrs. Lennox is callous about other people's sufferings.

4. LITERARY ELEMENTS:
Suspense
What is the effect of cutting to a different scene? The effect is to prolong the suspense about why Captain Lennox is sick.

---

1 is damp with perspiration and he looks ill. He suddenly looks up to see his wife's flirtation. Camera cuts back to show MARY looking through the slats of the door. CAPT. LENNOX reaches for his glass of wine and can barely raise it. He is obviously very sick. Camera on MARY. Angry at her mother for humiliating her father, MARY leaves the door and returns to her room.

14. Int. Mary's bedroom—night
As MARY enters and moves to the bed, she vents her anger at her mother on her absent nurse.

2 MARY: I'll fix Saidie in the morning! I'll put a snake in her millet![8]

[MARY sits in a chair with one of her dolls in her lap. She speaks to the doll.]

MARY: I'm going to read this lovely story about a rajah[9] and a tiger.

Cut to:

15. Int. dining room—night
MRS. LENNOX is speaking animatedly.

MRS. LENNOX: I just had the most marvelous idea! After the Governor's Ball, why don't we go for a breakfast picnic along the river?

[MRS. CRAWFORD, one of the dinner guests, speaks out.]

MRS. CRAWFORD: I doubt I'll feel much like a picnic after dancing all night.

MRS. LENNOX: Nonsense.

MRS. CRAWFORD: Besides, I shan't be going to the ball. Steven's booked passage for me to England. He says there's some kind of plague in the provinces.

3 MRS. LENNOX: (*gaily*) Oh, there's always some kind of plague in the provinces, Mrs. Crawford. I wouldn't let that stop me from going to the ball.

[MRS. LENNOX lifts the small bell next to her plate. Rings it. CAPT. LENNOX wipes perspiration from his brow. CAPT. LENNOX rises. He stares blindly at his wife, then pitches face-down on the table. Everyone with the exception of MRS. LENNOX races to be of help.]

Cut to: 4

16. Ext. blazing sky—sunset
A horn is being blown against the blood-red setting sun.

17. Ext. street outside compound wall[10]—day
Natives are fleeing the city, some on foot, others in carts pulled by bullocks.[11] Dust stirred up by the exodus[12] casts a yellow haze. The sound is that of the bullocks, the creaking carts, and the whips of the drivers. The frightened natives have

---

8. **millet** (mil'it): here, cereal.
9. **rajah** (rä'jə): Indian prince.
10. **compound wall:** wall built around the officers' compound, or community, where Mary and her family live.
11. **bullocks** (bool'əks): steers or oxen.
12. **exodus** (ek'sə·dəs): departure of a large group of people.

1 only one thought: to escape the cholera that kills.

18. Int. Mary's bedroom—day
MARY awakens and calls out for her nurse.

MARY: Saidie . . . Saidie!

[*There is no response and* MARY *moves to the window. From her point of view we again see the hundreds of natives fleeing the city.*]

Cut to:

19. Int. servants' quarters—day
MARY'S nurse lies dead on the bed.

2 MARY *is curious but not frightened. She's seen death before. Beggars often die in the streets of New Delhi.*

20. Int. parents' room—day
MARY'S *father is lying comatose[13] on the bed. Her mother, lying at the foot of the bed, is also feeling the final deadly effects of cholera.* MARY *enters the room.*

MARY: Mama, Saidie is dead and there's no one to dress me or give me breakfast.

[MRS. LENNOX *groans.*]

3 21. Int. dining room—day
The remains of the interrupted dinner are scattered on the table. Flies buzz around the platters of food. Some of the wineglasses are full, others have spilled and stained the damask cloth.[14]

---

13. **comatose** (kō′mə·tōs′): in a coma (an unconscious state).
14. **damask** (dam′əsk) **cloth:** fine table linen.

There's evidence of hasty departure: a woman's wrap, a fan, an overturned chair.

MARY *comes into shot. She helps herself to food off the plates and drinks a glass of wine. Still thirsty, she drinks another.*

22. Int. Mary's bedroom—day
MARY *enters. The wine has gone to her head. She can barely walk and looks as if she is about to be sick. She stumbles toward the bed.*

MARY: I'm sick.

[*She plops herself down on the bed and goes to sleep.*]

23. Ext. bungalow compound—day
Natives are busily burning furniture, which people believed had been contaminated by the cholera. COL. MCGRAW *and* LIEUT. BARNEY *enter the compound.*

LIEUT. BARNEY: The servants may have **4** taken the child with them. (*Suddenly spotting* MARY *standing in the doorway of her home*) She's here, Colonel . . . she's alive!

MARY: (*annoyed*) Of course I'm alive, but Saidie is dead, so I shall need a new ayah.

COL. MCGRAW: (*distressed*) Poor child . . .

MARY: (*haughty*) I am not a poor child. I am Mary Lennox and my father has a very important position at Government House.

LIEUT. BARNEY: (*shaken*) She doesn't know, Colonel.

[COL. MCGRAW *hesitates, trying to find a way to soften the blow.*]

The Secret Garden, Act One **481**

---

1. GUIDED READING:
Recognizing Cause and Effect
Why do the natives flee the city? They want "to escape the cholera that kills."

2. LITERARY ELEMENTS:
Characterization
Note that this shows us Mary's inner strength, which she will rely on repeatedly as the play continues.

3. GUIDED READING:
Recognizing the Author's Purpose
Why do you think the author includes this scene? The author wants to contrast the life that once filled the home with the illness and death that now dominate.

4. GUIDED READING:
Making Inferences
What did Lieutenant Barney think had happened to Mary? He thought she had died.

1. GUIDED READING:
Interpreting Meaning
Why do you think Mary's doll is so important to her? What does its burning represent? The doll is important because it is familiar and represents security and love. To Mary, the doll is all she has left. Its destruction represents her total separation from the life she knew, and the complete absence of love from her life.

2. GUIDED READING:
Making Inferences
What do you suppose Mary is feeling at this point? She is probably feeling grief about her parents' death, anxiety and confusion about her future, and a need to defend herself from a world she perceives as threatening.

3. GUIDED READING:
Making Inferences About Setting
What does the dialogue tell you about the setting? The setting has moved from India to England.

COL. MCGRAW: (*compassionate*) I'm afraid there's no easy way to tell you this, child. I'm very sorry, my dear, but your parents are dead.

[*In the turmoil surrounding the three of them,* MARY *accidentally drops her favorite doll. She tries to go back for it, but a native scoops it up and the doll is thrown into the fire.*]

1 MARY: (*screaming*) My doll . . . no, stop . . . give me my doll!

LIEUT. BARNEY: She doesn't understand, Colonel.

COL. MCGRAW: Well, it's hardly surprising. Look, we'll take you to Mrs. Crawford. She can look after you until other arrangements can be made.

MARY: (*screaming*) Give me my doll, my doll!

[MARY *looks back in tears as her doll begins to burn. Riding off on horseback with* COL. MCGRAW, *she continues to stare back at the burning doll.*]

Cut to:

24. Int. hotel dining room—dusk

MARY *and* MRS. CRAWFORD *are seated at a table.* MARY *is ignoring her food as she stares ahead, stone-faced. She wears mourning,[15] a black jumper and black shoes and stockings. Her thin black coat is across the back of her chair and her black bonnet hangs from a spindle[16] by its ribbons.* MRS. CRAWFORD *is in a smart traveling suit and hat, and has a small fur around her shoulders.*

MRS. CRAWFORD: (*kind*) Mary, you haven't touched your tea. Aren't you hungry?

MARY: (*curt*) No.

[*A woman in her late sixties, tall and spare, enters the room and speaks to the head waiter. She is* MRS. MEDLOCK, *and at first glance she's a formidable-looking[17] woman. She approaches the table where* MRS. CRAWFORD *and* MARY *are seated.*]

MRS. MEDLOCK: Mrs. Crawford?

MRS. CRAWFORD: (*warmly*) You must be Mrs. Medlock. Please, do sit down.

[*As* MRS. MEDLOCK *seats herself, she glances at* MARY, *curious about her.*]

MRS. CRAWFORD: (*continuing*) Mary, this is **2** Mrs. Medlock, who is going to take you to Yorkshire tomorrow.

[MARY *ignores the introduction.* MRS. MEDLOCK *manages to hide her annoyance at* MARY'S *rudeness, but only barely.*]

MRS. MEDLOCK: (*to* MRS. CRAWFORD) Mr. Craven said to thank you for bringing the little girl, ma'am.

MRS. CRAWFORD: It would have been un- **3** kind not to since I was returning to England anyway.

---

15. **mourning:** black clothes worn as an expression of grief for the dead.

16. **spindle:** knob on the chair.
17. **formidable** (fôr′mi·də·bəl): causing fear or dread.

482 Plays

[MARY *looks at* MRS. CRAWFORD *with contempt.*]

MRS. CRAWFORD: (*continuing*) Will you have some tea?

MRS. MEDLOCK: No, thank you.

MRS. CRAWFORD: What time will you be calling for Mary tomorrow?

MRS. MEDLOCK: The train leaves at seven, so I'll be here at six.

MRS. CRAWFORD: So early?! Mary, will you be good enough to ask the desk clerk to send a porter up for your trunk a little before six?

[*Rising*, MARY *stares directly at* Mrs. Medlock *without saying a word. She then moves from the table.*]

1 MRS. CRAWFORD: She's a difficult child, Mrs. Medlock. But to be fair, it's not entirely her fault. If her mother had carried her pretty face into the nursery more often, Mary might not be quite so recalcitrant.[18]

MRS. MEDLOCK: Neglected her, did she?

MRS. CRAWFORD: I know one shouldn't speak ill of the dead, but Mrs. Lennox was a very silly and shallow woman. She was embarrassed that Mary was plain, at least in her eyes, and Mary knew it.

MRS. MEDLOCK: Pity.

MRS. CRAWFORD: Yes. (*Warmly*) It's kind of Mr. Craven to take Mary, especially since they're not related.

2 MRS. MEDLOCK: There's no living relatives, but since Mr. Craven's and Capt. Lennox's father were dear friends till they both passed on, young Mr. Craven felt obliged to give the little girl a home.

Cut to:

25. Ext. English countryside—long shot—train—day

Though it's March and the fields are still fallow,[19] the gently rolling landscape is lovely.

MRS. MEDLOCK'S VOICE: I've got some nice watercress sandwiches. Would you like one?

MARY'S VOICE: (*curt*) I don't like English food, only Indian.

3 MRS. MEDLOCK'S VOICE: Well, English food is all you'll be getting at Misselthwaite Manor, so you'd better get used to it.

Cut to:

26. Ext. roadway—dusk

Carriage carrying MARY *and* MRS. MEDLOCK *to Misselthwaite Manor.*

MRS. MEDLOCK'S VOICE: Oh, it was different when Mrs. Craven was alive. She had cook make all sorts of foreign dishes. They took the recipes out of a book.

27. Int. carriage—dusk

MRS. MEDLOCK: (*continuing*) Mr. Archibald—Mr. Craven, that is—didn't mind. She was such a sweet pretty thing. Nobody thought she'd marry him, not with that hump on his back, but she did.

[MARY's *intrigued in spite of herself.*]

---

18. **recalcitrant** (ri·kal′sə·trənt): stubbornly disobedient.

19. **fallow:** plowed, but not planted for the summer.

---

1. GUIDED READING:
Interpreting Meaning
Why do you think Mrs. Crawford feels the need to make excuses for Mary's conduct? She wants Mrs. Medlock to like Mary.

2. LITERARY ELEMENTS:
Exposition
This dialogue provides the explanation for Mr. Craven's taking Mary in.

3. LITERARY ELEMENTS:
Tone
In what tone of voice do you think Mrs. Medlock said these words? Possible answers include annoyed, angry, matter-of-fact.

> **TRANSPARENCIES 29 & 30**
> **Fine Art**
> Theme: *Bring Your Imagination with You* – invites students to explore artworks that highlight acting and the imagination.

1. GUIDED READING:
Making Inferences About Character
What does Mary's dialogue reveal about her? Mary is well read and well educated, and has some lurking element of human sympathy.

2. BACKGROUND
A moor is a wide area of open, rolling boggy land, covered with coarse grass, heather, and other wild plants. A moor is something like a prairie, but it is wetter and has different vegetation. There are many beautiful moors in northern England, Scotland, and Ireland.

3. LITERARY ELEMENTS:
Foreshadowing
What may Mrs. Medlock's dialogue foreshadow? It may foreshadow difficult times at Misselthwaite Manor for Mary.

---

1 MARY: That's like a French fairy tale I once read, "Riquet de la Houppe."[20] It was about a hunchback and a beautiful princess.

MRS. MEDLOCK: So there is something that interests you.

MARY: (*coldly*) I didn't say I was interested.

28. Ext. roadway—dusk

2 MRS. MEDLOCK: These are the moors.
MARY: The moors are ugly!

[MRS. MEDLOCK's *patience is wearing thin, though she tries to cover.*]

MRS. MEDLOCK: Did your father ever tell you about Misselthwaite Manor?
MARY: (*bitter*) Why should he? He didn't know he was going to die and I'd have to live there.
MRS. MEDLOCK: Very well . . . I will. Misselthwaite Manor is a grand place. It was built ages ago and has over one hundred rooms.
MARY: (*caustic*) I don't care how many rooms there are.
MRS. MEDLOCK: (*dryly*) Your manners could use improving.
MARY: (*curt*) I don't have to be polite to servants.
MRS. MEDLOCK: (*sharp*) Mind yourself, Missy. I'm Mr. Craven's housekeeper and servant to no one. I'll overlook your bad manners for now, seeing you've gone through so much sadness. Not that you'll **3** find much joy at Misselthwaite Manor. Mr. Archibald still grieves for his wife and won't trouble himself with anyone.

29. Ext. Misselthwaite Manor—night
Various shots of the carriage as it approaches the main entrance of Misselthwaite Manor.

30. Ext. Misselthwaite Manor—night
As the carriage pulls into shot, JOHN, *a young footman, hurries out of the house.*

JOHN: Have a good trip, Mrs. Medlock?
MRS. MEDLOCK: I've had worse. Fetch Miss Mary's trunk. (*Stern*) And use the back stairs.
JOHN: (*grinning*) I'll tiptoe all the way. Wouldn't want to wake the dead.

[MRS. MEDLOCK's *too tired to chastise* JOHN *for his flippant remark. She also knows what lies behind it.*]

31. Int. manor—entry hall—night
The hall, though richly furnished, has a cold, unlived-in look. Dimly lit, the tapestries on the walls recede into darkness. A staircase leads to the upper floors, and PITCHER, *an elderly, too-thin man, descends the stairs. He doesn't waste any time on amenities.*[21]

PITCHER: You're to take her directly to her

---

20. **"Riquet de la Houppe"** (ri·kā′ de la ōōp): Riquet is the hunchback's name. *Houppe* literally means "tuft."

21. **amenities** (ə·men′ə·tēz): niceties of conversation; good manners.

484 Plays

rooms. He doesn't want to see her, and he'll be leaving for London in the morning.
Mrs. Medlock: As long as I know what's expected of me, Mr. Pitcher.
Pitcher: (*terse*) What's expected, Mrs. Medlock, is that you make certain Mr. Archibald is not disturbed and that he doesn't see what he doesn't want to see.

Mrs. Medlock: (*dryly*) Well . . . there's a revelation. (*To* Mary) Come on.

[Mary *and* Mrs. Medlock *start up the stairs.*]

32. Int. bedroom—night

Mary *and* Mrs. Medlock *enter from the hall corridor.*

The Secret Garden, Act One 485

FOR STUDY AND DISCUSSION

Identifying Facts

1. The three settings are Misselthwaite Manor, Yorkshire, in 1918; British India near the beginning of the century; the Manor near the beginning of the century.

2. Mary is taken to England because both her parents died in a cholera epidemic.

3. Mary's mother neglected her because Mary was plain, and her mother was silly and shallow.

4. Archibald Craven lives alone in a huge manor; he is a hunchback; he was married to a beautiful woman who is now dead and for whom he still grieves; he is a recluse and doesn't want to see Mary.

Interpreting Meanings

5. Our very first picture of Mary is as a beautiful young Red Cross nurse. Our first impression of her as a character comes in the opening flashback, where she appears as a haughty little girl full of "arrogance and [an] imperious manner" (page 479), who is rude to servants. She is a lonely child, but not likable.

6. Mary may be unpleasant to Mrs. Medlock because she has been raised to treat servants carelessly, or because grief for

485

> **TRANSPARENCY 32**
> **Literary Elements**
> *Suspense* – invites students to consider suspense and foreshadowing as elements of plot.

her parents has made her irritable. She is also feeling scared and alone, and takes refuge in a haughty and rude manner.

7. What will happen to Mary at Misselthwaite Manor? What is Archibald Craven like, and why doesn't he want to see Mary? Who is the crying child? How does Mary grow up to become a beautiful young woman?

Applying Meanings
8. At this point in the play, Mary probably feels desolate, abandoned, frightened, sad, resentful, angry. She probably also feels curious about what is going to happen to her.

MRS. MEDLOCK: This is where you're going to live, Miss Mary. This is your bedroom, and the sitting room's just through there.

[MARY *makes no response.*]

MRS. MEDLOCK: (*continuing*) The rooms were especially prepared for you.

[*Still no reaction from* MARY.]

MRS. MEDLOCK: (*continuing*) I see a little supper has been laid out for you. You must be tired, so eat it and go to bed.

[MARY *looks at* MRS. MEDLOCK *with barely veiled contempt.* MRS. MEDLOCK *has had her fill of* MARY *for the moment.*]

MRS. MEDLOCK: (*continuing*) Good night.

[MRS. MEDLOCK *moves to the door, opens it, pauses, then turns to* MARY. *She's grim now and her words carry a veiled threat.*]

MRS. MEDLOCK: (*continuing*) You can go anywhere you like in this wing of the house, but you're not to go poking about anywhere else. Mr. Archibald won't have it and neither will I. Is that understood?

[*Over the eerie, disembodied sound of a child crying:*]

Cut to:
33. Ext. the moors—night
The pale moon, high in the sky now, <u>illuminates</u> the Martian-like landscape.

34. Int. Mary's bedroom—night
MARY, *lying awake in bed, suddenly hears the sound of a crying child. As the sound, filled with pain and despair, rises to a crescendo,*[22] MARY *sits up and listens, obviously somewhat frightened.*

Fade-out.

---

22. **crescendo** (krə·shen′dō): the peak of a gradual increase in loudness.

For Study and Discussion

IDENTIFYING FACTS
1. Act One takes place in three different times and places. What are these three different **settings**?

2. Explain why Mary is taken to England.

3. According to Mrs. Crawford, why has Mary's mother neglected Mary?

4. What do we learn about Archibald Craven in Act One?

INTERPRETING MEANINGS
5. What is our first picture of Mary Lennox? List some of her **character traits**, or qualities. (Is she a likable character?)

6. Why do you think Mary is so unpleasant toward Mrs. Medlock? (How might Mary feel about what has just happened to her?)

7. List all the **questions** you have about the story so far.

APPLYING MEANINGS
8. How would you feel if you were Mary at this point in the play?

Act Two

Fade-in:

35. Ext. the moors—day—(dawn)

DICKON, *a boy of about twelve, sits near the moor path, fingering a panpipe.*[1] *A crow is perched on* DICKON'S *shoulder, a little lamb snuggles against him, a small red fox lies at his feet, and a squirrel is nestled in his pocket. There's a sweetness about* DICKON, *a forever-innocence, yet we sense in him a wisdom that transcends time.*

DICKON: (*beaming*) Mornin', Mr. Weatherstaff.

BEN: Mornin', Dickon. (*Teasing*) Wishin' the day in with a song?

DICKON: Just sayin' hello to the mornin'. (*Eager*) If you got a minute, I'll show you a trick I just learned.

BEN: I've work waitin' on me at the Manor.

DICKON: Please . . .

[DICKON *looks disappointed.* BEN *hesitates. Despite his dour appearance and usually gruff manner,* BEN *is fond of* DICKON *and finds it hard to disappoint him.*]

BEN: (*continuing*) Guess the work will wait till I get there.

[DICKON'S *delighted.*]

DICKON: (*to crow*) Take yourself elsewhere, Soot.

---
1. **panpipe:** a musical instrument made of tubes of different sizes. It is played by blowing across the tubes.

[*The crow obligingly hops down from* DICKON'S *shoulder and settles on a rock.* DICKON *puts the panpipe in his mouth and plays a one-note "song" as he walks on his hands. He moves a few feet and falls over.*]

BEN: (*laughing*) Good trick, especially the last part.

[DICKON *grins.*]

BEN: (*continuing*) I'm off. See you around, Dickon.

DICKON: See you about, Mr. Weatherstaff.

36. Ext. establishing shot—Misselthwaite Manor—day

37. Int. sitting room—day

MARTHA, *a pretty, fresh-faced girl of about seventeen, wearing a starched white pinafore and a little ruffled cap, is setting out breakfast on the table. As* MARY *enters from the bedroom,* MARTHA *greets her with a warm smile.*

MARTHA: Mornin', miss.

MARY: Who are you?

MARTHA: Martha. Martha Sowerby.

MARY: Are you going to be my servant?

MARTHA: (*amused*) I'm to do the cleanin' up here an' a bit of waitin' on you, though judgin' on your size, you won't need much waitin' on, will ya?

MARY: (*curt*) Of course I'll need to be waited on. Someone has to dress me.

MARTHA: (*confused*) Can you not dress yourself?

MARY: Of course I can, but in India my ayah dressed me!

The Secret Garden, Act Two

MEETING INDIVIDUAL NEEDS

ESL/LEP • Martha's Yorkshire dialect may be challenging for those students learning standard English. Call attention to grammatical variations, and ask the class to suggest standard forms.

1. GUIDED READING:
Distinguishing Between Fact and Opinion
Is it a fact or an opinion that the garments are lovely? It is Martha's opinion, and only her stated opinion at that. Mary may think they are ugly. Martha may be anticipating that.

2. GUIDED READING:
Making Inferences About Plot
What might the fact that Martha becomes flustered and that she changes the subject so rapidly suggest? Mary may be onto something that Martha doesn't want to discuss.

3. LITERARY ELEMENTS:
Characterization
The author is using indirect characterization, telling us what Dickon is like by giving us another character's view of him. Since the character is his sister, the view is probably accurate.

4. LITERARY ELEMENTS:
Characterization
Lead students to realize that Mary's childish haughtiness is more a sign of loneliness than of hostility.

MARTHA: (*wry*) Well, you're in Yorkshire now, an' here children dress themselves soon's they're out of nappies.² You'll find some lovely new garments in the cupboard, warm ones bought by Mrs. Medlock on Mr. Archibald's orders.

MARY: (*sarcastic*) I thought he troubled himself with no one.

MARTHA: He don't. It was Mrs. Medlock who told him you'd not have proper clothing for the cold since you was comin' from India. An' it was she who had these rooms fixed up all pretty for ya. (*Kind*) I know you was wore out from your journey, so I hope you had a good sleep.

MARY: (*caustic*) How could I sleep with all that crying and moaning. This is a haunted house, isn't it?

MARTHA: (*flustered*) It was the wind you heard wutherin'³ across the moors. It often makes a mournful sound. You best eat your breakfast 'fore it gets cold.

MARY: I don't like English food.

MARTHA: (*cajoling*) I've nine little brothers an' sisters who'd eat the table clean in a minute.

MARY: (*startled*) Nine brothers and sisters?

MARTHA: No doubt there'd be more if my dad hadn't died in his prime.⁴ Feedin' that brood's hard on my mother, but Dickon's a help.

MARY: Who's Dickon?

MARTHA: He's one of our gaggle of children. He leaves what food there is for the others an' feeds hisself out on the moors. He says the wild goats give him their milk, an' there's lovely greens an' berries his for the takin'.

MARY: (*dryly*) He sounds peculiar.

MARTHA: (*laughing*) He's a rare boy, Dickon. He talks to animals an' they talk back.

MARY: That's the silliest thing I ever heard.

[MARTHA's *enjoying herself too much to stop now.*]

MARTHA: And when he plays his panpipe, wild animals stop and listen.

MARY: (*contemptuous*) Animals can't talk and they don't listen to music.

MARTHA: (*teasing*) I told ya Dickon was a rare boy.

[MARTHA *starts toward the bedroom.*]

MARY: (*curt*) I didn't dismiss you.

MARTHA: (*innocently*) You'll be makin' your own bed up then.

MARY: (*haughty*) You have my permission to go on with your work.

MARTHA: (*admiring*) The Queen couldn't of said it better herself.

[As MARTHA *starts out:*]

MARY: I have nothing to do.

[MARTHA *reappears.*]

MARTHA: There's plenty of gardens you can go and play in, except for the one that's locked.

MARY: (*sarcastic*) How can a garden be locked?

---

2. **nappies:** British term for diapers.
3. **wutherin':** *wuthering* is Yorkshire dialect meaning "blowing with a dull roar."
4. **in his prime:** at the peak of his life, probably in his thirties.

1 **MARTHA:** It can if there's a high wall 'round it. Dress warm if you're goin' out. March can be a cruel month in Yorkshire.

Cut to:
38. Ext. vegetable garden—Ben—day
BEN is using a shovel to break the still-frozen ground. A wheelbarrow and other garden tools are nearby. MARY comes into shot. She's wearing her new warm coat and matching bonnet.

MARY: What are you doing?
BEN: (*testy*) You got eyes. I'm turnin' the earth for plantin' vegetables when spring comes.
2 **MARY:** (*haughty*) It doesn't surprise me you're rude. All the servants here seem to be rude.
BEN: (*dryly*) I take it you're the little wench just come from India.
MARY: I'm not a little wench. I'm Mary Lennox, and you may call me Miss Mary, if you like. Where are the flower gardens?
BEN: (*curt*) Other side, but naught blooms this time of year.
MARY: Where's the locked-up garden?
BEN: (*glaring*) There's no door into it, so you can save yourself the trouble of lookin'!
MARY: (*contemptuous*) Of course there's a door. If there wasn't, it wouldn't be locked.
BEN: Don't go pokin' your nose where it's no cause to go!
MARY: I think everyone in Yorkshire's mad as a hatter . . .

[*A robin sitting in a tree begins to chirp. BEN addresses the bird affectionately.*]

BEN: Ho, ho, you cheeky little beggar. Has **3** you started courtin' this early in the season?

[*The robin chirps in response. MARY's astounded.*]

MARY: He answered you!
BEN: (*gruff, but pleased*) Considers hisself my friend.
MARY: I never had any friends.
BEN: (*dryly*) Then we're a good deal alike, neither of us good-lookin' an' both as sour as we look.

[*MARY ignores the insult. For the first time she lowers her guard.*]

MARY: (*wistfully*) Do you think he'd mind being my friend too? (*To the robin*) If you'll be my friend, I'll be yours.
BEN: (*grudging*) You said that as nice an' human as Dickon talks to his wild creatures.
MARY: You know Dickon?
BEN: The very blackberries an' heather-bells know Dickon. The foxes show him where their cubs lie an' the skylarks don't hide their nests from him (*Embarrassed*) Off with you. I've work to do.
MARY: I think I shall look for the door into the locked garden.
BEN: All you'll find are brambles and thorns.
MARY: We shall see . . . shan't we?

[*A series of shots follows: MARY skip-* **4** *ping along the moor, tossing a rock into the water; MARY walking slowly through various gardens; MARY sitting quietly next to the fire in her bedroom.*]

The Secret Garden, Act Two 489

---

1. GUIDED READING:
Predicting Outcomes
What will Mary do? What makes you think so? Mary will play in the garden that is locked. It is the one place that is specifically forbidden to her, so naturally, she is determined to find it.

2. LITERARY ELEMENTS:
Irony
Explain the irony in what Mary says. It is the opposite of what is true. In fact, it is Mary and not the servants who are rude.

3. LITERARY ELEMENTS:
Theme
Ben's tenderness to the bird after his gruffness to Mary highlights a major theme of the play: that everyone has a loving and an unloving side. A secondary theme highlighted here is the way English country people love and identify with nature.

4. GUIDED READING:
Identifying the Author's Purpose
By depicting Mary in a series of solitary actions, the author conveys Mary's loneliness.

39. Ext. the moors—day

MARY *walks along the shore of the moors. Suddenly* MARY *spots* DICKON *and his animal friends.*

MARY: You're Dickon, aren't you?
DICKON: Aye. (*Smiles*) I was waitin' for you, Miss Mary.
MARY: (*confused*) How do you know my name? And how did you know I was going to be here when I didn't know it myself?
1 DICKON: (*matter-of-fact*) Sometimes wishin' makes things happen. (*Introducing his "creatures"*) The crow is Soot, the fox is Captain, the lamb is Lady, the squirrel is Nut. (*Grins*) The rabbit just happened to be passin'.
MARY: Those are strange names for animals.
DICKON: It's what they asked to be called.
MARY: (*sarcastic*) Animals and birds can't talk.
2 DICKON: There's ways of talkin' that don't take words. (*Rising*) I've gathered some wild mustard seeds for Ben Weatherstaff, so if you don't mind company, I'll walk back to the Manor with you . . .

[DICKON *pauses.*]

DICKON: (*gently*) You're sad an' lonely now, but in time, you'll find happiness in Misselthwaite Manor.
MARY: No . . . I shall never be happy there! And I don't want your company nor anyone else's!

[MARY *moves off swiftly. She fights to hold back her tears, too proud to admit even to herself that she is lonely and unhappy.*]

Cut to:

40. Int. sitting room—Mary—night

The wind is howling. MARY, *in her nightgown, stands at the window looking out.* MARTHA *emerges from the bedroom.*

MARTHA: (*cheerful*) Your bed's turned down an' the room's all cozy. Listen to that wind!
MARY: I looked for the door into the locked garden again today, but I couldn't find it.
MARTHA: Why trouble yourself when there's so many other gardens you can go and play in?
MARY: I like to know about things. Why **3** was the garden locked up?
MARTHA: (*sobering*) But for the garden, Mr. Archibald wouldn't be the way he is.
MARY: What do you mean?

[MARTHA *hesitates; then:*]

MARTHA: You'll not repeat what I tell you? **4**
MARY: You know I've no one to talk to except you!
MARTHA: All right, then. But mind you, I'm only tellin' what Mrs. Medlock said 'cause this happened long before I came to work here. Mrs. Craven had that garden made when she first came to Misselthwaite as a bride. She an' Mr. Archibald would shut themselves inside for hours an' hours, like two lovebirds.
MARY: Well, if the garden was such a happy place, why was it locked up?

The Secret Garden, Act Two **491**

---

1. GUIDED READING:
Interpreting Meaning
What does Dickon mean by this rather mystical statement? Opinions may vary, but he may mean that both he and Mary wished for the meeting and acted in such a way as to make it happen.

2. GUIDED READING:
Interpreting Meaning
What are some ways people "talk" without using words? People "talk" by their actions and by using facial expressions, gestures, and body language.

3. LITERARY ELEMENTS:
Characterization
This line shows us Mary's determined, intelligent curiosity. Ask students to guess how she might use that trait in the acts to come. Many will correctly guess that she will find the locked garden.

4. GUIDED READING:
Making Inferences
What can you infer about the relationship between the two girls? Mary and Martha have developed something of a friendship. Mary feels comfortable talking to Martha, and Martha trusts Mary enough to confide secrets to her.

1. LITERARY ELEMENTS:
Exposition
Martha's speech tells us a very important fact we must know in order to understand Archibald Craven and the bizarre way of life at Misselthwaite Manor.

2. GUIDED READING:
Self-Questioning
Students should note Martha's reaction when Mary questions her about the crying noise. They should recall that Martha reacted similarly the last time the topic was raised (Act Two, scene 37, page 488). Students' curiosity should be piqued, and they should be asking themselves what is making the noise.

3. LITERARY ELEMENTS:
Suspense
The quick cut from the talk about the crying to the actual sound of it heightens our suspense about who or what is crying.

---

1 MARTHA: Because it's where the accident happened. There was an old tree in the garden with a high branch bent like a seat. Mrs. Craven—Lilias was her name—she loved to climb up an' sit on the branch an' read when she was alone. One day the branch broke an' she fell an' she hurt so bad she died the next day.

MARY: (*dramatically*) And Mr. Craven was so wild with grief that he locked up the garden and threw away the key!

MARTHA: (*startled*) That's what Mrs. Medlock said, but how did you know?

MARY: (*triumphantly*) I didn't, you just told me. And if there's a key, there must be a door, and I intend to find it . . .

[*Suddenly a great draft blows the door open. As* MARTHA *hurries to the door, for a fleeting moment we hear the sound of a crying child.* MARTHA *closes the door.*]

MARTHA: Someone must have left the door downstairs open to cause such a terrible draft!

MARY: You heard it, too, didn't you?

MARTHA: I heard what?

MARY: Someone crying.

2 MARTHA: (*flustered*) I told you the wind often makes a mournful sound . . .

MARY: (*coldly*) No, it wasn't the wind. It was human . . . and if it wasn't human, it was a ghost.

MARTHA: (*nervous*) It was the wind you heard wutherin' across the moors. Good night, Miss Mary.

[*As* MARTHA *hurries to the door and exits,* MARY *looks after her, unconvinced.*]

Cut to:

41. Int. Mary's bedroom—Mary—night **3**

MARY, *shaken, is sitting up in bed listening to the distant, heart-rending sound of a child crying.* MARY *gets out of bed, opens the door, and looks down the corridor.*

42. Int. corridor outside Mary's room—night

Dimly lit by a single gas lamp, the corridor stretches off into darkness. MRS. MEDLOCK *emerges out of the darkness. She's in her nightgown, a shawl over her shoulders. She hurries to the stairway and starts down.* MARY *steps into the corridor and listens, and the sound of a child crying grows louder.*

Cut to:

43. Ext. manor house—Dickon and Ben—day

BEN *sits at the base of a tree as* DICKON *approaches.* DICKON *hands a small napkin-covered basket to* BEN.

DICKON: Mornin', Mr. Weatherstaff. From my mother. She baked this mornin'.

[BEN *takes the napkin off, revealing a small loaf of bread.*]

BEN: (*pleased*) My thanks to her. There's nobody bakes better bread than Susan Sowerby.

DICKON: (*grinning*) She'll be pleased to hear it.

MEETING INDIVIDUAL NEEDS
ESL/LEP • As Mary explores various rooms in the manor, new vocabulary is introduced, including *gallery, scullery, tapestry, inlaid, gilt,* and *Aubusson*. You may want to have students look up these words and write them in their vocabulary notebooks. You could also have students compile a separate list of vocabulary words for each setting. Settings could include India, Misselthwaite Manor, the moors, and the secret garden.

[DICKON *looks off. Sobers.* BEN *follows his gaze.*]

44. **Ext. manor house—day—point of view—long shot—Mary**
MARY *has just emerged from the manor and is moving away swiftly.*

45. **Ext. manor house—day**
DICKON *and* BEN *looking after* MARY.

1 BEN: There's not a day she don't go lookin' for the door into the locked garden, but she'll not find it. (*Bitter*) An' 'tis better so.
DICKON: Have you been in the garden, Mr. Weatherstaff?
BEN: (*grim*) We'll not talk about that garden.
DICKON: (*thoughtful*) Well, Miss Mary won't give up. There's a stubbornness in her, but there's also a need. I'm off. See you about, Mr. Weatherstaff.

46. **Int. sitting room—day**
MARY *stands at the window watching the rain come down in sheets.* MARTHA *is dusting the furniture.* MARY *turns to her.*

2 MARY: I've nothing to do when it rains.
MARTHA: Mrs. Medlock has wool to spare. You could knit.
MARY: I don't know how.
MARTHA: You could read.
MARY: I haven't any books.
MARTHA: There's thousands of books in Mr. Archibald's library.
MARY: (*caustic*) Mrs. Medlock said I wasn't to go anywhere except in this wing.
MARTHA: The library's in this wing, but findin' it is a bit trickish, so I'll tell you how.

47. **Int. portrait gallery—day**
MARY *slowly enters the portrait gallery. The walls of the long gallery are hung with portraits of people long gone; men, women, and children in sixteenth- and seventeenth-century garb.* MARY *slowly looks up at the various portraits. The gallery interests her. She pauses, studies a portrait of a* **3** *boy about twelve years old. He's a beautiful child with a pale, sensitive face and shock of black hair. He wears a velvet suit with a lace collar, the elegant apparel of seventeenth-century children. Intrigued,* MARY *studies the portrait for a long moment, then continues on.*

48. **Int. Lilias's bedroom—day—Mary's point of view**
MARY *enters the elegant bedroom. Maintained as though it were a shrine,*[5] **4** *the room is exquisitely feminine. The furniture is inlaid and the bed is draped in pastel silk. Gilt chairs are done in needlepoint. A rare Aubusson carpet covers the floor. A silk-draped dressing table is crowded with crystal perfume bottles. Against one wall, a tall, glass-fronted curio cabinet displays its treasures. Everywhere vases and bowls are filled with hothouse flowers.*

Entranced, MARY *moves slowly around the room. She pauses as she reaches the dressing table, picks up one of the perfume bottles, and shakes*

---
5. **shrine:** sacred place.

The Secret Garden, Act Two **493**

---

1. GUIDED READING:
Predicting Outcomes
Do you think Mary will find the door to the locked garden? Why or why not? Most students will say that Mary will, because she is so persevering. Also, the garden is in the play's title.

2. GUIDED READING:
Making Inferences
Do you think Mary might purposely be making a show of being bored? If so, why? It's possible Mary hopes that she will be given permission to explore.

3. LITERARY ELEMENTS:
Characterization
As in Scene 11 earlier in the play, Mary's portrait-viewing is a sign of her loneliness, her yearning for companionship. It is the dramatist's way of showing us this trait without using dialogue.

4. GUIDED READING:
Making Inferences About Character
What can you infer about Lilias Craven from the description of her bedroom? She had fine taste and liked to be surrounded by beautiful things.

1. GUIDED READING:
Identifying the Author's Purpose
Why did the author put this flashback here? It shows us that the visit to Lilias's bedroom makes Mary remember her own mother. It helps us sympathize with Mary: She was hurt by her mother.

2. LITERARY ELEMENTS:
Motivation
Why do you think Mrs. Medlock is so angry? For one thing, Mary had disobeyed her orders. More importantly, though, Mrs. Medlock knows Mary is on the brink of discovering the source of the crying.

3. LITERARY ELEMENTS:
Tone
In what tone of voice do you think Mary replied? She is probably disbelieving and quizzical.

---

it. The bottle is empty. MARY takes the stopper out of the bottle and sniffs it. The scent still lingers. MARY seems shaken now. As she stares into the mirror remembering another time, another place:

1 *Flashback: parents' bedroom—(New Delhi)—night*
MRS. LENNOX, *wearing a lacy peignoir,[6] sits at her dressing table touching perfume to her throat and ears.* MARY, *in her nightgown, appears in the mirror behind her mother.* MARY *smiles, taking pride in her pretty mother. As* MRS. LENNOX *sees her in the mirror, she gestures impatiently that* MARY's *to go away.*

Lilias's bedroom—day
MARY *stares at the mirror, hurt by the remembrance. As she replaces the perfume bottle, it clinks against another bottle and the sound triggers another memory:*

Flashback: dining room—(New Delhi)—night
CAPT. LENNOX, *his face damp with perspiration, his hand trembling, lowers his wineglass and it clinks against another glass.*

Lilias's bedroom—day
MARY, *remembering, hurts for her father.*

Dissolve to:
49. Int. tapestry corridor—day

---

6. **peignoir** (pān·wär′): robe.

A ceiling-to-floor tapestry hangs on the wall at the end of the short corridor. MARY *comes into shot. She pauses, aware she's reached a dead end.* MARY *freezes. The sound seems to be coming from behind the tapestry. As* MARY *moves slowly, nervously, toward the tapestry,* MRS. MEDLOCK *emerges from behind it. The shock is mutual. Then:*

MRS. MEDLOCK: (*furious*) What are you **2** doing here?!
MARY: (*coldly*) You don't have to shout. I got lost going to the library. (*Looking at the tapestry*) I heard someone crying . . .
MRS. MEDLOCK: Old houses are full of strange sounds.
MARY: (*softly*) I know what I heard, and it was someone crying.

[MRS. MEDLOCK, *aware* MARY's *not to be put off, manages a smile of sorts.*]

MRS. MEDLOCK: Perhaps you're right. Betty, who works in the scullery,[7] has been carrying on all day because she has a toothache. Come. I'll take you to your rooms.
MARY: Toothache? **3**

Cut to:
50. Int. manor—back stairs—Betty—day
BETTY, *a perky girl of about eighteen, carrying a breakfast tray, is going up the stairs.*

51. Int. Mary's sitting room—day
MARY, *still in her nightgown, stands at the window looking out.* BETTY *enters.*

---

7. **scullery** (skul′ər·ē): in big old-fashioned houses, a room off the kitchen where the dirty work is done.

BETTY: Mornin', miss.

MARY: Who are you?

BETTY: Betty. It's Martha's free day an' she's gone to the cottage to give her mum a hand.

[As BETTY *starts to lay out* MARY's *breakfast*, MRS. MEDLOCK *enters*.]

MARY: (*dryly, to* BETTY) Is your toothache gone?

BETTY: (*confused*) Toothache?

MARY: (*too sweetly*) The toothache you didn't have.

MRS. MEDLOCK: Betty, cook wants you at the scullery.

[BETTY *takes the empty tray and hurries out.*

The exchange about BETTY's *nonexistent toothache has made* MRS. MEDLOCK *somewhat uncomfortable. She manages a smile of sorts to cover.*]

MRS. MEDLOCK: (*continuing*) It's terribly muddy out because of the rain. I thought we'd go into the village this morning and buy you a sturdier pair of shoes.

[MARY *studies* MRS. MEDLOCK, *her face expressionless.*]

MRS. MEDLOCK: (*continuing*) It will be a nice little outing for you as well. I know you're lonely. When Mr. Archibald comes back, I shall speak to him. I'll ask him to get a governess[8] for you.

---

8. **governess** (guv'ər·nis): a woman who teaches children in a private home.

MARY: (*curt*) I had governesses in India. None of them stayed very long. They didn't like me.

MRS. MEDLOCK: Well, I'm sure that's not true.

MARY: Well, I don't lie, you do.

MRS. MEDLOCK: What a dreadful thing to say!

MARY: It's true! You lied to me yesterday about Betty having a toothache! There's something behind that tapestry and you don't want me to know about it.

[MARY *and* MRS. MEDLOCK *stare at one another.*]

Fade-out.

For Study and Discussion

IDENTIFYING FACTS

1. Who is Dickon?

2. Tell what you've learned about the secret garden in this act.

3. As Mary walks around Lilias Craven's bedroom, she experiences a **flashback** within the flashback of the main action of the play. What is she reminded of?

4. What mysterious sound does Mary hear at Misselthwaite Manor? How does Mrs. Medlock explain the noise?

INTERPRETING MEANINGS

5. Dickon says about Mary, "There's a stubbornness in her, but there's also a need." What do you think he means? (What might Mary need or want?)

The Secret Garden, Act Two

FOR STUDY AND DISCUSSION

Identifying Facts

1. Dickon Sowerby, the maid Martha's brother, is a member of a large family of poor cottagers. He is a good, sensitive person who spends most of his time on the moors, playing his panpipe, and talking to animals.

2. The secret garden is a mysterious, locked garden in which Archibald and Lilias Craven used to spend a lot of time. Archibald had it locked after Lilias was killed in a fall from a tree branch.

3. She is reminded of her parents in India. She remembers a scene in which her mother rejected her.

4. Mary hears a mysterious crying.

   Mrs. Medlock says it is Betty, a scullery maid, complaining about a toothache.

Interpreting Meanings

5. Dickon probably means that Mary needs love, friendship, kindness, and understanding.

FOCUS/MOTIVATION
Ask students which major character in the teleplay they haven't met yet. (It is Archibald Craven, the owner of Misselthwaite, and they will meet him in this act.)

Prereading Journal. Invite students to pretend they are Mary and Dickon, writing diary entries on the day they first met.

READING ACT THREE
Make sure students give close attention to the key scenes in this act that occur without dialogue: the description of the garden (Scene 54), Mary's first view of Archibald (Scene 60), and Mary's nighttime wanderings, which lead her to discover Colin (Scenes 62–65).

TEACHING RESOURCES C
Teacher's Notes, p. 118
Reading Check, p. 120
Study Guide, p. 121
Language Skills, pp. 147, 150, 153
Building Vocabulary, p. 122
Selection Vocabulary Test, p. 124
Selection Test, p. 132

---

1. GUIDED READING:
Interpreting Meaning
What does this passage reveal about Mary? How do you know? Mary is changing. She is not nasty to Ben. She is capable of good-natured teasing. She has found an enjoyable activity—jumping rope—and even laughs.

2. GUIDED READING:
Predicting Outcomes
What key is this? It is probably the key to the locked garden.

Act Three

Fade-in:

1 **52. Ext. fountain garden—day**
   MARY *is seen skipping rope in the garden, counting as she skips. She comes upon* BEN WEATHERSTAFF, *who is pruning trees.*

MARY: (*proudly*) I only got the skipping rope from Martha last night and I'm already very good at it.

BEN: (*dryly*) Maybe there's some child's blood in your veins after all.

[MARY's *too pleased with herself to take offense.*]

MARY: I have decided to skip one hundred times now without stopping.

[*As* MARY *skips away,* BEN *calls after her:*]

BEN: Pride goeth before a fall!

53. Ext. path outside the secret garden
   MARY *skips into shot, counting aloud:*

MARY: Ninety-five, ninety-six, ninety-seven . . .

[*As* MARY *approaches the stone bench under the tree:*]

MARY: (*counting; teasing*) Have you begun courting yet, you cheeky little beggar?

[*A robin is on the ground pecking at a small mound of dirt.*]

MARY: (*counting; laughing*) Are you looking for food?

[*The robin flies off. The wind suddenly blows away the leaves from the ground and a small rusted ring protrudes from the mound.* MARY *picks up the ring; a* **2** *rusted key encrusted with dirt* <u>emerges</u>. MARY *brushes the dirt away. Stares at the key.*]

MARY: The key . . . (<u>*Elated*</u>) And if there's a key, there *must* be a door!

[*A sudden gust of wind hurls leaves into* MARY's *face. Looking up, she sees that the wind has separated the ivy surrounding the secret garden. Elated, she spots the door leading to the garden.* MARY *races to the door, pushes aside the ivy, and inserts the key. The door to the secret garden slowly opens and* MARY *sneaks inside.*]

54. Ext. the secret garden—day
   Once inside, we see a nightmare. The high walls are covered with dead ivy, and the thorny, leafless stems of dead rose vines are so thick they're matted. Dead brown grass chokes dead bushes. The branches of dead-looking trees are gaunt against the sky. Soggy leaves, the <u>accumulation</u> of years, form a spongy, rotting carpet. Everywhere, what were once climbing roses have spread and fastened themselves to trees and bushes, creating an ugly, thorny web. Stone urns that once held flowers are now filled with rotting <u>debris</u>. MARY slowly, carefully walks around the garden, when something suddenly catches her eye. A tiny green shoot has poked

Plays

1. GUIDED READING:
Understanding Contrast
What is the important difference between the green shoot and the other plants in the garden? The shoot is the only sign of new, flourishing life. The other plants are dead or decaying.

2. GUIDED READING:
Using Context Clues
Lead students to use context clues to deduce that a niche is a hollow place in a wall.

3. LITERARY ELEMENTS:
Teleplay
The cut between Scenes 55 and 56 shows us that time has passed since Mary found the garden. It is night, and Mary is concealing her discovery from Martha.

4. LITERARY ELEMENTS:
Tone
There's a note of humorous exaggeration in Martha's remark, but at the same time it's essentially true.

---

1 through the layers of dead rotting leaves. Camera pulls back to include MARY staring down at the shoot. It's the first living thing she's seen in the garden. She kneels and scoops the dead leaves away until the dead choking grass around the shoot is revealed.

A dozen or so tender young shoots are now revealed. Camera pulls back to include MARY looking down at the shoots. MARY smiles. In the midst of death, she found life . . . <u>minimal</u>, fragile . . . but life.

55. *Ext. secret garden path—garden door—day*

MARY emerges from the garden. As she closes the door, pulling it firmly, a small piece of mortar falls from one of the bricks in the wall <u>adjacent</u> to the door.

MARY: It's my garden now. My own secret garden.

2 [MARY tugs the brick and it comes loose. She's found a place to hide the key. She puts the key in the niche and replaces the brick. Then she pulls the ivy over the door and steps back to study the result. The door is now completely hidden again.]

Cut to:

3 56. *Int. sitting room—Mary and Martha—night*

MARY, *in her long white nightdress, sits at the small table eating her supper.* MARTHA *sits beside her.*

MARY: Is Dickon good at making things grow?

MARTHA: (*laughing*) He can make things **4** grow just by whisperin' to them.

MARY: When will it be spring?

MARTHA: Spring comes on sudden in Yorkshire. You'll wake up one mornin' an' the moors'll be all purple with heather. I'll go and turn down your bed now . . .

[*As* MARTHA *starts toward the bedroom:*]

MARY: I wish I had a little spade.

[MARTHA *pauses, surprised.*]

MARY: (*casually*) If I had a spade, I could make a garden. (*Quickly*) A vegetable garden. I'd make it next to the big vegetable garden. It would give me something to do.

MARTHA: There's a little shop in Thwaite Village has garden sets for children, a spade an' rake an' fork all tied together, but it would cost two shillings.

MARY: Oh, I've got more than that. Much more. My mother always gave me money on my birthday so I could buy a present for myself, but I never did.

[MARTHA *barely manages to contain her anger at a mother who had so little interest in her child.*]

MARTHA: Well, if you give me the two shillings, I'll give it to the butcher boy when he comes an' he'll pass it on to Dickon. Dickon'll go and get your garden set for you.

[*As* MARTHA *goes into the bedroom,* MARY *looks after her, elated now. With*

498 Plays

the garden tools, she can accomplish much more in her secret garden.]

57. Ext. secret garden path—day
DICKON *sits under the tree next to the bench playing his pipe. The garden set, tied with a string, is on the ground beside him. As* MARY, *eager and filled with anticipation, hurries into shot,* DICKON *stops playing, picks up the garden set, and rises.*

DICKON: (*beaming*) I've brought your garden set. If you'll show me where you want to make your garden, I'll be pleased to help you start it.

[MARY *hesitates. She hates lying, and there's a sweetness and openness about* DICKON *that makes it even more difficult.*]

1 MARY: If I tell you a secret, will you promise not to tell anyone else?
DICKON: Aye, if it's what you want.
2 MARY: I've stolen a garden.

[DICKON *looks confused.*]

MARY: (*continuing*) I had to. It was locked up and no one's taken care of it for ages and ages and I'm not giving it back!
DICKON: A garden's not for givin' or takin'. A garden belongs to all. (*Studying* MARY) You found the door.

[MARY *nods.*]

3 DICKON: (*continuing*) It was meant to be.

58. Ext. the secret garden—day
MARY *and* DICKON *enter the garden.*

MARY: I was hoping it would look different than before, but it doesn't. Everything still looks dead.

[DICKON's *eyes move over the garden.*]

DICKON: It's how I thought it'd be . . .

[DICKON *moves to a bush and snaps off a cutting. He shows the cutting to* MARY.] **4**

DICKON: (*continuing*) If you look deep, you'll see it still has a green heart. (*Looking around*) Could be others is wick, too.
MARY: (*confused*) Wick?
DICKON: In Yorkshire, *wick* means 'live.
MARY: Even the thorny ones?!
DICKON: Aye. They've run wild an' attached themselves everywhere an' some will've died. But the strong ones will be wick, an' once the dead wood's cut away, there'll be roses.

[MARY's *eyes move over the "dead" garden. She's filled with wonder now, already visualizing the roses.*]

MARY: There'll be roses . . .

59. Int. sitting room—Mrs. Medlock—day
MRS. MEDLOCK *paces and* MARY *enters.*

MRS. MEDLOCK: Where have you been? Mr. Archibald is back and he wants to see you!

[MARY *tenses, fearful her guardian's discovered she's been inside the locked garden.*]

MARY: (*almost afraid to ask*) Why? Why does he want to see me?

---

1. GUIDED READING:
Interpreting Meaning
What does it mean when two people share secrets with each other? It usually means they are comfortable enough with each other to do so—in other words, they are friends.

2. GUIDED READING:
Interpreting Meaning
What does Mary mean by saying she's stolen a garden? She means she has taken it for her own. No one else was using it, but she is determined to.

3. GUIDED READING:
Interpreting Meaning
Why was it meant to be? Dickon probably means that hidden, locked-up beauty must eventually be brought into the open—with application to both gardens and people. (He is also referring to Mary's determination.)

4. LITERARY ELEMENTS:
Symbolism
How is the bush a symbol for some of the human characters in this play? Like the plant, Mary, Colin, and Archibald sometimes seem to be emotionally dead or hardened, but their inner hearts are still alive and can respond to proper care.

The Secret Garden, Act Three 499

MRS. MEDLOCK: I imagine it's about the governess. I mentioned it to Mr. Pitcher and he said he'd pass it on to Mr. Archibald.

60. Int. library—evening

Ever so slowly, MARY opens the door to the library and quietly enters. She walks farther into the room, staring at the beautiful overhead ceiling. She places her small hand on the arm of a chair. Suddenly an adult hand reaches out from the chair and clasps her hand. MARY jumps back in fright. ARCHIBALD CRAVEN slowly rises from the chair. Tall and gaunt to the point of emaciation,[1] his black coat strains against the hump on his back. Though he's not yet forty, his dark hair is streaked with white. His skin is pale and chalky. Pain from a debilitating

---

1. **emaciation** (ĭ·mā′sē·ā′shən): abnormal thinness.

500 Plays

illness[2] has etched his face with lines and created dark smudges under his eyes. A closer look would reveal fine, sensitive features.

MARY stands frozen, unable to take her eyes from ARCHIBALD. He beckons her.

ARCHIBALD: Come here . . .

[MARY *stands rooted, unable to move.*]

ARCHIBALD: (*continuing*) Don't be afraid. (*Bitter*) I know children usually find me frightening, but I'm quite harmless, I assure you.

[MARY *edges forward nervously.* ARCHIBALD *studies her.*]

ARCHIBALD: (*continuing*) You're too thin . . .

1 MARY: (*frantic*) I'm getting fatter!

[ARCHIBALD *continues to study* MARY. *Finally:*]

ARCHIBALD: You resemble your father. I only met him once, when we were boys, but I remember him. I envied him because he was on his way to Harrow[3] and I was too ill to go away to school.

[ARCHIBALD *moves slowly to the fireplace. He holds his forehead.*]

ARCHIBALD: (*continuing*) Ill. I have always been ill . . .

[MARY *manages to find her voice.*]

---

2. **debilitating** (di·bil′ə·tāt·ing) **illness:** illness that has made him weak and feeble.
3. **Harrow:** a famous preparatory school for boys in England.

MARY: I'm sorry.

ARCHIBALD: Yes. Are they taking good care of you?

[MARY *looks away.* ARCHIBALD *moves to the winged chair next to the fireplace and seats himself.*]

ARCHIBALD: (*continuing*) You find me repulsive, don't you?

[MARY *is shaken, but from somewhere inside herself she finds the courage to speak honestly.*]

MARY: You . . . you look different from other people . . . not repulsive.

ARCHIBALD: (*bitter*) Different. Yes, I look different. If we met in the dark, would you scream and run away?

[*Again,* MARY *finds it impossible to be anything but honest.*]

MARY: I might, but it would only be because it was the first time.

[ARCHIBALD *manages a shadow of a smile.*] **2**

ARCHIBALD: Honesty is rare. I value it. (*Beat*) Are you happy here?

MARY: I like India better.

[ARCHIBALD *stares into the fire. After a long moment:*]

ARCHIBALD: This is a sad house for a child . . . (*Beat*) We accept what we must. (*Beat*) **3** Oh, I meant to get a governess for you, I forgot. I'll see to it now.

[MARY *tries to hide her distress. She doesn't want a governess. A governess*

---

1. LITERARY ELEMENTS:
Dialogue
Why does Mary say this line frantically? She is so frightened of Archibald that even his comment about her thinness sounds like a threat to her.

2. GUIDED READING:
Comparing and Contrasting Characters
How are Mary and Archibald similar? Despite the obvious differences of age, gender, size, and wealth, both are lonely and griefstricken and find it hard to share affection. Both value honesty. In this scene, they begin to understand and help each other.

3. GUIDED READING:
Interpreting Meaning
Here, Archibald is talking as much about himself as about Mary.

The Secret Garden, Act Three

FOR STUDY AND DISCUSSION

Identifying Facts

1. The secret garden looks neglected and decayed.

Mary smiles because it is a sign of life in the garden.

2. Mary shares her secret with Dickon, because she wants to tell someone and because he has a welcoming and caring manner.

3. At first Mary is shocked by Archibald's appearance, but during their conversation they come to like each other.

Archibald is impressed with Mary's honesty.

4. Mary discovers that the crying behind the tapestry comes from a twelve-year-old boy.

Interpreting Meanings

5. Mary is snobbish toward people, so she doesn't make friends with them as readily as she might.

6. Mary becomes more trusting, more friendly, and less haughty in this act.

Sharing the secret with Dickon and her sympathy for Archibald mark the change.

7. Mary wants to find the secret garden and make it her own.

In this act, she has explored and found the key, opened the door, obtained a gardening set, obtained

---

would restrict her movements and she wouldn't be free to work in the secret garden.]

MARY: (*nervous*) Please, could I go without a governess for a while?

ARCHIBALD: Why?

[MARY *searches for a safe answer.*]

MARY: Well, I'm just getting used to being here. And when I came here, I wasn't very well . . . but now I'm getting better. And it's because I'm out a lot. And, well, if I had lessons, I wouldn't be out as much. And besides, I'm ahead on my studies. I know French, I'm good at history, and I read a lot.

ARCHIBALD: Very well. The governess can wait. Is there anything you need or want?

[ARCHIBALD *has given* MARY *an opportunity to ease her conscience about the secret garden.*]

MARY: Please, could I have a bit of earth to make a garden? I love gardens.

[ARCHIBALD *looks at* MARY *with shocked disbelief. Then he rises, moves to the window, and stands with his back to the room.* MARY'S *shaken. She's upset, perhaps angered, her guardian and she doesn't know why. After a long moment,* ARCHIBALD *turns to* MARY. *Pain and grief are mirrored in his face. He finds it difficult to speak.*]

ARCHIBALD: There was once someone, someone very dear to me, who loved gardens, too. Take your bit of earth wherever you like. (*Turning back to the window*) Go now. Leave me . . .

[MARY *understands.*]

MARY: (*whispers*) Thank you.

[*She hurries out of the room.* ARCHIBALD *watches her go, fighting to hold back his tears.*]

61. Int. corridor outside library—day

As MARY *moves into the corridor, she meets* MRS. MEDLOCK.

MRS. MEDLOCK: Miss Mary . . .

[MARY *simply stares up at her.*]

MRS. MEDLOCK: Well . . .

MARY: I think he's the saddest man I've ever seen, like the Hunchback of Notre Dame who died because he loved Esmerelda.[4]

[MRS. MEDLOCK *looks at* MARY *with surprise. This is the first time she's heard* MARY *express concern or compassion for another.*]

Cut to:

62. Int. Mary's bedroom—night

MARY *stands by her nightstand, listening once again to the sound of the child crying. Though frightened, she is now determined to find the source of the weeping. Taking a candle, she steps out into the corridor.*

---

4. **The Hunchback of Notre Dame** is a famous novel written in 1831 by the French writer Victor Hugo. The hunchback, called Quasimodo, is a handicapped bell-ringer. **Esmerelda** is a beautiful gypsy dancer.

63. Int. portrait gallery—night

The pale light from MARY's candle precedes her as she enters the gallery. In the wavering half-light, the portraits seem alive and menacing. A sudden clap of thunder followed by lightning frightens MARY even more. The crying of the child gets louder. The entire house is now filled with the menacing thunder and lightning.

64. Int. tapestry corridor—night

The sound of weeping is close. MARY appears at the top of the stairs. She looks toward the tapestry. A thin line of light is visible at the bottom of the tapestry. Suddenly the wind blows out the candle. Now, only the lightning is left to light up the corridor. Slowly, MARY inches toward the tapestry. Taking a moment to gather her courage, she pulls the tapestry aside and slowly moves inside.

65. Int. Colin's bedroom—night

The large room is crowded with handsome old furniture. MARY's eyes focus on the bed. The crying comes from someone rolling on the bed, covered by the bedcovers. Suddenly, the crying stops. Whoever is in the bed slowly drops the covers. MARY finds herself staring at a boy of about twelve. It is the boy who has been crying. As the boy sees MARY, he stares at her in shocked disbelief. MARY, equally shocked, stares back.

Fade-out.

For Study and Discussion

IDENTIFYING FACTS
1. Describe the **setting** of the secret garden when Mary first enters it. Why does Mary smile when she finds the green shoot?
2. Whom does Mary finally share her secret with? Why?
3. Describe Mary's meeting with Archibald Craven. Why is he impressed with her?
4. Besides the secret garden, what other **discovery** does Mary make in this act?

INTERPRETING MEANINGS
5. Ben calls after Mary, as she is skipping rope, "Pride goeth before a fall!" Ben is warning Mary that bragging can sometimes be followed by failure. In what other ways does Mary's pride get in her way—with making friends, for instance?
6. Mary's **character** begins to **change** in Act Three. How does it change? What important incident in this act marks the change?
7. In a play, the action moves forward when a character wants something and takes steps to get it. What does Mary want? What steps has she taken in this act to get what she wants?
8. What **questions** do you have at the end of this act?

APPLYING MEANINGS
9. Do you know people like Mary? What has happened in her life to make her the way she is?

permission to garden from Archibald, and shared her wish with Dickon.

8. Who is the boy? What relationship will he and Mary have later in the play? Will Mary get away with restoring the secret garden? Will Archibald find out, and if he does, what will he do about it?

Applying Meanings

9. Students may or may not know people like Mary. Most will agree that neglect, the death of her parents, and the displacement from her home have made her arrogant and lonely.

The Secret Garden, Act Three

Act Four

Fade-in:

66. Int. Colin's bedroom—Mary and Colin—night

For a long moment, MARY *and* COLIN *stare at each other. Then:*

COLIN: (*frightened*) Are you a ghost?
MARY: No. I thought you were.

[*As* MARY *starts toward the bed:*]

COLIN: Stay away from me!
MARY: (*continuing to the bed*) I'm Mary Lennox. I came here from India so Mr. Archibald Craven could be my guardian.
COLIN: (*trembling*) Are you sure you're not a ghost?

[MARY *extends her hand as she moves to the side of the bed and sits.*]

MARY: Touch me. If I'm a ghost, your hand will go right through mine.

[COLIN's *hand trembles as it touches* MARY's.]

COLIN: You feel real . . .
MARY: I am. Who are you?
COLIN: Colin Craven. My father's master of Misselthwaite Manor.
MARY: Your father?! Why didn't somebody tell me he had a son?!
COLIN: Because no one's allowed to talk to me!
MARY: Why?
COLIN: Because I won't have it . . . neither will my father.
MARY: Why?
COLIN: Because I'm going to have a hump on my back like he has!
MARY: Is that why you cry all the time?
COLIN: Yes.
MARY: Don't you ever go out of this room?
COLIN: No. If people look at me, I have a fit and get a fever.
MARY: I'm looking at you and you're not having a fit.
COLIN: (*glaring*) I might.
MARY: Well, you can save yourself the trouble. Now that I know you're human, not a spirit or a ghost, I'm going back to bed.
COLIN: (*imperious*) You'll stay. I've no one to talk to except my nurse, and she's away on holiday.
MARY: I don't have to stay if I don't want to.
COLIN: You said you came from India. I want to know about India.
MARY: You can read about India in books.
COLIN: (*petulant*) Reading makes my head ache.
MARY: (*tartly*) Well, if I were your father, I'd make you read so you could learn about things.
COLIN: No one can make me do anything!
MARY: Why not?
COLIN: Because I'm sick and I probably won't live to grow up!
MARY: (*interested now*) Do you want to live?

[COLIN *bursts into tears.*]

COLIN: Not if I'm going to have a lump on my back like my father . . .

1. GUIDED READING:
Making Inferences
What kind of person is Colin? He is self-pitying, demanding, spoiled, and manipulative. He is also lonely.

2. GUIDED READING:
Drawing Conclusions
Why is Colin pleased even though he didn't get his way? For the first time he has been treated as an equal, not as an invalid.

3. GUIDED READING:
Interpreting Meaning
What do we learn in this silent scene? We learn that Archibald loves his son.

4. GUIDED READING:
Paraphrasing
What is Martha worried about? She is worried she might lose her job.

5. GUIDED READING:
Drawing Conclusions
How serious is this fight? Are Mary and Colin as hostile toward each other as they sound? While they're genuinely angry, they're behaving like normal children in a momentary quarrel and like equals. This represents considerable progress for Colin.

MARY: You are the cryingest boy I've ever seen! I'm going back to bed!

[COLIN's *so angry he stops crying and glares at* MARY.]

1 COLIN: You'll stay till I say you can go!
MARY: (*haughty*) You can't make me stay if I don't want to.
COLIN: Yes, I can! Everyone has to do as I say because I'm going to die!
MARY: People who always talk about dying are boring. I'm going.

[As MARY *starts toward the door,* COLIN *realizes he's met his match.*]

COLIN: (*grandly*) You may go now, but you will come again tomorrow.
MARY: (*shrugging*) I might if I don't have anything else to do.

2 [MARY *exits. Despite the heated exchange,* COLIN *is pleased and excited.* MARY *is his first contact with another child.*]

67. Int. Colin's bedroom—night
Angle on ceiling as a large shadow looms into view. The shadow belongs to ARCHIBALD, COLIN's *father.*

3 ARCHIBALD *stands next to the bed, looking down at his sleeping son. He grieves for* COLIN . . . *but there's bitterness as well.*

Cut to:
68. Int. Mary's bedroom—Mary and Martha—day (morning)
MARY *sits on the bed tying her shoelaces.* MARTHA *is* <u>distraught</u>.

MARTHA: You shouldn't 've done it, Miss Mary! You shouldn't 've gone looking for Master Colin!
MARY: (*tartly*) Well, if you'd told me Mr. Craven had a boy, I wouldn't have gone looking for who was crying.
MARTHA: But no one's allowed to talk about him or see him!
MARY: (*dryly*) Then how do you know I saw him?
MARTHA: Because Master Colin told me! I'm the one has to look after him when his nurse is away.

[MARTHA's *on the verge of tears now.*]

4 MARTHA: (*continuing*) I'll be blamed for tellin' you an' I'll lose my place here.
MARY: (*impatient*) You won't lose your place because I won't tell anyone I saw him. No one's going to know except you.
MARTHA: But Master Colin said if you don't come now, he'll scream and scream till he brings the house down!
MARY: (*outraged*) We'll see about that!

69. Int. Colin's room—day

5 COLIN: (*furious*) You said you'd come!
MARY: (*just as furious*) I said I might! Might is only *maybe,* and I don't care if you scream till you're blue in the face!

[COLIN *turns away. He looks so* <u>frail</u>, *so miserable,* MARY's *moved in spite of herself.*]

MARY: (*continuing*) I suppose as long as I'm here I might as well stay.
COLIN: (*eager now*) Bring a stool and sit next to me.

[MARY *moves to get the stool.*]

MARY: I never had to do anything for myself in India. English people are the lords and masters there, you know.
COLIN: No, I didn't know.
MARY: (*dryly*) You don't know anything, do you?

[MARY *looks between* COLIN's *back and the pillows.*]

COLIN: (*depressed*) You're trying to see the lump on my back, aren't you?
MARY: Bother your lump. I was just thinking how different you are from Dickon.
COLIN: (*confused*) Dickon?
MARY: He's Martha's brother. If she wasn't so scared of you, she probably would have told you about him. Dickon's not like anyone in the world.
COLIN: Why?
MARY: Because he can charm animals and birds. He talks to them and they talk back.
COLIN: (*overwhelmed*) That's magic.
MARY: (*proudly*) Dickon's my friend, the first friend I've ever had.
COLIN: (*imperious*) Then I shall order him to be my friend, too.
MARY: (*contemptuous*) You don't know anything, do you? You can't order someone to be your friend. They have to want to be . . .

[*Suddenly,* MRS. MEDLOCK *and* DR. CRAVEN *enter.* MRS. MEDLOCK *is stunned, speechless, as she sees* MARY. DR. CRAVEN, *a tall, sensitive-looking man in his early forties, holds his medical bag. A gifted and dedicated physician, he barely manages to contain his anger now.*]

DR. CRAVEN: (*to* MRS. MEDLOCK) How dare you permit a stranger in the sickroom?

[*Before* MRS. MEDLOCK *can defend herself:*]

COLIN: She's not a stranger and I want her here!
DR. CRAVEN: (*stern*) Calm yourself, Master Colin. You know excitement makes you ill.
COLIN: You're the one who's making me so ill, so go away!

[*Though* DR. CRAVEN *is sensitive to* COLIN's *rudeness, his first concern is for his patient. A confrontation will do* COLIN *more harm than good.*]

DR. CRAVEN: You're to rest now. I insist. (*To* MRS. MEDLOCK) The vicar's ailing, so I'll get on to him and return tomorrow.
MRS. MEDLOCK: Yes, Doctor.

[MRS. MEDLOCK *looks back at* MARY *and* COLIN. *She is still shocked as she leaves the bedroom.*]

70. Int. kitchen—day
    MRS. MEDLOCK *sits at the table drinking a cup of tea to settle her frazzled nerves.* BETTY *stands nearby.* MRS. GORDY, *the cook, a plump, middle-aged woman, looks dismayed.*

MRS. GORDY: So Miss Mary found our little tyrant . . .
MRS. MEDLOCK: Master Colin actually wanted her there.

The Secret Garden, Act Four 507

---

1. GUIDED READING:
Understanding Slang
"Bother your lump" is British slang for "The heck with your lump" or "Who cares about your lump?"

2. LITERARY ELEMENTS:
Plot
The scene with Dr. Craven is important because it enables Mrs. Medlock to find out that Mary has discovered Colin. The incident reinforces the conflict between Mrs. Medlock and Mary. Also, the scene establishes an alliance between Mary and Colin.

507

1. GUIDED READING:
Finding the Main Idea
What do Betty and Mrs. Gordy agree about? They agree that Colin's problems are caused by the way he was raised, though they differ in their emphasis and proposed solutions.

2. GUIDED READING:
Making Inferences
What does Mrs. Medlock's response to Betty tell you about her? Mrs. Medlock is loyal to her employer and, by extension, to his family.

3. LITERARY ELEMENTS:
Characterization
Mrs. Sowerby's comment shows us how wise she is, even in the act of demurring about her wisdom.

4. GUIDED READING:
Interpreting Meaning
What message does Mrs. Sowerby convey to Mrs. Medlock? That there is a reason why Mary behaves poorly and that Mrs. Medlock will gain Mary's trust only if she treats her kindly and gently.

---

1 **BETTY:** I always said what Master Colin needs is the company of another child.

MRS. GORDY: (*tartly*) What Master Colin needs is a father who don't treat him like another plague that's been visited on him.

MRS. MEDLOCK: Anyway, it's done, and to tell the truth, I'm relieved in a way. It's been no easy thing trying to keep Miss Mary from finding out about Master Colin. Still, it's fortunate Mr. Archibald left for Cornwall this morning. Dr. Craven saw Miss Mary with Master Colin.

BETTY: He won't tell. He's Mr. Archibald's cousin an' down to inherit the manor someday, so he's not about to get Mr. Archibald angry.

2 **MRS. MEDLOCK:** (*sharp*) We'll have none of that. I've known Dr. Craven since he and Mr. Archibald were boys. (*Continues*) It was seeing Mr. Archibald suffer that turned Dr. Craven to medicine. So you just watch yourself, my girl.

71. Ext. church—day

The church bells are pealing as parishioners stream out of the church. MRS. SOWERBY, *a motherly-looking woman in her forties, wearing a neat but shabby dress, walks from the church with two of her children.*

MRS. SOWERBY: Go and see what's keepin' your brothers and sisters.

[*As the older boy starts back toward the church,* MRS. MEDLOCK *approaches* MRS. SOWERBY.]

MRS. SOWERBY: (*continuing warmly*) Mornin', Mrs. Medlock.

MRS. MEDLOCK: Good morning, Mrs. Sowerby.

MRS. SOWERBY: How's the little girl gettin' on, Mrs. Medlock? The one who come from India. (*To daughter*) Go and help your brother.

MRS. MEDLOCK: (*grim*) There are times when her rudeness and arrogance make me wish she had never left India, but I'm sure Martha's told you that.

MRS. SOWERBY: My Martha don't gossip about what's goin' on up at the manor, though she did ask my advice about how to deal with the little girl.

MRS. MEDLOCK: I could use your advice, Mrs. Sowerby. After all, you have had ten children.

3 **MRS. SOWERBY:** No two are alike.

MRS. MEDLOCK: Yes, but even so.

MRS. SOWERBY: Well, then, if I'm not bein' too forward, I'll tell you what I told Martha. A firm hand is needed, but there's also the need to see what's behind it when a child acts up. From what Martha said, there's a lot of hurt inside the little girl. **4** Seems to me she's like one of those wild creatures my Dickon sometimes finds out on the moors caught in a snare or trap. It strikes out at Dickon whilst he's tryin' to help it, but in the end he wins their trust with his gentleness.

MRS. MEDLOCK: (*politely*) The carriage is waiting, so I'll be running along. Good morning, Mrs. Sowerby.

[*As* MRS. MEDLOCK *moves off,* MRS. SOWERBY *looks after her. She knows that although* MRS. MEDLOCK *"got the message," she's not quite ready as yet to take* MARY *to her bosom.*]

72. Ext. secret garden—day
The garden glistens from a recent rain. Some of the dead branches on the trees and bushes have been cut away and lie in neat piles on the ground. MARY *and* DICKON, *holding hands, move quickly into the garden.*

MARY: How did you get so much done?! It's been raining for two days!
DICKON: I like the rain. So does the garden. Come. I've somethin' to show you.

[*The daffodils, crocuses, and snowdrops have bloomed.*]

MARY: (*joyfully*) They bloomed!
DICKON: Aye. Crocuses an' snowdrops an' daffydowndillies is always the first to say spring's on the way.
MARY: (*eager*) When will the roses bloom?
DICKON: Not till June.
MARY: (*disappointed*) It's only the beginning of April. June's such a long way away.
DICKON: Aye, but when they bloom, there'll be curtains an' fountains of roses.
MARY: (*overwhelmed*) Curtains and fountains of roses?
DICKON: Aye, but not unless the dead wood's cut away an' the earth is softened so it can drink in the rain. (*Surveying the garden*) There's lots to be done . . .
MARY: Well, tell me what you want me to do and I'll do it.
DICKON: If you'll clean out the flower urns, I'll bring fresh earth to put in 'em.

[*As* MARY *and* DICKON *move off, the camera moves with them.*]

MARY: I'm going to tell you another secret, Dickon. There's a sick boy who lives in Misselthwaite Manor and no one is allowed to see him, but I saw him.
DICKON: It's Master Colin you're talkin' about.

[MARY *pauses, astonished.*]

MARY: You know about him?
DICKON: Aye.
MARY: Did Martha tell you?
DICKON: My mother. Mrs. Craven fell from a tree an' the fall brought on her baby too soon. My mother knows midwifin',[1] so she was called in to help the doctor with the birthin'. It was a miracle, my mother said, how Mrs. Craven held on to life long enough to bring her baby into the world.

73. Ext. path outside secret garden—day
DICKON *closes and locks the garden door, and the children move off.* MARY's *lost in thought.*

DICKON: You're still thinkin' about Master Colin . . .
MARY: He said he's going to have a lump on his back like his father and he'd rather be dead.
DICKON: I doubt he means that, though he probably wishes he'd never been born, an' that's just as bad.
MARY: Why?

---
1. **midwifin'** or **midwifing:** A midwife helps women in childbirth.

---

1. GUIDED READING:
Understanding Dialect
Daffydowndilly is a British dialect name for daffodil.

2. GUIDED READING:
Finding the Main Idea
How do these words show a change in Mary? At one time, Mary would never have asked anyone to tell her what to do. Rather, she told others what to do.

1. GUIDED READING:
Interpreting Meaning
Discuss what Dickon means and whether students feel he is right. Note that he doesn't say "never"—he says "scarce ever." He is very likely right, but Mary has the inner strength to be one of the few who thrive despite feeling unwanted.

2. GUIDED READING:
Interpreting Meaning
Give students a few moments to think about the meaning of Colin's words, asking themselves whether or not they agree. Allow volunteers to discuss their responses.

FOR STUDY AND DISCUSSION
Identifying Facts
1. Colin's problem is psychological. He thinks he is dying and cannot walk.

   He stays in bed because he has been told he will develop a hunchback and may not even survive to maturity.

2. In general, the servants are glad that Mary has found out, although Martha is worried she might lose her job. Mrs. Medlock is glad she no longer has to keep the secret; Betty thinks that Colin needs the company of another child; and Nurse Boggs thinks that maybe Mary will shape Colin up.

510

---

1 DICKON: Those that feel unwanted scarce ever thrive.

MARY: I thrived and I didn't feel wanted. My mother didn't like me.

2 DICKON: Did you like yourself? It's where likin' has to begin.

MARY: I didn't like myself. I wasn't pretty, and I wanted to be because my mother only liked pretty things. Colin thinks he's ugly, too, and that's why his father can't bear to look at him and never comes to see him.

DICKON: Poor lad. There's not been much joy in his life. Have you told him about your secret garden?

MARY: No. (*Suddenly decisive*) But I'm going to, Dickon. It will give him something to think about besides feeling sorry for himself. (*Concerned*) What time do you think it is?

[DICKON *looks up at the sun.*]

DICKON: Well past three.

MARY: I've been out all day without stopping for lunch! Someone may be looking for me! (*As she runs*) Bring your animals tomorrow!

DICKON: If they don't want to play on the moors again like today!

74. Int. manor house—entry hall—angle to Martha—day

MARTHA *is hurrying down the stairs as* MARY *runs up the stairs. In the background, we can hear* COLIN *shouting for* MARY.

MARTHA: Master Colin is causin' a terrible fuss 'cause you've not been to see him all day!

MARY: I don't have to see him if I don't want to!

MARTHA: (*pleading*) Nurse Boggs is just back from her holiday an' has things to see to. You'd be doin' her a kindness.

75. Int. Colin's room—on Colin—day

COLIN *is pounding his bed and shouting.* MARY *is furious as she enters.*

COLIN: I waited and waited! Where were you all day?!

MARY: With Dickon.

COLIN: If you go to him instead of coming to me, I'll have him banished![2]

MARY: Who do you think you are, the Rajah of Punjab?![3]

COLIN: If you don't come, I'll have you dragged here! You're mean and selfish!

MARY: You're the one who's selfish! All you think about is yourself and feeling sorry for yourself!

COLIN: You'd feel sorry for yourself too, if you had a lump on your back and you were going to die!

MARY: You say things like that because you want people to feel sorry for you!

[COLIN, *outraged, throws his pillow at* MARY.]

MARY: (*continuing*) I was going to tell you something special . . . and now I'm not!

COLIN: I hate you!

MARY: Good! Now I don't have any reason to come and see you again and I won't!

---

2. **banished:** sent away from one's home or country.
3. **Rajah of Punjab:** prince of Punjab, a large region in northwest India.

[MARY, *fuming, emerges from behind the tapestry. She runs right into Nurse Boggs, who has been listening to the embattled children.*]

NURSE BOGGS: I'm Master Colin's nurse.
MARY: (*sarcastic*) I feel sorry for you.
NURSE BOGGS: (*wryly*) If he had a vixen of a sister like you, he might get well.
MARY: I don't care if he doesn't get well! If we were in India, I'd put a snake in his bed!

Fade-out.

For Study and Discussion

IDENTIFYING FACTS
1. What is Colin's **conflict,** or problem? Why does he stay in bed all day?
2. How do the servants feel about Mary's discovery of Colin? Describe the reactions of Mrs. Medlock, Martha, Betty, and Nurse Boggs.
3. What advice does Mrs. Sowerby give Mrs. Medlock about Mary?
4. Do Colin's tantrums "work" on Mary? What does Mary do when he has a fit?

INTERPRETING MEANINGS
5. In what ways is Colin like Mary when we first met her?
6. When Dickon says, "Those that feel unwanted scarce ever thrive," what truth does Mary **discover** about herself? What does she discover about Colin?
7. What do you think Colin's real **problem** is? What does he really want?

APPLYING MEANINGS
8. "You can't order someone to be your friend," says Mary. "They have to want to be." How do you think friends are made? How do you make someone *want* to be your friend? Or can you?

3. She advises Mrs. Medlock to treat Mary kindly.
4. Colin's tantrums don't work on Mary.
   She responds by shouting unpleasant truths at him and then leaving.

Interpreting Meanings
5. Both Colin and Mary, when we first meet them, are arrogant, imperious, lonely, friendless, and feeling unloved.
6. Mary discovers that she herself was unwanted by her mother, thought herself ugly, and didn't like herself.
   She discovers that Colin has very similar feelings. He feels unwanted by his father.
7. Colin's real problem is that he is lonely and feels unloved. He has been pampered and obeyed without truly being accepted.
   He probably wants love, friendship, and acceptance.

Applying Meanings
8. Most students will agree that we can make friends, and make others want to be our friends, by treating people considerately.

The Secret Garden, Act Four 511

FOCUS/MOTIVATION
Ask students whether they're beginning to like Mary more as time goes on. They're likely to, because she has acted decently toward Dickon and Archibald and because Colin has taken over the spoiled-and-arrogant role. Note that Frances Hodgson Burnett put many daringly new psychological theories about health and disease and childrearing in *The Secret Garden*. Interested students might want to talk about the idea that emotional deprivation can cause physical illness, just as it did with Colin.

Prereading Journal. Have students write their predictions about what will happen to Colin in this act.

> **TEACHING RESOURCES C**
> Teacher's Notes, p. 134
> Reading Check, p. 136
> Study Guide, p. 137
> Language Skills, pp. 147, 150, 153
> Building Vocabulary, p. 138
> Selection Vocabulary Test, p. 140
> Selection Test, p. 159

1. GUIDED READING:
Making Inferences About Character
The fact that Colin *asks* Mary to tell him the secret instead of demanding that she do so signals a change, a softening, of character.

Act Five

Fade-in:
76. *Int. Mary's sitting room—night*
   MARY, *in her nightgown and robe, sits on the floor in front of the fire, reading. At the sound of screams, hurrying feet, and slamming doors,* MARY *hurries to the door, opens it, and looks out.*

77. *Int. corridor outside Mary's sitting room—night*
   NURSE BOGGS *is hurrying toward* MARY'S *room.*

NURSE BOGGS: (*agitated*) Master Colin's worked himself up into a terrible state and I can't calm him! I'm afraid he's going to do himself harm!

78. *Int. Colin's room—Colin and Mrs. Medlock—night*
   COLIN *is screaming and struggling with* MRS. MEDLOCK, *who is trying to hold him down as he thrashes around the bed.* MARY *runs into the room and to the bed,* NURSE BOGGS *after her.*

MARY: (*screaming at the top of her lungs*) Stop it, you nasty, hateful boy! It would be a good thing if everyone went away and let you scream yourself to death!

[COLIN'S *so* astounded *he stops screaming.*]

MARY: (*continuing; grim*) That's better. If you scream again, I'll scream, too, and I can scream much louder and longer than you can.

COLIN: (*weeping*) I only screamed because I felt the lump on my back growing bigger.
MARY: (*to* MRS. MEDLOCK) Can I feel the lump?
MRS. MEDLOCK: (*horrified*) Certainly not!
COLIN: I want her to!
NURSE BOGGS: (*grim*) Oh, let her, Mrs. Medlock, or there'll be no end to this.
MARY: (*to* COLIN) Turn over.

[COLIN *turns on his side.* MARY *draws her hand across and down* COLIN'S *back.*]

MARY: (*continuing*) There's no lump.
COLIN: Yes, there is!
MARY: You've just got a knobby spine and knobby ribs like I have, so if you ever talk about lumps again, I'm going to laugh.
COLIN: I'm going to die!
MARY: (*to* NURSE BOGGS) Is he?
NURSE BOGGS: The specialist from London said Master Colin would improve if he ate well and got out into the air.
COLIN: (*to* MRS. MEDLOCK) You tell her!
MRS. MEDLOCK: You've been frail and sickly since you were born, Master Colin, and that's all I know. I've always hoped you'd outgrow your ailments, and I still hope. (*To* NURSE BOGGS) I'm worn out. Can you manage without me now?
COLIN: I want you to go! (*To* NURSE BOGGS) You, too! Only Mary can stay!
MRS. MEDLOCK: That's up to Miss Mary to decide.
COLIN: (*pleading*) Will you stay with me, Mary? Please?
MARY: Well, since you said please. But if

512 Plays

READING ACT FIVE
Encourage students to predict correctly that Mary, Dickon, and Colin will become a trio of friends in this act. The major silent scenes, 88 and 89, are important in the development and frustrations of the friendship.

---

you scream again, I'll smother you with a pillow!

NURSE BOGGS: (*sotto*)¹ And she would, too.

MRS. MEDLOCK: Thank God Mr. Archibald's still away or we'd be answering to him for this brouhah.²

NURSE BOGGS: Thank God, indeed. I'd just as soon be spared this distressing business.

[MRS. MEDLOCK *and* NURSE BOGGS *exit.* COLIN, *exhausted from his tantrum, lies back on his pillow.*]

COLIN: You said you had something wonderful to tell me. Will you tell me now?

MARY: (*tart*) You don't deserve to be told, but I will if you swear not to tell anyone else.

[COLIN *nods.*]

MARY: (*continuing*) Nodding doesn't count.

COLIN: All right. I swear.

MARY: There's a secret garden and I've been in it.

COLIN: (*confused*) A secret garden?

MARY: Yes. The door was hidden and it took me forever to find it but I did. No one had taken care of it for so long that it became a wild tangle. Everything looked dead, but Dickon said some of the roses were still alive, and that when they bloomed, there'd be curtains and fountains of roses.

[COLIN's *overwhelmed.*]

---

1. *sotto* as in *sotto voce* (sot′ō vō′chā): Italian for "in a quiet voice"; "under one's breath."
2. **brouhah** (broō′hä): uproar.

MARY: (*continuing*) The first time I saw it, it was like an evil witch's garden, ugly and scary. But Dickon and I have worked and worked and now it's beginning to get beautiful.

[COLIN *tries to picture the garden in his mind's eye.*]

MARY: (*fading*) Everything was gray, but now it's like a green veil hanging over the garden. A robin's made his nest there . . . in one of the trees. I call him "Beggar" . . .

[*Reaction shot of* COLIN *smiling brightly.*]

79. Ext. the secret garden—day
   MARY *and* DICKON *are busily knocking away dead brush and logs.*

MARY: There are holy men in India called dervishes who whirl and whirl until they go mad.³ That's what Colin was like last night.

DICKON: It's bein' lonely that makes him act like he does.

MARY: I was lonely in India, but I didn't have fits like that . . . (*Continuing*) That's not true. If my ayah or governesses didn't do what I wanted, I'd have terrible fits. (*Sighs*) No wonder they didn't like me.

Cut to:

80. Int. Colin's room—Colin—day
   COLIN, *propped up in bed, studies the*

---

3. **dervishes** (dûr′vish·əs): members of various Muslim orders, who whirl themselves into a religious frenzy.

---

1. GUIDED READING:
Making Inferences
How do you think Mary feels about the garden work she's describing? She feels proud.

2. GUIDED READING:
Identifying the Author's Purpose
Why do you think the author includes this scene? To show that Mary understands herself better than she used to. Mary understands part of the source of her loneliness. She is maturing.

The Secret Garden, Act Five

pages of a large book filled with beautifully illustrated flowers. Under each flower is its Latin name. MARY *enters and moves to the bed.*

1 MARY: I thought reading makes your head ache.
COLIN: I'm just looking at the pictures. I told Nurse to get me a book with flowers, and she brought this one from the library. But I can't tell what the names are.
MARY: Flower books always use the Latin names.
COLIN: Do you know Latin?
MARY: No, but I know a poem that was first written in Latin. (*Beat*) "I do not love thee, Doctor Fell. The reason why I cannot tell. But this alone I know full well, I do not love thee, Doctor Fell."
COLIN: (*delighted*) I like that. Do you know any other poems?
MARY: Oh, there are lots of other poetry books in your father's library.
COLIN: Will you read some of the poems to me?
MARY: I'll think about it.
COLIN: You smell nice.
MARY: It's the wind from the moors you smell. It's the springtime an' out-o-doors as smells so graidely.
COLIN: (*confused*) I never heard you talk that way before.
2 MARY: I'm givin' thee a bit o' Yorkshire. (*Sternly*) Tha's a Yorkshire lad. Tha' should understand Yorkshire talk. It's a wonder tha's not ashamed o' thy face.

[COLIN *bursts into laughter.*]

MARY: Sometimes Dickon forgets and talks Yorkshire to me. I like it.
COLIN: (*eager*) I'd like to hear him talk Yorkshire.
MARY: How can you if you don't want anyone to look at you?

[COLIN *stares at* MARY. *This is a big decision and it doesn't come easy. Then slowly, after a long moment:*]

COLIN: I don't think I'd mind if Dickon **3** looked at me . . .
MARY: You mean that?
COLIN: (*firmly now*) Yes. Yes.
MARY: (*awed*) Well, wonders never cease.

Cut to:
81. *Int. Colin's room—day*
   COLIN *is propped up on the sofa.* MARY *enters, followed by* DICKON. *They both carry* DICKON'S *animals.*

MARY: Colin . . . Dickon's here!
DICKON: I've brought along my creatures.

[DICKON *moves to sofa and puts the lamb in* COLIN'S *lap.*]

DICKON: Speak gentle and he'll take to you. **4**

[COLIN *looks down at the lamb with wonder. Then he looks up at* DICKON *and smiles* radiantly. MARY *smiles, happy for* COLIN. *The protective wall she built around her emotions is coming down. As they pet the animals, all three youngsters smile broadly.*]

COLIN: The squirrel looks sleepy. I didn't know animals are so friendly, Dickon.

The Secret Garden, Act Five **515**

---

1. GUIDED READING:
Identifying the Author's Purpose
Did the author include this dialogue in order to teach us about flowers and Latin? No, the scene is included to show that Mary's and Colin's friendship is developing.

2. LITERARY ELEMENTS:
Understanding Dialect
Although Mary does not usually speak Yorkshire dialect, she has a finely tuned ear and can imitate the local speech when she wants to.

3. GUIDED READING:
Recognizing Main Events
Why is this such an important decision? It is important because it is the first time he expresses an interest in meeting someone new. Colin is finally coming out of his self-imposed isolation.

4. GUIDED READING:
Understanding Idioms
"He'll take to you" is idiomatic for "he'll like you."

1. **GUIDED READING:**
Making Inferences
Why is Colin acting angry instead of glad about going inside? The point is that he is acting. The next scene makes clear that he is only pretending to be angry to trick the adults.

2. **GUIDED READING:**
Predicting Outcomes
What do you think will happen when Archibald returns and sees what has been going on? He might be angry and order Colin to remain alone and indoors. He might be happy that Colin is becoming normal.

3. **GUIDED READING:**
Visualizing
Have students compare this description of the garden with the one in scene 54 on page 496. Discuss how the garden has changed and why.

Cut to:

82. Ext. manor house—day

A wicker carriage chair (wheelchair) sits in the driveway. MARY and DICKON walk up to the wheelchair, followed by JOHN, the footman, who is carrying COLIN in his arms. NURSE BOGGS and MRS. MEDLOCK follow behind JOHN. As JOHN sets COLIN in the wheelchair:

1 COLIN: (glaring) You hurt me!
MARY: Stop being such a crybaby!

[NURSE BOGGS tucks the blanket around COLIN.]

NURSE BOGGS: (firm) This is your first time out, so it's to be only for an hour.
COLIN: It'll be for as long as I want! (To DICKON) Don't stand there like a stick! Push me!

[DICKON moves off, pushing the carriage chair, MARY walking alongside. MRS. MEDLOCK, NURSE BOGGS, and JOHN look after the retreating children.]

NURSE BOGGS: I'm all for it. It's wrong for the boy to be locked away like he wasn't fit to be seen.
2 MRS. MEDLOCK: John is right, Nurse. Master Colin can't spend his whole life in a world of his own making.
JOHN: (grim) His making or his father's?
MRS. MEDLOCK: It comes to the same thing. (Continuing) One thing is sure. Mary Quite Contrary isn't about to take any guff from Master Colin.

83. Ext. driveway—day

The children come into shot, with DICKON pushing the carriage chair.

COLIN: All clear?
MARY: Safe as churches!
COLIN: I wasn't really yelling at you, Dickon . . .
MARY: (giggling) We talked it over and decided if we were nasty, no one would get suspicious.
DICKON: (grinning) Ah, I figured that out myself.

84. Ext. secret garden path—day

The children approach the secret garden. DICKON is pushing the carriage chair slowly.

COLIN: (impatient now) Go faster, Dickon!
MARY: No! In case someone happens to see us, we don't want them to know we're going somewhere special!

85. Ext. secret garden path and doorway—day

DICKON opens the door and MARY pushes the carriage chair through.

86. Ext. the secret garden—day **3**

It's April and the spring flowers have all bloomed: pink and lavender, yellow and white. The tender green of new ivy covers the high walls. Bushes and trees wear a "green veil." Though the roses haven't bloomed, the "curtains and fountains" are greening. The fruit trees are budding. Much still remains to be done—there's still wild growth and tangle—but the garden is already *lovely.* MARY *watches* COLIN, *waiting for his reaction.* COLIN'S *eyes move over the garden and his face lights up.*

1 **COLIN:** This is a magic garden. It will make me well and I will live forever and ever.

Cut to:

87. Int. scullery—Betty—night

BETTY *stands at the table polishing brass pots.* MARTHA *enters.*

MARTHA: I'm done turnin' down the beds, so I'll give you a hand if you like.
BETTY: I'm not about to say no.

[MARTHA *gets a towel and joins in the polishing.*]

2 **MARTHA:** Ya know, I was lookin' at Miss Mary tonight. She was all plain an' scrawny an' she's gettin' pretty.
BETTY: It's our Yorkshire rain. Makes the flowers an' children bloom.
MARTHA: (*thoughtful*) She's changin' in other ways, too. She's still haughty sometimes, but not nearly as much.
BETTY: Her airs come from bein' spoiled when she lived in India.
MARTHA: I think it was the other way 'round. I think it was hurt and neglect made her act so badly.
BETTY: (*teasing*) You're deep as a river an' twice as murky . . .

[JOHN *enters the scullery.*]

JOHN: Mr. Archibald's back.
BETTY: (*tartly*) If you can't bring good news, don't bring any.
JOHN: (*grinning*) Well, this'll cheer you. Mr. Pitcher said they'll be off again soon.

Montage:

88. Ext. the secret garden—day   **3**

MARY *picks some flowers from the now-blossoming garden. She trots over to* COLIN, *who is sitting cheerfully in his carriage chair, and hands him the flowers. He smiles broadly.*

DICKON *discovers a bluejay feather and runs over to show it to* COLIN *and* MARY. *He points to a tree, where we see a robin's nest with several newly hatched fledglings.* DICKON *happily tries to balance the feather on his nose.*

DICKON *and* MARY *are dueling with branch stocks.* MARY *runs off, and* DICKON *runs, trying to catch her.* COLIN *sits in his chair, smiling. The smile suddenly turns to a look of sorrow as* COLIN *realizes he is unable to run with the others.*

End montage

89. Int. Colin's room—night

Moonlight streams into the room. COLIN *lies in bed, sleepless, unhappy because he can't be a part of* MARY'S *and* DICKON'S *world.* COLIN *suddenly senses that someone has entered the room.* ARCHIBALD *enters and quietly moves to a covered portrait hanging on the wall. He pulls the cord and the drape over the portrait parts. The portrait is one of Lilias Craven, an* exquisite *young woman.* ARCHIBALD *stares at the painting, agonizing over his loss. Slowly he closes the drapes again. As he exits,* ARCHIBALD *looks*

The Secret Garden, Act Five 517

---

1. GUIDED READING:
Interpreting Meaning
In what way is Colin right? Being out in the fresh air will improve Colin's physical health. The beauty of the garden will make Colin focus his attention on something other than himself.

2. LITERARY ELEMENTS:
Characterization
The author uses indirect characterization, telling us about Mary by letting us hear other characters' opinions of her.

3. GUIDED READING:
Summarizing
Summarize what has occurred in the silent scenes 88 and 89. The three children go to the garden. At first they play cheerfully. Then Colin becomes sad because Mary and Dickon are playing together while he's stuck in the chair. That night, because Colin cannot sleep, he sees his father enter the bedroom and grieve for Colin and for Lilias. Colin is in deep despair at the scene's end.

1. GUIDED READING:
Making Inferences
What can you infer from this dialogue? Archibald's distress causes him to lose sleep.

2. GUIDED READING:
Making Inferences
What does this tell you about Dickon? He is patient.

3. GUIDED READING:
Understanding Time Order
These words were spoken by the little girl's voice in Act One, Scene 9. Now we know the source of this line.

4. GUIDED READING:
Understanding Contrast
How is this Colin different from the one you were introduced to earlier in the play? Colin used to insist on his being handicapped in order to get his own way.

---

down at COLIN *with a <u>forlorn</u> look on his face.* COLIN *buries his face in his pillow and begins to weep.*

90. Ext. driveway—day

ARCHIBALD *enters his carriage. The driver takes his seat up top.* MRS. MEDLOCK *walks to the carriage together with* PITCHER. PITCHER *is also dressed for traveling.*

1 MRS. MEDLOCK: Mr. Pitcher, did you find the sleeping powders?
PITCHER: Fortunately, or there'd be no rest for him tonight.
MRS. MEDLOCK: Any idea when you'll be returning?
PITCHER: It may be months. We're to travel on the Continent.[4] Italy. Spain. Wherever.
MRS. MEDLOCK: (*sighs*) He'd rather be anywhere than here.
PITCHER: (*bitter*) With good reason. (*Glancing toward carriage*) The trunks are strapped. Good-bye, Mrs. Medlock.
MRS. MEDLOCK: Safe journey, Mr. Pitcher.

[MRS. MEDLOCK *looks on sadly as the carriage pulls away.*]

Cut to:

91. Ext. the secret garden—day

COLIN *sits in his chair watching* MARY *and* DICKON *working in the garden. He appears unhappy that he can't work with them.*

MARY: Do you think we'll ever get finished, Dickon?

---
4. **Continent:** Europe, apart from the British Isles.

DICKON: What's been left undone for years **2** can't be done in weeks.
COLIN: I wish I could help . . .

[COLIN *turns away. He's close to tears and doesn't want* MARY *to see. Suddenly, he spots* BEN WEATHERSTAFF *at the top of the garden wall.*]

COLIN: (*continuing; angry*) We're being spied on! (*To* BEN) Come in here!
MARY: He knows now. We'll be driven out **3** like from the Garden of Eden . . .
DICKON: (*to* BEN) This way . . . look at all the work we've done.
BEN: The hours you must have put in. I was up on the ladder . . . (*Turning to* COLIN) Poor crippled boy . . .
COLIN: (*furious*) I'm not a poor crippled **4** boy!

[*Holding the arms of the carriage chair,* COLIN *struggles to his feet, stands for a fraction of a moment, then falls back in the chair.*]

MARY: (*numbly*) You stood up . . .
BEN: You're frail, but you're no cripple, an' you're not dimwitted . . .
COLIN: (*outraged*) Who said I was dimwitted?

[BEN *pulls himself together.*]

BEN: Fools, that's who! But why've you locked yourself away . . .
COLIN: I thought I was going to have a lump on my back and my father hates me.
BEN: (*distressed*) Your father doesn't hate you, Master Colin.
COLIN: (*bitter*) Then why doesn't he come

to see me except when he thinks I'm sleeping?
BEN: (*gently*) Maybe it's because he wants to spare you his pain an' grief.

[COLIN *stares at* BEN; *then:*]

COLIN: I want you to promise me that you won't tell anyone else about our secret garden.

BEN: It was me that worked beside your mother to make the garden, an' I'll work again to make it like it once was.
MARY: You mean you'll help us?!
BEN: Aye.
COLIN: (*defeated*) Now I'm the only one who can't help.
DICKON: (*to* MARY) Get the little spade an' the rose I potted this mornin'.

1. LITERARY ELEMENTS:
Motivation
This passage explains Ben's motivation for helping work on the garden. He was apparently devoted to Lilias Craven.

1. GUIDED READING:
Self-Questioning
How does Mary know what's in Dickon's mind? Mary and Dickon understand each other because they are friends. Point out that Mary has used Colin's previous remark as a context clue to Dickon's meaning.

2. GUIDED READING:
Making Inferences
How do you think Mary and Colin feel at this moment? Colin feels proud of having done something useful. Mary feels proud of having helped someone. They probably also feel close to each other.

3. GUIDED READING:
Making Inferences
Why does Colin dislike Dr. Craven? The doctor is partly responsible for sheltering and restricting him, for participating in his imagined disability.

---

1 [MARY *understands what's in* DICKON'S *mind and she smiles as she hurries away.* DICKON *lifts* COLIN *out of the carriage chair and puts him on the ground.*]

COLIN: (*confused*) What are you doing? . . .

[MARY *hurries into shot. She gives* DICKON *the potted rose, then hands the spade to* COLIN.]

MARY: Dig a little hole. The earth's soft.

[COLIN'S *confused, but he digs the little hole.* DICKON *shakes the plant out of the pot and hands the plant to* COLIN.]

DICKON: Hold it firm with one hand, push the earth around it, an' tamp it down.

[COLIN *follows the instructions, then looks up.*]

2 MARY: You just planted your first rose.

Cut to:

92. Int. Colin's room—day

COLIN *is propped up on the sofa, the doctor and* NURSE BOGGS *standing next to him.*

DR. CRAVEN: (*concerned*) Nurse Boggs tells me you've been going out every day. You mustn't overdo, Master Colin.

COLIN: (*curt*) I'll do as I please.

93. Int. tapestry corridor—day

The door to COLIN'S *room is ajar and* MARY *stands next to the tapestry waiting to go in.*

DR. CRAVEN'S VOICE: Your father has entrusted me with your care, Master Colin.

COLIN'S VOICE: Well, I don't trust you, so **3** go away!

NURSE BOGGS'S VOICE: (*distressed*) I'll see you out, Doctor . . .

[MARY *quickly presses herself into the corner next to the tapestry, reluctant to let the doctor and* NURSE BOGGS *know she's been* eavesdropping. DR. CRAVEN *and* NURSE BOGGS *emerge from behind the tapestry. As they move off:*]

DR. CRAVEN: (*hopelessly*) Why does he dislike me so? I only want him to be well. It's all I've wanted since the day I brought him into the world and breathed life into him . . .

[MARY *looks at the doctor leaving, touched by his* anguish. *She runs back to* COLIN'S *room.*]

94. Int. Colin's room—day

MARY: You're wrong about Dr. Craven. He wants you to get well. He wouldn't let you be so rude to him if you weren't such a poor, pitiful thing.

COLIN: I'm not a poor, pitiful thing! I stood up for a whole minute yesterday, didn't I?! (*Continues*) And from now on, I'm going to try to stand every day, and when I'm good at it, I'm going to try walking!

MARY: (*sanguine[5]*) It's about time.

---

5. **sanguine** (sang′gwin): cheerful, hopeful.

Cut to:

95. *Ext. the secret garden—day*

Mary *and* Dickon *are supporting* Colin *as he tries to walk.* Colin's *feet drag uselessly on the ground.*

Mary: Pick up your feet, Colin! It won't work unless you pick up your feet!
Colin: I'm trying!
Mary: Try harder.
Colin: I'm tired. Take me back to my chair.

[Mary *and* Dickon *continue to half drag* Colin *back to the carriage chair and ease him down.* Ben *watches the three youngsters in amazement.*]

Dickon: It comes hard 'cause your muscles are soft from not bein' used. We've a neighbor, Bob Haworth, whose legs was all spindly once, an' now he's a champion runner. Came from the exercises he done.

[Colin *stares at* Dickon.]

Colin: Could you show me how to do the exercises? Could you, Dickon!
Dickon: Aye! Give me your leg. Now push against me.
Colin: Ow . . . that hurts, Dickon.

[Mary *looks at the birds' nest. The babies have grown bigger and* Mary *giggles in delight.*]

96. *Ext. the secret garden—day*

Mary *and* Dickon *are again supporting* Colin *as he tries to walk.* Colin *is obviously having a tough go of it.*

Dickon: Come on, Colin . . .

Colin: Wait . . . wait . . . wait a minute.

[Colin *slowly removes his arms from around* Mary *and* Dickon's *shoulders. He begins walking on his own—takes several steps and falls forward. In frustration,* Colin *pounds the ground with his fists.* Mary *and* Dickon *rush over to him.*]

Mary: Stop . . . no, you can't get mad . . . you've got to try harder.

Fade-out.

For Study and Discussion

IDENTIFYING FACTS
1. What trick do the children play on the adults to hide their trip to the secret garden?
2. According to Ben Weatherstaff, why doesn't Colin's father come to see him very often?
3. What **discovery** does Mary make about Colin's lump?
4. Colin has finally found some friends and begins to go out. Why is he still unhappy?

INTERPRETING MEANINGS
5. How does Colin's **character** begin to change in Act Five? Does he become more likable?
6. How is Mary also changing?

APPLYING MEANINGS
7. Betty thinks Mary is difficult because she was spoiled. Martha thinks Mary is difficult because she was hurt and neglected. What do you think?

The Secret Garden, Act Five

FOR STUDY AND DISCUSSION

Identifying Facts
1. The children pretend that Colin is angrily bossing Mary and Dickon, so the adults won't be suspicious.
2. Colin's father wants to spare Colin his grief and pain.
3. Colin's lump is illusory—he merely has a knobby spine.
4. Colin is unhappy because he still can't walk and run with his friends.

Interpreting Meanings
5. Colin becomes more likable in this act. He makes friends with Mary and Dickon and is delighted by the secret garden. He is trying to overcome his disability and seclusion.
6. Mary is becoming more sensitive and affectionate. She delights in nature and in friendship.

Applying Meanings
7. Betty and Martha are both right. Mary was spoiled in the sense of having servants do her bidding, but she was neglected and hurt by her mother.

FOCUS/MOTIVATION

Define *foreshadowing*—the hints the author gives about what will happen later in a work. Discuss what possible foreshadowings of events in Act Six the author may have planted in the preceding acts.

Prereading Journal. Have students write a prediction of how the play will end.

READING ACT SIX

The key event in this act is that Colin teaches himself to walk. He reveals his accomplishment to the others and, in an emotional scene, to his father. Make sure students recognize that in Scene 115 the long flashback ends.

Act Six

Fade-in:

97. Int. Colin's room—day

1 COLIN *has taken to his bed again. He is withdrawn, detached. Camera pulls back to include* MARY *standing next to the bed.*

MARY: (*brightly*) It's nice out. You're not going to stay in bed all day, are you, Colin?

[COLIN *doesn't respond.*]

98. Ext. the moors—day

MARY *and* DICKON *walk slowly across the moor.*

MARY: (*despondent*) Colin doesn't care anymore if I come to see him or not. I don't know what to do, Dickon.

[DICKON *pauses. Looks off. He seems to be searching beyond this time and place. After a long moment:*]

DICKON: Colin'll find his way, an' you'll be the one that helps him find it. (*Smiles at* MARY) The way will come to you.

Cut to:

99. Int. Colin's room—day

NURSE BOGGS *helps* COLIN *into the chair.*

COLIN: (*listless*) What're you doing . . . ?

2 MARY: We're just gonna go up and down the corridors because it's raining and I don't have anything else to do.

[MARY *pushes* COLIN *out of the room.* NURSE BOGGS *looks after them.*]

NURSE BOGGS: (*distressed*) He'd been doing so well . . .

100. Int. portrait gallery—day

COLIN *sits looking at the portrait of the boy in the velvet suit.*

MARY: The boy in the picture looks like you. That's why I thought you were a ghost the first time I saw you. He's dead, of course, but you're alive.

[COLIN *glances at the portrait, then turns away indifferently.*]

Dissolve to:

101. Int. Lilias's bedroom—day

COLIN: (*whispers*) I smell roses . . .

MARY: This was your mother's room, Colin. She loved the secret garden, so she must have loved roses.

[COLIN *looks up at* MARY. *His eyes fill.*]

MARY: (*continuing*) Sometimes it's all right to cry, Colin . . .

102. Int. Colin's room—day

MARY *has just drawn the drape over the fireplace open and is looking up at Lilias's portrait.*

MARY: She's beautiful, Colin. As beautiful as a princess in a fairy tale. (*Turning to* COLIN) Why did you let your father cover your picture?

3 COLIN: I'm the one had it covered. I didn't want my mother to see the lump growing on my back.

MARY: Oh, Colin, she would've loved you even if you did have a lump. But I think

The Secret Garden, Act Six **523**

TEACHING RESOURCES C

Teacher's Notes, p. 141
Reading Check, p. 144
Study Guide, pp. 145, 146
Language Skills, pp. 147, 150, 153
Building Vocabulary, p. 156
Selection Vocabulary Test, p. 158
Selection Test, p. 159

1. LITERARY ELEMENTS:
Plot
Colin's setback is a complication in the plot. It prolongs our suspense, even though we suspect it will work out all right.

2. GUIDED READING:
Interpreting Meaning
Mary is using her boredom as an excuse to be with Colin and to get him out of his room.

3. GUIDED READING:
Interpreting Meaning
That Colin thinks his own mother would not love him if he were physically deformed is a sign of his poor self-image.

1. GUIDED READING:
Making Inferences About Character
What do his actions in this scene tell you about Colin? Colin is not giving up. The thought of his mother inspires him to keep trying.

2. GUIDED READING:
Interpreting Meaning
Pause and ask students what they think is the meaning behind Ben's words. They will learn Mary's interpretation in the next scene.

3. GUIDED READING:
Interpreting Meaning
Why do Mary and Colin repeat "thistles and roses"? They are sharing their understanding that it is up to them to choose to fill their minds—their inner gardens—with ugly thoughts or with beautiful ones.

---

she wants you to try to keep on walking, too.

103. Int. Colin's room—Colin—night
Moonlight illuminates the room and portrait. COLIN *lies in bed looking at the portrait. The moments pass, then* COLIN *pushes his light covers aside and swings his legs over the side of the bed. Holding on to the nightstand, he stands. He releases his hold, takes a step, and he falls. He crawls to a chair and pulls himself up. Again and again, until he's soaked with perspiration, falling, pulling himself up, clinging to chairs and tables for support,* COLIN *struggles to walk until, finally, exhausted, he reaches the fireplace. Holding on to the mantle, he looks up at his mother's portrait.*

COLIN: Till I can walk, really walk, no one will know but you . . .

Cut to:

104. Ext. the secret garden—day
The roses have bloomed, a still-wild but glorious profusion of pink, coral, and deep velvet red. DICKON *pushes* COLIN's *chair as* BEN *works in the garden.*

MARY: Well . . . the roses bloomed even though it's been raining for days and days!
DICKON: They knew it was June.
BEN: Where you tend a rose, a thistle[1] canna' grow.

---
1. **thistle** (this′əl): prickly plant.

[MARY *glances at* BEN *as though sensing something beyond his words.*]

105. Ext. outside garden—day
COLIN *sits in his chair with* MARY *at his side.*

MARY: I'm just thinking about what Ben Weatherstaff said about roses and thistles. He was talking about us.
COLIN: (*confused*) About us?
MARY: Yes. Ugly thoughts are like thistles, and beautiful thoughts are like roses. As long as my head was filled with ugly thoughts, I didn't have room for pretty ones and I was mean all the time. As long as you thought about a lump growing on your back, you were nasty and rude.

[COLIN *considers this, then he smiles.*]

COLIN: Thistles and roses.
MARY: Thistles and roses.

Cut to:

106. Ext. the secret garden—day
It's July and the roses and summer flowers are in full bloom. BEN *and* DICKON *look around, admiring the fruits of their hard work.* MARY *walks over to* COLIN, *who is seated in his chair. She carries the fox in her arms and sings.*

MARY: (*singing*)
"She is coming, my dove, my dear;
She is coming, my life, my fate . . .
The red rose cries, she is near.
She is near, and the white rose weeps, she is late."

524 Plays

Cut to:

1 107. *Int. Colin's room—night*

   COLIN *lies on the bed.* MARY *sits next to him and continues to sing.*

MARY: (*singing*)
"The larkspur listens
I hear, I hear . . ."

COLIN: (*whispering*)
"And the lily whispers, I wait."

[COLIN *and* MARY *smile at one another.*]

Cut to:

108. *Ext. the secret garden—day*

   COLIN *sits in his chair with* MARY, DICKON, *and* BEN *standing nearby.*

COLIN: Come here, everyone . . . hurry up . . . come on. I have an announcement to make. I have decided that when I grow up, I am going to do important experiments with magic. (*To* MARY) You know a little bit about magic because you grew up in India, where there are fakirs.² (*To* DICKON) You can charm animals, so you know some magic, too. (*Beat*) I am now going to show you my first magic experiment.

[COLIN *rises from the carriage chair.* **2** *As* MARY, DICKON, *and* BEN *watch, astounded,* COLIN, *though somewhat unsteady, walks a few feet to a flower bush, picks a flower, brings it to* MARY, *then sinks down in his chair, tired but triumphant.*]

---

2. **fakirs** (fə·kirz′): Muslim or Hindu holy men who are beggars. Many claim they can perform miracles.

COLIN: (*continuing*) That is my first experiment!

MARY: (*numb*) You walked. You walked all by yourself . . .

COLIN: (*elated*) I've been practicing! Every night after Nurse Boggs went to bed, I practiced!

[DICKON *smiles.* BEN'S *eyes fill.*]

BEN: Praise God . . .

[*Unnoticed,* MRS. SOWERBY *has entered the garden.*]

MRS. SOWERBY: (*overcome by emotion*) Amen.

DICKON: (*to his mother, wryly*) You're in, so you might as well come all the way . . .

[*As* MRS. SOWERBY *moves forward:*]

MRS. SOWERBY: I was passin' an' heard voices, but never did I envision what I just saw—Master Colin up an' walkin'!

3 DICKON: (*to* COLIN) No cause to worry. She's my mother, Susan Sowerby.

COLIN: Since you're Dickon's mother, I guess I don't mind your knowing I can walk now. I don't want anyone else to know.

BEN: (*dismayed*) Surely, you wants your father to know.

COLIN: Not yet. I want to surprise him. When he comes home, I shall walk to him and say, "I can walk now, Father, and I shall grow up and make you proud of me!" (*Firmly*) It has to be that way. That's part of the magic.

BEN: (*moved*) I never knew it by that name, but what does a name matter? Call

---

1. LITERARY ELEMENTS:
Foreshadowing
What does this scene foreshadow about Mary and Colin? They will fall in love.

2. GUIDED READING:
Interpreting Meaning
Why do you think Colin's first action once on his feet is to bring a flower to Mary? He wants to acknowledge that she is responsible for changing his life.

3. GUIDED READING:
Making Inferences
What do you think was Colin's reaction to Mrs. Sowerby's presence? How do you know? Colin was alarmed. Dickon tells him not to worry.

1. GUIDED READING:
Self-Questioning
Ask students to discuss what Mrs. Sowerby might mean by "the Good Big Thing," aside from possibilities already mentioned. She might mean hope, faith, love, the ability to make one's life better.

2. GUIDED READING:
Making Inferences
Who else used to be rude and no longer is? Mary herself used to be rude. She could be talking about her own past behavior, in a veiled way.

3. GUIDED READING:
Interpreting Meaning
What commitment do you think Mary and Colin have made? Mary and Colin are committed to helping each other in the future. They may also have made a romantic commitment.

---

it magic or a miracle or the touch of God's hand . . .

1 **MRS. SOWERBY:** (*loving*) It's the Good Big Thing, Master Colin, an' I hope you'll never stop believin' in it.

MARY: Oh, he won't.

[DICKON *smiles.*]

Cut to:

109. *Int. Colin's room—night*

NURSE BOGGS *is turning down the bed.* COLIN *is propped on the sofa.* MARY *sits on the low stool beside him, books scattered on the floor around her.* NURSE BOGGS *finishes and moves toward the door.*

NURSE BOGGS: I'll be back in a little while to put you to bed, Master Colin.

[NURSE BOGGS *exits.*]

COLIN: (*worried*) I hope Dr. Craven isn't getting suspicious. When he was here before, he noticed my legs look stronger and that I'm getting fatter. (*Hoping*) Maybe he'll think I'm bloated.³ Sick people get bloated, don't they?

MARY: Dead people get bloated when they're left out in the sun. I once saw a dead beggar in India who was so bloated he looked like a melon about to burst.

COLIN: I don't like to talk about dead people or dying.

2 **MARY:** I know, but you used to. You're not rude to Dr. Craven anymore, either.

COLIN: I know. I used to think he wanted me to die, and now I know he doesn't.

---
3. **bloated:** puffed up, swollen.

(*Hesitates*) Mary, do you like Dickon more than you like me? (*Quickly*) I don't mind if you like Dickon. I just want you to like me, too.

MARY: I like you the same but different.

Cut to:

110. *Ext. the secret garden—angle to Dickon—day*

DICKON *marches around the garden playing his panpipe. Soot is on his shoulder, the squirrel peeps out of his pocket.*

MARY *and* COLIN *sit under a tree watching* DICKON, *delighted with the "performance."* COLIN *suddenly reaches into his pocket.*

COLIN: (*suddenly shy*) I have a present for you.

[COLIN *takes a small velvet box out of his pocket, hands it to* MARY, *and she opens it. Inside the box is a small heart-shaped locket suspended from a thin gold chain.* MARY *is absolutely astonished.*]

MARY: Oh, Colin . . . it's beautiful.

COLIN: (*proudly*) I picked it out myself from a catalogue, and Mrs. Medlock ordered it for me all the way from London.

[MARY *puts the locket on.*]

MARY: I shall wear it always.

[COLIN *smiles and* MARY *responds. Though neither fully understands,* 3 *both seem to sense they've made a commitment to each other.*]

Cut to:

111. Ext. sanitarium⁴—day

ARCHIBALD *is asleep on a lounge, covered with a blanket. Several medicine bottles, a water carafe,⁵ and glass are on the low table beside the lounge.* ARCHIBALD *stirs in his sleep. He dreams. The picture distorts, and as though through a clouded mirror, we share his dream:*

112. Ext. secret garden—day

We see LILIAS *standing in the garden.* LILIAS *is lovely in her airy white dress.* ARCHIBALD *takes her in his arms and they're lost in a kiss. Then* LILIAS *frees herself, smiles, and moves off. She pauses abruptly and turns to* ARCHIBALD, *deeply troubled now. The picture distorts. When it comes into focus:*

113. Ext. sanitarium balcony—day

ARCHIBALD *is suddenly awakened by the sound of* PITCHER *calling to him. He holds a letter in his hand.*

PITCHER: It's time for your medicine, Mr. Archibald. Also, this letter just arrived from your solicitor.⁶ Shall I see what it is?

[ARCHIBALD *nods, still caught up in his dream.* PITCHER *opens the envelope and takes out a smaller envelope.*]

---

4. **sanitarium** (san′ə·târ′ē·əm): a place where people live and receive treatment while recovering from illnesses. Archibald has gone to a sanitarium in Europe.
5. **carafe** (kə·raf′): glass bottle used to hold water, wine, or another drink.
6. **solicitor** (sə·lis′ə·tər): British term for lawyer.

PITCHER: (*continuing; confused*) Another letter is enclosed. Shall I read it?

[ARCHIBALD *nods indifferently.* PITCHER *takes the letter out of the envelope, puts on his spectacles, then reads:*]

PITCHER: (*continuing; reading*) "Dear Sir: I am Susan Sowerby who is Martha's mother who works for you in Misselthwaite Manor. I am making bold to speak to you. Please sir, I would come home if I were you. I think you would be glad you came, and if you will excuse me, sir, I think your lady would want you to come if she were here. Your obedient servant, Susan Sowerby."

[ARCHIBALD *stares at* PITCHER *in shocked disbelief.*]

PITCHER: (*continuing; frightened*) What is it?

ARCHIBALD: (*whispers*) I dreamed of Lilias . . .

Cut to:

114. Ext. the secret garden—day

Summer is drawing to a close. Petals from the overblown roses are scattered on the ground. COLIN *sits cheerfully in his carriage chair as* MARY *picks some flowers.*

DICKON: I've an errand to run, so I'm off to Thwaite Village now.

COLIN: (*concerned*) You'll come back, won't you? You have to push me back to the house.

The Secret Garden, Act Six 527

1. GUIDED READING:
Paraphrasing
What does Dickon mean? This is a colorful phrase for "The day's not over yet" or "It's not time to go back yet."

2. LITERARY ELEMENTS:
Foreshadowing
The dialogue may foreshadow Dickon's death or simply reflect his awareness of class differences.

3. BACKGROUND
The schools they're referring to are what we would call private schools, for well-to-do youngsters. In England, such schools are called "public schools" (in comparison to private tutors). At one time, these were the only schools in England.

---

1 **DICKON:** Aye, I'll be back. (*Teasing*) The game's not played out yet.

COLIN: (*laughing*) I like that. The game's not played out. I'm glad you're my friend, Dickon. You'll always be my friend, won't you?

[*For a fleeting moment, a shadow falls across* DICKON's *face, as though the sun's gone behind a cloud.*]

2 **DICKON:** (*quietly*) We'll be parted, you an' me, but remembrance will keep us friends.

COLIN: (*frowning*) Mary, why did Dickon say we'd be parted? How can he know that?

MARY: Dickon knows things no one else knows.

[COLIN *gets up from the carriage chair and walks with* MARY *through the garden. As they circle the garden,* MARY *looks at the overblown roses with regret.*]

MARY: Summer's almost over.

COLIN: I know. What will we do all winter, Mary?

MARY: We'll probably go to school. We're both too old for governesses, and you're well now.

COLIN: (*hoping*) Perhaps we can go to the same school.

MARY: No. Girls go to girls' schools and boys to boys'.

COLIN: I suppose there's no help for it.

MARY: You better sit down for a bit . . .

[COLIN *seats himself in the carriage chair.*]

COLIN: I wish we didn't have to go to different schools . . . **3**

MARY: We'll write letters to each other.

COLIN: (*disconsolate*) But it won't be the same. And we won't be able to come to our secret garden.

MARY: Oh, our garden will be here when we come back. And while we're away, we can think about how beautiful it is. And how it's waiting for us.

[*Suddenly* ARCHIBALD *walks into the garden. His eyes are fixed on* COLIN *with stunned disbelief.* MARY, COLIN, *and* ARCHIBALD *are frozen in place. Immobilized. The shock is mutual.* ARCHIBALD's *eyes fill.*]

ARCHIBALD: (*whispers*) Colin . . . son . . .

[COLIN *stares at his father. This is the moment he's been waiting for, and he's rigid. Unable to move.* MARY *whispers to* COLIN.]

MARY: (*desperately*) Get up. Get up and walk! Come on, you know you can do it.

[COLIN *remains rigid, his eyes fixed on his father.*]

MARY: (*continuing*) You know you can. Please, Colin . . . go. Come on, go.

[COLIN *stirs. Then slowly, his eyes fixed on his father,* COLIN *rises out of the carriage chair. As* COLIN *moves slowly, tentatively, toward his father,* ARCHIBALD *is overcome with emotion. Weeping tears of joy, he opens his arms to receive* COLIN. *Enfolds him.*]

ARCHIBALD: (*weeping*) My boy . . . my son . . .
COLIN: Don't cry, Father. I'm well now! I can walk, and I'm going to live forever!

[MARY *smiles in delight.*]

1 COLIN: (*continuing*) It was the secret garden that made me well, Father. My mother's garden. And it was Mary who made me walk.

[MARY *walks over to* ARCHIBALD. *He clasps her hand in appreciation.*]

ARCHIBALD: (*to* MARY) Thank you.
COLIN: Come see our garden.

[*Hand in hand,* ARCHIBALD *and the two youngsters begin to stroll through the garden.*]

2 Cut to:
115. Ext. vegetable garden—day (1918)
MARY, *the lovely young woman in the Red Cross uniform, is seated on a bench under a tree. Suddenly, a gnarled hand reaches out and touches her shoulder. She turns, rises, and embraces* BEN WEATHERSTAFF.

MARY: Ben! Ben Weatherstaff!

[BEN *holds out the rusted key for the secret garden.*]

BEN: You'll be needin' this to unlock the garden.
MARY: (*overjoyed*) Ben, it's been so long!
BEN: I didn't know you, you've changed so . . .
MARY: (*laughing*) I grew up.

[*A shadow crosses* BEN's *face.*]

BEN: (*somber*) You know about Dickon?
MARY: Mrs. Medlock wrote to me. She **3** wrote with such love. Such compassion.
BEN: You touched her heart an' warmed it . . . (*Heavily*) Killed in the war. Dickon. In a forest called the Argonne[7] . . .
MARY: If Dickon had to die, he would have chosen a place where there were green and growing things.
BEN: Aye. But to die so young. Who was to know . . .
MARY: (*gently*) Dickon knew.
BEN: (*managing a smile while fighting back tears*) Aye. Dickon knew. Come. I'll unlock the garden for you.

116. Ext. the secret garden—day **4**
The garden is as we have never seen it before, a mystical and magical place. Roses cascade *like waterfalls. Bushes have been transformed into the exquisite forms of woodland creatures. Low-growing flowers are a pink and lavender carpet. Lilies are massed against the walls and the walls are covered with tender green ivy. Pastel flowers tumble out of the stone urns. A little stream* meanders *through the garden; violets grow in the damp and shadowed crevices of the lichen-covered[8] rocks that border it.* MARY *is filled with wonder, beyond words. Finally:*]

---

7. **Argonne** (är·gän'): the site in France of a famous and bloody battle during World War I.
8. **lichen** (lī'kən): mosslike plant that grows on rocks and trees.

---

1. LITERARY ELEMENTS:
Symbolism
The secret garden represents life. Just as the garden is reclaimed from a state of ugliness and disrepair, so too are Mary, Colin, and Archibald transformed.

2. LITERARY ELEMENTS:
Flashback
The flashback ends. The action moves forward to the time in which the play opened.

3. LITERARY ELEMENTS:
Characterization
Mrs. Medlock is yet another character whose initial coldness has thawed during the course of the play.

4. GUIDED READING:
Visualizing
Have students compare and contrast this description of the garden with the descriptions in scenes 54 and 86. (See Annotation 3 on page 516.) This trio of garden shots shows the symbolic progress from death, decay, and gloom to life, rebirth, and love that is a central theme of the play.

CLOSURE

Write on the chalkboard these items, followed by blanks:
1. Characters: _____
2. What the characters want: _____
3. What steps they take in trying to get what they want: _____
4. What happens: Do they get what they want? _____

Have students work with you to fill in the blanks on the chalkboard. Then write the word *theme* on the chalkboard. Ask three students to explain what the play revealed to them. Finally, have one student explain to the class how *The Secret Garden* is a quest story. (Do not do this if you have not taught Unit Two.)

FOR STUDY AND DISCUSSION

Identifying Facts

1. Where beautiful thoughts are, there's no room for ugly ones.
2. Colin stands up out of his chair, walks across the garden, picks a flower, and gives it to Mary.
3. Archibald returns because Susan Sowerby wrote him a letter urging him to.
4. In 1916, Mary returns to the manor and finds Ben, who is now very old and who has made the garden more beautiful than ever. We learn that Dickon has been killed in the war. Colin greets Mary and repeats his marriage proposal, which she accepts.

Interpreting Meanings

5. Archibald weeps from happiness when he sees his son walking toward him.
   Most students will agree that he ameliorates his attitude toward his son, his manor, and himself.
6. Dickon's death is foreshadowed on page 528, when he says, "We'll be parted."
7. It was Mary who promised to wear the locket, and it was Colin she promised it to.
8. Student opinions will probably be evenly split. Colin seems a more appro-

---

MARY: I dreamed about the garden, but even in my dreams, it was never this beautiful . . .

[MARY *smiles tremulously at* BEN.]

MARY: (*continuing*) You did it, Ben. All these years . . .
BEN: There was a promise to be kept. As Mr. Archibald lay dyin', he said to me, "Tend the garden, Ben. Someday the children'll be comin' back an' when they do, their garden must be a magic place . . ."
MARY: (*loving*) And it is.
MAN'S VOICE (COLIN): Where you tend a rose, a thistle cannot grow . . .

[MARY *wheels toward the door.*]

MARY: (*joyful*) Colin!

[COLIN *stands in the garden door. Twenty-five now,* COLIN *is tall and handsome. He wears the uniform of a British officer and is leaning on a cane.* MARY *moves to* COLIN; *they embrace and kiss.*]

MARY: I wasn't sure the hospital would release you!
COLIN: (*teasing*) Did you think I'd let a little shrapnel⁹ stop me?

[COLIN *studies* MARY, *sober now.*]

COLIN: (*continuing*) When I was at Oxford,¹⁰ I asked you to marry me. When I was in France, I wrote and asked you to marry me. Why wouldn't you give me an answer, Mary?
MARY: I wanted you to ask me here, in our garden.

[COLIN *looks at* MARY *with love.*]

COLIN: I should have known. Will you marry me, Mary Lennox?
MARY: Of course.

[MARY *and* COLIN *join hands and stroll in the garden as* BEN *moves forward to congratulate them both. Camera pulls back as the three of them enjoy the sights and memories of the secret garden.*]

For Study and Discussion

IDENTIFYING FACTS

1. What meaning does Mary discover behind Ben's words: "Where you tend a rose, a thistle canna' grow"?
2. Describe Colin's first "magic experiment."
3. Explain why Archibald returns to Misselthwaite Manor.
4. Summarize what happens when we return to the present, 1918.

INTERPRETING MEANINGS

5. Why does Archibald weep when his son walks toward him? Do you think Archibald changed his attitudes toward Colin, Misselthwaite, and his own life?
6. **Foreshadowing** is the use of hints or clues to suggest what will happen later on in a

---

9. **shrapnel** (shrap′nəl): an artillery shell that explodes in the air and shatters a quantity of small metal balls.
10. **Oxford:** Oxford University, a well-known university in England.

EXTENSION AND ENRICHMENT

Art. Have students choose a scene from *The Secret Garden* to draw or paint. Display the finished artwork on the bulletin board, in the order in which the scenes appear in the play. Students may enjoy writing captions for each scene.

Social Studies. For extra credit, a group of volunteers may wish to prepare an oral report on England during the first two decades of this century through World War I. Topics could include the English class system; the British Empire and its colonies; the fashions, technology, pastimes, and ideas of the time; and the impact of World War I.

---

story. *Foreshadowing* literally means "shadows of things to come." In Act Six, what details foreshadow Dickon's death? Were you surprised when you heard this news?

7. Early in Act One, we hear a little girl's voice saying, "I shall wear it always." By the end of the play, what do you discover this means?

8. Did you **predict** that Mary would marry Colin? Or did you think she really loved Dickon?

APPLYING MEANINGS

9. Do you like the way the story ends? If you were the director and screenwriter, would you change the last scene at all? Exchange your ideas in class.

The Play as a Whole

INTERPRETING MEANINGS

1. Why are Mary and Colin (who are rich) so unpleasant, while Martha and Dickon (who are poor) are so cheerful? What might the play be saying about what makes people happy? You might talk about this remark made by Dickon in Act Four (page 510): "Those that feel unwanted scarce ever thrive."

2. Think of what the secret garden stands for in this story. How is the **transformation** (or change) of the garden like the transformations that take place in Colin and Mary? The children break through the wall that protects and hides the garden. What "walls" have Colin and Mary built around themselves?

3. In the Bible, the Garden of Eden is an enclosed world where the first human beings are perfectly happy. There they live forever and are loved by God. Is the secret garden at all like the Garden of Eden, in your opinion? Where in Acts One and Five does Mary compare their garden to Eden?

4. The **theme** of a story is its meaning—the main idea it reveals about our lives. What does this play reveal to you about the power love has to change our lives and open us up to others—just as love transforms and opens up the secret garden?

5. The novel doesn't tell us what happens to Mary, Dickon, and Colin when they grow up. What do you think of the way the play changes the book?

APPLYING MEANINGS

6. Do you think children with Colin's problems exist today? Do you know of any people who are "thistles," like Mary? What makes people that way?

7. The garden is very important in helping Mary and Colin discover their true selves. Do you think people can live without nature? How important are flowers and green things to people today?

Writing About Literature

WRITING ABOUT CHARACTERS

The secret garden is an important influence on both Mary's and Colin's **characters**. Write a paragraph in which you explain how the garden helped change both Mary and Colin. Did the garden help them focus on something else besides their own problems? Did priate match largely because of social class, but also because both he and Mary had to struggle to overcome lovelessness and arrogance.

Applying Meanings
9. Answers will vary.

THE PLAY AS A WHOLE
Interpreting Meanings
1. Mary and Colin, despite the fact that they are rich and have servants to do their every bidding, are both lonely, feel unloved, and are always bad-tempered. Dickon and Martha, on the other hand, come from a poor family where there is often not enough to eat, but they are always cheerful and loving. The play is making the point that all the wealth in the world won't make people happy unless they like and respect themselves and know how to care for others.

Dickon's remark is a key statement of the play's idea that people—just like animals and plants—need to be wanted and nurtured in order to thrive.

2. Like the garden, Colin and Mary have been neglected or mistreated, and allowed to become unpleasant. Nevertheless, with the right kind of attention from others they can still thrive.

The walls in Colin's and

PORTFOLIO ASSESSMENT

This unit provides a wealth of material for dramatic readings. Interested groups of students could choose and rehearse a scene from one of the plays and have a technical crew videotape their reading. Remind students to read with emotion and expression. Small props may be used, and students should be encouraged to use appropriate arm gestures. Videotapes can be added to student portfolios. Consult with individual students in the planning stages to agree on how their participation will be assessed. Ask students to write a paragraph self-assessing their participation. (For more information on student portfolios, see the *Portfolio Assessment and Professional Support Materials* booklet in your teaching resources.)

Mary's lives are arrogance, hostility, and isolation.

3. Most students will agree that the secret garden resembles the Garden of Eden in some ways. In Act One, the adult Mary remembers herself, in a voiceover, saying, "We'll be driven out, like from the Garden of Eden" (page 479). In Act Five, we see Mary making that same statement in the flashback, as a child (page 518).

4. The theme is that love has the power to heal our hurts and change our lives.

5. Student opinions will vary. Urge someone who has read the book to report to the class.

Applying Meanings

6. There certainly (and sadly) are many children who have been unwanted, neglected, or mistreated, and whose emotional lives and personalities have been affected by their experiences.

"Thistles" like Mary probably become that way because they fear, or are used to, rejection by others.

7. Opinions will vary. Ask what city people do to show they need to feel a part of nature. Ask what things inside our houses show that we need to be aware of the world of na-

bringing new life to the garden encourage them to find new life in themselves?

Before you write, you might organize your ideas by filling out the charts below.

Mary:

Three adjectives describing Mary when she first arrives at Misselthwaite Manor.	1. 2. 3.
How Mary changes after finding the garden.	
Meaning of the garden to Mary.	

Colin:

Three adjectives describing Colin when we first meet him.	1. 2. 3.
Actions Colin takes to help with the garden that change his life.	
Meaning of the garden to Colin.	

Making a Diorama

A **diorama** is a box in which you place miniature characters and objects so that they re-create a scene. The box stands on its side, so that when you look inside, the diorama looks like a real stage set. Construct a diorama to illustrate a setting from *The Secret Garden*. It could be a setting in Misselthwaite Manor (remember the tapestries, the gloom, all the furniture), or in the garden, before or after its magical transformation. Before you begin, list all the details from the play that describe this setting. If your class acts out the play, you can use your diorama as a model for a stage set.

Acting It Out

(A Group Activity)

Many words in the stage directions tell how the characters are feeling as they say their lines. For example, in scene 23 (Act One) we read that Mary feels *annoyed* and *haughty,* Col. McGraw feels *distressed* and then *compassionate,* and Lieut. Barney feels *shaken.* How could the actors use their voices to suggest these feelings?

Form groups and let each group select a scene to present to the class. Look for words in the stage directions that tell how the characters are feeling. Practice saying the lines aloud until you think you have found the best way to express these feelings. Present the scenes in front of the class to see if your audience can interpret the characters' emotions. Here are some scenes you might try: 28, 37, 38, 60, and 69.

Language and Vocabulary

**A SEMANTIC CHART
(A Group Project)**

On page 472 you saw how to do a semantic

chart. A **semantic chart** helps you compare the meanings of several words. It helps you see how the words are both similar and different.

Here are some words from the first scenes of *The Secret Garden*. They are all words telling how the various characters feel. Working with a partner or group, make a semantic chart for each group of words.

Group 1:	Group 2:
angered	arrogant
frustrated	superficial
annoyed	indifferent

1. Your first step is to write out a brief definition of each word. (You'll find most of the words defined in the Glossary at the back of this book. Some words you will already be very familiar with. If necessary, use a dictionary.)
2. List some of the features or meanings shared by the words across the top of your chart. You might add situations in which you would have a particular feeling.
3. List your words at the left.
4. Check off the features or meanings that apply to each word.

Do these charts help you see how the words are both alike and different? Be sure to compare your charts with those done by your classmates.

About the Author

Frances Hodgson Burnett (1849–1924) was born in England to a well-to-do family. When she was sixteen years old, an event occurred that changed her life: She and her family

moved to Knoxville, Tennessee, to join an uncle who owned a store there. The family now lived, not in a comfortable house off a city square, but in a log cabin, and without servants. Frances began earning money from her writing when she was only eighteen years old. Her first big success was a novel called *Little Lord Fauntleroy,* the story of a poor American boy who later inherits his noble father's title. Her novel *A Little Princess* is about an orphaned girl from India who lives in a cruel boarding school in London until it is discovered she is an heiress.

As for gardens, Frances Burnett always found them fascinating and mysterious, especially the overgrown gardens behind walls she longed to explore as a child in England. She also loved gardening: "I love to dig. I love to kneel down on the grass at the edge of a flower bed and pull out the weeds fiercely and throw them into a heap by my side. . . . And when at last . . . it seems as if I had beaten them . . . , I go away feeling like an army with banners."

ture (floral prints, plants, windows opening to the outside).

LANGUAGE AND VOCABULARY
A Semantic Chart
For answers, see the **Teaching Guide** at the beginning of the unit. You can expand this assignment to include many other words describing feelings.

FOCUS ON WRITING A SCENE
Using Improvisation to Explore a Scene
If cassette recorders are available, you might suggest that students record their improvisations. With the recordings to refer to, students can accurately write down the dialogue they used.

MAKING A DIORAMA
Settings inside the manor include Colin's bedroom, the tapestry corridor, Mary's room, Archibald's room, the portrait gallery, and the kitchen. Exterior settings include the fountain garden, the secret garden, and the moors. The New Delhi interior and exterior would also be good settings for dioramas.

ACTING IT OUT
As acting preparation, encourage students to think about times when they themselves have felt the given emotions.

OBJECTIVES
Students will read to enjoy the play; they will then enact the play in a classroom theater.

VISUAL CONNECTIONS
Have students look at this picture of Gollum and volunteer the descriptive words they wrote in their journals. Then have them share predictions as to what kind of character he will be. Remind them to be on the lookout to see whether, and how, their predictions are fulfilled.

The feature-length animated movie *Lord of the Rings,* directed by noted animator Ralph Bakshi, was released in 1978. It covered the first half of Tolkien's trilogy. Actor Peter Woodthrope provided the hissing voice of Gollum.

FOCUS/MOTIVATION
The headnote provides plenty of information that can be used for motivation. The focus of this incident from the play is the gold ring, which makes its wearer invisible. The focus in terms of character is the disgusting Gollum, a creature students will have much fun with. Before they start reading, talk about quests and perilous journeys taken to win something of value (see Unit Two). Ask students what they know of elves, dwarves, caves, magic rings, wizards, riddles, tests, and talking animals from the books they've read and from TV and movies they've seen.

NO QUESTIONS ASKED: A SCENE FOR CLASSROOM THEATER

Riddles in the Dark

Dramatized by PATRICIA GRAY
Based on the novel The Hobbit *by* J. R. R. TOLKIEN

Prereading Journal. Have students write down three words telling how they feel about the illustration of Gollum on page 535.

READING THE SELECTION
Assign parts, making sure that everyone in class has a chance to read at least a portion of one part. You might also assign one good reader to read aloud the stage directions.

Before You Read

This scene is from Act One of a play version of *The Hobbit*. *The Hobbit* takes place in Middle Earth, an imaginary world of long ago that is populated by wizards, dwarves, elves, trolls, goblins, dragons, and—hobbits. Hobbits are small furry-footed folk who live in a place called the Shire. They love peace, comfort, and food (not necessarily in that order). They avoid adventure and danger.

The hero of this tale, Bilbo Baggins, is a hobbit who finds himself in a very un-hobbit-like situation. The mysterious wizard Gandalf has persuaded Bilbo to join him and thirteen dwarves on a dangerous quest. Their aim is to retrieve the dwarves' ancient treasure from the evil dragon Smaug.

At this point in the play, Bilbo, Gandalf, the dwarf Thorin, and the other dwarves have narrowly escaped being eaten by hungry trolls. Now, resting in a cave in the Misty Mountains, they are about to be attacked by goblins. This portion of the play is adapted from Chapter 5 in the original novel. (Tolkien continues his tales of Middle Earth in his trilogy—a series of three related books—*The Lord of the Rings*.)

As you read, use the stage directions to help you visualize the strange setting. Try to picture the stage and what the characters are doing on it. When you produce the play for your classroom theater, you will want to assign someone to design sets and provide "props," those movable objects that the actors use on stage. One prop you'll need, for example, is a book that can serve as Bilbo's diary.

The character Gollum has a peculiar way of speaking. Once you "hear" his voice, with its strange hissing sounds and unusual grammar, you'll never forget it. As you read the play, first try to imagine what Gollum's voice should sound like. Then practice acting out some of his lines with a friend.

Gollum in the movie *The Lord of the Rings* (1978). All stills are from this Saul Zaentz production.

TEACHING RESOURCES C
Teacher's Notes p. 161

Riddles in the Dark

MEETING INDIVIDUAL NEEDS
ESL/LEP • Gollum's unusual speech may be confusing for students. Prior to assigning the story, you may want to discuss the following patterns:
1. Substitution of *it* for *you*
2. Substitution of *we* for *I*
3. Substitution of *us* for *me*
4. Use of singular instead of plural verb form
5. Forming plurals with unnecessary *-es* endings

Explain that the author has used these unusual speech forms to help characterize Gollum. Gollum's use of *it* to refer to Bilbo shows his indifference toward Bilbo; his use of plural pronouns to refer to himself shows his inflated view of his own importance; and the use of singular verb forms and the addition of *-es* endings contribute to the hissing quality of Gollum's speech.

1. LITERARY ELEMENTS:
Drama
Compare and contrast these stage terms with the teleplay terms on page 476.

Stage Terms

Stage plays contain special directions that the director and actors must understand and follow. Stage directions usually appear in parentheses or brackets. They tell actors where to stand on stage, when to enter and exit, how to say their lines, and so on. Theater people use a large vocabulary of stage direction terms; some of the most common ones are listed below. A hint: "left" and "right" always refer to the actor's left and right as he or she is facing the audience.

R (stage right).
L (stage left).
C (center): the center of the stage.
D (downstage): toward the audience.
U (upstage): away from the audience.
UC (upstage center): the center of the stage, farthest from the audience.
DC (downstage center): the center of the stage, closest to the audience.
UR (upstage right): the upper right-hand corner of the stage, farthest from the audience.
Off (offstage): those parts of the stage that are outside the boundaries of the setting.
ad lib: a term that comes from a Latin phrase meaning literally "at pleasure." To *ad lib* means to "improvise, or make up." Usually, actors ad lib in scenes in which many characters are talking at once.

Cast of Characters

BILBO BAGGINS: a hobbit.
THORIN: a dwarf, grandson of the old dwarf king from whom Smaug stole the treasure long ago.
GLOIN, BALIN, BOFUR, OIN AND ORI: other dwarves.
GANDALF: a mysterious wizard who is leading the quest for the dragon's treasure.
GOBLINS: evil creatures who want to destroy the dwarves.
GOLLUM: a fishlike creature who lives in a cave.

MEETING INDIVIDUAL NEEDS

ESL/LEP • A series of action verbs (*gnash, squash, smash, clash,* and *crash*) are presented on this page. Write them on the chalkboard, and ask the class the following questions:
Which verb has a silent letter? (*gnash*)
Which verb is also a noun that refers to a vegetable? (*squash*)
Which verb means "to grind"? (*gnash*)
Have students look in dictionaries to find the origins of *smash, clash,* and *crash*. What do these three words have in common? (They are all imitative in origin. That is, the words imitate the sounds made by the actions they name.)

SCENE:

A cave in the Misty Mountains. Lightning flashes. Sounds of thunder.

At rise of curtain:

Lights come up on platform at stage L. The DWARVES *and* GANDALF *are huddled together, talking in hushed tones.* BILBO *sits downstage on platform, writing in his diary. He scribbles industriously, then holds book off and reads impressively.*

1 BILBO: (*reading his entry*) "This is the first chance I've had to write in ages. We've been driven before the storm for twelve days and nights." (*There is a distant roll of thunder and more lightning.*) "The mountain path is steep and long. We are now resting in a smelly cave." (*He again scribbles rapidly.*)

THORIN: (*in a low voice*) This is awful!

GLOIN: (*holding his nose*) Phew!

BALIN: At least it's dry!

GANDALF: (*to* THORIN) If you know a better place, take us there!

2 BILBO: (*holding his script off and reading again*) "We don't dare to talk too loud—there are goblins in these mountains. All this misery for their gold—and my pride—hardly seems worthwhile. The next time anyone calls me a coward, I'll agree with him and stay home. I'd gladly trade my share of the treasure this minute for a steaming bowl of mutton soup!"

GANDALF: Keep your voices down! Thorin, look, your blade glows—that means goblins are nearby. Keep your eyes and ears open. Goblins are swift as weasels in the dark and make no more noise than bats. (*They huddle together, peering in all directions; lightning flashes and sounds of thunder.*) Are your guards posted?

THORIN: (*nodding*) Four of them, Gloin north, Bofur south, Oin east, and Ori west.

[*Lights dim on platform L and come up on platform R. Drumbeats are heard off. The* GREAT GOBLIN *steps out on the platform, followed by an attendant.*]

GREAT GOBLIN: (*bellowing in a stony voice*) Who are those miserable persons?

ATTENDANT GOBLIN: (*bowing and scraping*) **3** Dwarves, I believe, O Truly Tremendous One.

GREAT GOBLIN: What are they doing in my domain?

ATTENDANT GOBLIN: (*shaking*) I'll go and ask them, O Truly Tremendous One.

GREAT GOBLIN: (*with an awful howl of rage*) Ask them? (*Kicks the* ATTENDANT GOBLIN *and bats him over the head*) Beat them! Gnash them! Squash them! Smash them! (*Gesturing L*) After them!

[*The drumbeats increase as many* GOBLINS *rush on R with bloodcurdling cries. As they reach C, the lights come up on platform L.*]

OIN: (*reporting*) Goblins coming!

ORI: I think they're going to rush us!

GOBLINS: (*chanting and cracking whips*)
   Swish, smack! Whip, crack!
   Clash, crash! Crush, smash!

THORIN: (*drawing his sword*) Ready, my Goblin-cleaver! (*He stands on the edge of the platform.*) Ready, Dwarves—and Mr. Baggins. (GANDALF, *arms folded, stands*

Riddles in the Dark 537

---

1. LITERARY ELEMENTS:
Exposition
By having Bilbo read his diary entry, the dramatist helps the audience learn something about where the characters have been and where they are now.

2. LITERARY ELEMENTS:
Characterization
This speech shows that Bilbo doesn't care about material wealth or traditional heroism. He cares about comfort and peace of mind. Many students will like him for this; others may disdain it.

3. LITERARY ELEMENTS:
Tone
Although the stage direction doesn't indicate how the attendant goblin is to say his line, it is most likely that his tone is one of humility laced with fear. From the audience's point of view, the line is comic. Have your student actors try the line aloud.

MEETING INDIVIDUAL NEEDS
Kinesthetic Learners • Bilbo keeps the magic ring in his pocket until he meets Gollum and discovers its power to make him invisible. Challenge students to use their imaginations and collect other items that they think might have been in Bilbo's pocket. Students may wish to bring the items to class and explain why they chose each one.

1. LITERARY ELEMENTS:
External Conflict
A physical battle is the clearest possible example of external conflict.

2. GUIDED READING:
Predicting Outcomes
This would be a natural point at which to pause and guess what happens next.

3. GUIDED READING:
Drawing Conclusions
Based on what they have read about the glowing sword and goblins, students should be able to conclude that if the sword does not glow at all, it means that there are no goblins around.

4. LITERARY ELEMENTS:
Drama
A stage whisper is an acting technique that projects a whisper loud enough for an audience to hear. (You or a volunteer can demonstrate this fairly easily in a classroom.)

---

1 *aloof watching intently. The* GOBLINS *rush at the* DWARVES. THORIN *stabs one with his blade. The other* DWARVES *back up* THORIN, *and there are hand-to-hand conflicts.* BILBO *trips up a* GOBLIN *who is about to stab* THORIN *from behind.* THORIN *stabs another. All conflicts must be rehearsed with extra care so that the tempo is very fast. The* GOBLINS *fall, howling.*)

GOBLINS: (*ad lib*) Aie! He's got a Goblin-cleaver! Watch out! Stay back! (*The* GOBLINS *back off in terror.*)
GANDALF: (*to* DWARVES *and* BILBO) Quick. Now's our chance! Everyone follow me! (*Runs off L. Others follow,* BILBO *last. From off.*) Quicker, quicker! (GOBLINS *run after them, howling and hooting.*)

2 **Blackout**

[*Lights come up very dimly in cave.* BILBO *is discovered lying on the ground DC.*]

BILBO: (*sitting up, holding his head in pain*) Oooh! My head! Where am I! My head—I must have run into a tree! (*Groping*) It's so dark in here I can't see a thing. (*Calls loudly*) Anyone here?
ECHO: (*getting progressively fainter*) Here—here—here.
BILBO: (*getting frightened*) Who's that?

[*Now gleams appear in the darkness. They prove to be always in pairs, of yellow or green or red eyes. They seem to stare awhile and then slowly fade out and disappear and shine out again in another place. Sometimes they shine down from above. Some of them are bulbous.*]

BILBO: Now I remember. The goblins!
ECHO: 'Oblins, 'oblins—'oblins—'oblins.
BILBO: And what are those awful eyes watching me for? (*Lowers voice*) I was on Dori's back and someone tackled him and he dropped me!
ECHO: 'Opped me—'opped me—'opped me—'opped me.
BILBO: (*frightened, to the eyes*) Keep away from me, eyes! I wonder what happened to the dwarves? I hope the goblins didn't get them! (*Gasps*) My sword! (*Holding it up*) It hardly glows. That means the goblins **3** aren't near and yet they're still around. Ugh! What a nasty smell! Go away, you horrible eyes! (*Realizing, stage whisper*) I **4** know where I am. I'm still in the goblins' cave! They smell that way and these may be just the eyes of bats and mice and toads and slimy things like that. (*More naturally*) Cheer up, Bilbo. Fear always helps the thing you're afraid of. You're alive and you've been in holes before. You live in one. This is just an ordinary, black, foul, disgusting hole. So blah! (*The eyes begin to flicker out, pair by pair, until all are gone.* BILBO *brightens further.*) If this place were aired and decorated it would be nice and cozy. So now I'll just figure out how to get out of here. (BILBO *crawls around on his hands and knees toward stage R.*) Seems to be a lake over here—no use heading that way. Ouch! Something hurt my knee—— (*Picks up small object*) It's a ring! Someone's lost a ring. Well, finders keepers. I'll just stick it in my pocket so I don't lose it myself. (*Pockets ring. Lights come up a little*) I can see

COOPERATIVE LEARNING
Gollum and Bilbo challenge each other with difficult riddles. Ask students to share any riddles they have heard. Then have small groups of three or four students collaborate to invent two riddles. Have each group present its riddles aloud for the rest of the class to guess. Students may wish to invite another class to guess their riddles as well.

1. LITERARY ELEMENTS:
Drama
Note how the stage directions take into account the requirements of performance. The description includes costume notes such as, "touched up with vaseline to make it glisten."

2
Guttural means "of or produced in the throat." Ask a volunteer to demonstrate what a guttural voice would sound like.

better now. (*Stands and turns toward stage L*)

1 [*An unobtrusive black rubber float is pulled on stage R. On it sits a slimy creature, dressed in black tights or a shiny rubber diving suit, touched up with vaseline to make it glisten, complete with cap and goggles painted a pale watery green. He sits with a leg dangling over each side of the raft, or with knees bent, and holds a short paddle as if rowing.*]

GOLLUM: (*making a swallowing sound as he is pulled on*) Gollum! Gollum!
BILBO: (*whirling around*) What's that!
GOLLUM: It's me—Gollum!
BILBO: (*peering nervously in Gollum's direction*) Who's there?
GOLLUM: (*in full view now*) Bless us and splash us, my preciousss! Here's something to eat! (*Guttural*) Gollum! **2**
BILBO: (*brandishing his blade, while shaking and backing off*) Stay back!
GOLLUM: (*swaying his head from side to*

Riddles in the Dark 539

1. LITERARY ELEMENTS:
Dialect
Have two or three students try reading Gollum's lines to demonstrate his weird speech patterns. Notice how he uses plurals and pronouns and the hissing *s* sound.

2. LITERARY ELEMENTS:
Conflict
Unlike the earlier conflict between dwarves and goblins, this conflict takes the form of mental competition rather than physical combat. Nevertheless, it is a conflict and the stakes are high. Bilbo is playing for his life.

3. GUIDED READING:
Making Inferences
Gollum's lack of patience suggests that he is very hungry.

---

side as he talks) What's he got in his handses, hmmm?

BILBO: (*as fiercely as possible*) A sword, an elvish blade! It came out of Gondolin.[1]

GOLLUM: (*taken aback, hissing*) S-s-s-s-s What *iss* he, my preciouss? Hic! (*More politely*) Whom have we the pleasure of meeting?

BILBO: (*rapidly*) I am Mr. Bilbo Baggins, a hobbit. I've lost the dwarves and the wizard and I don't know where I am—but then I don't want to know where I am. The only thing I want to know is how to get out of here!

GOLLUM: (*hissing*) S-s-s-s-s s'pose we sits here and chats with it a bitsy, my preciousss— A Bagginsess! (*Rubs his stomach*) It likes riddles, p'raps it does, does it? S-s-s-s-s.

BILBO: You mean me?

GOLLUM: Yesssss—

BILBO: Well, I'd love to, but I'm expected somewhere else—— (*To himself*) I hope. (*To* GOLLUM) So if you'd kindly direct me to the nearest exit——

GOLLUM: (*cutting in*) S-s-s-s-s stop. First a riddle, yesss?

BILBO: (*resigned*) Very well, if you insisssst! After you—

GOLLUM: S-s-s-s-s say,
What has roots as nobody sees,
Is taller than trees,
   Up, up it goes,
   And yet never grows?

---
1. Bilbo's sword is one of several that he and his friends stole from the evil trolls. Some friendly elves have told them that these swords were made in Gondolin, an ancient elvan city, for goblin-wars.

BILBO: Easy! Mountain. Now if you'll kindly—

GOLLUM: (*cutting in*) S-s-s-s-s so does it guess easy? It must have a competition with us, my preciouss. If we wins we eats it—it tastes better if we earns it. If it wins we shows it the way out. Yessss.

BILBO: (*resigned*) Well—all right. Only, how many of them are you? Who's this "Precious" you keep talking to?

GOLLUM: Our Preciouss Self! We has to talk to someone, doesn't we? We are alone here—forever.

BILBO: So, I see. It's a dreadful place.

GOLLUM: We likes it! We generally passes the time feasting on fishesss and gobbling goblins. S-s-s.

BILBO: Goblins! Ick! I didn't think anyone ate them!

GOLLUM: We acquired the taste. Hic! S-s-s-s-s. (*Impatient*) Your turn. Riddle! Riddle!

BILBO: Just a minute— (*Thinking hard*) Ah!—
Thirty white horses on a red hill,
   First they champ,
   Then they stamp,
      Then they stand still.

GOLLUM: Easy! Teethes! Teethes! My preciouss, but we has only *six*. Now! Sssss.
Voiceless it cries,
Wingless flutters,
Toothless bites,
Mouthless mutters.

BILBO: Half a moment! (*Straining*) Wind! Wind, of course!

GOLLUM: (*disappointed*) Sssssss. Your turns!

TRANSPARENCIES 29 & 30	TRANSPARENCY 32
Fine Art Theme: *Bring Your Imagination with You* – invites students to explore artworks that highlight acting and the imagination.	**Literary Elements** *Suspense* – invites students to consider suspense and foreshadowing as elements of plot.

BILBO: Uh—
 A box without hinges, key, or lid,
 Yet golden treasure inside is hid.

1 GOLLUM: (*having great difficulty*) S-s-s-s-s. (*Whispers*) What iss it? Sssssss. (*Takes a fish out of his pocket and wipes his brow with it*)

BILBO: Well—what is it? The answer's not a kettle boiling over, as you seem to think from the noise you are making!

GOLLUM: Give us a chance; let it give us a chance, my preciousss—

BILBO: Well?

GOLLUM: (*wiping his brow with fish; suddenly*) Eggses! Eggses it is! Ssssssss— here's a choice one!
 Alive without breath,
 As cold as death;
 Never thirsty, ever drinking,
 All in mail, never clinking!

BILBO: (*stumped*) Ahem—ahem—well now. Just a minute—

GOLLUM: (*starting to emerge from the raft*) S-s-s-s-s-s.

BILBO: (*panic stricken*) Wait! I gave you a long time to guess!

2 GOLLUM: (*settling back in raft, hissing with pleasure*) Is it nice, my preciousss? Is it juicy? Is it crunchable?

BILBO: (*stalling for time*) Actually, I never gave a thought to how I'd taste cooked until I set out on this horrid adventure. But I'm sure I'd be terribly indigestible. (*False laughter*) Ha, ha!

GOLLUM: S-s-s-s-s—the riddle, answer it! It must make haste. We is hungry! (*Wipes his brow with the fish*)

BILBO: (*pointing wildly at the fish*) Fish! That's the answer! Fish!

GOLLUM: (*angry*) S-ss-ss—rotten luckses! It's got to ask us a question, my preciouss, yes, yess, just one more, yesss. Ask uss!

3 BILBO: (*frantic*) Oh, dear! I can't think— (*Grabs for his sword, puts his hand in his pocket. To himself*) What have I got in my pocket?

GOLLUM: (*taking this for the question*) Ssss—not fair! Not fair, my preciouss, to ask us what it's got in its nassty little pocketses!

BILBO: (*explaining*) But I— (*Thinks better of it*) Well, why not? (*Boldly*) What have I got in my pocket?

GOLLUM: S-s-s-s-s. It must give us three guesseses, my preciouss, three!

BILBO: Very well! Guess away!

GOLLUM: Handses!

BILBO: Wrong. Guess again!

GOLLUM: S-s-s-s-s—knife!

BILBO: Wrong! Last guess!

4 GOLLUM: (*wiggling and squirming, hissing and sputtering, rocking sideways and slapping his feet on the floor*) S-s-s-s-s.

BILBO: (*trying to sound bold and cheerful*) Come on! I'm waiting! Time's up!

GOLLUM: (*shrieking*) String or nothing!

BILBO: (*relieved*) Both wrong. (*Brandishes his sword*)

GOLLUM: (*eyeing the sword*) S-s-s-s-s.

BILBO: (*shivering*) Well? Show me the way out. You promised!

GOLLUM: Did we say so, preciouss? Show the nassty little Baggins the way out, yes, yess. But what's it got in its pocketses, eh? (*Starts to get up*) Not string, preciouss, but not nothing. Oh, no! Gollum!

BILBO: Never you mind. A promise is a promise!

1. GUIDED READING:
Making Inferences
The stage directions suggest that Gollum is getting nervous for fear that he will not guess the answer to the riddle and will have to show Bilbo the way out.

2. GUIDED READING:
Making Inferences
Gollum's persistence suggests a confidence that he will triumph over Bilbo.

3. GUIDED READING:
Understanding Cause and Effect
Make sure students grasp that Bilbo's chance, nervous question, "What have I got in my pocket?" saves the day, because Gollum mistakes it for a deliberate test question.

4. GUIDED READING:
Making Inferences
Now Gollum seems panic-stricken and very frustrated.

Riddles in the Dark **541**

PORTFOLIO ASSESSMENT

A character sketch, a composition in which a literary character is described, may include a description of physical characteristics, temperament, intelligence, demeanor, and facets of his or her personality that make the character individual. Students might enjoy writing a one-paragraph character sketch of Gollum, Bilbo, or Gandolf. Some students may want to include a drawing of what they think the character looks like, particularly if their idea does not conform to the illustrations here. Consult with students individually to agree on how their character sketches will be assessed. (See *Portfolio Assessment and Professional Support Materials*, especially the section entitled **Suggestions for Portfolio Projects**.)

1. BACKGROUND

Gollum's dialogue suggests that his birthday present and the ring that Bilbo found are one and the same. The dialogue also reveals the reason that the ring is special: It causes its wearer to become invisible.

2. GUIDED READING: Interpreting Meaning

The stage direction "light dawns" is a figure of speech meaning that Gollum now guesses that it is his lost ring that Bilbo has in his pocket.

GOLLUM: Cross it is. The Baggins is getting cross, preciouss, but it must wait, yes, it must. We can't go up the tunnels so hasty. We must go and get somethings first, yess,
1 things to help us. My birthday present, that's what we wants now—then we'll be quite safe! (*He steps out of his raft and waddles UR.*) We slips it on and it won't see us, will it, my preciouss. No, it won't see us and its nassty little sword will be useless, yess—Ssssss. (*Exits R*)
BILBO: (*calling*) Hurry up!
GOLLUM: (*off, letting out a horrible shriek*) Aaaaaah! Where iss it! Lost! Lost!

BILBO: What's the matter?
GOLLUM: (*offstage, wailing*) Gone—must find it! Lost! Lost!
BILBO: Well, so am I!

[GOLLUM *waddles on from R, on his hands and knees, searching wildly.*]

GOLLUM: Cursesss! Must find it!
BILBO: You can look for whatever it is later. You never guessed my riddle. You promised!
GOLLUM: Never guessed—never guessed—— (*Light dawns*) What has it got in its 2 pocketses? Tell us! (*Advances toward* BILBO)
BILBO: What have you lost?
GOLLUM: We guesses, we *guesses*, precious, only guesses. He's got it and the goblinses will catch it and take the present from it. (*Makes a lunge at* BILBO) They'll find out what it can do. The Baggins doesn't know what the present can do. It'll just keep it in its pocketses. It's lost itself, the nassty, nosey thing.
BILBO: I better put that ring on or I'll lose it. (*Puts his hand into his pocket and slips the ring on his finger and holds it up.*) This?
GOLLUM: (*rushing right past* BILBO, *wailing*) Cursess, the Baggins is *gone*—my precious. It has my ring! The ring of *power!*
BILBO: (*alone on stage*) He ran right past—as if he didn't see me—as if I weren't there— Maybe I'm not! The ring! I wonder if it made me invisible! (*Inspects himself*) I can still see me.

[GOLLUM *rushes on again from L.*]

542 Plays

LIBRARY LINK
Encourage students who enjoy fantasy literature to read other books from the genre. Imaginary kingdoms are featured in *The Lion, the Witch and the Wardrobe* by C. S. Lewis and *The Phantom Tollbooth* by Norton Juster. Fantastic characters appear in *The Borrowers* by Mary Norton and *James and The Giant Peach* by Roald Dahl. You may want to ask students to suggest additional fantasy stories they have enjoyed.

GOLLUM: Give it back like a good Baggins! Where isss it? (*Rushes off R*)

BILBO: A magic ring! I've heard of such things in Gandalf's stories—but to *find* one! What luck!

GOLLUM: (*offstage, shrieking*) Thief!

1 BILBO: I could stab him with my blade, but that would be wrong when he can't see me.

[GOLLUM *waddles on R, worn out and weeping.*]

GOLLUM: (*sitting downstage*) It's gone! (*Guttural sobs*) Gollum! Gollum! Thief! Thief Baggins! We hates it, we hates it, hates it forever! S-s-s-s-s. (*Recovering*) But he doesn't know the way out—he said so. (BILBO *nods silently and sits beside him.*) But he's tricksy. He doesn't say what he means—like what was in his pocketses—he knows! He knows a way *in*. He must know a way *out*! Yesss—he's off to the back door, that's it! (*Springs up*) After him! Make haste! (*Runs off L*) Gollum! Gollum!

BILBO: I'll follow him to the exit. Then with luck I can slip out the door! (*Runs off L after* GOLLUM)

2   **Curtain**

About the Author

John Ronald Reuel Tolkien (tōl′kēn) (1892–1973) was born to English parents in South Africa. As a child he was fascinated by the sounds and meanings of words. Early in life he tried to learn all he could about such languages as Latin, Greek, German, Welsh, and Old English. Like many highly imaginative children, he also made up his own

imaginary languages. In adulthood, Tolkien became a noted professor of the languages and literature of the Middle Ages at Oxford University in England. One of his friends was C. S. Lewis, the author of the Narnia series (see page 10 of this book).

Tolkien was not only a brilliant scholar. He was also an imaginative storyteller who loved myths and fantastic tales. Throughout Tolkien's life, part of him remained a child who "desired dragons with a profound desire." Eventually, he combined his knowledge of myths and languages with his keen imagination to create perhaps the most famous fantasies of the twentieth century, *The Hobbit* and the trilogy called *Lord of the Rings*. These books tell of an epic battle between good and evil fought long ago in the quiet of Middle Earth. They have been read and loved by millions of readers, young and old.

Riddles in the Dark   **543**

---

1. GUIDED READING:
Using Prior Knowledge
Bilbo's own words reveal that he has a strict moral sense. Have students compare and contrast him to other fantasy heroes who share this trait but are more muscularly imposing and self-important, such as Superman, Batman, or the Ninja turtles. (Would these heroes use the blade in this situation?)

2. GUIDED READING:
Predicting Outcomes
Here students can offer predictions about what might happen to Bilbo later in the work. Advanced readers may wish to read Tolkien and find out.

OBJECTIVES
The overall aim is for students to make inferences about characters, situations, and setting in a scene from a play. For a complete list of objectives, see the **Teacher's Notes**.

PRESENTATION
Before reading the passage in the text, define *inference* (an educated guess based on known facts) and discuss how students make inferences in their daily lives. Then read each section of dialogue aloud and have students make notes about what they infer. After you have read all the dialogue, ask students to share their responses orally.

DRAWING INFERENCES
Students should be aware that when they analyze a reading passage and make inferences, they should be careful to draw valid conclusions that are based on specific details in the selection. They should avoid making invalid conclusions which cannot be supported by logical evidence.

Answers
Answers will vary.
1. Colin is afraid that Dr. Craven has noticed that Colin's condition is improving.
2. She means that if Mr. Craven's wife were still alive, she would want him to be home where he is needed.
3. Even when Dickon goes away, he will always remember his friend, Colin.
4. Ben infers that the garden has powers that will bring the children back and help them.

FOCUS ON *Reading and Critical Thinking*

DRAWING INFERENCES

Many writers rely on you to make **inferences,** or educated guesses, about the characters, situations, and setting in a story or play. For example, if you were watching the first scene of *The Secret Garden* on television, you would not be told directly when and where the story's opening scene is set. However, you could use clues from details like the touring car, the characters' costumes, and the house to draw an inference about the time and place of the action.

Reread the passages from Act Six of *The Secret Garden* below. Then use a separate sheet of paper to answer the question marked with this symbol ■ after each passage.

1. **COLIN:** *(worried)* I hope Dr. Craven isn't getting suspicious. When he was here before, he noticed my legs look stronger and that I'm getting fatter.
   - What inference is Colin afraid that Dr. Craven has drawn?

2. **PITCHER:** *(continuing; reading)* "Dear Sir: I am Susan Sowerby who is Martha's mother who works for you in Misselthwaite Manor. I am making bold to speak to you. Please sir, I would come home if I were you. I think you would be glad you came, and if you will excuse me, sir, I think your lady would want you to come if she were here. Your obedient servant, Susan Sowerby."
   - What do you infer Susan Sowerby really means in her letter?

3. **DICKON:** *(quietly)* We'll be parted, you an' me, but remembrance will keep us friends.
   - What inference do you draw about Dickon's real meaning here?

4. **BEN:** There was a promise to be kept. As Mr. Archibald lay dyin', he said to me, "Tend the garden, Ben. Someday the children'll be comin' back an' when they do, their garden must be a magic place . . ."
   - What inference do you think Mr. Archibald has drawn about the importance of the magic garden?

OBJECTIVES

The overall aim is for students to write a dramatic scene which uses the basic elements of drama. For a complete list of objectives, see the **Teacher's Notes**.

PRESENTATION

Have students reread one of the scenes from *The Secret Garden* that focuses on a conflict, such as the scene on page 489 in the vegetable garden, where Mary and Ben decide they can be friends. Then tell students they will write a similar scene, but they will draw from their own experiences of making friends for the conflict, characters, setting, and dialogue. You might want to discuss with students the range of experiences that would be appropriate to include in their scenes. Students can write their scenes independently, or you might want to have students create small-group scenes. This collaborative effort may help weaker students or students who

FOCUS ON Writing

WRITING A SCENE

A **play** is a story acted out on a stage by actors and actresses who take the parts of characters. A play is different from a short story because in a play the writer has to use dialogue, rather than description or narration, to move the plot forward. In this unit you have studied some of the basic elements of drama. Now you will have the chance to write a dramatic scene of your own.

Prewriting

1. Just like a good short story, a dramatic scene explores a **conflict** or struggle. To find an idea for a scene, get together with a small group of classmates and brainstorm to fill in a chart like the one below. Some sample ideas have been filled in for you.

Idea Chart for a Dramatic Scene		
Character A	Character B	Conflict
Father	Daughter	Why can't you keep your room neat?
Space Alien	Earth Host	Why can't I stay with you forever?

2. Join with a group of partners and use **improvising** to explore one of the ideas on your chart. Assign each role in advance. Then relax and make up lines that you think are appropriate for your character and for the situation. If you wish, ask one group member to take notes on the dialogue. See if your improvisation leads to a turning point and a resolution for the conflict. [See **Focus** assignment on page 531.]

3. Write an **outline** for your scene. On your outline, cover the points listed on the diagram below:

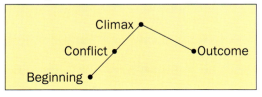

4. Make notes for the **setting** of your scene—the specific time and place of the action. Decide if the setting may be related to the atmosphere or mood of the scene.

HOLT WRITER'S WORKSHOP

This computer program provides help for all types of writing through guided instruction for each step of the writing process. (Program available separately.)

See **Elements of Writing, Introductory Course,** Chapter 5, for more instruction on creative writing.

WRITING A SCENE

Writing a scene should convey to students the dramatic impact of dialogue on a story. When students master the skill of writing dialogue in a scene, they may see how they can use dialogue to enhance other kinds of writing they do.

Prewriting

You might want to help students brainstorm many ideas before they fill in their charts. Also, the chart can be expanded to include possible settings. Do some listing with your students of all the characters, conflicts, and settings they can think of, and write these on the chalkboard. Students might even consult newspapers and magazines for potential conflicts, especially features like "Dear Abby." Then students can

Focus on Writing 545

might have trouble putting all the parts of a scene together and in the correct format. If students perform their scenes for the class, you might consider videotaping them. They can then evaluate themselves.

CLOSURE

Have students identify and explain the dramatic elements of a scene.

make choices from the list for their charts. You may need to work closely with students on the climax of their scenes.

Writing

As students write, remind them that the dialogue their characters speak must make the conflict clear to the audience, as there is no narrator to fill in between the lines. You might encourage students to write a first draft with dialogue only, and then to write a second draft in which they include their stage directions. Caution students not to get bogged down in the format of their scenes. They should simply get their ideas written now and worry about form in the next stage of the process.

Evaluating and Revising

Students should read their scenes aloud several times and try to do so for a variety of audiences who can give them ideas for improvement. They might even tape their scenes and listen to them as they use the **Checklist for Evaluation and Revision** questions. Students can then revise any parts that are weak.

Writing

1. Use **stage directions** to describe the scenery, lighting, and characters that the audience will see at the beginning of your scene. As a model, you can use the stage directions at the beginning of *Riddles in the Dark* (see page 537).

2. Follow your outline and write the **dialogue** for your scene. Remember to use the rules for identifying speakers and punctuating dialogue in drama. Here is an example from *The Monsters Are Due on Maple Street* (page 468):

    STEVE: I don't understand it. It was working fine before—

    DON: Out of gas?

    STEVE: *(shakes his head)* I just had it filled up.

3. Here are some guidelines to use when you write dialogue:

    - Be sure that the dialogue moves the plot forward.
    - Make the speeches sound natural—the way people speak in real life. Say your dialogue out loud to see that it meets this test.
    - Make the dialogue suit the speaker's character. For example, in *The Secret Garden* Dickon is gentle and patient. Notice that his speeches are never bossy or sarcastic.

4. Write **stage directions** to show information about the characters' feelings or emotions, tones of voice, movements, and gestures. Stage directions can also refer to props and important elements of scene design. When you write your stage directions, try to **visualize** how your scene would actually be played on stage in a theater.

5. Give your scene a title that hooks the reader's interest and sums up the action or problem.

Evaluating and Revising

1. When you have finished a first draft, put your scene aside for a while. Then try to evaluate it as objectively as you can. If you wish, join with a group of classmates. Organize a group reading of each member's scene. Give each other suggestions on how to improve dialogue and stage directions.

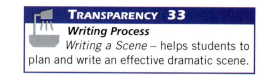

Here is how one writer revised part of a dramatic scene:

Writer's Model

(On the ^school^ playground: late morning.)

PAUL: (^glaring^ ~~looking~~ at Jeff) You were never really my friend, were you? Why'd you tell Mr. Samuels about the missing money?

JEFF: (feeling torn) Come off it, Paul. You know we shouldn't have taken the money. Samuels was always nice to us. He even let us use his garage ^for the club headquarters.^

PAUL: (losing his confidence and feeling ashamed) I guess you're right. I don't feel so good about having taken that money now. What ^, ya^ ~~do you~~ think we should do?

2. You may wish to use the following checklist as you revise your scene:

Checklist for Evaluation and Revision

- ✓ Have I clearly identified the setting and the characters?
- ✓ Does the scene explore a strong conflict?
- ✓ Does the scene have a high point and a resolution?
- ✓ Does the dialogue sound natural? Is this the way the characters would speak in real life?
- ✓ Do the stage directions give important information?
- ✓ Have I used the proper format?

Proofreading and Publishing

Proofread your scene and correct any errors you find in grammar, usage, and mechanics. (Here you may find it helpful to refer to the **Handbook for Revision** on pages 750–785.) Then prepare a final version of your scene by making a clean copy.

Consider some of the following ways to share your scene:

- illustrate your scene and post it on the class bulletin board
- join with a group to present a dramatic reading of your scene
- prepare a full staging of your scene, complete with scenery, costumes, and props

Portfolio If your teacher approves, you may wish to keep a copy of your work in your writing folder or portfolio.

Focus on Writing

UNIT 7 ◆ TEACHING GUIDE

MYTHS AND FOLK TALES

OVERVIEW OF THE UNIT

This unit focuses on the myths and folk tales of several different cultures. Students will enjoy the fanciful events and clever heroes in these ancient stories, which have been passed along orally from generation to generation and which contain truths and ideas that are still important today.

OBJECTIVES OF THE UNIT

The aims of this unit for students are
- To monitor their own reading
- To recognize the characteristics of myths and folk tales
- To identify similar elements in myths, "how and why" stories, fairy tales, and quest stories
- To summarize
- To identify major events and put them in chronological order
- To identify the main idea and supporting details
- To distinguish between realistic and supernatural events
- To make inferences and draw conclusions
- To trace the origins of words
- To determine word meaning from prefixes and roots
- To identify pronoun referents
- To recognize and use sound devices
- To recognize and analyze anecdotes
- To tell and dramatize stories
- To analyze a narrative for cause-and-effect relationships
- To write critically and creatively in relation to the selections
- To research and use foreign words
- To identify words with positive and negative connotations
- To make connections between cultures and between literature and geography
- To write a book report

CONCEPTS AND SKILLS

CLOSE READING OF A FOLK TALE
Guidelines for Close Reading 550
One Reader's Response 551
Looking at Yourself as a Reader 555

THINKING ABOUT WORDS
Using Context Clues 556

FOCUS ON READING AND CRITICAL THINKING
Identifying Pronoun Referents 564
Identifying Major Events 573
Finding the Main Idea 583
Anecdotes 593
Cause and Effect 616
Summarizing 629
Identifying the Main Idea 640

LITERARY ELEMENTS
Metamorphosis 564
Myths and Origins 574
Connections Between Myths 584
The Supernatural in Folk Tales 617
Common Features in Folk Tales 630

LANGUAGE AND VOCABULARY
Connotations 565   A Prefix Game 617
Words from Mexico 584   Japanese Words 630
Sound Effects 599   Praise Names 637

OPPORTUNITIES FOR WRITING
Focus on Writing a Book Report
Taking Notes on a Book 574   Organizing a Book Report 637
Deciding on the Main Idea 584   Writing a Book Report 641
Supporting the Main Idea 617

Writing About Literature
Making Up Your Own Tale 588
Making Up a "How and Why" Story 605
Extending the Story 630

CONNECTIONS
Literature and Geography 593
Connecting Cultures 593

ART
Drawing a Picture of a Hero 565
Illustrating the Myth 575
Illustrating the Tale 600

TRANSPARENCIES

The following unit support materials with specific correlations to literature selections are available in the **Fine Art and Instructional Transparencies with Teacher's Notes and Blackline Masters** section of your *Audiovisual Resources Binder*.

FINE ART TRANSPARENCIES
Theme: Traditional Tales
34 *A mon seul desir: Tapestry from the Lady with the Unicorn,* Anonymous
35 *The Legend Teller,* Jerome Tiger

READER RESPONSE
36 What's in the Box?

LITERARY ELEMENTS
37 Exploring Myths and Folk Tales

WRITING PROCESS
38 Writing a Book Report

547A

PLANNING GUIDE

FOR UNIT PLANNING
- Transparencies 34–38: *Audiovisual Resources Binder*
- *Portfolio Assessment and Professional Support Materials*
- Test Generator
- Mastery Tests: Teaching Resources D, pp. 131, 133
- Analogy Test: Teaching Resources D, p. 136
- Revision Worksheet: Teaching Resources D, p. 137

SELECTION (Pupil's Page)	Teacher's Notes	Reading Check	Reading Focus	Study Guide	Language Skills	Building Vocabulary	Selection Vocab. Test	Selection Test	AV BINDER Audio-cassette
MYTHS AND FOLK TALES *Introduction* (p. 549)	1								
Close Reading of a Folk Tale Retold by Kim So-un *The Pheasant's Bell* (p. 551)	1								
Retold by Richard Erdoes and Alfonso Ortiz *Glooscap Fights the Water Monster* (p. 558)	2	4	5	6	7	10	13	14	
Retold by Robert Graves *Perseus* (p. 567)	16	18	19	20, 21	22	25	27	28	
Retold by Amy Cruse *Quetzalcoatl* (p. 576)	30	33	34	35, 36	37	40	43	44	
Retold by Zora Neale Hurston *How the Possum Lost the Hair on Its Tail* (p. 586)	46	47		49				51	
Retold by Harold Courlander *Paul Bunyan's Cornstalk* (p. 589)	53	55		57				59	
Rudyard Kipling *How the Whale Got His Throat* (p. 595)	61	64		65	66	69	71	72	TAPE 3 SIDE B
Chinua Achebe *Why Tortoise's Shell Is Not Smooth* (p. 601)	74	77		78, 79	80	83	85	86	TAPE 3 SIDE B
Retold by Elisabeth Gille *Ali Baba and the Forty Thieves* (p. 609)	88	91	92	93, 94	95	99	101	102	
Retold by Yoshiko Uchida *Momotaro: Boy-of-the-Peach* (p. 618)	104	106	107	108, 109	110	113	115	116	TAPE 3 SIDE B
Retold by Hans Baumann *Nana Miriam* (p. 633)	118	120		121, 122		123	125	126	TAPE 3 SIDE B
Jenny Leading Cloud *The End of the World* (p. 638)	128								

INTRODUCING THE UNIT

Ask students to discuss the myths and folk tales that they are already familiar with. Have them tell what they liked or did not like about each one. Encourage them to explore the value that these tales had for people long ago and still have for people today.

PORTFOLIO ASSESSMENT

Suggestions for use of portfolios as support for this unit are described in the **Portfolio Assessment and Professional Support Materials** booklet accompanying this program. Specific suggestions are provided for a variety of student projects that may

547B

be suitable for inclusion in a portfolio. In addition, copying masters are provided for guides that may be used for evaluation and assessment of student projects.

SELECTION NOTES

"Glooscap Fights the Water Monster" (page 558)

Vocabulary

regulate(ing)	bloat(ed)	ferocious	confront(ed)
cherish(ed)	protrude(ing)	utter(ed)	gouge(ing)
council			

Reading Check

1. The villagers want to find out why the spring is dry.   **True**
2. A monster wants all the water.   **True**
3. Glooscap fights the monster.   **True**
4. The monster changes into a squirrel.   **False**

Language and Vocabulary: Connotations (page 565)

In each pair, the first word or phrase has positive connotations and the second has negative connotations. Words supplied to fill in the blanks will vary. Possibilities include these terms:
 1. shining, golden   2. well-rounded   3. a quiet lisp

Perseus (page 567)

Vocabulary

descend(ed)	oblige	impudence	vengeance
furious	pester(ing)	competition	constellation(s)
mortal(s)	snatch(ed)		

Reading Check

1. Perseus says he will bring Medusa's head to Polydectes.   **True**
2. Atlas changes into poisonous snakes.   **False**
3. The gods reward Perseus for his actions.   **True**
4. Acrisius is able to escape his fate.   **False**

Language and Vocabulary: Words from the Myths (page 574)

Responses will vary. Here are some possibilities.
 1. He moves swiftly and is messenger for the gods.
 2. Today an atlas is a book of maps. The name arose because early atlases often carried on the front page a picture of Atlas supporting the globe.
 3. a. Mars is the fourth planet from the sun. b. Venus is the second planet. Venus is also part of the name of a marine animal (Venus's girdle), a sponge (Venus's flower basket), and several plants, e.g., Venus's flytrap. c. Saturn is both the sixth planet and a type of rocket. d. Pluto is both the ninth planet and a cartoon dog. e. Apollo was the name for the United States series of astronaut flights to the moon. f. Uranus is the seventh planet. (*Uranium* comes from the name of the planet.) g. Mercury is both the first planet and a metallic element. h. Jupiter is the fifth and largest planet. i. The name of the Greek city Athens comes from *Athena*. j. The words *volcano* and *vulcanize* (to refine elastic materials) come from *Vulcan*.
 4. A medusa has tentacles that are armed with stinging cells to paralyze its prey. These tentacles resemble the poisonous snakes on Medusa's head.

"Quetzalcoatl" (page 576)

Vocabulary

prosperous	induce	resolve	lamentation
abundant	strife	entreaty(ies)	summit

Reading Check

1. The Toltecs lived in Peru.   **False**
2. Quetzalcoatl's enemies gave him wine.   **True**
3. Quetzalcoatl demands payment for his secrets.   **False**
4. The Aztecs believed that Cortés was Quetzalcoatl returning to them.   **True**

Language and Vocabulary: Words from Mexico (page 584)

The Nahuatl spelling is given in brackets.
chili [chilli]: hot pepper.
chocolate [xocatl]: a food made from cacao beans.
cocoa [cacahuatl]: a beverage made from cacao beans.
coyote [coyotl]: a doglike animal of western North America related to the North American wolf.
mesquite [mizquitl]: a spiny bush or tree found in Mexico and the southwestern United States.
tamale [tamalli]: ground meat that is seasoned (usually with chili), rolled in cornmeal dough, wrapped in corn husks, and steamed.
tomato [tomatl]: a red or yellow fruit eaten like a vegetable.

"How the Possum Lost the Hair on Its Tail" (page 586)

Reading Check

Have students respond with a short sentence or phrase.
 1. When did the possum have the bushy tail with long silk hair? **Before the big flood**
 2. What did Ham use to make his banjo? **A cigar box and hair from the possum's tail**
 3. What did the possum see when he woke up from his nap? **Ham playing banjo made with possum's tail hairs**
 4. How did Ham remove the hair on the possum's tail? **Shaved tail while possum slept**
 5. Why does the possum still feel bad about his hairless tail? **Knows it isn't what it used to be**

"Paul Bunyan's Cornstalk" (page 589)

Vocabulary

fell(ed)	phenomenal	veer(ed)	drought	hogshead

Reading Check

Have students respond with a short sentence or phrase.
 1. What was the only way to kill the cornstalk? **Cut its top off**
 2. What happened to Babe's eyelids when ice accumulated on his tail? **His eyes were pulled wide open.**
 3. Describe the *little* pumpkins that grew on Paul Bunyan's vine. **About the size of hogsheads**
 4. What was Paul Bunyan's first method of trying to kill the cornstalk? **Chopping it down**
 5. How were the men and boys on the ground able to communicate with Paul Bunyan when he was up in the cornstalk? **All yelled at once.**

"How the Whale Got His Throat" (page 595)

Vocabulary

| generous | mariner | infinite | resource | solitary |

Reading Check

1. The fish tells the Whale where he can find a man to eat.   True
2. The human in this story is foolish.   False
3. The Mariner makes the Whale laugh.   False
4. The suspenders tie the grating.   True

Language and Vocabulary: Sound Effects (page 599)

Answers will vary; look for choices similar to these.
1. Rhyme and onomatopoeia are illustrated in this passage: ". . . he banged and he clanged, and he hit and he bit, and he leaped and he creeped, and he prowled and he howled . . ." (page 598). Alliteration is illustrated in "Nice but nubbly" and "Best Beloved" (page 596). Repetition occurs in repeated use of the phrase "a man of infinite-resource-and-sagacity."
2. Example: The car *rattled* and *hissed* as it *buzzed* along.
3. Example: *K*im *k*ept crashing and clanging the *k*ettles.

"Why Tortoise's Shell Is Not Smooth" (page 601)

Vocabulary

| preparation(s) | famine | plumage | eloquent | delectable |

Reading Check

1. Tortoise is an excellent speaker.   True
2. The sky people dislike Tortoise.   False
3. Parrot tricks Tortoise.   True
4. Tortoise's crash kills him.   False

"Ali Baba and the Forty Thieves" (page 609)

Vocabulary

refuge	procure(d)	sumptuous	intact
obstinate(ly)	intricate	verify	moderation
resistance	sinister		

Reading Check

1. This tale takes place in the United States.   False
2. The magic words are "Open Barley."   False
3. Ali Baba frees Morgiana.   True
4. Ali Baba kills no one.   True

Language and Vocabulary: A Prefix Game (page 617)

1. *re*opened   (b)
2. *re*compense   (e)
3. *dis*persed   (a)
4. *re*tiring   (d)
5. *dis*mounted   (c)
6. *re*treat   (f)

"Momotaro: Boy-of-the-Peach" (page 618)

Vocabulary

| thrust | stalk(ing) | plunder(ing) | shriek(ed) | laden |

Reading Check

1. The old woman sings to the peach.   True
2. Inside the peach is a tiny dog.   False
3. Three animals help Momotaro.   True
4. Momotaro defeats the ogres.   True

Language and Vocabulary: Japanese Words (page 630)

Answers will vary. In order, here are the French, Spanish, and German translations. German is often the most like English.
1. thank you: *merci, gracias, danke*
2. mother: *mère, madre, Mutter*
3. father: *père, padre, Vater*
4. yes: *oui, sí, ja*
5. no: *non, no, nein*
6. good morning: *Bonjour, Buenos días, Guten Tag* (all mean "Good day")
7. please: *s'il vous plaît, por favor, bitte*
8. Mr./Mrs.: *Monsieur/Madame, Señor/Señora, Herr/Frau*
9. goodbye: *au revoir* ("till we meet again"), *adios* ("Go with God"), *auf wiedersehen* ("till we meet again")
10. good: *bon, bueno, gut*

"Nana Miriam" (page 633)

Vocabulary

| devour(ed) | despair | recoil(ed) | hurl(ed) | summon |

Reading Check

1. The monster takes the form of a pig.   False
2. The monster causes disease.   False
3. Nana Miriam uses magic against the monster.   True
4. Nana Miriam throws the monster across the river.   True

Language and Vocabulary: Praise Names (page 637)

1. Look for answers such as these: Anne Frank—Of noble promise; Abraham Lincoln—Strong worker; Momotaro—Generous one; Morgiana—Clever servant.
2. Students might choose such names as "Star athlete," "Good friend," or "One who succeeds."
3. Responses will vary.

Student Learning Options

Myths and Folk Tales
1. Sculpting Medusa
Have students make papier-mâché sculptures of Medusa's head. They can blow up a balloon to serve as the base for the head and paint the head to look like Medusa. You can put their work on display in the classroom.

2. Making a Scrapbook
Have students use discarded copies of magazines, such as *Smithsonian Magazine* and *National Geographic,* to find pictures related to mythology and folklore. They can clip the pictures and write brief captions explaining them.

3. Exploring American Folk Tales
Have students find information about heroes of American folk tales, such as Johnny Appleseed, Pecos Bill, and Annie Christmas. Let them read some of the tales and report on them to the class.

Cultural Diversity

Folk tales, handed down by word of mouth for generations, reflect the cultures that produce them. After students have read each of the folk tales in this unit, lead a discussion by asking students what they can infer about the culture and people who created and preserved each tale. For example, students might surmise that the culture which produced "The Pheasant's Bell" values and rewards good deeds done for others.

VISUAL CONNECTIONS

You can tell students that *Shahnamah* means "Book of Kings" in English. This kind of decorated manuscript is called "illuminated" manuscript. The term originated because the use of gold and silver made these manuscripts look "lit up." Today we use the term *illuminated* to refer to any decorated manuscript, whether or not it has gold or silver. The subjects of these beautiful manuscripts were chiefly religious, and they were done in all parts of Europe in the Middle Ages. Distinctive styles developed, but they all had these forms of decoration in common: (1) animals, (2) branches with leaves or berries, (3) geometric designs, (4) ornamental letters, (5) braids, and (6) scrollwork. Ask students to find some of these elements in this manuscript page.

Isfandiyar Slays the Dragon by Qasim (c. 1525–1530). From the Persian manuscript of the *Shahnamah*. Silver, gold, and ink on paper.

MEETING INDIVIDUAL NEEDS
ESL/LEP • The introduction discusses heroes with supernatural powers. You may want to point out that *supernatural* simply means "beyond or above what is natural or normal." As a prefix, *super–* may also be used to mean "greater or better than others of its kind." Ask the class to think of words that use the prefix *super–*. (Answers may include *superman, superhighway, superstar, supermarket*.)

The Metropolitan Museum of Art, New York City. Gift of Arthur A. Houghton, Jr., 1970. (1970.301.51)

UNIT SEVEN
Myths and Folk Tales

The first stories that people ever told are called myths. **Myths** are stories about gods—stories that ancient people once believed were true. Myths were probably first told to explain natural mysteries, such as the changes in the seasons. Myths also explained why people had certain rituals. By suggesting that the gods paid attention to them, myths made human beings feel a bit more important in a world where survival was difficult.

Folk tales are entertaining stories that people have handed down, mostly by word of mouth, from generation to generation. Folk tales have much in common with myths. Just like myths, folk tales are often about magic transformations or about people with supernatural powers. Like myths, folk tales are exaggerated. But there is one big difference between myths and folklore. Myths are religious stories: folk tales are not. Myths explain the relationships between gods and humans. Folk tales are fantastic stories told mostly to teach lessons and to entertain.

TEACHING RESOURCES D
Teacher's Notes, p. 1

INTRODUCING THE MYTH AND THE FOLK TALE
Students may be curious as to why they are studying tales that originated so long ago. You might discuss with them the idea that myths, especially, told these ancient people who they were and what kinds of lives they should lead. The myths explained natural phenomena, why people live and die, how the earth began, who the first people were. We study myths and folk tales today to learn about the people who told them—how they lived, what they ate, what they hoped for, what they feared. Myths and folk tales have been passed along many generations because they have continued to speak to all peoples, in all lands.

Before students begin reading the tales in this unit, you might ask them to name myths or folk tales they already know. (They may not realize how familiar they are with these tales.) For instance, you might ask if they have read any Grimm fairy tales, any tales from *The Thousand and One Nights*, and Greek myths (they might know the one about Pandora, for instance, or Hercules, or King Midas).

FOCUS/MOTIVATION

Building on Prior Knowledge. Have students discuss the human qualities that people give animals. For example, in real life as well as in literature dogs are usually described as loyal, trusting, brave, and faithful. Ask students what human qualities are often attributed to owls? lambs? mules?

Prereading Journal. Ask students to jot down the human qualities that we often give to birds and to snakes. Then tell students that a bird and a snake are two of the characters in this folk tale. As they read, ask students to notice if the Korean storytellers gave these animals the same qualities that we give them.

TEACHING RESOURCES D
Teacher's Notes, p. 1

1. BACKGROUND
Locate Korea on a world map. Tell students that Korea is about the size of the state of Utah. As a result of war, Korea was divided into two countries, North Korea and South Korea. The same language is spoken in both Koreas. There are many tales about animals and ghosts or spirits in Korea. Some of these tales date back to a time long ago when Koreans believed that everything in nature, animals as well as rivers and mountains, had a spirit which must be pleased—or at least treated considerately. Many Korean folk tales include the theme that all living creatures are related.

Close Reading OF A FOLK TALE

The oldest folk tales belong to oral tradition. No one knows who composed them. They were passed down from generation to generation by being recited. Many folk tales existed for centuries before they were collected and published. As you might expect, details of the stories changed as the tales were told and retold. This is why you will often find different versions of the same tale.

Guidelines for Close Reading

1. Read actively, asking yourself questions about characters and situations. Try to draw inferences as you read.
2. Make predictions about what will happen next.
3. Try to figure out unfamiliar words from context and other clues.
4. Look for qualities or traits that the characters represent. The characters in folk tales may be animals who speak and behave like people, yet retain their identity as animals.
5. Think about the message or point of the tale and how it applies to your own life.

1   The following tale about a pheasant (fĕz′ənt) is from Korea. The notes alongside the selection represent one reader's response.

550   Myths and Folk Tales

📁 **PORTFOLIO ASSESSMENT**
Students may find fascinating the stories that are handed down from one generation to the next by word of mouth. Some families have a tradition of handing stories down, particularly stories they tell their children at bedtime. Some students may want to make a collection of traditional stories to publish in booklet form as a portfolio project. Suggest that students edit, sort, select, and publish their collections toward the end of the unit of study. Allow enough time for peer editing, as well as time for students to decorate their covers and entries. Ask students to write a short paragraph explaining the criteria they used for making their choices. (See *Portfolio Assessment and Professional Support Materials* for additional information on student portfolios.)

The Pheasant's Bell
A Korean Folk Tale
Retold by KIM SO-UN

Deep in a lonely forest there once lived a woodcutter. One day the woodcutter was at work felling trees, when he heard the cry of a pheasant and the fluttering of wings nearby. He wondered what was happening and went to see what the commotion was about. Under the shade of a bush he saw a pheasant nest with many eggs inside it. A great snake was poised to strike at a mother pheasant, who was bravely trying to defend her nest. The woodcutter picked up a stick and tried to scare the snake away, crying: "Go away! Go away!" But the snake wouldn't move, so the woodcutter struck it with his stick and killed it.

Some years after this, the woodcutter one day set out on a distant journey. Twilight found him walking along a lonely mountain path. Soon it became completely dark. He was hungry and tired. Suddenly, far ahead of him in the woods he saw a dim light. He walked toward this light and came to a large and beautiful straw-thatched house. The woodcutter was surprised, for he had never expected to find such a fine house so deep in the forest. He knocked on the door, and a beautiful girl, about nineteen or twenty years of age, came out.

"I am hungry and tired," the woodcutter told her. "I have walked a long way today and have no place to stay. I wonder if you would put me up for the night?"

The girl answered in a kind tone: "I am alone in this house, but please do come in."

She welcomed the woodcutter inside and spread out a grand feast for him. But the woodcutter felt very ill at ease. He could not understand why such a beautiful young girl

Korean bell with dragon on top (9th century). Bronze. Central Historical Museum, P'yongyang, Korea.

ONE READER'S RESPONSE

1 *This sounds like the beginning of a fairy tale. I like stories set in lonely forests.*
A pheasant must be a kind of bird. (It has wings.)

So far this is just like a realistic story. All of these events could happen in real life.

2 *Is there something magical about this house?*

3 *There is something wrong. He feels ill at ease. I wonder what it is?*

Close Reading of a Folk Tale 551

1. BACKGROUND
Students might enjoy discussing why so many fairy tales take place in forests. (The forest represents a deep fear—being lost in a foreign and often hostile environment. The setting provides a good opportunity to express a hope—that something magical will happen to rescue us.) *What other fairy tales take place in a forest? How are these settings scary? How do the characters escape?* One example is Hansel and Gretel, who get lost in the forest and have to outsmart the evil witch.

2. GUIDED READING:
Making Inferences
Note that the reader is making an inference based on the unusual sight of a "large and beautiful house" deep inside a forest.

3. LITERARY ELEMENTS:
Suspense
This comment indicates that the storyteller has created suspense effectively.

VISUAL CONNECTIONS
This bell was cast during the period in Korean history known as the Unified Silla period (668–935 A.D.), which was the golden age of Korean art.

1. GUIDED READING:
Visualizing
The reader has used this descriptive detail to help visualize the girl.

2. BACKGROUND
Magical changes, often from human to animal or animal to human, are found in the folk tales of many different peoples. Write *metamorphosis* on the board. Explain that the word means a change in form. Tell students that this word is used in both literature and science. Example: A caterpillar undergoes metamorphosis when it becomes a butterfly.

Close Reading
OF A FOLK TALE

1 Why does she have a great red mouth? I get a weird picture of this girl.

2 This is magic. The snake turned into a girl.

She's set a test for him that is impossible to pass. This often happens in fairy tales.

---

should be living all alone in the middle of a forest. He couldn't help wondering if he hadn't entered a haunted house. But he was so hungry that he ate the fine food put before him and asked no questions. Only when he was quite full did he finally speak.

"Why should such a young person as you live all alone here in such a large house?" he asked.

"I am waiting to take my revenge against my enemy," the girl answered.

"Your enemy?" he asked. "Where would he be?"

"He is right here," she said. "See, you are my enemy!" Then she opened a great red mouth and laughed loudly.

The woodcutter was astounded and asked her why he should be her enemy.

The girl reminded him of the time he had saved the mother pheasant and her nest, and added: "I am the snake you killed that time. I've waited a long long time to meet up with you. And now I'm going to take your life. Then finally I'll have the revenge I've dreamed of so long."

When the woodcutter heard this, his heart sank. "I had nothing against you at that time," he said in a quavering voice. "It was simply because I couldn't bear to see helpless beings hurt by someone strong like you were. That's why I saved the pheasant. But I really didn't mean to kill you. Don't say I'm your enemy. Please, please spare my life."

At first the girl kept laughing at him and would not listen to his pleas. But he kept on pleading, from bended knees, with tears flowing down his cheeks.

"All right then," the girl said, "I'll give you one chance. Deep in the forest and high in the mountains there is a temple ruin. Not a single soul lives there. However, a huge bell hangs in that temple. If, before dawn, you are able to ring that bell without moving from the place where you're sitting now, then I'll spare your life."

When the woodcutter heard this, he was even more frightened. "How can I ring that bell while I'm still sitting here in this room?" he sighed. "You're unfair. I'm no better off than

552 Myths and Folk Tales

A Korean Temple.

before. Please don't say such a cruel thing. It's the same as killing me right now. Please let me go home."

The girl firmly refused: "No! You are the enemy I've waited for so long. Yes, I've waited a long time for this chance to avenge myself. Now that I have you in my hands, why

1. GUIDED READING:
Interpreting Meaning
The bell was probably one of those circular-shaped brass bells (or gong) that rang when it was hit with a cloth-covered stick. The pheasant probably threw herself against the bell, making it ring but dying from the impact.

Close Reading
OF A FOLK TALE

What happened? How did it ring?

What is "gnashed her teeth"?

More magic. The house and girl disappear.

1 **Well, what happened? Why is the pheasant dead? Did the pheasant ring the bell? How? The story has a good moral: The man's kindness to the pheasant was rewarded.**

should I let you go? If you can't ring the bell, resign yourself to death. I shall eat you up."

The woodcutter gave up all hope. He realized that he was as good as dead.

Suddenly, the quiet night air vibrated with the sound of a distant bell. "Bong!" the bell rang. Yes, it was the bell in the crumbling old mountain temple!

When the girl heard the bell, she turned white and gnashed her teeth. "It's no use," she said. "You must be guarded by the gods."

No sooner had she said this than she disappeared from sight. The fine house in which the woodcutter was sitting also disappeared in a puff of smoke.

The woodcutter, whose life had been so miraculously saved, could hardly wait for daylight to break. With the first sign of dawn he set off toward the mountains in search of the ruined temple, filled with gnawing curiosity.

Sure enough, as he had been told, there he found a temple in which hung a great bell. But there was not a single soul in sight. The woodcutter looked at the bell in wonder. On it he noticed a stain of blood. He looked down to the floor. There, with head shattered and wings broken, lay the blood-stained body of a pheasant.

CLOSURE
Call on a volunteer to summarize the folk tale. Remind students that a folk tale often teaches a "lesson." Ask students what lesson this folk tale teaches.

Looking at Yourself as a Reader

Compare your own responses with those in the notes alongside the selection. Using the **Guidelines** on page 550, evaluate the reader's responses. Do you agree or disagree with any of the reader's ideas?

1. Which of these statements do you think most accurately states the moral or lesson of this folk tale? Discuss your choice with a partner.
    a. A person's act of kindness will be rewarded.
    b. If you have faith, even the most hopeless situation can come to a good end.
    c. A person who is harmed will always seek revenge.

2. Magical events often occur in folk tales. Name two magical events in "The Pheasant's Bell."

A Pair of Birds on a Cinnamon Tree by Ch-i Bai-Shih (1940). Ink and color on paper.

Close Reading of a Folk Tale **555**

LOOKING AT YOURSELF AS A READER
1. Students will probably choose the first statement as the moral of the folk tale. Have students support their choices with examples from the folk tale.
2. Responses will vary. Possibilities include the changing of a snake into a girl and the disappearance of the girl and house.

Using Context Clues
Discuss with students the following types of context clues:
- Experience Clues—in which readers draw on their own experiences. Students use experience clues to figure out the meaning of *savage*.
- Synonym Clues—in which the writer provides a synonym or near synonym for the word. Students use this type of clue in part to figure out the meaning of *prosperous*. The fact that it is paired with *happy* indicates that being *prosperous* is a good thing.
- Example Clues—in which the writer provides an example of the word. Students use example clues to figure out the meaning of *prospered*.

THINKING ABOUT WORDS

USING CONTEXT CLUES

In a myth in this unit, you will read that a king

> ... locked ... his only daughter in a tower with brass doors, guarded by a *savage* dog. ...

If you didn't know that *savage* means "wild and fierce," the context would give you clues to uncover its meaning. Let's think about how you could have figured out that meaning.

Thinking It Out. The words *locked* and *brass doors* provide strong clues that the king does not want his daughter to get out, or anyone to get in. In fact, the door is *guarded* by some kind of dog. Certainly, a sweet and friendly dog would not stop someone from going in or out. So *savage* has to describe the kind of dog that could prevent someone from entering or exiting. A wild and fierce dog could do that.

Below are two passages from "Quetzalcoatl," another myth you will read in this unit. The passages provide some good clues to help you get a general sense of what the underscored words mean. (They are related.) Use context clues to try to uncover their meanings. Check with the Glossary at the back of this book or a dictionary to see how close you got.

> They were ruled by Quetzalcoatl, the great god of the sun and the wind, who had left his home in the land of the Sunrise so that he might teach the Toltecs and help them to become a happy and prosperous nation. ...

> ... while he reigned over them, the Toltecs were very happy. Everything in the country prospered. The maize crops were more abundant than they had ever been before; the fruits were larger and more plentiful. ...

Myths and Folk Tales

COOPERATIVE LEARNING

Before students read the hero myths in the text, you might want them to think about what their definition of a hero includes. To help them consider this, you might divide the class into three or four groups and have each group discuss what makes a hero. Each group could then come up with a set of criteria and name a person (or several) that the group believes exemplifies the definition.

You might allow each group to present their ideas to the class, and as they do, list the characteristics they mention on the chalkboard. Keep the list available as you read the myths in the textbook and assess the heroes on the criteria. Ask students if the definition of a hero differs from culture to culture or from the past to the present.

THREE HEROES OF MYTH

In the world of myth, heroes do the things we wish we could do and the things we are glad we don't have to do. Heroes in myths represent the hopes and fears of the people who create them.

Heroes in myths are often helped by gods. Sometimes they are even gods themselves. The heroes usually have supernatural powers, and they are always opposed by monsters and other difficulties. Often the mythic hero saves a whole society from ruin. In many myths, the people wait for their hero to return someday, to help them again in their hour of need.

INTRODUCING THE THREE HEROES OF MYTH

You may want to borrow from the library and bring to class several books of myths from various parts of the world. *Keepers of the Earth*, by Michael J. Caduto and Joseph Bruchac, is an excellent book of Native American myths which has related environmental activities. The best introduction to Greek myths is the classic *D'Aulaire's Book of Greek Myths* by Ingri and Edgar D'Aulaire.

Emphasize to students that although myths are very old, they are meaningful even today. As students read about the three mythical heroes in this section—Glooscap (Native American), Perseus (Greek), Quetzalcoatl (Mexican)—have them look for expressions of human hopes and fears that are still important today.

Hercules shown on a Greek plate (5th century B.C.).

Etruscan Museum in the Vatican, Rome.

Three Heroes of Myth 557

OBJECTIVES
Students will recognize examples of metamorphosis, identify pronoun referents, and identify positive and negative connotations of words.

FOCUS/MOTIVATION
Establishing a Purpose for Reading. Ask students to think about how Glooscap feels about his people.

Prereading Journal. Have students list the qualities a great teacher or leader should have.

TEACHING RESOURCES D
Teacher's Notes, p. 2
Reading Check, p. 4
Reading Focus, p. 5
Study Guide, p. 6
Language Skills, p. 7
Building Vocabulary, p. 10
Selection Vocabulary Test, p. 13
Selection Test, p. 14

1. BACKGROUND
Glooscap is also the hero of myths told by Northeast Woodlands Indians in the United States: the Maliseets, Penobscots, Passamaquaddy, and Eastern Algonquins. Some of the many other names for Glooscap are Gluscabi, Koluscap, Odzihozo, and Ksiwhambeh.

Glooscap Fights the Water Monster
A Micmac Myth

Retold by RICHARD ERDOES *and* ALFONSO ORTIZ

Micmac medicine doll. Wood.
Courtesy of the National Museum of the American Indian, Smithsonian Institution.

Before You Read

1 Many myth-makers tell stories about a god-teacher who teaches the people all the skills they need to survive on Earth. The great friend and teacher of the Micmac people of North America was a divine being called Glooscap. Glooscap taught his people all that was wise and good.

The Micmacs still live in eastern Canada, and they still tell Glooscap stories. The Micmacs say that when the famous Admiral Peary finally discovered the North Pole on April 6, 1909, he found Glooscap sitting on top of it.

After you read the first paragraph of this story about one of Glooscap's adventures, pause to discuss how the people felt about Glooscap. How would these beliefs comfort the Micmac people?

558 Myths and Folk Tales

READING THE SELECTION
This myth is easy to read. You might want to have students read it silently first. Then, assign the three individual speaking parts (Glooscap, the villager, and the monster) and have students prepare to read the myth in class. Assign the role of narrator to good readers, giving each one a page to narrate. Half of the remaining students could read together the speeches of Glooscap's people; the other half could read together the speeches of the monster's people.

Language and Vocabulary

Connotations (kǎn′ə·tā′shəns) are all the feelings and associations that become attached to a word as it is used over a period of time. For example, suppose you wanted to describe a wet creature with a word that would make your readers' flesh creep. You might use the word *slimy*. But suppose, instead, that you liked this creature and you wanted your readers to like it too. Then you might describe it as *slippery*. As you read this myth, look for descriptions of the water monster that make you feel it is very disgusting.

Courtesy of the National Museum of the American Indian, Smithsonian Institution.

Glooscap yet lives, somewhere at the southern edge of the world. He never grows old, and he will last as long as this world lasts. Sometimes Glooscap gets tired of running the world, ruling the animals, regulating nature, instructing people how to live. Then he tells us, "I'm tired of it. Good-bye; I'm going to make myself die now." He paddles off in his magic white canoe and disappears in misty clouds. But he always comes back. He cannot abandon the people forever, and they cannot live without him.

Glooscap is a spirit, a medicine man,[1] a sorcerer. He can make men and women smile. He can do anything.

Glooscap made all the animals, creating them to be peaceful and useful to humans. When he formed the first squirrel, it was as big as a whale. "What would you do if I let you loose on the world?" Glooscap asked, and the squirrel attacked a big tree, chewing it to pieces in no time. "You're too destructive for your size," said Glooscap, and remade him small. The first beaver also was as big as a whale, and it built a dam that flooded the country from horizon to horizon. Glooscap said, "You'll drown all the people if I let you loose like this." He tapped the beaver on the back, and it shrank to its present size. The first moose was so tall that it reached to the sky and looked altogether different from the way it looks now. It trampled everything in its path—forests, mountains, everything. "You'll ruin everything," Glooscap said. "You'll step on people and kill them." Glooscap tapped the moose on the back to make it small, but the moose refused to

---
1. **medicine man:** someone with supernatural powers over the natural world.

Glooscap Fights the Water Monster 559

1. LANGUAGE AND VOCABULARY
Word connotations in this myth help readers to feel positively toward the hero Glooscap and negatively toward his adversary, the monster. The Language and Vocabulary box on this page focuses on word connotations. Students will find practice with connotations in the Language and Vocabulary exercise on page 565.

2. GUIDED READING:
Using Context Clues
The definition of "medicine man" in the footnote gives students a clue about the meaning of the word *sorcerer*—someone who can do magic.

3. GUIDED READING:
Identifying Implied Ideas
What ideas about large and small animals are implied by Glooscap's words and actions? Large animals tend to be destructive, so they must be made smaller. When large creatures are free to do what they like, they cause harm.

ART LINK

If you have students read this myth as a group presentation, you might want to have another group of students design a simple setting for the classroom that would set the mood for the myth. They could make masks or other decorative items to place at the front of the classroom, or they could design a mural scene as a background, with shelters, canoes, and a landscape characteristic of the northeast woodlands.

1. GUIDED READING:
Making Inferences
Why do you think the wise men and elders decide to send someone else to investigate the problem rather than go themselves? They probably believe that, because of their wisdom and experience, they are unexpendable to the community.

2. LITERARY ELEMENTS:
Descriptive Details
What details help you to picture the brook? Details include "widened out," "a little" water, "slimy, yellowish, and stinking" water.

become smaller. So Glooscap killed it and re-created it in a different size and with a different look. In this way Glooscap made everything as it should be.

Glooscap had also created a village and taught the people there everything they needed to know. They were happy hunting and fishing. Men and women were happy in love. Children were happy playing. Parents cherished their children, and children respected their parents. All was well as Glooscap had made it.

The village had one spring, the only source of water far and wide, that always flowed with pure, clear, cold water. But one day the spring ran dry; only a little bit of slimy ooze issued from it. It stayed dry even in the fall when the rains came, and in the spring when the snows melted. The people wondered, "What shall we do? We
1 can't live without water." The wise men and elders held a council and decided to send a man north to the source of the spring to see why it had run dry.

The man walked a long time until at last he came to a village. The people there were not like humans; they had webbed
2 hands and feet. Here the brook widened out. There was some water in it, not much, but a little, though it was slimy, yellowish, and stinking. The man was thirsty from his walk and asked to be given a little water, even if it was bad.

"We can't give you any water," said the people with the webbed hands and feet, "unless our great chief permits it. He wants all the water for himself."

"Where is your chief?" asked the man.

Micmac Indians by an unknown Canadian artist (c. 1850).

560 Myths and Folk Tales

GEOGRAPHY LINK
Have students locate on a map the area of the United States where the various northeast woodlands native peoples lived. You might want to locate a reference that shows the territory of the various Native American groups for students to use. Then, you might point out which groups maintain contemporary communities in the United States.

VISUAL CONNECTIONS
Have students imagine they are one of the people in the canoes. Ask them to imagine the smell of the air, the color of the trees, and the sound of the birds. Then have students write a paragraph in which they describe their feelings about their environment, using details that appeal to the senses.

National Gallery of Canada, Ottawa.

TRANSPARENCY 36

Reader Response
What's in the Box? – invites students to write about the supernatural elements in a myth or folk tale.

1. GUIDED READING:
Recognizing Cause and Effect
What caused the stream to dry up? The monster sat in it and created a dam with his body.

2. GUIDED READING:
Connotations
Which words make you feel that the monster is disgusting? The negative words are *dull, bloated, warts, dully, protruding,* and *fearsome.*

3. LITERARY ELEMENTS:
Figurative Language
What is the noise of the monster's smacking his lips compared to? Is this a simile or a metaphor? How do you know? It is compared to the sound of thunder. It is a simile; it uses the word *like.*

"You must follow the brook farther up," they told him.

The man walked on and at last met the big chief. When he saw him, he trembled with fright, because the chief was a monster so huge that if one stood at his feet, one could not see his head. The monster filled the whole valley from end to end. He had dug himself a huge hole and dammed it up, so that all the water was in it and none could flow into the stream bed. And he had fouled the water and made it poisonous, so that stinking mists covered its slimy surface.

The monster had a mile-wide grinning mouth, going from ear to ear. His dull yellow eyes started out of his head like huge pine knots. His body was bloated and covered with warts as big as mountains. The monster stared dully at the man with his protruding eyes and finally said in a fearsome croak, "Little man, what do you want?"

The man was terrified, but he said, "I come from a village far downstream. Our only spring ran dry, because you're keeping all the water for yourself. We would like you to let us have some of this water. Also, please don't muddy it so much."

The monster blinked at him a few times. Finally he croaked:

Do as you please,
Do as you please,
I don't care,
I don't care,
If you want water,
If you want water,
Go elsewhere!

The man said, "We need the water. The people are dying of thirst." The monster replied:

I don't care,
I don't care,
Don't bother me,
Don't bother me,
Go away,
Go away,
Or I'll swallow you up!

The monster opened his mouth wide from ear to ear, and inside it the man could see the many things that the creature had killed. The monster gulped a few times and smacked his lips with a noise like thunder. At this the man's courage broke, and he turned and ran away as fast as he could.

Back at his village the man told the people, "Nothing can be done. If we complain, this monster will swallow us up. He'll kill us all."

The people were in despair. "What shall we do?" they cried. Now, Glooscap knows everything that goes on in the world, even before it happens. He sees everything with his inward eye. He said, "I must set things right. I'll have to get water for the people!"

Then Glooscap girded himself for war. He painted his body with paint as red as blood. He made himself twelve feet tall. He used two huge clamshells for his earrings. He put a hundred black eagle feathers and a hundred white eagle feathers in his scalp lock. He painted yellow rings around his eyes. He twisted his mouth into

562 Myths and Folk Tales

"Crooked Mouth" mask of False Face Society, Seneca, New York.

Courtesy of the National Museum of the American Indian, Smithsonian Institution.

a snarl and made himself look ferocious. He stamped, and the earth trembled. He uttered his fearful war cry, and it echoed and re-echoed from all the mountains. He grasped a huge mountain in his hand, a mountain composed of flint, and from it made himself a single knife sharp as a weasel's teeth. "Now I am going," he said, striding forth among thunder and lightning, with mighty eagles circling above him. Thus Glooscap came to the village of the people with webbed hands and feet.

"I want water," he told them. Looking at him, they were afraid. They brought him a little muddy water. "I think I'll get more and cleaner water," he said. Glooscap went upstream and confronted the monster. "I want clean water," he said, "a lot of it, for the people downstream."

Ho! Ho!
Ho! Ho!

All the waters are mine!
All the waters are mine!

Go away!
Go away!

Or I'll kill you!

"Slimy lump of mud!" cried Glooscap. "We'll see who will be killed!" They fought. The mountains shook. The earth split open. The swamp smoked and burst into flames. Mighty trees were shivered into splinters.

The monster opened its huge mouth wide to swallow Glooscap. Glooscap made himself taller than the tallest tree, and even the monster's mile-wide mouth was too small for him. Glooscap seized his great flint knife and slit the monster's bloated belly. From the wound gushed a mighty stream, a roaring river, tumbling, rolling, foaming down, down, down, gouging out for itself a vast, deep bed, flowing by the village and on to the great sea of the east.

"That should be enough water for the people," said Glooscap. He grasped the monster and squeezed him in his mighty palm, squeezed and squeezed and threw him away, flinging him into the swamp. Glooscap had squeezed this great creature into a small bullfrog, and ever since, the bullfrog's skin has been wrinkled because Glooscap squeezed so hard.

1. LITERARY ELEMENTS:
Conflict
What is the conflict? The conflict between the monster and Glooscap involves ownership of the water. The monster says that the water is his. Glooscap believes that clean water belongs to everyone.

2. LITERARY ELEMENTS:
Exaggeration
You may wish to have students discuss the purpose of exaggerating the details of combat.

CLOSURE
Call on a volunteer to define *metamorphosis* and to list the metamorphoses from this myth. Call on other volunteers to give examples from other myths and folk tales. Ask students how the metamorphoses in "Glooscap" add to the story.

EXTENSION AND ENRICHMENT
Science. Ask students to choose one of these questions to research and answer: (1) Where does the water for your town come from? (2) Who owns the water? How much do people pay for it? (3) What are some of the ways that people can conserve water? (4) What happens to water after you use it (in the shower, for instance)? (5) Why are some dams constructed? What are some benefits of dams?

FOR STUDY AND DISCUSSION
Identifying Facts
1. Glooscap is a supernatural being who rules the world, can do anything, and will "last as long as this world lasts." He always comes back because the people cannot live without him.
2. A water monster at the source of the brook is hoarding all the water.
3. The water monster threatens the man's life.
4. Glooscap makes himself twelve feet tall and decorates his body with bright red paint, his eyes with yellow rings, his ears with clamshell earrings, and his head with one hundred black and one hundred white eagle feathers.
5. Glooscap makes himself taller than the water monster and slits the monster's belly with his flint knife. From the wound gushes a great river. He then squeezes the monster into a small bullfrog.

Interpreting Meanings
6. He seems to identify with elements of nature that are large (clamshells and mountain), swift (eagle), and strong (mountain of flint).
7. Glooscap has great affection for his people. They love and respect him.

For Study and Discussion

IDENTIFYING FACTS
1. According to the first two paragraphs, who is Glooscap and why does he always come back?
2. Explain why the people's water supply has run dry.
3. Why can't the man sent by the villagers solve their water problem?
4. Describe how Glooscap looks as he goes to fight the monster.
5. Tell how Glooscap not only conquers the monster but also gets water for his people.

INTERPRETING MEANINGS
6. Heroes are often associated with the world of nature. Look at the way Glooscap dressed for battle. What elements in nature do you think he identifies with?
7. How does Glooscap feel about his people? How do they feel about him?

APPLYING MEANINGS
8. Many myths are told to explain in imaginative ways events that really happened at one time. The problem posed by the monster in this myth could be based on a real event. What might that event be? What details must be totally imaginary?

Focus on Reading

IDENTIFYING PRONOUN REFERENTS
Pronouns are words used in place of nouns. Some commonly used pronouns are *I, me, you, he, she, it, they, them, those, who, whom, what.* A pronoun always refers to a noun; the noun it refers to is called its **referent.** Usually, the referent comes *before* the pronoun.

Sometimes a writer is careless in using pronouns, so the reference is confusing. For example, read this sentence: "After the children read the magazines, they were thrown away." What was thrown away, the magazines or the children?

In the following passage, can you identify the referents to the italicized pronouns *they* and *it*?

"The people there were not like humans; *they* had webbed hands and feet. Here the brook widened out. There was some water in *it*, not much, but a little, though *it* was slimy, yellowish, and stinking."

Literary Elements

METAMORPHOSIS
A **metamorphosis** (met′ə·môr′fə·sis) is a fantastic change in shape or form. We call the change from a larva to a butterfly a metamorphosis. The ugly larva undergoes a fantastic change in form to become a beautiful butterfly. A tadpole goes through a metamorphosis to become a frog. Metamorphosis is very important in mythology and folklore. You might remember myths about people who are changed into flowers or trees or animals.

How many metamorphoses can you find in this myth? Describe the changes.

Here are some questions about metamorphoses in other popular folk tales. Do you know the answers to the questions?

1. In what story does a toad turn into a prince?
2. In what story do these changes take place: a pumpkin turns into a carriage, mice turn into footmen, and a ragged dress turns into a ball gown?
3. In what story does a king's golden touch turn everything into gold?

Language and Vocabulary

CONNOTATIONS

All words have strict dictionary definitions. In addition, some words carry **connotations**, or certain feelings or associations. If you describe a used car as a "gas guzzler," you are using a term with strong negative connotations. If you call a suit *cheap*, you are using a word with strong negative connotations. If you describe the same suit as *reasonable*, or *a bargain*, you have chosen a word with more favorable connotations.

Each word in the following pairs means the same thing. But the words have very different connotations. Which word in each pair has positive or favorable connotations? Which has negative or unfavorable connotations?

> young / immature
> slim / skinny
> senior citizen / old lady

The first sentence in the following pairs is how the myth-makers actually describe the monster's eyes, body, and voice. Fill in the blanks in the second sentence in each pair with more positive, friendly words that make the monster seem sweet and lovable.

1. He had dull yellow eyes.
   He had _____ _____ eyes.
2. His body was bloated.
   His body was _____.
3. He spoke in a fearsome croak.
   He spoke in _____ _____ _____.

Drawing a Picture of a Hero

On pages 562–563 is a fantastic description of Glooscap as he is dressed to do battle with the water monster. Working alone or in a group, illustrate Glooscap in his terrifying costume. In your illustration try to show every detail described here. You might want to create a **collage.**

About the Authors

Alfonso Ortiz is an anthropologist and **Richard Erdoes** is an artist and storyteller. Together they collected 166 tales from 80 tribal groups in a book called *American Indian Myths and Legends.* The work took them 25 years. Some of the stories, they say, "were jotted down at powwows, around campfires, even inside a moving car."

The **Micmacs,** who speak a variety of the Algonkian language, live in eastern Canada. The Micmacs once fished from spring to fall and hunted for game in the winter. They lived in tepees made of animal skins or birchbark. Their landscape of hills and rivers, ocean and forest was supposedly shaped by the god Glooscap. In the 1700s, the British took control of most of the Micmac land. The English made settlements along the Atlantic coast and forced the Micmacs to retreat to remote sections of Eastern Canada.

Glooscap Fights the Water Monster 565

Applying Meanings
8. The myth could be based upon a hero's having cleared the source of a river that was blocked by a rockfall, dirt slide, log jam, or beaver dam.

Imaginary details in the myth include the size and looks of the water monster and Glooscap, and the unusual webbed limbs of the people living near the monster.

FOCUS ON READING
Identifying Pronoun Referents
They refers to *people.* The first *it* refers to *brook.* The second *it* refers to *water.*

LITERARY ELEMENTS
Metamorphosis
Metamorphoses include a whale-sized beaver and a sky-high moose changing into smaller animals. A mountain becomes a flint knife, and a monster becomes a small bullfrog.
1. A toad turns into a prince in "The Frog Prince."
2. A pumpkin, mice, and a ragged dress are transformed in "Cinderella."
3. A touch turns everything to gold in the Greek myth about King Midas.

LANGUAGE AND VOCABULARY
For answers, see the **Teaching Guide** at the beginning of the unit.

565

OBJECTIVES
Students will identify elements of the quest myth; identify major events; and identify words from Greek myths.

FOCUS/MOTIVATION
Building on Prior Knowledge. Have students identify ways people foretell the future today.
Prereading Journal. Have students write about why they would or would not want to know their future.

READING THE SELECTION
This myth moves quickly. It will be easy for students to read it at home or silently in class. Read the cast of characters on page 568 in class. Ask volunteers to pronounce the Greek names, using the diacritical marks as guides. Explain that this list includes only the most important char-

566 Myths and Folk Tales

acters in the selection; other characters will be introduced in footnotes. After they have read the story silently, ask students to prepare to read the dialogue in class. The "speaking" characters are Zeus, Danaë, Acrisius, Polydectes, Perseus, Atlas, Cassiopeia, Cepheus, and the king of Tyre. Ask volunteers to read or summarize the parts of the myth that do not include dialogue.

Perseus
A Greek Myth

Retold by ROBERT GRAVES

Before You Read

There are four great quest myths in Greek mythology. You might know some of them. One tells about the strong man Hercules, whose quests consisted of twelve horrible labors. One is about the hero of Athens called Theseus (thē′sē·əs), who killed the half-man, half-bull called the Minotaur. One is about a hero named Jason, who paid dearly for the Golden Fleece. And one is about Perseus (pur′sē·əs), who "faced" the gorgon Medusa (mə·doo′sə), a famous female monster living in Libya. You can see her face on the opposite page.

The idea of fate is important in the Perseus story. You learn right away that a king has been told by an *oracle* (a priest or priestess who could foretell the future) that one day he will be killed by his own grandson. Think about this for a minute or two. In your journal, write down two or three sentences telling what *you* would do if you had learned this was to be your fate. Then read this myth to see what King Acrisius did.

A relief sculpture of Medusa's head at the temple at Didyma, Turkey (Greco-Turkish, 2nd century A.D.).

TEACHING RESOURCES D
Teacher's Notes, p. 16
Reading Check, p. 18
Reading Focus, p. 19
Study Guide, pp. 20, 21
Language Skills, p. 22
Building Vocabulary, p. 25
Selection Vocabulary Test, p. 27
Selection Test, p. 28

1. LITERARY ELEMENTS:
Quest
What is another word for quest? *Synonyms for* quest *might be* journey *or* adventure. Remind students that in literature a quest is a dangerous journey that a hero takes to seek something of great value. (See Unit Two.)

PORTFOLIO ASSESSMENT
Some students interested in Greek mythology may want to read about and react to one of the other four quests listed in the **Before You Read** section on page 567. Reactions may take the form of artwork, written or oral reports, or a combination of the three. Other interested students may want to write and illustrate their own "Greek" myth, using the style found in "Perseus." Suggest that students carefully plan what they will do before they begin. Consult with students individually to agree on how their reactions will be assessed. (See *Portfolio Assessment and Professional Support Materials,* especially the section entitled **Suggestions for Portfolio Projects.**)

1. LANGUAGE AND VOCABULARY
The Language and Vocabulary box on this page focuses on English words that are derived from ancient Greek and Roman myths. The Language and Vocabulary exercise on page 574 gives students additional help in understanding these words.

Language and Vocabulary

1 Even though they are over two thousand years old, the ancient myths from Greece and Rome still live today. You will find traces of the myths even in your own language. The planets are named for mythic gods and goddesses. When the people in NASA want to name a new space project, they often go to mythology. Animals, fish, birds—all have been given names from mythology. Towns, mountains, products, and businesses use names from the myths. Do you know what sea creature is named for the monster Medusa?

Cast of Characters

Acrisius (ə·krē′sē·əs): king of Argos.

Danaë (dan′ə·ē): the king's daughter, mother of Perseus.

Zeus (zōōs): king of the gods, father of Perseus. Though he is married to Hera, queen of the gods, Zeus is often attracted to mortal women.

Polydectes (pol·ē·dect′ēs): wicked king of Seriphos. He wants Danaë to be his wife.

Athene (ə·thē′nē): goddess of wisdom. She helps Perseus on his quest.

Three Gray Sisters: three old women who live in the Garden of the Hesperides (hes·per′ə·dēz), at the outer reaches of the world. They have only one eye and one tooth to share among them.

Andromeda (an·drom′ə·də): a beautiful princess who has been chained to a rock by her parents, **Cepheus** (sē′fē·əs) and **Cassiopeia** (kas′ē·ə·pē′ə), king and queen of the Philistines.

A relief of the goddess Athena on a gravestone.
Museum of the Acropolis, Athens.

MEETING INDIVIDUAL NEEDS

ESL/LEP • Before assigning "Perseus," you may want to review pronunciations given for the cast of characters (page 568), as well as the names of characters footnoted throughout the story. Model the correct pronunciations for these names, and have students repeat them several times. Modeling correct pronunciations and giving students the opportunity to practice them will help students' confidence when reading and discussing the myth.

---

1 An oracle had warned Acrisius, king of Argos, that his grandson would kill him. "Then I shall take care to have no grandchildren," Acrisius grunted. Going home, he locked Danaë, his only daughter, in a tower with brass doors, guarded by a savage dog, and brought all her food with his own hands.

Zeus fell in love with Danaë when he saw her, from far off, leaning sadly over the battlements. To disguise himself from Hera, Zeus became a shower of golden rain and descended on the tower. Danaë hurried downstairs, the rain trickled after her, and then Zeus changed back into his own shape. "Will you marry me?" he asked Danaë.

2 "Yes," she answered, "I am very lonely here."

A son was born to her. She named him Perseus. Hearing a baby cry behind the brass door, Acrisius grew furious.

"Who is your husband?"

"The god Zeus, Father. Dare to touch your grandchild, and Zeus will strike you dead!"

"Then I will put you both out of his reach."

Acrisius locked Danaë and Perseus in a wooden chest, with a basket of food and a bottle of wine, and threw the chest into the sea. "If they drown, it will be Poseidon's fault,[1] not mine," he told his courtiers.

Zeus ordered Poseidon to take particular care of the chest. Poseidon kept the sea calm, and presently a fisherman from the island of Seriphos saw the chest floating on the water. He caught it with his net and towed it ashore. When he knocked off the lid, out stepped Danaë, unhurt, carrying Perseus in her arms.

The friendly fisherman took them to Polydectes, king of Seriphos, who at once offered to marry Danaë. "That cannot be," she said. "I am already married to Zeus."

"I daresay, but if Zeus may have two **3** wives, why not have two husbands yourself?"

"Gods do as they please. Mortals may marry only one wife or husband at a time."

Polydectes constantly tried to make Danaë change her mind. She always shook her head, saying, "If I married you, Zeus would kill us both!"

When Perseus was fifteen years old, Polydectes called him and said, "Since your mother will not be my queen, I shall marry a princess on the Greek mainland. I am asking each of my subjects to give me a horse, because her father needs fifty of them as a marriage fee. Will you oblige?"

Perseus answered, "I have no horse, Your Majesty, nor any money to buy one. However, if you promise to marry that princess and stop pestering my mother, I will give you whatever you want—anything **4** in the world—even Medusa's head."

"Medusa's head will do very well," said Polydectes.

This Medusa had been a beautiful woman whom Athene had once caught kissing Poseidon in her temple. Athene was so angered by his bad manners that she

---

1. **Poseidon** (pə·sī′dən): the god in charge of the seas.

---

1. GUIDED READING:
Making Inferences
What can you infer about Acrisius's feelings for his daughter? Since he locks her up, he seems to care little for her.

2. GUIDED READING:
Recognizing Cause and Effect
Although Acrisius does not want Danaë to marry, how does his treatment of her indirectly cause her to marry Zeus? Danaë marries Zeus because she is lonely in the tower where Acrisius has imprisoned her.

3. GUIDED READING:
Understanding Contrasts
How does Danaë's attitude toward Zeus differ from Polydectes'? Danaë fears Zeus, but Polydectes is bold and disrespectful toward him.

4. GUIDED READING:
Making Inferences
The phrase "anything in the world—even Medusa's head" is a clue to the head's value.

Perseus

MEETING INDIVIDUAL NEEDS
Auditory Learners • To help students keep track of the cast of characters, you might want to list on a poster the characters as they occur in the myth. The major characters with speaking parts should be listed with an explanation of who they are beside their names. Because many of the Greek characters will be unfamiliar to sixth grade students, you might want to include minor characters who are mentioned but are not integral to the story on a separate list.

1. GUIDED READING:
Making Inferences About Character
What does this passage reveal about the human qualities of Athene? She is jealous, and she gets angry.

2. GUIDED READING:
Making Inferences About Character
What does this passage reveal about the heroic qualities of Perseus? He is brave and clever.

3. GUIDED READING:
Comparing and Contrasting
What is similar about the way Perseus gets what he wants from the Gray Sisters and from the Naiads? In both cases, he uses a form of blackmail to force them to cooperate with him.

---

1 changed Medusa into a gorgon—a winged monster with glaring eyes, huge teeth, and snakes for hair. Whoever looked at her would turn to stone.

Athene helped Perseus by handing him a polished shield to use as a mirror when he cut off Medusa's head, so as not to be turned into stone; and Hermes[2] gave him a sharp sickle.[3] But Perseus still needed the god Hades's[4] helmet of invisibility, also a magic bag in which to put the head, and a pair of winged sandals. All these useful things were guarded by the Naiads of the River Styx.[5]

2 Perseus went to ask the Three Gray Sisters for the Naiads' secret address. It was difficult enough to find the Three Gray Sisters, who lived near the Garden of the Hesperides, and had only a single eye and a single tooth between them. When Perseus eventually reached their house, he crept up behind them as they passed the eye and the tooth from one to the other. Then he <u>snatched</u> both these treasures and refused to return them until the Gray Sisters gave him the Naiads' address.

3 He found the Naiads in a pool under a rock near the entrance of Tartarus, and threatened to tell all the world about them, unless they lent him the helmet, the sandals, and the bag. The Naiads hated anyone to know that, though otherwise good-looking, they had dogs' faces; so they did as Perseus asked.

Perseus, now wearing the helmet and the sandals, flew unseen to Libya. Coming upon Medusa asleep, he looked at her reflection in the polished shield and cut off her head with his sickle. The only unfortunate accident was that Medusa's blood, trickling from the bag in which the head lay, turned into poisonous snakes as it hit the earth. This made the land of Libya unsafe forever afterward. When Perseus stopped to thank the Three Gray Sisters, the Titan Atlas[6] called out, "Tell your father Zeus that unless he frees me pretty soon, I shall let the heavens fall—which will be the end of the world."

Perseus showed Medusa's head to Atlas, who at once turned to stone and became the great Mount Atlas.

As he flew on to Palestine, Perseus saw a beautiful princess named Andromeda chained to a rock at Joppa, and a sea serpent, sent by the god Poseidon, swimming toward her with wide-open jaws. Andromeda's parents, Cepheus and Cassiopeia, the king and queen of the Philistines, were ordered by an oracle to chain her there as food for the monster. It seems that Cassiopeia had told the Philistines, "I am more beautiful than all the Nereids[7] in the sea"— a boast which angered the Nereids' proud

---

2. **Hermes** (hûr′mēz): messenger of the gods.
3. **sickle**: a kind of sword with a curved blade.
4. **Hades** (hā′dēz): god of the underworld, or **Tartarus** (tär′tər·əs).
5. **Naiads** (nā′ads) **of the River Styx** (stiks): nymphs who live in the river that surrounds the underworld.
6. **Atlas**: a member of a race of giants called Titans. Atlas has been made to hold up the sky by Zeus.
7. **Nereids** (nir′ē·ids): the fifty sea nymphs who attend the sea god Poseidon.

570 Myths and Folk Tales

ART LINK
You might get students involved in creating a mural for the classroom that shows the pantheon of Greek gods, goddesses, and mortals involved in this story. Students could work individually on their assigned or chosen characters if they are given a size range to use for the character. Encourage students to find out more about their assigned persons or gods and to include clues to their characteristics in the artwork.

Students might all use a similar medium to create their work, such as colored chalk, pastels, or charcoal. After they have completed their work, students could paste each character on a long strip of paper in the style of a Greek fresco or of a tapestry, depending upon the background students choose to use.

VISUAL CONNECTIONS
You might tell students that the red-figure style of pottery was invented in Greece in 520 B.C. In this style, the outer parts of the vase or pot are covered in black, and the decorative figures are exposed red clay. The inner markings were first drawn with pen and then in black glaze. The style is known for its graceful and ornamental design. The subjects of the red-figure style were usually drawn from mythology, as in this painting of Medusa and Perseus.

Perseus carrying Medusa's head (5th century B.C.). Red figure vase painting.

father, the god Poseidon. Perseus dived at the sea serpent from above and cut off its head. Afterward he unchained Andromeda, took her home, and asked permission to marry her. King Cepheus answered, "Impudence! She is already promised to the king of Tyre."

"Then why did the king of Tyre not save her?"

"Because he was afraid to offend Poseidon."

"Well, I feared no one. I killed the monster. Andromeda is mine."

As Perseus spoke, the king of Tyre arrived at the head of his army, shouting, "Away, stranger, or we shall cut you into little pieces!"

Perseus told Andromeda, "Please shut your eyes tight, Princess!"

Andromeda obeyed. He pulled Medusa's head from his bag and turned everyone but Andromeda to stone.

Perseus 571

CLOSURE

Discuss the heroic qualities of Perseus with the class. Have students give one example from the myth of each quality.

EXTENSION AND ENRICHMENT

Social Studies. Ask volunteers to locate the following places on a map: Argos, Seriphos (Serifos in the Cyclades), Libya, Atlas Mountains, Palestine, Joppa (Tel Aviv), Tiryns (southeast of Argos), and Mycenae (Mikinai).

1. GUIDED READING:
Drawing Conclusions
From this myth, what can you conclude about the qualities that the early Greeks admired? They admired respect for the gods, gratitude, bravery, intelligence, common sense, loyalty, and obedience.

FOR STUDY AND DISCUSSION
Identifying Facts

1. King Acrisius throws Perseus and his mother into the sea in a chest because an oracle told him that his grandson (Perseus) will kill him. Zeus orders Poseidon to keep the sea calm, and a fisherman catches the chest and pulls it ashore on Seriphos.
2. Anyone who looks at Medusa turns to stone.
3. Perseus is assisted by Athene and Hermes.
   Athene gives Perseus a polished shield to use as a mirror; Hermes donates a sharp sickle.
4. The Three Gray Sisters share among them a single eye and a single tooth.
   Perseus needs the secret address of the Naiads.
5. With the winged sandals, Perseus can fly. With the helmet of invisibility and the polished shield, he can approach Medusa unseen and not have to

Andromeda chained to her rock. A mosaic on the floor of the House of the Stags at Herculaneum, Italy.

When Perseus flew back to Seriphos, carrying Andromeda in his arms, he found that Polydectes had cheated him after all. Instead of marrying the princess on the mainland, he was still pestering Danaë. Perseus turned him and his whole family to stone, and made the friendly fisherman king of the island. Then he gave Medusa's head to Athene, and asked Hermes would he kindly return the borrowed helmet, bag, and sandals to the Naiads of the Styx? In this way Perseus showed far greater sense than Bellerophon,[8] who had gone on using the winged horse Pegasus after killing the Chimera. The gods decided that Perseus deserved a long, happy life. They let him marry Andromeda, become king of Tiryns, and build the famous city of Mycenae near by.

As for King Acrisius, Perseus met him one afternoon at an athletic competition. "Good day, Grandfather! My mother Danaë asks me to forgive you. If I disobey her, the Furies will whip me, so you are safe from my vengeance."

Acrisius thanked him, but when Perseus took part in the quoit-throwing competition, a sudden wind caught the quoit he had thrown and sent it crashing through Acrisius's skull. Later Perseus and Andromeda were turned into constellations, and so were Andromeda's parents, Cepheus and Cassiopeia.

---

8. **Bellerophon** (bə-ler′ə-fon): a hero who killed the dreaded monster called **Chimera** (kə-mir′ə), using the magical winged horse **Pegasus** (peg′ə-səs). Bellerophon got into trouble when he dared to ride Pegasus up to Olympus, home of the gods. The gods made him wander alone on Earth till he died.

572 Myths and Folk Tales

For Study and Discussion

IDENTIFYING FACTS
1. Like many heroes, Perseus's life is threatened as a child. Explain how Perseus and his mother came to be on the island of Seriphos.
2. The evil King Polydectes tricks Perseus into going on a **quest** for the head of the gorgon named Medusa. Why is Medusa so dangerous?
3. Heroes of myth and folklore often receive **supernatural** help on their quests. What gods assist Perseus? What **magic objects** do they donate to his project?
4. Describe what is very odd about the Three Gray Sisters. What information does Perseus need from them?
5. The Naiads give three **magic objects** to Perseus. Explain how these objects, plus the shield given to him by Athene, help Perseus accomplish his quest.
6. At the end of a fairy tale, the evildoers are usually punished and good is triumphant. What happens at the end of this myth?

INTERPRETING MEANINGS
7. Do you think that this myth proves that no one can escape fate? What do you think of the idea that everything in life is preordained (determined in advance) by fate?

APPLYING MEANINGS
8. Movie and TV quest stories are closely related to the ancient quest myths. Can you think of any movies or TV shows that are like this story of Perseus? Talk about these features:
   a. The hero threatened at birth
   b. The woman or girl who is in danger
   c. The awful monster
   d. The role played by magic
   e. The people who help the hero
   f. The perils of the journey
   g. The triumph of good at the end
9. The people who go on heroic quests in most of the ancient myths are men. Could a woman be cast in the role of Perseus? What heroes of quest movies and TV shows today are women?

Focus on Reading

IDENTIFYING MAJOR EVENTS
Can you remember the important events in this quest story? Test yourself by filling in the blanks that follow with the missing events.

1. Acrisius is told he will be killed by his grandson.
2.
3. Zeus visits Danaë as a shower of gold.
4. Perseus and his mother are cast out to sea.
5.
6. Perseus tells King Polydectes that he will bring back Medusa's head.
7.
8. Perseus finds the Three Gray Sisters.
9.
10. Perseus visits the Naiads.

look directly at her. In the magic bag, he can safely carry Medusa's severed head.

6. The evil King Polydectes is turned to stone, and the good fisherman becomes king of Seriphos. Perseus marries Andromeda, becomes a king, and builds a great city. King Acrisius is killed in a freak accident. Perseus, Andromeda, and her parents later become constellations.

Interpreting Meanings
7. The myth suggests that fate is inescapable: Acrisius is foiled when he tries to prevent Danaë from having a son, and Perseus accidentally kills Acrisius as the oracle foretold.

Opinions will differ, but many students will argue that people create their own fates by their choices and actions.

Applying Meanings
8. Look for answers such as these:
a. Superman
b. Lois Lane
c. Science fiction aliens
d. Superpowered beings
e. Robin in the show "Batman"
f. Hostile environments or aliens, as in science fiction
g. Success of the hero as

Perseus 573

COOPERATIVE LEARNING

Encourage ingenuity and foster group cooperation by having students use Greek names to create advertisements for modern products. You could divide the class into four or five groups and have each group work on an advertising campaign for a product, using a mythological name to boost its sales of related products.

You could ask each group to design an advertisement for a product—either visual (magazine or billboard) or auditory (radio) or both (television). You might assign product names such as these: Athene School of the Arts, Poseidon Snorkeling and Scuba Diving Equipment, Demeter's Bakery and Fruit Stand, Aphrodite Cologne and Cosmetics, and Apollo Suntan Lotion.

You might want to award prizes for the cleverest designs or most entertaining advertisements. As Zeus's representative in the classroom, you could make aluminum-foil-covered thunderbolts with the group members' names and their award name to

in the *Indiana Jones* or *Star Wars* movies.

9. A woman could be cast as Perseus, for his success depends not on male attributes but on supernatural assistance, bravery, and cleverness.

The heroes of quest movies and TV shows today are more often than not still men.

FOCUS ON READING

Identifying Major Events

These are the events:

2. Acrisius locks Danaë in a tower.
5. A fisherman rescues Danaë and Perseus and takes them to King Polydectes.
7. Athene and Hermes give Perseus a shield and a sickle, respectively.
9. Perseus gets the Naiads' address from the Three Gray Sisters.
11. The Naiads give Perseus the helmet, sandals, and bag.
13. Perseus beheads Medusa.
15. Perseus beheads the sea monster and frees Andromeda.
17. Perseus turns King Polydectes and his family to stone and returns the magical objects to their owners.
19. King Acrisius is killed when Perseus throws a quoit that crashes accidentally through Acrisius's skull.

11.
12. Perseus finds Medusa asleep.
13.
14. Perseus sees Andromeda chained to a rock.
15.
16. Perseus changes the king of Tyre's army to stone.
17.
18. Perseus marries Andromeda and builds the city of Mycenae.
19.

Literary Elements

MYTHS AND ORIGINS

Like many myths, this one explains the **origins** of several natural features of the world.

1. Why is Libya full of poisonous snakes? (Is it, really?)
2. What is the origin of Mount Atlas? (A real mountain in northwest Africa)
3. How did four of the constellations come to be in the heavens?

Language and Vocabulary

WORDS FROM THE MYTHS

The god Hermes has several names. The Romans called him Mercury, which is where we got the name for the chemical element.

1. Perhaps you've seen the figure of Hermes in his winged helmet and winged sandals, and carrying his staff entwined with serpents (snakes), used by various messenger services. Why is Hermes a good emblem for such businesses?
2. The sight of Medusa's face changed the giant Atlas into a mountain. How is the word *atlas* used today? Can you find out why it came to be used this way?
3. The Greek and Roman names for the gods have been borrowed to name many things in modern life. Discuss how these gods' and goddesses' names have been used. Are some names used for more than one thing?

    a. Mars   e. Mercury
    b. Venus   f. Jupiter
    c. Saturn   g. Athena
    d. Apollo   h. Vulcan

4. In the natural world, what does the jellyfish called medusa look like? (Why is the name a good one?)

Focus on Writing a Book Report

TAKING NOTES ON A BOOK

In a **book report**, you summarize the contents of a book and discuss a main idea of your own about it.

When you prepare to write a book report, you will find it helpful to take close-reading **notes** on the book as you read it. At least some of these notes should be related to the major literary elements of the book. For example, if "Perseus" were part of a collection of myths you were reading, you might take notes on the major story events and on the character of the hero.

Choose a short book that you would like to read: for example, a collection of myths, a brief novel, or a book of essays. Use a

574   Myths and Folk Tales

present to the winning groups.

sheet of paper to make a chart with the following headings:

Major Elements	Reactions/Notes
————————	————————
————————	————————

As you read the first twenty pages or so of the book, fill out the chart. Save your notes.

Illustrating the Myth

Many famous artists have been inspired by the myth of Perseus. Some have drawn pictures of the agonized face of Medusa. Others have painted or sculpted figures of Perseus holding up the dripping snaky head. Draw or paint Medusa as you visualize her. Write a caption for your illustration.

About the Author

Robert Graves (1895–1985) was a British poet and novelist who was always very interested in mythology and in the history of Greece and Rome. Two of his popular novels, *I, Claudius* and *Claudius the God*, are about an emperor of ancient Rome. Graves's story of Claudius was later made into a popular TV miniseries. Claudius was a very efficient emperor whose life made exciting drama. Some historians believe he was murdered by his wife so that his corrupt nephew Nero could become ruler. Graves's retelling of the Perseus myth appears in *Greek Gods and Heroes*, a paperback book written especially for young adults. In that book, you'll also find retellings of the other great quest myths of Greece.

LITERARY ELEMENTS
Myths and Origins
1. The poisonous snakes of Libya are said to come from drops of Medusa's blood that trickled from Perseus's bag.

The greater number of poisonous snakes are found farther south in central and southern Africa.

2. Atlas threatened to drop the world from his shoulders, so Perseus turned him to stone by showing him Medusa's head.

3. The gods rewarded Perseus, Andromeda, Cassiopeia, and Cepheus by turning them into constellations.

LANGUAGE AND VOCABULARY
Words from the Myths
For answers, see the **Teaching Guide** at the beginning of the unit.

FOCUS ON WRITING A BOOK REPORT
Taking Notes on a Book
To give students some ideas for taking notes, you may want to review the major literary elements. Write the following terms on the chalkboard: *Characters, Plot, Setting,* and *Meaning.* Then, using a portion of a story that students have read, demonstrate how you might take notes about each of the elements.

OBJECTIVES

Students will identify similarities between myths; identify the main idea and supporting details of a passage; and define "English" words that come from the Nahuatl language.

TEACHING RESOURCES D

Teacher's Notes, p. 30
Reading Check, p. 33
Reading Focus, p. 34
Study Guide, pp. 35, 36
Language Skills, p. 37
Building Vocabulary, p. 40
Selection Vocabulary Test, p. 43
Selection Test, p. 44

1. BACKGROUND

Ask a student to locate Mexico on the map. The Aztec empire was the last in a series of great Indian civilizations in Mexico. The tribal name of the Aztec people was "Mexica." They came from the northwest, from an area they called Aztlán. Aztec society was dominated by the worship of more than sixty gods. Aztec armies were large and highly skilled, but their soldiers were trained to take prisoners (for slaves and sacrifices), not to fight battles or to kill. The Spanish had guns and horses, neither of which the Aztecs had ever seen.

FOCUS/MOTIVATION

Establishing a Purpose for Reading. Have students think about why the Aztecs were waiting for Quetzalcoatl.

Prereading Journal. Have students list the qualities they most admire in heroes. Also, have them write a few sentences about someone alive today whom they consider heroic.

Quetzalcoatl
A Mexican Myth

Retold by AMY CRUSE

Aztec mask representing Quetzalcoatl. Turquoise mosaic (12th–16th century).

British Museum, London.

Before You Read

It is 1519. The great Spanish explorer Hernando Cortés (kor·tez′) has landed on the coast of Mexico. He is marching with his soldiers inland, to the mountain cities of the Aztecs. Cortés is looking for one thing: gold. He is willing to slaughter the Aztecs to get their fabled treasures. But when Cortés and his soldiers reach the palace of the Aztec king Montezuma, they are amazed to find that they are received with respect, even awe. What can this mean?

It seems that Montezuma thought Cortés was the god Quetzalcoatl (ket·säl′kwäht′′l), returning at last to save his people. Why did the great Aztec king make such a mistake? Montezuma's god was identified with the sun: Cortés was white and his armor glittered like the sun. The Aztecs had never seen such a man. Perhaps, to them, he looked like a sun god.

The myth that follows will tell you about this famous sun god who was worshipped by almost every civilization in Mexico. The Toltecs first told the myth of Quetzalcoatl. The Toltecs were an older group of people who first brought civilization to Mexico; the Aztecs took over the Toltec religion.

Talk for a few minutes about heroes. Do you know of any people or group of people today who wish that a hero would return to help them in time of trouble? Do any heroes in movies or even in cartoons return to help a people in need?

576 Myths and Folk Tales

READING THE SELECTION

Some students may have difficulty with the descriptive passages and long sentences of the myth. You might want to read aloud the beginning of the myth (up to Tezcatlipoca's first speech, top of column 1, page 580). Mature readers then will be able to finish the myth at home. You might have less mature readers read each page silently in class. Then have a volunteer summarize each page.

Xipe (zī′pē), the Toltec god of spring (left), and Quetzalcoatl as a serpent (right) (15th century). From an Aztec calendar.

The Bibliothèque Palais Bourbon, Paris.

VISUAL CONNECTIONS

You might suggest that students use an encyclopedia to look up these topics related to the Toltecs and Aztecs and report on them to the class:

1. Montezuma
2. Mexico City's origins
3. The Toltecs
4. Aztec calendar stone

Students will also be interested in doing research on the Aztec religion. You might tell them that the priests would climb the stairs of temples like the one on page 582 to offer sacrifices at the top. The Aztecs made human sacrifices to the gods. Often they sacrificed the prisoners they took in warfare. They felt that such sacrifices kept the gods strong and strengthened the people as well.

ART LINK

You might offer students a variety of art projects in connection with this myth. They could make masks with mosaics of bits of colored plastic or of torn colored magazine pages. They could design and paint a fresco with a scene from the story, using tempera paint on heavyweight, nubby paper. They could use clay to make a statuette of Tezcatlipoca or Quetzalcoatl. Or they could make a pyramid of cardboard or plastic building blocks like the Pyramid of the Sun, the Temple of Quetzalcoatl, or the Pyramid of the Moon.

1. LANGUAGE AND VOCABULARY

The Language and Vocabulary box on this page focuses on words that have come into the English language from Mexico. The Language and Vocabulary exercise on page 584 invites students to find meanings of some of these words.

2. BACKGROUND

Another reason why the Aztecs believed that Cortés might be the god Quetzalcoatl is that Cortés had a beard. Quetzalcoatl's beard was remarkable because the Toltecs had little facial hair.

3. GUIDED READING: Understanding Cause and Effect

Why did the god teach his people how to work? He knew that taking pride in good work makes people happy. Also, if everyone did some work, there would be plenty of time for all to enjoy life.

Language and Vocabulary

1 Today, Mexican words are entering the English language very rapidly, especially words relating to food. You all know what chili is, and tamale, tortilla, taco, and mesquite. Many Mexican words come from the Spanish language (tortilla, taco); others come from an older language spoken in Mexico called Nahuatl (nä′wät′l). The name of the hero of this myth is from the Nahuatl language. *Quetzalcoatl* means "plumed or feathered serpent." The word *quetzal* is still used to name a bird native to Central America. The bird is brilliantly colored with emerald green and crimson feathers, and the male has a three-foot train. One legend about this bird says that it loves freedom too much to survive captivity.

Long, long ago, hundreds of years before the people of Europe knew anything about the great land of America, a race of people called the Toltecs lived in the southern part of that country which we now call Mexico. They were ruled by Quetzalcoatl, the great god of the sun and the wind, who had left his home in the land of the Sunrise so that he might teach the Toltecs and help them to become a happy and <u>prosperous</u> nation.

2 He was an old man with a flowing white beard, and he wore a long black robe fringed with white crosses. He was kind and wise, and while he reigned over them, the Toltecs were very happy. Everything in the country prospered. The maize[1] crops were more <u>abundant</u> than they had ever been before; the fruits were larger and more plentiful. It is even said that the cotton grew in all sorts of colors, richer and rarer than could be produced by any dyes. The hills and valleys were gay with flowers, and bright-colored birds flitted through the air, filling the land with joyous song.

3 But the god Quetzalcoatl knew that if his people were to be really happy, they must not spend their days in the idle enjoyment of all this loveliness and plenty. They must work, and learn to take a pride in working as well as they possibly could. So he taught them many useful arts—painting and weaving and carving and working in metals. He taught them how to <u>fashion</u> the gold and silver and precious stones (which were found in great abundance

---

1. **maize** (māz): corn.

578   Myths and Folk Tales

A fresco from the Temple of Cazacol, Teotihuacán, Mexico (Toltec).

Museum of Anthropology, Mexico City.

1. GUIDED READING:
Understanding Comparisons
How are the people of the neighboring states and their gods alike? Both are savage and jealous.

throughout the country) into beautiful vessels and ornaments, and how to make marvelous many-tinted garments and hangings from the feathers of birds. Everyone was eager to work, and because each man did his share, there was plenty of leisure for all. No one was in want, and no one was unhappy. It seemed as if, for these fortunate Toltecs, the Golden Age had really come.

1 The people of the neighboring states, who were living almost like savages, were very jealous when they saw the prosperity of the Toltecs. The gods of these people were fierce and warlike, and they hated Quetzalcoatl because he was so unlike themselves. They plotted together to destroy the peace and good government which he had established.

Tezcatlipoca,[2] the chief of these gods,

---

2. **Tezcatlipoca** (tez′kat·lē·pō′kə).

Quetzalcoatl 579

SOCIAL STUDIES LINK

To encourage students to apply original thinking and to gain insights into ancient cultures, you might have them pretend to be archaeologists who have just acquired the illustrated Aztec calendar on page 577. Tell students that you know many things about ancient calendars by studying the calendars of other Mexican cultures, such as the Maya, but you have not been able to determine how the Aztec's calendar was designed. Their part in studying the calendar is to propose ideas.

Have them locate Xipe and Quetzalcoatl and after they find the gods, you might ask them to examine the remaining designs. Do students think the designs are decorative only, or could they be pictographs, like rebuses? Have students examine the designs carefully. What animals or plants do they find? Have them search for common elements, such as the balls. Could balls be used on a calendar to signify the number of days? Could some of the designs stand for the name of the year, month, or day?

1. GUIDED READING:
Making Inferences
Students should be able to infer from this passage that alcohol can be dangerous and, furthermore, that something that tastes good may, in fact, be harmful. This ancient myth may have aimed to warn people of the dangers of alcohol.

2. GUIDED READING:
Predicting Outcomes
What do you think Tezcatlipoca will do now? He will take over the country and try to destroy Quetzalcoatl's work.

3. GUIDED READING:
Recognizing Multiple Meanings of Words
What do the words train *and* pages *mean here? What does Quetzalcoatl take with him?* He takes a train, which is a following or group, of pages, or servants who are usually young people.

---

disguised himself as a very old man and went to the palace of Quetzalcoatl.

"I desire to speak with your master, the King," he said to the page who admitted him.

"That you cannot do," replied the page, "for the King is at present ill, and can see no one."

"Nevertheless, go and take my message," said Tezcatlipoca, "and come back and tell me what he says."

The page soon returned, saying that the King would see his visitor, and Tezcatlipoca went in. He bowed low and respectfully before the god, and said that he had come to bring him a drug that would at once cure him of his illness.

"I have been expecting you for some days," answered Quetzalcoatl, "and I will take your medicine, for my illness troubles me exceedingly."

Then Tezcatlipoca poured out a cupful of his medicine, which was really nothing but the strong wine of the country. Quetzalcoatl tasted it, and liked it very much; he did not know what it was, for he never drank wine. After drinking the cupful, he declared that he already felt better, so that it was easy to induce him to drink cupful after cupful of this new, pleasant-tasting medicine. Very soon the wine had its effect, and he could no longer think clearly or act wisely, or take his usual place as the ruler of the country. Tezcatlipoca took care to keep him supplied with plenty of the tempting drink, so that he remained for some time in this state of intoxication.

This was Tezcatlipoca's opportunity, and he used it to the full. He set to work to bring upon the happy Toltecs every kind of misery that he could devise. He stirred up strife between them and their neighbors, and in many cunning ways he used his magic arts to lure large numbers of them to destruction. He brought plagues³ upon them, and disasters in which many lost their lives; until at last, by his wicked devices, the once happy land was brought to a state even worse than that of its barbarous⁴ neighbors.

When Quetzalcoatl shook off the evil influence of the wine given to him by his enemy and came to his true self once more, the grief which he felt at seeing all his work undone made him resolve to leave the Toltecs and go back whence he had come. But first he determined to destroy what he could of the gifts he had given to the people. He burned the houses he had built, and changed the cacao trees⁵ from which the Toltecs had obtained so much valuable food into useless mesquites.⁶ He buried his treasures of gold and silver in one of the deep valleys. All the bright-plumaged birds he commanded to follow him back to his own country; and, full of anger and grief, he set out on his long journey, taking with him a train of pages and musicians to lighten the way with their flute playing. On the road, as he passed through the neigh-

---

3. **plagues** (plāgz): horrible, deadly illnesses.
4. **barbarous** (bär′bər·əs): like barbarians, or uncivilized and rough savages.
5. **cacao** (kə·kā′ō) **trees**: Cocoa and chocolate are made from the seeds of these trees.
6. **mesquites** (mes·kēts′): thorny bushes or trees found in the southwestern United States and Mexico.

580   Myths and Folk Tales

boring states, he was met by some of the gods of the land. These gods were his enemies, and were glad to see him depart; but before he went, they hoped to gain from him some of his secrets.

"Why are you going away," asked one, "and whither are you bound?"

"I am going back to my own country," Quetzalcoatl answered.

"But why?" the other asked again.

"Because my father, the Sun, has called for me."

"Go then," replied the gods. "But first tell us some of the secrets, which are known to you alone, concerning the arts you practice; for we know there is no one who can paint and weave and work in metals as you can."

1 "I will tell you nothing," replied Quetzalcoatl. He took all the treasures he had brought with him and cast them into a fountain nearby, which was called the Water of Precious Stones; and he went on his way, paying no heed to the entreaties of the disappointed gods.

As they journeyed on, the road grew ever harder and more dangerous, but Quetzalcoatl, his staff in his hand, pressed steadily forward; and his train, though they were weary and nearly exhausted, followed him. Only once did they stop to rest, and that was when an enchanter met Quetzalcoatl and gave him a cup of wine. The wine sent the god into a deep sleep, but in the morning he had recovered from its effects and was ready to set out once more.

That day was a terrible one for the wayfarers. At each step, it grew colder and

Xipe, the Toltec god of spring. Ceramic. Museum of Anthropology, Mexico City.

1. GUIDED READING:
Understanding Cause and Effect
What human feelings are the causes for Quetzalcoatl's actions? The feelings are sadness, anger, and disappointment.

PORTFOLIO ASSESSMENT

Ruins of the Western Hemisphere's ancient but sophisticated civilizations have been discovered in both Mexico (the Aztecs) and Peru (the Incas). Some students may want to organize a future search by compiling a bibliography of sources that provide information about one of the civilizations. Provide a format for each type of entry, such as book, film, or magazine. Students may want to enter their information in a database to facilitate sorting. Bibliographies will provide ample suggestions for future independent reading. (See *Portfolio Assessment and Professional Support Materials* for additional information on student portfolios.)

1. GUIDED READING:
Understanding Cause and Effect
What causes the pages' deaths? The intense cold kills them.

FOR STUDY AND DISCUSSION
Identifying Facts
1. The Toltecs paint, weave, carve, and work metals. No one wants for anything, and there are peace and leisure for all.
2. They are fierce, warlike, and destructive.
3. They are human strife, disease, and disasters.
4. Quetzalcoatl says that he has been called by his father, the Sun. He cannot bear to see the destruction of his work.
5. The road is hard and dangerous, the cold is intense, mountains must be climbed, and a sea must be crossed.

Interpreting Meanings
6. Their hope for their god's return was so strong that it clouded their judgment. When they saw Cortés in all his gold and glittering splendor, they mistook him for Quetzalcoatl. Believing that they must show their god respect and obedience, the Aztecs unwittingly acceded to Cortés's demands.
7. He sails on a raft made of entwined serpents.

582

Plumed serpent heads decorate the staircase at the Pyramid of the Sun, Teotihuacán, Mexico (6th–8th century A.D.). Built by either the Olmecs or the Aztecs.

colder, and the poor pages, used to the sunny skies of their native land, felt their limbs gradually becoming numb and useless. At length, Quetzalcoatl led the way through a narrow valley between a volcano and the Sierra Nevada, or Mountain of Snow. Here the cold was so intense that the pages, one by one, sank down and died. Quetzalcoatl mourned over them with many tears and sang wild songs of lamentation; then sadly he went on his way, still weeping bitterly.

He had now to cross a great mountain. He climbed up one side, then, when he had reached the summit, he slid down the opposite slope to the bottom. After this, he soon reached the seashore, and there, awaiting him, was a raft. It was not made of timber, as most rafts are, but of serpents, twined together, with writhing bodies and lifted, hissing heads. Onto this strange raft Quetzalcoatl stepped, and was borne away back to his own land.

The Mexicans believe that one day he will come again, and once more rule over his people and bring back to them the Golden Age. When Cortés and his companions, in 1519, landed at Veracruz, which was the very place from which Quetzalcoatl was supposed to have departed centuries before, the people believed that here was their god returning to help them. Only slowly and reluctantly did they come to understand that he was a Spaniard, bent on conquest.

582   Myths and Folk Tales

CLOSURE
Ask students to think of another myth they know that is like "Quetzalcoatl." Have them identify the points of similarity. You may wish to write these on the chalkboard for later discussion.

RETEACHING
Have students compare Quetzalcoatl with Perseus and Glooscap. Ask them to tell which of these heroes they would choose to visit their school. Have them tell what they would discuss with the hero and what they would ask the hero to do.

EXTENSION AND ENRICHMENT
Speaking/Listening. Ask volunteers to debate the question of whether Quetzalcoatl should have destroyed the gifts he had given to the Toltecs. Have them consider whether his behavior was fair or unfair, reasonable or unreasonable.

For Study and Discussion

IDENTIFYING FACTS
1. The sun god Quetzalcoatl brings a Golden Age to the Toltecs. Describe some of the ways in which the Toltecs prosper under his rule.
2. How are the gods of the Toltecs' neighbors different from Quetzalcoatl?
3. Like many myths, this one explains the origin of evil on earth. What evils are explained by Tezcatlipoca's cunning and Quetzalcoatl's anger?
4. Why does Quetzalcoatl leave the Toltecs?
5. Describe the hardships of Quetzalcoatl's perilous journey back to his own land.

INTERPRETING MEANINGS
6. One of the tragic episodes in history is the way the Aztecs allowed Cortés into their mountain city and then were brutally conquered by him. Explain how their hope for their god's return led to their destruction.
7. Quetzalcoatl is often shown with serpents. According to this myth, why would this be?

APPLYING MEANINGS
8. Why did the people look forward to Quetzalcoatl's return? Have other people wished for heroes to return and save them?
9. According to their myths, the Toltecs are destroyed for two reasons: (a) their neighbors are jealous of their prosperity, and (b) the neighbors hate the Toltec god because he is so different from their own gods. Have other people in history been threatened for these same reasons? Talk about your answers in class.

Focus on Reading

FINDING THE MAIN IDEA
Most paragraphs are written around at least one main idea. This main idea is often directly stated in one sentence in the paragraph, usually at its beginning or its end. The rest of the paragraph contains details to support this main idea, or to explain it.

The second paragraph of this myth provides a good example of a paragraph organized around one main idea. Go back now and reread that paragraph.

When you come to a sentence like the last one in that paragraph, it is most important to stop and ask yourself a question: "Now, *how* was this a Golden Age? Did I catch all the details that lead up to this summarizing statement?"

Find at least four details in the paragraph that explain what made this age "golden."

Applying Meanings
8. The people believed that the return of Quetzalcoatl would mean a return to a Golden Age of civilization.

Stories of returning heroes exist worldwide. For example, it is said that King Arthur will return to the British Isles.

9. Although students' answers will depend upon their knowledge of history and current events, most will say yes. They might discuss the conflicts that stem from religious differences in Northern Ireland and the Middle East.

FOCUS ON READING
Finding the Main Idea
Details that explain why the Toltecs are living in a Golden Age include their mastery of several different practical arts, the pride they take in their work, and the facts that all do their share, no one is in want, and there is leisure for all.

LITERARY ELEMENTS
Connections Between Myths
1. Quetzalcoatl teaches weaving, painting, metalworking, and working with feathers. Glooscap teaches hunting, fishing, and "everything they needed to know" (page 560).
2. Quetzalcoatl teaches

Cultural Diversity

Quetzalcoatl returns to his own land on a raft made of serpents, or snakes. In the myth of Perseus, Medusa's blood turns into poisonous snakes, making the land of Libya unsafe forever (page 570). Ask students how they usually react to thinking about or seeing snakes. What do snakes symbolize? Invite students to discuss myths involving snakes from their own and other cultures. What role does the snake play in each myth? How similar are these roles across cultures?

his people agriculture in order to keep them safe; Glooscap saves his people from dying of thirst by killing the water monster.

3. Quetzalcoatl is "the great god of the sun and the wind" (page 578); Glooscap rules the world, created people and animals, and will last as long as the world lasts.

4. In both societies the people's needs are met and there is no strife. The people are happy.

5. "Mexicans believe that one day [Quetzalcoatl] will come again" (page 582). Glooscap paddles off into misty clouds, but "he always comes back" (page 559).

LANGUAGE AND VOCABULARY
Words from Mexico
For answers, see the **Teaching Guide** at the beginning of the unit.

FOCUS ON WRITING A BOOK REPORT
Deciding on Your Main Idea
To find a main idea, students might look back over their notes for recurring observations or reactions such as the dialogue seeming realistic or the main character changing for the better. You may want to model for students how such an observation can be restated to identify a main idea for a report.

Literary Elements

CONNECTIONS BETWEEN MYTHS
Many myths from different parts of the world show similar features. The myths of Quetzalcoatl and of Glooscap show some resemblances. Following are five statements about similarities between these two great hero stories. What details in the myths support these statements?

1. Both heroes teach the people skills.
2. Both save their people from danger.
3. Both have supernatural powers.
4. Both create a "Golden Age" or paradise for the people.
5. Both are expected to return some day.

Language and Vocabulary

WORDS FROM MEXICO
In the seventeenth century, as the settlers in America pushed westward, they picked up many new words. They needed these words to name all the strange new things they saw—things that they had not known back East or in Europe. Several of the new words they picked up came from the native languages, including Nahuatl, the principal Aztec tongue. All of these "English" words are from the Nahuatl language. What does each word mean?

chili	mesquite
chocolate	tamale
cocoa	tomato
coyote	

A good dictionary will tell you how each word was spelled in Nahuatl.

Focus on Writing a Book Report

DECIDING ON YOUR MAIN IDEA
To give your book report a focus, you need to identify a **main idea** for your writing. Here are some examples of main ideas:

an overall evaluation or judgment of the book

an opinion about an important element, such as plot, characters, or setting

a statement that identifies or clarifies a unifying theme in the book

For example, a possible main idea for a book report discussing a collection of myths like "Quetzalcoatl" might be: "All these myths try to explain the origin of evil."

Take notes on some more of the book you started reading for the assignment on page 574, or choose another short book for a report. Experiment with two or three one-sentence statements of a main idea for your report. Save your writing.

Art Link

You might explain a little about the Navajo sand painting used to introduce "how and why" stories. Tell students that the paintings are part of a ceremony designed to heal. The sand picture is believed to absorb the illness of the sick man in the center. You could demonstrate the difficulty of executing the artwork by dying salt with food color and having students try to spread the sand precisely where they want it.

"HOW AND WHY" STORIES

"How and why" tales give us entertaining explanations of unexplainable things. Here you will learn how the possum lost the hair on its tail, how the whale got its peculiar throat, and why the tortoise has a cracked-looking shell. "How and why" stories often have animal characters. As you read these stories, think of how these animals are like the cartoon characters you see on television or in comics today.

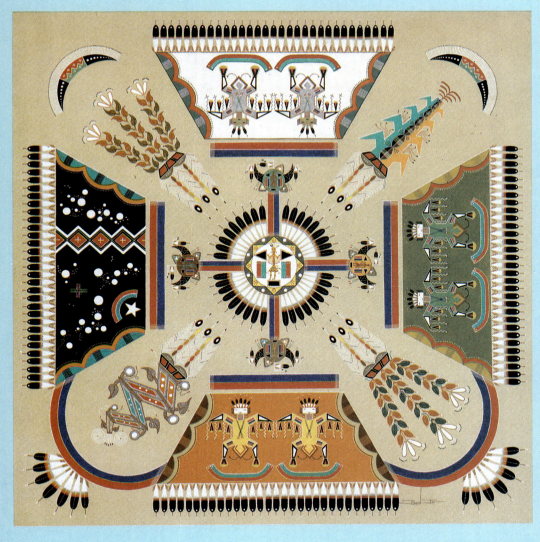

Navajo sand painting by Joe Ben, Jr., showing the harmony between humans and nature.

INTRODUCING "HOW AND WHY" STORIES

Introduce this section by discussing with students the fact that storytellers often use "how and why" tales as a means of giving their listeners practical advice about how they should behave. People realized that the animal characters in these stories represented various types of human beings.

In today's cartoons and comic strips, students often see the same kinds of characters, plots, and lessons that are in the old folk tales. Ask volunteers to describe briefly the typical plot of any cartoon that features animals as characters (the little underdog, such as Bugs Bunny, Tweety the Canary, Mighty Mouse, or Garfield, who manages to outwit a big enemy).

As students read the folk tales in this section, have them identify the lessons in behavior. Ask them to explain how valid they think the lessons are today.

"How and Why" Stories

OBJECTIVES

Students will analyze an animal from a folk tale in terms of human characteristics and create their own folk tales.

FOCUS/MOTIVATION

Establishing a Purpose for Reading. Ask students to speculate about what might have caused the possum to have a hairless tail. You might write their ideas on the chalkboard for students to refer to when they work on the **Writing About Literature** activity on page 588. **Prereading Journal.** Ask students to read the headnote and then to write a few sentences describing the characteristics of a good oral story.

TEACHING RESOURCES D
Teacher's Notes, p. 46
Reading Check, p. 47
Study Guide, p. 49
Selection Test, p. 51

1. BACKGROUND

Many cultures tell "how and why" stories. Some are told simply to entertain. Others teach a lesson. Still others point out that life is not always fair.

How the Possum Lost the Hair on Its Tail
An African American Folk Tale

Retold by ZORA NEALE HURSTON

Before You Read

Although most folk tales now appear in written form, you need to remember that they were created for speaking. As you read this tale, think of the storyteller face to face with an audience. How does the tale capture the actual speech of the storyteller?

586 Myths and Folk Tales

Language and Vocabulary

Dialect is the language spoken in a certain place or by a certain group of people. The dialect in this folk tale was recorded by Zora Neale Hurston, who make field trips and collected oral narratives in her native state of Florida. As you will see, she is careful to preserve the speech patterns of her storyteller.

Yes, he did have hair on his tail one time. Yes, indeed. De possum had a bushy tail wid long silk hair on it. Why, it useter be one of de prettiest sights you ever seen. De possum struttin' 'round wid his great big ole plumey tail. Dat was 'way back in de olden times before de big flood.

But de possum was lazy—jus' like he is today. He sleep too much. You see Ole Nora[1] had a son name Ham and he loved to be playin' music all de time. He had a banjo and a fiddle and maybe a guitar too. But de rain come up so sudden he didn't have time to put 'em on de ark. So when rain kept comin' down he fretted a lot 'cause he didn't have nothin' to play. So he found a ole cigar box and made hisself a banjo, but he didn't have no strings for it. So he seen de possum stretched out sleeping wid his tail all spread 'round. So Ham slipped up and shaved de possum's tail and made de strings for his banjo out de hairs. When dat possum woke up from his nap, Ham was playin' his tail hairs down to de bricks and dat's why de possum ain't got no hair on his tail today. Losin' his pretty tail sorta broke de possum's spirit too. He ain't never been de same since. Dat's how come he always actin' shame-faced. He know his tail ain't whut it useter be; and de possum feel mighty bad about it.

---

1. **Ole Nora:** Noah was told to build an ark so that he, his family, and pairs of living creatures might survive the flood (Genesis 6-9).

How the Possum Lost the Hair on Its Tail 587

CLOSURE
Call on a volunteer to define dialect and to explain the effect it can have on a story. Encourage students to tell whether the dialect in "How the Possum Lost the Hair on Its Tail" added to or detracted from their enjoyment of the story.

EXTENSION AND ENRICHMENT
Drama. Divide students into small groups to prepare this comical tale for a classroom theater. Each group will have to designate characters, write out the dialogue, list the needed props, and design costumes. Allow each group class time to stage its presentation.

FOR STUDY AND DISCUSSION
Identifying Facts
1. He has no time to put them on the ark because the rain starts so suddenly.
2. Possum is sleeping with his bushy tail spread out.

Interpreting Meanings
3. He no longer has a beautiful, bushy tail to be proud of.
4. The possum might be compared to a lazy person who puts great stock in appearance.

Applying Meanings
5. From the selection, students might determine that the expression came about because possum is lazy. Actually, when threatened by a predator an opossum will close its eyes and lie completely limp as though dead.

WRITING ABOUT LITERATURE
Making Up Your Own Tale
Students' tales should illustrate an understanding of cause and effect while incorporating exaggeration. You may want to have students work in pairs to read aloud and revise their tales before reading them aloud to the class.

588

For Study and Discussion

IDENTIFYING FACTS
1. Why is Ham without his musical instruments?
2. Why does Ham choose the possum's tail for his banjo strings?

INTERPRETING MEANINGS
3. Why was the possum's spirit broken?
4. The animals in folk tales often talk and act like people. What type of person does the possum remind you of?

APPLYING MEANINGS
5. "To play possum" is to pretend to be dead or asleep. How do you think this expression came about?

Writing About Literature

MAKING UP YOUR OWN TALE
Many of the stories Zora Neale Hurston collected in *Mules and Men* are called "lies"—wild exaggerations. After a speaker concludes a tale, someone else takes up the challenge of telling another tale that contains even greater exaggerations. Try your hand at "besting" the story about the possum's tail. Write your own folk tale explaining how the possum lost the hair on its tail. Then read your story out loud to the class.

About the Author

Zora Neale Hurston (1891–1960) was born in Eatonville, Florida, the first incorporated black township in the United States. She became interested in African American folk traditions while she was attending Barnard College in New York City. After graduation she returned to Florida to study oral traditions. Her research was published in *Mules and Men* (1935). Hurston, who wrote plays, novels, short stories, and articles, is best known for her second novel, *Their Eyes Were Watching God* (1937).

588 Myths and Folk Tales

Paul Bunyan's Cornstalk

An American Tall Tale

Retold by HAROLD COURLANDER

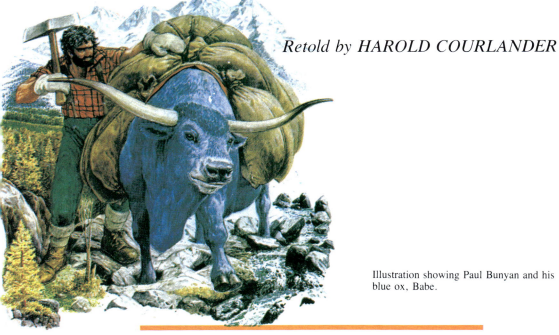

Illustration showing Paul Bunyan and his blue ox, Babe.

Before You Read

Paul Bunyan is an American folk hero known for his superhuman size and strength. Tales about Paul Bunyan were first told in the northern lumber camps. In these tales Paul accomplishes incredible feats with the help of his gigantic blue ox, Babe. Many legends tell how he changed the geography of North America.

The following story is an example of a *tall tale*, a wildly exaggerated and humorous story. As you read, ask yourself why tales about Paul Bunyan appeal so strongly to the imagination.

at home for homework.

> **TEACHING RESOURCES D**
> Teacher's Notes, p. 53
> Reading Check, p. 55
> Study Guide, p. 57
> Selection Test, p. 59

1. GUIDED READING:
Making Inferences About Character
How does Paul Bunyan compare with other lumberjacks? He is bigger, stronger, and faster.

2. BACKGROUND
The Grand Canyon is a deep gorge of the Colorado River located in northwest Arizona. It is over two hundred miles long.

3. GUIDED READING:
Transitional Elements
Generally, each new anecdote begins with a transitional phrase or sentence that ties it to the preceding anecdote.

4. LITERARY ELEMENTS:
Simile
The author compares a pumpkin vine to a Massauga rattlesnake.

---

1 Paul Bunyan was the fellow who invented the ax with two edges so a man could stand between two trees and chop them both down at the same time. As it turned out, Paul was the only man who could do that trick, but the other lumberjacks used the double-bitted ax anyway, because they didn't have to sharpen the blades so often. Paul Bunyan also had other tricks. Most lumberjacks used to cut off the tops of the pines before they felled them. But when Paul was in a hurry, he'd wait till a tree started falling; then he'd get set with his ax and lop off the top of the tree as it came down.

Nothing Paul Bunyan ever did was small. He had an ox named Babe, who used to help him with his logging work. Babe was just about the most phenomenal ox in Michigan. His color was blue, and he stood ninety hands high. If you happened to hang on the tip of one horn, it's doubtful if you could have seen the tip of the other, even on a clear day. One day when Paul had Babe out plowing, the ox was stung by a Michigan deer fly about the size of a bushel basket. Babe took off across the country dragging the plow behind him, right across Indiana, Illinois, and Missouri, with the deer fly bringing up the rear. After a while Babe veered south and didn't stop till he got to the Rio Grande. The plow that Babe was hitched to dug a furrow four miles wide and two hundred miles long. You can check 2 it in your own geography book. They call it Grand Canyon nowadays.

3 Even the storms that Paul was in were big. The biggest of all was the one they call the Big Blue Snow. It snowed for two months straight, and the way the drifts piled up only the tops of the tallest pines were showing. Lumberjacks went out that winter on their snowshoes and cut off all the pine tops. It saved them a lot of time when spring came around. Babe the blue ox didn't get a wink of sleep, though, from December till the first of March. It seems that standing out there in the weather the way he was, the snow that fell on his back melted and ran down his tail, and once it got there it froze into ice. Babe's tail kept getting heavier and heavier, and it drew on his hide so hard it just pulled his eyelids wide open and kept them that way. Babe never did get his eyes closed until the spring thaw came and melted the ice off his tail.

But the Big Blue Snow wasn't anything compared to the big drouth that started in Saginaw County and spread out as far as the Alleghenies in the East and the Rockies in the West. It all started with Paul Bunyan's vegetable garden. Paul planted some corn and some pumpkins. One of those cornstalks was six feet high before the others had sprouted. In two weeks it was tall as a house and growing like crazy. About the time it was as big as a fifty-year-old pine, people began to come in from all over the county to see it. It was growing out of the ground so fast it was pulling up stones that even the frost couldn't heave out. Same kind of thing, 4 more or less, happened to one of the pumpkin vines. It grew so fast it just darted around like a Massauga rattlesnake. It

590   Myths and Folk Tales

climbed into any place where there was an opening. People had to keep their windows closed. The ones that didn't had to cut their way out of their beds with a brush knife. Sometimes that vine would grow into one window and out another between sunset

Paul Bunyan by William Gropper (1939). Lithograph.

Paul Bunyan's Cornstalk   591

**5. LITERARY ELEMENTS:
Simile**
The author compares pumpkins on a vine to crab apples on a string.

**6. GUIDED READING:
Recognizing Cause and Effect**
What were some of the effects of Paul's oversized garden soaking up water? The fields, springs, and wells on farms for sixty miles went dry; the pine woods turned yellow; the Au Sable River became dry mud; the water in the Great Lakes went down, causing fish to hang in the air.

**7. LITERARY ELEMENTS:
Alliteration**
Names are alliterative.

**FOR STUDY AND DISCUSSION:
Identifying Facts**
1. They did not have to sharpen blades so often.
2. After being stung by a huge deer fly who was still in pursuit, Babe took off across the country, dragging a plow behind him. The plow furrowed out the Grand Canyon.
3. Its roots were soaking up all the water from the ground and causing a drought.

Interpreting Meanings
4. Speaker's tone of voice is probably tongue-in-cheek. Ask students to explain the reasoning behind their picture of the narrator.

592

---

and sunrise. Things weren't too bad until the vine blossomed and the pumpkins came out. They were about the size of hogsheads—the *little* pumpkins, that is—and when the vine whipped back and forth looking for someplace to grow it just snapped the pumpkins around like crab apples on a string. People had to be mighty alert to keep from getting hit by those pumpkins. One man lost a team of horses that way, and half a dozen good barns and one silo were stoved in.

But the real problem started when the corn and pumpkin roots began to soak up all the water out of the ground. Farms for sixty miles around went dry—fields, springs, and wells. The pine woods turned yellow from lack of moisture. The Au Sable River just turned into a trickle, and pretty soon there wasn't anything there but dry mud. The next thing that happened was that the water in the Great Lakes began to go down. It went down so fast in Lake Huron it left the fish hanging in the air. When things began to look real bad, folks came and told Paul Bunyan he'd just have to get rid of his corn and pumpkins. Paul was reasonable about it. First he went after the pumpkin vine. He spent four hours racing around trying to catch hold of the end, and finally did it by trapping it in a barn. He hitched Babe up to the end of the vine, but as fast as Babe pulled the vine grew. Babe ran faster and faster, and he was near Lake Ontario before he had the vine tight enough to pull it out.

Then Paul sized up his cornstalk. He figured he'd have to chop it down. He sharpened up his ax and spit on his hands. He made a good deep cut in that stalk, but before he could chip out a wedge the stalk grew up six feet, cut and all. Every time he made a cut it would shoot up out of reach before he could swing his ax again. Pretty soon he saw there wasn't any use going on this way. "Only way to kill this stalk is to cut off the top," he said. He hung his ax in his belt and started climbing. In about two hours he was completely out of sight. People just stood around and waited. They stood around two and a half days without any sight of Paul. Lars Larson called, "Paul!" but there was no answer. Erik Erikson and Hans Hanson called, "Paul!" But there wasn't any word from Paul Bunyan. So they waited some more. Two more days went by. No word from Paul. They decided that if everyone yelled at once maybe the sound would carry. So all together the two thousand eight hundred men and boys hollered, "Paul!" And sure enough, they heard his faint voice from up above.

"When you going to top that cornstalk?" they yelled back at him.

"Hasn't that top come down yet?" Paul hollered back. "I cut it off three days ago!"

And it was the truth, too. The stalk stopped growing, the water in the Great Lakes stopped falling, the Au Sable River began to run, the springs began to flow again, and things came back to normal. But it was a narrow escape.

592 Myths and Folk Tales

CLOSURE

Ask students to identify some of Paul's superhuman feats. Were any of the feats believable, or were they all wildly exaggerated?

EXTENSION AND ENRICHMENT

Geography. Have students use a map of the United States to locate the places mentioned in the tall tale. Have students trace Babe's cross-country trip that ended at the Grand Canyon.

For Study and Discussion

IDENTIFYING FACTS
1. Why did the other lumberjacks decide to use the double-bladed ax that Paul invented?
2. According to this story, how was the Grand Canyon created?
3. Why was it necessary for the giant cornstalk to be cut down?

INTERPRETING MEANINGS
4. What is the speaker's tone of voice (serious, sarcastic, humorous?)

APPLYING MEANINGS
5. What do you think is the reason for Paul Bunyan's popularity as a folk hero? Can you think of other characters like him?

Focus on Reading

ANECDOTES
An **anecdote** is a brief, entertaining narrative. The narrator tells a number of anecdotes that lead up to the incident with the cornstalk. Identify the different anecdotes in "Paul Bunyan's Cornstalk." How does each one relate to the final episode of the tale? How do these anecdotes contribute to your understanding of Paul Bunyan's character?

Literature and Geography

Changing Landscapes
In this tall tale Paul Bunyan gets credit for changing the American landscape. In other stories Paul digs a canal that turns out to be the Mississippi River and uses the dirt to create the Rocky Mountains and the Appalachians.

Making Connections: Activities
Read additional tales about Paul Bunyan and find out how he affected the geography of North America. Some sources to consult are *Ol' Paul* by Glen Rounds, *Paul Bunyan* by Esther Shepherd, and "Paul Bunyan: An American Hercules" by James Stevens.

Connecting Cultures

Tales About Giants
Some historians believe that the Paul Bunyan stories originated in Canada. They may have been adaptations of old French folk tales about giants. There are myths and legends about giants from many cultures around the world.

Making Connections: Activities
1. In your library locate tales about the following figures:
    Jack the Giant Killer
    Goliath
    Cyclops

    How do the stories about these giants compare with those about Paul Bunyan?
2. Read "A Voyage to Lilliput" in *Gulliver's Travels* by Jonathan Swift. How does Lemuel Gulliver seem to become a giant? What does he discover about people when he is bigger than they are?

Applying Meanings
5. His superhuman feats and his undaunted spirit are appealing. Other tall tale characters are Tony Beaver, the West Virginia super-lumberman, and Pecos Bill, the cowboy hero.

FOCUS ON READING
The different anecdotes include the use of Paul's invention—the double-bitted ax, Babe's furrowing of the Grand Canyon, the Big Blue Snow, and the problems caused by Paul's garden.

The initial anecdotes give background information about Paul and Babe. As the tales progress, so does the degree of exaggeration, leading up to the final, most exaggerated tale.

The tales highlight Paul's superhuman size and strength, his tenacity, and the awe and respect with which others regard him.

LITERATURE AND GEOGRAPHY
As an alternative activity, suggest that students write additional tales about how Paul Bunyan might have affected the geography around their own area.

TEACHING RESOURCES D
Teacher's Notes, p. 61
Reading Check, p. 64
Study Guide, p. 65
Language Skills, p. 66
Building Vocabulary, p. 69
Selection Vocabulary Test, p. 71
Selection Test, p. 72

AV RESOURCES BINDER
Audiocassette 3, Side B

594

Less mature readers may have some trouble at first with Kipling's long sentences and unusual vocabulary. The meanings of most of the unfamiliar words will be clear from the context. Before you begin the story, ask students to read the Language and Vocabulary box on page 596, and then have them listen for the sound effects mentioned in this section as you read aloud the first paragraph of the story. While they read the rest of the story in class or at home, ask them to write down any words they don't know. After they have finished reading, compile a master list of the unfamiliar words. Divide students into groups and give each group an equal number of words to research and define.

How the Whale Got His Throat

RUDYARD KIPLING

The illustrations for this story are the original drawings done by Rudyard Kipling for his *Just So Stories*.

Before You Read

Before you read about this Mariner (sailor) and the Whale, look up the word *whale* in an encyclopedia. You should discover that there are two kinds of whales, baleen and toothed. Instead of teeth, the baleens have hundreds of tiny "plates" that hang down from their upper jaws. Big as it is, a baleen whale can eat only tiny fish and plants, which it must sift through these plates (they are made of material like our fingernails). This story explains how whales came to have this "screen" in their mouths (Kipling calls it a "grating").

"How the Whale Got His Throat" is one of the *Just So Stories* that Kipling wrote for his own three children. As you read this story (or listen to a good reader read it aloud), look for places where the person telling the tale seems to be speaking as a parent to a child.

1. BACKGROUND

Whales are the largest animals on this planet. Like human beings, they are warm-blooded mammals. Large whales may migrate from one ocean to another twice a year.

The two suborders of whales are toothed whales (which include dolphins, porpoises, and sperm whales) and baleen whales (see Before You Read on this page) which are, in general, much larger than toothed whales. Baleen whales swim with their mouths open to take in and "strain" tiny fish and plankton. The largest baleens are more than 100 feet long and weigh more than 150 tons.

How the Whale Got His Throat 595

MEETING INDIVIDUAL NEEDS

ESL/LEP • Kipling uses several expressions that require explanation:
to be **out of harm's way** (page 596)
(out of danger)
He had his mummy's **leave** *to paddle,* (page 597)
(permission)
He swallowed them . . . into his . . . **inside cupboards** (page 598)
(stomach; belly)

1. LANGUAGE AND VOCABULARY

The Language and Vocabulary box focuses on the sound effects that Kipling uses in the story—rhyme, repetition, alliteration, and onomatopoeia. The Language and Vocabulary exercise on pages 599–600 gives students practice in identifying and using these techniques.

2. LITERARY ELEMENTS:

Sound Effects
What evidence can you find in this passage that the author likes to play with the sounds of words? Students may mention the rhyming words, the spelling twists, the alliteration, or the repetition of "silly" phrases like "small 'Stute."

Language and Vocabulary

1 Kipling loved words and all the funny sound effects he could create with them. In the second sentence of this story, for example, you will find a list of fish. All of these are real fish, though you probably have not heard of many of them. Notice that Kipling has found the names of fish that **rhyme** (*starfish* and *garfish, crab* and *dab*). And sometimes he twists the spelling of a name just a little bit so that it has a funnier sound (*pickereel* and *mackereel*). Like many old storytellers, Kipling uses **repetition** (notice how he repeats the clipped word *'stute* in the first paragraph). He also uses **alliteration**—the repetition of consonant sounds in words close together ("*N*ice but *n*ubbly"). You'll also hear **onomatopoeia** (on'ə·mat'ə·pē'ə)—words whose sounds echo their meaning (listen for the Whale "smacking" its lips). You'll enjoy this famous story best if you read it aloud to hear all its comical sound effects.

---

2 In the sea, once upon a time, O my Best Beloved, there was a Whale, and he ate fishes. He ate the starfish and the garfish, and the crab and the dab, and the plaice and the dace, and the skate and his mate, and the mackereel and the pickereel, and the really truly twirly-whirly eel. All the fishes he could find in all the sea he ate with his mouth—so! Till at last there was only one small fish left in all the sea, and he was a small 'Stute[1] Fish, and he swam a little behind the Whale's right ear, so as to be out of harm's way. Then the Whale stood up on his tail and said, "I'm hungry."

And the small 'Stute Fish said in a small 'stute voice, "Noble and generous Cetacean,[2] have you ever tasted Man?"

"No," said the Whale. "What is it like?"

"Nice," said the small 'Stute Fish. "Nice but nubbly."[3]

"Then fetch me some," said the Whale, and he made the sea froth up with his tail.

"One at a time is enough," said the 'Stute Fish. "If you swim to latitude Fifty North, longitude Forty West [that is magic], you will find, sitting *on* a raft, *in*

---

1. **'Stute** (stoot): short for *astute*, meaning "clever" or "shrewd."
2. **Cetacean** (si·tā'shən): the name of a group of fish and mammals, including the whale.
3. **nubbly**: lumpy.

596 Myths and Folk Tales

GEOGRAPHY LINK
Encourage students to use a globe or world map to locate the latitude and longitude marks mentioned in the story (latitude Fifty North, longitude Forty West). Have students place a symbol representing the raft on the map. Where is it? Is it in the middle of the sea as Kipling states?

the middle of the sea, with nothing on but a pair of blue canvas breeches, a pair of suspenders [you must *not* forget the suspenders, Best Beloved], and a jackknife, one shipwrecked Mariner, who, it is only fair to tell you, is a man of infinite-resource-and-sagacity.''[4]

So the Whale swam and swam to latitude Fifty North, longitude Forty West, as fast as he could swim, and *on* a raft, *in* the middle of the sea, *with* nothing to wear except a pair of blue canvas breeches, a pair of suspenders (you must particularly remember the suspenders, Best Beloved), *and* a jackknife, he found one single, solitary shipwrecked Mariner, trailing his toes in the water. (He had his mummy's leave to paddle, or else he would never have done it because he was a man of infinite-resource-and-sagacity.)

Then the Whale opened his mouth back and back and back till it nearly touched his tail, and he swallowed the shipwrecked Mariner, and the raft he was sitting on, and

---

4. **sagacity** (sə·gas′ə·tē): wisdom; judgment.

1. GUIDED READING:
Visualizing
These details help students picture the whale in their minds. By repeating the word *back*, Kipling emphasizes the enormous size of the whale.

2. VISUAL CONNECTIONS
Have students imagine that they are the person being swallowed by the whale. Tell them to freewrite about what is going through their minds.

MEETING INDIVIDUAL NEEDS
ESL/LEP • Students will encounter the word *hiccough* on this page. Point out that the *–gh* ending is pronounced as a *p*. This word can be used as a departure point to demonstrate several different pronunciations in English for the *–ough* ending. Write the following words on the chalkboard, and invite the class to suggest correct pronunciations: *through, thorough, enough, hiccough,* and *bought.*

1. GUIDED READING:
Understanding Cause and Effect
What is the cause of the whale's unhappiness? The Mariner's actions are the cause.

2. GUIDED READING:
Making Inferences
What can you infer about how the whale might have been able to swim if he did not have the hiccoughs? The whale would have been able to swim faster.

---

his blue canvas breeches, and the suspenders (which you *must* not forget), *and* the jackknife. He swallowed them all down into his warm, dark, inside cupboards, and then he smacked his lips—so, and turned around three times on his tail.

But as soon as the Mariner, who was a man of infinite-resource-and-sagacity, found himself truly inside the Whale's warm, dark, inside cupboards, he stumped and he jumped and he thumped and he bumped, and he pranced and he danced, and he banged and he clanged, and he hit and he bit, and he leaped and he creeped, and he prowled and he howled, and he hopped and he dropped, and he cried and he sighed, and he crawled and he bawled, and he stepped and he lepped, and he danced hornpipes⁵ where he shouldn't, and the Whale felt most unhappy indeed. (*Have you forgotten the suspenders?*)

So he said to the 'Stute Fish, "This man is very nubbly, and besides he is making me hiccough. What shall I do?"

"Tell him to come out," said the 'Stute Fish.

So the Whale called down his own throat to the shipwrecked Mariner, "Come out and behave yourself. I've got the hiccoughs."

"Nay, nay!" said the Mariner. "Not so, but far otherwise. Take me to my natal shore and the white cliffs of Albion,⁶ and I'll think about it." And he began to dance more than ever.

"You had better take him home," said the 'Stute Fish to the Whale. "I ought to have warned you that he is a man of infinite-resource-and-sagacity."

So the Whale swam and swam and swam, with both flippers and his tail, as hard as he could for the hiccoughs; and at last he saw the Mariner's natal shore and the white cliffs of Albion, and he rushed halfway up the beach, and opened his mouth wide and wide and wide, and said, "Change here for Winchester, Ashuelot, Nashua, Keene, and stations on the *Fitchburg* Road"; and just as he said "Fitch," the Mariner walked out of his mouth. But while the Whale had been swimming, the Mariner, who was indeed a person of infinite-resource-and-sagacity, had taken his jackknife and cut up the raft into a little square grating all running crisscross, and he had tied it firm with his suspenders (*now you know why you were not to forget the suspenders!*), and he dragged that grating good and tight into the Whale's throat, and there it stuck! Then he recited the following *Sloka*,⁷ which, as you have not heard it, I will now proceed to relate:

> *By means of a grating*
> *I have stopped your ating.*

For the Mariner, he was also a Hi-ber-

---

5. **hornpipes:** lively dances, originally danced by sailors.
6. **natal shore . . . cliffs of Albion:** the natal shore is the shore where he was born; Albion is another word for England.

7. ***Sloka*** (slō′kə): a couplet of Sanskrit verse. Kipling is being humorous here in describing his slangy rhyming couplet as classical formal verse in the ancient language of India.

598 Myths and Folk Tales

CLOSURE

Discuss with students the role of the trickster in folk literature. Call on volunteers to suggest the personal qualities of these characters and to describe tricksters they know from other folk tales.

EXTENSION AND ENRICHMENT

Geography. Have students use a globe to find the latitude and longitude of their own community. Continue by asking them to tell what country or place in the world they would most like to visit and why. Have students use the globe to find the latitude and longitude of that place.

---

ni-an.[8] And he stepped out on the shingle, and went home to his mother, who had given him leave to trail his toes in the water; and he married and lived happily ever afterward. So did the Whale. But from that day on, the grating in his throat, which he could neither cough up nor swallow down, prevented him eating anything except very, very small fish. And that is the reason why whales nowadays never eat men and boys or little girls.

The small 'Stute Fish went and hid himself in the mud under the Door Sills of the Equator. He was afraid that the Whale might be angry with him.

The Sailor took the jackknife home. He was wearing the blue canvas breeches when he walked out on the shingle. The suspenders were left behind, you see, to tie the grating with; and that is the end of *that* tale.

When the cabin portholes are dark and green
  Because of the seas outside;
When the ship goes wop *(with a wiggle between)*
And the steward falls into the soup tureen,
  And the trunks begin to slide;
When Nursey lies on the floor in a heap,
And Mummy tells you to let her sleep,
And you aren't waked or washed or dressed,
Why, then you will know (if you haven't guessed)
You're "Fifty North and Forty West!"

---

8. **Hi·ber·ni·an** (hī·bûr′nē·ən): Irishman. (They are said to be great bards, or poets.)

For Study and Discussion

IDENTIFYING FACTS

1. The 'Stute Fish suggests that the Whale go for a new food, Man. Why does this new food give the Whale hiccoughs?
2. Why does the storyteller keep reminding his listeners to remember the Mariner's suspenders?
3. How does the Mariner change the Whale's throat? How does this explain why the Whale doesn't eat people today?

INTERPRETING MEANINGS

4. Who is the **trickster** in this story? Is it the 'Stute Fish, the Mariner, or the Whale? Give a reason for your opinion.
5. Which of these statements is an important idea in the story?
   a. Advice is easy to give, but hard to take.
   b. Human beings may seem weak, but they can use their wits to defeat the biggest animal in the sea.
   c. No one is as smart as the Whale.

APPLYING MEANINGS

6. What other stories do you know of in which a person is swallowed whole by a sea monster? What happened to these people? Are these other stories also told to teach lessons?

Language and Vocabulary

SOUND EFFECTS

Kipling's prose often sounds like poetry. He uses **alliteration**, words close together that contain the same consonant sound. He uses

How the Whale Got His Throat

---

1. GUIDED READING:
Making Inferences About Character
In addition to his being "a man of infinite-resource-and-sagacity," what else can you infer about the Mariner? He is brave and he thinks quickly.

FOR STUDY AND DISCUSSION
Identifying Facts
1. The Mariner jumps and bumps and dances a hornpipe inside the whale.
2. The narrator is arousing suspense about what will be done with the suspenders.
3. The Mariner makes a grating from his raft and suspenders and sticks it in the whale's throat.
   The holes in the grating are too small to let a human being through.

Interpreting Meanings
4. Arguments can be made for either the 'Stute Fish or the Mariner.
   The 'Stute Fish, who knows the Mariner's abilities, talks the Whale into eating him anyway and then watches to see what will happen. The Mariner is clever enough to make himself indigestible, get a ride home, and prevent the Whale from ever eating another human being.
5. Idea **b** is the idea best illustrated by the story.

SCIENCE LINK

Suggest that students find out more about the varieties of fish mentioned in Kipling's story. You could assign several students to look up the varieties and to find one interesting or unusual fact about each fish. Encourage them to look for photographs or pictures to share with the class.

Applying Meanings

6. Many students will know the Biblical account of Jonah or the story of Pinocchio, in which an animated wooden puppet is swallowed by a whale.

In those accounts, the heroes are coughed up on shore.

Each of the heroes learns a lesson about his own behavior.

LANGUAGE AND VOCABULARY
Sound Effects
For answers, see the **Teaching Guide** at the beginning of the unit.

ILLUSTRATING THE TALE

Look for a breakdown of the story into approximately seven frames or scenes: the Whale saying, "I'm hungry"; the 'Stute Fish saying to the Whale, "Have you ever tasted Man?"; the Whale swallowing the Mariner, raft and all; the Mariner dancing inside the Whale; the conversation between the Whale and the Mariner; the Mariner making a grating; and the Mariner stuffing the grating in the Whale's throat as he steps ashore in England.

600

---

onomatopoeia, words whose sounds echo their meaning. He **repeats** words and phrases for a rhythmic effect. He even uses words that **rhyme**.

1. Find and read aloud four passages that use some of these techniques.

2. Write one sentence (it can be a silly sentence) in which you use at least three onomatopoetic words. Here are some words for ideas:

buzz	drip	lap	slurp
cluck	hiss	lick	snap
crack	holler	pop	squawk
crash	hoot	purr	whir
crunch	hum	rattle	whisper

3. Write one sentence in which you repeat one consonant sound at least four times. (It can be a silly sentence.)

Illustrating the Tale

Make a comic strip of "How the Whale Got His Throat." First decide which incidents you will illustrate; each incident will get one frame. Then write the dialogue that will be in those "conversation bubbles." You can't use all of Kipling's dialogue, so you will have to decide which parts of it are most important.

About the Author

Rudyard Kipling (1865–1936) was born in Bombay, India. His father, an illustrator, taught at the Lahore School of Industrial Art. One of Rudyard's earliest memories was of listening to his Indian baby sitters as they told him folk tales about jungle animals.

600 Myths and Folk Tales

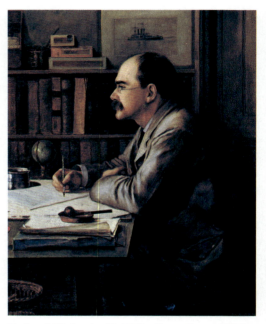

Rudyard Kipling by Sir Philip Burne-Jones (1899). Oil on canvas.

National Portrait Gallery, London.

When Rudyard was five years old, his parents sent him and his younger sister to England. They did this to protect them from the fevers that killed so many youngsters in India. For the next twelve years, Rudyard lived a very hard life, first in a foster home, where he was cruelly treated, and then at a boarding school, where he was bullied and beaten. When he was seventeen, he returned to India and began publishing humorous poems and short stories. By the time he returned to England, only a few years later, he was already famous. Kipling married an American and lived in Vermont for four years. There he wrote his best-known books for children: *The Jungle Books* and a novel called *Captains Courageous*. Kipling won the Nobel Prize for literature in 1907.

OBJECTIVES
Students will identify the problem in a folk tale and its important ideas.

FOCUS/MOTIVATION
Establishing a Purpose for Reading. Ask students to decide what is the most important idea of this folktale.
Prereading Journal. Have students jot down their answer to the question posed in the title.

Why Tortoise's Shell Is Not Smooth

An African Folk Tale

CHINUA ACHEBE

TEACHING RESOURCES D
Teacher's Notes, p. 74
Reading Check, p. 77
Study Guide, pp. 78, 79
Language Skills, p. 80
Building Vocabulary, p. 83
Selection Vocabulary Test, p. 85
Selection Test, p. 86

AV RESOURCES BINDER
Audiocassette 3, Side B

VISUAL CONNECTIONS
A tortoise is a turtle that lives on land. Its reputation for cleverness may stem from the fact that it protects itself by hiding inside its shell. Tortoises also live a long time, some for more than 150 years. You may wish to have students research tortoises in an encyclopedia or other reference source.

READING THE SELECTION
You may want to read aloud the beginning of the story, down to Ezinma's comment "But he had no wings" (middle of column 2, page 602). Have students read the story silently until they reach the trick that Tortoise plays on the birds (middle of column 3, page 603). Then ask students to summarize what has happened up to this point and predict what might happen in the rest of the story. Have students finish reading the story on their own.

1. BACKGROUND
Have a student locate Nigeria on a map of Africa. Explain that the Ibo are a major ethnic group among the more than two hundred groups that have their own culture and traditions in Nigeria. More than twelve million people speak the language Ibo.

2. VISUAL CONNECTIONS
Benin was a West African kingdom that flourished in the mid-1400s to the mid-1600s. Benin sculptures from this period are world famous. Many of these sculptures honored the king of Benin. Benin was conquered by the British in 1897.

3. GUIDED READING:
Drawing Conclusions
Based on this conversation, what conclusion can you draw about Tortoise's past? He has caused trouble.

4. GUIDED READING:
Interpreting Meaning
What ability does Tortoise's "sweet tongue" imply? He is a persuasive speaker.

Before You Read

1 This folk tale comes from the Ibo people of eastern Nigeria. It is taken from a novel that describes Ibo life in the early 1900s.

In this part of the novel, a mother tells her little girl a story. The mother learned this story from her own mother, and now she is passing it on. The story gives an answer to the question: Why isn't the tortoise's shell smooth? As you read, think about why parents passed this story on to their children for hundreds of years. What is this folk tale really about? What are some of the things it teaches?

Head of a woman. Benin (be·nēn') bronze sculpture. Made in Nigeria before 1600.

Low voices, broken now and again by singing, reached Okonkwo from his wives' huts as each woman and her children told folk stories. Ekwefi and her daughter, Ezinma, sat on a mat on the floor. It was Ekwefi's turn to tell a story.

"Once upon a time," she began, "all the birds were invited to a feast in the sky. They were very happy and began to prepare themselves for the great day. They painted their bodies with red cam wood and drew beautiful patterns on them with *uli*.

"Tortoise saw all these preparations and soon discovered what it all meant. Nothing that happened in the world of the animals ever escaped his notice; he was full of cunning. As soon as he heard of the great feast in the sky, his throat began to itch at the very thought. There was a famine in those days and Tortoise had not eaten a good meal for two moons. His body rattled like a piece of dry stick in his empty shell. So he began to plan how he would go to the sky."

"But he had no wings," said Ezinma.

"Be patient," replied her mother. "That is the story. Tortoise had no wings, but he went to the birds and asked to be allowed to go with them.

" 'We know you too well,' said the birds when they had heard him. 'You are full of cunning and you are ungrateful. If we allow you to come with us, you will soon begin your mischief.'

" 'You do not know me,' said Tortoise. 'I am a changed man. I have learned that a man who makes trouble for others is also making it for himself.'

"Tortoise had a sweet tongue, and within a short time all the birds agreed that

602 Myths and Folk Tales

MEETING INDIVIDUAL NEEDS

ESL/LEP • The main adjective used to describe and introduce the tortoise is *cunning*. Although this word appears twice on page 602, neither context offers much help to students in guessing its meaning. Therefore, before assigning the story, write *cunning* on the chalkboard and ask the class to provide a definition or synonyms. Most important, ask students to give examples of cunning behavior.

---

he was a changed man, and they each gave him a feather, with which he made two wings.

"At last the great day came, and Tortoise was the first to arrive at the meeting place. When all the birds had gathered together, they set off in a body. Tortoise was very happy and voluble[1] as he flew among the birds, and he was soon chosen as the man to speak for the party because he was a great orator.

" 'There is one important thing which we must not forget,' he said as they flew on their way. 'When people are invited to a great feast like this, they take new names for the occasion. Our hosts in the sky will expect us to honor this age-old custom.'

"None of the birds had heard of this custom but they knew that Tortoise, in spite of his failings in other directions, was a widely traveled man who knew the customs of different peoples. And so they each took a new name. When they had all taken names, Tortoise also took one. He was to be called *All of you*.

"At last the party arrived in the sky and their hosts were very happy to see them. Tortoise stood up in his many-colored plumage and thanked them for their invitation. His speech was so eloquent that all the birds were glad they had brought him, and nodded their heads in approval of all he said. Their hosts took him as the king of the birds, especially as he looked somewhat different from the others.

"After kola nuts had been presented and eaten, the people of the sky set before their guests the most delectable dishes Tortoise had ever seen or dreamed of. The soup was brought out hot from the fire and in the very pot in which it had been cooked. It was full of meat and fish. Tortoise began to sniff aloud. There was pounded yam and also yam pottage[2] cooked with palm oil and fresh fish. There were also pots of palm wine. When everything had been set before the guests, one of the people of the sky came forward and tasted a little from each pot. He then invited the birds to eat. But Tortoise jumped to his feet and asked, 'For whom have you prepared this feast?'

" 'For all of you,' replied the man.

"Tortoise turned to the birds and said, 'You remember that my name is *All of you*. The custom here is to serve the spokesman first and the others later. They will serve you when I have eaten.'

"He began to eat and the birds grumbled angrily. The people of the sky thought it must be their custom to leave all the food for their king. And so Tortoise ate the best part of the food and then drank two pots of palm wine, so that he was full of food and drink and his body filled out in his shell.

"The birds gathered around to eat what was left and to peck at the bones he had thrown all about the floor. Some of them were too angry to eat. They chose to fly home on an empty stomach. But before they left, each took back the feather he had lent to Tortoise. And there he stood in his

---

1. **voluble** (vol′yə·bəl): talkative.
2. **pottage** (pot′ij): stew or thick soup.

---

1. GUIDED READING:
Interpreting Meaning
What is another way of saying that they "set off in a body"? They set off together.

2
An *orator* is a speaker.

3. GUIDED READING:
Drawing Conclusions
Based on the way they treat guests, what conclusions can you draw about the people of the sky? They are good hosts and excellent cooks. They are polite. To make sure that the food is good, they even taste a bit from each pot.

TRANSPARENCIES 34 & 35
Fine Art
Theme: *Traditional Tales* – invites students to explore artworks that portray traditional tales handed down through the generations.

1. GUIDED READING:
Drawing Conclusions
What conclusion do you draw from the fact that Tortoise is tricked by Parrot? What lesson about cleverness does this story teach? You can be too clever for your own good, or, as Tortoise says, someone "who makes trouble for others is also making it for himself."

hard shell, full of food and wine, but without any wings to fly home. He asked the birds to take a message for his wife, but they all refused. In the end, Parrot, who had felt more angry than the others, suddenly changed his mind and agreed to take the message.

" 'Tell my wife,' said Tortoise, 'to bring out all the soft things in my house and cover the compound[3] with them so that I can jump down from the sky without very great danger.'

1 "Parrot promised to deliver the message, and then flew away. But when he reached Tortoise's house, he told his wife to bring out all the hard things in the house.

3. **compound**: a fenced yard with buildings in it.

And so she brought out her husband's hoes, machetes, spears, guns, and even his cannon. Tortoise looked down from the sky and saw his wife bringing things out, but it was too far to see what they were. When all seemed ready, he let himself go. He fell and fell and fell until he began to fear that he would never stop falling. And then, like the sound of his cannon, he crashed on the compound."

"Did he die?" asked Ezinma.

"No," replied Ekwefi. "His shell broke into pieces. But there was a great medicine man in the neighborhood. Tortoise's wife sent for him, and he gathered all the bits of shell and stuck them together. That is why Tortoise's shell is not smooth."

604 Myths and Folk Tales

CLOSURE

Have students list the human qualities of the characters in this tale. Then ask them to briefly state the message the tale has for people today.

EXTENSION AND ENRICHMENT

Social Studies. Divide the class into groups. Ask each group to choose a different African country to research. Let each group decide if it will present its findings in an oral or a written report.

For Study and Discussion

IDENTIFYING FACTS

1. Why is Tortoise especially eager to go to the feast in the sky?
2. What **problem** does he have in getting to the feast? How does he solve it?
3. Why does Tortoise say that everyone needs a new name? What name does he take?
4. Why does Tortoise have to jump down from the sky? How does Parrot trick him?

INTERPRETING MEANINGS

5. At the beginning of the folk tale, what is the birds' opinion of Tortoise? Does the story show that this opinion is right or wrong? Explain why you think so.
6. Which of the following statements expresses an important **idea** in this story?
   a. Everyone deserves a second chance.
   b. A person who makes trouble for others is also making it for himself or herself.
   c. A generous person will be rewarded.

APPLYING MEANINGS

7. What is it about a tortoise that might make people think it could be a good **trickster**? What is it about birds that might make people think they could be easily fooled? What other animals would be good tricksters?

Writing About Literature

MAKING UP A "HOW AND WHY" STORY

Think of three things in nature that might seem mysterious to a young child. Write a how or why question a child might ask about each of these things. Here are some examples: Why do dogs wag their tails? How did the giraffe get its long neck? Why do mosquitoes buzz?

After you've written three questions, ask a classmate to choose one of them to answer. Then you choose one of your classmate's three questions to answer. Let your imagination supply the answer, not science. Write your answer in one or two paragraphs. Try to think of a young child as your audience.

About the Author

Chinua Achebe (chin′yōō·ä a·chē′bē) (1930–) grew up during the time when Nigeria was ruled by the British. He was born in Ogidi, a large village in eastern Nigeria. He graduated from University College and worked in radio broadcasting for several

Why Tortoise's Shell Is Not Smooth 605

FOR STUDY AND DISCUSSION

Identifying Facts

1. There is a famine at the time, and Tortoise's body rattles in his shell because he has not eaten well for two months.
2. The feast will be in the sky, and Tortoise has no wings.

   By insisting that he is a changed person, Tortoise persuades the birds to give him feathers from which he makes wings.
3. Tortoise plans to use his new name to get first choice of the food when he asks the hosts, "For whom have you prepared this feast?" (page 603).

   Tortoise calls himself "All of you" (page 603).
4. The angry birds take back their feathers, destroying Tortoise's wings.

   Parrot tricks Tortoise by telling Tortoise's wife to put out all the hard things in the house instead of all the soft things.

Interpreting Meanings

5. At the beginning of the folk tale, the birds consider Tortoise a cunning troublemaker.

   The story shows that this opinion is right, because Tortoise cunningly deprives the birds of their feast.

MEETING INDIVIDUAL NEEDS

Visual and Auditory Learners • Before students write a "how and why" story on their own, you might want to review the "how and why" stories students have read so far. You might want to have students work in four groups with each group preparing a critical presentation of one of the "how and why" stories. Ask each group to prepare a list with the name of the story, the country of origin, the setting, the characters, the plot or the conflict, and the theme. Then, have the groups select a spokesperson and share their information with the class. Recorders from each group could write the information in columns on the chalkboard so that the stories could be easily compared.

---

6. Idea **b** expresses an important idea in the story. Ideas **a** and **c** are not supported by the story.

Applying Meanings

7. Answers will vary; these are representative:

A tortoise might appear to be a good trickster because it can hide within its shell.

Birds might appear easily fooled because their small size and their hopping and pecking movements make them look silly.

Other animals that would be good tricksters are the fox, monkey, snake, and rabbit.

WRITING ABOUT LITERATURE

Making Up a "How and Why" Story

Paragraphs will vary greatly. Evaluate them on the basis of how well they meet these criteria: The story fully answers the classmate's question in an imaginative way; it has characteristics typical of "how and why" stories; it is told in terms a young child can understand.

---

years in Lagos, the former capital of Nigeria. His first and most famous novel, which he wrote for adults, is called *Things Fall Apart.* This story is set in a village of the Ibo people in Nigeria in the early 1900s. In the novel, Achebe shows how folklore helps to keep things from falling apart, as the modern world forces changes on traditional ways of life. Achebe's other works include the novels *No Longer at Ease* and *Arrow of God,* and a collection of short stories, *Girls at War and Other Stories.*

Behind the Scenes

Rapping About Story Forms

A popular African American writer talks about the origin of stories:

One of the earliest forms of the story that we made up in Africa was the fable. A fable is a tale about animals . . . but really about people. It instructs us; it teaches us something about human behavior. But people do not like to be told straight out about themselves, so the storyteller acts as if he's just talking about buzzards or rabbits or something. When we came to these shores years ago, we brought these tales along. We even made up new ones, for there was much peculiar behavior on the part of people here to talk about and to teach about. So often, while drumming in the yard, we would tell stories about crafty foxes or sly monkeys or big dumb bears. We were often talking about our situation as slaves, trying to survive through our wits, trying to instruct each other through a "code" language.

This technique—this way of talking about one thing while really talking about another—is called "signifyin'." For instance, a beautiful sister in her beautiful Afro walks past a group of brothers. Right away they start signifyin'.

"Mmmm, what a fine spring day, right, Joe?"

"Sure is. Can't remember when we've had such beautiful weather."

"Yesirree. Such a lovely day, I feel I could fly."

"Well fly, brother, fly."

In other words—the girl is fine.

—Toni Cade Bambara

Myths and Folk Tales

TALES THAT AMUSE AND AMAZE

Tales told to amuse and amaze come from all parts of the world. The most popular of these tales is the fairy tale. For generations, fairy tales have given form to our nightmares and our hopes. Most of all, of course, fairy tales have amused and amazed us with their extraordinary imagination. This is the imagination of the human family, the imagination of the "folk," who cannot resist the magic of the words "Once upon a time . . ."

Bluebeard gives his wife the keys to the castle. Colored engraving by Gustave Doré (1867).

The Granger Collection, New York.

INTRODUCING THE TALES THAT AMUSE AND AMAZE

Fairy tales are perhaps the kind of story that students are most familiar with. You might want to introduce this section by having students list familiar fairy tales, such as "Snow White and the Seven Dwarfs," "Cinderella," "Rumplestiltskin," and "Bluebeard." Have students make generalizations from their list about characteristics of the fairy tale. These are sample generalizations.

1. The tale usually pits good against evil (Snow White vs. the wicked queen).
2. Good wins in the end.
3. The hero or heroine often must undergo a test of virtue or courage.
4. A magical metamorphosis is often involved.

OBJECTIVES

Students will distinguish realistic from supernatural events; identify major events and put them in chronological order; and identify words formed with prefixes and roots.

FOCUS/MOTIVATION

Building on Prior Knowledge. Review with students the meaning of suspense, the curiosity and tension we feel when we don't know how a conflict or contest will turn out or how a problem will be solved.

Prereading Journal. Have students write one sentence that creates suspense. ("Gil's foot suddenly stepped out into thin air." "Lenore opened her eyes to see a hairy face in front of her.")

Illustration for "The Story of the King of the Ebony Isles" from *The Arabian Nights*. Watercolor by Edmund Dulac (1882–1953).

© British Museum.

608 Myths and Folk Tales

READING THE SELECTION

Ask a student to list on the chalkboard the names of the characters in the story as you introduce them: Ali Baba, a poor but honest woodcutter; Cassim, Ali's rich brother; Forty Thieves and their Leader; Ali's wife; Cassim's wife; the Cobbler, who cannot keep a secret; Morgiana, Ali's faithful slave; and Ali's son. Tell students that the events in the plot alternate between two general settings, the forest and the city. Suggest that students draw a story map as they read. Tell them to draw a new rectangle whenever the general setting changes. Inside each rectangle they might write a summary (one or two sentences) telling what happens there. Ask students to use numbers or arrows to show the order of events.

Ali Baba and the Forty Thieves
A Middle Eastern Folk Tale

Retold by ELISABETH GILLE

Before You Read

This folk tale is from a collection of Persian, Indian, and Arabian stories called *The Thousand and One Nights* (also known as *The Arabian Nights*). The first tale in the collection tells about Scheherazade (shə·her′ə·zäd′), the daughter of the king's adviser. This king hated all women because his beloved first wife had betrayed him. And so the king killed his first wife. Then, to get even with females in general, he married a different girl every day and had her killed the next morning. Scheherazade eventually was married to the king. But being clever as well as beautiful, she thought of a plan to stay alive. On the night of her marriage, Scheherazade began telling her husband a story. When she got to the most exciting part, she told him he must wait until the following night to find out what happened next. Because her stories hooked his interest, the king didn't want to kill his storyteller. And so the clever Scheherazade went on telling part of a story every night for a thousand and one nights. By that time, the king had fallen in love with her, and "they lived happily ever after."

"Ali Baba and the Forty Thieves" is set in ancient Persia (modern-day Iran). As you read this story of Scheherazade's, notice how it rises to one exciting point after another. There are at least four places in this story where Scheherazade might have stopped. Can you find them?

TEACHING RESOURCES D
Teacher's Notes, p. 88
Reading Check, p. 91
Reading Focus, p. 92
Study Guide, pp. 93, 94
Language Skills, p. 95
Building Vocabulary, p. 99
Selection Vocabulary Test, p. 101
Selection Test, p. 102

1. BACKGROUND

Ask students to find Iran, Iraq, Saudi Arabia, Afghanistan, and Turkey on a world map. Explain that the stories in *The Arabian Nights* came from the area that was once part of the Persian Empire. In the 900s, the Persian Empire included most of the lands from Turkey to India, plus northern Africa, Spain, and Portugal. After the tales were gathered, they were translated into Arabic, which is why the collection is called *The Arabian Nights*.

MUSIC LINK
To give students a musical introduction to this Middle Eastern folk tale, you might bring a recording of the music from the ballet *Scheherazade* by Nicolai Rimsky-Korsakov. You might even be able to find a copy of a children's version that narrates the tale along with the music.

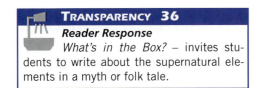

TRANSPARENCY 36
Reader Response
What's in the Box? – invites students to write about the supernatural elements in a myth or folk tale.

1. GUIDED READING:
Contrasting Characters
The disparity in the economic status of the two brothers is highlighted. It is Cassim's greed that ultimately leads to his death.

2. LITERARY ELEMENTS:
Fairy Tale
What supernatural event— an event that could not happen in real life—happens here? A cave opens and closes when someone says magic words.

3
Bolts are rolls.

Language and Vocabulary

A prefix is a group of letters added to the beginning of a word or word root to change its meaning. (A **root** is the basic part of the word from which other words can be built.) You can figure out the meaning of some new words if you know what their prefixes mean. Many prefixes came into English from the Latin language. For example, the prefix *dis-* comes from a Latin word meaning "apart" or "away." It also signals "opposite meaning." When you put the prefix *dis-* in front of the root *like*, you get *dislike*, the opposite of *like*. Another useful Latin prefix is *re-*, meaning "back" or "again." You'll find the prefixes *dis-* and *re-* as you read this story.

1 **O**nce upon a time in ancient Persia, there were two brothers. One, named Cassim, having married an heiress,¹ had become one of the richest merchants in the city. The other, Ali Baba, having married a young girl as poor as he was, had as his only means of livelihood whatever he could earn chopping wood in the nearby forest, loading it onto the three donkeys which were his only worldly goods, and bringing it to the city to sell. One day, while working in the forest, Ali Baba saw a large troop of horsemen galloping toward him. Fearing they might be thieves, he dispersed² his donkeys and climbed a tall tree from which he could watch, yet not be seen. The horsemen dismounted, each unloading a bag from behind his saddle. Their leader walked over to a great rock close to the tree where Ali Baba had taken refuge, and **2** pronounced these words: "Open Sesame!"³ Instantly, a door swung open, and the whole troop disappeared through it.

Half an hour later, the door reopened. The thieves (there were forty of them) came out of the cave and the door closed behind them as the leader pronounced the words: "Close Sesame!"

As soon as they were out of sight, Ali Baba climbed down the tree and out of curiosity walked over and stood in front of the rock. Barely had he spoken the magic words "Open Sesame!" when the door opened wide. Ali Baba entered the cave. To his amazement, he discovered heaps of rich merchandise, bolts of fine silks and **3** brocades,⁴ carpets of great worth, leather purses full of gold and silver! Here was the

---

1. **heiress:** a woman who has inherited a lot of money.
2. **dispersed:** scattered.
3. **sesame** (ses′ə·mē): a plant. (You've probably tasted food coated with sesame seeds.)
4. **brocades** (brō·kāds′): rich woven fabrics.

610   Myths and Folk Tales

MEDIA LINK
After you have introduced the background for this tale from *The Arabian Nights,* you might want to tell students that one of the tales from this collection has been made into a movie. See if they can guess that *Aladdin* was taken from *The Thousand and One Nights* and has been one of the most popular of the tales. If you have time and students have not seen the movie, you might arrange a viewing for the class.

---

1 treasure the thieves had collected during many years. Without hesitating, Ali Baba gathered up as much as his three donkeys could carry, strapped the bags on their backs, and placed some firewood on top in order to conceal the gold. He then returned to the city and told his wife of his adventure. As he emptied the sacks in front of her, great piles of gold pieces lay at her feet. She could hardly believe her eyes. As soon as she recovered from her surprise, she ran over to her sister-in-law's to borrow a scale to determine the exact value of this fortune.

But Cassim's wife, wondering what the poor Ali Baba could possibly own worth weighing, secretly coated the scale with tallow[5] before giving it to her. When her sister-in-law returned the scale, one goldpiece had indeed stuck to the tallow. His wife told Cassim of her trick and he **2** ran to his brother, who had to tell him how he happened to discover the thieves' hideout, and where it was. Cassim immediately saddled ten mules, loaded them with huge chests, and went to the forest. Standing in front of the rock Ali Baba had described, he pronounced the magic words and the door opened. But alas! When he was ready to leave, the door which he had closed would not open. He could no longer remember the necessary words! In vain he shouted, "Open Barley!" "Open Millet!"[6] The door obstinately remained shut.

---

5. **tallow:** the fat of certain animals, used to make candles and soap (a sticky substance).
6. **barley . . . millet** (mil′it): other kinds of grasses whose seeds are used for food.

The thieves soon returned. They discovered Cassim, killed him, and cut his body into four pieces which they placed at the entrance to the cave in order to frighten off anyone else. Ali Baba, worried by his brother's long absence, went to find him. Horrorstruck when he saw what had happened, he carried the corpse back to his house. There he ordered his faithful slave, Morgiana, to have the body sewn together by a skillful cobbler so that the neighbors would believe Cassim had died a natural death, and the thieves would not recognize him. Actually, finding that the body had been removed, the thieves realized somebody now knew the location of their retreat. The leader came to the city to inquire about the missing body, and the cobbler, who could not keep a secret, blurted out the whole story. **3**

Returning to his comrades, the leader said, "A certain person named Ali Baba knows of our secret hiding place. He must die! Here is my plan. I will go to him disguised as an honest merchant. I'll take with me twenty mules, each carrying two enormous oil jars. Of these forty jars, only one will be filled with oil; the others will each hide one of you, armed to the teeth. Ali Baba will certainly offer me shelter for the night, and I will have the jars placed in rows in the courtyard. Once darkness has fallen, and when all in the house are asleep, I'll toss some pebbles down from my window. At this signal, you are to split open your jars with the knives with which you will have been provided. Then, fully armed, we will throw ourselves upon Ali

---

1. **GUIDED READING:**
Making Inferences About Character
What can you infer about Ali Baba's character so far? He is curious and brave; he is also cautious and intelligent.

2. **GUIDED READING:**
Identifying Pronoun Referents
To whom does the pronoun him refer in "who had to tell him"? To whom does the he refer in "how he happened"? "Him" is Cassim. "He" is Ali.

3. **GUIDED READING:**
Understanding Cause and Effect
What two mistakes does Ali Baba make that cause the thieves to connect him with Cassim? He takes the corpse home. He trusts the cobbler.

MEETING INDIVIDUAL NEEDS
ESL/LEP • This page contains several idiomatic expressions that may require explanation. Write the following expressions on the chalkboard, and ask the class to restate them in simple terms:
put me up for the night, the time was ripe, took to his heels, struck up a friendship, showered her with gifts.

1. LITERARY ELEMENTS:
Suspense
It is likely that Scheherazade would have stopped telling the story after the leader's speech to his gang or after his speech to Ali Baba. Earlier, she might have stopped at the point at which Cassim is trapped in the cave.

2. GUIDED READING:
Recognizing Multiple Meanings
Have students give the different meanings of *draw*. In this sentence *draw* means "take out," as with a cup or bowl.

3. GUIDED READING:
Making Inferences About Character
What does this passage reveal about Morgiana? She is hard-working. She is calm in the face of danger. She thinks for herself. She is clever and loyal. She can be cold-blooded.

---

1 Baba and his servants, who, taken thus by surprise, will not offer much resistance."

Accordingly, twenty mules were loaded with two jars apiece. Thirty-nine jars held a thief, and the last jar was filled with oil. The leader then led them to the city. They arrived about an hour after sundown, as had been planned, and went at once to Ali Baba's house. They found him outside his doorway enjoying the evening air. The leader said, "My lord, I'm taking these oil jars to sell in the market. But darkness has overtaken me, and I do no know where to seek lodging. I would be most grateful if you could put me up for the night."

Ali Baba, suspecting nothing, courteously welcomed the false merchant, offered him supper, had a bed prepared, and ordered his slaves to set the jars in the courtyard. Before retiring, Morgiana wanted to make preparations for next morning's breakfast. But her lamp went out. As there was no more oil in the house, **2** she decided to draw some from one of the jars in the courtyard. She had barely reached the first jar when she heard a whisper: **3** "Has the time come?" Sensing danger, but without showing alarm, she calmly answered, "No, not yet." She then guessed the truth, that probably only one of the jars contained oil. Cleverly locating it, she drew off enough to fill a large caldron⁷ and put it on the stove to boil.

When it was ready, she carried it to the courtyard and silently poured enough boiling oil into each jar to suffocate and kill the thief inside. A little later, the leader, feeling the time was ripe, gave the agreed signal. When there was no response, he thought his comrades must have fallen asleep and he came down to wake them up himself. Overcome when he saw what had happened, he took to his heels and fled.

Next morning, Morgiana told her master everything. Ali Baba, deeply impressed and filled with gratitude, said, "I pledge you my word that before I die I will recompense⁸ you as you deserve. In the meantime, I grant you your freedom as of this moment. But let us hurry to bury the thieves secretly so that no one may suspect their fate. For if any hint of this were to leak out, it might easily be connected with my new riches."

Meanwhile the leader of the thieves had gone back to the forest and was thinking up a plan of revenge. He found one before long. At dawn he put on clean clothes, procured a horse upon which he packed all sorts of fine silks and linens, and went back to the city. Here he rented a shop directly across the street from the one which Ali Baba had recently bought for his son and struck up a friendship with him. He showered him with gifts, ingratiating⁹ himself so well that Ali Baba's son invited him to dine at his father's house.

---

7. **caldron** (kôl′drən): large kettle or pot.

8. **recompense** (rek′əm·pəns): reward.
9. **ingratiating** (in·grā′shē·āt′ing): pleasing someone to gain favor.

Myths and Folk Tales

Illustration for "The Magic Horse" from *Tales from the Arabian Nights*. Watercolor by Edmund Dulac (1882–1953).

Harry Ransom Humanities Research Center, The University of Texas at Austin.

Illustration for "Ali Baba and the Forty Thieves" from *Tales from the Arabian Nights*. Watercolor by Edmund Dulac (1882–1953). Harry Ransom Humanities Research Center, The University of Texas at Austin.

The leader had disguised himself so successfully that Ali Baba didn't recognize him as the imposter who, only a few days before, had tried to murder him. He welcomed him warmly, thanked him for all his kindness to his son, and led him into a great hall where a feast had been prepared.

Morgiana, however, while serving the meal, noticed the gleam of a dagger hidden under the guest's robe. Taking a closer look, she saw through his disguise and became suspicious.

When dinner was over, she put on a dancing costume and a suitable headdress, and buckled on a silver-gilt belt in which she slipped a dagger of the same metal. She then requested the honor of dancing before her master. Delighted at this opportunity of providing such entertainment for his guest, he accepted heartily. Morgiana ranked second to none among dancers. She drew the dagger from her belt and performed so many different motions, so many airy gestures, and so many intricate steps that her audience was enchanted. At times she waved the dagger in front of her as if to strike, at times she waved it as if to stab herself. Suddenly, she sprang upon the false merchant and, without allowing him time to move, sank the dagger up to the hilt into his heart! Ali Baba and his son, utterly dismayed, cried out, "Oh, wretched creature! What have you done?"

Whereupon Morgiana drew back the merchant's robe, pointed to the dagger with which he was armed, and said, "I only did this to save you. Examine more closely the face of the man whom you welcomed at your table. You will recognize the false oil merchant, the leader of the forty thieves! I saw through his disguise while I was serving him, and I devised this means of preventing him from carrying out his sinister plans."

Ali Baba gratefully embraced Morgiana and said, "When I freed you, Morgiana, I promised my favors would not stop there. I am now so deeply indebted that I see only one way of repaying you; namely, to present you in marriage to my son. He, too, owes you his life. I feel sure he will gladly accede to my wishes."

Ali Baba's son, far from opposing this marriage, replied that he consented, not only in order to obey his father, but also because, having fallen in love with Morgiana, he could ask for nothing better.

A few days later, Ali Baba celebrated their wedding with pomp and splendor. There was a sumptuous banquet, followed by dancing and pageantry.[10]

At the end of a year, Ali Baba went back to the cave and pronounced the words "Open Sesame!" which he had not forgotten. He was able to verify that the treasure was intact, and that no one else had any hint of its existence.

He passed the secret words on to his son, who, in turn, passed them on to his own children. Ali Baba and his heirs used the fortune with wisdom and moderation, and thus were able to live out their lives in comfort and in luxury.

---

10. **pageantry** (paj′ən·trē): splendid display.

---

1. GUIDED READING:
Drawing Conclusions
Based on the outcome, which qualities lead to great rewards? Rewarded qualities are loyalty, daring, courage, caution, intelligence, and moderation.

FOR STUDY AND DISCUSSION
Identifying Facts
1. Ali Baba uses magic words.
He finds treasures.
2. Cassim's death causes Ali Baba to rescue Cassim's body and the thieves to seek out and plot to kill the man who knows the location of their hideout.
The story might have focused on Ali Baba's efforts to conceal his break-ins from the thieves.
3. The leader of the thieves disguises himself as a merchant, hides his men in oil jars, and begs Ali Baba for hospitality.
Morgiana hears one thief asking if it is "time" and deduces what is happening.
4. Ali Baba grants Morgiana her freedom and presents her to his son in marriage.
She is freed for killing the thirty-nine thieves. She is wedded to Ali Baba's son for killing their leader.
5. The leader of the thieves disguises himself

CLOSURE
Recall with students the difference between realistic events and supernatural events. Have them cite examples of each kind of event from other stories they have read or from TV shows or movies they have seen.

EXTENSION AND ENRICHMENT
Drama. You might ask volunteers to dramatize "Ali Baba and the Forty Thieves" for students in a lower grade.

twice, as a merchant and as a shopkeeper. The thirty-nine thieves disguise themselves by hiding in oil jars. Morgiana disguises her intended use of the knife by making it part of her dance.

Interpreting Meanings
6. Ali Baba is immediately willing to feed a merchant, give him a bed for the night, and have his oil jars unloaded.
7. Most students will think the story was told for entertainment.
 Others may see a lesson of loyalty.

Applying Meanings
8. Ali Baba might be charged with burglary and Morgiana with murder.
 Students may suggest that they could make the goods from the cave available to their owners, requesting a reward for their services. They could have sealed the jars and guarded the thieves until they could call the authorities.

FOCUS ON READING
Cause and Effect
1. He uses the words to open the cave door also.
2. She coats the scale and discovers gold. She tells Cassim, who gets the secret from Ali Baba.
3. He is trapped and then killed by the thieves when they return.

616

For Study and Discussion

IDENTIFYING FACTS
1. How does Ali Baba get into the cave? What does he find inside?
2. How is Cassim's death important to the **plot**? That is, if he had not been killed, what might have happened in the story?
3. What plan does the leader of the thieves make to sneak his thirty-nine followers into Ali Baba's courtyard? How does the clever Morgiana find out the truth?
4. Ali Baba gives Morgiana two rewards. What are those rewards? What had Morgiana done to get each?
5. **Disguises** which hide a person's true nature are often found in folk tales. Find three places in this story where characters disguise themselves.

INTERPRETING MEANINGS
6. What details show that hospitality to strangers was an important value to the people who told this story?
7. Do you think this story was told mostly to entertain listeners? Or does it also teach a **moral lesson**? If you think it does, what is that moral?

APPLYING MEANINGS
8. In this story, as in almost all folk tales, the good are rewarded and the evil are punished. Judged by the standards of their own people, Ali Baba and Morgiana are admirable and heroic. Suppose that the setting of this story was not ancient Persia, but twentieth-century America.

616   Myths and Folk Tales

What criminal charges might Ali Baba and Morgiana have to face? If you were in their place, what would you have done to solve the problems without committing any "crimes"?

Focus on Reading

CAUSE AND EFFECT
The events that take place in a story are connected by **cause and effect**. This means that one event causes another event to happen. This event in turn causes another event to happen. See if you can answer these questions about cause and effect in Scheherazade's expertly plotted story.

1. Ali Baba sees the thieves open the cave door by saying the magic words.
 Effect:
2. Cassim's wife wonders why Ali Baba's wife wants to weigh something on her scale.
 Effect:
3. Cassim gets into the cave but can't remember the magic words to get out again.
 Effect:
4. The thieves return to find Cassim's body missing.
 Effect:
5. Morgiana's lamp runs out of oil.
 Effect:
6. The leader of the thieves strikes up a friendship with Ali Baba's son and is invited to dine at Ali Baba's house.
 Effect:

PORTFOLIO ASSESSMENT
Some students may want to write an elaborate tale such as one that Scheherazade might have told the king. Suggest that they include several high points of interest, so the king will remain curious; elements of the supernatural; and cause-and-effect reasoning. They may want to make one or all of their characters animals that are familiar in the Middle East. Ask students to write a statement of purpose before they begin their actual story writing. Consult with students individually to agree on how their stories will be assessed. (See *Portfolio Assessment and Professional Support Materials* for additional information on student portfolios.)

Literary Elements

THE SUPERNATURAL IN FOLK TALES

All folk tales contain elements of the supernatural. This means that things happen in folk tales that could not happen in the world as we know it. Our world is governed by certain laws of nature. Our laws of nature, for example, do not allow a cave door to open when it hears certain words.

1. List the events in this story that *definitely* could not happen in real life.
2. Which key events or situations in the story are perfectly realistic and could exist in real life?

Language and Vocabulary

A PREFIX GAME

A **prefix** is a group of letters added to the beginning of a word or word root. A prefix changes the meaning of a word. Many prefixes came into English from the Latin language. Here are two such prefixes:

dis- meaning "apart, away, opposite"
re- meaning "again, back"

Below, six mystery words or word parts are listed at the left, *without* their prefixes. At the right, in scrambled order, is a list of what the words mean *after* the correct prefix has been added (*dis-* or *re-*). All of the mystery words come from the story. See how many you can complete by using one of the prefixes. Then match the words to their correct meanings.

1. —opened
2. —compense
3. —persed
4. —tiring
5. —mounted
6. —treat

a. Scattered or spread apart
b. Opened again
c. The opposite of "climbed on"
d. Going back to bed
e. Pay back
f. Hiding place to go back to

Focus on Writing a Book Report

SUPPORTING THE MAIN IDEA

You need to support your main idea in a book report with **details.** You can use the following details in a book report.

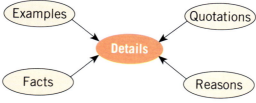

Suppose, for example, that you were presenting an opinion that Morgiana was the true hero of "Ali Baba." You might use a framework like the one below to support your opinion:

> In my opinion, the true hero of "Ali Baba" is Morgiana. My reasons for believing this are _____ and _____. One example of Morgiana's heroism is _____.

Write a one-sentence statement of a main idea for a book report. Then list as many specific details as you can to support and develop this idea. Save your notes.

---

4. The thieves learn that Ali Baba knows the secret of the cave.
5. She goes to the jars of oil and discovers the hidden thieves.
6. Morgiana recognizes him and kills him.

LITERARY ELEMENTS
The Supernatural in Folk Tales
Answers will vary; these are representative:
1. Besides a cave's responding to "Open Sesame," a cobbler could not make a mutilated body look natural. It is unlikely that thirty-nine men could silently hide in oil jars and silently die with no one noticing.
2. Realistic events are the spying of Cassim's wife on Ali Baba's wife; Ali Baba's concealing a new source of wealth; and a criminal's getting into someone's house by befriending his son.

LANGUAGE AND VOCABULARY
A Prefix Game
For answers, see the **Teaching Guide** at the beginning of the unit.

FOCUS ON WRITING A BOOK REPORT
Supporting the Main Idea
You may want to discuss the need for quotation marks when exact words from the book are used. Now would be a good time to review paraphrasing.

OBJECTIVES

Students will identify the quest motif in the folk tale; compare the heroes of folk tales; and summarize. They will also use context clues to determine the meanings of Japanese words.

TEACHING RESOURCES D
Teacher's Notes, p. 104
Reading Check, p. 106
Reading Focus, p. 107
Study Guide, pp. 108, 109
Language Skills, p. 110
Building Vocabulary, p. 113
Selection Vocabulary Test, p. 115
Selection Test, p. 116

AV RESOURCES BINDER
Audiocassette 3, Side B

1. BACKGROUND
This tale is as well known in Japan as the story of Cinderella is here.

Elicit from students what they already know about Japan. Ask a volunteer to locate Japan on a globe or world map. Japan is made up of four large islands and several small ones. The land area of all of Japan is about the same as that of New Mexico or Montana, but Japan has roughly half the population of the entire United States.

Japanese inventions and products are a part of most of your students' lives. They will probably be able to name several kinds of cars, TVs, VCRs, and other electronic equipment made in Japan.

FOCUS/MOTIVATION

Building on Prior Knowledge. Have students discuss some important values that people believe in and try to live by. Explain that in the upcoming story they will learn some of the values that the people of ancient Japan held dear.

Prereading Journal. Have students write down one value that is important to them. Remind them to explain why the value is important.

Momotaro: Boy-of-the-Peach
A Japanese Folk Tale

ももたろう

Retold by YOSHIKO UCHIDA

Before You Read

1 In Japan, people love to listen to the old tales told by professional storytellers. At one time, whole families would go to the *yose* to hear the storyteller, or *Hanashi-ka*, tell his tale—just as American families go to the movies today. A favorite story of Japanese children is this story of the boy who was born from a peach—Momotaro. As you read this tale, look for places where the storyteller would act out the story, or where he would change his voice to scare or amuse his listeners. Notice also what the folktale teaches about human values and family love. Before you read, talk about how we teach values to children today. Do parents still use stories to teach children what is important in life?

The illustrations for this story were done by Akasaka Sanko for a children's book written in Japanese.

© Miyoshi Akasaka

618 Myths and Folktales

READING THE SELECTION

This folk tale is easy to read. Except for a few Japanese words, the vocabulary is simple, and there is a great deal of dialogue. Slower students may have some trouble reading this story in one sitting. For these students, you may want to divide the story into two parts. You might have the first part end on page 621 with the sentence, "They spent many happy years together, and before long Momotaro was fifteen years old" (middle of column 2).

You may want students to reread the story aloud in class. If so, call on volunteers to take the various speaking roles. The characters who have dialogue are the old woman, the old man, Momotaro, the dog, the monkey, the pheasant, the ogres, and the Chief of the Ogres. You will also need to assign the role of narrator.

1. LITERARY ELEMENTS:
Fairy Tale
The opening is characteristic of fairy tales. Note that the setting, both time and place, and the main characters are established here.

2. GUIDED READING:
Making Inferences About Character
What can you infer about the old woman's feelings about her husband? She must love him because she immediately thinks of giving him the peach.

3. GUIDED READING:
Making Inferences
The old woman is determined and resourceful.

Language and Vocabulary

English has borrowed many words from other languages. Some of the words borrowed from Japanese are *judo*, *kimono*, and *tycoon*. Other words more recently borrowed from Japanese name many kinds of things, from foods (*sushi*) to furniture (*futon*). You probably know of at least three cars that have Japanese names. As you read this story, look for two Japanese words. You will find one of them easily. It is printed in italic type. Can you guess what this Japanese word means from the **context**, that is, from the rest of the sentence?

1 Once long, long ago, there lived a kind old man and a kind old woman in a small village in Japan.

One fine day they set out from their little cottage together. The old man went toward the mountains to cut some firewood for their kitchen, and the old woman went toward the river to do her washing.

When the old woman reached the shore of the river, she knelt down beside her wooden tub and began to scrub her clothes on a round, flat stone. Suddenly she looked up and saw something very strange floating down the shallow river. It was an enormous peach, bigger than the round wooden tub that stood beside the old woman.

Rumbley-bump and a-bumpety-bump . . . Rumbley-bump and a-bumpety-bump. The big peach rolled closer and closer over the stones in the stream.

"My gracious me!" the old woman said to herself. "In all my long life I have never seen a peach of such great size and beauty. What a fine present it would make **2** for the old man. I do think I will take it home with me."

Then the old woman stretched out her hand just as far as she could, but no matter how hard she stretched, she couldn't reach the big peach.

"If I could just find a long stick, I would be able to reach it," thought the old woman, looking around, but all she could see were pebbles and sand.

"Oh, dear, what shall I do?" she said **3** to herself. Then suddenly she thought of a way to bring the beautiful big peach to her side. She began to sing out in a sweet, clear voice:

The deep waters are salty!
The shallow waters are sweet!
Stay away from the salty water,
And come where the water is sweet.

She sang this over and over, clapping her hands in time to her song. Then, strangely enough, the big peach slowly be-

620 Myths and Folk Tales

gan to bob along toward the shore where the water was shallow.

Rumbley-bump and a-bumpety-bump . . . Rumbley-bump and a-bumpety-bump. The big peach came closer and closer to the old woman and finally came to a stop at her feet.

The old woman was so happy she picked the big peach up very carefully and quickly carried it home in her arms. Then she waited for the old man to return so she could show him her lovely present. Toward evening the old man came home with a big pack of wood on his back.

"Come quickly, come quickly," the old woman called to him from the house.

"What is it? What is the matter?" the old man asked as he hurried to the side of the old woman.

"Just look at the fine present I have for you," said the old woman happily as she showed him the big round peach.

"My goodness! What a great peach! Where in the world did you buy such a peach as this?" the old man asked.

The old woman smiled happily and told him how she had found the peach floating down the river.

"Well, well, this is a fine present indeed," said the old man, "for I have worked hard today and I am very hungry."

Then he got the biggest knife they had so he could cut the big peach in half. Just as he was ready to thrust the sharp blade into the peach, he heard a tiny voice from inside.

"Wait, old man! Don't cut me!" it cried, and before the surprised old man and woman could say a word, the beautiful big peach broke in two, and a sweet little boy jumped out from inside. The old man and woman were so surprised they could only raise their hands and cry out, "Oh, oh! My goodness!"

Now the old man and woman had always wanted a child of their own, so they were very, very happy to find such a fine little boy, and decided to call him "Momotaro," which means boy-of-the-peach. They took very good care of the little boy and grew to love him dearly, for he was a fine young lad. They spent many happy years together, and before long Momotaro was fifteen years old.

One day Momotaro came before the old man and said, "You have both been good and kind to me. I am very grateful for all you have done, and now I think I am old enough to do some good for others too. I have come to ask if I may leave you."

"You wish to leave us, my son? But why?" asked the old man in surprise.

"Oh, I shall be back in a very short time," said Momotaro. "I wish only to go to the Island of the Ogres,[1] to rid the land of those harmful creatures. They have killed many good people, and have stolen and robbed throughout the country. I wish to kill the ogres so they can never harm our people again."

"That is a fine idea, my son, and I will not stop you from going," said the old man.

So that very day Momotaro got ready

---

[1] **ogres** (ō′gərs): in fairy tales, giants or monsters that eat people.

**1. LITERARY ELEMENTS:
Fairy Tale**
What supernatural events have happened already in this tale? The peach is as big as the woman's wash tub; the peach floats in the water; it comes to her when she sings.

**2. GUIDED READING:
Drawing Conclusions**
What values did the people of ancient Japan hold dear? They valued goodness and kindness. They also valued a strong sense of obligation and responsibility.

SOCIAL STUDIES LINK

You might get students involved in learning about both contemporary Japan and the folk tale of Momotaro by assigning students a project that requires some knowledge of both. You might tell students to pretend that they have been hired to design a set of posters for American children to use to learn about Japan. A set of four will be hung in American libraries and schools. Some of the posters should tell about Japanese stories like "Momotaro." Others should tell about the country of Japan and its people.

Students could work in teams of two or three while gathering information, but after they finish their research, they should decide individually what would go on the four posters. Ask each student to divide a piece of paper into four parts and to sketch out the ideas they have for the posters. Remind them that the posters need not be too detailed because they are meant to be eye-catching and to be read quickly by younger children.

VISUAL CONNECTIONS

Call students' attention to the symbols on the banner. Very early in their history, the Japanese adopted as their script the Chinese orthographic system called kanji. Because kanji symbols are squarish and complicated in shape, they are difficult to write. As a result, the Japanese began writing kanji symbols in a cursive and simplified way, which, in the ninth century, came to be known as hiragana. Hiragana bears little or no resemblance to the original kanji.

to start out on his journey. The old woman prepared some millet[2] cakes for him to take along on his trip, and soon Momotaro was ready to leave. The old man and woman were sad to see him go and called, "Be careful, Momotaro! Come back safely to us."

"Yes, yes, I shall be back soon," he answered. "Take care of yourselves while I am away," he added, and waved as he started down the path toward the forest.

He hurried along, for he was anxious to get to the Island of the Ogres. While he was walking through the cool forest where

---

2. **millet** (mil'it): a kind of grass. Millet seeds are used to make certain foods in Asia.

the grass grew long and high, he began to feel hungry. He sat down at the foot of a tall pine tree and carefully unwrapped the *furoshiki* which held his little millet cakes. "My, they smell good," he thought. Suddenly he heard the tall grass rustle and saw something stalking through the grass toward him. Momotaro blinked hard when he saw what it was. It was a dog as big as a calf! But Momotaro was not frightened, for the dog just said, "Momotaro-san,³ Momotaro-san, what is it you are eating that smells so good?"

"I'm eating a delicious millet cake which my good mother made for me this morning," he answered.

---

3. In Japanese, the suffix *san* is often added to names as a mark of respect.

The dog licked his chops and looked at the cake with hungry eyes. "Please, Momotaro-san," he said, "just give me one of your millet cakes, and I will come along with you to the Island of the Ogres. I know why you are going there, and I can be of help to you."

"Very well, my friend," said Momotaro, "I will take you along with me." And he gave the dog one of his millet cakes to eat.

As they walked on, something suddenly leaped from the branches above and jumped in front of Momotaro. He stopped in surprise and found that it was a monkey who had jumped down from the trees.

"Greetings, Momotaro-san!" called the monkey happily. "I have heard that you

1. GUIDED READING:
Using Context Clues
Based on the rest of the sentence, what do you think a furoshiki is? It is a knapsack or bundle.

2. LITERARY ELEMENTS:
Fairy Tale
What supernatural qualities does the dog have? It is extraordinarily large. It can speak.

3. GUIDED READING:
Making Inferences About Character
What qualities in Momotaro can you infer from his meeting with the dog? Momotaro shows that he is brave and generous. He is also humble; he is willing to accept help.

623

1. GUIDED READING: Distinguishing Between Fantasy and Reality
In addition to its supernatural qualities, what realistic qualities does the dog have? It growls and barks. It is aggressive and jealous.

2. GUIDED READING: Identifying Purpose
Why do you think this passage is included in the tale? It is included to show that Momotaro is a wise and tactful leader and peacemaker. It also shows that, without Momotaro's leadership, the animal helpers would be able to accomplish nothing.

3. GUIDED READING: Understanding Cause and Effect
Why does Momotaro send the pheasant into the ogres' stronghold? Only the pheasant can fly over the walls with Momotaro's message.

---

are going to the Island of the Ogres to rid the land of these plundering creatures. Take me with you, for I wish to help you in your fight."

1 When the dog heard this, he growled angrily. "Grruff," he said to the monkey. "*I* am going to help Momotaro-san. We do not need the help of a monkey such as you! Out of our way! Grruff, grruff," he barked angrily.

2 "How dare you speak to me like that?" shrieked the monkey, and he leaped at the dog, scratching with his sharp claws. The dog and the monkey began to fight each other, biting, clawing, and growling. When Momotaro saw this, he pushed them apart and cried, "Here, here, stop it, you two! There is no reason why you both cannot go with me to the Island of the Ogres. I shall have two helpers instead of one!" Then he took another millet cake from his *furoshiki* and gave it to the monkey.

Now there were three of them going down the path to the edge of the woods—the dog in front, Momotaro in the middle, and the monkey walking in the rear. Soon they came to a big field, and just as they were about to cross it, a large pheasant[4] hopped out in front of them. The dog jumped at it with a growl, but the pheasant fought back with such spirit that Momotaro ran over to stop the dog. "We could use a brave bird such as you to help us fight the ogres. We are on our way to their island this very day. How would you like to come along with us?"

"Oh, I would like that indeed, for I would like to help you rid the land of these evil and dangerous ogres," said the pheasant happily.

"Then here is a millet cake for you, too," said Momotaro, giving the pheasant a cake, just as he had the monkey and the dog.

Now there were four of them going to the Island of the Ogres, and as they walked down the path together, they became very good friends.

Before long they came to the water's edge and Momotaro found a boat big enough for all of them. They climbed in and headed for the Island of the Ogres. Soon they saw the island in the distance, wrapped in gray, foggy clouds. Dark stone walls rose up above towering cliffs, and large iron gates stood ready to keep out any who tried to enter.

3 Momotaro thought for a moment, then turned to the pheasant and said, "You alone can wing your way over their high walls and gates. Fly into their stronghold[5] now, and do what you can to frighten them. We will follow as soon as we can."

So the pheasant flew far above the iron gates and stone walls and down onto the roof of the ogres' castle. Then he called to the ogres, "Momotaro-san has come to rid the land of you and your many evil deeds. Give up your stolen treasures now, and perhaps he will spare your lives!"

When the ogres heard this, they laughed and shouted, "HO, HO, HO! We

---

4. **pheasant** (fez′ənt): a long-tailed bird.

5. **stronghold**: fortress.

624 Myths and Folk Tales

are not afraid of a little bird like you! We are not afraid of little Momotaro!"

The pheasant became very angry at this, and flew down, pecking at the heads of the ogres with his sharp, pointed beak. While the pheasant was fighting so bravely, the dog and monkey helped Momotaro to tear down the gates, and they soon came to the aid of the pheasant.

"Get away! Get away!" shouted the ogres, but the monkey clawed and scratched, the big dog growled and bit the ogres, and the pheasant flew about, pecking at their heads and faces. So fierce were they that soon the ogres began to run away. Half of them tumbled over the cliffs as they ran, and the others fell pell-mell into the sea. Soon only the Chief of the Ogres remained. He threw up his hands, and then bowed low to Momotaro. "Please spare me my life, and all our stolen treasures are yours. I promise never to rob or kill anyone again," he said.

Momotaro tied up the evil ogre, while the monkey, the dog, and the pheasant carried many boxes filled with jewels and treasures down to their little boat. Soon it was laden with all the treasures it could hold, and they were ready to sail toward home.

When Momotaro returned, he went from one family to another, returning the many treasures which the ogres had stolen from the people of the land.

"You will never again be troubled by the ogres of Ogre Island!" he said to them happily.

---

1. GUIDED READING:
Making Inferences
What does the ogres' answer reveal about them? They are boastful bullies. They believe, mistakenly, that they do not have to fear anything that is smaller than they are.

2. GUIDED READING:
Understanding Cause and Effect
What effect does the pheasant's advance attack have? It distracts the ogres so that Momotaro and the others can get in.

3. GUIDED READING:
Interpreting Meaning
The significance of Momotaro's victory over the ogres suggests that the combination of intelligence, cooperation, and bravery can triumph over even the greatest of evils. It suggests that size alone does not necessarily determine the outcome of conflicts.

1. LITERARY ELEMENTS:
Fairy Tale
Note the traditional fairy tale ending.

And they all answered, "You are a kind and brave lad, and we thank you for making our land safe once again."

Then Momotaro went back to the home of the old man and woman with his arms full of jewels and treasures from Ogre Island. The old man and woman were so glad to see him once again, and the three of them lived happily together for many, many years.

For Study and Discussion

IDENTIFYING FACTS

1. Right away, this storyteller plunges us into the fabulous world of folklore. What miraculous thing does the old woman find in the stream?
2. Describe the **quest** that Momotaro goes on. Why does he undertake it?
3. As often happens in folk tales, the hero meets characters along the way who assist him on the quest. Who assists Momotaro? Tell exactly how each friend helps the Peach Boy get what he wants.
4. This is truly a tale that "amazes." Make a list of all the things in this tale that couldn't happen in real life.

INTERPRETING MEANINGS

5. What is the outcome of Momotaro's **quest**? Who benefits from his quest?
6. Many folk tales are stories of wish fulfillment. What wishes or fantasies come true for the people in this story?

APPLYING MEANINGS

7. Uchida's grandfather was a samurai in Japan before he became a teacher. The samurai were military leaders who had a strict code of conduct. In some ways, the samurai were like the knights of King Arthur's Round Table. The samurai code stressed bravery, loyalty, self-discipline, politeness, and respect for anyone in authority (such as parents, ancestors, and rulers). Which of these qualities does Momotaro have? Which of these qualities are important in our world today?

Focus on Reading

SUMMARIZING

When you **summarize** a story, you tell about its most important events. Here are some steps you can follow:

1. Divide the story into a beginning, a middle, and an end.
2. Look for a major event in each part of the story.
3. Tell about each major event in your own words. Use a complete sentence to describe each. If there are two major events in a part of the story, you may want to put both of them into one sentence.
4. Reread your summary. Have you used **transitions**—words and phrases like *then, after, as a result of* that help your reader know when and where events happened?

In the following summary, every other sentence has been left out. What sentences would you add to make a complete summary of the story?

  a. An old woman finds a large peach and takes it home. _____
  b. _____
  c. When Momotaro is fifteen, he leaves the old people because he wants to rid the land of ogres. _____
  d. _____
  e. The animals go with him, and they all become good friends. _____
  f. _____
  g. Momotaro returns home. _____
  h. _____

FOR STUDY AND DISCUSSION

Identifying Facts

1. The old woman finds a peach, bigger than her wash tub, which contains "a sweet little boy."
2. Momotaro proposes to rid the land of a group of ogres who have been robbing people and killing them.

Momotaro says that he is grateful for the old couple's goodness and wishes "to do some good for others too."

3. Momotaro is assisted by a dog, a monkey, and a pheasant.

The pheasant flies over the ogres' stronghold, taunts the ogres, and pecks at them, while the dog and the monkey help Momotaro tear down the gates. Then the monkey claws and scratches the ogres, and the dog growls and bites them. All three animals help carry treasures to the boat.

4. Answers may vary. Here are a few possibilities: peach floats; peach is as big as washtub; peach comes to the woman when she sings; boy is discovered in peach; animals talk; ogres exist.

CLOSURE
Have students summarize the main values about life that this tale presents. What does it say about family? leadership? community?

RETEACHING
Have students define *quest* and tell how this is a quest story. They should define the hero, the object of the quest, the perils faced by the hero, and the outcome.

EXTENSION AND ENRICHMENT
Social Studies. Ask volunteers to prepare and present an oral report on some aspect of Japanese history or culture. Here are some possible subjects: samurai warriors, the martial arts, Japanese gardens, and sumo wrestling.

Interpreting Meanings
5. The outcome is that Momotaro defeats the Ogres, making the land safe again, and returns home laden with the recovered treasures.
All the villagers benefit.
6. The wish of the old man and woman to have a child is fulfilled. The wish of the villagers for a safe and peaceful life is also fulfilled, as is the wish of Momotaro and his parents for a happy life.

Applying Meanings
7. Momotaro has all five qualities. Especially clear are *bravery* (taking on a quest against the ogres) and *respect for authority* (the old couple who raised him). He is also *loyal* and *polite* to his foster parents, the people of the land, and his helpers. He is *self-disciplined* in not hoarding but sharing his millet cakes and the treasures.
Many people today prize all five qualities; others prize bravery and loyalty more than politeness, self-discipline, or respect for authority.

FOCUS ON READING
Summarizing
These are the missing sentences:
b. The peach contains a little boy whom the old couple love and raise as their son.

Literary Elements

COMMON FEATURES IN FOLK TALES
One of the supernatural elements in this story has to do with the unusual origin of the hero—he was found in a large peach.

1. Can you think of any other hero who has strange or mysterious origins? (Where did Superman come from? Where do the Ninja turtles come from?)
2. Do you recall other heroes or heroines who have unusual friends who help them accomplish a difficult task? (Think of Dorothy's helpers as she journeys to Oz. How about Luke Skywalker in *Star Wars*?)

Language and Vocabulary

JAPANESE WORDS
Japanese and English look and sound quite different. For example, Japanese is spoken with an even beat on each syllable. Instead of stressing certain syllables the way English speakers do, Japanese speakers vary the pitch of their voice. Here are some Japanese words and their English meanings:

1. *arigato* (ä·re·gä·to)—thank you
2. *ha-ha* (hä·hä)—mother
3. *otoh* (au·to)—father
4. *hai* (hi)—yes
5. *iye* (yeh)—no
6. *ohayo* (o·hi·o)—good morning
7. *dozo* (do·zo)—please
8. *san* (sähn)—a word that, added to a person's name, shows respect, like Mr., Mrs., or Ms. in English.
9. *sayonara* (si·o·nä·rä)—good-bye (means "if it must be so")
10. *yoi* (yoy)—good

Choose three of the English meanings from the list above. Then find out how to say these words in another language. If you know people who speak a foreign language, you may ask them. If you can speak a foreign language yourself, of course, you won't have to ask anyone! See how many different foreign words you and your classmates can find for these English meanings. Do any of the words resemble English or Japanese?

Writing About Literature

EXTENDING THE STORY
Where did the Peach Boy come from? How did he get into the huge juicy peach? How long had he been inside the peach, floating down the river? How did he know he had to go on his quest? Write three or four sentences in which you tell the beginning of the story.

About the Author

Yoshiko Uchida (1921–1992) was born in Alameda, California, and grew up in Berkeley. Her parents were Japanese immigrants and leaders in the Japanese American community. Uchida attended the University of California at Berkeley, but just before she graduated, World War II broke out. She and her family, along with most other Japanese living on the West Coast, were sent to internment camps like the one where she was in Topaz, Utah. Several of Uchida's books tell about the hardships that the Japanese

Americans endured in these camps. Uchida heard the story of Momotaro from her own mother. Uchida wrote many books for young people, among them *The Dancing Kettle, A Jar of Dreams, and Other Japanese Folk Tales* and *The Invisible Thread: A Memoir.*

A Writer's Journal

Behind the Scenes

It seems to me I've been interested in books and writing for as long as I can remember. I was writing stories when I was ten, and being the child of frugal[1] immigrant parents, I wrote them on brown wrapping paper which I cut up and bound into booklets, and because I am such a saver, I still have them. The first is titled, "Jimmy Chipmonk and His Friends: A Short Story for Small Children."

I not only wrote stories, I also kept a journal of important events which I began the day I graduated from elementary school. Of course my saver self kept that journal as well, and even today I can read of the special events of my young life, such as the times my parents took us to an opera or concert in San Francisco, or the day I got my first dog, or the sad day it died, when I drew a tombstone for him in my journal and decorated it with floral wreaths.

By putting these special happenings into words and writing them down, I was trying to hold on to and somehow preserve the magic as well as the joy and sadness of certain moments in my life, and I guess that's really what books and writing are all about.

—Yoshiko Uchida

1. **frugal** (frū′gəl): careful with money.

OBJECTIVES
Students will recognize heroic qualities and analyze common elements of folk tales. They will also make up praise names.

FOCUS/MOTIVATION
Building on Prior Knowledge. Have students discuss natural disasters that they may have experienced themselves or have seen in films or on TV. Have them talk about the effects of these disasters on the land and people.

Prereading Journal. Ask students to write about experiencing a natural disaster. Have them explain how they might react. Tell them to also explain a cause for the disaster.

READING THE SELECTION

The story is easy to read. It is short enough to read in one class sitting. After students have read about the monster's defeat of the hunter Kara-Digi-Mao-Fosi-Fasi (bottom of column 2, page 635), you might have them summarize the events up to that point and predict what will happen in the rest of the story. (Tell students that the name Kara-Digi-Mao-Fosi-Fasi should be pronounced the way it is spelled.)

Nana Miriam
An African Folk Tale

Retold by HANS BAUMANN

Before You Read

Many folk tales tell about the deeds of a hero who saves the people from a great evil. Long ago, some of these stories may have had some basis in fact. For example, suppose that in years of drought, there was not enough water to grow crops. Suppose somebody figured out how to get water from a river to the fields. The people then praised their hero in songs and stories. As time passed, the tale changed—and became more interesting. The hero might have gained supernatural power. The drought might have become a monster.

As you read this folk tale from Nigeria, notice how it combines events that could happen with magic events that could never happen. Can you imagine what real disaster the story might be based on?

1

TEACHING RESOURCES D
Teacher's Notes, p. 118
Reading Check, p. 120
Study Guide, pp. 121, 122
Building Vocabulary, p. 123
Selection Vocabulary Test, p. 125
Selection Test, p. 126

AV RESOURCES BINDER
Audiocassette 3, Side B

1. BACKGROUND

Ask a volunteer to locate Nigeria on a map or a globe.

Nigeria is the largest of the West African coastal nations. The capital of the country was Lagos, and now Abuja; the official language is English, although there are many tribal dialects.

The Songai people, from whom this tale comes, speak their own language. The Songai names in this folk tale appear to be anglicized; that is, they are spelled the way they sounded to the translator.

1. GUIDED READING:
Drawing Conclusions
Based on the details in this passage, what do the Songai admire about Fara Maka? The Songai admire him because he's tall and strong. They also admire his teaching; he is patient and thorough.

2. GUIDED READING:
Making Inferences
Based on the details in this paragraph, what real natural disaster might have caused the famine? The river might have flooded its banks and destroyed the crops. (Less likely causes might be a drought, a great storm, or a volcanic eruption).

Language and Vocabulary

In most African groups, there are no family names, but people may get two or three more names as they become older. The additional names usually tell how someone looks, what one believes in, or what one stands for. Among the Yoruba, people may be given names that tell about something outstanding they have done. The Yoruba call these additional names "praise names." As you read this African folk tale, be thinking of a good praise name for Nana Miriam.

---

1 Fara Maka was a man of the Songai tribe, who lived by the River Niger.[1] He was taller than the other men and he was also stronger. Only he was very ugly. However, no one thought that important, because Fara Maka had a daughter who was very beautiful. Her name was Nana Miriam and she too was tall and strong. Her father instructed her in all kinds of things. He went with her to the sandbank and said, "Watch the fish!" And he told her the names of all the various kinds. Everything there is to know about fish he taught her. Then he asked her, "What kind is the one swimming here, and the other one over there?"

"This is a so-and-so," replied Nana Miriam. "And that is a such-and-such."

"Male or female?" asked Fara Maka.

"I don't know," said Nana Miriam.

"This one is a female, and so is the other one," explained Fara Maka. "But the third one over there is a male." And each time he pointed to a different fish.

That was how Nana Miriam came to learn so much. And in addition she had magic powers within her, which no one suspected. And because her father also taught her many magic spells, she grew stronger than anyone else in the Land of the Songai.

Beside the great river, the Niger, there lived a monster that took the form of a hippopotamus. This monster was insatiable.[2] It broke into the rich fields and devoured the crops, bringing famine to the Songai people. No one could tackle this hippopotamus, because it could change its shape. So the hunters had all their trouble for nothing and they returned to their villages in helpless despair. Times were so bad that many died of hunger. **2**

One day, Fara Maka picked up all his lances and set out to kill the monster. When he saw it, he recoiled in fear, for huge pots of fire were hung around the animal's neck. Fara Maka hurled lance after lance, but

---

1. **Niger** (nī′jər): river in West Africa, flowing from Guinea through Mali, Niger, and Nigeria.
2. **insatiable** (in·sā′shə·bəl): never getting enough; greedy.

634 Myths and Folk Tales

each one was swallowed by the flames. The hippopotamus monster looked at Fara Maka with scorn. Then it turned its back on him and trotted away.

Fara Maka returned home furious, wondering who he could summon to help him. Now there was a man of the Tomma tribe who was a great hunter. His name was Kara-Digi-Mao-Fosi-Fasi, and Fara Maka asked him if he would hunt the hippopotamus with his one hundred and twenty dogs. "That I will," said Kara-Digi-Mao-Fosi-Fasi.

So Fara Maka invited him and his one hundred and twenty dogs to a great banquet. Before every dog, which had an iron chain around its neck, was placed a small mound of rice and meat. For the hunter, however, there was a huge mound of rice. None of the dogs left a single grain of rice uneaten, and neither did Kara-Digi-Mao-Fosi-Fasi. Well fortified,³ they set out for the place where the monster lived.

As soon as the dogs picked up the scent, Kara-Digi-Mao-Fosi-Fasi unchained the first one. The chain rattled as the dog leaped forward towards its quarry.⁴ One chain rattled after the other, as dog after dog sprang forward to attack the hippopotamus. But the hippopotamus took them on one by one, and it gobbled them all up. The great hunter Kara-Digi-Mao-Fosi-Fasi took to his heels in terror. The hippopotamus charged into a rice field and ate that too.

When Fara Maka heard from the great hunter what had happened, he sat down in the shadow of a large tree and hung his head.

"Haven't you been able to kill the hippopotamus?" Nana Miriam asked him.

"No," said Fara Maka.

"And Kara-Digi-Mao-Fosi-Fasi could not drive it away either?"

"No."

"So there is no one who can get the better of it?"

"No," said Fara Maka.

"Then I'll not delay any longer," said Nana Miriam. "I'll go to its haunts and see what I can see."

"Yes, do," said her father.

Nana Miriam walked along the banks of the Niger, and she soon found the hippopotamus eating its way through a rice field. As soon as it saw the girl it stopped eating, raised its head and greeted her.

"Good morning," replied Nana Miriam.

"I know why you have come," said the hippopotamus. "You want to kill me. But no one can do that. Your father tried, and he lost all his lances. The great hunter Kara-Digi-Mao-Fosi-Fasi tried, and all his dogs paid with their lives for his presumption.⁵ And you are only a girl."

"We'll soon see," answered Nana Miriam. "Prepare to fight with me. Only one of us will be left to tell the tale."

---

3. **fortified** (fôr′tə·fīd): strengthened (by the food).
4. **quarry**: an animal that is being hunted.
5. **presumption** (pri·zump′shən): here, the hunter's too great confidence that he could kill the monster.

1
Scorn means "contempt and disgust."

2. GUIDED READING:
Predicting Outcomes
Based on what you know about the hunter and his dogs, predict what will happen when the hunter meets the monster. Most students will predict that the hunter will win.

3. GUIDED READING:
Recognizing the Author's Purpose
Why do you think the storyteller included this paragraph? It summarizes the story thus far and increases suspense.

CLOSURE
Discuss the story, asking students to list Nana Miriam's heroic qualities. Then have them name other fairy tales with which they are familiar. What qualities do the heroes of these tales reveal through their actions?

EXTENSION AND ENRICHMENT
Social Studies. Ask students to research and then to report orally on a heroic American woman. They should include in their reports a description of this woman's achievements and an explanation of why they chose her as their subject.

TRANSPARENCIES 34 & 35
Fine Art
Theme: *Traditional Tales* – invites students to explore artworks that portray traditional tales handed down through the generations.

FOR STUDY AND DISCUSSION

Identifying Facts

1. Her father, Fara Maka, "instructed her in all kinds of things" such as "everything there is to know about fish."
   She is stronger than anyone else because she has magic powers, and her father taught her magic spells.
2. The monster could change its shape at will.
   It was greedy, like some people, caring nothing about others.
3. The monster brought famine on the land by devouring the people's crops.
   If Nana Miriam had not killed the monster, the Songai might have starved.
4. The monster is fought by Fara Maka, the great hunter Kara-Digi-Mao-Fosi-Fasi, and Nana Miriam.
   The monster defeats Fara Maka and the great hunter, but Nana Miriam triumphs.
5. The Songai depend on rice, hunt with lances and with dogs, eat meat and fish, and make up songs about their heroes.

Interpreting Meanings

6. Nana Miriam uses magic powder to turn flames to water, a magic

---

"Right you are!" shouted the hippopotamus and with its breath it set the rice field afire. There it stood in a ring of flame through which no mortal could pass.

But Nana Miriam threw magic powder into the fire, and the flames turned to water.

"Right!" shouted the hippopotamus, and a wall of iron sprang up making a ring around the monster. But Nana Miriam plucked a magic hammer from the air, and shattered the iron wall into fragments.

Now for the first time the hippopotamus felt afraid, and it turned itself into a river that flowed into the Niger.

Again Nana Miriam sprinkled her magic powder. At once the river dried up and the water changed back into a hippopotamus. It grew more and more afraid and when Fara Maka came up to see what was happening, the monster charged him blindly. Nana Miriam ran after it, and when it was only ten bounds away from her father, she seized it by its left hind foot and flung it across the Niger. As it crashed against the opposite bank, its skull was split and it was dead. Then Fara Maka, who had seen the mighty throw, exclaimed, "What a daughter I have!"

Very soon, the whole tribe heard what had happened, and the Dialli, the minstrel[6] folk, sang the song of Nana Miriam's adventure with the hippopotamus, which used to devastate[7] the rice fields. And in the years that followed, no one in the Land of the Songai starved any more.

---
6. **minstrel:** musician.
7. **devastate** (dev′ə·stāt′): destroy.

For Study and Discussion

IDENTIFYING FACTS

1. Explain how Nana Miriam came to learn so much. In what two ways is she stronger than anyone else?
2. What **magic** power did the monster have? In what way was it like a human being?
3. Folk tales often tell about a people in danger, who need someone to save them. Why was the monster a terrible threat to the Songai? If Nana Miriam had not killed the monster, what might have happened to the Songai?
4. In folk tales the world over, things often happen in **threes.** (Three is thought of as a "mystical" number.) Name the three people who fight this monster. Who wins each **conflict**?
5. List three **facts** about the Songai that you learned from this tale. For example, what crop did they depend on?

INTERPRETING MEANINGS

6. What magic tools does Nana Miriam use? In what other folk tales does a character use a magic tool, such as a wand that grants wishes, or boots that can travel a great distance?
7. In many folk tales, we are surprised at the person who turns out to be the hero. Often the hero starts out as an unknown orphan, or as the youngest child. Is Nana Miriam an unlikely hero? Why?

APPLYING MEANINGS

8. What qualities did the Songai admire? Which of these qualities is most important to you? Which is least important?

636   Myths and Folk Tales

PORTFOLIO ASSESSMENT
A ballad is often a folk story told in poetic form and set to music. Musically inclined students may be interested in writing and producing a recording of a ballad that they compose about one of the stories in this unit. Suggest that students work in groups to write and to set their story to music. Provide a student-volunteer film crew to videotape the ballads and to present the recording to the class. Ask students to evaluate the merits of each of the ballads. Ask which they prefer, the sung ballad or the short story, and ask the reasons for their preference. Consult with student groups to agree on how their ballads will be assessed. (See *Portfolio Assessment and Professional Support Materials* for additional information on student portfolios.)

Language and Vocabulary

PRAISE NAMES
Many young people in the United States have names from African languages. Here are some African names and their meanings. These names were often added to a person's original name as a praise name.

Girls' Names

Aisha (ä·ē'shä)
    (Swahili, E. Africa)   Life
Amadi (ä·mä'dē)
    (Ibo, Nigeria)   Rejoicing
Femi (fē'mē)
    (Yoruba, Nigeria)   Love me
Naila (nä·ē'lä)
    (Arabic, N. Africa)   One who succeeds
Shani (shä'nē)
    (Swahili, E. Africa)   Marvelous

Boys' Names

Akiiki (ä·kē·ē'kē)
    (Muneyankole, Uganda)   Friend
Andwele (än·dwē'lē)
    (Nyakysa, Tanzania)   God brought me
Bakari (bä·kä'rē)
    (Swahili, E. Africa)   Of noble promise
Kamau (kä·mä'o͞o)
    (Kikiyu, Kenya)   Quiet warrior
Mudada (mo͞o·dä'dä)
    (Shona, Zimbabwe)   The provider

1. Make up praise names for three of the heroes in this book.
2. Suppose you are in your thirties. You are living in a society that adds praise names to the name you were given at birth. What three praise names would you like?
3. Make up praise names for three friends.

Focus on Writing a Book Report

ORGANIZING A BOOK REPORT
When you write your book report, follow an outline like the one below.

    I. Identify book's author and title
   II. Summarize book's contents briefly
  III. State your main idea and support it with details
  IV. Conclude with brief restatement of main idea

Write an outline for a book report. State your main idea for the report in a complete sentence and list your supporting details in a logical order. Save your notes.

About the Authors

The real authors of this story are the **Songai**. Songai (also spelled Songhay and Songhai) was a great empire that controlled the trade routes from North Africa through the Sahara Desert. Songai was at its height from the eleventh to the sixteenth century. The capital of the empire was Gao, on the River Niger. The empire included cities and vast grasslands, which were farmed by tribespeople. On the empire's eastern boundary, the principal city was Timbuktu (tim·buk·to͞o'), a center of wealth and learning. Today the Songai people, who now number about 900,000, live mostly in the Republic of Mali.

---

hammer to shatter an iron wall, and magic powder to dry up a river.

In "Cinderella," a fairy godmother uses a wand. In "The Seven-Leagued Boots," each of a giant's steps measures seven leagues (a league is longer than a mile).

7. Nana Miriam might be considered an unlikely hero.

People usually expect a strong man, not a beautiful girl, to act heroically. As the monster says, "you are only a girl" (page 635).

Applying Meanings
8. The Songai admire physical strength, feminine beauty, useful knowledge, skill in hunting, courage, and heroism.

Students will differ in identifying the qualities most and least important to them.

LANGUAGE AND VOCABULARY
Praise Names
For answers, see the **Study Guide** at the beginning of the unit.

FOCUS ON WRITING A BOOK REPORT
Organizing a Book Report
If possible, show students a completed book report that has followed this outline. Help students to compare the outline with the finished product.

NO QUESTIONS ASKED

The End of the World
A Sioux Myth

JENNY LEADING CLOUD

Before You Read

Myth makers have always told stories about the end of the world. But in most of these stories, a renewed world eventually is born from the old one. The Native Americans in particular have many of these end-of-the-world myths. In almost all of these stories, a dreaded event is prevented from happening, or the destruction is followed by renewal. Perhaps these myths remind us that optimism and courage and faith are the most human of all our characteristics—no matter where we live, or when.

Read the first paragraph of this myth. Then stop, and write in your journal your own prediction of what lies in this mysterious hidden cave. Write your own myth about the "end of the world."

(Opposite page) Painted buffalo robe (1875). Made by the Dakota Cheyenne or the Sioux.

Courtesy Colter Bay Indian Arts Museum, Grand Teton National Park, Wyoming.

Saddle blanket made out of beaded and fringed leather (c. 1875–1900). Made by the Northern Cheyenne or the Sioux.

Courtesy Colter Bay Indian Arts Museum, Grand Teton National Park, Wyoming.

638 Myths and Folk Tales

Somewhere at a place where the prairie and the Maka Sicha, the Badlands, meet, there is a hidden cave. Not for a long, long time has anyone been able to find it. Even now, with so many highways, cars, and tourists, no one has discovered this cave.

In it lives a woman so old that her face looks like a shriveled-up walnut. She is dressed in rawhide, the way people used to be before the white man came. She has been sitting there for a thousand years or more, working on a blanket strip for her buffalo robe. She is making the strip out of dyed porcupine quills, the way our ancestors did before white traders brought glass beads to this turtle continent. Resting beside her, licking his paws, watching her all the time is Shunka Sapa, a huge black dog. His eyes never wander from the old woman, whose teeth are worn flat, worn down to little stumps, she has used them to flatten so many porcupine quills.

A few steps from where the old woman sits working on her blanket strip, a huge fire is kept going. She lit this fire a thousand or more years ago and has kept it alive ever since. Over the fire hangs a big earthen pot, the kind some Indian peoples used to make before the white man came with his kettles of iron. Inside the big pot, *wojapi* is boiling and bubbling. *Wojapi* is berry soup, good and sweet and red. That soup has been boiling in the pot for a long time, ever since the fire was lit.

Every now and then the old woman gets up to stir the *wojapi* in the huge earthen pot. She is so old and feeble that it takes her a while to get up and hobble over to the fire. The moment her back is turned, the huge black dog starts pulling the porcupine quills out of her blanket strip. This way she never makes any progress, and her quillwork remains forever unfinished. The Sioux people used to say that if the old woman ever finishes her blanket strip, then at the very moment that she threads the last porcupine quill to complete the design, the world will come to an end.

About the Authors

This myth was told to Alfonso Ortiz and Richard Erdoes (see the note on page 565) in White River, South Dakota, by a Sioux woman named **Jenny Leading Cloud.**

The great **Sioux** people, lords of the Northern Plains, were fantastic horsemen and buffalo hunters and famed for their bravery. The Sioux produced the heroes Red Cloud, Sitting Bull, and Crazy Horse. In 1876, the Sioux defeated General George Custer at the bloody Battle of Little Bighorn in Montana. The Sioux fought their last battle against overwhelming odds, and in the face of cannon, at Wounded Knee, South Dakota, in 1891.

OBJECTIVES

The overall aim is for students to identify the main idea in a fable. For a complete list of objectives, see the **Teacher's Notes.**

PRESENTATION

Introduce this activity by explaining to students that a moral and main idea are synonymous with theme, the idea about life revealed in a literary work. Also, remind students that when we state a theme, moral, or main idea, we use a generalization. Then divide the class into small groups to read the fable and answer the questions that follow. After students have had time to read and discuss the questions, have group leaders share their group's ideas orally.

IDENTIFYING THE MAIN IDEA

To discover the main idea in a literary work, students should think about their feelings as they read it and after they have read it. If they were in the characters' places, how would they act? Do the events remind students of things that have happened to them? As they think about the answers to such questions, thoughtful readers often will understand what the writer is trying to say.

Answers

Answers may vary.
1. One frog gives up; the other keeps trying.
2. He keeps swimming around and around until the milk turns to butter.
3. If people don't give up, they will usually succeed, or "when the going gets tough, the tough get going."

FOCUS ON Reading and Critical Thinking

IDENTIFYING THE MAIN IDEA

A **generalization** is a universal statement. That means it's a statement that applies to many individuals or experiences.

A **fable** is a brief story, usually with animal characters, that teaches a practical lesson about how to behave in life. The fable's lesson is called a **moral.** This moral might be considered the **main idea** of the fable. Some fables, like those by Aesop, state the moral directly. Other fables present the moral indirectly. As you read the following fable, think about the lesson it teaches. What is its main idea?

Two Frogs and the Milk Vat

CLAUDE BROWN

There were two frogs sitting on a milk vat one time. The frogs fell into the milk vat. It was very deep. They kept swimming and swimming around, and they couldn't get out. They couldn't climb out because they were too far down. One frog said, "Oh, I can't make it, and I'm going to give up." And the other frog kept swimming and swimming. His arms became more and more tired, and it was harder and harder and harder for him to swim. Then he couldn't do another stroke. He couldn't throw one more arm into the milk. He kept trying and trying; it seemed as if the milk was getting hard and heavy. He kept trying; he knew that he was going to die, but as long as he had that little bit of life in him, he was going to keep on swimming. On his last stroke, it seemed as though he had to pull a whole ocean back, but he did it and found himself sitting on a vat of butter.

Identifying the Main Idea

1. What is the difference between the two frogs in the fable?
2. The frog who keeps on struggling to survive succeeds in getting out of the vat. How does he manage to solve his problem?
3. Make up a sentence that expresses the main idea of the fable. Here are some possibilities to consider:
   - If you keep on struggling and keep your optimism, you can triumph over life's problems.
   - Sometimes just when things seem darkest, the light shines through.

Myths and Folk Tales

OBJECTIVES

The overall aim is for students to write a report on a book of their choice. For a complete list of objectives, see the **Teacher's Notes**.

PRESENTATION

Ask students if any of them have read any books lately. Then ask any who have to tell whether they enjoyed the books or not and to explain what made reading the books a good or bad experience. Now explain to students that they will choose a book to read and then write a book report on it.

You might want to take students to the library to look for books. Encourage students to examine several books and skim through each one before they make a final choice. Give students plenty of time to read and take close-reading notes. You might incorporate reading into each class period and then develop some reader-

FOCUS ON Writing

WRITING A BOOK REPORT

In a **book report,** you present information about a book and present a main idea or evaluation of your own. In this unit you have had a chance to study some of the important elements of a book report. Now you will write your own report on a book of your choice.

Prewriting

1. For your report, select a book that you think you would enjoy reading. Before you choose a book, ask yourself:
   - What subjects do I really like? What issues are important?
   - What are my favorite types of reading? Myths? Poetry? Novels?
   - Can I get some ideas from movies or magazines?
   - Can my friends or classmates recommend a good book?

2. As you start to read, take close-reading **notes** on the book you have chosen. You may find it helpful to prepare a chart for your notes like the one below.

Major Elements of a Book	Reactions/ Notes
Plot _____	Opinions _____
Characters _____	Quotations _____
Setting _____	Questions _____
Theme _____	Evaluation _____

[See **Focus** assignment on page 574.]

3. Develop a **main idea** to focus your report. Use one or two sentences to state this idea as clearly as you can. Your main idea could be one of the following:

   - an overall evaluation of the book

   Example: Ashley Bryan's *Lion and the Ostrich Chicks and Other African Tales* is a wide-ranging collection of legends that never fails to entertain the reader.

   - an opinion about one of the book's major elements

   Example: In *The Rainbow People,* a collection of tales originally told by Chinese immigrants in California, Laurence Yep shows a flair for creating a magical, mysterious atmosphere.

   - a statement that identifies an important or unifying theme in the book

   Example: The myths of the Greek heroes in this collection often feature a seemingly impossible task or quest.

[See **Focus** assignment on page 584.]

4. Gather **details** to support your main idea. Fill out a chart like the one below:

Main Idea: _____
Supporting Details
Facts: _____
Examples: _____
Reasons: _____
Quotations: _____

[See **Focus** assignment on page 617.]

This computer program provides help for all types of writing through guided instruction for each step of the writing process. (Program available separately.)

See **Elements of Writing, Introductory Course,** Chapter 8, for more instruction on writing about literature.

WRITING A BOOK REPORT

Students should avoid the temptation to devote too much time to the synopsis of their books. They should be aware that too much summary is not the best kind of report. They should show through their evaluations, opinions, and statements of main idea how much thinking the book made them do.

Prewriting

You might need to work closely with students as they take their close-reading notes. You might want to create some open-ended questions for students to consider if they use the chart in the text: How are the characters like real people? How do they change or grow? Why do events in the book happen? How does the novel's main idea apply to real

Focus on Writing

response questions to help students focus on the literary elements of their books. Students should keep a special place in their journals for their book notes. Some students might like to buy or find paperback copies of a book so that they can highlight passages and write notes in the margins. During the prewriting stage, have students share their notes and tell about their books in small groups. Students might benefit from examining reviews of children's literature in magazines or local newspapers before they begin the writing stage.

life? How does the book keep the reader's interest? What importance does setting have in the book?

Writing

Students may need help incorporating quotations into their reports. You might want to do a mini-lesson on using quotations in writing. Encourage students not to overuse quotations but to include only a few well-chosen ones.

Evaluating and Revising

You might have students do a self-evaluation of the content of their reports by highlighting with different colors the information they should have included: title and author, brief summary, main idea, supporting details, quotations.

Then students can revise any gaps they find in their papers. For a final evaluation, students should work in small groups with the **Checklist for Evaluation and Revision** for additional suggestions for improvement.

Writing

1. Follow an outline like the one below when you write your report.

   I. Identify book's author and title
   II. Briefly summarize book's contents
   III. State main idea and give supporting details
   IV. Restate main idea in conclusion

   [See **Focus** assignment on page 637. If you need help with summarizing, see **Focus on Reading** on page 629.]

2. Remember to use **transitions** to make the relationship of events and ideas clear. Here are some helpful transition words:

after	next
as a result	then
finally	therefore
first	when
most important	

Evaluating and Revising

1. After you finish your first draft, exchange papers with a partner and read each other's book report. Share ideas with your partner about how to improve your reports. For example, ask your partner to tell you if you have given a clear summary of your book's contents. Also ask if you have stated your main idea clearly and supported it convincingly.

   Finally, ask what kind of impression your description and evaluation made on the reader. Did reading your book report stimulate your classmate's interest enough so that he or she would want to read the book?

   Here is an example of how one student writer revised a paragraph in a book report on the novel *Sounder* by William Armstrong.

TRANSPARENCY 38
Writing Process
Writing a Book Report — helps students plan and write an effective book report.

CLOSURE
Ask students to explain the process of writing a book report. (Prewrite—choose a book, take close-reading notes, develop a main idea, gather details to support main idea; write a draft—be careful of transitions; evaluate and revise; proofread and publish.)

Proofreading and Publishing
Remind students that they need to underline the title of their book wherever it appears in their reports. Also, make students aware that they do not underline their own titles for their reports. Have students work in small editing groups to correct each other's reports for spelling, punctuation of quotations, and pronoun usage.

Writer's Model

The novel's main character is the boy. The boy has to grow up ~~when~~ *during the years* his father *from place to place in the chain gang.* ~~The boy~~ is taken ~~to prison.~~ He helps his mother with crops so the family will not ~~lose~~ *be put off* the farm. He learns about kindness and hope *the value of education. He also learns* when a teacher helps him and gives him a chance to go to school. The boy's character development is related to one of the novel's main themes. Armstrong's story reveals how some people have the faith never to give up, *or become bitter* no matter how hard life may be.

2. You may find the following checklist helpful as you revise your report:

Checklist for Evaluation and Revision

✔ Do I identify the book's author and title at the beginning?
✔ Do I give a brief summary of the contents?
✔ Do I clearly state my main idea in the report?
✔ Have I supported the main idea with examples, facts, reasons, and quotations from the book?
✔ Have I arranged my supporting details clearly?
✔ Do I end with a strong conclusion?

Proofreading and Publishing

1. Proofread your report and correct any errors you find in grammar, usage, and mechanics. (Here you may find it helpful to refer to the **Handbook for Revision** on pages 750–785.) Then prepare a final version of your report by making a clean copy.

2. Consider some of the following publication methods for your report:
   - deliver your report orally to the class
   - make your report the centerpiece of an illustrated poster for the book
   - organize a round table with a few classmates and take turns discussing each other's books and reports

Portfolio If your teacher approves, you may wish to keep a copy of your work in your writing folder or portfolio.

Focus on Writing 643

UNIT 8 ◆ TEACHING GUIDE

THE NOVEL

OVERVIEW OF THE UNIT

This unit focuses on the novel. Like short stories, novels come out of a writer's imagination. Novels consist of the same basic elements as short stories: character, plot, setting, theme, and point of view.

HOW ARE NOVELS DIFFERENT FROM SHORT STORIES?

Short stories range in length from a page to more than fifteen pages. Most novels go on for at least a hundred pages, and some are more than a thousand pages long. A novel is much more than an overgrown short story, however.

A short story is designed to be read in a single sitting. A novel may take several days or even weeks to read. To keep you coming back for more, novelists make you care about the characters and keep you in suspense about what will happen next.

A novel is broader in scope than a short story. A novel usually gives you several interesting characters, a complicated plot, and several settings. Most short stories develop one theme, while a novel may develop several themes. Instead of having a single effect, a novel may move you to tears or anger in one chapter and then make you laugh in the next.

WHY DO PEOPLE READ NOVELS?

Most young people who develop the habit of reading for pleasure enjoy reading novels. But novels offer more than entertainment and escape. Good novels, like all good literature, are revelations: They show us how we live, what we live for, what kind of world we want to live in.

When we read a novel, we share the author's view of life. Reading novels is one of the few ways in which we can get outside our own feelings and understand the minds, hearts, and experiences of other people—even though they are fictional characters. Well-written novels help us understand what it means to be human.

HISTORY OF THE NOVEL

Poetry and drama are thousands of years old, but novels are a recent development. Although some narratives written by the Greeks and Romans resemble the modern novel, most critics believe that the first true novel was written about four hundred years ago. *Don Quixote* (1605) by the Spanish writer Miguel de Cervantes was the first book-length story with a true-to-life plot and characters who make mistakes just as real people do.

The first novel written in English is one that your students may have heard about. *Robinson Crusoe* (1719) by Daniel Defoe tells the story of a shipwrecked sailor. The oldest novel represented in this literature book is *The Adventures of Tom Sawyer* (1876) by the great American writer Mark Twain.

FANTASTIC AND REALISTIC NOVELS

There are many different types of novels, but the two kinds that most young people favor are modern fantasy, including science fiction, and contemporary realistic fiction. Fantasies such as C. S. Lewis's *The Lion, the Witch and the Wardrobe* (page 10) deal with imaginary worlds, while contemporary realistic fiction portrays life in the real world of today.

THE SUMMER OF THE SWANS

The Summer of the Swans is a contemporary realistic novel written especially for young people. Students will enjoy the story because the important characters are young people like themselves. As in most of the novels by Betsy Byars, adults tend to play background roles. Byars focuses on the feelings of young people and—although she never "preaches"—she emphasizes the positive effects that youngsters can have on one another.

Sixth graders will find it easy to identify with the main character, Sara Godfrey, who is, at the beginning of the novel, a confused and unhappy fourteen-year-old. Like many youngsters today, Sara and her sister and brother are not part of a traditional "nuclear family," but they love and support one another. The novel gives young readers the opportunity to experience vicariously what it might be like to live with someone who has special needs. Sara's love for her brother Charlie, who is mentally disabled, suggests to youngsters that they, like Sara, could be capable of loyalty, compassion, and selfless love.

Young readers will enjoy the dialogue in *The Summer of the Swans,* which, they will probably say, sounds just the way real people talk. The humor in the novel is conveyed mostly through dialogue and through characterization of Aunt Willie, the well-meaning relative who takes care of the Godfrey children.

Although *The Summer of the Swans* deals with serious themes, the plot moves quickly. Within twenty-four hours, Charlie becomes lost and is found. As a result of her quest for Charlie, Sara changes dramatically. She finds out what is truly important in her life and becomes a more self-confident, happy person. Adult readers—especially those who are teachers and parents of teenagers—may find these dramatic changes in Sara somewhat miraculous, but young readers will find them believable and satisfying.

The Summer of the Swans is a distinguished example of contemporary realistic fiction for young people. The quest story that is central to its plot and theme makes it an appropriate conclusion for this literature textbook.

OBJECTIVES OF THE UNIT

The aims of this unit for students are
◆ To read a novel
◆ To respond to the characters, events, and ideas in a novel, orally and in writing
◆ To make inferences and to draw conclusions
◆ To predict outcomes
◆ To recognize cause and effect
◆ To compare and contrast characters
◆ To identify and analyze the elements of the novel: character, setting, plot, theme, point of view

PLANNING GUIDE

FOR UNIT PLANNING
- Transparencies 39–44: *Audiovisual Resources Binder*
- *Portfolio Assessment and Professional Support Materials*
- Test Generator
- Mastery Tests: Teaching Resources D, pp. 193, 195
- Analogy Test: Teaching Resources D, p. 198
- Revision Worksheet: Teaching Resources D, p. 199

SELECTION (Pupil's Page)	Teacher's Notes	Reading Check	Reading Focus	Study Guide	Language Skills	Building Vocabulary	Selection Vocab. Test	Selection Test	AV BINDER Audio-cassette
THE NOVEL *Introduction* (p. 645)	138								
Betsy Byars *The Summer of the Swans, Part 1* (p. 648)	139	142	143	144, 145	146	149	151	152	
The Summer of the Swans, Part 2 (p. 670)	154	156		157, 158	159	162	164	165	
The Summer of the Swans, Part 3 (p. 690)	167	169		170	171	174	176	177	
The Summer of the Swans, Part 4 (p. 703)	179	181		182, 183, 184, 185		186	188	189	

- To write creatively and critically in relation to the novel
- To explore the use of slang and exaggeration in a novel
- To distinguish between facts and opinions
- To write a persuasive essay

CONCEPTS AND SKILLS

The following concepts and skills are treated in this unit:

CLOSE READING OF A NOVEL
Guidelines for Reading a Novel 646

THINKING ABOUT WORDS
How to Own a Word 647

FOCUS ON READING AND CRITICAL THINKING
Distinguishing Between Facts and Opinions 718

LITERARY ELEMENTS
Character 669
Point of View 688
Theme 712

LANGUAGE AND VOCABULARY
Dialogue 712

OPPORTUNITIES FOR WRITING
Focus on Persuasive Writing
Choosing a Topic and Writing an Opinion Statement 669
Supporting Your Opinion 689
Organizing a Persuasive Paper 714
Writing a Persuasive Essay 719

Writing About Literature
Using Another Point of View 713
Analyzing a Change in Character 713

TRANSPARENCIES

The following unit support materials with specific correlations to literature selections are available in the **Fine Art and Instructional Transparencies with Teacher's Notes and Blackline Masters** section of your *Audiovisual Resources Binder*.

FINE ART TRANSPARENCIES
Theme: An Expanded Story
39 *Nakht with His Family Hunting in the Nile Marshes*, Anonymous
40 *Baseball at Night*, Morris Kantor

READER RESPONSE
41 Check the Stars
42 Letter to an Author

LITERARY ELEMENTS
43 Understanding and Evaluating a Novel

WRITING PROCESS
44 Writing a Persuasive Essay

643B

INTRODUCING THE UNIT

You might begin the unit with activities designed to interest students in reading novels.

1. Discussing Novels Young People Like. Bring in several young people's novels that you think your students may have read and liked. (You might want to ask students to find these in a library and bring them to class.) Include at least one novel by Betsy Byars, another by Judy Blume, and at least one work of fantasy, such as Lloyd Alexander's *The High King.* You may also want to include a popular mystery novel (Hardy Boys or Nancy Drew); a science fiction novel, such as one of those based on the *Star Trek* series; some sports novels by Matt Christopher; and whatever else any of your students enjoy reading. Ask students to discuss any of the novels they have read. Encourage them to tell about novels they have liked.

2. Keeping a Record. Encourage students to keep a record of the novels they read. Suggest that they buy a small notebook to record their impressions of novels. Each entry might include the title and author and the student's opinion of the novel. They might also want to copy sentences from the novels that they find especially interesting, funny, or beautifully written. A notebook like this, even if it is kept for just a month or two, serves as an important record of thoughts and feelings at a particular time.

3. Writing to Authors. You might have each student compose a letter to an author. Most authors of books for young people do answer letters from their readers. If students write their letters before you begin *The Summer of the Swans,* many of them will receive answers within three or four weeks. You can then make a copy of each answer and have several students create a bulletin-board display of them. Students may write to an author in care of the company that publishes the author's book. You can find the addresses of publishers in a publication called *Literary Market Place,* at most public libraries.

4. Selling and Trading Novels. You might want to organize a book fair. The easiest way to do this is to have students bring to class books (including novels) in good condition that they want to sell or trade. You can have students sell and trade within their own class, with another class at your school, or with classes at other schools.

5. Looking at the Illustrations. Allow class time for students to browse through the novel and look at the illustrations. List on the chalkboard questions generated by the pictures.

PORTFOLIO ASSESSMENT

Suggestions for use of portfolios as support for this unit are described in the **Portfolio Assessment and Professional Support Materials** booklet accompanying this program. Specific suggestions are provided for a variety of student projects that may be suitable for inclusion in a portfolio. In addition, copying masters are provided for guides that may be used for evaluation and assessment of student projects.

SELECTION NOTES

Following are vocabulary lists of words from each part of the novel that are included in the Building Vocabulary Worksheets and Selection Vocabulary Tests; Reading Check tests (which are also available in blackline masters); and answers to questions in the Language and Vocabulary exercise.

THE SUMMER OF THE SWANS (PAGES 650–668)

Vocabulary

pathetic	pry	indignation	persist
lanky	grimace(d)	taunt(ing)	
detest(ed)	emphatic(ally)	clamor(ing)	

Reading Check

Have students judge each statement as true or false.
1. Sara likes the way she looks.   **False**
2. Charlie is mentally disabled because of a motorcycle accident.   **False**
3. One of Charlie's favorite possessions is his watch.   **True**
4. Charlie is unable to speak.   **True**
5. The Godfreys live with Aunt Willie.   **True**

THE SUMMER OF THE SWANS (PAGES 670–688)

Vocabulary

splendor	logical	elongate(d)	accusation
feverish	discourage(d)	testify	
chide	agitation	sustain	

Reading Check

Have students judge each statement as true or false.
1. Charlie leaves the house to find the dog.   **False**
2. Sara thinks that Charlie was looking for the swans when he got lost.   **True**
3. Aunt Willie says that Sara is too revengeful.   **True**
4. Aunt Willie telephones Sara's father.   **True**
5. Joe apologizes for stealing Charlie's watch.   **False**

THE SUMMER OF THE SWANS (PAGES 690–702)

Vocabulary

indestructible	finality	flail(ing)	engulf
constructive(ly)	envelope(d)	compulsion	
impetuous(ly)	distract(ed)	expanse	

Reading Check

Have students judge each statement as true or false.
1. Sara finds out that Joe did not take Charlie's watch.   **True**
2. Mary breaks her ankle and has to give up the search.   **False**
3. Joe Melby finds a button from Charlie's pajamas.   **False**
4. Sara and Joe argue.   **False**
5. Sara and Joe climb to the top of a hill.   **True**

THE SUMMER OF THE SWANS (PAGES 703–710)

Vocabulary

frenzy	dreadful	beacon	foliage
routine	associate	shrill	
procedure	urgent	mute	

Reading Check

Have students judge each statement as true or false.
1. Charlie calls Sara's name.   **False**
2. Joe gives Charlie his watch to wear.   **True**
3. Someone in the search party shoots at the swans.   **False**
4. Joe asks Sara to go to a party with him.   **True**
5. Sara talks to her father on the phone.   **True**

Language and Vocabulary: Dialogue (page 712)

Slang
Answers will vary. Examples are given.
1. annoying, silly, irritating, aggravating
2. sticky, disgusting, messy
3. beautiful, lovely, stylish

Exaggeration
Students' explanations will vary. Examples are given.
1. Aunt Willie has been holding him tightly because she is so afraid.
2. Her sneakers make her feet look large and ridiculous.
3. Her life since third grade has been disappointing.

Student Learning Options

THE NOVEL

1. Designing a Dust Jacket
Ask students to design a dust jacket for *The Summer of the Swans*. It should feature an illustration on the cover, a brief summary of the plot on the flaps, and comments by "critics" on the back. It can also include quotations from the text that represent the work's theme or significant turning points in the action.

2. Composing a Letter
Ask students to write a letter from Sara's father to Sara, expressing his feelings for his children and explaining why he is unable to spend more time with them.

3. Researching Swans
Many legends about swans exist. Ask students to look up swans in an encyclopedia or other reference book and to report their findings to the class. Students could focus on characteristics of real swans or on fictional and legendary swans.

4. Performing Reader's Theater
Have students select a scene from the novel and turn it into a play for a Reader's Theater presentation. Encourage students to select scenes that have a good bit of dialogue already, but assure them that they are free to write as much dialogue as they like.

5. Planning a Rescue
Have students work in groups to plan how they would conduct the rescue of a lost child in your area. They should consider who would be involved in the effort, how they would coordinate the search, and what kind of equipment they would need.

6. Learning About Missing Persons
Invite a representative of a local law enforcement agency to talk to the class about how the police search for missing persons. To prepare for the speaker's visit, ask each student to write down a question for the police officer. Have a committee of students select a few of the best questions, and let the students who wrote the questions ask them after the talk.

7. Proposing a New Title
Ask students to propose a new title for *The Summer of the Swans*. Remind them that a title should catch the interest of readers and that many titles of literary works give clues to the theme of the works.

8. Illustrating a Scene
At the end of the novel, Sara has a mental picture of life as a set of steps. Ask students to draw and color an illustration of this mental picture. They can cut out pictures from magazines to represent the people Sara sees, or they can draw them.

643D

VISUAL CONNECTIONS

This painting, typical of Lawrence's interest in social realism, captures the intense interest and concentration of people reading in a library. The row upon row of books in the background suggests the tremendous wealth of knowledge available in free public libraries. The titles of many of the books gleam like beacons on the shelves. Ask students what they think of the painting's unusual title.

About the Artist
Jacob Lawrence (1917–) captures feelings and ideas with warm, vibrant colors, and exaggerated, yet simple, shapes. Much of Lawrence's work deals with the experiences and history of African Americans. A series by Lawrence depicting the life of Harriet Tubman is included in his picture biography for children, *Harriet and the Promised Land* (Windmill: Simon & Schuster, 1968). (See one of the paintings on page 32.)

The Libraries Are Appreciated by Jacob Lawrence (1943). Gouache on watercolor on paper.

Philadelphia Museum of Art.
The Louis E. Stern Collection.

UNIT EIGHT

The Novel

Novels are long stories about characters who face **conflicts** of some kind. These conflicts might be **external:** that is, they might involve the characters in physical struggles with forces like fire-breathing dragons or sub-zero temperatures. Or, the conflicts might be **internal:** the characters might have to struggle with feelings like fear, doubt, or loneliness. Most novels include both kinds of conflicts.

Like a short story, a novel reveals a theme. **Theme** is a truth about life that we discover by watching the characters and the way they respond to the things that happen to them.

As you probably have already discovered, the most satisfying elements in most novels are the **characters** themselves. In a successful novel, we care deeply about the fates of the main characters. We worry about them. We cheer when they succeed, and we weep when they fail. Some characters in fiction, in fact, are so vivid that we add them to that endless parade of real, live people we will never forget.

PORTFOLIO ASSESSMENT

Students may want to keep a reading journal as they study *The Summer of the Swans*. In their journals, they might keep summaries of events, a vocabulary list, doodle art, phrases that interest them, evaluations of characters, and notes about how the novel is reflective of its title. Suggest that students pay particular attention to changes that occur in Sara's attitude as the novel progresses. Ask if other characters show as much change as Sara. Students may want to complete their journals by binding them and decorating their covers. Consult with students individually to agree on how their journals will be assessed. (See *Portfolio Assessment and Professional Support Materials* for additional information on student portfolios.)

Almost every student has visited the public library, but some may never have entered a bookstore. Try to arrange a field trip to a bookstore that has a well-stocked children's section. Shiny new books attractively displayed are most appealing. You may even be able to find a store that also sells used children's books at greatly reduced prices.

Help students find books they will like by asking any young book addict you know to explain how he or she predicts that a book is worth reading. (Find an author you like, pull the book from the shelf, glance through the pictures, if any, read the table of contents, and skim a page or two.)

Close Reading OF A NOVEL

You read a novel in almost the same way you read a short story or play or biography. You take pleasure in experiencing a good story, told by a talented storyteller. You enjoy the feeling of suspense building up. You enjoy watching the characters perform for you. When you're busy washing the dishes, you think, "I can't wait to get back to that novel."

Guidelines for Reading a Novel

1. **Ask questions as you read.** Ask about unfamiliar words or terms. Ask about situations or references that puzzle you. Ask questions when the writer drops clues.
2. **Make predictions.** Think about what might happen next.
3. **Relate what you read to your own life.** Compare the characters and events with people and situations in your own experience. Are the characters believable?
4. **Think about the underlying meaning or theme.** Relate the theme to life as you know it. Decide if it's a good theme or if it's overworked.

You might have a pad of paper and pencil handy as you read the following novel. Write down your questions and your responses to the problems faced by Sara, Wanda, and Charlie on this extraordinary day that starts out in such an ordinary way.

THINKING ABOUT WORDS

HOW TO OWN A WORD

In an earlier unit (page 76), you were introduced to the notion of "owning" a word. The idea is that when you know a lot about a word, you "own it" because you can use it comfortably in many ways. *Astute* is a marvelous word that is well worth "owning."

In the last unit, in "How the Whale Got His Throat" (page 595) you read about a 'stute fish. At the bottom of the page on which the 'stute fish is introduced, there is a little note explaining that *'stute* is short for *astute,* meaning "clever." *Clever* is a good synonym for *astute,* but someone who is astute is often more than clever. People who are astute are clever at understanding behavior and situations and at using this knowledge to their own advantage. That is certainly what the 'stute fish was like.

Below is a chart that organizes some ideas about *astute.* Think of ideas you might add.

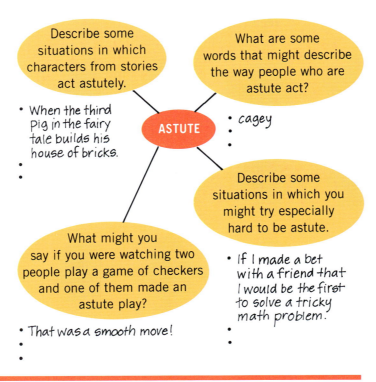

Thinking About Words
Here are some words from *The Summer of the Swans* that sixth graders might enjoy owning: *pathetic* (page 650), *inscrutable* (page 650), *indignation* (page 657), *agitation* (page 680), *compulsion* (page 700).

Assign one word to each of five groups. Ask each group to make up a cluster chart similar to the one on this page. Each chart should contain five questions about the word or any of its forms (for example, *compulsion, compulsive, compulsively*). Some questions might require a drawing or a mimed answer. Students will have to use dictionaries to make sure they have the correct forms.

Groups might then trade charts and try to answer the questions that another group has made up.

OBJECTIVES
Students will make inferences about a character based on the character's actions, words, and thoughts. They will choose a persuasive writing topic and write an opinion statement.

TEACHING RESOURCES D
Teacher's Notes, p. 139
Reading Check, p. 142
Reading Focus, p. 143
Study Guide, pp. 144, 145
Language Skills, p. 146
Building Vocabulary, p. 149
Selection Vocabulary Test, p. 151
Selection Test, p. 152

1. BACKGROUND
The Newbery Award is presented annually to the author who wrote the "most distinguished book for children" in the preceding year. A committee of twenty-three members from the American Library Association chooses the winner. The first Newbery was given in 1922. For more about the author's acceptance of the Newbery Award, see "Behind the Scenes," pages 715–717.

FOCUS/MOTIVATION
Establishing a Purpose for Reading. Tell students that the main character in this novel, Sara Godfrey, is a teenager. As they get to know Sara, ask them to decide if they think she has the feelings and problems that real teenagers might have.

Prereading Journal. Have students write a few sentences telling what they think they might enjoy most about being a teenager. Also have them write what they think they might like least about being a teenager.

The Summer of the Swans

BETSY BYARS

Before You Read

1 This novel, which won the Newbery Award in 1971, is an example of realistic fiction. It's fiction because it came out of Betsy Byars's imagination. It's realistic because it shows life as it really is. All of the events that occur in *The Summer of the Swans* could really have happened. The story is set in a realistic small town in West Virginia, where abandoned coal mines dot the outlying hills. The characters in the story experience the needs, wishes, and fears of real people.

The main character in *The Summer of the Swans* is fourteen-year-old Sara Godfrey. The whole story covers a crisis in the Godfrey family that is over in just a little more than twenty-four hours. Yet in that time, Sara's feelings about herself and her whole outlook on life change.

This is also a story about a ten-year-old boy who has very special needs. Charlie is mentally handicapped, and his problems are often a trial to his sisters and aunt. But Charlie is the one who helps the family understand the tragedy of loss and the value of love.

Before you read, write a few sentences in your journal telling how you think families can be affected by special children in their midst. How might they have to adjust their lives to accommodate a child with special needs?

The Novel

READING THE SELECTION
For teaching purposes, the novel has been divided into four parts. The first part (pages 648–668) introduces the characters and the basic situation. Most students who read on grade level will be able to read these pages silently in three or four class periods. After you introduce the story and read the headnote in class, you might want to assign the reading to be done at home.

In either case, you may want to divide up this part as follows: Day 1: pages 648–654; Day 2: page 655 to the break in the right-hand column of page 659; Day 3: page 659 to the break in the right-hand column of page 662; Day 4: pages 662–668.

For slower students, you may need to assign fewer pages each day. You may have students read from one break to the next.

VISUAL CONNECTIONS
Artist and illustrator Robert Heindel has illustrated this story so as to reflect the perceptions of the characters. (Here, it's Sara, probably as seen by other people.) You might want to compare this approach to illustration with point of view in literature. You might ask students to tell you how feelings affect what people see. For example, a parent might see a "broken, useless" toy and want to throw it away. A child might see a "favorite" toy, connected with good times in the past, and not be willing to throw it away.

Later you might ask students how they think Sara would see herself.

649

(Since there are eight breaks, the reading would then take students eight days.)

You may need to help slower students understand that the narrator can tell what all of the characters are thinking and feeling. They should especially watch for shifts between Sara's feelings and Charlie's feelings.

MEETING INDIVIDUAL NEEDS
Kinesthetic Learners • To get students quickly involved in the characters and their lives in this novel, you might want to have two students act out the opening scene between Sara and her sister Wanda. You might have the actors use a stuffed animal, if one can be located, to represent the family dog Boysie.

1. LANGUAGE AND VOCABULARY:
Dialogue
Note that the dialogue adds humor to the story, moves the plot forward, and reveals character.

When students see a slang word or phrase in this novel, they might ask themselves if this slang is still "in" today. If it is no longer used, what word or phrase has replaced it?

2

Inscrutable means "not easily understood" or "mysterious."

3. GUIDED READING:
Making Inferences
What can you infer about the way Sara and Wanda feel about one another? They like each other and care about each other's feelings.

4. LITERARY ELEMENTS:
Exaggeration
What examples of exaggeration—making something much bigger or worse than it is in real life—do you find? Some examples of exaggeration are "I can't do anything around here" and "This place smells like a perfume factory." You might point out that Sara's exaggerated language helps you know that she is feeling intensely confused and unhappy.

650

Language and Vocabulary

1 **Dialogue refers to the characters' quoted conversation.** If a story is to be believable, its dialogue has to sound just the way people talk in real life. If you're like many readers, you'll immediately realize that Betsy Byars has a great talent for writing dialogue that is natural, realistic, even witty. Her young characters, and her older ones, all are able to say things in ways that make us laugh, or cry.

Sara Godfrey was lying on the bed tying a kerchief on the dog, Boysie. "Hold your chin up, Boysie, will you?" she said as she braced herself on one elbow. The dog was old, slept all the time, and he was lying on his side with his eyes closed while she lifted his head and tied the scarf.

Her sister Wanda was sitting at the dressing table combing her hair. Wanda said, "Why don't you leave Boysie alone?"

"There's nothing else to do," Sara answered without looking up. "You want to see a show?"

"Not particularly."

"It's called 'The Many Faces of Boysie.'"

"Now I know I don't want to see it."

Sara held up the dog with the kerchief neatly tied beneath his chin and said, "The first face of Boysie, proudly presented for your entertainment and amusement, is the Russian Peasant Woman. Taaaaaa-daaaaaa!"

"Leave the dog alone."

"He likes to be in shows, don't you, Boysie?" She untied the scarf, refolded it and set it carefully on top of the dog's head. "And now for the second face of Boysie, we travel halfway around the world to the mysterious East, where we see Boysie the Inscrutable Hindu, Taaaaaaa-daaaaaa!" **2**

With a sigh Wanda turned and looked at the dog. "That's pathetic. In people's age that dog is eighty-four years old." She shook a can of hair spray and sprayed her hair. "And besides, that's my good scarf."

"Oh, all right." Sara fell back heavily **3** against the pillow. "I can't do anything around here."

"Well, if it's going to make you that miserable, I'll watch the show."

"I don't want to do it any more. It's **4** no fun now. This place smells like a perfume factory." She put the scarf over her face and stared up through the thin blue material. Beside her, Boysie lay back down and curled himself into a ball. They lay

650 The Novel

SOCIAL STUDIES LINK
Because this novel was written more than twenty-five years ago, students may find many of the references to people, products and activities, television programs, and slang expressions either out of date or unknown to them. You might suggest that as they read, they make a list of dated customs, references, or expressions. As you discuss the novel with students, you could make a master list of things they found. Then, take the opportunity to discuss how our culture has changed.

---

without moving for a moment and then Sara sat up on the bed and looked down at her long, lanky legs. She said, "I have the biggest feet in my school."

"Honestly, Sara, I hope you are not going to start listing all the millions of things wrong with you because I just don't want to hear it again."

"Well, it's the truth about my feet. One time in Phys Ed the boys started throwing the girls' sneakers around and Bull Durham got my sneakers and put them on and they fit perfectly! How do you think it feels to wear the same size shoe as Bull Durham?"

"People don't notice things like that."

"Huh!"

"No, they don't. I have perfectly terrible hands—look at my fingers—only I don't go around all the time saying, 'Everybody, look at my stubby fingers, I have stubby fingers, everybody,' to *make* people notice. You should just ignore things that are wrong with you. The truth is everyone else is so worried about what's wrong with *them* that—"

"It is very difficult to ignore the fact that you have huge feet when Bull Durham is dancing all over the gym in your shoes. They were not stretched the tiniest little bit when he took them off either."

1 "You wear the same size shoe as Jackie Kennedy Onassis if that makes you feel any better."

"How do you know?"

"Because one time when she was going into an Indian temple she had to leave her shoes outside and some reporter looked in them to see what size they were." She leaned close to the mirror and looked at her teeth.

"Her feet *look* littler."

"That's because she doesn't wear orange sneakers."

"I like my orange sneakers." Sara sat on the edge of the bed, slipped her feet into the shoes, and held them up. "What's wrong with them?"

"Nothing, except that when you want **2** to hide something, you don't go painting it orange. I've got to go. Frank's coming."

She went out the door and Sara could hear her crossing into the kitchen. Sara lay back on the bed, her head next to Boysie. She looked at the sleeping dog, then cov- **3** ered her face with her hands and began to cry noisily.

"Oh, Boysie, Boysie, I'm crying," she wailed. Years ago, when Boysie was a young dog, he could not bear to hear anyone cry. Sara had only to pretend she was crying and Boysie would come running. He would whine and dig at her with his paws and lick her hands until she stopped. Now he lay with his eyes closed.

"Boysie, I'm crying," she said again. "I'm really crying this time. Boysie doesn't love me."

The dog shifted uneasily without opening his eyes.

"Boysie, Boysie, I'm crying, I'm so sad, Boysie," she wailed, then stopped and sat up abruptly. "You don't care about anybody, do you, Boysie? A person could cry herself to death these days and you wouldn't care."

The Summer of the Swans 651

---

1. BACKGROUND
Jackie Kennedy Onassis (1929–1994) was the wife of John F. Kennedy, the thirty-fifth President of the United States. After his death, she married Aristotle Onassis, a Greek shipping magnate who died in 1975. Mrs. Onassis was considered a very stylish woman. Wanda is complimenting Sara by suggesting that stylish women sometimes have big feet.

2. GUIDED READING:
Distinguishing Between Fact and Opinion
Is this a fact or an opinion? How do you know? This is an opinion. It makes good sense and sounds factual, but it cannot be proved true or false.

3. GUIDED READING:
Interpreting Meaning
Do you think Sara is really crying here? How does she feel? She is just pretending to cry because she wants to make Boysie respond to her. Sara is bored, but she also feels confused and sorry for herself.

MEETING INDIVIDUAL NEEDS
ESL/LEP • Sara's conversation with Charlie includes two slang words, *finky* and *gross*, which may require explanation. Ask the class to supply synonyms or to describe in their own words what these words mean. Write students' responses on the chalkboard. You might also want to ask students to suggest other slang words that have similar meanings.

1. GUIDED READING:
Making Inferences
Why does Sara change her mind about going into the kitchen? She does not want to hear her aunt and Wanda argue.

2. GUIDED READING:
Drawing Conclusions
What clues lead you to the conclusion that there might be something wrong with Charlie? He does not answer Sara's question. He can't put his candy back onto the stick, and Sara reminds him to be careful with it.

3. GUIDED READING:
Identifying the Author's Purpose
Since neither Boysie nor Charlie speaks, what good does it do to have Sara talk to them? Sara's speeches to Boysie and Charlie help readers find out what she is thinking and feeling. They help readers get to know and like Sara.

She got up and left the room. In the hall she heard the tapping noise of Boysie's feet behind her and she said without looking at him, "I don't want you now, Boysie. Go on back in the bedroom. Go on." She went a few steps farther and, when he continued to follow her, turned and looked at him. "In case you are confused, Boysie, a dog is supposed to comfort people and run up and nuzzle them and make them feel better. All you want to do is lie on soft things and hide bones in the house because you are too lazy to go outside. Just go on back in the bedroom."

1 She started into the kitchen, still followed by Boysie, who could not bear to be left alone, then heard her aunt and Wanda arguing, changed her mind, and went out onto the porch.

Behind her, Boysie scratched at the door and she let him out. "Now quit following me."

Her brother Charlie was sitting on the top step and Sara sat down beside him. She held out her feet, looked at them, and said, "I like my orange sneakers, don't you, Charlie?"

2 He did not answer. He had been eating a lollipop and the stick had come off and now he was trying to put it back into the red candy. He had been trying for so long that the stick was bent.

"Here," she said, "I'll do it for you." She put the stick in and handed it to him. "Now be careful with it."

She sat without speaking for a moment, then she looked down at her feet and said, "I hate these orange sneakers. I just *hate* them." She leaned back against the porch railing so she wouldn't have to see them and said, "Charlie, I'll tell you something. This has been the worst summer of my life."

She did not know exactly why this was true. She was doing the same things she had done last summer—walk to the Dairy Queen with her friend Mary, baby-sit for Mrs. Hodges, watch television—and yet everything was different. It was as if her life was a huge kaleidoscope, and the kaleidoscope had been turned and now everything was changed. The same stones, shaken, no longer made the same design.

But it was not only one different design, one change; it was a hundred. She could never be really sure of anything this summer. One moment she was happy, and the next, for no reason, she was miserable. An hour ago she had loved her sneakers; now she detested them.

3 "Charlie, I'll tell you what this awful summer's been like. You remember when that finky Jim Wilson got you on the seesaw, remember that? And he kept bouncing you up and down and then he'd keep you up in the air for a real long time and then he'd drop you down real sudden, and you couldn't get off and you thought you never would? Up and down, up and down, for the rest of your life? Well, that's what this summer's been like for me."

He held out the candy and the stick to her.

"Not again!" She took it from him. "This piece of candy is so gross that I don't even want to touch it, if you want to know

652 The Novel

the truth." She put the stick back in and handed it to him. "Now if it comes off again—and I mean this, Charlie Godfrey—I'm throwing the candy away."

Charlie looked at the empty sucker stick, reached into his mouth, took out the candy, and held them together in his hand. Sara had said she would throw the candy away if this happened again and so he closed his fist tightly and looked away from her.

1 Slowly he began to shuffle his feet back and forth on the step. He had done this so many times over the years that two grooves had been worn into the boards. It was a nervous habit that showed he was concerned about something, and Sara recognized it at once.

"All right, Charlie," she said wearily. "Where's your sucker?"

He began to shake his head slowly from side to side. His eyes were squeezed shut.

"I'm not going to take it away from you. I'm going to fix it one more time."

He was unwilling to trust her and continued to shake his head. The movement was steady and mechanical, as if it would continue forever, and she watched him for a moment.

Then, with a sigh, she lifted his hand and attempted to pry his fingers loose. "Honestly, Charlie, you're holding onto this grubby piece of candy like it was a crown jewel or something. Now, let go." He opened his eyes and watched while she took the candy from him and put the stick in. The stick was now bent almost double, and she held it out to him carefully.

"There."

He took the sucker and held it without putting it into his mouth, still troubled by the unsteadiness of the bent stick. Sara looked down at her hands and began to pull at a broken fingernail. There was some- **2** thing similar about them in that moment, the same oval face, round brown eyes, brown hair hanging over the forehead, freckles on the nose. Then Charlie glanced up and the illusion was broken.

Still holding his sucker, he looked across the yard and saw the tent he had made over the clothesline that morning. He had taken an old white blanket out into the yard, hung it over the low clothesline, and then got under it. He had sat there with the blanket blowing against him until Sara came out and said, "Charlie, you have to fasten the ends down, like this. It isn't a tent if it's just hanging in the wind."

He had thought there was something wrong. He waited beneath the blanket until she came back with some clothespins and hammered them into the hard earth, fastening the edges of the blanket to the ground. "Now, *that's* a tent."

The tent had pleased him. The warmth **3** of the sun coming through the thin cotton blanket, the shadows of the trees moving overhead had made him drowsy and comfortable and now he wanted to be back in the tent.

Sara had started talking about the summer again, but he did not listen. He could tell from the tone of her voice that she was

The Summer of the Swans 653

---

1. GUIDED READING:
Interpreting Meaning
Point out that Sara and Charlie communicate very well even though Charlie does not speak.

2. GUIDED READING:
Making Inferences
What can you infer about Charlie's expression as compared to Sara's? Charlie's expression is different from Sara's. Hers is probably quite lively; she seems to be interested in many things. He may look worried and confused or just blank.

3. LITERARY ELEMENTS:
Point of View
Students should notice that here the **narrator,** the person telling the story, tells what Charlie is thinking and feeling. Earlier in the story, the reader found out mostly what Sara was thinking and feeling. This point of view is called **omniscient,** which means "all-knowing." The narrator knows and can tell the thoughts and feelings of any character.

COOPERATIVE LEARNING

To help students understand one way that a novel is different from a short story, you might ask them to analyze the main characters at the beginning of the novel and then to compare the character traits they see at the end of the novel. By listing these traits at both times, students can see how a character is allowed to grow in a longer work, a process not easily accomplished in a short story.

During this first section of the story, you could divide the class into cooperative groups of five or six and have each group write a list of five or six adjectives to describe Sara, Wanda, Charlie, and Aunt Willie. Ask the groups to share their lists with the class and perhaps to keep track of all the adjectives they come up with on the chalkboard. Then, after you finish reading the novel, have students get back together with their groups and make another list of character traits. Which characters have changed? How have they grown?

1. VISUAL CONNECTIONS
Through whose eyes do you see this sight of Charlie in his tent? How does Charlie feel in this protected world? (See page 653.)

2. GUIDED READING:
Predicting Outcomes
What do you think might be wrong with Charlie? At this point students will probably predict that Charlie is mentally retarded to some extent.

not really talking to him at all. He got up slowly and began to walk across the yard toward the tent.

2   Sara watched him as he walked, a small figure for his ten years, wearing faded blue jeans and a striped knit shirt that was stretched out of shape. He was holding the sucker in front of him as if it were a candle that might go out at any moment.

Sara said, "Don't drop that candy in the grass now or it's really going to be lost."

She watched while he bent, crawled into the tent, and sat down. The sun was behind the tent now and she could see his silhouette. Carefully he put the sucker back into his mouth.

Then Sara lay back on the hard boards of the porch and looked up at the ceiling.

In the house Wanda and Aunt Willie were still arguing. Sara could hear every word even out on the porch. Aunt Willie, who had been taking care of them since the death of their mother six years ago, was saying loudly, "No, not on a motorcycle. No motorcycle!"

Sara grimaced. It was not only the loudness of Aunt Willie's voice that she disliked. It was everything—the way she bossed them, the way she never really listened, the way she never cared what she said. She had once announced loud enough for everyone in Carter's Drugstore to hear that Sara needed a good dose of magnesia.

"It isn't a motorcycle, it's a motor *scooter*." Wanda was speaking patiently, as if to a small child. "They're practically like bicycles."

"No."

"All I want to do is to ride one half mile on this perfectly safe motor scooter—"

"No. It's absolutely and positively no. No!"

"Frank is very careful. He has never had even the tiniest accident."

No answer.

"Aunt Willie, it is perfectly safe. He takes his mother to the grocery store on it. Anyway, I am old enough to go without permission and I wish you'd realize it. I am nineteen years old."

No answer. Sara knew that Aunt Willie would be standing by the sink shaking her head emphatically from side to side.

"Aunt Willie, he's going to be here any minute. He's coming all the way over here just to drive me to the lake to see the swans."

"You don't care *that* for seeing those swans."

"I do too. I love birds."

"All right then, those swans have been on the lake three days, and not once have you gone over to see them. Now all of a sudden you *have* to go, can't wait one min-

The Summer of the Swans 655

1. GUIDED READING: Identifying Cause and Effect
Why are the Godfreys living with their aunt? Their mother died six years ago.

2. GUIDED READING: Drawing Conclusions
What kind of person do you think Aunt Willie is? Remember that this is what *Sara* thinks of Aunt Willie. Students will see as they read on that Aunt Willie is a very good person and loves the children very much.

3. LITERARY ELEMENTS: Conflict
This humorous dialogue between Aunt Willie and Wanda is the kind of minor conflict that you would not have in a more tightly plotted short story. (You might explain that "tightly plotted" means that everything in a story is important to the outcome of the plot.) Here the conflict adds comic relief and reveals the characters of Aunt Willie and Wanda.

1. GUIDED READING:
Forming Valid Opinions
Although Wanda is quite rude to her aunt, with whom does the author seem to sympathize? How do you know? Byars seems to sympathize with Wanda. She presents Aunt Willie as a somewhat foolish, old-fashioned figure. You might ask students if they think *their* parents would let them ride on somebody's motor scooter.

2. GUIDED READING:
Interpreting Meaning
Why do you think Sara has never before used the word retarded? It is possible that she has never before accepted the fact that Charlie is retarded. Also, she is extremely loyal to Charlie and knows how unique and lovable he is. She does not like the idea of his being "labeled"—as if that were the most important thing about him.

---

ute to get on this devil motorcycle and see those swans."

1 "For your information, I have been dying to see them, only this is my first chance." She went out of the kitchen and pulled the swinging door shut behind her. "And I'm going," she said over her shoulder.

Wanda came out of the house, slammed the screen door, stepped over Boysie, and sat by Sara on the top step. "She never wants anyone to have any fun."

"I know."

"She makes me so mad. All I want to do is just ride down to see the swans on Frank's motor scooter." She looked at Sara, then broke off and said, "Where did Charlie go?"

"He's over there in his tent."

"I see him now. I wish Frank would hurry up and get here before Aunt Willie comes out." She stood, looked down the street, and sat back on the steps. "Did I tell you what that boy in my psychology class last year said about Charlie?"

Sara straightened. "What boy?"

"This boy Arnold Hampton, in my psychology class. We were discussing children who—"

"You mean you talk about Charlie to perfect strangers? To your class? I think that's awful." She put her feet into the two grooves worn in the steps by Charlie.

2 "What do you say? 'Let me tell you all about my retarded brother—it's so interesting'?" It was the first time in her life that she had used the term "retarded" in connection with her brother, and she looked quickly away from the figure in the white tent. Her face felt suddenly hot and she snapped a leaf from the rhododendron bush by the steps and held it against her forehead.

"No, I don't say that. Honestly, Sara, you—"

"And then do you say, 'And while I'm telling you about my retarded brother, I'll also tell you about my real hung-up sister'?" She moved the leaf to her lips and blew against it angrily.

"No, I don't say that because you're not all that fascinating, if you want to know the truth. Anyway, Arnold Hampton's father happens to be a pediatrician and Arnold is sincerely interested in working with boys like Charlie. He is even helping start a camp which Charlie may get to go to next summer, and all because I talked to him in my psychology class." She sighed. "You're impossible, you know that? I can't imagine why I even try to tell you anything."

"Well, Charlie's our problem."

"He's everybody's. There is no— Oh, here comes Frank." She broke off and got to her feet. "Tell Aunt Willie I'll be home later."

She started quickly down the walk, waving to the boy who was making his way slowly up the street on a green motor scooter.

"**W**ait, wait, you wait." Aunt Willie came onto the porch drying her hands on a dish

656 The Novel

towel. She stood at the top of the steps until Frank, a thin boy with red hair, brought the motor scooter to a stop. As he kicked down the stand she called out, "Frank, listen, save yourself some steps. Wanda's not going anywhere on that motorcycle."

"Aw, Aunt Willie," Frank said. He opened the gate and came slowly up the walk. "All we're going to do is go down to the lake. We don't even have to get on the highway for that."

"No motorcycles," she said. "You go break your neck if you want to. That's not my business. Wanda, left in my care, is not going to break her neck on any motorcycle."

"Nobody's going to break his neck. We're just going to have a very uneventful ride down the road to the lake. Then we're going to turn around and have a very uneventful ride back."

"No."

"I tell you what," Frank said. "I'll make a deal with you."

"What deal?"

"Have you ever been on a motor scooter?"

"Me? I never even rode on a bicycle."

"Try it. Come on. I'll ride you down to the Tennents' house and back. Then if you think it's not safe, you say to me, 'Frank, it's not safe,' and I'll take my motor scooter and ride off into the sunset."

She hesitated. There was something about a ride that appealed to her.

Sara said against the rhododendron leaf, "I don't think you ought to. You're too old to be riding up and down the street on a motor scooter."

She knew instantly she had said the wrong thing, for at once Aunt Willie turned to her angrily. "Too old!" She faced Sara with indignation. "I am barely forty years old. May I grow a beard if I'm not." She stepped closer, her voice rising. "Who says I'm so old?" She held the dish towel in front of her, like a matador taunting a bull. The dish towel flicked the air once.

"Nobody said anything," Sara said wearily. She threw the leaf down and brushed it off the steps with her foot.

"Then where did all this talk about my age come from, I'd like to know?"

"Anyway," Frank interrupted, "you're not too old to ride a motor scooter."

"I'll do it." She threw the dish towel across the chair and went down the steps. "I may break my neck but I'll do it."

"Hold on tight, Aunt Willie," Wanda called.

"Hold on! Listen, my hands never held on to anything the way I'm going to hold on to this motorcycle." She laughed, then said to Frank, "I never rode on one of these before, believe me."

"It's just like a motorized baby carriage, Aunt Willie."

"Huh!"

"This ought to be good," Wanda said. She called, "Hey, Charlie," waited until he looked out from the tent, and then said, "Watch Aunt Willie. She's going to ride the motor scooter."

Charlie watched Aunt Willie settle herself sidesaddle on the back of the scooter.

---

1. GUIDED READING:
Making Inferences
What does this passage tell you about Aunt Willie? What do you think of Aunt Willie as a parent? She has a streak of adventure in her. She has several different qualities that make her an interesting and realistic character. Although she is imperfect—like all people—she is a loving person who means well.

**1. GUIDED READING:
Drawing Conclusions**
What clues lead you to the conclusion that Charlie has not been keeping track of what is happening? When he hears Aunt Willie scream, he thinks she is being hurt. He did not come out of his tent when Frank arrived on the motor scooter.

2
Spigot is another word for *faucet*.

**3. GUIDED READING:
Identifying Cause and Effect**
What causes Sara's abrupt change in mood? When Aunt Willie suggests that Sara may soon be dating, Sara gets depressed. Sara thinks she is not as attractive as Wanda.

"Ready?" Frank asked.

"I'm as ready as I'll ever be, believe me, go on, go on."

Her words rose into a piercing scream as Frank moved the scooter forward, turned, and then started down the hill. Her scream, shrill as a bird's cry, hung in the still air. "Frank, Frank, Frank, Frankeeeeee!"

1 At the first cry Charlie staggered to his feet, staring in alarm at Aunt Willie disappearing down the hill. He pulled on one side of the tent as he got to his feet, causing the other to snap loose at the ground and hang limp from the line. He stumbled, then regained his balance.

Wanda saw him and said, "It's all right, Charlie, she's having a good time. She *likes* it. It's all right." She crossed the yard, took him by the hand, and led him to the steps. "What have you got all over yourself?"

"It's a gross red sucker," Sara said. "It's all over me too."

2 "Come on over to the spigot and let me wash your hands. See, Aunt Willie's coming back now."

In front of the Tennents' house Frank was swinging the scooter around, pivoting on one foot, and Aunt Willie stopped screaming long enough to call to the Tennents, "Bernie, Midge, look who's on a motorcycle!" Then she began screaming again as Frank started the uphill climb. As they came to a stop Aunt Willie's cries changed to laughter. "Huh, old woman, am I! Old woman!" Still laughing, she stepped off the scooter.

"You're all right, Aunt Willie," Frank said.

Sensing a moment of advantage, Wanda moved down the walk. She was shaking the water from her hands. "So can I go, Aunt Willie?"

"Oh, go on, go on," she said, half laughing, half scolding. "It's your own neck. Go on, break your own neck if you want to."

"It's not her neck you have to worry about, it's my arms," Frank said. "Honest, Aunt Willie, there's not a drop of blood circulating in them."

"Oh, go on, go on with you."

"Come on, Little One," Frank said to Wanda.

Aunt Willie came and stood by Sara, 3 and they watched Wanda climb on the back of the motor scooter. As Wanda and Frank drove off, Aunt Willie laughed again and said, "Next thing, *you'll* be going off with some boy on a motorcycle."

Sara had been smiling, but at once she stopped and looked down at her hands. "I don't think you have to worry about that."

"Huh! It will happen, you'll see. You'll be just like Wanda. You'll be—"

"Don't you see that I'm nothing like Wanda at all?" She sat down abruptly and put her lips against her knees. "We are so different. Wanda is a hundred times prettier than I am."

"You are just alike, you two. Sometimes in the kitchen I hear you and I think I'm hearing Wanda. That's how alike you are. May my ears fall off if I can hear the difference."

"Maybe our *voices* are alike, but

that's all. I can make my voice sound like a hundred different people. Listen to this and guess who it is. 'N–B–C! Beautiful downtown Burbank.'"

"I'm not in the mood for a guessing game. I'm in the mood to get back to our original conversation. It's not how you look that's important, let me tell you. I had a sister so beautiful you wouldn't believe it."

"Who?"

"Frances, that's who."

"She wasn't all that beautiful. I've seen her and—"

"When she was young she was. So beautiful you wouldn't believe it, but such a devil, and—"

"It is *too* important how you look. Parents are always saying it's not how you look that counts. I've heard that all my life. It doesn't matter how you look. It doesn't matter how you look. Huh! If you want to find out how much it matters, just let your hair get too long or put on too much eye makeup and listen to the screams." She got up abruptly and said, "I think I'll walk over and see the swans myself."

"Well, I have not finished with this conversation yet, young lady."

Sara turned and looked at Aunt Willie, waited with her hands jammed into her back pockets.

"Oh, never mind," Aunt Willie said, picking up her dish towel and shaking it. "I might as well hold a conversation with this towel as with you when you get that look on your face. Go on and see the swans." She broke off. "Hey, Charlie, you want to go with Sara to see the swans?"

"He'll get too tired," Sara said.

"So walk slow."

"I never get to do anything by myself. **1** I have to take him everywhere. I have him all day and Wanda all night. In all this whole house I have one drawer to myself. *One drawer.*"

"Get up, Charlie. Sara's going to take you to see the swans."

Sara looked down into his eyes and said, "Oh, come on," and drew him to his feet.

"Wait, there's some bread from supper." Aunt Willie ran into the house and came back with four rolls. "Take them. Here. Let Charlie feed the swans."

"Well, come on, Charlie, or it's going to be dark before we get there."

"Don't you rush him along, hear me, Sara?"

"I won't."

Holding Sara's hand, Charlie went slowly down the walk. He hesitated at the **2** gate and then moved with her onto the sidewalk. As they walked down the hill, his feet made a continuous scratching sound on the concrete.

When they were out of earshot Sara said, **3** "Aunt Willie thinks she knows everything. I get so sick of hearing how I am exactly like Wanda when Wanda is beautiful. I think she's just beautiful. If I could look like anyone in the world, I would want to look like her." She kicked at some high grass by the sidewalk. "And it does too matter how you look, I can tell you that." She walked

1. GUIDED READING:
Making Inferences
What feelings in Sara does this passage reveal? She feels sorry for herself because she doesn't have enough freedom or privacy. She sometimes feels that people take advantage of her.

2. LITERARY ELEMENTS:
Foreshadowing
Why do you think Charlie hesitates at the gate? He has probably been repeatedly told never to go outside the gate alone. This hesitation foreshadows the one on page 672.

3. GUIDED READING:
Identifying Pronoun Referents
To whom does the pronoun they *refer?* They refers to Sara and Charlie.

The Summer of the Swans

1. GUIDED READING:
Self-Questioning
Students might ask themselves if they agree or disagree with Sara. They might want to write a few sentences about this in their journals. *Suppose that Sara were the most beautiful girl in her school. How do you think this change would affect the novel up to this point?*

2. GUIDED READING:
Drawing Conclusions
What seems to be the author's opinion of strip mining? How do you know? She doesn't like strip mining. She thinks it has made the hills ugly: "hacked away, leaving unnatural cliffs . . ."
(Strip mining is a technique used to remove coal and other minerals that lie near and along the earth's surface. Strip mining destroys trees and other vegetation and leaves behind ugly, dangerous pits and piles of waste.)

---

ahead angrily for a few steps, then waited for Charlie and took his hand again.

1   "I think how you look is the most important thing in the world. If you *look* cute, you *are* cute; if you *look* smart, you *are* smart, and if you don't look like anything, then you aren't anything.

"I wrote a theme on that one time in school, about looks being the most important thing in the world, and I got a D—a D! Which is a terrible grade.

"After class the teacher called me up and told me the same old business about looks not being important, and how some of the ugliest people in the world were the smartest and kindest and cleverest."

They walked past the Tennents' house just as someone inside turned on the television, and they heard Eddie Albert singing, "Greeeeeeen acres is—" before it was turned down. Charlie paused a moment, recognizing the beginning of one of his favorite programs, looked up at Sara, and waited.

"Come on," Sara said. "And then there was this girl in my English class named Thelma Louise and she wrote a paper entitled 'Making People Happy' and she got an A. An *A*! Which is as good as you can get. It was sickening. Thelma Louise is a beautiful girl with blond hair and naturally curly eyelashes, so what does she know? Anyway, one time Hazel went over to Thelma Louise's, and she said the rug was worn thin in front of the mirror in Thelma Louise's room because Thelma Louise stood there all the time watching herself."

She sighed and continued to walk. Most of the houses were set close together as if huddled for safety, and on either side of the houses the West Virginia hills rose, black now in the early evening shadows. The hills were as they had been for hundreds of years, rugged forest land, except that strip mining had begun on the hills to the north, and the trees and earth had been hacked away, leaving unnatural cliffs of pale washed earth. 2

Sara paused. They were now in front of Mary Weicek's house and she said, "Stop a minute. I've got to speak to Mary." She could hear Mary's record player, and she longed to be up in Mary's room, leaning back against the pink dotted bedspread listening to Mary's endless collection of records. "Mary!" she called. "You want to walk to the pond with me and Charlie and see the swans?"

Mary came to the window. "Wait, I'm coming out."

Sara waited on the sidewalk until Mary came out into the yard. "I can't go because my cousin's here and she's going to cut my hair," Mary said, "but did you get your dress yesterday?"

"No."

"Why not? I thought your aunt said you could."

"She did, but when we got in the store and she saw how much it cost she said it was foolish to pay so much for a dress when she could make me one just like it."

"Disappointment."

"Yes, because unfortunately she can't make one *just* like it, she can only make one *kind of* like it. You remember how the

660   The Novel

stripes came together diagonally in the front of that dress? Well, she already has mine cut out and I can see that not one stripe meets."

"Oh, Sara."

"I could see when she was cutting it that the stripes weren't going to meet and I kept saying, 'It's not right, Aunt Willie, the stripes aren't going to meet,' and all the while I'm screaming, the scissors are flashing and she is muttering, 'The stripes will meet, the stripes will meet,' and then she holds it up in great triumph and not one stripe meets."

"That's awful, because I remember thinking when you showed me the dress that it was the way the stripes met that looked so good."

"I am aware of that. It now makes me look like one half of my body is about two inches lower than the other half."

"Listen, come on in and watch my cousin cut my hair, can you?"

"I better not. I promised Aunt Willie I'd take Charlie to see the swans."

"Well, just come in and see how she's going to cut it. She has a whole book of hair styles."

"Oh, all right, for a minute. Charlie, you sit down right there." She pointed to the steps. "Right there now and don't move, hear me? Don't move off that step. Don't even stand up." Then she went in the house with Mary, saying, "I really can't stay but a minute because I've got to take Charlie down to see the swans and then I've got to get home in time to dye my tennis shoes—"

"Which ones?"

"These, these awful orange things. They make me look like Donald Duck or something."

Charlie sat in the sudden stillness, hunched over his knees, on the bottom step. The whole world seemed to have been turned off when Sara went into the Weiceks' house, and he did not move for a long time. The only sound was the ticking of his watch.

The watch was a great pleasure to him. He had no knowledge of hours or minutes, but he liked to listen to it and to watch the small red hand moving around the dial, counting off the seconds, and it was he who remembered every morning after breakfast to have Aunt Willie wind it for him. Now he rested his arm across his legs and looked at the watch.

He had a lonely feeling. He got this whenever he was by himself in a strange place, and he turned quickly when he heard the screen door open to see if it was Sara. When he saw Mrs. Weicek and another woman he turned back and looked at his watch. As he bent over, a pale half circle of flesh showed between the back of his shirt and his pants.

"Who's the little boy, Allie?"

Mrs. Weicek said, "That's Sara's brother, Charlie. You remember me telling you about him. He's the one that can't talk. Hasn't spoken a word since he was three years old."

"Doesn't talk at all?"

---

1. GUIDED READING:
Making Inferences
What does Sara's answer reveal about her? She values a promise. Even though she wants to spend time with Mary, she obeys Aunt Willie.

2. GUIDED READING:
Predicting Outcomes
What do you think will happen next? Students may predict that Charlie will get up and leave without Sara.

3. LITERARY ELEMENTS:
Point of View
As students read this passage, ask them to notice how the author's choice of omniscient point of view gives an unusual insight into how it might feel to be Charlie.

The Summer of the Swans

**1. GUIDED READING:
Identifying the Author's Purpose**
What is the purpose of this dialogue? It gives the reader more information about Charlie's condition.

**2. GUIDED READING:
Interpreting Meaning**
Since Charlie can't tell time, why does he like the watch? He likes the sound it makes. The ticking calms him. He finds most of what goes on around him very confusing. The watch is always the same, so it comforts him.

**3. GUIDED READING:
Self-Questioning**
Students might ask themselves how they would feel if they were Sara.

---

1 "If he does, no one's ever heard him, not since his illness. He can understand what you say to him, and he goes to school, and they say he can write the alphabet, but he can't talk."

Charlie did not hear them. He put his ear against his watch and listened to the 2 sound. There was something about the rhythmic ticking that never failed to soothe him. The watch was a magic charm whose tiny noise and movements could block out the whole clamoring world.

Mrs. Weicek said, "Ask him what time it is, Ernestine. He is so proud of that watch. Everyone always asks him what time it is." Then without waiting, she herself said, "What time is it, Charlie? What time is it?"

He turned and obediently held out the arm with the watch on it.

"My goodness, it's after eight o'clock," Mrs. Weicek said. "Thank you, Charlie. Charlie keeps everyone informed of the time. We just couldn't get along without him."

The two women sat in the rocking chairs on the porch, moving slowly back and forth. The noise of the chairs and the creaking floor boards made Charlie forget the watch for a moment. He got slowly to his feet and stood looking up the street.

"Sit down, Charlie, and wait for Sara," Mrs. Weicek said.

Without looking at her, he began to walk toward the street.

"Charlie, Sara wants you to wait for her."

"Maybe he doesn't hear you, Allie."

"He hears me all right. Charlie, wait for Sara. Wait now." Then she called, "Sara, your brother's leaving."

Sara looked out the upstairs window and said, "All right, Charlie, I'm coming. Will you wait for a minute? Mary, I've got to go."

She ran out of the house and caught 3 Charlie by the arm. "What are you going home for? Don't you want to see the swans?"

He stood without looking at her.

"Honestly, I leave you alone for one second and off you go. Now come on." She tugged his arm impatiently.

As they started down the hill together she waved to Mary, who was at the window, and said to Charlie, "I hope the swans are worth all this trouble I'm going to.

"We'll probably get there and they'll be gone," she added. They walked in silence. Then Sara said, "Here's where we cut across the field." She waited while he stepped carefully over the narrow ditch, and then the two of them walked across the field side by side, Sara kicking her feet restlessly in the deep grass.

There was something painfully beautiful about the swans. The whiteness, the elegance of them on this dark lake, the incredible ease of their movements made Sara catch her breath as she and Charlie rounded the clump of pines.

"There they are, Charlie."

She could tell the exact moment he saw them because his hand tightened; he

662 The Novel

PORTFOLIO ASSESSMENT

The style used by the artist to paint the swans below is impressionistic. Students may notice the soft lines and muted color tones and may want to react to the painting by writing either a paragraph or a poem about their feelings. Other students may want to use a different art style and paint their own group of swans. Have students publish their reactions, and post them in designated areas of the room. Ask students how their reactions to the swans differ from Charlie's reaction. Consult with students individually to agree on how their reactions will be assessed. (See *Portfolio Assessment and Professional Support Materials* for additional information on student portfolios.)

BACKGROUND

The swans in this novel are Mute, or European, swans. They are quite large, up to five feet from bill to tail, with a wingspan of six or seven feet. The Mute is the only swan that makes an S-curve with its neck. Most people consider it the most beautiful swan. The Mute swan grunts, hisses, and snorts, but it does not call or "sing" like other swans. In flight its wings make a throbbing, cello-like sound that can be heard at great distances. Swans can fly at speeds of up to seventy mph.

Most swans mate for life. The male guards the nest and sometimes keeps the eggs warm. The baby swans, called *cygnets,* hatch after five weeks and can swim within two days. They are born with gray and brown feathers, which they lose gradually. By the end of their first year, they are all white. The young swans stay with their parents through the first winter. Mute swans have been known to live to the age of seventy.

1. GUIDED READING:
Interpreting Meaning
Why do you think Sara feels this way? It gives her pleasure to know that she is the one who has introduced Charlie to the swans. She feels that she and Charlie are connected somehow through the swans because they are both so impressed by their beauty.

---

really held her hand for the first time since they had left Mary's. Then he stopped.

"There are the swans."

The six swans seemed motionless on the water, their necks all arched at the same angle, so that it seemed there was only one swan mirrored five times.

1 "There are the swans," she said again. She felt she would like to stand there pointing out the swans to Charlie for the rest of the summer. She watched as they drifted slowly across the water.

"Hey, Sara!"

She looked across the lake and saw Wanda and Frank, who had come by the road. "Sara, listen, tell Aunt Willie that Frank and I are going over to his sister's to see her new baby."

"All right."

"I'll be home at eleven."

She watched as Wanda and Frank got back on the motor scooter. At the roar of the scooter, the startled swans changed direction and moved toward Sara. She and Charlie walked closer to the lake.

"The swans are coming over here, Charlie. They see you, I believe."

They watched in silence for a moment as the sound of the scooter faded. Then Sara sat down on the grass, crossed her legs yoga style, and picked out a stick which was wedged inside one of the orange tennis shoes.

"Sit down, Charlie. Don't just stand there."

Awkwardly, with his legs angled out in front of him, he sat on the grass. Sara pulled off a piece of a roll and tossed it to the swans. "Now they'll come over here," she said. "They love bread."

She paused, put a piece of roll into her own mouth, and sat chewing for a moment.

"I saw the swans when they flew here, did you know that, Charlie? I was out on our porch last Friday and I looked up, and they were coming over the house and they looked so funny, like frying pans with their necks stretched out." She handed him a roll. "Here. Give the swans something to eat. Look, watch me. Like that."

She watched him, then said, "No, Charlie, small pieces because swans get things caught in their throats easily. No, that's *too* little. That's just a crumb. Like *that*."

She watched while he threw the bread into the pond, then said, "You know where the swans live most of the time? At the university, which is a big school, and right in the middle of this university is a lake and that's where the swans live. Only sometimes, for no reason, the swans decide to fly away, and off they go to another pond or another lake. This one isn't half as pretty as the lake at the university, but here they are."

She handed Charlie another roll. "Anyway, that's what Wanda thinks, because the swans at the university are gone."

Charlie turned, motioned that he wanted another roll for the swans, and she gave him the last one. He threw it into the water in four large pieces and put out his hand for another.

"No more. That's all." She showed him her empty hands.

One of the swans dived under the

664 The Novel

water and rose to shake its feathers. Then it moved across the water. Slowly the other swans followed, dipping their long necks far into the water to catch any remaining pieces of bread.

Sara leaned forward and put her hands on Charlie's shoulders. His body felt soft, as if the muscles had never been used. "The swans are exactly alike," she said. "Exactly. No one can tell them apart."

She began to rub Charlie's back slowly, carefully. Then she stopped abruptly and clapped him on the shoulders. **1** "Well, let's go home."

He sat without moving, still looking at the swans on the other side of the lake.

"Come on, Charlie." She knew he had heard her, yet he still did not move. "Come *on*." She got to her feet and stood looking down at him. She held out her hand to help him up, but he did not even glance at her. He continued to watch the swans.

"Come on, Charlie. Mary may come up later and help me dye my shoes." She looked at him, then snatched a leaf from the limb overhead and threw it at the water. She waited, stuck her hands in her back pockets, and said tiredly, "Come on, Charlie."

He began to shake his head slowly back and forth without looking at her.

"Mary's coming up to help me dye my shoes and if you don't come on we won't have time to do them and I'll end up wearing these same awful Donald Duck shoes all year. Come *on*."

He continued to shake his head back and forth.

"This is why I never want to bring you anywhere, because you won't go home when I'm ready."

With his fingers he began to hold the long grass on either side of him as if this would help him if she tried to pull him to his feet.

"You are really irritating, you know that?" He did not look at her and she sighed and said, "All right, if I stay five more minutes, will you go?" She bent down and showed him on his watch. "That's to right there. When the big hand gets *there*, we go home, all right?"

He nodded.

"Promise?"

He nodded again.

"All right." There was a tree that hung over the water and she went and leaned against it. "All right, Charlie, four more minutes now," she called.

Already he had started shaking his **2** head again, all the while watching the swans gliding across the dark water.

Squinting up at the sky, Sara began to kick her foot back and forth in the deep grass. "In just a month, Charlie, the summer will be over," she said without looking at him, "and I will be so glad."

Up until this year, it seemed, her life had flowed along with rhythmic evenness. The first fourteen years of her life all seemed the same. She had loved her sister without envy, her aunt without finding her coarse, her brother without pity. Now all that was changed. She was filled with a discontent, an anger about herself, her life, her family, that made her think she would never be content again.

The Summer of the Swans

---

1. LITERARY ELEMENTS:
Foreshadowing
Charlie's fixation on the swans foreshadows his future adventure when he tries to find them.

2. LITERARY ELEMENTS:
Conflict
What two kinds of conflict do you find in the right-hand column? There are external conflict (Sara vs. Charlie) and internal conflict (Sara vs. her feelings of discontent and confusion).

MEETING INDIVIDUAL NEEDS

ESL/LEP • In the darkness, Wanda *stumbled* over the stool, an accident which left her *hobbling* on one foot. To familiarize students with the difference between these verbs, ask for volunteers to demonstrate the actions they describe. You may also want to challenge students to look for other verbs that describe ways of walking or moving, such as *clomping*. How does *clomping* compare to *stumbling* and *hobbling*? What does *clomping* look like? Sound like? You could have students compile ongoing lists of such words as they read the novel.

1. GUIDED READING:
Interpreting Meaning
What does Sara mean? She means that Frank is not attractive and that anyone who looks like him is to be pitied. She's being sarcastic and is joking.

She turned and looked at the swans. The sudden, unexpected tears in her eyes blurred the images of the swans into white circles, and she blinked. Then she said aloud, "Three minutes, Charlie."

Sara was lying in bed with the lights out when Wanda came into the bedroom that night. Sara was wearing an old pair of her father's pajamas with the sleeves cut out and the legs rolled up. She watched as Wanda moved quietly across the room and then stumbled over the dressing-table stool. Hobbling on one foot, Wanda opened the closet door and turned on the light.

"You can put on the big light if you want. I'm awake," Sara said.

"*Now* you tell me."

"Did you have a good time, Wanda?"

"Yes."

"Did you get to see the baby?"

"He was so cute. He looked exactly like Frank. You wouldn't have believed it."

1 "Poor baby."

"No, he was darling, really he was, with little red curls all over his head." She undressed quickly, turned off the closet light, and then got into bed beside Sara. She smoothed her pillow and looked up at the ceiling. "Frank is so nice, don't you think?"

"He's all right."

"Don't you like him?" She rose up on one elbow and looked down at Sara in the big striped pajamas.

"I said he was all right."

"Well, what don't you like?"

"I didn't say I didn't like him."

"I know, but I can tell. What don't you like?"

"For one thing, he never pays any attention to Charlie. When he came up the walk tonight he didn't even speak to him."

"He probably didn't see him in the tent. Anyway, he likes Charlie—he told me so. What else?"

"Oh, nothing, it's just that he's always so affected, the way he calls you Little One and gives you those real meaningful movie-star looks."

"I love it when he calls me Little One. Just wait till someone calls *you* Little One."

"I'd like to know who could call me Little One except the Jolly Green Giant."

"Oh, Sara."

"Well, I'm bigger than everyone I know."

"You'll find someone."

"Yes, maybe if I'm lucky I'll meet somebody from some weird foreign country where men value tall skinny girls with big feet and crooked noses. Every time I see a movie, though, even if it takes place in the weirdest, foreignest country in the world, like where women dance in gauze bloomers and tin bras, the women are still little and beautiful." Then she said, "Anyway, I hate boys. They're all just one big nothing."

"Sara, what's wrong with you?"

"Nothing."

"No, I mean it. What's really wrong?"

"I don't know. I just feel awful."

"Physically awful?"

"Now don't start being the nurse."

"Well, I want to know."

"No, not physically awful, just plain awful. I feel like I want to start screaming and kicking and I want to jump up and tear down the curtains and rip up the sheets and hammer holes in the walls. I want to yank my clothes out of the closet and burn them and—"

"Well, why don't you try it if it would make you feel better?"

"Because it wouldn't." She lifted the top sheet and watched as it billowed in the air and then lowered on her body. She could feel the cloth as it settled on the bare part of her legs. "I just feel like nothing."

"Oh, everybody does at times, Sara."

"Not like me. I'm not anything. I'm not cute, and I'm not pretty, and I'm not a good dancer, and I'm not smart, and I'm not popular. I'm not anything."

"You're a good dishwasher."

"Shut up, Wanda. I don't think that's funny."

"Welllll—"

"You act like you want to talk to me and then you start being funny. You do that to me all the time."

"I'm through being funny, so go on."

"Well, if you could see some of the girls in my school you'd know what I mean. They look like models. Their clothes are so tuff and they're invited to every party, every dance, by about ten boys and when they walk down the hall everybody turns and looks at them."

"Oh, those girls. They hit the peak of their whole lives in junior high school. They look like grown women in eighth grade with the big teased hair and the eye liner and by the time they're in high school they have a used look."

"Well, I certainly don't have to worry about getting a used look."

"I think it is really sad to hit the peak of your whole life in junior high school."

"Girls, quit that arguing," Aunt Willie called from her room. "I can hear you all the way in here."

"We're not arguing," Wanda called back. "We are having a peaceful little discussion."

"I know an argument when I hear one, believe me. That's one thing I've heard plenty of and I'm hearing one right now. Be quiet and go to sleep."

"All right."

They lay in silence. Sara said, "The peak of my whole life so far was in third grade when I got to be milk monitor."

Wanda laughed. "Just give yourself a little time." She reached over, turned on the radio, and waited till it warmed up. "Frank's going to dedicate a song to me on the Diamond Jim show," she said. "Will the radio bother you?"

"No."

"Well, it bothers me," Aunt Willie called from her room. "Maybe you two can sleep with the radio blaring and people arguing, but I can't."

"I have just barely got the radio turned on, Aunt Willie. I have to put my head practically on the table to even hear it."

The Summer of the Swans

CLOSURE
Divide students into groups. Ask each group to decide on one quality that they think Sara Godfrey has. Then have a spokesperson from each group give examples of Sara's actions, words, or thoughts that reveal this quality.

RETEACHING
Ask students to compare and contrast Sara with youngsters of the same age that they know. Are Sara's actions, words, and thoughts realistic? Are teenagers different from Sara in this community? If so, how, and why?

EXTENSION AND ENRICHMENT
Art. Ask students to draw a place, an animal, or an article of clothing in two ways. First, draw it in a way that shows they like it; then in a way that shows they dislike it.

FOR STUDY AND DISCUSSION
Identifying Facts
1. She dislikes her height and big feet.
    She feels bored and restless.
2. Wanda tells Sara she will eventually find a boyfriend who cares for her.
3. Aunt Willie is taking care of them because their mother died six years ago.
4. At three Charlie had two illnesses that damaged his brain. He has not spoken since.
    Charlie likes to listen to its ticking sound and watch the small red hand move.

Interpreting Meanings
5. Students may call her bored, restless, self-conscious, impatient.
    Feelings about Sara will vary.
6. She is patient with Charlie and helps him with the candy and tent. She confides her inner feelings to Charlie.
7. Charlie is delighted by the swans and doesn't want to leave.
    Students may suggest that Charlie may feel a certain kinship with them.

Applying Meanings
8. He might say it's important to have a normal brain or to be able to talk.
    Some will say that looks are superficial.

She broke off abruptly. "What was that dedication, did you hear?"

"It was to all the girls on the second floor of Arnold Hall."

"Oh."

"I mean what I say now," Aunt Willie called. "You two get to sleep. Wanda, you've got to be up early to get to your job at the hospital on time, even if Sara can spend the whole day in bed."

"I'd like to know how I can spend the whole day in bed when she gets me up at eight o'clock," Sara grumbled.

"Aunt Willie, I just want to hear my dedication and then I'll go to sleep."

Silence.

Sara turned over on her side with the sheet wrapped tightly around her body and closed her eyes. She was not sleepy now. She could hear the music from the radio, and the sound from the next room of Charlie turning over in his bed, trying to get settled, then turning over again. She pulled the pillow over her head, but she could not block out the noises. Oddly, it was the restless sounds from Charlie's room which seemed loudest.

Charlie was not a good sleeper. When he was three, he had had two illnesses, one following the other, terrible high-fevered illnesses, which had almost taken his life and had damaged his brain. Afterward, he had lain silent and still in his bed, and it had been strange to Sara to see the pale baby that had replaced the hot, flushed, tormented one. The once-bright eyes were slow to follow what was before them, and the hands never reached out, even when Sara held her brother's favorite stuffed dog, Buh-Buh, above him. He rarely cried, never laughed. Now it was as if Charlie wanted to make up for those listless years in bed by never sleeping again.

Sara heard his foot thump against the wall. It was a thing that could continue for hours, a faint sound that no one seemed to hear but Sara, who slept against the wall. With a sigh she put the pillow back beneath her head and looked up at the ceiling.

"That was my dedication. Did you hear it?" Wanda whispered. "To Little One from Frank."

"Vomit."

"Well, I think it was sweet."

The thumping against the wall stopped, then began again. It was a sound that Sara had become used to, but tonight it seemed unusually loud. She found herself thinking how this had been Charlie's first movement after his long illness, a restless kicking out of one foot, a weak movement then that could hardly be noticed beneath the covers, but now, tonight, one that seemed to make the whole house tremble.

"Don't tell me you don't hear that," she said to Wanda. "I don't see how you can all persist in saying that you don't hear Charlie kicking the wall."

Silence.

"Wanda, are you asleep?"

Silence.

"Honestly, I don't see how people can just fall asleep any time they want to. Wanda, are you really asleep?"

She waited, then drew the sheet close about her neck and turned to the wall.

668 The Novel

Social Studies. Ask a group of interested students to find out how special students are educated in your community. How many students are enrolled in special classes? How many students are mainstreamed? Contact teachers of special classes to see if some of your students might volunteer in their classrooms—or share a field trip.

For Study and Discussion

IDENTIFYING FACTS
1. What does Sara dislike about herself? Why is she having a miserable summer?
2. Describe how Wanda tries to console Sara when they're talking in bed.
3. Explain why Sara, Wanda, and Charlie are living with Aunt Willie.
4. Describe Charlie's handicap. Explain why Charlie loves his watch.

INTERPRETING MEANINGS
5. What three adjectives would you use to describe how Sara feels most often in this part of the novel? How do you feel about Sara so far?
6. How do you know that Sara loves Charlie? What are some of the other feelings she has about Charlie?
7. How does Charlie feel about the swans? Why do you think he feels this way about them?

APPLYING MEANINGS
8. Sara tells Charlie that the most important thing in the world is how you look. If Charlie were able to speak, what do you think he would tell Sara? What do you think about her opinion?

Literary Elements

CHARACTER
You can get to know a character by thinking about his or her **actions, words,** and **thoughts.** Describe what you find out about Sara from each of these clues.

1. Sara tells Wanda that she likes her orange sneakers. Later, Sara tells Charlie she hates her orange sneakers.
2. When Charlie doesn't want to leave the pond, Sara gives him more time to look at the swans.
3. Sara thinks she is ugly.

Notice that Sara, like a real person, has many different qualities. Also, like a real person, she is not perfect. Which of Sara's qualities do you like? Which do you dislike?

Focus on Persuasive Writing

CHOOSING A TOPIC AND WRITING AN OPINION STATEMENT
Wanda and Frank use several arguments to persuade Aunt Willie that Frank's motor scooter is safe. In **persuasive writing** you state your opinion on an issue. Then you support that opinion with facts, reasons, and expert opinions.

When you choose a topic for persuasive writing, make sure your subject is a matter of opinion, not a fact. An *opinion* states a personal belief. (Motor scooter riders should wear helmets.) A *fact* is a statement that can be tested and proved true. (Statistics show that safety helmets save lives.)

Together with a small group, brainstorm some topics for a persuasive essay. For example, you could discuss some issues in your school or neighborhood that the group cares about. For one of these issues, write a one-sentence **opinion statement** that presents your view. (Hint: Persuasive writers often use the word *should* in an opinion statement.) Save your notes.

The Summer of the Swans 669

LITERARY ELEMENTS
Character
1. Sara doesn't really know what she likes; her likes and dislikes change quickly.
2. This suggests that Sara is very fond of Charlie and is patient and gentle with him.
3. Sara is self-conscious and lacks confidence.

FOCUS ON PERSUASIVE WRITING

Choosing a Topic and Writing an Opinion Statement
As stated in the activity, students should choose topics that they care about. In addition, explain to students that a suitable topic is one with which some other people disagree. If everyone has the same opinion about a subject, persuasion is unnecessary.

OBJECTIVES
Students will distinguish between first-person and omniscient points of view. They will also write and answer questions based on the information given in the novel.

FOCUS/MOTIVATION
Building on Prior Knowledge. Ask students to summarize why Sara thinks she is having a miserable summer. Discuss what makes a summer vacation fun or miserable.
Prereading Journal. Ask students to write a few sentences telling what they think will happen next. Do they think Sara's summer will take a turn for the better? Could it get worse?

TEACHING RESOURCES D
Teacher's Notes, p. 154
Reading Check, p. 156
Study Guide, pp. 157, 158
Language Skills, p. 159
Building Vocabulary p. 162
Selection Vocabulary Test, p. 164
Selection Test, p. 165

1. BACKGROUND
Clark Gable was a popular film star during the 1940s and 1950s. He played Rhett Butler in *Gone with the Wind*.

2. GUIDED READING:
Identifying Pronoun Referents
To what does the pronoun *it* refer? It refers to the place where the button is missing.

3
Puce (pyo͞os) is brownish purple. The person who made up this word must have thought that fleas were this color because *puce* is the French word for *flea*!

4. GUIDED READING:
Interpreting Meaning
Why is the missing button such a worry to Charlie? Changes in his usual routine or in something he expects to be always the same—and suddenly finds different—make Charlie extremely anxious. This symptom is typical of several kinds of brain damage.

In his room Charlie lay in bed still kicking his foot against the wall. He was not asleep but was staring up at the ceiling where the shadows were moving. He never went to sleep easily, but tonight he had been concerned because a button was missing from his pajamas, and sleep was impossible. He had shown the place where the button was missing to Aunt Willie when he was ready for bed, but she had patted his shoulder and said, "I'll fix it tomorrow," and gone back to watching a game show on television.

"Look at that," Aunt Willie was saying to herself. "They're never going to guess the name. How can famous celebrities be so stupid?" She had leaned forward and shouted at the panelists, "It's Clark Gable!" Then, "Have they never heard of a person who works in a store? A person who works in a store is a *clerk*—Clerk Gable—the name is *Clerk Gable*!"

Charlie had touched her on the shoulder and tried again to show her the pajamas.

"I'll fix it tomorrow, Charlie." She had waved him away with one hand.

He had gone back into the kitchen, where Sara was dyeing her tennis shoes in the sink.

"Don't show it to me," she said. "I can't look at anything right now. And Mary, quit laughing at my tennis shoes."

"I can't help it. They're so gross."

Sara lifted them out of the sink with two spoons. "I know they're gross, only you should have told me that orange tennis shoes could not be dyed baby blue. Look at that. That is the worst color you have ever seen in your life. Admit it."

"I admit it."

"Well, you don't have to admit it so quickly. They ought to put on the dye wrapper that orange cannot be dyed baby blue. A warning."

"They do."

"Well, they ought to put it in big letters. Look at those shoes. There must be a terrible name for that color."

"There is," Mary said. "Puce."

"What?"

"Puce."

"Mary Weicek, you made that up."

"I did not. It really is a color."

"I have never heard a word that describes anything better. Puce. These just look like puce shoes, don't they?" She set them on newspapers. "They're—Charlie, get out of the way, please, or I'm going to get dye all over you."

He stepped back, still holding his pajama jacket out in front of him. There were times when he could not get anyone's attention no matter what he did. He took Sara's arm and she shrugged free.

"Charlie, there's not a button on anything I own, either, so go on to bed."

Slowly, filled with dissatisfaction, he had gone to his room and got into bed. There he had begun to pull worriedly at the empty buttonhole until the cloth had started to tear, and then he had continued to pull until the whole front of his pajama top was torn and hung open. He was now holding the jacket partly closed with his hands and looking up at the ceiling.

670 The Novel

READING THE SELECTION
You might have students read this next part of the novel silently in two class periods or two homework sessions: Day 1, page 670 to the break on page 679; Day 2, pages 679–688. For slower students, read aloud page 670 to the break on page 675. Then assign the next four pages for silent reading. Pages 679–688 are easy to read.

Because there is so much dialogue in this novel, it might be fun for students to take parts and read some of the scenes aloud, after they have had a chance to prepare.

1. GUIDED READING:
Identifying Cause and Effect
What is the cause of Charlie's inability to sleep (and, therefore, his subsequent adventure)? He can't sleep because he's holding his pajamas closed because he has a button missing. The button is missing because no one would sew it on for him. (You might want to point out that many of the events in a well-plotted story, like events in real life, are connected by cause and effect.)

2. GUIDED READING:
Predicting Outcomes
What do you think Charlie will do next? Given Charlie's persistence (putting the lollipop on the stick, trying to find someone to sew on his pajama button), students might predict that Charlie will try to find the swans.

1 It was one o'clock and Charlie had been lying there for three hours.

He heard a noise outside, and for the first time he forgot about his pajamas. He stopped kicking his foot against the wall, sat up, and looked out the window. There was something white in the bushes; he could see it moving.

He released his pajamas and held onto the window sill tightly, because he thought that he had just seen one of the swans outside his window, gliding slowly through the leaves. The memory of their soft smoothness in the water came to him and warmed him.

He got out of bed and stood by the **2** other window. He heard a cat miaowing and saw the Hutchinsons' white cat from next door, but he paid no attention to it. The swans were fixed with such certainty in his mind that he could not even imagine that what he had seen was only the cat.

Still looking for the swans, he pressed his face against the screen. The beauty of them, the whiteness, the softness, the si-

The Summer of the Swans   **671**

1
Banister is another word for *railing*.

**2. LITERARY ELEMENTS:
Symbol**
Advanced students might be interested to know that in literature and art, a cat can stand for something sinister or evil, while a swan usually stands for innocence and purity. You might have students discuss the qualities in these animals that caused people to give them such symbolic meanings.

**3. GUIDED READING:
Drawing Conclusions**
What two clues up to this point lead you to the conclusion that Charlie is becoming confused and worried? He shuffles his feet on the step and pulls at his torn pajamas.

**4. GUIDED READING:
Contrasting**
What is being contrasted in this paragraph? The author is contrasting the worlds of daytime and night. Notice that she appeals to two senses: sight and sound. (Your students might want to try a contrast like this in their journals.)

---

lent splendor had impressed him greatly, and he felt a longing to be once again by the lake, sitting in the deep grass, throwing bread to the waiting swans.

It occurred to him suddenly that the swan outside the window had come to find him, and with a small pleased smile he went around the bed, sat, and slowly began to put on his bedroom slippers. Then he walked out into the hall. His feet made a quiet shuffling sound as he passed through the linoleumed hall and into the living room, but no one heard him.

The front door had been left open for coolness and only the screen door was latched. Charlie lifted the hook, pushed open the door, and stepped out onto the porch. Boysie, who slept in the kitchen, heard the door shut and came to the living room. He whined softly when he saw Charlie outside on the porch and scratched at the door. He waited, then after a moment went back to the kitchen and curled up on his rug in front of the sink.

Charlie walked across the front porch and sat on the steps. He waited. He was patient at first, for he thought that the swans would come to the steps, but as time passed and they did not come, he began to shuffle his feet impatiently back and forth on the third step.

Suddenly he saw something white in the bushes. He got up and, holding the **1** banister, went down the steps and crossed the yard. He looked into the bushes, but the swans were not there. It was only the cat, crouched down behind the leaves and looking up at him with slitted eyes.

He stood there, looking at the cat, unable to understand what had happened to the swans. He rubbed his hands up and down his pajama tops, pulling at the torn material. The cat darted farther back into the bushes and disappeared.

After a moment Charlie turned and began to walk slowly across the yard. He went to the gate and paused. He had been told again and again that he must never go out of the yard, but those instructions, given in daylight with noisy traffic on the street, seemed to have nothing to do with the present situation.

In the soft darkness all the things that usually confused him—speeding bicycles, loud noises, lawn mowers, barking dogs, shouting children—were gone, replaced by silence and a silvery moonlit darkness. He seemed to belong to this silent world far more than he belonged to the daytime world of feverish activity.

Slowly he opened the gate and went out. He moved past the Hutchinsons' house, past the Tennents', past the Weiceks'. There was a breeze now, and the smell of the Weiceks' flowers filled the air. He walked past the next house and hesitated, suddenly confused. Then he started through the vacant lot by the Akers' house. In the darkness it looked to him like the field he and Sara had crossed earlier in the evening on their way to see the swans.

He crossed the vacant lot, entered the wooded area, and walked slowly through the trees. He was certain that in just a moment he would come into the clearing and see the lake and the white swans gliding on the dark water. He continued walking, looking ahead so that he would see the lake as soon as possible.

The ground was getting rougher. There were stones to stumble over now and rain gullies and unexpected piles of trash. Still the thought of the swans persisted in his mind and he kept walking.

Charlie was getting tired and he knew something was wrong. The lake was gone. He paused and scanned the field, but he could not see anything familiar.

He turned to the right and began to walk up the hill. Suddenly a dog barked behind him. The sound, unexpected and loud, startled him, and he fell back a step and then started to run. Then another dog was barking, and another, and he had no idea where the dogs were. He was terribly frightened and he ran with increasing awkwardness, thrashing at the weeds with his hands, pulling at the air, so that everything about him seemed to be running except his slow feet.

The sound of the dogs seemed to him to be everywhere, all around him, so that he ran first in one direction, then in another, like a wild animal caught in a maze. He ran into a bush and the briers stung his face and arms, and he thought this was somehow connected with the dogs and thrashed his arms out wildly, not even feeling the cuts in his skin.

He turned around and around, trying to free himself, and then staggered on, running and pulling at the air. The dogs' barking had grown fainter now, but in his terror he did not notice. He ran blindly, stumbling over bushes and against trees, catching his clothing on twigs, kicking at unseen rocks. Then he came into a clearing and was able to gain speed for the first time.

He ran for a long way, and then suddenly he came up against a wire fence that cut him sharply across the chest. The surprise of it threw him back on the ground, and he sat holding his hands across his bare chest, gasping for breath.

Far down the hill someone had spoken to the dogs; they had grown quiet, and now there was only the rasping sound of Charlie's own breathing. He sat hunched over until his breathing grew quieter, and then he straightened and noticed his torn pajamas for the first time since he had left the house. He wrapped the frayed edges of the jacket carefully over his chest as if that would soothe the stinging cut.

After a while he got slowly to his feet, paused, and then began walking up the hill beside the fence. He was limping now because when he had fallen he had lost one of his bedroom slippers.

The fence ended abruptly. It was an old one, built long ago, and now only parts remained. Seeing it gone, Charlie felt relieved. It was as if the fence had kept him from his goal, and he stepped over a trailing piece of wire and walked toward the forest beyond.

Being in the trees gave him a good feeling for a while. The moonlight coming through the leaves and the soft sound of the wind in the branches were soothing,

1
Gullies are ditches made by running water.

2
Thrashing means "hitting hard; beating."

3. LITERARY ELEMENTS:
Imagery
This description is especially vivid and moving because the author makes you feel, hear, and see what Charlie is experiencing. The details appeal to the senses of touch, sound, and sight.

4. GUIDED READING:
Identifying Key Details
Why do you think losing a bedroom slipper might be an important detail? It could be a clue to where Charlie has gone.

The Summer of the Swans

TRANSPARENCY 41
Reader Response
Check the Stars – invites students to give advice and warnings to characters from a point in time before the story starts.

VISUAL CONNECTIONS
Through whose imagination do you see these fierce dogs? (Charlie's. See page 673.) *What feeling has the artist tried to create in this illustration?* (A sense of Charlie's terror)

674 The Novel

but as he went deeper into the forest he became worried. There was something here he didn't know, an unfamiliar smell, noises he had never heard before. He stopped.

He stood beneath the trees without moving and looked around him. He did not know where he was. He did not even know how he had come to be there. The whole night seemed one long struggle, but he could not remember why he had been struggling. He had wanted something, he could not remember what.

His face and arms stung from the brier scratches; his bare foot, tender and unused to walking on the rough ground, was already cut and sore, but most of all he was gripped by hopelessness. He wanted to be back in his room, in his bed, but home seemed lost forever, a place so disconnected from the forest that there was no way to get from one to the other.

He put his wrist to his ear and listened to his watch. Even its steady ticking could not help him tonight and he wrapped the torn pajamas tighter over his chest and began to walk slowly up the hill through the trees. As he walked, he began to cry without noise.

In the morning Sara arose slowly, letting her feet hang over the edge of the bed for a moment before she stepped onto the floor. Then she walked across the room, and as she passed the dressing table she paused to look at herself in the mirror. She smoothed her hair behind her ears.

The Summer of the Swans 675

1. LITERARY ELEMENTS:
Conflict
What external conflict facing Charlie makes the plot suspenseful? The external conflict is Charlie's struggle against his unfamiliar surroundings. He wants to go home but is totally lost.

2. GUIDED READING:
Identifying Cause and Effect
What is the effect of Charlie's struggle? He feels increasingly confused and hopeless.

3. LITERARY ELEMENTS:
Dramatic Irony
This complete and sudden shift in scene and mood is very effective because the reader knows what is happening to Charlie—but Sara doesn't know yet. Advanced students who enjoy learning "sophisticated" terms may be interested in knowing that this technique is called **dramatic irony**.

1. GUIDED READING:
Making Inferences
What does Sara think about as soon as she gets up? What does this tell you about her? She thinks about how she looks. At this point in the novel, she is, to some extent, self-centered and preoccupied with the idea that she isn't "beautiful."

2. LITERARY ELEMENTS:
Flashback
This dialogue may confuse some students who will not realize at first that it took place some time in the past. You may want to introduce the term **flashback,** a scene that interrupts the present action of the plot to show something that happened earlier. Another example of flashback is on page 670.

3. BACKGROUND
Gentle Ben was the brown bear featured in the TV adventure show of the same name. Before that, Gentle Ben was the animal hero of an exciting young adult novel set in Alaska: *Gentle Ben* by Walt Morey (Dutton, 1965).

---

1 One of her greatest mistakes, she thought, looking at herself critically, was cutting her hair. She had gone to the beauty school in Bentley, taking with her a picture from a magazine, and had asked the girl to cut her hair exactly like that.

"And look what she did to me!" she had screamed when she got home. "Look! Ruined!"

"It's not that bad," Wanda had said.

"Tell the truth. Now look at that picture. Look! Tell the truth—do I look anything, anything at *all,* even the tiniest little bit, like that model?"

Wanda and Aunt Willie had had to admit that Sara looked nothing like the blond model.

2 "I'm ruined, just ruined. Why someone cannot take a perfectly good magazine picture and cut someone's hair the same way without ruining them is something I cannot understand. I hope that girl fails beauty school."

"Actually, your *hair* does sort of look like the picture. It's your face and body that don't."

"Shut up, Wanda. Quit trying to be funny."

"I'm not being funny. It's a fact."

"I didn't make smart remarks the time they gave you that awful permanent."

3 "You did too. You called me Gentle Ben."

"Well, I meant that as a compliment."

"All right, girls, stop this now. No more arguing. Believe me, I mean it."

Sara now looked at herself, weighing the mistake of the hair, and she thought suddenly: I look exactly like that cartoon cat who is always chasing Tweetie Bird and who has just been run over by a steam roller and made absolutely flat. This hair and my flat face have combined to make me look exactly like—

"Sara!" Aunt Willie called from the kitchen.

"What?"

"Come on and get your breakfast, you and Charlie. I'm not going to be in here fixing one breakfast after another until lunch time."

"All right."

She went into the hall and looked into Charlie's room.

"Charlie!"

He was not in his bed. She walked into the living room. Lately, since he had learned to turn on the television, he would get up early, come in, and watch it by himself, but he was not there either.

"Charlie's already up, Aunt Willie."

In the kitchen Aunt Willie was spooning oatmeal into two bowls.

"Oatmeal again," Sara groaned. "I believe I'll just have some Kool-Aid and toast."

"Don't talk nonsense. Now, where's Charlie?"

"He wasn't in his room."

She sighed. "Well, find him."

"First I've got to see my shoes." She went over to the sink and looked at the sneakers. "Oh, they look awful. Look at them, Aunt Willie. They're gross."

"Well, you should have left them alone. I've learned my lesson about dyeing

676 The Novel

clothes, let me tell you. You saw me, I hope, when I had to wear that purple dress to your Uncle Bert's funeral."

"What color would you say these were?"

"I haven't got time for that now. Go get your brother."

"No, there's a name for this color. I just want to see if you know it."

"I don't know it, so go get your brother."

"I'll give you three choices. It's either, let me see—it's either pomegranate, Pomeranian, or puce."

"Puce. Now go get your brother."

"How did you know?"

"Because my aunt had twin Pomeranian dogs that rode in a baby carriage and because I once ate a piece of pomegranate. Go get your brother!"

Sara put down the shoes and went back into the hall. "Charlie!" She looked into his room again. "Oh, Charlie!" She went out onto the front porch and looked at Charlie's tent. It had blown down during the night and she could see that he wasn't there.

Slowly she walked back through the hall, looking into every room, and then into the kitchen.

"I can't find him, Aunt Willie."

"What do you mean, you can't find him?" Aunt Willie, prepared to chide the two children for being late to breakfast, now set the pan of oatmeal down heavily on the table.

"He's not in his room, he's not in the yard, he's not anywhere."

"If this is some kind of a joke—" Aunt Willie began. She brushed past Sara and went into the living room. "Charlie! Where are you, Charlie?" Her voice had begun to rise with the sudden alarm she often felt in connection with Charlie. "Where could he have gone?" She turned and looked at Sara. "If this is a joke . . ."

"It's not a joke."

"Well, I'm remembering last April Fool's Day, that's all."

"He's probably around the neighborhood somewhere, like the time Wanda took him to the store without saying anything."

"Well, Wanda didn't take him this morning." Aunt Willie walked into the hall and stood looking in Charlie's room. She stared at the empty bed. She did not move for a moment as she tried to think of some logical explanation for his absence. "If anything's happened to that boy—"

"Nothing's happened to him."

"All right, where is he?"

Sara did not answer. Charlie had never left the house alone, and Sara could not think of any place he could be either.

"Go outside, Sara. Look! If he's not in the neighborhood, I'm calling the police."

"Don't call until we're sure, Aunt Willie, please."

"I'm calling. Something's wrong here."

Sara was out of her pajamas and into her pants and shirt in a minute. Leaving her pajamas on the floor, she ran barefoot into the yard.

The Summer of the Swans 677

---

1. LITERARY ELEMENTS: Suspense
Aunt Willie tells Sara four times: "Go get your brother," but Sara keeps talking, thus delaying the discovery that Charlie is missing, and heightening the suspense.

2. GUIDED READING: Making Inferences
Why do you think Sara doesn't want Aunt Willie to call the police? At this point in the novel, it is clear that Sara is concerned about appearances. If Charlie really isn't missing, and Aunt Willie has called the police, Sara thinks that the family will look foolish.

3. GUIDED READING: Making Inferences
What does this paragraph suggest about how Sara feels? In spite of her attempts to calm Aunt Willie, Sara is getting worried about Charlie.

1. GUIDED READING:
Understanding Time Order
What do you find out about Charlie's behavior? What time clue tells you when he behaved like this? Charlie was so reluctant to leave the swans that Sara had to drag him home screaming. The time clue is "last night."

2. GUIDED READING:
Identifying the Author's Purpose
Why do you think the author gives you this information about Charlie's behavior now? Why do you think the author didn't describe this behavior on page 666? The information makes you sympathize with Sara. On page 666, the author wanted to emphasize Sara's feelings of closeness and love for Charlie.

3. GUIDED READING:
Interpreting Meaning
What's the point of this story about the old man? Just because somebody is missing doesn't mean something terrible has happened. Note that this was a true incident that Byars read about in a newspaper. See "About the Author," page 715.

"Charlie! Charlie!" She ran around the house and then stopped. Suddenly she remembered the swans and ran back into the house.

"Aunt Willie, I bet you anything Charlie went down to the lake to see the swans."

Aunt Willie was talking on the telephone and she put one hand over the receiver and said, "Run and see."

"You aren't talking to the police already?" Sara asked in the doorway.

"I'm not talking to the police, but that's what I'm going to do when you get back. Now quit wasting time."

"Just let me get my shoes."

She ran back into the kitchen and put on the sneakers, which were still wet. Then she ran out of the house and down the street. As she passed the Weiceks', Mary came out on the porch.

"What's the hurry?" she called.

"Charlie's missing. I'm going to see if he's down at the lake."

"I'll go with you." She came down the steps, calling over her shoulder, "Mom, I'm going to help Sara look for Charlie."

"Not in those curlers you're not."

"Mom, I've got on a scarf. Nobody can even tell it's rolled."

"Yeah, everyone will just think you have real bumpy hair," Sara said.

"Oh, hush. Now what's all this about Charlie?"

"We couldn't find him this morning and I think he might have got up during the night and gone to see the swans. He acted awful when we had to leave."

"I know. I saw you dragging him up the street last night."

"I had to. It was the only way I could get him home. It was black dark. You couldn't even see the swans and he still wouldn't come home."

"I hope he's all right."

"He's probably sitting down there looking at the swans, holding onto the grass, and I'm going to have to drag him up the hill screaming all over again. He's strong when he wants to be, you know that?"

"Hey, you've got your shoes on."

"Yeah, but they're still wet."

"You'll probably have puce feet before the day's over."

"That's all I need."

They turned and crossed the field at the bottom of the hill.

"Let's hurry because Aunt Willie is at this moment getting ready to call the police."

"Really?"

"She's sitting by the phone now. She's got her little card out with all her emergency numbers on it and her finger is pointing right to *POLICE*."

"Remember that time the old man got lost in the woods? What was his name?"

"Uncle somebody."

"And they organized a posse of college boys and the Red Cross brought coffee and everything, and then they found the old man asleep in his house the next morning. He was on a picnic and had got bored and just went home."

"Don't remind me. Probably as soon

as Aunt Willie calls the police we'll find Charlie in the bathroom or somewhere."

They came through the trees and into the clearing around the lake. Neither spoke.

"Yesterday he was sitting right here," Sara said finally. "Charlie! Charlie!"

There was no answer, but the swans turned abruptly and began to glide to the other side of the lake. Sara felt her shoulders sag and she rammed her hands into her back pockets.

"Something really has happened to him," she said. "I know it now."

"Probably not, Sara."

"I *know* it now. Sometimes you just know terrible things. I get a feeling in my neck, like my shoulders have come unhinged or something, when an awful thing happens."

Mary put one hand on her arm. "Maybe he's hiding somewhere."

"He can't even do that right. If he's playing hide-and-seek, as soon as he's hidden he starts looking out to see how the game's going. He just can't—"

"Maybe he's at the store or up at the Dairy Queen. I could run up to the drugstore."

"No, something's happened to him."

They stood at the edge of the water. Sara looked at the swans without seeing them.

1 Mary called, "Charlie! Charlie!" Her kerchief slipped off and she retied it over her rollers. "Charlie!"

"I was so sure he'd be here," Sara said. "I wasn't even worried because I knew he would be sitting right here. Now I don't know what to do."

"Let's go back to the house. Maybe he's there now."

"I know he won't be."

"Well, don't get discouraged until we see." She took Sara by the arm and started walking through the trees. "You know who you sound like? Remember when Mary Louise was up for class president and she kept saying, 'I know I won't get it. I know I won't get it.' For three days that was all she said."

"And she didn't get it."

"Well, I just meant you sounded like her, your voice or something," Mary explained quickly. "Now, come on."

When Sara entered the house with Mary, Aunt Willie was still sitting at the telephone. She was saying, "And there's not a trace of him." She paused in her conversation to ask, "Did you find him?" and when Sara shook her head, she said into the telephone, "I'm hanging up now, Midge, so I can call the police. Sara just came in and he wasn't at the lake."

She hung up, took her card of emergency phone numbers and began to dial.

There was something final about calling the police and Sara said, "Aunt Willie, don't call yet. Maybe—"

"I'm calling. A hundred elephants couldn't stop me."

"Maybe he's at somebody's house," Mary said. "One time my brother went in the Hutchinsons' to watch TV and we—"

1. LITERARY ELEMENTS:
Descriptive Details
You might point out that this is an example of a tiny but important detail that makes the difference between a well-written novel and one that is poorly written. Such details help you visualize the scene and even make you feel as if you are experiencing it.

1
Grudgingly means "reluctantly" or "unwillingly."

2. GUIDED READING:
Interpreting Meaning
What does Aunt Willie mean? What is her tone here? She means that Charlie is much more important than television. Her tone is sarcastic. (Advanced students might enjoy knowing that another word for *sarcastic* is *ironic*.) She is saying just the opposite of what she means.

3. LITERARY ELEMENTS:
Exaggeration
Aunt Willie's exaggerated statements provide some comic relief in a stressful situation. Some examples of her exaggerated statements are "My tongue should fall out on the floor . . ." and "There are a hundred things that could have happened to him."

"Hello, is this the police department? I want to report a missing child."

She looked up at Sara, started to say something, then turned back to her telephone conversation. "Yes, a missing child, a boy, ten, Charlie Godfrey. G-o-d-f-r-e-y." Pause. "Eighteen-oh-eight Cass Street. This is Willamina Godfrey, his aunt. I'm in charge." She paused, then said, "Yes, since last night." She listened again. "No, I don't know what time. We woke up this morning, he was gone. That's all." She listened and as she answered again her voice began to rise with concern and anger. "No, I could not ask his friends about him because he doesn't have any friends. His brain was injured when he was three years old and that is why I am so concerned. This is not a ten-year-old boy who can go out and come home when he feels like it. This is not a boy who's going to run out and break street lights and spend the night in some garage, if that's what you're thinking. This is a boy, I'm telling you, who can be lost and afraid three blocks from home and cannot speak one word to ask for help. Now are you going to come out here or aren't you?"

She paused, said, "Yes, yes," then **1** grudgingly, "And thank you." She hung up the receiver and looked at Sara. "They're coming."

"What did they say?"

"They said they're coming. That's all." She rose in agitation and began to walk into the living room. "Oh, why don't they hurry!"

"Aunt Willie, they just hung up the telephone."

"I know." She went to the front door and then came back, nervously slapping her hands together. "Where can he *be*?"

"My brother was always getting lost when he was little," Mary said.

"I stood right in this house, in that room," Aunt Willie interrupted. She pointed toward the front bedroom. "And I promised your mother, Sara, that I would look after Charlie all my life. I promised your mother nothing would ever happen to Charlie as long as there was breath in my body, and now look. Look! Where is this boy I'm taking such good care of?" She threw her hands into the air. "Vanished without a trace, that's where."

"Aunt Willie, you can't watch him every minute."

"Why not? Why can't I? What have I got more important in my life than looking after that boy? Only one thing more im- **2** portant than Charlie. Only one thing—that devil television there."

"Aunt Willie—"

"Oh, yes, that devil television. I was sitting right in that chair last night and he wanted me to sew on one button for him but I was too busy with the television. I'll tell you what I should have told your mother six years ago. I should have told her, 'Sure, I'll be glad to look after Charlie except when there's something good on television. I'll be glad to watch him in my spare time.' My tongue should fall out on the **3** floor for promising to look after your brother and not doing it."

She went back to the doorway. "There are a hundred things that could have hap-

PORTFOLIO ASSESSMENT
Self-portraits can often tell quite a bit about the artists themselves and what they think is important. Some students may be interested in painting their own self-portrait. Suggest that they list the three most important things in their lives and make sure that these are portrayed in their portrait. For example, they might put themselves in a significant setting or show themselves dressed in their favorite clothing. They may also want to include a special pet. Consult with students individually to agree on how their self-portraits will be assessed. (See *Portfolio Assessment and Professional Support Materials* for additional information on portfolios.)

pened to him. He could have fallen into one of those ravines in the woods. He could be lost up at the old mine. He could be at the bottom of the lake. He could be kidnapped." Sara and Mary stood in silence as she named the tragedies that could have befallen Charlie.

Sara said, "Well, he could not have been kidnapped, because anybody would know we don't have any money for ransom."

"That wouldn't stop some people. Where are those policemen?"

Sara looked down at the table beside the television and saw a picture Charlie had drawn of himself on tablet paper. The head and body were circles of the same size, the ears and eyes overlapping smaller circles,

1
Ravines are deep, narrow holes in the earth.

2. VISUAL CONNECTIONS
What can you tell about Charlie from the way he drew himself? He draws the way a much younger child might draw. Notice his precious watch.

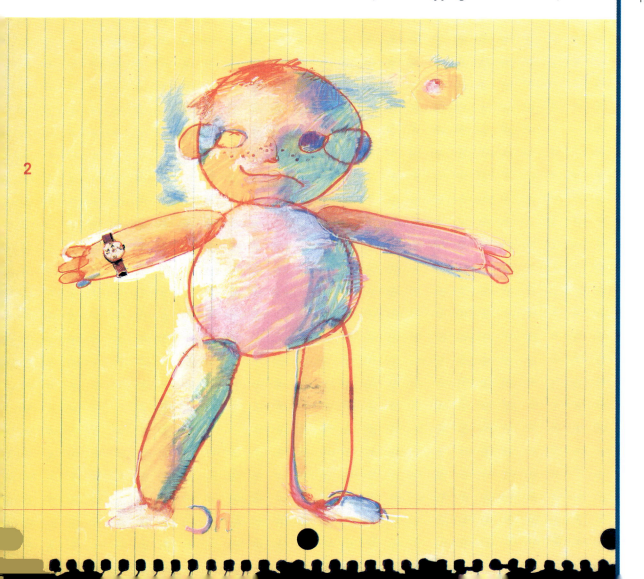

1. LITERARY ELEMENTS:
Subplot
Byars recognizes the importance of introducing a romantic conflict to make the novel more interesting to some middle-school readers. Unlike a short story, a novel may include several minor conflicts that add suspense and develop the characters. Some sixth graders will become more interested in the boy/girl conflict of Sara vs. Joe than in the main conflict of the novel, the more subtle conflict of values that goes on inside Sara. Ask students to notice the way this subplot is cleverly woven into the main plot.

2. GUIDED READING:
Contrasting
How is Sara's opinion of Joe different from Aunt Willie's? Sara dislikes Joe because she thinks he stole Charlie's watch. Aunt Willie says that he did not steal the watch but brought it back.

3. GUIDED READING:
Self-Questioning
What questions might you have as a result of this difference of opinion? Students might wonder who Joe Melby is and what really happened.

---

the arms and legs were elongated balloons. He had started printing his name below the picture, but had completed only two letters before he had gone out to make the tent. The *C* was backward.

Wanda had bought him the tablet and crayons two days ago and he had done this one picture with the brown crayon. It gave Sara a sick feeling to see it because something about the picture, the smallness, the unfinished quality, made it look somehow very much like Charlie.

Aunt Willie said, "When you want the police they are always a hundred miles away bothering criminals."

"They're on their way. They said so," Mary said.

"All right then, where are they?"

Mary blinked her eyes at this question to which she had no answer, and settled the rollers beneath her scarf.

"I still can't get it out of my head that Charlie went back to see the swans," Sara said.

"He really was upset about having to go home. I can testify to that," Mary said.

Aunt Willie left the room abruptly. When she came back she was holding a picture of Charlie in one hand. It was a snapshot of him taken in March, sitting on the steps with Boysie in front of the house.

"The police always want a photograph," she said. She held it out so Mary and Sara could see it. "Mrs. Hutchinson took that with her Polaroid."

"It's a real good picture of him," Mary said.

Sara looked at the picture without speaking. Somehow the awkward, unfinished crayon drawing on the table looked more like Charlie than the snapshot.

"It was his birthday," Aunt Willie said mournfully, "and look how proud he was of that watch Wanda bought him, holding his little arm straight out in the picture so everyone would notice it. I fussed so much about Wanda getting him a watch because he couldn't tell time, and then he was so proud just to be wearing it. Everyone would ask him on the street, 'What time is it, Charlie? Have you got the time, Charlie?' just to see how proud he was to show them."

"And then those boys stole it. I think that was the meanest thing," Mary said.

"The watch was lost," Aunt Willie said. "The watch just got lost."

"Stolen," Sara snapped, "by that crook Joe Melby."

"I am the quickest person to accuse somebody, you know that. You saw me, I hope, when I noticed those boys making off with the Hutchinsons' porch chairs last Halloween; but that watch just got lost. Then Joe Melby found it and, to his credit, brought it back."

"Huh!"

"There was no stealing involved."

Mary said, giggling, "Aunt Willie, did Sara ever tell you what she did to Joe?"

"Hush, Mary," Sara said.

"What did she do?"

"She made a little sign that said *FINK* and stuck it on Joe's back in the hall at school and he went around for two periods without knowing it was there."

"It doesn't matter what I did. Nobody's going to pick on my brother and I mean it. That fink stole Charlie's watch and then got scared and told that big lie about finding it on the floor of the school bus."

"You want revenge too much."

"When somebody *deserves* revenge, then—"

"I take my revenge same as anybody," Aunt Willie said, "Only I never was one to keep after somebody and keep after somebody the way you do. You take after your Uncle Bert in that."

"I hope I always do."

"No, your Uncle Bert was no good in that way. He would never let a grudge leave him. When he lay dying in the hospital, he was telling us who we weren't to speak to and who we weren't to do business with. His dying words were against Jeep Johnson at the used-car lot."

"Good for Uncle Bert."

"And that nice little Gretchen Wyant who you turned the hose on, and her wearing a silk dress her brother had sent her from Taiwan!"

"That nice little Gretchen Wyant was lucky all she got was water on her silk dress."

"Sara!"

"Well, do you know what that nice little Gretchen Wyant did? I was standing in the bushes by the spigot, turning off the hose, and this nice little Gretchen Wyant didn't see me—all she saw was Charlie at the fence—and she said, 'How's the *retard* today?' only she made it sound even uglier, 'How's the *reeeeetard*,' like that. Nothing ever made me so mad. The best sight of my whole life was nice little Gretchen Wyant standing there in her wet Taiwan silk dress with her mouth hanging open."

"Here come the police," Mary said quickly. "But they're stopping next door."

"Signal to them," Aunt Willie said.

Before Mary could move to the door, Aunt Willie was past her and out on the porch. "Here we are. This is the house." She turned and said over her shoulder to Sara, "Now, God willing, we'll get some action."

Sara sat in the living room wearing her cut-off blue jeans, an old shirt with *Property of State Prison* stamped on the back which Wanda had brought her from the beach, and her puce tennis shoes. She was sitting in the doorway, leaning back against the door with her arms wrapped around her knees, listening to Aunt Willie, who was making a telephone call in the hall.

"It's no use calling," Sara said against her knees. This was the first summer her knees had not been skinned a dozen times, but she could still see the white scars from other summers. Since Aunt Willie did not answer, she said again, "It's no use calling. He won't come."

"You don't know your father," Aunt Willie said.

"That is the truth."

"Not like I do. When he hears that Charlie is missing, he will . . ." Her voice trailed off as she prepared to dial the telephone.

The Summer of the Swans 683

1
Remoteness means "being far away"; that is, "being cold and uninvolved."

2. GUIDED READING:
Identifying Cause and Effect
What do you think might have caused the change in Sara's father? Charlie's illness and his wife's death seem to have been the causes.

3
Sober means "serious."

Sara had a strange feeling when she thought of her father. It was the way she felt about people she didn't know well, like the time Miss Marshall, her English teacher, had given her a ride home from school, and Sara had felt uneasy the whole way home, even though she saw Miss Marshall every day.

1 Her father's remoteness had begun, she thought, with Charlie's illness. There was a picture in the family photograph album of her father laughing and throwing Sara into the air and a picture of her father holding her on his shoulders and a picture of her father sitting on the front steps with Wanda on one knee and Sara on the other.

2 All these pictures of a happy father and his adoring daughters had been taken before Charlie's illness and Sara's mother's death. Afterward there weren't any family pictures at all, happy or sad.

When Sara looked at those early pictures, she remembered a laughing man with black curly hair and a broken tooth who had lived with them for a few short golden years and then had gone away. There was no connection at all between this laughing man in the photograph album and the gray **3** sober man who worked in Ohio and came home to West Virginia on occasional weekends, who sat in the living room and watched baseball or football on television and never started a conversation on his own.

Sara listened while Aunt Willie explained to the operator that the call she was making was an emergency. "That's why I'm not direct dialing," she said, "because I'm so upset I'll get the wrong numbers."

"He won't come," Sara whispered against her knee.

As the operator put through the call and Aunt Willie waited, she turned to Sara, nodded emphatically, and said, "He'll come, you'll see."

Sara got up, walked across the living room and into the kitchen, where the breakfast dishes were still on the table. She looked down at the two bowls of hard, cold oatmeal, and then made herself three pieces of toast and poured herself a cup of cherry Kool-Aid. When she came back eating the toast Aunt Willie was still waiting.

"Didn't the operator tell them it was an emergency, I wonder," Aunt Willie said impatiently.

"Probably."

"Well, if somebody told me I had an emergency call, I would run, let me tell you, to find out what that emergency was. That's no breakfast, Sara."

"It's my lunch."

"Kool-Aid and toast will not sustain you five minutes." She broke off quickly and said in a louder voice, "Sam, is that you?" She nodded to Sara, then turned back to the telephone, bent forward in her concern. "First of all, Sammy, promise me you won't get upset—no, promise me first."

"He won't get upset. Even *I* can promise you that," Sara said with her mouth full of toast.

"Sam, Charlie's missing," Aunt Willie said abruptly.

Unable to listen to any more of the

conversation, Sara took her toast and went out onto the front porch. She sat on the front steps and put her feet into the worn grooves that Charlie's feet had made on the third step. Then she ate the last piece of toast and licked the butter off her fingers.

In the corner of the yard, beneath the elm tree, she could see the hole Charlie had dug with a spoon; all one morning he had dug that hole and now Boysie was lying in it for coolness. She walked to the tree and sat in the old rope swing and swung over Boysie. She stretched out her feet and touched Boysie, and he lifted his head and looked around to see who had poked him, then lay back in his hole.

"Boysie, here I am, look, Boysie, look."

He was already asleep again.

"Boysie—" She looked up as Aunt Willie came out on the porch and stood for a minute drying her hands on her apron. For the occasion of Charlie's disappearance she was wearing her best dress, a bright green bonded jersey, which was so hot her face above it was red and shiny. Around her forehead she had tied a handkerchief to absorb the sweat.

Sara swung higher. "Well," she asked, "is he coming?" She paused to pump herself higher. "Or not?"

"He's going to call back tonight."

"Oh," Sara said.

"Don't say 'Oh' to me like that."

"It's what I figured."

"Listen to me, Miss Know-it-all. There is no need in the world for your father to come this exact minute. If he started driving right this second he still wouldn't get here till after dark and he couldn't do anything then, so he just might as well wait till after work and then drive."

"Might as well do the sensible thing." Sara stood up and really began to swing. She had grown so much taller since she had last stood in this swing that her head came almost to the limb from which the swing hung. She caught hold of the limb with her hands, kicked her feet free, and let the swing jerk wildly on its own.

"Anyway," Aunt Willie said, "this is no time to be playing on a swing. What will the neighbors think, with Charlie missing and you having a wonderful time on a swing?"

"I knew he wouldn't come."

"He is going to come," Aunt Willie said in a louder voice. "He is just going to wait till dark, which is reasonable, since by dark Charlie will probably be home anyway."

"It is so reasonable that it makes me sick."

"I won't listen to you being disrespectful to your father, I mean that," she said. "I know what it is to lose a father, let me tell you, and so will you when all you have left of him is an envelope."

Aunt Willie, Sara knew, was speaking of the envelope in her dresser drawer containing all the things her father had had in his pockets when he died. Sara knew them all—the watch, the twenty-seven cents in change, the folded dollar bill, the brown

---

1. GUIDED READING:
Making Inferences
What course of action do you think Sara wishes her father would take? Why? She wants him to come immediately and help find Charlie. She thinks he doesn't care what happens to Charlie (or to her).

2. GUIDED READING:
Drawing Conclusions
Based on the clues you have been given, do you think Sara is right about her father, or is she too hard on him? Even if Sara's father doesn't mean to hurt her feelings, Sara genuinely feels rejected by him. Sara probably doesn't know all the facts, and therefore doesn't understand why he lives so far away.

3. GUIDED READING:
Comparing
How is Aunt Willie like Sara? Who is Aunt Willie trying to protect here? Aunt Willie is loyal to her brother and protective of him just as Sara is loyal to Charlie and protects him.

1. GUIDED READING:
Self-Questioning
Aunt Willie and Sara are not communicating very well. If you were Aunt Willie, what would you have said to Sara that might have made her feel better? Aunt Willie might have said, "I know that you feel that your father doesn't love you and Charlie, but his staying away has nothing to do with you. I wish he would come here more often too, because he's missing out on a lot of happiness seeing how well you and Charlie and Wanda are doing."

2. GUIDED READING:
Making Inferences
What kind of person does Joe seem to be? He seems to be helpful and interested in Charlie.

---

plaid handkerchief, the three-cent stamp, the two bent pipe cleaners, the half pack of stomach mints.

1 "Yes, wait till you lose your father. Then you'll appreciate him."

"I've already lost him."

"Don't you talk like that. Your father's had to raise two families and all by himself. When Poppa died, Sammy had to go to work and support all of us before he was even out of high school, and now he's got this family to support too. It's not easy, I'm telling you that. *You* raise two families and then I'll listen to what you've got to say against your father."

Sara let herself drop to the ground and said, "I better go. Mary and I are going to look for Charlie."

"Where?"

"Up the hill."

"Well, don't *you* get lost," Aunt Willie called after her.

From the Hutchinsons' yard some children called, "Have you found Charlie yet, Sara?" They were making a garden in the dust, carefully planting flowers without roots in neat rows. Already the first flowers were beginning to wilt in the hot sun.

"I'm going to look for him now."

"Sawa?" It was the youngest Hutchinson boy, who was three and sometimes came over to play with Charlie.

"What?"

"Sawa?"

"What?"

"Sawa?"

"*What?*"

"Sawa, I got gwass." He held up two fists of grass he had just pulled from one of the few remaining clumps in the yard.

"Yes, that's fine. I'll tell Charlie when I see him."

Sara and Mary had decided that they would go to the lake and walk up behind the houses toward the woods. Sara was now on her way to Mary's, passing the vacant lot where a baseball game was in progress. She glanced up and watched as she walked down the sidewalk.

The baseball game had been going on for an hour with the score still zero to zero and the players, dusty and tired, were playing silently, without hope.

She was almost past the field when she 2 heard someone call, "Hey, have you found your brother yet, Sara?"

She recognized the voice of Joe Melby and said, "No," without looking at him.

"What?"

She turned, looked directly at him, and said, "You will be pleased and delighted to learn that we have not." She continued walking down the street. The blood began to pound in her head. Joe Melby was the one person she did not want to see on this particular day. There was something disturbing about him. She did not know him, really, had hardly even spoken to him, and yet she hated him so much the sight of him made her sick.

"Is there anything I can do?"

"No."

"If he's up in the woods, I could help

CLOSURE
Divide students into groups. Ask each group to collaborate on rewriting any five-to-ten lines from pages 670–688, using first-person point of view. Let each group decide whether they will rewrite from the viewpoint of Sara, Aunt Willie, Mary, or Joe.

RETEACHING
Give each student a novel (preferably paperback) for young people. Have them glance through their novels and tell whether the point of view is first-person or omniscient. You might also give them two minutes to review the table of contents, illustrations (if any), and information about the author. Then have students tell whether they might like to read this novel and why—or why not.

---

look. I know about as much about those hills as anybody." He left the game and started walking behind her with his hands in his pockets.

"No, thank you."

"I *want* to help."

She swirled around and faced him, her eyes blazing. "I do not want your help." They looked at each other. Something twisted inside her and she felt suddenly ill. She thought she would never drink cherry Kool-Aid again as long as she lived.

Joe Melby did not say anything but moved one foot back and forth on the sidewalk, shuffling at some sand. "Do you—"

"Anybody who would steal a little boy's watch," she said, cutting off his words, and it was a relief to make this accusation to his face at last, "is somebody whose help I can very well do without." Her head was pounding so loudly she could hardly hear her own words. For months, ever since the incident of the stolen watch, she had waited for this moment, had planned exactly what she would say. Now that it was said, she did not feel the triumph she had imagined at all.

1 "Is that what's wrong with you?" He looked at her. "You think I stole your brother's watch?"

"I know you did."

"How?"

"Because I asked Charlie who stole his watch and I kept asking him and one day on the school bus when I asked him he pointed right straight at you."

"He was confused—"

"He wasn't that confused. You probably thought he wouldn't be able to tell on you because he couldn't talk, but he pointed right—"

"He *was* confused. I gave the watch *back* to him. I didn't take it."

"I don't believe you."

"You believe what you want then, but I didn't take that watch. I thought that matter had been settled."

"Huh!"

She turned and started walking with great speed down the hill. For some reason she was not as sure about Joe Melby as she had been before, and this was even more disturbing. He did take the watch, she said to herself. She could not bear to think that she had been mistaken in this, that she had taken revenge on the wrong person.

Behind her there were sudden cheers as someone hit a home run. The ball went into the street. Joe ran, picked it up, and tossed it to a boy in the field. Sara did not look around.

"Hey, wait a minute," she heard Joe call. "I'm coming."

She did not turn around. She had fallen into that trap before. Once when she had been walking down the street, she had heard a car behind her and the horn sounding and a boy's voice shouting, "Hey, beautiful!" And she had turned around. She! Then, too late, she had seen that the girl they were honking and shouting at was Rosey Camdon on the opposite side of the street, Rosey Camdon who was Miss Batelle District Fair and Miss Buckwheat

The Summer of the Swans **687**

---

1. GUIDED READING:
Making Inferences
Do you believe Joe? How do you think he feels about Sara? Joe is quite believable. Even though he knows Sara is angry with him, he doesn't become angry. He just keeps stating the truth as he sees it. He leaves the game to talk with her, and, in spite of her rejection, he seems to like her, and he wants to help her find Charlie.

EXTENSION AND ENRICHMENT
Art. Ask students to draw a map showing where Charlie went. Have them label and number each place to show the correct sequence. (They will have to reread pages 672–675 to do this accurately.)
Research. Advanced students might be able to do some research on mental retardation and present their findings to the class. An excellent book written for young people is *Mental Retardation* by Robert E. Dunbar (Franklin Watts, 1978).

Here's another approach: Ask each student to write one question about mental retardation. Let the questions serve as a guide to the students who will do the research.

FOR STUDY AND DISCUSSION
Identifying Facts
1. He cannot sleep because a button is missing from his pajama top.
   He leaves the house to see one of the swans.
2. Once their father had been happy; he started becoming remote when Charlie became ill. He works in Ohio and visits occasionally but, according to Sara, doesn't pay attention to them even when he is there.
3. He doesn't seem to feel Charlie's absence is an emergency. He is waiting for more news before he makes the long trip to West Virginia. He says he will call back later.
4. Joe Melby is a classmate of Sara's at school.
   She dislikes him because she thinks he stole Charlie's watch.

Interpreting Meanings
5. Sara thinks her father has paid little attention to his children.
   Aunt Willie defends Sam by explaining that he has raised two families all by himself.
6. Students might suggest (a) Will Charlie be found? (b) Will the conflict between Sara and her father be resolved? (c) How will Sara treat Joe Melby when he offers to help?

688

Queen and a hundred other things. Sara had looked down quickly, not knowing whether anyone had seen her or not, and her face had burned so fiercely she had thought it would be red forever. Now she kept walking quickly with her head down.

"Wait, Sara."

Still she did not turn around or show that she had heard him.

"Wait." He ran, caught up with her, and started walking beside her. "All the boys say they want to help."

She hesitated but kept walking. She could not think of anything to say. She knew how circus men on stilts felt when they walked, because her legs seemed to be moving in the same awkward way, great exaggerated steps that got her nowhere.

She thought she might start crying so she said quickly, "Oh, all right." Then tears did come to her eyes, sudden and hot, and she looked down at her feet.

He said, "Where should we start? Have you got any ideas?"

"I think he's up in the woods. I took him to see the swans yesterday and I think he was looking for them when he got lost."

"Probably up that way."

She nodded.

He paused, then added, "We'll find him."

She did not answer, could not, because tears were spilling down her cheeks, so she turned quickly and walked alone to Mary's house and waited on the sidewalk until Mary came out to join her.

688 The Novel

For Study and Discussion

IDENTIFYING FACTS
1. Explain why Charlie is unable to sleep. Why does he leave the house?
2. What further details do you learn in this section about the children's father?
3. How does Sara's father react to Charlie's disappearance?
4. Who is Joe Melby? Why does Sara dislike him?

INTERPRETING MEANINGS
5. Why does Sara say she's already "lost" her father? How does Aunt Willie respond to Sara's complaint?
6. Charlie's disappearance immediately creates **suspense**. It makes us anxious to find out what will happen next. List three questions you hope the rest of the novel will answer.
7. How do you feel about Charlie so far?

APPLYING MEANINGS
8. What's your opinion of the way Sara punished Gretchen Wyant for her cruelty to Charlie? If Charlie were your brother, how would you have handled this incident?
9. This novel does not have chapter titles. Choose any one of the chapters you've read so far. Make up an interesting title for that chapter.

Literary Elements

POINT OF VIEW
Point of view is the vantage point from which a story is told. There are two main points of

MEETING INDIVIDUAL NEEDS

Visual Learners • As students discuss the conflict between Sara and her father, you might want to draw a family tree for the Godfrey family that would include the father's family as he was growing up. You could start with Mr. Godfrey's family when he was a child and then add his wife and his children on another branch of the tree.

---

view: first person and omniscient (om·nish'ənt).

1. **First-person point of view:** The story is told by a character inside the story. Suppose that Sara were telling this story. She would refer to herself as "I," which is called the first-person pronoun. ("You" is the second-person pronoun. "He, she, it" are third-person pronouns.) If Sara were telling the story, we would not be able to share Charlie's private thoughts and feelings. We would only know what Sara could tell us.

2. **Omniscient point of view:** The narrator is someone outside the events of the story. This all-knowing narrator knows everything about the story and can take us back and forth in time. An omniscient narrator can tell us the unspoken thoughts of all the characters.

The point of view in *The Summer of the Swans* is omniscient. Whose private thoughts and feelings does the narrator tell about in each of the following passages?

1. "The beauty of them, the whiteness, the softness . . . had impressed him greatly, and he felt a longing to be once again by the lake, sitting in the deep grass, throwing bread to the waiting swans." (Pages 671–672)

2. "The whole night seemed one long struggle, but he could not remember why he had been struggling." (Page 675)

3. "One of her greatest mistakes, she thought, looking at herself critically, was cutting her hair." (Page 676)

Whose thoughts and feelings does the narrator of this novel tell you most about?

Focus on Persuasive Writing

SUPPORTING YOUR OPINION

How would you convince Sara that Joe Melby didn't take Charlie's watch? You would probably need to use supporting arguments. At the beginning of the next section, you will see how Mary persuades Sara (see pages 690–691).

To persuade your readers or listeners to agree with your opinion on a topic, your argument needs **support**. Here are some types of support you can use:

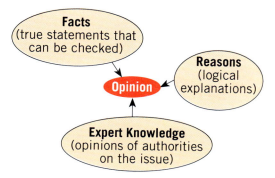

Choose a topic for a persuasive speech to your classmates. For example, you might want to persuade your listeners to support recycling or to start a pen pal program. Write a one-sentence opinion statement. Then list as many facts, reasons, and expert opinions as you can to support your view. Save your notes.

---

7. Most students will feel sympathetic to Charlie.

Applying Meanings

8. Some may think Gretchen deserved Sara's treatment; others may say Sara was too eager to get revenge.

Ask students to explain and defend their various suggestions.

9. Encourage students to be imaginative and to think of titles that will hook readers' interest.

LITERARY ELEMENTS

Point of View
1. Charlie
2. Charlie
3. Sara

The narrator tells us most about Sara's thoughts and feelings.

FOCUS ON PERSUASIVE WRITING

Supporting Your Opinion

For some opinion statements, students will be able to use supporting reasons and facts that come from common knowledge and their own observations. For other issues, students will need to find support in books, magazines, and other library resources. These sources will also provide expert opinions to quote, but remind students not to forget about people in their school or community who know something about their topics.

OBJECTIVES

Students should be able to recognize external and internal conflict. They should be able to make inferences and draw conclusions about the characters and events in the novel.

FOCUS/MOTIVATION

Building on Prior Knowledge. Elicit and list the conflicts facing Sara. Ask students to identify each as external or internal. For example, Sara vs. her own feelings and thoughts (internal); Sara vs. Joe (external); Sara vs. Aunt Willie (external).

Prereading Journal. Tell students to imagine that they are Sara. Then have them write a few sentences telling what they would do to solve one of their conflicts.

TEACHING RESOURCES D
Teacher's Notes, p. 167
Reading Check, p. 169
Study Guide, p. 170
Language Skills, p. 171
Building Vocabulary p. 174
Selection Vocabulary Test, p. 176
Selection Test, p. 177

---

1. GUIDED READING

Drawing Conclusions
Based on what you know about Aunt Willie, what conclusion do you draw about why she went to see Joe's mother? She probably wanted Joe to be punished for taking Charlie's watch.

2. GUIDED READING:

Forming Valid Opinions
Do you agree with Sara that it was terrible of Aunt Willie to visit Joe's mother? Why? Young people will probably think it *was* terrible. Is Sara upset mostly because Aunt Willie didn't tell her about the visit? Or that she "interfered"?

She and Mary were almost across the open field before Sara spoke. Then she said, "Guess who just stopped me and gave me the big sympathy talk about Charlie."

"I don't know. Who?"

"Joe Melby."

"Really? What did he say?"

"He wants to help look for Charlie. He makes me sick."

"I think it's nice that he wants to help."

"Well, maybe if he'd stolen your brother's watch you wouldn't think it was so nice."

Mary was silent for a moment. Then she said, "I probably shouldn't tell you this, but he didn't steal that watch, Sara."

"Huh!"

"No, he really didn't."

Sara looked at her and said, "How do you know?"

"I can't tell you how I know because I promised I wouldn't, but I *know* he didn't."

"How?"

"I can't tell. I promised."

"That never stopped you before. Now, Mary Weicek, you tell me what you know this minute."

"I promised."

"Mary, tell me."

"Mom would kill me if she knew I told you."

"She won't know."

1 "Well, your aunt went to see Joe Melby's mother."

"What?"

"Aunt Willie went over to see Joe Melby's mother."

"She didn't!"

"Yes, she did too, because my mother was right there when it happened. It was about two weeks after Charlie had gotten the watch back."

"I don't believe you."

"Well, it's the truth. You told Aunt Willie that Joe had stolen the watch—remember, you told everybody—and so Aunt Willie went over to see Joe's mother."

2 "She wouldn't do such a terrible thing."

"Well, she did."

"And what did Mrs. Melby say?"

"She called Joe into the room and she said, 'Joe, did you steal the little Godfrey boy's watch?' And he said, 'No.'"

"What did you expect him to say in front of his mother? 'Yes, I stole the watch'? Huh! That doesn't prove anything."

"So then she said, 'I want the truth now. Do you know who did take the watch?' and he said that nobody had *stolen* the watch."

"So where did it disappear to for a week, I'd like to know."

"I'm coming to that. He said some of the fellows were out in front of the drugstore and Charlie was standing there waiting for the school bus—you were in the drugstore. Remember it was the day we were getting the stamps for letters to those pen pals who never answered? Remember the stamps wouldn't come out of the machine? Well, anyway, these boys outside the store started teasing Charlie with some candy, and while Charlie was trying to get

690 The Novel

READING THE SELECTION
Some students will quickly finish reading the novel at home. Slower students may need to spend two class periods or two homework sessions on this part. You may want to assign page 690 up to the break on page 697 for one class period or homework session. Then read pages 697–698 aloud in class, and assign pages 699–702 for silent reading in class or for homework.

---

the candy, one of the boys took off Charlie's watch without Charlie noticing it. Then they were going to ask Charlie what time it was and when he looked down at his watch, he would get upset because the watch would be gone. They were just going to tease him."

"Finks! *Finks!*"

"Only you came out of the drugstore right then and saw what they were doing with the candy and told them off and the bus came and you hustled Charlie on the bus before anybody had a chance to give back the watch. Then they got scared to give it back and that's the whole story. Joe didn't steal the watch at all. He wasn't even in on it. He came up right when you did and didn't even know what had happened. Later, when he found out, he got the watch back and gave it to Charlie, that's all."

"Why didn't you tell me before this?"

"Because I just found out about it at lunch. For four months my mother has known all about this thing and never mentioned it because she said it was one of those things best forgotten."

"Why did she tell you now?"

"That's the way my mom is. We were talking about Charlie at the dinner table, and suddenly she comes up with this. Like one time she casually mentioned that she had had a long talk with Mr. Homer about me. Mr. Homer, the principal! She went over there and they had a long discussion and she never mentioned it for a year."

"That is the worst thing Aunt Willie has ever done."

"Well, don't let on that you know or I'll be in real trouble."

"I won't, but honestly, I could just—"

"You promised."

"I know. You don't have to keep reminding me. It makes me feel terrible though, I can tell you that." She walked with her head bent forward. "Terrible! You know what I just did when I saw him?"

"What?"

"Accused him of stealing the watch."

"Sara, you didn't."

"I did too. I can't help myself. When I think somebody has done something mean to Charlie I can't forgive them. I want to keep after them and keep after them just like Aunt Willie said. I even sort of suspected Joe Melby hadn't really taken that watch and I still kept on—"

"Shh! Be quiet a minute." Mary was carrying her transistor radio and she held it up between them. "Listen."

The announcer was saying: "We have a report of a missing child in the Cass section—ten-year-old Charlie Godfrey, who has been missing from his home since sometime last night. He is wearing blue pajamas and brown felt slippers, has a watch on one wrist and an identification bracelet with his name and address on the other. He is a mentally handicapped child who cannot speak and may become alarmed when approached by a stranger. Please notify the police immediately if you have seen this youngster."

The two girls looked at each other, then continued walking across the field in silence.

---

1. GUIDED READING:
Identifying the Author's Purpose
What purpose does this passage serve? It shifts your attention from one conflict (Sara vs. Joe) to another (Charlie vs. the forest), and increases the suspense.

2. GUIDED READING:
Predicting Outcomes
What do you think will happen next between Sara and Joe? What would you do if you were Sara? Answers will, of course, vary. Some students may suggest that Sara will seek out Joe and apologize to him. Others may say she will avoid him.

The Summer of the Swans

MEETING INDIVIDUAL NEEDS
Visual Learners • To prepare students for the climax of the story and to compare Sara's and Joe's climb to the top to the rising action in the plot, you might want to draw a diagram of the plot on the chalkboard. Use a wide space so that you can add along the way events that lead to the climax. Explain that a plot creates interest by leading a reader to a peak, or *climax*, and then moves to a conclusion by resolving the conflicts between the characters. You might then show the resolution of the conflicts as events following the climax. Compare the plot to the excitement that builds as the two characters climb uphill to search for Charlie.

1
Strained means "forced" or "unnatural."

2. GUIDED READING:
Making Inferences
How does Mary feel about the search? She wants to turn back. It's hot, she's tired, and she thinks they've gone too far.

3. GUIDED READING:
Making Inferences
Why do you think Mary keeps mentioning Bennie Hoffman's party? She is quite proud that she has a date; it may be her first date—and Sara has never had a date. There is probably some natural competition between the two girls.

Mary and Sara were up in the field by the woods. They had been searching for Charlie for an hour without finding a trace of him.

Mary said, "I don't care how I look. I am taking off this scarf. It must be a hundred degrees out here."

"Charlie!" Sara called as she had been doing from time to time. Her voice had begun to sound strained, she had called so often. "Charlie!"

"Sara, do you know where we are?" Mary asked after a moment.

"Of course. The lake's down there and the old shack's over there and you can see them as soon as we get up a little higher."

"*If* we get up a little higher," Mary said in a tired voice.

"You didn't have to come, you know."

"I wanted to come, only I just want to make sure we don't get lost. I have to go to Bennie Hoffman's party tonight."

"I know. You told me ten times."

"So I don't want to get lost." Mary walked a few steps without speaking. "I still can't figure out why I was invited, because Bennie Hoffman hardly knows me. I've just seen him two times this whole summer at the pool. Why do you think he—"

"Come on, will you?"

"It seems useless, if you ask me, to just keep walking when we don't really know which way he went. Aunt Willie thinks he went in the old coal mine."

"I know, but she only thinks that because she associates the mine with tragedy because her uncle and brother were killed in that coal mine. But Charlie wouldn't go in there. Remember that time we went into the Bryants' cellar after they moved out, and he wouldn't even come in there because it was cold and dark and sort of scary."

"Yes, I do remember because I sprained my ankle jumping down from the window and had to wait two hours while you looked through old *Life* magazines."

"I was not looking through old magazines."

"I could hear you. I was down there in that dark cellar with the rats and you were upstairs and I was yelling for help and you kept saying, 'I'm going for help right now,' and I could hear the pages turning and turning and turning."

"Well, I got you out, didn't I?"

"Finally."

Sara paused again. "Charlie! Charlie!" The girls waited in the high grass for an answer, then began to walk again. Mary said, "Maybe we should have waited for the others before we started looking. They're going to have a regular organized posse with everybody walking along together. There may be a helicopter."

"The longer we wait, the harder it will be to find him."

"Well, I've got to get home in time to bathe and take my hair down."

"I know. I *know*. You're going to Bennie Hoffman's party."

"You don't have to sound so mad about it. I didn't *ask* to be invited."

"I am not mad because you were invited to Bennie Hoffman's party. I couldn't

692 The Novel

care less about Bennie Hoffman's party. I'm just mad because you're slowing me up on this search."

"Well, if I'm slowing you up so much, then maybe I'll just go on home."

"That suits me fine."

They looked at each other without speaking. Between them the radio began announcing: "Volunteers are needed in the Cass area in the search for young Charlie Godfrey, who disappeared from his home sometime during the night. A search of the Cheat woods will begin at three o'clock this afternoon."

Mary said, "Oh, I'll keep looking. I'll try to walk faster."

Sara shrugged, turned, and started walking up the hill, followed by Mary. They came to the old fence that once separated the pasture from the woods. Sara walked slowly beside the fence. "Charlie!" she called.

"Would he come if he heard you, do you think?"

Sara nodded. "But if they get a hundred people out here clomping through the woods and hollering, he's not going to come. He'll be too scared. I know him."

"I don't see how you can be so sure he came up this way."

"I just know. There's something about me that makes me understand Charlie. It's like I know how he feels about things. Like sometimes I'll be walking down the street and I'll pass the jeweler's and I'll think that if Charlie were here he would want to stand right there and look at those watches all afternoon and I know right where he'd stand and how he'd put his hands up on the glass and how his face would look. And yesterday I knew he was going to love the swans so much that he wasn't ever going to want to leave. I know how he feels."

"You just think you do."

"No, I *know*. I was thinking about the sky one night and I was looking up at the stars and I was thinking about how the sky goes on and on forever, and I couldn't understand it no matter how long I thought, and finally I got kind of nauseated and right then I started thinking, Well, this is how Charlie feels about some things. You know how it makes him sick sometimes to try to print letters for a long time and—"

"Look who's coming," Mary interrupted.

"Where?"

"In the trees, walking toward us. Joe Melby."

"You're lying. You're just trying to make me—"

"It is him. Look." She quickly began to tie her scarf over her rollers again. "And you talk about *me* needing eyeglasses."

"Cut across the field, quick!" Sara said. "No, wait, go under the fence. Move, will you, Mary, and leave that scarf alone. Get under the fence. I am not going to face him. I mean it."

"I am not going under any fence. Anyway, it would look worse for us to run away than to just walk by casually."

"I cannot walk by casually after what I said."

"Well, you're going to have to face

1
Notice the use of *like* here, and the long, run-on sentence that makes this dialogue sound realistic.

2. GUIDED READING:
Forming Valid Opinions
Do you think anyone can know how another person feels? Answers will vary. Students may realize that it is because Sara loves Charlie—in spite of the trouble he causes her—that she feels so closely connected to him.

3. GUIDED READING:
Making Inferences
What can you infer about Mary's feelings toward Joe? She wants to impress him.

The Summer of the Swans

VISUAL CONNECTIONS
Through whose eyes do you catch this glimpse of Charlie's slipper? Joe's, or perhaps this is what Sara thinks when Joe hands her the slipper.

him sometime, and it might as well be now when everyone feels sorry for you about your brother." She called out, "Hi, Joe, having any luck?"

He came up to them and held out a brown felt slipper and looked at Sara. "Is this Charlie's?"

Sara looked at the familiar object and forgot the incident of the watch for a moment. "Where did you find it?"

"Right up there by the fence. I had just picked it up when I saw you."

She took the slipper and, holding it against her, said, "Oh, I *knew* he came up

this way, but it's a relief to have some proof of it."

"I was just talking to Mr. Aker," Joe continued, "and he said he heard his dogs barking up here last night. He had them tied out by the shack and he thought maybe someone was prowling around."

"Probably Charlie," Mary said.

"That's what I figured. Somebody ought to go down to the gas station and tell the people. They're organizing a big search now and half of the men are planning to go up to the mine."

There was a pause and Mary said,

The Summer of the Swans

---

1. GUIDED READING:
Making Inferences
What can you infer about how helpful Joe will be in looking for Charlie? He seems to have started his search quite intelligently. He has been looking for clues on the ground and he has talked to someone to find out if they heard anything last night.

2. GUIDED READING:
Interpreting Meaning
Notice that Joe is clever enough not to suggest directly to Mary that she should be the one to go down to the gas station!

1
Cicadas are large insects that make a shrill sound.

2
A *guru* is a spiritual leader.

"Well, I guess I could go, only I don't know whether I'll have time to get back up here." She looked at Joe. "I promised Bennie Hoffman I'd come to his party tonight. That's why my hair's in rollers."

"Tell them I found the slipper about a half mile up behind the Akers' at the old fence," Joe said.

"Sure. Are you coming to Bennie's tonight?"

"Maybe."

"Come. It's going to be fun."

Sara cleared her throat and said, "Well, I think I'll get on with my search if you two will excuse me." She turned and started walking up the hill again. There seemed to be a long silence in which even **1** the sound of the cicadas in the grass was absent. She thrashed at the high weeds with her tennis shoes and hugged Charlie's slipper to her.

"Wait a minute, Sara, I'll come with you," Joe Melby said.

He joined her and she nodded, still looking down at the slipper. There was a picture of an Indian chief stamped on the top of the shoe and there was a loneliness to the Indian's profile, even stamped crudely on the felt, that she had never noticed before.

She cleared her throat again. "There is just one thing I want to say." Her voice did not even sound familiar, a tape-recorded voice.

He waited, then said, "Go ahead."

She did not speak for a moment but continued walking noisily through the weeds.

"Go ahead."

"If you'll just wait a minute, I'm trying to think how to say this." The words she wanted to say—I'm sorry—would not come out at all.

They continued walking in silence and then Joe said, "You know, I was just reading an article about a guru over in India **2** and he hasn't spoken a word in twenty-eight years. *Twenty-eight years* and he hasn't said one word in all that time. And everyone has been waiting all those years to hear what he's going to say when he finally does speak because it's supposed to be some great wise word, and I thought about this poor guy sitting there and for twenty-eight years he's been trying to think of something to say that would be the least bit great and he can't think of anything and he must be getting really desperate now. And every day it gets worse and worse."

"Is there supposed to be some sort of message in that story?"

"Maybe."

She smiled. "Well, I just wanted to say that I'm sorry." She thought again that she was going to start crying and she said to herself, You are nothing but a big soft snail. Snail!

"That's all right."

"I just found out about Aunt Willie going to see your mother."

He shrugged. "She didn't mean anything by it."

"But it was a terrible thing."

"It wasn't all that bad. At least it was different to be accused of something I *didn't* do for a change."

"But to be called in like that in front

of Aunt Willie and Mary's mother. No, it was terrible." She turned and walked into the woods.

"Don't worry about it. I'm tough. I'm indestructible. I'm like that coyote in 'Road Runner' who is always getting flattened and dynamited and crushed and in the next scene is strolling along, completely normal again."

"I just acted too hastily. That's one of my main faults."

"I do that too."

"Not like me."

"Worse probably. Do you remember when we used to get grammar-school report cards, and the grades would be on one part of the card, and on the other side would be personality things the teacher would check, like 'Does not accept criticism constructively'?"

Sara smiled. "I always used to get a check on that one," she said.

"Who didn't? And then they had one, 'Acts impetuously and without consideration for others,' or something like that, and one year I got a double check on that one."

"You didn't."

"Yes, I did. Second grade. Miss McLeod. I remember she told the whole class that this was the first year she had ever had to give double checks to any student, and everyone in the room was scared to open his report card to see if he had got the double checks. And when I opened mine, there they were, two sets of double checks, on acting impetuously and on not accepting criticism, and single checks on everything else."

"Were you crushed?"

"Naturally."

"I thought you were so tough and indestructible."

"Well, I am"—he paused—"I think." He pointed to the left. "Let's go up this way."

She agreed with a nod and went ahead of him between the trees.

There was a ravine in the forest, a deep cut in the earth, and Charlie had made his way into it through an early morning fog. By chance, blindly stepping through the fog with his arms outstretched, he had managed to pick the one path that led into the ravine, and when the sun came out and the fog burned away, he could not find the way out.

All the ravine looked the same in the daylight, the high walls, the masses of weeds and wild berry bushes, the trees. He had wandered around for a while, following the little paths made by dirt washed down from the hillside, but finally he sat down on a log and stared straight ahead without seeing.

After a while he roused enough to wipe his hands over his cheeks where the tears and dirt had dried together and to rub his puffed eyelids. Then he looked down, saw his bare foot, put it on top of his slipper, and sat with his feet overlapped.

There was a dullness about him now. He had had so many scares, heard so many frightening noises, started at so many shadows, been hurt so often that all his senses

---

1. GUIDED READING:
Interpreting Meaning
Why is Joe going on about how badly behaved he was in second grade? He is trying to make Sara feel more comfortable about jumping to conclusions about him. He is really quite mature for his age.

2. LITERARY ELEMENTS:
Point of View
Now we are back to Charlie, finding out what is happening to him and what he is thinking and feeling.

The Summer of the Swans 697

1
Enveloped means "surrounded" (like a letter snugly in an envelope). Aunt Willie probably picked up Charlie, held him close, and hugged him.

2
The *stem* of a watch is the tiny knob on top that you turn or wind. Most wristwatches today run on battery power, but as recently as ten years ago, most watches ran on power generated by a mainspring that had to be wound up. Charlie's watch stopped because the mainspring wound down.

3. LITERARY ELEMENTS:
Imagery
This description is powerful because it appeals to three senses: sight, touch, and hearing.

---

were worn to a flat hopelessness. He would just sit here forever.

It was not the first time Charlie had been lost, but never before had there been this finality. He had become separated from Aunt Willie once at the county fair and had not even known he was lost until she had come bursting out of the crowd screaming, **1** "Charlie, Charlie," and enveloped him. He had been lost in school once in the hall and could not find his way back to his room, and he had walked up and down the halls, frightened by all the strange children looking out of every door, until one of the boys was sent out to lead him to his room. But in all his life there had never been an experience like this one.

He bent over and looked down at his watch, his eyes on the tiny red hand. For the first time he noticed it was no longer moving. Holding his breath in his concern, he brought the watch closer to his face. The hand was still. For a moment he could not believe it. He watched it closely, waiting. Still the hand did not move. He shook his hand back and forth, as if he were trying to shake the watch off his wrist. He had seen Sara do this to her watch.

Then he held the watch to his ear. It was silent. He had had the watch for five months and never before had it failed him. He had not even known it could fail. And now it was silent and still.

He put his hand over the watch, covering it completely. He waited. His breathing had begun to quicken again. His hand on the watch was almost clammy. He waited, then slowly, cautiously, he removed his hand and looked at the tiny red hand on the dial. It was motionless. The trick had not worked.

Bending over the watch, he looked closely at the stem. Aunt Willie always **2** wound the watch for him every morning after breakfast, but he did not know how she did this. He took the stem in his fingers, pulled at it clumsily, then harder, and it came off. He looked at it. Then, as he attempted to put it back on the watch, it fell to the ground and was lost in the leaves.

A chipmunk ran in front of him and scurried up the bank. Distracted for a moment, Charlie got up and walked toward it. The chipmunk paused and then darted into a hole, leaving Charlie standing in the shadows trying to see where it had gone. He went closer to the bank and pulled at the leaves, but he could not even find the place among the roots where the chipmunk had disappeared.

Suddenly something seemed to ex- **3** plode within Charlie, and he began to cry noisily. He threw himself on the bank and began kicking, flailing at the ground, at the invisible chipmunk, at the silent watch. He wailed, yielding in helplessness to his anguish, and his piercing screams, uttered again and again, seemed to hang in the air so that they overlapped. His fingers tore at the tree roots and dug beneath the leaves and scratched, animal-like, at the dark earth.

His body sagged and he rolled down the bank and was silent. He looked up at the trees, his chest still heaving with sobs, his face strangely still. After a moment, his eyelids drooped and he fell asleep.

"Charlie! Charlie!"

The only answer was the call of a bird in the branches overhead, one long tremulous whistle.

"He's not even within hearing distance," Sara said.

For the past hour she and Joe Melby had been walking deeper and deeper into the forest without pause, and now the trees were so thick that only small spots of sunlight found their way through the heavy foliage.

"Charlie, oh, Charlie!"

She waited, looking down at the ground.

Joe said, "You want to rest for a while?"

1 Sara shook her head. She suddenly wanted to see her brother so badly that her throat began to close. It was a tight feeling she got sometimes when she wanted something, like the time she had had the measles and had wanted to see her father so much she couldn't even swallow. Now she thought that if she had a whole glass of ice water—and she was thirsty—she probably would not be able to drink a single drop.

2 "If you can make it a little farther, there's a place at the top of the hill where the strip mining is, and you can see the whole valley from there."

"I can make it."

"Well, we can rest first if—"

"I can make it."

She suddenly felt a little better. She thought that if she could stand up there on top of the hill and look down and see, somewhere in that huge green valley, a small plump figure in blue pajamas, she would ask for nothing more in life. She thought of the valley as a relief map where **3** everything would be shiny and smooth, and her brother would be right where she could spot him at once. Her cry, "There he is!" would ring like a bell over the valley and everyone would hear her and know that Charlie had been found.

She paused, leaned against a tree for a moment, and then continued. Her legs had begun to tremble.

It was the time of afternoon when she usually sat down in front of the television and watched game shows, the shows where the married couples tried to guess things about each other and where girls had to pick out dates they couldn't see. She would sit in the doorway to the hall where she always sat and Charlie would come in and watch with her, and the living room would be dark and smell of the pine-scented cleaner Aunt Willie used.

Then "The Early Show" would come on, and she would sit through the old movie, leaning forward in the doorway, making fun, saying things like, "Now, Charlie, we'll have the old Convict Turning Honest scene," and Charlie, sitting on the stool closer to the television, would nod without understanding.

She was good, too, at joining in the dialogue with the actors. When the cowboy would say something like, "Things are quiet around here tonight," she would join in with, "Yeah, *too* quiet," right on cue. It seemed strange to be out here in the woods with Joe Melby instead of in the living room with Charlie, watching *Flame of Ar-*

The Summer of the Swans   699

---

1. GUIDED READING:
Making Inferences
What does this detail reveal about how Sara used to feel about her father? She used to love him very much; she yearned to see him when she was sick.

2. GUIDED READING:
Contrasting
How is Sara's search with Joe different from her search with Mary? With Mary, Sara was the leader; now Joe is the leader. He knows the hills, and he seems to know where they are going. Mary was afraid they would become lost.

3
A *relief map* shows hills and valleys.

CLOSURE
Ask students to define conflict and give an example of any conflict in the novel. Then have them tell how the events in pages 690–702 made the conflict they chose more or less suspenseful. (Some of the conflicts may not have been affected.)

RETEACHING
Discuss and list on the board some of the conflicts in your state, community, or school. (Advanced students may be able to come up with a list of conflicts by reading a local newspaper. For slower students you may want to deal with just one major conflict.) Who or what are the forces on each side? What is being done to resolve the important conflicts?

1. GUIDED READING:
Identifying the Author's Purpose
Why does the author spend so much time describing the climb uphill? The description adds to the suspense in the story. It also develops the relationship between Sara and Joe. He is considerate and supportive, helping and encouraging her.

2. LITERARY ELEMENTS:
Plot
Tell students that the series of related events in the **plot** of a novel follows a pattern that looks like the side of a hill. Your interest in the outcome goes up and up, like Sara and Joe climbing to the top. The most exciting points in the plot, when your interest is greatest, are called the **climaxes.** The major climax in a novel occurs toward the end, when you find out how the conflict will end.

Ask students to summarize the plot up to this point. Have them show how each event is related to the event that came before it.

3
Wryly means "with grim humor."

---

aby, which was the early movie for that afternoon.

Her progress up the hill seemed slower and slower. It was like the time she had won the slow bicycle race, a race in which she had to go as slow as possible without letting a foot touch the ground, and she had gone slower and slower, all the while feeling a strong compulsion to speed ahead and cross the finish line first. At the end of the race it had been she and T. R. Peters, and they had paused just before the finish line, balancing motionless on their bicycles. The time had seemed endless, and then T. R. lost his balance and his foot touched the ground and Sara was the winner.

She slipped on some dry leaves, went down on her knees, straightened, and paused to catch her breath.

"Are you all right?"

"Yes, I just slipped."

She waited for a moment, bent over her knees, then she called, "Charlie! Charlie," without lifting her head.

"Oh, Charleeeeee," Joe shouted above her.

Sara knew Charlie would shout back if he heard her, the long wailing cry he gave sometimes when he was frightened during the night. It was such a familiar cry that for a moment she thought she heard it.

She waited, still touching the ground with one hand, until she was sure there was no answer.

"Come on," Joe said, holding out his hand.

He pulled her to her feet and she stood looking up at the top of the hill. Machines had cut away the earth there to get at the veins of coal, and the earth had been pushed down the hill to form a huge bank.

"I'll never get up that," she said. She leaned against a tree whose leaves were covered with the pale fine dirt which had filtered down when the machines had cut away the hill.

"Sure you will. I've been up it a dozen times."

He took her hand and she started after him, moving sideways up the steep bank. The dirt crumbled beneath her feet and she slid, skinned one knee, and then slipped again. When she had regained her balance she laughed wryly and said, "What's going to happen is that I'll end up pulling you all the way down the hill."

"No, I've got you. Keep coming."

She started again, putting one foot carefully above the other, picking her way over the stones. When she paused, he said, "Keep coming. We're almost there."

"I think it's a trick, like at the dentist's when he says, 'I'm almost through drilling.' Then he drills for another hour and says, 'Now, I'm really almost through drilling,' and he keeps on and then says, 'There's just one more spot and then I'll be practically really through.'"

"We must go to the same dentist."

"I don't think I can make it. There's no skin at all left on the sides of my legs."

"Well, we're really almost practically there now, in the words of your dentist."

She fell across the top of the dirt bank on her stomach, rested for a moment, and then turned and looked down the valley.

700 The Novel

EXTENSION AND ENRICHMENT
Art. Students who enjoy art might want to draw what Sara sees from the top of the hill. Suggest that they use the colors that the author mentions on page 701. They should not include Sara in the drawing, but draw only what Sara sees. After they have finished their drawings, have them write one-sentence captions.

If students prefer to draw people, they might illustrate any scene in pages 690–702. They should include at least two people in their drawings. Have them decide what the characters might be saying to each other, and put the dialogue in dialogue bubbles. (They can make up words or use the words in this book.)

---

1 She could not speak for a moment. There lay the whole valley in a way she had never imagined it, a tiny finger of civilization set in a sweeping expanse of dark forest. The black treetops seemed to crowd against the yards, the houses, the roads, giving the impression that at any moment the trees would close over the houses like waves and leave nothing but an unbroken line of black-green leaves waving in the sunlight.

Up the valley she could see the intersection where they shopped, the drugstore, the gas station where her mother had once won a set of twenty-four stemmed glasses which Aunt Willie would not allow them to use, the grocery store, the lot where the yellow school buses were parked for the summer. She could look over the valley and see another hill where white cows were all grouped together by a fence and beyond that another hill and then another.

She looked back at the valley and she saw the lake and for the first time since she had stood up on the hill she remembered Charlie.

Raising her hand to her mouth, she called, "Charlie! Charlie! Charlie!" There was a faint echo that seemed to waver in her ears.

"Charlie, oh, Charlie!" Her voice was so loud it seemed to ram into the valley.

Sara waited. She looked down at the forest, and everything was so quiet it seemed to her that the whole valley, the whole world was waiting with her.

"Charlie, hey, Charlie!" Joe shouted.

"Charleeeeee!" She made the sound of it last a long time. "Can you hear meeeeee?"

With her eyes she followed the trail she knew he must have taken—the house, the Akers' vacant lot, the old pasture, the forest. The forest that seemed powerful enough to engulf a whole valley, she thought with a sinking feeling, could certainly swallow up a young boy.

"Charlie! Charlie! Charlie!" There was a waver in the last syllable that betrayed how near she was to tears. She looked down at the Indian slipper she was still holding.

"Charlie, oh, Charlie." She waited. There was not a sound anywhere. "Charlie, where are you?"

"Hey, Charlie!" Joe shouted.

They waited in the same dense silence. A cloud passed in front of the sun and a breeze began to blow through the trees. Then there was silence again.

"Charlie, Charlie, Charlie, Charlie, Charlie."

She paused, listened, then bent abruptly and put Charlie's slipper to her eyes. She waited for the hot tears that had come so often this summer, the tears that had seemed so close only a moment before. Now her eyes remained dry.

I have cried over myself a hundred times this summer, she thought, *I have wept over my big feet and my skinny legs and my nose, I have even cried over my stupid shoes, and now when I have a true sadness there are no tears left.*

She held the felt side of the slipper against her eyes like a blindfold and stood

The Summer of the Swans 701

---

1. GUIDED READING:
Visualizing
Ask students to tell what this excellent description makes them see. Point out that although most of the details appeal to the sense of sight, there are details that appeal to the senses of hearing and touch.

FOR STUDY AND DISCUSSION
Identifying Facts
1. Aunt Willie wanted to find out if Joe took Charlie's watch.
2. Some boys teased Charlie by taking his watch. Before they could return it, Sara rushed Charlie onto the bus. Joe got the watch back from the boys and returned it.
3. She fears that the noise and commotion will frighten Charlie.

Interpreting Meanings
4. Mary is most concerned about getting home in time to get ready for the party that night.
   Sara cares only about finding Charlie. Mary is much more self-centered than Sara.
5. Students should mention Charlie's feelings of confusion and nausea, and his difficulty in concentrating.
6. Sara herself is lonely and sad; maybe she is imagining Charlie's loneliness and confusion.

7. Joe may be saying indirectly that if we hesitate to say something important, it may never get said. Remember also that Charlie cannot speak.
8. The watch is a symbol of orderly routine and Charlie's link with the outside world. (Many people ask him what time it is.) When the watch stops, it is as if Charlie's ordered world is shattered.
Most students will feel for Charlie.
9. She realizes she has been self-centered.

Applying Meanings
10. Students may suggest that cruelty is caused by fear of the strange or different or abnormal. (That fear may be the source of most prejudice.)

---

there, feeling the hot sun on her head and the wind wrapping around her legs, conscious of the height and the valley sweeping down from her feet.

"Listen, just because you can't hear him doesn't mean anything. He could be—"

"Wait a minute." She lowered the slipper and looked down the valley. A sudden wind blew dust into her face and she lifted her hand to shield her eyes.

"I thought I heard something. Charlie! Answer me right this minute."

She waited with the slipper held against her breasts, one hand to her eyes, her whole body motionless, concentrating on her brother. Then she stiffened. She thought again she had heard something—Charlie's long high wail. Charlie could sound sadder than anyone when he cried.

In her anxiety she took the slipper and twisted it again and again as if she were wringing water out. She called, then stopped abruptly and listened. She looked at Joe and he shook his head slowly.

She looked away. A bird rose from the trees below and flew toward the hills in the distance. She waited until she could see it no longer and then slowly, still listening for the call that didn't come, she sank to the ground and sat with her head bent over her knees.

Beside her, Joe scuffed his foot in the dust and sent a cascade of rocks and dirt down the bank. When the sound of it faded, he began to call, "Charlie, hey, Charlie," again and again.

For Study and Discussion

IDENTIFYING FACTS
1. Why did Aunt Willie visit Joe Melby's mother?
2. Explain what really happened to Charlie's watch.
3. Why does Sara want to find Charlie before the search party starts out?

INTERPRETING MEANINGS
4. What is Sara's friend Mary most concerned about? How is Sara different from Mary at this point in the novel?
5. On page 693, Sara says to Mary that she knows how Charlie *feels*. Reread the passage beginning "No, I *know*." In your own words, explain how Charlie feels about some things.
6. Why do you think Sara feels that the picture of the Indian chief on Charlie's slipper is so lonely? (See page 696.)
7. Why do you think Joe tells Sara the story about the guru who hadn't spoken for twenty-eight years? (See page 696.)
8. Charlie undergoes a crisis when his watch stops. Why does this minor event affect him so strongly? How did this description of Charlie's anguish make you feel about him? (See page 698.)
9. When Sara and Joe stand on the hill overlooking the valley, Sara wants to cry but can't. What does she realize about herself? (See page 701.)

APPLYING MEANINGS
10. Why do you think some people are cruel to people like Charlie?

OBJECTIVES
Students should be able to identify the theme of the novel; they should also be able to narrate an event in the novel using first-person point of view, analyze how a character has changed, and write a poem expressing how one of the characters feels.

FOCUS/MOTIVATION
Building on Prior Knowledge. Ask volunteers to summarize the main events in the plot. Tell students that they are about to reach the climax of the novel, the most exciting point, when they will know how the most important conflict (and some of the minor ones too) will come out.

Prereading Journal. Ask students to write a few sentences telling what they think the climax of the novel will be and how the novel will end.

Charlie awoke, but he lay for a moment without opening his eyes. He did not remember where he was, but he had a certain dread of seeing it.

1 There were great parts of his life that were lost to Charlie, blank spaces that he could never fill in. He would find himself in a strange place and not know how he had got there. Like the time Sara had been hit in the nose with a baseball at the Dairy Queen, and the blood and the sight of Sara kneeling on the ground in helpless pain had frightened him so much that he had turned and run without direction, in a frenzy, dashing headlong up the street, blind to cars and people.

By chance Mr. Weicek had seen him, put him in the car, and driven him home, and Aunt Willie had put him to bed, but later he remembered none of this. He had only awakened in bed and looked at the crumpled bit of ice-cream cone still clenched in his hand and wondered about it.

2 His whole life had been built on a strict routine, and as long as this routine was kept up, he felt safe and well. The same foods, the same bed, the same furniture in the same place, the same seat on the school bus, the same class procedure were all important to him. But always there could be the unexpected, the dreadful surprise that would topple his carefully constructed life in an instant.

The first thing he became aware of was the twigs pressing into his face, and he put his hand under his cheek. Still he did not open his eyes. Pictures began to drift into his mind; he saw Aunt Willie's cigar box which was filled with old jewelry and buttons and knickknacks, and he found that he could remember every item in that box—the string of white beads without a clasp, the old earrings, the tiny book with souvenir fold-out pictures of New York, the plastic decorations from cakes, the turtle made of sea shells. Every item was so real that he opened his eyes and was surprised to see, instead of the glittering contents of the box, the dull and unfamiliar forest.

He raised his head and immediately felt the aching of his body. Slowly he sat up and looked down at his hands. His fingernails were black with earth, two of them broken below the quick, and he got up slowly and sat on the log behind him and inspected his fingers more closely.

Then he sat up straight. His hands dropped to his lap. His head cocked to the side like a bird listening. Slowly he straightened until he was standing. At his side his fingers twitched at the empty air as if to grasp something. He took a step forward, still with his head to the side. He remained absolutely still.

3 Then he began to cry out in a hoarse excited voice, again and again, screaming now, because he had just heard someone far away calling his name.

At the top of the hill Sara got slowly to her feet and stood looking down at the forest. She pushed the hair back from her forehead and moistened her lips. The wind dried them as she waited.

The Summer of the Swans 703

TEACHING RESOURCES D
Teacher's Notes, p. 179
Reading Check, p. 181
Study Guide, pp. 182, 183, 184, 185
Building Vocabulary, p. 186
Selection Vocabulary Test, p. 188
Selection Test, p. 189

1. GUIDED READING:
Identifying the Main Idea
What is the main idea of this paragraph? Sometimes Charlie cannot remember what has happened to him, especially if he has had an unpleasant experience. You might ask students if they sometimes wish they could forget unpleasant experiences. What's good about remembering them?

2. GUIDED READING:
Making Inferences
What happens when Charlie's routine is changed? He feels confused, endangered, and ill.

3. GUIDED READING:
Identifying Cause and Effect
Why do you think Charlie hears someone calling him now? He just woke up. He has been asleep for a while.

READING THE SELECTION
Most students should be able to read the rest of the novel silently in one sitting. You might want to read page 703 aloud for slower students.

1. LITERARY ELEMENTS:
Figurative Language: Similes
You might ask students to find some of the **similes** (comparisons using *like* or *as*) that make this description so vivid: Similes: "shoes slapping the ground like rubber paddles"; "She felt like a wild creature who had traveled through the forest this way for a lifetime"; "her legs were as useless as rubber bands"; "sirenlike cry."

Joe started to say something but she reached out one hand and took his arm to stop him. Scarcely daring to believe her ears, she stepped closer to the edge of the bank. Now she heard it unmistakably—the sharp repeated cry—and she knew it was Charlie.

"Charlie!" she shouted with all her might.

She paused and listened, and his cries were louder and she knew he was not far away after all, just down the slope, in the direction of the ravine.

"It's Charlie, it's Charlie!"

A wild joy overtook her and she jumped up and down on the bare earth and she felt that she could crush the whole hill just by jumping if she wanted.

She sat and scooted down the bank, sending earth and pebbles in a cascade before her. She landed on the soft ground, ran a few steps, lost her balance, caught hold of the first tree trunk she could find, and swung around till she stopped.

She let out another whoop of pure joy, turned and ran down the hill in great strides, the puce tennis shoes slapping the ground like rubber paddles, the wind in her face, her hands grabbing one tree trunk after another for support. She felt like a wild creature who had traveled through the forest this way for a lifetime. Nothing could stop her now.

At the edge of the ravine she paused and stood gasping for breath. Her heart was beating so fast it pounded in her ears, and her throat was dry. She leaned against a tree, resting her cheek against the rough bark.

She thought for a minute she was going to faint, a thing she had never done before, not even when she broke her nose. She hadn't even believed people really did faint until this minute when she clung to the tree because her legs were as useless as rubber bands.

There was a ringing in her ears and another sound, a wailing sirenlike cry that was painfully familiar.

"Charlie?"

704   The Novel

Charlie's crying, like the sound of a cricket, seemed everywhere and nowhere.

She walked along the edge of the ravine, circling the large boulders and trees. Then she looked down into the ravine where the shadows lay, and she felt as if something had turned over inside her because she saw Charlie.

He was standing in his torn pajamas, face turned upward, hands raised, shouting with all his might. His eyes were shut tight. His face was streaked with dirt and tears. His pajama jacket hung in shreds about his scratched chest.

He opened his eyes and as he saw Sara a strange expression came over his face, an expression of wonder and joy and disbelief, and Sara knew that if she lived to be a hundred no one would ever look at her quite that way again.

She paused, looked down at him, and

1. LITERARY ELEMENTS:
Climax
Sara's reunion with Charlie marks the major climax of the novel. This is the plot's most exciting event, when we feel the highest intensity of suspense. Charlie's conflict with a hostile environment is now over. More important to the theme of the novel, the crisis with Charlie helped break Sara's shell of moodiness and ended her preoccupation with her appearance. If Sara had *not* found Charlie, her life might also have changed, but in a negative way. Of course, Sara might have changed anyway as she matured. (Some people respond negatively to crisis. Sara's father never recovered from the double blow of his son's illness and his wife's death.)

VISUAL CONNECTIONS
Through whose eyes do you catch this glimpse of Charlie? (Sara's) You might ask what Charlie sees, from his point of view.

1. LITERARY ELEMENTS:
Resolution
Tell students that the part of the novel following the climax is called the resolution. In these final scenes, minor conflicts will be resolved or settled, and the novel will be brought to a close. The resolution should answer any important questions that we have about the plot.

2. GUIDED READING:
Interpreting Meaning
Why is Charlie so anxious to have his watch work again? What meaning does the watch hold for him? As long as the watch is ticking steadily, Charlie feels secure. Now, even though Sara has rescued him, he feels that things are not quite right because his watch isn't ticking.

---

then, sliding on the seat of her pants, went down the bank and took him in her arms.

"Oh, Charlie."

His arms gripped her like steel.

"Oh, Charlie."

She could feel his fingers digging into her back as he clutched her shirt. "It's all right now, Charlie, I'm here and we're going home." His face was buried in her shirt and she patted his head, said again, "It's all right now. Everything's fine."

She held him against her for a moment and now the hot tears were in her eyes and on her cheeks and she didn't even notice.

"I know how you feel," she said. "I know. One time when I had the measles and my fever was real high, I got lost on my way back from the bathroom, right in our house, and it was a terrible feeling, terrible, because I wanted to get back to my bed and I couldn't find it, and finally Aunt Willie heard me and came and you know where I was? In the kitchen. In our kitchen and I couldn't have been more lost if I'd been out in the middle of the wilderness."

She patted the back of his head again and said "Look, I even brought your bedroom slipper. Isn't that service, huh?"

She tried to show it to him, but he was still clutching her, and she held him against her, patting him. After a moment she said again, "Look, here's your slipper. Let's put it on." She knelt, put his foot into the shoe, and said, "Now, isn't that better?"

He nodded slowly, his chest still heaving with unspent sobs.

"Can you walk home?"

He nodded. She took her shirttail and wiped his tears and smiled at him. "Come **1** on, we'll find a way out of here and go home."

"Hey, over this way," Joe called from the bank of the ravine. Sara had forgotten about him in the excitement of finding Charlie, and she looked up at him for a moment.

"Over this way, around the big tree," Joe called. "That's probably how he got in. The rest of the ravine is a mass of brier bushes."

She put one arm around Charlie and led him around the tree. "Everybody in town's looking for you, you know that?" she said. "Everybody. The police came and all the neighbors are out—there must be a hundred people looking for you. You were on the radio. It's like you were the President of the United States or something. Everybody was saying, 'Where's Charlie?' and 'We got to find Charlie.'"

Suddenly Charlie stopped and held up **2** his hand and Sara looked down. "What is it?"

He pointed to the silent watch.

She smiled. "Charlie, you are something, you know that? Here we are racing down the hill to tell everyone in great triumph that you are found, *found*, and we have to stop and wind your watch first."

She looked at the watch, saw that the stem was missing, and shook her head. "It's broken, Charlie, see, the stem's gone. It's broken."

He held it out again.

"It's *broken*, Charlie. We'll have to take it to the jeweler and have it fixed."

706 The Novel

He continued to hold out his arm.

1 "Hey, Charlie, you want to wear my watch till you get yours fixed?" Joe asked. He slid down the bank and put his watch on Charlie's arm. "There."

Charlie bent his face close and listened.

"Now can we go home?" Sara asked, **2** jamming her hands into her back pockets.

Charlie nodded.

They walked through the woods for a long time, Joe in the lead, picking the best path, with Charlie and Sara following. From time to time Sara turned and hugged Charlie and he smelled of trees and dark earth and tears and she said, "Everybody's going to be so glad to see you it's going to be just like New Year's Eve."

3 Sara could not understand why she suddenly felt so good. It was a puzzle. The day before she had been miserable. She had wanted to fly away from everything, like the swans to a new lake, and now she didn't want that any more.

Down the hill Mr. Rhodes, one of the searchers, was coming toward them and Joe called out, "Mr. Rhodes, Sara found him!"

4 "Is he all right?" Mr. Rhodes called back.

"Fine, he's fine."

"Sara found him and he's all right. He's all right." The phrase passed down the hill from Dusty Rhodes, who painted cars at the garage, to Mr. Aker to someone Sara couldn't recognize.

Then all the searchers were joining them, reaching out to pat Charlie and to say to Sara, "Oh, your aunt is going to be so happy," or "Where *was* he?" or "Well, now we can all sleep in peace tonight."

They came through the woods in a big noisy group and out into the late sunlight in the old pasture, Sara and Charlie in the middle, surrounded by all the searchers.

Suddenly Sara sensed a movement above her. She looked up and then grabbed Charlie's arm.

The swans were directly overhead, flying with outstretched necks, their long wings beating the air, an awkward blind sort of flight. They were so low that she thought they might hit the trees, but at the last moment they pulled up and skimmed the air just above the treetops.

"Look, Charlie, look. Those are the swans. Remember? They're going home."

He looked blankly at the sky, unable to associate the heavy awkward birds with the graceful swans he had seen on the water. He squinted at the sky, then looked at Sara, puzzled.

"Charlie, those are the swans. Remember? At the lake?" she said, looking right at him. "They're going home now. Don't you remember? They were—"

"Hey, there's your aunt, Charlie. There's Aunt Willie coming."

Sara was still pulling at Charlie's arm, directing his attention to the sky. It seemed urgent somehow that Charlie see the swans once again. She said, "Charlie, those are—"

He looked instead across the field and

The Summer of the Swans 707

---

1. GUIDED READING:
Making Inferences
What does this passage tell you about Joe? He is, as we have already suspected, very good at dealing with people. He thinks quickly and is a very kind person.

2. LITERARY ELEMENTS:
Resolution
The loan of the watch brings one of the subplots to an ironic but satisfactory conclusion. It is ironic (just the opposite of what you would expect) that the person Sara accused of stealing Charlie's watch understands why the watch is important to Charlie and gives him the watch he needs to be completely happy.

3. GUIDED READING:
Making Inferences
How do you know that Sara's outlook on life has changed? She feels good, even though she can't understand why.

4. GUIDED READING:
Making Inferences
What can you infer about the community in which Sara lives? The community is close-knit. The people are mostly kind and helpful.

1. GUIDED READING:
Making Inferences
How do you think Sara feels about Aunt Willie now? How do Aunt Willie's actions and words on this page make you feel? Sara probably feels somewhat relieved that Aunt Willie will now take over responsibility for Charlie. She realizes that Charlie and Aunt Willie love each other too. (He breaks away from Sara, and, after taking two steps, she lets him go.) We feel sympathy for Aunt Willie, who has, after all, lost several people that she loved; unlike Sara's father, she is still a warm, loving person.

2. LITERARY ELEMENTS:
Symbolism
How is Sara like the swans? Sara is sometimes awkward (as the swans are when they fly). At the beginning of the novel, she wanted to "fly away" from everything. Now the swans are returning to their lake to settle down, just as Sara is returning home after completing her quest for Charlie, having found both her brother and herself.

---

1 he broke away from Sara and started running. She took two steps after him and then stopped. Aunt Willie in her bright green dress seemed to shine like a <u>beacon</u>, and he hurried toward her, an awkward figure in torn blue pajamas, shuffling through the high grass.

There was a joyous yell that was so <u>shrill</u> Sara thought it had come from the swans, but then she knew that it had come from Charlie, for the swans were <u>mute</u>.

"Here he is, Willie," Mrs. Aker called, running behind Charlie to have some part in the reunion.

Aunt Willie was coming as fast as she could on her bad legs. "I never thought to see him again," she was telling everyone and no one. "I thought he was up in that mine. I tell you, I never thought to see him again. Charlie, come here to your Aunt Willie."

Charlie ran like a ball rolling downhill, bouncing with the slope of the land.

"I tell you this has been the blackest day of my life"—Aunt Willie was gasping—"and I include every day I have been on earth. Charlie, my Charlie, let me look at you. Oh, you are a sight."

He fell into Aunt Willie's arms. Over his head Aunt Willie said through her tears to Mrs. Aker, "May you never lose your Bobby, that's all I got to say. May you never lose your Bobby, may none of you ever lose anybody in the woods or in the mine or anywhere."

Sara stood in the pasture by the old gray shack and watched the swans disappear over the hill, and then she watched Charlie and Aunt Willie disappear in the crowd of people, and she felt good and loose and she thought that if she started walking down the hill at that moment, she would walk with the light movements of a puppet and never touch the ground at all.

She thought she would sit down for a moment now that everyone was gone, but when she looked around she saw Joe Melby still standing behind her. "I thought you went with the others."

"Nope."

"It's been a very strange day for me." She looked at the horizon where the swans had disappeared.

"It's been one of my stranger days too."

"Well, I'd better go home."

Joe walked a few steps with her, cleared his throat, and then said, "Do you want to go to Bennie Hoffman's party with me?"

She thought she hadn't heard him right for a moment, or if she had, that it was a mistake, like the boy who shouted, "Hey, beautiful," at Rosey Camdon.

"What?"

"I asked if you wanted to go with me to the party."

"I wasn't invited." She made herself **2** think of the swans. By this time they could probably see the lake at the university and were about to settle down on the water with a great beating of wings and ruffling of feathers. She could almost see the long perfect glide that would bring them to the water.

"I'm inviting you. Bennie said I could

The Novel

bring somebody if I wanted to. He begged me to bring someone, as a matter of fact. He and Sammy and John and Pete have formed this musical group and they're going to make everybody listen to them."

1 "Well, I don't know."

"Why not? Other than the fact that you're going to have to listen to some terrible guitar playing. Bennie Hoffman has had about one and a half lessons."

"Well . . ."

"It's not any big deal, just sitting in Bennie Hoffman's back yard and watching him louse up with a two-hundred-dollar guitar and amplifier."

"I guess I could go."

"I'll walk over and pick you up in half an hour. It won't matter if we're late. The last fifty songs will sound about the same as the first fifty."

"I'll be ready."

2 When Sara came up the walk Wanda was standing on the porch. "What is going on around here, will you tell me that? Where is Charlie?"

"We found him. He's with Aunt Willie, wherever that is."

"Do you know how I heard he was lost? I heard it on the car radio when I was coming home. How do you think that made me feel—to hear from some disc jockey that my own brother was missing? I could hardly get here because there are a hundred cars full of people jamming the street down there."

"Well, he's fine."

"So Mr. Aker told me, only I would like to see him and find out what happened."

"He got up during the night sometime—this is what I think happened—to go see the swans and ended up in a ravine crying his heart out."

Wanda stepped off the porch and looked across the street, leaning to see around the foliage by the fence. She said, "Is that them over there on the Carsons' porch?"

Sara looked and nodded.

3 "Honestly, Charlie still in his pajamas, and Aunt Willie in her good green dress with a handkerchief tied around her forehead to keep her from sweating, and both of them eating watermelon. That beats all."

"At least he's all right."

Wanda started down the walk, then paused. "You want to come?"

"No, I'm going to a party."

"Whose?"

"Bennie Hoffman's."

"I didn't think you were invited."

"Joe Melby's taking me."

"Joe Melby? Your great and terrible enemy?"

"He is not my enemy, Wanda. He is one of the nicest people I know."

"For three months I've been hearing about the evils of Joe Melby. Joe Melby, the thief; Joe Melby, the fink; Joe Melby, the—"

"A person," Sara said coldly, "can occasionally be mistaken." She turned and went into the living room, saw Boysie sleeping by the door and said, "Boysie, we

The Summer of the Swans

---

1. LITERARY ELEMENTS:
Resolution
Do you think Joe has admired Sara for some time, or is he attracted to her because of the courage, persistence, humor, and compassion that he saw in her while they were searching for Charlie? And what do you think Sara sees in Joe? Answers will vary. Joe's invitation and Sara's acceptance nicely wind up the conflict between them.

2. GUIDED READING:
Making Inferences
Why do you think the author brings Wanda back into the novel at the end? Here is another loose strand that needs to be tied up in the resolution.

3. GUIDED READING:
Making Inferences
What does this passage tell you about Wanda? Wanda hasn't gone through a crisis. She is still concerned with appearances. Sara knows that the important thing is that Charlie is all right.

1. LITERARY ELEMENTS:
Resolution
What other strand of subplot is wound up on this page? Sara's conflict with her father is about to be resolved. Be sure students evaluate the resolution. Are they satisfied with it? Or disappointed?

2. GUIDED READING:
Recognizing the Author's Purpose
What is the purpose of this paragraph? The author wants to show that Sara has become tolerant and understanding of others, and that she realizes her potential is unlimited. Sara also is aware that she has changed. Ask students if, considering what is happening to Sara, the prison shirt has some significance.

3. LITERARY ELEMENTS:
Resolution
The final paragraph winds up the final subplot strand—Sara vs. her tennis shoes—and ends the novel on a humorous note. Ask students what they think Sara is thinking now.

---

found Charlie." She bent and rubbed him behind the ears. Then she went into the kitchen, made a sandwich, and was starting into the bedroom when the phone rang.

"Hello," she said, her mouth full of food.

"Hello, I have a long-distance call for Miss Willamina Godfrey," the operator said.

"Oh, she's across the street. If you'll wait a minute I'll go get her."

1 "Operator, I'll just talk to whoever's there," Sara heard her father say.

She said quickly, "No, I'll go get her. Just wait one minute. It won't take any time. She's right across the street."

"Sara? Is this Sara?"

"Yes, this is me." The strange feeling came over her again. "If you wait a minute I'll go get Aunt Willie."

"Sara, did you find Charlie?"

"Yes, we found him, but I don't mind going to get Aunt Willie. They're over on the Carsons' porch."

"Is Charlie all right?"

"He's fine. He's eating watermelon right now."

"Where was he?"

"Well, he went up into the woods and got lost. We found him in a ravine and he was dirty and tired and hungry but he's all right."

"That's good. I was going to come home tonight if he hadn't been found."

"Oh."

"But since everything's all right, I guess I'll just wait until the weekend."

"Sure."

"So I'll probably see you Saturday, then, if nothing turns up."

"Fine."

"Be sure to tell Willie I called."

"I will."

2 A picture came into her mind of the laughing, curly-headed man with the broken tooth in the photograph album, and she suddenly saw life as a series of huge, uneven steps, and she saw herself on the steps, standing motionless in her prison shirt, and she had just taken an enormous step up out of the shadows, and she was standing, waiting, and there were other steps in front of her, so that she could go as high as the sky, and she saw Charlie on a flight of small difficult steps, and her father down at the bottom of some steps, just sitting and not trying to go further. She saw everyone she knew on those blinding white steps and for a moment everything was clearer than it had ever been.

"Sara?"

"I'm still here."

"Well, that was all I wanted, just to hear that Charlie was all right."

"He's fine."

"And I'll see you on Saturday if nothing happens."

"Sure."

"Good-bye."

3 She sat for a minute still holding the receiver and then she set it back on the telephone and finished her sandwich. Slowly she slipped off her tennis shoes and looked down at her feet, which were dyed blue. Then she got up quickly and went to get ready for the party.

710 The Novel

Meeting Individual Needs

Visual Learners • To introduce students to the concept of literary allusion (without the necessity of their learning the term), you might have students find the similarities between this story's theme and symbols and those of the tale "The Ugly Duckling." Ask students to look back at the illustration of Sara on page 649. In the muted and soft tints in this picture, what stands out? How does Sara feel about her feet? On page 711, the illustration shows that Sara is still concerned about her feet, but now she has a reason. Is she more worried or less concerned about her feet now than she was at the beginning of the story?

Ask students to recall "The Ugly Duckling" or other stories from their childhoods in which a character who feels ugly and lonely grows up into a beautiful, graceful creature. Then, ask students whether they think the author used swans in this story to remind readers of "The Ugly Duckling."

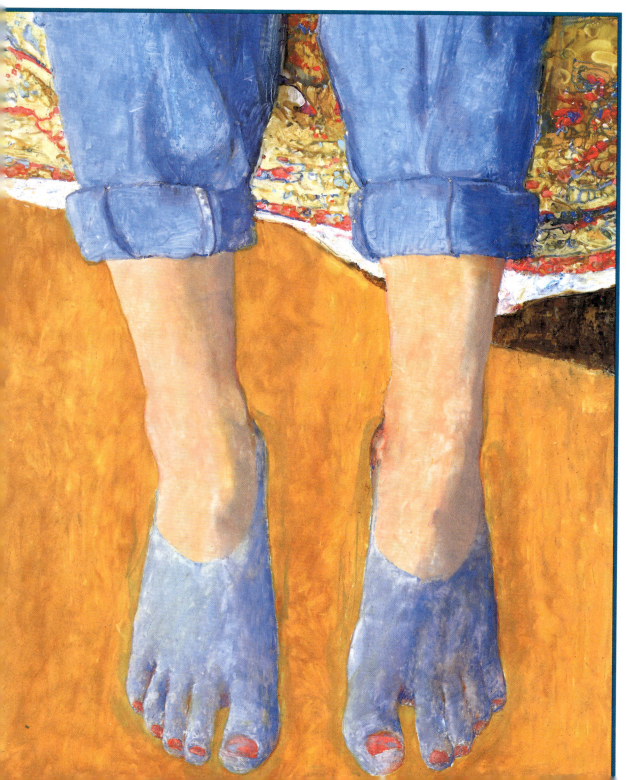

FOR STUDY AND DISCUSSION

Identifying Facts

1. Routine reassures Charlie about his own safety and security. On the other hand, ". . . always there could be the unexpected, the dreadful surprise that would topple his carefully constructed life in an instant" (page 703).

2. At the top of the hill, Sara hears Charlie's loud cries from the direction of the ravine. Walking along the edge of the ravine, Sara sees him, shouting.

3. Joe asks Sara to go to Bennie Hoffman's party that evening.

4. (a) the paragraph beginning "Sara could not understand why she suddenly felt so good" (page 707); (b) the paragraph beginning "A picture came into her mind . . ." (page 710).

Interpreting Meanings

5. The climax of the novel is the discovery of Charlie.
   Most will say that the climax made them feel relief and joy.

6. Charlie's steps are small and difficult. (He won't go "very far" or change very much. His life is limited.) Sara's steps are huge and uneven. She's just moved an enormous distance on the steps, out of the shadows. Her steps go all the way to the sky.

711

> **TRANSPARENCY 43**
> **Literary Elements**
> *Understanding and Evaluating a Novel* – invites students to explore the various elements of fiction that affect a reader's experience of the novel.

Sara's father sits at the bottom of his flight of steps, not trying to go further. (He won't try to change.)

7. Sara has a clearer picture of her own character and of her relationships to her family. She realizes that life consists of a series of challenges, the "steps" in the various flights of stairs. Sara realizes that her own possibilities differ from Charlie's and even her father's. She knows that meeting challenges is more important than her petty worries about her own looks.

8. Charlie has not changed. (Can he ever be "cured"? No.) Some students may argue that Charlie is worse off. He has had a frightening experience. More and more as he grows older, he will realize how different he is and he will be more and more frustrated. He will also, inevitably, discover more of the frightening aspects of life (like those dogs in the woods).

9. A number of the conflicts are certainly resolved: the crisis of Charlie's disappearance, Sara's internal conflicts of restlessness and confusion, and Sara's external conflict with Joe Melby. The close of the novel implies, however, that Sara's conflict involving her father

For Study and Discussion

IDENTIFYING FACTS

1. Why is routine so important to Charlie?
2. Explain how Charlie is found.
3. After the crowd of people leaves them alone, what does Joe ask Sara?
4. At the end of the novel, Sara seems quite different from the person she was at the beginning. Find the passages that describe how Sara feels she has **changed**.

INTERPRETING MEANINGS

5. The **climax** of a novel is that exciting or emotional moment when you find out how the main problem will turn out. What is the climax of this novel? How did you feel at this moment?
6. On page 710 Sara compares life to a series of steps. How is her flight of steps different from Charlie's? What is her father's flight of steps like?
7. At the end of this passage, Sara sees that "everything was clearer than it had ever been." What do you think is now clear to Sara?
8. Is Charlie different from the person he was at the beginning of the novel? Give a reason for your answer.
9. Are all the problems or **conflicts** in the story resolved by the end of the novel? For example, is Sara's problem concerning her father resolved?

APPLYING MEANINGS

10. Suppose Sara had not experienced the loss of her brother. Do you think she would have come to realize what was of true worth in life anyway? What other experiences could make a person "see life clearly"?

Literary Elements

THEME

Theme is the idea or truth about human life revealed in a story or novel. Here are some questions that will help you identify the theme in *The Summer of the Swans*.

1. The **title** of a novel often has something to do with its theme. What are some characteristics of the swans? In what ways is Charlie like the swans?
2. How does Sara, the main character, **change** in the story? What causes the change?
3. Think of how Sara's search for Charlie is like a **quest**. Even before Charlie leaves the house on his own quest for the swans, what is Sara searching for? Sara finds Charlie, but what else has she **discovered** at the end of the novel?

Discuss in class what the novel has revealed to you. As part of your discussion, compose two possible statements of the novel's theme. (Remember that there is no one true way to state a theme.)

Language and Vocabulary

DIALOGUE

Byars's witty dialogue sounds, to most readers, exactly the way real people talk. Among the characteristics of her dialogue are the use of slang and exaggeration.

Slang is a kind of informal language that is usually spoken by a particular group of people. Teenagers are particularly good at making up new slang words.

Two of Sara's favorite slang words are *fink* and *gross.* Sometimes she makes an adjective out of *fink* and says *finky.* Can you write a dictionary definition for each of these slang words? After each definition, write a sentence using the word. Identify each word's part of speech.

One characteristic of slang is that it is not welcome in formal situations. Someone delivering a formal speech to the School Board would not use slang. What words could you use in these sentences to replace the slang words *finky, gross,* and *tuff?*

1. "You remember when that *finky* Jim Wilson got you on the seesaw?"
2. "This piece of candy is so *gross* that I don't even want to touch it . . ."
3. "Their clothes are so *tuff* and they're invited to every party . . ."

Exaggeration stretches the truth by describing things as much greater than they really are. Sometimes the characters in this novel use exaggeration for comic effect. Sometimes they use exaggeration to emphasize how they feel. Explain why the characters use exaggeration in each of these speeches. (What point is each one making?)

1. After Aunt Willie gets off the motor scooter, Frank says "there's not a drop of blood circulating" in his arms. (Page 658)
2. Sara complains to Mary that her awful orange sneakers make her look "like Donald Duck." (Page 661)
3. Sara tells Wanda, "The peak of my whole life so far was in third grade when I got to be milk monitor." (Page 667)

Writing About Literature

USING ANOTHER POINT OF VIEW
Suppose Charlie is telling his own story. Charlie can't speak, but he certainly can think and he certainly has feelings. Narrate the events that take place in one part of this novel, but let Charlie tell the story, using the first-person pronoun *I.* You might have Charlie tell about the time he sees the swans; the time he loses his way; the time his watch breaks; the day after he is found.

ANALYZING A CHANGE IN CHARACTER
Betsy Byars says that early in her career, a teacher told her that in a good children's novel, the main character had to be different by the end of the book. "That made instant sense to me," said Byars. "If what happened to your character was important enough, then the person would be changed . . . I take characters, ordinary people, and throw them into a crisis, and I think that is one reason I haven't done a sequel—I feel one crisis is enough for anybody."

Write at least one paragraph in which you explain how Sara has changed in this novel, and why she changed. Before you write, you might fill out a chart like the one on page 714 to gather your details.

lack of attention to the family is not yet resolved.

Applying Meanings
10. Sara might have achieved a more balanced sense of values anyway because she is intelligent and loyal.

Examples: travel to new places, making new friends, coping with success or failure in school, the example of grandparents, the death of a loved one, loss, falling in love, meeting people less fortunate than oneself.

LITERARY ELEMENTS
Theme
1. Whiteness, gracefulness, silence, fragile beauty.

Charlie is also fragile and cannot speak.
2. Sara becomes less concerned about the superficial value of appearance and more concerned about what is truly important in life: truth, friendship, and love.

The change in Sara is caused by Charlie's disappearance and by her acceptance of Joe's help after she had falsely accused him.
3. Sara is searching for happiness, stability, love, confidence.

By the end of the novel, Sara has discovered the enduring values of love,

CLOSURE
Have students define theme and tell one idea about people or life that the novel reveals.

RETEACHING
Discuss *The Summer of the Swans* as a quest novel. (See Unit Two.) What is the object of Sara's quest? Who does she think are her enemies? (Most people, particularly Joe) Who is her only real enemy? (Herself) In her ordeal to find Charlie, what does she find out about herself?

TRANSPARENCY 42
Reader Response
Letter to an Author – invites students to write a letter directly to the author of a selection, using a variety of prompts.

---

trust, and respect for others.

Two possible statements of the novel's theme might be: (a) It is only when we forget our own needs and recognize the humanity of others that we can find genuine happiness. (b) How we behave toward others is far more important than how we look.

LANGUAGE AND VOCABULARY
Dialogue
For answers, see the **Teaching Guide** at the beginning of the unit.

WRITING ABOUT LITERATURE
Using Another Point of View
Check to see that students' accounts are told in the first person and from Charlie's point of view. The vocabulary should be simple and the sentences short, in keeping with Charlie's limited intellectual ability. (Good readers might be directed to the story "Flowers for Algernon," Daniel Keyes's account of a young man with a mental disability, told by the young man himself in journal form.)

Analyzing a Change in Character
Check to see that students' paragraphs are focused on how and why

Sara	Story at start	Story at end
1. Feelings about Charlie.		
2. Feelings about Joe.		
3. Feelings about herself.		
4. Feelings about her father.		
Crisis in Sara's life:		

Open your paragraph with a sentence that states your general topic. Note that the example below includes the title and author.

> In *The Summer of the Swans* by Betsy Byars, Sara is a character who changes as a result of a crisis in her life.

Focus on Persuasive Writing

ORGANIZING A PERSUASIVE PAPER
Use an outline like the one below to organize your ideas for a persuasive essay:

I. Introduction
   A. Attention grabber
   B. Opinion statement
II. Body
   Supporting reasons, facts, expert opinions
III. Conclusion
   A. Restatement of opinion
   B. Call to action (if appropriate)

Organize your supporting details in a logical way. You may want to use **order of importance**. In this method, you present details from least to most important, or the reverse.

Remember to use **transitions** to help your readers or listeners understand the connections between ideas. Here are some helpful transitions for order of importance:

first   mainly   second
last   most important   third

Choose a topic for a persuasive paper. Write a one-sentence opinion statement that expresses your view. Then prepare an outline for your essay, using the one above as a guideline. Next, exchange outlines with a partner. Give each other suggestions for making your papers clearer and more persuasive. Save your notes.

About the Author

Betsy Byars (1928–), one of the most popular of all young adult novelists, was born in Charlotte, North Carolina, and graduated from Queens College there. She began writing mystery stories and magazine articles when her husband was in graduate school in Illinois and her children were very young. Her first successful children's novel was *The Midnight Fox* (1968), a realistic story about a city boy who overcomes his fear of animals.

Byars says that she always asked her four children to read her manuscripts, and she admits that they were not tactful about what they didn't like.

Many of her books began with a newspaper story or an event from her own children's lives. The character of Charlie in

EXTENSION AND ENRICHMENT

Drama. Ask a group of three students to dramatize what might happen when Sara, Joe, and Mary meet later at the party. Assume that Mary hasn't heard that Charlie has been found, and that she doesn't expect to see Sara at the party.

---

her most famous novel, *The Summer of the Swans,* grew out of some volunteer work she was doing with children with mental retardation. The plot for the novel came from an article that Byars read in a local newspaper. The article told about the search for an elderly man who wandered away from a picnic and got lost. The swans, she says, came from an article about swans at the university in Greenville, South Carolina, who "persist in leaving their beautiful lake and flying to less desirable ponds." *The Summer of the Swans* not only won the Newbery Award, but also was named a Junior Literary Club book, a *Horn Book* honor book, and an American Library Association Notable Book. Her other works include *Seven Treasure Hunts, Wanted . . . Mud Blosson,* and *McMummy.*

Byars now lives in Clemson, South Carolina. "There is no activity in my life," she has said, "which has brought me more pleasure than my writing." How does it feel to have a mother who is a famous young adult novelist? When one of Byars' daughters was fourteen years old and was asked this question, she replied, "Well, it's no big deal."

Behind the Scenes

Winning the Newbery

In 1968, I participated in a volunteer program sponsored by West Virginia University. Anybody who was interested—truck drivers, housewives, miners—signed up to help kids who were having learning difficulties in school. I got a third-grade girl and a first-grade boy.

This was a stunning experience for me. Up until this time I had never been around kids who were having real problems in learning. I had not been aware of how much they suffered, not only because they had learning difficulties, but—more importantly—because of the way other kids treated them.

Charlie, the character in *The Summer of the Swans,* was neither of the kids I tutored, but I would never have written the book if I had not known them.

I did a lot of research on the character of Charlie in the Medical Library of W.V.U. I found three case histories of kids who had had brain damage because of high-fevered illnesses when they were babies, and that's where Charlie

---

Sara has changed in the novel. Look for details from the novel that support their assertions. Paragraphs should be well organized and clearly written; there should be smooth transitions between sentences within a paragraph and between paragraphs. Check to see that the title of the novel and the name of the author are mentioned. Finally, evaluate paragraphs for errors in grammar, usage, punctuation, capitalization, and spelling.

FOCUS ON PERSUASIVE WRITING

Organizing a Persuasive Paper

Before students write their outlines, you may want to discuss and model various ways to grab a reader's attention. First, choose a topic and write an opinion statement on the board. Next, show students how to write attention grabbers for that topic by using a startling fact, an anecdote, and a question. Then, you could circulate throughout the room to offer suggestions as students write their own attention grabbers.

PORTFOLIO ASSESSMENT

Students may want to write a sequel to *The Summer of the Swans* in which they tell what happens at Bennie Hoffman's party. What shoes will Sara wear? Will Sara and Joe have a good time? What will Mary's hair look like? Will the music be entertaining? Suggest that students begin with a plan of what will happen, so their sequels do not ramble. Also, remind them to use vividly descriptive words to maintain the readers' interest. Sequels may be bound within a student-decorated cover. Consult with students individually to agree on how their sequels will be assessed. (See *Portfolio Assessment and Professional Support Materials* for additional information on student portfolios.)

1. BACKGROUND

The Caldecott Medal is awarded to the most distinguished American picture book for children.

---

came from. All the details of his life were from those three case histories. I made nothing up.

I worked hard on the book and I was proud of it. It was published in April of 1970 to a sort of resounding thud. It didn't sell well, it didn't get great reviews; in some papers it didn't get reviewed at all.

I went through a very discouraging period. Maybe, I thought, I am just not going to make it as a first-rate writer. Maybe I never will be good enough. Maybe I should consider doing something else. That fall I enrolled at West Virginia University to get my master's degree in special education.

I had now published seven books, but I had never had one of those long editorial lunches at a swanky New York restaurant that you read about. I had never been in a publisher's office. I had never even met an editor. My contacts with my editors had consisted of long letters and brief phone calls. I did not know a single other writer. Despite having published seven books, I was as green as grass.

I was leaving for class one morning in January when the phone rang. I answered it, and a woman's voice said, **1** "This is Sara Fenwick and I'm Chairman of the Newbery-Caldecott Committee." My heart rose. "We've been in Los Angeles for the past week going over possible Newbery-Caldecott winners." My heart sank. I realized what she wanted now. She wanted to ask me some questions about writing *The Summer of the Swans,* and I would not be able to answer the questions intelligently and she would go back to the committee and say, "The woman is an idiot."

"And," she continued, "I am so pleased to tell you that your book *The Summer of the Swans* has won the Newbery Award."

I was stunned. I went blank. I couldn't say a word. She said, "Mrs. Byars, are you there?"

I managed to say, "Yes."

She said, "Mrs. Byars, have you ever heard of the Newbery Award?"

I said, "Yes."

Obviously, it was not one of my shining hours. At the end of the conversation, she said, "We're having a champagne reception on Thursday and we wish you could be with us."

I uttered my first complete sentence of the conversation. "I wish I could too."

It was midafternoon before my editor called. She said, "What time are you leaving for Los Angeles?"

I said I wasn't planning to go.

She said, "Of course you're going. Get your reservations and call me back."

I got the reservations, rushed downtown and bought two Newbery Award-type outfits. The next morning at seven o'clock I was on my way to Los Angeles. I was a nervous wreck.

When I got out there, it turned out that I had to be hidden for a day and a half to keep people from suspecting I was the new winner. Actually I could have passed freely among all the librarians, not once falling under suspicion. In fact, one of the things someone said after the announcement was, "It's so refreshing to have someone win that nobody ever heard of."

The announcement of the Newbery Award literally changed my life overnight. Up until this time I had had a few letters from kids. Now we had to get a bigger mailbox. I got tapes, questionnaires, invitations to speak, invitations to visit schools, requests for interviews. For the first time in my life, I started feeling like an author.

—Betsy Byars

OBJECTIVES

The overall aim is for students to distinguish between facts and opinions. For a complete list of objectives, see the **Teacher's Notes**.

PRESENTATION

To introduce the difference between facts and opinions, you might create a list of five facts and five opinions. Mix them up and write the list on the chalkboard. Ask students to identify the facts and then the opinions, and engage students in a discussion of the difference by referring to the information in the text. Now you might read the passage by Seymour Simon aloud as students listen and look for facts and opinions. Have volunteers share their answers orally.

DISTINGUISHING BETWEEN FACTS AND OPINIONS

The key to effective persuasion is being able to support opinions with facts. Understanding how facts and opinions work together will help students be better readers, writers, and listeners. As listeners, students can better evaluate the opinions and facts that someone else might use in trying to persuade them to agree with a certain point of view or to go along with some action.

Answers

1. The first paragraph contains all facts.
2. Students might mention any statement from paragraph 1; or in paragraph 2, the wetlands act like sponges, protecting against floods; they recycle decaying plant and animal materials; wetlands filter pollutants.
3. In the last paragraph, the author wants people to help save the wetlands by learning about them and telling other people how important wetlands are.
4. Answers will vary, but students will probably say that wetlands are important to the environment and to people as places of wonder and enjoyment.

FOCUS ON

Reading and Critical Thinking

DISTINGUISHING BETWEEN FACTS AND OPINIONS

A **fact** is something that has happened or is true. An **opinion** is a statement of belief or judgment. Facts can be checked or verified. People can (and do) disagree about opinions. For example, the statement that Washington, D.C., is our nation's capital is a fact. The statement that Washington is a beautiful city, on the other hand, is an opinion.

Good readers are able to distinguish between facts and opinions. Read the passage below from the essay "Wetlands" by Seymour Simon. Then use a separate sheet of paper to answer the questions that follow.

    Wetlands range in size from those that cover only a fraction of an acre to the huge swamps and marshes of Florida, the Carolinas, Georgia, and Louisiana. The large prairie potholes of the midwestern United States and Canada provide nesting places for two-thirds of the more than ten million North American ducks and other waterfowl, while millions more nest in the swamps and marshes of the southeastern United States.

    Wetlands are important to people. They act like natural sponges, helping protect against floods. They recycle decaying plant and animal materials and allow the chemicals in them to be used again by living things. Wetlands filter pollutants and cleanse fresh waters better than any sewage-treatment plant ever built. Wetlands are places for fishing and small boats and are also spots of peace and quiet beauty. . . .

    Many people and nature organizations are working to save our remaining wetlands. All of us can help, too, by learning about our local wetlands and telling our friends and families how wonderful wetlands really are and how they need to be protected. You may not want to live in a swamp or a bog, but wetlands are some of the world's most interesting places to explore and treasure.

Distinguishing Between Facts and Opinions—from *Wetlands*

1. Which paragraph consists entirely of facts?
2. List four facts from the passage about wetlands.
3. In which paragraph does the author try to persuade you to do something? What does he want you to do?
4. Use a sentence of your own to state the author's opinion about wetlands.

OBJECTIVES

The overall aim is for students to apply the key elements of persuasion in a persuasive essay. For a complete list of objectives, see the **Teacher's Notes.**

PRESENTATION

To stimulate students' interest in persuasive writing, you might begin by asking students to name the kinds of persuasion they encounter every day (TV, radio, magazine, newspaper ads; store displays; signs; school programs and presentations; peer pressure; discussion with family members). Then, explain to students that they will have an opportunity to develop their persuasive skills in an essay. You might want to engage students in a brainstorming session for topics. Students can do some individual listing and then share orally one or two of their best ideas with the class. You may need to give students time outside class to consult re-

---

FOCUS ON Writing

WRITING A PERSUASIVE ESSAY

What do a campaign speech, a movie advertisement, and a sermon have in common? They are all examples of persuasion. In **persuasive writing** you state an opinion on an issue and then try to convince your audience. In the writing assignments in this unit, you have learned some of the key elements of persuasion. Now you will have a chance to write a persuasive essay of your own.

Prewriting

1. List some topics that you care about. Then jot down your opinion on each one. The topic you choose for your paper should be a subject about which people can disagree, rather than a matter of fact. Remember how to distinguish between facts and opinions:
    - A **fact** is something that has happened or is true.
    - An **opinion** is a statement of belief or judgment.

   For your persuasive essay, choose an issue that you think is important and that also matters to your audience.

2. Use one sentence to state your opinion on the issue. This **opinion statement** will be the **main idea** of your essay. [See **Focus** assignment on page 669.]

3. Think about how to make the best appeal to your **audience.** Ask yourself questions like these:
    - What are my readers likely to know already about the topic?
    - What opinions are they likely to have?
    - What reasons will appeal to them most?
    - Will I ask them to take an action?

4. Find support for your opinion. Here are some kinds of support you can use in a persuasive essay or speech:
    - facts ■ reasons ■ expert opinions

   [See **Focus** assignment on page 689.]

5. Evaluate your support. The following are two misleading types of support that you should avoid in your paper:
    - **Bandwagon:** urging people to think or do something simply because "everybody" believes or does it. Example: "Don't be the only holdout. Join the In-Line Skating Club today!"
    - **Testimonial:** using the statement of a celebrity or another person who doesn't know very much about the topic. Example: "Singer Paul Lorenzo thinks in-line skates are cool!" [Notice that testimonial is an emotional appeal quite different from the logical appeal of *expert* opinion.]

 HOLT WRITER'S WORKSHOP

This computer program provides help for all types of writing through guided instruction for each step of the writing process. (Program available separately.)

See **Elements of Writing, Introductory Course,** Chapter 7, for more instruction on persuasive writing.

WRITING A PERSUASIVE ESSAY

Because persuasion focuses so much on logical reasoning and well-chosen evidence, students will benefit from writing their own persuasive essays. They will learn to think critically as they write persuasively. Also, since persuasion is so dependent on audience, students can develop a better awareness of the importance of audience and purpose in writing.

Prewriting

Encourage students to choose topics of immediate concern to them, maybe something related to school, home, or community that they feel needs changing. Remind students that the issues they choose should have at least two sides. Students might create lists of

Focus on Writing   719

sources for information to support their opinions. Before students begin writing, you may want to do a quick check of their opinion statements and support elements. You might want to extend the revision stage by spending several class sessions to help students work with different components of their writing: content and organization, language (connotation and denotation), and sentence structure.

pros and cons for their topics before they decide on their own opinion statements. Students might work in small groups to help each other with the questions on audience. Be sure students have time to collect plenty of evidence to support their opinions.

Writing

Students might benefit from writing their body paragraphs first. They should write their opinion statement at the top of their first draft and then compose the body of their essay. Then they can "see" what they have said and experiment with introductions and conclusions until they find the most effective ones.

Evaluating and Revising

Students will find the **Checklist for Evaluation and Revision** helpful during this stage. Students should read their essays aloud to a partner who should respond to the argument as a whole. Students might work with different partners to get different suggestions for improvement. Encourage students to begin their evaluations of each other's essay with positive comments. Then, using the **Checklist for Evaluation and Revision** on page

Writing

1. When you write your first draft, use an **outline** like the one below.

   I. Introduction
      A. Attention-grabber
      B. Opinion statement
   II. Body
      A. Most important fact, reason, or expert opinion
      B. Next supporting detail
      C. Additional support, if necessary
   III. Conclusion
      A. Restatement of opinion
      B. Call to action (if appropriate)

   (If you wish, you can reverse the order in the body of your paper, starting with the least important supporting argument and ending with the most important detail.)

2. **Word choices** are especially important for a persuasive writer. As you work on your draft, pay special attention to the impact your choice of words might have on your audience. For example, if you were trying to persuade a parents' association to buy new uniforms for a sports team, would you refer to the uniforms as *hot*, *comfortable*, *fashionable*, or *neat*? If you were giving a speech about recycling to a community group, would you use the pronouns *you* and *your* or the pronouns *we*, *us*, and *our*? When you choose your words, remember that the purpose of persuasive writing and speaking is to convince your audience to identify with you and to adopt your point of view.

3. Use **transitions** to make the relationship of your ideas clear. Some helpful **transitional words and phrases** include the following:

also	first	second
another	last	then
but	mainly	therefore
finally	most important	third

[See **Focus** assignment on page 714.]

Evaluating and Revising

1. When you revise your essay, pay special attention to evaluating your reasons. Have you presented strong, specific evidence to support your opinion? Have you arranged your ideas clearly?

   Here is how one writer revised a paragraph in a persuasive paper about recycling.

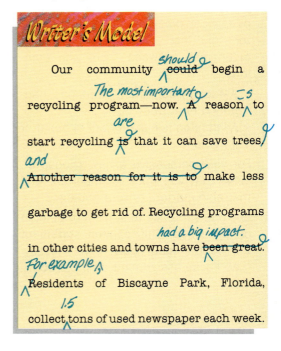

2. You may find the following checklist helpful as you revise your essay.

Checklist for Evaluation and Revision

- Does the beginning grab the reader's attention?
- Do I state my opinion clearly?
- Do I use supporting details such as facts, reasons, and expert opinions?
- Is my reasoning sound?
- Have I organized my support in a logical way?
- Do I end with a strong conclusion?

Proofreading and Publishing

1. Proofread your persuasive essay and correct any errors you find in grammar, usage, and mechanics. (Here you may find it helpful to refer to the **Handbook for Revision** on pages 750–785.) Then prepare a final version of your essay by making a clean copy.

2. Consider some of the following ways to publish and share your essay:
   - post your essay on the class bulletin board
   - organize a debate with one or more classmates
   - deliver your essay as a speech in class
   - send your essay as an editorial to the school or local paper

Portfolio If your teacher approves, you may wish to keep a copy of your work in your writing folder or portfolio.

Books for Further Reading

Some selections in this anthology (such as *Julie of the Wolves* by Jean Craighead George on page 3) are taken from novels or other book-length works. If you enjoy these excerpts, you will enjoy reading the books they come from. Here are some other books that will almost certainly give you a lot to think about.

CHARACTERS

Byars, Betsy, *Cracker Jackson* (Viking, 1985; paperback, Puffin)

When a twelve-year-old boy gets an anonymous note, he realizes that his former babysitter is in big trouble. You can't make a bad choice reading any of Byars's novels. She takes young people seriously and makes you feel that you too can make a difference.

Lord, Bette Bao, *In the Year of the Boar and Jackie Robinson* (Harper & Row, 1984)

This novel tells about a spunky Chinese girl who emigrates with her family to the United States in 1947. Shirley Temple Wong finds acceptance when she excels at baseball.

Mohr, Nicholasa, *Going Home* (Dial, 1986)

In this sequel to *Felita,* a twelve-year-old girl learns a lot about herself when she visits her parents' birthplace in Puerto Rico. You will especially enjoy Felita's warm and caring family.

Soto, Gary, *Baseball in April* (Harcourt Brace Jovanovich, 1990)

These stories are based on Soto's experiences growing up Latino in central California.

QUESTS

Alexander, Lloyd, *The High King* (Henry Holt, 1968; paperback, Dell)

This is the final book in the Prydain series. The others are *The Book of Three, The Black Cauldron, The Castle of Llyr,* and *Taran Wanderer.* In *The High King,* Taran, an orphan and former pigkeeper, completes his marvelous quest to save Prydain from its evil enemies. After you read this series, if you're hungry for more high fantasy, try *The Dark Is Rising* (Harcourt Brace Jovanovich, 1966), the first in a wonderful six-book series by Susan Cooper.

L'Engle, Madeline, *A Wrinkle in Time* (Farrar, Straus & Giroux, 1962; paperback, many editions)

This is the first of four fascinating fantasies about three young people whose quest for a kidnapped scientist (the father of two of them) takes them into a time warp. The other books in this series are *A Wind in the Door, A Swiftly Tilting Planet,* and *Many Waters.*

O'Dell, Scott, *Island of the Blue Dolphins* (Houghton Mifflin, 1960; paperback, Dell)

> You won't be able to forget Karana, a nineteenth-century Native American girl who survives all alone on an island for eighteen years. This novel is based on real historical events.

Rawls, Wilson, *Where the Red Fern Grows* (Doubleday, 1961; paperback, Bantam)

> A ten-year-old boy saves for two years to buy hunting dogs. This is an exciting and sad story of a boy's coming-of-age.

Speare, Elizabeth, *The Sign of the Beaver* (Houghton Mifflin, 1983; paperback, Dell)

> This gripping quest for survival is set in Maine before the Revolutionary War. Matt's father has to leave him alone to guard the family's cabin. Winter sets in and Matt has very little food left. Will the Penobscot boy he meets save his life—or take it?

SHORT STORIES

Aiken, Joan, *The Last Slice of Rainbow, and Other Stories* (Harper, 1988)

> Joan Aiken's imaginative stories are always different from anything you have read before.

Singer, Isaac Bashevis, *Stories for Children* (Farrar, Straus & Giroux, 1984)

> This fine collection includes more than 30 stories set long ago in the Jewish district of Warsaw, in Poland.

Yolen, Jane, Martin B. Greenberg, and Charles G. Waugh, *Dragons & Dreams: A Collection of New Fantasy and Science Fiction Stories* (Harper & Row, 1986)

> Some of the best-known writers of science fiction and fantasy contributed stories to this collection.

POETRY

Atwood, Ann, *Haiku: The Mood of the Earth* (Scribner, 1971)

> Each of the twenty-five haiku in this collection is illustrated with two full-color photographs. Atwood teaches you about haiku, as well as providing beautiful examples of it.

Giovanni, Nikki, *Spin a Soft Black Song* (Hill & Wang, 1985)

> This popular collection includes poems about family relationships and events that are important to all children.

Silverstein, Shel, *Where the Sidewalk Ends* (Harper, 1974) and *A Light in the Attic* (Harper, 1981)

> Silverstein needs no introduction. Both of these collections are more popular than the fiction books at many libraries. This poet seems to know exactly how to appeal to young people.

Sneve, Virginia Driving Hawk, *Dancing Teepees* (Holiday House, 1989)

> This beautifully illustrated collection combines traditional Native American

poetry and poems written by tribal poets today.

BIOGRAPHY AND AUTOBIOGRAPHY

Kerr, M. E., *Me Me Me Me Me: Not a Novel* (Harper & Row, 1983)

> A well-known author of young adult novels tells about her teenage years. If you think you want to become a writer some day, you should read this often humorous autobiography.

Lawson, Robert, *Ben and Me* (Little, Brown, 1939; paperback, Dell)

> This book is told from the unique point of view of a mouse, Amos, who enjoyed the friendship of the great Ben Franklin.

HISTORY

Fisher, Leonard Everett, *Pyramid of the Sun, Pyramid of the Moon* (Macmillan, 1988)

> If you want to know more about the Indian civilizations of Mexico, this is the book for you. It takes you through the invasion of Cortés in 1520.

SCIENCE

Macaulay, David, *The Way Things Work* (Houghton Mifflin, 1988)

> This clearly written text explains complicated machinery in a fascinating way. Look also for his book *Pyramid* (Houghton Mifflin, 1975).

PERSONAL ESSAYS

Bombeck, Erma, *Family: The Ties That Bind . . . and Gag* (McGraw-Hill, 1987)

> These wise and witty essays about family life are fun for all ages to read.

PLAYS

George, Richard, *Roald Dahl's Charlie and the Chocolate Factory: A Play* (Penguin, 1983)

> A sixth-grade teacher did this adaptation of the well-known story by Roald Dahl, and his class enacted it. Dahl liked the adaptation so much that he wrote an introduction for it.

Winther, Barbara, *Plays from Folktales of Africa and Asia* (Plays, Inc., 1975)

> This collection includes six plays based on folktales from Africa, six based on folktales from India and the Near East, and seven from the Far East.

MYTHS AND FOLK TALES

Bryan, Ashley, *Lion and the Ostrich Chicks and Other African Tales* (Macmillan, 1986)

> This book contains retellings of legends from the Bushman, Masai, Hausa, and Angolan peoples of Africa.

Caduto, Michael J., and Joseph Bruhac, *Keepers of the Earth* (Fulcrum, Inc., 1988)

> This collection unites each Native American folktale with related environmental activities. If you are interested in ecology, and if you want to understand more about how Native

Americans respected and celebrated nature, you must read this book.

D'Aulaire, Ingri, and Edgar Parin, *D'Aulaire's Book of Greek Myths* (Doubleday, 1962)

This beautifully illustrated book contains the best-known Greek myths. If you are interested in Norse, or Scandinavian, mythology, see *D'Aulaire's Norse Gods and Giants* (Doubleday, 1986).

Riordan, James, *The Woman in the Moon and Other Tales of Forgotten Heroines* (Dial, 1985)

These traditional stories feature strong, capable women.

Yep, Laurence, *The Rainbow People* (Harper & Row, 1989)

Yep retells twenty magical and mysterious tales originally told by Chinese immigrants in Oakland, California.

NOVELS

Babbitt, Natalie, *Tuck Everlasting* (Farrar, Straus & Giroux, 1975)

Ten-year-old Winnie meets the mysterious Tuck family and learns their amazing secret—but what will she do with it? This novel raises some profound questions.

Banks, Lynn Reid, *The Indian in the Cupboard* (Doubleday, 1981; paperback, Avon)

Omri isn't too excited about his birthday present—a little plastic Indian figure. Then, he finds out how to make the toy come to life. The sequel is *The Return of the Indian* (Doubleday, 1986).

Boyd, Candy Dawson, *Forever Friends,* originally titled *Breadsticks and Blessing Places* (Penguin, 1986)

A sixth grader has trouble accepting her best friend's death in an accident, but her family helps her when she needs it most. This is the second book by an African American writer who grew up in Chicago.

Cleaver, Bill, and Vera Cleaver, *Where the Lilies Bloom* (Lippincott, 1969; paperback, New American Library)

A fourteen-year-old girl in Appalachia struggles to keep her brother and three sisters together. After their father dies, the children pretend to the neighbors that he is still alive and taking care of them.

Howe, James, *Bunnicula: A Rabbit Tale of Mystery* (Atheneum, 1974; paper, Avon)

This is the first in a comical series featuring a family cat and dog who talk like humans. The cat suspects that the new pet, a rabbit, is a vampire. Other books in this series are *The Celery Stalks at Midnight, Howliday Inn,* and *Nighty Nightmare.*

Taylor, Mildred, *Roll of Thunder, Hear My Cry* (Dial, 1976; paperback, Bantam)

This unforgettable novel tells about a close-knit African American family that endures prejudice during the 1930s. It is also about bravery and love. The sequel is *Let the Circle Be Unbroken* (Dial, 1981).

WRITING ABOUT LITERATURE

Reasons for Writing About Literature

You will often be asked in English class to write about the literature you read. Sometimes you will be given a topic to work on: for example, as a homework assignment or in response to an examination question. At other times you may have to choose your own subject.

Writing about a literary work is a good way of getting to know it better. Before you write a composition about a story, a poem, or a play, you must study the selection carefully. Usually, you will want to examine its literary elements, such as characters, setting, point of view, conflict, and suspense. Your appreciation and enjoyment of a work will grow as your understanding of it deepens.

Another reason for writing about literature is that it develops your skills in critical thinking. In writing an analysis or an evaluation of a work, you sharpen your ability to think in certain ways, such as identifying cause and effect or comparing and contrasting. Before you write, you must sort out your thoughts and reach conclusions. You will find all these skills valuable in many areas throughout your life.

Finally, writing about literature can be a way to explore your own ideas and feelings and to express your personal reactions. How do you respond to a certain character, and why? What are the reasons for your own evaluation, or judgment, of a work? How would you persuade your family or friends to read a certain piece of literature (or *not* to read it)? When you write about literature, these are some of the questions you can ask and answer.

Using the Writing Process

Writing is called a *process* because it involves several steps, or stages. Here is a summary of the stages of the writing process.

1. *Prewriting.* Gather your information and organize your ideas.

2. *Writing.* Put your ideas down on paper or on a word processor.

3. *Evaluating and Revising.* Look critically at your writing and decide how it can be made clearer and more forceful. Then make changes to improve your writing.

4. *Proofreading and Publishing.* Correct errors in grammar, usage, punctuation, capitalization, and spelling. Then share your work with others, either in written form or orally.

As you write, you will move freely back and forth among these stages. When you are proofreading, for example, you may find that you need to add some new ideas in a part of your essay. Then you will have to move back to the prewriting stage.

The following pages contain more information about each step in the writing process.

PREWRITING

The first stage, prewriting, can be divided into three important steps.

1. *Be sure you understand the assignment.* Words such as *analyze, describe, discuss, explain, compare,* and *contrast* often appear in writing assignments. These words describe your *purpose* in writing. Before you begin to write, make certain that you understand what these words mean.

Often, your teacher will ask you to write about the elements of a story, poem, or play. You might be asked to write about *plot, setting, character,* or *theme*. You will find these elements defined in *Literary Terms and Techniques,* pages 738–749.

2. *Gather your ideas.* You might gather ideas by brainstorming or clustering. *Brainstorming* means jotting down ideas as quickly as they come to you. Do not stop to decide if the ideas are helpful. (You can evaluate your ideas later.) If your teacher approves, brainstorm with a classmate. If you brainstorm in a small group, one person should write down all the ideas that the group members suggest.

In *clustering,* you use a visual kind of brainstorming. Write your subject in the center of a piece of paper and draw a circle around it. Then, around the subject, write related ideas and circle these. Draw lines to connect them with the subject or with each other. Keep going by writing additional ideas, circling them, and drawing lines to show connections.

Here is an example of a cluster diagram about Sara in Betsy Byars' novel *The Summer of the Swans* (page 648).

You can also gather ideas by using *character wheels* (see page 733) or *reporter's questions* (Who? What? When? Where? Why? How?).

3. *Organize your ideas.* Next, think about how you are going to organize all your information. One way to do this is to look over your material and write a sentence that states the main idea you want to focus on. A *topic sentence* states the main idea of a paragraph; a *thesis statement* states the main idea of an essay or report. A topic sentence or thesis statement should be followed up with details that support the main idea. For example, here is a rough outline for a paragraph on Ray Bradbury's story, "All Summer in a Day" (page 194).

Topic Sentence: In "All Summer in a Day" by Ray Bradbury, the children have strong reasons for disliking Margot.
Reason 1: She stays separate and alone.
Reason 2: She's the only one who remembers the sun.

Reason 3: She has acted strangely, and her parents plan to take her back to Earth.

The topic sentence usually comes at the beginning of a paragraph, but it can also come at the end.

WRITING

Use your prewriting plan and notes to write a first draft of your essay. As you write, don't worry about correcting mistakes. You can do that at several later stages of the process—for example, when you revise and proofread. The important thing now is just to get your ideas down on paper or on a word processor.

EVALUATING AND REVISING

When you *evaluate* your writing, you decide what changes you need to make in your first draft. You may evaluate your writing alone, or you may exchange papers with a classmate and evaluate each other's work. It's a good idea to reread your first draft at least twice.
The first time, evaluate your *content:*

1. Have you answered the question or done what the assignment asks?

2. Have you stated your main idea clearly?

3. Have you supported or explained the main idea with specific details?

On your second reading, evaluate your *writing style:*

4. Is the order of your ideas clear and logical?

5. Have you included a conclusion that states the main idea again or that summarizes the main points?

6. Are your ideas clearly stated and easy to understand?

7. Have you used transitional words and phrases to show relationships of ideas?

8. Have you been too wordy or unnecessarily repetitious?

9. Does your paragraph (or essay) read smoothly?

When you *revise,* you write your changes on your first draft. Evaluating and revising often occur at the same time. You actually make the changes as you decide what needs to be done. Here are four helpful methods you can use to revise an essay.

1. You can add details or restate them.

2. You can delete (take out) details.

3. You can move details around.

4. You can replace some details with others.

PROOFREADING AND PUBLISHING

When you *proofread* your paper, you correct errors in grammar, usage, punctuation, capitalization, and spelling. Keep these rules in mind as you proofread.

1. Titles of short stories, poems, and essays should have quotation marks around them. Titles of long works like plays and novels should be underlined.

2. Each sentence should begin with a capital letter.

3. Each sentence should end with a period, a question mark, or an exclamation point.

4. Proper nouns and proper adjectives should be capitalized.

5. All words should be spelled correctly.

6. Verb forms should be correct.

7. Verbs should agree with their subjects.

8. Pronouns should be used correctly. The referents or pronouns should be clear (see page 564).

9. Quotation marks should be placed around direct quotations from a story, poem, play, essay, or novel.

10. Commas or periods should go *inside* the closing quotation marks.

Below is a chart showing some useful proofreading symbols.

Symbol	Example	Meaning of Symbol
≡	Pine street	Capitalize a lowercase letter.
∧	fabulus	Insert a word, letter, or punctuation mark.
ℒ	I am am here.	Cut a word, letter, or punctuation mark.
⌒	Here is my key.	Leave out and close up.
tr	Please give us and them the books.	Transfer the circled material.
¶	It was early.	Begin a new paragraph.
⊙	Take this pen	Add a period.
∧	Oh, I'm not so sure.	Add a comma.

Writing About Literature

The paragraph below shows the changes that one writer made while revising and proofreading an essay about "All Summer in a Day." Notice that the writer has added some details, changed some wording, and moved a sentence around. The writer has also corrected some spellings and punctuation marks.

In "All Summer in a Day" the children have strong reasons for dislikeing Margot. She keeps to herself, she refuses to play games with them "in the echoing tunnels of the underground city." She is different from them in many ways. *separated and alone.* Margot looks strange, too she is pale, *and thin and washed-out looking.* But the children hate Margot most of all for two reasons. First, she is different because she remembers Earth, *and what the sun is like.* Second, her parents plan to take her back to Earth. Bradbury sums up there *the children's* reasons for hatred by saying: They hated her pale snow face, her waiting silence, her thinness, and her possible future."

[For additional examples of revising and proofreading, see the model essays on pages 734–737, and in the *Handbook for Revision,* pages 750–785.]

When you *publish* your writing, you share it with an audience. Here are some publication methods you can consider:

1. Submitting your paper in an essay contest or to the school or community newspaper

2. Reading your essay aloud, either in class or to another appropriate audience

Using the Writing Process 731

3. Joining with classmates to create an illustrated booklet or anthology of essays
4. Posting your essay on the class or hall bulletin board
5. Making your essay the basis for a performance, a slide show, or a video

Writing on a Topic of Your Own: A Character Sketch

A *character* in literature is usually a person, but characters may also be animals (like Hank the Cowdog) or fantasy creatures (like Heath the dragon). A *character sketch* describes someone's personality traits. A **trait** is a quality, such as intelligence, humor, stubbornness, or shyness. A character sketch answers the question, "What is this character like?"

Writers reveal a person's character in several ways:
1. By letting us hear what a character says
2. By letting us know a character's thoughts
3. By describing the appearance of a character
4. By describing the actions of a character
5. By letting us know what others say about the character
6. By telling us directly what a character is like (nasty, sweet, naive, stupid, wacky, and so on)

ASSIGNMENT: Write a short character sketch of Becky in "Becky and the Wheels-and-Brake Boys" by James Berry (page 220). Mention at least two of Becky's character traits.

PREWRITING Reread James Berry's story. Find passages where the author reveals something about Becky. Look at her words and thoughts and actions. Examine what other people say about her.

Then you could make a *character wheel* like the one on the opposite page. In your wheel, write a few of the character's important traits in wider sections. Underneath each section, list details and events from the story that illustrate each trait. (You could also gather ideas by using a cluster diagram.)

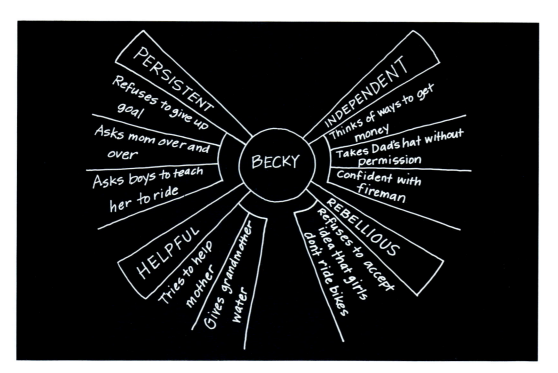

WRITING In a short character sketch, you should discuss only two or three character traits. Begin by writing a topic sentence that names the story or play you are writing about. In your first paragraph, identify the character you are describing, as well as the traits which you will discuss. Then explain or illustrate each trait with specific details, events, examples, or quotations.

On the next two pages is a model essay that presents a character sketch of Becky. The notes in the margin show important parts or features of the essay.

MODEL ESSAY

Final Copy

Title

GETTING HER OWN WAY

Introduction

In "Becky and the Wheels-and-Brake Boys" by James Berry, Becky's words and actions show that she is a strong character who is determined to get her own way. When Becky sets out to get the bicycle she wants so badly, three of her character traits are especially important. She is persistent, independent, and rebellious.

Thesis

Body

Topic sentence

First, Becky shows her persistence by refusing to give up her goal—a bike of her own. Becky asks her mother over and over for a bike, and she refuses to take "no" for an answer. When her mother asks Becky if she still thinks about "that foolishness," Becky honestly answers, "I can't get rid of it, mam."

Supporting details

Quotations

Topic sentence

When Becky thinks of a way to earn money, she shows her independence. Without asking anyone's permission, she takes her father's sun helmet to sell, and she approaches the fireman all on her own. Becky knows exactly what she wants, and her instincts tell her to go straight to the top. Typically, when she arrives at the fire station she says, "I'd like to talk to the head man." Both her mother and the fireman seem

Supporting details

Quotation

amazed at Becky's behavior, but neither one scolds or punishes her.

Topic sentence

Becky is also rebellious. She refuses to accept the idea that there is "proper behavior" for a girl, although her mother, grandmother, and the boys all believe that girls should restrict themselves to traditional roles like sewing and washing clothes. Although she risks the disapproval of her family and the boys, Becky still clings to making her dream of a bike come true.

Supporting details

Conclusion

Becky's persistence, independence, and rebelliousness pay off, because she gets what she wants in the end. She may have had a one-track mind about her bike, but it is hard not to admire her spirit.

EVALUATING AND REVISING

Use these questions to help you evaluate and revise your character sketch.

1. Do you begin with a strong topic sentence? In your introduction, do you name the work, the character, and two or three character traits?
2. Do you use specific details from the story to show how each trait is developed?
3. Have you arranged all your details in logical order?
4. Have you used transitional words and phrases to help your readers understand the connections between events and ideas?
5. Do you end with a strong conclusion?

PROOFREADING AND PUBLISHING

Use the guidelines on page 730 to proofread your work. Then write or type a clean copy and proofread *that* version as well. Finally, think of an appropriate way to share your writing.

Below you will find a rough draft of the essay that appears on pages 734–735. The notes in the margin show revision techniques, as well as the reasons for proofreading corrections. Study the two versions of the essay. Notice how the writer has revised the draft for greater clarity and accuracy.

MODEL ESSAY

Rough Draft

Title

GETTING HER OWN WAY

Comma after introductory phrases

In "Becky and the Wheels-and-Brake Boys" by James Berry, Becky's words and actions show that she is a strong character who is determined to get her own way. When Becky sets out to get the bicycle *she wants so badly*, three of her character traits are especially important. She is persistent, independent, and rebellious.

Additional detail

Transition

First, Becky shows her persistence by refusing to give up her goal—a bike of her own. Becky asks her mother over and over for a bike, and she refuses to take "no" for an answer. When her mother asks Becky if she still thinks about "that foolishness," Becky answers honestly, *"I can't get rid of it, mam."*

Direct quote

Transition; Sentences combined

When Becky thinks of a way to earn money, she shows her independence. Without asking anyone's permission, she takes her father's sun helmet to sell, and she approaches the fireman *all on her own.* Becky knows exactly what she wants, and her instincts tell her to go straight to the top. Typically, when

Added for clarity

Spelling

| | she arrives at the fire station she says, "I'd like to talk to the head man."
Subject-verb agreement | Both her mother and the fireman seem*s*, amazed at Becky's behavior, but neither one scolds or punishes her.
Transition | Becky is *also* rebellious. She refuses to accept the idea that there is
Commas with series | "proper behavior" for a girl, although her mother, grandmother, and the
Spelling | boys all believe that girls should restrict themselves to trad*i*tonal roles like sewing and washing clothes. Although she risks the disapproval of
Comma after introductory adverb clause | her family and the boys, Becky still clings to making her dream of a bike come true.
Added for clarity | Becky's persistence, independence, and rebelliousness pay off, *because she gets what she wants in the end.* She may have had a one-track mind about her bike, but it is hard not to admire her spirit.

LITERARY ELEMENTS TRANSPARENCIES

In the *Audiovisual Resources Binder,* you will find **Literary Elements** transparencies with accompanying **Teacher's Notes** and student activity pages. You may want to use these audiovisual materials when discussing the specific literary elements identified on the following pages.

Alliteration: See Sound Effects in Poetry, Transparency 22.

Literary Terms and Techniques

ALLITERATION *The repetition of the same, or very similar, sounds in words that are close together.* Alliteration usually occurs at the beginning of words, as in the phrase "*busy* as a *bee.*" It can also occur within or at the ends of words. The following poem repeats the sounds of "s" and "p."

January

In January
it's so nice
while slipping
on the sliding ice
to sip hot chicken soup
with rice.
Sipping once
sipping twice
sipping chicken soup
with rice.
—Maurice Sendak

Alliteration can establish a mood, emphasize words, and serve as a memory aid. If you ever twisted your tongue around a line like "Suzy sells shells by the sea shore" or "How much wood could a woodchuck chuck if a woodchuck could chuck wood," you have already had some fun experiences with alliteration.

See page 300.

ALLUSION *A reference to something, such as a statement, a person, a place, or an event, that is known from literature, history,* religion, mythology, politics, sports, or science. Writers expect readers to recognize an allusion and to think almost at the same time about the literary work it comes from. In the excerpt from *The Lion, the Witch and the Wardrobe* (page 10), Mr. Tumnus calls Lucy "daughter of Eve." The Narnian faun is making an allusion to the Biblical story of Adam and Eve. The cartoon below makes an allusion you will recognize right away.

"Someone's been sleeping in my bed, too, and there she is on Screen Nine!"

Drawing by Shanahan; © 1989 The New Yorker Magazine, Inc.

AUTOBIOGRAPHY *An account of the writer's own life, or part of it.* The Diary of a Young Girl, a journal kept by Anne Frank as she and her family hid from the Nazis during World War II, is a well-known autobiographical work (see page 393). Bill Cosby's hilarious account of his own experiences parenting is called *Fatherhood* (see page 453). Roald Dahl (you might know him as the author of *Charlie and the Chocolate Factory*) writes about his experiences growing up in England in *Boy*. Benjamin Franklin tells the story of his own life in his famous *Autobiography*.

> See pages 385, 393.
> See also *Biography*.

BIOGRAPHY *An account of a real person's life, or part of it, written or told by another person.* A classic American biography is Carl Sandburg's life of Abraham Lincoln. In a library or bookstore you can find biographies of movie stars, television personalities, politicians, sports figures, self-made millionaires, and artists. Today, biographies are among the most popular forms of literature.

> See pages 385, 393.
> See also *Autobiography*.

CHARACTER *A person or an animal in a story, play, or other literary work.* In some works, such as the tales told by African Americans when they labored as slaves, animals are characters. In other works, such as fairy tales, a fantastic creature like a dragon is a character (see "Dragon, Dragon" on page 166). In still other works, a character is a god or a hero (see "Quetzalcoatl" on page 576). Most often, a character is an ordinary human being, as in *The Summer of the Swans* (page 648).

The way a writer reveals the personality of a character is called **characterization**. A writer can reveal character in six ways:

1. By describing how the character looks and dresses.
2. By letting us hear the character speak.
3. By showing us how the character acts.
4. By letting us know the character's inner thoughts and feelings.
5. By revealing what other people in the story think or say about the character.
6. By telling us directly what the character's personality is like (cruel, kind, sneaky, brave, and so on).

> See pages 1, 157, 645.

CONFLICT *A struggle or clash between opposing characters or between opposing forces.* In an **external conflict,** a character struggles against some outside force. This outside force might be another character, a society as a whole, or a natural force like bitter cold weather or a ferocious shark. An **internal conflict,** on the other hand, takes place within the character's own mind. A character with an internal conflict might be struggling against fear or loneliness or even being a sore loser.

> See pages 95, 157, 645.

CONNOTATION *Emotions or associations that have come to be attached to certain words.* For example, the words *inexpensive, cheap,* and *a bargain* all are used to describe something that is not costly. Their dictionary definitions, or **denotations,** are roughly the same. However, a manufacturer of VCR's would not use *cheap* when advertising its latest model, since the word *cheap* is asso-

---

Character: See Characterization, Transparency 5. See also Story Map, Transparency 16.

Conflict: See Transparency 10.

Literary Terms and Techniques 739

Description: For information on appeal to the senses, see Imagery, Transparency 27.

Dialogue: See Characterization, Transparency 5.

---

ciated with something that is not well made. *Bargain* would be a better choice. Connotations can be especially important in poetry.

See page 565.

DESCRIPTION *Writing intended to create a mood or emotion, or to recreate a person, a place, a thing, an event, or an experience.* Description works through **images,** words that appeal to the senses of sight, smell, taste, hearing, or touch. Writers use description in all forms of writing—in fiction, nonfiction, and poetry. Here is a description of a famous character who has wormed her way into the hearts of readers everywhere. The writer's description appeals to our sense of sight, but it also gives us a hint of the girl's character. Viewing this lone figure in a deserted train station, an "ordinary observer" would see:

> A child of about eleven, garbed in a very short, very tight, very ugly dress of yellowish gray wincey. She wore a faded brown sailor hat and beneath the hat, extending down her back, were two braids of very thick, decidedly red hair. Her face was small, white, and thin, also much freckled; her mouth was large and so were her eyes, that looked green in some lights and moods and gray in others.
> —from *Anne of Green Gables,* L. M. Montgomery

See page 100.

DIALECT *A way of speaking characteristic of a particular region or of a particular group of people.* A dialect may have a distinct vocabulary, pronunciation system, and grammar. In a sense, we all speak dialects. The dialect that is dominant in a country or culture becomes accepted as the standard way of speaking. Writers often reproduce regional dialects, or dialects that reveal a person's economic or social class. The characters in *Sounder* (page 114) use an African American dialect spoken in the rural South. In "Jody's Discovery" (page 129), the characters speak a dialect common in the backwoods of Florida. Below, a spunky young girl gets up the courage to ask her uncle a hard question (she is speaking an African American urban dialect):

> So there I am in the navigator seat. And I turn to him and just plain ole ax him. I mean I come right on out with it . . . And like my mama say, Hazel—which is my real name and what she remembers to call me when she bein serious—when you got somethin on your mind, speak up and let the chips fall where they may. And if anybody don't like it, tell em to come see your mama. And Daddy look up from the paper and say, You hear your mama good, Hazel. And tell em to come see me first. Like that. That's how I was raised.
>
> So I turn clear round in the navigator seat and say, "Look here, . . . you gonna marry this girl?"
> —from "Gorilla, My Love," Toni Cade Bambara

See pages 126, 230, 587.

DIALOGUE *Conversation between two or more characters.* Most plays consist entirely of dialogue. Dialogue is also an important element in most stories and novels. Dialogue is very effective in revealing character. It can also add realism and humor to a story.

In the written form of a play, dialogue appears without quotation marks. In prose or poetry, however, dialogue is normally enclosed in quotation marks.

See pages 464, 712.

DRAMA *A story written to be acted in front of an audience.* (A drama can also be appreciated and enjoyed in written form, however.) The action of a drama is usually caused by a character who wants something very much, who takes steps to get it, and who then meets with complications.

See page 463.
See also *Dialogue*.

ESSAY *A short piece of nonfiction prose.* An essay usually examines a subject from a personal point of view. Most essays are short. The French writer Michel de Montaigne (1533–1592) is supposed to have invented the essay. James Thurber, also in this book (page 446), is one of America's greatest humorous essayists.

See page 446.

FABLE *A very brief story in prose or verse that teaches a moral or a practical lesson about how to succeed in life.* The characters of most fables are animals that behave and speak like human beings. Some of the most popular fables are those supposedly told by Aesop, who was a slave in ancient Greece. You may have heard his fable about the sly fox who praises the crow for her beautiful voice. The fox begs the crow to sing for him, which she does. But when the crow opens her mouth, she lets fall the piece of cheese in her beak that the fox had been after the whole time.

See page 640.

FANTASY *Imaginative writing that carries the reader into an invented world where the laws of nature as we know them do not operate.* In fantasy worlds, supernatural forces are often at play. Characters may wave magic wands, cast spells, or appear and disappear at will. These characters may seem almost like ordinary human beings—or they may be witches, Martians, elves, giants, or fairies. Some of the oldest fantasy stories are called **fairy tales.** "Cinderella" and "The Emperor's New Clothes" are fairy tales. A newer type of fantasy, which deals with the changes that science may bring in the future, is called **science fiction.** "All Summer in a Day" (page 194) is Ray Bradbury's science fiction story about life as he imagines it on the planet Venus.

See page 18.
See also *Science Fiction*.

FICTION *A prose account that is basically made-up rather than factually true.* The term usually refers to novels and short stories.

See also *Fantasy, Nonfiction, Science Fiction*.

FIGURE OF SPEECH *A word or phrase that describes one thing in terms of something*

Fable: See Exploring Myths and Folk Tales, Transparency 37.

Fantasy: See Exploring Myths and Folk Tales, Transparency 37.

Fiction: See Understanding and Evaluating a Novel, Transparency 43. For basic elements of fiction, see Story Map, Transparency 16.

Figure of Speech: For information on simile and metaphor, see Imagery, Transparency 27.

Literary Terms and Techniques

Folk Tale: See Exploring Myths and Folk Tales, Transparency 37.

Free Verse: See Sound Effects in Poetry, Transparency 22.

Imagery: See Transparency 27.

else and is not literally true. Figures of speech always involve some sort of imaginative comparison between seemingly unlike things. Some 250 different types of figures of speech have been identified. The most common by far are the **simile** ("My heart is like a singing bird"), the **metaphor** ("The road was a ribbon of moonlight"), and **personification** ("The leaves were whispering to the night").

See page 443.
See also *Metaphor, Personification, Simile.*

FLASHBACK *Interruption in the present action of a plot to flash backward and tell what happened at an earlier time.* A flashback breaks the normal chronological movement of a narrative. A flashback can be placed anywhere in a story, even at the very beginning. There it usually gives background information. *The Secret Garden* (page 474) is almost one entire flashback. Although it starts out in the present when the main character is an adult, it soon flashes back to her childhood.

See pages 474, 495.

FOLK TALE *A story with no known author that originally was passed on from one generation to another by word of mouth.* Folk tales generally differ from myths in that they are not about gods and they were never connected with religion or belief. "The Pheasant's Bell" (page 551), and "Momotaro: Boy-of-the-Peach" (page 618) are both folk tales. Some folk tales tend to travel. The old European folk tale of Cinderella has turned up in hundreds of other cultures (see "The Algonquin Cinderella" on page 147.)

See pages 549, 617, 630.

FORESHADOWING *The use of clues or hints suggesting events that will occur later in the plot.* Foreshadowing builds suspense or anxiety in the reader or viewer. In a movie, for example, strange alien creatures glimpsed among the trees may foreshadow later danger for the exploring spacemen.

See pages 165, 470.

FREE VERSE *Poetry that is "free" of a regular meter and rhyme scheme.* Poets writing in free verse try to capture the natural rhythms of ordinary speech. The following poem is written in free verse.

The City
If flowers want to grow
right out of the concrete sidewalk cracks
I'm going to bend down to smell them.
—David Ignatow

See pages 358, 362, 366.

IMAGERY *Language that appeals to the senses.* Most images are visual—that is, they create pictures in our minds by appealing to our sense of sight. Images can also appeal to our senses of hearing, touch, taste, or smell. Images can appeal to several senses at once. While imagery is an element in all types of writing, it is especially important in poetry. The following poem is full of rainy images:

FROM The Rainy Day

The day is cold, and dark, and dreary;
It rains, and the wind is never weary;
The vine still clings to the moldering wall,
But at every gust the dead leaves fall,
And the day is dark and dreary.
—Henry Wadsworth Longfellow

See page 250.

IRONY *A contrast between what appears to be true and what is really true, or a contrast between expectation and reality.* Irony can create powerful effects, from humor to horror. Here are some examples of situations that would make us feel irony:

1. We would feel irony if the shoemaker goes around with holes in his shoes.
2. We would feel irony if the children of a famous dancer trip over their own feet.
3. We would feel irony if it rains on the day the weather forecasters schedule their picnic.
4. We would feel irony if someone asks "How's my driving?" after going through a stop sign.
5. We would feel irony if a huge Great Dane runs away from a tiny mouse.
6. We would feel irony if a person who lives in the desert keeps a boat in the yard.
7. We would feel irony if the relative of a law enforcer is a bank robber.
8. We would feel irony if someone walked out in the midst of a hurricane and said "Nice day."

See page 408.

LEGEND *A story, usually based on some historical fact, that has been handed down from one generation to the next.* Legends often grow up around famous figures or events. The stories about King Arthur and his knights are legends based on the exploits of a real Celtic warrior-king who probably lived in Wales in the 500s. The story "Where the Buffaloes Begin" (page 252) is about a legend told around the campfires of the Native Americans of the Great Plains. As you can tell from that story, legends often make use of fantastic details.

METAPHOR *A comparison between two unlike things in which one thing becomes another thing.* A metaphor is an important type of figure of speech. Metaphors are used in all forms of writing and are common in ordinary speech. When you say about your grumpy friend, "He's such a bear today," you do not mean that he is growing bushy black fur. You mean that he is in a bad mood and taking his feelings out on everybody else.

Metaphors differ from **similes,** which use specific words to make their comparisons (words such as *like, as, than,* and *resembles*). "He is behaving like a bear" would be a simile.

The following famous poem compares fame to an insect:

> Fame is a bee.
> It has a song—
> It has a sting—
> Ah, too, it has a wing.
> —Emily Dickinson

See pages 44, 53.
See also *Figure of Speech, Simile.*

Literary Terms and Techniques

Metaphor: See Imagery, Transparency 27.

Myth: See Exploring Myths and Folk Tales, Transparency 37.

Novel: See Understanding and Evaluating a Novel, Transparency 43.

MOOD *The overall emotion created by a work of literature.* Mood can often be described in one or two adjectives, such as eerie, dreamy, mysterious, depressing. The mood created by the poem below is sad and lonely:

Since Hanna Moved Away
The tires on my bike are flat.
The sky is grouchy gray.
At least it sure feels like that
Since Hanna moved away.

Chocolate ice cream tastes like prunes.
December's come to stay.
They've taken back the Mays and Junes
Since Hanna moved away.

Flowers smell like halibut.
Velvet feels like hay.
Every handsome dog's a mutt
Since Hanna moved away.

Nothing's fun to laugh about.
Nothing's fun to play.
They call me, but I won't come out
Since Hanna moved away.

—Judith Viorst

See page 112.

MYTH *A story that usually explains something about the world and involves gods and other supernatural beings.* Myths are deeply connected to the traditions and religious beliefs of the culture that produced them. Myths often explain certain aspects of life, such as what thunder is or where sunlight comes from or why people die. **Creation myths** explain how the world came to exist. Most myths are very old and were handed down orally for many centuries before being put in writing. The story of the hero Perseus on page 567 is a famous Greek myth. "Quetzalcoatl" (page 576) is a Mexican myth, and "Glooscap Fights the Water Monster" (page 558) is a popular Native American myth.

See page 549.
See also *Folk Tale*.

NARRATION *The kind of writing that tells "what happened."* Narration (also called *narrative*) is the form of writing most used by storytellers. Narration is also used in nonfiction, whenever a series of events are related.

See pages 63–65.

NONFICTION *Prose writing that deals with real people, events, and places without changing any facts.* Popular forms of nonfiction are the autobiography, the biography, and the essay. Other examples of nonfiction include newspaper stories, magazine articles, historical writing, travel writing, scientific reports, and personal diaries and letters.

See page 385.
See also *Fiction*.

NOVEL *A long fictional story, whose length is normally somewhere between one hundred and five hundred book pages.* A novel uses all the elements of storytelling—**plot, character, setting, theme,** and **point of view.** Because of its length, a novel usually has a more complex plot and more characters, settings, and themes than a short story has.

See page 645.

ONOMATOPOEIA (on′ə·mat′ə·pē′ə) *The use of a word whose sound imitates or suggests its meaning.* Onomatopoeia is so natural to us that we begin using it at a very early age. *Boom, bang, sniffle, rumble, hush, ding,* and *snort* are all examples of onomatopoeia. Onomatopoeia helps create the music of poetry. In the following poem, the poet had a lot of fun using onomatopoeia:

Our Washing Machine
Our washing machine went whisity whirr
Whisity whisity whisity whirr
One day at noon it went whisity click
Whisity whisity whisity click
Click grr click grr click grr click
  Call the repairman
  Fix it . . . quick.
—Patricia Hubbell

See pages 337, 596, 600.
See also *Alliteration*.

PARAPHRASE *A restatement of a poem or a story, in which the meaning is expressed in other words.* You might be asked to paraphrase a work of literature to be sure you have understood exactly what it says. When you paraphrase a poem, you should tell what it says, line by line, in your own words. When you paraphrase a work of prose, you should give a brief summary of the major events or ideas. Here is the first stanza of a very famous poem, followed by a paraphrase:

Once upon a midnight dreary, while I
  pondered, weak and weary,
Over many a quaint and curious volume
  of forgotten lore—
While I nodded, nearly napping, suddenly there came a tapping,
As of someone gently rapping, rapping
  at my chamber door.
"'Tis some visitor," I muttered, "tapping at my chamber door—
  Only this, and nothing more."
—from "The Raven,"
Edgar Allan Poe

One midnight, I was tired but I stayed up late to read some interesting old books that I hadn't looked at in a while. As I was dozing off, I suddenly heard a sound as if someone were tapping at the door. "Just someone stopping by," I said, annoyed, "knocking at the door—that's all."

Notice that the paraphrase is neither as eerie nor as elegant as the poem.

PERSONIFICATION *A special kind of metaphor in which a nonhuman thing or quality is talked about as if it were human.* You are using personification if you say, "The leaves danced along the sidewalk." Of course leaves don't dance—only people do. The poem below personifies the night wind.

Rags
The night wind
rips a cloud sheet
into rags,
then rubs, rubs
the October moon
until it shines
like a brass doorknob.
—Judith Thurman

See also *Figure of Speech, Metaphor, Simile*.

Onomatopoeia: See Sound Effects in Poetry, Transparency 22.

Plot: See Transparency 15.

Poetry: See Sound Effects in Poetry, Transparency 22.

Point of View: For point of view in fiction, see Story Map, Transparency 16.

Literary Terms and Techniques

PLOT *The series of related events that make up a story.* Plot tells "what happens" in a short story, novel, play, or narrative poem. Most plots are built on these bare bones: An **introduction** tells us who the characters are and what their **conflicts,** or problems, are. **Complications** arise as the characters take steps to resolve their conflicts. Eventually, the plot reaches a **climax,** the most exciting moment in the story, when the outcome of the conflict is decided one way or another. The final part of the story is the **resolution.** This is when the characters' problems are solved and the story is closed.

See page 157.

POETRY *A kind of rhythmic, compressed language that uses figures of speech and imagery to appeal to our emotions and imaginations.* Poetry often has a regular pattern of rhythm, and it may have a regular rhyme pattern. **Free verse** is poetry that has no regular pattern of rhythm or rhyme.

See page 281.
See also *Alliteration, Figure of Speech, Free Verse, Imagery, Refrain, Rhyme, Speaker, Stanza.*

POINT OF VIEW *The vantage point from which a story is told.* Two common points of view are the omniscient (om·nish'ənt) and the first person.
1. In the **omniscient,** or "all-knowing," point of view, the narrator knows everything about the characters and their problems. This all-knowing narrator can tell us about the past, the present, and the future. Below is an example of the omniscient point of view:

Once upon a time, in a small village, there were three houses built by three brother pigs. One was made of straw, one was made of twigs, and one was made of brick. Each pig thought his house was the best and the strongest. A wolf—a very hungry wolf—lived just outside of town. He was practicing his blowing techniques and trying to decide which pig's house was the weakest.

2. In the **first-person point of view,** one of the characters is telling the story, using the personal pronoun *I*. We become very familiar with this narrator, but we can only know what this character knows. We can observe only what this character observes. All our information about the story must come from this one narrator. In some cases the information this narrator gives us is not correct.

As soon as I found out some new pigs had moved into the neighborhood, I started to practice my blowing. I like to blow down houses and eat whoever is inside. The little pigs have built their houses out of different materials—but I know I can blow 'em down in no time. That brick house looks especially weak.

See page 229.

PROSE *Any writing that is not poetry.* Essays, short stories, novels, news articles, and letters are all usually written in prose.

PUN *A play on words.* Puns are based on either (1) the multiple meanings of a word, or (2) two words that sound alike but have different meanings. There's a pun in the famous "Knock Knock" joke: Who's there? *Orange.* Orange who? *Orange you glad I came?* Puns are often used by poets. Here is a "prehistoric riddle" that uses a pun.

Question: Why did dinosaurs turn into fossils?

Answer: When the band started to play, the music made the dinosaurs rock.

This riddle puns on two meanings of the word *rock:* (1) a hard substance, and (2) a slang term for dancing to music.

REFRAIN *A repeated sound, word, phrase, line, or group of lines.* Refrains are usually associated with songs and poems, but they are also used in speeches and other forms of literature. Refrains are often used to create rhythm. Refrains are also used for emphasis and emotional effects.

See pages 300, 304.

RHYME *The repetition of accented vowel sounds and all sounds following them, in words that are close together in a poem.* Trouble and *bubble* are rhymes, as are *clown* and *noun.* Rhymes in poetry help create rhythm, they lend a songlike quality to the poem, they emphasize ideas, they provide humor or delight, and they aid memory.

End rhymes are rhymes at the ends of lines. **Internal rhymes** are rhymes within lines. Here is an example of a poem with both kinds of rhymes.

In days of *old* when knights caught *cold,*
They were not quickly *cured;*
No aspirin *pill* would check the *ill,*
Which had to be *endured.*
— from "Thoughts on Progress," David Daiches

See pages 300, 319, 596, 600.

RHYTHM *A musical quality produced by the repetition of stressed and unstressed syllables or by the repetition of other sound patterns.* Rhythm occurs in all language—written and spoken—but it is particularly important in poetry. The most obvious kind of rhythm is the regular repetition of stressed and unstressed syllables called **meter.** If you say the following lines aloud you'll hear a strong, regular rhythm. (Crowns, pounds, and guineas are British currency.)

When I was one-and-twenty
I heard a wise man say,

Refrain: See Sound Effects in Poetry, Transparency 22.

Rhyme: See Sound Effects in Poetry, Transparency 22.

Rhythm: See Sound Effects in Poetry, Transparency 22.

Setting: For setting in fiction, see Story Map, Transparency 16.

Short Story: For basic elements of fiction, see Story Map, Transparency 16.

Simile: For comparison using simile, see Imagery, Transparency 27.

Literary Terms and Techniques

"Give crowns and pounds and guineas
But not your heart away . . ."
—from "When I Was One-and-Twenty," A. E. Housman
See pages 292, 300, 316.

SCIENCE FICTION *A kind of fantasy usually based on changes that science or technology may bring in the future.* While science fiction creates imaginary worlds—often on other planets or in Earth's future—these worlds are usually governed by physical laws as we know them. "All Summer in a Day" (page 194) is Ray Bradbury's science fiction story about life on the planet Venus. It is based on the idea that someday our space technology will be advanced enough for people to set up civilizations on distant planets. Popular young adult science fiction books include *The Martian Chronicles* by Ray Bradbury, *A Wrinkle in Time* by Madeleine L'Engle, and *Sweetwater* by Laurence Yep.

See also *Fantasy.*

SETTING *The time and place of a story or play.* The setting can help create mood or atmosphere in a story. Some examples of vivid settings are the bleak and spooky mansion in *The Secret Garden* (page 474), the empty, vast tundra in *Julie of the Wolves* (page 3), the deserted wilderness in *Hatchet* (page 99), and the crumbling Fadgin house in "Nancy" (page 233).

See pages 157, 233, 262.

SHORT STORY *A short fictional prose narrative that usually takes up less than twenty book pages.* Short stories are usually built on a plot that consists of these elements: **introduction, conflict, complications, climax,** and **resolution.** Short stories are more limited than novels. They usually have only one or two major characters and one setting.

See page 157.
See also *Fiction, Plot.*

SIMILE (sim′ə·lē) *A comparison between two unlike things, using a word such as* like, as, resembles, *or* than. The simile is an important type of figure of speech. "His voice is as loud as a trumpet" and "Her eyes are like the blue sky" are both similes. In the following poem, the poet uses a simile to help us see a winter scene in a new way:

Scene
Little trees like pencil strokes
black and still
etched forever in my mind
on that snowy hill.
—Charlotte Zolotow

See pages 36, 40, 196, 204, 333.
See also *Figure of Speech, Metaphor.*

SPEAKER *The voice talking to us in a poem.* Sometimes the speaker is identical to the poet, but often the speaker and the poet are not the same. A poet may speak as a child, a woman, a man, a whole people, an animal, or even an object. In "Life Doesn't Frighten Me" (page 303), the speaker is a little girl. The unexpected speaker of "Interview" (page 370) is Cinderella's stepmother.

See pages 304, 362.

STANZA *A group of lines in a poem that form a unit.* A stanza in a poem is something like a paragraph in prose; it often expresses a unit of thought. The word *stanza* is an Italian word meaning "stopping place" or "place to rest."

SUSPENSE *The uncertainty or anxiety we feel about what will happen next in a story.* Any kind of writing that has a plot evokes some degree of suspense. Our sense of suspense is awakened in "Jody's Discovery" (page 129), for example, when Penny gets bitten by the rattlesnake. Jody's horror and disbelief make us anxious to read on to see whether his father will live or die.

>See pages 443, 470, 688.
>See also *Plot*.

THEME *An idea about life revealed in a work of literature.* A theme is not the same as a subject. A subject can usually be expressed in a word or two—love, childhood, death. A theme is the idea the writer wishes to reveal about that subject. Theme has to be expressed in a full sentence. A work can have more than one theme. A theme is usually not stated directly in the work. Instead, the reader has to think about all the elements of the work and then make an inference, or educated guess, about what they all mean. One theme of *The Secret Garden* (page 474) might be stated this way: "We cannot like ourselves until we learn to respect and care about others."

>See pages 157, 204, 274, 645, 712.

TONE *The attitude a writer takes toward an audience, a subject, or a character.* Tone is conveyed through the writer's choice of words and details. A tone can be light and humorous, serious and sad, friendly or hostile toward a character, and so forth. The poem "The Sneetches" (page 285) is light and humorous in tone. The excerpt from *Sounder* (page 114) has a serious tone.

>See pages 371, 400.

WRITING PROCESS TRANSPARENCIES

In the *Audiovisual Resources Binder,* you will find **Writing Process** transparencies with accompanying **Teacher's Notes** and student activity pages. You may want to use these audiovisual materials when discussing specific aspects of the writing process or of particular types of writing.

HANDBOOK FOR *Revision*

Contents

Part 1: **MODEL ESSAYS** 751
- Persuasive Essay
- Informative Essay

Part 2: **SENTENCE STRUCTURE** 760
- Sentence Fragments
- Run-on Sentences
- Comparisons

Part 3: **PRONOUNS** 761
- Pronoun-Antecedent Agreement
- Case Forms of Personal Pronouns

Part 4: **VERBS** 762
- Missing or Incorrect Verb Endings
- Subject-Verb Agreement
- Sequence of Tenses

Part 5: **COMMA USAGE** 765
- Compound Structure
- Items in a Series
- Two or More Adjectives
- Nonessential Elements
- Introductory Elements
- Interrupters

Part 6: **STYLE** 767
- Sentence Variety
- Stringy Sentences
- Overwriting
- Creative Use of Synonyms
- Vivid Words
- Clichés
- Levels of Language

Part 7: **GLOSSARY OF USAGE** 769

Part 8: **GRAMMAR REFERENCE GUIDE** 775

Part 9: **MECHANICS** 778
- Capitalization
- Punctuation
- Letters

Part 1: Model Essays
- Persuasive Essay
- Informative Essay

Each of the essays on pages 752–759 is shown in two versions: a rough draft and a final copy. In the draft, the writer has evaluated and revised the essay for logic, clarity, style, and specific support. The writer has also proofread the essay for errors in grammar, usage, punctuation, spelling, and capitalization. The writer's corrections are shown on the draft. The reasons for many of the changes are shown in the margin. Marginal annotations in the final copy identify important parts of each essay.

Symbols for Revising and Proofreading

Symbol	Example	Meaning of Symbol
≡	Pine street	Capitalize a lowercase letter.
/	Mae's Mother	Lowercase a capital letter.
/	revizing	Change a letter.
∧	fabulus	Insert a word, letter, or punctuation mark.
℘	I am am here.	Cut a word, letter, or punctuation mark.
⌒	Here is my key.	Leave out and close up.
ⓣⓡ	Please give us the books and them.	Transfer the circled material.
¶	It was early.	Begin a new paragraph.
⊙	Take this pen	Add a period.
⋀	Oh I'm not so sure.	Add a comma.
⋁	Tanyas voice	Add an apostrophe.
⊙	as follows	Add a colon.
⋀	Rob Pinzio, Jr. Paula Fong, M.D.	Add a semicolon.

Handbook for Revision

Model Essays

WRITING PROCESS TRANSPARENCIES

In the *Audiovisual Resources Binder,* you will find **Writing Process** transparencies with accompanying **Teacher's Notes** and student activity pages. You may want to use these audiovisual materials when discussing specific aspects of the writing process or of particular types of writing, such as the transparency listed below.

Writing a Persuasive Essay: See Transparency 44.

Handbook for Revision

MODEL 1: A PERSUASIVE ESSAY
Rough Draft

EARTHLINGS, UNITE!

What happened on April 22, 1970, to bring people all over the world together? That date marked the first celebration of Earth Day. Every April 22 since then, people in record-breaking numbers have used this day to show their common concern for our environment. Our school should organize a full schedule of Earth Day activities for students, parents, and other members of the community.

The most important reason for observance of Earth Day is that the holiday draws attention to environmental problems on our planet. Toxic chemicals, hazardous wastes, and other pollutants are choking our air and water. Many of our fellow creatures on earth, including some of the rarest animals and plants, may die out completely because they are losing their natural surroundings. Celebration of Earth Day would help to make us all more aware of environmental problems and how we might solve them.

A second reason for our school to observe this holiday is that Earth Day activities would allow students, parents, teachers, and community

Margin annotations: Question mark; Commas with series; Transition; Spelling; Run-on sentence; Capital letter needed; Transition

752 Handbook for Revision

MODEL 1: A PERSUASIVE ESSAY
Final Copy

EARTHLINGS, UNITE!

What happened on April 22, 1970, to bring people all over the world together? That date marked the first celebration of Earth Day. Every April 22 since then, people in record-breaking numbers have used this day to show their common concern for our environment. Our school should organize a full schedule of Earth Day activities for students, parents, and other members of the community.

The most important reason for observance of Earth Day is that the holiday draws attention to environmental problems on our planet. Toxic chemicals, hazardous wastes, and other pollutants are choking our air and water. Many of our fellow creatures on earth, including some of the rarest animals and plants, may die out completely because they are losing their natural surroundings. Celebration of Earth Day would help to make us all more aware of environmental problems and how we might solve them.

A second reason for our school to observe this holiday is that Earth Day activities would allow students, parents, teachers,

Title

Introduction

Opinion statement

Body

Supporting reasons

Additional support

Sentence fragment	members, To be involved together on an issue that concerns
Apostrophe	everyone. Students could benefit from the adults knowledge and
	practical experience on environmental topics. Adults would be
	exposed to the ideas of teachers and students. Fresh solutions
	would be the result.
Style; Question mark	What are some possible projects for an Earth Day program*and activities*.
Comma with interrupter	you ask. Students and adults could work together in teams for
Sentence fragment	example to clean up trash, plant young trees, Or learn more about
	recycling. Community members could share slides and
Spelling	videocasettes about remote but important areas of the earth's
	environment, such as tropical rain forests. Teachers could
	organize special classes on topics such as the destruction of the
	rain forest and the recycling of garbage.
	So, Earthlings, unite! If you agree that we can help to make
Pronoun reference	a difference by celebrating Earth Day at your *our* school, write a letter
	to the school board or the administration today. All of us take life
Contraction	from the earth. Now lets start to give something back in return.

and community members to be involved together on an issue that concerns everyone. Students could benefit from the adults' knowledge and practical experience on environmental topics. Adults would be exposed to the ideas of teachers and students. Fresh solutions would be the result.

What are some possible projects and activities for an Earth Day program? Students and adults could work together in teams, for example, to clean up trash, plant young trees, or learn more about recycling. Community members could share slides and videocassettes about remote but important areas of the earth's environment, such as tropical rain forests. Teachers could organize special classes on topics such as the destruction of the rain forest and the recycling of garbage.

So, Earthlings, unite! If you agree that we can help to make a difference by celebrating Earth Day at our school, write a letter to the school board or the administration today. All of us take life from the earth. Now let's start to give something back in return.

Practical suggestions

Conclusion

Call to action

Handbook for Revision

Model Essays

WRITING PROCESS TRANSPARENCIES

In the *Audiovisual Resources Binder*, you will find **Writing Process** transparencies with accompanying **Teacher's Notes** and student activity pages. You may want to use these audiovisual materials when discussing specific aspects of the writing process or of particular types of writing, such as the transparency listed below.

Writing an Informative Paper: See Transparency 28.

MODEL 2: AN INFORMATIVE ESSAY
Rough Draft

IN THE LAND OF THE GWICH'IN

In northeast Alaska, amid the tall peaks and the winding river valleys of the Brooks Range, stands the small town of Arctic Village. This collection of log houses, together with a school, a church, and a community center, *is* ~~are~~ home to one of the most endangered peoples on earth. They are the Gwich'in.

The nother*n*most Indians of North America, the Gwich'in live in fifteen settlements*, that* ~~These settlements~~ stretch from Alaska into Canada, roughly a hundred miles south of the Arctic *O*cean. Although experts believe humans have lived here for more than 25,000 years*,* today the Gwich'in number only about 5,000.

Their*~~'s~~* is a harsh land, frozen and dark for much of the year. There is an even ~~more~~ harsher prospect for the Gwich'in, however: they may lo*s*e their traditional way of life.

For thousands of years, these ~~The~~ people have depended on the caribou, or reindeer. Caribou meat*,* for example*,* provides 75 percent of the protein in the Gwich'in diet. Skins are sewn into boots and clothing, and bones are made into tools. *A*ccording to traditional stories the Gwich'in

Revision marks (left margin):
- Subject-verb agreement
- Spelling
- Combine sentences
- Capital letter needed
- Comma after introductory clause
- Possessive pronoun
- Double comparison
- Spelling
- Transition
- Commas with interrupter
- Capitalization

Handbook for Revision

756   Handbook for Revision

MODEL 2: AN INFORMATIVE ESSAY
Final Copy

IN THE LAND OF THE GWICH'IN | Title

In northeast Alaska, amid the tall peaks and the winding river valleys of the Brooks Range, stands the small town of Arctic Village. This collection of log houses, together with a school, a church, and a community center, is home to one of the most endangered peoples on earth. They are the Gwich'in. | **Introduction**

The northernmost Indians of North America, the Gwich'in live in fifteen settlements. These settlements stretch from Alaska into Canada, roughly a hundred miles south of the Arctic Ocean. Although experts believe that humans have lived here for more than 25,000 years, today the Gwich'in number only about 5,000. Theirs is a harsh land, frozen and dark for much of the year. There is an even harsher prospect for the Gwich'in, however: they may lose their traditional way of life. | **Body** / **Specific details**

For thousands of years, these people have depended on the caribou, or reindeer. Caribou meat, for example, provides 75 percent of the protein in the Gwich'in diet. Skins are sewn into boots and clothing, and bones are made into tools. According to | **Additional details**

Subject-verb agreement

still tell, long ago they and the caribou was [were] one. After humans and animals became separate beings, they say, every caribou kept some of the human heart, and every human kept some of the caribou heart.

It is oil exploration that threatens to end the close ties of the Gwich'in and the caribou. After oil was discovered in Prudhoe Bay

Spelling; Apostrophe

in 1968, the Gwich'in suceeded [succeeded] for a while in protecting the caribous [caribou's] grazing lands. Some of the world's leading oil companies, however, want to drill in the lands where the herds raise their young. This

Capitalization

land lies within the arctic national wildlife refuge [Arctic National Wildlife Refuge]. Aside from the direct threat to the caribou calves, the Gwich'in worry about the

Sentence fragment

dangers of oil spills. And [, and] toxic chemicals if the companies' plan is approved.

The Gwich'in have organized themselves to protect their way of life. They have the strongest motivation of all, their own survival.

Commas with appositive

As Sarah James[,] a Gwich'in leader[,] put it: "Caribou are not just what

Close quotation marks

we eat; they are who we are. Without caribou we wouldn't exist.["]

758 Handbook for Revision

traditional stories the Gwich'in still tell, long ago they and the caribou were one. After humans and animals became separate beings, they say, every caribou kept some of the human heart, and every human kept some of the caribou heart.

It is oil exploration that threatens to end the close ties of the Gwich'in and the caribou. After oil was discovered in Prudhoe Bay in 1968, the Gwich'in succeeded for a while in protecting the caribou's grazing lands. Some of the world's leading oil companies, however, want to drill in the lands where the herds raise their young. This land lies within the Arctic National Wildlife Refuge. Aside from the direct threat to the caribou calves, the Gwich'in worry about the dangers of oil spills and toxic chemicals if the companies' plan is approved.

The Gwich'in have organized themselves to protect their way of life. They have the strongest motivation of all, their own survival. As Sarah James, a Gwich'in leader, put it: "Caribou are not just what we eat; they are who we are. Without caribou we wouldn't exist."

LANGUAGE SKILLS WORKSHEETS

In the *Teaching Resources* booklets, you will find **Language Skills** worksheets that address specific grammar, usage, and mechanics skills and show how these are applied by the writers of particular literary selections. The topics discussed and the **Language Skills** worksheets that discuss them are indicated on the pages that follow.

Sentence Fragments: See Teaching Resources B, page 69.

Run-on Sentences: See Teaching Resources B, page 24.

For definitions of grammatical terms, see The Grammar Reference Guide on pages 775–778.

Part 2: Sentence Structure
- Sentence Fragments
- Run-on Sentences
- Comparisons

SENTENCE FRAGMENTS

A **sentence** is a group of words that expresses a complete thought. A sentence has a subject and a predicate. A group of words that looks like a sentence but that doesn't make sense by itself is a **sentence fragment**.

1. **Correct a fragment by adding the necessary sentence parts. Usually you will need to add a verb, a subject, or both.**

    Fragment
    By running to get help from the Forresters, Jody. [verb missing: What about Jody, or what did he do?]

    Sentence
    By running to get help from the Forresters, Jody **shows** responsibility.

    Fragment
    In the dream, is making a fire at a barbecue pit. [subject missing: Who is making a fire?]

    Sentence
    In the dream, Brian's friend **Terry** is making a fire at a barbecue pit.

    Fragment
    Acting like a young dog again. [subject and verb missing]

    Sentence
    Acting like a young dog again, **Sounder rushes** to greet his master.

2. **Correct a fragment by connecting it to an independent clause.**

    Fragment
    Because Tom hates to go to school, especially on Monday mornings. He pretends to be sick.

    Sentence
    Because Tom hates to go to school, especially on Monday mornings, **he** pretends to be sick.

RUN-ON SENTENCES

A **run-on sentence** consists of two complete sentences run together as if they were one sentence. Most run-ons are *comma splices*—or two complete thoughts separated only by a comma. Other run-ons are *fused sentences*—two complete thoughts separated by no punctuation.

1. **Correct a run-on sentence by using a period to form two complete sentences.**

    Run-on
    During his childhood, Abraham Lincoln lived in Kentucky and Indiana he had less than a year of formal schooling.

    Corrected
    During his childhood, Abraham Lincoln lived in Kentucky and Indiana**. He** had less than a year of formal schooling.

2. **Correct a run-on by using a comma and a coordinating conjunction (such as *and, but,* or *yet*) to create a compound sentence.**

    Run-on
    Cinderella's stepmother treated her badly life turned out well for her because she married a handsome prince and lived with him happily ever after.

    Corrected
    Cinderella's stepmother treated her badly**, but** life turned out well for her because she married a handsome prince and lived with him happily ever after.

COMPARISONS

1. Avoid incomplete comparisons.

Incomplete
The team played better today. [better than what?]

Complete
The team played better today **than it did yesterday.**

2. Avoid double comparisons.

Nonstandard
Nana Miriam is **more stronger** than anyone else because she has magic powers.

Standard
Nana Miriam is **stronger** than anyone else because she has magic powers.

Part 3: Pronouns
- Pronoun-Antecedent Agreement
- Case Forms of Personal Pronouns

PRONOUN-ANTECEDENT AGREEMENT

The noun or pronoun to which a pronoun refers is called its **antecedent**.

1. A pronoun must agree with its antecedent in number and in gender.

Example
Ali Baba frees Morgiana and also rewards **her**.

2. Use a singular pronoun to refer to an antecedent that is a singular indefinite pronoun. Use a plural pronoun to refer to an antecedent that is a plural indefinite pronoun.

Examples
Each of the daughters has **her** own hobbies.

Some of these poets use metaphors in **their** works.

3. When the antecedent may be either masculine or feminine, rephrase the sentence to avoid an awkward construction, or use both the masculine and the feminine forms.

Standard
All the heroes were known for **their** great deeds.

Standard
Each of the heroes was known for **his or her** great deeds.

4. Use a plural pronoun to refer to two or more antecedents joined by *and*.

Nonstandard
In the end, **Ben** and the other **boys** allowed Becky to join **his** group.

Standard
In the end, **Ben** and the other **boys** allowed Becky to join **their** group.

5. Use a singular pronoun to refer to two or more singular antecedents joined by *or* or *nor*.

Nonstandard
Neither **Gwendolyn Brooks** nor **Maya Angelou** wrote **their** poems in the nineteenth century.

Standard
Neither **Gwendolyn Brooks** nor **Maya Angelou** wrote **her** poems in the nineteenth century.

Sentences of this type can sound awkward if the antecedents are of different genders. If a sentence sounds awkward, revise it to avoid the problem.

Comparisons: See Comparison of Adjectives and Adverbs, *Teaching Resources D,* page 37. See also Making Comparisons, *Teaching Resources B,* page 179.

Pronoun-Antecedent Agreement: See *Teaching Resources C,* page 147.

Case Forms of Personal Pronouns: See Subject and Object Pronouns, *Teaching Resources C,* page 150. See also Pronouns, *Teaching Resources A,* page 42.

Missing or Incorrect Verb Endings: See Verb Tenses, *Teaching Resources D,* page 7. See also Irregular Verbs, *Teaching Resources D,* page 22.

Handbook for Revision

Awkward
Each of the rich children in *The Secret Garden* has **his or her** internal conflicts.

Revised
Both the rich children in *The Secret Garden* have **their** internal conflicts.

CASE FORMS OF PERSONAL PRONOUNS

Use the correct case for personal pronouns that are part of compound constructions.

Nonstandard
Wanda says that **her** and Frank are going for a ride on the scooter. [object form used as subject]

Standard
Wanda says that **she** and Frank are going for a ride on the scooter.

Nonstandard
Did Mr. Ramos ask you and **she** to give a report on Vietnamese refugees? [subject form used for direct object]

Standard
Did Mr. Ramos ask you and **her** to give a report on Vietnamese refugees?

Nonstandard
Between you and **I,** did you think ''The Jumblies'' was funny? [subject form used for object of preposition]

Standard
Between you and **me,** did you think ''The Jumblies'' was funny?

Part 4: Verbs
- Missing or Incorrect Verb Endings
- Subject-Verb Agreement
- Sequence of Tenses

MISSING OR INCORRECT VERB ENDINGS

1. A *regular verb* forms the past and past participle by adding *-d* or *-ed* to the infinitive form. Don't make the mistake of leaving off or doubling the *-d* or *-ed* ending.

Nonstandard
Sara was **suppose** to take Charlie to see the swans.

Standard
Sara was **supposed** to take Charlie to see the swans.

Nonstandard
During their attempt to escape, some refugees **drownded.**

Standard
During their attempt to escape, some refugees **drowned.**

2. An *irregular verb* forms the past and past participle in some other way than by adding *-d* or *-ed* to the infinitive form. Irregular verbs form their past and past participle by
- changing a vowel
- changing consonants
- adding *-en*
- making no change at all

Examples

Infinitive	Past	Past Participle
catch	caught	(have) caught

762 Handbook for Revision

know	knew	(have) known
speak	spoke	(have) spoken
cut	cut	(have) cut

When you proofread your writing, check your sentences to determine which form—past or past participle—is called for. Remember that many nonstandard verb forms sound quite natural. Keep a dictionary handy to check any verb forms you're not sure about.

Nonstandard
The Mexicans did not believe that Quetzalcoatl **had went** away for good.

Standard
The Mexicans did not believe that Quetzalcoatl **had gone** away for good.

Nonstandard
When he was driving down the road, Maibon **seen** an old man hobbling along.

Standard
When he was driving down the road, Maibon **saw** an old man hobbling along.

Nonstandard
Brian **throwed** his hatchet at the porcupine.

Standard
Brian **threw** his hatchet at the porcupine.

SUBJECT-VERB AGREEMENT

1. **A verb must agree with its subject in number—either singular or plural.**

   Nonstandard
   Beterli **try** to bully Keevan, and the two **boys quarrels.**

   Standard
   Beterli **tries** to bully Keevan, and the two **boys quarrel.**

2. **When a sentence contains a verb phrase, the first helping verb in the verb phrase agrees with the subject.**

   Nonstandard
   The **actors has** memorized their parts.

   Standard
   The **actors have** memorized their parts.

3. **The number of a subject is not changed by a phrase or clause coming between the subject and the verb.**

   Nonstandard
   The **effects** of the volcano's eruption **was** serious.

   Standard
   The **effects** of the volcano's eruption **were** serious.

4. **Use a singular verb to agree with the following singular indefinite pronouns:** *anybody, anyone, each, either, everybody, everyone, neither, nobody, no one, one, somebody,* **and** *someone.*

   Nonstandard
   Everyone in the play **grow** to love the secret garden.

   Standard
   Everyone in the play **grows** to love the secret garden.

   Nonstandard
   Rena likes those poems because **each** of them **use** clever rhymes.

   Standard
   Rena likes those poems because **each** of them **uses** clever rhymes.

5. **Use a plural verb to agree with the following plural indefinite pronouns:** *both, few, many,* **and** *several.*

   Nonstandard
   Many of E. E. Cummings' poems **has** unusual punctuation.

   Standard
   Many of E. E. Cummings' poems **have** unusual punctuation.

   Nonstandard
   Several of my classmates **has** seen the movie version of *The Yearling.*

   Standard
   Several of my classmates **have** seen the movie version of *The Yearling.*

Handbook for Revision

Subject-Verb Agreement: See *Teaching Resources B,* page 83. For practice matching subjects and predicates, see Subject and Predicate, *Teaching Resources A,* page 117. See also Compound Subjects and Compound Verbs, *Teaching Resources A,* page 146.

Verbs

Sequence of Tenses: See Verb Tenses, *Teaching Resources D,* page 7. For principal parts of irregular verbs, see Irregular Verbs, *Teaching Resources D,* page 22.

6. **The following indefinite pronouns are singular when they refer to singular words and plural when they refer to plural words:** *all, any, most, none,* **and** *some.*

   Nonstandard
   Most of the story **are** easy to read.
   Standard
   Most of the story **is** easy to read.
   Nonstandard
   Most of these poems **has** lively rhythms.
   Standard
   Most of these poems **have** lively rhythms.
   Nonstandard
   All of these novels **is** available at the public library.
   Standard
   All of these novels **are** available at the public library.

7. **Subjects joined by** *and* **usually take a plural verb.**

   Nonstandard
   Frank and **Wanda goes** to his sister's house.
   Standard
   Frank and **Wanda go** to his sister's house.

8. **Singular subjects joined by** *or* **or** *nor* **take a singular verb.**

   Nonstandard
   At the beginning of the play, neither **Mary** nor **Colin are** happy.
   Standard
   At the beginning of the play, neither **Mary** nor **Colin is** happy.

9. **When a singular subject and a plural subject are joined by** *or* **or** *nor,* **the verb agrees with the subject nearer the verb.**

   Nonstandard
   Neither **Roger** nor the other **boys knows** that Jerry sold Rollie Tremaine the card.
   Standard
   Neither **Roger** nor the other **boys know** that Jerry sold Rollie Tremaine the card.

10. **When the subject follows the verb, as in questions and in sentences beginning with** *here* **and** *there,* **identify the subject and make sure that the verb agrees with it.**

    Nonstandard
    Here **are** a **list** of the world's tallest volcanoes.
    Standard
    Here **is** a **list** of the world's tallest volcanoes.
    Nonstandard
    When **does** summer **classes** start?
    Standard
    When **do** summer **classes** start?

11. **A verb should always agree with its subject, not with its predicate nominative.**

    Nonstandard
    Grandfather's **words was** a precious legacy.
    Standard
    Grandfather's **words were** a precious legacy.

12. **The contractions** *don't* **and** *doesn't* **must agree with their subjects.**

    Examples
    At the beginning of James Berry's story, the **Wheels-and-Brake Boys don't** allow Becky to join them.

    According to James Thurber, **Rex doesn't** hesitate to jump fences.

SEQUENCE OF TENSES

Changing verb tense in mid-sentence or from sentence to sentence without good reason creates awkwardness and confusion. Be sure that the verb tenses in a single sentence or in a group of related sentences are consistent.

Awkward
When Jody **searches** for the abandoned fawn, he **risked** the danger of an attack by a rattlesnake or a panther.

Better
When Jody **searches** for the abandoned fawn, he **risks** the danger of an attack by a rattlesnake or a panther.

Part 5: Comma Usage

- Compound Structure
- Items in a Series
- Two or More Adjectives
- Nonessential Elements
- Introductory Elements
- Interrupters

COMPOUND STRUCTURE

Use a comma before a coordinating conjunction *(and, but, or, nor, for, so,* and *yet)* that joins two independent clauses. If the clauses are very short, you may omit the comma.

Examples
The voice was as loud as an earthquake, **and** the eldest son's knees knocked together in terror.
 —Gardner, "Dragon, Dragon" (p. 169)

Little Wolf was only ten years old, **but** he could run faster than any of his friends.
 —Baker, "Where the Buffaloes Begin" (p. 254)

He felt perfectly sure he could slay the dragon by simply laying into him, **but** he thought it would be only polite to ask his father's advice.
 —Gardner, "Dragon, Dragon" (p. 171)

The President cards were a roaring success **and** the cowboy cards were quickly forgotten.
 —Cormier, "President Cleveland, Where Are You?" (p. 184)

ITEMS IN A SERIES

Use commas to separate words, phrases, and clauses in a series.

Examples
Thousands of people came to **hike, picnic, camp, fish, paint, bird watch, or just enjoy the scenery.**
 —Lauber, "Volcano" (p. 435)

Maibon **flung down the stone, spun around, and set off as fast as he could.**
 —Alexander, "The Stone" (p. 215)

My seven sisters helped by **working in the garden, gathering eggs, or taking water to the cattle.**
 —Nhuong, "The Land I Lost" (p. 413)

In front, behind, and on both sides of him, a heaving mass of buffaloes billowed like the sea.
 —Baker, "Where the Buffaloes Begin" (p. 260)

All the floors were full of greenish light reflected from the maple trees outdoors; **the floors were dark and gleaming, the carpets had been taken up for the summer, and the furniture had linen dresses on.**
 —Enright, "Nancy" (p. 235)

TWO OR MORE ADJECTIVES

Use a comma to separate two or more adjectives preceding a noun. However, do *not* use a comma before the final adjective in a series if the adjective is thought of as being part of a noun. Determine if the adjective and noun form a unit by inserting the word *and* between the adjectives. If *and* fits sensibly, use a comma.

Examples
"We need **warm, soapy** water," the teacher said. [warm *and* soapy; comma needed]
 —Armstrong, from *Sounder* (p. 119)

Meg got her **large chocolate** milkshake and I had a small one. [*And* sounds awkward.]
 —Namioka, "The All-American Slurp" (p. 272)

NONESSENTIAL ELEMENTS

A *nonessential* (or *nonrestrictive*) clause or participial phrase contains information that is not necessary to the meaning of the sentence. Use commas to set off nonessential clauses and nonessential participial phrases. An *essential* (or *restrictive*) clause or participial phrase is not set off by commas, because it contains information that is necessary to the meaning of the sentence.

Compound Structure: See Compound Subjects and Compound Verbs, *Teaching Resources A,* page 146.

Items in a Series: See Commas, *Teaching Resources B,* page 9. See Using Phrases in Sentences, *Teaching Resources C,* page 83.

Comma Usage

Nonessential Clause
I have relations, aunts and uncles, **who are darlings too,** a good home, no—I don't seem to lack anything. [The clause can be omitted without changing the main idea.]
—Frank, from *The Diary of a Young Girl* (p. 394)

Essential Clause
That particular egg was the one **Beterli had marked as his own.** [The clause is necessary to identify which egg is meant.]
—McCaffrey, "The Smallest Dragonboy" (p. 82)

Nonessential Phrase
That selection, **written by Marjorie Kinnan Rawlings,** comes from her novel *The Yearling*.

Essential Phrase
The selection **written by Marjorie Kinnan Rawlings** comes from her novel *The Yearling*.

INTRODUCTORY ELEMENTS

Use a comma after *yes, no,* or any mild exclamation such as *well* or *why* at the beginning of a sentence. Also use a comma after an introductory participial phrase, after two or more introductory prepositional phrases, and after an introductory adverb clause.

Examples
Yes, being the smallest candidate was not an enviable position.
—McCaffrey, "The Smallest Dragonboy" (p. 81)

"**Well,** has there ever been a case where a dragon didn't choose?"
—McCaffrey, "The Smallest Dragonboy" (p. 85)

In the still darkness of the shelter in the middle of the night, his eyes came open and he was awake and he thought there was a growl.
—Paulsen, from *Hatchet* (p. 103)

Whenever she thought of the handbills, she walked faster. [introductory adverb clause]
—Petry, "Harriet Tubman" (p. 29)

INTERRUPTERS

1. **Nonessential appositives and appositive phrases are usually set off by commas.**

We had been invited to dinner by our neighbors, **the Gleasons.**
—Namioka, "The All-American Slurp" (p. 265)

Yet Little Wolf knew well that his enemies, **the Assiniboins,** could come creeping along the hollows of the prairie like wolves.
—Baker, "Where the Buffaloes Begin" (pp. 255–256)

I told her that this was America and yelled that Debbie, **my sister,** didn't have a jacket like mine.
—Soto, "The Jacket" (p. 39)

She told her of the panic-stricken talk in the quarter, told her that the slaves were afraid that the master, **Dr. Thompson,** would start selling them.
—Petry, "Harriet Tubman" (p. 24)

2. **Words used in direct address are set off by commas.**

Examples
"**Father,** have you any advice to give me?" he asked.
—Gardner, "Dragon, Dragon" (p. 172)

"And may I ask, **O Lucy, daughter of Eve,**" said Mr. Tumnus, "how you have come into Narnia?"
—Lewis, "Mr. Tumnus" (p. 12)

"Thanks, **Jerry,**" he said. "I hate to take your last cent."
—Cormier, "President Cleveland, Where Are You?" (p. 182)

3. **Use commas to set off parenthetical expressions.**

Examples
And then, **of course,** the biggest crime of all was that she had come here only five years ago from Earth.
—Bradbury, "All Summer in a Day" (p. 197)

Yes, I'm still alive, **indeed,** but don't ask where or how.
—Frank, from *The Diary of a Young Girl* (p. 395)

But even if she fell asleep, **she thought,** the Lord would take care of her.
—Petry, "Harriet Tubman" (p. 26)

Part 6: Style

- Sentence Variety
- Stringy Sentences
- Overwriting
- Creative Use of Synonyms
- Vivid Words
- Clichés
- Levels of Language

SENTENCE VARIETY

1. **Create sentence variety in length and rhythm by using different kinds of clauses, as well as simple sentences.**

   Little Variation
   In ''Becky and the Wheels-and-Brake Boys,'' Becky wants a bike badly. Her mother says no. The family is too poor. Becky does not give up. She tries to raise some money. She takes her father's sun helmet to the fire station. She wants to sell the helmet to the fireman, Mr. Dean. Mr. Dean laughs. He drives Becky home.

   More Variation
   In ''Becky and the Wheels-and-Brake Boys,'' Becky wants a bike badly. Her mother says no, telling Becky that the family is too poor. Becky does not give up, however, and she tries to raise some money by taking her father's sun helmet to the fire station. When she tells the fireman, Mr. Dean, that she wants to sell the helmet to him, he laughs and drives Becky home.

2. **Expand short, choppy sentences by adding details.**

   Choppy
   Lensey Namioka was born in China. She came to America. She now lives in Seattle, Washington. She has written several novels. Her autobiography is called *Life with Chaos*.

   More Detailed
   Lensey Namioka was born in 1929 in Beijing, China. She came to America with her parents and now lives in Seattle, Washington. She has written several novels about the adventures of Japanese samurai warriors. The title of her autobiography, *Life with Chaos*, is a pun on Namioka's Chinese family name, *Chao*.

3. **Vary sentence openers by using appositives, single-word modifiers, phrase modifiers, clause modifiers, and transitional words.**

   Little Variation
   Harriet's brothers force her to return on the first attempt to escape. Harriet decides to go North alone. She tells her sister Mary of her decision. She slips away from the plantation in the middle of the night. She comes to the farmhouse where the white woman lives. Harriet approaches carefully. The woman opens the door. She does not seem surprised to see Harriet.

   More Variation
   Because Harriet's brothers force her to return on the first attempt to escape, Harriet decides to go North alone. **After telling her sister Mary of her decision,** she slips away from the plantation. **In the middle of the night,** she comes to the farmhouse where the white woman lives and approaches carefully. **When the woman opens the door,** she does not seem surprised to see Harriet.

STRINGY SENTENCES

Simplify stringy sentences by writing as concisely as you can. Cut down your use of prepositional phrases. Reduce clauses to phrases, if possible. If you can, reduce clauses and phrases to single words.

Stringy
Tom Sawyer experienced misery on Monday morning because he didn't want to go to school, so he thought for a while and then he decided to create a pretense that he was sick, and he started to groan so that Sid would wake up.

Style 767

Sentence Variety: See Varying Sentence Beginnings, *Teaching Resources D*, page 171. For practice with sentences, see Writing Effective Sentences 1, *Teaching Resources D*, page 146, and Writing Effective Sentences 2, *Teaching Resources D*, page 159.

Overwriting: See Repetition and Wordiness, *Teaching Resources D,* page 95.

Handbook for Revision

Better
Tom Sawyer was miserable on Monday morning. He didn't want to go to school, so after thinking for a while, he decided to pretend to be sick. He started to groan so that Sid would wake up.

OVERWRITING

1. Get rid of unnecessary words.

Wordy
That poem has a lively **rhythm and beat.**
Better
That poem has a lively **rhythm.**

Wordy
At the end of the story, the boy's father **unexpectedly and surprisingly** returns.
Better
At the end of the story, the boy's father **unexpectedly** returns.

2. Avoid complicated words where plain, simple ones will do.

Pretentious
Langston Hughes was the author of many distinguished literary **creations.**
Simpler
Langston Hughes was the author of many distinguished literary **works.**

CREATIVE USE OF SYNONYMS

Avoid awkward repetition by using synonyms creatively.

Awkward
While Brian looks at the **bear,** he wonders if the **bear** will attack him.
Better
While Brian looks at the **bear,** he wonders if the **beast** will attack him.

VIVID WORDS

1. Whenever possible, replace vague words with specific ones.

Vague
The light in the forest and the sound of the trees were nice, but as he went along he became worried.
Specific
The moonlight coming through the leaves and the soft sound of the wind in the branches were soothing, but as he went deeper into the forest he became worried.
—Byars, *The Summer of the Swans* (p. 673)

2. Replace abstract words with vivid, concrete words that appeal to the senses.

Abstract
Her pallor was striking, and if she spoke her voice would be tiny.
Concrete/Sensory
She was an old photograph dusted from an album, whitened away, and if she spoke at all, her voice would be a ghost.
—Bradbury, "All Summer in a Day" (p. 197)

CLICHÉS

A **cliché** is a tired expression. Replace clichés in your writing with fresh, vivid expressions.

Cliché
They were as fast as lightning.
Vivid
They were as fast as sprinting cheetahs.

LEVELS OF LANGUAGE

Depending on your purpose, audience, and form of writing, you should use an appropriate level of language. For example, *formal English* **is appropriate for serious essays, reports, and speeches on solemn occasions.** *Informal English* **is suitable for personal letters, journal entries, and many articles. The following chart gives an outline of formal and informal levels of language.**

	Formal	Informal
Words	longer, rare, specialized	shorter, colloquial

768 Handbook for Revision

Spelling	in full	contractions
Grammar	complex, complete	compound, fragmentary

Formal English usually creates a serious tone. Informal English tends to have a friendlier, more personal tone.

Formal
Once on Sunday after the usual slow, massive dinner, as Fiona lay in the extremity of boredom counting mosquito bites and listening to herself yawn, she heard another sound: a new one that might promise much.

—Enright, "Nancy" (p. 236)

Informal
"Oh! Given themselves a name as well, have they? Well, Becky, answer this. How d'you always manage to look like you just escaped from a hair-pulling battle? Eh? And don't I tell you not to break the backs down and wear your canvas shoes like slippers? Don't you ever hear what I say?"

—Berry, "Becky and the Wheels-and-Brake Boys" (p. 223)

Part 7: Glossary of Usage

a, an Use the indefinite article *a* before words beginning with a consonant sound. Use the indefinite article *an* before words beginning with a vowel sound.

Examples
Lucy finds herself in *a* dark wood.

Jamaica is *an* island in the Caribbean Sea.

accept, except *Accept* is a verb meaning "to receive." *Except* may be either a verb or a preposition. As a verb, *except* means "to leave out." As a preposition, *except* means "excluding."

Examples
Do you *accept* the idea that everything is determined by fate in advance?

No one *except* Margot remembers the sun clearly. [preposition]

The swift, destructive mudflows from the volcano *excepted* no obstacle in their path. [verb]

affect, effect *Affect* is a verb meaning "to influence." As a verb, *effect* means "to bring about" or "to accomplish." As a noun, *effect* means "the result of an action."

Examples
How did Gwendolyn Brooks's description *affect* your opinion of Narcissa?

Maibon's magic stone *effected* some mysterious changes on his farm. [verb]

In "Nancy," the house in which Fiona lived with her grandparents had a confining *effect* on her. [noun]

all, all of The word *of* can usually be omitted, except before some pronouns.

Examples
All my friends liked reading "Ali Baba and the Forty Thieves." [preferable to *all of*]

All of us wanted to see the movie. [*Of* is necessary.]

among, between Use *between* when you are referring to two things at a time. Use *among* when you are referring to more than two items.

Examples
Bruce wanted to memorize a short poem, but he couldn't decide *between* "The Sea" and "Dream Variations."

Among the folktales we read, which did Reggie like best?

amount, number Use *amount* to refer to a singular word. Use *number* to refer to a plural word.

Examples
Tom Sawyer had a great *amount* of ingenuity.

Glossary of Usage

Robert Cormier has written a *number* of novels for young adults.

anxious, eager *Anxious* means "worried" or "uneasy." *Eager* means "feeling keen desire or strong interest."

Examples
Aunt Willie becomes *anxious* about Charlie when no one can find him.

Bharati liked "Perseus" so much that she is *eager* to read more ancient Greek myths about heroes.

as, like *Like* is a preposition. In formal situations, do not use *like* for the conjunction *as* to introduce a subordinate clause.

Examples
Poets *like* Shel Silverstein create funny verses about unusual subjects.

Did C. S. Lewis' story "Mr. Tumnus" end *as* you expected?

awhile, a while *Awhile* is an adverb meaning "for a short time." *A while* is made up of an article and a noun and means "a period or space of time."

Examples
Shirl and Nikki read *awhile* in the library.

Mark Twain worked for *a while* as a cub pilot.

bad, badly *Bad* is an adjective. *Badly* is an adverb. In standard English, only the adjective form should follow a sense verb, such as *feel, see, hear, taste, look,* or another linking verb.

Examples
Sara thinks that Joe Melby has played a *bad* trick on Charlie by taking his watch.

In "The Smallest Dragonboy," the bully Beterli behaved *badly* to Keevan.

When he sits by his father's bed and thinks of the motherless fawn, Jody feels *bad*.

because In formal situations, do not use the construction *reason . . . because*. Instead, use *reason . . . that*.

Informal
The reason nothing frightens the speaker is *because* she has a magic charm.

Formal
The reason nothing frightens the speaker is *that* she has a magic charm.

beside, besides *Beside* is a preposition meaning "by the side of" or "next to." *Besides* may be used as either a preposition or an adverb. As a preposition, *besides* means "in addition to" or "also." As an adverb, *besides* means "moreover."

Examples
Did you sit *beside* Dihundra at the play rehearsal?

Besides "Habits of the Hippopotamus," which other poems did you enjoy? [preposition]

Langston Hughes was a poet and playwright; he was an outstanding writer of fiction, *besides*. [adverb]

between See **among, between.**

bring, take *Bring* means "to come carrying something." *Take* means "to go carrying something."

Examples
"Please *bring* your textbooks to class tomorrow," said Ms. Owens.

Mr. Ortega said, "Please *take* these books to Room A302."

compare to, compare with Use *compare to* when you want to stress either the similarities or the differences between two things. Use *compare with* when you wish to stress both similarities and differences.

Examples
The metaphor in the first line of James Reeves's poem compares the sea *to* a hungry dog.

770 Handbook for Revision

Stu's report compared Rudyard Kipling's "How the Whale Got His Throat" *with* Chinua Achebe's "Why Tortoise's Shell Is Not Smooth."

convince, persuade *Convince* means "to win someone over through argument." *Convince* is usually followed by *that* and a subordinate clause. *Persuade* means to move someone to act in a certain way. *Persuade* is often followed by *to*.

Examples
Frank wants to convince Aunt Willie *that* his motor scooter is safe.

Frank *persuades* Aunt Willie *to* take a ride on the scooter.

could of Do not write *of* with the helping verb *could*. Write *could have*. Also avoid *had of, ought to of, should of, would of, might of,* and *must of*.

Example
Jerry *could have* [not *could of*] spent the money himself, but he gave it to his brother Armand.

different from, different than Use *different from*, not *different than*.

Example
An autobiography is *different from* a biography because in an autobiography the writer tells about his or her own life.

doesn't, don't *Doesn't* is the contraction of *does not*. *Don't* is the contraction of *do not*. Use *doesn't*, not *don't*, with *he, she, it, this, that,* and singular nouns.

Examples
Sarah Cynthia Sylvia Stout *doesn't* like dealing with the garbage.

Harriet Tubman's three brothers *don't* want to escape with her.

eager See **anxious, eager.**

effect See **affect, effect.**

everyday, every day *Everyday* is an adjective meaning "daily" or "common." *Every day* is an adverbial phrase meaning "each day."

Examples
Moderate exercise should be part of *everyday* life.

Sara thinks that *every day* of the summer has been awful.

everyone, every one *Everyone* is an indefinite pronoun. *Every one* consists of an adjective and a pronoun and means "every person or thing of those named."

Examples
Everyone in my class loved "The Sneetches."

Every one of my friends enjoys science fiction.

except See **accept, except.**

farther, further *Farther* refers to geographical distance. *Further* means "in addition to" or "to a greater degree."

Examples
The boat was taking Tran to Thailand, but Tran's mother wanted him to travel even *farther*, all the way to America.

Because the sudden eruption puzzled scientists, they researched its causes *further*.

fewer, less Use *fewer*, which tells "how many," to modify a plural noun. Use *less*, which tells "how much," to modify a singular noun.

Examples
With each passing year, the buffaloes on the plain grew *fewer* and *fewer*.

If Mary had possessed *less* curiosity, she might not have discovered the secret garden.

good, well *Good* is an adjective. *Well* may be used either as an adjective or an adverb. The

Glossary of Usage

expressions *feel good* and *feel well* mean different things. *Feel good* means "to feel happy or pleased." *Feel well* means "to feel healthy."

Examples
At the end of the novel, Sara feels *good* about Joe.

Tom Sawyer pretends to Sid and Aunt Polly that he doesn't feel *well*.

Avoid using *good* to modify an action verb. Instead, use *well* as an adverb meaning "capably" or "satisfactorily."

Nonstandard
John Gardner uses humor *good* in "Dragon, Dragon."

Standard
John Gardner uses humor *well* in "Dragon, Dragon."

had of   See **could of.**

hardly, scarcely   The words *hardly* and *scarcely* convey negative meanings. Never use with another negative word.

Example
The people *can* [not *can't*] *hardly* believe that Momotaro has saved them from the ogres.

Abe Lincoln's family *had* [not *hadn't*] *scarcely* any money.

he, she, they   Do not use an unnecessary pronoun after the subject of a clause or a sentence. This error is called the *double subject*.

Nonstandard
At the end of the story, Mr. Dean *he* will probably marry Becky's mother.

Standard
At the end of the story, Mr. Dean will probably marry Becky's mother.

how come   In informal situations, *how come* is often used instead of *why*. In formal situations, *why* should always be used.

Informal
How come the narrator says that her family disgraced themselves at the dinner party with the Gleasons?

Formal
Why does the narrator say that her family disgraced themselves at the dinner party with the Gleasons?

imply, infer   *Imply* means "to suggest something indirectly." *Infer* means "to get a certain meaning from a remark or an action."

Examples
Writers often do not directly state the theme of a story or poem; instead, they *imply* it.

Did you *infer* from the end of Robert Cormier's story that Jerry would eventually feel better about his actions?

in, into, in to   *In* means "within." *Into* means "from the outside to the inside." *In to* refers to motion with a purpose.

Examples
"Jody's Discovery" takes place *in* the Florida backwoods.

The porcupine stuck some of its quills *into* Brian's leg.

Did Ms. Lopez come *in to* your classroom to make the announcement?

its, it's   *Its* is a possessive pronoun. *It's* is the contraction for *it is* or *it has*.

Examples
Anne McCaffrey's story is enjoyable because of *its* use of fantasy.

It's clear in the play that both Mary and Colin are very unhappy children.

kind(s), sort(s), type(s)   With the singular form of each of these nouns, use *this* or *that*. With the plural form, use *these* or *those*.

Examples
Do you like *this type* of essay?

Those kinds of tales are about a leader who instructs the people in survival skills.

lay, lie The verb *lay* means "to put (something) in a place." *Lay* usually takes an object. The past tense of *lay* is *laid*. The verb *lie* means "to rest" or "to stay in one position." *Lie* never takes an object. The past tense of *lie* is *lay*.

Examples
Please *lay* [place] those books on the table.

After Wanda leaves the room, Sara *lies* [rests] on her bed and complains to the dog Boysie.

leave, let *Leave* means "to go away." *Let* means "to permit" or "to allow."

Nonstandard
Please *leave* us watch TV till 9:00!

Standard
Please *let* us watch TV till 9:00!

Standard
The bus was supposed to *leave* at 6:30.

less See **fewer, less**.

might of, must of See **could of**.

number See **amount, number**.

on, onto, on to *On* refers to position and means "upon," "in contact with," or "supported by." *Onto* implies motion and means "to a position on." Do not confuse *onto* with *on to*.

Examples
The waves broke *on* the seashore.

The crocodile dragged Lan's body *onto* an island.

The author goes *on to* discuss the eruption itself.

or, nor Use *or* with *either*. Use *nor* with *neither*.

Examples
Consuelo's report will be *either* on Leroy V. Quintana *or* on Pat Mora.

Neither Sara *nor* Aunt Willie can find Charlie.

ought to of See **could of**.

principal, principle *Principal* is an adjective meaning "first" or "main." It can also be a noun meaning the head of a school. *Principle* is a noun meaning "rule of conduct" or "a fact or general truth."

Examples
The *principal* characters in "President Cleveland, Where Are You?" are Jerry, Rollie, Roger, and Jerry's brother Armand.

Tricksters like Tortoise have very few *principles*.

real In informal situations, *real* is often used as an adverb meaning "very" or "extremely." In formal situations, *very* or *extremely* is preferred.

Informal
The speaker in "Abuelito Who" feels *real* close to her grandfather.

Formal
The speaker in "Abuelito Who" feels *very* close to her grandfather.

rise, raise *Rise* means "to go up" or "to get up." *Rise* never takes an object. The past tense of *rise* is *rose*. *Raise* means "to cause (something) to rise" or "to lift up." *Raise* usually takes an object. The past tense of *raise* is *raised*.

Examples
When the volcano erupted, the magma *rose* to the surface.

Fiona *raised* herself to her elbows and saw that Nana was asleep.

scarcely, hardly See **hardly, scarcely**.

should of See **could of**.

sit, set *Sit* means "to rest in an upright, seated

Glossary of Usage 773

position." *Sit* seldom takes an object. The past tense of *sit* is *sat*. *Set* means "to put (something) in a place." *Set* usually takes an object. The past tense of *set* is *set*.

Examples
In fine weather, Ben likes to *sit* outside and read.

Ali Baba orders his slaves to *set* the jars in the courtyard.

some, somewhat   In writing, do not use *some* for *somewhat* as an adverb.

Nonstandard
The end of that story surprised me *some*.
Standard
The end of that story surprised me *somewhat*.

than, then   *Than* is a conjunction used in comparisons. *Then* is an adverb telling *when*.

Examples
Nana Miriam was stronger *than* anyone else in two ways.

Quetzalcoatl mourns for the dead pages and *then* goes on his way.

that   See **who, which, that**.

this here, that there   The words *here* and *there* are unnecessary after *this* and *that*.

Example
This [not *this here*] figure of speech is a simile, but *that* [not *that there*] one is a metaphor.

try and   In informal situations, *try and* is often used instead of *try to*. In formal situations, *try to* should be used.

Informal
Try and draw inferences from clues in the story.
Formal
Try to draw inferences from clues in the story.

use to, used to   Be sure to add the *d* to *use*.

Example
Many different peoples around the world *used to* [not *use to*] tell myths and folk tales orally.

well   See **good, well**.

when, where   Do not use *when* or *where* to begin a definition.

Nonstandard
Onomatopoeia is *when* you use a word whose sound imitates or suggests its meaning.
Standard
Onomatopoeia is the use of a word whose sound imitates or suggests its meaning.
Nonstandard
A pun is *where* there is a play on words.
Standard
A pun is a play on words.

where   Do not use *where* for *that*.

Nonstandard
Roxy read *where* James Thurber grew up in Columbus, Ohio.
Standard
Roxy read *that* James Thurber grew up in Columbus, Ohio.

who, which, that   *Who* refers to persons only. *Which* refers to things only. *That* may refer to either persons or things.

Examples
The poet *who* wrote "Cynthia in the Snow" was Gwendolyn Brooks.

The strange land, *which* was called Narnia, was ruled by the White Witch.

A writer *that* Jay enjoyed was Lensey Namioka.

One poem *that* uses an ingenious shape is "Concrete Cat."

who, whom   *Who* is used as the subject of a verb or as a predicate nominative. *Whom* is used as an object of a verb or as an object of a preposition. The use of *who* or *whom* in a subordinate clause depends on how the pronoun functions within the clause.

Examples

Who wrote "The Sneetches"?

Armand, *who* is Jerry's older brother, wants to take Sally to a dance.

The writer *whom* Carlos liked best was Bill Cosby.

Of *whom* were the children jealous in Bradbury's story?

whose, who's *Whose* is the possessive form of *who*. *Who's* is a contraction for *who is* or *who has*.

Examples

Whose son is Jody?

Who's the true hero of the tale, Ali Baba or Morgiana?

would of See **could of.**

your, you're *Your* is the possessive form of *you*. *You're* is the contraction of *you are*.

Examples

Is *your* class putting on a play this spring?

You're a Ray Bradbury fan, aren't you?

Part 8: Grammar Reference Guide

SUBJECT-VERB AGREEMENT

A verb should agree with its subject in number—singular or plural.

The **waves were** not big now.
—Ashabranner, "The Most Vulnerable People" (p. 424)

The **slaves were** right about Dr. Thompson's intention.
—Petry, "Harriet Tubman" (p. 24)

Among these people **were** many natural **scientists.**
—Lauber, "Volcano" (p. 442)

If a **family wants** to get through the day with a minimum of noise and open wounds, the **parents have** to impose order on the domestic scene.
—Cosby, "Fatherhood" (p. 454)

NOUNS

A **noun** is a word used to name a person, place, thing, or idea. Nouns can function in sentences as subjects, direct objects, indirect objects, objects of prepositions, predicate nominatives, and appositives.

The **king's knights** were all **cowards** who hid under their **beds** whenever the **dragon** came in **sight,** so they were of no **use** to the **king** at all.
—Gardner, "Dragon, Dragon" (p. 167)

Dian Fossey studied the **behavior** of **Coco** and **Pucker,** orphan **gorillas.**

To fling my **arms** wide
In some **place** of the **sun,**
To whirl and to dance
Till the white **day** is done.
—Hughes, "Dream Variations" (p. 350)

PRONOUNS

A **pronoun** is a word used in place of a noun or of more than one noun. **Personal pronouns** refer to the person speaking (first person), the person spoken to (second person), or the person, place, or thing spoken about (third person).

	Singular		
	Subject Form	Object Form	Possessive Form
First Person	I	me	my, mine
Second Person	you	you	your, yours
Third Person	he	him	his
	she	her	her, hers
	it	it	its

Grammar Reference Guide 775

Subject-Verb Agreement: See *Teaching Resources B,* page 83. For practice with subject-verb agreement using pronouns, see Pronoun Agreement, *Teaching Resources D,* page 66.

Nouns: See *Teaching Resources A,* page 9. For review of parts of speech, see Parts of Speech, *Teaching Resources A,* page 69.

Pronouns: See *Teaching Resources A,* page 42.

Verbs: See *Teaching Resources A,* page 27. See also Verb Phrases, *Teaching Resources B,* page 40.

Handbook for Revision

	Plural		
	Subject Form	Object Form	Possessive Form
First Person	we	us	our, ours
Second Person	you	you	your, yours
Third Person	they	them	their, theirs

They stopped running and stood in the great jungle that covered Venus, that grew and never stopped growing, tumultuously, even as **you** watched **it.**
—Bradbury, "All Summer in a Day" (p. 201)

"Pray that **we** reach the refugee camp," the woman told **him.**
—Ashabranner, "The Most Vulnerable People" (p. 426)

He licked at our hands and, staggering, fell, but got up again.
—Thurber, "Snapshot of a Dog" (p. 450)

A **reflexive pronoun** ends in *-self* or *-selves* and refers back to the subject of a verb.

On the other side of the wardrobe, Lucy finds **herself** in Narnia.

A **relative pronoun** is used to introduce adjective and noun clauses.

It was difficult enough to find the Three Gray Sisters, **who** lived near the Garden of the Hesperides.
—Graves, "Perseus" (p. 570)

At this signal, you are to split open your jars with the knives with **which** you will have been provided.
—Gille, "Ali Baba and the Forty Thieves" (p. 611)

The catastrophe **that** might take his father had made it motherless.
—Rawlings, "Jody's Discovery" (p. 139)

An **interrogative pronoun** is used to begin questions.

who knows if the moon's
a balloon, coming out of a keen city
in the sky—filled with pretty people?
—Cummings, "who knows if the moon's" (p. 314)

"**What**'s the matter?" I asked.
—Cormier, "President Cleveland, Where Are You?" (p. 182)

A **demonstrative pronoun** is used to point out a specific person or thing.

"Well, well, **this** is a fine present indeed," said the old man.
—Uchida, "Momotaro: Boy-of-the-Peach" (p. 621)

These he knew because there were some raspberry bushes in the park and he and Terry were always picking and eating them when they biked past.
—Paulsen, from *Hatchet* (p. 100)

An **indefinite pronoun** is used to refer to people or things in general.

Dickon's not like **anyone** in the world.
—Hanalis, *The Secret Garden* (p. 507)

VERBS

A **verb** is a word that expresses action or a state of being. An **action verb** tells what action someone or something is performing.

Wandering wolves **caught** it, **threw** their long noses to the moon, and **howled** an answering cry.
—Baker, "Where the Buffaloes Begin" (p. 259)

A **linking verb** helps to make a statement by serving as a link between two words (for example, subject with predicate nominative or predicate adjective). The most commonly used linking verbs are forms of the verb *be.*

This monster **was** insatiable.
—Baumann, "Nana Miriam" (p. 634)

He never **grows** old.
—Erdoes and Ortiz, "Glooscap Fights the Water Monster" (p. 559)

A **helping verb** is a verb that can be added to another verb to make a verb phrase.

The people of the neighboring states, who **were living** almost like savages, were very jealous when they saw the prosperity of the Toltecs.
—Cruse, "Quetzalcoatl" (p. 579)

776 Handbook for Revision

ADJECTIVES

An **adjective** is a word used to modify a noun or pronoun. Adjectives tell *what kind, which one,* or *how many.*

> But McBean was quite **wrong.** I'm quite **happy** to say
> That the Sneetches got really quite **smart** on **that** day.
> —Dr. Seuss, "The Sneetches" (p. 291)

The articles *the, a,* and *an* are adjectives. *An* is used before a word beginning with a vowel sound or with an unsounded *h.*

ADVERBS

An **adverb** is a word used to modify a verb, an adjective, or another adverb. Adverbs tell *how, when, where,* and *to what extent.*

> Let me put it **more clearly,** since no one will believe that a girl of thirteen feels herself **quite** alone in the world, nor is it so.
> —Frank, from *The Diary of a Young Girl* (p. 394)

PREPOSITIONS

A **preposition** is a word that shows the relationship of a noun or a pronoun to some other word in the sentence. Prepositions are almost always followed by nouns or pronouns. A group of words that begins with a preposition and ends with a noun or pronoun is called a **prepositional phrase.**

> The look **in Pierre's eyes** stopped him.
> —Reynolds, "A Secret for Two" (p. 161)

> They went **to sea in a Sieve,** they did.
> **In a Sieve** they went **to sea:**
> **In spite of all their friends could say,**
> **On a winter's morn, on a stormy day,**
> **In a Sieve** they went **to sea!**
> —Lear, "The Jumblies" (p. 295)

The two dogs eventually worked their way **to the middle of the car tracks,** and **after a while** two or three streetcars were held up **by the fight.**
—Thurber, "Snapshot of a Dog" (p. 448)

CONJUNCTIONS

A **conjunction** is a word used to join words or groups of words. **Coordinating conjunctions** join equal parts of a sentence or similar groups of words.

> That winter the elbows began to crack **and** whole chunks of green began to fall off.
> —Soto, "The Jacket" (p. 39)

Correlative conjunctions are used in pairs to join similar words or groups of words.

> **Both** Tezcatlipoca **and** Quetzalcoatl were Toltec gods.

A **subordinating conjunction** is used to introduce a clause that has less importance than the main clause in a sentence.

> I was twelve years old **when** I made my first trip to the jungle with my father.
> —Nhuong, "The Land I Lost" (p. 413)

A **conjunctive adverb** is an adverb used as a conjunction to connect ideas.

> **Besides,** no one knew exactly what impressed the baby dragons as they struggled from their shells in search of their lifetime partners.
> —McCaffrey, "The Smallest Dragonboy" (p. 81)

INTERJECTIONS

An **interjection** is a word that expresses emotion and has no grammatical relation to other words in the sentence.

> "**Oh,** Mr. Tumnus—I'm so sorry to stop you, and I do love that tune—but really, I must go home."
> —Lewis, "Mr. Tumnus" (p. 15)

> Mary was silent for a moment. Then she said, "I probably shouldn't tell you this, but he didn't steal that watch, Sara."
> "**Huh!**"
> —Byars, *The Summer of the Swans* (p. 690)

PHRASES

A **phrase** is a group of words that does not contain a subject and a verb.

Handbook for Revision

Adjectives: See *Teaching Resources A,* page 57.

Adverbs: See *Teaching Resources A,* page 60.

Prepositions: See Prepositions and Prepositional Phrases, *Teaching Resources A,* page 99. See also Identifying Phrases, *Teaching Resources B,* page 97.

Interjections: See Conjunctions and Interjections, *Teaching Resources A,* page 114.

Phrases: See Identifying Phrases, *Teaching Resources B,* page 97. See also Verb Phrases, *Teaching Resources B,* page 40. See Using Phrases in Sentences, *Teaching Resources C,* page 83.

Grammar Reference Guide

Capitalization: See *Teaching Resources A,* page 12.

A **prepositional phrase** is a group of words that begins with a preposition and ends with a noun or pronoun.

in the story   **to** the lake
outside the house   **with** them

An **appositive** is a noun or pronoun placed beside another noun or pronoun to identify or explain it. An **appositive phrase** is made up of an appositive and its modifiers.

"We have a report of a missing child in the Cass section—**ten-year-old Charlie Godfrey**."
—Byars, *The Summer of the Swans* (p. 691)

A **participial phrase** consists of a participle and its complements or modifiers. The entire participial phrase acts as an adjective.

Bad dogs **barking loud**
Big ghosts in a cloud
Life doesn't frighten me at all.
—Angelou, "Life Doesn't Frighten Me" (p. 303)

Now Maibon began to be truly distressed, not only for the toothless baby, the calfless cow, the fruitless tree, and the hen **sitting desperately on her eggs**, but for himself as well.
—Alexander, "The Stone" (p. 213)

The mighty voice rolled out upon the valley, each flutelike bark **echoing from slope to slope**.
—Armstrong, from *Sounder* (p. 125)

His tongue, **stained with berry juice**, stuck to the roof of his mouth and he stared at the bear.
—Paulsen, from *Hatchet* (p. 100)

An **infinitive phrase** consists of an infinitive together with its modifiers and complements. The entire phrase can be used as a noun, an adjective, or an adverb.

Monday was the best day **to buy the cards.** [infinitive phrase used as an adjective modifying *day*]
—Cormier, "President Cleveland, Where Are You?" (p. 181)

CLAUSES

A **clause** is a group of words that has a subject and a verb. An **independent clause** expresses a complete thought and can stand by itself as a sentence.

The rattler struck him from under the grapevine without warning.
—Rawlings, "Jody's Discovery" (p. 131)

A **subordinate clause** does not express a complete thought and cannot stand by itself as a sentence.

When the woman opened the door, she did not seem at all surprised to see her.
—Petry, "Harriet Tubman" (p. 28)

Part 9: Mechanics
- Capitalization
- Punctuation
- Letters

CAPITALIZATION

1. FIRST WORDS

▮ **Capitalize the first word of every sentence.**

Examples
My clothes have failed me.
—Soto, "The Jacket" (p. 36)

When Tom reached the little isolated frame schoolhouse, he strode in briskly, with the manner of one who had come with all honest speed.
—Twain, from *The Adventures of Tom Sawyer* (p. 48)

▮ **Capitalize the first word of a direct quotation when the word begins with a capital letter in the original. If the writer has not** used a capital letter, do not capitalize the first word of the quotation.

Examples
Penny shouted, "**G**it back! Hold the dogs!"
—Rawlings, "Jody's Discovery" (p. 131)

"**I**t's only just round the corner," said the faun, "**a**nd there'll be a roaring fire—and toast—and sardines—and cake."
—Lewis, "Mr. Tumnus" (p. 13)

▌ Traditionally, the first word in a line of poetry is capitalized, although some writers do not follow this rule for reasons of style.

Examples
The sea is a hungry dog,
Giant and gray.
He rolls on the beach all day.
—Reeves, "The Sea" (p. 335)

Abuelito who throws coins like rain
and asks who loves him
who is dough and feathers . . .
—Cisneros, "Abuelito Who" (p. 345)

2. THE PRONOUN *I*

▌ Capitalize the pronoun *I*.

Example
This here phizzog—somebody handed it to you
—am **I** right?
—Sandburg, "Phizzog" (p. 368)

3. PROPER NOUNS AND PROPER ADJECTIVES

▌ A *proper noun* names a particular person, place, or thing. A *proper adjective* is formed from a proper noun. Capitalize proper nouns and proper adjectives.

Examples
| Jamaica | Spain | Japan | Poland |
| Jamaican | Spanish | Japanese | Polish |

▌ In proper nouns consisting of two or more words, do not capitalize articles (*a, an, the*), short prepositions (those with fewer than five letters, such as *at, of, for, with*), and coordinating conjunctions (*and, but, for, nor, or, so, yet*).

Examples
San **A**ntonio	**I**sle of **M**an
Caribbean **S**ea	**P**resident **C**linton
Mayor **R**uiz	**T**ruth or **C**onsequences

If you are not sure whether to capitalize a word, check in an up-to-date dictionary.

4. NAMES OF PEOPLE

▌ Capitalize the names of people. Note that some names may contain more than one capital letter.

Examples
Blanche **H**analis	**S**cott **O**'**D**ell
L. **M**. **M**ontgomery	**N**ikki **G**iovanni
Leroy **V**. **Q**uintana	**H**arriet **T**ubman

5. GEOGRAPHICAL NAMES

▌ Capitalize geographical names, such as towns, cities, counties, townships, states, regions, countries, continents, islands, mountains, bodies of water, parks, roads, highways, and streets.

Examples
San **F**rancisco	**A**lbemarle **S**ound	**I**nterstate 90
North **A**merica	**C**atalina **I**sland	**D**ade **C**ounty
Panama **C**anal	**L**ake **H**uron	**T**hird **A**venue
Michigan	**R**oute 110	**C**osta **R**ica

▌ Note that words such as *south, east,* and *northwest* are *not* capitalized when they indicate direction.

Examples
east of the Rockies   northwest of the airport
west of Tulsa   southeast of the mall

6. ORGANIZATIONS

▌ Capitalize the names of organizations, teams, businesses, institutions, buildings, and government bodies.

Proper Nouns and Proper Adjectives: For proper nouns, see Nouns, *Teaching Resources A,* page 9. See also Adjectives, *Teaching Resources A,* page 57. For practice with capitalizing proper nouns and proper adjectives, see *Teaching Resources B,* page 55.

Historical Events: For practice with capitalization, see Capitalization, *Teaching Resources A,* page 12.

Examples

Chicago Bulls	Girl Scouts
Willis Intermediate School	General Electric
	Holiday Inn
Regent Hotel	Treasury Department
University of Texas	Empire State Building

7. HISTORICAL EVENTS

▌ Capitalize the names of historical events and periods, special events, and calendar items.

Examples

New Deal	Middle Ages	Flag Day
Stone Age	Wednesday	Tulip Festival
Earth Day	World Series	Korean War

8. NATIONALITIES, RACES, AND RELIGIONS

▌ Capitalize the names of nationalities, races, and peoples.

Examples

Chippewa	Bantu	Turkish
Aztec	African American	Navajo
Dominican	Micronesian	Vietnamese

▌ Capitalize the names of religions and their followers, holy days, sacred writings, and specific deities.

Examples

Islam	the Talmud	the Koran
Lutheran	Taoism	Pentecost
Good Friday	Presbyterian	Purim
the Bible	Lent	Hindu
Judaism	Allah	
Lakshmi	Potlatch	

9. BRAND NAMES

▌ Capitalize the brand names of business products. Do not capitalize the noun that often follows a brand name.

Examples

Chevrolet cars	**Canon** cameras
Ritz crackers	**Tide** detergent

10. PARTICULAR PLACES, THINGS, AND EVENTS

▌ Capitalize the names of ships, trains, airplanes, spacecraft, monuments, buildings, awards, planets, and any other particular places, things, or events.

Examples

Voyager 2	Tower of London	*Monitor*
Nobel Prize	Silver Crescent	*Concorde*
Uranus	*Pinta*	Niagara Falls

11. SPECIFIC COURSES, LANGUAGES

▌ Do *not* capitalize the names of school subjects, except for languages and for course names followed by a number.

Examples

chemistry	history	mathematics
biology	Spanish	Science 2

12. TITLES OF PEOPLE

▌ Capitalize a title belonging to a particular person when it comes before a person's name.

Examples

President Suharto	Professor Stern
General Powell	Principal Larson
Ms. Oates	Dr. Rao

▌ Do not capitalize a title used alone or following a person's name, especially if the title is preceded by *a* or *the*.

Examples

Rosa Santos, **m**ayor of Galveston
the **g**overnor's **m**ansion
a **d**uke's title

▌ Capitalize a word showing a family relationship when the word is used with a person's name but *not* when it is preceded by a possessive.

Examples

Aunt Pia	**U**ncle Roger	their **a**unt Dot

Handbook for Revision

13. TITLES OF LITERARY AND OTHER CREATIVE WORKS

▌ **Capitalize the first and last words and all important words in titles of books, magazines, newspapers, short poems, stories, historical documents, movies, television programs, works of art, and musical compositions.**

Unimportant words within titles are articles (*a, an, the*), short prepositions (fewer than five letters, such as *at, of, for, to, from, with*) and coordinating conjunctions (*and, but, for, nor, or, so, yet*).

Examples
The Summer of the Swans
The Secret Garden
"Life Doesn't Frighten Me"
"Nancy"
"Nana Miriam"
"Volcano"
Newsweek
Beauty and the Beast

▌ **The word *the* written before a title is capitalized only when it is the first word of a title.**

Examples
"The Jacket"   *Julie of the Wolves*

PUNCTUATION

1. END MARKS

▌ **End marks—*periods, question marks,* and *exclamation points*—are used to indicate the purpose of a sentence. (A period is also used at the end of many abbreviations.) Use a period to end a statement (or declarative sentence).**

Example
He was fourteen, three years older than I, and a freshman at Monument High School.
—Cormier, "President Cleveland, Where Are You?" (p. 181)

▌ **A question (or interrogative sentence) is followed by a question mark.**

Examples
Did your father ever tell you about Misselthwaite Manor?
—Hanalis, *The Secret Garden* (p. 484)

"Then why did the king of Tyre not save her?"
—Graves, "Perseus" (p. 571)

You'll not repeat what I tell you?
—Hanalis, *The Secret Garden* (p. 491)

▌ **Use an exclamation point after an exclamation.**

Examples
"My goodness! What a great peach!"
—Uchida, "Momotaro: Boy-of-the-Peach" (p. 621)

"Bless you!" cried the king.
—Gardner, "Dragon, Dragon" (p. 169)

"Pa! You'll bleed to death!"
—Rawlings, "Jody's Discovery" (p. 134)

▌ **An imperative sentence may be followed by either a period or an exclamation point.**

Examples
Hold it firm with one hand, push the earth around it, an' tamp it down.
—Hanalis, *The Secret Garden* (p. 520)

"Well, don't wait around here!" cried the boy savagely.
—Bradbury, "All Summer in a Day" (p. 198)

▌ **Use a period after an abbreviation.**

Examples
Personal Names: M. R. Cox
Titles Used with Names: Rev., Dr., Mr., Mrs., Ms.
States: N.M., S.D., N.C., Ala.
Time of Day: A.M., P.M.
Years: B.C., A.D.
Addresses: St., Ave.
Organizations and Companies: Co., Inc.
Units of Measure: lb., oz., in., ft., yd., mi.

▌ **No periods are used in abbreviations with states when the zip code is included.**

Example
NC 28211

End Marks: See *Teaching Resources A,* page 131.

Mechanics

Commas: Conventional Uses: See Commas, *Teaching Resources B,* page 9.

- Abbreviations in the metric system are often written without periods: for example, km for kilometer, kg for kilogram, ml for milliliter. Abbreviations for government agencies and international organizations and some other frequently used abbreviations are written without periods: for example, NBA, NAACP, FBI, PTA.

2. COMMAS: CONVENTIONAL USES

- Use a comma to separate items in dates and addresses.

  Examples
  I wrote to Darlene on June 26, 1995.
  I sent the letter to 450 Springs Blvd., Scottsdale, AZ 85258.

- Notice that a comma also separates the final item in a date and in an address from the words that follow it. A comma does *not* separate the month from the day, the house number from the street name, or the state name from the ZIP code.

- Use a comma after the salutation of a friendly letter and after the closing of any letter.

  Examples
  Dear Rev. Sanchez,   My dear Gloria,
  Sincerely yours,   Love,

For other uses of commas, see **Part 5** (pp. 765–766).

3. SEMICOLONS

- Use a semicolon between independent clauses that are closely related in thought and that are not joined by *and, but, or, nor, for, so,* or *yet.*

  Example
  The maize crops were more abundant than they had ever been before; the fruits were larger and more plentiful.
  —Cruse, "Quetzalcoatl" (p. 578)

4. COLONS

- Use a colon before a list of items, especially after expressions like *as follows* and *the following.*

  Example
  Marcia's favorite writers were the following: Maya Angelou, Pat Mora, Robert Cormier, and Elizabeth Enright.

- Use a colon in certain conventional situations: between the hour and the minute, between chapter and verse in a Biblical citation, and after the salutation of a business letter.

  Examples
  10:30 A.M.   Exodus 4:10   Dear Dr. Long:

5. ITALICS

- When writing or typing, indicate italics by underlining. Use italics for titles of books, plays, periodicals, films, television programs, long musical compositions, ships, aircraft, and spacecraft.

  Examples
  BOOK: *Island of the Blue Dolphins*
  PLAY: *Carousel*
  PERIODICAL: *People*
  FILM: *The Last Emperor*
  TELEVISION PROGRAM: *Safari*
  LONG MUSICAL COMPOSITION: *A Little Night Music*
  SHIP: *Queen Mary*
  AIRCRAFT: *Spirit of St. Louis*
  SPACECRAFT: *Discovery*

- Use italics for words, letters, and figures referred to as such.

  Examples
  All right should always be written as two words.

  Double the *p* and add *-ed* to form the past participle of the verb *hop.*

  Many people think that *7* is a lucky number.

  Vaca is Spanish for cow.

6. QUOTATION MARKS

■ **Use quotation marks to enclose a direct quotation—a person's exact words.**

Example
"Maibon, it's the fault of that stone!" wailed his wife.
— Alexander, "The Stone" (p. 212)

■ **Do not use quotation marks to enclose an indirect quotation—a rewording of a direct quotation.**

Example
I wondered what was happening to me, because I did not know whether to laugh or cry.
— Cormier, "President Cleveland, Where Are You?" (p. 183)

■ **Begin a direct quotation with a capital letter.**

Example
Sara looked down into his eyes and said, "**O**h, come on," and drew him to his feet.
— Byars, *The Summer of the Swans* (p. 659)

■ **When an expression identifying the speaker interrupts a quoted sentence, the second part of the quotation begins with a small letter.**

Example
"Okay," I said, "what do *you* want for breakfast?"
— Cosby, "Fatherhood" (p. 454)

■ **A direct quotation is set off from the rest of the sentence by a comma or by a question mark or an exclamation point.**

Examples
"Janice Gordon has a bike," I reminded her.
— Berry, "Becky and the Wheels-and-Brake Boys" (p. 226)

"Did he die?" asked Ezinma.
— Achebe, "Why Tortoise's Shell Is Not Smooth" (p. 604)

"Charlie!" she shouted with all her might.
— Byars, *The Summer of the Swans* (p. 704)

■ **Commas and periods are always placed inside closing quotation marks.**

Examples
"I am going back to my country," Quetzalcoatl answered.
— Cruse, "Quetzalcoatl" (p. 581)

At last he said, "I want to go home."
— Ashabranner, "The Most Vulnerable People"

■ **Question marks and exclamation points are placed inside closing quotation marks if the quotation is a question or an exclamation. Otherwise, they are placed outside.**

Examples
"A girl from the North Side?" I asked, incredulous.
— Cormier, "President Cleveland, Where Are You?" (p. 186)

"Babes don't give orders to candidates around here, babe!"
— McCaffrey, "The Smallest Dragonboy" (p. 88)

Did you like Edward Lear's "The Jumblies"?

Let's all read "Habits of the Hippopotamus"!

■ **When you write dialogue (conversation), begin a new paragraph every time the speaker changes, and enclose each speaker's words in quotation marks.**

Example
   The cobbler scratched his chin and considered it. "It's not enough," he said at last. "It's a good enough kingdom, you understand, but it's too much responsibility."
   "Take it or leave it," the king said.
   "I'll leave it," said the cobbler. And he shrugged and went home.
— Gardner, "Dragon, Dragon" (pp. 168–169)

■ **When a quotation consists of several sentences, place quotation marks at the beginning and at the end of the whole quotation.**

Example
"Why, it is she that has got all Narnia under her thumb. It's she that makes it always winter. Always winter and never Christmas—think of that!"
— Lewis, "Mr. Tumnus" (p. 16)

Quotation Marks: See Punctuation and Capitalization in Quotations, *Teaching Resources C,* page 53. See also End Marks, *Teaching Resources A,* page 131.

Mechanics 783

Apostrophes—Possessive Case: See Punctuation 3: Apostrophes, *Teaching Resources B,* page 143.

- **Use single quotation marks to enclose a quotation within a quotation.**

  Example
  Donna reminded us, "At the end of the play, Colin's exact words are, 'When I was at Oxford, I asked you to marry me.' "

- **Use quotation marks to enclose titles of short works, such as short stories, short poems, articles, songs, episodes of television programs, and chapters and other parts of books.**

  Examples
  SHORT STORY: "Dragon, Dragon"
  SHORT POEM: "Beach Stones"
  ARTICLE: "Splendors of Coral"
  SONG: "Yankee Doodle"
  TV EPISODE: "Nest of Vipers"

7. APOSTROPHES

POSSESSIVE CASE

- **To form the possessive of a singular noun, add an apostrophe and an *s*. Add only the apostrophe to a proper noun ending in an *s* sound if the addition of '*s* would make the name awkward to pronounce.**

  Examples
  the **sun's** rays   **Roberta's** bike
  a **bird's** wings   Mr. **Rodriguez'** class

- **To form the possessive of a plural noun that does not end in *s*, add an apostrophe and an *s*.**

  Examples
  the **children's** toys   **women's** hats

- **To form the possessive of a plural noun ending in *s*, add only the apostrophe.**

  Examples
  the **trees'** leaves   the **jars'** lids

- **Do not use an apostrophe with possessive personal pronouns.**

  Incorrect
  Are these hats **our's**?

  Correct
  Are these hats **ours**?

- **To form the possessive of some indefinite pronouns, add an apostrophe and an *s*.**

  Examples
  Everyone's vote counts.
  Someone's books are on that table.

CONTRACTIONS

- **Use an apostrophe to show where letters or numerals have been left out in a contraction.**

  Examples
  We're here. [We are]   **I'm** not sure. [I am]
  Let's go. [Let us]   **He'd** arrived. [He had]
  in the **'90s** [1990s]   **You'll** see. [You will]

PLURALS

- **Use an apostrope and an *s* to form the plurals of letters, numerals, signs, and of words referred to as words.**

  Examples
  That word has four *s***'s**.
  Write your *4***'s** more clearly, please.
  Use *@***'s** on the invoice.
  Take out some of the *and***'s** in that sentence.

8. HYPHENS

- **Use a hyphen to divide a word at the end of a line.**

  Example
  Many of Anne McCaffrey's books are **available** in foreign languages.

- **Divide a word only between syllables.**

  Incorrect
  Rawlings' *The Yearling* became a very succe-ssful movie.

  Correct
  Rawlings' *The Yearling* became a very **success-ful** movie.

- **Do not divide a one-syllable word.**

Incorrect
Nonfiction deals with real people and events: fa-cts are not changed.

Correct
Nonfiction deals with real people and events: **facts** are not changed.

▮ **Do not divide a word so that one letter stands alone.**

Incorrect
Language that appeals to the sense is called i-magery.

Correct
Language that appeals to the senses is called **im-agery.**

▮ **Use a hyphen with compound numbers from *twenty-one* to *ninety-nine* and with fractions used as modifiers.**

Examples
fifty-two cards   a **two-thirds** vote

LETTERS

1. PERSONAL AND SOCIAL LETTERS

▮ **Follow the format below for a personal or social letter.**

                    Your Address
                    Today's Date

Dear _____,

_____

_____

_____

             _____,
             (Your Signature)

2. BUSINESS LETTERS

▮ **Use either of the two formats below for a business letter.**

Block Style
Heading (Your Address and Today's Date)

Inside Address (Name and Address of the Person or Company You Are Writing)

(Salutation):

_____

_____

_____.

_____

_____

_____.

(Closing),
(Your Signature and Typed Name)

Modified Block Style
                Heading (Your Address
                and Today's Date)

Inside Address (Name and Address of the Person or Company You Are Writing)

(Salutation):

_____

_____

_____.

_____

_____

_____.

              (Closing),
              (Your Signature and Typed Name)

Glossary

The words listed in this Glossary are found in the selections in this book. Use this Glossary as you would a dictionary—to look up unfamiliar words. Strictly speaking, the word *glossary* means a collection of technical, obscure, or foreign words found in a certain field of work. The words in this Glossary are not "technical, obscure, or foreign," but are those that might present difficulty as you read the selections in this book.

Many words in the English language have several meanings. This Glossary gives the meanings that apply to the words as they are used in the selections in the book. Words closely related in form and meaning are generally listed together in one entry (**arrogance** and **arrogant**), and the definition is given for the first form. Regular adverbs (ending in *-ly*) are defined in their adjective form; the adverb form is shown at the end of the definition.

The following abbreviations are used:

adj., adjective *n.*, noun
adv., adverb *v.*, verb

For more information about the words in this Glossary, consult a dictionary.

A

abrupt (ə·brupt′) *adj.* **1.** Sudden; hasty. **2.** Rude or curt, as in speech.
abundant (ə·bun′dənt) *adj.* Existing in plentiful supply.
accede (ak·sēd′) *v.* To give consent or agreement; say yes.
accommodation (ə·kom′ə·dā′shən) *n.* A willingness to help or oblige.
accompany (ə·kum′pə·nē) *v.* To come or go along with. —**accompaniment** *n.*
accord (ə·kôrd′) *v.* To give as due or earned. —**of one's own accord** By one's own choice.
accumulation (ə·kyōōm′yə·lā′shən) *n.* A collecting or gathering together.
accurate (ak′yər·it) *adj.* Making no error; exact; true. —**accurately** *adv.*
acquaintance (ə·kwān′təns) *n.* A person with whom one is slightly familiar.
acquire (ə·kwīr) *v.* To come into possession of; to get.
adjacent (ə·jā′sənt) *adj.* Lying near or close by.
adjoin (ə·join) *v.* To be next to. —**adjoining** *adj.*
affected (ə·fek′tid) *adj.* Not natural; artificial.
aggravate (ag′rə·vāt′) *v.* **1.** To make

worse, more serious, more unpleasant. **2.** To make angry; annoy.
aghast (ə·gast′) *adj.* Shocked; horrified.
agony (ag′ə·nē) *n.* A terrible suffering of body or mind.
ailment (āl′mənt) *n.* An illness.
albeit (ôl·bē′it) *conj.* Even though.
alert (ə·lurt′) **1.** *v.* To warn or prepare, as if for danger or attack. **2.** *adj.* Very watchful and ready.
alleviate (a·lē′vē·āt′) *v.* To make lighter or easier to bear; relieve.
aloof (ə·loof′) *adj.* Cool or distant in manner or action; unsympathetic.
altitude (al′tə·tood) *n.* Height.
amateur (am′ə·choor) *n.* A person who does something without sound training or skill.
ambush (am′boosh) **1.** *n.* A concealed place where troops, or others, lie hidden to attack. **2.** *v.* To hide in order to attack.
anchorage (ang′kər·ij) *n.* Something that gives support or steadiness.
anguish (ang′gwish) *n.* Great suffering of mind or body; agony.
animated (an′ə·mā′tid) *adj.* Having spirit or zest; lively. —**animatedly** *adv.*
animosity (an′ə·mos′ə·tē) *n.* Strong dislike or hatred.
antic (an′tik) *n.* *(usually plural)* A prank or funny act.
anvil (an′vil) *n.* A heavy block of iron or steel on which heated metal is hammered into shape.
apparatus (ap′ə·ra′təs) *n.* All the devices or equipment for a particular use.
apparent (ə·par′ənt) *adj.* Obvious.
application (ap′li·kā′shən) *n.* **1.** Something put on, especially a medicine or treatment. **2.** A formal request.
arrogance (ar′ə·gəns) *n.* Too much pride and too little regard for others. — **arrogant** *adj.*
aspire (ə·spīr′) *v.* To have great hope or ambition for something; seek.
assent (ə·sent′) *v.* To agree or consent.
assortment (ə·sôrt′mənt) *n.* A collection or group of various things; variety.
astound (ə·stound′) *v.* To stun with amazement.
attire (ə·tir′) *n.* Clothing.
avenge (ə·venj′) *v.* To get revenge for.
avid (av′id) *adj.* **1.** Enthusiastic; eager. **2.** Greedy. —**avidly** *adv.*
awe (ô) *n.* A feeling of fear and wonder, as at the size or power of something.
awry (ə·rī′) *adj.* **1.** Leaning or turned to one side. **2.** Not right; amiss.

B

baleful (bāl′fəl) *adj.* Evil or threatening.
banish (ban′ish) *v.* To drive away; get rid of; dismiss.
bawl (bôl) *v.* **1.** To call out loudly; shout. **2.** To cry or sob noisily.

a	add	i	it	oo	took	oi	oil
ā	ace	ī	ice	oo	pool	ou	pout
â	care	o	odd	u	up	ng	ring
ä	palm	ō	open	û	burn	th	thin
e	end	ô	order	yoo	fuse	th	this
ē	equal					zh	vision

ə = { a in *above*, e in *sicken*, i in *possible*, o in *melon*, u in *circus* }

Glossary 787

beacon (bē′kən) *n.* Any light for warning or guiding.
beckon (bek′ən) *v.* To summon or signal by a movement of the hand or head.
bellow (bel′ō) *v.* To utter a loud, hollow cry.
betray (bi·trā′) *v.* **1.** To fail, desert, or be unfaithful to. **2.** To give away; disclose.
bewilder (bi·wil′dər) *v.* To puzzle or confuse.
billow (bil′ō) *v.* To rise or roll in waves; swell.
bison (bī′sən) *n.* A large wild animal related to the ox. The North American bison is called a buffalo.
blistering (blis′tər·ing) *adj.* Extremely strong or intense.
bloat (blōt) *v.* To puff up; swell.
blurt *v.* To say abruptly or without thinking.
bog 1. *n.* Wet and spongy ground, such as a swamp. **2.** *v.* To sink or cause to sink in, as if in a bog.
boisterous (bois′tər·əs) *adj.* Noisy and wild. —**boisterously** *adv.*
brandish (bran′dish) *v.* To wave triumphantly or threateningly.
brier (brī′ər) *n.* A prickly bush or shrub.
brisk *adj.* Acting or moving quickly; lively. —**briskly** *adv.*
brood *n.* All of the young of the same mother.
buffet (buf′it) *v.* To strike over and over.
bulbous (bul′bəs) *adj.* Shaped like a bulb.

C

cajole (kə·jōl′) *v.* To coax or persuade by flattery or deceit.
callous (kal′əs) *adj.* **1.** Thickened and hardened. **2.** Unfeeling; hardhearted.
candidate (kan′də·dāt′) *n.* A person who seeks, or is proposed for, an office or honor.
canvass (kan′vəs) *v.* To examine, discuss, or debate.
carcass (kar′kəs) *n.* The dead body of an animal.
cascade (kas·kād′) *n.* **1.** A small waterfall. **2.** Something that looks like a waterfall.
casual (kazh′ōō·əl) *adj.* **1.** Happening by chance; not planned. **2.** Informal and relaxed.
catastrophe (kə·tas′trə·fē) *n.* A sudden and widespread misfortune or disaster.
caustic (kôs′tik) *adj.* **1.** Capable of eating or burning away living tissue. **2.** Sarcastic; biting.
cautious (kô′shəs) *adj.* Careful not to take chances or make mistakes. —**cautiously** *adv.*
cavern (kav′ərn) *n.* A large cave.
ceaseless (sēs′lis) *adj.* Going on without pause; continual. —**ceaselessly** *adv.*
chastise (chas′tīz) *v.* To punish, scold, or condemn.
chide (chīd) *v.* To scold mildly.
clamber (klam′bər) *v.* To climb up or down with effort, using both hands and feet.
clamor (klam′ər) *n.* A loud and contin-

uous noise, especially a loud protest or outcry.

commend (kə·mend′) *v.* To speak highly of; praise.

commitment (kə·mit′mənt) *n.* A pledge; promise.

commotion (kə·mō′shən) *n.* Great confusion; excitement; disturbance.

compassion (kəm·pash′ən) *n.* Pity for the suffering or distress of another and the desire to help. —**compassionate** *adj.*

compensation (kom′pən·sā′shən) *n.* Something paid, given, or done to balance something else.

complement (kom′plə·mənt) **1.** *n.* Something that completes or perfects. **2.** *v.* To make complete.

complexion (kəm·plek′shən) *n.* The color and appearance of the skin, especially of the face.

compose (kəm·pōz′) *v.* **1.** To make up; form. **2.** To create. **3.** To make calm.

compound (kom·pound′) *v.* To mix; put together.

compulsion (kəm·pul′shən) *n.* An irresistible, sometimes irrational, urge.

comrade (kom′rad) *n.* A close companion or friend.

concealment (kən·sēl′mənt) *n.* A place or means of hiding.

conceivable (kən·sē′və·bəl) *adj.* Imaginable; capable of being thought of.

conduct 1. *n.* (kon′dukt) A person's behavior. **2.** *v.* (kən·dukt′) To act or behave.

confront (kən·frunt′) *v.* To stand face to face with; face boldly. —**confrontation** *n.*

conquest (kon′kwest′) *n.* The act of winning over or defeating by force.

consciousness (kon′shəs·nis) *n.* The condition of being awake and aware.

consensus (kən·sen′səs) *n.* Agreement of a majority or of everyone; general opinion.

console (kən·sōl′) *v.* To comfort in sorrow or disappointment; cheer.

constellation (kon′stə·lā′shən) *n.* A group of stars to which a name has been assigned.

constrict (kən·strikt′) *v.* To draw together; make narrower; squeeze. —**constriction** *n.*

constructive (kən·struk′tiv) *adj.* Helping to build up or improve. —**constructively** *adv.*

consumption (kən·sump′shən) *n.* The act of using up or destroying.

contempt (kən·tempt′) *n.* The feeling that a person, act, or thing is low, dishonorable, or disgusting.

contemptuous (kən·temp′chōō·əs) *adj.* Full of scorn; disdainful.

contortion (kən·tôr′shən) *n.* The act of twisting.

a	add	i	it	ōō	took	oi	oil
ā	ace	ī	ice	ōō	pool	ou	pout
â	care	o	odd	u	up	ng	ring
ä	palm	ō	open	û	burn	th	thin
e	end	ô	order	yōō	fuse	th	this
ē	equal					zh	vision

ə = { a in *above* e in *sicken* i in *possible*
      o in *melon* u in *circus* }

Glossary **789**

contraption (kən·trap′shən) *n.* An odd or puzzling device or gadget.

conventional (kən·ven′shən·əl) *adj.* **1.** Established by custom; usual. **2.** Behaving in an expected way.

converse (kən·vûrs′) *v.* To take part in a conversation.

convict 1. *n.* (kon′vikt) A person found guilty of a crime and serving a prison sentence. **2.** *v.* (kən·vikt′) To prove guilty.

cordial (kôr′jəl) *adj.* Warm and hearty; sincere.

corridor (kôr′ə·dər) *n.* A long hallway.

courteous (kûr′tē·əs) *adj.* Polite and considerate. —**courteously** *adv.*

cradle (krād′əl) *v.* To hold and rock as if in a baby's cradle.

crane *v.* To stretch out (one's neck), especially to try to look at something.

crater (krā′tər) *n.* **1.** A bowl-shaped hollow around an opening of a volcano. **2.** A hole made by an explosion.

crave (krāv) *v.* To want very much.

crestfallen (krest′fô′lən) *adj.* Low in spirits; downcast.

crevice (krev′is) *n.* A narrow opening due to a crack or split, as in a rock or wall.

crouch *v.* To bend down in a shrinking or cowering position.

crude (krōōd) *adj.* **1.** Lacking good taste; uncouth. **2.** Roughly made; not well finished. —**crudely** *adv.*

curt (kûrt) *adj.* Short and somewhat rude in tone or manner.

D

dam *n.* A wall or other barrier that is built to hold back flowing water.

debris (də·brē′) *n.* **1.** Scattered fragments or remains; rubble. **2.** Something discarded; rubbish.

decisive (di·sī′siv) *adj.* Showing decision; firm.

dedicate (ded′ə·kāt′) *v.* **1.** To set aside or devote to a special purpose. **2.** To write or say publicly that a thing has been done as a sign of affection or respect for a person named.

defiant (də·fī′ənt) *adj.* Boldly resisting to obey or submit.

dejection (di·jek′shən) *n.* Lowness of spirits; sadness.

delectable (di·lek′tə·bəl) *adj.* Delicious.

deliberation (di·lib′ə·rā′shən) *n.* Long and careful thought.

delve *v.* **1.** To dig with a spade. **2.** To make a careful search for information.

demote (di·mōt′) *v.* To reduce to a lower grade, rank, or position. —**demotion** *n.*

deposit (di·poz′it) *v.* **1.** To set down; place. **2.** To give over for safekeeping. **3.** To make a partial payment.

descend (di·send′) *v.* To go or move from a higher to a lower point; to go down.

descent (di·sent′) *n.* The action of going down or coming down to a lower point.

desolate 1. *adj.* (des′ə·lit) Dreary; empty. **2.** *v.* (des′ə·lāt′) To make sorrowful or miserable. —**desolation** *n.*

desperation (des′pə·rā′shən) *n.* A state of despair that causes reckless behavior.

despondent (di·spon′dənt) *adj.* Discouraged or depressed.

destination (des′tə·nā′shən) *n.* The place toward which someone is going; goal.

destruction (di·struk′shən) *n.* Ruin or great damage.

detached (di·tacht′) *adj.* **1.** Standing alone; separate. **2.** Not favoring a certain side.

detest (di·test′) *v.* To hate.

devastate (dev′ə·stāt′) *v.* To leave in ruins; destroy.

device (di·vīs′) *n.* **1.** An instrument or tool. **2.** A scheme or plan. **—leave to his or her own devices** To let someone do as he or she pleases.

dignity (dig′nə·tē) *n.* **1.** The quality of character or worth that commands respect. **2.** Stately manner.

dimension (di·men′shən) *n.* Any measurable extent, as length, width, depth.

diminish (di·min′ish) *n.* To make smaller or less; decrease.

disastrous (di·zas′trəs) *adj.* Causing great distress or damage.

discard (dis·kärd′) *v.* To throw away or get rid of.

discourse (dis′kôrs) *n.* **1.** A formal speech. **2.** Conversation.

disdain (dis·dān′) *n.* Scorn or haughty contempt, especially toward someone considered inferior.

disembodied (dis′em·bod′ēd) *adj.* Existing apart from a body.

disgrace (dis·grās′) **1.** *n.* A condition of shame or dishonor. **2.** *v.* To bring shame or dishonor to.

dismal (diz′məl) *adj.* **1.** Very bad. **2.** Dark, gloomy, and depressing. **3.** Sad and miserable.

dismantle (dis·man′təl) *v.* **1.** To remove all equipment or furnishings from. **2.** To take apart.

dismay (dis·mā′) **1.** *n.* Alarm, uneasiness, and confusion. **2.** *v.* To fill with uneasiness and alarm.

disoblige (dis′ə·blīj′) *v.* To act against the wishes of.

disposition (dis′pə·zish′ən) *n.* Someone's usual mood or spirit; temperament.

dispute (dis·py o͞o t′) **1.** *v.* To quarrel. **2.** *n.* An argument or debate.

disrepair (dis′rə·pâr′) *n.* A run-down condition due to neglect.

dissipate (dis′ə·pāt′) *v.* To break up and scatter or dissolve.

distort (dis·tôrt′) *v.* **1.** To twist out of normal shape. **2.** To alter in a way that creates a false impression.

a	add	**i**	it	o͞o	took	**oi**	oil
ā	ace	**ī**	ice	o͞o	pool	**ou**	pout
â	care	**o**	odd	**u**	up	**ng**	ring
ä	palm	**ō**	open	**û**	burn	**th**	thin
e	end	**ô**	order	**yo͞o**	fuse	**th**	this
ē	equal					**zh**	vision

ə = {a in *above* e in *sicken* i in *possible*
     {o in *melon* u in *circus*

Glossary **791**

distraught (dis·trôt′) *adj.* Extremely upset; crazed.
distress (dis·tres′) **1.** *n.* Extreme suffering or its cause. **2.** *v.* To cause to suffer or worry.
divulge (dī·vulj′) *v.* To tell; reveal.
domain (dō·mān′) *n.* **1.** Land belonging to one ruler or government. **2.** Any field of action, interest, or knowledge.
dome (dōm) *n.* A round roof shaped somewhat like an upside-down cup.
domestic (də·mes′tik) *adj.* Of or having to do with the home or family.
dominate (dom′ə·nāt′) *n.* To control or rule over.
dour (door) *adj.* Gloomy and sullen.
dreary (drir′ē) *adj.* Full of or causing sadness or gloom.
drone *v.* **1.** To make a deep humming or buzzing sound. **2.** To speak in a dull manner.
drought (drout) *n.* A lack of rain for a long period; a severe dry spell.
drouth (drout) *n.* Another word for **drought.**
drowsy (drou′zē) *adj.* Sleepy.
dwarf (dwôrf) *n.* **1.** In fairy tales, a tiny person having some special skill or magical power. **2.** A person, animal, or plant that is much smaller than normal size.

E

eavesdrop (ēvz′drop′) *v.* To listen secretly to things being said in private.
ebullient (i·bool′yənt) *adj.* Bubbling over with high spirits.
edible (ed′ə·bəl) *adj.* Fit to eat.
eerie (ir′ē) *adj.* Causing or arousing fear; weird; strange. —**eerily** *adv.*
elate (i·lāt′) *v.* To cause to feel full of joy or pride.
elegant (el′ə·gənt) *adj.* Tasteful, luxurious, and beautiful.
elicit (i·lis′it) *v.* To call forth or draw out.
eligible (el′ə·jə·bəl) *adj.* Capable of or legally qualified for something.
eliminate (i·lim′ə·nāt′) *v.* **1.** To get rid of. **2.** To remove from competition.
elixir (i·lik′sər) *n.* A sweetened liquid.
elongate (i·long′gāt′) *v.* To increase in length; stretch out.
eloquent (el′ə·kwənt) *adj.* Effective or skillful in expressing feelings or ideas.
elude (i·lood′) *v.* To escape from by quickness or cleverness.
emaciated (i·mā′shē·āt′id) *adj.* Abnormally thin. —**emaciation** *n.*
embed (im·bed′) *v.* To set firmly in a surrounding substance.
emerge (i·mûrj′) *v.* To come forth or come out, so as to be visible.
emigrate (em′ə·grāt′) *v.* To move from one country or section of a country to settle in another.
emit (i·mit′) *v.* To send forth or give off.
emphatic (em·fat′ik) *adj.* Spoken or done with emphasis. —**emphatically** *adv.*
endure (in·door′) *v.* To put up with; bear; tolerate.

engulf (in·gulf′) *v.* To swallow up; overwhelm completely.

enhance (in·hans′) *v.* To add to; increase.

ensue (in·sōō′) *v.* To follow in time; to come next.

entice (in·tīs′) *v.* To attract by tempting with something attractive or desirable.

entreaty (in·trē′tē) *n.* An earnest request or plea.

enviable (en′vē·ə·bəl) *adj.* So excellent as to be envied or much desired.

envious (en′vē·əs) *adj.* Feeling discontent or jealousy because of someone else's good fortune. —**enviously** *adv.*

epidemic (ep′ə·dem′ik) *n.* The sudden spread of a disease among many people.

epitome (i·pit′ə·mē) *n.* A person or thing that possesses all of the qualities or characteristics of something.

erect (i·rekt′) *adj.* Upright; not stooping or leaning.

erupt (i·rupt′) *v.* To cast forth (as lava or steam).

etiquette (et′ə·kət) *n.* The rules established for behavior in polite society or in official or professional life.

evasion (i·vā′zhən) *n.* The act of getting away from, especially the avoiding of something unpleasant by tricks or cleverness.

evoke (i·vōk′) *v.* To call forth.

exasperation (ig·zas′pə·rā′shən) *n.* The feeling of being annoyed or irritated almost to the point of anger.

exceedingly (ik·sē′ding·lē) *adv.* Extremely; very.

exertion (ig·zûr′shən) *n.* Great effort.

exhalation (eks′hə·lā′shən) *n.* The process of breathing out.

exhaust (ig·zôst′) *v.* **1.** To make extremely tired. **2.** To use up entirely. **3.** To study or discuss thoroughly.

exhilarate (ig·zil′ə·rāt′) *v.* To fill with happiness or high spirits.

exquisite (eks′kwi·zit) *adj.* **1.** Finely and delicately made. **2.** Extremely beautiful.

extravagant (ik·strav′ə·gənt) *adj.* **1.** Going beyond reason or proper limits. **2.** Spending too much.

extremity (ik·strem′ə·tē) *n.* **1.** The most distant point or part. **2.** Something extreme, such as distress, need, or danger.

F

facet (fas′it) *n.* One of the small, smooth surfaces cut upon a gem. —**faceted** *adj.*

falter (fôl′tər) *v.* To hesitate, be uncertain.

famine (fam′in) *n.* A widespread lack of food which causes starvation.

a	add	i	it	ōō	took	oi	oil
ā	ace	ī	ice	ōō	pool	ou	pout
â	care	o	odd	u	up	ng	ring
ä	palm	ō	open	û	burn	th	thin
e	end	ô	order	yōō	fuse	th	this
ē	equal					zh	vision

ə = { a in *above* e in *sicken* i in *possible* o in *melon* u in *circus* }

fate *n.* What happens to a person; fortune.
favoritism (fā′vər·ə·tiz′əm) *n.* An unfair favoring of one or a few out of a group.
feeble (fē′bəl) *adj.* **1.** Lacking strength; weak. **2.** Not adequate or effective.
fell (fel) *v.* To cut down.
ferocious (fə·rō′shəs) *adj.* Extremely fierce or savage.
filter (fil′tər) *v.* **1.** To act as a device that strains out impurities from a liquid or gas. **2.** To leak out slowly.
fleeting (flēt′ing) *adj.* Passing quickly.
flexible (flek′sə·bəl) *adj.* **1.** Capable of being bent or twisted without breaking. **2.** Easily changed; adaptable.
flippant (flip′ənt) *adj.* Not respectful or serious; too smart or pert.
flirt (flûrt) *v.* To act in an affectionate or loving way without being serious. —**flirtation** *n.*
flourish (flûr′ish) *v.* To wave about.
fluster (flus′tər) *v.* To make confused or upset.
foal (fōl) *n.* A young horse, donkey, zebra, or similar animal.
foliage (fō′lē·ij *or* fo′lij) *n.* The leaves of trees or plants.
forlorn (fôr·lôrn′) *adj.* Sad or pitiful because alone or neglected.
fracture (frak′chər) *v.* To break or crack.
frail (frāl) *adj.* Easily damaged in body or structure; weak.
frantic (fran′tik) *adj.* Wild with fear, worry, pain, or rage.
frazzle (fraz′əl) *v.* To tire out, exhaust.
frenzied (fren′zēd) *adj.* Wildly excited. —**frenziedly** *adv.*
frenzy (fren′zē) *n.* A wild, excited fit or condition.
frustrate (frus′trāt′) *v.* To baffle the efforts of or bring to nothing.
furtive (fûr′tiv) *adj.* Done in secret; stealthy.
futile (fyoō′təl) *adj.* Useless.

G

gape (gāp) *v.* To stare with the mouth open, as in surprise.
garb *n.* Clothing.
garish (gâr′ish) *adj.* Too showy or bright; gaudy.
gaunt (gônt) *adj.* Very thin and bony, as from illness.
genuine (jen′yoō·in) *adj.* **1.** Being as it appears; not false. **2.** Sincere.
gesture (jes′chər) *n.* A motion of the hands or other part of the body that expresses some feeling or idea.
gingerly (jin′jər·lē) *adv.* In a cautious, careful, or reluctant manner.
gird (gûrd) *v.* To get ready for action.
glisten (glis′ən) *v.* To shine or sparkle.
gnarled (närld) *adj.* Knotty or twisted.
gnash (nash) *v.* To grind or strike the teeth together, as in a rage.
gnaw (nô) *v.* **1.** To bite or eat away little by little. **2.** To trouble persistently.
goad (gōd) *v.* To drive into action; to urge on.
gouge (gouj) *v.* To scoop out.
gratify (grat′ə·fī′) *v.* To satisfy; indulge.

gratitude (grat′ə·tōōd′) *n.* Thankfulness for a gift or favor; appreciation.

grimace (gri·mās′) *n.* A twisting of the face expressing pain, annoyance, disgust, or other feelings.

grudging (gruj′ing) *adj.* Reluctant; unwilling. —**grudgingly** *adv.*

guarantee (gar′ən·tē′) *n.* **1.** A pledge to repair, replace, or refund payment for something. **2.** A promise.

gusto (gus′tō) *n.* Keen enjoyment.

guttural (gut′ər·əl) *adj.* Having a throaty, grating sound; harsh.

H

habituate (hə·bich′ōō āt′) *v.* To accustom or make used to.

hallucination (hə·lōō′sə·nā′shən) *n.* The impression of seeing or hearing something that is not really present.

hamper *v.* To interfere with the movements of.

harass (hə·ras′) *v.* To trouble, as with cares or worries.

hasty (hās′tē) *adj.* **1.** Quick. **2.** Acting or done on impulse; rash.

haughty (hô′tē) *adj.* Satisfied with one's self and scornful of others; arrogant.

haze *n.* **1.** Fine droplets, as of water or dust particles, suspended in air. **2.** Mental confusion; muddle.

heartily (här′tə·lē) *adv.* Sincerely and enthusiastically.

heir (âr) *n.* A person who inherits or is likely to inherit property upon the death of the person possessing it.

hogan (hō′gən) *n.* A Navaho hut made of sticks and branches and covered with earth.

hogshead (hogz′hed′ *or* hôgz′hed′) *n.* A barrel or cask large enough to hold from 63 to 140 gallons.

hoist *v.* To raise or lift, especially by mechanical means.

homage (hom′ij) *n.* Respect or honor given or shown.

hostile (hos′təl) *adj.* **1.** Having to do with the enemy. **2.** Showing dislike; unfriendly.

humiliate (hyōō·mil′ē·āt′) *v.* To strip of pride or self-respect; embarrass.

hysterical (his·ter′ə·kəl) *adj.* Showing uncontrolled excitement or emotion.

I

idle (īd′əl) *adj.* **1.** Not busy. **2.** Lazy; unwilling to work.

ignite (ig·nīt′) *v.* To set on fire.

illuminate (i·lōō′mə·nāt′) *v.* **1.** To light up. **2.** To make clear.

illusion (i·lōō′zhən) *n.* A deceiving appearance or the false impression it gives.

imperative (im·per′ə·tiv) *adj.* Urgently necessary; unavoidable.

a	add	i	it	ōō	took	oi	oil
ā	ace	ī	ice	ōō	pool	ou	pout
â	care	o	odd	u	up	ng	ring
ä	palm	ō	open	û	burn	th	thin
e	end	ô	order	yōō	fuse	th	this
ē	equal					zh	vision

ə = { a in *above*, e in *sicken*, i in *possible*, o in *melon*, u in *circus* }

imperious (im·pir′ē·əs) *adj.* Proud and haughty.

impetuous (im·pech′ōō·əs) *adj.* Acting on impulse and without thought; rash. —**impetuously** *adv.*

imposing (im·pō′zing) *adj.* Impressive, as in manner, appearance, or size.

impostor (im·pos′tər) *n.* A person who deceives, especially one who pretends to be someone else.

impudence (im′pyə·dəns) *n.* Offensive boldness; rudeness.

impulse (im′puls) *n.* **1.** A driving force. **2.** A sudden desire or feeling which makes one want to act.

incision (in·sizh′ən) *n.* A cut or gash, especially one made in surgery.

incoherent (in′kō·hir′ənt) *adj.* Not clear; confused. —**incoherently** *adv.*

incompetent (in·kom′pə·tənt) *adj.* Lacking in ability or skill.

inconsolable (in′kən·sō′lə·bəl) *adj.* Not to be comforted or cheered; broken-hearted.

incredulous (in·krej′ə·ləs) *adj.* Feeling, having, or showing doubt or disbelief. —**incredulously** *adv.*

indebted (in·det′id) *adj.* Owing gratitude or thanks, as for a favor.

indifference (in·dif′rəns) *n.* Lack of interest; unconcern. —**indifferent** *adj.*

indignant (in·dig′nənt) *adj.* Angry because of something that is not right, just, or fair. —**indignation** *n.*

indistinct (in′dis·tingkt′) *adj.* Not clear; vague; dim.

indomitable (in·dom′ə·tə·bəl) *adj.* Not easily defeated or overcome; persevering.

induce (in·dōōs′) *v.* To persuade.

industrious (in·dus′trē·əs) *adj.* Working hard.

inevitable (in·ev′ə·tə·bəl) *adj.* Certain; unavoidable.

inexplicable (in·eks′pli·kə·bəl) *adj.* Impossible to explain.

infest (in·fest′) *v.* To overrun or occupy in large numbers so as to be annoying or dangerous.

infinite (in′fə·nit) *adj.* Having no limits; endless. —**infinity** *n.*

ingest (in·jest′) *v.* To swallow.

inhabit (in·hab′it) *v.* To live in; occupy.

initial (in·ish′əl) *adj.* Coming at the beginning; earliest; first.

inquisitive (in·kwiz′ə·tiv) *adj.* Full of questions; curious.

inscrutable (in·skrōō′tə·bəl) *adj.* Incapable of being understood; mysterious; puzzling.

inseparable (in·sep′ər·ə·bəl) *adj.* Incapable of being separated.

integrity (in·teg′rə·tē) *n.* Great sincerity, honesty, and virtue; strength of character.

intense (in·tens′) *adj.* Very strong, great, or deep. —**intensity** *n.*

intent (in·tent′) *adj.* Firmly directed or fixed; earnest. —**intently** *adv.*

intention (in·ten′shən) *n.* Plan, purpose.

intermix (in′tər·miks′) *v.* To mix together.

interspecific (in′tər·spi·sif′ik) *adj.* Relating to similar behavior patterns among different species.

intervene (in′tər·vēn′) *v.* **1.** To come in to change a situation. **2.** To come or be between two places or times.

intricate (in′tri·kit) *adj.* Complicated or involved.

intrigue 1. *v.* (in·trēg′) To arouse the interest of. **2.** *n.* (in′trēg) A secret, crafty plot or scheme.

intrude (in·trōōd′) *v.* To come in without being invited or wanted. —**intrusion** *n.*

J

jaunty (jôn′tē) *adj.* Having a lively or self-confident air or manner.

jeer (jir) *v.* To make fun of with insulting words; mock.

jostle (jos′əl) *v.* To push or crowd against; shove; bump.

jubilant (jōō′bə·lənt) *adj.* Expressing great joy. —**jubilation** *n.*

K

kaleidoscope (kə·lī′də·skōp′) *n.* **1.** A tubelike device containing loose bits of colored glass. **2.** Any changing pattern, view, or scene.

kerchief (kûr′chif) *n.* A piece of fabric, usually square, worn over the head or around the neck.

L

labor (lā′bər) *v.* To work hard.

laden (lād′ən) *adj.* Weighed down; loaded; burdened.

lair (lâr) *n.* The den of a wild animal.

lamentation (lam′ən·tā′shən) *n.* The act of expressing great sorrow; wail; moan.

larva (lar′və) *n., pl.* (lar′vē) The early stage of an insect's life after hatching; for example, a caterpillar before it turns into a moth.

lavish (lav′ish) *adj.* **1.** Generous or too generous. **2.** Provided or used up in great supply. —**lavishly** *adv.*

legitimate (lə·jit′ə·mit) *adj.* **1.** Lawful. **2.** Logical; reasonable; justified.

leisurely (lē′zhər·lē) *adj.* Relaxed and unhurried. —**leisureliness** *n.*

linger (ling′gər) *v.* To stay on as if unwilling to go.

listless (list′lis) *adj.* Lacking energy or interest in anything.

lofty (lôf′tē) *adj.* **1.** Very high. **2.** Proud.

lull 1. *n.* A time of quiet or calm during a period of noise or activity. **2.** *v.* To quiet or put to sleep by soothing sounds or motions.

luminous (lōō′mə·nəs) *adj.* Full of light; glowing.

lunge (lunj) *v.* To make a quick movement or plunge forward.

lure (lōor) *v.* To attract, especially into danger.

luscious (lush′əs) *adj.* **1.** Very good to

a	add	i	it	ŏŏ	took	oi	oil
ā	ace	ī	ice	ōō	pool	ou	pout
â	care	o	odd	u	up	ng	ring
ä	palm	ō	open	û	burn	th	thin
e	end	ô	order	yōō	fuse	th	this
ē	equal					zh	vision

ə = { a in *above*   e in *sicken*   i in *possible*
      o in *melon*   u in *circus* }

taste and smell; delicious. **2.** Pleasing to any sense or to the mind.

M

malice (mal′is) *n.* A desire to injure someone; ill will.

maneuver (mə·nōō′vər) **1.** *n.* Any skillful move or action. **2.** *v.* To use planned moves skillfully.

manifest (man′ə·fest′) *v.* To reveal; show.

meander (mē·an′dər) *v.* To wander aimlessly.

meek *adj.* Lacking courage or spirit.

melancholy (mel′ən·kol′ē) **1.** *adj.* Very gloomy; sad. **2.** *n.* Low spirits; sadness; depression.

mellow (mel′ō) *adj.* **1.** Rich and soft in quality, as colors or sounds. **2.** Made gentle by age or experience.

menace (men′is) **1.** *n.* A threat. **2.** *v.* To threaten with evil or harm.

merchandise (mûr′chən·dīs′) *n.* Goods bought and sold for profit.

merely (mir′lē) *adv.* Nothing more than; only.

mimic (mim′ik) *v.* To imitate the speech or actions of someone, usually to make fun.

minimal (min′ə·məl) *adj.* Smallest or least possible in size, amount, or degree.

mire (mīr) **1.** *n.* Swampy ground or deep mud. **2.** *v.* To sink or stick in mire.

moderation (mod′ə·rā′shən) *n.* The condition of not being extreme or excessive.

modify (mod′ə·fī) *v.* To change moderately.

molest (mə·lest′) *v.* To harm or bother.

monarch (mon′ərk) *n.* A ruler, as a king or queen.

mooring *n.* The line, cable, or anchor that holds something in place.

mope *v.* To be gloomy and depressed; sulk.

mortify (môr′tə·fī′) *v.* **1.** To deprive of self-respect or pride; humiliate. **2.** To become dead or decayed.

mottle (mot′′l) *v.* To mark with spots of different colors; blotch.

mournful (môrn′fəl) *adj.* Showing or causing grief; sorrowful.

muddle (mud′′l) *n.* A condition of confusion; mix-up.

murky (mûr′kē) *adj.* **1.** Dark, gloomy. **2.** Foggy, misty.

mutual (myōō′chōō·əl) *adj.* Having the same attitude toward or relationship with each other or others.

N

nectar (nek′tər) *n.* **1.** A sweet liquid found in flowers, collected by bees to make honey. **2.** A sweet drink.

niche (nich) *n.* A hollow in a wall.

nobility (nō·bil′ə·tē) *n.* The condition of showing outstanding or impressive qualities.

noncommittal (non′kə·mit′əl) *adj.* Not binding one to an opinion or plan of action.

nymph (nimf) *n.* In Greek and Roman myths, any of a group of lesser goddesses who lived in woods, fountains, or trees.

O

oblige (ə·blīj′) *v.* **1.** To compel; force. **2.** To do a favor or service for.

oblivious (ə·bliv′ē·əs) *adj.* Not conscious or aware.

obscure (əb·skyŏor′) *v.* To make dim or indistinct.

obsess (əb·ses′) *v.* To fill or trouble the mind of excessively; haunt.

obstinate (ob′stə·nit) *adj.* **1.** Stubbornly holding to one's opinions. **2.** Hard to overcome or control. —**obstinately** *adv.*

offensive (ə·fen′siv) *adj.* Unpleasant or disagreeable.

officious (ə·fish′əs) *adj.* Too forward in offering service or advice; meddlesome. —**officiously** *adv.*

ooze *v.* To flow or leak out slowly or gradually.

optimistic (op′tə·mis′tik) *adj.* Full of hope and cheerfulness.

orator (ôr′ə·tər) *n.* A person who delivers a public speech.

ostentation (os′tən·tā′shən) *n.* Too great a display of something in order to attract attention or admiration.

outrageous (out·rā′jəs) *adj.* Fantastic; unbelievable. —**outrageousness** *n.*

overwhelm (ō′vər·welm′) *v.* To overcome completely.

P

pallid (pal′id) *adj.* Pale in appearance; lacking in color or strength; weak.

pant *v.* To breathe quickly and jerkily.

paralysis (pə·ral′ə·sis) *n.* **1.** The loss of the power of movement or feeling in a part of the body. **2.** Any stopping of normal activities.

parasite (par′ə·sīt′) *n.* A plant that lives on and gets its food from another. —**parasitic** *adj.*

parch *v.* **1.** To make or become dry with heat. **2.** To make or become thirsty.

pathetic (pə·thet′ik) *adj.* Arousing, expressing, or deserving pity or sympathy.

perennial (pə·ren′ē·əl) *adj.* Everlasting.

perky (pûr′kē) *adj.* Lively.

persistent (pər·sis′tənt) *adj.* Enduring or continuing.

perturb (pər·tûrb′) *v.* To disturb greatly; alarm; agitate.

petulant (pech′ōō·lənt) *adj.* Showing annoyance over little things; fretful.

phenomenal (fi·nom′ə·nəl) *adj.* Marvelous; extraordinary.

philosophy (fi·los′ə·fē) *n.* **1.** Wisdom and strength in dealing with difficult experiences.

pinion (pin′yən) *v.* To bind or hold the

a	add	i	it	ōō	took	oi	oil
ā	ace	ī	ice	ōō	pool	ou	pout
â	care	o	odd	u	up	ng	ring
ä	palm	ō	open	û	burn	th	thin
e	end	ô	order	yōō	fuse	th	this
ē	equal					zh	vision

ə = { a in *above* e in *sicken* i in *possible*
      o in *melon* u in *circus* }

Glossary **799**

arms of (someone) to make the person helpless.
piteous (pit′ē·əs) *adj*. Arousing or deserving pity.
pivot (piv′ət) **1.** *n*. A point, shaft, or pin on which something turns. **2.** *v*. To turn as if on a pivot.
placate (plā′kāt′) *v*. To calm the anger of; soothe.
plague (plāg) **1.** *v*. To trouble, torment. **2.** *n*. A contagious, often fatal, disease that spreads rapidly.
plaintive (plān′tiv) *adj*. Expressing sadness; mournful.
plight (plīt) *n*. An awkward, bad, or dangerous situation.
plumage (plōō′mij) *n*. The feathers of a bird.
plunder (plun′dər) *v*. To rob of goods or property by force.
ply (plī) *v*. To work at; be engaged in.
pollen (pol′ən) *n*. A yellow powder containing the male reproductive cells of plants.
pomegranate (pom′gran′it) *n*. A tropical fruit about the size of an orange, having many seeds.
pomp *n*. Magnificent display; splendor.
posse (pos′ē) *n*. A force of people summoned by a sheriff to help in some official duty.
precede (pri·sēd′) *v*. To be, go, or come before.
prestige (pres·tēzh′) *n*. Fame, importance, or respect based on a person's reputation or power.
prey (prā) *n*. Any animal killed by another for food.

primate (prī′māt′) *n*. An order of mammals including apes, monkeys, lemurs, and humans.
procure (prō·kyŏŏr′) *v*. To get by some effort or means; acquire.
profile (prō′fīl′) *n*. **1.** The outline of a human face as seen from the side. **2.** A short biographical sketch.
profusion (prə·fyōō′zhən) *n*. A large supply.
propellers (prə·pel′ərs) *n*. Rotating blades that move an aircraft or vessel through the air or water.
prospect (pros′pekt′) *n*. The act of looking ahead; expectation.
prosperous (pros′pər·əs) *adj*. Successful; thriving.
protrude (prō·trōōd′) *v*. To jut out; project.
provoke (prə·vōk′) *v*. To cause or bring about.
prowess (prou′is) *n*. **1.** Great skill or ability. **2.** Strength and courage.
psyche (sī′kē) *n*. The human soul or mind.
psychiatry (sī·kī′ə·trē) *n*. The branch of medicine that deals with the treatment of mental illness.
puce (pyōōs) *adj*. A dark brownish purple or purplish brown.
punctual (pungk′chōō·əl) *adj*. Acting, finished, or arriving on time.
pursuit (pər·sōōt′) *n*. A chase.

Q

quaver (kwā′vər) *v*. To tremble or shake in an uncertain way, as a voice.

queasy (kwē′zē) *adj.* Sick or causing sickness at the stomach.

quiver (kwiv′ər) *v.* To make a slight trembling motion; vibrate.

R

radiant (rā′dē·ənt) *adj.* **1.** Beaming, as with joy, love, or energy. **2.** Very bright and shining; brilliant.

rancid (ran′sid) *adj.* Having the bad taste or smell of spoiled fat or oil.

random (ran′dəm) *adj.* Not planned or organized; chance.

ransom (ran′səm) *n.* The price demanded or paid for the release of a person held captive.

ravage (rav′ij) *v.* To hurt or damage severely; destroy.

recess (rē′ses) *n.* **1.** A short period of time when work is stopped. **2.** A hollow place.

recoil (ri·koil′) *v.* To react suddenly, as to pain or fear, by leaping or shrinking back.

reconcile (rek′ən·sīl′) *v.* **1.** To bring back to friendship after a quarrel. **2.** To make adjusted to; resign.

recover (ri·kuv′ər) *v.* **1.** To get back after losing. **2.** To make up for, as a loss. **3.** To get well.

recreation (rek′rē·ā′shən) *n.* Amusement, relaxation, or play.

reference (ref′ər·əns) *n.* **1.** The act of calling attention. **2.** Something that provides information or help.

reflective (ri·flek′tiv) *adj.* Thoughtful.

refuge (ref′yōoj) *n.* Shelter or protection from danger or distress.

register (rej′is·tər) *v.* **1.** To show; express. **2.** To enter one's name in an official record; enroll.

regulate (reg′yə·lāt′) *v.* To control according to certain rules.

relent (ri·lent′) *v.* To become gentler or more compassionate.

relentless (ri·lent′lis) *adj.* **1.** Without pity; unforgiving; harsh. **2.** Continuing; persistent.

reluctant (ri·luk′tənt) *adj.* Unwilling; not eager.

remote (ri·mōt′) *adj.* Distant in time or relationship.

render (ren′dər) *v.* **1.** To perform; do. **2.** To cause to be or become.

replenish (ri·plen′ish) *v.* To provide with a new supply; fill up again.

reproach (ri·prōch′) *v.* To blame for some wrong.

repulsive (ri·pul′siv) *adj.* Disgusting or horrifying.

resent (ri·zent′) *v.* To feel or show anger or ill will based on real or imagined wrong or injury.

resign (ri·zīn′) *v.* To give up; submit.

resilient (ri·zil′yənt) *adj.* Springing back to former shape or position.

resound (ri·zound′) *v.* To be filled with sound or echo back.

a	add	i	it	o͞o	took	oi	oil
ā	ace	ī	ice	o͞o	pool	ou	pout
â	care	o	odd	u	up	ng	ring
ä	palm	ō	open	û	burn	th	thin
e	end	ô	order	yo͞o	fuse	th	this
ē	equal					zh	vision

ə = { a in *above* e in *sicken* i in *possible*
      o in *melon* u in *circus* }

resource (ri·sôrs′) *n.* **1.** The ability to act usefully and well in a difficulty. **2.** A supply of something.

restless (rest′lis) *adj.* Unable to rest or be still; nervous; uneasy.

restore (ri·stôr′) *v.* To bring back to a former or original condition.

resume (ri·zo͞om′) *v.* To begin again after stopping.

reticent (ret′ə·sənt) *adj.* Reserved; quiet.

retort (ri·tôrt′) *v.* To reply sharply.

retrieve (ri·trēv′) *v.* To get back; regain.

revelation (rev′ə·lā′shən) *n.* Something made known, especially something surprising.

reverberation (ri·vûr′bə·rā′shən) *n.* A reflecting, as of sound waves, light, or heat.

rigor (rig′ər) *n.* Harshness or discomfort.

riotous (rī′ət·əs) *adj.* Loud; uproarious. —**riotously** *adv.*

rival (rī′vəl) *n.* A person who tries to outdo another; competitor.

rivulet (riv′yə·lit) *n.* A brook.

S

sanctuary (sangk′cho͞o·er′ē) *n.* A place of safety and peace.

scald (skôld) *v.* To burn with hot liquid or steam.

scour (skour) *v.* **1.** To clean by washing and rubbing hard. **2.** To clean or clear, as by flowing water.

seizure (sē′zhər) *n.* A sudden, violent attack, as of a disease.

shear (shir) *v.* **1.** To cut the hair or fleece from. **2.** To take something away from; deprive.

sheepish (shē′pish) *adj.* Awkwardly shy or embarrassed.

shingle (shin′gəl) *n.* A pebbly beach.

shorn An alternative past participle of *shear.*

sidle (sīd′′l) *v.* To move sideways, especially in a cautious or sly manner.

silhouette (sil′o͞o·et′) *n.* The outline of a person or object seen against a light or a light background.

sinister (sin′is·tər) *adj.* **1.** Wrong, wicked, or evil. **2.** Threatening evil, trouble, or bad luck.

skirmish (skûr′mish) *n.* A brief fight or encounter between small groups.

skirt *v.* To go around, not through; pass along the edge of.

slacken (slak′ən) *v.* To make or become slower, less active, or less forceful.

sluggish (slug′ish) *adj.* Not active or energetic; lazy or dull. —**sluggishly** *adv.*

sly (slī) *adj.* Clever in a secret, stealthy, or sneaky way; crafty; cunning. —**slyly** *adv.*

smolder (smōl′dər) *v.* To burn slowly with smoke but no flame.

snarl *v.* To growl, showing the teeth.

sober (sō′bər) *adj.* **1.** Serious, calm, thoughtful, and well-balanced. **2.** Solemn.

sociable (sō′shə·bəl) *adj.* Liking to be with people; pleasant in company; social.

solitary (sol′ə·ter′ē) *adj.* **1.** Living, being, or going alone. **2.** Single; sole.
sorrowful (sor′ə·fəl) *adj.* Sad, distressed. —**sorrowfully** *adv.*
souvenir (soo′və·nir′) *n.* Something that is kept as a reminder of the past.
spasm (spaz′əm) *n.* A sudden, involuntary contraction of a muscle.
spate *n.* **1.** A sudden flood or rush. **2.** A large number occurring or appearing together.
speculation (spek′yə·lā′shən) *n.* The act of thinking or wondering seriously.
sprite *n.* A fairy, elf, goblin, or similar creature.
stagger (stag′ər) *v.* To walk or run unsteadily; sway; reel.
stalk (stôk) *v.* **1.** To approach secretly or stealthily. **2.** To walk in a stiff or angry manner.
stampede (stam·pēd′) *n.* A sudden rushing off or flight through panic, as of a herd of cattle or horses.
stealthy (stel′thē) *adj.* Done in a secret or underhand way. —**stealthily** *adv.*
strenuous (stren′yoo·əs) *adj.* Taking much effort or energy.
strife (strīf) *n.* Angry fight, quarrel, or conflict.
sturdy (stûr′dē) *adj.* Vigorous; strong.
substantial (səb·stan′shəl) *adj.* **1.** Actual; real; having substance. **2.** Solid; strong; firm.
succession (sək·sesh′ən) *n.* A group of things or persons that follow one after another.
sullen (sul′ən) *adj.* Glumly silent because ill-humored or resentful. —**sullenly** *adv.*
sultry (sul′trē) *adj.* Uncomfortably hot, humid, and still.
summit (sum′it) *n.* The highest point; top.
summon (sum′ən) *v.* To send for or order to come.
sumptuous (sump′choo·əs) *adj.* Very expensive and luxurious.
superficial (soo′pər·fish′əl) *adj.* **1.** Of, on, or affecting only the surface; not deep. **2.** Not genuine.
suspicious (sə·spish′əs) *adj.* Having a feeling or idea, not based on real proof, that something is wrong.

T

tactic (tak′tik) *n.* A device or maneuver used to achieve a specific goal.
tantalize (tan′tə·līz′) *v.* To torment by making something desirable almost but never quite available.
tapestry (tap′is·trē) *n.* A heavy ornamental cloth with designs or pictures woven into it, usually hung on a wall.
tart *adj.* **1.** Having a sharp, sour taste. **2.** Sharp and biting in meaning or tone.

a	add	i	it	oo	took	oi	oil
ā	ace	ī	ice	o͞o	pool	ou	pout
â	care	o	odd	u	up	ng	ring
ä	palm	ō	open	û	burn	th	thin
e	end	ô	order	yoo	fuse	th	this
ē	equal					zh	vision

ə = { a in *above*   e in *sicken*   i in *possible*
       o in *melon*   u in *circus* }

taunt (tônt) *v.* To insult or make fun of with scornful, mocking, or sarcastic remarks.

tempo (tem′pō) *n.* **1.** The pace or rate of activity. **2.** The speed at which a piece of music is played.

tenacious (ti·nā′shəs) *adj.* **1.** Holding or grasping firmly. **2.** Not forgetting.

tentative (ten′tə·tiv) *adj.* Hesitant; halfhearted. —**tentatively** *adv.*

terrorist (ter′ə·rist) *n.* A person who uses threats and violence to frighten others.

terse (tûrs) *adj.* Short and to the point.

testify (tes′tə·fī) *v.* To give evidence; bear witness.

testy (tes′tē) *adj.* Easily made angry.

thicket (thik′it) *n.* A thick, dense growth, as of trees or bushes.

threadbare (thred′bâr′) *adj.* So badly worn that the threads show, as a rug or garment.

thrive *v.* **1.** To prosper or be successful. **2.** To grow vigorously; flourish.

timid (tim′id) *adj.* Fearful or shy.

toil *v.* To work hard.

token (tō′kən) *n.* A sign or symbol.

tolerate (tol′ər·āt′) *v.* **1.** To allow to be or permit without opposition. **2.** To bear or endure.

torrent (tôr′ənt) *n.* Water flowing with great speed and violence.

totter (tot′ər) *v.* To walk feebly and unsteadily.

tranquil (trang′kwil) *adj.* Calm; serene. —**tranquillity** *n.*

transcend (tran·send′) *v.* To go beyond; overstep the limits of.

transfix (trans·fiks′) *v.* To make motionless, as with horror or fear.

traverse (trə·vûrs′) *v.* To pass or travel over, across, or through.

tremor (trem′ər) *n.* **1.** A quick, vibrating movement. **2.** A quivering feeling.

tremulous (trem′yə·ləs) *adj.* Showing fear; timid. —**tremulously** *adv.*

trench *n.* A long, narrow opening dug into the earth; ditch.

trundle (trun′dəl) *v.* To roll or propel as if by rolling.

turmoil (tûr′moil) *n.* A condition of great agitation; disturbance.

tyrant (tī′rənt) *n.* **1.** A ruler having absolute power. **2.** Any person who exerts power in such a way.

U

unconscious (un·kon′shəs) *adj.* Not able to feel or think; not awake.

unison (yōō′nə·sən) *n.* Agreement.

unobtrusive (un′əb·trōō′siv) *adj.* Not demanding notice; inconspicuous.

unwieldy (un·wēl′dē) *adj.* Hard to handle or manage; awkward.

urgency (ûr′jən·sē) *n.* Need or demand for prompt action or attention.

urn *n.* A large vase used for flowers and plants.

V

vacancy (vā′kən·sē) *n.* An empty place.

vacant (vā′kənt) *adj.* Empty or unfilled.

vague (vāg) *adj.* Not definite, clear, precise, or distinct.

vain (vān) *adj.* Unsuccessful; useless. —**in vain** Without success.

veer (vir) *v.* To change direction.
vengeance (ven′jəns) *n.* Punishment inflicted in return for a wrong done; revenge.
venomous (ven′əm·əs) *adj.* Poisonous.
vent *v.* To relieve or express freely.
veranda (və·ran′də) *n.* A long, open, outdoor porch, usually roofed.
verge (vûrj) *n.* **1.** The edge of something. **2.** The point at which some action is likely to occur.
verify (ver′ə·fī) *v.* To prove to be true or accurate.
vessel (ves′əl) *n.* **1.** A hollow container, as a bowl. **2.** A ship or boat larger than a rowboat.
vicious (vish′əs) *adj.* **1.** Dangerous or likely to attack. **2.** Spiteful or mean.
vigil (vij′əl) *n.* The act of staying awake to observe or protect; watch.
vinyl (vī′nəl) *n.* A plastic used in making records, combs, floor coverings, and other items.
vital (vīt′′l) *adj.* **1.** Lively and energetic. **2.** Necessary or essential to life.
vitality (vī·tal′ə·tē) *n.* Physical or mental energy.
vixen (vik′sən) *n.* An ill-tempered, quarrelsome person.
vocalize (vō′kəl·īz′) *v.* To make sounds with the voice. —**vocalization** *n.*
vulnerable (vul′nər·ə·bəl) *adj.* Capable of being hurt, injured, or wounded.

W

waive (wāv) *v.* To give up voluntarily, as a claim or right.
waver (wā′vər) *v.* **1.** To sway; flutter. **2.** To be uncertain or undecided.
wayfarer (wā′fâr′ər) *n.* A traveler.
weary (wir′ē) *adj.* Tired; fatigued. —**wearily** *adv.*
whimper (wim′pər) *v.* To cry with low, mournful, broken sounds.
whittle (wit′əl) *v.* To cut or shave bits from wood.
wilt *v.* To lose or cause to lose freshness or energy; to become limp.
wily (wī′lē) *adj.* Sly; cunning.
wince (wins) *v.* To shrink or draw back, as from a blow or a pain.
wistful (wist′fəl) *adj.* Wishful; longing. —**wistfully** *adv.*
witness (wit′nis) *n.* A person who has seen or knows something and can give evidence concerning it.
writhe (rīth) *v.* To twist or distort the body or part of the body, as in pain.
wry (rī) *adj.* **1.** Bent or twisted. **2.** Grim, bitter, or ironic. —**wryly** *adv.*

Y

yield (yēld) *v.* **1.** To give up; surrender. **2.** To give forth; produce.

a	add	i	it	o͝o	took	oi	oil
ā	ace	ī	ice	o͞o	pool	ou	pout
â	care	o	odd	u	up	ng	ring
ä	palm	ō	open	û	burn	th	thin
e	end	ô	order	yo͞o	fuse	**th**	this
ē	equal					zh	vision

ə = { a in *above*   e in *sicken*   i in *possible*
       o in *melon*   u in *circus* }

Outline of Concepts and Skills

LITERARY SKILLS

Acrostic poems 375
Alliteration 299, 300, 319, 596, 599, 738
Allusion 738
Audience 443
Autobiography 385, 393, 738
Biography 23, 385, 393, 739
Character 1, 7, 19, 32, 40, 52, 53, 145, 157, 190, 451, 645, 669, 713, 739
Character traits 32, 249, 486
Cinquains 381
Climax 712
Conflict 95, 111, 157, 428, 645, 739
Connotations 559, 565, 739
Couplets 355, 378
Description 100, 254, 263, 420, 447, 740
Dialect 116, 126, 131, 145, 222, 230, 587, 740
Dialogue 54, 145, 464, 650, 712, 740
Drama 463, 741
Essay 446, 741
Exaggeration 175, 451, 713
Extended metaphor 336, 342
External conflict 428, 645
Fable 741
Fairy tales 166, 607

Fantasy 18, 741
Fiction 741
Figures of speech 443, 741
First-person point of view 229, 689, 746
Flashback 474, 495, 742
Folk Tales 549, 617, 630, 742
Foreshadowing 165, 470, 530, 742
Free verse 358, 362, 366, 742
Graphic aids 431, 443
Haiku 330, 332
Hero 420, 557, 565
Homophones 339
"How and why" stories 585, 605
Imagery 234, 250, 321, 324, 332, 443, 742
Internal conflict 428, 645
Internal rhyme 319
Irony 408, 743
Japanese-lantern poems 375
Legend 743
Limericks 379
Main ideas 353, 368
Message 355, 362, 550
Metamorphosis 564
Metaphors 44, 53, 333, 336, 337, 342, 346, 743
Mood 112, 744
Moral 292, 640

Myths 549, 557, 573, 584, 744
Narration 744
Narrative 63–65, 262, 420
Narrator 278
Nonfiction 385, 744
Nonsense 295, 298, 307
Novel 645, 744
Omniscient point of view 229, 689, 746
Onomatopoeia 300, 337, 596, 600, 745
Paraphrase 745
Parts-of-speech poems 377
Personification 745
Plays 463
Plot 157, 175, 204, 274, 277, 746
Poetry 281, 746
Point of view 229, 231, 263, 688, 713, 746
Prose 746
Pun 746
Quests 67, 573, 629, 712
Refrain 300, 304, 747
Repetition 283, 596, 600
Rhyme 292, 300, 319, 596, 600, 747
Rhyme scheme 308
Rhythm 292, 300, 316, 747
Science 431, 445
Science fiction 748
Sense poems 376
Sensory details 263

Setting 157, 233, 252, 262, 748
Short story 157, 748
Similes 36, 40, 196, 204, 333, 346, 374, 748
Sound effects 300, 313, 596, 599
Speaker 362, 748
Stanza 748
Story map 175
Story poems 284
Supernatural 573, 617
Suspense 443, 470, 688, 749
Theme 157, 194, 204, 216, 274, 645, 712, 749
Title 165, 250, 712
Tone 371, 400, 749
Trickster 599, 605

READING/CRITICAL THINKING SKILLS

Comparing and contrasting 18
Distinguishing between fact and opinion 250, 400
Distinguishing between realism and fantasy 18
Drawing conclusions 95, 144, 190
Evaluating a book 641
Identifying cause and effect 616
Identifying facts 400, 408, 573
Identifying major events 573
Identifying pronoun referents 564
Identifying the main idea 584
Identifying the sequence of events 32, 111, 262
Making generalizations 62
Making inferences 40, 52, 544
Predicting outcomes 2, 203, 216
Stating a theme 274
Summarizing 629
Supporting general statements 126
Visualizing descriptions 420

Focus on Reading and Critical Thinking
(End-of-unit activities)

Distinguishing between facts and opinions 718
Drawing inferences 544
Exploring connotations 152
Evaluating short stories 274–276
Identifying the main idea 640
Making generalizations 62
Relating sound to meaning 380
Understanding cause and effect 458

LANGUAGE AND VOCABULARY SKILLS

Action words 167, 176
African praise names 634, 637
Alliteration 299, 300, 319, 596, 599
Antonyms 179
Concrete words 329
Connotations 559, 565, 739
Context clues 8, 80, 179, 191, 412, 420, 556
Description 100, 112, 254, 263
Dialect 116, 126, 131, 145, 222, 230, 587
Exact words 112
Footnotes 12, 19
Glossary 12, 19
Homophones 339
Imagery 250
Japanese words 620, 630
Metaphors 44, 53
Multiple meanings 24, 32
Names in other languages 346, 634, 637
Onomatopoeia 300, 337, 596, 600
Owning a word 76, 647
Portmanteau words 308
Prefixes 217, 342, 394, 610, 617
Rhyme 596, 600
Semantic features 472, 532
Sensory details 263
Similes 36, 40, 196, 204
Slang 316, 713
Sounds and spellings 312
Spanish words 362
Stage terms 536
Suffixes 207, 217, 403
Synonyms 179
Teleplay terms 476
Word histories 432
Wordplay 292
Words from Mexico 578, 584
Words from mythology 568, 574

Outline of Concepts and Skills **807**

Outline of Concepts and Skills

Words from other languages 346, 362, 578, 584, 620, 630
Words in science 445

SPEAKING AND LISTENING SKILLS

Acting it out 532
Classroom theater 147, 535
Dramatizing a selection 53, 176
Group reading 310
Reading aloud 56, 97, 126, 131, 145, 222, 230, 265, 285, 307
Reading dialect aloud 145
Recording familiar stories 218

COMPOSITION SKILLS

Creative and Response-Centered Writing
  Creating metaphors 337
  Describing a fantasy character 19
  Describing a place 420
  Describing a wish that goes wrong 217
  Describing and illustrating a fantastic creature 292
  Describing your phizzog 369
  Extending a metaphor 342
  Extending the story 630
  Imitating the poem 358
  Letting an object speak 339
  Making a list 112
  Making up a "how and why" story 605
  Planning a poem 320
  Playing with words 308
  Portraits of imagination: writing your own poems 374
  Using your own dialect 230
  Writing your own snapshot 451
  Writing a description 96, 111, 126, 145, 153–155
  Writing a journal entry 355
  Writing a letter 97
  Writing a personal narrative 19, 32, 41, 54, 63–65
  Writing a poem 299, 304, 308, 313, 317, 320, 324, 329, 332, 342, 347, 358, 366, 374–379, 381–383
  Writing an interview 363
  Writing from another point of view 263, 713

Critical Writing
  Analyzing a change in character 713
  Supporting an opinion 689
  Writing a book report 574, 584, 617, 637, 641–643
  Writing a letter 97
  Writing an informative paper 401, 409, 428, 444, 459–461
  Writing a scene for a play 532, 545–547
  Writing a summary 629

Focus on Writing (End-of-unit activities)
  Writing a book report 641–643
  Writing a description 153–155
  Writing an informative paper 459–461
  Writing a personal narrative 63–65
  Writing a persuasive essay 719–721
  Writing a poem 381–383
  Writing a scene for a play 545–547
  Writing a short story 277–279

ART AND OTHER ACTIVITIES
Creating a travel brochure 205
Drawing a picture of a hero 565
Group activities 34, 53, 145, 176, 229, 532
Illustrating a fantastic creature 292

Illustrating the selection 327, 420, 600
Interviewing an older person 363
Library research 97, 205, 445, 593
Making a collage 327, 565
Making a diorama 532
Planning costumes 177
Setting a poem to music 351

LITERATURE AND HISTORY
The Underground Railroad 34

LITERATURE AND SCIENCE
Fact Versus Fiction 205
Myths and Scientific Words 445

CONNECTING CULTURES
Myths About Dragons 96
Tales About Giants 593

Index of Fine Art Transparencies by Type

In the *Audiovisual Resources Binder*, you will find **Fine Art** transparencies that relate to the literature units in the textbook. Each **Fine Art** transparency is accompanied by **Teacher's Notes** and student activity pages. Although these **Fine Art** transparencies are arranged in unit order, you may want to relate them to a variety of selections by literary type, such as those listed below.

Myths, Fables, Folk Tales: For artwork that depicts generations sharing traditional tales, see Transparencies 34 and 35.

Nonfiction: See Transparencies 12, 13, 24, 25, 39, and 40 for artwork depicting real people or real events. See also Transparencies 7 and 8 for examples of people involved in dangerous pursuits while attempting to meet a goal.

The Novel: For practice on interpreting stories through artwork, see Transparencies 12, 13, 39, and 40.

Plays: See Transparencies 29 and 30 for a view of an actor and a dramatic performance.

Index of Contents by Types

Myths and Folk Tales

Ali Baba and the Forty Thieves, retold by Elisabeth Gille 609
End of the World, The, Jenny Leading Cloud 638
Glooscap Fights the Water Monster, retold by Richard Erdoes and Alfonso Ortiz 558
How the Possum Lost the Hair on Its Tail, from *Mules and Men*, Zora Neale Hurston 586
How the Whale Got His Throat, Rudyard Kipling 595
Momotaro: Boy-of-the-Peach, retold by Yoshiko Uchida 618
Nana Miriam, retold by Hans Baumann 633
Paul Bunyan's Cornstalk, Harold Courlander 589
Perseus, retold by Robert Graves 567
Pheasant's Bell, The, retold by Kim So-un 551
Quetzalcoatl, retold by Amy Cruse 576
Two Frogs and the Milk Vat, Claude Brown 640
Why Tortoise's Shell Is Not Smooth, Chinua Achebe 601

Nonfiction

Backwoods Boy, A, Russell Freedman 402
Diary of a Young Girl, The, from, Anne Frank 393
Fatherhood, Bill Cosby 453
Gorillas in the Mist, from, Dian Fossey 387
Harriet Tubman, Ann Petry 22
Jacket, The, Gary Soto 35
Land I Lost, The, Huynh Quang Nhuong 411
Most Vulnerable People, The, Brent Ashabranner 422
Snapshot of a Dog, James Thurber 446
Volcano, Patricia Lauber 431
Wetlands, from, Seymour Simon 718

Novel, The, and selections from

Adventures of Tom Sawyer, The, from, Mark Twain 42
Anne of Green Gables, from, L. M. Montgomery 740
Carlota, from, Scott O'Dell 69
Hank the Cowdog, from, John R. Erickson 56
Hatchet, from, Gary Paulsen 99
Jody's Discovery, from *The Yearling*, Marjorie Kinnan Rawlings 129
Julie of the Wolves, from, Jean Craighead George 3
Mr. Tumnus, from *The Lion, the Witch and the Wardrobe*, C. S. Lewis 10
Sounder, from, William Armstrong 114
Summer of the Swans, The, Betsy Byars 648

Plays

Monsters Are Due on Maple Street, The, from, Rod Serling 465
Riddles in the Dark, based on the novel *The Hobbit* by J. R. R. Tolkien 534
Secret Garden, The, based on the novel by Frances Hodgson Burnett 474

Index of Contents by Types

Poetry

Abuelito Who, Sandra Cisneros 345
Beach Stones, Lilian Moore 323
City, The, David Ignatow 742
Concrete Cat, Dorthi Charles 328
Cynthia in the Snow, Gwendolyn Brooks 301
Darkling Elves, The, Jack Prelutsky 282
Dream Variations, Langston Hughes 350
Fame is a bee, Emily Dickinson 743
Habits of the Hippopotamus, Arthur Guiterman 307
Haiku, Shōha, Taigi, Bonchō, Ryōta 330
Inside a Poem, Eve Merriam 281
Interview, Sara Henderson Hay 370
January, Maurice Sendak 738
Jumblies, The, Edward Lear 295
Knoxville, Tennessee, Nikki Giovanni 365
Legacy II, Leroy V. Quintana 360
Life Doesn't Frighten Me, Maya Angelou 303
Minor Bird, A, Robert Frost 354
Narcissa, Gwendolyn Brooks 318
Our Washing Machine, Patricia Hubbell 745
Petals, Pat Mora 326
Phizzog, Carl Sandburg 368
Rags, Judith Thurman 745
Rainy Day, The, from, Henry Wadsworth Longfellow 743
Raven, The, from, Edgar Allan Poe 745
Rum Tum Tugger, The, T. S. Eliot 310
Sarah Cynthia Sylvia Stout Would Not Take the Garbage Out, Shel Silverstein 372
Scene, Charlotte Zolotow 748
Sea, The, James Reeves 335
Since Hanna Moved Away, Judith Viorst 744
Sneetches, The, Dr. Seuss (Theodor Geisel) 285
That Day, David Kherdian 356
Things to Do If You Are a Subway, Bobbi Katz 340
Thoughts on Progress, from, David Daiches 747
Toaster, The, William J. Smith 338
Waking, The, Theodore Roethke 380
When I Was One-and-Twenty, from, A. E. Housman 748
who knows if the moon's, E. E. Cummings 314

Short Stories

Algonquin Cinderella, The, M. R. Cox 147
All-American Slurp, The, Lensey Namioka 264
All Summer in a Day, Ray Bradbury 194
Becky and the Wheels-and-Brake Boys, James Berry 220
Dragon, Dragon, John Gardner 166
Gorilla, My Love, from, Toni Cade Bambara 740
Nancy, Elizabeth Enright 233
President Cleveland, Where Are You?, Robert Cormier 178
Rolls for the Czar, Robin Kinkead 275
Secret for Two, A, Quentin Reynolds 159
Smallest Dragonboy, The, Anne McCaffrey 78
Stone, The, Lloyd Alexander 206
Where the Buffaloes Begin, Olaf Baker 252

Poetry: For images and objects which invoke poetic response, see Transparencies 18 and 19.

Short Stories: See Transparencies 12 and 13 to explore characters adjusting to new settings or challenges. For an example of shared moments between generations, see Transparency 35.

Index of Fine Art and Illustrations

Andromeda chained to her rock. Mosaic, Herculaneum, Italy 572
Athena, relief on a gravestone, Acropolis, Athens 568
Baynes, Pauline, illustrations for *The Lion, the Witch and the Wardrobe* 18, 20
Bearden, Romare, *Maudelle Sleet's Magic Garden* 364
Ben, Joe Jr., Navajo sand painting 585
Benson, Frank Weston, *Gertrude* 237
Benton, Thomas Hart, *The Wreck of the Ole '97* 156–157
Bierstadt, Albert, *The Shore of the Turquoise Sea* 334–335
Bradford, William, *Whalers Trapped in Arctic Ice* 384–385
Burne-Jones, Sir Philip, *Rudyard Kipling* 600
Cat, The, by an unknown American painter 311
Catlin, George, *Buffalo Hunt* 258–259
    Chee-ah-ka-tchee, Wife of Not-to-way 260
    Mint, a Pretty Girl 151
Ch-i Bai-Shih, *A Pair of Birds in a Cinnamon Tree* 555
Crite, Allan Rohan, *Marble Players* 319
Crowe, Eyre, *Slave Market in Richmond, Virginia* 27
Doré, Gustave, Bluebeard gives his wife the keys to the castle. Colored engraving 607
    Cinderella. Colored engraving 308
Dulac, Edmund, illustrations from *The Arabian Nights* 608, 613, 614
Geisel, Theodor (Dr. Seuss), illustrations for "The Sneetches" 285–292
Gropper, William, *Paul Bunyan*. Lithograph 591
Henri, Robert, *Irish Girl (Mary O'Donnell)* 244
Henry, Edward Lamson, *Kept In* 302
Hercules shown on a Greek plate 557
Hessler, Alexander, *Abraham Lincoln* 405
Hokusai, *Mt. Fuji from Kajikazawa in the Province of Kai* 280–281
    View of Kondrai 331
Holmes, G. L., illustrations for *Hank the Cowdog* 56, 57, 60
Hurd, Peter, *The Dry River* 361
    Eve of St. John, The 1
Kemble, E. W., *The Romantic Outcast, Huck Finn*. Illustration 52
Kipling, Rudyard, drawings for *Just So* stories 594, 595, 597
Lawrence, Jacob, *Harriet Tubman worked as a water girl* 32
    The Libraries Are Appreciated 644–645
Lear, Edward, illustrations for "The Jumblies" 294–298
Luks, George, *Boy with Baseball* 357
Medusa, head of, relief sculpture at temple in Didyma, Turkey 566
Micmac Indians, by an unknown Canadian artist 560–561
O'Keeffe, Georgia, *The Lawrence Tree* 283
Paul Bunyan and his blue ox Babe, illustration 589
Perseus carrying Medusa's head. Vase painting 571
Pious, Robert Savon, *Harriet Tubman* 22
Plumed serpent heads, Pyramid of the Sun, Teotihuacan, Mexico 582
Qasim, *Isfandiyar Slays the Dragon* 548–549
Rivera, Diego, *Flower Day* 326
Rockwell, Norman, illustration for *The Adventures of Tom Sawyer* 43
Rousseau, Henri, *A Carnival Evening* 315
Sanko, Akasaka, illustrations for a children's book written in Japanese 618–619, 622–623, 625, 626–627, 628
Savage, Augusta, *La Citadella-Freedom* 351
Shields, Charles, illustrations for "Dragon, Dragon" 170, 173
Silverstein, Shel, illustrations from *Where the Sidewalk Ends* 372
Simon, Luke, *Cradled in the Wind* 151
Steichen, Edward, *Carl Sandburg* 369
Temple of Cazacol, Mexico, fresco from 579
Thurber, James, sketches of dogs 446, 450, 452
Uccello, Paolo, *St. George and the Dragon* 66–67
Walrus, Eskimo ivory carving 3
Webber, Charles T., *The Underground Railroad* 30
Wyeth, N. C., illustrations for *The Yearling* 140, 143

Photo Credits

Abbreviations: AP—Associated Press/Wide World Photos; AR—Art Resource, NY; BA—The Bettmann Archive; BCI—Bruce Coleman, Inc.; CP—Culver Pictures, Inc.; GC—The Granger Collection, New York; PR—Photo Researchers, Inc.; SM—The Stock Market; TIB—The Image Bank.

Illustrators: Rosekrans Hoffman, pp. 10-11, 14-15; Charles Reid, pp. 78-79, 82-83, 87, 90-91, 94; Alan Cober, pp. 194-195, 199, 200-201; Andy San Diego, pp. 206, 208, 210-211, 212, 214-215; Tom Leonard, pp. 338, 433, 438; Steve Cieslawski, p. 471; Robert Heindel, pp. 649, 654-655, 663, 671, 674-675, 681, 694-695, 704-705, 711.

Title Page and Back Cover images, William S. Nawrocki/Nawrocki Stock Photos.

TABLE OF CONTENTS: vi, Chris Arend, Courtesy of Alaska State Council/Alaska Stock Images; vii, Michael Giannechini/PR; viii, E. R. Degginger/ColorPic; ix-a, Robert Bornemann/PR; ix-b, Frontera Fotos/Michelle Bridwell; x, Martha Swope Photography; xi, Courtesy Rosemary Thurber; xii, Richard Haynes; xiii, Ronald Sheridan's Photo Library; xiv, Mike Yamashita/Woodfin Camp & Associates; xv, Richard Gross/SM

2, HRW Photo by Sam Dudgeon; 3, Chris Arend, Courtesy of Alaska State Council/Alaska Stock Images; 4, Larry B. Jennings/PR; 5, Stephen J. Krasemann/DRK Photo; 7, Lawrence Migdale/PR; 8, Michael Giannechini/PR; 21, Burt Glinn/Magnum; 33, CP; 35, Jules Zalon/TIB; 38, HRW photo by Sam Dudgeon; 41, Carolyn Soto; 43, © Richard Cerretti Photography for Mark Twain Museum; Hannibal, Missouri; 46, The Kobal Collection/Superstock; 51, Illustration House, Inc.; 55, CP; 61, © John R. Erickson: Maverick Books, by Gulf Publishing; 68, HRW Photo by Sam Dudgeon; 69, Alese & Mort Pechter/SM; 71, Chris McClaughlin/SM; 73, Tom McHugh/PR; 74, Richard Gross/SM; 96, Virginia Kidd Literary Agent/Photo by Greg Preston; 98-99, William Curtsinger/PR; 99, Gabe Palmer/Mug Shots; 100, William J. Jahoda/PR; 101, Pat & Tom Leeson/PR; 104 Superstock; 109, Richard B. Peacock/PR; 111, Alan D. Carey/PR; 112, CP; 113, Vickie Kettlewell/Grand Forks Herald; 115-126, Movie Still Archives; 128, AP; 129, BA; 130, Leonard Lee Rue III/PR; 132, Movie Still Archives; 137, BA; 140-143, Charles Scribner's Sons, an imprint of Macmillan Publishing Company from "The Yearling" by Marjorie Kinnan Rawlings. Illustrations by N.C. Wyeth; 145, The Kobal Collection/ Superstock; 146, BA; 147-149 Photos by Jerry Jacka; 150, Philip L. Greene; 151a, AR; 151b, Photo by Jerry Jacka; 158, HRW Photo by Sam Dudgeon; 161, McCord Museum of Canadian History, Notman Photographic Archives; 163a, Will Rhyins/Woodfin Camp & Associates; 163b, Francisco Hidalgo/TIB; 166(l). AR; 166(r), E.R. Degginger/Color Pic; 170-173, Reprinted by permission of Alfred A. Knopf, Inc.; 176, Giraudon/AR; 177, BA; 178a,b, Stephen St. John; 179, BA; 180a,b, Stephen St. John; 181, BA; 184, Stephen St. John; 185, BA; 188 FPG; 192, Finkle Photography/Random House, Inc.; 205, 219, AP; 220, Andre Gallant/TIB; 221, Mel di Giacomo/TIB; 225, Baron Wolman/Woodfin Camp, Associates; 226, Jay Freis/TIB; 228, Andre Gallant/TIB; 229, Tony Aruzza/BCI; 230, S.L. Craig, Jr./BCI; 231, Orchard Books; 232-233, David Hamilton/TIB; 240-241, Jonathan Pratt; 251, Courtesy Oliver Gillham; 253, Werner Forman Archive; 254, Werner Forman Archive/Plains Indian Museum; Buffalo Bill Historical Center, Cody, Wyoming; 256, Jeff Foott/BCI.; 261, Werner Forman Archive/Glenbow Museum; Calgary, Alberta; 263, National Museum of the American Indian, Smithsonian Institution; 264, Jeffrey W. Meyers/FPG; 265, John Lei-Omni-Photo Communications, Inc.; 269, Roy Morsh/SM; 272, Lawrence Migdale; 273a, Ruth Cohen Agency; 273b, Bill Dykes; 282, HRW by Sam Dudgeon; 284, Thomas Braise/SM; 285-292, Reprinted by permission of Random House, Inc.; 293, BA; 294-298, Frederic Warne & Co. Ltd.; 299, Topham/The Image Works; 300-301, Andre Gallant/TIB; 305, Nancy Crampton; 306-307, M.P.L. Fogden/BCI; 308, GC; 309, Louise Sclove; 312, Martha Swope Photography; 313, UPI/Bettmann Newsphotos; 314, W. Adams/FPG; 316, J. Zehrt/FPG; 317, AP; 320a, Nancy Crampton; 320b, Robert Bornemann/PR; 321, Alvin Upitis/TIB; 322-325, Tom Bean/ SM; 325a, Courtesy Lilian Moore; 327, Jody Schwartz Photography/Arte Publico Press; 332, V. Gardner/FPG; 333, Walter Bibikow/TIB; 336, Cliff Feulner/TIB; 337, William Heinemann, London; 338, Gary Gay/TIB; 340-341, Louis Goldman/PR; 340a, Spencer Jones/BCI; 343a, Courtesy Bobby Katz; 343b, Copyright United Media; 344, Guido Alberto Rossi/TIB; 347, Frontera Fotos/Michelle Bridwell; 348, Ruben Guzman, copyright Sarah Wells, 1990; 352, BA; 353, Claudia Parks/SM; 354a, Barth Schorre/BCI; 354b, Frank W. Mantlik/PR, 355, BA; 358, Connie Hanson/SM; 359, H. L. Hoffmaster; 363, LaVerne H. Clark; 364, Collection of Mr. and Mrs. Gerhard Stebich. Courtesy the Estate of Romare Bearden; 366, Gary Gay/TIB; 367, Nancy Crampton; 369, AR, with permission of Joanna T. Steichen; 386, HRW photo by Sam Dudgeon; 389, 390, 391, Robert M. Campbell/National Geographic Society; 392, © 1990, Anne Frank-Fonds, Basel, Switzerland; 397, BA; 398, Tom McHugh/PR; 402, Illinois State Historical Library, Springfield; 409, Clarion Books; 410-411, 414-415, SuperStock; 413-419, Robert Nickelsberg/Gamma-Liaison; 421, Harper Collins Publishers, Inc.; 423, Christopher Morris/Black Star; 424-425, Peter Turnley/Black Star; 427, Brent Jones; 429, Jennifer Ashabranner/The Putnam and Grosset Group; 430, U. S. Geological Survey, Cascades Volcanic Observatory, Vancouver, Washington; 434, U. S. Forest Service, Vancouver, Washington; 436-437, Gary Rosenquist; 439, 440-441, 442, U. S. Geological Survey, Cascades Volcanic Observatory, Vancouver, Wasington; 445, Macmillan Publishing Company; 452, Courtesy, Rosemary Thurber; 453, Vinnie Zuffante/Star File; 456, Shooting Star; 462-463, Martha Swope Photography; 464, HRW photo by Sam Dudgeon; 475, 478, 485, 490, 497, 500, 505, 511, 514, 519, 522, From the TV Production, "The Secret Garden" (11/30/87), Rosemont Productions, Ltd. and CBS-TV Reading Program; 533, BA; 534, 535, Movie Stills Archives; 536, Richard Haynes; 539, 542, From "The Lord of the Rings" (1978), Saul Zaentz Production/Movie Stills Archives; 543, AP; 550, HRW photo by Sam Dudgeon; 553, Hyung Rok Lee/TIB; 554, Kenneth Fink/BCI; 555, Werner Forman Archive; 557, Scala/AR; 566, Ronald Sheridan's Photo Library; 568, Scala/AR; 571, 572, Ronald Sheridan's Photo Library; 575, The Image Works; 576, Lee Boltin; 577, AR; 578, Ronald Sheridan's Photo Library; 579, AR; 581, Lee Boltin; 582, Ronald Sheridan's Photo Library; 583, 584, Dover Publications, Inc.; 585, Jerry Jacka; 586, C. C. Lockwood/DRK; 587, John R. Hicks/DRK; 588, Harry West/AP; 589, From Booklet of Franklin Philatelic Society, Pennsylvania, 1978/New York Public Library Picture Collection; 601, George Holton/PR; 602, 604, Marc & Evelyn Bernheim/Woodfin Camp & Associates; 605, William Heinemann, Ltd., London; 607, GC; 613, 614, Harry Ransom Humanities Research Center, The University of Texas at Austin; 618-619, 622-623, 625, 626-627, 628, Illustration by Akasaka Sanko, Courtesy Shogakukan Publisher, Tokyo, copyright Miyoshi Akasada; 631, Scribner Book Co., Inc.; 632-633, Victor Englebert/PR; 633, Eric Wheater/TIB; 638, 639, Jerry Jacka; 646, Mike Yamashita/Woodfin Camp & Associates; 715. Edward Byars, Courtesy Viking Penguin, Inc.

Index of Authors and Titles

The numbers in italics refer to pages on which author biographies appear.

Abuelito Who 345
Achebe, Chinua 601, 605
Adventures of Tom Sawyer, The, from 42
Alexander, LLoyd 206, *218*, 219
Algonquin Cinderella, The 147
Algonquins 151
Ali Baba and the Forty Thieves 609
All Summer in a Day 194
All-American Slurp, The 264
Angelou, Maya 303, *305*
Anne of Green Gables, from 740
Armstrong, William 114, *127*, 128
Ashabranner, Brent 422, *429*

Backwoods Boy, A 402
Baker, Olaf 252, *263*
Bambara, Toni Cade 606, 740
Baumann, Hans 633
Beach Stones 323
Becky and the Wheels-and-Brake Boys 220
Berry, James 220, *231*
Bonchō, Nozawa 330
Bradbury, Ray 194, *205*
Brooks, Gwendolyn 301, 318, *320*
Brown, Claude 640

Burnett, Frances Hodgson 474, *533*
Byars, Betsy 648, *714*, 715

Carlota, from 69
Charles, Dorthi 328, *329*
Cisneros, Sandra 345, *347*, 348
City, The 742
Concrete Cat 328
Cormier, Robert 178, *191*, 192
Cosby, Bill 453, *457*
Courlander, Harold 589
Cow, The 378
Cox, M. R. 147
Cruse, Amy 576
Cummings, E. E. 314, *317*
Cynthia in the Snow 301

Daiches, David 747
Darkling Elves, The 282
Diary of a Young Girl, The, from 393
Dickinson, Emily 743
Dragon, Dragon 166
Dream Variations 350
Duck, The 378

Eliot, T. S. 310, *313*
End of the World, The 638
Enright, Elizabeth 233, *251*
Erdoes, Richard 558, *565*
Erickson, John R. 56, *61*

Fame is a bee 743
Fatherhood 453
Fossey, Dian 387
Frank, Anne 393, *401*
Freedman, Russell 402, *409*
Frost, Robert 354, *355*

Gardner, John 166, *177*
Geisel, Theodor 285, *293*
George, Jean Craighead 3
Gille, Elizabeth 609
Giovanni, Nikki 365, *367*
Glooscap Fights the Water Monster 558
Gorilla, My Love, from 740
Gorillas in the Mist, from 387
Graves, Robert 567, *575*
Gray, Patricia 534
Guiterman, Arthur 307, *309*

Habits of the Hippopotamus 307
Haiku 330
Hanalis, Blanche 474
Hank the Cowdog 56
Harriet Tubman 22
Hatchet, from 99, 152
Hay, Sara Henderson 370, *371*
Housman, A. E. 748
How the Whale Got His Throat 595
Hubbell, Patricia 745
Hughes, Langston 350, *352*
Hurston, Zora Neale 586, *588*

Ignatow, David   742
Inside a Poem   281

Jacket, The   35
January   738
Jody's Discovery   129
Julie of the Wolves, from   3
Jumblies, The   295

Katz, Bobbi   340, *343*
Kherdian, David   356, *359*
Kipling, Rudyard   595, *600*
Knoxville, Tennessee   365

Land I Lost, The   411
Lauber, Patricia   431, *444*, 445
Leading Cloud, Jenny   638
Lear, Edward   295, *299*
Legacy II   360
Lewis, C. S.   10, *20*, 21
Life Doesn't Frighten Me   303
Longfellow, Henry Wadsworth   743

McCaffrey, Anne   78, *96*
Merriam, Eve   281
Micmacs   565
Minor Bird, A   354
Momotaro: Boy-of-the-Peach   618
Monsters Are Due on Maple Street, The, from   465
Montgomery, L. M.   740
Moore, Lilian   323, *324,* 325
Mora, Pat   326, *327*
Most Vulnerable People, The   422
Mr. Tumnus   10
Mules and Men, from   586

Namioka, Lensey   264, *273*
Nana Miriam   633
Nancy   233
Narcissa   318
Nash, Ogden   378
Nhuong, Huynh Quang   411, *421*

O'Dell, Scott   69
Ortiz, Alfonso   558, *565*
Our Washing Machine   745

Paul Bunyan's Cornstalk   589
Paulsen, Gary   99, *112,* 113
Perseus   567
Petals   326
Petry, Ann   22, *33*
Pheasant's Bell, The   551
Phizzog   368
Poe, Edgar Allan   745
Prelutsky, Jack   282
President Cleveland, Where Are You?   178
Prinderella and the Cinch   309

Quetzalcoatl   576
Quintana, Leroy V.   360, *363*

Rags   745
Rainy Day, The, from   743
Raven, The, from   745
Rawlings, Marjorie Kinnan   129, *146*
Reeves, James   335, *337*
Reynolds, Quentin   159
Riddles in the Dark   534
Roethke, Theodore   380
Rum Tum Tugger, The   310
Ryōta, Ōshima   330

Sandburg, Carl   368, *369*
Sarah Cynthia Sylvia Stout Would Not Take the Garbage Out   372
Scene   748
Sea, The   335
Secret Garden, The   474
Secret for Two, A   159
Sendak, Maurice   738
Serling, Rod   465
Seuss, Dr.   285, *293*
Seymour, Simon   718
Shōha, Kuroyanagi   330
Silverstein, Shel   372, *373*
Since Hanna Moved Away   744
Sioux   639
Smallest Dragonboy, The   78
Smith, William Jay   338, *339*
Snapshot of a Dog   446
Sneetches, The   285
So-un, Kim   551
Songai   637
Soto, Gary   35, *41*
Sounder, from   114
Stone, The   206
Storm, The   743
Summer of the Swans, The   648

Taigi, Tan   330
That Day   356
Things To Do If You Are a Subway   340
Thoughts on Progress, from   747
Thurber, James   446, *452*
Thurman, Judith   745
Toaster, The   338
Tolkien, J. R. R.   534, *543*
Twain, Mark   42, *54,* 55

Two Frogs and the Milk Vat 640

Uchida, Yoshiko 618, *630,* 631

Viorst, Judith 744
Volcano 431

Waking, The 380
Wetlands, from 718
When I Was One-and-Twenty, from 747
who know's if the moon's 314
Where the Buffaloes Begin 252
Why Tortoise's Shell Is Not Smooth 601

Zolotow, Charlotte 748